The World Economy

The World Economy

History & Prospect

University of Texas Press Austin & London

Publication of this book was made possible by a grant from the Sid W. Richardson Foundation.

Library of Congress Cataloging in Publication Data

Rostow, Walt Whitman, 1916–
The world economy.

Includes bibliographical references and index.
1. Economic history. 2. Economic forecasting.
I. Title.
HC51.R67 330.9 77-24053
ISBN 0-292-79008-2

Set in Primer by G & S Typesetters, Inc.
Printed in the United States of America

Grateful acknowledgment is made to the following for permission to quote copyrighted materials:

Academic Press, Inc., and Glenn R. Hueckel, for material from Glenn Hueckel, "War and the British Economy, 1793–1815: A General Equilibrium Analysis," *Explorations in Economic History*, vol. 10, no. 4 (Summer 1973), p. 388.

Almqvist & Wiksell and Östen Johansson, for material from Östen Johansson, *The Gross Domestic Product of Sweden and Its Composition, 1861–1955*.

American Philosophical Society and John D. Durand, for material from John D. Durand, "The Modern Expansion of World Population," *Proceedings of the American Philosophical Society*, vol. 111, no. 3 (June 22, 1967).

Arthavijnana (Journal of the Gokhale Institute of Politics and Economics) and Morris David Morris, for material from Morris David Morris and Clyde B. Dudley, "Selected Railway Statistics for the Indian Subcontinent (India, Pakistan and Bangladesh), 1853–1946–47," *Arthavijnana*, vol. 17, no. 3 (September 1975).

Association Internationale des Sciences Economiques, for material reproduced from a paper by Witold Langrod in the International Economic Association conference volume *Economics of International Migration*, edited by Brinley Thomas, published by Macmillan & CO Ltd., London, and the St. Martin's Press, New York, 1958.

Banca Nazionale del Lavoro, for material from Angus Maddison, "Growth and Fluctuation in the World Economy, 1870–1960," *Quarterly Review*, no. 61 (June 1962).

Thomas Senior Berry, for unpublished data furnished by Thomas Senior Berry of the University of Richmond, Virginia.

The Brookings Institution, for material from:

Why Growth Rates Differ: Postwar Experience in Nine Western Countries, by Edward F. Denison assisted by Jean-Pierre Poullier, © 1967 by the Brookings Institution, Washington, D.C.

Trade in Primary Commodities: Conflict or Cooperation? a tripartite report by fifteen economists from Japan, the European Community, and North America, © 1974 by the Brookings Institution, Washington, D.C.

Cooperative Approaches to World Energy Problems, a tripartite report by fifteen experts from the European Community, Japan, and North America, © 1974 by the Brookings Institution, Washington, D.C.

Higher Oil Prices and the World Economy: The Adjustment Problem, Edward R. Fried and Charles L. Schultze, editors, © 1975 by the Brookings Institution, Washington, D.C.

Barry Bosworth, James S. Duesenberry, and Andrew S. Carron, *Capital Needs in the Seventies* (Brookings Institution, 1975), Table 2-11, page 38.

Curtis Brown, Ltd., for world rights to material from Lester R. Brown, *In the Human Interest*. Reprinted by permission of Curtis Brown Ltd. Copyright © 1974 by W. W. Norton Co., Inc.

Cambridge University Press, for material from the following, all published by Cambridge University Press:

Burn, D. L., *The Economic History of Steel-Making, 1867–1939*, p. 399 and Fig. 1.

Butlin, N. G., *Australian Domestic Product, Investment and Foreign Borrowing, 1861–1938/39*, pp. 10–11, 460–461.

Butlin, N. G., *Investment in Australian Economic Development, 1861–1900*, p. 51.

Cairncross, A. K., *Home and Foreign Investment, 1870–1913*, Chart 1.

Chaudhuri, K. N., *The Economic Development of India under the East India Company, 1814–58*, p. 26.

Feinstein, C. H., *National Income, Expenditure, and Output of the United Kingdom, 1855–1965*.

Habakkuk, H. J., and Postan, M., *The Cambridge Economic History of Europe*, vol. VI, pt. 1, "The Industrial Revolutions and After," pp. 68–69 from D. V. Glass and E. Grebenik, "World Population, 1800–1950."

Thomas, Brinley, *Migration and Economic Growth*, p. 176.

Allen, R. G. D., "The Immediate Contributors to Inflation," *The Economic Journal*, vol. 85, no. 339, p. 610.

Commission on Critical Choices for Americans, for material from Volume I of a major project of the Commission on Critical Choices for Americans. The fourteen volumes of this project have been published by Lexington Books, D. C. Heath and Company. Volume I is entitled *Vital Resources*. Reprinted by the permission of the publisher. All rights reserved. © 1976 The Third Century Corporation.

East-West Center and Lee-Jay Cho, for material from Lee-Jay Cho, *The Demographic Situation in the Republic of Korea*.

The Economic History Association and Nathaniel H. Leff, for material from Nathaniel H. Leff, "Long-term Brazilian Economic Development," *The Journal of Economic History*, vol. 29, no. 3 (September 1969).

The Economic History Society, for material from E. W. Cooney, "Long Waves in Building in the British Economy of the Nineteenth Century," *The Economic History Review*, 2d ser., vol. 13, no. 2 (December 1960).

The Economist, for material from *The Economist*, London.

The Ford Foundation, for material reprinted from *Exploring Energy Choices* with permission of the Energy Policy Project of The Ford Foundation.

Harcourt Brace Jovanovich, Inc., for material from Stuart Bruchey, *Cotton and the Growth of the American Economy: 1790–1860*.

Harper & Row, Publishers, Inc., for material:

Abridged from pp. 410, 411 and 422 in *Business Fluctuations*, 2nd Edition by Robert A. Gordon. Copyright © 1961 by Robert Aaron Gordon. Reprinted by permission of Harper & Row, Publishers, Inc.

From *The Reinterpretation of American Economic History* edited by Robert William Fogel and Stanley L. Engerman: Table 1 (p. 26) by Robert E. Gallman and Edward S. Howle; Table 1 (pp. 123–4) by Robert Brooke Zevin. Harper & Row, 1971.

Hart Schaffner & Marx, for material from the 1930 Hart Schaffner & Marx Prize Essay by Simon S. Kuznets, *Secular Movements in Production and Prices*.

Harvard University Press, for material from the following, all published by Harvard University Press:

Albert Feuerwerker, *China's Early Industrialization*, Copyright © 1958 by the President and Fellows of Harvard College.

Albert H. Imlah, *Economic Elements in the Pax Britannica: Studies in British Foreign Trade in the Nineteenth Century*, Copyright © 1958 by the President and Fellows of Harvard College.

Simon S. Kuznets, *Economic Growth of Nations*, Copyright © 1971 by Simon Kuznets; The Belknap Press of Harvard University Press.

Wilfred Malenbaum, *The World Wheat Economy, 1885–1939*, Copyright © 1953 by the President and Fellows of Harvard College.

Stanley J. Stein, *The Brazilian Cotton Manufacture*, Copyright © 1952 by the President and Fellows of Harvard College.

The Hudson Institute, for material from *1973 Synoptic Context on the Corporate Environment: 1973–1985*, vol. 2, © The Hudson Institute, Croton-on-Hudson, NY 10520.

International Association for Research in Income and Wealth and O. J. Firestone, for material from O. J. Firestone, *Canada's Economic Development, 1867–1953*, Income and Wealth, Series VII.

International Economic Association, for material from Walther G. Hoffmann, "The Take-off in Germany," Chapter 6 in *The Economics of Take-off into Sustained Growth*, ed. W. W. Rostow (New York: St. Martin's Press, 1963); and from J. Marczewski, "The Take-off Hypothesis and French Experience," in ibid.

Richard D. Irwin, Inc., for:

Material by Miyohei Shinohara and Hisao Kanamori, reproduced with permission from *Economic Growth: The Japanese Experience since the Meiji Era*, Klein and Ohkawa, eds. (Homewood, Ill.: Richard D. Irwin, Inc., 1968 c.), pp. 284, 323.

Material from Henry William Spiegel, *The Brazilian Economy*, 1949, p. 123.

The Johns Hopkins University Press, for material from Hans H. Landsberg et al., *Resources in America's Future*, published for Resources for the

Future by the Johns Hopkins University Press, 1963. © 1963, The Johns Hopkins Press, Baltimore 18, Maryland.

The Journal of Economic History, for material from Jeffrey G. Williamson, "Urbanization in the American Northeast, 1820–1870," originally published in *The Journal of Economic History*, December 1965.

W. Arthur Lewis, for material from "The Terms of Trade," a pedagogical note.

LiberLäromel Lund (formerly CWK Gleerup), for material from Lennart Jörberg, *A History of Prices in Sweden, 1732–1914*.

Lloyds Bank Review, for material from F. W. Paish, "Inflation, Personal Incomes and Taxation," *Lloyds Bank Review*, no. 116 (April 1975).

The London School of Economics and Political Science, for material from "Seven Centuries of the Price of Consumables, Compared with Builders' Wage-Rates," by E. H. Phelps Brown and Sheila V. Hopkins, *Economica*, November 1956.

Longman Australia Pty Limited, for material from E. A. Boehm, *Twentieth Century Economic Development in Australia*.

McGraw-Hill Publications Company, for material from McGraw-Hill Publications' Economics Department's Special Table on Capital Spending Plans of the Energy Industry, May 7, 1976.

Macmillan Publishing Co., Inc., for material from *History of the National Economy of Russia to the 1917 Revolution* by Peter Lyashchenko; translated by L. M. Herman. Copyright, 1949, by American Council of Learned Societies.

Methuen & Co., Ltd., publishers, for material from M. M. Postan, *An Economic History of Western Europe, 1945–1964*.

M.I.T. Press, for material from W. W. Rostow et al., *The Prospects for Communist China*.

Mitre Corporation and Charles A. Zraket, for material from *Energy Resources for the Year 2000 and Beyond*, MTP-401, March 1975, C. A. Zraket, Mitre Corp.

Motor Vehicle Manufacturers Association (formerly Automobile Manufacturers Association), for material from *Automobile Facts and Figures*, 21st edition, 1939.

National Association of Business Economists and Geoffrey H. Moore, for material from Geoffrey H. Moore, "The State of the International Business Cycle," *Business Economics*, vol. 9, no. 4 (September 1974).

National Bureau of Economic Research, for material as follows:

Permission granted by National Bureau of Economic Research to reprint from O. J. Firestone, "Development of Canada's Economy, 1850–1900," *Trends in the American Economy in the Nineteenth Century*, Copyright © 1960 by National Bureau of Economic Research, Inc.

Permission granted by National Bureau of Economic Research to reprint from Solomon Fabricant, *The Output of Manufacturing Industries, 1899–1937*, Copyright © 1940 by National Bureau of Economic Research, Inc.

Permission granted by National Bureau of Economic Research to reprint from Richard A. Easterlin, *Population, Labor Force, and Long Swings in Economic Growth*, Copyright © 1968 by National Bureau of Economic Research, Inc.

Permission granted by National Bureau of Economic Research to reprint from Oskar Morgenstern, *International Financial Transactions and Business Cycles*, Copyright © 1959 by National Bureau of Economic Research, Inc.

Permission granted by National Bureau of Economic Research to reprint from Arthur F. Burns, *The Business Cycle in a Changing World*, Copyright © 1969 by National Bureau of Economic Research, Inc.

Permission granted by National Bureau of Economic Research to reprint from Ilse Mintz, *Trade Balances during Business Cycles: U.S. and Britain since 1880*, Copyright © 1959 by National Bureau of Economic Research, Inc.

Permission granted by National Bureau of Economic Research to reprint from G. Warren Nutter, assisted by Israel Borenstein and Adam Kaufman, *The Growth of Industrial Production in the Soviet Union*, Copyright © 1962 by National Bureau of Economic Research, Inc.

Permission granted by National Bureau of Economic Research to reprint from William H. Shaw, *Value of Commodity Output since 1869*, Copyright © 1947 by National Bureau of Economic Research, Inc.

National Tax Journal and Joseph E. Pluta, for material from Joseph E. Pluta, "Growth and Patterns in U.S. Government Expenditures, 1956–1972," *National Tax Journal*, vol. 27, no. 1 (March 1974).

The New York Times Company, for material from *The New York Times*, December 24, 1975, © 1975 by The New York Times Company. Reprinted by permission.

North-Holland Publishing Company, Hollis B. Chenery, and Lance Taylor, for material from Hollis Chenery and Lance Taylor, "Development Patterns: Among Countries and over Time," *Review of Economics and Statistics*, vol. 50, no. 4 (November 1968).

W. W. Norton & Company, Inc., for material reprinted from *In the Human Interest* by Lester R. Brown. By permission of W. W. Norton & Company, Inc. Copyright © 1974 by W. W. Norton & Company, Inc.

OECD Observer, for material reprinted from the *OECD Observer*, February 1971; August 1972; August 1974; October–November 1974; and July–August 1975.

Organization for Economic Cooperation and Development, for material from Mo-Huan Hsing, "Taiwan: Industrialization and Trade Policies," in *Industry and Trade in Some Developing Countries: The Philippines and Taiwan*, © Copyright OECD, published by Oxford University Press, U.K.

Oxford University Press, for material from:

E. H. Phelps Brown and Sheila V. Hopkins, "The Course for Wage-Rates in Five Countries, 1860–1939," *Oxford Economic Papers*, vol. 2 (1950), by permission of the Oxford University Press.

World Population: Past Growth and Present Trends, 1936, by A. M. Carr-Saunders, published by the Oxford University Press.

Pacific Affairs, for material from Fred W. Riggs, *Formosa under Chinese Nationalist Rule*.

Praeger Publishers (now a division of Holt, Rinehart & Winston), for material from Robert E. Looney, *The Economic Development of Iran*. © 1973 by Praeger Publishers, Inc.

Prentice-Hall, Inc., for material from Douglass C. North, *The Economic Growth of the United States, 1790–1860*, © 1961, pp. 74, 93, 95, 137. Reproduced by permission of Prentice-Hall, Inc., Englewood Cliffs, New Jersey.

Princeton University, International Finance Section, and Arthur I. Bloomfield, for material from Arthur I. Bloomfield, *Patterns of Fluctuation in International Investment before 1914*, Princeton Studies in International Finance No. 21. Copyright © 1968, by International Finance Section, Department of Economics, Princeton University.

Princeton University Press, for:

Selection from Table 121 in Irene B. Taeuber, *The Population of Japan* (copyright © 1958 by Princeton University Press), p. 311. Reprinted by permission of Princeton University Press.

Selections from Table 1 in Ansley J. Coale and Melvin Zelnik, *New Estimates of Fertility and Population in the United States* (copyright © 1963 by Princeton University Press), pp. 21–23. Reprinted by permission of Princeton University Press.

The Royal Society, Joel Darmstadter, and Sam H. Schurr, for material from J. Darmstadter and S. H. Schurr, "World Energy Resources and Demand," *Philosophical Transactions of the Royal Society of London*, 1974, A.276, p. 413 (extracts).

Stanford University Press, for material:

Reprinted from *Japanese Economic Growth: Trend Acceleration in the Twentieth Century* by Kazushi Ohkawa and Henry Rosovsky with the permission of the publishers, Stanford University Press. © 1973 by the Board of Trustees of the Leland Stanford Junior University.

Reprinted from *China's Modern Economy in Historical Perspective*, edited by Dwight H. Perkins, with the permission of the publishers, Stanford University Press. © 1975 by the Board of Trustees of the Leland Stanford Junior University.

Statistical Publishing Society, Calcutta, for material from M. Mukherjee, *National Income of India: Trends and Structure*.

Universe Books, for material from *THE LIMITS TO GROWTH: A report for THE CLUB OF ROME's Project on the Predicament of Mankind*, by Donella H. Meadows, Dennis L. Meadows, Jørgen Randers, William W. Behrens III. A Potomac Associates book published by Universe Books, New York, 1972. Graphics by Potomac Associates.

University of California Press, for material from:

Morris David Morris, *The Emergence of an Industrial Labor Force in India: A Study of the Bombay Cotton Mills, 1854–1947*, Copyright © 1965 by The Regents of the University of California; reprinted by permission of the University of California Press.

James W. Wilkie, *The Mexican Revolution: Federal Expenditure and Social Change since 1910*, rev. ed. Copyright © 1967, 1970 by The Regents of the University of California; reprinted by permission of the University of California Press.

The University of Chicago Press, for material from:

Nathaniel H. Leff, "Tropical Trade and Development in the Nineteenth Century: The Brazilian Experience," *The Journal of Political Economy*, vol. 81, no. 3 (May/June 1973). © 1973 by the University of Chicago.

Charles Issawi (ed.), *The Economic History of Iran, 1800–1914*. © 1971 by the University of Chicago.

University of Michigan Press, for material from Alexander Eckstein, *China's Economic Development*. Copyright © by The University of Michigan 1975.

University of Ottawa Press, for material from O. J. Firestone, *Industry and Education: A Century of Canadian Development*.

University of Toronto Press, for material from Kenneth Buckley, *Capital Formation in Canada, 1896–1930*.

Verlag Weltarchiv GmbH, for material from *Intereconomics*, no. 1 (January 1975), p. 31.

Wadsworth Publishing Company, Inc., for material from *The Management of Market-Oriented Economies: A Comparative Perspective* by Philip A. Klein. © 1973 by Wadsworth Publishing Company, Inc., Belmont, California 94002. Reprinted by permission of the publisher.

The Wharton Magazine, for material reprinted with permission from "Resource Shortage in an Expanding World" by Wilfred Malenbaum, *Wharton Quarterly*, © 1973.

John Wiley & Sons, Inc., for material from:

Is the Business Cycle Obsolete? edited by Martin Bronfenbrenner. Copyright © 1969 by John Wiley & Sons, Inc. Reprinted by permission of John Wiley & Sons, Inc.

Albert Fishlow, "The American Common School Revival: Fact or Fancy?" in *Industrialization in Two Systems: Essays in Honor of Alexander Gerschenkron by a Group of His Students*, edited by Henry Rosovsky. Copyright © 1966, by John Wiley & Sons, Inc. Reprinted by permission of John Wiley & Sons, Inc.

John C. Fisher, *Energy Crises in Perspective*. Copyright © 1974, by John Wiley & Sons, Inc. Reprinted by permission of John Wiley & Sons, Inc.

Charles P. Kindleberger, *The Terms of Trade: A European Case Study*. Copyright © 1956 by The Massachusetts Institute of Technology. Reprinted by permission of John Wiley & Sons, Inc.

Yale University Press, for:

Material reprinted by permission of the Yale University Press from *Modern Economic Growth* by Simon S. Kuznets. Copyright © 1966 by Yale University.

Permission granted by Yale University Press to reprint from *The Mexican Economy* by Clark W. Reynolds, Copyright © 1970 by Yale University.

Permission granted by Yale University Press to reprint from *Essays on the Economic History of the Argentine Republic* by Carlos F. Díaz Alejandro. Copyright © 1970 by Yale University.

To Lois Nivens

Contents

Tables

Charts

Preface

I began as an economic historian in the 1930's by studying the British economy of the nineteenth century. It soon became clear that its development could not be fully understood except as part of the evolution of an expanding world economy. I decided, therefore, to study and teach economic history as the interaction between pervasive forces generated in the world economy and the stories of national growth. For some twenty years my graduate students and I turned the saga of the world economy, thus conceived, around in our hands. In 1972 I concluded it was time to try to put between covers this way of looking at things and to do so in a form which might help illuminate present and future problems in the world economy. The first result of this exercise in summation was *How It All Began*, initially planned as the opening chapter to the present volume; but the subject took on a life of its own and emerged as a separate book.

The present study is both an essay in history and a challenge to conventional neoclassical and neo-Keynesian economic theory. With all their virtues, neither provides, nor do both together, a sufficient framework for understanding the dynamic past or the character of the economic problems the world economy now confronts. Part Six, dealing with the latter, is something of a tract for the times. In this aspect, as well as in its challenge to conventional theory, the book belongs with an old tradition among economic historians, a tradition reaching back to the origins of the subject in both Adam Smith and the German historians who took exception to some of Smith's policy precepts.

As the book fell into perspective, I found that its applications to current policy were more numerous than I had originally perceived. To include these applications fully in Part Six, however, would have distorted the proportions of the study. I have chosen, therefore, to write a separate volume addressed wholly to policy matters. Part Six seeks, therefore, to define an appropriate framework for policy rather than offer detailed prescriptions.

I have aimed here at a level of exposition accessible to interested nonprofessional readers and upper-level undergraduates, to whom I have, in fact, taught much of the substance of the book over the past several years. Professional issues in contention among economic historians and analysts of economic growth are mainly confined to the notes. Although there are a good many tables and charts for those who find them useful, the major conclusions to be drawn from them are stated in the text.

In filling gaps in the data required for this study, many helped: Moses Abramovitz, Stephen Baer, Thomas Berry, T. G. Beynon, Herbert J. Bickel, William Braisted, Hollis Chenery, Howard Cottam, L. J. Deman, Alexander Eckstein, O. J. Firestone, Edward Fried, Robert Gallman, William Glade, S. A. Goldberg, Kermit Gordon, Doreen Goyer, James Grant, Walter Heller, Hans Heyman, John Holsen, Frances James, Tomasson Jannuzi, Herman Kahn, Charles P. Kindleberger, Philip Klein, Simon Kuznets, Wassily Leontief, W. Arthur Lewis, Vitaly P. Lomykin, Robert McPheeters, Wilfred Malenbaum, Edwin Martin, Ilse Mintz, B. K. Nehru, Douglass North, H. D. Potter, Stanley Roe, Paul Rosenstein-Rodan, Henry Rosovsky, Anna Schwartz, Gary Walton, Anthony Wiener, Charles Zraket, economic officers in the Australian, British, Indian, and Turkish embassies in Washington, and the OECD in Paris.

I wish to thank, in particular, Professor Berry for making available unpublished United States national income calculations and Professor Kuznets for permitting me to use unpublished national income worksheets for thirty-two countries.

I am grateful also to the following for reading in draft and criticizing portions of the text: Hossein Askari, Harley Browning, Paul English, Hafez Farmayan, O. J. Firestone, Lincoln Gordon, Richard Graham, Charles Hitch, David Kendrick, Robert McGinnis, Robert McNamara, Elspeth Rostow, J. H. Warren, and Sidney Weintraub. The detailed critiques of Part Six by Professor Gordon and Professor Rostow were particularly valuable.

Pamela Grisham, Virginia Fay, and Lois Nivens typed the various drafts of the manuscript with good cheer. In addition, Miss Nivens was, as always, a devoted editor. Carolyn Cates Wylie, of the University of Texas Press, was extraordinarily helpful and meticulous in preparing the final copy for publication.

The National Endowment for the Humanities generously provided assistance in mobilizing the data which underlie the twenty national economic histories summarized in Part Five. I had experimented in *The Process of Economic Growth* (Appendix I) with assembling and charting aggregate and sectoral data on national economies. In the course of extending that procedure, in the present study, Stuart Greenfield, my research assistant in 1975, suggested that we put the data into a computer. The N.E.H. agreed that we divert a portion of its grant for this purpose. James Peach designed a flexible interacting computer program. At various times, Joseph Pluta and Terri

Hempe, as well as Stuart Greenfield, helped mobilize the data. Frederick Fordyce and then Faisal Nasr checked the data against original sources and consolidated Appendix D. Gerald Fay designed the method and format for reducing the computerized charts of Part Five to their present form. Stephen Chase worked with the Visual Instruction Bureau of The University of Texas at Austin to complete the job and, in addition, made a good many of the charts this book contains. The Bureau of Business Research of The University of Texas at Austin kindly assisted in the reproduction of the charts used in other parts of the book.

Sources for the data charted in Part Five are given in Appendix D. The data and information on the manipulations permitted by the computer program are available from: Project Mulhall, Economics Department, Room 400 B.E.B., The University of Texas at Austin, Austin, Texas 78712. Some of my colleagues and I are now expanding the initial historical data base with respect to both the number of countries and the range of statistical series embraced, and sharing it with all who may be interested.

Publication of this study at its full length has been made possible by a grant from the Sid W. Richardson Foundation to the University of Texas Press. I am indebted, therefore, both to the generosity of the Richardson Foundation and to the enthusiasm and technical skill of my colleagues at the Press.

June 1977 W. W. Rostow
Austin, Texas

Introduction

I have chosen to tell the story of the world economy since the eighteenth century by surveying that era from five successive perspectives: the demographic transition; the overall sweep of production, trade, and price movements; the more or less regular sequence of trend periods or Kondratieff cycles; the timing and character of more conventional business cycles; and then an account of how twenty economies have thus far moved through the stages of growth, economies embracing about two-thirds of the world's population, 80 percent of its output. Each of the first five parts of the book thus marches up to the present, ending with problems that the world economy now faces. When these problems are collected, they form the policy agenda addressed in Part Six.

Contrary to the view presented in formal analyses of the limits to growth, the most critical period for industrial civilization emerges as the next quarter-century, rather than the first half of the twenty-first century. The framework for policy developed in Part Six embraces not only the fields of population, agriculture, energy, raw materials, and the environment, but also the return to regular full employment and the achievement of price stability in the advanced industrial countries.

I have structured the book in ways which deal with the past two centuries as an analytic unit because I have gradually become convinced it is possible and useful to view the saga of modern economic growth as a whole. I hope this book encourages further studies from this long perspective. Similarly, I hope the exercise of trying briefly to tell the story of twenty national economies in Part Five will convince readers that it is not impossible to get to know each of them (and others) like old friends. Put another way, I believe we need a somewhat broader and less parochial view of economic history, less chopped up by periods and nations, less reduced to statistical averages, to see clearly where we have come from and what we, as a human community, confront in the times ahead.

All works in history and the social sciences are rooted in theory. The theory used by the author determines the facts selected as relevant, the book's structure, and, ultimately, its conclusions. It is important, I believe, for an author to be explicit about his theory.

From beginning to end this book is shaped by a particular dynamic, disaggregated theory of production and prices. Portions of that theory are stated in the opening chapters of Parts Three, Four, and Five. The interested reader can find it elaborated as a whole in *The Process of Economic Growth*. It may, nevertheless, be useful briefly to summarize its character, because it differs, to a degree, from the theory of production and prices which we conventionally teach our students and which pervades the way we look at economic phenomena beyond the classroom.

At its hard core, conventional economic theory excludes or deals only abstractly with what economists call long-run economic change. That means it does not embrace effectively within its structure changes in population, in technology, or in the willingness of private or public entrepreneurs to innovate. Those exclusions permit elegant statements of static equilibrium; but such theory is of limited use, either to historians or to economic practitioners, both of whom must live in a world where the economists' long-run forces are in motion every day.

A second difficulty is that the modern theory of growth is formulated in highly aggregated terms which do not permit growth to be related to the critical technological changes taking place in particular sectors.

I believe it is possible to bring within the structure of a dynamic, disaggregated theory the forces making for population change, as well as the generation of scientific knowledge and invention, and the process of innovation. It is then possible to conceive of a dynamic equilibrium path for a peaceful, closed economy and all its sectors. Those overall and sectoral optimum paths imply that investment resources are allocated to the sectors without error or lag, taking into account changes in technology as well as demand. We can thus formulate abstractly a disaggregated, moving, rather than static, equilibrium. In fact, of course, the economies we study were not closed; they were often at war or affected by war; and investment was subject to systematic errors and lags. Moreover, the coming of new technologies and the opening of new sources of food and raw-materials supply often took the form of large discontinuous changes in the economy and its structure. And, even in the most capitalist of societies, the economic role of government was significant. What we observe, then, are dynamic, interacting national economies, trying rather clumsily to approximate optimum sectoral equilibrium paths, tending successively to undershoot and overshoot those paths.

If these various economies more or less regularly absorbed the technologies generated by the world's investment in science and invention, they grew; that is, with many irregularities and vicissitudes, their average income per capita tended to rise at rates which generally followed an S-shaped path of acceleration and deceleration once take-off occurred. That process of growth, accompanied as it regularly was by increased urbanization, education, and other social changes, underlies the demographic transition analyzed in Part One. Where investment lags were particularly long, as they have historically tended to be in expanding output from new sources of foodstuffs and raw materials, the dynamics of growth yielded the trend periods analyzed in Part Three, generally marked by rather massive undershooting and overshooting of optimum sectoral paths. Part Three reflects my theory of the cycles which Kondratieff identified but for which he offered no systematic explanation. When the lags were shorter, and investment errors more quickly corrected, the business cycles of Part Four emerged. When national growth is analyzed with particular attention to the effective absorption of the lumpy sequence of major technologies, the stages of growth of Part Five move to the center of the stage. It is this dynamic, disaggregated theory of production and prices which equally determines the emphasis in Part Six on changed directions of investment as the primary instrument for regaining momentum in the world economy and recapturing a structural balance lost since the end of 1972.

I have never regarded discussions of method as likely to be highly productive. A method is as good as the results it helps achieve. Nevertheless, a few words about method may be useful, since the self-consciousness on the subject of some contemporary economic historians has placed the issue inescapably on the agenda, where it has appeared from time to time since the field of economic history took shape.

For some forty-three years I have been trying to bring to bear modern economic theory and statistical methods in economic history. (My first exercise, as a sophomore at Yale, was the application of Keynes' *Treatise on Money* to the British inflation of 1793–1815.) I have found two dangers in this exciting and challenging line of endeavor. First, there is the danger of cutting the problem down to the size of the orderly statistical data that happen to be available. I have tried here to keep the problem, with all its sharp edges, before the reader and to bring to bear on it whatever relevant quantitative data (and qualitative evidence) I could mobilize. And where a gap remains between the problem and the insights quantitative analysis can generate (as, for example, with respect to the determinants of birth rates in various societies), I have tried to be explicit about our residual areas of ignorance or uncertainty. The second danger arises from a little-understood trade-off between complexity of method and simplicity of usable theory. Generally speaking, the fancier the method the more simple the usable theory. (I discuss and illustrate this problem in *The Journal of Economic History*, March 1971, pp. 76–86.) As a historian as well as an economist, my loyalty must be to the full complexity of the story, as nearly as I can perceive it, rather than to the formal elegance sophisticated but over-simple models can provide. The dynamic disaggregated theory of production and prices applied throughout this book is somewhat more complex than, say, a Walrasian model of equilibrium or a Harrod-Domar or neoclassical model of economic growth. I believe it produces a better framework for dealing with the realities of, say, long cycles, business cycles, or sequences of national growth than more aggregated models, and a better framework for analysis of the present state and prospects for the world economy. But it does not lend itself easily to high-powered econometric exercises, in part because the data are not available in appropriate forms. I have gladly used formal quantitative exercises when they bore in a relevant way on a particular subject; e.g., Robert Brooke Zevin on New England cotton textile production after 1815, Simon Kuznets and Hollis Chenery on average economic and social patterns in relation to GNP per capita, Ilse Mintz on business cycle patterns. But if one is trying to capture in a reasonably coherent way the evolution of the world economy over the past two centuries and the major stories of national growth (each interwoven inextricably with noneconomic history), one must, I believe, opt, on balance, for complexity of analysis rather than complexity of manipulation.

I do believe, however, that a good many of the issues raised here can be isolated and pursued with more rigorous statistical methods; for example, the relative role in trend-period phenomena of impulses from relative prices, leading sector retardation, and migration; the comparative aggregate and sectoral analysis of pairs of countries at similar stages of economic growth (Turkey-Mexico, Venezuela-Iran). I hope one effect of this study is to stimulate such further research. But, evidently, that is for others to decide.

Any effort to tell the story of the world economy over two centuries must inevitably be governed by the old academic dictum: in limitation lies mastery. There are a good many aspects of modern economic history which are not dealt with systematically here; for example, the evolution of corporations and labor unions, banks and social legislation. My *Politics and the Stages of Growth* deals with some dimensions of economic as well as social and political history set aside in the present study.

For some, at least, monetary affairs will also appear to have been slighted. In the analysis of the pre-1914 era, monetary factors appear only when I believe they left a significant impact on the course of events; e.g., in transmitting the effects of bad harvests in the eighteenth and nineteenth centuries; in helping create the setting for cyclical crises and then (in Britain, at least) cushioning their impact; in making it easier or more difficult (via interest rates) for housing booms to develop; in stimulating, under the gold standard, the inflationary diversion of resources to gold mining. In the post-1918 world of more conscious monetary policies, they emerge on stage in the 1920's with the French devaluation and the British return to the gold standard at the old rate, as well as the failure of the United States to accept its responsibilities for the trade and monetary structure of the world economy. After 1945, the rise and fall of the Bretton Woods system forms, of course, part of the narrative.

Nevertheless, it should be underlined that the view taken here of the course of production and prices—in cycles, trend periods, and the process of growth itself—would regard the nonmonetary factors as paramount. (This is a perspective I have elaborated in my essays in *The British Economy of the Nineteenth Century* and in passages for which I bear primary responsibility in A. D. Gayer et al., *Growth and Fluctuation of the British Economy, 1790–1850*, including the preface to the 1975 edition.) Men and societies have devised and evolved monetary systems which more or less met their deeper needs and purposes as they conceived them. Different monetary policies, at different times and places, might have yielded somewhat different results than history now records. The same could be said with equal or greater strength about fiscal policies. But down to 1914 modern concepts of monetary and fiscal policy did not exist, except, perhaps, in a few unorthodox minds; and prevailing notions rendered the monetary system substantially passive and responsive.

Between the wars, men and governments began to move toward more active policies designed to influence the level of demand. And since 1945 our virtuosity in these matters has considerably increased. I would certainly not deprecate the current importance of fiscal and monetary policy. But I regard them as grossly inadequate instruments for dealing with the tasks that lie ahead—a perspective that strongly colors Part Six of this book. And historically, too, a demand-oriented analysis does not suffice. So powerful were the forces operating from the side of supply that no rational or politically supportable monetary policy could have prevented, say, the rise of prices during the French Revolutionary and Napoleonic Wars (*pace* David Ricardo), their trend decline after 1873 (*pace* William Jennings Bryan and Milton Friedman), or their explosive rise in 1972–1974. Conventional macroeconomics would tend to regard supply forces operating on particular commodities as affecting relative prices but not the general price level. It took the events of the past few years to evoke from Paul Samuelson, for example, this unorthodox expostulation: "Microeconomic commodity inflation . . . refuses to remain microeconomic" ("Worldwide Stagflation," *Intermountain Economic Review*, vol. 6, no. 2 [Fall 1975], p. 9). But that is the way it has been, with both inflations and deflations, since, say, the dreadful British harvests of 1710–1712.

I introduce here this apparently narrow and parochial debate among economists because the issue at stake comes close to the heart of this book and its purpose: to contribute to a unity of view as between the dynamics of demand and supply (the aggregates and the sectors) that we require both to understand the past and to make our way through the next quarter-century with reasonable success.

Part One

The Demographic Transition

1

Two Centuries of Expansion in World Population

We begin with some important numbers. Table I-1 and Chart I-1 show how the world's population more than tripled in the two centuries after 1750 and is likely to be more than twice its 1950 level by the year 2000, unless a demographic catastrophe intervenes.[1] Chart I-1 exhibits the rise in the world's population on a geometric scale, in which a constant rate of increase would appear as a straight line. Its visual effect is to underplay the scale of the demographic revolution now under way. Chart I-2, including estimates reaching back to 8000 B.C., uses an arithmetic scale and catches better the drama of modern experience with population growth.[2]

The difference in the impression imparted by Charts I-1 and I-2 goes to the heart of the issue with which Part Six of this book ultimately grapples: Is the global industrial civilization created by man in the past two centuries viable? If so, under what conditions? Chart I-1 imparts an impression of gradually increasing growth rates, with future projections within the range of prior experience. If one carries in one's head a sense that progress is normal and man's technological virtuosity is capable of dealing with the economic challenges of the future as well as it did with those of the past, Chart I-1 does not evoke an image of impending doomsday. But Chart I-2 with its longer sweep of history and its measurement of absolute numbers of men, women, and children, rather than growth rates, suggests immediately the grandiose nature of man's performance since 1750 and his magnificent (or, perhaps, tragic) arrogance in programming, as it were, for a six-billion-plus population level by the year 2000. One is led automatically to ask: How many human beings can a finite planet support? When and how will that frightening, almost vertical curve level off?

For the moment, however, the question is retrospective. How did the human race get to a position where it has already produced the mothers of the children who, along with survivors from the present, appear to guarantee a population of more than six billion by the year 2000? As Chart I-1 shows, the result emerges from rather simple arithmetic: a gradually rising rate of increase on a progressively

TABLE I-1. *"Medium" Estimates of Population of the World and Major Areas, 1750–1950, and Projections to 2000*

Areas	Population (Millions)					
	1750	1800	1850	1900	1950	2000
World total	791	978	1,262	1,650	2,515	6,130
Asia (exc. USSR)	498	630	801	925	1,381	3,458
China (Mainland)	200	323	430	436	560	1,034
India and Pakistan	190	195	233	285	434	1,269
Japan	30	30	31	44	83	122
Indonesia	12	13	23	42	77	250
Remainder of Asia (exc. USSR)	67	69	87	118	227	783
Africa	106	107	111	133	222	768
North Africa	10	11	15	27	53	192
Remainder of Africa	96	96	96	106	169	576
Europe (exc. USSR)	125	152	208	296	392	527
USSR	42	56	76	134	180	353
America	18	31	64	156	328	992
Northern America	2	7	26	82	166	354
Middle and South America	16	24	38	74	162	638
Oceania	2	2	2	6	13	32

Source: John D. Durand, "The Modern Expansion of World Population," *Proceedings of the American Philosophical Society*, vol. 111, no. 3 (June 22, 1967), p. 137. It should be noted that the 1973 "medium" United Nations estimate of world population in the year 2000 was 6.4 billion.

Note: Figures have been rounded; totals do not in all cases equal the sums of component figures.

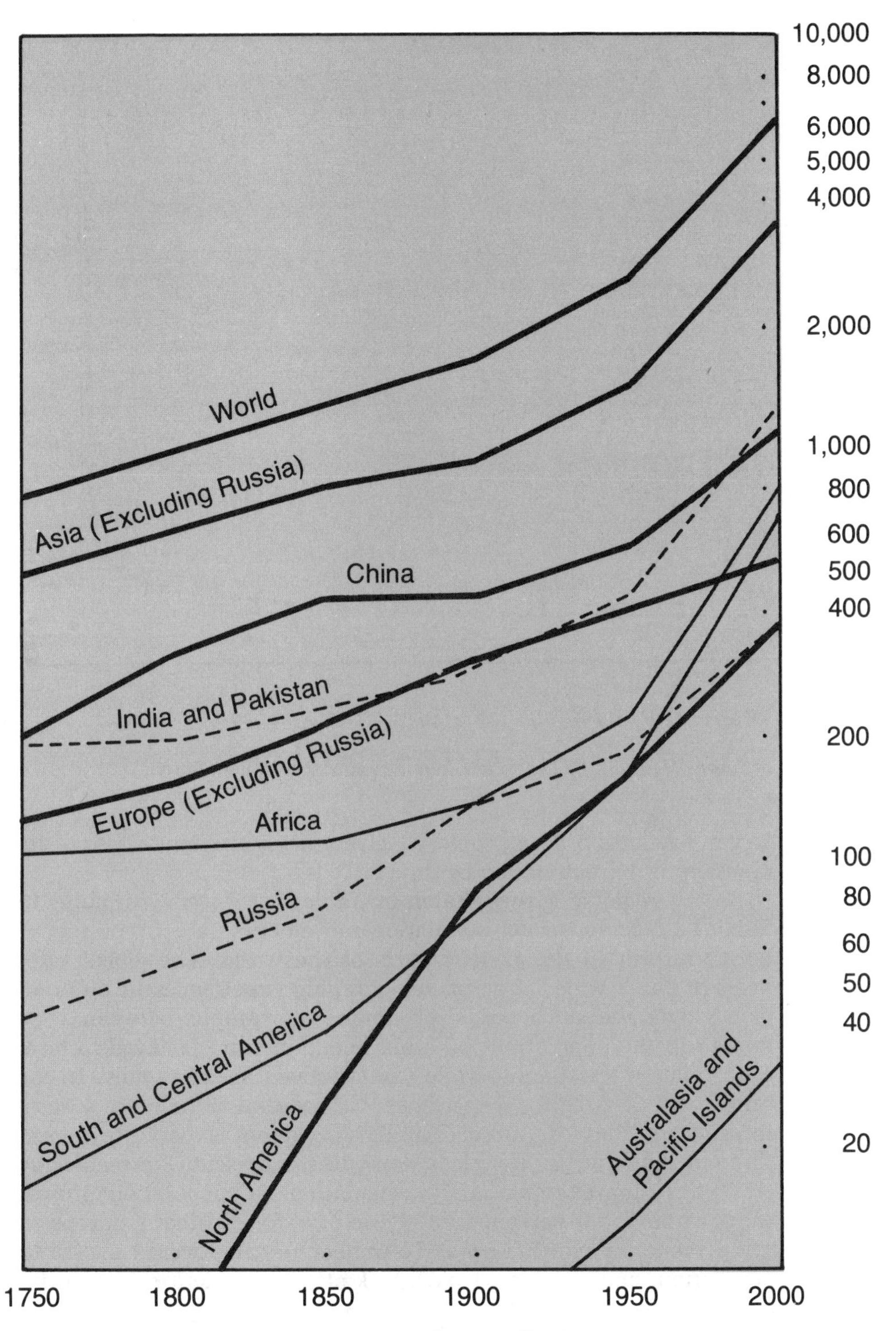

CHART I-1. *Population: The World and Major Regions, 1750–2000*

Source: E. A. Wrigley, *Population and History*, p. 207, from data of Durand, "The Modern Expansion of World Population," p. 137.

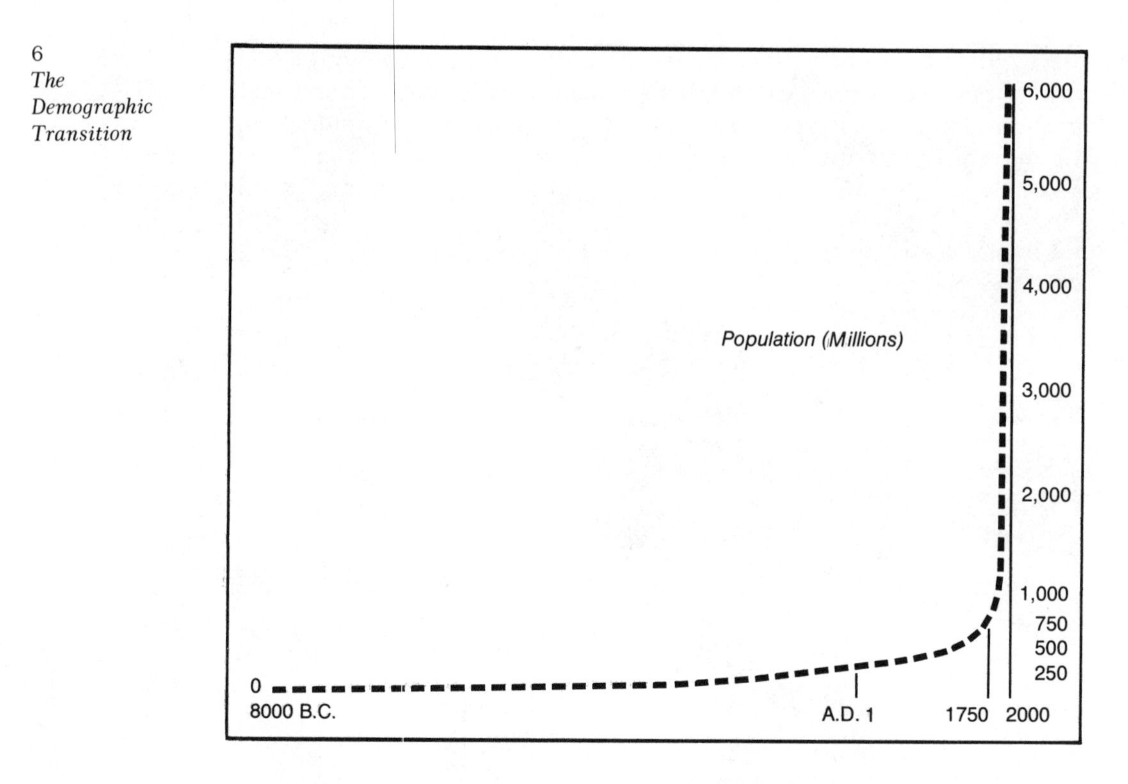

CHART I-2. *Long-Range Trend of World Population Growth*

Source: Durand, "The Modern Expansion of World Population," p. 139.

larger population base. Table I-2 gives the approximate rate of increase in world population by time periods.

As the regional growth rates in Table I-3 (based on figures in Table I-1) demonstrate, population movements have by no means been uniform in the various parts of the world. The global rates average out a wide range of demographic experiences in different places over the same period of time. For example, between 1750 and 1800 the populations of India and Japan are believed to have been relatively stagnant, while China moved ahead rapidly. In the same period, America experienced a population increase almost three times that of Europe. Similar ranges of experience persist through the other time periods down to the present. Between 1965 and 1971, for example, U.N. calculations of population growth range from a 0.6 percent rate of increase for Northern Europe to 3.1 percent for North Africa. To understand the overall course of population, one must, obviously, look at the experience of the principal nations and regions.

Before doing so, however, it may be useful to note four major forces, operating widely if not universally, which leave a strong imprint on the global population growth rates in Table I-2.

1. *The Eighteenth-Century Population Surge.* The latter half of

the eighteenth century was marked in China and Europe by a pervasive increase in population based on release from population constraints of the previous century, associated with war and epidemic; the introduction of certain new crops derived from the Western

TABLE I-2. *Approximate World Population Growth Rates, 1750–1970 (Annual Percentage Rate of Increase)*

1750–1800	0.4
1800–1850	0.5
1850–1900	0.5
1900–1920	0.6
1920–1930	1.1
1930–1940	1.0
1940–1950	1.0
1950–1960	1.8
1960–1970	1.9

Sources: Durand, "The Modern Expansion of World Population," pp. 137, 140, and U.N. data for 1950–1960, 1960–1970 (*United Nations Demographic Yearbook, 1974* [New York, 1974], p. 105).

TABLE I-3. *Approximate Regional Population Growth Rates, 1750–2000 (Annual Percentage Rate of Increase)*

	1750–1800	1800–1850	1850–1900	1900–1950	1950–2000
World total	0.4	0.5	0.5	0.8	1.8
Asia (exc. USSR)	0.5	0.5	0.3	0.8	1.9
China (Mainland)	1.0	0.6	0.0	0.5	1.2
India and Pakistan	0.1	0.3	0.4	0.8	2.2
Japan	0.0	0.1	0.7	1.3	0.8
Indonesia	0.2	1.2	1.2	1.2	2.4
Remainder of Asia (exc. USSR)	0.1	0.5	0.7	1.3	2.5
Africa	0.0	0.1	0.4	1.0	2.5
North Africa	0.2	0.5	1.2	1.4	2.8
Remainder of Africa	0.0	0.0	0.2	0.9	2.5
Europe (exc. USSR)	0.4	0.6	0.7	0.6	0.6
USSR	0.6	0.6	1.1	0.6	1.4
America	1.1	1.5	1.8	1.5	2.2
Northern America	—	2.7	2.3	1.4	1.5
Middle and South America	0.8	0.9	1.3	1.6	2.8
Oceania	—	—	—	1.6	1.8

Source: Durand, "The Modern Expansion of World Population," p. 137.

Hemisphere; significant expansion of acreage in certain regions; improved commerce in agricultural products; and a decline in certain infectious diseases which had operated earlier to constrict population growth. So far as Europe is concerned this increase was not merely the prelude to modern population growth. It was also the third major upswing in a sequence that began with the population expansion of the twelfth and thirteenth centuries, followed by the decline of the fourteenth and first half of the fifteenth centuries. A second wave of expansion then began which was checked in the seventeenth century, yielding decline or relative stagnation, until expansion began again in the second quarter of the eighteenth century. In seventeenth-century Spain, population declined; in France and Italy, on balance, it stagnated; in England, there was a sharp deceleration of population growth from about 1630. We know somewhat less about the long-term history of the Chinese population; but it is likely that, as in Western Europe, it moved cyclically, both reflecting and playing an active role in the undulating sequence of China's political dynasties. The demographic crisis of China in the nineteenth century (with population approximately stagnant between 1850 and 1900) suggests that, without the coming of the industrial revolution at the end of the eighteenth century, Europe might have also experienced a demographic setback; for it was the American railroads that opened up new food supplies for Europe in the third quarter of the nineteenth century, and Europe's new industrial virtuosity that permitted enlarged food imports to be financed.

2. *The Initial Impact of the Industrial Revolution.* In the nineteenth century the population of the nations first caught up in the industrial revolution generally increased more rapidly than the population in those nations temporarily left behind. Infant mortality and the ravages of infectious disease remained powerful forces in the industrializing West; but improvements in food, shelter, clothing, water supply, and sanitation gradually brought down death rates; and this decline outweighed the usually somewhat later decline in birth rates and family size that also accompanied industrialization. Urban life and the rise in per capita incomes systematically set up constraints and incentives to limit the size of families. Meanwhile, population moved out of Europe to the Western Hemisphere and Australasia, where the economic environment permitted even more rapid increases in population.

3. *The Explosive Impact of Modern Medicine.* In the nineteenth century, only smallpox yielded to new medical insight among the major diseases; but starting round about 1900 modern science, galvanized by the earlier work of Pasteur, Koch, and others, began to make direct, systematic, and statistically significant inroads on infant mortality and infectious disease. The first impact of these developments came in the more economically advanced countries; but the death rate began to fall significantly in India in the 1920's; and, after the Second World War, the death rate was brought down

dramatically by DDT, antibiotics, and other medical innovations. The sequence is clearly suggested in Table I-4, showing the movement of death rates in the Indian subcontinent between the periods 1911–1921 and 1965–1971. India experienced in thirty years, from the 1930's to the 1960's, a decline in death rates it took British society about a century and a quarter to achieve. The Indian death rate now approximates that of the more advanced parts of Western Europe at the opening of the twentieth century. But over the past fifty years the Indian birth rate has fallen only from 49 per thousand to, perhaps, 35. This kind of relative movement of death and birth rates is typical of Asia (except Japan), the Middle East, Africa, and Latin America. Thus, the current radical increase in population in the developing world.

The decline in death rates in the more advanced part of the world has been, during the twentieth century, more modest, as the reasonably typical figures for the United Kingdom in Table I-5 indicate.

TABLE I-4. *Death Rate (per 1,000 of Population), 1911–1974, Indian Subcontinent*

1911–1921	47
1921–1931	36
1931–1941	31
1950–1955	25
1965–1974	17

Sources: D. V. Glass and E. Grebenik, "World Population, 1800–1950," p. 84; and U.N. data for 1965–1974 (*United Nations Demographic Yearbook 1974*, p. 105).

TABLE I-5. *Death Rate (per 1,000 of Population), 1896–1971, United Kingdom*

1896–1900	17.7
1906–1910	14.7
1911–1915	14.3
1916–1920	14.4
1921–1925	12.1
1926–1930	12.1
1931–1935	12.0
1936–1940	12.5
1941–1945	12.8
1946–1950	11.8
1951–1955	11.7
1967–1971	11.7

Sources: TABLE I-7, below; and U.N. data for 1967–1971 (*United Nations Demographic Yearbook, 1971* [New York, 1972], p. 694).

War and acute depression have left their marks on these figures, breaking or decelerating a decline rendered inherently slow, as the infectious diseases were conquered and the hard-core problems of cancer and circulatory diseases remained. Over this seventy-year span the British birth rate per thousand declined from 29.3 to 16.7: thus, the deceleration in population growth typical of the advanced industrial world in the twentieth century.

4. *The Movement toward Stagnant Population in the Advanced Industrial Societies: the 1930's and the 1960's.* As the 1970's began, world population as a whole was expanding at an annual rate of 2 percent; but at just this time there was a rather dramatic change in population prospects in certain of the more advanced societies. They began to move toward a position of prospective population stagnation or decline. This is best seen by examining net reproduction rates for the female populations. This rate measures the number of daughters who would be born to a group of girl babies by the end of their child-bearing period, assuming that current rates and patterns of fertility and mortality remain fixed. A net reproduction rate of 1.00 implies that in the long term population will remain stable. During the depression of the 1930's net reproduction rates in a number of advanced countries fell below this level. After the war, there was a widespread increase in birth rates as well as a resumed decline

TABLE I-6. *Net Reproduction Rates, Selected Advanced Industrial Countries, 1935–1939, 1955–1959, and Latest Figure*

	1935–1939	1955–1959	Latest Figure
Austria	—	1.12	0.90 (1974)
Belgium	0.96 (1939)	1.14	1.04 (1971)
Bulgaria	—	1.03	1.07 (1968)
Canada	1.16	1.82	0.91 (1973)
Czechoslovakia	—	1.23	1.02 (1972)
Denmark	0.94	1.19	0.91 (1973)
Finland	0.99 (1936–1939)	1.31	0.81 (1971)
France	0.86 (1935–1937)	1.27 (1956–1960)	1.10 (1973)
Germany (Federal Republic)	—	1.04	0.80 (1972)
Germany (GDR)	—	1.11 (1959)	1.00 (1971)
Hungary	1.04 (1930–1931)	1.07	0.90 (1973)
Italy	1.18 (1936–1939)	1.08 (1959)	1.14 (1967)
Japan	1.49	0.96	1.05 (1967)
Luxembourg	—	0.98	0.99 (1968)
Netherlands	1.15	1.46	1.29 (1968)
Norway	0.81	1.32	1.02 (1974)
Poland	1.15 (1932–1934)	1.52	1.05 (1973)
Sweden	0.78 (1936–1939)	1.06	0.90 (1974)
United Kingdom (England and Wales)	0.79	1.13	0.96 (1973)
United States	0.96	1.73	0.89 (1974)
USSR	1.53 (1938–1939)	1.29 (1958–1959)	1.14 (1972–1973)
Yugoslavia	—	1.55 (1950–1954)	1.06 (1972)

Source: *Population Index*, April 1973, April 1974, April 1975, and April 1976.

in death rates. A rise in net reproduction rates reflected both factors. During the 1960's, however, birth rates fell off in a good many countries, again bringing net reproduction rates down toward 1.00, or below. This sequence is indicated in Table I-6.[3] In the thirteen countries where comparison is possible (excepting Japan), an average increase in net reproduction rates of about 25 percent, from the late 1930's to the late 1950's, was just about canceled out by the decline of birth rates in the 1960's and early 1970's. Birth rates in modern times have proved surprisingly volatile in advanced industrial societies and have several times belied predictions. The postwar surge in birth rates in Europe, North America, and other advanced industrial societies was unpredicted.[4] It reflected in part, of course, a return to normal life of men and women in the armed forces; but it persisted longer than that process can account for. Then the interwar trend resumed. No one can predict the future course of birth rates with confidence. We have as much still to learn about the dynamics of fertility in advanced industrial societies as in developing nations.

2

Population Dynamics among the Early-Comers to Industrialization

Against the background of these four general observations, we turn to a brief but more detailed view of demographic experience over the past two centuries in the major regions of the world. In particular, we shall focus on the demographic transition; that is, the sequence of declining death and birth rates that accompanied economic and social modernization, yielding a phase first of increasing then of decelerating rates of population increase. It is the incomplete stage of the demographic transition in the developing regions of the world that accounts for the urgency of the population problem now and over the coming several generations.

The heart of European population experience has been a slow fall in death rates, accelerating after 1900 as the economic and social environment, and then medical virtuosity, improved, followed in time by a decline in birth rates, yielding a majestic population surge which may have largely run its course by the 1970's. The movement of birth and death rates was, of course, not continuous. Short-term movements were in some areas still sensitive to the harvests as well as to business fluctuations and international conflict. Moreover, the experience among the various European states was not uniform, as Table I-7 reveals.[5]

Major variations in Table I-7 relate both to the timing of industrialization and to special circumstances in particular European societies.

The uniformities and variations of the European demographic revolution are roughly captured in Table I-8, which exhibits the timing of four critical population benchmarks for twenty European countries over the period 1825–1971.

In general, the benchmarks occur in sequence; that is, the fall in the death rate below 20 per thousand is followed by the decline below 30 per thousand in birth rates. A further decline of the birth rate below 20 per thousand generally precedes a fall in the death rate close to or below 10 per thousand.

As Table I-8 makes clear, the demographic revolution unfolded in broad synchronization with the diffusion of industry and the shift from rural to urban life. The European countries of Northern and Western Europe, experiencing take-off from 1783 to about 1890, form a quite distinct group, as do the relative late-comers of Southern and Eastern Europe, whose take-offs were completed in the twentieth century. Data for the USSR, the United States, and Japan, discussed at a later point in the chapter, are included.

The average birth rate in 1906–1910 for a sample of eleven nations in the former group, coming early to industrialization, was 27 per thousand; for a sample of eight of the European late-comers, 37 per thousand, not far below the maximum rates in traditional societies.[6] For death rates the comparable figures were 16 and 24, respectively. The dramatic narrowing of the demographic gap in Europe and Japan in the next sixty years, under the joint impact of industrialization and the medical revolution of the twentieth century, is indicated by the United Nations figures for 1965–1971 shown in Table I-9.[7] For the first time since the latter part of the eighteenth century, the European demographic experience became approximately homogeneous and quite similar to that of both North America and Japan; and this relative homogeneity emerged at a time when the levels of GNP per capita among these regions still varied over a considerable range. As we shall see in Part Six, hopes for future world population stabilization hinge on a similar narrowing of birth-rate differentials among nations which entered into sustained economic growth at different time periods, in an era where modern medicine has already greatly narrowed the gap in death rates.

Along the way there were a number of special cases in Europe. A precocious adoption of birth control by the French peasantry, to avoid excessive parcelization of the land, kept the birth rate systematically lower in France than in most of Western Europe from the end of the eighteenth century down to the First World War. In fact, contrary to the usual pattern, the decline of French birth rates slightly preceded the decline in death rates, beginning as early as 1776–1780. Birth control also came early to Switzerland. Although data are not provided in the tables, the traumatic famine of the 1840's led to a pattern of emigration and foregone and late marriages in Ireland, yielding a protracted period of population decline which stabilized during the interwar years at a level about half that of 1840, as emigration slackened off. Birth rates and population increase in the Netherlands remained somewhat above those of the rest of Western Europe, due, apparently, to a sense of political and social competition between the two major religious communities in the country combined with a precociously low death rate. Perhaps most important for the strategic and military history of Europe, German birth rates and population increase remained significantly above those of France and the rest of Western Europe until the interwar years.

The demographic transition in Russia and the USSR can be less clearly documented than that for most of the rest of Europe. Data are more scanty; boundaries shift; terrible war losses are suffered;

TABLE I-7. *Crude Birth and Death Rates of European Countri 1841–1850 to 1951–1955 (Rates per 1,000 Total Populatio*

		1841–1850	1851–1860	1861–1870	1876–1880	18 18
Austria[a]	BR	—	—	39.6	41.0	4(
	DR	—	—	31.5	33.2	3(
Belgium	BR	30.5	30.4	32.2	32.0	29
	DR	24.4	22.6	23.8	21.8	2(
Bulgaria	BR	—	—	—	—	–
	DR	—	—	—	—	27
Czechoslovakia	BR	—	—	—	—	–
	DR	—	—	—	—	–
Denmark	BR	30.5	32.5	30.8	32.1	31
	DR	20.5	20.5	19.9	19.4	18
Finland	BR	35.5	35.9	34.7	36.9	34
	DR	23.5	28.6	32.6	22.7	20
France	BR	27.3	26.1	26.1	25.3	23
	DR	23.2	23.7	23.6	22.5	22
Germany	BR	36.1	35.3	37.2	39.2	36
	DR	26.8	26.4	26.9	26.1	24
Greece	BR	—	—	—	—	–
	DR	—	—	—	—	–
Hungary	BR	—	—	—	—	–
	DR	—	—	—	—	–
Italy	BR	—	—	37.9	37.0	37
	DR	—	—	30.9	29.5	27
Netherlands	BR	33.0	33.3	35.7	36.4	33
	DR	26.2	25.6	25.4	22.9	20
Norway	BR	30.7	33.0	30.8	31.8	30
	DR	18.2	17.1	18.0	16.6	17
Poland	BR	—	—	—	—	–
	DR	—	—	—	—	–
Portugal	BR	—	—	—	33.3	32.
	DR	—	—	—	23.2	22
Rumania	BR	—	—	41.8	40.9	39.
	DR	—	—	26.6	28.7	30.
Spain	BR	—	—	37.8	—	36.
	DR	—	—	30.6	—	31.
Sweden	BR	31.1	32.8	31.4	30.3	28.
	DR	20.6	21.7	20.2	18.3	16.
Switzerland	BR	29.8	27.8	30.2	31.3	27.
	DR	22.8	22.4	23.0	23.1	20.
United Kingdom (England and Wales)[k]	BR	32.6	34.1	35.2	35.3	31.
	DR	22.4	22.2	22.5	20.8	18.
Scotland	BR	—	34.1[l]	(35.0)	34.8	31.
	DR	—	20.8[l]	(22.1)	20.6	18.
Yugoslavia	BR	—	—	—	—	—
	DR	—	—	—	—	—

[a] Austria-Hungary before 1906. [b] 1945–1947. [c] 1951–1954. [d] 1940–19
[e] West Germany. [f] 1946–1949. [g] 1935–1938. [h] 1953. [i] 1948–1950. [j] 1947–19
[k] Birth rates before 1876 not corrected for under-registration. [l] 1855–1860.
Source: Glass and Grebenik, "World Population, 1800–1950," pp. 68–69.

96–00	1906–1910	1911–1915	1916–1920	1921–1925	1926–1930	1931–1935	1936–1940	1941–1945	1946–1950	1951–1955
3.2	34.0	22.1	16.0	21.9	17.7	14.4	14.7	19.1	16.7	15.0
5.6	22.5	18.3	21.1	15.6	14.5	13.3	13.9	14.4	15.4	12.2
9.0	24.7	20.9	14.7	20.5	18.6	16.9	15.5	13.9	17.3	16.7
3.2	15.9	14.6	51.8	13.4	13.7	13.0	13.2	15.1	13.5	12.2
1.3	42.1	38.8	26.5	39.0	33.1	29.3	24.2	22.1	24.6[b]	20.7[c]
4.1	23.8	22.3	23.1	20.8	17.8	15.5	13.9	13.2	14.0[b]	10.1
—	—	—	24.6	27.1	23.2	19.6	17.1	20.8	22.4	22.0
—	—	—	18.6	16.1	15.3	13.3	13.2	14.3	13.4	10.9
9.9	28.2	25.7	24.0	22.2	19.4	17.8	17.9	20.3	21.6	17.9
5.4	13.7	12.8	13.1	11.2	11.1	10.9	10.6	10.0	9.6	9.0
3.5	30.6	27.3	23.3	23.1	21.1	18.4	20.2	20.1	27.0	22.8
9.5	17.2	16.0	19.5	14.1	13.9	12.6	13.2	17.1	11.7	9.6
1.9	20.2	17.4	13.2	19.3	18.2	16.5	15.1	14.7	20.7	19.5
9.6	19.1	21.5	22.1	17.2	16.8	15.7	13.2	17.9	13.8	12.8
5.0	31.6	26.3	17.8	22.1	18.4	16.6	19.4	17.4[d]	16.6[ef]	15.8[e]
1.3	17.5	17.7	19.1	13.2	11.8	11.2	11.9	12.2[d]	11.2[ef]	10.5[e]
—	—	—	—	21.0	29.9	29.5	26.8	19.6	25.5	19.4
—	—	—	—	15.1	16.4	16.5	14.5	17.3	10.8	7.1
—	36.7	32.8	16.0	29.4	26.0	22.5	20.1	19.3[d]	19.9	21.1
—	25.0	24.2	22.4	19.9	17.0	15.8	14.3	13.9[d]	14.8	11.4
3.9	32.6	31.2	23.0	29.6	26.7	23.9	23.2	20.6	21.2	18.4
2.9	21.1	19.6	24.3	17.3	15.9	14.0	13.9	14.6	11.7	9.9
2.2	29.6	27.8	26.1	25.6	23.2	21.1	20.3	21.8	25.9	22.2
7.2	14.3	12.8	13.7	10.3	9.9	8.9	8.7	10.2	9.5	7.5
9.3	26.0	24.9	24.5	22.1	17.9	15.2	15.0	17.7	20.8	18.7
4.6	13.7	13.2	14.1	11.5	11.0	10.4	10.2	10.7	9.3	8.7
—	39.8	—	—	34.7	32.3	27.6	25.4[g]	—	27.9[f]	30.1
—	22.8	—	—	18.5	16.7	14.6	14.0	—	11.4[j]	11.1
1.6	30.9	33.7	30.6	33.3	30.9	29.0	27.1	24.5	25.6	23.9
3.2	20.0	20.4	26.6	20.7	18.4	16.9	15.9	15.8	13.8	11.7
9.3	40.3	42.0	—	37.9	35.2	32.9	30.2	23.2	—	23.7[h]
5.8	26.0	24.5	—	23.0	21.2	20.6	19.6	19.1	—	11.5[h]
4.5	33.2	30.8	28.8	29.8	28.5	27.0	22.0	22.0	22.3	20.3
9.0	24.0	22.1	24.6	20.2	17.9	16.3	17.9	15.3	11.9	10.2
5.9	25.4	23.1	21.2	19.1	15.9	14.1	14.5	17.7	19.0	15.5
5.1	14.3	14.1	14.5	12.1	11.8	11.6	11.7	10.8	10.4	9.8
3.4	26.0	22.7	19.2	19.5	17.5	16.4	15.4	17.9	19.4	17.3
3.1	16.0	14.3	15.0	12.5	12.1	11.8	11.6	11.4	11.2	10.1
9.3	26.3	23.6	20.1	19.9	16.7	15.0	14.7	15.9	18.0	15.2
7.7	14.7	14.3	14.4	12.1	12.1	12.0	12.5	12.8	11.8	11.7
9.0	27.6	25.4	22.8	23.0	20.0	18.2	17.6	17.8	19.8	17.8
7.9	16.1	15.7	15.0	13.9	13.6	13.2	13.5	13.8	—	12.1
—	39.0	—	—	34.9	34.2	31.9	27.9	—	28.3	28.8
—	24.7	—	—	20.1	20.0	18.0	15.9	—	13.3[i]	12.5

and only in relatively recent times is there evidence on population dynamics among the Asian populations of the Soviet Union.

Birth rates for prerevolutionary Russia suggest a rise from 40 per thousand in 1811–1820 to figures over 50 as late as 1881–1890. But with the Russian take-off in the 1890's, and increased urbanization, the figure began to fall, reaching 47 per thousand in 1901–1910. The postwar settlement divested Russia of some eleven western provinces where birth rates were generally lower than the average. Birth rates thus remained extraordinarily high in the European portion of the Soviet Union well into the 1920's, with levels of 47 per thousand in rural areas, 39 in urban areas, and an overall figure of 43, as late as 1926.[8] Accelerated urbanization and policies encouraging abortion brought the birth rate down to 30 per thousand in 1935. A reversal of policy in the period 1934–1936 may have lifted the

TABLE I-8. *Timing of the Demographic Transition in Europe, the United States, and Japan (Rates per 1,000 Total Population)*

	Death Rate Falls below 20	Birth Rate Falls below 30	Birth Rate Falls below 20	Death Rate Falls below 10
Norway	Pre-1841	1906–1910	1926–1930	1946–1950
Denmark	1861–1870	1896–1900	1926–1930	1946–1950
Sweden	1876–1880	1886–1890	1921–1925	1951–1955
England and Wales	1886–1890	1896–1900	1921–1925	(11.6, 1971)
Scotland	1886–1890	1906–1910	1931–1935	(11.8, 1971)
Switzerland	1896–1900	1841–1850	1916–1920	post-1955
Finland	1896–1900	1911–1915	1931–1935	1951–1955
Netherlands	1896–1900	1906–1910	post-1955	1926–1930
Belgium	1896–1900	1886–1890	1926–1930[a]	(12.2, 1971)
France	1906–1910	1831–1835	1911–1915	(10.7, 1971)
Germany	1906–1910	1911–1915	1926–1930[a]	(11.7, 1971)
Austria	1911–1915	1911–1915	1926–1930[a]	(13.0, 1971)
Italy	1911–1915	1921–1925[a]	1951–1955	1951–1955
Poland	1921–1925	1931–1935	post-1955	post-1955
Hungary	1921–1925	1921–1925[a]	1946–1950[a]	(11.9, 1971)
Portugal	1926–1930	1931–1935	1969	(10.4, 1970)
Spain	1926–1930	1916–1920	1969	post-1955
Bulgaria	1926–1930	1931–1935[a]	post-1955	post-1955
Yugoslavia	1931–1935	1936–1940	1967	post-1955
Rumania	1936–1940	1951–1955[a]	(21.1, 1970)	post-1955
USSR[b]	1938	1945–1950	1964	1950–1955
United States[c]	1868–1872	1920	1932	1948
Japan[d]	1926	1938–1940	1955	1950–1955

[a] War-time aberrant figures set aside.
[b] For discussion, see pp. 13, 16–17.
[c] For discussion, see below, pp. 22–24.
[d] For discussion, see below, pp. 24–25.
Sources: TABLE I-7, above; and *United Nations Demographic Yearbook, 1971*.

TABLE I-9. *European, North American, and Japanese Birth and Death Rates, 1965–1971, in Relation to GNP per Capita (Rates per 1,000 Total Population)*

	Births	Deaths	GNP per Capita, (U.S. $, 1967)
Western Europe	17	11	$1,625
Southern Europe	19	9	604
Eastern Europe	17	10	914
Northern Europe	17	11	2,073
USSR	18	8	970
North America	18	9	3,553
Japan	18	7	1,000

Sources: Birth and death rates from *United Nations Demographic Yearbook, 1971*, p. 111; 1967 GNP per capita calculated from Thorkil Kristensen, *Development in Rich and Poor Countries* (New York: Praeger, 1974), pp. 156–157 (World Bank data).

figure to 38 per thousand by 1938.[9] This was a transient phenomenon. In the post-1945 period, birth rates held during the 1950's at about 25 but then fell rapidly in the first half of the 1960's to a level of 17, with an urban-rural spread in 1967 of 15.5–19.7 per thousand. The surge of births in the immediate postwar period yielded a population structure in recent years which is experiencing some slight increase in birth rates. The demographic transition in Russian birth rates—from over 40 to under 20 per thousand—is, thus, a rather brisk phenomenon, covering forty years at most.

Evidence on Russian death rates becomes available only from 1899. Death rates in those parts of Czarist Russia which remained in the Soviet Union declined from 33.1 (1899–1901) to 29.6 (1911–1913).[10] There is no direct evidence for a death rate decline preceding (as in a typical demographic transition) the birth rate decline which began in the 1890's. But the accelerated increase of the Russian population in the second half of the nineteenth century suggests that this may have been the case. By the mid-1920's, Soviet death rates were appreciably below pre-1914 levels. The fall below 20 per thousand came, as in Rumania, in the late 1930's. After the Second World War, the Soviet death rate fell again, averaging 8 per thousand for the period 1967–1971.

The interplay of Soviet birth and death rates, against the background of the population's age structure, yielded a sharp decline in the rate of increase in the 1960's: an annual rate of increase of 1.8 percent in 1958 had fallen almost in half a decade later. The rate of population increase has been much higher in the Central Asian republics than in the European portion of the Soviet Union. Thus, between 1959 and 1970 the proportion of the three major Slavic groups in the population (Great Russians, Ukrainians, and Belorussians) fell from 76.3 percent to 74.0 percent of the total.

Demographic history, as well as history in general, has been significantly affected by migration. The movement of slaves across the South Atlantic; the colonial settlement of Europeans in the Americas, Australia, and New Zealand; the flow of Chinese to overseas communities in Southeast Asia and of Europeans and Indians to Africa all left abiding marks on the racial structure of populations and on the political and social life of nations. But the most significant population movement, in both scale and demographic consequence, was the European emigration of the nineteenth and early twentieth centuries.

Table I-10 and Chart I-3 suggest its scale, composition, and timing.[11]

It is by no means easy to measure the demographic effect of population movement on this scale. As Table I-11 shows, net immigration played a fluctuating but increasing role in the white population increase in the United States, down to the First World War.[12] In a mood anticipating Thomas Malthus, Benjamin Franklin as early as 1751 took the view that immigration would, in time, "eat the natives out";[13] that is, the pressure of population increase would raise death

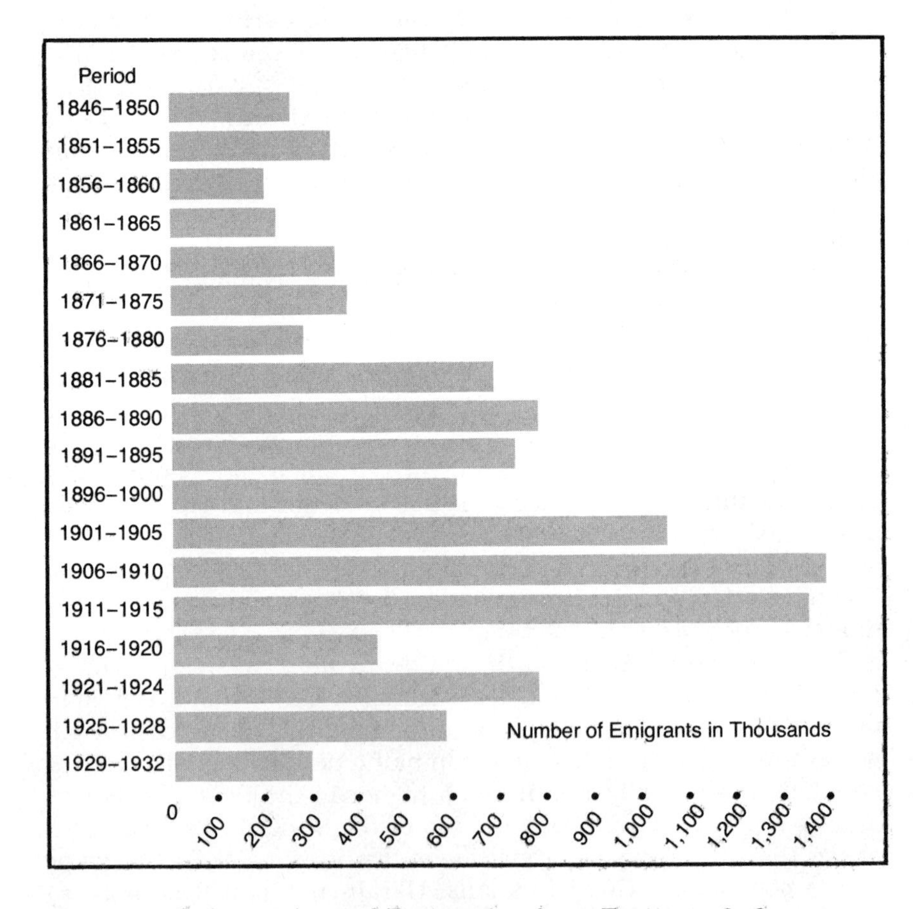

CHART I-3. *Intercontinental Emigration from Europe, 1846–1932 (Annual Averages in Five- and Four-Year Periods)*

Source: A. M. Carr-Saunders, *World Population: Past Growth and Present Trends*, p. 51.

TABLE I-10. *World Intercontinental Migration, 1821–1932*

Emigration, 1846–1932

Country of Emigration	Period Covered	Total (Thousands)
Europe:		
Austria-Hungary	1846–1932	5,196
Belgium	1846–1932	193
British Isles	1846–1932	18,020
Denmark	1846–1932	387
Finland	1871–1932	371
France	1846–1932	519
Germany	1846–1932	4,889
Italy	1846–1932	10,092
Malta	1911–1932	63
Holland	1846–1932	224
Norway	1846–1932	854
Poland	1920–1932	642
Portugal	1846–1932	1,805
Russia	1846–1924	2,253
Spain	1846–1932	4,653
Sweden	1846–1932	1,203
Switzerland	1846–1932	332
Total (Europe)		51,696
Other Countries:		
British India	1846–1932	1,194
Cape Verde	1901–1927	30
Japan	1846–1932	518
St. Helena	1896–1924	12
Grand total		53,450

Immigration, 1821–1932

Country of Immigration	Period Covered	Total (Thousands)
America:		
Argentina	1856–1932	6,405
Brazil	1821–1932	4,431
British West Indies	1836–1932	1,587
Canada	1821–1932	5,206
Cuba	1901–1932	857
Guadeloupe	1856–1924	42
Dutch Guiana	1856–1931	69
Mexico	1911–1931	226
Newfoundland	1841–1924	20
Paraguay	1881–1931	26
United States	1821–1932	34,244
Uruguay	1836–1932	713
Total (America)		53,826
Asia:		
Philippines	1911–1929	90
Oceania:		
Australia	1861–1932	2,913
Fiji	1881–1926	79
Hawaii	1911–1931	216
New Caledonia	1896–1932	32
New Zealand	1851–1932	594
Africa:		
Mauritius	1836–1932	573
Seychelles	1901–1932	12
South Africa	1881–1932	852
Grand total		59,187

Source: Carr-Saunders, *World Population*, p. 49.

TABLE I-11. *Estimated Growth of the White Population from Natural Increase and Net Immigration, by Decades, United States, 1800–1930*

Decade	White Population Growth (Thousands)	Natural Increase	
		Thousands	% of Population Grow
1800–1810	1,556	1,494	96.0
1810–1820	2,005	1,934	96.5
1820–1830	2,671	2,548	95.4
1830–1840	3,658	3,165	86.5
1840–1850	5,357	3,937	73.5
1850–1860	7,369	4,811	65.3
1860–1870	7,415	5,341	72.0
1870–1880	9,066	6,486	71.5
1880–1890	11,581	6,617	57.1
1890–1900	11,708	8,019	68.5
1900–1910	14,923	8,680	58.2
1910–1920	13,089	10,864	83.0
1920–1930	15,466	12,131	78.4

Source: Warren S. Thompson and P. K. Whelpton, *Population Trends in the United States*, p. 303. For somewh modified estimates of the growth of the United States white population, 1855–1960, see Ansley J. Coale a Melvin Zelnik, *New Estimates of Fertility and Population in the United States* (Princeton: Princeton Univers Press, 1963).

rates or reduce birth rates and, therefore, immigration could not be counted a net accretion to population. Late in the nineteenth century Francis Walker echoed this view, arguing that immigration "simply resulted in a replacement of native by foreign elements."[14] Assessing this argument in more sophisticated terms, Thompson and Whelpton considered the possible effects of immigration on the accelerated exploitation of arable land and on the pace of industrialization and urbanization, all of which might bring down the birth rate more rapidly than otherwise.[15] They concluded that, in fact, the decline in the American birth rate did not appear highly sensitive, decade by decade, to the flow of immigration; that immigration had to be reckoned a net positive force in the growth of the American population; but that some limited but unmeasurable allowance should be made for the Franklin-Walker replacement hypothesis. One can assume similar results would hold for immigration to Canada, New Zealand, Australia, Argentina, Brazil, and other countries with a comfortable balance between natural resources and population.[16]

The net demographic effect of emigration on Europe is also obscure. Ireland is, of course, a famous case: the traumatic effects of the famine of 1845–1847 caused not only a protracted surge of emigration but also a decline in birth rates.[17] Although one might look for the Franklin-Walker theory to operate in reverse (with rising population in the country of emigration compensating for the outflow, as population pressure was reduced), the Irish case does not conform. On the contrary, the cause of emigration was also a cause of demographic changes which led to reduced, not expanding, popu-

mmigration		Adjustment (%)
Thousands	% of Population Growth	
62	4.0	4.4
71	3.5	5.2
123	4.6	4.7
493	13.5	5.3
,420	26.5	3.4
,558	34.7	3.6
,074	28.0	5.3
,580	28.5	2.7
,964	42.9	4.0
,689	31.5	2.4
,243	41.8	2.8
,225	17.0	1.6
,335	21.6	0.7

lation. The Irish case is, however, not typical. On balance, it is probably true that emigration from Britain and other rapidly industrializing nations weakened to some degree the incentives to invest at home. This was notably true in urban construction, for emigration was a kind of substitute for rural migration to native cities. But whatever losses were suffered were compensated for, in time, by the enlarged supplies of foodstuffs and raw materials generated in the immigrant-receiving regions. Where emigration came from less industrialized countries, faced with acute domestic population pressure, the net gain was even less ambiguous; e.g., in the south-to-north movement of European labor in the 1950's and 1960's, as well as in the increased relative flow of labor across the Atlantic from southern and eastern Europe from the 1880's to 1914, reflected in Chart I-4.[18] Here, on balance, the country of emigration almost certainly gained.

One's general impression is that, putting the Irish case aside, emigration, in narrow population terms, represented a net loss to the European populations involved, and a net accretion to overseas populations; but the movement did not significantly alter, in either region, the long-term course of birth rates and death rates, which were primarily determined by the pace of industrialization and urbanization. On the other hand, the transfer to regions whose environment decreed a relatively higher rate of natural population growth almost certainly caused a more rapid increase in total world population than would otherwise have taken place; and the transfer to regions where the agricultural and industrial productivity of labor was higher de-

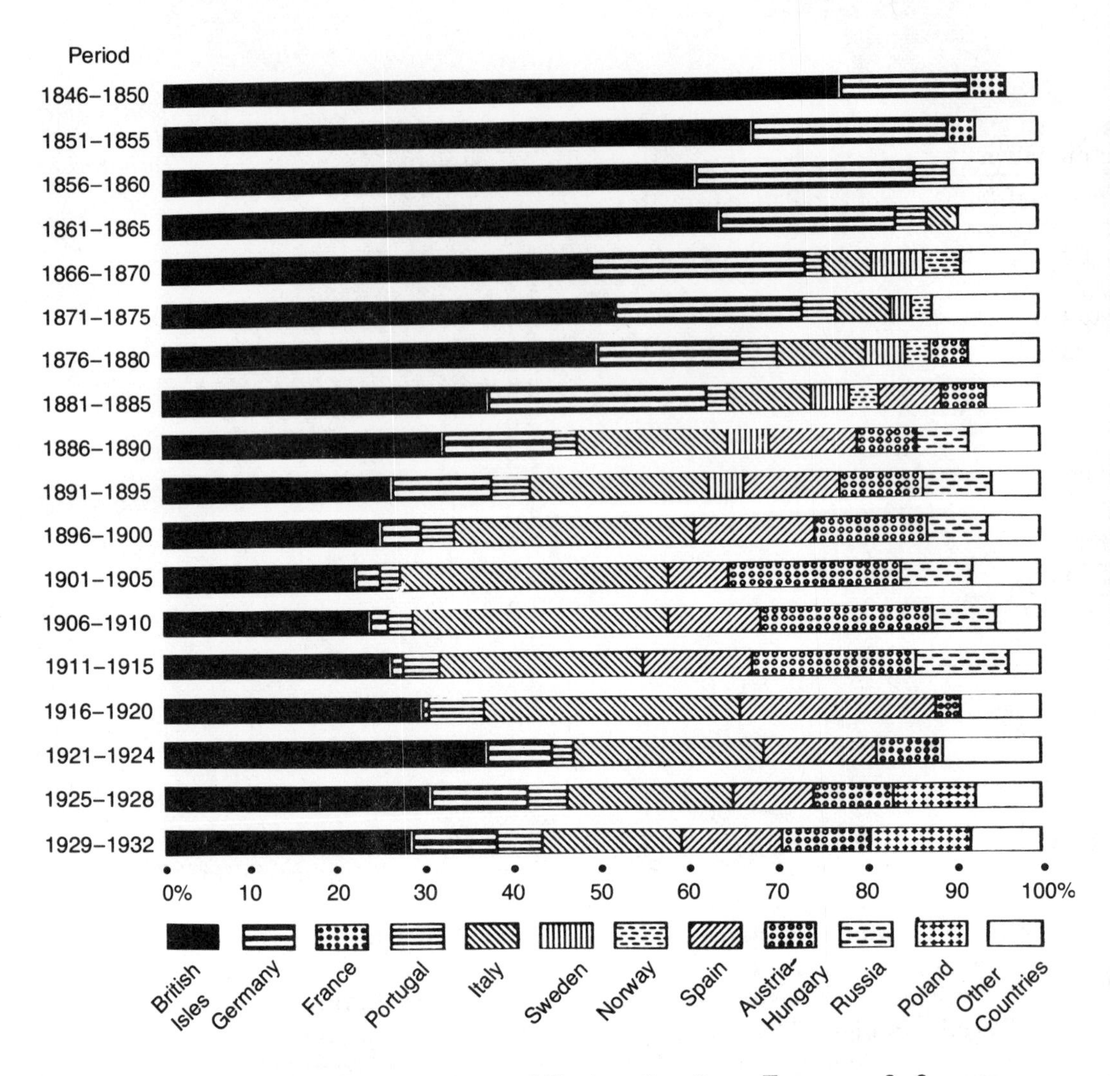

CHART I-4. *Intercontinental Emigration from Europe, 1846–1932 (Percentage Distribution of the Average Annual Emigration from the Major Countries of Emigration in Five- and Four-Year Periods)*

Source: Carr-Saunders, *World Population*, p. 53.

creed a more rapid increase in total world output than would otherwise have occurred.

The economic forces that appear to have directly determined fluctuations in the flow of emigration and the economic consequences of these fluctuations are considered in Part Three.

Reasonably reliable census data exist for the United States from 1790; and approximations have been developed for earlier years.[19] The census data also provide information on regional population movements, age composition, the relative increase of the white and negro populations and (from 1850) the foreign-born. On the other hand, official death-rate statistics are available only from 1900, from a restricted, gradually widening sample beginning with 26 percent of the population, embracing the whole only in 1933. Massachusetts data, however, were collected sporadically from 1789. Official birth-rate statistics begin only in 1910, again from a restricted but widening sample. The census data, however, permit estimates for earlier years.[20]

Table I-12 puts together the crude birth- and death-rate data available.

The course of death rates for whites in the United States approximates that in the more advanced countries in Western Europe; for example, Denmark. A systematic gap existed between white and

TABLE I-12. *The Demographic Transition of the United States, 1789–1971*

	Birth Rate (per 1,000)			Death Rate (per 1,000)			
	National			Massachusetts	National		
	Total	White	Negro	Total	Total	White	Negro
1789	—	—	—	27.8	—	—	—
1800	—	55.0	—	—	—	—	—
1810	—	54.3	—	—	—	—	—
1820	55.2	52.8	—	—	—	—	—
1830	—	51.4	—	—	—	—	—
1840	—	48.3	—	—	—	—	—
1850	—	43.3	—	—	—	—	—
1855	—	— (42.8)	—	21.4	—	—	—
1860	44.3	41.4 (41.8)	—	—	—	—	—
1870	—	38.3 (37.1)	—	19.5 (1868–1872)	—	—	—
1880	39.8	35.2 (33.6)	—	19.2 (1878–1882)	—	—	—
1890	—	31.5 (31.2)	—	19.8 (1888–1892)	—	—	—
1900	32.3	30.1 (28.5)	—	17.3 (1898–1902)	17.2	17.0	25.0
1910	30.1	27.4 (27.3)	—	15.6 (1908–1912)	14.7	14.5	21.7
1920	27.7	26.1 (25.0)	35.0	14.6 (1918–1922)	13.0	12.6	17.7
1930	21.3	20.1 (19.4)	27.5	11.9 (1928–1931)	11.3	10.8	16.3
1940	19.4	18.6 (17.8)	26.7	—	10.8	10.4	13.8
1950	24.1	23.0 (22.4)	33.3	—	9.6	9.5	11.2
1960	23.7	22.7 (22.2)	32.1	—	9.5	9.5	10.1
1970	18.4	17.4	25.1	—	9.5	9.5	9.4
1971	17.2	16.2	24.7	—	9.3	9.4	9.2
1972	15.6	14.6	22.9	—	9.4	9.5	9.2
1973	14.9	13.9	21.9	—	9.4	9.4	9.1
1974	15.0	—	—	—	9.1	9.2	8.6

Sources: 1789–1960, *Historical Statistics of the United States: Colonial Times to 1970* (Washington, D.C., 1975), pp. 51–52, 59, except Massachusetts data on the death rate which are from Thompson and Whelpton, *Population Trends in the United States*, p. 231. The birth-rate figures in parentheses in the second column are the more refined estimates of Coale and Zelnik, *New Estimates of Fertility and Population in the United States*, pp. 21–23. The slightly lower Coale and Zelnik rates stem from their correction of U.S. census data for underenumeration of the total population. 1970–1974 data from National Center of Health Statistics (HEW), *Monthly Vital Statistics Report*: birth rates, vol. 23, no. 11, Supplement (January 30, 1975); death rates, vol. 23, no. 13, Annual Summary for the United States, 1974 (May 30, 1975). "Negro" data for these years are for "non-whites."

negro death rates, narrowing with the passage of time, disappearing in the 1970's, when the age structure of the nonwhite population decreed lower rates than for whites. Over the period 1900–1960, negro death rates approximated those in Southern and Eastern Europe; for example, those of Poland.

The special features of American demography were the extraordinarily high birth rates of whites during the period down to about the 1880's (when they begin to approximate those of Western Europe) and, of course, the scale of immigration. Taken together, they account for the persistence of a population growth rate of about 3 percent down to the Civil War. This figure almost matches the peak figures for population growth in the contemporary developing world; e.g., Algeria. The American rate of population increase declined from 1870 to 1910 from 2.4 percent to 2.0 percent, a rate which subsided rapidly thereafter, except for the birth-rate surge of the 1950's. Nonwhite birth rates followed a similar path at a higher level, again approximating that of Poland for the period 1910–1970. The falling away of the birth rate from 1800 forward (except for a brief surge after the Civil War) yielded a declining natural rate of increase throughout the nineteenth century. This pattern differed from that in Europe, where the interplay of death and birth rates caused a phase of rising rates of natural increase.

As in the case of Russia, reliable population data in Japan become available only in the 1920's. This is so despite the existence of a remarkable system of annual registration of households, births, and deaths, launched by a law of 1871, as well as quinquennial summations, which cover the years 1898, 1903, 1908, 1913, and 1918.[21] These permit, with some adjustment, adequate estimates of overall and regional population size and growth rates; but incomplete registration of births and deaths of infants, a deficiency only slowly remedied, makes it impossible to analyze with confidence the Japanese demographic transition before 1920, when the first modern census was taken.

As of 1920, the Japanese birth rate was 36 per thousand, the death rate 25. The last year of the old registration system (1919) showed figures of 32 and 23, respectively, suggesting the order of magnitude of underenumeration at that time, a deficiency that had probably narrowed considerably over the period 1875–1919. Working backward from population structure as of the 1920's, and using analogy with population patterns in societies similar to Meiji Japan, Irene B. Taeuber concludes as follows:

—late Tokugawa Japan was under severe population pressure, contained by high rates of infanticide and abortion; the birth rate, excluding infanticide, may have been about 40;

—the initial impact of the opening of Japan to international commerce and the expansion of urban and industrial life was to increase fertility up to, perhaps, the 1890's, when a typical decline of the birth rate under conditions of rapid industrialization set in;

—the opening of Japan to the West and its first phase of mod-

TABLE I-13. *The Japanese Demographic Transition, 1920–1971*

	Birth Rate (per 1,000)	Death Rate (per 1,000)
1920–1924	34.6	26.9
1925–1929	34.0	19.8
1930–1934	31.8	18.1
1935–1939	29.2	17.3
1940–1943	30.2	16.0
1947–1949	33.6	12.7
1950–1954	23.7	9.4
1960	17.2	7.4
1967–1971	18.9	6.8

Sources: 1920–1954, Irene B. Taeuber, *The Population of Japan*, p. 311; 1960, 1967–1971, *United Nations Demographic Yearbook, 1971*, pp. 637 and 692.

ernization probably had divergent effects on mortality: increased food availabilities and improved public health measures counterposed against contact with new disease strains and accelerated urbanization. On balance, the evidence suggests some slow decline in death rates, from the 1890's, at least.[22]

The upshot was an initially slow, but gradually accelerating population increase, from the relative stability of the late Tokugawa period to, say, 0.75 percent per annum in the 1870's and 1880's, 1 percent in the 1890's, reaching a peak of almost 1.5 percent in the decade 1925–1935.

If this portrait is roughly correct, Japan as of 1920 was well into the demographic transition; that is, death rates were well below their Tokugawa and early Meiji level and were falling rapidly, as Japan moved forward toward technological maturity. The decline in the birth rate had proceeded to a lesser degree. By 1926, the death rate fell below 20 per thousand; the birth rate dipped under 30 per thousand in the period 1938–1940, but came definitively below that level in the remarkable decline of the 1950's. In 1949 the birth rate was 33; in 1955, 19. As in many other societies, the decline in the death rate below 10 per thousand was a phenomenon of the 1950's. Table I-13 exhibits the Japanese demographic transition from 1920 to 1971, including the brief postwar surge in birth rates.

3

Population Dynamics among the Late-Comers to Industrialization

The population history and dynamics of Asia, overall, are suffused with uncertainty if not total ignorance. As noted earlier, reasonably good data on India become available from 1871; and in Japan the registrations under the law of 1871 permit some insight into the evolution of its population since that time, although we can be confident of birth and death rates only from the 1920's. The troubled political history of China, however, leaves us with a broad aggregate sketch, at best, which Ping-ti Ho has summarized as follows:

> China's population increased from about 150,000,000 around 1700 to perhaps 313,000,000 in 1794, more than doubling in one century. Because of later growth and the lack of further economic opportunities, the population reached about 430,000,000 in 1850 and the nation became increasingly impoverished. The great social upheavals of the third quarter of the nineteenth century gave China a breathing spell to make some regional economic readjustments, but the basic population-land relation in the country as a whole remained little changed. Owing to the enormous size of the nineteenth-century Chinese population, even a much lowered average rate of growth has brought it to its reported 583,000,000 by 1953.[23]

Ho's painstaking study contains only one reference to birth rates: the result of a 1954 limited sample which suggests a birth rate of 37 per thousand and annual population growth of 2 percent.[24] For more recent times, the estimation of Chinese population has become a major demographic sport, since the government does not publish data and may not even know with confidence the country's demographic pattern.[25] The three major players are the Population Division of the United Nations Secretariat, John S. Aird of the Foreign Demographic Analysis Division of the United States Department of Commerce, and Leo A. Orleans of the Library of Congress. Their results and projections are compared in Table I-14.

Evidently, the greatest differences as of the early 1970's lie in judgments about the extent of the decline in birth rates since 1954;

although there is also a significant difference with respect to death rates as between the United Nations experts, on the one hand, and Aird and Orleans, on the other.

In effect, the United Nations experts imply that the demographic transition in China is far in advance of typical behavior for its income per capita; Aird, that its performance is more or less typical; Orleans is in between. The United Nations estimates for 1970–1975, for example, conform approximately to the average behavior of birth rates for a society which has attained a GNP-per-capita level of well over $500 (U.S., 1964); of death rates, about $400 (see below, Chart I-7 and Table II-3, panel 10). Orleans' estimates for 1975 would also conform to average performance at over $500, his death-rate estimate, to a society at $200–300 per capita. Aird's figures approximate the average at $200 per capita. The best current estimate of Chinese GNP per capita, for 1974, is $243, in 1973 U.S. dollars.[26] Given U.S. price changes since 1964, this is the equivalent of only $171, U.S., 1964. Average birth rates at that level in the 1960's were 39.4 per thousand, death rates 18.2. But it is precisely in this range of birth rates and precisely at this low but expanding level of real income per capita (between $100 and $300, U.S., 1964) that the decline in fertility is, on the average, most rapid, as Table II-3 indicates.

The United Nations experts have not published the analytic bases for their estimates. But Aird has expressed his reserve about excessively high hopes for a very rapid reduction in birth rates in a society still 80 percent rural. Orleans takes a somewhat more optimistic view of the effectiveness of the current family planning policy in China, although he is evidently less sanguine than the United Nations experts. With respect to the death rate, both Aird and Orleans credit China with an exceedingly rapid decline in the past generation.

Whatever the precise demographic position in China may be, the outcome is the result of a decline in the death rate, interrupted during the grave economic difficulties of the early 1960's; a decline in the birth rate, reflecting some net increase in urbanization, improved literacy, and, perhaps, more equitable income distribution; plus a vacillating official policy toward birth control. There have been three periods of official, purposeful encouragement of family limitation: 1954–1958, when agricultural difficulties overcame an initial doctrinaire Marxist anti-Malthusianism; 1962–1966, in the wake of the failure of the Great Leap Forward, a period also shadowed by bad harvests; 1969 to the present, in the wake of the disarray of the Cultural Revolution, when a serious and sustained program has been in effect.

The most recent phase of emphasis on late marriages, combined with the availability of increasingly sophisticated birth-control devices, has captured the attention of Western visitors to China. There is no doubt that a major national effort to limit the size of the population is under way; but Chinese officials have warned against excessive optimism: "Actually, we have achieved some progress but we do not regard it as very great progress. When we hear from our friends that it is great progress, we look at such talk as something bigger than reality, or as courteous talk."[27] There is no way of establishing with confidence exactly where between, say, 1.5 percent and 2.4 percent the annual rate of population increase lies. But it may be that the figure of "approximately 2 percent" casually thrown out by Chinese officials is about right.

In a vast nation, more than 80 percent rural, with a literacy rate of about 25 percent, and a modest average rate of increase in real income (say, 4–5 percent), one might assume that the decline in the birth rate is likely to proceed at a fairly slow pace, despite the resources of administrative control and propaganda available to the authorities in Peking. But we have seen birth rates spiral down rapidly elsewhere at equivalent levels of real income; and one should keep an open mind about this possibility in China until reliable estimates supplant thoughtful speculation.

The demographic transition, by United Nations estimates, has proceeded considerably further in China than in India. United Nations data show an Indian population increase from 462 to 563 million in the period 1965–1970, an annual rate of increase of 2.2 percent, with a 1972 crude birth rate of 42.8 per thousand, a death rate of 16.7. Indian planners, however, estimate that the birth rate in 1974 may have fallen to about 35 per thousand, from a level of 39 five years earlier.[28] They had hoped India would achieve a level of about 32 by 1974; but they have now set a target of 30 by 1979, 25 by 1984. Their estimate for 1971 is a crude death rate of 15.1 per thousand.[29] The 1974 birth- and death-rate figures would approximate those of Orleans for China in 1970. Although higher birth rates exist in Asia, the demographic transition in the first half of the 1970's thus moved more slowly than expected, despite the Indian government's strong declaratory policy of family planning and the considerable efforts undertaken to implement it.[30] It is possible, however, that the heightened Indian effort in 1976 to induce

TABLE I-14. *Alternative Estimates of China's Population: United Nations, Aird, and Orleans*

	Birth Rates (per 1,000)			Death Rates (per 1,000)		
Period	United Nations	Aird	Orleans	United Nations	Aird	Orleans
1954	—	45.0	43	—	21.2	22
1960	—	39.8	38	—	23.7	21
1970	26.7 (1970–1975)	39.5	32	10.2 (1970–1975)	15.5	16
1975	—	37.1	27	—	13.2	12
1980	22.9 (1980–1985)	34.3	22	8.6 (1980–1985)	11.2	10
2000	18.2 (1995–2000)	29.6 (1990)	—	7.6 (1995–2000)	7.6 (1990)	—

Source: Leo A. Orleans, "China's Population: Can the Contradictions Be Resolved?" The United Nation estimates are those of 1974, medium variant, and include the "Province of Taiwan," at 12 million (official PRC figure). Taiwan's population in 1975 was, in fact, about 16 million.

vasectomies and generally to force on the citizens' attention the public interest in smaller families may bring about an accelerated decline in birth rates.

The sheer scale of the task is suggested by these figures. As of 1975 the Indian population was about 600 million. Two-thirds of the population was under thirty years of age, 42 percent under fifteen. The married women currently in their reproductive years are slightly outnumbered by females under fifteen, never married. During the 1970's, 20 million married women will pass out of their childbearing years, but they will be replaced by more than 60 million females entering the fertile age group. If past patterns persist, at least 45 million of these will be married by 1980. Eighty percent of the population exists in some 600,000 rural settlements, where the cultural environment and economic and social incentives still create a strong bias toward large families, despite government efforts. As of 1971 the urban-rural differential may have been about as follows: crude birth rates, rural 38.9 per thousand, urban 30.1; crude death rates, rural 16.4, urban 9.7.

Although not formulated in vivid ideological terms, Indian government policy, like China's, has varied over the past quarter-century. In 1974 a period of frustration and disillusion with the methods and results of the 1960's appeared to have given way to a determination of the government to press forward for the long pull on three fronts: the development of birth-control devices more relevant to the Indian scene than those used in the past; a strengthening of the quality of social services in the villages; and an improvement in efforts to strengthen the motives for limiting family size. This intent is reflected in the integrated program outlined in the Fifth Five Year Plan (1974–1979), which embraces health and nutrition as well as family planning. The achievement of a birth rate of 30 per thousand is judged to require an increase from 15 to 42 million couples protected against conception.[31] In 1976 the intensity of the government's family planning campaign sharply increased, with results that cannot yet be estimated. The birth-control

tural Increase (%)			Total Population (Millions)		
ited Nations	Aird	Orleans	United Nations	Aird	Orleans
	2.38	2.1	—	589	588
	1.61	1.7	—	679	663
5 (1970–1975)	2.40	1.6	772	827	788
	2.39	1.5	838	931	850
3 (1980–1985)	2.31	1.2	907	1,046	911
6 (1995–2000)	2.20 (1990)	—	1,152	1,307 (1990)	—

devices used in India (sterilization, intrauterine coils, and condoms) have all raised problems of acceptability; but a hopeful note was sounded in 1975 when the Indian government announced a "recent scientific breakthrough of great potential significance": a discovery by the All-India Institute of Medical Sciences which "relates to the development of a contraceptive vaccine for mass use."[32]

Piecing together census data from 1920 and plausible speculation, John D. Durand produced the rough historical estimates of Indonesian population incorporated in Table I-1.[33] What is clear is that, after undergoing for some time under the Dutch a maximum population growth rate of 1–1.5 percent and a setback due to Second World War circumstances, Indonesia, like many other developing nations, experienced a sharp acceleration in the quarter-century after 1945. As of 1971 the United Nations shows a death rate which had fallen to 19.4 per thousand, a birth rate still extraordinarily high at 48.3, and a 2.8 percent population increase for the period 1963–1971.

Quite aside from the recent experience of Japan, however, it is clear that a rapid decline in birth rates is possible in the cultural setting of modern Asia under conditions of rapid economic and social progress, accelerated urbanization, and high levels of literacy. Table I-15 summarizes four dramatic cases where the annual decline in birth rates exceeded 1 per thousand for a decade. The cases of Taiwan and South Korea are particularly impressive, since they are not as urbanized as Hong Kong and Singapore. The crude birth rate on Taiwan was as high as 46.6 per thousand in 1952. Sri Lanka brought its birth rate down from about 39 per thousand in the first half of the 1950's to a level of 29.4 in 1971. Charts I-5 and I-6 exhibit visually the downward shift in fertility rates by age groups of some of the success stories of the 1960's, in Asia and elsewhere.

The dramatic case of South Korea is worth further comment because the data permit some insight into the complex of forces at work in the demographic transition of the contemporary developing world under relatively optimum circumstances.

TABLE I-15. *Asian Countries Exhibiting a Rapid Decline in Birth Rates in Recent Years (Crude Birth Rates per 1,000)*

	1960	1961	1962	1963	1964	1965	1966	1971
Hong Kong	36.0	34.3	33.3	32.8	30.1	27.7	24.9	19.0
Singapore	38.7	36.5	35.1	34.7	33.2	31.1	29.9	22.8
Taiwan	39.5	38.3	37.4	36.3	34.7	32.7	32.5	28.1
South Korea	42.9	—	—	—	—	—	33.7	29.0

Sources: Wrigley, *Population and History*, p. 216, for 1960–1966. *United Nations Demographic Yearbook, 1971* for Hong Kong and Singapore, 1971. John S. Aird, "Population Policy and Demographic Prospects," p. 326, for Taiwan; "1971" is provisional estimate for 1970. South Korean data from Lee-Jay Cho, *The Demographic Situation in the Republic of Korea*, Honolulu, Papers of the East-West Population Institute, no. 29 (December 1973), p. 5.

Rough estimates suggest that the population of the Korean peninsula in 1669 was about 5 million; in 1753, 7.3 million; in 1807, 7.6 million; and in 1904, 13 million. The increase over these two and a third centuries is approximately proportionate to that in China, with the Korean population remaining in the range of about 3 percent of the Chinese. Censuses conducted under Japanese occupation and in South Korea after 1949 indicate the subsequent expansion; and they permit also estimates of the evolution of crude birth and death rates (see Table I-16). We observe here not merely a decline in the death rate below 10 per thousand, but a fall in the birth rate from over 40 per thousand to under 30 within a single decade. The decline began in the wake of an intense baby boom in the period 1957–1960, after the Korean Army was substantially pulled back from the front.

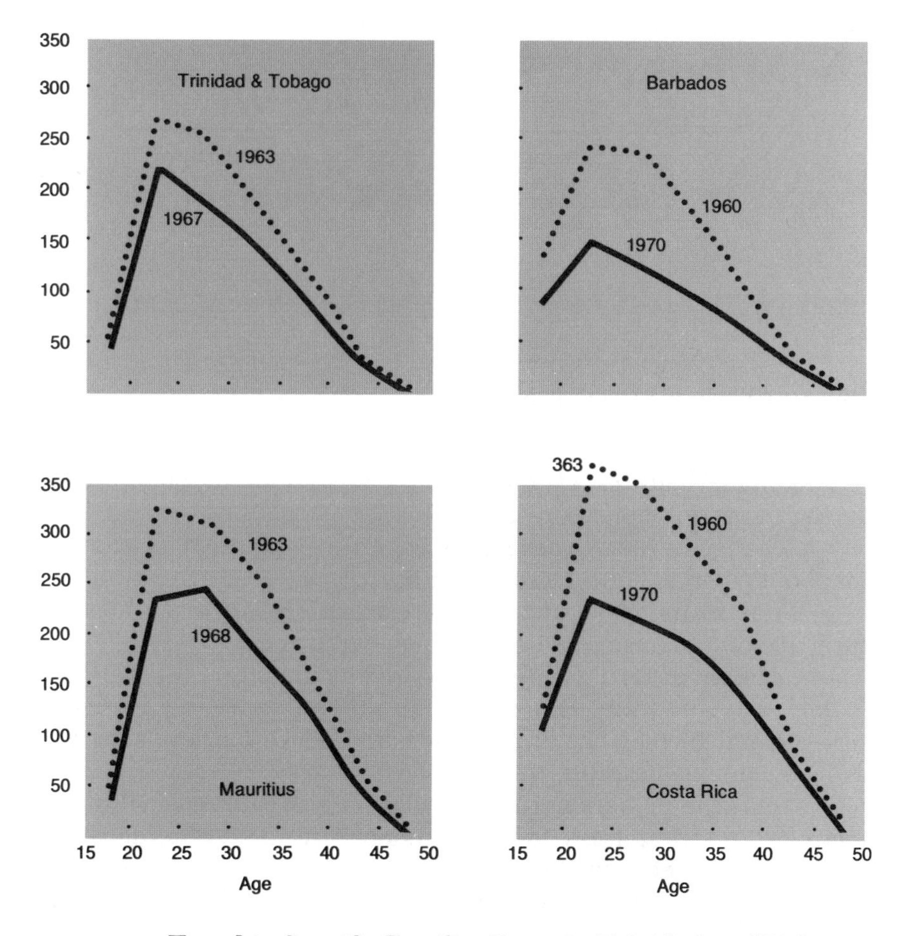

CHART I-5. *Trend in Specific Fertility Rates in Trinidad and Tobago, Barbados, Mauritius, and Costa Rica*

Source: World Bank Staff Report (Timothy King, coordinating author), *Population Policies and Economic Development*, p. 167.

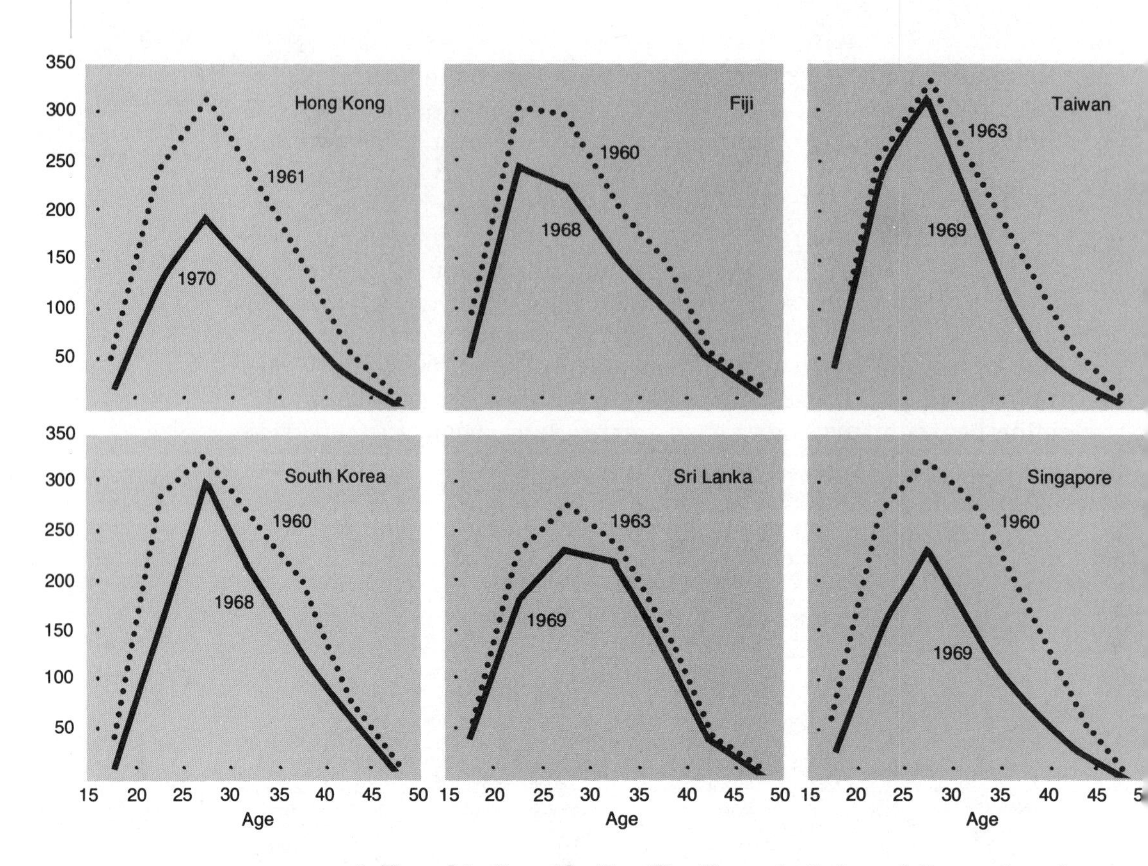

CHART I-6. *Trend in Specific Fertility Rates in Selected Countries of Asia*

Source: World Bank Staff Report, *Population Policies and Economic Development*, p. 168.

The main features of the decline in fertility in South Korea during the 1960's appear to be:

—a change in the age-sex structure of the population, accounting for about 9 percent of the fall in fertility;

—a rise in marriage age, for both urban and rural women, the rural age of marriage remaining somewhat lower;

—a decline of fertility in rural as well as urban areas at approximately the same rate, although rural birth rates remain higher;

—a rapid increase in urbanization and education levels, as well as in income per capita;

—a purposeful national family planning program, reaching effectively into rural areas, including nonenforcement of antiabortion laws (formally abolished in February 1973): surveys indicate abortion played a substantial role in the decline of the birth rate in the 1960's.

As in other societies, there is in South Korea a sharp inverse correlation between the education level of women and the size of their families, as well as the usual income and urban-rural differentials. On the basis of present knowledge it is impossible to assign

TABLE I-16. *Population, Growth Rates, and Crude Birth and Death Rates: All Korea, 1925–1944, and Republic of Korea, 1945–1970*

Year	Population	Intercensal Growth Rate (%)	Crude Birth Rate Estimated (per 1,000)	Crude Death Rate Estimated (per 1,000)
All Korea				
1925 (October 1)	19,020,030			
		1.44	45.4	27.9
1930 (October 1)	20,438,108			
		1.66	45.3	25.5
1935 (October 1)	22,208,102			
		1.17	43.5	20.2
1940 (October 1)	23,547,465			
		1.41	41.0	u
1944 (May 1)	25,120,174			
Republic of Korea				
1949 (May 1)	20,166,756			
		1.20	u	u
1955 (September 1)	21,502,386			
		2.70	43.3	16.3
1960 (December 1)	24,954,290		42.9	
		2.49	35.8	10.9
1966 (October 1)	29,159,640		33.7	
		2.16	30.0	8.4
1970 (October 1)	31,438,768		29.0	7.5–8.0

u: unavailable.

Source: Lee-Jay Cho, *The Demographic Situation in the Republic of Korea*, pp. 3 and 5, where detailed sources are indicated.

firm weights to each of the factors producing this decline in South Korean fertility. One can only conclude that a high rate of economic and social modernization, a sharp decline in infant mortality, a determined national family planning program addressed especially to rural areas, and a culture and government tolerant of abortion somehow converged to produce a remarkably brisk movement through the demographic transition.

As we shall see (Part Six), the fact that death rates in China, India, Indonesia, Pakistan, and Bangladesh still have some distance to fall before they reach practical minima means that, barring demographic catastrophes in the region, very large further increases in Asia's population are inevitable, even if birth rates should move downward as fast as they have done on (say) Taiwan in the past generation. And as of 1971 birth rates were still above 40 per thousand in Afghanistan, Burma, India, Indonesia, Iran, Iraq, the Khmer Republic, Laos, Mongolia, Nepal, Pakistan, the Philippines, Syria, Thailand, and Yemen. They were just below that level in Turkey and in Malaysia as a whole, although receding quite rapidly in the more advanced western region of the latter country.

The long-term history of population in Africa is even more obscure and fragmentary than in China, since no central imperial government attempted even sporadic and incomplete registrations.[34] Writing in the 1930's, Carr-Saunders concluded that in tribal Africa ancient customs kept birth rates so low that perhaps "the Africans are not fated to pass through a prolonged period characterized by the unlimited family which has brought a threatening situation into being among many Asiatic peoples."[35] But he also noted that, in the cities of the Union of South Africa, where tribal patterns were broken, a population revolution was under way: birth rates of 50 per thousand were recorded, along with death rates of 20. Moreover, a history of relatively high population increase had marked Egypt and Algeria in the nineteenth and early twentieth centuries, as shown in Table I-17.[36] For the period 1907–1931 Egyptian birth rates may have averaged about 44 per thousand, death rates about 26. And, since the 1930's, Carr-Saunders' hope has been belied:

TABLE I-17. *Annual Average Rate of Growth of Population in Egypt and Algeria, 1800–1931 (%)*

	Egypt		Algeria	
1800–1846	1.29	(including nomadic Arabs)	—	
1846–1882	1.05[a]	" " "		
1882–1897	2.41[a]	" " "	1850–1901	1.3
1897–1907	1.52	(excluding nomadic Arabs)		
1907–1917	1.24	" " "		
1917–1927	1.11	" " "	1901–1931	1.1

[a] Census of 1882 may have involved substantial underestimate.
Source: Carr-Saunders, *World Population*, pp. 280 and 284.

tribal Africa has been fully caught up in the population revolution sweeping the less-developed regions of the world, as Table I-18 reveals.[37]

The regional averages reflect in lower death rates the relatively more advanced stage of economic development of Northern and Southern Africa; and, in the case of the latter, the beginnings of a decline in birth rates can be detected. Birth rates in South Africa and Rhodesia show clearly this trend, as well as significant racial distinctions in both birth and death rates.[38] In rapidly industrializing and urbanizing South Africa colored and Asiatic birth rates are coming close together; but a considerable gap remains between both groups and the birth rate of the European population.

Although birth rates remain extraordinarily high in Africa, there are indications that their decline has at least begun in some coun-

TABLE I-18. *Africa: Annual Average Rate of Population Increase, Birth Rates, and Death Rates, 1965–1971*

	Population Increase (%)	Birth Rate (per 1,000)	Death Rate (per 1,000)
Africa	2.6	47	21
Western Africa	2.5	49	24
Eastern Africa	2.5	46	22
Northern Africa	3.1	47	17
Middle Africa	2.1	45	24
Southern Africa	2.4	41	17

Source: *United Nations Demographic Yearbook, 1971*, p. 111.

TABLE I-19. *South Africa and Rhodesia: Birth and Death Rates by Race, 1967–1971*

	South Africa			Rhodesia		
	Asiatic	Colored	European	Asiatic	Colored	European
Birth Rate (per 1,000)						
1967	30.0	43.3	22.9	24.3	35.9	18.7
1968	32.3	40.0	23.6	22.2	33.4	18.0
1969	35.7	38.2	22.9	21.6	33.8	17.8
1970	33.8	36.7	23.6	23.0	32.5	18.3
1971	—	—	—	21.8	—	18.0
Death Rate (per 1,000)						
1967	7.6	15.7	9.0	7.5	6.4	7.0
1968	7.4	14.5	8.8	5.3	5.3	7.4
1969	7.3	14.2	8.7	5.1	5.4	7.1
1970	7.0	14.2	8.1	5.3	5.6	6.9
1971	—	—	—	4.7	—	7.1

Source: *United Nations Demographic Yearbook, 1971*, pp. 635 and 690.

tries; e.g., Algeria, Egypt, Tunisia, and the island states of Mauritius, Réunion, and Seychelles. But, evidently, they still have a long way to go: in none of the three North African nations cited above has the birth rate yet fallen below 30 per thousand.

Although the long sweep of population history in Latin America cannot be well documented, the accelerating growth rates set out in Table I-3 probably convey a reasonably accurate impression of the story.[39] Immigration and the existence of some open arable land permitted a higher rate of population growth in the century and a half before 1900 than in any other major region except North America. The overall acceleration of population growth between 1920 and 1970 and regional deviations are captured in Table I-20.[40]

In tropical South America and Middle America (including Mexico) this outcome is the result of a rapid decline in death rates accompanied by birth rates which remain close to maximum levels. The data on four Middle American countries in Table I-21 represent a Latin American version of the general experience of the developing regions; that is, high, or even rising birth rates down to 1960 accompanied by rapidly falling death rates, with some decline in birth rates setting in during the 1960's. The rapid decline of birth rates in Costa Rica during the 1960's places it among the success stories of the developing world.

The demographic dynamics of temperate South America (Argentina, Uruguay, Chile, and Paraguay) have been distinctively different. Argentina and Uruguay experienced large if irregular flows of immigration. Along with Chile, they also underwent significant declines in birth rates, as their predominantly European populations urbanized rapidly at relatively high levels of income and social services. Between 1925–1929 and the late 1960's, the Argentine crude birth rate (already modest) fell from 30 to 22 per thousand; that of Chile, from 40 to 25. Uruguay has followed a pattern similar to that of Argentina; but very high birth rates, well over 40, have persisted in less-developed Paraguay.

In some islands of the Caribbean the demographic transition is under way in a fairly classical sequence; that is, falling death rates

TABLE I-20. *Latin America: Decennial Rates of Increase of Population, 1920–1970 (%)*

	1920–1930	1930–1940	1940–1950	1950–1960	1960–1970
Latin America	19.9	20.9	25.0	30.9	32.9
Tropical South America	19.4	22.5	26.0	33.7	33.1
Middle America (mainland)	15.5	19.67	29.2	34.9	37.0
Temperate South America	27.3	18.2	20.3	22.1	17.2
Caribbean	19.9	19.8	20.2	21.9	23.1

Sources: 1920–1960, *World Population Prospects as Assessed in 1963*, p. 138. 1960–1970, calculated from "Recent Population Trends and Future Prospects," secretariat paper prepared for Item 7 of the Provisional Agenda, United Nations World Population Conference, Bucharest, 19–30 August 1974, Annex II, p. 5.

TABLE I-21. *Crude Birth and Death Rates in Four Middle American Countries, 1930–1970 (per 1,000 Population)*

Period	Birth Rate	Death Rate	Birth Rate	Death Rate
	Mexico		Guatemala	
1930–1934	44.5	25.6	51.6	26.1
1935–1939	43.5	23.3	47.7	26.5
1940–1944	44.2	22.1	47.2	27.8
1945–1949	44.4	17.8	50.6	23.8
1950–1954	44.9	15.5	51.4	21.4
1955–1959	45.9	12.5	49.1	19.9
1960	46.0	11.5	49.5	17.5
1970	43.4	9.9	39.0	15.0
	El Salvador		Costa Rica	
1930–1934	43.3	23.0	45.7	22.1
1935–1939	42.7	21.1	45.0	20.0
1940–1944	43.3	20.5	44.9	18.3
1945–1949	44.4	17.1	45.1	14.0
1950–1954	49.4	15.2	49.2	11.6
1955–1959	50.0	13.2	50.0	9.6
1960	49.9	11.0	50.2	8.6
1970	40.0	9.9	33.8	6.6

Sources: 1930–1960, *World Population Prospects as Assessed in 1963*, pp. 110–111; 1970 data from *United Nations Demographic Yearbook, 1971*.

(from the 1920's, at least)[41] have been followed in the 1950's (for Puerto Rico) and the 1960's by declining birth rates which, by the late 1960's, yielded levels as low as 22–24 per thousand for Netherlands Antilles, Barbados, Puerto Rico, and Trinidad and Tobago; 35 for Jamaica.

The United Nations summary portrait of the region for the period 1965–1971 roughly measures these distinctive subregional experiences (see Table I-22).

TABLE I-22. *Latin American Population Growth, 1965–1971*

	Annual Growth Rate (%)	Birth Rate (per 1,000)	Death Rate (per 1,000)
Latin America	2.9	38	10
Tropical South America	3.0	40	10
Middle America (mainland)	3.4	43	10
Temperate South America	1.8	25	8
Caribbean	2.2	35	11

Source: *United Nations Demographic Yearbook, 1971*, p. 111.

As the results of the 1970 census were absorbed and the Latin American governments began to measure the implications of population growth rates for future levels of unemployment, agricultural production, and education and other social service outlays, residual religious and nationalist resistances to policies of family planning eroded to a degree, notably in Mexico.

4

The Contemporary Scene: A Preliminary View

What can be said, in general, about the state of the demographic transition in the various regions of the contemporary world?

In a bold exercise in fertility analysis, Lee-Jay Cho has estimated, for the period 1955–1960, the degree to which the countries of the world had completed the demographic transition.[42] His results can be translated into the summary set out in Table I-23. It exhibits, for each region of the world as of 1960, the degree to which the demographic transition had been completed.[43] Chart I-7 provides a somewhat different picture of the demographic transition during the 1950's and 1960's. It exhibits the average relationship between GNP per capita (in U.S. 1964 dollars) and crude birth and death rates for some one hundred countries. The data are from United Nations sources over the period 1950–1970. The pattern of behavior that emerges is statistically significant but averages out a quite wide range of national demographic experiences.[44] The measurement of standard error on the chart indicates that there is a wider range of behavior in birth than in death rates with respect to GNP per capita.

Formal correlation analysis shows what we have already observed in the regional statistics; that is, an initially more rapid decline in death than birth rates; a deceleration in the decline of death rates, particularly marked above $300 per capita, as hard-core diseases

TABLE I-23. *Percentage Demographic Transition Completed, 1960*

Region	%
World	43.5
Africa	19.9
North America	79.0
Middle America	26.3
South America	35.4
Asia	39.3
Europe	91.4
USSR	80–90

Source: D. J. Bogue, *Principles of Demography*, p. 672.

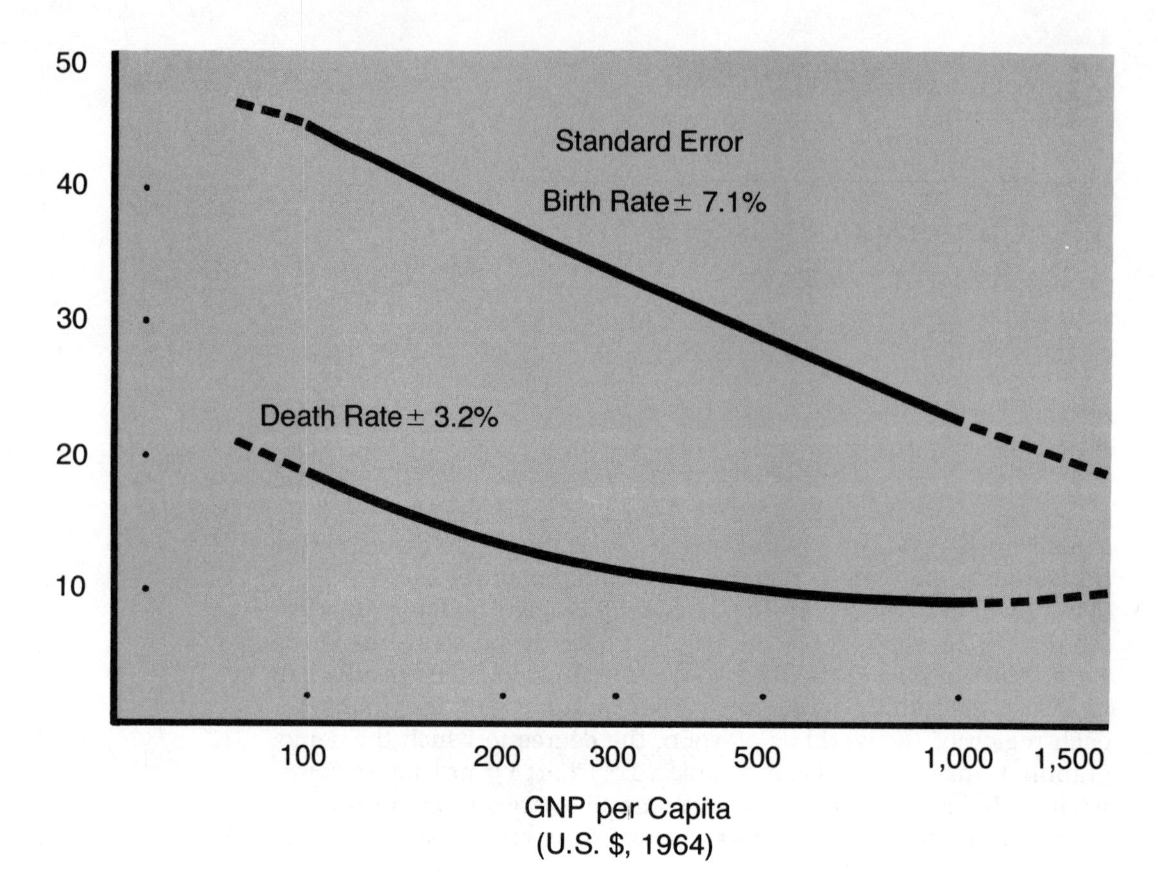

CHART I-7. *The Demographic Transition: A Cross-Sectional View (1950–1970): Birth and Death Rates per Thousand; GNP per Capita*

Source: Hollis B. Chenery and Moises Syrquin, assisted by Hazel Elkington, *Patterns of Development, 1950–1970* (London: Oxford University Press [for the World Bank], 1975), p. 57.

(cancer, circulatory disorders, etc.) come to dominate the mortality statistics; and then a possible slight rise in death rates in rich nations as the age structure of the population yields increasing proportions of older people. Meanwhile, birth rates move downward at a slower, but also decelerating, rate with the increase of GNP per capita. Some evidence suggests this net movement may be the result of conflicting forces: a rise in per capita income may cause an initial rise in birth rates; but a persistence of improved income brings about circumstances (including a reduction in infant mortality) which, on balance, cause a reduction in birth rates. The result is a maximum gap between birth and death rates in the range of $100–$300 (1964) per capita (despite the rapid decline of birth rates) causing the high rates of population growth to be observed in the least developed nations of the world.[45] As we have already noted, the higher rates of population increase in the contemporary developing world than in pre-1914 Europe and Japan stem primarily from the medical and public health revolution of the twentieth century. This has permitted more rapid reductions in death rates than in earlier times in societies at equivalent levels of economic and social development.[46]

When we move from generalizations of this broad kind to efforts to explain why, on balance, birth rates behave the way they do, there is much less knowledge and agreement among experts. This should not be surprising. It is evidently easier to diffuse and gain acceptance for measures which save and prolong life than to induce action reducing birth rates. We are talking about all the complex forces which lead individual men and women to alter the number of children they have and the size of families they seek. To this inherent complexity must be added the statistical problems which are set aside when crude birth and death rates are compared on a national basis.[47] Ideally, one should work with birth and death rates for each age group in the population, broken down by regions, race, income level, social setting, etc. One should also take into account the element of dependence of birth rates on prior and current death rates; for example, a decline in death rates can yield an increase of birth rates in developing societies as a larger proportion of women come to live out their child-bearing years. But even now such age-group data are systematically available for relatively few nations.

This combination of intellectual complexity and inadequate data accounts for many unanswered questions in the field of demography. After generations of study and debate, for example, the causes and mechanisms of the population increase in Europe of the eighteenth century and, indeed, of Europe's demographic transition of the nineteenth century remain in question. Some of the best contemporary analyses of these problems still conclude with a call for further historical research.

In dealing with the post-1945 world, with its wealth of relatively uniform statistical data generated by the United Nations, analysts have sought to go beyond rough inverse correlations of GNP per capita and birth rates (putting aside the temporary baby boom in rich countries of the 1950's) to approximate statistically the human calculus involved in the tendency of family size to diminish as economic growth and social modernization proceed.[48]

A great many hypotheses have been explored.[49] The most important would relate the decline in the birth rate in developing nations not merely to increases in income per capita but also to the degree of urbanization, the level of education, and the equity of income distribution.[50] But these hypotheses, in turn, open up for examination, rather than settle, the ultimate human and social calculus involved.

The question is: Why, precisely, does the calculation about family size differ as between rural and urban life? Is it because the cost of raising a child is greater in an urban setting; because a child can contribute less to a family's income in a city than on a farm; because (in modern times) medical services are better in the cities, death rates are lower, and fewer children need to be born to complete a family of a given size; because urban life offers wider (but more expensive) opportunities for education and social advance and, therefore, having fewer children permits greater investment in each child's future; because social services available in urban life may reduce the tendency to have children as a form of old-age and disability insurance; because housing is more expensive and overcrowding leads to family limitation; because there are more families in cities who enjoy incomes above the minimum levels of farmers in traditional agriculture in particular, rural life in general?

Similarly, the question is: How, precisely, does a higher level of education tend to reduce birth rates in developing societies? Is it because better-educated people can more easily absorb and apply information on birth control; because they are more likely to be sensitive to the possibilities of improving the opportunities for each child if the family size is reduced; because education may widen tastes in ways which diminish the relative value attached to a large family; because better-educated people more easily understand the social need in developing nations for smaller families; because better-educated people are to be found in urban areas and are already subject to the influences urban life engenders, making for lower family size?

There are no lucid and agreed answers to these questions; and it is likely that answers will be found only when analysts go beyond the manipulation of national statistical data and examine in great detail all manner of relevant evidence in regions or small communities. But there is a consensus that when variables reflecting degrees of urbanization and educational levels are introduced, in addition to levels of per capita income (or consumption), the inverse correlation with birth rates improves in countries with relatively low per capita income.

This result flows, in part, from the fact that GNP per capita (or, even, consumption per capita) is an imperfect index of the kind of social modernization believed to influence decisions on family size. Take the extreme cases of oil-rich nations of the Middle East. Libya, Kuwait, and Saudi Arabia now enjoy extremely high levels of GNP per capita; Kuwait, well over $3,000 per capita, exceeding the highest levels in Western Europe even before the 1973 rise in the price of oil; but, understandably, social modernization has lagged. Birth rates for those three countries were, respectively, 46, 43, and 50 per thousand as of 1971. Compare, for example, Venezuela and Cyprus, at almost identical levels of GNP per capita ($923 and $933, in 1971). Oil-rich Venezuela has made considerable social progress in the past generation, starting from an acute stage of general underdevelopment when its oil deposits were first systematically exploited. Cyprus, less rural, part of the Mediterranean world, long under British administration, has enjoyed more protracted social development. In 1971 the Venezuelan birth rate was still over 40 per thousand, while that of Cyprus was 23, with identical low death rates (8 per thousand).

Moreover, high growth rates do not appear, in themselves, to guarantee a rapid decline of birth rates. Mexico, for example, has enjoyed high and relatively steady economic expansion since about 1940. Its birth rate, however, remains well over 40 per thousand. South Korea has also experienced a high rate of growth in the past decade, although its GNP per capita in 1971 was less than half that of Mexico ($265 versus $632). Nevertheless, the South Korean birth rate appears to be falling quite rapidly and fell below 30 per thousand by 1970. Is this kind of differential due to a more homogeneous population in Korea, a longer tradition of literacy, a more even pattern of development, a greater sense of social discipline, more equitable income distribution, or, simply, a culture more permissive of abortion? Despite analyses of increasing refinement, we cannot yet answer this kind of question with confidence. What we can say is that the reduction of birth rates is not a simple function of levels of income or consumption per capita; and that, in addition to the vigor of public policies of family planning, the degree of urbanization, levels of education, income distribution, the availability of medical services, and other aspects of political and social policy help determine the outcome, along, perhaps, with cultural residues from the past, imperfectly understood.

Of all the major problems confronting the world economy over the next quarter-century, surveyed in Part Six, the pace of the demographic transition is, I believe, the greatest. It raises, in the context of the world's agricultural situation, immediate problems of possible starvation and worsened levels of nutrition on a massive scale, longer-run problems of the global population in the next century which, from all current indications, will attempt to consolidate and maintain an industrial civilization. While the world's population is not highly sensitive in the short run to current declines in fertility, due to time lags, it is highly sensitive over the longer run.

The approaches taken by governments to this problem are not directly geared to this global perspective. And they usually respond to short-run rather than long-run impulses. Their current policies vary widely and are now determined by perceptions of relatively narrow and immediate national interests: economic, social, political, and strategic. There is, thus, a spectrum of national positions ranging from pronatalist through nuances of neutrality to antinatalist policies of varying degrees of purposefulness.[51] Pronatalist countries include some moved by religious considerations (e.g., Spain); some by the continued availability of arable land (e.g., a good many smaller African countries); at least one by a combination of available land and strategic concern for a larger neighbor (Argentina); some by a concern about the economic and strategic consequences of a stagnant or declining population (e.g., Bulgaria, Czechoslovakia, Hungary, Rumania). The antinatalist countries embrace some of the more advanced nations (e.g., Sweden, United Kingdom, Japan) and a lengthening list of developing nations which have concluded that their economic and social prospects would be best served by an accelerated decline in birth rates. The number of developing countries with family planning programs increased from four in 1960 to fifty-three in 1974.[52] The proportion of developing nations with family planning programs is lowest in Africa (19 percent), around 50 percent in Latin America and Asia.

This spectrum of national interests and responses was faithfully reflected in the debates at Bucharest in August 1974 at the first United Nations World Population Conference. The initial result was a sturdy affirmation of national sovereignty in this field, tempered to a degree by this phrase: ". . . taking into account universal solidarity in order to improve the quality of life of the people of the world."[53] Beneath the surface of a good deal of enflamed North-South as well as some East-West rhetoric, the main thrust of the consensus reached was that a rapid reduction of birth rates must be envisaged as part of accelerated economic and social development in the developing nations. Considerable efforts were made at Bucharest (as at other United Nations gatherings of 1974–1975) to increase the explicitness of the commitment of the more advanced industrial nations to allocate enlarged resources to this objective. As we shall see in Part Six, whether such enlarged flows in fact take place in the years ahead depends on the manner in which both the industrialized and developing countries solve or fail to solve a range of other problems placed on their agenda by the course of recent history. What can be said as of the spring of 1977 is that, since the Bucharest Conference, a number of governments have intensified their national efforts in family planning, and the peak rate of global increase in population may have been transited, but the task of accommodating some two billion additional human beings on the planet over the next quarter-century remains.

Part Two

Growth since the Eighteenth Century: An Overall View

5

Industrial Growth and Its Diffusion

A human being is an unambiguous statistical unit: a man, woman, or child counted in the eighteenth century can be compared with one counted in the twentieth; a human being in one country can be equated statistically with one in another. In dealing with production, structural change, trade, and the prices of goods and services, we are in a more slippery business. The quality of commodities changes; new products and services are created; prices change and the prices of the same commodities vary among countries, affected by transport costs as well as by tariffs and other kinds of government policies. And these price differences affect the weights to be assigned to them when we try to add them up—oranges and apples and everything else—into a production, trade, or national-income index. Moreover, the relative values of currencies change and are also subject to the influence of public policy, so that it is often difficult to compare the value of output or trade in one country with that in another. Finally, as in the case of population data, the availability of statistics varies and their quality changes with the passage of time. Nevertheless, we can say with some confidence that the world's population more than tripled between 1800 and 1970; from, say, 978 million to, say, 3,632 million. Both figures are subject to margins of error; but we know what the figures are meant to represent, and we can have reasonable confidence in the order of magnitude of the expansion they reflect. We are in a considerably less certain world of numbers as we examine the growth of production and trade, and the fluctuations of prices over the past two centuries.

Nevertheless, it is possible to piece together an index showing the trend of world industrial production covering the century and a half from 1820 to 1971; and still rougher calculations can push the estimate back to the first decade of the eighteenth century. The composite index is presented in Chart II-1, and its components and construction are described in Appendix A.

It should be noted that what we are measuring here, after 1785, is primarily modern industry, excluding, for example, the large

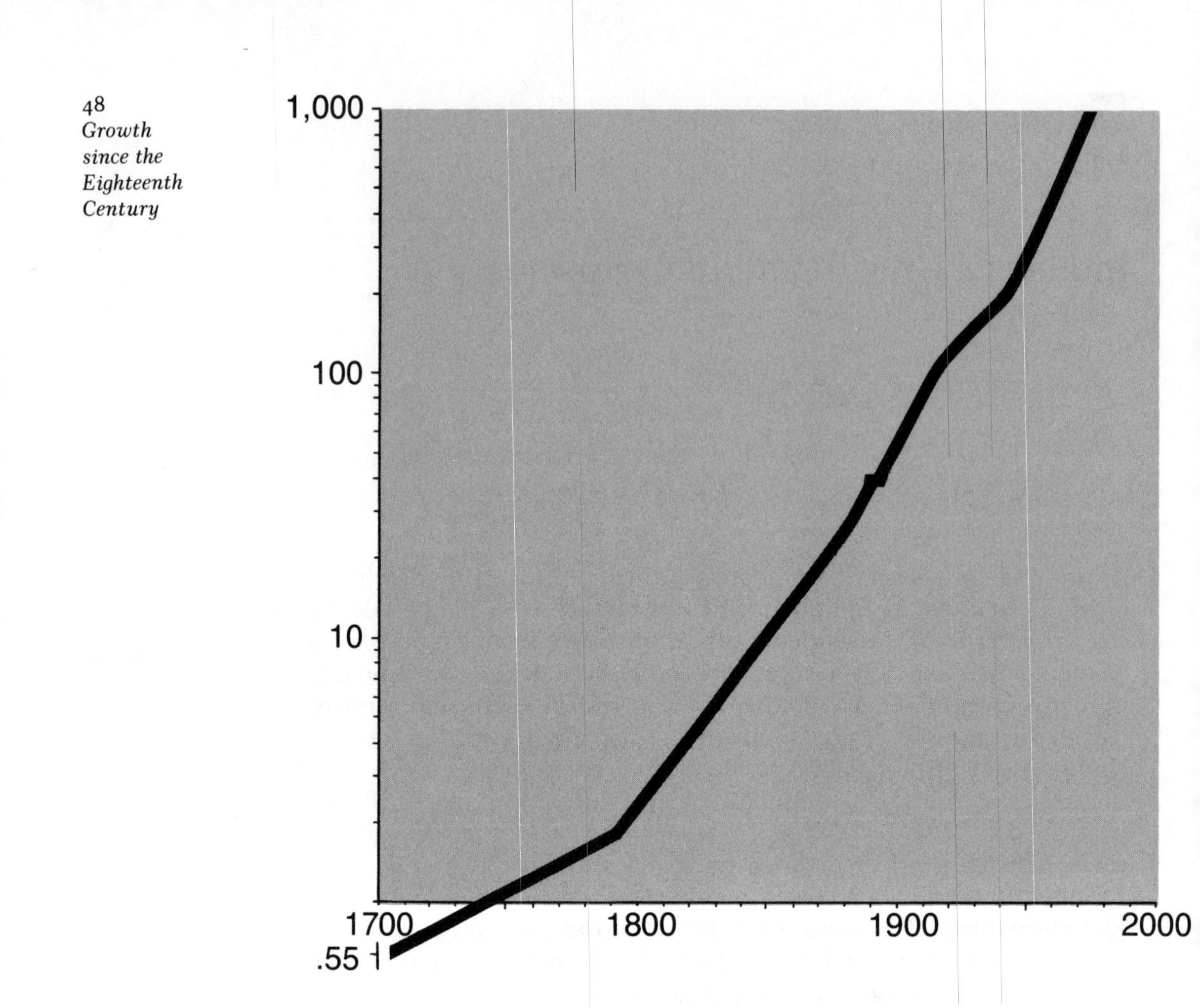

CHART II-1. *World Industrial Production, 1700–1971 (1913 = 100)*

Source: See Appendix A.

volume of handicraft production in India, China, and elsewhere in preindustrial societies. Taken at face value, the quantity of manufacturing production in the world increased about 1,730 times over this span. This improbable figure takes on a certain proportion and plausibility if it is expressed as an annual average rate of growth. For the whole period, the figure is 2.84 percent per annum, about half the rate the world experienced in the period 1948–1971. Table II-1 shows the growth rate for major subperiods.

Much more is, of course, involved in economic growth and the modernization of societies than industrial production. Nevertheless, the diffusion of industry is at the heart of the process; and the changing rates of growth in Table II-1 reflect a good deal of modern economic history which will be explored at greater length elsewhere in this book.

The positive but relatively low rate of increase down to the 1780's (1.5 percent) catches the final period of the preconditions for take-off in Western Europe. The British take-off, starting in the 1780's,

TABLE II-1. *Index of World Industrial Production, 1705–1971*

	Annual Average Growth Rates (%)
1705–1785	1.5
1785–1830	2.6
. . .	. .
1820–1840	2.9
1840–1860	3.5
1860–1870	2.9
1870–1900	3.7
1900–1913	4.2
1913–1929	2.7
1929–1938	2.0
1938–1948	4.1
1948–1971	5.6

Source: Appendix A.

the post-1815 recovery on the Continent, notably in textiles, and the surge of New England factory production of cottons in the 1820's all play their part in the higher rate (2.6 percent) down to 1830. After 1830 railroadization begins, while cotton maintains its momentum. The Belgian take-off starts in the 1830's as does that of France. There is a strong industrial boom in Britain, as well as continued momentum in the New England textile industry during part of that decade. Cotton produced and consumed in the world during the 1820's is 1.6 million tons; in the 1840's, 5.2 million tons.[1] World iron production is estimated at 1.01 million tons in 1820, 2.68 million tons in 1840.[2]

The accelerated rate for 1840–1860 (3.5 percent) captures the sharp impact of the American take-off combined with those concurrent in Belgium, France, and Germany. The British rate holds steady at a high level in the 1840's, declines somewhat in the 1850's.

The lower rate for the 1860's reflects contrary tendencies: the slow-down in the United States, due to the Civil War; the forward surge of Germany and France, as they complete their take-offs; and continued industrial growth at a high level in Britain.

From 1870 to 1900, the United States and Germany move forward rapidly, but a new class of nations comes vigorously into take-off: notably, the Scandinavian states, Japan, parts of Eastern Europe, Italy, and Russia. They are joined from the mid-1890's by an exuberant Canada, lifted by a rise in the wheat price, at last beginning to fulfill its great promise. The continued high momentum of the newcomers and their greater weight in the index, down to the First World War, compensate for some deceleration in Western Europe and the United States, in the period 1900–1913.

The lower average figures for 1913–1929 and for 1929–1938 reflect, of course, the impact of the First World War and its difficult immediate aftermath in Europe and, then, the Great Depression. The sharp rise between 1938 and 1948 reflects the greater promptness of recovery after the Second World War, as compared with the First, but, even more, the full recovery from the depression experienced by the United States during the war and its continued postwar prosperity.

The uniquely high rate over the period 1948–1971 is the product of the movement of Western Europe and Japan into two decades of sustained rapid growth, as they fully enjoy at last the stage of high mass-consumption; the high postwar industrial growth rates in the Soviet Union and Eastern Europe; and, latterly, the maintenance of a quite extraordinary rate of industrial expansion in the developing regions of Asia, the Middle East, Africa, and Latin America, taken as a whole. Their weight is relatively modest, but they proceed between 1955 and 1971 at 7.5 percent per annum, a rate which more than doubles industrial output each decade. The setback of 1974–1976 (discussed in later chapters) is not reflected in this series. As with the rate of population increase, we may have just passed, as we move through the difficult mid-1970's, the maximum rate of increase in world industrial growth in history.

At first sight, the line on Chart II-1 suggests a smooth and almost steady expansion. But, as the above comments on that index suggest, its course, looked at more closely, reflects not only great traumatic events, such as war and the Great Depression of the 1930's, but also the shifting leadership in economic growth as industrialization moves out across the face of Europe, North America, and then to other continents. Simon Kuznets once put the matter this way:

> The picture of economic development suffers a curious change as we examine it first in a rather wide sphere, then in a narrower one. If we take the world from the end of the eighteenth century, there unrolls before us a process of uninterrupted and seemingly unslackened growth. We observe a ceaseless expansion of production and trade, a constant growth in the volume of power used, in the extraction of raw materials, in the quality and quantity of finished products.
>
> But if we single out the various nations or the separate branches of industry, the picture becomes less uniform. Some nations seem to have led the world at one time, others at another. Some industries were developing most rapidly at the beginning of the century, others at the end. Within single countries or within single branches of industries (on a world scale) there has not been uniform, unretarded growth.[3]

The shifting leadership among industries is best observed by examining the sectoral paths of development followed by individual nations, which is done in Part Five, where the issues in the debate over the stages of economic growth are also explored (Chapter 27). But Chart II-2, based on both the sectoral and aggregate analysis conducted in Part Five, suggests the time that various major nations came into modern industrialization, moving forward thereafter, with many vicissitudes, in the further stages of economic growth,

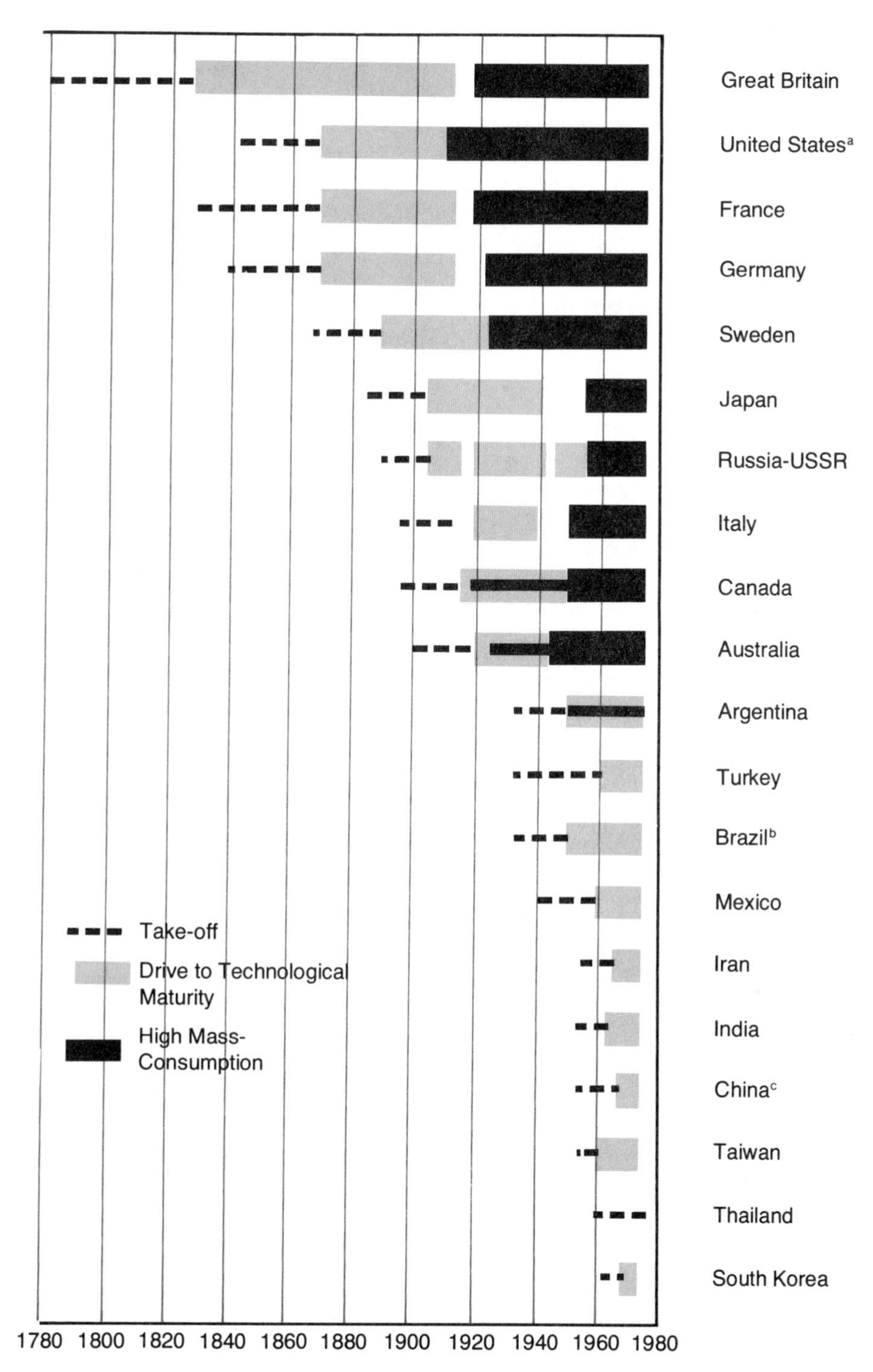

CHART II-2. *Stages of Economic Growth: Twenty Countries*

[a]New England regional take-off, 1815–1850.
[b]São Paulo regional take-off, 1900–1920.
[c]Manchuria regional take-off, 1930–1941.
Source: Part Five.

leaving their mark on the world index of industrial production.[4] The sequence in Chart II-2 helps shape Table II-2, which puts together estimates of the percentage distribution of the world's industrial production at different dates, from 1820 to 1971.[5]

In the pre-1860 period, the sharpest movement is the rise of American industry in the period 1840–1860. Its surge forward during those two U.S. take-off decades reduces, on Mulhall's calculations, the proportion of industry in Europe from 94 percent to 86 percent. As for the three major European economies, all lose relatively between 1820 and 1860. Despite the French and German take-offs, during the period 1840–1860, Britain holds its own in Europe, according to this index.

The data from 1870 to 1913, in which we can have higher confidence, show the relative decline of Britain, whose peak proportion may, indeed, have been around 1870; the movement forward of Germany to a relative peak just before the turn of the century; the decline of France and Belgium, held off in the last golden years before 1914; the decelerating but continuing rise in the relative position of the United States; and the movement into take-off, at a sufficient pace to shift the proportions their way, of Sweden, Italy, Canada, Russia, and Japan.

TABLE II-2. *Distribution of World's Industrial Production, 1820–1963 (in Percentages)*

Year	Europe									North America		
	Total	U.K.	France	Germany	Russia	Belgium	Scandinavia	Italy	Rest of Europe	Total	USA	Can
1820	96	24	20	15					37		4	
1840	94	21	18	17					38		5	
1860	86	21	16	15					34		14	
1870		32	10	13	4	3	[a]	2		24	23	1
1881–1885		27	9	14	3	3	1	2		30	29	1
1896–1900		20	7	17	5	2	1	3		31	30	1
1906–1910		15	6	16	5	2	1	3		37	35	2
1913		14	6	16	6	2	1	3		38	36	2
1913[b]		14	7	14	4[c]	2	1	3		38	36	2
1926–1929		9	7	12	4[c]	2	1	3		44	42	2
1936–1938		9	5	11	19[c]	1	2	3		34	32	2
1963	53	5	4	6[d]	19[c]	1	2	2	14[e]	34	32	2
1968		5	3	4[d]	16[c]	1	2	2		37	34	3
1971		4	3	5[d]	16[c]	1	2	2		36	33	3

[a] Less than 0.5 percent.
[b] The second line for 1913 represents the distribution according to the frontiers established after the First World War.
[c] USSR.
[d] Federal Republic of Germany.
[e] Eastern Europe, 10 percent; other European, 4+ percent.
[f] Central American weight is 0.74, of which Mexico is 0.64.
[g] Brazil's weight is 0.85; Argentina's, 0.72.
[h] For Brazil, the 1968 percentage is 0.66; for Argentina, 0.55. In 1971, the two figures were 0.67 and 0.59, respectively.

Sources: 1820–1860, Mulhall calculations; 1870 to 1936–1938, Hilgerdt calculations; 1963–1971, United Nations calcu tions (see note 5 for explanation of sources).

A comparison of the data for 1913 and 1926–1929 exhibits crudely the relative impact of the First World War as well as the pattern of industrial growth. The impact of the Great Depression is quite different: the United States loses ground relatively, as the rise of Soviet industry (perhaps somewhat exaggerated in these data) dominates the redistribution of manufacturing, while Western Europe holds its own fairly well, and Japan continues its relative movement forward.

We lack, unfortunately, an estimate for the early years after the Second World War. Such an estimate would exhibit a phase of extraordinary but transient primacy for the undamaged American economy, as Western Europe, the Soviet Union, and Japan, gravely set back, find their feet and resume their growth at rates generally higher than that of the United States.

The pattern that emerges in the 1960's, after the vicissitudes of the postwar years, has significant new features. Industrialization on a scale sufficient to impress itself on the distribution calculations is now a feature of every continent. The process to be observed between 1870 and 1913, when a new group of nations moved into take-off, is repeated on a wider canvas, as industrialization moves forward in the southern regions. Western Europe, which accounted for

n. America		South America			Rest								World
tal	Mexico	Total	Brazil	Argen-tina	Middle East	Rest of Asia	Japan	India	China	Africa	Oceania	Other Countries	
													100
													99
													100
												11	99
												12	101
						2	1	1				12	100
						2	1	1				12	99
						2	1	1				12	100
						2	1	1				14	99
						4	3	1				13	99
						5	4	1				12	101
	1[f]	3	1[g]	1[g]	[a]	6	4	1		1	1		99
	1	2	1[h]	1[h]	1	7	4	2		2	1	15	100
	1	2	1[h]	1[h]	1	8	5	1		2	1	15	100

almost two-thirds of industrial production as late as 1870, and about a third in 1936–1938, produces only 24 percent as of 1963, despite its remarkable postwar recovery and growth. Within Europe, Britain falls back, France holds its own, Western Germany moves relatively ahead. Meanwhile, the whole southern region, from Spain to Turkey, moves into rapid growth, a process aided by a remarkable south-north labor migration. The USSR settles down at about the same proportion as Western Europe as a whole (excluding Spain, Austria, Greece, and Turkey). The U.S. proportion remains about a third of the total, a proportion which was reached by about the turn of the century. Japan emerges in Asia as the third industrial power of the world; but elsewhere in Asia, in Eastern Europe, Latin America, Africa, and the Middle East a good many nations have by 1963 moved into take-off, and a few are beyond, in the drive to technological maturity. The early-comers to industrialization—Britain, the United States, Western Europe, Russia, and Japan—whose take-offs occurred before 1900, still dominate the industrial world. In 1963 the United Nations calculated that the nations of the world, excluding the USSR and Eastern Europe, produced 71 percent of total industrial production. Of that percentage, the advanced industrialized nations produced 62 percent, the developing nations, 9 percent. Put another way, the developing nations produced only 13 percent of the industrial output of the noncommunist world. But those who experienced take-off in the twentieth century are generally moving forward more rapidly than the average, with the exception of India and China, which have experienced special problems examined in Part Five. The average annual rate of growth of industrial production for the world between 1955 and 1971 is 6.2 percent; for the "developing market economies," 7.5 percent. For the "developed market economies" of Western Europe, North America, and Japan, where increasing resources are moving into services, as opposed to manufactures, the figure is only 5.0 percent.

6

Growth and Structural Change

We have broken into the analysis of modern growth by examining the expansion and diffusion of industry because the generation and absorption of new technologies in industry are central to the process at work in the world economy over the past two centuries. This approach is, of course, too limited. Invention and innovation were by no means confined to industry. They affected agriculture, communications, and various kinds of services as well. Moreover, the process of modernization carried with it wide-ranging structural changes in the economy, in social life, and, indeed, in politics.[6] The analysis of the demographic transition in Part One is, substantially, an exercise in the linkage between economic change and critical aspects of social change, as income per capita rises, education expands, and urbanization goes forward. In general, the wider economic and social changes that occur are not merely the result of industrialization but also play back on that process; for societies are interacting phenomena.

Table II-3, developed at the World Bank, is a useful, compressed portrait of how, in the course of this interacting process, certain key economic and social phenomena varied with levels of income per capita in the period 1950–1970.[7] We begin with this relatively contemporary table because data are both more abundant and more comparable than over long periods in the past. After summarizing the main features of Table II-3, we shall comment on some of the major similarities and differences between historical and contemporary experience under each heading.

Investment. In the contemporary world, the poorest countries (under $100 per capita) exhibit higher average levels of saving, investment, and capital imports than would be found in most cases in the past for societies at these minimum income levels. A gross investment rate of almost 14 percent of GNP (line 1b in Table II-3) is likely to yield an annual average increase of almost 5 percent in GNP itself. This implies that the marginal productivity of investment is around 33 percent; that is, an annual gross investment rate of 3 percent results in an increase of GNP of 1 percent. On average,

TABLE II-3. *Normal Variation in Economic Structure with Level of Development, 1950–1970*

Process	Mean[a] under $1
Accumulation processes	
1. Investment (% GNP)	
a. Saving	10.3
b. Investment	13.6
c. Capital inflow	3.2
2. Government revenue (% GNP)	
a. Government revenue	12.5
b. Tax revenue	10.6
3. Education	
a. Education expenditure (% GNP)	2.6
b. School enrollment ratio (% relevant age group)	24.4
Resource-allocation processes	
4. Structure of domestic demand (% GNP)	
a. Private consumption	77.9
b. Government consumption	11.9
c. Food consumption	41.4
5. Structure of production (% value added)	
a. Primary share	52.2
b. Industry share	12.5
c. Utilities share	5.3
d. Services share	30.0
6. Structure of trade (% GNP)	
a. Exports	17.2
b. Primary exports	13.0
c. Manufactured exports	1.1
d. Services exports	2.8
e. Imports	20.5
Demographic and distribution processes	
7. Labor allocation (% working force)	
a. Primary share	71.2
b. Industry share (including utilities)	7.8
c. Services share	21.0
8. Urbanization (% total population)	
a. Urban	12.8
9. Income distribution (% gross rates)	
a. Highest 20%	50.2
b. Lowest 40%	15.8
10. Demographic transition	
a. Birth rate	45.9
b. Death rate	20.9

[a] Approximately $70. Mean values of countries with per capita GNP under $100 va slightly according to composition of the sample.

[b] Approximately $1,500. Mean values of countries with per capita GNP over $1,000 va

NP per Capita in U.S. $, 1964									
.00	$200	$300	$400	$500	$800	$1,000	Mean over $1,000	Total Change	GNP per Capita at Midpoint
.5	17.1	19.0	20.2	21.0	22.6	23.3	23.3	13.0	$ 200
.8	18.8	20.3	21.3	22.0	23.4	24.0	23.4	9.8	$ 200
.3	1.6	1.2	1.0	0.9	0.6	0.6	0.1	– 3.1	$ 200
.3	18.1	20.2	21.9	23.4	26.8	28.7	30.7	18.2	$ 380
.9	15.3	17.3	18.9	20.3	23.6	25.4	28.2	17.6	$ 440
.3	3.3	3.4	3.5	3.7	4.1	4.3	3.9	1.3	$ 300
.5	54.9	63.7	69.4	73.5	81.0	84.2	86.3	61.9	$ 200
.0	68.6	66.7	65.4	64.5	62.5	61.7	62.4	–15.5	
.7	13.4	13.5	13.6	13.8	14.4	14.8	14.1	2.2	
.2	31.5	27.5	24.8	22.9	19.1	17.5	16.7	–24.7	$ 250
.2	32.7	26.6	22.8	20.2	15.6	13.8	12.7	–39.5	$ 200
.9	21.5	25.1	27.6	29.4	33.1	34.7	37.9	25.4	$ 300
.1	7.2	7.9	8.5	8.9	9.8	10.2	10.9	5.6	$ 300
.8	38.5	40.3	41.1	41.5	41.6	41.3	38.6	8.6	
.5	21.8	23.0	23.8	24.4	25.5	26.0	24.9	7.7	$ 150
.7	13.6	13.1	12.5	12.0	10.5	9.6	5.8	– 7.2	$1,000
.9	3.4	4.6	5.6	6.5	8.6	9.7	13.1	12.0	$ 600
.1	4.2	4.8	5.1	5.3	5.6	5.7	5.9	3.1	$ 250
.8	23.4	24.3	24.9	25.4	26.3	26.7	25.0	4.5	$ 250
.8	55.7	48.9	43.8	39.5	30.0	25.2	15.9	–55.3	$ 400
.1	16.4	20.6	23.5	25.8	30.3	32.5	36.8	29.0	$ 325
.1	27.9	30.4	32.7	34.7	39.6	42.3	47.3	26.3	$ 450
.0	36.2	43.9	49.0	52.7	60.1	63.4	65.8	53.0	$ 250
.1	55.7	55.4	54.7	53.8	51.1	49.4	45.8	– 4.4	
.0	12.9	12.7	12.8	13.0	13.8	14.3	15.3	– 0.5	
.6	37.7	33.8	31.1	29.1	24.9	22.9	19.1	–26.8	$ 350
.6	13.5	11.4	10.3	9.7	9.1	9.0	9.7	–11.2	$ 150

ghtly according to composition of the sample.

Source: Hollis Chenery and Moises Syrquin with the assistance of Hazel Elkington, *tterns of Development, 1950–1970*, pp. 20–21.

then, the poorest countries of the world are growing faster than their rates of population increase, and most of them have broken out of the relative stagnation which they experienced over previous centuries.

But there is an important conceptual problem embedded in the use of such averages, which will emerge more clearly in Part Five. GNP per capita is an inadequate measure of stages of growth. There can be relatively comfortable nations, with both good resource endowments and relatively high GNP per capita, which have not entered take-off; for example, to take an extreme case, contemporary Libya or, historically, the United States before the New England textile expansion of the 1820's. There can also be very poor countries which have entered take-off; for example, India and South Korea of the mid-1960's. Finally, there can be very poor countries which have not entered take-off, e.g., a good many of the new African states, Yemen, and Burma. In short, countries with GNP per capita of less than $100 can be either in the preconditions for take-off or in take-off and, in averaging them together, we conceal that critical distinction.

Despite this important proviso, it is a fact that economic growth is now an endemic phenomenon and investment rates in the poorest countries are higher than they generally were in such countries during the interwar years or before 1914. Capital imports, in the form of regular institutionalized assistance from richer to poorer nations, are also a special feature of the post-1945 world. Whatever its inadequacies, the provision of 3 percent of GNP to the poorest nations of the world in capital imports is remarkable by historical standards, although that percentage (line 1c) includes private as well as intergovernmental capital flows.

The great rise in the investment rate comes between countries under $100 per capita and those in the $200 per capita category. After that point the average investment rate rises more slowly, leveling off at $1,000 per capita. The initial jump, both historically and in the contemporary world, is generally associated with take-off,[8] although high investment rates tended to exist in the preconditions for take-off in countries requiring large railway or other infrastructure investment before a national market could be created (e.g., Canada, Argentina, Australia). These levels of investment were often sustained by large capital imports. In the 1880's, for example, the net capital inflow to Australia was almost half of gross domestic capital formation. As domestic saving and investment rates rise with the process of growth, and income per capita rises, the role of capital imports falls off (line 1c). This is both a contemporary and a historical phenomenon.

Government Revenue. The tendency of government revenue (and expenditure) as a proportion of GNP to rise with increases in per capita income has long been noted and incorporated in Wagner's Law, the creation of Adolph Wagner, published first in 1883 in Leipzig. As lines 2a and 2b indicate, the tendency broadly holds for the contemporary world. There is deceleration as GNP per capita rises, but it is not as marked as in investment rates, as Table II-4 shows. What Table II-4 broadly suggests is that as nations become richer they are content to accept a relatively constant rate of economic growth but continue to demand an increasing proportion of total output in the form of governmental services. Historically it is possible to show in a number of now advanced nations, from Bismarck's Germany forward, that it is in a post–take-off stage, the drive to technological maturity, that social welfare expenditures expand to a sufficient scale, backed by reasonably efficient administrative organizations, to begin to have a major impact on the life of the citizen.[9] The relatively higher rates of increase in government revenues than investment in the $200–$500 per capita range appear to reflect this phenomenon on the contemporary scene.

Where historical GNP data exist (as well as public finance data) we can derive some sense of how these proportions moved in the past; although technical and philosophic difficulties make it treacherous to try to express GNP-per-capita data in contemporary U.S. dollars. It is wiser, using Chart II-2, to relate these historical proportions to each other via stages of growth. We can somewhat arbitrarily relate the figures in Table II-3 (in U.S. 1964 dollars) to stages of growth as follows:

Under $100–$200 per capita	—	Take-off
$200–$500 per capita	—	Drive to technological maturity
$500 per capita and over	—	High mass-consumption

It should be borne in mind that accelerated inflation since 1965 would alter these relationships, raising the dollar equivalents by up to 90 percent. Table II-5 summarizes the result for five major nations. More detailed data are presented in a note.[10]

These figures require some comment. The proportions given for the British take-off (11–19 percent) are for the two peacetime years 1792 and 1822. The high wartime figures (1800, 24 percent;

TABLE II-4. *Rates of Increase with Rising GNP per Capita: Investment and Government Revenue (in Percentage Rate of Growth)*

	Investment	Government Revenue
Under $100–$100	16	22
$100–$200	19	18
$200–$300	8	12
$300–$400	5	8
$400–$500	3	6
$500–$800	2	5
$800–$1,000	1	3
$1,000–over $1,000	– 0.03	7

Source: Calculated from TABLE II-3.
Note: Rates are calculated per $100 increase in GNP per capita.

TABLE II-5. *Stages of Growth and Public Revenue-Expenditure: Contemporary and Historical Ranges (% GNP)*

Stage	Contemporary	Great Britain	France	Germany	Japan	United States
Take-off	12–18	11–19	15	—	10–20	—
Drive to technological maturity	18–25	11–14	20–21	9–18	20–40	7–9
Interwar years and Great Depression	—	24–30	24–39	25–43	—	21–22
High mass-consumption	31[a]	38–44	46–47	41–44	30+	12–35

[a] Mean over $1,000 per capita.
Sources: "Contemporary" column derived from TABLE II-3. For historical sources, see note 10.

1814, 29 percent) are excluded. The Japanese take-off proportion is inflated by the high military expenditures undertaken by Japan in its early stage of modern growth. But, by and large, contemporary and historical figures for take-off fall in the same range, despite the fact that Britain and France probably enjoyed higher levels of income per capita during take-off than Japan and most contemporary nations in that stage.

In the drive to technological maturity contemporary nations allocate more of their resources to government and governmental services than did Britain, Germany, and the United States. (The relatively constant French figure is enigmatic and has not been fully analyzed by historians and public finance experts.) There is no doubt that government plays a larger economic and social role in contemporary nations at this intermediate stage of development (e.g., in Latin America) than in pre-1914 Britain, Germany, and the United States. The Japanese figure remained abnormally high (by historical, not contemporary, standards), again because of its large military establishment rather than economic or social outlays. The pre-1914 social reforms and arms expansion in Europe lifted the proportions in Britain and Germany, but only to modest levels by contemporary standards; from 9 percent to 13 percent in Britain between 1890 and 1910; from 13 percent to 18 percent in Germany between 1891 and 1913. In the United States the pre-1914 proportions also rose, but at a lower level: from 7 percent in 1890 to 9 percent in 1913.

The interwar and depression years are a special story. In Europe the political pressures on government moved public expenditures into new high ranges, coming close to or over 40 percent in France and Germany, to 29 percent in 1931–1932 in Britain, at the bottom of depression and before rearmament began. In the United States, during the prosperous 1920's, the figures were also higher than in prewar times, but still low: only 12 percent in 1927. Depression and the New Deal raised the figure to 21 percent in 1932, 22 percent in 1940. During years of acute depression the proportion rose, in part because GNP fell more than public expenditures; but, in those difficult and frustrating times, the political process pressed democratic governments to try to compensate for the unsatisfactory workings of the private sectors.

In the two prosperous phases of high mass-consumption (1920–1929, 1946–1957) the U.S. figure is at quite different levels: 12–13 percent in the 1920's; 23–29 percent in the 1940's and 1950's, reflecting higher public outlays brought about permanently by the New Deal as well as higher military expenditures than a generation earlier. The lift in the 1960's is wholly attributable to nonmilitary outlays, notably for education and medical care, since expenditures for military purposes, space, foreign aid, etc., rose at just about the rate of increase of GNP.

Education. After an initial sharp expansion when income rises to $100 per capita, the proportion of GNP allocated to education increases slowly indeed with the rise of income per capita (Table II-3, line 3a). From such scattered evidence as is available, it appears that current outlays for education in poor countries enjoy higher priority than those in the historical past. In Germany, for example, only 1.3 percent of GNP was spent from public resources on education in 1881, and 2.6 percent as late as 1913, a proportion about equal to that in the poorest countries on the contemporary scene. The British proportion rose from under 0.8 percent in 1884 to 1.3 percent at the turn of the century to 2.4 percent in 1913. Reflecting a general postwar trend in Europe, the German figure was about 4 percent in 1958. The United States proportion rose from something like 0.9 percent in 1881 to about 1.3 percent in 1900 to perhaps 1.4 percent in 1913.[11]

The strong contemporary thrust for literacy is reflected also in the school enrollment ratio (line 3b), which more than doubles between under $100 per capita and $200 per capita, increasing more slowly thereafter. Working with United Nations data for 1950, Simon Kuznets assembled the data in Table II-6 showing the percentage of population, fifteen years and over, illiterate; to the right are added the approximate dates when the indicated proportion of British males were unable to sign at marriage registries and the dates for the equivalent U.S. (white) illiteracy proportions.[12] The U.S. illiter-

TABLE II-6. *Illiteracy Rates: Contemporary and Historical*

Income per Capita	% Contemporary Population Illiterate	United Kingdom	United States
Under $100	71	—	—
$100–$200	49	ca. 1815	—
$200–$350	30	1850	—
$350–$575	19	1870	1870
$575–$1,000	6	1893	1920
$1,000 and over	2	1903	1952

Sources: See notes 12 and 13.

acy rates are relatively higher than Britain's, due, in part, to large-scale immigration.

Structure of Domestic Demand. The categories measured under the "Structure of Domestic Demand" in Table II-3 reflect different forces at work in the process of growth. The relative decline in the proportion of private consumption results from both the rise in saving and investment and the increasing proportionate role of government in the society as income per capita expands. These are characteristics already suggested by lines 1a and 1b, 2a and 2b. Line 4c, food consumption, indicates a quite different aspect of rising income per capita; that is, the tendency of families to spend a declining proportion of income on food, as income expands. Here we are dealing, again, with an insight first generalized by a nineteenth-century German statistician—Ernst Engel—from an initial study of 153 Belgian family budgets.[13] In the contemporary world, the decline is relatively slight between those under $100 per capita and at $100 per capita. Among very poor families, in fact, a rise in income yields initially a disproportionate increase in outlays on food. The greatest decline occurs between $100 and $200 per capita.

Structure of Production. The major feature of lines 5a–5d is the oldest and best-documented characteristic of modern economic growth, both historically and on the contemporary scene; that is, the relative decline in the role of agriculture (primary sector) and the rise of industry.[14] The greatest proportional expansion of industry comes between $100 and $200 per capita, generally during take-off. The relative increase in industry then decelerates. The pattern in the decline of the primary sector is symmetrical but a bit less sharp in its movement. The pattern in the services sector is less consistent: a rise to a peak proportion at about $800 per capita; a slight decline; a second rise (not shown in Table II-3) at very high levels of per capita income, as both private and public outlays shift disproportionately toward outlays on education, health, travel, recreation, etc.[15] The concept of a service sector is highly ambiguous. It contains many kinds of activities subject to quite different patterns of demand and supply.[16] Within the service sector are hairdressers and generals, surgeons, waiters, bankers, insurance salesmen, professors, and gas-station attendants. Generalizations about services should be treated with extreme caution unless the components are disaggregated and we know what we are talking about.

Structure of Trade. All the structural characteristics of growing economies generalized in Table II-3 and in our discussion of it are, of course, subject to wide variation. This is particularly true of international trade, where the size of a country and the character of its natural resources (or lack of them) can produce great differences. In the 1950's, for example, the proportion of foreign trade in commodities and services to national product ranged from 9 percent for the United States to 77 percent for Norway. Section 6 in Table II-3 is to be read with this in mind.

As in many other cases, the greatest relative structural change comes in moving up to $200 per capita—that is, during the take-off. Exports and imports then expand at diminishing rates until a decline emerges at over $1,000 per capita, although trade in services (notably tourism) continues to expand rapidly as a proportion of income per capita. Exports of primary products rise in the earliest stage of growth (up to $100 per capita) and are then replaced by rising exports of industrial products, which decelerate slowly.

Labor Allocation. As one would expect, the proportions of the working force move broadly in the same direction as the structure of production, when broken down into primary, industrial, and service sectors. As income per capita rises, the proportion of the working force in agriculture declines, while that in both industry and services rises. This has been true historically as well as in the contemporary world. A comparison of the shift in production (value added) and labor proportions at different income-per-capita levels tells us something about productivity. The share of services in value added, for example, rises only from 30.0 percent to 38.6 percent in line 5d (after peaking at 41.6 percent). That modest increase is accompanied by more than a doubling of the working force in services, from 21.0 percent to 47.3 percent. There are serious difficulties in measuring productivity in certain services; but, as nearly as we can measure it, productivity in services in richer societies is much lower than the average, drawing an increasing proportion of the working force, while the share in value added actually declines. On the other hand, in countries with income per capita over $1,000, industry plus utilities contributes about half of value added with 37 percent of the working force.

As compared with historical experience, a major difference in labor allocation relates to agriculture.[17] Presently advanced industrial nations exhibited lower proportions of their working forces in agriculture at equivalent stages of growth than contemporary developing nations; and they have experienced remarkable increases in agricultural productivity since the end of the Second World War. Put another way, a number of contemporary developing nations are marked by vast agricultural sectors, where productivity increases slowly, while their industrial sectors move forward quite rapidly as modern enclaves. This duality appears more acute than in Western Europe and the United States at early stages of growth. It emerges statistically as a less rapid movement of labor out of agriculture than the rise of value added in industry and services, as well as in per capita income, would suggest. The diffusion to an economy of what modern technology and organization can provide does not take place evenly; and some of the most difficult and recalcitrant problems in the developing world lie within agriculture, a problem discussed in Part Six.

Urbanization. The proportion of the population in cities rises with the increase in income per capita, as one would expect, both historically and in a cross-section view of the contemporary world. Adequate, comparable historical data on urbanization do not exist which would permit fine-grained comparisons with the past; but the sluggish movement of labor out of agriculture, cited above, suggests that the urban proportions would prove lower at similar stages of growth for those societies where the dualism between modern industrial and quasi-traditional agricultural sectors is particularly acute; e.g., India and China.

Income Distribution. Lines 9a and 9b of Table II-3 suggest an initially painful aspect of the growth process; that is, the changes wrought in the early stages of growth, up to $200 per capita, cause a shift in income in favor of those in the highest income brackets, a proportion that subsequently declines. The proportion flowing to those in the lowest income brackets declines until $300 per capita, then rises slowly. It is the middle class that relatively gains most from modern growth. After $200 per capita the proportion going to the 40 percent in middle income brackets rises from 31.4 percent to 38.9 percent of the total. Over the whole sequence, the middle 40 percent gains at the expense of both the upper 20 percent and the lower 40 percent. These averages conceal considerable variation in income distribution within contemporary countries at early stages of growth: from, say, 20 percent of GNP to the poorest 40 percent of the population to 7 percent.[18] Historical data are insufficient to permit useful comparisons with past experience, although an initial widening and later narrowing of income differentials is likely to emerge if we can generate useful evidence.

Income-distribution calculations on a national basis conceal an important aspect of the problem; i.e., regional differences in income levels. Since growth is inherently an uneven process, proceeding by sectors, certain regions have tended to enter modern growth sooner than others. In many cases the northern regions have been industrialized first, although in Brazil it was the south. Initially, regional income differentials widen; but as nations move to industrial maturity, regional differences diminish. The relative rise of the American Sunbelt since 1940 is a quite typical phenomenon.

Demographic Transition. The data incorporated in lines 10a and 10b are presented below in Chart II-3 and discussed above in Chapter 4.

There are, then, significant similarities, as well as differences, in contemporary as opposed to historical patterns and sequences of growth. Contemporary nations at early stages of growth carry a heavier burden of population increase than in the past, but they have a larger pool of unapplied technologies available for incorporation into their economic structures, and they are driven forward by more purposeful public policies, notably in education, on which the pace at which technologies can efficiently be absorbed heavily depends.

7

International Trade and Its Changing Distribution

Against the background of this terse survey of the structural changes that accompany the process of growth, we turn to international trade. It is possible, after a fashion described in Appendix B, to put together an index of the volume of world trade covering the period 1720–1971. That index is presented in Chart II-3. It exhibits an expansion of 460 times over the period, or an annual growth rate of 2.47 percent. Table II-7 sets out annual average growth rates for the volume of world trade for periods parallel to those for the world manufacturing index presented in Table II-1. (The data from Table II-1 are repeated in Table II-7 for purposes of quick comparison.) Since international trade statistics have been more regularly mobilized by governments than industrial production data, the former can be broken down over shorter periods for the pre-1945 era.

Table II-7 catches some of the major developments in the evolution of the world economy over the past two and a half centuries:

—Trade expanded quite rapidly in the period 1720–1750, at a slightly higher rate than our industrial production index.

—There is an exaggerated slowdown between 1750 and 1780, because 1780 is a distorted benchmark. Anglo-American trade was severely damped by the War of Independence. British trade, for example, expanded at an annual rate of 1.35 percent between 1750 and 1774. This is probably a fair measure of the pace of international commerce in the third quarter of the century.

—The French Revolutionary and Napoleonic Wars cut back the growth of trade, while shifting it toward Britain, both because its control of the major sea routes permitted a virtual monopoly in the re-export trade and because the first phase of the industrial revolution provided Britain with the capacity to export cotton textiles on a large scale, also expanding trade in raw cotton across the Atlantic.

—From 1815 to 1870 the rate of expansion of world trade fluctuated about a much higher level than during the eighteenth century, averaging 4.2 percent between 1820 and 1870.[19] This rate slackened off down to the mid-1890's, but then rose again, reaching particularly high rates in the pre-1914 decade, when massive capital ex-

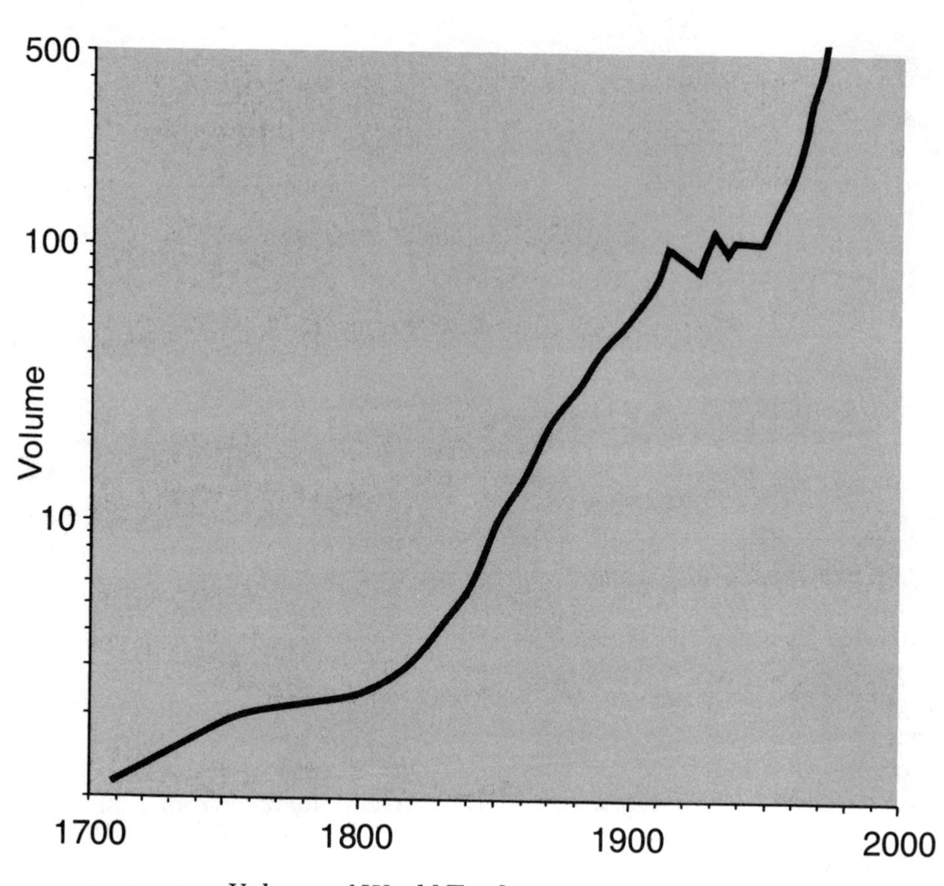

CHART II-3. *Volume of World Trade, 1720–1971*

Sources: See Appendix B.

ports helped open up new areas (e.g., Western Canada) and brought their products onto world markets.

—The protectionist pathology of the interwar years and the Great Depression of the 1930's is reflected in relatively sharper setbacks in the trade index than in the industrial index, although there was a brief rapid revival of trade in 1925–1929.

—The post-1945 world down to the early 1970's emerges as unique, in the growth of trade, as in the growth of industry.

Table II-8 sets out the approximate distribution of world trade by countries and regions for selected years from 1720 to 1971. The method of its construction is also described in Appendix B. Bracketed figures [ ] provide, for convenient comparison, selected data drawn from Table II-2 showing the proportionate share of industrial production for key countries and dates.

The nature of the data underlying Table II-8 justifies conclusions drawn only from large and obvious changes.

Great Britain (United Kingdom). The British trade proportion in 1720 was large for a nation of only six million people, a third the size of France. But, contrary to a widely held image, Britain did not

TABLE II-7. *World Trade and Industrial Production: Growth Rates, Selected Periods, 1705–1971 (Annual Average Percentage Rate of Growth)*

		World Trade		World Industry	
1720–1750	1.75	1720–1780	1.10	1705–1785	1.5
1750–1780	0.46				
1780–1800	0.27	1780–1830	1.37		2.6
1800–1820	1.50				
1820–1830	3.33	1820–1840	2.81		2.9
1830–1840	2.30				
1840–1850	6.46	1840–1860	4.84		3.5
1850–1860	3.25				
1860–1870	5.53		5.53		2.9
1870–1876 to 1880	2.94				
1881–1885	4.84	1870–1900	3.24		3.7
1886–1890	2.97				
1891–1895	1.75				
1896–1900	3.50				
1901–1905	3.29	1900–1913	3.75		4.2
1906–1910	3.87				
1911–1913	4.34				
. . . . .					
1921–1925	−1.42	1913–1929	0.72		2.7
1926–1929	6.74				
1931–1935	−3.00	1929–1938	−1.15		2.0
1936–1938	3.32				
1938–1948	0.00	1938–1948	0.00		4.1
1948–1953	6.63				
1953–1958	5.66	1948–1971	7.27		5.6
1958–1963	7.40				
1963–1968	8.63				
1968–1971	8.51				

Sources: See Appendix B.

significantly expand its proportionate share until its take-off began in the 1780's. The relative trade advantage achieved down to 1792 became more marked during the French Revolutionary and Napoleonic Wars, when the cotton textile revolution combined with Britain's quasi-monopolistic control of the seas to push its trade proportion to something like a third of the world's total in 1800. After the war Britain lost its monopoly position, notably in the re-export trade. But the scale of its industrial and trading advantage in 1815, relative to its major potential rivals; its accelerated postwar industrial momentum; the fact that its major industry (cotton textiles) involved both large raw material imports and large exports; and its progressively increased reliance on grain imports all contributed to the fact that down to 1870 Britain conducted about a quarter of the world's trade. As northwestern continental Europe and the United

States moved forward in the drive to technological maturity, between 1870 and 1914, the relative British proportion fell to something like 16 percent. In the relatively stagnant trading environment of the interwar years, Britain lost ground relative to its pre-1914 position. After the Second World War, Britain emerged initially (see 1948 data) in a better position than the major war-torn continental nations and Japan; but from that point, once again, Britain's relative world role diminished, and it lost ground, as well, within Western Europe.

France. Throughout its modern history, foreign trade has played a somewhat lesser role in the economic life of France than was the case for Britain. In 1820, for example, Mulhall estimates the British and French industrial proportions as 24 percent and 20 percent, respectively, the trade proportions as 27 percent and 9 percent. If one looks at the trade and industrial data for 1963 in Table II-8 it is evident that this structural difference narrows, but persists.

Against that background, France began with 8 percent of the world's trade in 1720, but moved up relatively down to 1780. War and Britain's precocious industrialization set France back over the next forty years; but it gained a little ground during its take-off (1830–1860) until set back once again by the loss of important economic territory after the Franco-Prussian War. And its relative trading position suffered further attrition with the rise of Germany and the United States in the pre-1914 era. Decline continued during the interwar years, especially during the middle and late 1930's, when France failed to move forward as rapidly from the nadir of depression as its major trading partners. From 1958 to 1971, however, French economic growth yielded a somewhat expanded relative position in world trade.

Germany. It is difficult to know how Mulhall achieved his *tour de force* in producing a total trade estimate for the fragmented German states of the eighteenth and early nineteenth centuries. The rise between 1850 and 1870 is, however, a credible reflection of the strong German take-off of that period. The relative German trading position then slowly expanded down to the First World War. A physically somewhat diminished Germany lost relative position during the interwar years; and then after 1945, in a remarkable effort, truncated Western Germany expanded from 2 percent in 1948 to 6 percent in 1971. At the latter date it was the second largest trading nation in the world, the first European nation to surpass Britain since statistics were recorded.

Switzerland. The relative position of Switzerland in world trade is chiefly notable for its stability. In a highly dynamic environment, it held its own in trade and in the modernization of its economy in general. It is also, of course, a major example of a small nation whose foreign trade constitutes a very high proportion of its GNP (46 percent excluding services, 61 percent including services in the late 1950's).

Holland and Belgium. Something of the same can be said of what we now call the Benelux area, although its role in the European and world economy is more significant. The decline in the eighteenth century reflects Holland's dour rear guard struggle to sustain its status, as its seventeenth-century primacy waned in the face of the rise of Britain and France. In the second quarter of the nineteenth century Belgium moved into take-off on the basis of its coal, railroads, and engineering capacity, lifting the trading role of the region, a rise which continued down to about 1905, with steel and chemicals reinforcing its position. There was a deceleration in the pre-war decade. As for other regions based on heavy industry, the interwar years were difficult and saw some relative falling away. But the post-1945 boom on the European continent and the Common Market lifted Benelux, by 1971, above its relative trading position of 1913.

Scandinavia. Led by Sweden, with its important but (after 1720) restricted iron exports, Scandinavia played a modest but steady role in trade during the eighteenth century. Although its trading access to Britain varied during the war years, they were, by and large, a period of setback. After 1815, the region held its own, moving up, however, with the Swedish drive to technological maturity in the 1890's, its exports expanding beyond timber to pulp and paper, iron ore, and a widening range of engineering products. The British housing boom of the 1930's, German rearmament and, perhaps, domestic economies better sustained than most others combined to lift the Scandinavian trading proportion between 1928 and 1937–1938. In the post-1945 years, the vitality of continental Europe lifted Scandinavia in much the same way as Benelux.

Italy. The Italian trading proportion declined somewhat as Germany surged forward after 1850, and then held its own during the Italian take-off from the 1890's to the First World War. It declined with the autarchic 1930's but rose in the 1950's and 1960's as Italy made up considerable ground in relation to the rest of Western Europe.

Spain. The eighteenth-century revival of Spain under the Bourbons, after its grave crisis of the seventeenth century, permitted it to hold its own in the world trading arena, notably after 1750. The decision to cast its lot with France in 1796, however, opened a tragic era in Spanish life. There is no movement in Table II-8 quite as dramatic as the decline in the relative role of Spanish trade between the mid-eighteenth and mid-nineteenth centuries (from 10 percent to 1 percent). From the 1840's, however, Spain began slowly to recover. The Catalonian textile industry, modernizing in the 1780's at a pace surpassed only in Britain, found its feet. In the period 1856–1865 railroadization began the long process of overcoming the fragmentation of the national market imposed by Spanish geography, a phase reflected by a lift in its trading proportion down to about 1905. Bilboan iron ore significantly lifted the level of exports after 1875. Down to 1913, despite the vicissitudes imposed by the loss of Cuba and the Philippines, Spain managed proportionately to hold its own,

TABLE II-8. *World Trade and Its Distribution by Countries and Regions, 1720–1971*

Volume world trade (Index, 1913 = 100)	1.13	1.90	2.18	2.3
Annual average growth rate	—	1.75%	0.46%	0.27%
Year	*1720*(1)	*1750*(1)	*1780*(1)	*1800*(1)
Great Britain	13%	13%	12%	33%
France	8	10	12	9
Germany	9	11	11	10
Switzerland	1	1	2	1
Holland and Belgium	5	4	4	4
Scandinavia	2	2	3	1
Italy	4	4	4	3
Western Europe (total)	42	45	48	61
Spain	12	10	10	3
Portugal	2	2	2	1
Austrian Empire (Austria)	2	3	3	2
Turkish Empire	2	2	2	1
Eastern (communisty Europe	—	—	—	—
of which: Russia (USSR)	9	10	9	9
Total Europe	69	72	74	77
North America	—	—	—	—
of which: United States	—	—	2	5
Canada	—	—	—	—
Latin America	12	11	11	7
of which: Argentina	—	—	—	—
Brazil	—	—	—	—
Mexico	—	—	—	—
Asia	—	—	—	—
of which: Communist Asia	—	—	—	—
Noncommunist Asia	—	—	—	—
of which: Japan	—	—	—	—
India	11	7	5	3
Africa	—	—	—	—
British Colonies	2	2	a	1
Oceania	—	—	—	—
of which: Australia	—	—	—	—
Various	6	7	8	6
Total	100%	99%	100%	99%

[] indicates percentage industrial production, from TABLE-2.

[a] 0.54 percent.

[b] Under 0.5 percent.

[c] U.N. regional trade totals may differ from sum of national trade figures. Regional figures are rendered uniform: all imports measured C.I.F.; all exports, F.O.B. Certain categories of trade excluded in national statistics are also estimated in U.N. regional totals.

3.1	4.3	5.4	10.1	13.9	23.8	33.5	45.3
1.5%	3.3%	2.3%	6.5%	3.2%	5.5%	3.5%	3.4%
820[1]	*1830*[1]	*1840*[1]	*1850*[1]	*1860*[1]	*1870*[1]	*1880*[1]	*1889*[1]
27% [24]	24%	25%	22%	25%	25% [32]	23%	22%
9 [20]	10	11	11	11	10 [10]	11	9
11 [15]	11	8	8	9	10 [13]	10	11
2	2	2	2	2	2	2	2
6	7	7	7	6	6	8	9
2	2	2	2	2	2	2	2
4	5	5	5	3	3	3	3
61	61	60	57	58	58	59	58
3	2	2	1	2	2	2	2
1	1	1	1	1	b	b	1
3	4	4	3	3	4	4	3
2	2	2	2	2	3	2	2
—	—	—	—	—	—	—	—
6	7	5	5	3	5	4	3
76	77	74	69	69	72	71	69
—	—	—	—	—	—	—	—
6 [4]	5	7	7	9	8 [23]	10	9
—	—	—	—	—	—	—	—
8	8	8	8	6	6	5	5
—	—	—	—	—	—	—	—
—	—	—	—	—	—	—	—
—	—	—	—	—	—	—	—
—	—	—	—	—	—	—	—
—	—	—	—	—	—	—	—
—	—	—	—	—	—	—	—
—	—	—	—	—	—	—	—
3	2	3	4	3	4	4	4
—	—	—	—	—	—	—	—
1	2	3	5	7	6	7	9
—	—	—	—	—	—	—	—
—	—	—	—	—	—	—	—
7	7	6	6	5	5	4	4
01%	101%	101%	99%	99%	101%	101%	100%

Sources:
[1] indicates Mulhall used as source;
[2] indicates Kuznets, *Modern Economic Growth*, p. 307;
[3] indicates ibid., p. 308 (sources for both Kuznets tables given on p. 309); data on "Eastern (communist) :urope" include allowance for presently Communist Asia;
[4] indicates calculation from U.N. sources. For details see Appendix B.

TABLE II-8. *World Trade and Its Distribution by Countries and Regions, 1720–1971 (continued)*

Volume world trade (Index, 1913 = 100)	48	67	100	110
Annual average growth rate	1.5%	3.4%	4.1%	.64%
Year	*1891–1895*(2)	*1901–1905*(2)	*1913*(3)	*1928*(3)
Great Britain	18%	16%	16% [14]	14% [9]
France	9	7	7 [6]	6 [7]
Germany	11	12	12 [16]	9 [1
Switzerland	2	2	2	1
Holland and Belgium	10	11	7	5
Scandinavia	3	3	3	3
Italy	3	3	3	3
Western Europe	56	55	50	41
Spain	2	2	1	2
Portugal	—	—	b	b
Austrian Empire (Austria)	4	4	—	—
Turkish Empire	—	—	—	—
Eastern (communist) Europe	—	—	13	8
of which: Russia (USSR)	3	4	— [6]	— [4]
Total Europe	65	65	64	51
North America	12	13	14	18
of which: United States	(10.5)	(11)	(11) [36]	(14) [4
Canada	(1.5)	(2)	(3)	(4)
Latin America	—	—	8	9
of which: Argentina	—	—	—	—
Brazil	—	—	—	—
Mexico	—	—	—	—
Asia	—	—	9	13
of which: Communist Asia	—	—	—	—
Noncommunist Asia	—	—	—	—
of which: Japan	—	—	—	—
India	—	—	—	—
Africa	—	—	4	4
British Colonies	—	—	—	—
Oceania	—	—	2	3
of which: Australia	2	2	—	—
Various	21	20	—	3
Total	100%	100%	101%	101%

[] indicates percentage industrial production, from TABLE II-2.

[a] 0.54 percent.

[b] Under 0.5 percent.

[c] U.N. regional trade totals may differ from sum of national trade figures. Regional figures are rende uniform: all imports measured C.I.F.; all exports, F.O.B. Certain categories of trade excluded in natic statistics are also estimated in U.N. regional totals.

	103	103	187	269	520
.4%	—	−0.26%	6.1%	7.5%	8.6%
7[3]	*1938*[4]	*1948*[4]	*1958*[4]	*1963*[4]	*1971*[4]
% [9]	14%	12%	9%	8% [5]	7%
[5]	4	5	5	5 [4]	6
[11]	9	2	8	9 [6]	10
	1	2	2	2	2
	5	6	6	7	8
	5	6	4	5	5
	2	2	3	4	4
)	40	35	37	40	42
(0.5)	b	1 (0.71)	1 (0.6)	1 (0.8)	1 (1.1)
	b	b	b	b	b
	1	b	1	1	1
	—	—	—	—	—
	6	5	9	11	9
	(1)	(2)	(4)	(5) [19]	(4)
	47	41	48	53	53
	13	22[c]	19	17[c] [34]	18
)	(10)	(16)	(14)	(11) [32]	(13)
) [32]	(3)	(5)	(5)	(4) [2]	(5)
	7	12	9	7 [4]	6
	(1.6)	(2.63)	(1.0)	(0.74)	(0.51)
	(1.1)	(1.90)	(1.2)	(0.91)	(0.93)
	(0.50)	(0.85)	(0.84)	(0.70)	(0.54)
	17	13	14	14	15
	(2)	(1)	(2)	(1)	(1)
	(15)	(12)	(12)	(13)	(14)
	(4.1) [4]	(0.8)	(2.7)	(3.9) [4]	(6.2)
	(2.2)	(2.6)	(1.4)	(1.3)	(0.6)
	5	7	6	5	5
	—	—	—	—	—
	3	3	2	2 [1]	2
	(1.9)	(2.4)	(1.6)	(1.7)	(1.4)
	8	1	2	2	1
)%	100%	99%	100%	100%	100%

ources:
indicates Mulhall used as source;
indicates Kuznets, *Modern Economic Growth*, p. 307;
indicates ibid., p. 308 (sources for both Kuznets tables given on p. 309); data on "Eastern
nmunist) Europe" include allowance for presently Communist Asia;
indicates calculation from U.N. sources. For details see Appendix B.

aided, like France, by the possibilities of hydroelectric power which helped underpin its industrial development. After some recovery in the 1920's, Spain remained at a low and relatively stagnant level from the time of its Civil War to 1958. Its subsequent recovery is reflected in the rise of its trading proportion from 0.6 percent in 1958 to 1.1 percent in 1971, a rise damped (as in the case of Mexico) by the high proportion of its foreign exchange earned through tourism and workers' remittances, which are not included in the trade figures of Table II-8.

Eastern Europe. The political as well as economic vicissitudes of the countries of Eastern Europe make it impossible to track out in an orderly shorthand way the region's trading role and the major forces determining it. Poland had brief passages of independence over these two centuries and a half; but down to 1914 the region was mainly part of the Turkish, Austrian, and Russian empires. Between the two world wars the nations achieved national identity; but by 1948 they enjoyed, excepting Yugoslavia, varying (and changing) degrees of quasi-independence at best. Among the minor consequences of all this painful history is that continuous economic data are hard to come by, even in the most accessible category, foreign trade. One can only make a few tentative comments on the basis of the data in Table II-8. The Austrian and Turkish empires roughly held their own in eighteenth-century trade, if Mulhall's calculations are to be credited. We know this to have been a period of considerable vitality and reform in Vienna, at least. The war years undoubtedly saw a relative decline; but after 1815 parts of the Austrian empire began to move forward in industrialization (e.g., Bohemia), responding to impulses from the emergence of modern Germany; and late in the nineteenth century Hungary moved into take-off.[20] By 1913 Eastern Europe (excluding Russia) may have commanded about 8 percent of world trade.[21] This proportion fell off during the difficult interwar years. After 1945, under communist rule, with strong autarchic biases and, in most cases, under pressure to channel a high proportion of trade to the Soviet Union, the trading position of Eastern Europe declined despite rapid industrialization.

Russia (USSR). Russia, with its iron, timber and furs, was a great trading nation of the eighteenth century; but the coming of the new British iron technology in the 1780's and the rupture of trading ties after 1806 diminished its trading role down to the end of the Continental Blockade (1813) and beyond. With its own economic modernization moving forward slowly at best after 1815 and without export commodities closely linked to the dynamic industries of the West, the Russian trading proportion fell away irregularly to the mid-1890's. The rapid industrialization of Russia in the pre-1914 generation, backed by large capital imports and including the expansion of grain exports made possible by railroadization, lifted the Russian trading position at that time, despite the high rate of increase of world trade as a whole.

The slow recovery of the Soviet Union after the First World War, the highly autarchic character of the Five Year Plans of the 1930's, and disruptive agricultural policies left the USSR in 1938 with about 1 percent of world trade, as opposed to 4 percent for czarist Russia in 1913. The emergence of a communist trading bloc, after 1945, as well as increased Soviet interest in trade with the noncommunist world, raised the figure back to 4–5 percent in the period 1958–1971, a low proportion for the second economic power of the world, producing some 19 percent of industrial production in 1963.

North America. The slow but powerful rise of the United States as a trading partner in the world community emerges with clarity in Table II-8. There was a sharp jump from 2 percent in 1780 to 5 percent in 1800, as the United States enjoyed for a time both high prices for its export products in the wartime environment of the 1790's and, down to 1807, the advantages of neutrality. After 1815 cotton exports surged ahead, but the low prices of the 1820's slightly reduced the American proportion. The cotton boom of the 1830's left its mark on the figures, as did the low prices of 1850.[22] By 1860 wheat had joined cotton as a significant American export, and the United States, with 9 percent of world trade, ranked third, along with France. By Mulhall's calculations the United States in 1860 was, with its take-off complete, the fourth industrial power in the world (14 percent), just below France and Germany (16 percent and 15 percent, respectively). In relative trading status the United States did not move above that level until the pre-1914 generation. But then the modest increase in the American trading proportion concealed a revolutionary shift in the composition of United States exports, suggested in Table II-9.

The rise of manufactures (21 percent to 49 percent) more than outweighed the halving in the role of foodstuffs (42 percent to 21 percent), which reflected the ending of the frontier, not balanced, at that time, by compensating increases in agricultural productivity. Crude material exports fell less dramatically. It was in the early 1880's that the United States achieved industrial primacy, with 29 percent of the world industrial production. By 1913 the figure was

TABLE II-9. *Composition of United States Exports, 1890 and 1913 (%)*

	1890	1913
Crude materials	36.6	30.5
Crude foodstuffs	15.6	7.5
Manufactured foodstuffs	26.6	13.2
Semimanufactures	5.4	16.8
Finished manufactures	15.6	31.9
Total	99.8	99.9

Source: Jeffrey G. Williamson, *American Growth and the Balance of Payments, 1820–1913* (Chapel Hill: University of North Carolina Press, 1964), pp. 267–268.

36 percent, more than twice the levels for Britain and Germany (14 percent and 16 percent, respectively).

The relative American trading position rose slightly, relative to 1913, in the boom of the 1920's and fell slightly in the 1930's. After a transient interval of postwar dominance (see 1948 figures), the American trading proportion fluctuated during the great foreign trade boom of the 1950's and 1960's about a level (11–14 percent) not much above the 11 percent of 1913, whereas its position as an industrial power subsided a little to about 32 percent.

The story of Canada and its trading position differs significantly from that of the United States. In 1971 Canada, with about 3 percent of the world's industrial production, engaged in 5 percent of the world's trade. With a population about 10 percent that of the United States, its external trade was more than a third of the American level. Canada emerged significantly in the world's trading accounts in the pre-1914 generation. As in the United States of the 1850's, Canada's take-off into industrial growth converged with a period of railroadization sparked by a high wheat price providing the incentive to open up a new agricultural area (Western Canada). Canada somewhat expanded its trading position in the interwar years; and in the post-1945 decades it remained a major supplier to the world of foodstuffs and raw materials and enjoyed as well an increasing role as an exporter of manufactures, based on the technological maturity it achieved during and after the Second World War.

Latin America. From its large role in the export of precious metals in the eighteenth century, Latin American trade proportionately declined down to the 1890's. This decline was accompanied, however, by the emergence of a wide range of food and raw material exports which supplanted the attenuated gold and silver mines as a source of foreign exchange. With the rise of agricultural and raw-material prices in the pre-1914 generation and, in particular, the expansion of Argentine production and exports, the Latin American trading proportion rose from 5 percent in 1889 to 8 percent in 1913. But the extraordinary rise in the export of tropical products from Brazil and Colombia (notably, coffee) also played a significant role. The Latin American trading proportion rose again in the 1920's; but the region was disproportionately hit by the depression of the 1930's, its loss of foreign exchange constituting one major factor in the beginnings of serious and sustained industrialization in the region. Down to the early 1950's Latin America enjoyed a high range of export prices, and its trade proportion expanded; but the relative decline in the agricultural and raw-material prices in the twenty years after the Korean War damped the Latin American trade position. Only toward the end of the 1960's did Latin American industrialization begin to achieve levels of diversification and efficiency which permitted manufactured exports to expand significantly. But this important transition had not arrested the decline in the Latin American trading proportion by 1971.

Asia. Next to the decline of Spain as a trading nation, the decline of India from its great commercial role in the early eighteenth century is the most dramatic movement in Table II-8. As the British solved the problem of machine spinning of cotton and cheap factory-produced textiles flooded into India as elsewhere, the Indian capacity to earn foreign exchange declined. In the latter part of the nineteenth century, however, a modern cotton textile industry developed in India and the railroads permitted India to emerge as a significant wheat exporter. For a time India held its own as a trading nation in a dynamic world setting. But it did not move on to self-sustained industrial growth. The Indian trading proportion fell away to 2.2 percent in 1938, 1.4 percent in 1958. India's vicissitudes with economic development, including its difficulties in generating diversified manufactured exports from a rather sophisticated industrial establishment, pushed the figure as low as 0.6 percent in 1971.

A comparison of the approximate trading proportions of China and India between 1938 and 1971 illuminates something of the evolution of these two giant nations, both primarily oriented toward internal rather than external commerce (Table II-10).

India and China launched their first five-year plans (1953) with quite similar trading proportions. China initially moved ahead more vigorously, as the figures for 1958, the year of the Great Leap Forward, suggest. The sharp subsequent relapse, accompanied by the loss of Soviet aid, is reflected in the Chinese figure for 1963. India advanced between 1958 and 1963, but its trade expansion was slower than the world average. Both countries confronted acute problems in the mid-1960's: India, two years of famine (1965–1967); China, the economic consequences of the Cultural Revolution. The setback in relative trade was more severe for India. With the ending of the Cultural Revolution in 1968–1969, China moved ahead at a modest but steady pace, in trade as in production. Its rate of expansion, however, did not quite match that for the world as a whole, and its trading proportion slipped. In 1971, for example, Hong Kong conducted trade at a significantly higher level than the People's Republic of China, and Taiwan's trade alone was more than

TABLE II-10. *Proportion of World Trade: India and China, 1938–1971, Selected Years (%)*

	India	China
1938	2.5	2.3
1953	1.4	1.5
1958	1.4	1.8
1963	1.3	1.0
1968	0.9	0.9
1971	0.6	0.8

Source: United Nations Statistical Yearbook, 1972, pp. 404–405. Footnote 9, p. 404, should be noted.

half that of the PRC. India's chronic problem in agriculture, in all its complex ramifications, produced a sharper decline between 1968 and 1971 than in the case of China.

Given its somewhat lesser population, India is relatively more oriented toward world trade than China, at least down to the 1971 figures. Moreover, since 1953 India has generally enjoyed higher levels of external assistance than China, permitting imports to run substantially higher than exports. The simple fact, however, is that neither China nor India has kept up with the rapid expansion of world trade in the three post-1945 decades.

While the earlier history of China's role in world commerce is of considerable significance, the data available do not permit China to find an explicit place in the Mulhall and League of Nations calculations. A historical discussion of the China trade is, therefore, left for Chapter 44.

Japan is not accorded independent status in the Mulhall or League of Nations calculations. By 1938, however, its proportion of world trade had risen to about 4 percent. As its take-off began, foreign trade was about 10 percent of Japan's national product (1878–1887).[23] In the course of the drive to technological maturity, the proportion rose from about a third (1908–1913) to about 40 percent (1918–1927). The figure has declined, however, in Japan's extraordinary expansion since the mid-1950's, as it has moved into high mass-consumption. As of 1971 the proportion was about 20 percent. Japan's percentage of world trade (6.2 percent) was not much higher than its percentage of world industrial production (about 5 percent). The extent of Japan's postwar setback and the momentum of its subsequent recovery is suggested by the movement of its world trade proportion from under 1 percent in 1948 to over 6 percent in 1971. Contrary to a widespread image, however, Japanese foreign trade, as a proportion of its GNP, has emerged as relatively moderate: higher than that for the United States (and the USSR); much lower than that of the United Kingdom, West Germany, Canada, and a good many of the industrialized smaller nations; at about the same level as France. Table II-11 presents one measure of this relationship for the late 1950's.

Africa. Although it does not appear explicitly in Mulhall's calculations, the African slave trade and all the commercial activity that accompanied it was a significant component in the world trading system of the eighteenth century. In the period 1761–1780, for example, Britain exported from Africa some 28,000 slaves per year.[24] The average price paid in Africa was £16.08 per slave. The average price received in Jamaica was £37.73. Average outlays for slaves in Africa were, therefore, £450,240; average receipts in the West Indies, about £1,056,440. The average total value of British trade over these two decades was of the order of, say, £27 million. Thus, imports (slaves) plus exports to Africa may have been over 3 percent of total British trade; and slaves (as a kind of re-export) evidently played a large role in the West Indian trade. British imports from the West Indies averaged annually about £2.85 million. Thus, export of slaves from Africa may have financed about 37 percent of these imports. With the waning of the slave trade, Africa's role diminished, to revive with the gold and diamond trade and the rapid expansion in exports of tropical products toward the close of the nineteenth century. By 1913, the region's trading proportion was about 4 percent. It has since fluctuated in the range of 4–7 percent. Africa now includes a highly industrialized South Africa; a North Africa in the process of industrialization; a good many small preindustrial countries, with low levels of trade; and a few nations providing relatively large flows of oil, minerals, and foodstuffs to the world trading system.

Table II-12 indicates the regional structure of African trade as of 1971.

Oceania. The role of Oceania in world trade began with John Macarthur's perception of Australia's possibilities as a sheep-raising, wool-exporting area and his dogged and ultimately successful translation of that perception into reality between 1797 and 1813. From that time down to mid-century, wool dominated Australian growth. Then came the gold rush of 1851. By 1884, with gold tapered off, the Australian government shifted toward a policy of encouraging wheat production via railroadization; and, with the rise of the wheat price, from the mid-1890's wheat production began to rise, increasing by more than three times between 1894–1899 and 1909–1914 (see Table III-24). New Zealand, starting in the 1860's with gold, was sustained by a similar export sequence of land- or capital-

TABLE II-11. *Proportion of Foreign Trade to GNP: Developed Countries, Post–World War II Years*

Countries in Descending Order of GNP	Exports plus Imports as % of GNP: Commodities and Services (1)	Exports plus Imports as % of GNP: Commodities Only (2)	Commodities as % of Commodities and Services (Col. 2 ÷ Col. 1) (3)
1. United States	9.6	7.3	76
2. United Kingdom	41.7	30.4	73
3. France	26.5	19.0	72
4. West Germany	44.5	29.2	66
5. Canada	40.4	34.3	85
6. Japan	27.3	21.6	79
7. Australia	33.6	30.1	90
8. Belgium	65.5	57.5	88
9. Sweden	55.4	49.8	90
10. Netherlands	96.8	83.6	86
11. Switzerland	60.6	46.4	77
12. Denmark	67.3	53.1	79
13. Norway	88.7	52.9	60
14. New Zealand	53.0	46.1	87
15. Luxembourg	161.5	157.0	97

Source: Simon Kuznets, *Modern Economic Growth*, p. 301.

TABLE II-12. *African Trade, 1971 (% of Total)*

North Africa	28
South Africa	19
Nigeria	10
Zaire (1970)	4
Zambia	4
Rhodesia	2
Rest	33
	100

Source: United Nations Statistical Yearbook, 1973, pp. 398–399.

intensive agricultural activities: wool, wheat, and dairy products. By 1913 Oceania contributed about 2 percent to world trade from a narrow and surprisingly urbanized population base. Like Canada, Australia and New Zealand enjoyed high levels of income per capita before they were fully industrialized.

In the postwar decades a significant increase in trade (as well as in tourism) has developed in the islands of the region—notably, Papua New Guinea, New Caledonia, French Polynesia, Fiji, and Guam. The proportions of trade within Oceania since 1938 reflect this new element in the region. Australia, with its rich mineral resources and its new vital ties to the Japanese economy, has held its relative position somewhat better than New Zealand.

TABLE II-13. *Trade Proportions: Oceania, 1938, 1948, 1963, 1970 (%)*

	1938	1948	1963	1970
Australia	67	70	68	68
New Zealand	29	26	25	19
Developing island economies	4	4	7	13
	100	100	100	100

Source: United Nations Statistical Yearbook, 1973, pp. 400–401.

8

Prices

In their book on British economic growth Phyllis Deane and W. A. Cole provide, as an end-piece, Chart II-4.[25] It brings together movements in the overall British price level from four indexes, between 1661 and 1959. It has been here brought down to 1974.

Price levels are not uniform among the various countries due to transport costs, tariffs, differences in wage levels, and the immobility of certain goods and services. Moreover, public policy can directly control key prices in various ways or, indeed, price levels as a whole. The Soviet Union, for example, reports an absolutely constant wholesale price level between 1962 and 1966, and, again, between 1967 and 1970.[26] Nevertheless, the British price level over this span of more than three centuries catches well the general direction of prices in the world economy, as well as short-run fluctuations and medium-term trends because of Britain's large role as a trading nation and the relative openness of its economy.

The analysis of price movements is a complex art. First, prices do not all move together. Indexes like those used in Chart II-4 sum up many often-divergent short-period and trend movements in particular prices. Second, such indexes reflect all manner of forces affecting the course of demand and supply. On the side of demand, there are the special impulses arising from war finance and wartime requirements for particular goods, from eighteenth-century cannon, blankets, and uniforms to modern aircraft and missiles. There are also more or less regular cycles in overall demand of various lengths, changing rates of population increase, and changing demands for particular products as incomes rise. On the side of supply, there are changing technology, political and military disruptions in the normal flow of commerce, the opening up of new sources of supply, and the waning productivity of older sources of supply. Third, price movements contribute their own impulse to the dynamics of the world economy, signaling areas for profitable investment or oversupply, altering income distribution, affecting the course of interest rates as well as the real burden of debt and the real value of provisions for the future security of families. We shall explore aspects of

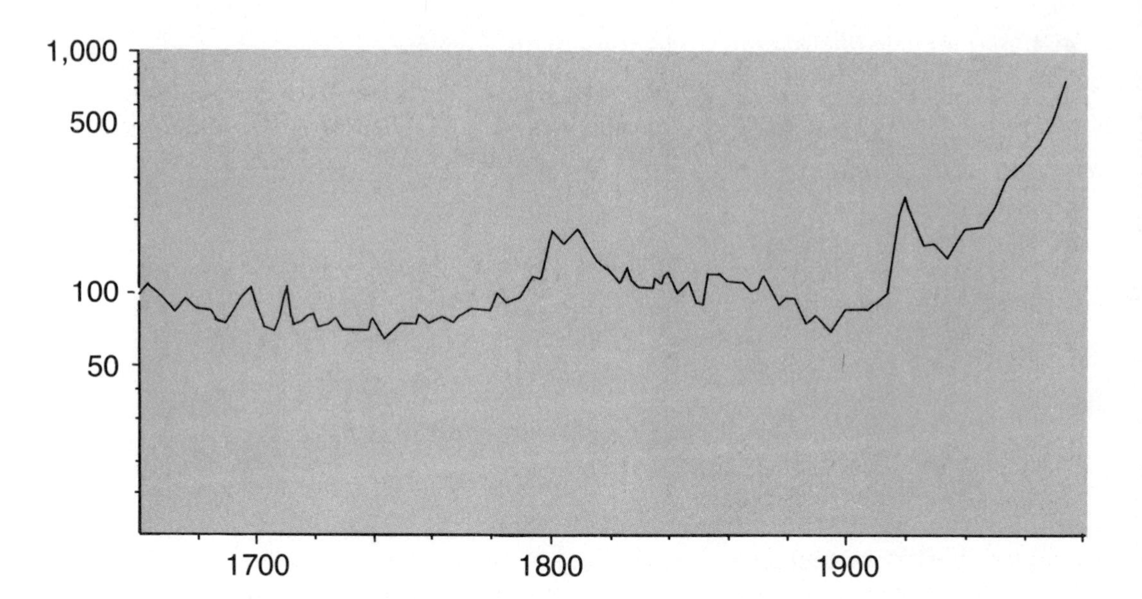

CHART II-4. *The British Price Level, 1661–1974*

Source: Phyllis Deane and W. A. Cole, *British Economic Growth, 1688–1959*, updated from official British data (*Board of Trade Journal*).

these phenomena in Parts Three, Four, and Five when we deal with the dynamics of the world economy and individual national economies. Here our purpose is limited to outlining, in a preliminary and introductory way, the major contours of overall price changes during the past three centuries.

In broad terms, the price curves in Chart II-4 reflect four major and reasonably distinct historical environments. First, the period 1661–1783. Short-term price movements over this century and a quarter's span are mainly to be understood in terms of harvest fluctuations, the incidence of war and peace, and the course of foreign trade, often affected by political as well as military affairs in a mercantilist age, but subject also to short inventory fluctuations of a more regular kind.[27] We shall have something more to say about these fluctuations in the early modern history of the world economy in Part Four. From 1783 to 1914, as industrialization begins in England and spreads out over the northern half of the world, a new element emerges: a major business cycle, averaging about nine years in length, dominated by the rhythm of long-term investment. Wars continue to leave a strong mark on the price curve, as do harvests and inventory fluctuations, although the latter two elements diminish in their relative role after, roughly, the mid-nineteenth century. There also emerges in this century and a quarter the phenomenon of long cycles or trend periods, the central subject matter of Part Three, in which price movements transcending major business cycles play a key role.

Although the interwar years (1920–1939) contain elements of

both major cycle fluctuations and a trend period, consonant with the pre-1914 world, they have their own pathology, also explored in Part Three.

The post-1945 years are marked, of course, by the public policies of a post-Keynesian era, where the political process systematically intervenes to prevent sustained periods of substantial unemployment. Largely in consequence of that fact, it is an inflationary era, since the political process in most of the world's societies fails to reconcile high rates of growth with relative price stability. Moreover, inflation accelerates in two waves, 1966–1972, and then the Price Revolution of 1972–1977, which bears, as we shall see in Part Three, a family relation to four trend-period turning points of the past.

Against this broad background, the major movements in Chart II-4 are to be understood along the following lines:

1. *1660–1783*. The underlying trend in British prices from 1660 to, roughly, the mid-eighteenth century is downward, broken mainly by the inflationary impact of the most intense stage of wars, which both expanded demand and obstructed supply. Between 1689 and 1713 Britain and France were at war with barely five years of respite; and there was war again from 1739 to 1748. Both periods of conflict left their mark on the price index, although the sharp rise in 1710–1712 was a result of two of the worst harvests in the century. The upward movement in 1740–1741 resulted from a similar cause. The peak at 1720, on the other hand, reflects a precarious cyclical movement in Western Europe, climaxed by the bursting of the South Sea Bubble and the failure of John Law's ambitious schemes in France. Recovery set in, however, in 1722, and some part of the subsequent rise in prices was a product of prosperity. From 1725 to 1729 the price index was sustained primarily by bad harvests, the business expansion having turned down in 1726.

Putting aside the impact of wars, harvests, and occasional strong peacetime booms, why should the underlying drift of prices have been downward between 1660 and the early 1750's? We cannot be sure, but in this preindustrial era the answer probably lies in the balance between population movements and agricultural production. In this Malthusian context the period we are considering falls into a useful perspective when placed in the grand setting of Charts II-5 and II-6, covering consumers' prices and real wages for English building craftsmen over seven centuries.[28] Chart II-5 shows the rise of prices that preceded the demographic setback of the fourteenth century, their low range down to the early sixteenth century, and the subsequent price revolution, which leveled off between the mid-seventeenth and mid-eighteenth centuries, with some tendency to sag away from the peak level of 1650. On an index-number basis (1451–1475 = 100), the price level for 1648–1652 is 756; for 1748–1752, 595. Chart II-6 demonstrates how, roughly speaking, real wages moved inversely to prices: a rise from the mid-fourteenth to the end of the fifteenth century; a massive decline to the end of

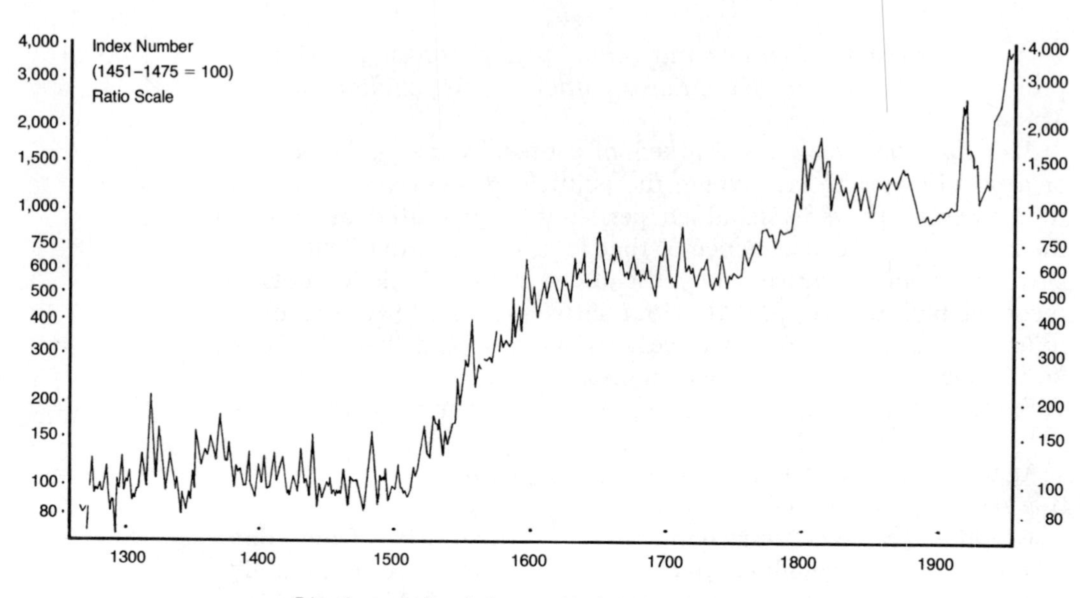

CHART II-5. *Consumers' Prices: England, 1264–1954*

Source: See note 28.

the sixteenth century; and a rise again to the mid-eighteenth century, which failed, however, to reattain the bounteous levels of the fifteenth century. Changes in agricultural and industrial technology were sporadic but not trivial over these four centuries of premodern history; but the critical element appears to have been the waxing and waning of tension between population, on the one hand, and arable land and the relatively fixed technological ceiling on productive employment, on the other. The population of England, for example, is believed to have risen from 1.1 to 3.8 million between 1086 and 1348. The Black Death reduced it by 20 percent in two years and the decline continued more gradually to a low point of 2.1 million in 1430. This low population range set the framework for the high real wages of the fifteenth century. As population rose again to 3.8 million (1603), real wages fell.

The seventeenth century is a less straightforward story, marked in Britain (as on the Continent and, indeed, in China) by severe wartime population losses. Nevertheless, on balance, population increased.[29] But as the eighteenth century began the increase was slow, at best, rising (for England and Wales) from 5.826 million in 1701 to 5.926 million forty years later—an annual average rate of growth of only 0.04 percent. But these were also years when British agriculture was capable of producing a grain export surplus. The rise in real wages down to mid-century is, therefore, not surprising.

With considerable variation, much of continental Europe shared this cyclical experience; that is, the decline of the fourteenth cen-

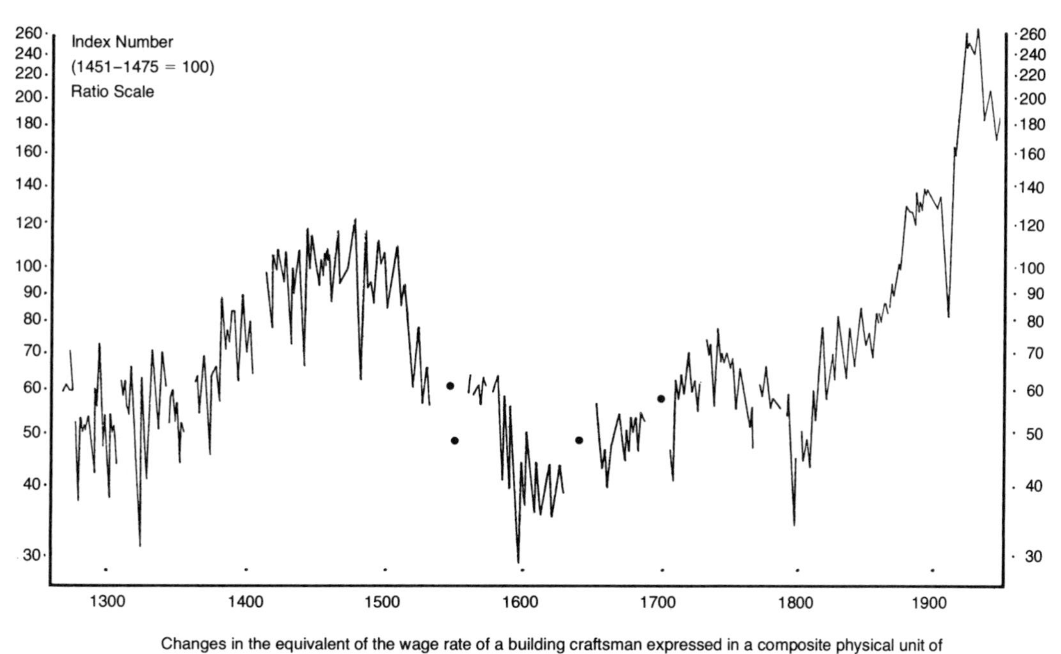

Changes in the equivalent of the wage rate of a building craftsman expressed in a composite physical unit of consumables in southern England, 1264–1954.

CHART II-6. *Real Wages: English Building Craftsmen, 1264–1954*

Source: See note 28.

tury was reversed by the third quarter of the fifteenth, with the 1300 population level regained by 1600, at the latest.[30] The relative experiences of the various European states varied more markedly in the seventeenth century, with the Dutch Republic achieving naval, commercial, and financial primacy, despite a heavy burden of defense expenditures; Britain rising as a commercial and colonial power, despite its Civil War, first challenging the Dutch, then joining under Dutch leadership to challenge the France of Louis XIV, strengthened by Colbert's policies after 1660; France rapidly gaining in commercial and military power, but taking on more than it could handle in the latter part of the century, suffering a setback that permitted Britain to move ahead in the period down to 1720; Spain spiraling into an economic morass, losing perhaps 25 percent of its population until its eighteenth-century recovery under the Bourbons began.

Douglass C. North and Robert Paul Thomas hold that the concurrence of rising populations and rising real wages in seventeenth-century Britain and Netherlands is definitive evidence that the Malthusian monster had there been overcome by the forces of modernization, notably, the acceptance of private property rights; and that the greater vicissitudes of Spain and France, which suffered population decline or stagnation in the seventeenth century, stemmed from the overriding of private property rights by absolutist rulers. Their argument can be challenged in terms of seventeenth-century history itself; but from the present narrow perspective the course of population and prices in the second half of the eighteenth century is evidence that their conclusion is premature. There was a tendency for both population and prices to rise from the 1750's to the early 1790's; and in Britain, at least, real wages again came under strain. Moreover, Britain shifted gradually from a grain-exporting to a grain-importing nation in that period. (In China, too, Malthusian pressures late in the century began to close in on a sustained period of prosperity.) As E. H. Phelps Brown and Sheila V. Hopkins conclude, comparing the decline of real wages in the sixteenth and late eighteenth centuries: "Do we not see here a Malthusian crisis, the effect of a rapid growth of population impinging on an insufficiently expansive economy; such as perhaps we see also in the fall [in real wages] that set in around 1750, until this time a commercial and industrial revolution came to save Britain from the fate of Ireland?"[31] They might well have added—and the fate of nineteenth-century China.

2. *1783–1914*. The upward drift of prices from mid-century became an explosive inflation in the decade after the outbreak of war between Britain and France in 1793. The great surge came in the years 1798–1801, after which prices fluctuated in a high range down to 1814 and the end of the Napoleonic Wars.[32]

From 1814 to 1851 the price trend was downward, despite brief upward breaks in the 1820's and 1840's and a more protracted phase of relatively high prices in the 1830's. The price increases of the mid-1820's and mid-1830's were, in part, cyclical phenomena, although the latter had structural features which ran counter to the trend period (see below, pp. 134–139). The sharp rise in 1846–1847 was primarily a result of bad harvests, including the traumatic failure of the Irish potato crop. As we shall see, the downward price trend was the normal outcome of the forces at work in the world economy between 1815 and 1914 at times of peace and agricultural abundance.

In 1852–1854 there was another great price lift, like that of 1798–1801. In the Rousseaux index the increase in those two years is 33 percent. Gold mining, war, and a worldwide business expansion all helped produce this convulsion. Prices fluctuated in this high range down to the crisis of 1873; but 91 percent of the total increase in this period came in 1852–1854.

As after 1815, a second protracted period of falling prices ensued, down to the trough of 1895. Again the trend was slowed or broken—during the cyclical expansion of the early 1880's and, more strongly, of the late 1880's, which, like that of the 1830's, was an authentic break in the trend period but one which confirms the basic mechanism at work (see below, pp. 163, 169–171). The decline from 1814 to 1851 was 55 percent; from 1872 to 1894, 44 percent. More than half the latter decline took place during the cyclical depression of the 1870's, from 1872 to 1879.

The trend of prices drifted upward from the mid-1890's to the outbreak of the First World War. Half the total increase was, again, concentrated in a few years, 1897–1900. As in the early 1850's, the convergence of gold mining, war, and cyclical expansion appears responsible, although the subsequently high and upward-drifting price trend reflects deeper forces at work, examined in Part Three. The First World War produced something like a doubling in the British price level, which continued to rise until the crisis of 1920, in an environment of postwar shortages.

3. *1920–1939.* Prices then fell away (despite the relative prosperity of the late 1920's) to a trough in 1933. Sixty percent of that decline came in two years, 1920–1922. There was an increase in prices for the second half of the 1930's, notably an 8 percent jump in 1935–1937.

After 1914 there were rather greater divergences in national economic experiences than earlier. U.S. retail prices, for example, rose less than Britain's during the First World War—about 50 percent. The peak of 1920 was shared; but the 1920–1922 decline was less drastic in the United States, so that British and American prices began by 1922 to bear a closer relative relationship to their pre-1914 levels. From 1922 to 1929 the American price level was relatively steady, rising a bit down to 1926, then falling back to a level only slightly above 1922. Under the weight of the 1925 return to the Gold Standard at the old parity, the British decline from 1925 to 1929 was more marked. On the other hand, the British decline from 1929 to 1933 was less severe than that in the United States, and the rise to 1937 more muted.

In broad terms, however, the interwar movement of Chart II-4 represents fairly well what happened to prices as a whole.

4. *1945–1976.* The Second World War produced, of course, another price convulsion. With the ending of price controls there was also a postwar surge, between 1945 and 1948. But this time there was no equivalent to the drastic break in prices of 1920. At varying rates, and with a few minor exceptions (1949, 1954), there was unbroken price inflation down to 1975. And this phenomenon occurred despite a decline in agricultural and certain raw-material prices from 1951 to about 1964. The Korean War played a part in this inflationary sequence, with a 6 percent consumers' price increase in 1950 and 1951 in the United States. The war in Southeast Asia had a less dramatic effect in the 1960's. But fundamentally this unique phenomenon was the product of an era where governments became committed to maintain a high level of employment without finding the societal self-discipline to supplant the harsh rigors of cyclical depression in containing money wages, a subject examined in Part Four.

Between the end of the Korean War and the mid-1960's the rate of inflation was relatively low. There was then a phase of quite general acceleration, running from 1966 to 1972. A second more acute phase of acceleration began late in 1972. The 1966–1972 acceleration stemmed from a phase of rapid growth (accompanied by the most intense phase of the war in Southeast Asia) which loosened wage-price discipline throughout the industrialized world, and from a cessation of the relative decline in food and raw-material prices. The 1972–1975 acceleration was the result of a convulsive rise in the price of energy and in agricultural and raw-material prices that ranks historically with those of 1798–1801, 1853–1855, 1897–1900, the late 1930's, and 1950–1951. As we shall see in Part Three, the world economy, with its underlying problem of inflation unsolved, exhibited an exacerbated version of the patterns which had dominated the other four protracted periods of high prices since the early 1790's.

The largest meaning of Chart II-4 is, perhaps, this: from the Napoleonic War price peak to 1913 the British price level fell from 190 to 100, standing at that time a bit below its pre-war level of the 1790's; despite two world wars it stood at only a little more than twice the 1913 level in 1946 (203.5); in the subsequent quarter-century, marked by relatively minor military conflict compared to the scale of the world economy, the British price level tripled. The annual average rate of price increase in the period 1946–1956 was 4.53 percent; 1956–1966, 2.97 percent; 1966–1972, 5.92 percent; 1972–1974, 12.5 percent, with inflation proceeding at an annual rate of almost 40 percent in the spring of 1975. By historical standards this is an odd story, indeed, even though the average annual rate of inflation was somewhat higher in Britain than in (say) the United States and Germany.[33] The annual average British price increase between 1946 and 1972 was 4.25 percent as opposed to 0.7 percent in the late eighteenth-century inflationary period (1754–1790), 2.17 percent in the pre-1914 phase of rising prices (1895–1913).

So much for the main features of Chart II-4. Now a major weakness of any such overall price index should be underlined: in an important sense, each commodity has a price history of its own. Charts II-7 and II-8 are designed to catch the extent to which certain basic commodity prices exhibited distinctive features over the period 1790–1945.[34]

Trends are presented here in the form of overlapping eleven-year averages, which effectively eliminate cyclical and other short-term movements. The most striking fact about the trend movements is that while, undoubtedly, these commodity prices were subject to a variety of common influences, notably during war periods, and while they were interrelated in subtle and complex ways, they widely diverge in their trend movements both over the period as a whole and over shorter intervals within it. Note, for example, over the whole period, the substantial net declines in the prices of cotton and sugar as compared with wheat, wool, and coal, which stand in the final decade not far from their initial positions, and as compared with timber, beef, and iron, whose price levels in 1935–1945 were well above the late-eighteenth century level. On firmer grounds of comparability in the quality of the commodities, note the movement

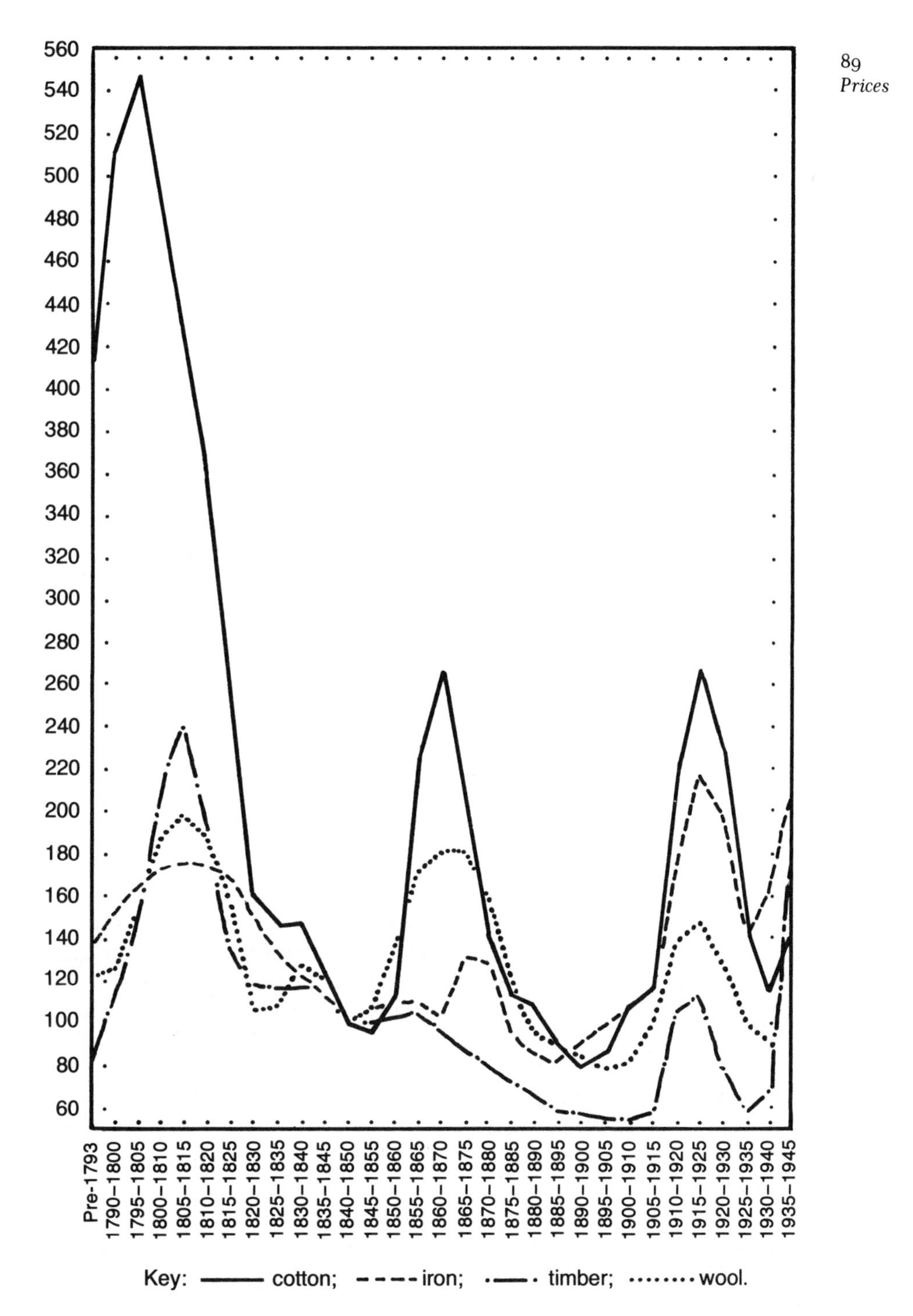

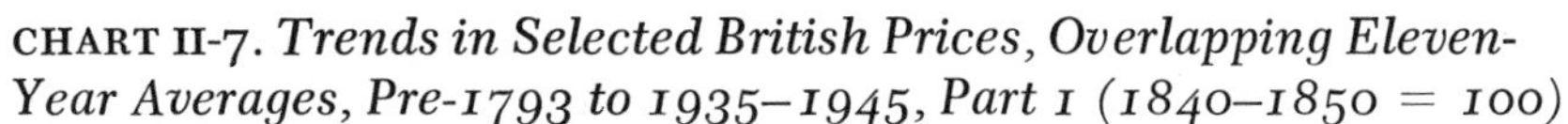

CHART II-7. *Trends in Selected British Prices, Overlapping Eleven-Year Averages, Pre-1793 to 1935–1945, Part 1 (1840–1850 = 100)*

Source: W. W. Rostow, *The Process of Economic Growth*, p. 198.

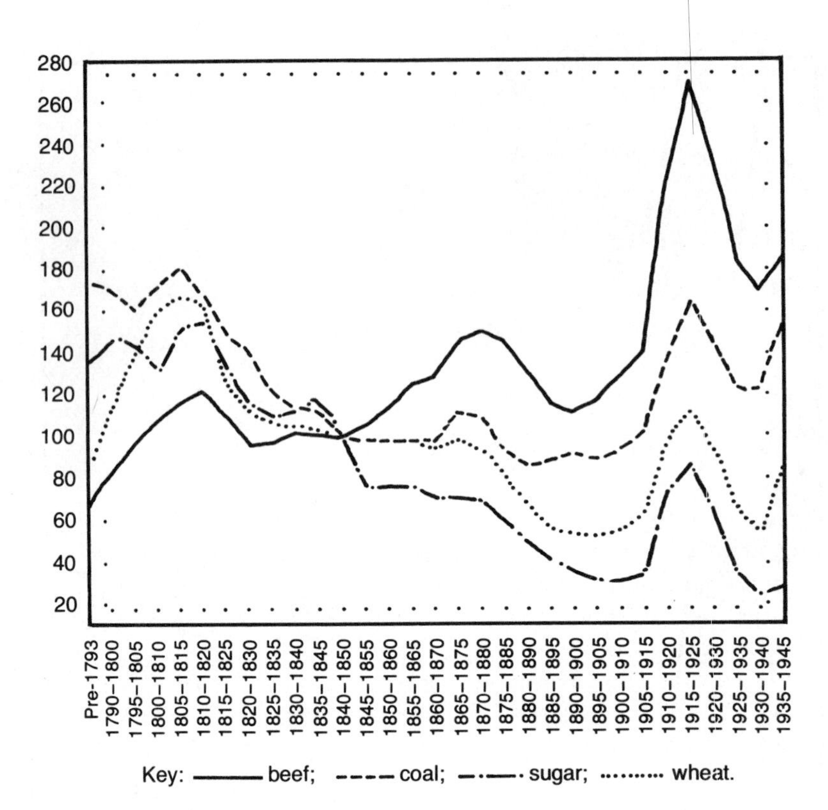

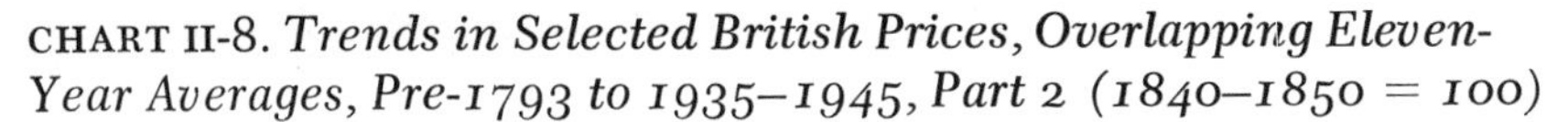

CHART II-8. *Trends in Selected British Prices, Overlapping Eleven-Year Averages, Pre-1793 to 1935–1945, Part 2 (1840–1850 = 100)*

Source: Rostow, *The Process of Economic Growth*, p. 199.

from the decade 1840–1850 to 1865–1875, embracing the famous price-level increase of the third quarter of the century: the absolute declines in sugar, timber, and wheat; the modest increases in coal, iron, and beef; the more substantial rises in cotton and wool. Excepting iron, these commodities might, under existing conventions, be lumped together under "foodstuffs and raw materials"; or, broken down further, a foodstuffs subindex might conceal strongly divergent trend movements in wheat and meat, and a raw-materials index might conceal the divergent movements of timber, coal, and the textile raw materials. For certain purposes, of course, notably in making real-wage calculations or estimates of changes in industrial costs, such indexes are useful and necessary. Further, the existence of such divergences does not deny the possibility of certain common forces operating upon wide categories of prices taken as a whole. But the prices within them cannot be assumed automatically to have moved together in the past; and, in fact, the divergences in trend movements within these categories have been substantial, and significant for important aspects of economic history and analysis.

9

Relative Prices and the Terms of Trade

Bearing in mind the wide diversity of individual price movements, we turn to a question which runs through economic thought and policy since Adam Smith at least; that is, the relative movement of prices of industrial products versus the prices of agricultural products and raw materials. In the first chapter of the *Wealth of Nations*, Smith noted that the potentialities for the division of labor seemed to be less in agriculture than in manufactures. He went on to foreshadow the notion that, in the long run, diminishing returns might yield a rise in the price of agricultural products and raw materials relative to those of manufactures, where progress could be expected to cause a decline in their real price; that is, in the "quantity of labour . . . requisite for executing any particular piece of work."[35] Thus began two centuries of indecisive analysis of the case of increasing returns to industry.[36]

The concern of the mid-1970's with the relative prices and supply prospects for food, energy, and raw materials is, as we shall see in Part Three, the fifth occasion over the past two centuries when the consequences of diminishing returns in the production of primary products have appeared a real and present danger. Future prospects for the relative prices of manufactured goods and primary products are by no means certain, intimately tied, as they are, to the whole question of the limits of growth, including the potentialities of new technologies—issues which are central to Part Six of this book. Historically, however, relative prices have been associated with fluctuations rather than an uninterrupted working out of diminishing returns to natural resources, increasing returns to manufactures. The world economy did not move directly into the impasse Malthus feared in the 1790's, not only because birth rates declined with the course of economic and social progress in the more advanced parts of the world but also because there was unused arable land to be opened up, new raw-material resources to be found and exploited, and remarkable reductions in transport costs. Moreover, primary production lent itself rather more than Adam Smith could perceive in 1776 to the application of science and technology. The upshot was sustained phases of relatively high and relatively low foodstuff and raw-material prices, as well as short-term changes, reflecting the luck of the harvests, business cycle oscillations, the traumatic impact of wars, technological innovations in production and transport, changes in trade policy—in fact, all the forces that might come to rest in a major way on the demand for and supply of primary commodities and manufactures. A full analysis of terms-of-trade movements for a particular country is a complicated piece of business indeed, conforming to no simple theoretical proposition.

The relative prices of British exports and imports (net barter terms of trade) are, nevertheless, a useful shorthand index of how this process proceeded because, from the 1790's forward, Britain was essentially an exporter of manufactures, an importer of foodstuffs and industrial raw materials, with the important exception of coal. Chart II-9 shows how the British terms have moved from 1796 to 1974.

The data begin in 1796, when the French Revolutionary War had been under way for three years. The initial net effect of wartime conditions—the obstructions to supply, rising freight rates, and the British quasi-monopoly in overseas trade—was to raise export prices somewhat more than import prices, although from year to year the terms of trade moved erratically.[37] The terms-of-trade peak in 1802, for example, was the product of contrary movements in import and export prices during the brief Peace of Amiens: peace both cut import costs and raised export prices in briefly opened Continental

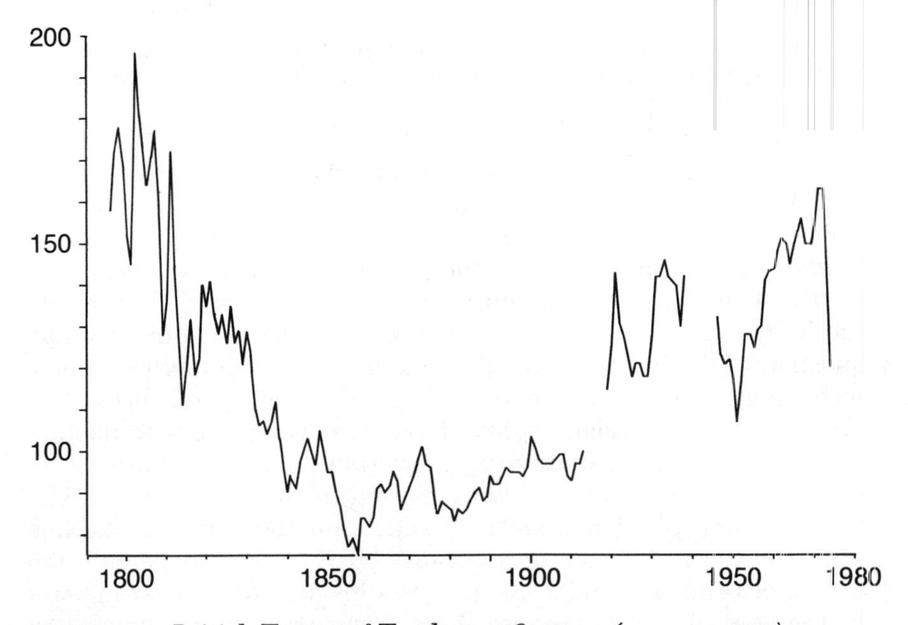

CHART II-9. *British Terms of Trade, 1796–1974 (1913 = 100)*

Source: Albert H. Imlah, *Economic Elements in the Pax Britannica*, updated from Board of Trade data (*Statistical Abstract of the United Kingdom*).

markets. From that peak to about mid-century, the trend in the British terms of trade was dominated by the dynamics of the cotton industry, which came to be the decisive force in British foreign trade. The downward trend was primarily the result of improvements in technology and efficiency in the manufacture of cotton goods, since the fall in the raw cotton price, if alone operating, might have produced a greater decline in the import than the export price index. Chart II-10 illustrates the resulting greater reduction, to about 1850, in the price of manufactures than in less-fabricated cotton yarn and in raw cotton, less subject to technological refinements.[38]

As the technological momentum in the cotton industry waned after mid-century, other factors came to shape the British terms of trade. For example, the sharp deterioration of the early 1850's reflects an extraordinary rise of the wheat price. The railroadization of Britain in the 1840's opened an era of expanding British coal exports. The sharp rise in the early 1870's reflects a temporary coal shortage in Britain which lifted the price of British steel and engineering exports much in demand in the United States, Germany, and Russia, as well as exports of coal itself, whose value more than doubled between 1871 and 1873; the subsequent rapid subsidence reflects the ending of the coal shortage and a sharp reduction in railway-related exports. British export profits were low and competition acute in the period 1873–1879. From the early 1880's, the dominant factor at work was the decline in a wide range of British

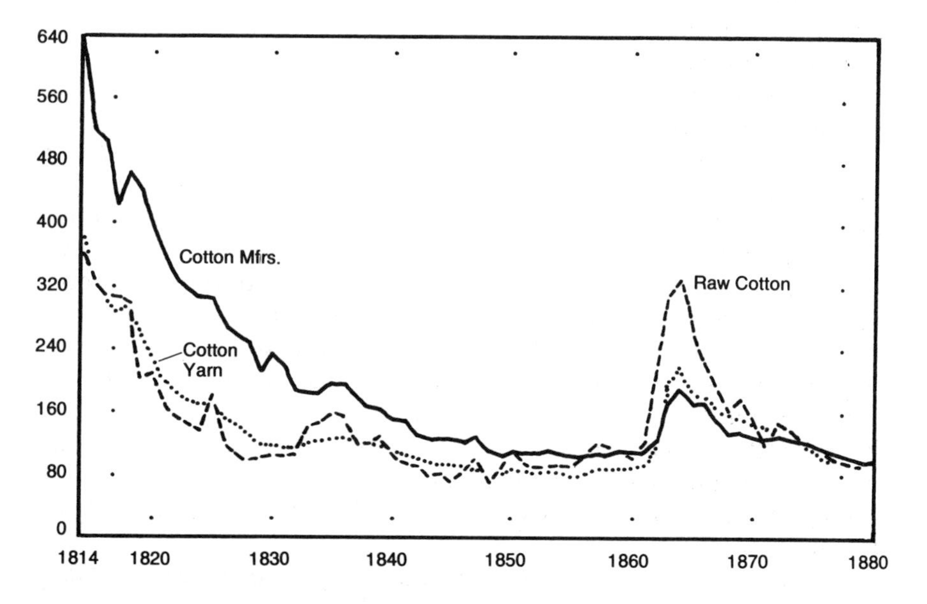

CHART II-10. *Weighted Average Prices of Exports of Cotton Manufactures and Yarn and of Net Imports of Raw Cotton, 1814–1880 (1880 = 100)*

Source: Imlah, *Economic Elements in the Pax Britannica*, p. 105.

import prices, assisted by the sharply reduced freight rates that accompanied the triumph of the efficient long-distance steel steamship. The sharp rise up to 1900 was, once again, induced by the favorable net effect on the British terms of trade of a relative coal shortage: between 1898 and 1900 the value of British coal exports again more than doubled. The net deterioration of the terms of trade to the eve of the First World War was a consequence of the relative rise of imported foodstuff and raw-material prices in that period, compounded by the rapid, general development of Canada, Argentina, and other foodstuff- and raw-material-producing areas, supported by large capital imports. This process lifted their price levels (and the prices of their exports) relative to the price levels in capital-exporting areas. The rise in British export prices, during this primarily external boom, was somewhat outweighed by the forces operating to raise import prices.

How did the erratic short-run movements of the terms of trade relate to business cycles in the era from 1796 to 1914? The answer is that there was no simple, consistent movement covering the whole period.[39] Before 1868, the price of wheat played a large role in these short-run movements, tending to be low in periods of depression and the early stages of revival, rising in the latter stages of expansion, with important effects on the value of imports, the balance of payments, and the state of the money markets. This tended to produce (with some exceptions) an inverse movement between the terms of trade and the British business cycle. From 1868 to 1914, with the exception of the cycle which peaked in 1883, the terms of trade moved in conformity with the business cycle; that is, export prices rose more rapidly in business expansions (and fell more rapidly in contractions) than import prices. This was also the tendency during the interwar years.

Between 1919 and 1938 the British terms of trade fluctuated in a high range, relative to the 1913 level, particularly marked after the price break of 1920 and during the worst years of the Great Depression. The favorable effects of relatively cheap imports were, however, largely dissipated in unemployment. Britain's traditional export markets were weak, due to the low range of foodstuff and raw-material prices. Diminished British earnings in shipping and from capital investment abroad further reduced the advantages of favorable terms of trade.[40] If Britain had restructured its economy rapidly, expanding domestic demand and shifting its export industries to supply that demand (which happened to a significant extent after 1931), it might have lost less of its gain from the terms of trade in unemployment.[41]

The British terms-of-trade index was 75 percent more favorable in 1920 than in 1913. After the Second World War, in 1947, it was 15 percent less favorable than it had been in 1938. With a slight break during the recession of 1949, the unfavorable trend, exacerbated by the Korean War, continued to 1951, when the terms of trade were 33 percent less favorable than in 1938. This price structure put considerable pressure on the British (and European) cost of living during the early postwar years; but it also eased the task of reviving European exports to overseas producers of foodstuffs and raw materials.

From 1951 to 1972 the British terms of trade moved up by more than 50 percent, reflecting both domestic inflation and the relatively low range of foodstuff and raw-material prices. This was the period when spokesmen for the developing world articulated their discontent with the terms of trade experienced in the less industrialized nations. Unlike the situation in the interwar years, however, the dynamism of domestic development, centered on the leading sectors of high mass-consumption, permitted Western Europe and Japan to enjoy high rates of growth and low levels of unemployment, despite the relative weakness of purchasing power derived from foodstuff and raw-material exports in Asia, the Middle East, Africa, and Latin America. That weakness was, of course, mitigated by flows of official development assistance, by large private investments, notably in oil production, by the rapid growth of the industrialized nations, and by purposeful growth generated in some of the developing nations which successfully translated itself into a capacity to export manufactured goods as well as primary products.

From 1972 to 1976 the terms of trade once again shifted dramatically against Britain and in favor of producers of foodstuffs and raw materials, a general movement greatly heightened by a rise in the oil price. The decline of about 25 percent was mildly reversed under the impact of the recession of 1974–1975, with its softening of raw-material prices.

Although the story of the terms of trade can be broadly told with reference to Britain and the relative prices of manufactures versus foodstuffs and raw materials, it is important to be aware of the range of variation in the experience of industrialized nations and of the extent to which the terms of trade calculated in current account (including services) may diverge from simple merchandise calculations. Charts II-11 and II-12, drawn from the work of C. P. Kindleberger, covering the period 1870–1952, suggest these variations.[42] Major points to be noted are: the extent to which agricultural protectionism denied Germany and France the benefits of cheap imported food down to the mid-1890's; Sweden's fortunate mixture of resource endowments and the uniquely favorable movement in the terms of trade they provided in the period 1900–1913; the effect of post-1918 inflation and, then, the extraordinary impact of the depth of the depression on German terms-of-trade movements.

Chart II-13 extends down to 1972 a famous set of calculations that relate closely to the relative prices of manufactures and primary products. It was presented in one of the final pieces of research done under the auspices of the League of Nations, *Industrialization and Foreign Trade*, written by Folke Hilgerdt. It shows the movement of two fractions. Line A is the quantum index of world trade in manufactured goods as a percentage of that in primary goods

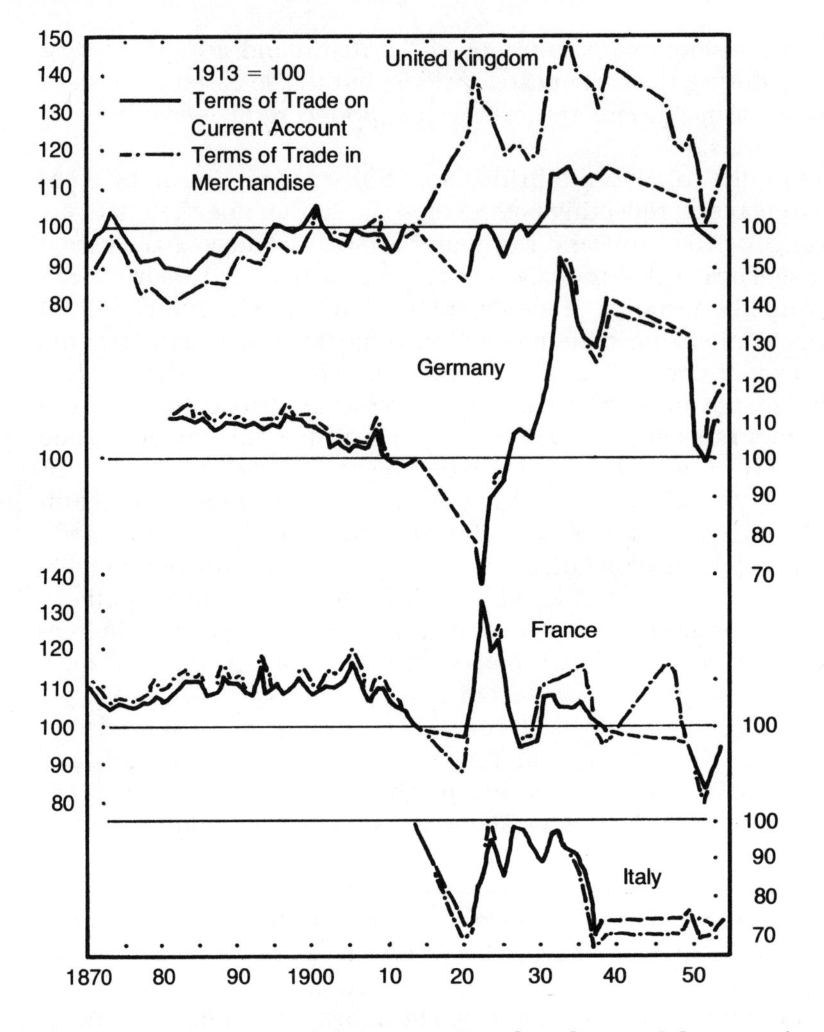

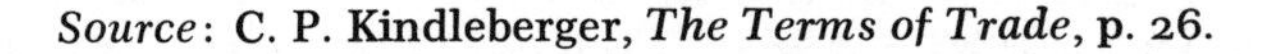

CHART II-11. *Industrial European Merchandise and Current-Account Terms of Trade, 1870–1952, Part 1*

Source: C. P. Kindleberger, *The Terms of Trade*, p. 26.

(foodstuffs and raw materials). Line B is a price index of manufactured goods as a percentage of that for primary goods. Hilgerdt demonstrated that, down to the 1920's, this price index conformed closely in its trend to the British terms of trade.

The striking fact about the movement of the quantity and price relationships, down to 1938, is, of course, that they moved inversely. When prices were moving favorably to manufactures—when the B curve rose—the A curve fell; that is, the volume of manufactures moving in world trade relative to primary materials declined. Hilgerdt showed that, in 1935, two-thirds of the manufactured articles exported by the highly industrialized countries flowed to the unindustrialized producers of primary products. His chart strongly suggested that the relative volume of manufactured exports was high when the incomes of primary producers were sustained by relatively

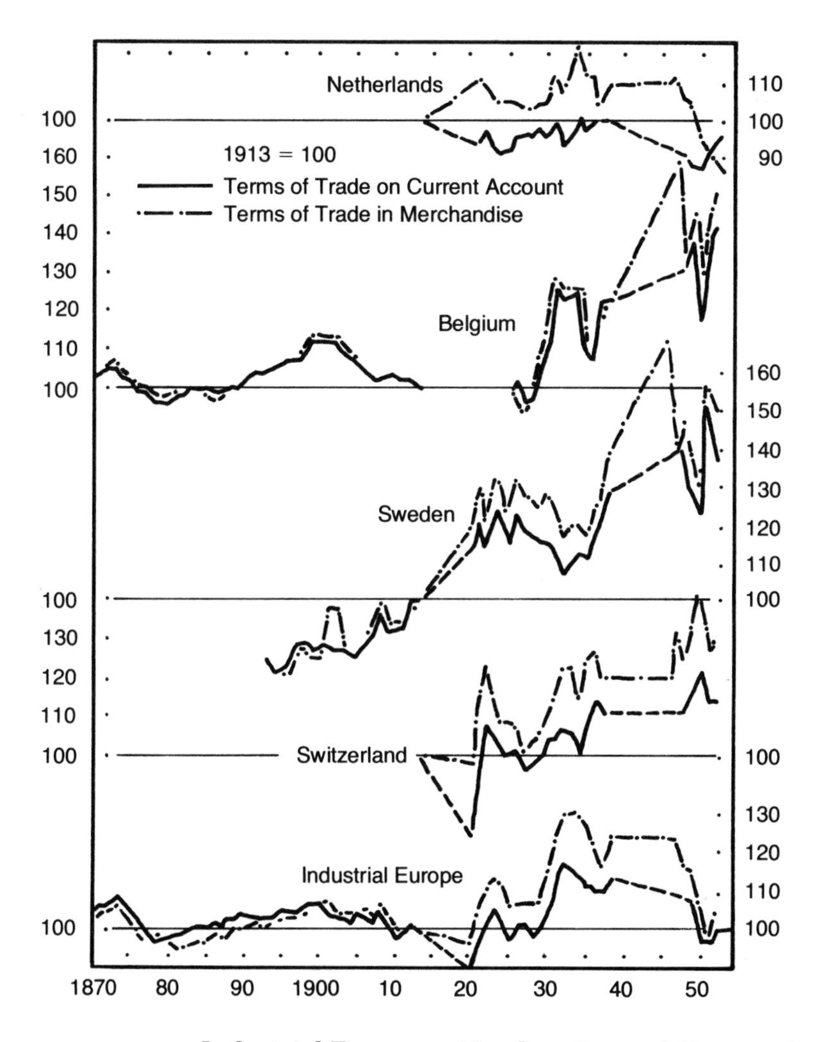

CHART II-12. *Industrial European Merchandise and Current-Account Terms of Trade, 1870–1952, Part 2*

Source: Kindleberger, *The Terms of Trade*, p. 27.

favorable prices for their products. And there is, of course, an important element of truth in this proposition, although the flow of capital to primary producers, levels of unemployment in industrialized countries, and other complexities affect the outcome.

After the Second World War the A and B curves lose their elegant reciprocity of movement.[43] The initial price shift between 1938 and 1948 does yield the expected result; that is, the price movement against manufactures, in favor of primary products, is accompanied by a radical upward shift in the quantity of manufactures in world trade relative to trade in primary products. But in the post–Korean War period, 1951–1972, when manufactured prices are rising relative to primary products, there is not the expected retardation or decline: trade in manufactures continues relatively to forge ahead until the Price Revolution of 1972–1976. In 1948, manufactured

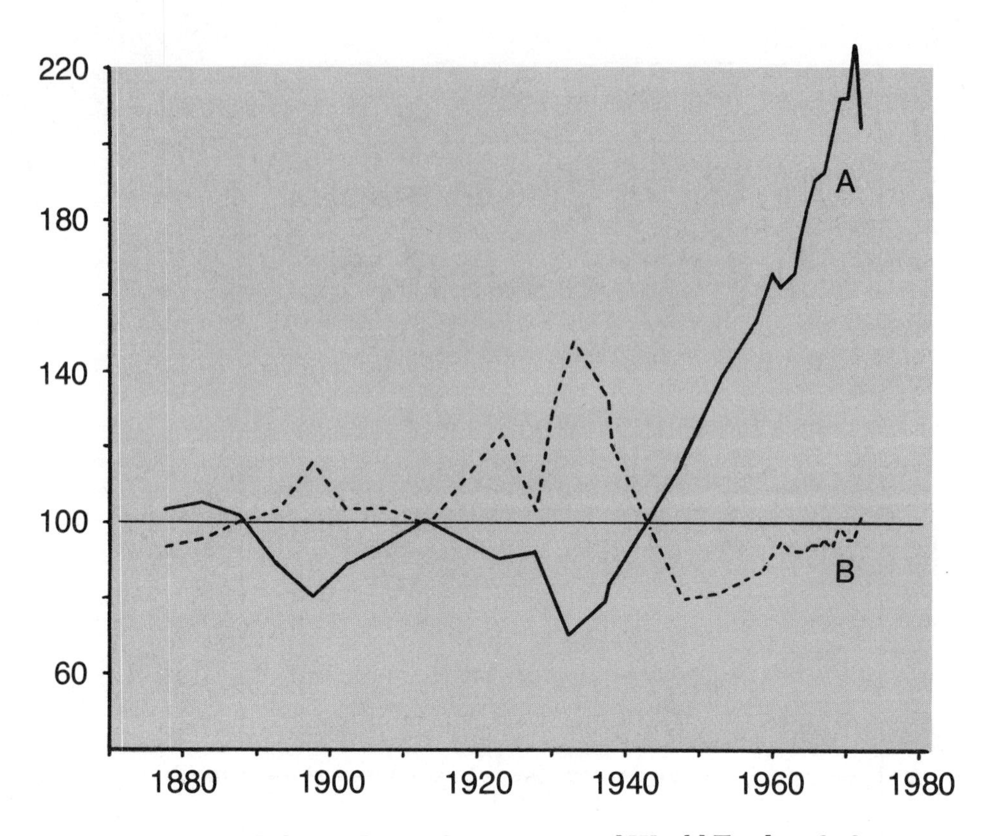

CHART II-13. *Relative Price Movements and World Trade, 1876–1880 to 1972*

A. Quantum index of world trade in manufactured goods as percentage of that in primary goods.
B. Price index of manufactured goods as percentage of that for primary goods.

Source: Folke Hilgerdt, *Industrialization and Foreign Trade*, p. 18, updated from *United Nations Statistical Yearbooks*, various years.

exports were 44 percent of the total value of world exports; in 1971, 66 percent.

A number of factors account for this significant structural change: the diminishing role of the less-developed nations in the grain trade, now dominated by the United States, Canada, and Australia; the extraordinary rise of trade in manufactures among the industrialized nations centered on automobiles, television sets, and other paraphernalia of high mass-consumption; economies in the use of raw materials in manufacturing plus a shift to industrial sectors using a lower proportion of raw materials; the increasing role of petroleum in world trade, responding to demand and supply conditions somewhat different from the classic circumstances governing trade in primary products between industrialized and nonindustrial countries. Between 1938 and 1971 trade in fuel rose in volume from

7.2 percent of total world trade to 10.3 percent (from 8.1 percent to 9.7 percent in value). In the same period, trade in food and raw materials declined from 49.1 percent to 23.4 percent in volume (from 46.4 percent to 22.9 percent in value). Between these dates there was, evidently, a slight favorable shift in food and raw material prices, an unfavorable shift in fuel prices.[44]

Between 1972 and 1977, of course, the pattern of both relative prices and world trade altered dramatically. The terms of trade shifted sharply in favor of oil exporters and against importers of both oil and food. The trade among industrialized countries, whose expansion dominated the post-1945 world, was constricted by an acute recession which also affected the volume and prices of trade in industrial raw materials. The proportion of world trade conducted by the oil exporters rose to an extraordinary degree. As we shall see in Part Three, the course of events in 1972–1977, while in many ways unique, bears a family relation to four previous periods over the past two centuries when major changes in relative prices occurred. In all these cases, including the most recent experience, these shifts in relative prices flowed from gross distortions in the balance between the demands of industry and consumers and the supply of raw materials and food necessary to match them.

Part Three

Trend Periods

10

Balanced and Unbalanced Growth

We concluded the discussion of movements in relative prices in Part Two by suggesting the possibility of deviations of production of raw materials and foodstuffs away from the requirements set up by the growth of world population, industrial production, and real income. This notion of normal or optimum requirements for balance in the world economy (and within national economies) must now be generalized, as we turn to examine certain major phases in the evolution of the world economy over the past two centuries.[1] Starting with the work of the Russian economist N. D. Kondratieff, the analysis of these phases has generated a vast literature addressed variously to long waves or cycles, secular movements or trend periods.[2] Economists have sought to explain the phenomena involved in various ways and, in some cases, focused narrowly on one or another of the processes at work in these phases.

Broadly speaking, there have been three approaches to long cycles: those emphasizing phases of agricultural and raw-material scarcity or abundance, and, in the former case, the bringing into the world economy of new territories; those seeking to link long cycles in prices, interest rates, and other value series to the sequence of great technological innovations; and those centered on fluctuations in overall growth rates, associated with changes in rates of international and domestic migration, linked, in turn, to accelerated investment in transport, housing, and urban infrastructure. I shall not here review the literature on long cycles directly, but proceed with my own exposition.[3] It embraces all three of these elements in the dynamics of growth.

We begin with the following question: If we assume as given, in a closed economic system, at peace, a certain steady overall rate of growth in the economy, how should the sectors expand smoothly to support that rate of growth? By assuming the rate of growth as given, we are setting aside for the moment what determines the rate of growth of population and the working force; the size and quality (e.g., education level) of the working force; the level of investment and its productivity. We are further assuming that relatively full employment is maintained and that investment is, somehow, perfectly and without lag directed into the channels appropriate for balance in the economy.

We shall focus initially on three key sectors which absorb in all societies a high proportion of total investment: the supply of industrial raw materials, including energy; the supply of food; the supply of housing and associated infrastructure (streets, sewerage, water, gas, etc.). Investment required to furnish industrial supplies would then be a function of the rate of industrial growth, corrected for changing economies in raw-material use and the changing structure of industry, as it relates to raw-material requirements. Investment in agriculture would be a function of the size of the population, its real income, and the manner in which the demand for food and tastes in food varied with the level of real income. The amount of investment required to sustain raw-material and food requirements would also be affected, of course, by the quality and availability of raw-material supplies and changing technologies in those industries: do diminishing returns operate or are diminishing returns being overcome by the exploitation of new resources, additional acreage, or new technologies? Investment in housing, etc., would be geared to the rate of family formation, the rate of urbanization, and the direction of migration within the economy.

On a simplified basis, the path of such an abstract system through time might look something like Chart III-1. Industrial production would normally increase in such a growing system faster than GNP, population less. The amount of investment required to sustain the three sectors (raw-material production, construction, and food production) would be determined by their upward slope and the productivity of investment (or marginal capital-output ratio) in those particular sectors. The productivity of investment varies greatly by sectors, being high in industry, for example, low in housing. (This means that the proportion of increase in capital investment to increase in output is low in the first case, high in the second.)

But what sustains industrial production itself? At any period of time in the life of a modern growing economy, industrial production is marked by widely diverging growth rates in the sectors. These variations reflect many factors but, most notably, on the side of supply, the pace of technological change within the sector; on the side of demand, population increase and changing tastes, as income increases and the range of consumers' goods available widens. Old sectors may be declining, others may be stagnant, others may be moving forward at about the average rate of industrial production as a whole (like raw-material production); but there will be one or more leading sectors, reflecting the introduction of major new technologies, moving ahead more rapidly than the average, absorbing a disproportionate volume of current investment and able entrepreneurs, stimulating requirements to sustain it, and, quite often, bringing about accelerated urban growth in new regions. Table III-1, showing the sectoral growth of manufactures in the United States from 1899 to 1937, exhibits how widely growth rates vary, as well as the extraordinary movement of a large leading sector of this period—automobiles.

Historically, the classic sequence of such great leading sectors was: cotton textiles; railroads and iron; steel, chemicals, and elec-

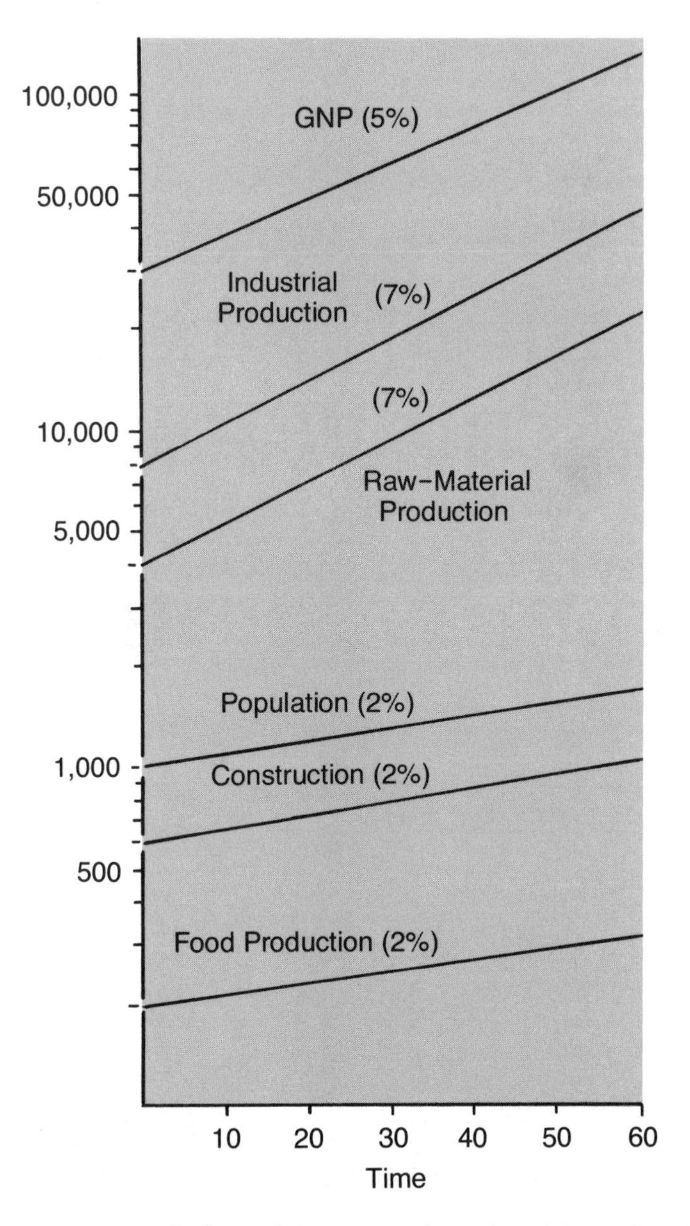

CHART III-1. *Balanced Optimum Growth in Three Key Sectors (Arbitrary Annual Growth Rates)*

TABLE III-1. *Individual Manufacturing Industries Ranked According to Percentage Change in Physical Output, United States, 1899–1937*

Industry	Percentage Change	Industry	Percentage Change
Automobiles	+180,100	Cotton goods	+101
Cigarettes	+4,226	Cane-sugar refining	+101
Petroleum refining	+1,920	Fish, canned	+96
Milk, canned	+1,810	Hats, wool-felt	+90
Beet sugar	+1,688	Shoes, leather	+87
Hosiery, knit	+1,202	Salt	+82
Cement	+838	Cane sugar, not elsewhere made	+67
Fruits and vegetables, canned	+792	Meat packing	+66
Chemicals, not elsewhere classified	+741	Cottonseed products	+63
Ice	+668	Leather	+61
Silk and rayon goods	+512	Woolen and worsted goods	+60
Pulp	+505	Liquors, malt	+60
Printing and publishing	+494	Underwear, knit	+52
Paper	+465	Carpet and rugs, wool	+52
Rice	+416	Lead	+51
Outerwear, knit	+393	Cordage and twine	+38
Paints and varnishes	+391	Hats, fur-felt	+26
Coke-oven products	+380	Gloves, leather	+16
Zinc	+318	Cigars	0
Liquors, distilled	+315	Pianos	−5
Steel-mill products	+313	Tobacco products, other	−6
Butter	+309	Flour	−8
Tanning and dye materials	+292	Clay products	−15
Copper	+272	Ships and boats	−17
Explosives	+267	Cars, railroad, not elsewhere made	−22
Wood-distillation products	+259	Lumber-mill products, not elsewhere classified	−32
Fertilizers	+248	Turpentine and rosin	−32
Blast-furnace products	+171	Linen goods	−44
Cheese	+158	Locomotives, not elsewhere made	−79
Jute goods	+134	Carriages, wagons, and sleighs	−95
Wool shoddy	+116		

Source: Solomon Fabricant, *The Output of Manufacturing Industries, 1899–1937* (New York: National Bureau of Economic Research, 1940),

tricity; and the automobile industry. The normal path of such sectors is one of progressive deceleration, as the initial technological breakthrough is exploited, followed by lesser refinements, while other damping forces operate on both supply and demand.[4]

Chart III-2 shows, by way of illustration, how certain key leading sectors moved in relation to overall industrial production in Britain, on a trend basis, with short-term fluctuations smoothed. (The analysis of sectoral and aggregate growth patterns for twenty countries is pursued in Part Five.) In an optimum world the new technologies on which the sequence of leading sectors is based would be regularly developed in response to the society's requirements and changing tastes,[5] promptly and smoothly introduced by innovators, and then diffused without interruption along their decelerating tracks, carrying with them without lag the sectors to which they were linked.

The fact is, of course, that the world economy and national economies did not develop in any such smooth way. National economies were not closed, but subject to all manner of impulses arising from the world economy. The world economy not only contained a wide variety of inhibitions on the movement of capital, populations, goods, and services across borders; it also was not fixed in size. Over the period we are considering, it gradually expanded to include virtually all of the world's nations and population. There were also wars, distorting the demands on the sectors and, for a time, changing the shape of the world economy, the possibilities and costs of movement within it, and the availability of critical supplies. Rates of population increase varied within the world economy and within its regions; large movements of population proved possible at certain times and in certain directions, responding to more or less ra-

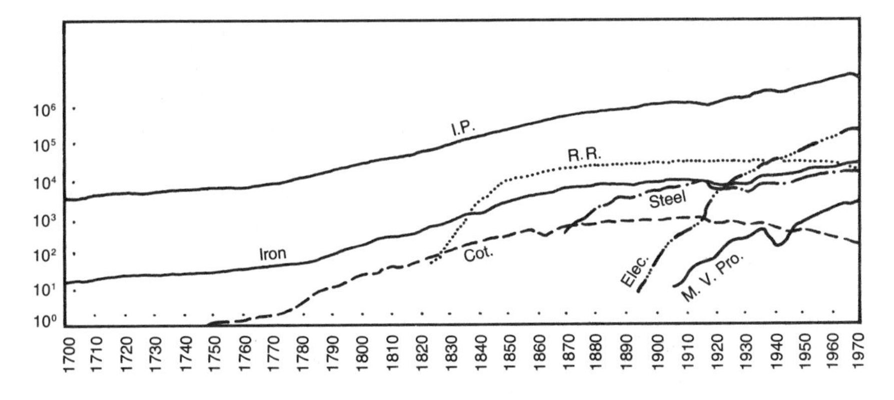

CHART III-2. *Aggregate and Sectoral Growth Patterns Illustrated: British Industrial Production and Six Major Sectors, 1700–1972*

Industrial production (I.P.); railroad mileage (R.R.); raw cotton consumption (Cot.); production of iron (Iron); steel (Steel); electricity (Elec.); and motor vehicles (M.V. Pro.).

Source: Part Five, Chapter 28, below.

tional economic criteria; but at other times and in other directions population movements were inhibited. The level of investment fluctuated, and with it the level of employment and output; and in many times and places total investment was at levels which did not permit the world's requirements in the various sectors to be met simultaneously. The level of interest rates in relation to expected profits in the various sectors helped conduct the necessary rationing. And there were lags: lags between the time opportunities for profitable investment, required for balance, were perceived and the time capital flowed in those directions; lags of various lengths between the initiation of investment and its completion, ranging from a year (for, say, a factory) to many years (for, say, an American or Canadian transcontinental railroad); lags between the completion of an act of investment and the time it yielded fully its productive results.

Moreover, the investment process did not yield smoothly the pattern of investment most appropriate to the requirements of balance in national economies or the world economy. For the bulk of our period, in most nations, the pattern of investment was determined by the assessment in private markets of where future profitability lay. These assessments were inherently distorted by three factors: they were determined by current indicators of profitability rather than rational long-range assessments; investors rarely took into account the fact that the indicators that moved them to act were also moving others to act in the same direction, so that they were unclear about the appropriateness of the total volume of investment flowing in particular directions; and there was, psychologically, a follow-the-leader tendency in capital markets tending to produce over-investment and then underinvestment (as compared to long-run optimum levels) in particular sectors. These characteristics of the investment process lay behind the cyclical fluctuations we shall consider in Part Four, as economies systematically overshot and undershot the sectoral optimum positions; but the same imperfections in foresight also influenced the trend phenomena considered here.

When, in the pre-1914 world, governments were involved in the process (for example, in railway building), their calculations were not always more rational than those of private markets. When socialist and other state-controlled economies emerged in some countries in the post-1914 world, their calculations were sometimes more forward-ranging than those of private markets, but quite often flawed in their assessment of future national requirements and governed by national or ideological criteria which complicated the task of maintaining balance in their own economies and in the world economy as a whole (e.g., agricultural policy in the Soviet Union).

Finally, there were gold and silver. These were, of course, commodities used for ornamentation as well as, latterly, for more mundane industrial purposes. But gold and sometimes silver were for almost all of our period linked to the value of key currencies. Governments or central banks were committed to buy bullion at prices fixed for particular periods of time, because bullion was, quite formally, a form of currency and banking reserve, as well as used directly in coins. Moreover, in many societies, bullion was viewed as a way to hold savings in a concentrated, easily transportable, and negotiable form, when the currency was in doubt or there were other kinds of insecurity. But, aside from ornamentation and industrial purposes, bullion had no normal positive human use. Its production was a kind of tax for the maintenance of the monetary systems or for the provision of insurance against monetary or other instability. Gold and silver production did not expand at a steady rate. Output fluctuated with the productivity of existing mines and the discovery of new sources. Moreover, with currencies tied to fixed amounts of bullion, the attractiveness of gold mining varied inversely with general trends in the price level. At times when new gold mines were discovered and exploited, the flow of investment in that direction and the infusion of new supplies into the world economy had disequilibrating effects.

These are the characteristics of the world economy that account for the fact that the overall and sectoral paths of growth were not as neat or smooth as those in Chart III-1. And, indeed, the leading sectors unfolded a good deal less continuously than the smoothed curves in Chart III-2 would indicate. The workings of the price system, the sequence of inventions and innovations, the directions of international migration, and the pattern of investment over periods of time all reflect responsiveness to the requirements of the world economy for sectoral balance; but their movement was lagged, erratic, and sometimes convulsive rather than prompt and smooth. Excepting the wars, there is a rough and ready economic rationality in the story of growth in the world economy over the past two centuries; but it is rough and ready. And the wars that did happen left powerful marks on the story of growth.

In turning now to consider secular trends (or long cycles) between 1790 and 1977, we shall focus, in particular, on the erratic adjustment of food and raw-material production to the requirements of population and industrial growth in the world economy; on the role of the sequence of great leading sectors which helped determine the structure of production, costs, and prices; and on fluctuations in the demand for housing as decreed, in particular, by population growth and migration. As we shall see, these three forces interact in complex ways, with consequences for the price level and relative prices; interest rates and patterns of investment; the distribution of income within nations and among them; and flows of capital across borders and the pattern of international trade.

What we have to explain, in particular, are these phenomena:

—Periods when the trend of prices in general, agricultural and raw-material prices in particular, and interest rates are rising or high, relative to previous and subsequent periods; agriculture is expanding rapidly; income distribution tends to shift in favor of agriculture and profits, while urban real wages are under pressure. The rough dating of these trend periods is:[6] 1790–1815; 1848–1873; 1896–1920; 1935–1951; 1972–1977, with the likelihood that the forces which asserted themselves in these five years will persist for some time, despite the raw-material price declines of 1974–1975.

—Periods when the trend of prices in general, agricultural and raw-material prices in particular, and interest rates are falling or low, relative to previous and subsequent periods; income distribution tends to shift in favor of urban real wages, while profits in industry and agriculture are under pressure. The rough dating of these trend periods is: 1815–1848; 1873–1896; 1920–1935. The period 1951–1972, a period of endemic inflation, shares some but not all the characteristics of previous phases when agricultural and raw materials were relatively low.

—Periods when massive waves of international or domestic migration (or other discontinuous population changes) raise the rates of family formation in certain countries or regions, yielding disproportionately strong expansion in housing construction and urban infrastructure. For the United States, for example, the periods concerned (so-called long-cycle peaks) are in intervals centered on 1880–1885; 1900–1905; and 1920–1925.[7]

Before plunging into the history of these phenomena, it is important to emphasize that the view presented here is not one of inevitably recurring smooth cycles. The trend periods broadly described above in terms of prices, relative prices, interest rates, etc., were uneven; and, in most cases, they were broken by intervals in which the trend movements were halted or temporarily reversed. For example, in the case of Great Britain, the course of affairs from 1803 to 1808, in the 1830's, in the 1860's, and in the late 1880's runs counter to the trend periods of which these intervals are a part. And there are other deviations from smooth long-cycle behavior; for example, as we have already seen (Chart II-4), the British (and world) price level rose during the period of relative weakness of food and raw-material prices 1951–1972. What is essential here is not the existence of long waves or cycles: it is the dynamic mechanism by which growing national economies and the world economy struggle toward a balance never actually attained. In that context the periods of deviation from smooth long-cycle behavior (e.g., the 1830's and late 1880's) become quite as explicable as the intervals of conformity.

Against this background, we shall now summarize how the trend periods unfolded, examining, successively, the situation in agriculture and raw-materials production; the state of the leading sectors which often link to rapidly increasing demands for specific raw materials; and, where relevant, the population and other impulses operating on the demand for housing and urban infrastructure, which, as we shall see, were often a function of the other two factors examined.

11

1790–1815

As we noted in Part One, there was an endemic rise in European population in the second half of the eighteenth century. The annual average rate of population growth in Great Britain, for example, moved as shown in Table III-2, coming to a peak rate of increase for British history in 1811–1821.

TABLE III-2. *Rate of Population Increase: Great Britain, 1731–1831 (Annual Average Rate of Growth [%])*

1731–1741	−0.03
1741–1751	0.36
1751–1761	0.68
1761–1771	0.71
1771–1781	0.66
1781–1791	0.91
1791–1801	1.05
1801–1811	1.29
1811–1821	1.58
1821–1831	1.43

Source: Phyllis Deane and W. A. Cole, *British Economic Growth, 1688–1959*, second edition (Cambridge: At the University Press, 1969), pp. 6 and 8.

Accompanying this increase, down to 1790, the price of wheat rose. Between 1741–1745 and the five years preceding the outbreak of the French Wars (1788–1792), the wheat price doubled (from 3.6 shillings per bushel to 7.2), and the price of bread in London increased by 50 percent. By 1800, only a decade later, the price of wheat was up to 16 shillings and the price of bread in London had also more than doubled. They fluctuated about relatively high levels down to the end of the wars, responding to the British harvests and changing access to imported supplies of grain. In short, protracted war struck Britain at a period of gathering tension between population increase and the food supply; and wartime circumstances

TABLE III-3. *Agricultural Capital: United Kingdom, Selected Dates, 1750–1887*

	£ Millions, Sterling				£ per Inhabitant
	Land	Cattle	Sundries	Total	
1750	498	25	58	581	55
1780	702	35	81	812	65
1814	1,470	74	172	1,716	95
1843	1,677	94	197	1,968	72
1850	1,705	104	201	2,010	72
1860	1,748	140	210	2,098	72
1868	1,925	170	233	2,328	75
1880	2,086	209	255	2,550	72
1887	1,873	185	229	2,287	61

Source: Michael G. Mulhall, *The Dictionary of Statistics* (London; George Routledge, 1892), p. 18.

gravely exacerbated the underlying situation. They did so mainly by causing erratic obstructions to the normal flow of grain imported from the Baltic and by sharply increasing shipping costs; for Britain had shifted slowly from food-exporting to food-importing status between the 1750's and the 1790's.

The wartime rise in agricultural prices yielded, as one would expect, a sharp expansion in production and investment in that sector. Mulhall provides a table (III-3), estimating changes in agricultural capital in the United Kingdom over the period 1750–1887. This table catches well the pre-war rise in agricultural investment during the period 1750–1780 and the acceleration during the war years. It also reflects later phases, which we shall discuss below.

The wartime surge in agricultural investment can be seen on a narrower but more precise basis in Table III-4, showing the number of acts of enclosure passed in the British parliament over the period 1788–1819.

There are, unfortunately, no reliable estimates of the actual increase in British agricultural production over these years.[8] What can be said is that the increase in agricultural output roughly matched the increase in population; that is, the level of wheat and

TABLE III-4. *British Acts of Enclosure, 1788–1819 (Annual Averages)*

1788–1792	35
1793–1797	74
1798–1802	82
1803–1807	79
1808–1814	114
1815–1819	50

Source: A. D. Gayer et al., *British Basic Statistical Data*, Table 41, p. 160.

flour imports averaged at roughly the same figure for the period 1793–1797 and the period 1810–1814 (2.2 million cwts. and 2.4 million cwts., respectively). From year to year, of course, imports varied with the state of the British harvests and the availability of external supplies. There were particular years of very high food prices and real shortage for the poorer groups in the population. Taken as a whole, the war years were a time of pressure on the real wages of the urban population. But the sectoral requirement for agricultural expansion was met by a shift in the pattern of investment responding to profit possibilities opened up by relative price movements.

Glenn Hueckel has constructed for this period indexes of agricultural and industrial prices which demonstrate clearly the relative rise in the former (Chart III-3 and Table III-5). The difference in trend is quite evident, as well as the impact of bad harvest years in widening the differential in 1800–1801 and 1812–1813. Wheat and oats carry a weight of 46 percent in Heuckel's agricultural price index. The industrial price index reflects both continued technological progress during the period and the fact that the industrial raw-materials supply from domestic sources was probably more elastic and certainly less volatile than the food supply; but it should be noted that the substantial rise in the price of wool was in part due to the pressure of enclosures for grain production on grazing land, a switch which had marked other wartime periods in British history.

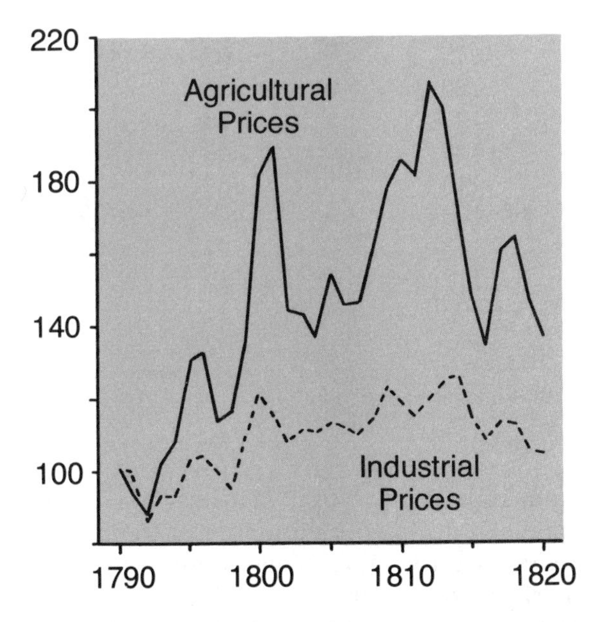

CHART III-3. *Indexes of Agricultural and Industrial Prices: Great Britain, 1790–1820 (1790=100)*

Source: Glenn Hueckel, "War and the British Economy, 1793–1815: A General Equilibrium Analysis," *Explorations in Economic History*, vol. 10, no. 4 (Summer 1973), p. 388.

TABLE III-5. *Indexes of Agricultural and Industrial Prices: Great Britain, 1790–1820 (1790 = 100)*

	(1) Agricultural Prices	(2) Industrial Prices	(3) Difference (1 – 2)
1790	100	100	0
1791	93	99	–6
1792	88	86	2
1793	102	93	9
1794	108	93	15
1795	130	103	27
1796	133	104	29
1797	113	100	13
1798	116	95	21
1799	135	109	26
1800	181	121	60
1801	189	115	74
1802	144	108	36
1803	143	111	32
1804	137	111	26
1805	154	113	41
1806	145	112	33
1807	146	110	36
1808	160	114	46
1809	178	123	55
1810	185	119	66
1811	182	115	67
1812	206	120	86
1813	200	124	76
1814	170	126	44
1815	148	114	34
1816	135	109	26
1817	160	113	47
1818	164	112	52
1819	147	106	41
1820	137	105	32

Source: Hueckel, "War and the British Economy," p. 388.

The cotton price rose more rapidly than that of wheat (or wool) down to 1799, and then actually declined, as a matter of trend, during the rest of the war years, as Eli Whitney's cotton gin worked its magic and the flow of American cotton expanded rapidly.

The major reason for the price differential between agricultural and industrial prices, however, was the continued technological momentum of the leading sectors of the British take-off, notably cotton textiles and iron. Indeed, the cotton gin was an invention induced by the momentum of British cotton textile production in the most direct way. The food component of R. S. Tucker's cost-of-living index, for example, rose by 131 percent between 1790 and 1813 (the peak year), whereas the clothing component rose by only 20 percent.[9] Pig iron rose from £64 per ton on the eve of the war with France to a peak as early as 1804 at £80, where the price, determined by monopolistic arrangements, remained down to the end of the struggle. Bar iron rose from £16 per ton to a peak of £22 in 1801 and then actually declined to £14 in 1815.

The movement of the leading sectors, with cost-reducing and dynamically unfolding technologies embedded within them, thus damped the inflationary impulses of the period, helping account for the relative movement of agricultural and industrial prices.

As for housing, the effects of war were what they had been over the previous century and would be over the century and three-quarters that followed; that is, house construction was depressed by wartime high interest rates and the high cost of building materials, notably imported timber, whose price rose by 219 percent between 1792 and the peak in 1814. British brick production and timber imports, for all but a few years, remained below the pre-war peak figure of 1792 until the postwar building boom of 1818–1819.

TABLE III-6. *Building Cycles in Great Britain: Eighteenth Century*

Trough	Peak	Trough	Years between	
			Peaks	Troughs
ca. 1698?	1705?	1711?	—	—
ca. 1711	1724	1727?	19	16
1727?	1736	1744	12	17
1744	1753	1762	17	18
1762	1776	1781	23	19
1781	1792	1798	16	17

Source: John Parry Lewis, *Building Cycles and Britain's Growth*, p. 14.

The housing and construction boom which peaked in 1792 was the sixth which can be roughly discerned in the course of the eighteenth century.[10] With the exception of the weakest of these expansions (peaking in 1736), all can be associated with the depressing effect of the wars of this period and the release of funds that intervals of peace afforded.[11] From 1730 forward there was a clear, if rough, inverse correlation between the yield on 3 percent consols and indicators of building activity (Chart III-4).

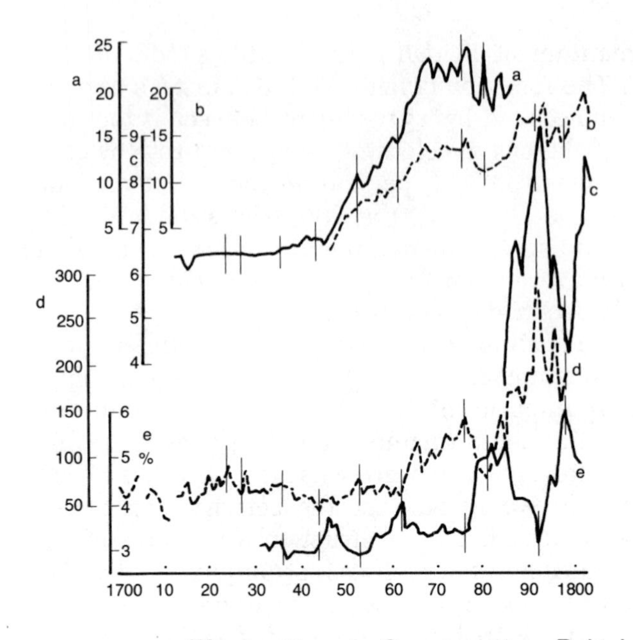

CHART III-4. *Fluctuations in Construction: Britain, 1700–1800*

a: Stained paper charged with duty (hundred thousand yards). Excise years.

b: Glass (excluding bottles, etc.) charged with duty (ten thousand cwts.). Excise years.

c: Bricks charged with duty (hundred millions). Excise years.

d: Imports of fir and deal (£ thousands).

e: Yield on 3 percent funds (reciprocal of average annual [July–June] prices).

Source: J. P. Lewis, *Building Cycles and Britain's Growth*, p. 12.

The volume of timber imports fluctuated about a relatively static level until the end of the Seven Years' War (1763); but it then moved sharply upward, a trend reflecting, no doubt, the increase in family formation that followed the mid-century increase in population, as well as the increase in transport construction and accelerated urbanization between 1783 and 1792.

During the war years there was a substantial expansion in the indicators of housing and construction from the depressed level of 1797–1798 to a peak around 1805; but, despite the intervening growth in population, brick production and timber imports barely exceeded the 1792 level at that time; and they were only slightly higher in the subsequent boom, peaking in 1810. They moved promptly to a quite different level in the peacetime expansions peaking in 1818 and 1825. The doubling in the scale of construction in the postwar decade suggests the power of the constraints operating even during the best of the wartime years.

What we observe in Britain from 1793 to 1815, then, is an economy dealing with a major protracted war at a time of accelerated

TABLE III-7. *Indicators of British Construction, 1792–1825*

Business Cycle Peak	Production of Bricks (in Millions)	Quantity of Sawn Timber Imports (1,000 Loads of 50 Cu. Ft.)
1792	858.4	289
1805	889.4	264
1810	945.1[a]	320[a]
1818	1,101.6[a]	415
1825	1,948.8	709

[a] Building indicator peaks exhibit lag of one year beyond business cycle peak.
Source: Gayer et al., *British Basic Statistical Data.*

increase in population stemming from forces that began to assert themselves in the mid-eighteenth century. If war had not come, with its obstructions to supply and increased transport costs, British food requirements would have been met by larger imports, a lesser expansion in domestic agriculture.

Aside from the artificial diversion of resources into agriculture, the war had real costs in other directions:

—The British military establishment was expanded by perhaps 400,000 over the peacetime level. The mobilized force was 3–5 percent of the total population, depending on the population base taken; a substantially higher proportion of the working force.

—As noted in the discussion of grain prices, the real cost of certain basic commodities rose: overseas imports, because of the circuitous and often dangerous routes followed, the necessity for convoys, and the consequent very large increases in freight rates; foodstuffs, timber, and other Baltic products, because of erratic access, notably after 1802.

—Large resources were diverted into shipbuilding and docks to support military operations and the artificially expanded requirements that went with Britain's quasi-monopolistic trading position; and into armament manufactures and other military supplies required by British and allied military forces.

Protracted war, combined with the pressures of an accelerating population increase, altered the optimum paths of investment away from those which had prevailed between 1783 and 1792 and which would have prevailed if peace had reigned. The British economy (and public policy) responded in ways which permitted its population to be fed, the war to be fought, and allies to be subsidized on a large scale, the transfer of resources being made by means of profits from re-exports and the rapidly expanding manufactures flowing from the cotton mills. The costs of the effort were met by an expansion in the rate of investment;[12] a rise in the real rate of tax collection; a radical damping in housing and infrastructure (including canals, turnpikes, etc.); and a decline in real income for the urban population.

The upshot was a pattern of price, relative price, interest rate, and income distribution movements that was broadly to characterize the four other such trend periods over the subsequent 160 years.

The experience of other nations during this trend period differed, of course, from that of Britain, which was alone in its experience of rapid industrialization, as well as in its quasi-monopolistic trading role.

Our information on the French economy between 1793 and 1815 is much less complete than in the case of Britain. Certain aspects of the experience of the two nations can, nevertheless, be compared.

On the eve of revolution and war the French population was expanding, but at a distinctly lower rate than in the case of Britain: say, 0.4 percent per annum, a rate which may have persisted to about 1801.[13] From that date, apparently, the French population, experiencing a high rate of mobilization and heavy war casualties, slowed in its rate of increase to, say, 0.1 percent until the end of the war, when a sharp rebound occurred.

The course of eighteenth- and early nineteenth-century French agriculture is the subject of unresolved debate.[14] In real terms, the output of French agriculture is estimated to have expanded at a rate of 0.6 percent per annum between 1781–1790 and the economically best years of the war (1803–1812).[15] This was somewhat higher than the rate of population increase. As in Britain, the relative price of agricultural products rose more than for industrial products. The former increased by 15 percent from 1781–1790 to 1803–1812, while the products of industry and handicrafts were virtually constant as between the two periods.[16] So far as leading sectors are concerned, France experienced no sustained phase of industrialization during this period equivalent to that in Britain. Nevertheless, there was some considerable progress in the cotton spinning industry, notably during the period of the Continental Blockade. There was less technological progress in woolens and some in chemicals, but a severe decline in the linen industry. Pig iron was relatively stagnant in both output and technology; but there was some advance in the metalworking trade.[17] Overall, French industrial production is estimated to have increased between 1781–1790 and 1803–1812 at an annual average rate of 0.5 percent by Markovitch, 2 percent by Marczewski.[18] Whatever statistical coverage and method are used, however, two things are clear: the French economy rebounded in the first decade of the century from its vicissitudes of the 1790's; but its overall industrial progress during the war years failed to match that experienced in Britain, widening the gap between them which had opened up between 1783 and 1792. As in the case of Britain, the industries reflecting housing and construction exhibited much lower rates of growth than the average; but they rebounded in the postwar decade.[19]

Whereas events in this trend period pushed France inward on the Continent, away from its eighteenth-century orientation toward overseas trade, the first impact of the war on the United States was to enlarge its role in the world trading system, as a neutral in a position to trade with all sides. The rapid increase in population (2.95 percent per annum in the 1790's) was easily fed despite an increase in the value of domestic exports of 142 percent between 1792 and 1801, as well as an expansion of re-exports from $2 million to $47 million, a figure slightly higher than that for U.S. domestic exports at the time. Relative price movements, as elsewhere, shifted in favor of agriculture; farm prices rose by 100 percent between 1791 and 1801; fuel by 67 percent; metals by 45 percent; building materials by 62 percent.[20] Despite Alexander Hamilton's powerful case to the Congress in 1791 for the development of manufactures in the United States, the first phase of the war drew capital in other directions: to agriculture, shipping, and commerce, where large profits were to be made.

The character of the war's impact on America emerged vividly during the brief Peace of Amiens:

> The worst depression in business thus far encountered [since 1790] took place between the end of 1801 and the spring of 1803. This was an interval of peace in Europe—the peace of Amiens—and of business readjustment in the United States. Prices both of imports and exports fell sharply with the news of peace. Business failures were numerous, sailing vessels lay idle in the docks from Salem to New Orleans. There was much unemployment.
>
> Underlying the depression was the reduced demand by foreigners for American exports. The English harvests of 1801 and 1802 were abundant. The resumption of English trade with the Baltic ports following the death of Emperor Paul of Russia made alternative supplies of grain available to Great Britain. Naval stores fell in price because of the "great surplussage of shipping." At the same time imported goods, such as copper, salt, hemp, duck, Swedish iron, cocoa, coffee, and sugar were declining. Prices seem to have fallen the world over. In England there was a mild commercial crisis which may have caused forced sales of some of these commodities in America.
>
> American business not only reflected the changed state of the markets for commodities, but also felt severely the decline in the demand for the services of her shippers. Europeans were once more able to do some of their own carrying.[21]

A second, lesser period of expansion followed the resumption of hostilities which gave way to the troubled period of the Embargo and then the War of 1812. Here, of course, the pattern of investment shifted away from international trade toward industry, with one important exception: the production and export of raw cotton. Exports were, of course, set back in the most acute phase of the

TABLE III-8. *U.S. Cotton Exports, 1794–1815 (Annual Averages in Millions of Lbs.)*

1794–1798	5.4
1799–1803	23.6
1804–1808	37.4
1809–1815	50.7

Source: *Historical Statistics of the United States*, 1960 ed., p. 547.

Embargo and War with Britain (i.e., 1808, 1812–1814); but the power of the upward trend created by the British demand and the cotton gin is suggested by the figures for U.S. raw cotton exports given in Table III-8.

In 1794 cotton was 7 percent of the value of U.S. exports; in 1815, 39 percent. This rise in proportion occurred despite the trend decline in the cotton price from 1799, which shifted the U.S. terms of trade "unfavorably" from that date to 1814.[22] Like the concurrent "unfavorable" movement of the British terms of trade, flowing from the cost-reducing effects of the new technology in textile manufacture, this American decline, stemming substantially from the cotton gin, was, economically, a positive factor in the growth of the United States as well as the world economy.

It is impossible to measure satisfactorily the scale of the shift to industry from 1806 to the end of the War of 1812; but a rise in the number of cotton spindles from 8,000 in 1808 to about 80,000 in 1811 suggests the reality of the impetus which, in fact, spread over a much wider range of manufactures than cotton textiles. One significant reflection of this shift in orientation toward manufactures is the course of U.S. patents granted, set out in Table III-9. Looked at closely, it was with the period of Embargo, 1807–1809, that the rate of patents granted moved up to a quite new level: from 99 to 203, a level which persisted, with year-to-year variations, until the end of the War of 1812 and the resumption of normal international commerce. It was not until the second half of the 1820's that the level of 1810–1814 was exceeded; but by then an industrial boom was under way in New England on a scale that dwarfed the efforts at import substitution during the Embargo and war years.

The extraordinary commercial prosperity of the period 1793–1808 led to an increase in the urban proportion of the population from 5.1 percent in 1790 to 7.3 percent in 1810; and the generally high range of real income per capita probably induced, in addition, increased outlays for public buildings and improved quality of housing for the most affluent. Immigration was not a significant demographic factor over this period, possibly averaging four to six thousand per year.

On balance, then, the United States was a beneficiary of both the wartime environment and the raw-material requirements of Britain's leading sector down to about 1808. The period of Embargo

TABLE III-9. *U.S. Inventions: Patents Issued, 1790–1829 (Annual Averages)*

Period	Patents
1790–1794	18
1795–1799	36
1800–1804	66
1805–1809	116
1810–1814	213
1815–1819	186
1820–1824	184
1825–1829	354

Source: *Historical Statistics of the United States*, 1960 ed., p. 608.

and war ended the abnormal prosperity of that phase, but set in motion a period of expansion in manufactures, often regarded as a wasteful diversion of national resources and a violation of comparative advantage.[23] And, indeed, as we are all taught, many of the war babies collapsed in 1816 with the coming of peace and the availability of cheap British manufactured imports. But it was during the War of 1812 that the New England cotton textile industry found its feet technologically, in Lowell and elsewhere, and, after a sharp setback, proceeded from 1817 forward into two decades of remarkable expansion.[24]

The price and relative-price phenomena to be observed down to 1806 are similar to those in Britain and France; but with a relatively smaller urban population, and that tied to a prosperous phase of expansion in commerce and shipping, the cities probably did not feel the weight of high living costs in the same degree as the urban populations of Europe.

It is difficult to speak with confidence about U.S. interest rates in this trend period. Data are scarce; the capital markets were thin and fragmented; but this was also a period of significant institutional development for banks and for corporations in the fields of insurance, turnpikes, and bridges. Industrial capital, however, was initially mobilized privately and subsequent investment financed mainly from the plowing back of profits.

The evidence available tends to suggest that, contrary to the situation in Britain, the trend of interest rates was downward. The value of fixed-interest 3 percent U.S. government bonds rose sharply in the period 1799–1802, fluctuating about the 1802 level, to fall, as one would expect, during the War of 1812. The price of these bonds revived, however, to a postwar level far above that of 1795–1799.[25] Bank-stock prices, with fluctuating yields, exhibited similar but less volatile fluctuations around a declining trend.[26] The inward turn of the American economy, from about 1808, was accompanied by a rise in the government bond prices, perhaps reflecting a flow of commercial capital to this form of savings, and by a rise also in bank-stock prices.

The short-run data available for these years do not permit us to trace the trend-period pattern in many countries. There are, however, good statistics on Swedish prices, wages, and real wages.[27] Like Britain (and most of Europe), Sweden experienced an expansion of population from the mid-eighteenth century: at an annual average rate of 0.5 percent between 1750 and 1775; 0.6 percent to 1800. Agricultural output expanded on the basis of the potato, land enclosure, and reclamation. From about the mid-1770's, however, the expansion fell behind the rate of population increase: grain prices rose slowly, and, with money wages relatively fixed until the years of war, real wages fell away in the 1780's and early 1790's. These trends were intensified, of course, in the most acute phases of conflict, since Sweden was linked to the international markets as an importer of grain, an exporter of timber and iron. Its prices moved similarly to those in Copenhagen and Amsterdam, as well as in London.[28] Relative prices in Sweden also followed the British and U.S. patterns; that is, the wartime rise in grain prices was greater than that in industrial products (e.g., iron, tar, and timber).

The period 1793–1815 is most clearly perceived in the behavior of the British economy, which alone was then experiencing sustained economic growth and which moved from a major to a dominant position in the world trading framework over those years. We can observe in a rather direct way the exacerbating effects of major protracted war on a food supply pressed since the mid-eighteenth century by an expanding European population. We can observe also the pressure on the supply of raw cotton generated by the leading sector of the British take-off. The upshot was an initial sharp rise in wheat and cotton prices. The former were contained by massive investment in British agriculture; the latter led to a major technological break-through, the cotton gin, which permitted the raw cotton price to fall from 1799, despite the inflationary and other disruptive forces at work in the world economy. There was an intense elevation of British prices in 1798–1800, after which prices fluctuated about a high level down to the end of the war; agricultural prices rose more than industrial prices; interest rates were high; urban real wages were under severe but uneven pressure. The Swedish data permit useful confirmation of these price and real-wage phenomena. In its phase of neutral trading, the United States responded as a region favored by its resource endowments, enjoying a precocious but transient high rate of growth in real income. From the Embargo forward, the United States entered (like France and Belgium from, say, 1800) a period of protected industrial expansion which helped prepare the way for the later passage of New England into sustained industrial growth.

12

1815–1848

There were no substantial wars in the period from 1815 to the mid-nineteenth century. We are examining, therefore, the workings of the world economy at a time of peace, of endemic population increase, and of an industrialization process which diffused beyond Britain to most of Western Europe and the United States.

Chart III-5 shows the price of wheat in Britain and the fluctuations in wheat imports from 1790 to 1850. The British harvests

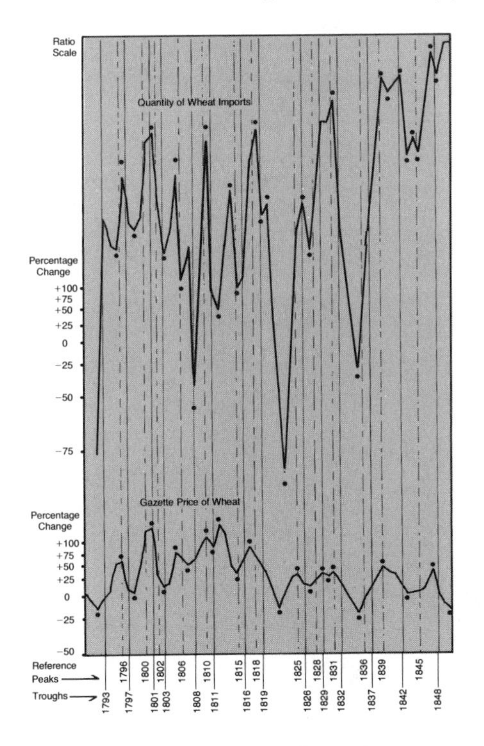

CHART III-5. *British Wheat Imports and Prices, 1790–1850*

Source: A. D. Gayer et al., *The Growth and Fluctuation of the British Economy, 1790–1850*, vol. 2, pp. 758 and 826.

Note: Peaks and troughs are for business cycles.

affect the movements of both curves, imports fluctuating over a very wide range, with significant effects on the money markets, interest rates, and the course of business cycles, as well as on domestic income distribution. After a sharp postwar decline to 1822, the trend in the wheat price was relatively constant down to mid-century; but this steadiness was maintained only by a rising trend in wheat imports, which, after 1815, had to transit a protective tariff. The tariff was lowered in 1828 and 1842, repealed in 1846. On the European continent, however, the price trend was gently upward from the early 1820's to the mid-1840's, when (1845–1847) Germany and Scandinavia, as well as Ireland, were hit by disastrous harvests which produced throughout the world trading area a sharp, transient increase in grain prices.[29]

Like the British wheat price, the American wheat price exhibits a sharp decline in the 1820's; a relatively steady trend down to mid-century broken by the relatively high prices of the late 1830's. Then comes the food crisis of the 1840's and, after a pause, a further large increase in the early 1850's. The American wheat price doubled between 1852 and 1854, as the Crimean War temporarily cut off Russian grain exports to Western Europe.

Thus, a European population increasing at an annual average rate of about 0.6 percent (and a North American, at about 2.7 percent) was fed during the first thirty-five years of peace at substantially lower prices than those which had generally prevailed during the war years; but the dynamics of demography and economic progress produced a turning point round about mid-century.

Since money wages fell much less than grain prices and the prices of imported foods and tobacco, and since the revolutionary decline in the prices of textiles and iron continued, real wages in Britain rose down to mid-century, most markedly, of course, in the adjustment from wartime peak prices to the low range of the early 1820's.[30] The basic evidence is presented in Chart III-6, again covering the whole period 1790–1850.

TABLE III-10. *Wheat Price: United States, 1810–1854 (Five-Year Averages: U.S. $ per Bushel)*

1810–1814	1.712
1815–1819	1.848
1820–1824	1.103
1825–1829	1.079
1830–1834	1.153
1835–1839	1.568
1840–1844	1.067
1845–1849	1.181
1850–1854	1.632

Source: *Historical Statistics of the United States*, 1960 ed., p. 124.

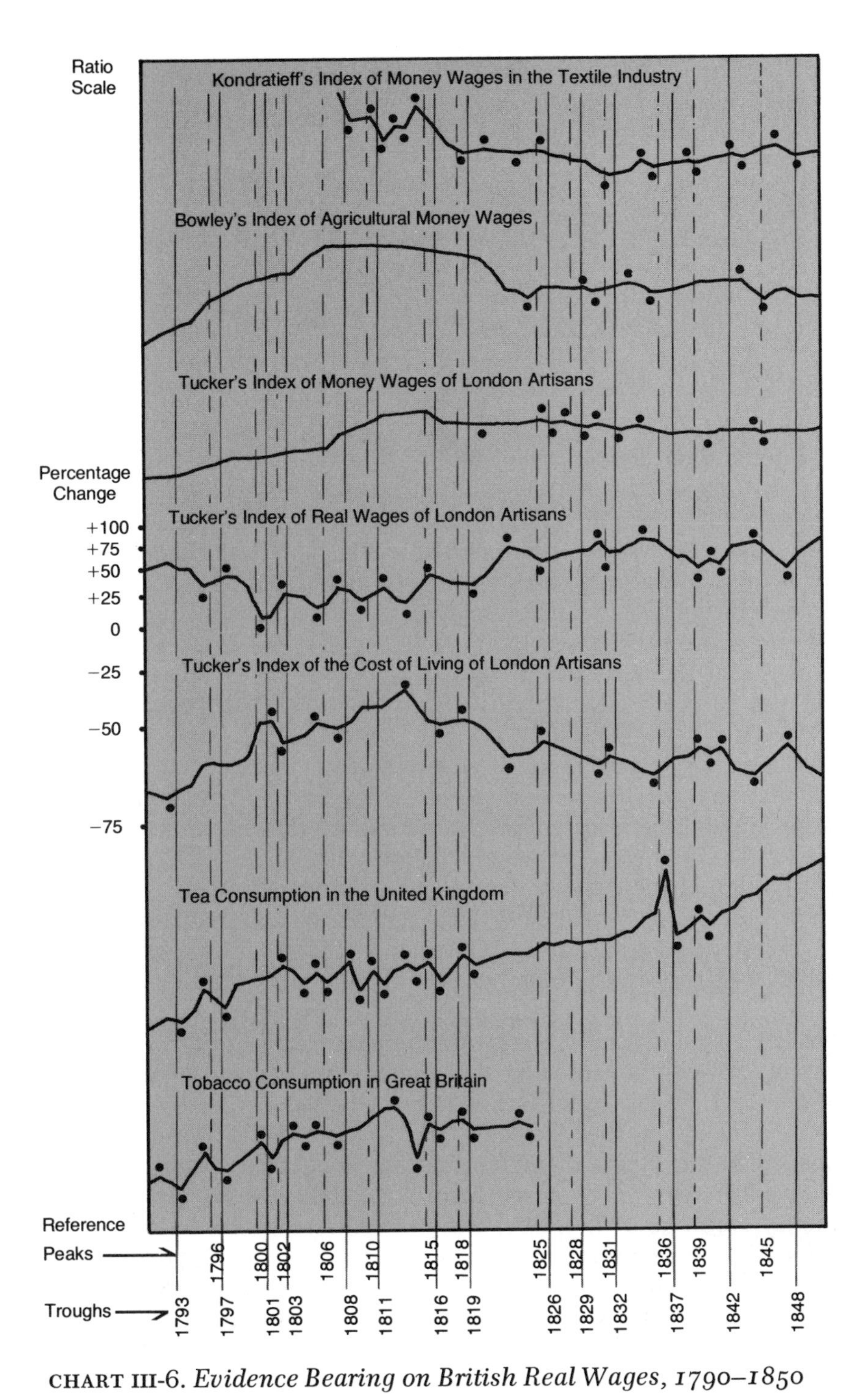

CHART III-6. *Evidence Bearing on British Real Wages, 1790–1850*

Source: Gayer et al., *The Growth and Fluctuation of the British Economy*, vol. 2, p. 950.
Note: Peaks and troughs are for business cycles.

TABLE III-11. *French Retail Prices and Money Wages, 1806–1860*

	Retail Prices (1914 = 100)	Annual Average Rate of Change (%)	Money Wages in Paris (1911 = 100)	Annual Average Rate of Change (%)
1806	—		40	
1820	68		—	
1830	71	0.43	40 (1828)	0.0
1840	72	0.14	47 (1842)	1.35
1850	73	0.14	51 (1852)	0.82
1860	81	1.04	63 (1860)	2.7

Source: *Annuaire Statistique de la France: Résumé Retrospectif*, 1966, pp. 422 and 405.

French data are more sparse, but also suggest a modest net rise in real wages between 1830 and 1850; that is, between those two dates, a slight rise in retail prices was outweighed by a 28 percent rise in money wages in Paris (Table III-11).[31] Jean Lhomme provides annual real-wage estimates for France from 1840 (see below, Table III-23). They exhibit clearly the pressure exerted on real wages in the bad harvest period 1846–1847; the response to good harvests at the turn of the decade; and then the depressing effect on real wages of the sharply rising prices of 1853–1856, which opened a new trend period.

Table III-12 and Chart III-7 show Alvin Hansen's U.S. real-wage calculations for the period 1820–1860. Year-to-year movements were, of course, affected by the course of the harvests and food prices. The real-wage movement by decades, however, is a striking affirmation of the trend-period mechanism which suffuses this analysis. The rise in the 1820's reflects the concentration of investment in industry and transport improvements, against the background of relative agricultural abundance. During the great land boom of the 1830's, however, real wages came under pressure, recovering to the level of 1830 only in 1840. During the 1840's, as in the 1820's, when capital flowed into industry and transport (notably in the northeast), real wages rose sharply, strengthened by the agricultural overextension of the previous decade. As the next trend period opened, in the 1850's, the pattern of the 1830's was repeated.

Swedish real wages (as measured by the relative movement of money wages and the price of rye) oscillated about a stagnant or even slightly declining trend, after sharing the initial postwar rise to the early 1820's.[32] The Belgian pattern may conform more nearly to the French. The data suggest some net increase in average money wages in industry between 1819 and 1846, when more or less comparable wage surveys are available.[33] Reliable price data are, unfortunately, only available from 1832. They exhibit the familiar increase of the late 1830's (1835–1841); a subsidence; the almost universal increase of 1845–1847; and the easing at the end of the

TABLE III-12. *U.S. Real Wages, 1820–1860 (1913 = 100)*

Year	Index of Money Wages	Index of Cost of Living	Index of Real Wages
1820	36	88	41
1821	36	84	43
1822	37	86	43
1823	37	82	45
1824	37	76	49
1825	37	78	47
1826	37	74	50
1827	36	77	47
1828	37	76	49
1829	37	78	47
1830	37	72	51
1831	38	75	51
1832	38	77	49
1833	39	75	52
1834	39	69	57
1835	39	81	48
1836	40	92	43
1837	40	97	41
1838	40	96	42
1839	40	96	42
1840	41	80	51
1841	41	81	51
1842	41	74	55
1843	40	69	58
1844	40	70	57
1845	41	72	57
1846	42	78	54
1847	42	78	54
1848	43	73	59
1849	43	69	62
1850	43	73	59
1851	42	81	52
1852	42	80	53
1853	43	86	50
1854	45	86	52
1855	46	90	51
1856	46	92	50
1857	47	94	50
1858	46	93	49
1859	46	85	54
1860	47	82	57

Source: Alvin H. Hansen, "Factors Affecting the Trend of Real Wages," *American Economic Review*, vol. 15 (March 1925), p. 32.

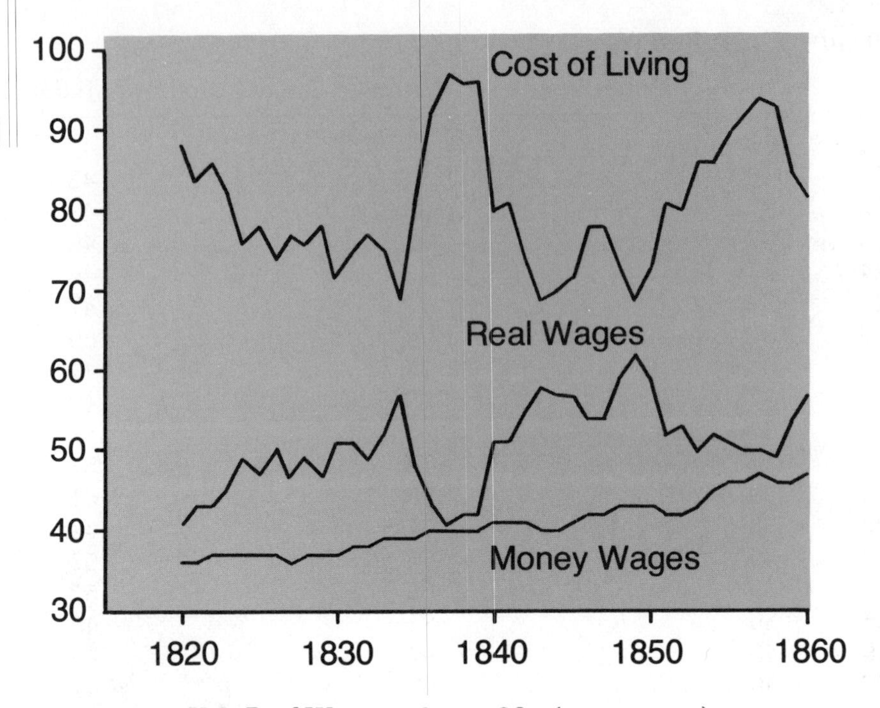

CHART III-7. *U.S. Real Wages, 1820–1860 (1913=100)*

Source: Hansen, "Factors Affecting the Trend of Real Wages," p. 32.

decade. A few money-wage series are also available for these two decades.[34] There is a considerable apparent increase in real wages, in mining, at least, and in hourly cotton wages as well, from 1841 to 1850. One can also assume that Belgium shared the initial post-war release of pressure on real wages down to the early 1820's. On balance, it is likely that there was some net increase in Belgian real wages between the war years and mid-century, although the increase must have been limited, the absolute level still very low, and the period marked, as elsewhere, by intervals of high food prices and of unemployment; e.g., in the period of adjustment after the achievement of Belgian independence in 1830.

So far as the European balance between food supply and demand is concerned, what one can observe is an expansion of agricultural production that does not quite keep up with expanding population, urbanization, and rising incomes, leading to an increasing dependence on imports.

In France, there was strong agricultural protection, with a sliding scale of duties permitting imports only in years of high domestic prices. After 1840 France became increasingly a grain importer. As elsewhere, bad harvests left a clear mark on year-to-year fluctuations; for example, 1846–1847, when imports were twice as high as during the three other years of the quinquennium. Within this framework, however, there were important increases in the production of meat and dairy products, as the cities grew and transport

TABLE III-13. *Annual Average Food Imports: France, 1827–1860 (in Millions of Old Francs)*

1827–1829	126
1830–1834	138
1835–1839	120
1840–1844	191
1845–1849	214
1850–1854	234
1855–1859	502

Source: *Annuaire Statistique de la France*, 1966, p. 350.

became more efficient. There was also, from the 1830's, a very rapid increase in sugar-beet production. Potatoes also expanded rapidly but were set back, as elsewhere, in the 1840's.[35] Overall, Marczewski estimates that the real value of French agricultural output may have expanded at a rate of about 1.5 percent per annum, from the end of the war years to mid-century.[36] In Britain, agriculture found its feet by the 1830's after a difficult postwar adjustment which protective tariffs could not wholly cushion. But widespread improvements in productivity permitted most farmers to prosper and, indeed, to survive the repeal of the corn laws. As Table III-3 suggests, there was a more rapid increase in the value of cattle than of land between 1814 and 1850.

Prussia began the postwar era with an agricultural depression. It was normally a grain exporter: but it found some of its normal markets in Western Europe blocked by tariffs designed to protect the situation created by wartime circumstances. But, as elsewhere, the trend in agricultural production and productivity was upward, with wheat production, for example, increasing at an average annual rate of about 2 percent between 1816 and 1852. Nevertheless, Germany's net exporting position gradually narrowed. It moved over to become a regular net importer of grain by 1860.

In Ireland, of course, there was less dynamism in the economy than in most of Western Europe. The population expansion was matched neither by an increase in agricultural productivity nor by an ability to finance enlarged food imports by manufactured exports. The capacity of the potato to feed the people on Irish soil reached its limit with the disastrous harvests of 1845–1847, yielding the loss of some 500,000 of the population by death or emigration in two years.

The case of Ireland thus clearly overdramatizes the point Europe had reached by mid-century in the balance between the demand for and the supply of food. By and large it had done pretty well in overcoming diminishing returns, as population increased, the cities expanded, and incomes rose. But the balance had reached a juncture where the price of grain moved into a range which, along with the new technologies of transport which had emerged, made profitable the opening up of the American West, an area where wheat could be produced at considerably less cost than in Europe, and whose absorption into the world economy is central to the next trend period.

The leading sectors in industrial growth between the end of the Napoleonic Wars and mid-century were, of course, cotton textiles and then the railroads, with the steam-powered ship playing an ex-

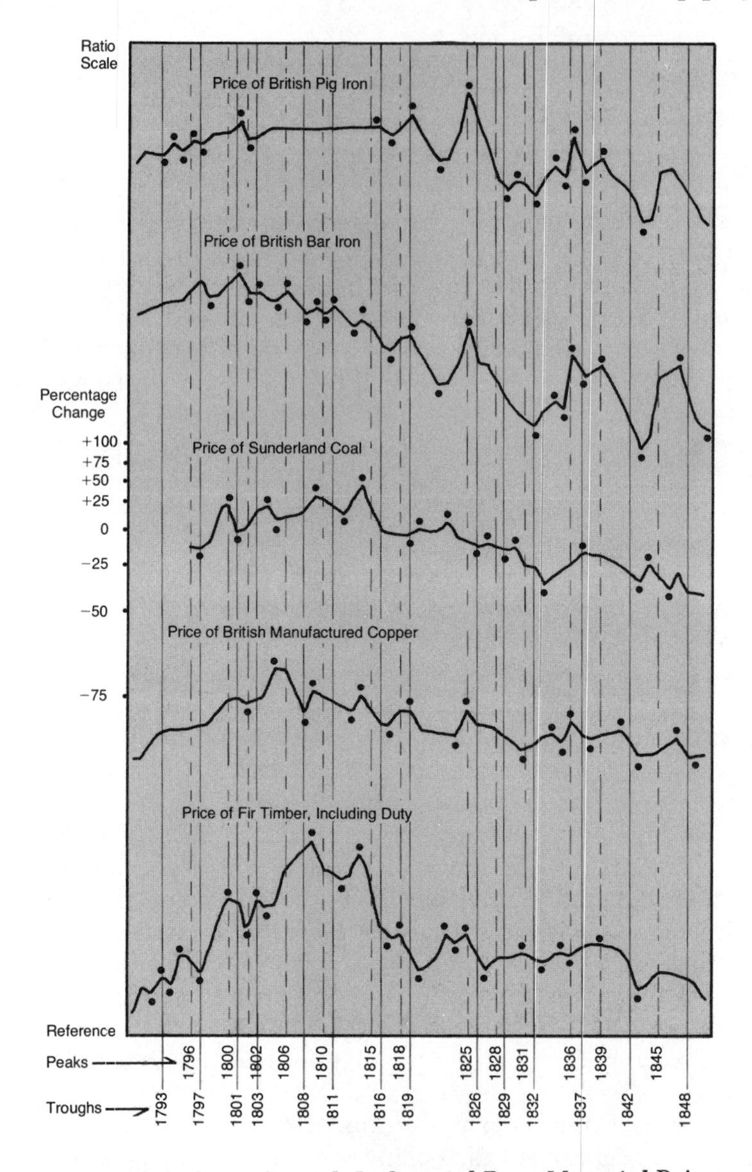

CHART III-8. *Some British Industrial Raw-Material Prices, 1790–1850*

Source: Gayer et al., *The Growth and Fluctuation of the British Economy*, vol. 2, p. 824.

Note: Peaks and troughs are for business cycles.

panding role on the rivers and on short passages at sea. Between 1815 and 1848 the still-evolving cotton textile technology had established itself throughout northwestern Europe as well as in the United States, although Britain maintained well the initial, virtually monopolistic status it had achieved as an exporter of cotton manufactures. By 1848, railway nets of considerable density had been laid down in Britain, Belgium, and the American Northeast; and they were in the process of being laid down in Germany and France, the latter a bit slower in its start. Up to this time railways were used primarily to link up existing urban centers. Their period of gestation was relatively short, and their cost-reducing effects were promptly felt.

Taken together, the leading sectors of this period were at a stage in their evolution where they contributed substantially to the declining general tendency in prices. The powerful decline in cotton textile prices was noted earlier (see above, Chart II-10); but the price trend in iron, coal, and copper was also downward, as indicated in Chart III-8. Aside from the railroads, there were other transport improvements of great importance in this period; e.g., canals and a drastic decline of ocean freight rates (Chart III-9). The latter owed little to the steamship, except perhaps on short-haul routes.[37] The reduction was primarily the combined result of improvements in ship construction, improved ship utilization, and improved navigation.[38]

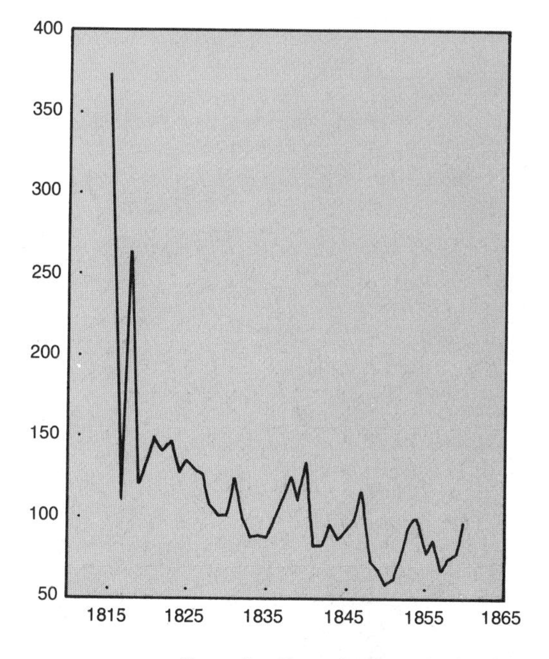

CHART III-9. *Freight Rate Index, U.S. Exports, 1815–1860 (Base 1830)*

Source: Douglass C. North, *The Economic Growth of the United States*, p. 95.

TABLE III-14. *Cotton Data, 1813–1860*

	(1) U.S. Cotton Production (1,000 Bales)	(2) U.S. Cotton Price (Cents per Lb.)	(3) U.S. Cotton Exports (Million Lbs.)	(4) U.S. Cotton Exports ($ Million)	(5) U.K. Total Co[tton] Consumption (Million Lbs.)
1813	305	12.5	19	2	78
1814	285	15.0	18	3	74
1815	364	21.0	83	18	81
1816	458	29.5	82	24	89
1817	461	26.5	86	23	107
1818	448	24.0	92	31	110
1819	598	24.0	88	21	109
1820	606	17.0	128	22	120
1821	647	14.3	125	20	129
1822	742	14.3	145	24	145
1823	621	11.4	174	20	154
1824	762	14.8	142	22	165
1825	892	18.6	176	37	167
1826	1,121	12.2	205	25	150
1827	957	9.3	294	29	197
1828	721	10.3	211	22	218
1829	870	9.9	265	27	219
1830	876	10.0	298	30	248
1831	1,038	9.7	277	25	263
1832	987	9.4	322	32	277
1833	1,070	12.3	325	36	287
1834	1,205	12.9	385	49	303
1835	1,254	17.5	387	65	318
1836	1,361	16.5	424	71	347
1837	1,424	13.3	444	63	366
1838	1,801	10.1	596	62	417
1839	1,361	13.4	414	61	382
1840	2,178	8.9	744	64	459
1841	1,635	9.5	530	54	438
1842	1,684	7.9	585	48	435
1843	2,379	7.3	792	49	518
1844	2,030	7.7	664	54	544
1845	2,395	5.6	873	52	607
1846	2,101	7.9	548	43	614
1847	1,779	11.2	527	53	441
1848	2,440	8.0	814	62	577
1849	2,867	7.6	1,027	66	630
1850	2,334	12.3	635	72	588
1851	2,454	12.1	927	112	659
1852	3,126	9.5	1,093	88	740
1853	3,416	11.0	1,112	109	761
1854	3,075	11.0	988	94	776
1855	2,983	10.4	1,000	88	839
1856	3,656	10.3	1,351	128	891
1857	3,084	13.5	1,048	132	826
1858	3,257	12.2	1,119	131	906
1859	4,019	12.1	1,386	161	977
1860	4,861	11.0	1,768	192	1,084

Sources: Col. 1, M. B. Hammond, *The Cotton Industry* (New York: Macmillan, 1897), table following p.
years ending Aug. 31; cols. 2, 3, and 4, *Historical Statistics of the United States*, 1960 ed., pp. 124 and
col. 5, B. R. Mitchell, with the collaboration of Phyllis Deane, *Abstract of British Historical Statistics*, p. 179 (
T. Ellison, *Cotton Trade of Great Britain*; col. 6, James A. Mann, *The Cotton Trade of Great Britain* (Lon

. Cotton Stocks llion Lbs.)	(7) U.K. Consumption / Stocks	(8) U.S. Receipts from Sales of Land in Five Southern States ($ Thousands)	(9) Price of Slaves (Prime Field Hands) (U.S. $) Virginia	(10) New Orleans
—	—	—	400	675
—	—	101	425	550
—	—	332	500	700
—	—	899	525	800
—	—	2,016	625	900
—	—	9,063	800	1,000
—	—	4,441	800	1,050
—	—	1,096	700	925
—	—	564	600	800
—	—	353	500	700
—	—	228	450	675
—	—	283	425	700
.5	1.45	539	400	800
.9	1.35	452	400	850
.8	1.20	590	400	775
.0	1.48	357	400	775
.5	1.90	830	400	800
.8	2.09	750	425	825
.4	2.30	1,016	450	925
.7	2.67	677	500	1,000
.4	3.04	1,544	525	1,050
.3	3.68	3,256	600	1,100
.6	3.55	7,159	650	1,150
.3	2.98	7,170	800	1,250
.6	3.17	1,568	1,100	1,300
.9	2.59	817	900	1,200
.8	3.04	1,297	1,000	1,250
.0	2.22	497	800	1,100
.7	2.02	299	600	875
.3	1.80	315	500	750
.0	1.51	481	500	700
.2	1.39	368	500	700
.5	1.34	299	550	700
.4	1.78	496	600	725
.4	2.39	601	650	900
.1	2.62	445	650	950
.3	2.62	413	650	1,050
.6	2.54	664	650	1,100
.9	2.92	776	700	1,150
.9	2.46	357	750	1,200
.9	2.48	1,023	875	1,250
.2	2.86	1,363	950	1,300
.9	4.02	927	950	1,350
.2	4.54	685	950	1,400
.7	3.90	808	950	1,500
.0	4.77	862	1,000	1,575
.3	4.24	1,164	1,100	1,650
—	—	1,089	1,200	1,800

o), p. 134; col. 7, col. 5 ÷ col. 6; col. 8, North, *The Economic Growth of the United States*, p. 256 (from ur H. Cole, "Cyclical and Sectional Variations in the Sale of Public Lands, 1816–1860," *Review of Economic tistics*, vol. 9, no. 1 [January 1927], p. 52; cols. 9 and 10, Ulrich B. Phillips, *American Negro Slavery* (New York London: D. Appleton, 1918), pp. 370–377.

The raw-material requirements of the leading sectors were, with one exception, easily met. Old and newly found European and American coal and iron deposits (e.g., in Belgium, Germany, and Pennsylvania) supported the railroads and the expanding metallurgical industries. The exception was cotton; for the dynamics of balancing cotton requirements and supply yielded the Atlantic boom of the 1830's, whose contours ran counter to those of the trend period as a whole, as the real-wage data already suggest. For our purposes the story of cotton in this period is also important because it illustrates well the recurring pattern by which new areas were brought within the working structure of the world economy between 1815 and 1914.

Although the causal mechanism at work has been the subject of considerable controversy, the basic facts, brought together in Table III-14 and Chart III-10, are clear enough.[39]

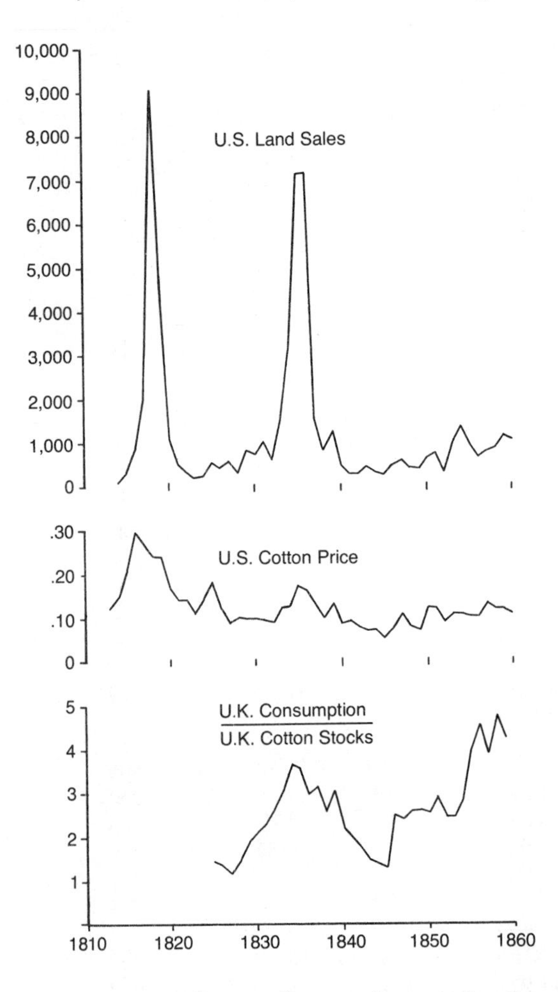

CHART III-10. *Cotton Data, 1814–1960: Land Sales in Five Southern States (in $ Thousands), U.S. Cotton Price (Cents per Lb.), and Proportion U.K. Cotton Consumption to Stocks*

Sources: See Table III-14.

1. There was an explosive rise in U.S. cotton prices, production, and exports (volume and value) in the wake of the Napoleonic Wars. It was accompanied by a massive opening of new cotton acreage, reflected in the sale of public lands in the southern states. U.S. cotton production doubled between 1814 and 1819.

2. From 1818, prices moved sharply downward from the high range of the two previous years; in 1819 land sales fell off and, briefly, even the volume of U.S. cotton exports fell. Cotton prices reached a trough in 1823, as did the value of cotton exports and land sales in the cotton-producing states. But the volume of cotton production (aside from harvest fluctuations) and the volume of exports continued to expand. Not only was British cotton production increasing rapidly, but so also was production on the European continent and in New England. The new acreage opened up in the immediate postwar boom was, evidently, brought effectively into production in the following years of lower prices.

3. Due to this background of newly available acreage, the great British boom of 1823–1825, accompanied by much plant expansion in cotton textiles, yielded only a modest increase in prices and a slight expansion in American land sales; but, on the American side, prices quickly fell away to a new low point after 1825.

4. From 1826 to 1832 the strong upward trend in the demand for cotton began gradually to catch up with supply, although the increase in output continued and remained profitable, notably in the lands newly opened to cotton production. Prices fluctuated in a relatively low range, but ceased to fall as a matter of trend; cotton land sales began to move erratically upward from a low point in 1828; and the proportion of British cotton consumption to British cotton stocks began to rise. Cotton stocks declined absolutely from 1828. Against this background, the cyclical expansion of 1833–1836 throughout the Atlantic world yielded the famous increase in prices and in cotton land sales of the Jacksonian period. (We shall see something very like this sequence repeated on a grander scale for grain and oil in the 1960's and early 1970's.)

5. As Table III-14 indicates, the increase of U.S. cotton production was greater in the second half of the 1830's than in the first, when prices were rising and land purchases were increasing rapidly. This phenomenon may well reflect the lag required to bring the new lands into production, notably the new acreage in Mississippi and Louisiana. The sequence of rising prices, expanded land sales, and subsequent increase in production is well captured in Douglass C. North's chart, dramatizing his hypothesis about this period (Chart III-11).

6. As in the early 1820's, cotton prices and land sales fell off in the first half of the 1840's; but output continued to increase and the British stock position was comfortable. In 1845, at the peak of their domestic railroad boom, the British had the benefit of a bumper American crop and the lowest cotton price in the 1815–1860

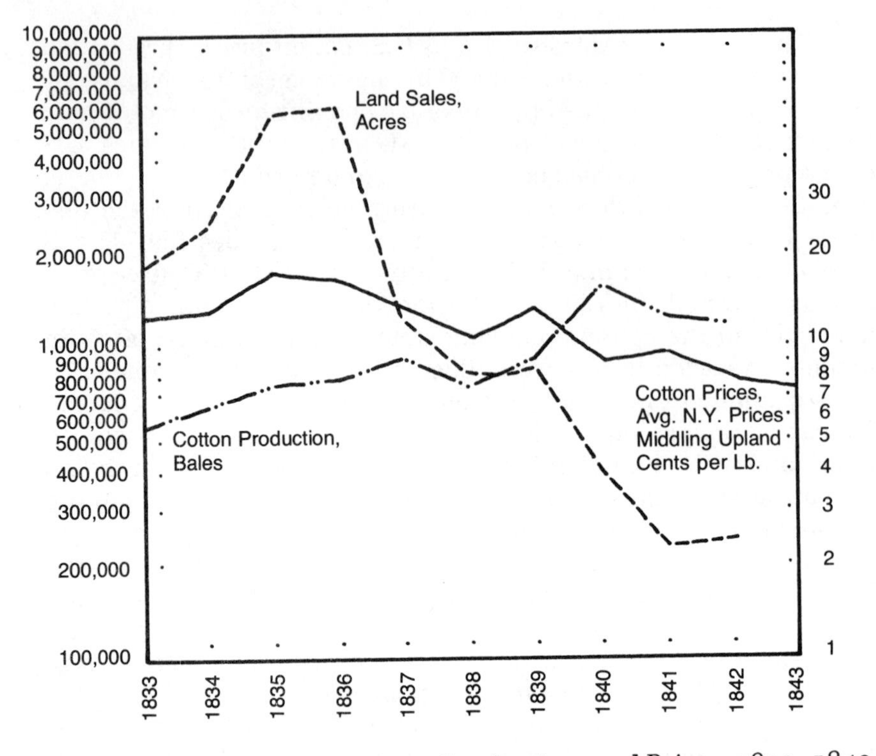

CHART III-11. *Land Sales, Cotton Production, and Prices, 1833–1843 (Alabama, Arkansas, Mississippi, Florida, Louisiana)*

Source: North, *The Economic Growth of the United States*, p. 74.

period. As in the second half of the 1820's, prices moved up unevenly in the period 1845–1850, as did land sales and the proportion of British consumption to stocks. There was also a sharp deceleration in American output. The stage was set for the third great period of cotton prosperity and acreage expansion—that of the 1850's, a decade that belongs with the next trend period.[40]

The U.S. cotton price was 15 cents a pound in 1814, almost 30 cents in 1816, 18 cents at its peak in the 1830's (1835), around 8 cents at the end of the 1840's. It conformed, then, to the general price pattern of the trend period, despite the price surge of the 1830's. The progressive expansion into fertile American lands thus permitted the cotton textile revolution to proceed on a widening geographic basis, its essential raw material moving downward in price as production expanded. On the other hand, by Phillips' famous calculations, the trend in the price of slaves was upward, although it moved closely with the cotton price in the short period. In the mid-1790's a prime field hand cost $300–400; on the eve of the Civil War the average price may have been about $1,200–1,800.[41] The United States was by no means the only producer of raw cotton; but its extraordinary expansion in acreage yielded by 1850 a situation where it supplied two-thirds of the world market, as indicated in Table III-15.

TABLE III-15. *Cotton Production by Areas and the U.S. Proportion, 1791–1860 (in Millions of Lbs.)*

Area	1791	1801	1811	1821	1831	1840	1850	1860
Brazil	22	26	35	32	38	30	40	36
West Indies	12	10	12	10	9	8	3	6
Egypt	—	—	1	6	18	25	30	34
Rest of Africa	45	46	44	40	36	34	34	35
India	130	160	170	175	180	185	210	450
Rest of Asia	190	160	146	135	115	110	120	132
Mexico and South America	68	56	57	44	35	35	40	57
Other Areas	—	15	11	8	4	13	15	100
United States	2	48	80	180	385	654	990	1,650
Total	469	531	556	630	820	1,044	1,482	2,500
Percentile share of United States	0.4	9.0	16.3	28.6	49.6	62.6	67.8	66.0

Source: S. W. Bruchey, *Cotton and the Growth of the American Economy, 1790–1860*, p. 7.

TABLE III-16. *Growth of the New England Cotton Industry: Yards of Cloth Produced, 1815–1860 (Annual Average Growth Rates [%])*

1815–1818	45.2
1818–1825	38.3
1825–1830	15.2
1830–1836	12.2
1836–1843	3.9
1843–1850	7.1
1850–1855	1.2
1855–1860	6.2

Source: Calculated from data in Robert Brooke Zevin, "The Growth of Cotton Textile Production after 1815," pp. 123–124.

What happened in the Atlantic world during the 1830's was much more than a surge of investment in the expansion of cotton acreage. There was, for the first time, a great increase in immigration to the United States; an expansion in housing and a rapid increase in urbanization; and substantial investments in transport. The cotton textile revolution in New England continued. Its pace decelerated in the 1830's (Table III-16); but this is the normal behavior of a leading sector as it exploits its initial revolutionary possibilities and moves toward maturity. Its rate of expansion remained extraordinarily high down to the cyclical peak in 1836.

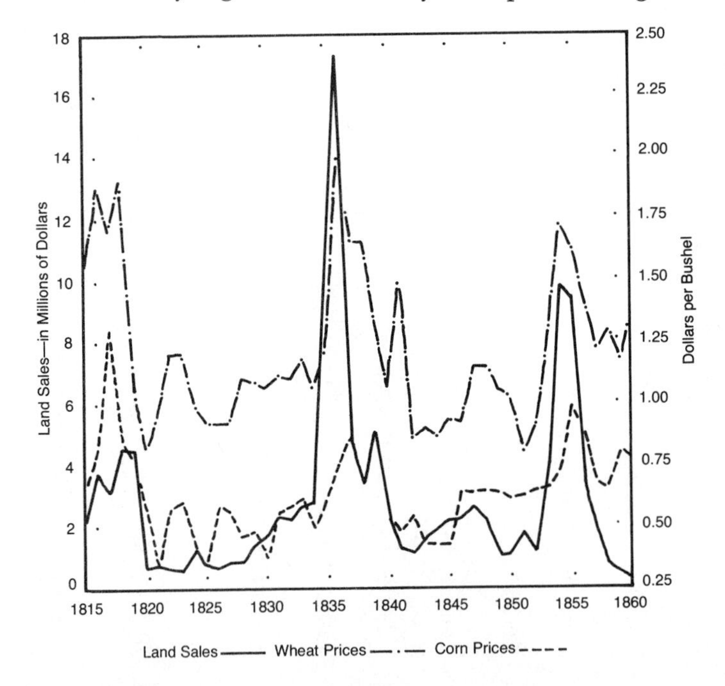

CHART III-12. *Land Sales in Seven Western States, 1815–1860 (Ohio, Illinois, Indiana, Michigan, Iowa, Wisconsin, Missouri)*

Source: North, *The Economic Growth of the United States*, p. 137.

As Chart III-12 indicates, the three periods of expansion in land sales between 1815 and 1860, noted for the southern states, are also evident in the western states: 1816–1819 more muted; the mid-1830's equally strong; the 1850's even more marked. There were large net capital imports in the 1830's: about $177 million between 1831 and 1839. This sum was 16 percent of the total value of American commodity imports over these years. Capital imports helped finance not only the expansion in cotton acreage and production but also (via state bonds) large infrastructure investments in the West.

The overall effect of this whole process was to produce a generalized expansion in the United States which caused a greater increase in domestic than in imported prices and a favorable shift in the American terms of trade—a pattern that marked also the post-1815 boom and that of the 1850's (Chart III-13). The terms of trade were less favorable in the 1820's and 1840's, when agricultural prices were relatively low and the pattern of American investment was more focused on industrial expansion in New England (the 1820's) and the building of the railway network in the Northeast (the 1840's).

As shall emerge, there is much in the course of events in the 1830's beyond the story of cotton that foreshadows the process by which other new areas were brought into the world economy in the pre-1914 era.

We turn now to the movement of population and housing construction.

First, Britain. Contrary to the longer rhythm that emerged between the 1870's and 1914, there were British construction booms

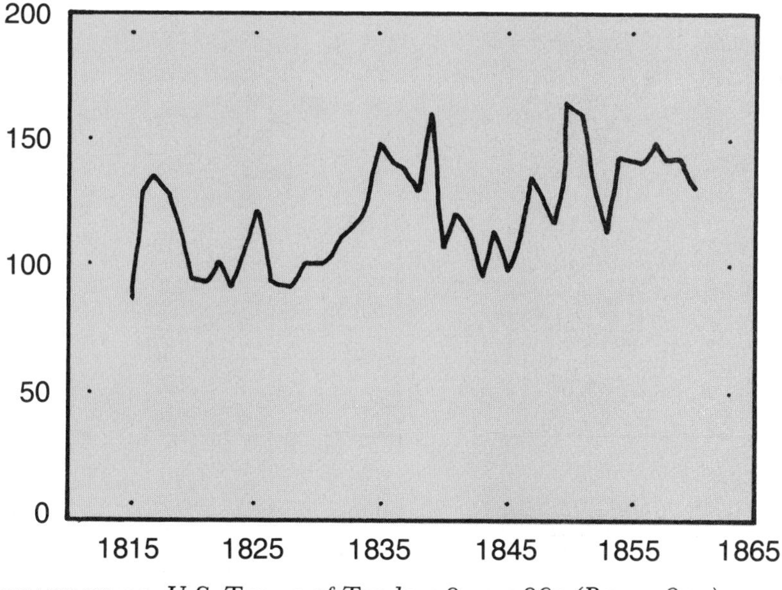

CHART III-13. *U.S. Terms of Trade, 1815–1860 (Base 1830)*

Source: North, *The Economic Growth of the United States*, p. 93.

in each of the post-1815 decades (see Chart III-14). In the trend period considered here, they peaked in 1825; 1835 and 1840 (a double peak); and 1846 or 1847, depending on the indicator used.[42]

The construction boom of the 1820's was a response to the general prosperity of the first half of the decade, accelerated urbanization, increased family formation reflecting prior acceleration in the expansion of population, and the housing deficit which accumulated during the war years. John Parry Lewis estimates that half the houses constructed between 1811 and 1831 may have been built in the eight postwar years 1817–1825.[43]

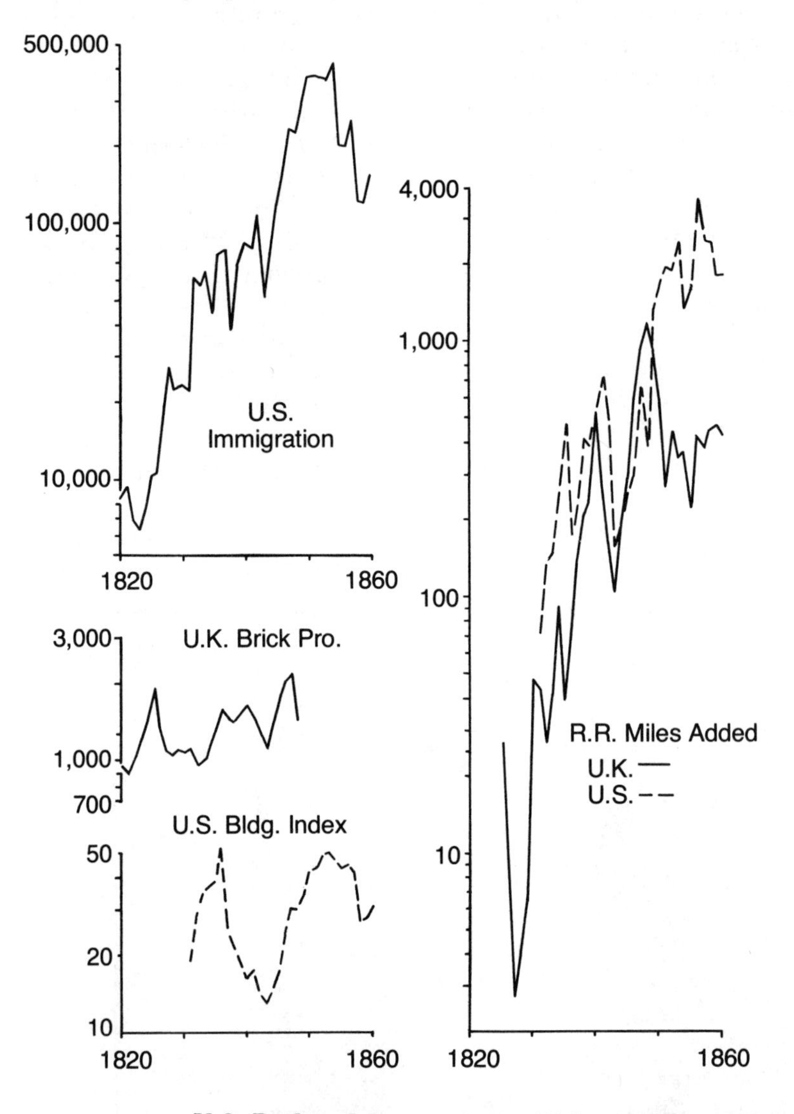

CHART III-14. *U.S. Railroad Construction (Miles Added), U.K. Brick Production, U.K. Railroad Construction, U.S. Building Index, and U.S. Immigration, 1820–1860*

Sources: See Table III-17.

The double-peaked construction cycle of the 1830's had a new element: the railways. As nearly as we can estimate from the regional data available on brick production, the second peak (1840) is probably related to the completion of railway lines earlier initiated, rather than to housing construction.[44]

Railway construction certainly played a large role in the construction boom of the 1840's. The evidence on housing is more complex. The net increase in houses in Britain was distinctly less in the 1840's than in the 1830's. But this evidence for a relative slowdown is inconclusive: some houses were torn down to make way for the railway lines; timber imports suggest a strong housing (as well as railroad) element in the boom of the 1840's; and the regional data indicate that certainly in Liverpool (and possibly in other cities of the region) the flow of immigration from Ireland produced a stronger building expansion than in the 1830's.

After a depression at the end of the 1840's, another brief building boom began. It may have run its course before the Crimean War intervened; that is, the 1854 peak in British timber imports could reflect an inventory build-up in anticipation of war (and of a cutoff in Russian timber) rather than a construction peak. But high wartime interest rates certainly accentuated any housing recession which might have been under way.[45]

For the United States, systematic building data begin in 1830.[46] In our period there are two major differences between American and British building patterns. First, 1836 stands alone: there is no second peak in the 1830's. This may reflect the fact that the U.S. index relates simply to housebuilding, not construction in general. As in Britain, railroad lines completed in the United States continued to rise beyond 1836 (to a peak in 1841). Second, the American building expansion of the 1840's (beginning from the trough in 1843) continued virtually unbroken to a peak in 1853. This overriding, as it were, of the depression of the late 1840's was, in part, almost certainly due to the extraordinary acceleration of immigration which occurred during the 1840's, peaking in 1854 (see Chart III-14). But, in general, the cyclical decline of the late 1840's was less marked in the United States than it was in Britain and on the Continent, where the revolutions of 1848 left a mark on economic as well as political life.

The expanded immigration to the United States during this trend period has within it all three of the elements which play their part, in differing proportions, in subsequent large international population movements. There is an element of "push": most notably, of course, from the Irish tragedy of the 1840's, but also from the Continental agricultural troubles of the period. There is the attraction of newly opened lands: in the Middle West, parts of Texas, and (after 1848) California. But there is also the pull of rapid industrial growth—in this case, notably, the textile factories of New England. The proportion of laborers among immigrants to the United States

TABLE III-17. *Series Related to Building: United States and United Kingdom, 1820–186(*

	U.S. Immigration	U.S. Building Index (Riggleman: per Capita, Real Terms, Value of Building Permits)	U.S. Railroad Construc (Miles Added)
1820	8,385	—	—
1821	9,127	—	—
1822	6,911	—	—
1823	6,354	—	—
1824	7,912	—	—
1825	10,199	—	—
1826	10,837	—	—
1827	18,875	—	—
1828	27,362	—	—
1829	22,520	—	—
1830	23,322	—	—
1831	22,633	19	72
1832	60,482	28	134
1833	58,640	35	151
1834	65,365	37	253
1835	45,374	39	465
1836	76,242	52	175
1837	79,340	25	224
1838	38,914	22	416
1839	68,069	19	389
1840	84,066	16.5	516
1841	80,289	17.5	717
1842	104,565	14.5	491
1843	52,496	13	159
1844	78,615	14.5	192
1845	114,371	17.5	256
1846	154,416	24	297
1847	234,968	30	668
1848	226,527	30	398
1849	297,024	34	1,369
1850	369,980	42	1,656
1851	379,466	44	1,961
1852	371,603	48.5	1,926
1853	368,645	50.5	2,452
1854	427,833	47.5	1,360
1855	200,877	44.5	1,654
1856	200,436	45	3,642
1857	251,306	42	2,487
1858	123,126	27	2,465
1859	121,282	28	1,821
1860	153,640	30.5	1,837

Sources: U.S. immigration, *Historical Statistics of the United States*, 1960 ed., pp. 56–57; U.S. Building In (Riggleman), reprinted accessibly in Brinley Thomas, *Migration and Economic Growth* (Cambridge: At University Press, 1954), p. 298; U.S. railroad construction, ibid., p. 288; U.K. brick production, Mitchell, v

K. Brick Production illions)	British Timber Imports (Official Value in £ Thousands)		U.K. Railroad Construction (Miles Opened)
	(G.B.)	(U.K.)	
949.2	591		—
899.2	602		—
019.5	609		—
244.7	672		—
463.2	768		—
948.8	979		26.75
350.2	738	1,026	11.25
103.3	658	823	2.75
078.8	634	836	4.00
109.6	657	896	6.25
091.3		772	46.50
125.4		875	42.50
971.9		898	26.00
011.3		870	42.25
152.4		858	89.75
349.3		1,011	39.75
606.1		1,009	65.50
478.2		1,029	137.00
427.0		1,059	202.25
568.7		1,190	227.25
677.8		1,228	527.75
423.8		1,147	277.50
271.9		820	163.75
158.9		1,032	105.00
420.7		1,128	192.00
820.7		1,587	293.00
039.7		1,740	595.00
193.8		1,442	909.00
461.0		1,375	1,182.00
462.7		1,202	904.00
—		1,265	590.00
—		1,653	269.00
—		1,447	446
—		1,801	350
—		1,879	368
—		1,389	226
—		1,706	427
—		—	387
—		—	448
—		—	460
—		—	431

ane, *Abstract of British Historical Statistics*, p. 235; timber imports, Great Britain, 1820–1829, d., p. 289; United Kingdom, 1826–1856, ibid., p. 291; U.K. railroad construction, 1825–1850, Gayer al., *British Basic Statistical Data*; 1851–1860, Mitchell, with Deane, *Abstract*, pp. 225 and 228.

(as opposed to merchants, mechanics, and farmers) rises as indicated in Table III-18. The rise in the proportion of farmers and mechanics from the first half of the 1820's to the first half of the 1850's is impressive, but less dramatic: from 27.4 percent of total immigrants to 47.3 percent.

What we observe, then, from the end of the Napoleonic Wars to mid-century, in the Atlantic world, is an increasingly industrialized economy moving forward at a time of peace. Its major leading sectors, cotton textiles and railroads (including the sectors required to sustain them), expand in the various economies at different times and rates depending on forces at work within each national society. Both leading sectors induce accelerated urbanization. The expanding population of this international economy is fed, the raw materials required for its rapidly growing industry are generated, its communications are enlarged and rendered more efficient in an environment in which prices generally tend to fall. Where industry is expanding rapidly, as in Britain, France, and Belgium, the evidence suggests a rise in real wages down to mid-century, broken during the extensive agricultural boom of the 1830's. In pre–take-off Sweden, there may have been relative stagnation, after the initial postwar favorable adjustment. And, as the marginal Malthusian case, Ireland moves toward disaster in the 1840's.

Twice in this period a relative shortage of raw cotton in relation to a rapidly expanding demand triggers periods of rising prices and expansion into new acreage: in 1817–1818 and the 1830's. In the case of the 1830's we have a major capital import boom in the United States, substantially, but not wholly, rooted in the expected profitability of cotton production. For most of the 1820's and 1840's, the cotton price is relatively low, reacting to excessive expansion in the previous booms. The overall trend in the cotton price is downward. The less elastic supply of slaves yields an upward trend in their price.

The wheat price falls rapidly from the end of the wars to the early 1820's. Depending on the degree of protection in the various countries, it then fluctuates around a relatively stable or slightly rising

TABLE III-18. *Proportion of Laborers among U.S. Alien Arrivals, 1820–1855 (Annual Average [%])*

1820–1824	8.4
1825–1829	16.0
1830–1834	12.4
1835–1839	22.4
1840–1844	27.0
1845–1849	36.0
1850–1855	42.3

Source: North, *The Economic Growth of the United States*, p. 98, from William J. Bromwell, *History of Immigration to the United States* (New York: Redfield, 1856).

trend. The bad harvests of 1845–1847 (and then of 1853–1854), however, signal a period of tension throughout the world trading area between the demand for and supply of grain.

Starting in the second half of the 1820's, the United States begins to draw from Europe an increasing flow of immigrants. Short-term business fluctuations leave some mark on this flow, but it reflects mainly the Irish disaster combined with the magnetism exercised over a much wider front by the relative attractiveness of both American agriculture and the nation's industrial prospects.

13

1848–1873

The environment of the world economy in the third quarter of the nineteenth century was quite different from that of the previous trend period. The most obvious difference lay in the behavior of prices. They lifted sharply and almost universally in 1853–1854; and the hitherto sluggish wage level lifted with them. They then fluctuated in this higher range down to the early 1870's, when a second brief interval of sharp inflation occurred.

Why were the normal cost-reducing processes of technological progress held for a time at bay? The answer lies in three factors, two of which were new to the post-1815 world.

First, there were wars: principally, the Crimean War (1854); the Indian Mutiny (1857–1858); the American Civil War; and the sequence of three Prussian campaigns that ended with the French defeat in 1870. Far to the east there was massive and protracted conflict as the Chinese reacted to Malthusian pressures and the challenge represented by the intruding West in the Taiping Rebellion (1850–1864); but this bloody conflict did not significantly disrupt the world economy. By post-1914 standards these wars, excepting the American and Chinese civil wars, were minor affairs. They undoubtedly wasted, however, a significant portion of the resources normally available for productive investment, in the years over which they took place, within the countries directly affected; and these effects were transmitted through the international markets to the rest of the world. For example, British military expenditures rose in 1855–1857 to an average annual rate of £35.9 million, an increase of £15.6 million over the average level for 1851–1854. This increase represents about 2.4 percent of British net national income of the period, 38 percent of gross and 57 percent of net domestic fixed capital formation. We are evidently dealing here with a meaningful diversion of resources and an inflationary impulse that was not trivial.[47]

Second, there was gold mining. As noted earlier, gold, for those who mined it, was a useful product, capable of exchange for goods and services, including imports. The United States financed a part of its trade deficit and capital imports by mining and exporting gold, as did Australia. India, which absorbed large quantities of the new-mined gold, surrendered for it exports of goods. The real effort required by Australia and the United States in mining gold was quite probably less than that necessary to purchase an equivalent volume of imports by growing and exporting, say, additional wheat or wool or cotton, although there were significant wastes of manpower and resources among the prospectors who did not strike it rich. But in terms of the mining areas the production of gold was a thoroughly reasonable enterprise in the nineteenth century; and it led, with significant time lags, to the bringing into the world economy of new regions on a wider basis than gold production. Gold mining in California and Australia, with the concurrent development of those territories in other directions, certainly constituted, at the time, a significant and attractive form of investment; but it was a form of investment tending to raise world prices, both because gold provided nothing significantly useful on the supply side and because of the considerable period of gestation involved in the opening up of new territories.

TABLE III-19. *World Wheat Production, 1831–1840 to 1888 (in Millions of Bushels)*

	1831–1840	1851–1860	1871–1880	1881–1887	1888
United Kingdom	120	121	85	78	76
France	190	223	275	290	275
Germany	50	70	94	98	103
Russia	110	130	224	250	258
Austria	65	85	109	151	138
Italy	60	75	115	105	141
Spain	58	70	114	133	170
Portugal	4	5	8	10	10
Sweden and Norway	1	2	4	4	6
Denmark	3	4	5	6	5
Holland	3	4	5	6	6
Belgium	8	13	16	17	16
Switzerland	1	1	2	2	2
Greece	2	2	3	4	6
Servia	2	2	3	4	4
Rumania	15	20	24	26	30
Turkey, etc.	20	30	40	47	50
Europe	712	857	1,126	1,231	1,296
United States	78	137	338	440	415
Canada	6	9	24	36	37
Australia	2	8	24	38	45
India, etc.	108	187	282	375	478
Total	906	1,198	1,794	2,120	2,271
Annual average rate of growth (%)		1.4	2.0	1.68	1.73

Source: Mulhall, *The Dictionary of Statistics*, p. 8.

Third, there was the story of wheat and the lags involved in bringing into the world economy new productive acreage, a factor similar to that we observed with respect to cotton in the period 1815–1850. The locus of this expansion is indicated in Table III-19.[48] In a rough-and-ready way Table III-19 shows the modest rate of increase in wheat production between the 1830's and the 1850's, the accelerated expansion down to the 1870's, and the deceleration in the next decade as cheap American (and Indian) wheat flooded the international market. The expansion in the third quarter of the century was, evidently, tied closely to developments in the United States and Russia. They contributed 29 percent and 13 percent, respectively, of the estimated total expansion between the 1830's and the 1870's. India became a major wheat exporter only in the 1870's and 1880's.[49]

Table III-20 and Chart III-15 suggest something of the anatomy of the process by which the wheat lands of the American West were brought into production to feed a population expanding at 2.7 percent per annum (1839–1879) while supplying also a critical margin

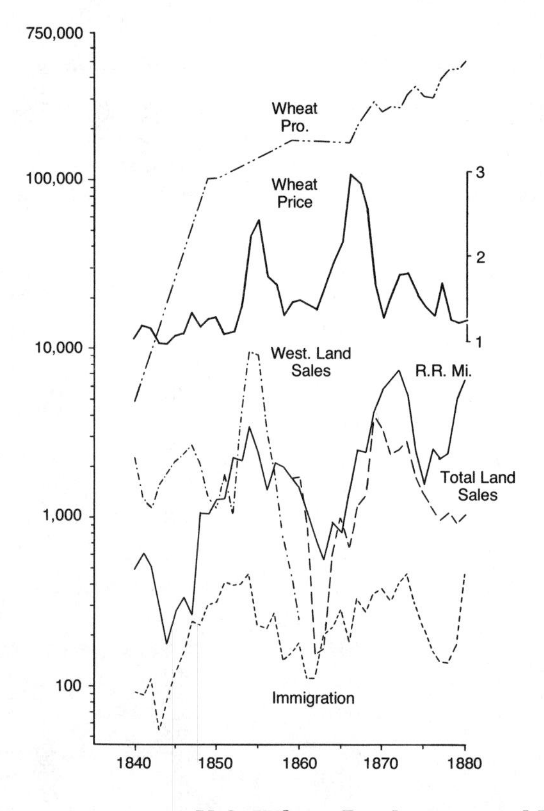

CHART III-15. *U.S. Wheat Production and Related Series, 1840–1880*

Western land sales in seven states, 1840–1860 ($ thousands); total land sales, 1859–1880 ($ thousands); railroad mileage added; immigration (thousands); wheat production (thousand bushels); annual wheat price ($ per bushel).

Source: Table III-20.

of exports to a world economy which had moved toward a precarious Malthusian balance as mid-century approached.

The wheat price began to move up in the mid-1840's and, after briefly falling away, more than doubled between 1851 and 1855. It fluctuated in a high range down to 1873, the actual peak coming as early as 1866. After 1873 the famous secular decline to the mid-1890's began.

Related to these price movements, there were three waves of expansion into new wheat lands: a minor surge in the mid-1840's, and the massive expansions of 1853–1855 and between 1866 and 1873, both closely linked to the great railway booms of those periods. U.S. wheat production increased at an annual rate of only 1.7 percent between 1839 and 1849; at 5.2 percent over the subsequent thirty years. Here was the basis for the U.S. emergence as a major wheat exporter. In the world food crisis of the mid-1840's the United States exported at the peak (1847) 4 million bushels. The average for the years 1870–1874 was 34 million bushels. From year to year exports fluctuated, of course, with the state of the harvests and markets on both sides of the Atlantic rather than with the interrelated process of railroad and wheat-acreage expansion. For example, exports were high during the Civil War years when wheat acreage and railroads expanded slowly, at best. This may have reflected the availability of a surplus normally exported to the southern states. But the underlying trend was evidently the result of the bringing of vast new areas into the world economy via the railroads.

As in the case of cotton in the 1830's, the process was strongly reinforced, in the 1850's and from 1864 to 1873, by massive net capital inflows: $193 million in the 1850's; $1,287 million between 1863 and 1873.[50] The wide-based industrial and agricultural boom of the 1850's, with capital imports holding at bay discipline from the balance of payments, yielded a greater increase in prices than in Europe and, as in the 1830's, a favorable shift in the terms of trade.[51] The period from the end of the Civil War to 1873 was more complex. As noted earlier, the American wheat price (with wheat now a significant item in U.S. exports) peaked as early as 1866, as U.S. acreage, output, and exports expanded at extraordinary rates. The cotton price, too, fell as the South began to resume its place in world markets. Moreover, U.S. import prices and terms of trade were affected by the sharp rise in British export prices in 1871–1873, which resulted from the coal bottleneck that emerged in that great international boom, affecting a wide range of British export prices.[52] Thus, although the American terms of trade rose from their low level of 1864–1866, they did not exhibit the kind of behavior usually associated with a major expansion supported by capital imports. Evidently, the British terms of trade also did not follow the textbook pattern for a phase of large capital exports.

In terms of leading sectors, this was an era of massive railroadization in Western Europe, Russia, India, and the United States, as Table III-21 indicates.

TABLE III-20. *U.S. Wheat Production and Related Series, 1840–1880*

	(1) Wheat Price (Dollars per Bushel) Annual	(2) Annual Average	(3) Wheat Production (1,000 Bushels)	(4) Annual Average Growth Rate (%)	(5) Western Land Sales Seven States ($ Thousands)
1840	1.055		84,823 (1839)		2,251
1841	1.185				1,212
1842	1.140	1840–1844: 1.067		1839–1849: 1.71	1,137
1843	0.981				1,568
1844	0.975				1,872
1845	1.040				2,163
1846	1.085	1845–1849: 1.181			2,386
1847	1.315				2,672
1848	1.175				2,088
1849	1.240		100,486		1,328
1850	1.275				1,124
1851	1.075				1,797
1852	1.105	1850–1854: 1.411		1849–1859: 5.59	1,031
1853	1.390				3,970
1854	2.210				9,771
1855	2.435				9,215
1856	1.755	1855–1859: 1.725			3,453
1857	1.675				1,895
1858	1.325				765
1859	1.435		173,105		450
1860	1.495				248
1861	1.425				
1862	1.390	1860–1864: 1.578		1859–1869: 5.28	
1863	1.640				
1864	1.942				
1865	2.160				
1866	2.945	1865–1869: 2.428	169,703		
1867	2.844		210,878		
1868	2.541		246,272		
1869	1.651		289,526		
1870	1.373		254,429		
1871	1.581		271,881		
1872	1.780	1870–1874: 1.608	271,482	1869–1879: 4.72	
1873	1.787		321,931		
1874	1.517		356,115		
1875	1.403		313,728		
1876	1.320	1875–1880: 1.356	309,116		
1877	1.685		395,510		
1878	1.252		449,175		
1879	1.223		459,234		
1880	1.253		502,257		

Sources: Cols. 1 and 2, *Historical Statistics of the United States*, 1960 ed., pp. 123–124; col. 3, ibid., p. 297; col. 5, No *The Economic Growth of the United States, 1790–1860*, p. 256 (from Arthur H. Cole); col. 6, *Historical Statistics*, p. 712; co ibid., p. 297; cols. 8 and 9, ibid., p. 547; col. 10, ibid., p. 428; col. 11, ibid., p. 62.

) otal Land Sales Thousands)	(7) Acreage Harvested (1,000 Acres)	(8) Volume of Wheat Exports (60-Lb. Bu. in Millions)	(9) Value of Wheat Exports ($ Millions)	(10) Railroad Mileage Added	(11) Immigration (Thousands)	
		2	2	491	92	1840
		1	1	606	88	1841
		1	1	505	111	1842
		—	—	288	57	1843
		1	1	180	85	1844
		—	—	277	120	1845
		2	2	333	159	1846
		4	6	263	239	1847
		2	3	1,056	229	1848
		2	2	1,048	300	1849
		1	1	1,261	315	1850
		1	1	1,274	409	1851
		3	3	2,288	397	1852
		4	4	2,170	401	1853
		8	12	3,442	460	1854
		1	1	2,453	230	1855
		8	15	1,471	224	1856
		15	22	2,077	272	1857
		9	9	1,966	145	1858
57		3	3	1,707	156	1859
79		4	4	1,500	180	1860
71		31	38	1,016	113	1861
52		37	43	720	114	1862
68		36	47	574	200	1863
88		24	31	947	222	1864
97		10	19	819	287	1865
65	15,408	6	8	1,404	186	1866
64	16,738	6	8	2,541	342	1867
49	19,140	16	30	2,468	282	1868
20	21,194	18	24	4,103	353	1869
50	20,945	37	47	5,658	387	1870
89	22,230	34	45	6,660	321	1871
76	22,962	26	39	7,439	405	1872
32	24,866	39	51	5,217	460	1873
52	27,310	71	101	2,584	313	1874
14	28,382	53	60	1,606	227	1875
29	28,283	55	68	2,575	170	1876
76	27,963	40	47	2,280	142	1877
30	33,379	72	97	2,428	138	1878
25	35,347	122	131	5,006	178	1879
17	38,096	153	191	6,706	457	1880

TABLE III-21. *The Expansion of World Railroad Mileage, 1840–1888*

	1840	1850	1860	1870	1880	1888
United Kingdom	838	6,620	10,430	15,540	17,930	19,810
France	360	1,890	5,880	9,770	14,500	20,900
Germany	341	3,640	6,980	11,730	20,690	24,270
Russia	16	310	990	7,100	14,020	17,700
Austria	90	960	2,810	5,950	11,500	15,610
Italy	13	270	1,120	3,830	5,340	7,830
Spain	—	80	1,190	3,200	4,550	5,930
Portugal	—	—	40	440	710	1,190
Sweden	—	—	375	1,090	3,650	4,670
Norway	—	—	40	170	690	970
Denmark	—	20	70	470	830	1,220
Holland	11	110	200	780	1,440	1,700
Belgium	210	550	1,070	1,800	2,400	2,760
Switzerland	—	15	650	890	1,600	1,870
Rumania	—	—	—	150	860	1,530
Servia	—	—	—	—	100	340
Bulgaria	—	—	—	—	200	430
Greece	—	—	—	—	10	370
Turkey	—	—	40	390	700	900
Europe	1,879	14,465	31,885	63,300	101,720	130,000
United States	2,820	9,020	30,630	53,400	93,670	156,080
Canada	16	70	2,090	2,500	6,890	12,700
Mexico	—	—	—	220	660	5,010
Peru	—	—	50	250	1,180	1,630
Chile	—	—	120	450	1,100	1,750
Brazil	—	—	135	505	2,175	5,580
Argentina	—	—	15	640	1,540	5,550
Uruguay	—	—	—	60	270	450
Japan	—	—	—	—	75	910
India	—	—	840	4,830	9,310	15,250
Australia	—	—	250	1,230	5,390	10,140
South Africa	—	—	—	—	1,010	2,010
Algeria	—	—	—	—	780	1,840
Egypt	—	—	275	550	1,120	1,260
West Indies	—	—	—	100	650	1,280
Various	—	—	—	200	900	2,870
World	4,715	23,555	66,290	128,235	228,440	354,310
Annual average rate of increase (%)		18.0	10.9	6.8	5.9	5.6

Source: Mulhall, *The Dictionary of Statistics*, p. 495.

The impact of the railroads was by no means uniform. Where existing commercial and industrial centers were being linked, the cost-reducing effects on transport volume were quickly felt. The short-run impact was more inflationary where the time for construction was longer and, especially, where the period before production in new areas could fully build up was more extended. In the United States and Western Europe, where the economic, social, and political foundations for an industrial society had already been laid, the railroads brought about a prompt general acceleration in growth focused on the heavy-industry sectors. Where such prerequisites were lacking (as, for example, in India), the spreading effects were more limited, although they generally accelerated the commercialization of agriculture.

The full revolutionary impact of railroadization is difficult to measure. It had powerful, multiple effects: it lowered transport costs; brought new areas and supplies into national and international markets; helped in some cases to generate new export earnings which permitted the whole process of development to move ahead at a higher rate; stimulated expansion in output and the accelerated adoption of new technologies in the coal, iron, and engineering industries; set up pressures (via the need for more durable rails) which helped give birth to the modern steel industry; altered and modernized the institutions of capital formation; and accelerated the pace of urbanization, with all its dynamic playback effects on economic as well as social and political development.[53] It has required an extraordinary willingness to ignore massive historical evidence, and exaggerated reliance on over-simple analytic techniques to attempt to remove the railroads from their central place in the modernization and growth of the world economy of the nineteenth century.

One limited but important part of the effects of railroadization is suggested by the expansion of coal, iron, and energy production (Table III-22).

In 1840, 30 percent of total steam power was used by railroads; in 1870 and 1888, about twice that proportion. Related to those figures was an expansion not merely in the output of rails (after 1870, increasingly made of steel) but also of the engineering industry manufacturing locomotives and railroad cars. As for the coal and iron industries, neither, of course, was created by the railways. Large iron industries existed in the eighteenth century in Russia, Britain, France, the United States, and Sweden. After the British pioneered the new coke-based methods for manufacturing iron in the 1780's, these methods slowly spread after 1815, in the pre-railroad age. They spread much more rapidly in the environment of increased iron demand generated by the coming of the railroads.

Dealing with the American case, Albert Fishlow concluded that reduced transport costs provided direct benefits to the American economy of the order of $175 million, about 4 percent of 1859 gross national product.[54] Railroad gross investment over the period 1849–1858 accounted for more than 15 percent of gross capital formation, reaching almost a fourth at the peak in 1854. As for sectoral inputs, railroad requirements for pig iron rose through the period, amounting to the order of 20 percent of net consumption for the 1850's; railroad demands "contributed heavily" to the critical transition of the pig iron industry to anthracite and then coke as a source of fuel; they "achieved still greater pre-eminence" in stimulating rolling mills; and (post–Civil War) rail requirements introduced the Bessemer process to the United States. As for machinery, the locomotive industry and repair shops (domestic from the beginning) had greater spreading effects in engineering than the textile and steamboat engine shops from which they initially stemmed. Fishlow believes that the railroads had a massive effect on agricultural output, population expansion (including immigration), and the growth of agricultural processing industries in the West in the 1850's.

Dealing with the British case, G. R. Hawke concludes that the coming of railroads lifted national income by 1865 to a level 10 percent higher than it would otherwise have reached.[55] This implies that almost a quarter of the expansion in British national income between (say) 1840 and 1865 derived from the introduction of the railroads.[56] Hawke finds that railroads significantly expanded the demand for iron, notably in South Wales (the peak figure for overall railway demand for pig iron being 12.6 percent for the period 1844–1851); contributed (along with competition from the Scottish iron industry) to an expansion in the scale of plants and (less certainly) an improvement of technology in the industry; brought new coal supplies into the market and helped break up the monopolistic coal Vend. Hawke also reaches out to catch some of the railroads' more oblique effects on British development, via external economies, even when they are difficult or impossible to quantify, concluding: ". . . the study of linkages from railways indicates that the quantitative measurement of the social returns to investment in railways results in an underestimate."[57]

Standing back from the details, the trend period we are examining, setting aside its military struggles and pursuit of gold, was dominated by a counterpoint between the opening up of new grain acreage and the installation of railroad networks, which accelerated the pace of the heavy-industry leading sectors which brought the United States, Belgium, France, and Germany into take-off. The achievement of maximum productivity, as measured by ton-miles per man employed by railroads, came, as one would expect, much more quickly in Britain (and, undoubtedly, on the Continent) than in the United States, where the railways, from the 1850's forward, played a critical role in the longer process of bringing new lands

TABLE III-22. *World Production of Coal, Iron, and Energy, 1800–1889*

	Coal (Millions of Tons)	Annual Average Growth Rate (%)	Pig Iron (Millions of Tons)	Annual Average Growth Rate (%)	Energy (Steam) (Million Horsepower)	Annual Average Growth Rate (%)
1800	11.6	—	0.4	—	—	—
1810	—	—	0.6	3.0	—	—
1820	17.2	2.0	1.0	5.2	—	—
1830	—	—	1.6	4.8	—	—
1840	44.8	4.9	2.7	5.4	1.6	—
1850	81.4	6.2	4.4	5.0	4.0	9.6
1860	142.3	5.7	7.2	5.1	9.4	8.9
1870	213.4	4.1	11.9	5.2	18.5	7.0
1880	340.0	4.8	18.1	4.3	34.2	6.3
1889	485.0	4.0	25.2	3.8	50.2	4.9

Source: Mulhall, *The Dictionary of Statistics*, p. 119 (coal); p. 332 (pig iron); p. 545 (energy).

and other natural resources into production.[58] There were, then, both cost-reducing and inflationary forces at work in the railroad extension of this period, depending on the economic character of the railroads and the initial functions they were designed to fulfill.

What was the upshot for real wages?

We have rough but reasonable annual estimates for Britain, France, and the United States (Table III-23 and Chart III-16).

In general, money wages in this period were less volatile than prices entering the worker's cost of living. They drifted upward over the period 1850–1873, with brief intervals of sharp advance during phases of intense inflation. The money-wage level in Britain, for example, rose sharply in 1852–1854, 1862–1864, and 1870–1873. Of the total increase in money wages between 1850 and 1873, 80 percent occurred in these seven years. In France, almost half the increase took place in the five years 1852–1854, 1860–1861, and 1871–1873. In the United States, 71 percent occurred during and immediately after the Civil War, between 1862 and 1867. Otherwise, short-run real-wage fluctuations (excluding the effects of cyclical unemployment) were determined by movements in the cost of living. For example, the high food prices of 1846–1847 drove down real wages in Britain and France, as they had in 1835–1837. In Britain and France the great price lift of 1852–1854, on balance, outpaced the rise in money wages. To a much lesser extent, the out-

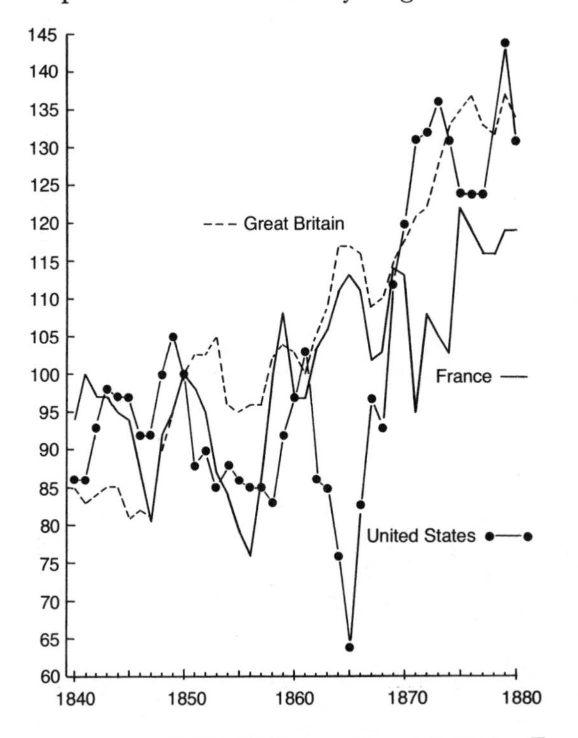

CHART III-16. *Real Wages: Great Britain, France, and the United States, 1840–1880 (1850=100)*

Source: See Table III-23.

TABLE III-23. *Real Wages: Great Britain, France, and the United States, 1840–1880*[59] *(1850 = 100)*

	(1) Great Britain	(2) France[60]	(3) United States[61]
1840	85	94	86
1841	83	100	86
1842	84	97	93
1843	85	97	98
1844	85	95	97
1845	82	94	97
1846	84	87	92
1847	81	81	92
1848	90	92	100
1849	95	95	105
1850	100	100	100
1851	102	98	88
1852	102	95	90
1853	105	87	85
1854	96	84	88
1855	95	79	86
1856	96	76	85
1857	96	86	85
1858	102	100	83
1859	104	108	92
1860	103	97	97
1861	100	97	103
1862	105	103	86
1863	109	106	85
1864	117	111	76
1865	117	113	64
1866	116	111	83
1867	109	102	97
1868	110	103	93
1869	115	114	112
1870	118	113	120
1871	121	95	131
1872	122	108	132
1873	128	105	136
1874	133	103	131
1875	135	122	124
1876	137	119	124
1877	133	116	124
1878	132	116	132
1879	137	119	144
1880	134	119	131

Sources: Col. 1, 1840–1850, R. S. Tucker, "Real Wages of Artisans in London"; 1850–1880, G. H. Wood, real wages at full work (in Walter T. Layton and Geoffrey Crowther, *An Introduction to the Study of Prices* [London: Macmillan, 1938], p. 273); col. 2, Jean Lhomme, "Le Pouvoir d'achat de l'ouvrier français au cours d'un siècle: 1840–1940," *Le Mouvement Social*, no. 63 (April–June 1968), p. 46; col. 3, Hansen, "Factors Affecting the Trend of Real Wages," p. 32.

come was the same in the United States. On the other hand, in all three countries real wages rose in the great boom of 1871–1873.

Setting aside these short-run patterns, real wages fell during the most prosperous period of the 1850's—down to 1856 in France, 1857 in Britain, 1858 in the United States. The 1860's, when British capital no longer flowed to expand acreage in the American West and South, was a good decade for British real wages, as it also was for the French; and, as noted above, the intensity of the boom of the early 1870's, with the British coal bottleneck shifting the terms of trade favorably despite large capital exports, permitted that increase to continue. In the United States, real wages also were set back in the 1850's, rising during the recession which preceded the Civil War. Real wages fell during the war years, but more than doubled between 1865 and 1873 as the cost of living declined rapidly and money wages rose almost 20 percent.

The French real-wage calculations show a lesser trend rise than in Britain and the United States between 1840 and 1850; and a similar net movement down to the eve of the Franco-Prussian War. The early 1870's were, of course, affected by the impact of the war, the revolution, and the reparation burden France assumed.

For purposes of trend-period analysis, the most significant aspect of this story is the pressure on British, French, and American real wages in the 1850's, as a critical margin of the world's resources moved into gold mining, the extensive investment in the American West, and the military outlays of that decade; and then the recovery of British and French real wages in the 1860's. The wartime and

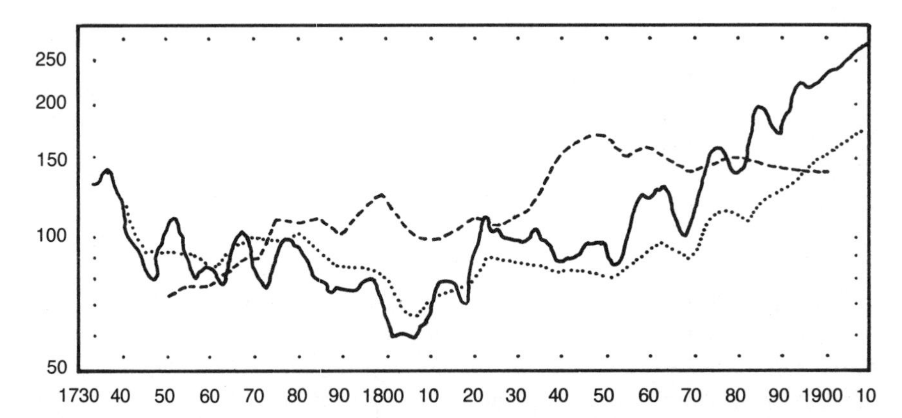

CHART III-17. *Sweden: Real Wages for Agricultural Workers, 1732–1910 (1860–1864 = 100), and the Number of Agricultural Workers, 1751–1900*

——— Nominal wages deflated by the price of rye, five-year moving averages.

. . . . . . Nominal wages deflated by a cost-of-living index, ten-year overlapping averages.

- - - - - - Number of farmhands, farmers' sons, etc. (thousands).

Source: Lennart Jörberg, *A History of Prices in Sweden*, vol. 2, p. 337.

postwar behavior of American real wages are roughly what one would expect, reinforced by the decline in grain prices from their peak in 1866.

Swedish real wages continued their decline from the peak in the early 1820's down through the first half of the 1850's.[62] The cost of living in Sweden fully reflected the global price revolution of 1852–1854. With a setback in the second half of the 1860's, however, real wages then moved upward, for the first time since the post-1815 years, to the end of this trend period. They subsequently accelerated, as elsewhere, after the price downturn of 1873. Chart III-17 catches vividly where this period fits in the long sweep of Sweden's development.

It was during this period that Sweden was, in my vocabulary, completing the preconditions for take-off—in Lennart Jörberg's, experiencing the "last period prior to the so-called industrial breakthrough." The period was marked by a shift to the production of oats, livestock, and dairy products, whose relative prices were favorable; an expansion in iron production; and, above all, an expansion of timber production and exports from steam-powered mills. These produced differential increases in real wages in particular regions and a reversal of the overall downward trend to be observed in Chart III-17. From 1850 the number of farmhands began its decline, drawn off primarily to nonagricultural activities in Sweden, with emigration to America playing a more substantial role after the Civil War.

Charts III-18 and III-19 exhibit for the period 1830–1948 two of the most widely discussed relationships in modern economic history: immigration to the United States in relation to U.S. building construction; U.S. building construction in relation to that in Britain. Although our focus here is 1850–1873, it may be useful to set that period in its broader historical context. Since the author of Chart III-18 (Brinley Thomas) used a rather inadequate measure of British building to cover the gap between 1850 and 1870 (railway miles open per million of population), E. W. Cooney's chart, III-19, using timber imports, is also presented.

The broad correlation between U.S. immigration and building is palpable in our period, although the decline of both in the first half of the 1860's is to be understood primarily as a common result of the Civil War. There are also two quite significant lags which suggest that more than the flow of immigrants affected U.S. building construction: housing peaked as early as 1853 and 1871; immigration, in 1854 and 1873. The high interest rates and the attraction of investment in other directions, toward the peak of these great expansions, may have damped housing construction despite the continued momentum of immigration.

British housing construction emerged as relatively low in the early 1850's, when U.S. capital imports were high. The Crimean War undoubtedly had the usual damping effect of military outlays on housing. There is the suggestion of an increase in the second half of the decade (in Chart III-19) and a twin-peaked boom in the 1860's which ended as the decade closed. In the period of maximum British capital exports, in the early 1870's, building was, once again, at a low level, but in the wake of the world-wide downturn of 1873 Britain enjoyed a famous countercyclical building expansion down to 1876 which also helped carry Sweden into take-off.

Thus, to a degree, British and American housing cycles moved out of phase: the great American housing expansions came in the early 1850's and after the Civil War, down to 1871; the great British housing expansions came in the 1860's and in the years following the 1873 peak. The major force operating here was, almost certainly, the effect on the availability of capital for housing in Britain, via interest rates, induced by periods of large and diminished flows of capital to the United States and elsewhere; but fluctuations in British emigration probably also left their mark on the demand for housing in Britain.

This much having been said in general terms, it is salutary to be reminded that the building cycles about which we generalize so easily in economic history took quite different paths in different regions. John Parry Lewis has laboriously examined the regional

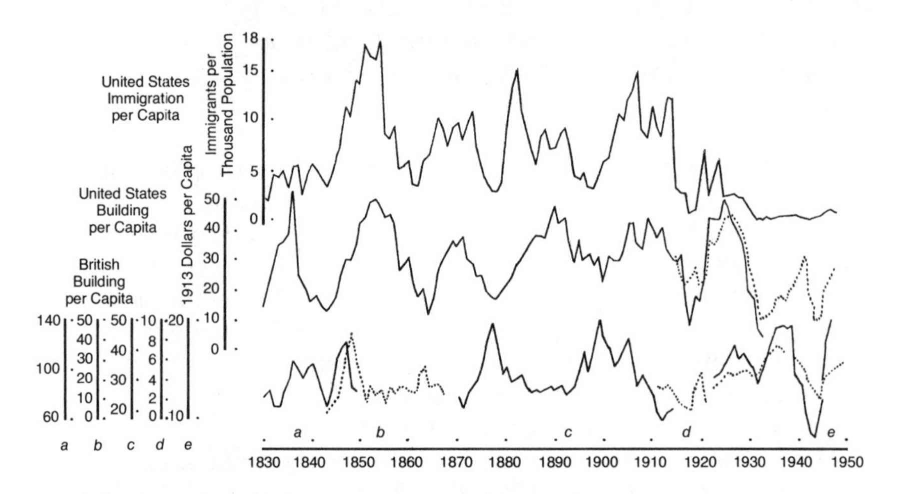

CHART III-18. *Building Activity per Capita in the United States and the United Kingdom, and Immigration to the United States per Thousand Annually, 1831–1948*

British building scales:
a: Bricks taxed per capita in England and Wales.
b: Railway miles opened per million of population in the United Kingdom.
c: Volume of building per capita in Great Britain (Cairncross index).
d: Volume of building per capita in Great Britain based on estimated cost of plans approved and Board of Trade index.
e: Building employment per thousand of population in the United Kingdom.

Source: Thomas, *Migration and Economic Growth*, p. 176.

differences in Britain.[63] The aggregate indexes for Britain sum up differences which could flow from the vicissitudes of particular industries or the opening up of new resources (like coal in South Wales, from the mid-1860's). These differences produce a wide variety of regional patterns despite the more general effects on building which flow from the level of interest rates, the availability of credit for housing construction, fluctuations in rates of family formation, and the course of business cycles, harvests, and real wages.

The world of 1873 looked quite different from that of 1850. It contained well over 100,000 more miles of railroads—a fivefold increase. Some six million immigrants had crossed the seas to a United States whose transport links now spanned the continent. The world economy had moved into dependence on the flow of a critical margin of American wheat as well as cotton. Coal production and the use of steam power had quintupled; pig iron output had tripled;

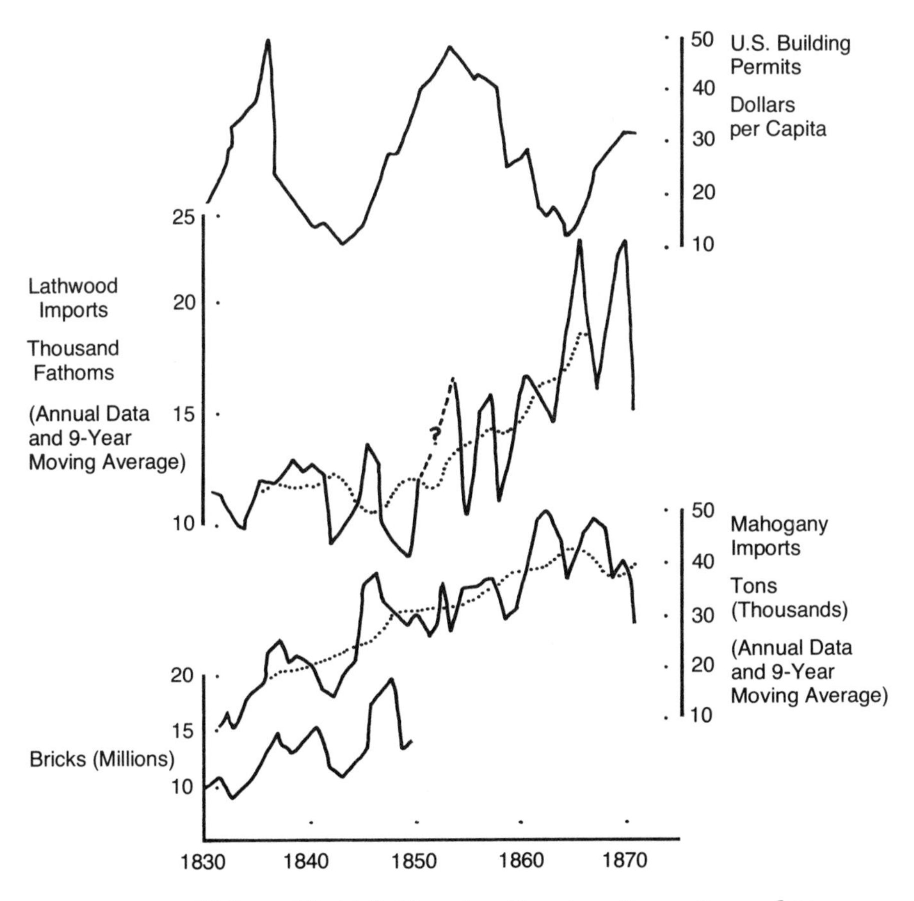

CHART III-19. *U.S. and British Housing Construction, 1830–1870*

Source: E. W. Cooney, "Long Waves in Building in the British Economy of the Nineteenth Century," *Economic History Review*, Second Series, vol. 13, no. 2 (December 1960), p. 261.

Western Europe and the United States had joined Britain in mastery of heavy industry; the age of steel had been born.

These productive transformations, however, were accompanied by intervals of war and by substantial diversions of resources to gold mining. Moreover, there were significant lags involved in opening up the trans-Mississippi West. On balance, the contending forces of expanding demand and expanding supply yielded an interval of relatively high prices and of strain on food supplies in the early 1850's, on coal in the early 1870's. Interest rates were relatively high, and farmers, by and large, prosperous. Real wages varied in Britain, France, and the United States by decades, as they had since 1820; but the net movement in both countries, after the setback of the 1850's (and the Civil War, for the United States), was upward.

14

1873–1920

The trend periods on either side of the mid-1890's are best dealt with in a single analysis.[64] That turning point was a true watershed; but whether one is examining the population-food balance, the leading sectors, or the character and scale of immigration flows (and construction cycles) the patterns of the pre-1914 generation are illuminated by observing them in the context of the two decades that followed the crisis of 1873.

The period from 1873 to the trough of the mid-1890's is one of the most fully analyzed and debated intervals in modern economic history. Like the period from the end of the Napoleonic Wars to mid-century it was, by and large, a period of peace; of falling prices and interest rates; of agricultural abundance; of rising real wages. As in that period also, there was a cylical expansion (like that of the 1830's) when the trend period characteristics briefly reversed; that is, the boom of the late 1880's. This time it was the economic attractiveness of the Argentine pampas rather than cotton lands in the American South that primarily caused the break in trends.

There is also a family relation between the following trend period, down to 1914, and that which got under way around mid-century. Again, there were wars: the Spanish-American, Boer, Russo-Japanese, and Balkan conflicts; prices and interest rates rose; new areas were brought into production and the world market to maintain Europe's food supply; farmers were generally prosperous; and urban real wages came under even more protracted pressure than during the trend period a half-century earlier.

Tables III-24 and III-25 show the changing pattern of wheat production and prices over the whole sweep from 1871 to 1919; Chart III-20 shows the annual price of wheat in Great Britain.

From its pre–Civil War peak, the wheat price moved erratically downward, with increases in 1870–1872, 1875–1877, 1889–1891. But in 1894 it was at only 35 percent of its 1867 level, an astounding transformation in the cost of man's most basic commodity. By the eve of the First World War, however, the price had risen sufficiently to wipe out almost a third of that decline; and at the postwar peak in 1920 it was a third higher than it had been in 1867.

As Tables III-24 and III-25 suggest, the increases in output in the United States and (then) Russia lay behind the period of price decline; but, from the 1890's to 1914, increases in Russian, Canadian, Australian, and Indian output failed to balance sufficiently the leveling off in U.S. output (and the decline of U.S. exports) to prevent a rise in the range within which the wheat price subsequently fluctuated.[65] The price decline to the mid-1890's was the result not only of the opening up of new grain-producing areas made possible by railroadization but also of a halving of ocean shipping rates be-

TABLE III-24. *World Wheat Production, 1871–1919 (in Millions of Bushels)*

	1871–1880	1881–1887	1885–1889	1889–189
United Kingdom	85	78	76	70
France	275	290	303	288
Germany	94	98	108	112
Russia[a]	224	250	358[a]	360
Austria[b]	109	151	181[b]	186
Italy	115	105	146	156
Spain	114	133	93	81
Portugal	8	10	6	7
Sweden and Norway	4	4	4	5
Denmark	5	6	5	4
Holland	5	6	6	5
Belgium	16	17	17	19
Switzerland	2	2	4	4
Greece	3	4	6	7
Servia	3	4	—	—
Rumania	24	26	46	55
Turkey, etc.	40	47	—	—
Other Europe	—	—	47	63
Europe	1,126	1,231	1,406	1,422
United States	338	440	516	628
Canada	24	36	38	41
Australia	24	38	26	31
India, etc.[c]	282	375	266[c]	247
Other Extra-Europe	—	—	138	171
Total	1,794	2,120	2,391	2,545
Annual average rate of change (%)	—	—	—	1.26
Annual average wheat price, Great Britain (1900 = 100)	212	140	117	110 (1894 = 8

[a] USSR boundaries, post-1945, from 1885–1889 forward.
[b] Austria and Hungary, from 1885–1889 forward.
[c] Indian peninsula only from 1885–1889 forward.
[d] Trough.
[e] Peak.

tween 1873 and the mid-1890's, a decline then interrupted (by the Boer War and high coal prices) which resumed to a trough in 1908 (Chart III-21).

The European governments reacted in different ways to the revolutionary changes in the availability and cost of overseas wheat in the 1870's, 1880's, and 1890's, as C. P. Kindleberger's terse summary indicates: "In Britain agriculture was permitted to be liquidated. In Germany large-scale agriculture sought and obtained protection for itself. In France, where the demography, pattern of resources, and small scale of industrial enterprise favored farming, agriculture as a whole successfully defended its position with tariffs.

4–1899	1899–1904	1904–1909	1909–1914	1914–1919
59	58	56	61	73
26	339	332	318	214
14	117	124	148	116
52	545	620	792	709
35	206	220	231	152
57	172	184	183	168
04	120	110	131	137
8	9	8	9	8
5	5	7	8	9
4	4	4	6	6
5	5	5	6	5
17	14	14	15	8
4	4	3	3	4
7	8	8	10	11
—	—	—	—	—
56	62	74	88	61
—	—	—	—	—
61	61	71	80	54
64	1,729	1,840	2,090	1,735
87	714	672	694	813
52	77	104	197	248
27	43	59	91	109
41	249	302	352	353
91	229	299	307	338
62	3,041	3,276	3,731	3,597
5	1.94	1.50	2.64	−0.73
03	101	117	123	246 (1920 = 315)[e]

Sources: 1871–1880, 1881–1887, Mulhall, *The Dictionary of Statistics*, p. 8; 1885–1919, Wilfred Malenbaum, *e World Wheat Economy, 1885–1939*, pp. 238–239; British wheat prices, Layton and Crowther, *An Introduction the Study of Prices*, p. 234.

Note: Due to rounding, totals may not equal sum of components.

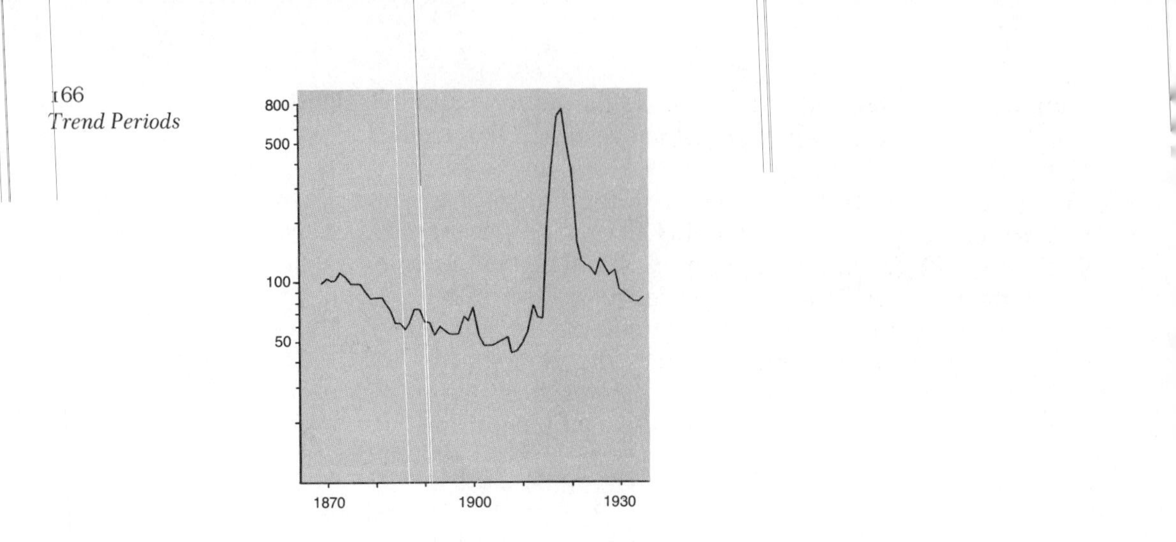

CHART III-20. *Index of Tramp Shipping Freights, 1869–1935*

Source: L. Isserlis, "Tramp Shipping Cargoes, and Freights," in Mitchell, with Deane, *Abstract of British Historical Statistics*, p. 224.

In Italy [despite the tariffs of 1887–1888] the response was to emigrate. In Denmark grain production was converted to animal husbandry."[66]

Continental tariff protection undoubtedly sustained the level of grain production at higher levels than would otherwise have prevailed; but European wheat output (*ex* Russia) was sluggish until the price turn-around of the 1890's caused expansion to resume.

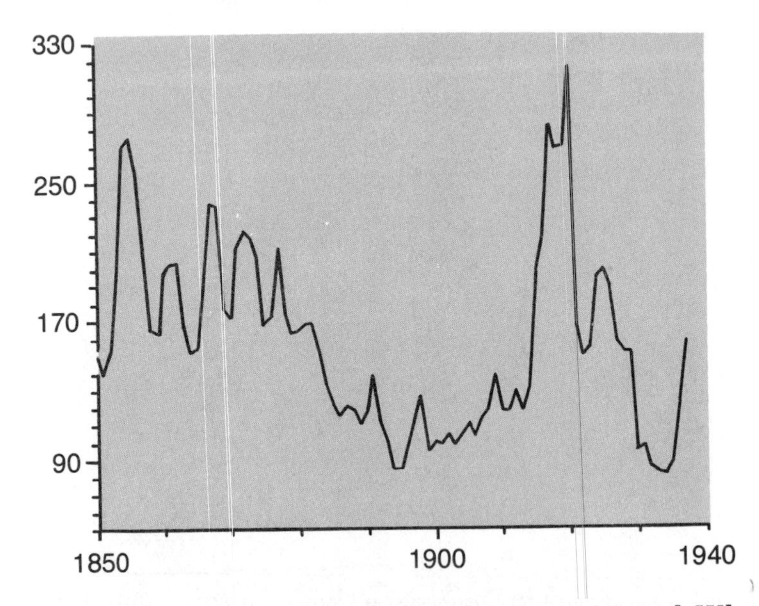

CHART III-21. *Annual Average Gazette Price of British Wheat per Quarter, 1850–1937*

Source: Layton and Crowther, *An Introduction to the Study of Prices*, p. 226.

TABLE III-25. *Wheat Production Growth Rates, 1885–1919 (Annual Average Rates of Change [%])*

	World	Europe except Russia	Russia	USA	Canada	Argentina	Australia	India
1885–1889/1889–1894	1.26	0.27	0.11	4.01	1.53	18.64	3.58	−1.47
1889–1894/1894–1899	1.65	0.92	4.66	1.81	4.87	5.01	−2.73	−0.49
1894–1899/1899–1904	1.94	1.26	3.81	0.77	9.17	9.16	9.75	0.66
1899–1904/1904–1909	1.50	0.60	2.61	−1.21	6.20	11.18	6.53	3.93
1904–1909/1909–1914	2.64	1.25	5.02	0.65	13.63	−1.43	9.05	3.11
1909–1914/1914–1919	−0.73	−4.59	−2.19	3.22	4.71	2.58	3.68	0.06

Source: Calculated from data in TABLE III-24.

Chart III-22 shows how protection kept the wheat price higher in certain European countries than in Free Trade Britain.

The price of meat and dairy products was subject to quite different supply and demand forces over this period than the price of grain. (Compare, for example, trends in beef and wheat prices in Chart II-8 above.) The opening of new lands and transport improvements did have their impact; but the effect was less substantial than in the case of grain. Moreover, the fall in the price of grain and other factors tending to raise urban real incomes increased the demand in Western Europe for meat and dairy products disproportionately; and in Britain and elsewhere there was a shift of agricultural production in these more profitable directions. Mulhall, for example, provides estimates of the European cattle population which indicate an annual average increase of 0.57 percent between 1850 and 1870, an increase of 0.74 percent over the subsequent seventeen years.[67]

The data on 1914–1919 in Tables III-24 and III-25 show how expansion in overseas areas during the First World War partially cushioned the war-induced decline (except in Britain) in European wheat production, helping to lay the basis for the chronic excess grain capacity of the 1920's.

The central feature of this story is the expansion and then deceleration of wheat output in the United States and the compensatory expansions in Argentina, Australia, Canada, and Russia. The Russian position in the European wheat market was, of course, an old story; but it took on a special character with the spread of the railroads from the 1860's, the Russian setbacks of 1879–1881 and 1892–1893 (due to the famine of 1891), and Russia's large role in the pre-1914 decade, strengthened by the Stolypin land reform of 1906. The other regions were brought into the world markets by a

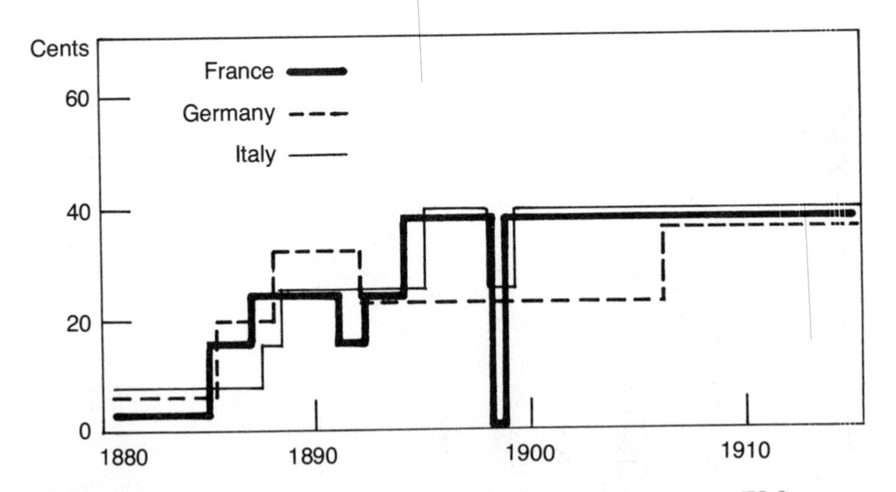

CHART III-22. *Effective Wheat Import Duties, 1880–1914 (U.S. Cents per Bushel)*

Source: Malenbaum, *The World Wheat Economy*, p. 162.

process similar to that which had induced the expansion of American cotton acreage in the 1830's and of wheat and cotton acreage in the 1850's. But there was a difference. The earlier booms had responded directly to changes in prices. The expansion to the trans-Mississippi West took place, and the expansions in Argentina, Canada, and Australia began, at least, in an environment in which the wheat price (and agricultural prices in general) were still subject to a downward trend. There is no great mystery as to why this happened. These regions were sufficiently productive to justify economic exploitation at current prices, given the economies in transport the railroads and the unfolding revolution in ocean shipping could provide. Other technical developments helped: refrigeration, barbed wire, new seed strains, agricultural machinery, and mining techniques to exploit nonagricultural resources the railroads also made accessible. Political changes in Argentina and new public policies in Canada and Australia converged with these economic possibilities to draw large flows of foreign capital and immigrants to permit these expansions. The rise in wheat prices from the mid-1890's mightily reinforced them.

The great surges of external investment relative to grain production (aside from the pre-1873 flows to the United States) were to Australia in 1883–1886, remaining high, however, until 1890; to Argentina in 1886–1890; and to Canada in 1905–1913. The massive build-up of foreign investment in Russia proceeded less erratically, but expansion was particularly marked in the 1890's and in the period 1904–1909.

In Australia, railroad mileage open more than doubled in the 1880's, a period when net capital inflow was about half of gross domestic capital formation.[68] This occurred at a time when wool dominated Australian exports, as gold production tapered off. In the 1880's Australia turned to domestic development and found the rather depressed London capital market in a mood to finance its enterprises.[69] There was no immediate expansion of Australian exports. But from 1884 Australian land policy changed in ways to encourage agricultural rather than pastoral activity. When wheat prices moved up in the mid-1890's, the combination of prior land policy and railroadization had set the stage for the expansion in output registered in Table III-25. As a contemporary remarked: "It is not so much a 15-inch rainfall and good lands which are essentials required to extend our cultivated area as it is the provision of cheap railway transport."[70] The linkage of acreage and railway expansion is roughly suggested in Chart III-23. The expansion of immigration came later, accompanied by some revival of capital imports in the years before 1914. But Australian capital imports never reached again the peak level of the mid-1880's.[71]

The Argentine case bears a family resemblance to that of Australia: there was an initial phase of capital imports and railroadization in the 1880's related to domestic developments in Argentina; a subsequent surge in exports, including wheat exports, starting in the 1890's, substantially dependent on prior railroadization; a second wave of capital imports accompanied by large net immigration in the years before 1914. Although Argentine capital imports never quite reachieved the peak level of 1888–1889, the expansion of 1905–1914 was stronger than in the Australian case.[72] The initiating impulse in this process was political: the consolidation of a firm central government by Julio Roca in 1880. At the time, Argentina, like Australia, was primarily an exporter of wool. The pampas were, however, obviously an area capable of profitable grain exploitation even at low world prices, if immigrants could be attracted and efficient transport provided. Unlike the case of Australia, immigrants came to Argentina in large numbers in the 1880's. As the railways moved out over the pampas and barbed wire permitted the segregation of pastoral areas, the immigrants put increased acreage into production. There was a spectacular surge of output and exports in the early 1890's, helping stabilize the Argentine economy after the Baring Crisis in the face of falling export prices which otherwise would have had disastrous consequences;[73] and then the price in-

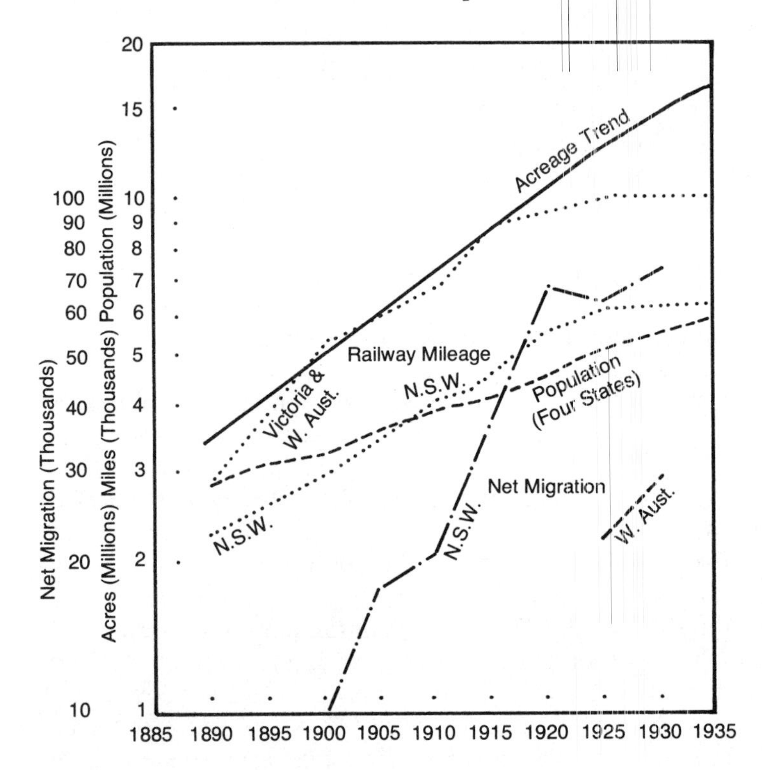

CHART III-23. *Australia: Wheat Acreage and Related Growth Factors, 1890–1935*

N.S.W.: New South Wales.
W. Aust.: West Australia.
Source: Malenbaum, *The World Wheat Economy*, p. 142.

crease, from the mid-1890's, induced the tripling in output to be observed in Chart III-24, accompanied by a quadrupling in wheat acreage (from 3.47 million acres in 1889–1894, to 16.05 million in 1909–1914), and a memorable period of general prosperity.

Chart III-24 catches in broad terms the linkage of the railways, wheat acreage, and population trends in Argentina over these years.[74]

The role of the turn-around in wheat prices in the mid-1890's is most dramatic in the Canadian case: "After thirty years of waiting and frustrated hopes, it was at last Canada's turn to be drawn into the world network of trade and investment."[75] But, as in the case of Australia and Argentina, a prior period of creative preparation was necessary. From the Land Act of 1868 and the Homestead Act of 1872, the Dominion government had been trying to bring the western acreage, with its palpable potential for low-cost wheat, effectively into production. But the railroads had to be built, the population expanded by substantial net immigration, the competition of American extension of the frontier overcome. In addition, there was some-

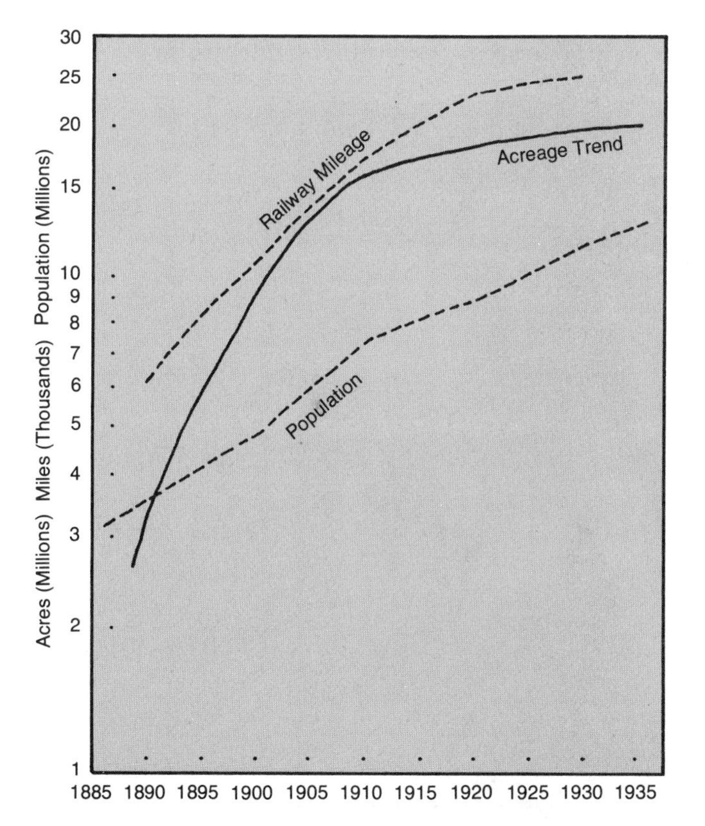

CHART III-24. *Argentina: Wheat Acreage and Related Growth Factors, 1885–1935*

Source: Malenbaum, *The World Wheat Economy*, p. 137.

thing of a lag in the adoption and full understanding of the dry-farming techniques pioneered in the United States. There were surges of immigration and capital imports (in support of railway building) in the early 1870's and 1880's; and, as Chart III-25 indicates,[76] some expansion of new homesteads, responding to transient wheat price increases in the early 1880's and a decade later; but only from the mid-1890's did the great expansion in western Canada take hold and net immigration rapidly increase. The extraordinary pre-1914 expansion in capital imports, however, came later, notably from 1905 to 1914. Capital inflows were at the astonishing level of 9.2 percent of GNP in 1906–1910, 12.4 percent in 1911–1915. Trends in wheat acreage, population in western Canada, and railway mileage are given in Chart III-26.[77]

The Russian case can be traced out in somewhat the same way, although the element of immigration is, of course, lacking (Table III-26 and Chart III-27). Nevertheless, once again massive capital imports played a critical role in the railroadization of the country, which, starting in a big way in the 1860's, prepared the way for and then lifted Russia into its take-off of the 1890's. Along with Stolypin's agricultural policy, these prior developments also made possi-

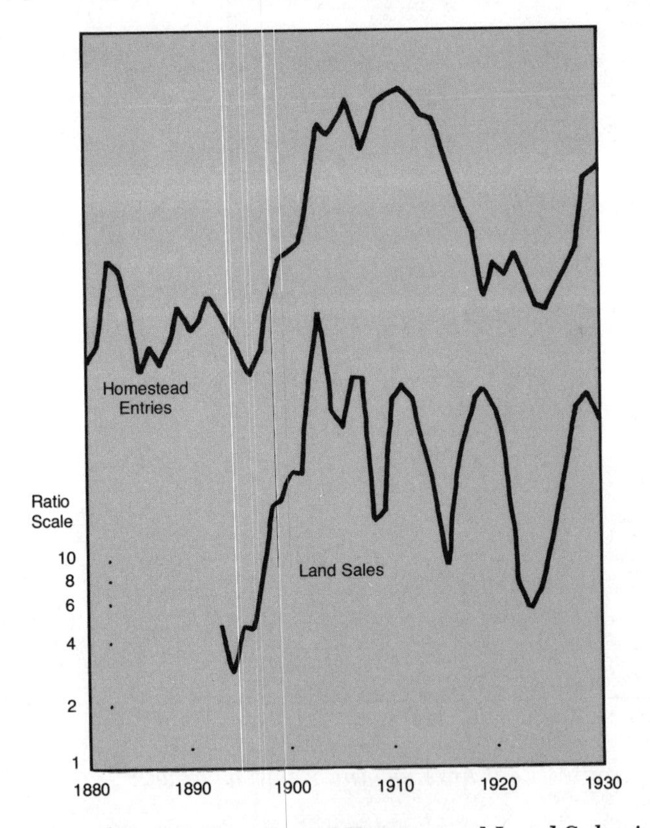

CHART III-25. *Homestead Entries and Land Sales in Western Canada, 1880–1930*

Source: Kenneth Buckley, *Capital Formation in Canada, 1896–1930*, p. 14.

ble the remarkable increase in wheat production in the eight years before 1914, although the relative role of the domestic market was increasing at this stage.[78] The flow of capital to Russia, notably from France, was motivated heavily by strategic considerations after the Franco-Prussian War. The French held about 80 percent of the Russian government debt in 1914 as well as one-third of the investment in Russian private enterprise. The total Russian government debt had reached 8.8 billion rubles by 1914.[79] Its servicing was rendered easier by the large increase and relatively high prices of Russian wheat exports after the mid-1890's.

In broad terms, the story of the food-population balance is straightforward enough. The spread of railroads, from the American West to Russia, India, and Australia, from Western Canada to the Argentine pampas, brought into production sufficient new acreage to generate a surplus capable of keeping Europe fed down to the First World War, despite a strong trend increase in the requirement for imported wheat. The upward movement of the international wheat price in the period 1895–1898 resulted from discontinuities in that process. For different reasons, export availabilities declined from India (1896–1897), Australia (1896–1898), and Russia (1898–1901), while Argentina did not sustain in 1896–1898 the export surge which had followed the collapse of its capital import

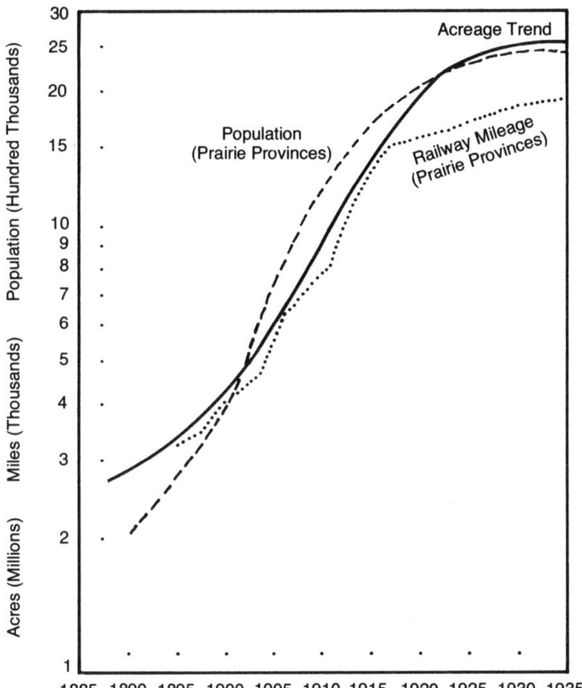

CHART III-26. *Canada: Wheat Acreage and Related Growth Factors, 1890–1935*

Source: Malenbaum, *The World Wheat Economy*, p. 145.

boom in 1890. Although U.S. and Canadian exports helped cover the gap, the wheat price rose in Britain by 50 percent between 1895 and 1898. After the turn of the century, a new and more persistent factor came into play; that is, the absolute decline in the American wheat surplus. But then Canada, Australia, Argentina, Russia, and India were, as a group, capable of responding. Their combined wheat exports to Britain doubled in the period 1901–1910 over the previous decade, while U.S. exports fell by about a quarter; the wheat price tended to rise; and the terms of trade pressed down on the urban nations and regions of the world.

This result was the outcome of a complex process that transcended the story of wheat itself. To keep the world's food supply in balance required vast capital exports from Western Europe, most notably from Great Britain. These flows diverted capital that might have flowed not only into housing but also into the expansion and refinement of the domestic capital stock of the capital-exporting nations, improving their real terms of trade by increasing the productivity of their export industries.

But the expansions in most of the capital-importing countries were much bigger affairs than mere increases in acreage, production, and exports of foodstuffs and raw materials. The railroads had their usual diffuse and powerful effects, including an increase in

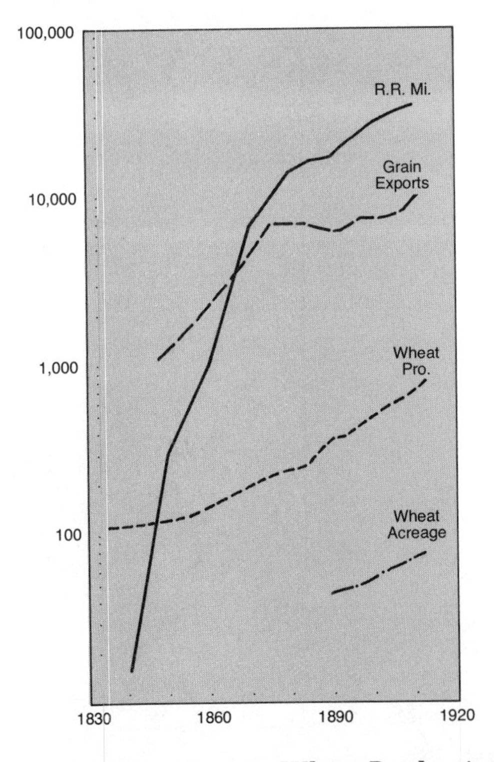

CHART III-27. *Russia: Wheat Production and Related Series, 1831–1914*

Source: Table III-26.

TABLE III-26. *Russia: Wheat Production—Acreage and Related Series, 1831–1914*

	(1) Wheat Production (Millions of Bushels)	(2) Wheat Acreage (Millions of Acres)	(3) Railway Mileage	(4) Annual Average Exports of Grain (Thousands of Metric Tons)	(5) Population (Millions)
1831–1840	110		16 (1840)		45.5 (1830)
1841–1850			303 (1850)	1,038 (1842–1850)	
1851–1860	130		986 (1860)	1,665	
1861–1870			6,763 (1870)	3,025	68.7 (1860)
1871–1880	224		14,024 (1880)	6,797	
1881–1887	250		16,061 (1885)	6,905	84.9 (1880)
1888	258			8,394	
1885–1889	358	44		6,231	
1889–1894	360	46	17,960 (1890)	6,386	92.0 (1890)
1894–1899	452	49	22,364 (1895)	7,496	
1899–1904	545	59	27,652 (1900)	7,508	
1904–1909	620	67	31,982 (1905)	8,079	
1909–1914	792	77	34,016 (1910)	10,192 (1909–1913)	

Sources: Col. 1, 1831–1888, Mulhall, *The Dictionary of Statistics*, p. 8; 1885–1914, Malenbaum, *The World Wheat Economy*, pp. 238–239; col. 2, ibid., pp. 236–237; col. 3, 1840, Mulhall, *The Dictionary of Statistics*, p. 495; 1850–1910, Jacob Metzer, "Railroad Development and Market Integration: The Case of Tsarist Russia," *Journal of Economic History*, vol. 34, no. 3 (September 1974), p. 536; col. 4, B. R. Mitchell, *European Historical Statistics*, pp. 338, 340, and 342.

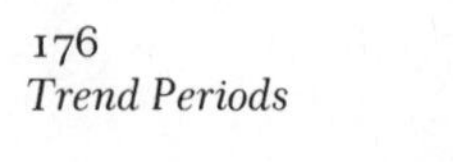

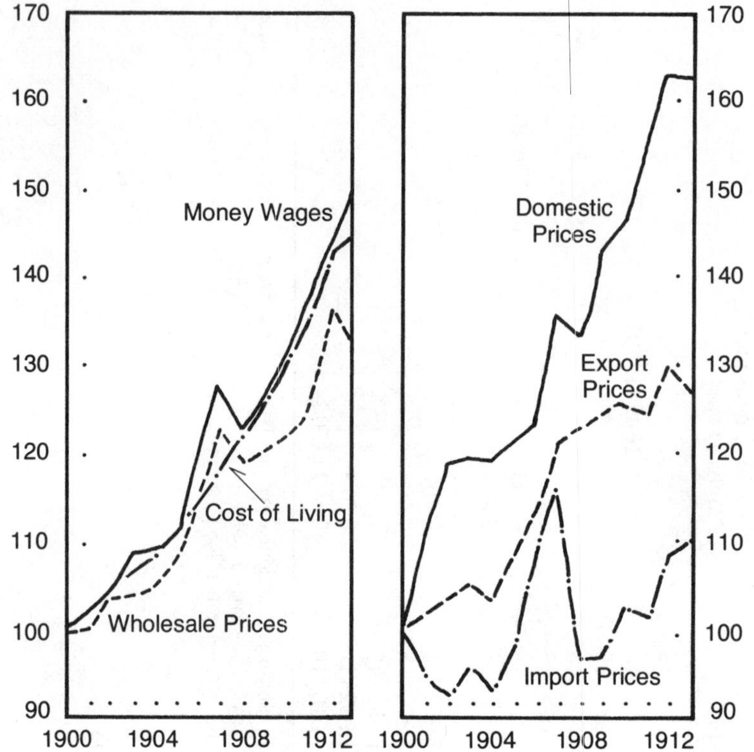

CHART III-28. *Canada:* Left, *Wages and Prices, 1900–1913;* Right, *Import, Export, and Domestic Prices, 1900–1913*

Source: A. K. Cairncross, "Investment in Canada, 1900–1913," p. 157.

urbanization. In Australia, Argentina, and Canada there were large flows of immigrants to absorb and house, as well as those moving internally to new areas. They had to be grubstaked: they required food, shelter, and clothing over the period when they were transferring their residences and finding productive employment. In varying degrees these booms, rooted in agriculture, stimulated the expansion of industry as well as cities, housing, and infrastructure.

Thus, there was a double effect. First, there was the underlying

TABLE III-27. *Raw-Material Prices: United Kingdom, 1870–1913 (1900 = 100)*

	Coal	Copper (Ore and Regulus)	Crude Zi
Peak: early 1870's	124 (1873)	103 (1872)	113 (1873)
Trough: 1890's	53 (1896)	56 (1894)	72 (1895)
1913	84	92	115

Source: William Page (ed.), *Commerce and Industry: Statistical Tables* (Lond

global supply-demand balance that caused the price turn-around in 1896 and thereafter; then there was the inflationary expansion in the new countries. The high export prices in those countries and the capital imports available permitted inflationary expansion and high levels of imports to proceed, without discipline from the balance of payments. The upshot was a relative increase in prices and wages in the new country, a tendency to draw labor away from as well as toward the export industries, and a kind of second shift in terms of trade against the capital-exporting nation. The breadth of these booms slowed the expansion of export products below the level they might otherwise have attained. A. K. Cairncross's price and wage data on Canada from 1900 to 1913 in Chart III-28 catch well what was involved.[80] Roland Wilson arrived at a similar conclusion about the relative movement of domestic and import prices in his study of Australia.[81] In this sense, we are during the pre-1914 generation back in the world of the 1830's and 1850's.[82]

A phase of capital exports and of unfavorable terms of trade for food-importing nations was a kind of tax that had to be paid by the world economy as a whole for maintaining a balance between the demand for and the supply of grain. The incidence of that tax, however, did not fall evenly. The expanding food-producing areas gained; the food importers as a whole enjoyed the long-run benefits of the expansion in food supplies; but Britain, the major capital exporter, paid a significant short-run price for which its rapid increase in exports was an inadequate compensation.[83]

It is, evidently, impossible here to trace out in the detail devoted to wheat the course of events between the 1870's and 1914 for all the major commodities. But, as Table III-27 makes clear, the irregular downward sweep from the early 1870's to a trough in the 1890's and the lift to a higher range in the pre-1914 generation suffused a good many raw-material prices. The wheat price is included for purposes of comparison. The fact that these prices are indexes in which 1900 equals 100 suggests the strength of the price lift of the late 1890's and the considerable range of subsequent individual price movements. A central fact is, of course, that in all cases they remained above the minima of the mid-1890's.

The effect of the lift in raw-material prices was exacerbated by

ock Tin	Lead	Cotton	Imported Wool	Wood and Timber	Imported Wheat
05	144	163	161	180	191
872)	(1873)	(1872)	(1875)	(1874)	(1873)
45	55	69	84	88	79
896)	(1894)	(1898)	(1897)	(1895)	(1894)
54	107	140	108	96	122

nstable, 1919), pp. 218, 222.

the evolution of the leading sectors in the most advanced economies. Chart III-29 shows the rise and fall of the railroad as a leading sector in American economic growth. It measures the number of miles of line added annually. The peak was reached in the 1880's, when feeder lines and double-tracking rounded out the transcontinental net whose basic structure had been earlier established. The peak increment had come as early as the 1840's in Britain, the 1860's in Belgium, and the 1870's in Germany. The French network was laid out at a more even rate with the decadal increments at a similar level from 1850 to 1890 (see Table III-21 above). From the 1870's onward, steel progressively took over the role of iron in railroads and in much else; e.g., ships, construction, machine tools. Charts III-30 and III-31 catch the scale and the power of the cost-reducing technological revolution in steelmaking in the United States. Typical of a leading sector incorporating a new technology (as well as newly exploited raw-material sources) steel's expansion decelerated; and, as early as the 1890's, cost reduction ceased, as measured by the price of steel rails.

Chart III-32 shows the evolution of steel production in Europe of four major producers. At the center of the story is the rise of Germany with the famous crossing of the British curve in 1893.[84] The critical invention (1879) was the Thomas-Gilchrist (basic) process which made possible the efficient exploitation of the abundant phosphoric iron ore on the Continent, notably in Lorraine and in Sweden.

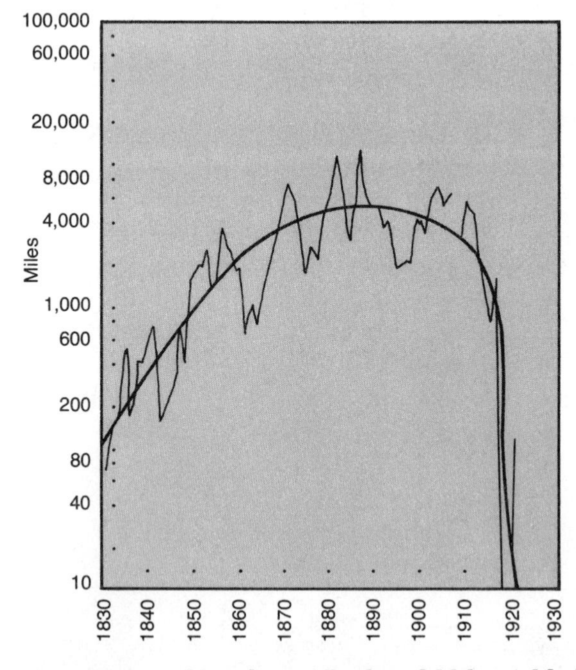

CHART III-29. *Number of Railroad Miles Added Annually, United States, 1831–1922: Original Data and Primary Trend Line*

Source: Simon S. Kuznets, *Secular Movements in Production and Prices* (Boston and New York: Houghton Mifflin Company, 1930), p. 191.

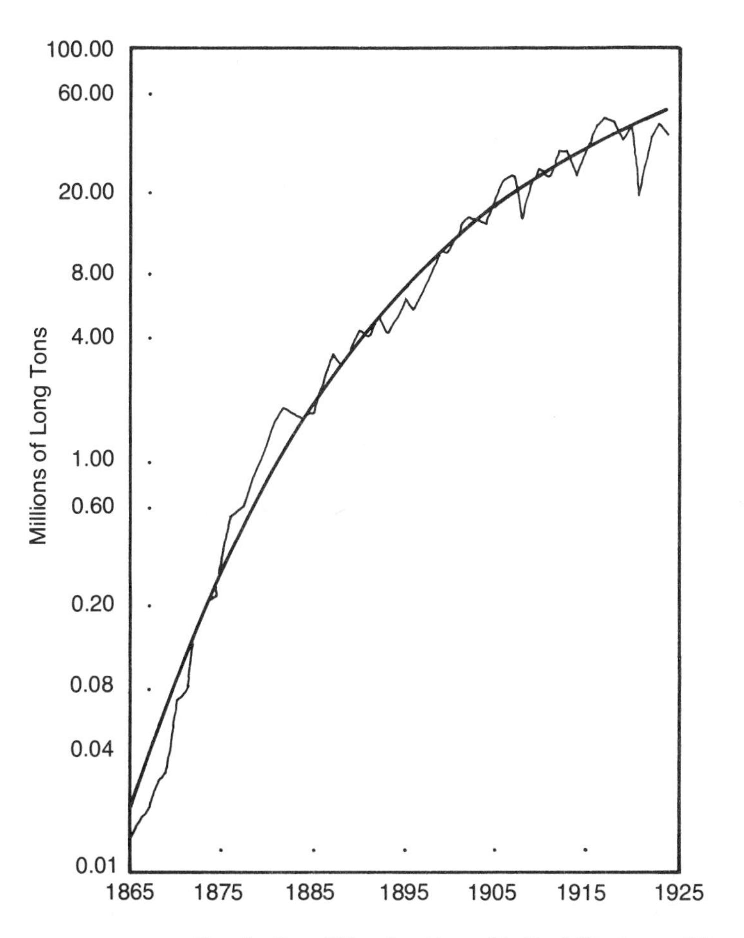

CHART III-30. *Crude Steel Production, United States, 1865–1924: Original Data and Primary Trend Line*

Source: Kuznets, *Secular Movements in Production and Prices*, p. 97.

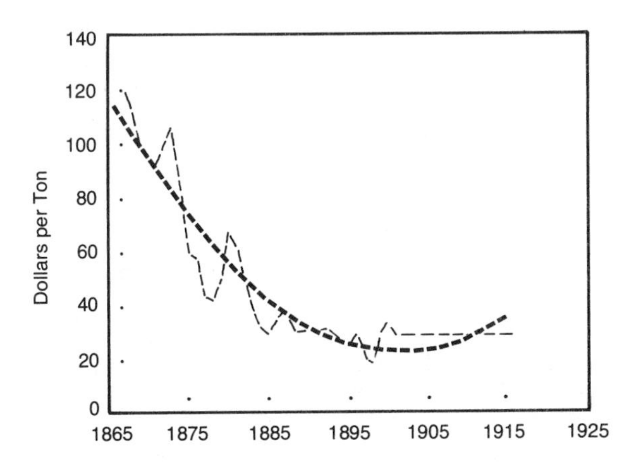

CHART III-31. *Price of Steel Rails, United States, 1867–1915: Original Data and Primary Trend Line*

Source: Kuznets, *Secular Movements in Production and Prices*, p. 98.

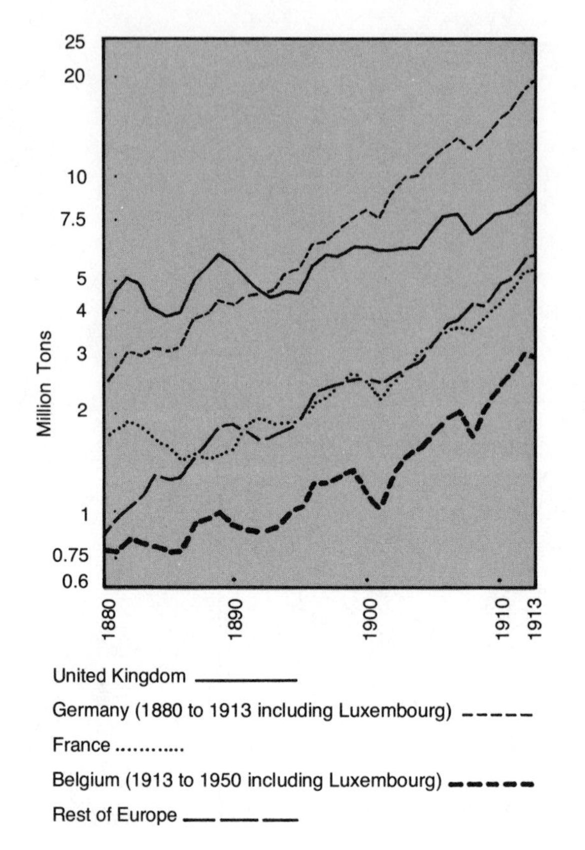

CHART III-32. *Production of Steel Ingots and Castings in European Countries, 1880–1913*

Source: Ingvar Svennilson, *Growth and Stagnation in the European Economy*, p. 122.

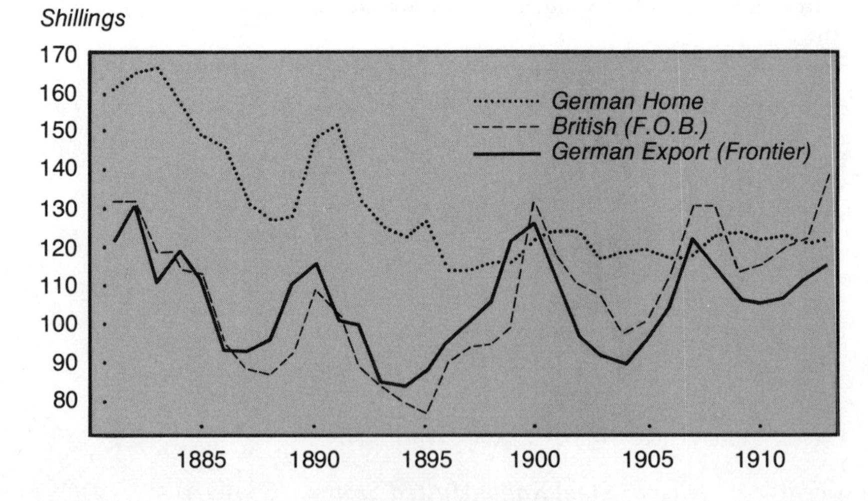

CHART III-33. *Rail Prices (Shillings), 1881–1913*

Source: D. L. Burn, *The Economic History of Steelmaking*, end paper.

The German industry seized on its possibilities promptly and with great vigor. Britain stayed with its hematite ores, including imports from Spain, reduced by Bessemer and Siemens-Martin (acid) processes. The net result was the emergence of larger units of higher productivity in Germany and, before 1914, the surpassing of British by German as well as U.S. steel exports. Economic historians still debate indecisively the extent to which the outcome was decreed by technology, resources, the scale and momentum of the domestic market, as opposed to less vigorous and imaginative British entrepreneurship and industrial organization. Although steel production decelerated in Germany between the mid-1890's and the eve of the First World War, it maintained a pace which more than doubled output each decade as it succeeded wrought iron and pioneered new usages in many directions.[85] But, as in the United States, the secular decline in steel prices ceased after the mid-1890's (Chart III-33); that is, the price lift of the late 1890's was succeeded by cyclical fluctuations in a higher range down to 1914.[86] While expanding impressively in scale, the steel industry, speaking generally, ceased after the mid-1890's to impart to the advanced economies of the North Atlantic the revolutionary cost reduction of the previous generation.

The pre-war years were, nevertheless, a period of technological innovation; but innovation did not proceed at a pace capable of overcoming the wastages of war and arms outlays and the slowing down in the technological momentum of the older leading sectors. These factors yield the deceleration of national income per occupied person in the United States, United Kingdom, and Germany, caught, for example, in Chart III-34 and Table III-28.[87] Along with the rise

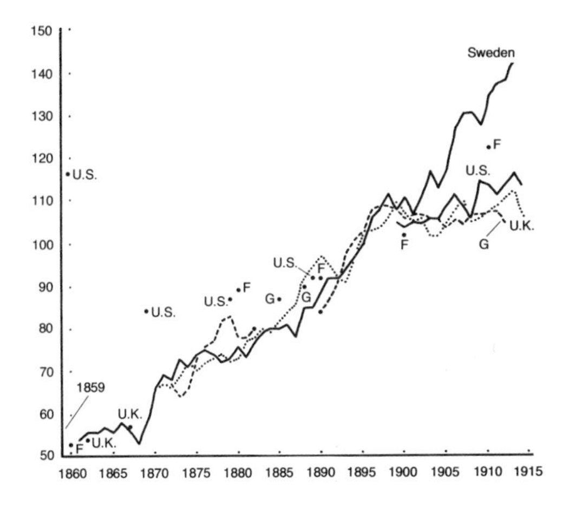

CHART III-34. *National Income (in Product Units) per Occupied Person: Five Countries, 1860 to 1913–1914 (1890–1899=100)*

F: France.
G: Germany.
Source: E. H. Phelps Brown, with Sheila V. Hopkins, "The Course of Wage-Rates in Five Countries, 1860–1939," p. 291.

in food costs this deceleration is also the cause of the deceleration or decline in real wage rates over this period (Table III-28 and Chart III-35) long noted in the United States, Britain, and Germany, with France a somewhat special case.[88]

The fact that Phelps Brown and Hopkins include the case of Sweden is useful in the present context. Sweden was at an earlier stage of growth than the other four countries charted. It had moved in the 1890's from take-off into a more diversified stage of growth, and was, over the years down to 1914, absorbing rapidly more sophisticated technology, notably in the pulp and paper and engineering sectors.[89] The fact that its national income per occupied person and real wage rate moved in a quite different way than that of the older industrial states is prima-facie confirmation of the role of the leading sector transition in the latter case. Something of the same is true of Japan.[90]

The role of the leading sector transition is further reinforced if one looks more closely at the four older industrial economies.

France, aided by the emergence of electric power, experienced a sharp acceleration of growth from about the mid-1890's to 1914, a surge notable in the final years of the period. This surge was rooted in what Jan Marczewski and François Crouzet designate as the

TABLE III-28. *Real Wages[a] and National Income per Capita,[b] 1890–1913: France, German United Kingdom, United States, and Sweden (1890–1899 = 100)*

	France				Germany	
	Real Wage	Average Annual Rate of Change (%)	National Income per Capita	Average Annual Rate of Change[c] (%)	Real Wage	Average Ann Rate of Change (%)
1870	75	—	89 (1880)	—	77	—
1890	96	1.24	92	0.33	97	1.16
1900	108	1.18	102	1.04	109	1.17
1910	114	0.54	123	1.89	107	0.19
1913	106	−2.40	—	—	110	0.93

	United States				Sweden	
	Real Wage	Average Annual Rate of Change (%)	National Income per Capita	Average Annual Rate of Change (%)	Real Wage	Average Ann Rate of Change (%)
1870	83	—	84 (1869)	—	59	—
1890	96	0.73	92 (1889)	0.46	88	2.02
1900	102	0.61	104	1.12	113	2.53
1910	108	0.57	114	0.92	140	2.17
1913	110	0.61	117	0.87	143	0.71

[a] Wage rate in consumption units.

[b] National income per occupied person in product units.

[c] The calculations of Lhomme, "Le Pouvoir d'achat de l'ouvrier français au cours d'un siècle: 1840–1940," 46, yield the following annual average rates of change for real wages in France: 1870–1890, 1.02 percent; 189 1900, 1.4 percent; 1900–1910, 0.77 percent; 1910–1913, −1.89 percent.

"new" industries.[91] On Crouzet's definition, this group rose in weight from 4.1 percent to 11.0 percent of industrial production between 1885–1894 and 1905–1913. The category includes rubber, gas, electricity, cement, and automobiles. France also moved briskly into aluminum production.

Next to France, the waning of the older sectors was best compensated for in the United States. The overall retardation in U.S. industrial growth after 1900 has been documented in detail since Arthur Burns' study of production trends.[92] The emergence of the new sectors is well delineated in Solomon Fabricant's study of U.S. manufacturing industries, which examines the subsectors in sufficient detail to derive some sense, at least, of the major changes wrought by new technology.[93]

The new sectors of high momentum for the United States in the period 1899–1914 were the automobile sectoral complex (embracing automobiles, petroleum, rubber products, etc.); canned foods and ice; cigarettes; chemicals (including, notably, fertilizers, paints, and varnishes); phonographs; and electrical machinery. Net production of electricity in central stations rose from 6 to 25 billion kilowatt-hours between 1902 and 1912. In 1899, nonelectric prime movers generated 9.8 million horsepower; in 1919, 20.0. Compara-

		United Kingdom			
tional Income r Capita	Average Annual Rate of Change[d] (%)	Real Wage	Average Annual Rate of Change (%)	National Income per Capita	Average Annual Rate of Change (%)
7 (1872)	—	61	—	66	—
4	1.26	97	2.35	97	1.94
5	2.35	103	0.60	107	0.99
3	0.19	97	−0.60	108	0.09
5 (1912)	−1.40	97	—	113	1.52

tional Income Capita	Average Annual Rate of Change (%)
3	—
3	2.11
1	2.35
5	1.98
3	1.94

The calculations of Gerhard Bry, assisted by Charlotte Boschan, *Wages in Germany, 1871–1945* (Princeton: nceton University Press, 1960), p. 71, yield the following annual average rates of change for gross real weekly nings in Germany: 1871–1890, 0.86 percent; 1890–1900, 1.20 percent; 1900–1913, 0.16 percent.
ource: Phelps Brown, with Hopkins, "The Course of Wage-Rates in Five Countries, 1860–1939," pp. 3–277.

ble figures for electric motors are 0.5 and 16.3.[94] The scale of the rise in the automobile sectoral complex is suggested by the fact that the percentage of value added by the automobile, petroleum, and rubber industries rose from 0.99 percent of total value added in manufactures in 1899 to 2.63 percent in 1909, to 8.6 percent in 1919, a significant underestimate since the impact of the automobile on steel, glass, battery, and other component production is not included.[95] The great surge came, of course, relatively late in the period with the emergence of Ford's mass-produced Model T, but growth accelerated from as early as 1904.

The overall deceleration in the first decade of the twentieth century of German industrial production (as well as in income per capita) emerges in both R. Wagenführ's and Walther G. Hoffmann's indexes.[96] In terms of broad industrial classification, the metals and metalworking sectors, chemicals, paper and printing, gas and electricity helped counter deceleration elsewhere.[97] As in the United States, steel production maintained a high momentum. In chemicals, the continued rapid expansion of sulphuric acid and rubber, joined by oil refining and coal derivatives, countered the slower growth in the soda and soap subsectors.[98] The rise of the German electrical manufacturing industry in the pre-1914 years (as well as the rapid exploitation of electric power) is, of course, a well-known story in economic history.[99] Between 1900 and 1913 Hoffmann's index of German electricity production rises from 12 to 100.[100] Only

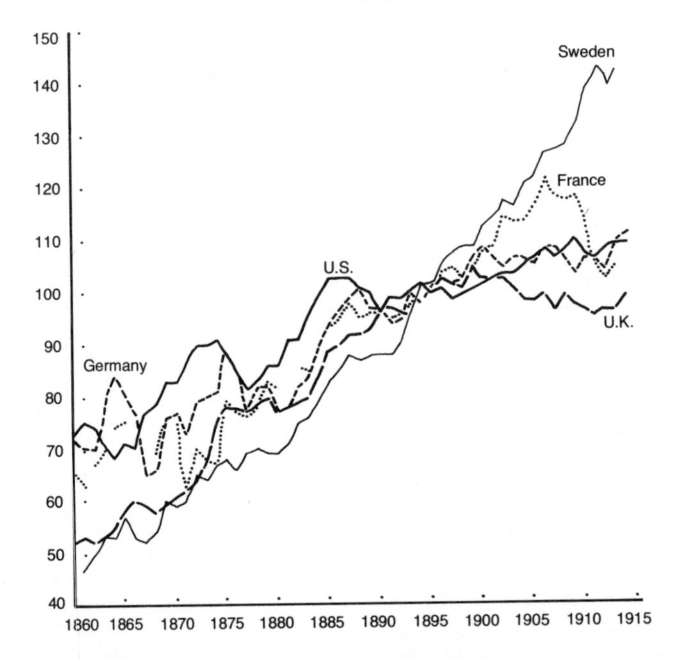

CHART III-35. *Wage Rate in Consumption Units: Five Countries, 1860 to 1913–1914 (1890–1899=100)*

Source: Phelps Brown, with Hopkins, "The Course of Wage-Rates in Five Countries," p. 287.

the fledgling automobile industry exhibits a more rapid rate of growth: from 2.5 in 1901 to 100 in 1913.[101]

Examining the deceleration of British industry and real income per capita in the period 1900–1914, E. H. Phelps Brown and S. J. Handfield-Jones conclude in terms consonant with the perspective here taken on the United States and Germany: ". . . the previous rise had been carried forward by the massive application of Steam and Steel, which now had not much scope for extension; while the new techniques, especially of electricity, the internal combustion engine, and the new chemical processes, did not attain massive application until during and after the First World War."[102] In general, the British absorption of the new technologies, including new methods of aluminum production, was not unimpressive, although Britain fell behind Germany and the United States in industrial chemistry and electrical equipment manufacture.[103] But its industrial pattern of these years was marked by two more basic characteristics as compared with its European competitors: first, a greater deceleration in the older industries, symbolized by the story of steel, referred to above (see pp. 178–181), second, the extraordinary rise of capital exports after the London capital market had worked off the burden of the Boer War and the consequently damped level of domestic investment.

As we have already noted (see above, pp. 171–172), 1896 is the hinge on which modern Canadian economic history turns. By all accounts and measurements, it was from 1896 to the eve of the First World War that Canadian economic growth accelerated, accompanied by expanded net immigration, a tripling in the rate of population increase, an extraordinary rise in capital imports, and greatly enlarged industrial as well as agricultural production. The period from 1867, when the Canadian confederation was formed, down to 1896 is generally viewed as a period of disappointment at best, stagnation at worst: agricultural prices were falling; the pull of growth in the United States outweighed the flow of immigration to Canada; the value of exports increased slowly; capital imports were modest, by later standards. But Penelope Hartland is right in protesting against the view that this was a wholly stagnant or sterile period in Canadian development.[104] The proportion of total investment in durable physical assets to gross national expenditure was high for a preindustrial society, averaging about 13 percent.[105] Capital imports contributed 30 percent to gross investment in 1870, 25 percent in 1900, before the great surge in capital imports began.[106] Industrial production expanded at something like 3.5 percent per annum, a rate doubled during the subsequent take-off period, but still substantial. Above all, the nation's basic railroad net was built. There were 2,213 miles of track in Canada at the time of confederation. The expansion of the early 1870's lifted the figure over 5,000. When British Columbia entered the confederation in 1871, pressure grew for a transcontinental line, which was set in motion two years later. The passage of the first train from Montreal to Vancouver in 1886 ranks with the driving of the gold spike in Utah in 1869. By 1895, 16,000 miles of track had been laid down. Over the next twenty years an additional 19,000 miles were added; but it was from a rather solid base of preparation that the prairie wheat lands were opened and the great pre-1914 Canadian boom occurred. In the most literal sense, Canada created the preconditions for take-off between 1867 and 1896.

As Chart III-36 shows, Canadian immigration, capital imports, and urban building moved cyclically and, more or less, together. But there were a few significant deviations from simple conformity:

—Down to the mid-1890's there was some tendency for housing to lead, capital imports to lag in cyclical turning points, with immigration fluctuating quite sensitively with business cycles, which were, in turn, closely tied to those in the United States.

—The urban housing boom of the late 1880's was not accom-

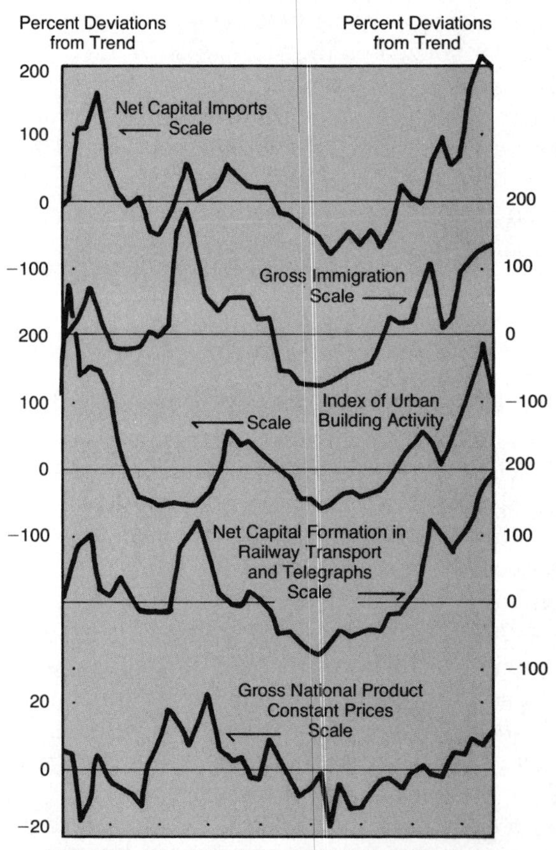

CHART III-36. *Canada: Cycles in Capital Imports, Immigration, Urban Building, Transport, and Gross National Product, 1870–1913*

Source: Arthur I. Bloomfield, *Patterns of Fluctuation in International Investment before 1914*, Princeton Studies in International Finance, no. 21 (Princeton, 1968), p. 25.

panied by a strong increase in net immigration or population. It was primarily a result of inner migration connected with prior railway extension and current agricultural depression.[107]

—The protracted expansion after 1896 in net immigration and housing (and the generally accelerated momentum of the Canadian economy) came much earlier than the great surge in capital imports, which got seriously under way in 1903 in the wake of the Boer War.

Although measurements via deviation from trend are unsatisfactory for many purposes, Arthur I. Bloomfield's portrait of Canada over these years catches well the elements of cyclical conformity and variation among these variables.[108]

Argentina's equivalent of confederation was the emergence of a central government capable of putting down the Indians and opening the pampas for cultivation. That objective was accomplished by 1881. Like Canada, Argentina experienced its first surge of immigration and capital imports in the period of falling price trend for agricultural products. The great boom of the late 1880's was followed by a protracted period of relatively low flows of human and capital resources from abroad. There was some mild revival from the worst days after the Baring Crisis of 1890 in the second half of the decade; but it was less marked than in the case of Canada. Immigration began to move up persuasively starting in 1904, capital imports in 1905. Like the parallel boom in Canada, the expansion in Argentina in the pre-war decade was well sustained, subject only to brief and relatively mild setbacks.

There is a certain independent perversity in the pattern of Australian economic development during these two trend periods. It tended at times to draw capital and immigrants when the attractions of the United States, Canada, and Argentina were relatively weak;[109] and a good deal of its transport and urban infrastructure was built in response to domestic needs and objectives rather than to support export expansion or in response to such expansion.[110] As Brinley Thomas notes: "Between 1863 and 1881 the flows to Australasia[111] and Canada are inverse to each other . . . Towards the end of the period a strong recovery in emigration to Australasia occurred in 1906, four years later than the beginning of the boom in Canadian immigration."[112] In between, there was the strong surge of capital imports,[113] immigration, and construction, running from the mid-1870's to the late 1880's, well caught in Bloomfield's smoothed cyclical curves (Chart III-37).

The much studied U.S. data on capital imports, railroadization, immigration, and housing construction can be briskly summarized.[114] First, there was a massive boom after the Civil War in railroad construction, accompanied by large inflows of capital and immigrants and by an extraordinary expansion in housing construction. The peaks in railroad mileage added and housing construction came in 1871, capital imports in 1872, immigration in 1873.

The severe depression that followed gave way to some increase in railway mileage in 1876, but the second major boom did not start until 1879, reaching a peak in 1882. At the trough in 1878–1879 the United States was a net capital exporter, paying out more on past borrowing than it was receiving from abroad; but it moved over again to a significant and sustained capital importing position by 1882. Immigration rose sharply again from a trough in 1878 to a peak in 1882. The trough in building came in 1878; but it continued to expand beyond the general cyclical peak in 1882 to a peak in 1890, with only a minor setback in 1888.

In 1882, railway mileage added was 57 percent above the previous peak; capital imports, only 42 percent of the previous peak; immigration, 72 percent above the previous peak. Clearly, these variables, although linked in subtle ways, were not rigorously related.

From a trough in 1885, railways moved on to their all-time peak in mileage added in 1887. A trough in capital imports came also in 1885, a peak in 1888, briefly above the 1872 level. Immigration, from a trough in 1886, moved up to a peak in 1888, fell away briefly, and moved on to a second peak in 1892, conforming to the general cyclical movement of the American economy. As noted earlier, housing construction peaked in 1890, but remained at a high level until 1892.

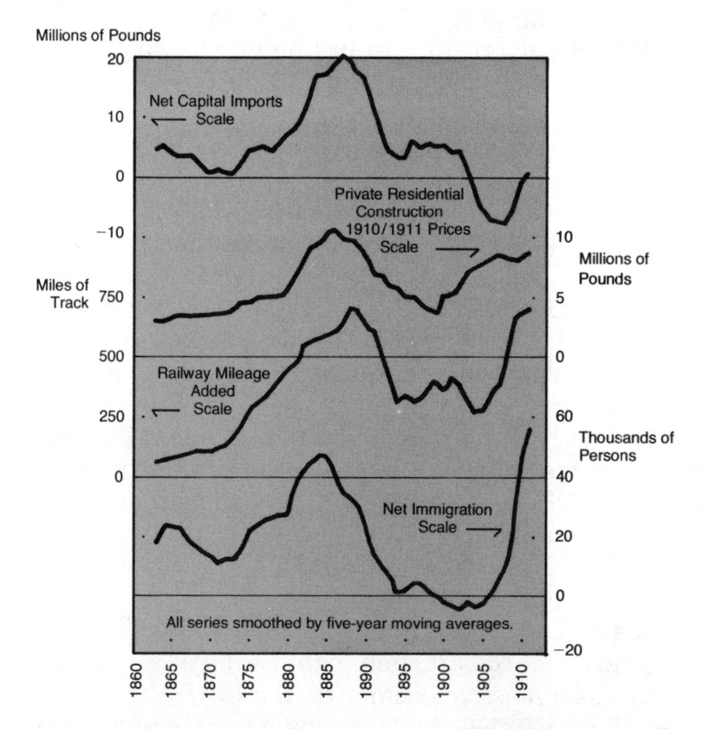

CHART III-37. *Australia: Cycles in Capital Imports, Residential Construction, Railway Mileage, and Immigration, 1860–1913*

Source: Bloomfield, *Patterns of Fluctuation in International Investment before 1914*, p. 28.

The 1887 peak in railway mileage was 11 percent above that in 1882; capital imports in 1888 were 160 percent above 1882; the immigration peak in 1892 was only 73 percent of the 1882 level.

In the depression (and structural watershed) of the 1890's, railroads fell away to a trough in 1895 lower (with the exception of one year) than any since the Civil War. There was a subsequent recovery to 1904 when, at the peak, mileage added was only slightly more than half that of 1887. That level was never again exceeded, as the automobile age began. Capital imports gave way in the 1890's to a protracted phase of net capital exports (1897–1905). Between 1906 and 1913, the massive industrial economy of the United States was again, on balance, a modest net capital importer, averaging $2.15 million per annum. Immigration, on the other hand, moved from a trough in 1898 to an unexampled peak in 1907: from a quarter million to a million and a quarter. The figure fell away but averaged over 900,000 each year for the period 1908–1913. The housing index, after fluctuating erratically far below the 1892 peak until 1903, responded to the consequences of this wave of immigration, with peaks in 1906, 1909, and 1912.

In general, then (and as one can observe elsewhere), the effects of massive immigration on population and family formation were systematically, if roughly, reflected in American housing construction over this period. On the other hand, the link between railroadization and immigration changed in character over this span, as did the role of capital imports in the American economy. Capital imports and railroadization were connected; but the relative role of capital imports diminished from the 1880's on, as one would expect in an economy moving on after the Civil War to technological maturity.

It is important to examine the movement of these variables by cycles over these two quite different trend periods to break up the image generated by the Kuznets effort to treat railroads as "population-sensitive," to lump them in with residential housing construction, and to relate them, thus grouped, to population fluctuations induced by immigration.[115] The American economy in the boom of the early 1870's and, indeed, down to 1890 partook of many of the characteristics of a country being newly opened for agricultural exploitation, like Canada, Argentina, and Australia, although even during that period there was a growing pull to industry as well as to the West. After the watershed of the 1890's, however, with the frontier gone, the pull was to American industrial centers—more like the pull of Western Europe on immigrants from Southern Europe in the 1950's and 1960's. We lose much more than we gain in confusing these phases in pursuit of an illusory long cycle.

The character of the structural change in the American economy is well captured in the Gallman and Howle decadal estimates in Table III-29.[116] They show how current price and real output trends moved in different directions in the early years of the twentieth century, with the relative role of industry accelerating in real terms

TABLE III-29. *Shares of Agriculture and Industry in Value Added: United States, 1879–1919*

	Current Prices		Constant Prices	
	Agriculture (%)	Industry (%)	Agriculture (%)	Industry (%)
1879	53	47	53	47
1889	39	61	41	59
1899	37	63	35	65
1909	38	62	26	74

Source: Robert E. Gallman and Edward S. Howle, "Trends in the Structure of the American Economy since 1840," p. 26.

as compared to the 1890's. Between 1900 and 1910 the labor force in agriculture increased by less than 1 percent; in nonagricultural tasks, by 48 percent.[117] It was primarily the higher pace of industrial expansion, and all associated with it, which drew the immigrants in the great pre-1914 influx, although there was something of a push from Russia and parts of Eastern Europe.

As the principal capital exporter of this period, Britain was a major actor in the drama of developing the various new areas brought within the world economy; and its pattern of domestic investment also responded to the process. As Table III-30 indicates, there were three clearly marked cycles in net capital exports, peaking in the early 1870's, at 1890, and on the eve of the First World War; and domestic fixed capital formation tended to move inversely with these cycles.

In the wake of the crisis of 1873, there was a boom in housing and other forms of domestic capital formation which waned only in 1876. The expansion of 1879–1883 was supported preponderantly by domestic investment; but, as Canada, Australia, Argentina, and other borrowers drew increasingly on London in the second half of the 1880's, the relative proportion of domestic investment fell away. From 1890 to 1903, however, domestic investment once again dominated, to decline again in the pre-war decade.

Investment in home building represented normally about 15–20 percent of gross domestic fixed capital formation, occasionally moving above or below that range. There were two clearly marked housing cycles in this period, peaking in 1876 and 1900, following broadly the path of domestic investment in general. British housing construction, as it had been over the two previous centuries, was sensitive to interest rates; but the decline in emigration during the 1890's and increase in family formation supported the boom of that decade.[118]

The total proportion of British resources invested over this period ranged roughly between 10 percent and 13 percent. The peak averages in Table III-30 come clearly in the three major periods of capital exports: 1870–1873, 1887–1890, and 1904–1913.[119]

These shifts in the proportion of British income invested almost certainly reflect changes in income distribution, while changes in the composition of investment helped reinforce income distribution shifts.

Modern studies of changes in British income distribution between 1870 and 1914 confirm the views of contemporaries and earlier analysts; i.e., there was, in the first trend period down to the end of the century, a net shift favorable to labor, unfavorable to profits; and there was a cessation of these trends down to 1913.[120] C. H. Feinstein's calculations for years averaged in about the same expansion phase of the business cycle emerge in Table III-31.

The sharp shift of income distribution against property (in favor of labor) during the first trend period must have operated to reduce, to some extent, the nation's rate of savings. The subsequent cessation of that shift and, especially, the rise in incomes derived from capital held abroad help account for Britain's capacity to mount, in the decade after the Boer War, a vast expansion in capital exports and an increase in the overall rate of investment. This capacity was probably supported by a sharp institutional shift in the proportion of profits of companies, as opposed to profits derived from self-employment. In 1889 (the first year for which data can be separated) company profits were 30 percent of the total; in 1913, 47 percent. One would expect a higher rate of plowback of profits in companies.

In addition, as noted earlier, the accelerated expansions in the new food-producing areas, fueled in part by Britain's capital exports, helped heighten the unfavorable shift in the terms of trade against Britain, pressing down particularly on the real wages of labor.

In general, then, it would appear that the forces at work from the early 1870's to the late 1890's by and large shifted income toward those with a high propensity to consume, a low propensity to save. In the pre-war generation these forces, notably the pressure on urban real wages, operated in the other direction.

It is against the background of the changing situation with respect to the supply of foodstuffs and raw materials and the transition from one group of leading sectors to another that one should view the migrations of this period and the patterns of investment, domestic and international.

The upshot can be stated quite simply:

—The new territories opened up for agricultural production in Canada, Argentina, and Australia drew, at different times, related to cyclical fluctuations, large flows of immigrants and capital.

—These set in motion expansions in housing and urban infrastructure as well as in agricultural output; altered the demographic structure of the societies; and, in the cases of Canada and Australia, helped launch the first stage of rapid industrial growth.

—The American case was more complex, involving also large cyclical immigration flows; but these were related both to the attrac-

TABLE III-30. *Foreign and Home Investment: United Kingdom, 1870–1913 (Annual Averages of Indicated Proportions, in £ Millions at Current Prices)*

	Net Investment Abroad / Gross National Product	Gross Domestic Fixed Capital Formation / Gross National Product	Total Capital Formation (Excluding Stocks) / Gross National Product
1870–1873	6.2%	6.5%	12.7%
1874–1876	4.0	8.4	12.4
1877–1879	1.6	8.2	9.8
1880–1883	3.6	6.9	10.5
1884–1886	5.1	5.9	11.0
1887–1890	6.2	5.3	11.4
1891–1894	3.8	6.1	9.9
1895–1899	2.5	7.7	10.2
1900–1903	1.4	9.4	10.8
1904–1908	5.1	7.4	12.5
1909–1913	7.6	5.6	13.2

Source: C. H. Feinstein, *National Income, Expenditure and Output of the United Kingdom, 1855–1965* (Cambridge: At the University Press, 1972), pp. T37–38 and T85–86.

TABLE III-31. *Income Distribution as a Proportion of GNP: United Kingdom, 1870–1913 (Average Annual Percentages)*

	(1) Income from Employment	(2) Gross Trading Profits of Companies	(3) Rent	(4) Net Property Income from Abroad	(5) Total of Columns (2), (3), (4)
1870–1873	46.1	37.6	12.4	3.9	53.9
1896–1899	50.4	30.6	12.4	6.2	49.2
1910–1913	49.4	29.5	11.1	8.4	49.0

Source: Feinstein, *National Income, Expenditure and Output*, pp. T4 and T5.

Note: Columns (1) plus (5) do not add up to 100 percent for 1896–1899 and 1910–1913 because the small but growing item (after 1889) for the "gross trading surplus of public enterprises" is not included in this breakdown.

tions of an expanding agriculture and to the high industrial momentum of the American economy, the latter factor increasing in relative importance, notably after the 1890's. As in the other cases, cycles in housing and urban infrastructure can be related to this process, as well as changes in demographic and social structure.

—The British economy, as the major supplier of international capital, played a central role in this sequence, the focus of its capital exports both fluctuating with the cycles and shifting in direction over this period. As one would expect, domestic investment (including housing and urban infrastructure) was relatively strong when the impulses to invest abroad were weakest and vice versa.

—Some demographic consequences can be detected, as a result of emigration, in Britain and in other nations which experienced an outflow of population to Canada, Australia, Argentina, and the United States.

How did the military outlays in the pre-1914 generation affect the outcome? In one case, the evidence is clear-cut; that is, the effects of the Boer War on the London capital market. Starting in October 1899, government wartime flotations of securities, combined with the psychological effects of war itself, drove interest rates up, reduced other forms of investment, and foreshortened the business expansion, which turned down in 1900. Increased taxes pressed in the same direction.

Both domestic and foreign investment declined. Although the war finally ended on May 31, 1902, it was not until well into 1904 that recovery began. A week-by-week reading of the London *Economist* makes clear that a significant part of the nation's savings had been diverted. Sir Robert Giffen estimated at the time that, over its three-year span, the war had dissipated a third of Britain's "surplus income."[121] A similar result emerges from a comparison of the increase in British military expenditures with modern capital-formation estimates. In the period 1895–1899 average annual British military expenditures were £39.7 million; for 1900–1903, £104.6 million; the difference is 33.8 percent of gross fixed domestic capital formation for 1900–1903, 3.7 percent of net national income.[122]

The Spanish-American War was a lesser strain on U.S. resources. American military outlays averaged $81 million in 1895–1897, $222 million in 1898–1899. The difference was about 3.6 percent of gross annual capital formation for the period, 0.8 percent of GNP.[123] In addition, of course, there was a significant expansion of military expenditures in Europe in the pre-war decade. German military expenditures rose from 979 million DM in 1903 to 1,909 million DM in 1913,[124] when they constituted almost 4 percent of GNP;[125] British naval expenditures rose from about £31 million in 1907 to over £44 million in 1913, when total military expenditures were about 3 percent of net national income. In both cases, the increase since the 1890's was about 0.5 percent of national product or income.

TABLE III-32. *Steel and Coal Production: United Kingdom, 1913–1921 (Million Tons)*

	Steel	Coal
1913	7.7	287
1914	7.8	266
1915	8.6	253
1916	9.0	256
1917	9.7	249
1918	9.5	228
1919	7.9	230
1920	9.1	230
1921	3.7	163[a]

[a] Affected by major strikes.
Source: B. R. Mitchell, *European Historical Statistics*, p. 137 (steel) and p. 116 (coal).

By the terrible standards of the times to come, these are small orders of magnitude; but, in terms of their effects on economies already feeling the consequences of a deceleration in leading sectors and increased relative prices of foodstuffs and raw materials, they represent not insignificant additional marginal pressures.

The First World War, in narrowly economic terms, was a kind of distorted completion of the trend period which began in the second half of the 1890's and the prelude to that which began in 1920 and ended in the years immediately preceding the Second World War. Its impact can be summarized in terms of the three concepts used throughout Part Three: the balance between the demand for and supply of food and raw materials; the movement of the leading sectors and the effective absorption of new technology; changes in population and migration and their impact on housing and urban infrastructure.

Like the French and Napoleonic Wars a century earlier, the First World War violated the pre-war pattern of international trade in

TABLE III-33. *Steel Ingot Production: The World and Major Regions, 1913–1925 (Million Tons)*

	Total	U.S.	Rest	Northwest Europe of which:			
				Total	Germany	Saar	Luxembou
1913	75	31	44	25	17.31		1.3
1917	81	45	36	19	15.3		1.1
1920	71	42	29	14	8.4	0.7	0.6
1921	44	20	24	14	8.9	0.9	0.7
1925	89	45	44	25	12.0	1.6	2.1
1929	118	56	62	34	16.0	2.2	2.7
1931	68	26	42	23	8.2	1.5	2.0

[a] To make the figures in these columns comparable throughout, the Russian figur
1913 has been reduced by 0.5 to allow for subsequent creation of Poland, while 1.0

agricultural products, damping production in some areas, stimulating it elsewhere, in an environment of rising prices. As Table III-24 shows, there were in the period 1914–1919 major expansions in wheat production in Australia, Canada, and the United States; there was also a substantial increase in production (without much acreage expansion) in Argentina. Together these four countries increased output by 18 percent compared to the period 1909–1914. On the other hand, output in Russia and Eastern Europe fell by 16 percent, in Western and Southern Europe by 18 percent, despite increases in Britain, Denmark, Finland, Greece, Norway, Spain, Sweden, and Switzerland. There were some increases in parts of Asia and Africa not affected by the war, as well as in Latin America, apart from Argentina. The price of wheat increased by about two and a half times between 1914 and 1920, when some revival in European production and a normalization of world trade, combined with the artificially expanded flow from overseas induced by the war, caused a price collapse similar to that which followed the end of the Napoleonic Wars. This occurred despite the disappearance of revolutionary Russia from among the grain exporters. The British wheat price declined by 48 percent from 1812 to 1815, by 52 percent between 1920 and 1922. In both cases, the rapid fall in agricultural prices opened a new and rather difficult phase for farmers throughout the world.

The course of industrial nonfarm raw materials varied; but, in general, they moved in similar ways during the war and in the post-1920 decline.

In terms of leading sectors, the character of the war required, and British conditions permitted, a sharp increase in steel production, accompanied by a decline in coal production, as exports fell by more than half. The expanded British steel industry geared itself in 1919–1920 for an export boom that never materialized.[126] Elsewhere in Europe steel production declined during the war, resuming the pre-war pattern almost exactly in 1925, with the exception of the shift of Lorraine from Germany to France; but, as Table III-33

ance	Belgium	Great Britain	Rest of British Empire	Japan	Russia	Rest of Europe
[illegible]	2.4	7.7	1.1	0.24	4.2[a]	5.4[a]
[illegible]	0.0	9.7	1.9	0.78	—	—
[illegible]	1.2	9.1	1.5	0.83	0.16	3.6
[illegible]	0.8	3.7	1.1	0.85	0.18	3.4
[illegible]	2.5	7.4	1.6	1.3	1.8	5.6
[illegible]	4.0	9.6	2.3	2.3	4.6	8.4
[illegible]	3.1	5.2	1.7	2.0	5.0	5.9

n added for the same reason to the Rest of Europe in 1913.
ource: Burn, *The Economic History of Steelmaking*, p. 399.

indicates, the world outside Europe had moved on, with notable increases in the United States and Japan.

Putting aside until later a general examination of the postwar trend period, it should be noted here that wartime industrial developments outside Europe had significant consequences for Europe in general, Britain in particular. In India, for example, domestic cotton textile production expanded by about a quarter during the war years. In addition, the Japanese moved in as cotton textile exporters in a substantial way.[127] Britain failed fully to recapture its old position in China, the Dutch East Indies, the Near East, and South America, as well as in India.

Even more fundamental was the wartime development of the American economy. It was precisely during the war years that the automobile revolution took hold as a mass phenomenon; and a leading sector emerged as powerful as railways proved to be in the nineteenth century. In the fiscal year 1910–1911 Henry Ford led the industry with sales of 34,528 Model T's, costing about $700 each.[128] In the fiscal year 1916–1917, he sold 730,041 cars at about $350 each. Retail prices had risen about 60 percent between 1911 and 1917; but the moving assembly line was under way, gathering momentum before direct U.S. engagement in the war, as Table III-34 indicates. The virtual tripling of motor car sales between 1914 and 1916 and the stimulus of wartime use of motor trucks emerge clearly. More generally, the accelerated emergence during the war years of the whole automobile sectoral complex (which embraced strip steel and other significant inputs, as well as rubber and petroleum)

TABLE III-34. *The Automobile as a Leading Sector: United States, 1909–1922*

	(1) Passenger Car Sales (Millions)	(2) Motor Truck and Bus Sales (Millions)	(3) U.S. Motor Vehicle Registrations (Millio
1909	0.12	0.003	0.31
1910	0.18	0.006	0.47
1911	0.20	0.017	0.64
1912	0.36	0.022	0.94
1913	0.46	0.023	1.26
1914	0.55	0.025	1.76
1915	0.90	0.074	2.49
1916	1.53	0.092	3.62
1917	1.75	0.128	5.11
1918	0.94	0.227	6.16
1919	1.65	0.224	7.58
1920	1.91	0.321	9.24
1921	1.47	0.148	10.48
1922	2.27	0.269	12.27

[a] Annual average rate of growth.
Sources: Cols. 1–3, *Historical Statistics of the United States*, 1960 ed., p. 462; col

is apparent, sparked by an astonishing average annual increase in motor vehicle registrations of 42 percent between 1909 and 1914, 34 percent between 1914 and 1919.

The point can be put more generally. A whole group of new technologies were germinating in the pre-1914 era which were widely if not quite uniformly shared among the most advanced nations of the Atlantic world. Aside from the automobile itself and the use of electricity, Ingvar Svennilson lists the following:

> Alloy steels, such as stainless steel; non-ferrous alloys; new low-cost methods of aluminum production; electric furnace technique (basic inventions, 1903–1906).
> The rotating cement kiln (first units in 1896).
> New electro-chemical processes.
> New methods for the fixation of atmospheric nitrogen.
> New methods for the bleaching of wood pulp; the use of pulp in chemical production; rayon (production passed experimental stage shortly before the first World War).
> New methods of oil refining (cracking); hydrogenation of carbon, followed by other synthetic methods for production of heavy organic chemicals.
> Synthetic solvents, plastics and rubber.
> Continuous rolling mills in the steel industry (first unit built in 1922); welding, for example in shipbuilding (first used during the first World War).
> Ball bearings.

) pital Invested in otor Car Industry 929 $ Millions)	(5) Crude Petroleum Production (Millions of 42-Gallon Barrels)	(6) Petroleum Refining: Capital Invested (1929 $ Millions)	(7) Rubber Products: Capital Invested (1929 $ Millions)
267	0.18	327	139
	0.21		
	0.22		
	0.22		
	0.25		
616 (18%)[a]	0.27	522 (11%)[a]	265 (14%)[a]
	0.28		
	0.30		
	0.33		
	0.36		
936 (26%)[a]	0.38	1,380 (20%)[a]	704 (22%)[a]
	0.44		
	0.47		
	0.56		

7, ibid., p. 412; col. 5, ibid., p. 360.

The use of diesel motors for large ships (first ship launched in 1912).
Electronic tubes; radio for domestic use (produced on large scale from the middle of the 'twenties).
Aircraft.
Office machinery of more efficient types.
New machinery in clothing industry.
Freezing technique; the domestic refrigerator (from middle of 'twenties).
New methods of canning (modern tin canning used from 1905–1908).
Prefabricated material for packing; machinery for packing.

A number of these new products and processes—canning, freezing, motor transport, office machinery, prefabricated packing—were of importance in promoting more efficient methods of distribution. The new methods of production of cheap standardized goods stimulated, and were stimulated by, new sales methods such as large-scale advertising and the chain store. These developments made possible a complete transformation of the distributive trade.[129]

The war years were by no means wholly barren for Europe with respect to the absorption of new technologies. Nitrogen fixation was carried forward in Germany on a large scale as well as aircraft production in Germany, France, and Britain. Despite the war, British electricity production continued to expand rapidly, at an annual rate of almost 14 percent between 1913 and 1918, higher even than the rate in the previous five years. French electricity production also increased. The British steel industry made improvements in technique and organization which left it stronger at the end of the war than at the beginning, if not strong enough to sustain a major export position during the interwar years. The postwar potential of the British automobile industry was also expanded by wartime developments.[130] The technologies of the telephone and radio were advanced in Europe as well as in the United States. But, clearly, the United States, undamaged, its growth proceeding at a relatively normal rate despite the distortions of the time, was in a vastly better position to absorb the new technologies efficiently than Western Europe. This advantage was strengthened because a good many of the new technologies (aside from the automobile itself) related to private consumption and distribution. The pace at which these were absorbed related to levels of income per capita in various economies and their rates of expansion. The United States had the advantage on both counts. In addition, of course, the war gravely ran down Europe's existing capital (including overseas holdings), while American physical capital was enhanced, and the United States became unambiguously a regular exporter of capital.

The shift in economic balance between the United States and Western Europe was echoed elsewhere. Canada moved on briskly from its pre-1914 take-off into an expansion and diversification of industrial production marking the early stage of the drive to technological maturity:

> The advent of World War I brought a notable acceleration of industrial diversification. For example, military exigencies were responsible for the establishment of new refining capacity for non-ferrous metals, e.g. copper, zinc, and magnesium. Previously, concentrates of zinc and copper matte had been processed in the United States. The development of a shell industry and heavy demand for steel products including rods, billets, bars, and other semi-fabricated or fabricated products and components were responsible for a substantial expansion of domestic steel capacity, from an estimated one million to one and one-quarter million ingot tons in 1914 to two and one-quarter million ingot tons in 1919. In fact, the level reached after World War I was so high that little further change occurred in steel capacity until the outbreak of World War II.
>
> Other manufacturing industries newly created or greatly expanded during World War I were the aircraft and shipbuilding industries. From a very modest beginning in 1917 the aircraft industry in the course of two years turned out some 3,000 training planes for British and Canadian forces. Shipyards were greatly expanded and produced close to one hundred ships, half the number steel and the other half wood, the total tonnage being about 350,000 dead weight tons. Plant facilities and equipment were expanded and managerial and technical knowledge acquired which enabled most industries in the post-World War I period to undertake more diversified, integrated, and efficient operations than they had previously been able to perform.[131]

This structural transition was accompanied by a sharp decline in capital imports and a shift from Britain to the United States as a major supplier of capital.[132] American capital flowed not to finance the railway net but to enter directly into manufacturing and mining, bringing with it management and, quite often, new technology. Canada proved capable of backing its war effort with a rise in the proportion of gross savings to GNP from 17.2 percent (1911–1915) to 27.1 percent (1916–1920) despite the decline in capital imports.[133]

Across the Pacific, Japan experienced an equally sharp acceleration in industrialization. The years of the First World War came at a time when Japan, unlike Canada, had already moved beyond take-off into the drive to technological maturity. That transition to a more diversified industrial structure is conventionally dated round about 1906, in the wake of the Russo-Japanese War.[134] The circumstances of the First World War accelerated that process, as Table III-35 indicates. Despite the relative decline of employment, there was a relative rise in output in Group II industries (textiles) during the war, reflecting Japan's exploitation of possibilities for expanding exports, mainly at the expense of Britain. The extraordinary proportional rise of employment in Group III industries reflects primarily the unavailability of heavy industry imports from Europe and, to a degree, from the United States, although Japanese imports from the United States rose from 18 percent to 38 percent of the total between 1914 and 1919, exports from 36 percent to 44 percent.[135] The shift to the United States as a source of Japanese imports, at the expense of Europe, proved to be a long-run phenomenon. As the data for 1927 indicate, the momentum and, to a degree, the direction of wartime structural changes somewhat altered in the post-1919 period.

Financially, Japan shifted from a current-account deficit (and capital-importing) position in the period 1908–1913 to a large current-account surplus (and capital-exporting) position in 1914–1919.[136] In the subsequent decade (1920–1931) Japan's current account shifted again to deficit, and it resumed capital-importing status.

The First World War brought about, of course, a drastic decline of intercontinental European emigration: from an annual rate of 1.3 million in 1911–1915 to 0.4 million in 1916–1920.[137] Immigration to the United States fell between these periods to 19 percent of its previous level; immigration to Canada fell to 24 percent. In Europe, the war had profound demographic consequences. The direct and indirect loss of population (that is, the whole deficit of births and the whole excess of deaths) is estimated at 22.4 million, a figure to be compared with the net increase of 26.9 million between 1900 and 1910, a period in which net emigration overseas was 4.6 million.[138] Taking war losses and the reduction in migration together, the increase in European population between 1910 and 1920 may have been only about 1 million; from 1913 to 1920 there was a decline of perhaps 2.3 million.[139] Meanwhile, despite the slowdown in immigration, the population of the United States continued to increase at an annual average rate of 1.3 percent, moving from 97.2 million in 1913 to 106.5 million in 1920. This was well

TABLE III-35. *Acceleration and Diversification of Industrial Production in Japan, 1909–1927*

	Employment in Industrial Sectors[a]			Proportion of Factory Employme[nt] to Total Manufacturing Employment (%)
	Group I (%)	Group II (%)	Group III (%)	
	(1)	(2)	(3)	(4)
1909	24.8	62.8	12.4	27.2
1914	24.9	59.4	15.7	32.9
1919	20.9	54.8	24.3	43.4
1927	21.4	52.7	25.9	40.7

[a] Group I includes predominantly food processing and similar industries; Group II, textile products; Group [III,] the heavier industries (e.g., chemicals, metals, machinery).

below the 2 percent rate of increase from 1880 to 1913, but still substantial.

As always, however, it was the claims of war, rather than demography, that mainly decreed a radical decline in housing construction on a scale sufficient to create the basis for a postwar housing boom. In the United States, building held up through 1916, fell away to about 28 percent of that level in 1918, recovering rapidly in the postwar years. In Canada, the national urban building index averaged only 26 percent of its 1911–1913 level for the whole period 1914–1918.[140] A somewhat less dramatic building boom emerged in the postwar years, exhibiting greater continued sensitivity to reduced immigration than in the United States.[141] In Britain there was a virtually complete cessation of housebuilding in the course of the war. In 1911–1913, annual average housing construction was fifty-eight thousand, only 37 percent of the level during the peak years 1902–1903.[142] From this modest pre-war level, housing fell to seventeen thousand units in 1916. None is recorded for 1917–1919. Feinstein estimates net disinvestment in housing for each year during the period 1914–1919.[143] On the continent, in the areas of combat, there was, of course, much physical destruction added to the imbalance created by the economics of wartime conditions.

The analysis of housing cycles can, thus, no more be disentangled from the traumatic impact of wars in the twentieth century than in the eighteenth. As Clarence D. Long concluded:

> . . . periods of severe war have been periods of severe building depression. For one thing, construction is usually expressly prohibited in order to conserve the economic resources of the nation. . . . But government prohibition is not the sole explanation for the wartime decline of building. . . . One is the fall in the flow of income or the failure of that income flow to increase at the same rate; this is naturally due to the diversion of a large amount of energy and resources to war purposes. This diversion is reflected in disproportionate increases in costs of construction and operation. . . . In addition, the un-

lanufacturing Output Million Yen at 1934–1936 Prices)	Annual Average Rate of Growth (%)
5)	(6)
742	6.1 (1905–1909)
533	5.2
100	11.5
043 (1925)	0.9

Source: Kazushi Ohkawa and Henry Rosovsky, *Japanese Economic Growth*, p. 83 (colnns 1–4); p. 81 (column 5).

certainty as to the outcome of the war should not be underestimated—uncertainty felt not only by the participants, but also by the non-belligerents who are rarely free from anxiety.[144]

In terms of trend period analysis, then, the First World War had these major effects, all of which left their mark on the troubled twenty interwar years:

—The pre-war expansion of agricultural and raw-material production in non-European areas was abnormally heightened.

—Industrial production into new leading sectors was encouraged in non-European areas, notably, but not exclusively, in the United States, Japan, and Canada. In the case of the United States, the stage of high mass-consumption can be said to have begun during the war years with the coming of Henry Ford's moving assembly line for the Model T.

—Immigration and housing construction were narrowly restricted by wartime conditions.

15

1920–1936

The century between 1815 and 1914 carried with it a strong sense of unity in economic as in political and diplomatic affairs. But it was certainly not a static time. The United States was the only major nation operating under the same constitutional arrangements in 1914 as those which framed its political life in 1815; and this continuity cost a great civil war. The Germany and Italy of 1914 had not existed a century earlier. The contracting Ottoman Empire gave way painfully to a new, narrower, modernizing Turkish nationalism. An industrial Japan, under the new political management of the Meiji Restoration, had emerged from its self-created womb in Asia, in response to the somewhat brutal midwifery of the West. The volume of world industrial production and international trade was of the order of thirty times greater than it had been as Napoleon went into final exile. In every major domain, with the possible exception of textiles, technologies were at work which had not been conceived of when this remarkable century began. Two facts account for the image of economic continuity: there was no major international war on the scale of the struggle from 1793 to 1815; and there was a considerable continuity in economic process.

In substantial part, the continuity of process stemmed from the role of Great Britain. Its proportionate stature in world manufacturing production may have fallen from, say, 24 percent to 14 percent; in world trade, from about a third to 16 percent. But Britain remained throughout the acknowledged center of the world economy. It had moved quickly after 1815 to translate its wartime role as a supplier of loans and subsidies to allies into the position of peacetime exporter of capital. It was still exporting capital massively on the eve of the First World War. After becoming during the years of the war with France the dominating international center for imports and re-exports, it retained a substantial part of that function, by moving progressively toward free trade and then holding to that policy despite the pressures for change that emerged from 1873 to the late 1890's. In particular, it accepted the costs as well as the benefits of the flow of cheapened grain its own lending and shipping technology had made possible, in the form of a painful structural adjustment in British agriculture. Despite acute financial crises, more or less from decade to decade, the British remained steadily on the gold standard from 1819 forward. The British pound and short-term balances held in London were universally regarded as a reliable form of financial reserves. Britain accepted the responsibilities as well as the rewards of this circumstance, the Bank of England altering its rate in response to changes in Britain's foreign balance. To some extent the British banking system as a whole learned to shield the domestic credit supply from international strain; but, when the attractions of lending abroad drew British savings out of the country on an increased scale, London rationed domestic capital through higher interest rates, the latter having a special importance for housing construction.

Finally, there was the continuity afforded by capitalism. None of the major economies of the world operated purely on the basis of private markets, not even Britain. In the United States and Canada, Belgium, France, and Germany, there were even deeper interventions, notably to get the railroads built, but in many other domains as well: the legal framework of the banking system; tariffs; land tenure arrangements; the acquisition and diffusion of new technologies. In Russia and Japan intervention was even more pervasive and intimate. Still, there was an international price system, modified as it might be by tariffs and other efforts to mitigate its rigors.

It was this significant degree of institutional and structural stability that gave to a century of extraordinary economic and political change its image of continuity. Within its framework business cycles undulated in a more or less regular way; and there was the alternating sequence of longer trend periods we have examined here, which have a clear family relation to each other, despite their unique features.

As we turn to the two interwar decades, much of this continuity is lost. We confront the adjustments of the immediate postwar years that brought with them in some countries fantastic inflations; then the brief return to a reasonably credible normality, from 1925 to 1929, although pathologically high levels of unemployment persisted in Western Europe, excepting France. Then came the depression of the early 1930's, proceeding to depths never known before; the recovery to 1937, uneven in its international impact; and a phase of rapid rearmament which gathered momentum from 1936 forward.

Clearly, the fluctuations of these years did not follow a simple pre-1914 cyclical pattern.

Institutionally, London was crippled, partially recovered, but never regained the economic strength to revive fully the pre-1914 system of international trade and finance. The United States, emerging, like Britain after 1815, from a wartime to a peacetime lender, fulfilled ad hoc down to 1929 some but not all of the functions performed by Britain during the pre-1914 century; but then it failed itself and the international system.

Despite the pathology of these years and the breakdown of the pre-1914 international economic order, the period 1920–1935 has some of the essential characteristics of a trend period, parallel to those which began in 1815 and 1873. Indeed, some of the much-studied special characteristics of the interwar period cannot be fully understood outside its trend-period framework.

This is the case, for example, with respect to the post-1920 course of foodstuff and raw-material prices, production, and stocks (Chart III-38).

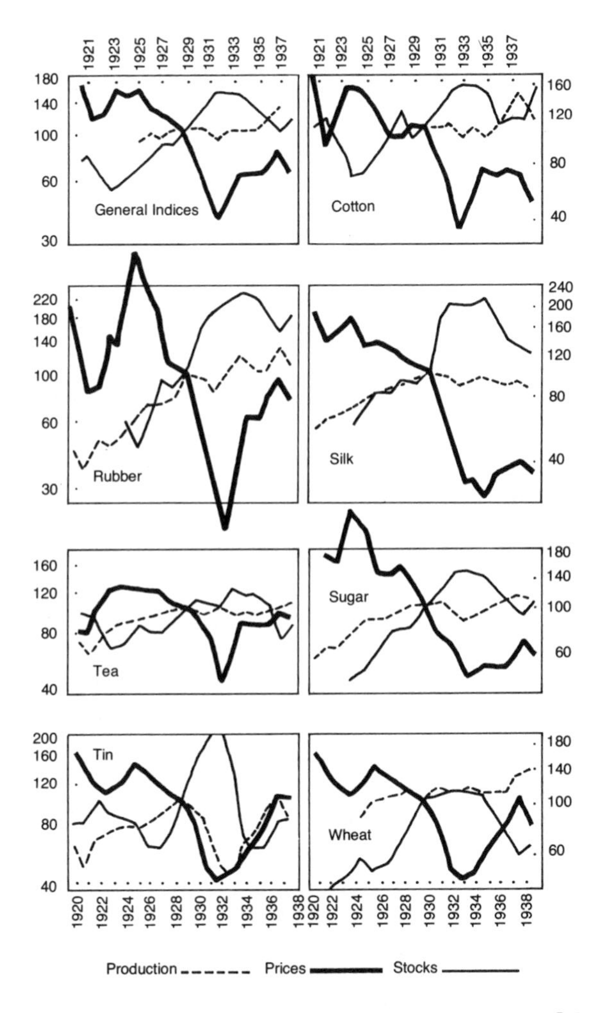

CHART III-38. *World Production, Prices, and Stocks of Primary Commodities, 1920–1938 (1929=100)*

Source: League of Nations, *Economic Instability in the Postwar World* (Geneva, 1945), p. 85, reproduced in C. P. Kindleberger, *The World in Depression, 1929–1939* (Berkeley and Los Angeles: University of California Press, 1973), p. 88.

As always there are elements of uniqueness in the story of each commodity;[145] but the general pattern is reasonably clear. Prices began to recover from the post-1920 collapse in 1921–1923. The recoveries were (excepting rubber) generally mild and short-lived. Prices turned downward again in the period 1925–1929, despite the industrial prosperity of those years. This occurred because the increase in agricultural and raw-material production during the 1920's was greater than the expansion in demand. Therefore, stocks rose, in some cases held off the markets by government financing to prevent still greater price declines. With these stocks overhanging the markets, the collapse of demand after 1929 produced a catastrophic further decline in prices and, initially, a further increase in stocks. During the years of most acute depression, production of food and textile raw materials generally stagnated; rubber, caught up in a long lag between tree planting and output, continued to rise; tin production, linked to an industrial demand spiraling downward, declined sharply. Then came the upturn from the pit of depression. Prices rose sharply down to 1937. The fall in stocks was generally greater than the increase in production. But almost without exception prices were lower at the cyclical peak in 1937 than they had been at the troughs of 1921–1923. There was, then, an authentic downward trend in basic commodity prices for this period.

The British terms of trade are a reasonably fair measure of the relative movements of industrial prices versus those of foodstuffs and raw materials. During the immediate postwar inventory boom, Britain's export prices rose even more rapidly than import prices. The price collapse of 1920 still further improved Britain's terms of trade. In 1922 they were 41 percent higher than in 1913.[146] They weakened somewhat down to 1929, but then improved radically during the worst of the depression. In 1933 they were 47 percent higher than in 1913. They fell away somewhat in the business expansion down to 1937; but the average level of the British terms of trade from 1919 to 1938 was 31 percent above the 1913 level.[147]

The American farm parity ratio is a kind of internal terms-of-trade measurement, exhibiting the ratio of prices received by farmers to prices paid, including interest, taxes, and wage rates. With only a few exceptions it moves from year to year over this period inversely to the British terms of trade, but the order of magnitude of its fluctuations and trend is different. At the trough in 1921, it was 21 percent lower than in 1913. The recovery of the twenties brought it back to a point 9 percent below 1913 in 1929. By 1932, however, it was a catastrophic 43 percent below 1913. Recovery and government policies of acreage restriction and subsidy brought the parity ratio slightly above the 1929 level by 1937. Like the British terms of trade, the farm parity ratio was extremely sensitive to the recession of 1938, moving, of course, in the opposite direction. From 1919 to 1938 the parity ratio averaged 15 percent lower than in 1913.

TABLE III-36. *Interwar World Wheat Production, 1914–1919 (Five-Year Averages: Millions of Bushels)*

	1914–1919	1919–1924	1924–1929	1929–1934	1934–1939
Overseas exporters	1,338	1,478	1,648	1,559	1,337
European exporters	943	695	1,099	1,250	1,686
European importers	792	831	926	1,090	1,152
World total	3,597	3,503	4,199	4,466	4,822

Source: Malenbaum, *The World Wheat Economy*, p. 239.

The position of continental Europe was different from that of Britain and the United States. Moreover, it presented patterns of considerable variety. There were the Eastern European grain exporters; the specialized exporters of dairy products and meat, notably Denmark, Ireland, and the Netherlands; and the countries of Southern Europe, importing grain, exporting citrus fruits, wine, and other high-value agricultural products.[148] Generalization is therefore difficult. By and large, however, governments sought to protect their agricultural sectors, increasingly so after 1929. In consequence, wheat production, for example, rose in Europe and declined after 1929 among the overseas exporters (Table III-36).

The sharp rise in the 1930's among European exporters reflects, in part, the expansion of production and return to an exporting position of the USSR as well as the bilateral trading relations developed between Germany and Eastern Europe. Among the European importers, the expansion of heavily protected French and German wheat production is notable. Chart III-39 shows how wheat import duties, which had risen during the 1880's and 1890's, leveled off in the pre-1914 phase of relatively high prices, then rose to extremely high levels in the 1930's in three major Continental countries. In short, the European continent, taken as a whole, denied itself the advantages of favorable terms of trade in order to cushion the position of agriculture.

These defensive policies toward agriculture had their cost: "From a productivity point of view, the protection of agriculture suffered from a double weakness. On the one hand, it was never able to restore the prosperity of the farmer to a level which would have given a stimulus to rapid modernization. On the other hand, it prevented —by maintaining incomes derived from less efficient production— an increase in productivity through elimination or regional specialization."[149] Moreover, the best approximations we have for the farm parity ratio on the Continent indicate that the cushioning policies of government did not prevent the terms of trade from turning against the farmer down to 1932 (Table III-37).

Ratios of this kind can only be suggestive. Their real meaning requires that productivity changes be taken into account as well as changes in the composition of farm production and what farmers

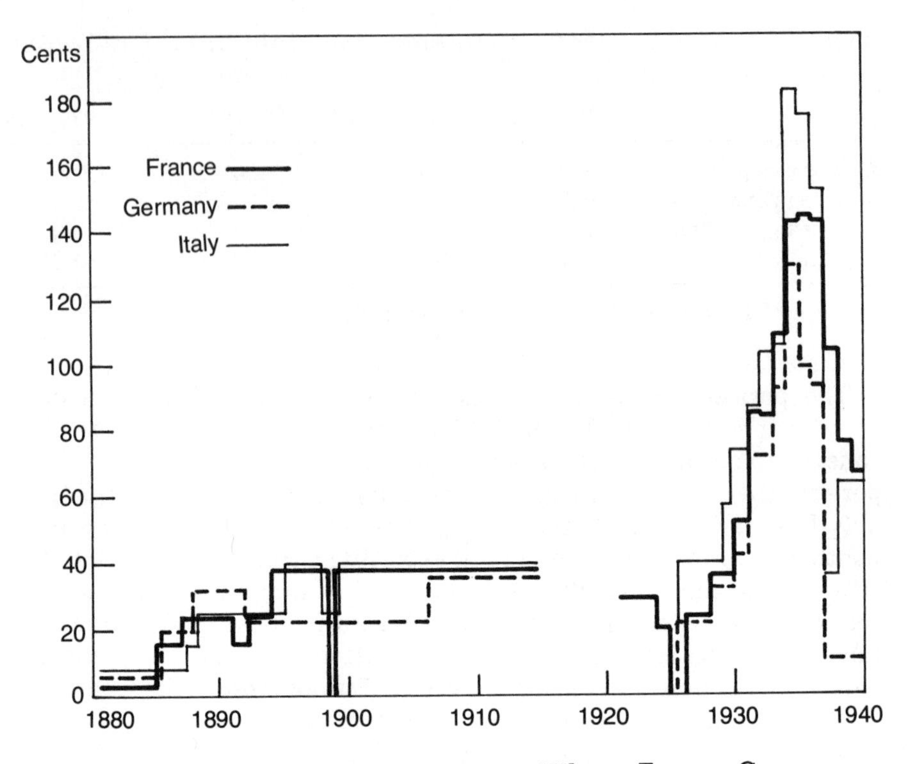

CHART III-39. *Effective Import Duties on Wheat: France, Germany, and Italy, 1880–1939 (U.S. Cents per Bushel)*

Source: Malenbaum, *The World Wheat Economy*, p. 162.

buy. But the story of these ratios does underline three basic characteristics of the interwar decades:

—It was a period of chronic surplus of agricultural products and raw materials, caused in part by the distortions of 1914–1918 and the immediate postwar years, in part by the chronically depressed state of demand.

—Producers of foodstuffs and raw materials, in general, suffered a relative decline in income, limiting their capacity to purchase industrial products and to invest in new methods and technologies. In particular, their catastrophic losses from 1929 to 1933 were one major factor accounting for the depth of the Great Depression throughout the world.

—On the other hand, industrial and other urban workers who were employed enjoyed an increase in real wages due to the decline in cost of living.

The distortions in foodstuff and raw-materials production generated by what transpired between 1913 and 1920 do not, however, wholly explain the pathology of the subsequent two decades. One must look also at the new leading sectors in the advanced industrial countries, how they evolved, and what was required to sustain their momentum.

The three great new leading-sector complexes which had emerged before the First World War continued to move forward in the erratic, distorted environment of the interwar years: the internal combustion engine, electricity, and chemicals. They supplied elements of growth and development to the most advanced part of the world economy; but, except in the United States of the 1920's, they could not by themselves bring about an environment of relatively full employment in any of the major economies.

The three complexes were related in significant ways. The automobile (and truck), for example, depended on rapidly evolving chemistries of oil refining and rubber manufacture, as well as on the battery, spark plugs, and other light electrical gear. Electric power played a large role in the production of many of the new chemicals.

Tables III-38 and III-39, showing automobile registrations and motor vehicle production, catch the main features of the story.

By the early 1920's, the automobile and truck revolution was a massive fact in the United States, at a much earlier stage in Europe. In 1921 European automobile registrations were only 10 percent of American; in 1924 the four leading European producers turned out only 11 percent of the number of motor vehicles manufactured in the United States. There was expansion in both areas in the 1920's, at a higher rate in Europe, as one would expect, given the earlier stage of the leading sector. By 1930 European automobile registrations were at 20 percent of the American level, vehicle production at 13 percent. The greater depth and intractability of the depression in the United States, as compared to most of Europe, and the lesser degree of pre-1939 recovery permitted Europe further to narrow the gap. Indeed, it was German policy explicitly to encourage the expansion of the motor vehicle industry through road building and incentives to promote sales. European registrations in 1938 were at 28 percent of the American level, vehicle production at 43 percent. But, as Charts III-40 and III-41 indicate, the intensity of motor vehicle use remained markedly greater in the United States; and there was an even greater spread among the countries of Europe.

TABLE III-37. *Ratio of Agricultural Prices to Cost of Living: Selected Countries, 1924–1938*

	Germany	France	Denmark	Hungary	United States[a]
1924	100	100 (1926)	100	—	100
1929	81	91	80	100	103
1932	71	80	55	83	65
1938	83	80	70	83	88

[a] Parity ratio.

Sources: Svennilson, *Growth and Stagnation in the European Economy*, p. 244, for Germany, France, Denmark, and Hungary; *Historical Statistics of the United States*, 1960 ed., p. 283, for U.S. farm parity ratio.

TABLE III-38. *Registered Motor Vehicles in European Countries and the United States, 1905–1938 (Thousands)*

	United Kingdom	Germany	France	Italy
1905	32	27[a]	22[b]	—
1910	108	56	54[b]	—
1913	208	93	125[c]	—
1921	464	91	236	54
1926	1,042	319	891	138
1930	1,524	679	1,460	293
1938	2,422	1,816	2,251	469

[a] 1906.
[b] Passenger cars only.
[c] Passenger cars, taxis, and buses only.
Source: Svennilson, *Growth and Stagnation in the European Economy*, p. 147. See al

The European motor-vehicle industry evolved behind high protective tariffs (20–45 percent) imposed in Britain, France, and Germany during the 1920's, to shield against the overwhelming initial U.S. advantage. Italy imposed even more forbidding barriers (over 100 percent) in the 1930's. To such protection were added horsepower taxes which, along with less spacious European geography,

TABLE III-39. *Production of Motor Vehicles in Four Leading European Producing Countries and the United States, 1923–1938 (Thousands)*

	United Kingdom	Germany	France	Italy	Four Leading European Producers	United States
Passenger Cars						
1923	71	31	—	—	—	3,625
1929	182	117	211	—	—	4,587
1937	390[a]	264	177	62	893	3,916
1938	341	277	200	59	877	2,001
Commercial Vehicles						
1923	24	9	—	—	—	409
1929	57	39	42	—	—	771
1937	118[a]	64	24	10	216	893
1938	104	65	27	8	204	488
Total						
1923	95	40	110	—	—	4,034
1929	239	156	253	54	702	5,358
1937	508[a]	328	201	72	1,109	4,809
1938	445	342	227	67	1,081	2,489

[a] 1927–1937, year ended 30 September.
Source: Svennilson, *Growth and Stagnation in the European Economy*, p. 149.

lgium, Luxembourg, etherlands, Switzerland, veden	Rest of Europe	Total Europe	Total United States
—	—	—	79
—	—	—	469
—	—	—	1,258
7	114	1,056	10,494
7	432	3,139	22,053
3	713	5,182	26,532
1	732	8,381	29,443

rman annual data for 1925–1931 and 1933–1938 in M. E. Falkus, "Cars, Roads, and onomic Recovery in Germany, 1932–1938," *Economic History Review*, Second Series, 28, no. 3 (August 1975), pp. 466–483. Annual data on the German motor vehicle ustry for the period 1907–1939 are given on p. 483.

helped encourage the production of smaller cars than in the United States.

The automobile age brought wide-ranging changes: from courting habits to the get-away methods of bank robbers. It stimulated road building, accelerated the relocation of urban population in the suburbs, and provided more flexible and efficient market transport for agricultural commodities as well as new forms of public passenger transport. But above all, motor vehicle manufacture set up a range of requirements which made its demands a major factor in the whole industrial structure. For example, by 1938 the automobile industry in the United States was the largest single consumer of the output of the following industries, absorbing the indicated percentages of their output.[150]

	(%)		(%)		(%)
Strip steel	51	Alloy steel	54	Plate glass	69
Bars	34	Steel,all forms	17	Nickel	29
Sheets	41	Gasoline	90	Lead	35
Malleable iron	53	Rubber	80	Mohair	40

The proportions were, of course, not as high in the major countries of Western Europe; but the emergence of this sectoral complex was a central economic fact. Beneath the surface of sluggishness and depression, down to 1933, it provided an important element of dynamism. And its subsequent expansion, down to the eve of the Second World War, helped sustain the recovery. Directly and indirectly, this sectoral complex was a continuing vital "spring of technical progress."[151]

As Chart III-42 demonstrates, the revolution in electricity production and consumption proceeded vigorously and almost universally over the interwar period. So powerful is the trend that the Great

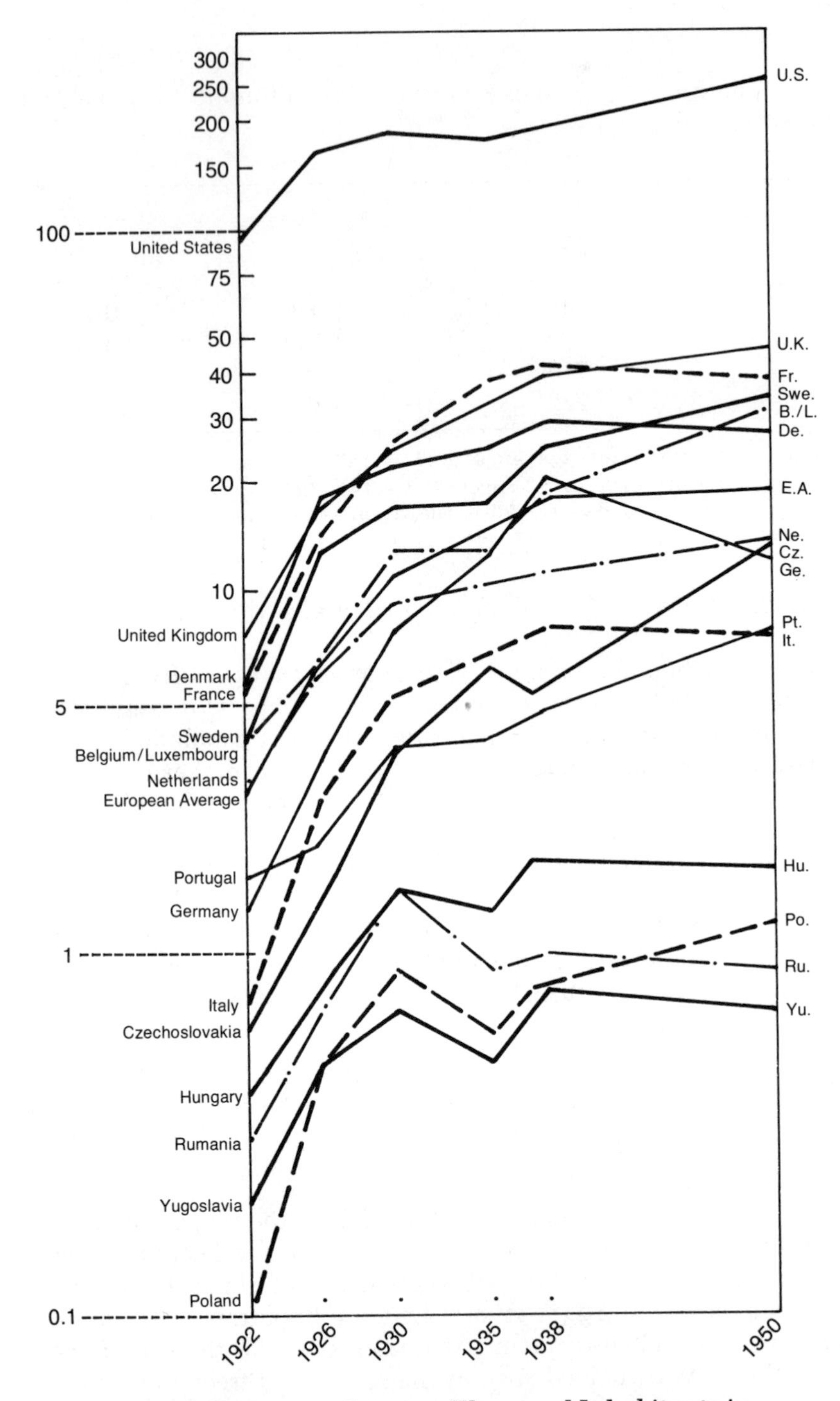

CHART III-40. *Passenger Cars per Thousand Inhabitants in European Countries and the United States, 1922–1950*

Source: Svennilson, *Growth and Stagnation in the European Economy*, p. 146.

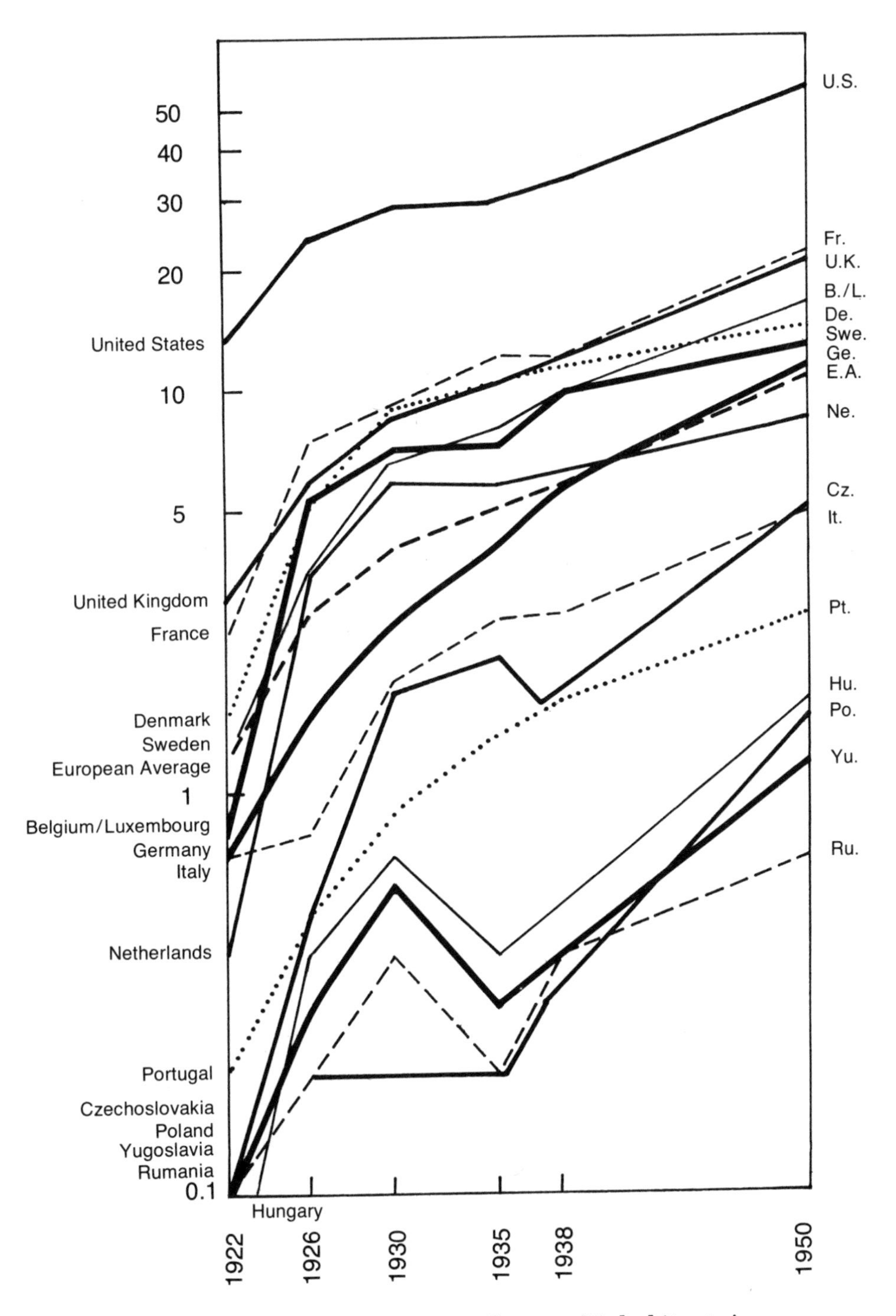

CHART III-41. *Commercial Vehicles per Thousand Inhabitants in European Countries and the United States, 1922–1950*

Source: Svennilson, *Growth and Stagnation in the European Economy*, p. 146.

Depression is reflected as a relatively mild decline (e.g., the United States) or as merely a retardation in the rate of growth. As Table III-40 shows, this process was accompanied and strengthened by a remarkable increase in the efficiency of electricity production. Here is the basis for the emergence of the mass market in electricity-consuming durable consumers' goods which proceeded rapidly in the United States, less rapidly elsewhere, except for the ubiquitous radio.[152] Although electricity production itself is (like oil refining) a highly capital-intensive industry, the whole sectoral complex, including the building of power stations and lines, generators, radios, vacuum cleaners, refrigerators, irons, and the other electric-powered household gadgetry of high mass-consumption, created substantial increases in employment.

The chemical industry is less easy to measure as a leading sector. It consists of a wide range of products subject to different technologies and supply conditions, linked to demands of quite different types: from chemical fertilizers to rayon, from pharmaceuticals to dyestuffs and plastics, the latter just emerging on a substantial scale toward the end of our period.

Table III-41 and Chart III-43 suggest the pace at which certain major chemicals continued their expansion during the interwar years.

TABLE III-40. *Number of Kilowatt-Hours Corresponding in Cost to One Ton of Coal, 1890–1949*

	United Kingdom		France
	Household Use	Industrial Purposes	Household Us[e]
1890	—	—	12
1900	—	—	14
1913	—	—	29
1925	51	194	84
1929	55	194	79
1935	80	233	64
1938	123	301	83
1948	390	598	—
1949	—	—	197

[a] 1912.

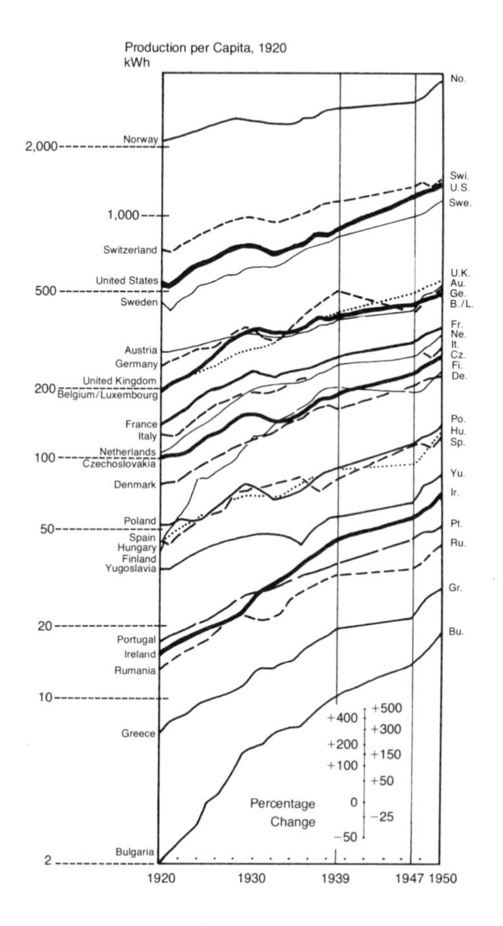

CHART III-42. *Electricity Production in European Countries and the United States, 1920–1950*

Source: Svennilson, *Growth and Stagnation in the European Economy*, p. 113.

Note: The curves represent changes in total production. They are arranged according to per capita production in each country in 1920.

		United States	
ther Purposes	Average	Household Use	Commercial and Industrial Purposes
—	15	—	—
—	25	—	—
)1	41	14[a]	50[a]
55	122	31	102
75	114	31	96
52	116	39	101
.8	162	52	116
—	342	183	383
15	349	181	361

Source: Svennilson, *Growth and Stagnation in the European Economy*, p. 113.

TABLE III-41. *Production of Major Chemicals, 1913–1938*

	Sulphuric Acid (Thousands of Tons of 100% Acid)			Superphosphates (Thousands of Tons)		
	1913	1929	1936–1938	1913	1928	1938
Total Europe	5,800	6,800	7,800	7,400	8,000	6,900
USSR	116	265	1,500[a]	158	151	1,572
United States	2,250	4,817	4,930[b]	3,248	4,071	3,244
Canada	40	100	240	—	—	—
Japan	70	819	2,051	549	926	1,284
Total world	8,300	13,100	17,100	11,750	14,650	15,300

	Calcium Carbide (Thousands of Tons)			Synthetic Dyestuffs (Thousands of Tons)		
	1918	1928	1938	1913	1927	1938
Total Europe	250	800	1,500	154	123	120
USSR	—	6	100	4	10	35
United States	50	183[d]	175[e]	3	43	37
Canada	16	—	—	—	—	—
Japan	—	—	400	—	—	28
Total world	325	1,300	2,500	161	184	220

[a] 1938.
[b] 1937.
[c] Chilean production is, respectively, 433, 354, and 215 thousand tons.
[d] 1927.

A few features of Table III-41 stand out:

—The global growth rates of the major chemicals varied greatly, from rayon, expanding at an annual average rate of 19 percent from 1913 to the late 1930's, to superphosphates and synthetic dyes, at not much over 1 percent.

—The rapidly expanded use of nitrogen brought into play a significant force making for an increase in agricultural productivity.[153]

—The comparative data for 1913 and 1926–1929 show the rapid but uneven advance of the American chemical industry in this period; those for 1926–1929 and 1936–1938 (excepting rayon), the greater relative impact of the Great Depression on the United States.

—It was in this period that Japan, the Soviet Union, and, to a degree, Canada, all in the drive to technological maturity, became significant producers of chemicals.

While these new leading sectors continued to move forward, the sectors which had dominated growth patterns in the pre-1914 industrial world decelerated rapidly, stagnated, or declined over the interwar years.[154] In Germany, for example, railway freight tonnage was increasing at an annual average rate of 4.5 percent between

]a Ash]ousands of Tons of Na_2CO_3)			Chemical Nitrogen (Thousands of Tons)		
)4	1929	1938	1913	1926–1928	1936–1937
00	2,300	3,200	278	1,071	1,415
82	231	532	3	3	136
20	2,346	2,647	36	170	324
—	—	—	12	27	45
—	44	251	4	54	353
00	5,000	6,700	767[c]	1,684[c]	2,510[c]

yon Yarn and Fiber]ousands of Tons)		
13	1926–1928	1936–1938
2	91.1	403.0
—	—	—
7	35.8	138.8
—	—	—
—	5.4	208.3
0	134.7	770.7

]937.
ource: Svennilson, *Growth and Stagnation in the European Economy*, pp. 287–291.
'ote: In some cases small producers have not been specified. Therefore, the world total
exceed specified subtotals.

1900 and 1913; between 1913 and 1937 the rate was 0.7 percent. This reflected not merely the reduced trend rate of industrial growth but also the beginning of the shift to the roads. European steel production, which had been increasing annually at a rate close to 8 percent over the thirty years before the war, fell to 1.3 percent between 1913 and 1936–1937. This retardation was, in part, natural in an aging sector; but it also reflected the relatively brief phases of prosperity (1925–1929, 1933–1938), the low levels of investment, and the delay, relative to the United States, in the coming in of the automobile sectoral complex on a massive scale. In the United States, steel production increased at an annual rate of 3 percent between 1913 and 1927–1928, about half the pre-1914 rate. The stagnation over the last decade of the period yields a rate of 1.9 percent average annual increase from 1913 to 1936–1937. In the United States, however, there was significant modernization and a shift in the composition of steel output to meet the requirements of the leading sectors of high mass-consumption. The most notable innovation was the continuous wide-strip mill to produce the thin steel plates required for motor vehicles, home appliances, and canning.

Such mills appeared in Europe only in the late 1930's and were not built on a large scale until after the Second World War. Nevertheless, concentration and improvements in efficiency yielded large increases in output per blast furnace in Germany and the United Kingdom (226 percent and 249 percent, respectively, between 1913 and the late 1930's), somewhat lesser increases in France and Belgium.

The deceleration in coal production was even more marked than that in steel as new sources of energy came in. Coal output in the major countries of Western Europe had been increasing at an annual average rate of 2.4 percent between 1880 and 1913, in the United States at 6.5 percent. In 1929 the Western European total was slightly below that for 1913, in 1938 fully 10 percent below. In the United States the 1929 figure was 7 percent above the 1913 level, in 1933, 31 percent below.

Thus, the most advanced industrial nations faced after 1920 a double structural adjustment: an adjustment to the potentialities

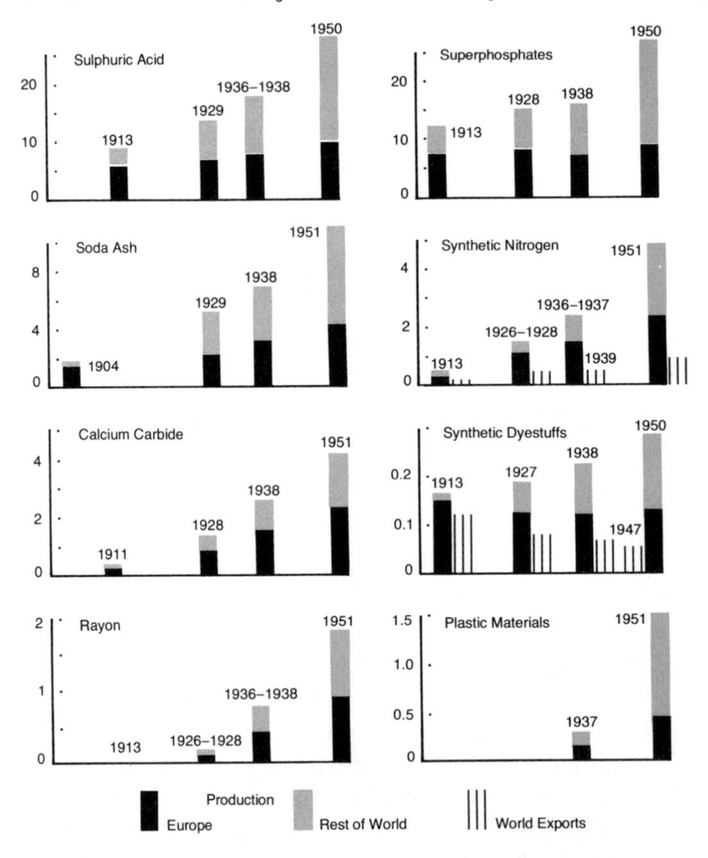

CHART III-43. *World and European Production and World Exports of Various Chemicals, 1913–1951 (Millions of Tons)*

Source: Svennilson, *Growth and Stagnation in the European Economy*, p. 166.

of cheapened supplies of foodstuffs and raw materials and an adjustment to the potentialities of the new leading sectors. The British took full benefit of the favorable terms of trade in the 1920's, even heightening their effect by returning to the gold standard at a rate which rendered their imports cheap, their exports at a competitive disadvantage. In such a framework it would have required massive action to increase domestic demand, in order for the new leading sectors to move forward at a pace which would have rapidly shifted labor and other industrial resources from exports to production for the domestic market. Intellectually and otherwise, the British (and other) governments were not prepared for such policies. The advantages of favorable terms of trade were, then, dissipated in chronically high levels of unemployment, as the older leading sectors stagnated and the new ones failed to move forward with sufficient momentum to yield full employment. On the Continent, France returned to gold with an undervalued currency and did well in the 1920's, shielding its agriculture to some degree, but enlarging its exports and expanding its industrial production, which was 37 percent over 1913 in 1929, as opposed to a 9 percent increase in Britain, 17 percent in Germany.

In general, Continental Europe countered the advantages of favorable terms of trade to some degree by policies of agricultural protection and, like Britain, failed to make the structural shift to the new leading sectors at a pace sufficient to avoid abnormally high levels of unemployment even during the best years of the 1920's, as Table III-42 indicates. In the whole period 1850–1914, British unemployment had exceeded 10 percent in only three years, at the pit of cyclical depressions (1858, 1879, 1888). And something like the British experience can be regarded as typical for industrialized countries of the pre-1914 era.

Only in the United States was income per capita sufficiently high to drive the new leading sectors forward at a pace which permitted relatively full employment in the 1920's without public intervention to expand the level of effective demand.

But there was something new and little understood about these leading sectors. Relative to cotton textiles, the purchase of the automobile and durable consumers' goods (and a suburban house) was postponable. Such goods were subject, unlike textiles, to a high income elasticity of demand. Unlike railroads or more efficient ships or the introduction of steel or machine tools—which cut costs—the new products and way of life required high and expanding levels of consumers' income, and a high degree of confidence about the future, to be rapidly diffused. Thus, the depression after 1929 hit the United States with peculiar force. The decline in incomes it induced sent the industrial system into a spiral which was not self-correcting, as such spirals had been in the pre-1914 world.[155] This lesson was never fully learned even during the New Deal. The United States still had 17 percent unemployment in 1939.

TABLE III-42. *Unemployment in Six European Countries and the United States, 1921–1938 (Unemployed as % of Labor Force)*

	United Kingdom	Germany	Sweden	Denmark	Norway	Austria	United States
1921	17.0	2.9	26.1	19.7	17.7	—	11.9
1922	14.3	1.5	22.7	19.2	17.1	—	7.6
1923	11.7	9.7	12.5	12.6	10.6	—	3.2
1924	10.3	14.2	10.1	10.7	8.5	—	5.5
1925	11.3	6.9	11.1	14.8	13.1	—	4.0
1926	12.5	18.1	12.2	20.6	24.3	—	1.9
1927	9.7	8.8	12.0	22.5	25.4	13.6	4.1
1928	10.8	8.4	10.6	18.5	19.2	12.1	4.4
1929	10.4	13.1	10.7	15.5	15.4	12.3	3.2
1930	16.1	22.2	12.2	13.7	16.6	15.0	8.7
1931	21.3	33.7	17.2	17.9	22.3	20.3	15.8
1932	22.1	43.7 (30.1)	22.8	31.7	30.8	26.1	23.6
1933	19.9	(26.3)	23.7	28.8	33.4	29.0	24.9
1934	16.7	(14.9)	18.9	22.1	30.7	26.3	26.7
1935	15.5	(11.6)	16.1	19.7	25.3	23.4	20.1
1936	13.1	(8.3)	13.6	19.3	18.8	22.9	16.9
1937	10.8	(4.6)	11.6	21.9	20.0	20.4	14.3
1938	12.9	(2.1)	11.8	21.3	22.0	—	19.0

Source: Svennilson, *Growth and Stagnation in the European Economy*, p. 31; *Historical Statistics of the United States*, 1960 ed., p. 73. Figures in parentheses are from Mitchell, *European Historical Statistics*, p. 170.

The national responses to depression varied among the nations, as they were thrown back on their own devices by the breakdown of the international trade and monetary systems and the failure of international cooperation. The British at last devalued the pound, set up an imperial trading preference system, and encouraged housing, as we shall see. France, deprived of its trading advantage of the 1920's by British devaluation, failed to revive vigorously from the bottom of depression, although unemployment itself was at relatively modest levels. Germany, after subjecting itself to an incredible unemployment rate of almost 44 percent in 1932, turned its fate over to the National Socialists, who conducted a relatively successful recovery policy and then moved into a large-scale arms program in 1936.

Excepting British imperial preferences and the German bilateral trading arrangements with Eastern Europe, there were no major international efforts to shield the producers of foodstuffs and raw materials from the burdens imposed by the combination of excessive supply and sluggish or depressed industrial demand. Their fortunes varied with their capacity to diversify and industrialize.

Canada, after weathering the postwar adjustment to a new lower range of agricultural prices and to a competitive setting for some of its war-built industry, enjoyed a quite rapid rate of growth during the 1920's. In constant dollars, net national product increased at an annual rate well below the 5.2 percent of the decade of the Canadian miracle (1900–1910), but still averaged a relatively satisfactory 3.2 percent.[156] This was due to three major factors: the many links to the boom in the United States; the continued diversification of Canadian industry; and a rise in manufacture and export of pulp and paper from British Columbia, nonferrous metals from northern Ontario and Quebec. These cushioned the relatively depressed state of the wheat sector. The depression struck hard, reducing net national product 32 percent by 1933. By 1939 it had risen 8 percent over 1929. These figures are similar to those for the United States, although the Canadian rise back to 1939 was relatively somewhat greater.

The deceleration of Australia during the 1920's was more marked than that of Canada. In the twelve pre-1914 years Australian gross domestic product (in constant pounds) expanded at an annual rate of about 4.5 percent; in the 1920's, 1.3 percent.[157] On the other hand, the depression struck less hard: at the trough, gross domestic product was 8 percent below the peak in the late 1920's and on the eve of the Second World War it was 20 percent above. In part these differences reflect the close links of Australia to Britain, whose boom of the 1920's was less marked than that of the United States but whose recovery from the slump began earlier and was more substantial. The differences also resulted from rapid Australian industrialization, an expansion in mining in the 1930's, and some diversification of agriculture.

The course of economic events during the interwar years varied among the Latin American countries. Mexico, for example, was caught up in the reorganization of its political life for the better part of a generation following the civil war of 1910–1920. In general one can say that, despite the price movements of 1920–1929, economic development moved forward, even in Mexico, but at slower rates than in the pre-1910 generation; the depression struck very hard at the balance-of-payment position of most Latin American countries; and, in consequence, a structural shift toward a more diversified industrialization, based on import substitution, began in the course of the 1930's and continued through the Second World War and beyond.

The experience of Argentina illustrates this pattern, although the relatively high level of its per capita income imparts a special character to its evolution. The First World War resulted in a severe decline in real output and real wages, of the order of 20 percent.[158] There was a sharp revival, aided by high export prices in the period 1918–1920; retardation in 1921–1926; and a phase of growth at 6 percent per annum in the late 1920's, when urban real wages were 40 percent above their 1914 level; real gross domestic product per capita, 26 percent. Structurally, the role of the agricultural and livestock sectors remained proportionally at about the same level in 1925–1929 as in 1910–1914; manufactures rose modestly; construction declined, with a slower rate of immigration, population growth, and railway construction. The rate of growth of acreage sown with crops was only 1.3 percent per annum, as compared with 8.3 percent in the pre-1914 era; of railroads, 1.4 percent versus 15.4 percent. Essentially, the limits of the pampas were reached. Between 1929 and 1933 gross domestic product declined by almost 10 percent. Recovery then moved forward in an erratic pattern of spurts and setbacks. Between the late 1920's and 1941–1943, gross domestic product averaged an annual increase variously estimated at from about 2 to 3 percent. The increase was almost wholly due

TABLE III-43. *Annual Manufacturing Production: Ten Economies, 191 1929, 1932, 1938 (Index Numbers: 1913 = 100)*

	United Kingdom	United States	USSR	Japan	Ita
1913	100	100	100 (100)[a]	100	10
1929	109	182	182 (102)[a]	279	18
1932	90 (1931)	94	337	273	12
1938	132	144	857 (232)[a]	541	19

[a] Measured by the consumption of industrial materials, the figures in parentheses refl G. Warren Nutter's estimate of growth rates in industrial production from 1913 to 19 and from 1928 to 1937 (*Growth of Industrial Production in the Soviet Union* [Princet Princeton University Press, 1962], p. 163).

to increases in manufacturing, oil and mining, electrical and other public utilities.[159] The course of agricultural development and, especially, world prices for Argentine products had not become irrelevant; on the contrary, they continued to determine foreign-exchange availabilities and thereby the setting for domestic investment. But, as in much of Latin America, the leading sectors had shifted to industry. The Argentine take-off can be dated from the post-1932 recovery, taking the form of three spurts when gross domestic product increased at 5 percent per annum or more—1932–1937, 1943–1948, and 1953–1958.[160]

Industrializing countries at stages of growth earlier than that of Western Europe and the United States fared variously in the setting of the interwar years. In general, those whose take-offs had occurred in the last third of the nineteenth century gained some ground in the process of industrialization, despite the setback of the early 1930's. As Table III-43 shows, this was most notably true of the Soviet Union and Japan, but was a more widespread phenomenon. Britain and the United States are included for purposes of comparison.

We turn now to international migration, demographic change, and housing construction as they affected the contours of the interwar trend period.

Chart III-44 shows the interwar decline of more than 50 percent in European emigration as compared to the levels attained in the period 1901–1915.

Within Europe, France absorbed some two million immigrants from the east and south until its prosperity faded in the 1930's and many of the migrant workers returned to their homelands. The episode foreshadowed, however, the massive intra-European migration of the 1950's and 1960's.

In the United States, policies of restriction were initiated in 1917, climaxed by the permanent quota system passed into law in 1924. The rate of alien immigration revived somewhat in the early 1920's,

therlands	Sweden	Czechoslovakia	Rumania	Spain
0	100	100	100	100
7	151	171	136	132
6	140	102 (1933)	112	117
3	232	165 (1937)	117	b

Civil War.

ources: Svennilson, *Growth and Stagnation in the European Economy*, pp. 304–305,
epting Japan. Japanese data are net domestic product for mining and manufacture at
istant prices (Ohkawa and Rosovsky, *Japanese Economic Growth*, p. 284).

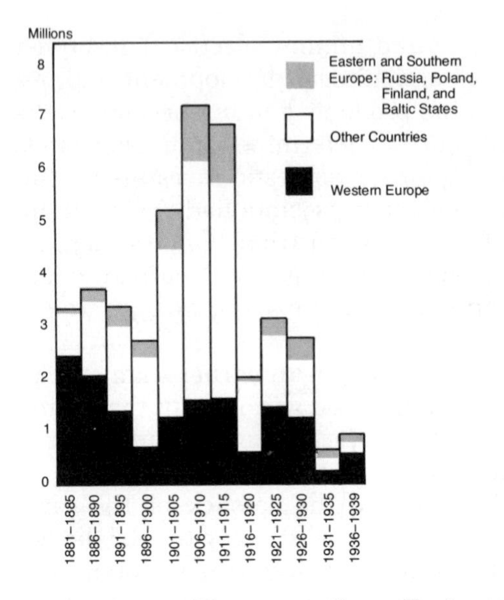

CHART III-44. *European Gross Emigration Overseas, 1881–1939*

Source: Svennilson, *Growth and Stagnation in the European Economy*, p. 65.

but never approached its pre-1914 level during the interwar period. The marked deceleration after 1924 probably contributed to the early (1925) peaking of the housing boom of the 1920's (Table III-44).

The rate of population increase in the United States was slowing down after the mid-1920's, with a faster decline in the birth than the death rate converging with the slowdown in immigration. Only reduced immigration would have had a prompt effect on the demand for housing, since the change in the birth rate did not immediately alter the rate of family formation. But there were three special forces working to strengthen the demand for houses in the 1920's: a reaction to the abnormally low level of housing construction during the war and immediate postwar years (1917–1920); the rapid

TABLE III-44. *Rate of Immigration and Housing Construction in the United States, 1910–1939*

	Immigrants per 1,000 Total Population: Annual Averages	Number of Dwelling Units Started (Thousands)
1910–1914	7.79	410
1915–1919	1.08	309
1920–1924	3.39	629
1925–1929	1.90	772
1930–1934	0.15	187
1935–1939	0.18	341

Source: Richard A. Easterlin, *Population, Labor Force, and Long Swings in Economic Growth*, pp. 208–209.

movement to suburbia permitted by the diffusion of the automobile and bus; and an accelerated absolute decline in the farm population accompanied by an increase in the growth rate of the nonfarm population. The depression of the 1930's struck at all the factors supporting the demand for housing: immigration almost ceased; the birth rate declined by 15 percent and marriages were postponed; the shift to the cities and suburbia sharply decelerated, as automobiles in use in relation to the size of the American population actually remained below the 1929 level until 1937.

Chart III-45 shows interwar housing construction in Britain, Germany, and France. Strong housing booms developed in all three cases during the 1920's, peaking as early as 1927 in Britain. Thereafter, patterns differed markedly: the decline in housing construction continued without significant interruption in France throughout the 1930's. British housing started up again in 1931, with devaluation and an easing of interest rates; in Germany, in 1933, with the beginnings of recovery. As in the United States, a reaction to wartime constraints and the expanding role of the motor vehicle played a role in all three cases: the former a larger, the latter a lesser role than in the United States. But public policy toward housing emerged in Europe for the first time as a positive factor in the housing market. This was particularly the case in Britain. The British government found that wartime control over rents could not, politically, be removed in the setting of acute shortage compounded by a typical wave of postwar marriages.[161] To counter the consequently reduced profitability of housing construction at a time of acute need, the government moved to subsidize construction carried

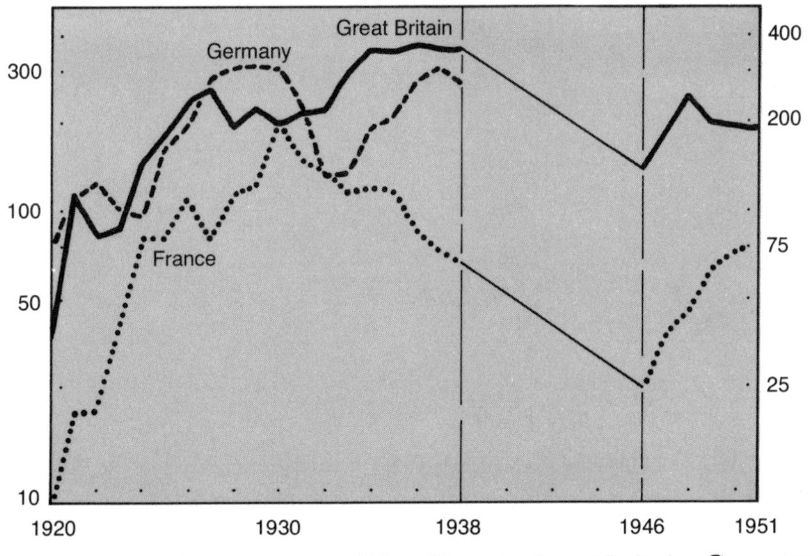

CHART III-45. *Construction of Dwellings in Great Britain, Germany, and France, 1920–1951 (Thousands)*

Source: Svennilson, *Growth and Stagnation in the European Economy*, p. 81.

out both by local authorities and private builders. The scale of the change brought about is suggested by the fact that expenditures by local authorities on housing rose from something like 0.5 percent of their total budgets in the pre-1914 years and 1919 to almost 10 percent in the period 1926–1928, remaining as high as 7 percent in 1937–1939 after the central government had made serious efforts to limit its commitment to the housing subsidy.[162] It was the low range of interest rates after 1931, combined with the forces making for suburbanization and the attractive power of the London area and the Midlands, as the locus of the new light-industry leading sectors, which mainly accounted for the building boom which sustained the British economy fairly well in the 1930's. The ultimate link of housing construction to population and family formation in Britain was not wholly broken. But, as Chart III-46 shows, while the direction of movement in housing reflected fluctuations in the rate of increase of the population, the scale of increased housing construction in the period 1921–1931 reflected other strengthening factors at work. These factors, related to the new leading sectors and public policy, bring to an end the more or less inverse British and American building cycles which had characterized the period 1865–1914.[163] The scale of the change is suggested by the fact that dwelling construction in Britain was 21 percent of net domestic fixed capital formation (at constant prices) during the housing boom of 1902–1905; it fell to 15 percent in 1910–1913, when capital exports were drawing British savings on a large scale and inter-

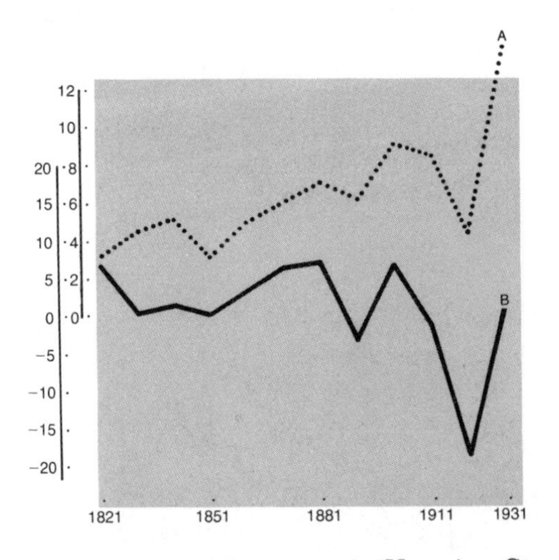

CHART III-46. *Increase in Housing Stock and Fluctuations in the Rate of Population Increase: Great Britain, 1821–1931*

A: Decennial increase in housing stock, Great Britain (hundred thousands).

B: Interdecennial second difference in population, Great Britain (hundred thousands).

Source: J. P. Lewis, *Building Cycles and Britain's Growth*, p. 165.

est rates were high; but the figure was 66 percent for 1925–1929, 84 percent in 1933–1936 (when there was considerable disinvestment in other directions), and still as high as 52 percent in 1938.[164] Clearly, housing construction played a large role in cushioning the British economy in both decades.

The analysis of the interwar years thus far is designed to serve a limited purpose: to explore the extent to which the method of analysis applied to the earlier trend periods can illuminate what was more or less typical of these years and what was unique. This was a time, down to the second half of the 1930's, of a falling price trend brought about by two factors: a relative surplus supply of foodstuffs and raw materials, and the cost-reducing effects of the new technologies being introduced, notably in the leading sectors of the most advanced economies: the motor vehicle, electricity, and a new range of chemicals. It was, in general, a period of relative depression for agriculture, although (as in the last quarter of the nineteenth century) those who shifted to meat and dairy products (plus citrus fruit and other high-value products for urban markets) could survive profitably. It was also a time of rising urban real wages for those who were employed. Finally, it was a period when capital ceased to flow on the old scale to expand the supplies of foodstuffs and raw materials. All this could also be said of the period 1873–1896; and a good deal would hold for 1815–1848. But, of course, there were critical differences:

—the pathologically high levels of unemployment which persisted in Europe even during the best years of the 1920's;

—the build-up of stocks of foodstuffs and raw materials during the 1920's, partially and reciprocally related to the damped rate of industrial growth and high unemployment;

—the large flows of international capital which moved within the industrialized world down to 1929;[165]

—and, above all, the great depression of the 1930's, unexampled in depth, in duration, and in its noneconomic consequences.

Strictly speaking, the depression of the 1930's belongs with the subject matter of Part Four, where the cyclical behavior of the world economy over the past three centuries is outlined. But that event was so closely interwoven with the distortions of this trend period that it requires some comment here.

In the rich literature on the depression of the 1930's there are differences of view and of emphasis as well as elements of consensus. Some would regard the depth and prolonged character of the depression as resulting from a simple failure of policy in the United States to sustain the money supply; others, from the convergence of a series of historical accidents; others would give great weight to the distorting and then depressing effects of the American stock exchange boom and bust of 1928–1929; to the deflationary impact on world trade of the exaggerated fall in the prices of basic commodities, rooted in the surpluses built up in the 1920's; to the slowness of European industry to adjust to the post-1920 environment of the world economy; to the failure of governments actively to stimulate the level of effective demand; to the breakdown of the pre-1914 system of international finance and trade, as Britain could no longer carry the responsibilities of leader, while the United States lacked the insight and will to assume fully after 1929 the role of leader. This would have required keeping its domestic markets open to cheap imports, accepting whatever domestic adjustments might be required, and providing both short-term discounting facilities at times of crisis and enlarged long-term lending abroad, even during cyclical depression. The best analyses of the period embrace, in different proportions, most or all of those elements.

From the present perspective, the clue to an answer capable of relating these partial insights to each other lies in the character of the new leading sectors in the advanced industrial regions of the world. They required high and expanding levels of real income to move forward rapidly, notably in an environment in which the demand for European exports was depressed by the low prices of basic commodities after 1920. As the undervalued French franc and the overvalued British pound indicated, it might have made sense for Europe to turn back a portion of its favorable terms of trade and, in effect, subsidize income (and its own exports) in overseas markets. The structural adjustment to the new leading sectors would have been somewhat less stark. But the maintenance of pre-1914 levels of employment required a more rapid expansion of real income (and a more rapid absorption of the new technologies) than the unaided working of the European economies could generate. There was nothing abnormal, by pre-1914 standards, in the coming of a cyclical downturn in 1929. Its timing recalls, in fact, the downturn of 1825, a decade after the ending of the Napoleonic Wars, which was also followed by a short-lived boom (1817–1818), a brief acute depression (1819), and a sustained cyclical expansion. Here, the role of the United States becomes crucial and, once again, the nature of the new leading sectors is decisive. In my view, the avoidance of severe and protracted depression in the United States required that, in one way or another, consumers' income be sustained by public policy: by some combination of expansionary fiscal and monetary policy with unemployment insurance, housing subsidies, farm supports, etc. The reserve position of the United States would have permitted such a policy. As a society, America was unprepared for such measures, in part because its economists (like their counterparts of the 1970's) did not understand the structural problems that underlay the day-to-day working of the markets. America acted on the implicit assumption that the new leading sectors, like those of the pre-1914 world, would automatically resume their upward course. And, of course, with the Smoot-Hawley Tariff of 1930 the United States signaled an unwillingness to lead the international community to a resolution of its interlocked trade and monetary problems on a cooperative basis. At a time when gold holdings mattered greatly in international finance, the United States pursued this policy, down to the pit of the depression, while its gold stock remained steadily higher than it had been in 1928–1929.

C. P. Kindleberger has recently analyzed afresh the process by which the failure of American leadership brought disintegration to the international trade and monetary system.[166] That essentially political fact, rooted in a failure of understanding as well as in misdirected impulses of raw nationalism, was without question a factor which drove the deflationary spiral downward throughout the world and forced nations to seek recovery on a national basis or through cooperation among limited groups of countries. Britain after 1931 and Germany after 1933 achieved considerable degrees of recovery by policies of income expansion even before armaments expenditures became a significant factor. European nations linked closely to the British and German economies also revived. Japan, like Germany, found its way to subtle policies of economic expansion later also corrupted by commitments to military expansion.

The simple point I would underline is this: only an America lucid and effective in cushioning and reversing its downward spiral in income and employment was likely also to command the perspective and poise to exercise the international leadership it alone was in a technical position to mount. It took time for economists and governments to accept the fact that, when growth had come to depend on the diffusion of the automobile, electrically powered durable consumers' goods, and the shift to suburbia, the level of income had to be sustained by public policy if the leading sectors of high mass-consumption were to move forward at a pace capable of sustaining relatively full employment. But by the time that lesson was at least partially learned, the political as well as economic character of the world community had altered; and men were in power in Berlin and Tokyo bent on war.

16

1936–1951

Somewhere round about 1936 a new trend period can be said to begin. It was then that the Spanish Civil War began and German rearmament accelerated. In 1937 there was a major expansion in British military expenditures, and Japan renewed its attack on China, initially launched in 1931. The demand for foodstuffs and raw materials had, of course, been increasing from, say, 1932; and prices were on the rise from their cyclical troughs, in some cases aided by production cutbacks. But by 1936 the increase in demand was sufficient to bring down stocks of most basic commodities. Price increases accelerated down to the cyclical peak in 1937. The British terms of trade declined by 8 percent between 1935 and 1937.[167]

One reason for taking the benchmark for a new trend period at about this phase of the 1930's is that the relative prices of foodstuffs and raw materials were to remain in a high range, profoundly affected by the Second World War, postwar adjustments, and the Korean War, down to the turning point in 1951. Both the British terms of trade and the American farm parity ratio, after almost two decades of fluctuations at a low level in the one case, a high level in the other, began a systematic period of reverse movement in 1952. Chart III-47 catches the terms-of-trade turning points in the 1930's and early 1950's as well as the gross unfavorable shift between the pre-war and immediate postwar years. It should be noted that in this chart the terms of trade are measured by import over export prices; a rise, therefore, represents an "unfavorable" movement.

A second reason for treating this interval as a unit is that, by its close, postwar reconstruction was about over in Europe, and the pattern set for two decades of remarkable sustained economic growth. Japan was a little behind; but the Korean War provided a stimulus that soon permitted the Japanese to mobilize their resources for a phase of sustained growth unique in modern history, whose inception is conventionally dated in 1955.[168]

It might also be added that, with the failure of the blockade of Berlin in 1949 and the opening of Korean peace negotiations in

1951, a period of relative international stability settled over the northern part of Eurasia which was to persist over the next quarter-century. Western Europe and Japan could move forward in an environment of security, although the former was burdened by somewhat increased defense outlays. Their life was by no means untouched by the crises in Southeast and South Asia, the Middle East, Africa, and Latin America; but they were able to concentrate their energies and resources predominantly on the tasks of economic and social progress.

Table III-45 supplies, on a rough but global basis, some insight into the impact of the Second World War and the postwar pattern of recovery and resumed growth.

The broad conclusions to be drawn from this table are clear enough.

—Direct and indirect war losses slowed the rate of population increase between 1938 and 1948; but world population quickly moved up toward a two percent annual rate of increase.

—Energy consumption increased modestly, on balance, between 1938 and 1948, lifted notably by the U.S. figures; but it then moved forward rapidly, with electricity, petroleum, and natural gas increasing their share of the total, as against coal.

—Like energy consumption, production of steel, cement, and sawn wood showed some net increase between 1938 and 1948; but

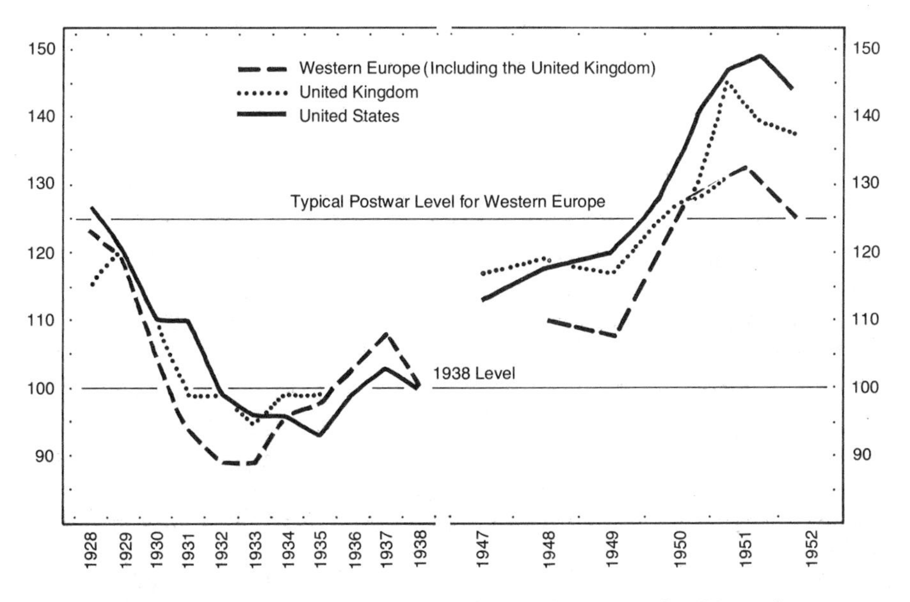

CHART III-47. *Terms of Trade of the United States, the United Kingdom, and Nineteen Western European Countries, 1928–1952 (1938=100)*

Source: Economic Commission for Europe, *Economic Survey of Europe since the War* (Geneva: United Nations, 1953), p. 12.

these three good indicators of the volume of investment then forged ahead at high rates reflecting the post-1948 momentum of Western Europe and Japan.

—Like electricity, the other interwar leading sectors (e.g., motor vehicles and chemicals) quickly re-emerged and moved forward at high rates, with the age of plastics coming into its own.

—On a world basis, agricultural production (except rice) was more gravely set back by the war than industrial production, slower to reattain 1938 levels; but after 1948, strengthened by accelerated production and application of chemical fertilizers and by increased use of farm machinery, agricultural production (including cotton) caught up sufficiently to yield the downward trend in prices after 1951.

The pattern of these global data was strongly affected, of course, by the postwar evolution of the Atlantic economy and, especially, by the manner and timing of European recovery.

Table III-46 shows the pace at which the economies of Western Europe and the United States moved forward after the Second World War in relation to 1938. In 1938, among the countries listed,

TABLE III-45. *World Production of Major Commodities: Selected Years, 1938–1955 (Millions)*

	1938	1948	1938–1948: Average Annual Grow[th] Rate (%)
Population	2,250	2,473	0.95
Total energy (metric-tons-of-coal equivalent)	1,910[a]	2,365[b]	1.80
Electric energy (kWh)	459	810	5.84
Crude petroleum (metric tons)	250	467	6.45
Natural gas (billions of cubic meters)	78.1[a]	168.9[b]	8.02
Coal and lignite (metric tons)	1,302	1,729	2.88
Crude steel (metric tons)	109.6	112.0	0.22
Aluminum (metric tons)	0.6	1.3	8.04
Cement (metric tons)	85.0	103.0	1.94
Plastics and resins (metric tons)	—	1.0	—
Sulphuric acid (metric tons)	14.4	15.1	0.48
Rubber (metric tons)	0.9	2.4	10.31
Motor vehicles (units)	3.8	6.7	5.83
Sawn wood (cubic meters)	200.1[a]	216.4	0.71
Cereals (metric tons)	640	673	0.50
Wheat (metric tons)	176.1	157.3	−1.12
Rice (metric tons)	132.3	158.4	1.82
Cotton lint (metric tons)	6.4	6.3	−0.16
Soybeans (metric tons)	13.5	13.0	−0.38
Milk (metric tons)	245.0	243.1	−0.08
Meat (metric tons)	37.0	35.4	−0.44

[a] 1937.
[b] 1949.

the recovery from depression of France and the United States had been least complete. The United States surged forward during the war, bringing its working force at last back to full employment. The French economy was damped and distorted during the war years, but, under the aegis of Monnet's modernization plan and supported by American aid, it moved rapidly beyond 1938 levels after 1948. Among the major belligerents, Britain initially fared best, quickly converting its war industries to production for the home market and exports, as Table III-47 demonstrates.

The numbers in Table III-47 tell quite a story. To fight the war, Britain more than quadrupled public outlays, which amounted to about half the gross domestic product in 1943–1944. War outlays were achieved at the expense of consumption and capital formation and despite a loss of income from abroad. Essential imports were sustained in these circumstances by Lend-Lease and the sale of assets abroad, despite a radical decline in exports. In the face of relatively unfavorable terms of trade (but strong overseas demand), British exports revived rapidly after the war, reaching a level more than 40 percent above that of 1938 in 1950; but the volume of im-

50	1948–1950: Average Annual Growth Rate (%)	1955	1950–1955: Average Annual Growth Rate (%)
517	1.78	2,758	1.85
607	10.23	3,290	4.76
957	8.7	1,545	10.05
523	5.83	772	8.10
195.9	7.70	298.8	8.81
318	2.54	2,133	3.25
189.3	30.01	269.3	7.30
1.5	7.42	3.2	16.36
133.0	13.63	217.0	10.29
1.4	18.32	3.3	18.71
24.4	27.12	38.1	9.32
2.9	9.92	3.6	4.42
10.5	25.19	13.7	5.46
245.7	6.56	303.6	4.32
578	0.37	825	4.20
167.2	3.10	206.8	4.34
164.7	1.97	209.7	4.95
6.6	2.35	9.7	8.01
17.0	14.35	21.0	4.32
265.3	4.47	299.9	2.48
41.8	8.66	51.0	4.06

Source: *United Nations Statistical Yearbook, 1969* (New York, 1970), p. xxxi.

TABLE III-46. *Gross National Product at Constant Prices: Western Europe and the United States after the Second World War (1938 = 100)*

	Belgium	Denmark	France	Germany	Italy
1938	100	100	100	100	100
1948	115	118	100	45	92
1950	124	135	121	64	104

Source: Angus Maddison, "Growth and Fluctuation in the World Economy, 1870–1960,"

ports was constrained below the 1938 level. Domestic capital formation moved well above the 1938 level. These developments were aided by the fact that, although capital formation in general and housing construction in particular had fallen sharply during the war, plant and machinery construction, much convertible to peacetime uses, had expanded: by 12 percent between 1938 and 1947.[169] Germany, in particular, shared this experience, France to a lesser degree. That is one reason French manufacturing production was 9 percent less than that of 1938 in 1947, British production 15 percent greater.[170]

Thus, by 1950 British consumers' expenditure, domestic capital formation, and gross national product were well above the 1938 level, and social services (notably health services) had been expanded. This result was achieved despite a net loss of property income from abroad and unfavorable terms of trade. This outcome was made possible by two major factors: unemployment was low, averaging 1.4 percent for 1946–1950, as opposed to 8.8 percent for 1936–1938; and American aid, at first bilateral, then through the Marshall Plan, permitted Britain to sustain its dollar imports, unavailable from any other source, while expanding its exports, including exports financed by sterling balances accumulated during

TABLE III-47. *Index Numbers of Expenditure and Gross National Produc at Constant Factor Cost: United Kingdom, 1938–1950 (1938 = 100 at Constant Market Prices)*

	Consumers' Expenditure	Public Authorities' Expenditure	Gross Domestic Fixe Capital Formation
1938	100	100	100
1944	85	438	28
1945	90	356	32
1946	100	195	81
1947	103	138	94
1948	104	132	101
1949	106	140	111
1950	109	140	117

Source: Feinstein, *National Income, Expenditure and Output of the United Kingdo* p. T22. It will be noted that Feinstein's estimate of GNP in 1950 relative to 1938 is slight

etherlands	Norway	Sweden	Switzerland	U.K.	Western Europe	U.S.
00	100	100	100	100	100	100
14	122	133	125	106	87	165
27	131	148	131	114	102	179

uarterly Review (Banca Nazionale del Lavoro), no. 61 (June 1962), p. 195.

the war. Britain's ability to pay off these debts re-established the continuity of the London capital market. American aid thus played a triple role: it supported European recovery, permitted a revival of Britain as a center for capital transactions, and indirectly financed an expansion in world trade.

Within this framework, the revival of Western Germany began relatively late: in 1948. This was not merely the result of war damage, the political disarray of occupation, and inflation. It was also the result of a conscious decision that German recovery should have lower priority than that of the rest of Europe. Coal (especially coking coal needed for steel) was in short supply; and, until Ruhr production was fully revived, it was allocated on a priority basis which discriminated against German recovery. But, with the currency reform of 1948, Germany moved forward; and the governments of Western Europe, as well as the United States, were prepared to acquiesce in or support a policy of rapid German growth.

Disaggregated data on housing construction, coal, steel, motor vehicles, and cement construction all confirm the greater promptness and vigor of British relative to French recovery, French relative to German.[171] As Table III-46 indicates, the smaller countries of

xports, Goods nd Services	Imports, Goods and Services	Net Property Income from Abroad	Gross National Product
00	100	100	100
68	90	22	119
55	86	21	111
93	86	21	110
93	87	30	107
14	85	43	111
26	91	39	114
44	92	62	119

gher than Maddison's, in Table III-46 above.

Western Europe revived even more promptly than Britain. Some had been at peace; others benefited from resource endowments in short supply after the war; most had acquired increased industrial capacity during the war; all were strengthened, directly or indirectly, by U.S. aid and the general European environment of recovery and full employment.

By 1951 industrial production in Western Europe was about 40 percent higher than in 1938; the engineering sector (including motor vehicles) 52 percent; chemicals, still higher.[172] The production of passenger cars in the major producing countries was 56 percent over that of 1938; of commercial vehicles, 150 percent.[173] On the other hand, textile production was only 19 percent over the 1938 level, although rayon leaped ahead everywhere.[174]

The whole process of European revival and the beginnings of postwar growth were framed by an American policy that earnestly sought to learn from the errors of the interwar years. The United States had been a high-tariff nation: it now encouraged imports and led the way in seeking a general reduction in tariff barriers, despite continuing protectionist pressures that had to be held at bay by efforts of the executive branch. It had withdrawn its capital from the world at a time when dollars were needed to maintain world trade: it now made dollars available by gift and loan on a generous scale, and it accepted trade discrimination against the dollar as long as there was a dollar shortage. It had permitted its economy to spiral into a depression which damaged other economies as well as its own: it now passed the Employment Act of 1946 and acted to sustain the level of employment. Above all, it had turned its back on Europe and the world after 1929: but now, despite strong political pressures to bring home its troops and concentrate on domestic matters in 1945–1946, it turned in 1947 to policies of long-term security and political as well as economic commitment in the world —policies which then commanded overwhelming bipartisan support.

The policies pursued by the United States, directly and indirectly, helped yield the revival of trade measured in Table III-48.

The basic situation confronted by Western Europe was one of both unfavorable postwar terms of trade and a shortage of dollars. Put another way, an essential margin of foodstuffs and raw materials required for European recovery could be acquired only from

TABLE III-48. *Volume of Exports and Imports: 1950 as Percentage of 1938*

	United Kingdom	France	Germany	Western Europe	United States	Third Countries	World
Volume of exports	173	167	64	123	181	104	124
Volume of imports	91	104	56	96	180	141	124

Source: Maddison, "Growth and Fluctuation in the World Economy," pp. 186 and 188.

the United States (or other dollar areas), given the levels of output elsewhere. For example, production and exports of grain had declined in Eastern Europe, the USSR, Argentina, Australia, New Zealand, South Africa, and the Indian subcontinent. Only the United States or Canada could supply Europe's essential grain imports. Similar shifts to dollar sources were required in cotton, vegetable oils, meat, dairy products, petroleum, and metals. The Marshall Plan and other policies which made dollars available helped cover that gap, while Western Europe expanded agricultural productivity, and shifted, where possible, from dollar to nondollar imports. By 1951–1952 Western European grain production, excepting the special case of Britain, had not yet fully caught up with 1934–1938 levels; but it was rising and the exaggerated immediate postwar dependence on dollar imports was declining.[175] During this period "third countries," including, especially, overseas exporters of foodstuffs and raw materials, were able to acquire a relatively greater quantity of European manufactured imports for a given quantity of their exports. This tendency was enhanced in some cases by their ability to enlarge imports by drawing down sterling balances and other reserves built up during the war. For example, the volume of Argentine exports actually declined slightly between 1940–1944 and 1945–1949; but the volume of its imports increased by 90 percent.[176] The upshot by 1950 was the pattern in Table III-48: an extraordinary surge in the volume of Western European exports (except for the delay in Germany); a lesser expansion in European imports; a disproportionate rise in imports to "third countries"; and, above all, a resurgence in the total volume of world trade which lifted it, for the first time in twenty years, above the levels of 1929.

Due mainly to the slow revival of German trade and the altered political and economic situation in Eastern Europe, intra-European trade was a lesser proportion of the total in 1950 than it had been in 1938, while trade with overseas countries was relatively greater.[177] On the other hand, the structural shift within manufactures toward trade in transport equipment, chemicals, and machinery could already be discerned by 1950 in the British, French, Italian, and U.S. trade figures (Chart III-48).

The evolution of the Soviet and Eastern European economies down to 1950 was, of course, less affected by the pattern of events in the world economy. The direct and indirect losses of the Soviet Union during the war yielded a decline of total population of fully 20 million between 1940 and 1945. The 1940 level (195.1 million) was not reattained until the mid-1950's. Although overall indexes of Soviet national income and industrial production of this period have a considerable upward bias, there is no doubt that the recovery of production was rapid; producers' goods expanded more rapidly than consumers' goods; agricultural production lagged significantly behind both. Table III-49 shows the movement of some official

Soviet indexes as between 1940 and 1950; Table III-50 shows, for certain sectors, the immediate postwar production level (1946) and the expansion over the four subsequent years.[178]

These data show three things: an intense concentration of resources on the reconstruction and expansion of the heavy industries; a considerable expansion of investment in agriculture, yielding mediocre results; and a reinstallation of something like the 1940 pattern of consumption by 1950, with real wages rising modestly, attaining a level perhaps 18 percent over that of 1940 by 1952.[179] As from 1906 to 1914 and from 1929 to 1940, Russia remained down to 1952 in a version of the drive to technological maturity. In Khrushchev's later phrase, the "steel-eaters" were evidently in command; that is, those advocating the plowing back of steel production into enlarged steel-producing capacity. This was also a time when the modernization of the armed forces, including their equipment

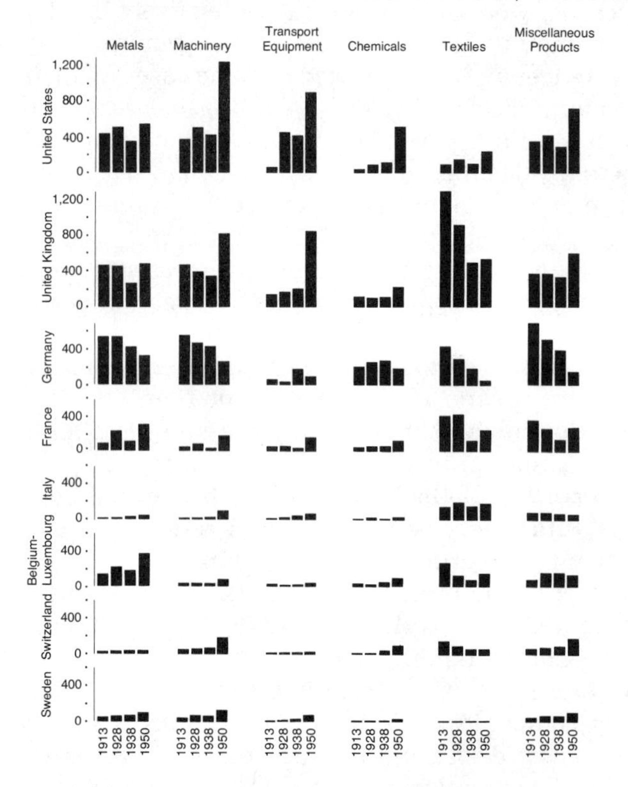

CHART III-48. *Export Volume of Manufactures from Seven European Countries and the United States, 1913, 1928, 1938, 1950 (Six Commodity Groups: Millions of Dollars at 1938 Prices)*[a]

[a] The volume figures have been obtained by deflating current values for each commodity group by its export price index of the United Kingdom. The figures are rough approximations.

Source: Svennilson, *Growth and Stagnation in the European Economy*, p. 184.

Note: Data refer to current territory.

TABLE III-49. *Official Soviet Economic Indexes: 1950 as Percentage of 1940*

National income	164
Gross industrial production	173
Producers' goods	205
Consumers' goods	132
Gross agricultural output	107
Plant	113
Animal	95
Sown area	97

Source: Economic Commission for Europe, *Economic Survey of Europe since the War*, p. 39.

with atomic weapons, engaged a high proportion of Soviet national income. But on these immediate postwar foundations the USSR proceeded into the 1950's with a high but decelerating rate of overall growth.

The course of postwar recovery in Eastern Europe was, of course, more complex. At different times these nations came under the control of communist governments which radically changed the organization of industry and agriculture. The degree of wartime damage (and wartime accretion of industrial capacity) varied greatly among them. In addition, they stood, in terms of their prior history, at quite different stages of growth. Eastern Germany and Czechoslovakia, for example, were technically ready to move into high mass-consumption, having acquired the requisite plants and technologies and, under normal conditions, appropriate levels of con-

TABLE III-50. *Production in the Soviet Union in Certain Sectors, 1940, 1946, 1950*

	1940	1946	1950
Coal and lignite (million tons)	166	162	260
Crude petroleum (million tons)	31.0	21.8	37.8
Electric power (billion kWh)	48.3	49.5	90.3
Crude steel (million tons)	18.3	13.3	27.3
Equipment for iron and steel mills (thousand tons)	28	—	134
Combine harvesters (thousands)	13	—	46
Mineral fertilizers (thousand tons)	2,608	—	5,100
Soap (thousand tons)	747	245	866
Cement (million tons)	5.8	3.3	10.3
Window glass (million square meters)	4.4	46.7	84.3
Cotton fabrics (million meters)	3,886	1,878	3,815
Leather shoes (million pairs)	205	78	205
Butter (thousand tons)	206	185	322
Meat (thousand tons)	1,184	—	1,267
Sugar (thousand tons)	2,150	467	2,522
Canned foodstuffs (billion tons)	1	0.5	1.5

Source: Economic Commission for Europe, *Economic Survey of Europe since the War*, pp. 42–43.

sumers' income per capita. At the other end of the spectrum, Rumania, Bulgaria, and Albania (in that order of relative development) were in a pre–take-off stage. In between were Poland, with new boundaries and enlarged industrial resources, ready to move forward in the drive to technological maturity, and Yugoslavia, on average at about that stage, but its regions representing a wider range, with an advanced north, an intermediate center, and a quite primitive south.

What can be said in general is that, under direct or indirect Soviet influence, they all moved toward higher levels of investment, concentrated in the producers' goods sectors; they all experienced grave difficulties with their newly collectivized agricultural arrangements; and standards of life recovered from immediate postwar levels but, by 1950, were probably not far above those levels. Trade between Eastern and Western Europe declined as compared to prewar levels, as the Soviet Union extracted reparations from some nations and reoriented trade away from the West for all.[180] From 1948 forward, after Tito's break with Stalin, Yugoslavia pioneered a new economic policy, moving toward strong private incentives in agriculture, significant degrees of decentralized decision-making in industry, and widened trade with the West.

Chart III-49 shows the relatively slow and incomplete recovery of agricultural production in Eastern Europe down to 1951–1952.

In Asia, excepting Japan, postwar recovery generally came slowly. New nations were being born out of colonialism. There was war in China down to 1949, in Indo-China down to 1954, and in Korea from 1950 to 1953. There were disruptive guerrilla wars in Burma, Malaya, the Philippines, and Indonesia. Taiwan was taken over from the Japanese by the defeated Chinese Nationalists and reorganized with considerable initial pain, but strengthened for the long pull by the land reform measures of 1949–1953. Hong Kong, its trade with the mainland attenuated, had to reorient its life while population almost doubled between 1946 and 1952, outpacing its incipient industrialization. Only Thailand moved forward without major trauma on the basis of its agricultural and raw-material resources, with agriculture 47 percent above the 1934–1938 level in 1951–1952.[181] The high prices of foodstuffs and raw materials down to 1951 and favorable terms of trade cushioned the position of some of the Asian countries, as did measures of external assistance.

At various times in the early 1950's, however, the economic situation stabilized. India and China began their first five-year plans; the industrialization of Taiwan and Hong Kong began in earnest; and other nations in the region as well began the long, erratic adventure of moving into purposeful modern economic growth.

Turning back to the more industrialized parts of the world and to the role of population movements and the construction of dwellings, we find once again postwar housing booms. The immediate postwar housing problem in Europe was compounded of four elements: the repair and replacement of direct war destruction; making up for the hiatus in new housing construction during the war; demography, as it affected the postwar rate of family formation; and public policy, as it affected goals for slum clearance and, in general, an elevation of housing standards. It was estimated in 1949 that, at the end of the war, the equivalent of 7.76 percent of total housing units had been lost through total and partial destruction or damage.[182] The figures ranged from 21.5 percent and 20.7 percent in Poland and Greece (about the same loss as in Germany) to 7.6

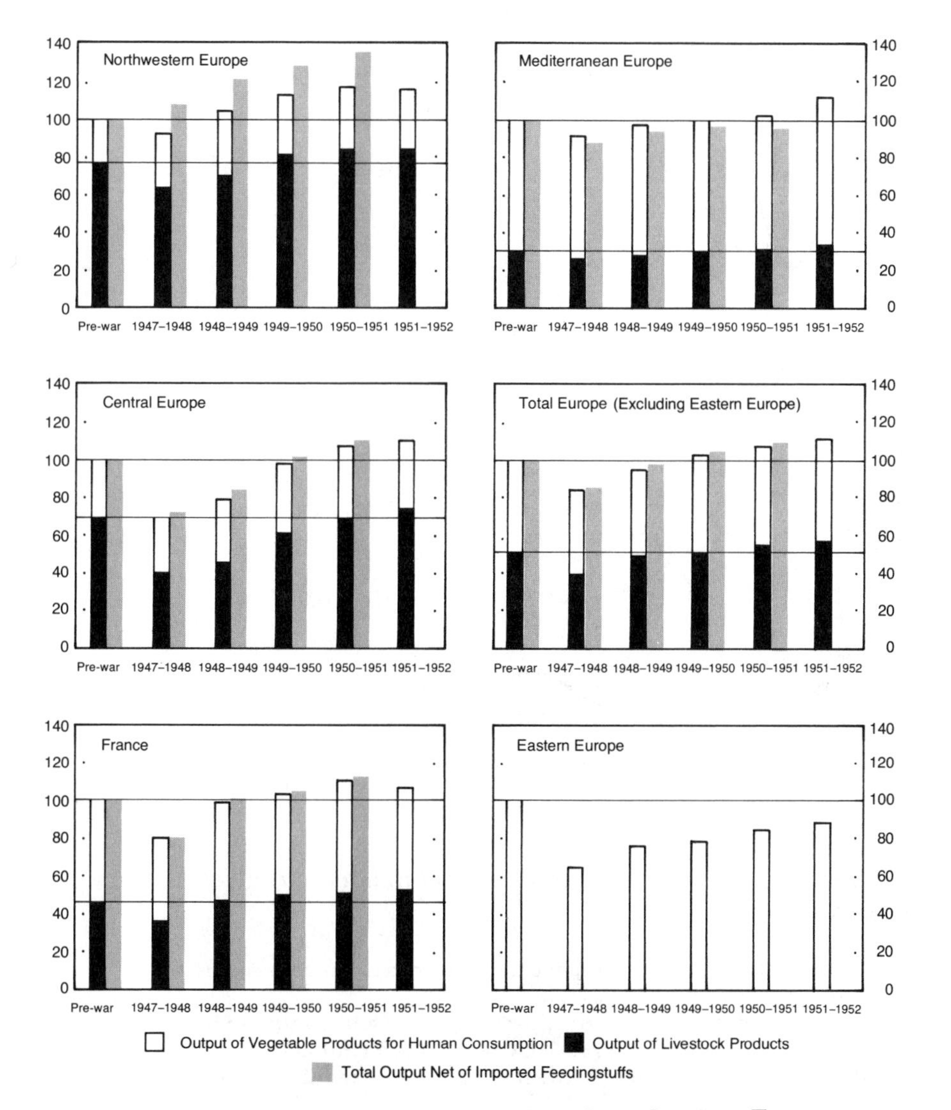

CHART III-49. *Index Numbers of Agricultural Production: Europe, Pre-war to 1951–1952 (Pre-war=100)*

Source: Economic Commission for Europe, *Economic Survey of Europe since the War*, p. 167.

percent and 6.5 percent in France and Britain, to zero in Denmark, Sweden, and Switzerland. It was also estimated, by explicit but arbitrary standards of decent housing, that 17 percent of total housing was overcrowded, unhealthy, or unsafe.[183] Only 2.5 million dwellings were built in Europe between 1940 and 1947, as opposed to more than a million annually before 1939. There was, evidently, a formidable initial backlog of demand for housing in 1945.[184] The demographic patterns of the past yielded different proportions of the population of an age likely to marry and set up new households; but there was a general tendency for the marriage rate to rise with the end of hostilities and demobilization.

Chart III-50 shows the evolution of construction in Britain from

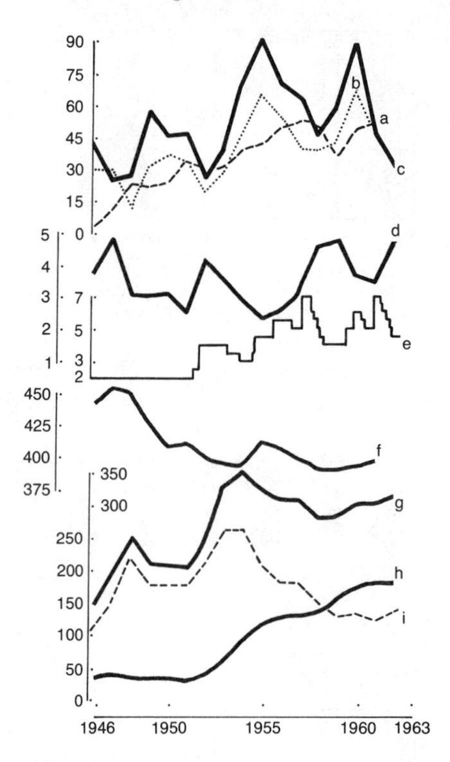

CHART III-50. *British Construction and Related Variables, 1946–1963*

a: Industrial building completed, Great Britain (million square feet). *Monthly Digests of Statistics.*

b: Industrial building started, Great Britain (million square feet). Ibid.

c: Industrial building approved, Great Britain (million square feet). Ibid.

d: Registered unemployed, Great Britain (hundred thousands). Monthly average. Ibid.

e: Bank rate (%). *Financial Statistics.*

f: Marriages, United Kingdom (thousands). *Annual Abstracts of Statistics.*

g: Permanent houses completed, United Kingdom (thousands). Ibid.

h: Permanent houses completed for private owners, United Kingdom (thousands). Ibid.

i: $g-h$.

Source: J. P. Lewis, *Building Cycles and Britain's Growth*, p. 242.

1946 to 1963. The post-1945 demand for houses was enlarged by the coming to maturity of those born in the surge of births after the First World War, as well as by the high level of marriages in 1946–1948.

For our purposes two features of Chart III-50 are particularly worth noting: the setback to the initial postwar housing surge in 1949–1951 (curve *g*) due to the higher priority accorded by the government to industrial construction (curves *a*, *b*, *c*); and the extraordinarily high proportion of houses initially completed under the aegis of public authorities (curves *g*, *h*, *i*). In 1938–1939, 31 percent of the houses built in England and Wales were for local authorities. The average for 1946–1950 was 79 percent.[185] The total number of new houses built in Britain averaged well below the immediate pre-war level; but, given the scale of housing reconstruction and repair, the comparative figures are somewhat deceptive. Outlays for housing repair and adaptation exceeded those for permanent housing in 1946, were 86 percent of the latter figure in 1947–1948.[186]

As Chart III-45 shows, the revival in housing construction was even more rapid in France than in Britain, exceeding the 1938 level by 1951; but housing in France had been greatly depressed in the 1930's and it was still far below the 1930 peak in the period 1946–1950.[187]

In the United States, on the other hand, where housing had also been depressed in the 1930's, new dwelling units constructed moved well above the average of the late 1920's by 1949–1950 (Table III-51).

Immediate postwar international population movements undoubtedly left some mark on housing demand; but, excepting the refugee flow to West Germany, they were not a major factor. In Britain over the period 1945–1954, emigration and immigration came close to balancing: the former slightly over 1.5 million, the latter about 1.25 million.[188] In West Germany, on the other hand, the census of 1946 showed 7.1 million persons whose residence had been outside the present boundaries of the Federal Republic; and by 1950 this group had grown by 2.5 million.[189] In France there was a modest influx of foreign workers: some 306,000 between 1946 and

TABLE III-51. *Permanent Dwelling Units Started in Nonfarm Areas: United States, 1925–1950 (Annual Averages in Thousands)*

1925–1929	772
1930–1934	187
1935–1939	359
1940–1944	400
1945–1950	847
(1948–1950)	(1,118)

Source: *Historical Statistics of the United States*, 1960 ed., p. 393.

1954.[190] In the United States, immigration, which had been running at less than 100,000 annually between 1931 and 1945, due to depression and war, averaged about 173,000 annually for the period 1946–1950; but this was only 59 percent of the 1925–1930 level, and a much lesser proportion of the typical rates before the legislation of 1924.[191] Renewed immigration added to the forces making for the postwar U.S. housing boom, but it was not a decisive factor. It is, nevertheless, worth noting that net migration was contributing almost 20 percent of the increase in the U.S. labor force by the 1950's; and there is a reasonably close relation in this period between labor force changes and the formation of households, with its rather direct bearing on housing demand.[192] In the postwar years publicly owned housing and private dwellings financed by the Federal Housing and Veterans Administrations became a significant feature of the American scene. FHA housing began in 1935, publicly owned low-rent housing in 1936.[193] They were joined from 1941 by a considerable volume of publicly owned war and defense housing. By 1951, some 400,000 private housing units were started under FHA and VA auspices and over 10,000 public units completed for low-rent occupancy—about 39 percent of total housing starts.

TABLE III-52. *Intercontinental Immigration: Selected Countries, Single Years, 1945–1954*

Country	Total	1945	1946	1947
A. Immigration, mainly of aliens				
Argentina[a]	742,259	989	4,422	38,
Australia[b]	868,768	5,752	15,759	28,
Brazil[a]	413,252	2,889	12,852	18,
Canada[a]	1,027,243	11,793	57,071	51,
Israel[bc]	547,520	12,398	20,525	19,
New Zealand[bd]	131,581	3,011	5,960	7,
Rhodesia[ae]	55,512	—	3,071	6,
United States[a]	1,444,806	14,116	106,854	126,
Union of South Africa[a]	153,212	2,100	9,074	25,
Venezuela[f]	150,000	—	—	
B. Immigration, mainly of nationals (return of former emigrants)				
Italy[g]	142,450	—	525	9,
Netherlands[b]	334,133	—	79,183	28,
Portugal[g]	42,613	1,704	5,367	7,
Spain[b]	106,205	2,591	5,107	6,
C. Immigration of nationals and aliens				
United Kingdom[b]	668,760	—	67,051	62,

[a] Aliens only.
[b] Nationals and aliens.
[c] The figure for 1954 refers to both intercontinental and continental immigration to Is
[d] Fiscal year ending 31 March of the following year.
[e] In 1954, ten months only.

Table III-52 presents a general picture of intercontinental immigration from 1945 to 1954. Its most striking feature, as compared to the past, was the high level of immigration to Australia, notably in the period 1949–1952.

In general, then, the postwar world economy moved from reconstruction into sustained growth without a traumatic setback like that of 1920–1921. The process took place in an environment of relatively high prices for foodstuffs and raw materials. In the advanced industrial world the leading sectors of high mass-consumption, which had given some strength to Western European growth during the interwar years (and supported the American boom of the 1920's), re-emerged quickly, despite the urgent general tasks of reconstruction. The Soviet Union also recovered quickly and resumed its particular version of the drive to technological maturity. Japan regained its pre-war level only a little more slowly than Western Europe but, with its military outlays constrained, faced the amiable task of moving over from the drive to technological maturity to high mass-consumption—a task for which it was about to exhibit a certain talent. The Latin American take-offs of the 1930's were carried forward in an environment of relatively high export prices. More

948	1949	1950	1951	1952	1953	1954
19,201	149,764	134,933	106,499	76,506	49,567	61,746
61,898	163,640	169,612	127,986	124,202	71,669	99,616
21,421	23,713	34,458	62,229	84,720	80,070	72,248
14,387	86,370	65,535	185,675	154,055	158,216	142,980
06,567	167,586	112,073	70,897	16,742	7,517	14,116[c]
9,590	14,386	14,372	20,563	22,725	18,922	14,240
10,550	6,340	4,885	6,846	8,566	5,139	3,211[e]
27,148	209,534	165,542	196,022	158,109	114,972	225,753
32,532	13,352	11,787	14,257	17,108	14,438	13,257
—	—	—	—	—	—	—
15,323	16,319	28,826	28,567	18,946	10,422	14,394
25,847	22,841	60,870	35,715	24,202	25,239	31,270
10,235	8,508	3,784	1,423	1,047	1,209	1,373
6,148	6,888	9,626	11,630	19,471	19,815	18,641
73,746	64,792	71,932	76,295	82,072	77,764	92,328

[f] Estimated.
[g] Nationals only.
Source: Witold Langrod, in Brinley Thomas (ed.), *Economics of International Migration*, p.
2.

complex readjustments were faced in Eastern Europe; but by 1950 these economies were also moving forward, although in patterns different from those which less constrained sovereignty would have decreed. In Asia, excepting Thailand, conflict and the transitions to independence impeded recovery; but by 1951 China, India, and a few others were about ready to launch, in reasonably stable political environments, purposeful policies of growth and modernization.

In this setting, then, population movements of a type long familiar resumed: from Europe to the Americas and Australia. They were substantially higher than during the depressed 1930's, but generally lower than in the 1920's or the pre-1914 decades. These left their impact on housing construction; but in most cases that impact was overwhelmed by the making good of direct and indirect war losses, by the surge of postwar family formation, and by the influence of public policies which, in one way or another, subsidized housing construction.

17

1951–1972

We turn now to consider, in terms of trend-period analysis, the most remarkable two decades of economic growth in modern history, running from the early 1950's to the price revolution that began in 1972. As emerged in Part Two (see above, Table II-7), the average annual rates of growth of both world industrial production (about 5.6 percent) and world trade (about 7.3 percent) in this period exceeded by a substantial margin any before experienced. This happened because the potentially depressing effects of relatively low terms of trade for producers of foodstuffs and raw materials were overridden by two factors: the rapid movement forward of the leading sectors, in an environment of relatively full employment, in the industrialized regions of the world; and the cushioning effects of a considerable flow of intergovernmental assistance to the less industrialized nations, most of whom were also governed by policies designed to accelerate economic growth. Trade among the industrialized nations expanded faster than between them and the less developed nations; but there was nothing like the interwar stagnation and collapse of the trade of the less developed regions. The process was strengthened, notably in Europe, by flows of migration from south to north, reinforcing the impulses to growth in both regions, and by movements within nations from rural to urban areas, accompanied by rapid increases in agricultural productivity. The whole period was framed by stable international monetary arrangements, with the dollar serving as the world's reserve currency down to 1971, and by increasingly liberal trade policies. It was also a time of unexampled price inflation for a time of relative peace.

Putting aside the question of inflation for consideration in Part Four, the major nations did all the things they should have done between the wars; and, in considerable part, this was because the lessons of the earlier period were well learned. Endemic inflation was, in part, a result of this great success. But, down to 1972, inflationary pressures were eased in most industrialized nations by the relatively low level of foodstuff and raw-material prices.

Tables III-53 and III-54 capture the movement of relative prices of commodities entering international trade and the terms of trade for the major regions of the world over the period 1938–1972. We have already considered the relatively favorable shift of foodstuff and raw-material prices from 1938 to 1951 and the consequently unfavorable movement of the terms of trade for the more industrialized nations. Broadly speaking, the movement reversed after 1951.

Given its later importance, the movement of fuel prices is worth particular note. The fuel price rose less between 1938 and 1948–1953 than prices of food and raw materials. Its net decline between

TABLE III-53. *World Export Prices, 1938–1972: Unit Value Index*

Exports	1938	1948	1951	1953	1958	1963
All commodities	39	102	108	100	100	100
Food and raw materials	35	111	125	109	101	100
Fuel	43	105	103	105	113	100
Manufactured goods	47	95	97	94	98	100

Source: *United Nations Statistical Yearbook, 1972*, p. 42, with 1972 data added a

TABLE III-54. *World Trade of Market Economies: Terms of Trade*[a] *(1963 = 100)*

Regions[b]	1938	1948	1951	1953	195
Developed market economies[c]	98	95	89	93	96
North America[d]	116	101	86	94	97
Europe	96	92	85	92	95
EEC	92	91	85	92	95
EFTA	97	87	84	91	97
Other Europe	127	107	101	93	94
Africa[e]	92	103	128	115	100
Asia[f]	84	85	95	95	99
Oceania	102	117	173	125	85
Developing market economies	79	95	118	106	104
Excluding petroleum	79	96	128	108	102
Africa	70	93	126	105	110
Asia	88	94	120	103	106
Asian Middle East	107	88	116	97	116
Excluding petroleum	90	62	138	100	106
Other Asia	86	96	122	105	100
Latin America	70	100	124	110	100
Excluding petroleum	67	98	134	112	100

[a] Unit value index of exports divided by the unit value index of imports.

[b] The geographical regions used in this table are in accordance with the United Natio Standard Country Code, Annex II, Country Classification for International Trade Statist (Statistical Papers, Series M, no. 49).

[c] Excluding the trade of Centrally Planned Economies.

1953 and 1963 was also less drastic. Between 1963 and 1969 it fell absolutely, while food and raw materials rose slightly. By 1972, however, the indexes were virtually together. As compared to the prices of manufactured goods, the price of fuel rose slightly more between 1938 and 1951; but it rose considerably less between 1951 and 1971–1972, actually declining significantly from 1953 to 1969, while the price of manufactured exports increased. This is a fact of considerable significance, given the character of the energy-consuming leading sectors in most industrialized parts of the world at that time. Comparing 1971 and 1938 prices, the greatest increase

963 = 100)

66	1967	1968	1969	1970	1971	1972
5	104	103	107	112	119	128
5	103	102	106	110	115	124
7	96	97	98	102	114	123
6	106	105	108	114	122	131

rections for 1971 made from 1973 edition, p. 55.

65	1966	1967	1968	1969	1970	1971	1972
0	100	101	101	101	102	101	102
1	102	103	104	104	103	102	98
0	100	101	100	101	102	103	105
0	99	99	100	100	102	103	104
2	103	103	104	104	104	104	105
2	103	106	102	100	98	96	99
9	97	96	99	99	98	88	85
4	93	96	98	102	103	105	111
5	97	90	88	88	83	79	92
9	101	100	101	100	101	102	100
1	104	102	103	106	106	101	100
0	104	104	105	108	103	103	98
8	99	98	100	100	99	103	99
7	95	96	97	92	89	96	81
5	95	99	97	95	94	83	—
9	100	99	100	102	104	104	100
3	103	100	99	100	101	101	102
5	107	102	102	104	106	103	105

Canada and the United States.
South Africa.
Israel and Japan.
ource: *United Nations Statistical Yearbook, 1972*, p. 42, data added and corrections 1969–1971 made from the 1973 edition, p. 54.

is in food and raw materials (3.29 times). Fuel and manufactured goods show similar movements (2.67 and 2.60 times, respectively). In 1972, a year of cyclical, demand-pull global inflation, food, raw-material, and energy prices rose 8 percent, manufactured goods exports, 7 percent.

The impact of these movements (and of particular commodities within them) determines the terms-of-trade movements of the various regions (Table III-54). Excepting South Africa and Australia (Oceania), there was a net favorable movement for all the more developed economies between 1953 and 1972. The fixed monetary price of gold and the foodstuff and raw-material exports of Australia and New Zealand mainly caused the apparent anomaly. As for the others, most of the favorable shift had taken place by 1965, except in Israel and Japan.

Putting aside the extraordinary price movements of 1951—a speculative boom after the outbreak of the Korean War—the fortunes of the developing regions varied. After some deterioration between 1953 and 1965, the African terms of trade almost recovered their 1953 level by 1971, but fell away again in 1972. Asia as a whole shows a similar pattern, with a trough in 1967. The figures for the Middle East (including and excluding petroleum) exhibit the powerful effect of oil prices on the outcome: the terms of trade, excluding petroleum, exhibited a considerable net deterioration down to 1971; the rise in the petroleum price in 1971, modest by what was shortly to occur, lifted the terms of trade for that year almost back to the 1953 level. The net deterioration of the Latin American terms of trade between 1951 and 1971 was most marked; but it was mainly confined to the period 1951–1958. The terms of trade fluctuated in a range generally above the 1958 level over the subsequent decade, although well below the 1953 (let alone the 1951) figure.

In general, then, this was a time of relatively cheap food, raw materials, and energy. The relative cheapening, however, took place in the period down to the mid-1960's, even earlier for Latin American exports. As the 1960's wore on, there was evidence of strain between the requirements of population increase and the food supply, between the requirements of industrial growth and the supply of raw materials and energy. The price explosion of 1972–1974 thus came against a background which signaled that things were changing.

As we know, this is a familiar phenomenon. The extraordinary price increase of 1799–1801 was preceded by a prior tendency for food prices to rise in the face of increasing population in Western Europe and, more proximately, by the increases of 1793–1796 associated with the first phase of the French Revolutionary War. The great cotton price rise of 1833–1835 was preceded by a phase when the price decline ceased and cotton stocks were drawn down in Britain, the major market. There was, in fact, some net price increase from 1828 to 1832. The surge of prices in 1852–1854 was preceded by the warning of 1845–1847, when the potato crop washed away in Ireland and elsewhere, signaling the precarious balance between food supply and demand. The extraordinary price increase of 1898–1900 was foreshadowed by the upward movement of prices from their deep trough of 1894. There was also a mild price turn-around from about 1933 which set the stage for the marked increases of 1935–1937.

Looking back on the period 1965–1971 we can also perceive a growing tension in the markets for certain key foodstuffs and raw materials. Food grains and petroleum were particularly important. This was the case not merely because of the large role of these commodities in the world economy but also because the real or believed reserve position of the United States as a supplier had powerful constraining effects on world prices until the precarious underlying position was revealed by events.

Tables III-55, III-56, and III-57 and Chart III-51 dramatize the setting of the 1960's out of which emerged the grain price explosion of 1972–1973. Their major features are these:

—North America filled the gap in grain exports as Asia, Eastern Europe and the USSR, Africa, and then Latin America shifted to increasingly deficit positions (Table III-55).

—This process was accompanied by an occasionally broken but powerful trend decline in world food reserves as measured by days of annual world grain consumption, including idle U.S. cropland (Table III-57 and Chart III-51).

—U.S. reserve stocks and idle cropland were drawn down as a matter of public policy to deal with the Indian harvest failures of 1965–1967; but they rose in 1968–1970, fell in 1971, and rose again in 1972 (Table III-57). A narrow view of the U.S. position as of 1972 would not have suggested the vulnerability of the global position. To understand that position required a sense of the longer trends toward food deficit in the various regions of the world and, especially, of the global reserve position measured in relation to rising world grain consumption.

TABLE III-55. *The Changing Pattern of World Grain Trade*

Region	1934–1938	1948–1952	1960	1966	1973 (Prel.)
	(Million Metric Tons)				(Fiscal Year)
North America	+5	+23	+39	+59	+88
Latin America	+9	+1	0	+5	−4
Western Europe	−24	−22	−25	−27	−21
Eastern Europe and USSR	+5	—	0	−4	−27
Africa	+1	0	−2	−7	−4
Asia	+2	−6	−17	−34	−39
Australia	+3	+3	+6	+8	+7

Source: Lester R. Brown, *In the Human Interest* (New York: W. W. Norton, 1974), p. 81. Based on U.S. Department of Agriculture data.

Note: Plus = net exports; minus = net imports.

TABLE III-56. *World Prices of Major Food Commodities, 1960–1973 (Unit Value of U.S. Exports)*

	Rice (Dollars per 100 Lbs.)	Wheat (Dollars per Bushel)	Soybeans (Dollars per Bushel)
1960	$ 6.62	$1.69	$2.27
1961	5.99	1.77	2.41
1962	6.62	1.81	2.41
1963	6.77	1.79	2.58
1964	7.02	1.80	2.71
1965	7.21	1.63	2.85
1966	7.79	1.69	3.09
1967	7.80	1.74	2.93
1968	8.61	1.68	2.75
1969	8.44	1.64	2.64
1970	8.48	1.58	2.79
1971	8.41	1.68	3.13
1972	9.40	1.75	3.38
1973 (Jan.–June)	12.00	2.12	5.35
1973 (July–Dec.) (prel.)	19.00	3.80	6.20

Source: Brown, *In the Human Interest*, p. 59. Based on IMF, *International Financial Statistics*, and U.S. Department of Agriculture data.

TABLE III-57. *Index of World Food Security*

	Reserve Stocks of Grain	Grain Equivalent of Idle U.S. Cropland	Total Reserves	Reserves as Days of Annual World Grain Consumption
	(Million Metric Tons)			
1961	154	68	222	95
1962	131	81	212	88
1963	125	70	195	77
1964	128	70	198	77
1965	113	71	184	69
1966	99	79	178	66
1967	100	51	151	55
1968	116	61	177	62
1969	136	73	209	69
1970	146	71	217	69
1971	120	41	161	51
1972	131	78	209	66
1973	103	20	123	37
1974 (proj.)	89	0	89	27

Source: Brown, *In the Human Interest*, p. 56. Based on U.S. Department of Agriculture data.

—The availability of U.S. stocks and reserve cropland kept wheat price fluctuations in a relatively narrow range from 1960 to 1972, although there was a rising trend in soybeans and, even more markedly, in rice (Table III-56 and Chart III-51).

—A convergence of bad harvests in the USSR and Asia, combined with the U.S. grain deal with the Soviet Union, produced the attenuation of stocks, the rise in prices, and the elimination of idle cropland to be observed in Table III-57.

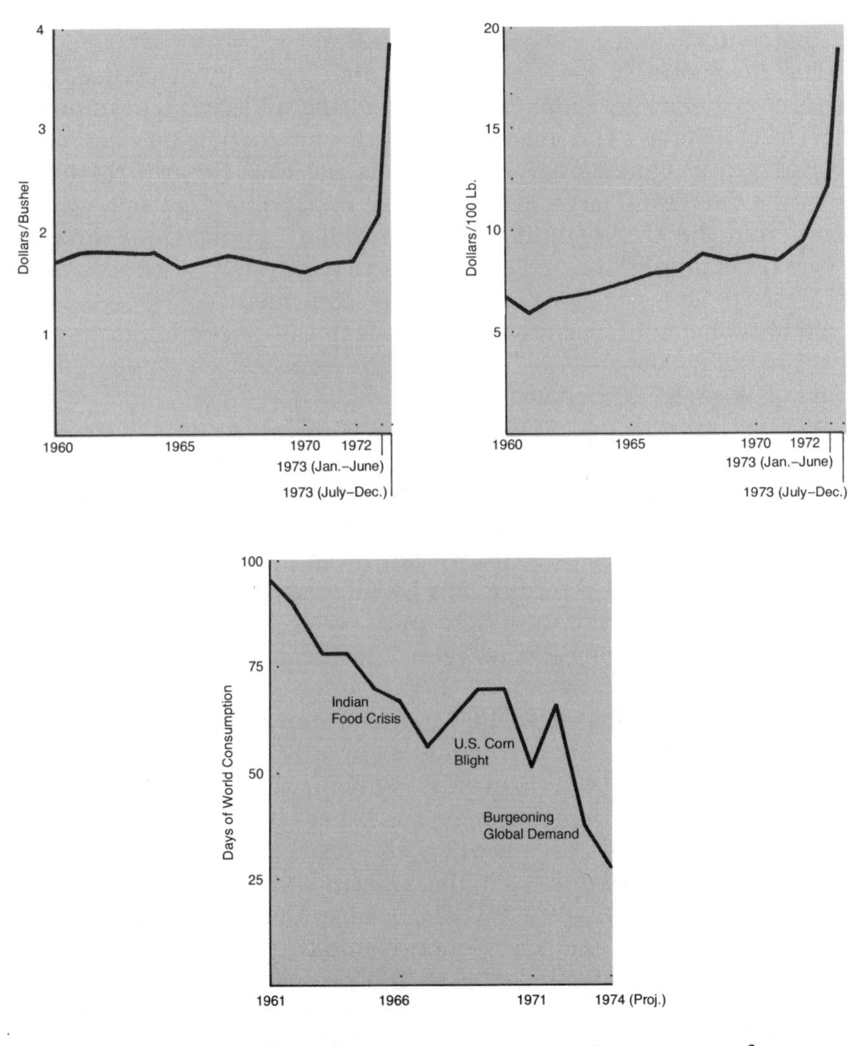

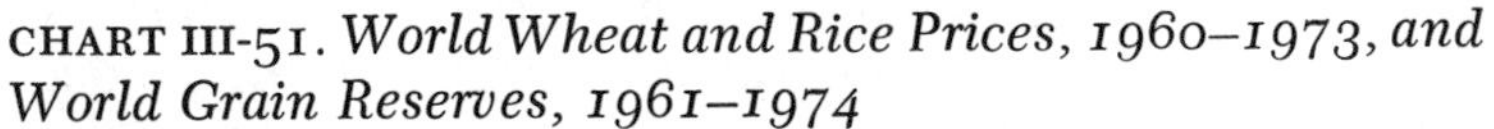

CHART III-51. *World Wheat and Rice Prices, 1960–1973, and World Grain Reserves, 1961–1974*

Upper left: world wheat price, 1960–1973 (unit value of U.S. exports).
Upper right: world rice price, 1960–1973 (unit value of U.S. exports).
Lower: world grain reserves as days of world consumption, 1961–1974 (includes production potential of idled U.S. cropland).
Source: Brown, *In the Human Interest*, pp. 58, 57, and 55. Based on U.S. Department of Agriculture data.

The rising level of demand for grain, which was the backdrop to these events, represented more than merely the rise in world population. In the poorer parts of the world increases in income were spent disproportionately on food in the form of grain; in some richer societies, increases in income were translated into new demands for grain-expensive meat. Thus, in the developing countries, where population increase averaged 2.5 percent per annum, the growth of effective demand for the 1970's was estimated at 3.6 percent; in the high-income countries, where population increase averaged annually about 1 percent, the increase in demand was estimated at about 1.7 percent.[194]

The revolution in petroleum prices in 1973 was, of course, the product of policy decisions by OPEC; but the underlying position of the United States with respect to energy production and reserves also played a significant role. This was the case for two reasons: first, the image of large and regularly expanding U.S. energy reserves and the U.S. potentiality as a residual supplier at a time of crisis in oil supplies helped contain petroleum prices; second, when the United States became increasingly dependent on imports, the scale of its demand was great, even though the proportion of its imports to total consumption was relatively modest as compared to those of Western Europe and Japan.

In effect, the United States behaved with respect to energy consumption the way the developing continents behaved with respect to population and the food supply: it permitted demands to develop which required an increasing reliance on imports; it permitted its ready energy reserves to be drawn down; and it failed to anticipate the consequences of this situation by altering its domestic policies and its patterns of consumption and investment, which (as with the developing nations) were geared to the notion of indefinitely low prices and world surpluses. OPEC perceived its opportunities in this situation and produced in 1973–1974 an exaggerated version of the kind of price increase the markets yielded in the case of grain. Perhaps the gravest American misjudgment, shared by government and the petroleum industry, was the belief that the oil producers were incapable of the organization and discipline required to exercise their monopolistic power in these circumstances.

The mechanism that gave OPEC its opportunity has been thoroughly described in the many energy studies which emerged after the crisis of 1973.[195] It is reflected in Table III-58.

As late as 1950 the United States was a net exporter of energy. In the 1950's the decline in coal production shifted American status to that of net importer, despite the rapid expansion in the production and use of natural gas. Two significant steps in public policy were taken in this decade: starting in 1954, the Federal Power Commission controlled the wellhead price of natural gas entering interstate commerce and held the price relatively constant; in 1959, in reaction to the curtailment of Middle East oil exports during the Suez Crisis of 1956–1957, quotas were imposed on imported oil which kept the U.S. price somewhat above the world price, encouraged the drilling of new wells, and for a time generated a margin of quickly available excess capacity in the form of production below the maximum efficient recovery rates arbitrarily set in the oil-producing states. But the real cost of establishing a unit of oil and gas reserves was rising rapidly.[196] By 1960, the United States was importing about 7 percent of its energy.

As the 1960's wore on, the energy market began to tighten. First, the increase in U.S. energy consumption accelerated with the increased pace and energy-intensive character of economic growth: from an annual average rate of 2.7 percent in the 1950's, to 3.79 percent for 1960–1965; 4.8 percent for 1965–1970. The volume of petroleum imports grew: from 10 percent of total crude petroleum consumption in 1960 to 28 percent in 1968. In response to the pressure of demand, older American wells moved up to their maximum efficient recovery rates, eliminating a reserve significant as a symbol in world markets as well as in substance. U.S. oil production increased, but suddenly peaked out in 1970, declining substantially over the subsequent five years. The only major new American oil discoveries were in Alaska and the Outer Continental Shelf, their exploitation delayed by controversy over environmental impact, as well as the lag which in any case exists between discovery and production. Enlarged American dependence on oil imports, with no short-term ready reserve, was dramatized for all to see. Prior to the embargo of October 1973, the United States was importing 36 percent of its petroleum consumption. Meanwhile, the Middle Eastern producers could observe a decline in immediately available reserve production capacity in Venezuela and Canada, as well as in the United States. Finally, the United States was proceeding to increase its reliance on natural gas at an astonishing rate. Between 1960 and 1970, gas consumption increased 5.7 percent per annum, while proved reserves increased only at about 1 percent. The administered low price made new drilling unprofitable. The decline of the 1950's in the production of bituminous coal and lignite reversed in the 1960's; but the increase was not sufficient to compensate for shortfalls elsewhere. Coal continued slowly to decline as a proportion of U.S. energy production, despite some increase in price and movement toward surface mining. The decline in coal as a proportion of U.S. energy consumption was even greater, since substantial amounts were exported to Japan and elsewhere.

U.S. petroleum policy made sense only if the supply of Middle Eastern oil would remain cheap and reliable; gas policy made no sense at all. Consumer prices of energy declined quite steadily relative to other consumer prices from 1960 to 1972, as Chart III-52 illustrates. And, indeed, the real cost of producing and distributing the marginal source of America's (and the world's) energy from the Middle East was low—lower, even, than the prices charged by the international oil companies which controlled the industry down to the end of the 1960's. But the political and economic temptation of

TABLE III-58. *United States Energy Production and Consumption: Mineral Fuels and Electricity, 1940–1975 (in Quadrillions of British Thermal Units, Unless Otherwise Indicated)*

	Total Production	Average Annual Rate of Growth (%)	Total Consumption	Average Annual Rate of Growth (%)	Net Energy Imports (Consumption minus Production)	Average Annual Rate of Growth (%)	Energy Imports: Total Consumption (%)
1940	25.1	—	23.9	—	−1.2	—	−4.9
1950	34.5	3.2	23.1	3.6	−0.4	—	−1.0
1960	41.5	1.9	44.6	2.7	3.1	—	6.8
1965	49.1	3.4	53.3	3.7	4.2	7.2	8.0
1966	52.6	7.2	56.8	6.5	4.2	−0.9	7.4
1967	54.8	4.2	58.3	2.5	3.5	−18.8	5.9
1968	56.6	3.2	61.8	6.1	5.2	51.0	3.4
1969	58.7	3.8	65.0	5.2	6.3	20.3	9.6
1970	61.8	5.3	67.1	3.3	5.3	−15.2	7.8
1971	61.1	−1.4	68.7	2.3	7.6	46.2	11.1
1972	62.2	1.9	72.1	4.9	9.9	28.1	13.8
1973	61.9	−0.6	74.7	3.7	12.8	27.7	17.1
1974	61.4	−0.8	71.8	−3.9	10.4	−17.8	14.5
1975	60.2	−1.9	71.1	−1.1	10.9	3.7	15.3

	Coal: Anthracite					Bituminous and Lignite				
	Production	Average Annual Rate of Growth (%)	% of Total Energy Production	Consumption	% of Total Energy Consumption	Production	Average Annual Rate of Growth (%)	% of Total Energy Production	Consumption	% of Total Energy Consumption
1940	1.3	—	5.2	1.24	5.2	12.1	—	48.1	11.3	47.2
1950	1.1	−1.5	3.2	1.01	3.0	13.5	1.1	39.2	11.9	34.8
1960	.48	−8.2	1.1	.45	1.0	10.7	−2.3	25.7	10.0	21.8
1965	.38	−4.6	0.8	.33	0.5	13.0	4.1	26.5	11.6	21.7
1966	.33	−13.0	0.6	.29	0.5	14.0	7.5	26.6	12.2	21.5

1970	.25	−7.1	0.4	.21	0.3	14.8	6.2	24.0	12.5	18.6
1971	.22	−10.1	0.4	.19	0.3	13.4	−9.7	22.0	11.9	17.3
1972	.18	−18.5	0.3	.15	0.2	14.3	7.0	23.0	12.3	17.1
1973	.17	−8.8	0.3	.14	0.2	14.2	−0.9	23.0	13.1	17.6
1974	.17	−3.4	0.3	.14	0.2	14.5	1.9	23.6	13.0	18.2
1975	.16	−6.5	0.3	.13	0.2	15.4	6.0	25.5	13.2	18.6

Crude Petroleum

	Production	Average Annual Rate of Growth (%)	% of Total Energy Production	Proved Reserves (Trillions of 42-Gal. Barrels)	Average Annual Rate of Growth (%)	Consumption	Average Annual Rate of Growth (%)	% of Total Energy Consumption
1940	7.8	—	31.3	19.0	—	7.5	—	31.4
1950	11.4	3.8	33.2	25.3	2.9	12.7	5.4	37.2
1960	14.7	2.5	35.3	31.6	2.3	18.6	3.9	41.8
1965	15.9	1.7	32.4	31.3	−0.2	21.4	2.8	40.1
1966	17.3	8.6	32.9	31.4	−0.3	22.4	4.7	39.5
1967	18.1	4.7	33.0	31.4	−0.2	23.3	4.0	40.0
1968	18.6	2.7	32.8	30.7	−2.1	24.8	6.5	40.2
1969	18.9	1.6	32.2	29.6	−3.5	26.0	4.6	39.9
1970	19.8	4.7	32.0	39.0[a]	31.6[a]	27.0	4.2	40.3
1971	19.3	−2.3	31.6	38.1	−2.4	30.6	13.0	44.4
1972	19.3	−0.1	31.1	36.3	−4.5	33.0	7.8	45.7
1973	18.8	−2.6	30.5	35.3	−2.9	34.8	5.7	46.6
1974	18.6	−1.6	30.2	34.2	−3.0	32.4	7.0	45.1
1975	17.7	−4.5	29.4	32.7	−4.6	32.7	0.9	46.0

[a] Increase in proved reserves reflects North Slope Alaska oil.

Memorandum: Total energy consumption in the first two quarters of 1976 was 2.3 percent higher than in the first two quarters of 1975.

Natural Gas

	Production	Average Annual Rate of Growth (%)	% of Total Energy Production	Proved Reserves (Trillions of Cu. Ft.)	Average Annual Rate of Growth (%)	Consumption	% of Total Energy Consumption
1940	3.0	—	11.9	85.0	—	3.0	12.4
1950	6.8	8.7	19.8	184.6	8.1	6.9	20.3
1960	14.1	7.5	34.0	262.3	3.6	14.1	31.7
1965	17.6	4.5	36.0	286.5	1.7	17.9	33.7
1966	18.9	7.0	35.9	289.3	1.0	19.3	33.9
1967	20.1	6.4	36.6	292.9	1.2	20.3	34.8
1968	21.5	7.3	38.1	287.3	−1.9	21.8	35.3
1969	22.8	6.0	38.9	275.1	−4.3	23.5	36.2
1970	24.1	5.8	39.0	290.7	5.7	24.5	36.5
1971	24.8	2.7	40.6	278.8	−4.1	22.8	33.2
1972	24.9	0.3	40.0	266.1	−4.6	23.1	32.1
1973	24.7	−0.5	40.0	249.9	−6.1	22.7	30.4
1974	23.7	−4.3	38.6	237.1	−5.1	21.7	30.2
1975	22.2	−6.3	36.8	228.2	−3.8	20.2	28.4

	Electricity: Production	Electricity: Average Annual Rate of Growth (%)	Electricity: % of Total Energy Production	Electricity: % of Total Energy Consumption	Crude Petroleum Price in Dollars (Average per Barrel at Wells)	Natural Gas Price in Cents (Average per 1,000 Cu. Ft.)
1940	—	—	—	—	—	—
1950	—	—	—	—	$2.5	6.5¢
1960	1.6	—	3.9	3.7	2.9	14.0
1965	2.1	5.4	4.3	3.9	2.9	15.6
1966	2.1	0.5	4.0	3.7	2.9	15.7
1967	2.4	15.1	4.4	4.1	2.9	16.0
1968	2.5	1.7	4.4	4.0	2.9	16.4
1969	2.8	13.2	4.7	4.3	3.1	16.7
1970	2.9	2.3	4.6	4.3	3.2	17.1
1971	3.3	14.2	5.3	4.8	3.4	18.2
1972	3.5	7.8	5.6	4.9	3.4	18.6
1973	3.9	10.8	6.3	5.2	3.9	21.3
1974	4.5	15.6	7.3	6.3	6.9	30.4
1975	4.8	7.1	8.0	7.7	7.7	44.5

Source: U.S. Department of the Interior, Bureau of Mines, *Minerals Yearbook*, annual volumes.

Note: Growth rates have been calculated from data expressed to three decimal places and may differ marginally from calculations from data rounded to one decimal place in this table.

exploiting their potentially monopolistic position, combined with a sense that their reserves might last only another generation or so at the existing global rate of increase in oil consumption (about 8 percent annually), proved too much for the Middle Eastern producers to resist; and they were soon joined by the other exporters.

The crises in food and agricultural prices of the early 1970's were, thus, both caused by a rate of increase in demand that drew down readily available reserves in the United States and rendered unrealistic the existing price level. The two cases differed sharply, however, in that there was no agricultural equivalent of the short- and medium-term reserve represented by Middle Eastern oil and there was no equivalent to OPEC operating among the three major agricultural exporters.

The relatively low prices of energy between 1951 and 1971 contributed to the momentum of the leading sectors which carried forward the growth of the advanced industrial nations. The automobile, chemicals, and many of the most rapidly diffusing durable consumers' goods depended, in different ways, on energy; and these sectoral complexes clearly played a key role in the great global boom of the 1950's and 1960's. Most analyses of growth in the United States, Western Europe, and Japan during these two decades, however, are conducted in highly aggregated terms which do not adequately portray the role of the leading sectors.[197] Overaggregation takes three forms. First, there is an effort to account for growth in terms of aggregate changes in labor and capital inputs combined with overall measures of change in labor and capital productivity.

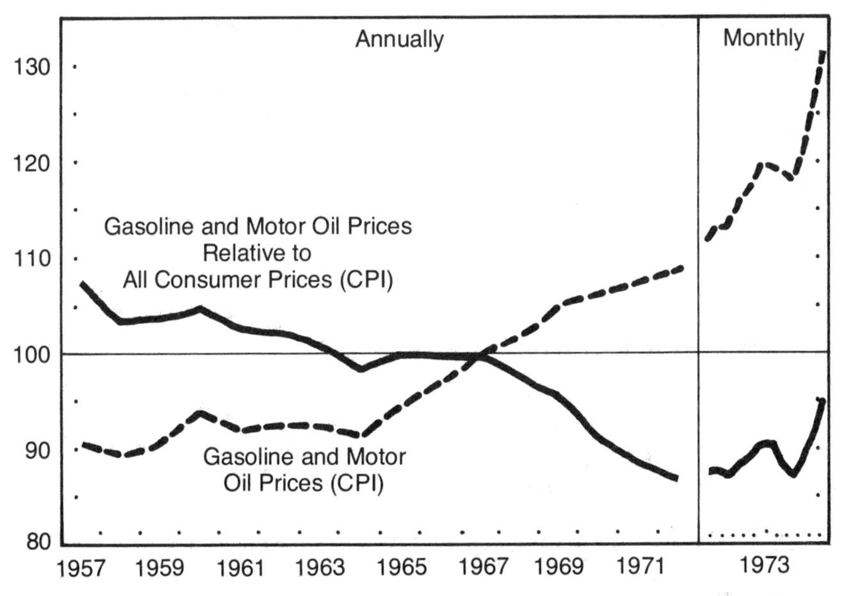

CHART III-52. *Consumers' Prices of Gasoline and Motor Oil Relative to All Consumers' Prices: United States, 1957–1973 (1967 = 100)*

Source: U.S. Department of Labor, in *Economic Report of the President* (February 1974), p. 113.

Second, the tripartite classification of economic activities is used in some cases—agriculture, industry, and services. Third, the standard international classification of industry is applied. All three of these analytic devices obscure the role of leading sectors in growth, because they are embedded in large aggregates where other components damp and conceal their movement. In dealing with Western Europe as a whole only M. M. Postan follows the good precedent of Ingvar Svennilson for the interwar years in disaggregating sufficiently to capture the linkage between the efficient introduction of new technologies, the scale and productivity of investment in particular sectors, and the quality of entrepreneurship.[198] He concludes as follows:

> . . . the links between investment and technology will also have to be dealt with here, if only because they may help us to identify some of the "other" factors behind the high rate of post-war investment.
>
> What these factors were and how they were linked with technological change is suggested by the very order in which industries arranged themselves in their demand for new capital. In almost every European country the industries heading the list, i.e., those with the largest infusion of capital, were the "modern" or the modernized industries. The chemical and petroleum industries, with their joint offspring in petrochemicals, plastics, and man-made fibres, developed a voracious appetite for new capital as they grew and renewed their equipment. Equally voracious for capital were the engineering and metal-working industries, especially their newer branches, such as electro-mechanical, electronic, and motor-car. On the other hand, new investment was low relatively to output, and also grew rather slowly, in such industries as cotton and wool, coal-mining (except where they were in the process of wholesale modernization as in the United Kingdom), wood-working, or in

TABLE III-59. *Indexes of Industrial Production by Sectors: Western Europe, 1950 and 1963 (1953 = 100)*

	1950	1963
Total industrial production	86	178
Mining and quarrying	88	114
Total manufactures	86	182
All metal products	83	196
Motor cars	78	427
All textiles	95	128
Cotton fabrics	96	100
Electric power	80	225
Chemical industry	78	260

Source: M. M. Postan, *An Economic History of Western Europe, 1945–1964*, p. 190.

such older branches of the engineering and metal-working industry as manufacture of railway equipment and milling machinery.[199]

Despite the statistical difficulties in isolating formally the role of the leading sectors, their critical importance can be quite firmly established. For Western Europe as a whole, for example, Table III-59 shows the disproportionate rise down to 1963 in the three leading sectors which had begun to emerge before 1914—motor vehicles, chemicals, and electricity—sectors which cushioned the stagnation of the interwar years, and finally carried Western Europe forward at relatively full employment in the 1950's and 1960's.

The unique surge in motor-car production emerges clearly. It helps substantially to account for a rise in metal products greater than the industrial average. It also helps produce the disproportionate rise in chemicals, through its effects on petroleum, rubber tire, and plastics production. The greater rise in "all textiles" than in "cotton fabrics" relates, of course, to the increasing role of synthetic textiles, also subsumed in the chemical industry. In 1964, chemical fibers had reached a level of 29.6 percent of total world consumption of textile fibers: by 1974 the figure was 42.5 percent. Even so redoubtable an aggregative analyst as Edward F. Denison finally breaks away from the inhibitions of his data with this perceptive observation on the sectoral pattern of growth in postwar Europe:

> What distinguishes postwar Europe is that increases in output in the fast-growing countries have systematically been particularly marked in those products that Europe produced only on a small scale and at high cost *compared to the United States* in the early 1950's, and for which techniques for lowering costs with an increase in the scale of production already existed in the United States and did not need to be developed gradually and expensively as markets expanded. As incomes rose in Europe, demand for and production of these income-elastic products rose sharply and their unit costs were reduced by applying American techniques that could not have been adopted until per capita incomes were sufficient to provide a market. . . .
>
> Automobiles and consumer durables provide classic and obvious examples of the process but it was quite pervasive and, I believe, applied to a great range of detailed products.[200]

Table III-60 carries Postan's and Denison's insights a bit further. It shows average annual growth rates for certain sectors of the five major market economies of the industrialized world over two periods: 1953–1963 and 1963–1972. The growth rates for industrial production as a whole are included for purposes of comparison. In all cases, chemicals as a whole moved forward more rapidly than the average. Certain textile fibers and plastics illustrate the kinds of new products of the chemical industry, with high momentum, that

TABLE III-60. *Some Leading Sector Indicators in Major Industrial Nations: 1963/1953; 1972/1963 (Annual Average Rates of Growth)*

	Total Industrial Production		Total Chemical Production		Noncellulosic Continuous Filaments (Nylon, etc.)		Nitrogeneous Fertilizers[a]		Plastics and Resins	
	1963/1953	1972/1963	1963/1953	1972/1963	1963/1953	1972/1963	1963/1953	1972/1963	1963/[b] 1953	1972/1963
United States	3.2%	4.7%	6.6%	7.5%	13.8%	16.3%	10.3%	8.7%	12.6%	9.1%
United Kingdom	3.1	2.6	12.7	6.5	27.1	13.2	7.1	4.2	10.1	8.8
France	6.0	6.3	10.2	11.7	27.6	9.4	11.6	5.5[c]	13.6	17.1
Federal Republic of Germany	7.6	5.6	8.3	12.0	30.1	20.7	6.7	1.7	13.5	15.6
Japan	13.6	12.6	20.9	13.9	51.5	11.8	8.6	7.3	24.4	27.6

	Aluminum (Primary and Secondary)		Tires		Passenger Car Production		Television Receiver Production	
	1963/1953	1972/1963	1963/1953	1972/1963	1963/1953	1972/1963	1963/1953	1972/1963
United States	5.7%	6.7%	3.8%	5.5%	2.5%	1.62%	1.33%	3.1%
United Kingdom	4.8	8.3	8.0	5.3	10.5	2.0	3.8	6.9
France	9.8	4.2	12.1	9.3	14.9	8.1	34.6	3.6
Federal Republic of Germany	9.6	8.1	15.9	8.6	20.1	4.3	46.9	5.4
Japan	18.9	19.1	27.8	14.9	47.3	29.0	79.7	12.3

[a] 1952–1953/1956–1957/1963–1964; 1972–1973/1963–1964.
[b] 1960–1963.
[c] 1971/1963.
Source: *United Nations Statistical Yearbook*, 1969 and 1973.

helped yield this result. The rise of aluminum emerges clearly, as does the extraordinary surge of automobile production in Western Europe and Japan, especially between 1953 and 1963, and of television production in France, Germany, and Japan. Both sectors rapidly decelerated down to 1972, excepting television production in Britain. The powerful popular appeal of television led to a remarkably swift and nearly universal diffusion, including the substitution of color for black-and-white receiving sets. The figures for automobile and television production were also affected, of course, by the relative success of each nation in export markets and its reliance on imports. Between 1963 and 1972, U.S. auto imports, for example, rose from 5 percent of domestic production to about 30 percent. Along with television a wide array of durable consumers' goods long familiar in North America were being diffused to the households of Western Europe and Japan. In France, for example, the proportion of households equipped with refrigerators rose from 7.5 percent in 1954 to 52 percent in 1964; in Britain, from 7 percent in 1954 to 40 percent by 1966. Half the families in Northwest Europe as a whole had refrigerators by 1964.[201]

The figures for the United States indicate the earlier arrival of the automobile age and of electric-powered durable consumers' goods in general. By 1957, 75 percent of American households owned automobiles; 81 percent, television sets; 96.0 percent, refrigerators; 66.7 percent, vacuum cleaners; 76.8 percent, washers. Increases over the next decade were inevitably modest: to 78 percent, 97.8 percent, 99.6 percent, 90.6 percent, and 88.2 percent, respectively. Only freezers, driers, and air conditioners remained still to be installed in 70 percent of American homes by 1967. By the late 1950's, the automobile and durable consumers' goods complexes, while massive elements in the American economy, lacked the momentum to qualify as leading sectors. American growth in the 1960's was carried forward by housing construction; by a surge in aerospace outlays early in the decade; by the rise of the computer industry; and, above all, by the rapid increase in outlays in certain service sectors. On the eve of the energy crisis, the gap in automobiles had been narrowed, but not closed, among the nations of the industrialized world. With less spacious geography and higher gasoline prices, it is, indeed, likely that automobile density in Western Europe and Japan would have leveled off on a lower plateau than in the United States and Canada.

The leading sectors are not, of course, the whole story of growth in the postwar industrialized world. The debate among the economists using more aggregative methods of analysis is clearly relevant. At some risk of oversimplification, it can be regarded as an argument about the relative roles of supply and demand. With regard to the former, C. P. Kindleberger states his proposition with admirable lucidity:

> The thesis of the book is that the major factor shaping the remarkable economic growth which most of Europe has experienced since 1950 has been the availability of a large supply of labor. The labor has come from a high rate of natural increase (the Netherlands), from transfers from agriculture to services and industry (Germany, France, Italy), from the immigration of refugees (Germany), and from the immigration of unemployed and underemployed workers from the Mediterranean countries (France, Germany, and Switzerland). Those countries with no substantial increase in the labor supply—Britain, Belgium, and the Scandinavian nations—on the whole have grown more slowly than the others.[202]

Kindleberger recognizes that there are two substantial exceptions to his Lewis[203] model, as Table III-61 indicates: Austria and France; and that the growth of Southern Europe, from Spain to Turkey, benefited from the flow of excess labor to the economies of Western Europe.

Kindleberger bypasses the question of how the process of rapid growth in postwar Europe was initially induced. His model can be set in motion from the side of either demand or supply. Once in motion, it continues until deceleration occurs due to a using up of the supply of surplus labor (from agriculture or abroad) and a consequent shift in income distribution against profits; or due to a failure of export earnings to increase fast enough to avoid balance-of-payments crises which slow down the rate of growth. The latter process can be brought about by the former; that is, the rise in wages due to labor shortage can reduce a nation's competitive position in export markets. But an inadequate increase in exports can also come about if, for other reasons, a nation's productivity increase in the production of exports falls behind that of its competitors.

Angus Maddison, on the other hand, places primary emphasis on the maintenance by government policies of a high level of effective demand:

> A striking characteristic of the postwar European economy has been the high level and continuous expansion of demand. Initially, this was a spontaneous aftermath of the war, but its continuance for almost two decades is mainly due to the success of an active governmental policy, both national and international. It is noteworthy that three of the slower-growing countries, the United States, Canada and Belgium, have had a less buoyant level of demand and that they, together with the fourth slow-growing country, the United Kingdom, have also had a much greater cyclical volatility of demand than the fast-growing countries.[204]

As noted earlier (p. 261), Denison's somewhat similar emphasis on demand draws him finally toward the leading sectors. He perceives

TABLE III-61. *Growth of Output, Labor Force and Labor Productivity, Average Gross Investment Ratio, and Incremental Capital/Output Ratio in Selected European Countries, 1949–1959*

Country	Gross Domestic Product Trend	GDP per Capita	Active Labor Force	Labor Productivity	Average Gross Investment Ratio (%)	Average Incremental Capital/Output Ratio (ICOR) (Coefficient)
	(Compound Annual Percentage Rates)					
A.						
Germany	7.4	6.3	1.6	5.7	24.2	3.3
Italy	5.9	5.4	1.1	4.8	22.0	3.7
Switzerland	5.2	3.8	1.5	3.7	23.7	4.5
Netherlands	4.8	3.5	1.2	3.6	24.3	5.2
B.						
Austria	6.0	5.8	1.1[a]	4.8	23.2	3.9
France	4.5	3.6	0.1	4.3	20.1	4.6
C.						
Norway	3.4	2.5	0.3	3.1	31.3	9.5
Sweden	3.4	2.8	0.5	2.9	21.3	6.3
Denmark	3.2	2.4	1.0	2.2	17.6	5.5
Belgium	3.0	2.4	0.3	2.7	17.6	5.6
United Kingdom	2.4	2.0	0.6	1.8	16.3	6.7
D.						
Greece	5.9	5.0	1.5	4.3	16.5	3.0
Turkey	5.9	2.9	2.4	3.4	15.0	2.6
Spain	5.2	4.3	0.8	4.3	16.3	3.1
Portugal	4.1	3.4	0.6	3.5	16.0	4.0

[a] This figure is subject to considerable doubt.

Source: Charles P. Kindleberger, *Europe's Postwar Growth: The Role of Labor Supply*, p. 25. Data from Economic Commission for Europe, *Some Factors in Economic Growth in Europe during the 1950's*, pp. 1, 12, 31.

that growth in output, investment, and productivity is highest in sectors with a high income elasticity of demand—notably, motor vehicles and durable consumers' goods. But he does not pursue his insight systematically or mobilize the statistical data which bear on it. Kindleberger's emphasis on the availability of labor supply yields only brief and casual reference to the pace of technological change in the sectors,[205] although, in his discussion of the impact of European growth on the U.S. balance of payments, there is a sudden reference to "European entry into products previously supplied from the United States, many of them highly income-elastic and supported by high growth rates."[206]

The difference between the European performance from 1919 to 1939 and after 1945 poses a question Kindleberger does not attempt to answer. Surely, there were ample supplies of labor in Europe between 1919 and 1939 capable of being drawn into industrial growth: unemployed, employed at low productivity on the land, or available (as France demonstrated in the 1920's) for intra-European migration. The story of European postwar growth is clearly incomplete without taking into account that this was a Keynesian age of growthmanship: "In all European countries economic growth became a universal creed and a common expectation to which governments were expected to conform. To this extent economic growth was the product of economic growthmanship."[207] Just how government policy played its part in the age of growthmanship, however, is by no means simple. R. C. O. Matthews, for example, thoughtfully explored this question with respect to the British experience.[208] Clearly, the outcome was not the direct result of government deficits of a classic Keynesian type. On the contrary, the British systematically ran budget surpluses and chronically faced the task of constraining effective demand. The high level of effective demand, in turn, arose initially from a rising proportion of income invested. The environment of full employment made private investment attractive in the leading-sector complexes, given the income elasticity of demand. In addition, government encouraged the investment process by tax incentives, support for housing construction, and direct investment outlays in nationalized industries, dealing with balance-of-payments pressures by methods which minimized the classic devices of general deflation; e.g., by limiting the flow of capital exports.

Behind all this was a new set of mind and the strongest kind of political pressure. Whatever the degree of formal planning introduced by the Western European governments, they all accepted some version of the Keynesian formulation; that is, the level of effective demand should be maintained, by some mixture of private and government consumption, private and government investment, at levels compatible with relatively full employment. The pursuit of policy in those terms was reinforced because, within each nation and internationally, political pressures operated on the government to maintain full employment. Political, labor, and business leaders knew that the government in power would pay promptly and severely at the polls for levels of unemployment that would have been regarded as eminently satisfactory in interwar Europe.

Such policies were technically possible because the direct and indirect role of governments in the economy was sufficient to influence the private as well as public flows of consumption and investment and because the experience of postwar growth itself strengthened private expectations that it would continue. Starting in France and then spreading in different forms (and with varying efficacy) throughout Europe, this public-private partnership was institutionalized by forms of investment sectoral planning, fitted into the analysis of the aggregate income flows required for full employment.

But behind it all was the fact that Western Europe had arrived at levels of income per capita which, under conditions of full employment, drove the leading sectors forward at high momentum, given the high income elasticity of demand for the products of those sectors.

In my view, Kindleberger is correct in the sense that the outcome for the individual countries of Western Europe, in terms of relative real growth rates, did partially depend, under the circumstances, on the reserves of labor available to be drawn into each economy; but without the high momentum, created basically by other circumstances, the flows of labor, notably from abroad, would not have been accepted or efficiently put to work. They could be put to work —and accelerate the growth process—because the leading sectors were not only the fastest-growing industries, but also those enjoying the greatest productivity increases and, for a time, also the greatest potentialities for export expansion, in part at the expense of the United States and those who did not keep up in the growthmanship race. Good investment management in France and the Austrian linkage to the German economy exhibited what could be done even without large increments to the industrial working force.

The most sophisticated statistical effort to account for Western European growth rates in aggregative terms—and for differences between Western Europe and the United States—is that of Denison.[209] Table III-62 sets out the comparative performance of the United States and Northwest European economies over the period 1950–1962; Table III-63 presents Denison's estimates of the relative determinants of the outcome.

Evidently, the problem to be explained is the slower growth of national income and, even more markedly, per capita income in the United States. By Denison's accounting, the major difference was between total factor inputs and output per unit of labor input in the two cases; that is, the contribution of productivity increases was much greater in Europe than in the United States.

With respect to labor, the growth of the U.S. working force was higher, as was the estimated contribution of education; but this

TABLE III-62. *National Income and per Capita Growth Rates: The United States and Northwest Europe, 1950–1962 (Annual Average Percentage Rate of Growth)*

	National Income		National Income per Capita	
	United States	N.W. Europe	United States	N.W. Europe
1950–1962	3.32	4.78	2.15	3.8
1950–1955	4.23	5.68	2.74	4.46
1955–1962	2.67	4.11	1.73	3.34

Source: Edward F. Denison, *Why Growth Rates Differ*, pp. 298 and 300.

TABLE III-63. *Northwest Europe and the United St per Person Employed, 1950–1962 (Contribution*

Sources of Growth
National income
Total factor input
Labor
Employment
Hours of work
Age-sex composition
Education
Capital
Dwellings
International assets
Nonresidential structures and equipment
Inventories
Land
Output per unit of input
Advances of knowledge
Changes in the lag in the application of knowledge, general efficiency, and errors and omissions
Reduction in age of capital
Other
Improved allocation of resources
Contraction of agricultural inputs
Contraction of nonagricultural self-employment
Reduction of international trade barriers
Balancing of the capital stock
Deflation procedures
Economies of scale
Growth of national market measured in U.S. prices
Income elasticities
Independent growth of local markets
Irregularities in pressure of demand
Irregularities in agricultural output

Source: Denison, *Why Growth Rates Differ*, pp. 298 and 300.

was partially compensated for by a greater reduction of hours worked (due to part-time employment) and a shift in the age-sex composition of the working force.

With respect to capital, the overall growth rates were similar for the period 1950–1962; but a much higher proportion of the U.S. increase was in dwellings and international assets, a lower proportion in nonresidential structures and equipment.

Turning to the productivity of these inputs, the major relative advantages of Europe are estimated to have been in the contraction

rces of Growth of Total National Income and National Income
wth Rate in Percentage Points and Percentages of Total)

thwest Europe				United States			
l National ome		National Income per Person Employed		Total National Income		National Income per Person Employed	
78	100	3.80	100	3.32	100	2.15	100
69	36	0.73	20	1.95	58	0.79	36
83	18	0.12	3	1.12	33	0.22	10
71	15	—	—	0.90	27	—	—
14	−3	−0.14	−4	−0.17	−5	−0.17	−8
03	1	0.03	1	−0.10	−3	−0.10	−5
23	5	0.23	6	0.49	15	0.49	22
86	18	0.65	17	0.83	25	0.60	27
07	1	0.04	1	0.25	7	0.21	10
03	−1	−0.04	−1	0.05	1	0.04	2
64	14	0.51	14	0.43	13	0.29	13
18	4	0.14	4	0.10	3	0.06	3
00	0	−0.04	−1	0.00	0	−0.03	−1
07	64	3.07	80	1.37	42	1.36	62
.76	16	0.76	20	0.76	23	0.75	34
—	12	—	15	—	—	—	—
.02	—	0.02	1	—	—	—	—
.54	11	0.54	14	—	—	—	—
—	14	—	16	—	9	—	13
.46	10	0.46	12	0.25	7	0.25	11
.14	3	0.14	4	0.04	1	0.04	2
.08	2	0.08	2	0.00	0	0.00	0
.08	2	0.08	2	—	—	—	—
.07	—	0.07	—	—	—	—	—
—	20	—	25	—	11	—	16
.41	9	0.41	11	0.30	9	0.30	14
.46	10	0.46	12	—	—	—	—
.06	1	0.06	2	0.06	2	0.06	3
.01	—	−0.01	—	−0.04	—	−0.04	—
.00	—	0.00	—	—	—	—	—

of agricultural inputs, the reduction of international trade barriers, and the components of economies of scale. The relatively higher level of American unemployment left its mark particularly on the subperiod 1955–1962.

As noted earlier, Denison has a pretty shrewd idea of where these differences mainly arise, although his method denies him the opportunity or the data to pursue the matter: "The estimates for . . . European countries . . . include . . . gains from economies of scale associated with the especially large magnitude of increases in income-elastic consumption components. The great expansion of markets for these products made possible special gains by adoption of existing techniques for large-scale production."[210]

What this argument comes to is that Europe moved toward U.S. patterns of consumption; that is, toward the diffusion to a higher proportion of the population of the automobile, durable consumers' goods, etc. This process made for the efficient absorption of technologies earlier applied in the United States. The leading sector complexes which expanded disproportionately both drew capital on a large scale and used it with the greatest relative efficiency. The accelerator operated powerfully; that is, an expansion of consumption outlays led to rapid increases in investment in the sectors with high income elasticity of demand and in the subsectors to which they were linked.

In the vocabulary of the stages of economic growth, Western Europe came fully into the stage of high mass-consumption. The United States had more nearly completed the process by the mid-1950's. It faltered and then moved forward in the 1960's, at higher momentum, with a different structural balance. The U.S. annual average rate of growth of national income, 3.23 percent for the period 1953–1964, rose to 4.54 percent for the period 1964–1969.[211]

In Denison's aggregative terms, it was the higher average level of employment which primarily accounted for the rise in the U.S. growth rate of the 1960's,[212] although an expansion in capital inputs also made a modest net contribution as compared to the earlier period. But this does not capture the character of the changes that occurred. First, the income elasticity of demand at the income per capita levels attained by the United States shifted significantly toward certain services through the process of the market place and through politics. This was one element in the more general shift in the working force toward the service sectors. As V. R. Fuchs states in the opening passage of his book *The Service Economy*:

> The United States is now pioneering in a new stage of economic development. During the period following World War II this country became the world's first "service economy"—that is, the first nation in which more than half of the employed population is not involved in the production of food, clothing, houses, automobiles, or other tangible goods.
>
> In 1947 total employment stood at approximately 57 mil-

lion; by 1967 it was about 74 million. Virtually all of the net increase occurred in institutions that provide services—such as banks, hospitals, retail stores, schools. The number of people employed in the production of goods has been relatively stable; modest increases in manufacturing and construction have been off-set by declines in agriculture and mining.[213]

Fuchs finds that employment grew 0.9 percent per annum faster in services than in industry from 1929 to 1965; but none of this increase can be explained by an overall shift of final output to services. He allocates half the differential to relatively shorter hours, lower labor quality, and less capital per worker in services: the other half of the differential he attributes to lesser technological change and economies of scale.[214]

The shift in employment toward services is, however, compounded of two elements: the slow rate of increase of productivity in the service sector taken as a whole; and the high income elasticity of demand for certain services. For our purposes, it is the latter which is of particular interest.

Over the whole sweep of this period a good many of the service subsectors with high rates of growth in real output (rather than merely in employment) are linked to the automobile–durable consumers' goods complex; e.g., auto repair, automobile dealers, gasoline stations, furniture and appliances.[215] And these subsectors decelerate with the passage of time.

On the other hand, there is a marked acceleration in the share of the consumers' real resources going to education, medical services, recreation equipment, foreign travel, religious and welfare expenditures.[216] Table III-64 shows the percentage increase of consumption expenditures between the censuses of 1960 and 1970.[217]

TABLE III-64. *Personal Consumption Expenditures by Product: United States, 1960–1970 (Ranked by Order of Percentage Increase)*

	1960–1970
1. Private education	181
2. Medical care	148
3. Personal business	122
4. Foreign travel	118
5. Recreation	113
6. Housing	97
7. Personal care	91
8. Clothing, accessories, and jewelry	89
9. Religious and welfare activities	87
10. Household operations	83
11. Transportation	81
12. Food, beverages, and tobacco	63

Source: Ben. J. Wattenberg, *The Real America*, p. 85, from U.S. Bureau of Economic Analysis.

It is the rise of these service subsectors that helps define the character of the shift from the 1950's to the 1960's in the United States.

On the public side, outlays for purposes other than defense rose disproportionately in the 1960's, despite the remarkable sustained surge in the economy as a whole and the fiscal burden of war in Southeast Asia: nonmilitary federal purchases of goods and services were 1.7 percent of GNP in 1960, 2.4 percent in 1968; state and local purchases were 9.1 percent in 1960, 11.3 percent in 1968.[218] In money terms, transfers by the federal government doubled in these years, moving relatively from 7.5 percent to 9.9 percent of GNP. In this process, grants-in-aid from the federal government to state and local governments rose from $6.5 billion in 1960 to $18.4 billion in 1968. As Table III-65 indicates, the rapid rise of GNP in these years masks a movement of resources to welfare purposes which, by normal standards of American politics, must be judged remarkable.[219]

The shift of American income elasticity of demand toward these service sectors, at a time of both fixed exchange rates and rising efficiency in Western European and Japanese production of automobiles and durable consumers' goods (and in the capital goods sectors connected with them), helps account for deterioration of the American trade balance over the past two decades. The expanding service sectors did not generate new sources of foreign exchange. Indeed, with foreign travel increasingly popular, the negative item in the U.S. balance of payments for net travel and transportation expenses moved from $361 million in 1956 to a peak of $2,853 million in 1972. The travel of American citizens abroad increased more than tenfold between 1950 and 1971, better than three times the rate of expansion of real national income. But it was the new virtuosity of Western Europe and Japan in producing the gadgetry of high mass-consumption (plus the new virtuosity of some less developed nations in textiles) that mainly eroded the American balance of payments: a shift of $7 billion in the trade balance between 1966 and 1971 is accounted for by the relative increase in U.S. im-

TABLE III-65. *Federal, State, and Local Expenditures as Proportions of Gross National Product: United States, 1959, 1963, 1968*

	1959 (%)	1963 (%)	1968 (%)
National security (including space, foreign aid, and veterans)	11.0	10.9	10.7
Interest payments	1.4	1.4	1.4
Law, order, and administration	2.2	2.5	2.5
Economic and environmental services	4.4	4.4	4.6
Social services	9.7	10.9	14.2
Total	28.7	30.1	33.4

Source: W. W. Rostow, *Politics and the Stages of Growth*, p. 233.

ports (and decrease in exports) of radio and television receiving sets, motor vehicles, steel, and textiles.

The extraordinary expansion of the Japanese economy from the mid-1950's to 1973 can be viewed as a heightened version of the experience of Western Europe but marked by certain features special to the Japanese situation. Once again we find growth carried forward by the rapid absorption of the hitherto unapplied technologies associated with the leading sector complexes of high mass-consumption; a disproportionate flow of capital into those sectoral complexes; a reserve of labor to be drawn down; an increase in agricultural productivity; and a surge in exports sustained by the same industries which had newly found a mass market at home.

But there were major differences. Japan could draw labor into high-productivity industrial activity not only from agriculture, but also from its semitraditional low-productivity industrial sector. On the other hand, there was no equivalent available to the flow of workers from Southern Europe unless one takes into account the farming out of component production to low-wage regions in Asia, e.g., South Korea. Starting from lower levels of income per capita than Western Europe and a larger unapplied backlog of technology, the pace of growth was higher. (Within Western Europe, the initially poorer nations, Italy and Spain, were most nearly in the Japanese category in this respect.) The rate of expansion and of plowing back of profits in the industrial private sector, the constraints on military expenditures, a relatively lower proportion of resources going to government, and the high level of private savings all conspired to permit a higher level of investment than in Western Europe.

In aggregated terms this story is well told by Kazushi Ohkawa and Henry Rosovsky in their *Japanese Economic Growth*. They view the Japanese economic experience in this century as marked by three long swings in the rate of growth, the spurts at successively higher levels (Chart III-53). Each was carried forward by high levels of private capital formation and the rapid absorption of unexploited Western technologies, a process subject to retardation. The first intervening period (1919–1931) was one of deceleration during the 1920's and the initial phase of the post-1929 depression, cushioned by enlarged government outlays for social overhead capital; the second (1939–1955) embraces the period of war and postwar recovery; the third spurt (1955–) gave way not to deceleration but to a fully sustained high level of growth down to 1973.[220] Ohkawa and Rosovsky are quite conscious that they are dealing with a sequence marked by traumatic political and military events and do not present their spurts and decelerations as a self-governing cycle.

As in other highly aggregated analyses, it is a bit difficult to detect the role of the leading sectors. In dealing with the nonagricultural segment of the economy, Ohkawa and Rosovsky generally confine themselves to four large sectors: manufacturing, facilitating sectors, construction, and services. (Facilitating sectors include primarily transportation, communications, and public utilities.) In the period we are now considering (the third spurt) the expansion in output and productivity of manufacturing and their related facilitating sectors dominate.[221] But, as in Denison's discussion of Western Europe, the role of the leading sectors occasionally breaks through in an ad hoc way. For example, in a footnote reminiscent of Postan's analysis of European investment (see above, pp. 260–261), it is noted that the highest rates of growth in capital formation for the period 1955–1961 were in metal products, transport machinery, other machinery, and petroleum and coal products.[222] At another point the authors address in an even more direct way the role of consumers' durables and motor vehicles in Japanese expansion.[223] They note that, from negligible levels, the Japanese had moved so rapidly into consumers' durables that, by 1964, 80 percent of wage earners' households had sewing machines; 55 percent, cameras; 91 percent, television sets; 59 percent, refrigerators; 72 percent, electric washing machines. Between 1941 and 1955 the proportion of "modern" as opposed to "traditional" goods in Japanese household assets rose from 13 percent to 50 percent.[224] On the question of motor vehicles, however, Ohkawa and Rosovsky are bearish as of the time their systematic data collection ends—about 1966. They observe that in 1964 only 8.8 percent of city households in Japan owned passenger automobiles; and in 1966, of a total motor vehicle production of 2.2 million, only 36 percent were passenger vehicles. This fits well their image of a Japanese consumer enticed

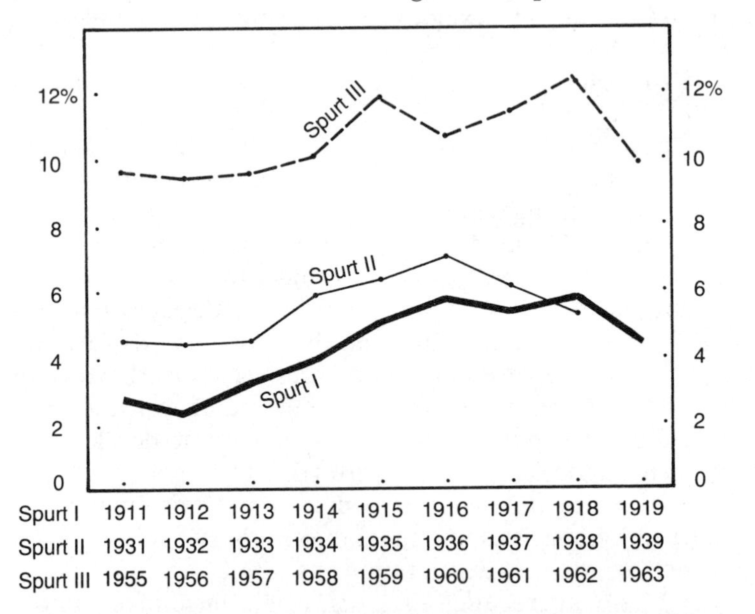

CHART III-53. *A Comparison of Three Growth Spurts: Japan, 1911–1963 (Average Annual Rates of Growth of GNP)*

Source: Ohkawa and Rosovsky, *Japanese Economic Growth*, p. 205.

by the small gadgetry of high mass-consumption but living still a rather traditional life, with traditional consumption outlays still substantial and savings at a high rate in a system which still counts heavily on the family's resources for social security. From this portrait they derive a picture of Japanese growth carried forward by "autonomous" investment, introducing the unused backlog of advanced technology to the industrial structure, generating an increase in consumption which, via the accelerator, stimulates an enlarged demand in quasi-traditional sectors with relatively low productivity (high capital-output ratios).

This portrait fails to anticipate the surge in the Japanese automobile sectoral complex in the late 1960's. The growth of passenger car production from 1966 to 1972 was at the astonishing rate of 28.9 percent per annum. In the latter year 64 percent of total motor vehicle production consisted of passenger cars, Japan having moved from sixth to second place as a producer. Passenger cars in use in Japan increased from 1.2 million in 1964 to 12.5 million in 1972, an annual rate of increase of 34 percent. To some extent the Ohkawa-Rosovsky portrait of the Japanese consumer and the workings of the damped accelerator was quickly outmoded in the late 1960's.

In connection with Japanese foreign trade, the linkage between a domestic market caught up in the adventure of high mass-consumption and the structure of exports is more clear. Ohkawa and Rosovsky's general proposition is that the export expansion required to finance Japan's extraordinary growth was based on its rapidly growing high-productivity sectors, in which relative prices declined. They conclude: "What this meant in terms of actual commodities sent abroad was a shift away from toys, sewing machines, clothing, etc., in the direction of plastics, business machines, and automobiles."[225]

Although his analysis only goes down to 1965, Miyohei Shinohara's more disaggregated view of the postwar Japanese economy reveals with greater clarity the role of the leading sectors. Shinohara calculates (Table III-66) the increase of production for some fifty-three major commodities in the first stage of postwar Japanese growth (1955–1961), as opposed to reconstruction. Durable consumers' goods, motor vehicles, and the newer chemicals evidently lead the parade. Textiles and the older chemicals bring up the rear.

Commenting on this period and the relative deceleration of 1961–1965, Shinohara observes:

> . . . the growth pattern during 1955–61 was highly investment or heavy industry–oriented. In machinery, the growth rate was 28.6 percent; in iron and steel, it was 19.3 percent; and in chemicals, 14.9 percent, on the one hand, but in textiles, it was only 9.1 percent. The growth rate in capital goods was 24.9 percent and that in consumer durables 37.2 percent, while that in consumer nondurables was only 7.9 percent. . . .

TABLE III-66. *Japan: Production of Major Commodities, 1961 (Ratios to 1955 Production)*

Commodity	Ratio	Commodity	Ratio
Electric refrigerators	50.48	Steel vessels (started)	2.58
Television sets	33.64	Electrolytic copper	2.44
Passenger cars	12.31	Cement	2.33
Chassis for trucks and buses	11.59	Paper pulp	2.29
Synthetic fabrics	11.37	Carbide	2.25
Synthetic fibers	9.72	Woven woolen fabrics	2.19
Radio receivers	7.60	Electricity	2.11
Corrugated cardboard	6.40	Crude oil	2.08
Machine tools	6.33	Foreign style paper	2.07
Standard induction motors	6.28	Sheet glass	2.00
Plastics	5.71	Caustic soda	1.84
Standard transformers	5.26	Sewing machines	1.72
Heavy oil	5.24	Woolen yarn	1.72
Electric washers	4.69	Rayon filament yarn	1.59
Hot roll special steel products	4.60	Looms	1.44
Steel frames	4.42	Sulfuric acid	1.42
Auto tires and tubes	4.13	Cotton fabrics	1.34
Paperboard	3.52	Cotton yarn	1.33
Pig iron	3.03	Rayon staple fabrics	1.30
Crude steel	3.00	Coal	1.28
Watches and clocks	2.97	Rayon fabrics	1.23
Gasoline	2.95	Ammonium sulfate	1.18
Hot roll ordinary steel products	2.94	Rayon staple yarn	1.09
Telegraph wire and cable	2.93	Raw silk	1.08
A.C. generators	2.91	Calcium super phosphate	1.05
Bicycles	2.84	Silk fabrics	1.00
Aluminum	2.65		

Source: Myohei Shinohara, "Patterns and Some Structural Changes in Japan's Postwar Industrial Growth," p. 284.

> an extraordinary expansion of consumer durables, e.g., television sets, refrigerators, etc., proceeed in parallel with the investment boom. . . .
>
> In the 1956–61 period, technological innovation proceeded in various fields of industry. For example, mass production was introduced into the automobile industry to such an extent that the monthly production of passenger cars per factory and per kind of car amounted to 8,000 by 1961, which means that the industry had already passed beyond the sharpest part of its decreasing-cost curve. . . .
>
> . . . Automobile plants, with a monthly production level of more than 10,000 units per plant per one kind of car, began to emerge and have almost successfully absorbed most of the advantages of cost reductions through mass production.[226]

Shinohara noted correctly that future Japanese export expansion was likely to be sustained by "steel, automobiles, and similar products" and that the long-run share of consumers' durables in the machinery industry would rise.[227]

Rather more than Ohkawa and Rosovsky, then, Shinohara is aware of the linkages between the rise of consumers' durables and the automobile and their part in the transformation of the Japanese industrial structure as a whole. His technical problem is that in Japan, as elsewhere, the conventional statistical data do not permit strict measurement of those linkages: "Although I have been using the 'conventional' concept, heavy industry, there remain some problems in this connection . . . It includes not only capital goods but also consumers durables and chemicals, as well as intermediate goods. This makes it a heterogeneous concept."[228]

Referring to Svennilson's analysis, Shinohara notes that postwar Japan made successfully the structural adjustment that Britain made so imperfectly in the 1920's and 1930's.[229] In one grandiose sweep (with minor retardations along the way) Japan moved from the stage of technological maturity, at a low level of income per capita, to high mass-consumption at a Western European level of income per capita. Meanwhile, Western Europe, its interwar problems overcome, was also moving through this stage, at a rapid but more decorous pace, with Spain and Italy (like Japan) relatively catching up with the industrial nations whose take-offs had come earlier.

In the case of both Japan and Western Europe, the direct and indirect consequences of this process yielded increases in foreign trade in precisely the areas of most rapidly expanding domestic demand. The Japanese linkage is illustrated in Table III-67.[230]

In Japan, as in Western Europe, the postwar expansion, led by energy-intensive sectors, and on a scale requiring vast increases in raw-material imports, was aided by the post-1951 decline in import prices. Its terms of trade, conventionally measured, improved down to 1960, then fell away somewhat; but in real terms Japan did very well, given the high rate of increase in productivity in its major export sectors. It was acquiring its food, raw-material, and energy imports at a decreasing cost in terms of Japanese resources. But its energy consumption was increasing at a rate of more than 10 percent per annum, while its production of energy was declining, providing in 1972 only 22 percent of total consumption. Like Western Europe, Japan was highly vulnerable to the unfavorable shift in the terms of trade and, especially, to the disproportionate rise in energy prices that was to come.

The proportion of total fixed capital formation devoted to housing construction in postwar Japan rose from around 9 percent in the period 1948–1950 to an average level of about 17 percent for 1955–1970.[231] This was a somewhat lower proportion than in Germany and Britain, about half that in the United States. The result emerges because of the extraordinarily high level of total capital formation in this period and the scale of industrial investment within it. The

TABLE III-67. *Japan: Classification of Goods According to the Rates of Increase of Exports and Domestic Demand (Annual Rate for 1955–1964)*

I. Goods with increasing domestic demand and increasing exports	
	(Export rate > 15 percent
	Domestic demand rate > 15 percent)
Radios and TV sets	Pumps
Business machinery	Metal-processing machinery
Pulp and paper manufacturing machinery	Watches
Automobiles	Dynamos and electric motors
Bearings	Motors
Sporting goods	Optical instruments
Plastics	Inorganic chemicals
Organic medicines	Wooden products
Insulated electric wire	Metallic products
Oil products	Artificial and synthetic fibers
Tile	Textile machinery
	Lace
II. Export-centered goods	
	(Export rate > 15 percent
	Domestic demand rate > 10 percent)
Footwear	
III. Domestic-demand-centered goods	
	(Export rate < 10 percent
	Domestic demand rate > 15 percent)
Sewing machines	Aluminum
Porcelain	Rolling stock
Veneer	Precious stones
IV. Goods with stagnant domestic demand and stagnant exports	
	(Export rate < 10 percent
	Domestic demand rate < 10 percent)
Woolen textiles	Cotton yarn
Chemical fertilizers	Raw silk
Cotton textiles	Tea
Cement	

Source: Hisao Kanamori, "Economic Growth and Exports," p. 323.

volume of investment in housing (in constant prices) rose at an annual average rate of 15 percent between 1950 and 1970. Aside from the rise of incomes and the rate of family formation, the very rapid movement of labor from agriculture to industry required outlays on this scale.[232]

There was, of course, more to the great expansion in Western Europe and Japan than automobiles, durable consumers' goods, and suburban houses. As in the United States there was an extraordinary increase in real outlays on higher education and in enrollments, captured in Table III-68. Chart III-54 suggests how, at high levels of per capita product, enrollment rates of the relevant age group in higher education rise disproportionately. In most cases the rate of increase in educational expenditures is two or three times the rate of increase of GNP.

The expansion of outlays for higher education in the richer nations was part of a more general tendency for citizens to receive a higher proportion of their consumption in the form of increased government benefits: old age pensions, health insurance, unemployment benefits, and other welfare allowances. This flow represented half the increased proportion of consumers' income taken in the form of taxes in OECD countries; that is, between 1955 and 1969 the direct taxes paid by consumers rose 5 percent of GNP, while transfers to consumers from governments rose by 2.5 percent.[233] The changed pattern of disposal of the total initial flow of income to consumers ("primary" income) and the variations among the OECD nations are shown in Table III-69.

So much for the role of relative prices and the leading sectors in the most advanced industrial regions of the world. Their historically unexampled and relatively sustained growth was the central economic fact in the world economy. But high rates of economic

TABLE III-68. *OECD: Comparative Growth of Expenditure on and Enrollments in Higher Education, 1950's to 1960's (Average Annual Growth Rates)*

Country	Period	Current Expenditure (%)	Enrollments (%)
Belgium	1958–1967	18.3	8.6
Canada	1954–1965	16.6	12.3[a]
Denmark	1955–1966	22	7.3
Finland	1950–1967	11.1	7.3
France	1958–1968	13.3	9.8[a]
Germany	1957–1966	16.3	5.0
Iceland	1950–1957	2.4	—
	1957–1967	16	—
Ireland	1951–1963	—	4.8
Italy	1950–1965	15	3.9
Japan	1950–1965	11.1	6.9
Netherlands	1950–1968	16.8	5.6
Norway	1950–1967	10	7.2
Spain	1950–1968	11.4	—
Turkey	1950–1967	5	7.1
United Kingdom (England and Wales)	1950–1966	9.8	5.1[a]
United States	1955–1967	11.4	7.5
Yugoslavia	1952–1967	18.2	9.6

[a] Universities only.
Source: *OECD Observer*, no. 50 (February 1971), p. 15.
Note: Current expenditures are deflated according to a cost-of-living index.

growth were endemic if not quite universal. In the present limited context it is impossible to trace out in equal detail the experiences of the other major economies. The following paragraphs are designed merely to suggest the pace and character of their growth.

In terms of the data accepted by the United Nations, the societies with communist governments ("centrally planned economies") moved ahead at high but decelerating overall rates of growth: averaging annually 9 percent in the 1950's, 6.5 percent in the 1960's. According to the data in Appendix D, the Soviet rate of increase in real GNP per capita declined from 5.2 percent per annum in the 1950's to 4.1 percent in the period 1960–1972. The Soviet Union and the more advanced countries of Eastern Europe were caught up, as growth proceeded, in the transition so briskly made by the Japanese; that is, from the drive to technological maturity to some version of high mass-consumption. In Khrushchev's phrase, they had to move out of the world of the "steel-eaters" to one in which steel (and the whole advanced industrial base) was turned more substantially toward consumers' durables and automobiles; for income per capita reached levels where this was possible, and there was every reason to conclude that the natural income elasticities of demand of the people would not have been significantly different from those in North America, Western Europe, and Japan, if con-

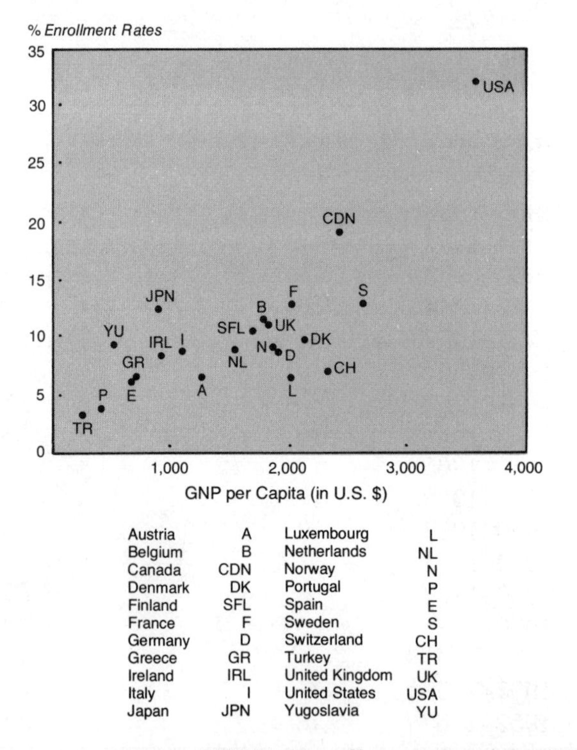

CHART III-54. *OECD: Enrollment Rates in Higher Education and Gross National Product per Capita, 1965–1966*

Source: *OECD Observer*, no. 50 (February 1971), p. 16.

sumers' sovereignty had reigned.[234] To some extent, for political reasons, but somewhat reluctantly, the authorities respected this fact. In the Soviet and other plans one can observe the rising priority for consumers' durables and, toward the end of the 1960's, an acceptance, to a degree, of the automobile revolution. Between 1963 and 1969 the average annual rate of growth of Soviet passenger car production was about 9 percent; for 1969 to 1972, over 35 percent, as newly constructed plants came into operation. On a scale about one-tenth that of the USSR, Polish production moved roughly in parallel. Between 1963 and 1972 private motor vehicles in use increased at an annual average rate of 13 percent in Czechoslovakia, 12 percent in East Germany, 19 percent in Hungary, 13 percent in Poland, 7 percent in less advanced Rumania, 27 percent in more free-wheeling Yugoslavia. These are rates calculated to bestow the mixed blessings of the automobile age on the people of the USSR and Eastern Europe quite rapidly, if they persist. On the other hand, the consumers' durables and automobile sectors had not attained a scale, by the early 1970's, to shape the Soviet economy to the same degree as those of North America, Western Europe, and Japan.

Aside from the inherent strains of reorienting planned and controlled economies from the build-up of heavy industry to the meeting of consumers' needs with reasonable efficiency, these governments had to deal with the inefficiency of their agricultural sectors. This problem became politically urgent as the high income elasticity of demand for meat asserted itself. In Eastern Europe modifications were made, in varying degree, to provide increased incentives to the farmers; and allocations to agricultural investment increased. But the Soviet Union and Eastern Europe as a whole moved over into a chronic food-importing position.

While the Soviet Union and most of Eastern Europe were making a somewhat awkward and incomplete transition from the heavy-industry sectors of the drive to technological maturity to the industrial and service complexes associated with high mass-consumption, Latin America, taken as a whole, was making an awkward and incomplete transition from the light, import-substitution industries of the take-off to the more capital-intensive sectors of the drive to technological maturity. By and large, the transition can be dated from the late 1950's. It occurred within a framework of overall annual average growth of about 5.5 percent in gross domestic product and 6.7 percent in the manufacturing sectors—high figures by pre-1914 (or pre-1939) historical standards.

In all the major Latin American countries one can observe retardation or decline in the light consumers' goods industries over the past two decades; e.g., in cotton textile production. In the 1950's, sulphuric acid and nitrogenous fertilizers came into production in Latin America; plastics and resins, in the second half of the 1960's. Automobile and truck assembly, component production, and full manufacture moved forward from the 1950's, notably in

Argentina, Brazil, and Mexico. Here one can observe clearly a general characteristic of Latin America's movement through technological maturity. Brazil and Mexico sustained high rates of growth through the period 1965–1972; but Argentina (actually the first in the automobile field) slowed down markedly.[235] This was also true of Argentine steel and sulphuric acid production as compared to that in Brazil and Mexico. The tendency for the absorption of new technology to take the form of a quick spurt followed by rapid deceleration or absolute decline can be observed in a number of modern, capital-intensive sectors in the smaller but technologically advanced Latin American countries; e.g., Colombia, Peru, and Venezuela. This phenomenon almost certainly results from the relatively small size of the domestic markets in relation to the minimum efficient scale of output in these sectors. A tour de force in

TABLE III-69. *OECD: From "Primary" Income to "Pure" Private Consumption (as Percentage of GNP, 1955 and 1969)*

	"Primary" Income		Net Current Transfers from Government		Direct Taxes	
	1955	1969	1955	1969	1955	1969
Major countries						
Canada	72.9	72.9	6.4	10.0	5.8	11.0
United States	79.3	78.8	4.2	6.1	11.5	16.2
Japan	78.0	72.0	2.7	3.2	5.4	7.6
France	74.5	73.4	12.3	17.0	13.4	19.5
Germany	71.3	71.9	12.2	13.3	14.4	19.2
Italy	77.3	77.1	8.5	13.7	10.3	16.5
United Kingdom	74.9	76.8	4.9	8.3	9.4	15.8
Other Northern European countries						
Austria	77.6	75.8	9.3	13.6	13.6	18.8
Belgium	78.6	77.3	9.1	13.6	11.4	17.6
Denmark	80.6	75.0	6.0	9.6	10.4	16.2
Finland	73.8	74.6	4.5	7.3	9.1	14.9
Ireland	78.7	75.4	5.7	7.5	3.3	7.4
Luxembourg	71.9	74.0	10.0	15.4	14.7	19.5
Netherlands	73.1	75.9	6.6	16.2	13.2	24.7
Sweden	77.5	76.5	5.4	10.0	13.5	26.1
Switzerland	77.3	75.3	3.1	6.9	10.0	13.4
Other Southern European countries						
Greece	84.7	77.2	4.0	8.3	6.2	8.6
Spain	79.0	78.1	1.1	4.2	3.6	7.7
OECD total	77.4	76.6	5.7	8.2	10.8	15.9
OECD excl. U.S.	75.4	74.2	7.3	10.5	10.0	15.6

Source: *OECD Observer*, no. 59 (August 1972), p. 5.

export promotion, as in Taiwan, South Korea, Hong Kong, and Singapore, would be required for these sectors to take hold efficiently. Import substitution does not suffice, especially against the background of habits and inefficiencies fostered in the first highly protectionist phase of Latin American industrialization. Only Brazil (after recovery from its setback of the first half of the 1960's) and Mexico appear to command domestic markets sufficient to proceed steadily forward with these new sectors unless effective Latin American economic integration is achieved or the tricks of exporting diversified manufactured exports are more effectively learned.

Latin America's performance in the growthmanship league of the less-developed regions emerges from Table III-70, lifted in 1967–1972 by the extraordinary pace of Brazilian expansion in those years. The regional averages attest to the high average momentum

[Ne]t Current [Tr]ansfers [fr]om Abroad		Disposable Income		Saving as a Percentage of GNP		Private Consumption		"Pure" Private Consumption	
[1]955	1969	1955	1969	1955	1969	1955	1969	1955	1969
0.2	−0.1	73.3	71.8	8.6	10.7	64.6	61.1	58.2	51.1
0.1	−0.1	71.9	68.6	7.9	7.3	63.9	61.3	59.7	55.2
0.1	0.0	75.2	67.6	13.4	16.1	62.1	51.5	59.4	48.3
0.1	−0.3	73.5	70.6	9.3	10.8	64.3	58.8	52.0	42.8
0.0	−0.7	69.1	65.3	9.2	10.4	59.8	54.9	47.6	41.6
0.7	0.8	76.2	75.1	9.8	12.3	66.4	62.8	57.9	49.1
0.4	−0.5	70.0	68.8	3.2	6.0	66.8	62.7	61.9	54.4
0.1	0.6	73.4	71.2	11.1	12.6	62.3	58.6	53.0	45.0
0.0	0.4	76.3	73.7	6.4	11.1	69.9	62.4	60.8	48.8
0.0	0.0	76.2	68.4	7.3	6.8	68.9	61.6	62.9	52.0
0.0	0.0	69.2	67.0	8.1	11.2	61.2	55.8	56.7	48.5
2.2	1.3	83.3	76.8	5.4	8.7	77.9	68.1	72.2	60.6
0.0	0.0	67.2	69.9	9.3	8.9	57.8	61.0	47.8	45.6
0.2	−0.1	66.7	67.3	7.5	10.4	59.2	56.8	52.6	40.6
0.0	0.0	69.4	60.4	7.5	6.0	61.7	54.2	56.3	44.2
0.6	−1.8	69.8	67.0	4.3	10.1	65.6	56.9	62.5	50.0
2.3	3.7	84.8	80.6	7.1	11.6	77.7	68.9	73.7	60.6
0.3	1.5	76.8	76.1	6.1	7.6	70.6	68.5	69.5	64.3
0.0	−0.1	72.3	68.8	8.3	9.0	63.9	59.8	58.2	51.6
0.1	−0.1	72.7	69.0	8.7	10.8	63.9	58.2	56.6	47.7

TABLE III-70. *Comparative Growth Rates, Developing Regions: Selected Regions, 1960–1970 (Annual Average Percentage Rate of Growth)*

	Gross Domestic Product		Agricultural Production		Manufacturing Production		Energy Production[a]	
	1960–1965	1966–1970	1960–1965	1966–1970	1960–1965	1966–1970	1960–1965	1966–1970
Developing countries	5.5	5.8	2.6	3.1	8.7	7.8	9.5	10.3
Africa	5.0	5.2	2.1	1.5	6.0	7.5	—	—
South Asia	3.8	4.4	1.0	4.1	9.1	3.1	—	—
East Asia	5.4	7.0	3.4	3.3	8.8	13.1	—	—
Southern Europe	7.3	6.3	2.8	3.7	11.7	9.5	—	—
Latin America	5.3	5.7	4.1	2.7	6.3	7.1	—	—
Middle East	8.2	7.8	6.1	1.5	11.0	10.1	—	—
Industrialized countries	5.2	4.6	1.7	2.1	6.3	5.4	7.6	7.6

	Primary School Enrollment[b]		Secondary School Enrollment[b]		Higher Education Enrollment[b]	
	1960–1965	1965–1970	1960–1965	1965–1970	1960–1965	1965–1970
Developing countries	6.8	4.8	9.0	—	—	—
Africa	6.2[c]	—	10.9	5.3	11.6	6.5
South Asia } East Asia	5.4[c]	4.0	7.5	3.3	11.7	7.8
Southern Europe	—	—	—	—	—	—
Latin America	5.2	4.5	11.5	9.9	9.5	11.3
Middle East	7.2[d]	3.7	12.4	9.2	12.3	7.5
Industrialized countries	2.3	0.3	4.9	1.9	9.5	7.5

[a] *United Nations Statistical Yearbooks*, annual volumes.
[b] *UNESCO Statistical Years*, annual volumes.
[c] Excluding Arab states.
[d] Arab states.
Source: World Bank calculations, unless otherwise indicated (World Bank, *World Tables*).

of industrial growth accompanied by a rapid expansion in the educational base. As noted earlier, the agricultural performance of these regions almost matches population growth, but fails to keep up with the demand for food, yielding a pervasive slide toward net food imports. There were also widespread harvest failures in 1972, producing an absolute decline of 0.9 percent in agricultural output in the developing countries. Among the regions, Africa and South Asia are the most sluggish, the former, by and large, in a pre–take-off stage, the latter hampered in this period by the successive weak monsoons of 1965–1967 and difficulties in generating adequate flows of foreign exchange. The southern fringe of Europe, from Spain to Turkey, and the Middle East exhibit the highest sustained momentum, the latter lifted by a surge in Iran from the mid-1960's forward. Iran's real national product increased at 6 percent per annum between 1960 and 1964 and at almost 12 percent from 1964 to 1972. There are success stories in each of these regional settings, cases of frustration, and unevenness in the distribution of benefits. But, in aggregate terms and by historical standards, the 1960's was, indeed, a decade of development.

The process was assisted by a unique feature of the post-1945 world: the commitment of governments of the more advanced industrialized countries to supply capital on a regular basis to less developed nations (see Table III-71). The origins of the commitment lie in the creation of the World Bank at Bretton Woods. The process was extended erratically in the 1950's and increasingly regularized in the 1960's, under the aegis of the Development Assistance Committee of the OECD. The net flows of official development assistance are set out in Table III-71. Given price and exchange rate move-

TABLE III-71. *Net Flow of Official Development Assistance*[a] *to Less Developed Countries and Multilateral Agencies, 1960–1973 (in Billions of U.S. Dollars)*

1960	4.7
1961	5.2
1962	5.5
1963	5.9
1964	6.0
1965	6.1
1966	6.3
1967	6.6
1968	6.4
1969	6.4
1970	6.8
1971	7.8
1972	8.7
1973	9.4

[a] From members of the Development Assistance Committee of the OECD only.
Source: OECD, *Reports of Development Assistance Committee*, annual.

ments over the period, and the expansion of income in the more advanced nations, the proportion of GNP devoted to this international function declined. The flow of intergovernmental capital nevertheless helped cushion the effect on foreign-exchange availabilities for many developing nations; encouraged the evolution of rational planning; and elevated the priority in recipient countries of development objectives. Although many (including this author) would regard the level of this flow as inadequate and its allocation as less equitable than it might have been, it represents by historical standards a considerable communal achievement in a world arena still predominantly governed by considerations of narrow national interest.

The world economy which emerged and moved forward in this rather remarkable way during the quarter-century after the Second World War generated four major vulnerabilities.

First, the rate of population increase in the less developed parts of the world began in the 1960's to outstrip the rate of increase in world agricultural production, a process exacerbated by faulty doctrines of economic growth in the less developed parts of the world, illusions about American agricultural surpluses, and inadequate allocations of resources to agricultural sectors.

Second, the rate of industrial expansion in the more developed parts of the world, pulled forward by energy-intensive leading sectors, began in the 1960's to draw down ready energy reserves in the Western Hemisphere and leave the world community doubly vulnerable: immediately vulnerable to monopolistic price setting by OPEC; and vulnerable over the span of a generation to the virtual exhaustion of the world's likely petroleum and natural gas reserves.

Third, there was a setting of endemic inflation in the more developed nations, as relatively high levels of employment, the expectation that such levels would be sustained, and the relative exhaustion of supplies of surplus rural and migrant labor caused the gap between money-wage increases and productivity increases to widen progressively, notably after 1965.

Fourth, the dollar eroded as reliable reserve currency under the Bretton Woods system as: (*a*) the increased virtuosity of Western Europe and Japan in the technologies of high mass-consumption reduced the U.S. trade surplus; (*b*) large net U.S. overseas security outlays exerted continuing strain on the dollar;[236] (*c*) the American economy drifted from the leading manufacturing sectors of high mass-consumption to the rapid expansion of certain services, the latter generating in the short run virtually no new technologies capable of sustaining U.S. exports; and (*d*) the wage-price guideposts, which had successfully protected the dollar over the previous five years, were gravely weakened from approximately the summer of 1966, to be abandoned in January 1969. Taken all together, these forces destroyed the Bretton Woods monetary system in 1971, yielding uneasy and unstable transitional arrangements, which, like other expedients, may persist for a long time.

18

The Price Revolution of 1972–1976

The price revolution of 1972–1976 was an immediate consequence of the first two of the four vulnerabilities of the world economy described at the end of Chapter 17; but its inflationary impact was exacerbated by the third and fourth. It broke the back of the great postwar boom by undercutting its leading sectors; and it exacerbated gravely the population-food balance, the problem of inflation, and the disarray of the international monetary system.

The experience with the price revolution of 1972–1976 conforms thus far, in a somewhat exaggerated way, to the opening phases of the four other trend periods marked by relatively rising prices of foodstuffs and raw materials. Each was marked, at or near its beginnings, by a brief, sharp price increase: 1798–1801; 1852–1854; 1897–1900; 1934–1937. The last, of course, was followed by general inflation during and immediately after the Second World War. As for the other three cases, 59 percent of the total price increase between 1793 and 1813 occurred from 1798 to 1801; 73 percent of the increase between 1850 and 1873, from 1852 to 1854; 48 percent of the increase between 1897 and 1913, from 1898 to 1900.[237] As our analysis has indicated, these dramatic surges did not strike the world economy out of the blue. They were preceded, like the sharp rise of cotton prices in the 1830's, by demand trends which put pressure on existing productive capacity; i.e., expanding European population in the second half of the eighteenth century; a catching up, once again, of population increase with agricultural capacity, including the carrying capacity of the potato in Ireland and elsewhere; the ending of the American frontier, accompanied by a rapidly enlarging and urbanizing American population. So, also, the crisis which began in 1972 had its preparatory history to be observed in the stock position of grains and the reserve position of American gas and oil.

Once under way the price rise quickly produced the familiar pattern: generalized inflation, as labor sought to redress the decline in real incomes with higher money wages; rising interest rates; radically shifted terms of trade within and between national economies; shifts in income distribution against the urban worker. But it also had the historically unique result of inducing a severe recession affecting virtually all nations except oil exporters.

Chart III-55 shows on a monthly basis how certain categories of wholesale prices moved in the United States during the period January 1972–December 1975; Table III-72 exhibits those movements on an annual basis.

Farm prices began to accelerate in December 1972; fuel prices moved up sharply in April 1973, then relatively stabilized before the increases which began in November. A 55 percent increase in fuel prices occurred over the following thirteen months. With somewhat improved harvests around the world, there was a tendency for farm prices to fall away from about February 1974, when they stood 75 percent over the January 1972 level. They rose again in 1975, responding to the effects of the poor Soviet harvest. Raw materials (other than food and fuel) also sagged away from a peak in April 1974, 86 percent above January 1972, under the impact of American (and world-wide) recession.

Taking wholesale prices overall, the 54 percent net increase between January 1972 and December 1975 compares to a 35 percent increase between 1940 and 1945, during the Second World War; and to the 52 percent postwar increase, from 1945 to 1948. As one would expect at a time of revolutionary change in agricultural, energy, and raw-material prices, prices of intermediate goods and finished goods rose less than those of crude materials, and, of course, they rose with a lag. Average gross weekly earnings in nonagricultural employment rose still less, at an average annual rate of 6.4 percent.

From these differential changes flowed significant shifts in terms

TABLE III-72. *Wholesale Prices by Stage of Processing: United States, 1972–1975, Annual (1967 = 100)*

	All Commodities	Annual Average Increase (%)	Crude Materials	
			Total	Foodstuffs a[nd] Feedstuffs
1972	119.1	—	127.6	127.5
1973	134.7	13.1	174.0	180.0
1974	160.1	18.9	196.1	189.4
1975	174.9	9.2	196.9	191.8
Annual average increase, 1972–1975		13.7%	15.6%	14.6%
Peak	Oct. 1975	Dec. 1975	Sept. 1975	Feb. 1974

Source: *Economic Report of the President* (Washington, D.C.: Government Prin[ting] Office, January 1976), pp. 227–228.

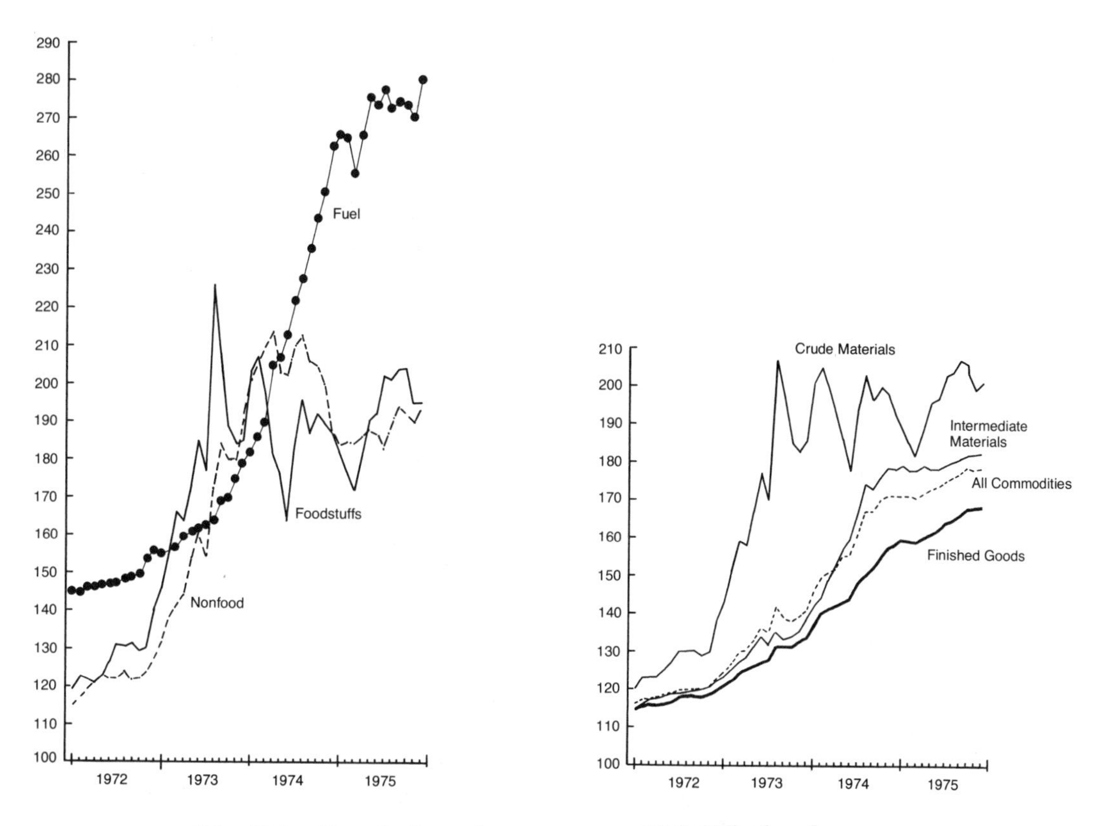

CHART III-55. *The Price Revolution of 1972–1975: U.S. Wholesale Prices, Monthly (1967=100)*

Source: *Economic Report of the President* (February 1975), pp. 301–302; ibid. (January 1976), pp. 227–228.

ıde Materials		Intermediate Materials (Total)	Finished Goods (Total)
nfood Materials ·ept Fuel	Fuel		
.9	148.7	118.7	117.2
.5	164.5	131.6	127.9
›.4	219.4	162.9	147.5
›.3	271.5	180.0	163.4
›.6%	22.2%	14.9%	11.7%
·il ·74	Dec. 1975	Nov. 1975	Oct. 1975

of trade and income distribution, within nations and among them. The American farm parity ratio moved up (on a basis unadjusted for government payments) from 75, as late as 15 November 1972 (1967=100) to a peak of 102 in mid-August 1973. By May-June 1975, the parity ratio was down as low as 69 due to the sag in farm prices plus the impact of energy and other increases in the prices farmers paid. At the close of 1975, the poor Soviet harvest and enhanced export prices brought the parity index back to just about where it had been three years earlier. But in 1976 once again good global harvests put the farmer under pressure.

The American farmer did relatively better, however, than the United States and the developed regions as a whole. The U.S. terms of trade fell away from 95 in 1972 (1963=100) to 84 in the third quarter of 1975.[238] For the developed areas as a whole the terms-of-trade deterioration was only slightly less: 102 in 1972, 92 in the third quarter of 1975. Due to the great changes in international petroleum prices, the terms of trade of the developing areas as a whole rose from 99 in 1972 to 132 in the third quarter of 1975; but the terms of trade for non–oil producers sharply deteriorated.

As Table III-73 and Chart III-56 indicate, the impact of all this on the industrialized nations was to produce a convergence of stagnation and inflation unique in modern economic history. From a situation where an average 5.2 percent annual rate of increase in output was accompanied by an average 4.1 percent rate of price increase, the OECD world moved to slight absolute reduction in output in 1974–1975 accompanied by 10–12 percent price increases. The recovery expected in 1976 for OECD as a whole (5.75 percent) was judged at the close of 1975 to be insufficient greatly to reduce unemployment (Chart III-56). Inflation would, it was estimated, moderate only to something still over 8 percent.

The mechanism at work in the various industrialized countries was similar, although its net impact varied:

—the terms of trade shifted adversely;

—acute balance-of-payments pressures stemming from the oil price increase led to policies of fiscal and monetary restraint (including high interest rates) as well as to more direct energy conservation measures;

—the rise in energy prices and reduced levels of employment led, in particular, to a decline in postponable consumption expenditures (notably on automobiles, durable consumers' goods, and housing), as well as to reduced consumption outlays in general, a decline that was promptly transmitted to related sectors;

—wage-push inflation accelerated, as those unions with bargaining leverage sought to compensate for reduced real wages;

—efforts of varying success were made to expand exports to the oil-rich nations and others, but these were inhibited in the short run by the limited absorptive capacity of some of the major oil producers and by the endemic world recession which gathered momentum in 1974;

—business expectations, particularly optimistic in the boom of 1972–1973, shifted toward caution or pessimism, exacerbating the decline in investment induced by high interest rates and reduced consumption outlays, while compensatory investment in alternative energy resources and conservation expanded only slowly;

—similarly, the dour expectations of private consumers, in an environment of both accelerated inflation and rising unemployment, led to a rise in savings.

Through this complex convergence of forces, the real losses in output suffered in 1974 by the OECD world were about twice the amount transferred to the oil producers due to the fourfold increase in their export prices.[239] Table III-74 summarizes the results of a sophisticated analysis of the forces at work on aggregate demand and GNP in the United States, Western Europe, and Japan in 1973–1974.[240] The ultimate cost would depend on the policies pursued in 1976 and beyond by the advanced industrial nations, a subject considered in Part Six.

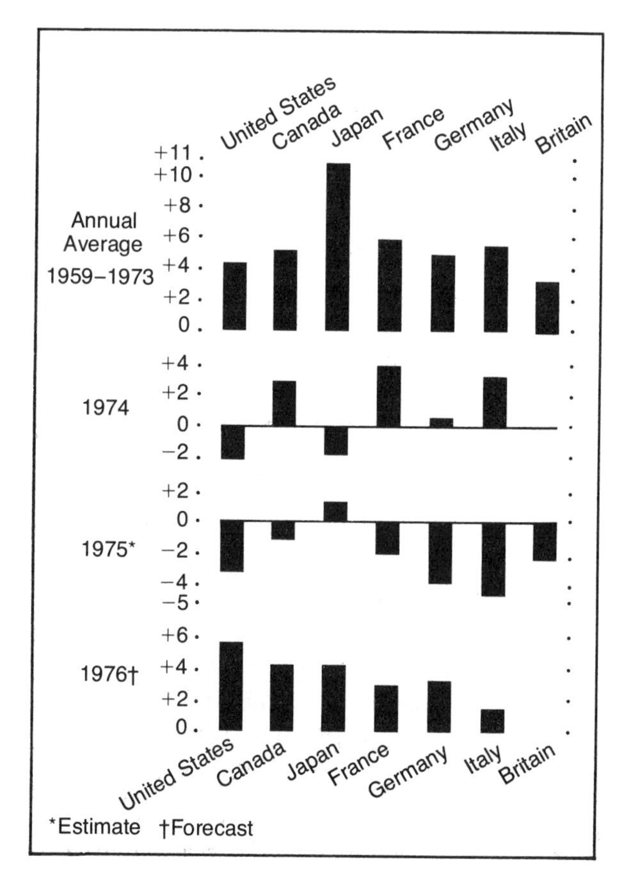

CHART III-56. *Growth of Real Gross National Product: Six Countries, 1959–1976 (% Changes)*

Source: *New York Times*, 24 December 1975. From the Organization for Economic Cooperation and Development.

TABLE III-73. *Gross National Products and Price Indexes:*
Adjusted at Annual Rates, Estimates and Forecasts)

Canada (GNP)
United States (GNP)
Japan (GNP)
France (GDP)
Germany (GNP)
Italy (GDP)
United Kingdom (GDP)
Total of above countries[a]
Other OECD countries
Total OECD
Total OECD excluding United States
GNP/GDP deflator: Total of above countries

Canada (GNP)
United States (GNP)
Japan (GNP)
France (GDP)
Germany (GNP)
Italy (GDP)
United Kingdom (GDP)
Total of above countries[a]
Other OECD countries
Total OECD
Total OECD excluding United States
GNP/GDP deflator: Total of above countries

D Countries, 1959–1975 (Percentage Changes Seasonally

owth of real GNP/GDP in Seven Major Countries

eights in otal[a] (%)	Average, 1959–1960 to 1971–1972 (%)	From Previous Year		
		1973 (%)	1974 (%)	1975 (%)
3.7	5.0	6.9	2.8	−0.25
0.0	4.1	5.9	−2.1	−3.75
2.9	11.0	9.9	−1.8	1.5
8.0	5.8	6.5	3.9	1.0
0.9	4.9	5.3	0.4	−2.0
4.3	5.5	6.3	3.4	−2.75
5.4	3.1	5.2	−0.2	0.5
5.3[c]	5.5	6.5	−0.6	−1.75
4.7	5.3	5.3	2.7	0.75
0.0	5.4	6.3	−0.1	−1.5
0.0	6.3	6.6	1.2	0.75
—	—	—	—	—

ivate Consumption Deflators in
even Major Countries

verage, 1959–1960 to 971–1972 (%)	From Previous Year		
	1973 (%)	1974 (%)	1975 (%)
3	6.5	10.6	10.5
4	5.6	11.4	8.0
5[b]	11.8	24.4	12.5
3[b]	7.1	13.7	11.75
0	7.1	7.3	6.0
1[b]	10.8	19.1	18.25
8	8.5	14.5	22.5
3	7.4	13.6	10.25
—	—	—	—
—	—	—	—
—	—	—	—
6	7.1	12.1	10.5

73 weights and exchange rates.
nsumer price index, not seasonally adjusted.
ure does not equal sum of components due to rounding.
rce: *OECD Observer*, no. 76 (July–August 1975), pp. 4 and 6, Tables 1 and 3.

TABLE III-74. *Changes in Real GNP, 1973–1974: United States, Western Europe, and Japan*

Country or Region	Pre-embargo Outlook (%)	Actual (%)	Change from Pre-embargo Outlook		
			Total (%)	Attributable to Oil (%)	Attributable to Other Factors (%)
United States	+2.6	−2.1	−4.7	−2.5	−2.2
Western Europe	+4.8	+2.3	−2.5	−2.7	+0.2
Japan	+5.2	−1.8	−7.0	−4.2	−2.8

Source: Edward R. Fried and Charles L. Schultze (eds.), *Higher Oil Prices and the World Economy*, p. 21, where detailed sources are indicated.

The impact of the price revolution of 1972–1976 was peculiarly acute for two reasons:

First, the industrialized world was enjoying a strong and virtually universal boom in 1972–1973. Effective demand for food, fuel, and raw materials was high and vulnerable, both to the bad harvests of 1972–1973 and to the action of OPEC in October 1973. It also seems clear that there would, in any case, have been some general recession or retardation in 1974. Second, the crisis occurred against a background of accelerating wage-push inflation. Phillips curves (measuring the change in prices associated with a change in the level of unemployment) were moving to the right, indicating that a given decline in unemployment yielded progressively higher rates of inflation; or, put the other way, a given rate of inflation was associated with higher levels of unemployment. In this setting the rise of international prices for basic materials in 1973–1974 yielded an especially prompt and sharp initial increase in inflation rates and accelerated increases in money wages. Its effects on real income, not fully compensated for by increases in energy-related investment, brought unemployment to a level of 14.5 million men and women within the OECD nations by the close of 1975.

In leading to a general recession, the price surge of 1972–1974 is unique among the five lower inflection points in price trends over the past two centuries. Such a recession did not happen in the 1790's, 1850's, 1890's, or mid-1930's. The mechanism by which it happened in the 1970's, however, is quite familiar in economic history. The non–oil exporters reacted to the price increases of 1972–1974 precisely the way the British economy reacted historically to bad domestic harvests and a sharp rise in wheat prices and imports: there were deflationary balance-of-payments and monetary effects combined with direct real-income effects, as higher import prices left less to be spent on other consumers' goods.

Taken altogether, the price revolution of 1972–1976 was the most traumatic economic event in the world economy since 1945. It struck directly at the energy-intensive leading sectors of the postwar expansions in Western Europe and Japan and caused, through the mechanism outlined above, declines in output and increases in unemployment on a scale which had not been experienced since the interwar years.

The impact of these events on Asia, the Middle East, Africa, and Latin America was less uniform, as Table III-75 indicates.

The immediately enhanced prospects for the oil producers are obvious. Their longer-run prospects will evidently depend on the energy policies pursued by the non-OPEC nations, future petroleum prices, and the rate of growth in the OECD world which emerges from the crisis of 1973–1975.

The other mineral exporters also enjoyed, for a time, relatively high export prices, which helped mitigate the increased cost of importing oil. The subsequent recession in the OECD world and weakening of their export prices dimmed their prospects in the course of 1974–1975.

The more advanced among the developing nations (above $200 per capita income) faced sharp increases in their foreign-exchange requirements; but a combination of their rather high reserves, access to borrowing, and capacity to export on a reasonably diversified basis initially yielded prospects for continued progress. These nations, however, were also adversely affected by the coming in 1974–1975 of acute recession in the more advanced nations of the industrial world. In Latin America, for example, the 7 percent average growth rates of 1973 and 1974 fell to 4 percent in 1975, less than 1 percent per capita. And these nations were left, in 1976, with a heavy debt burden, with uncertain prospects.

Those hardest hit were, of course, the poorest nations: under $200 per capita income. Their growth had been slowest in the period

TABLE III-75. *GDP Growth Rates by Groups of Developing Countries (Average Annual Percentage Growth Rate)*

	1961–1970 (%)	1971–1974 (%)	Population in 1970
Total GDP			(Millions)
Low-income countries	4.4	1.6	908
Middle-income countries	5.7	6.9	640
Subtotal (excl. OPEC)	5.2	5.3	1,548
OPEC members	6.6	7.7	251
Total developing countries	5.4	5.6	1,799
Per capita GDP			(% of Total)
Low-income countries	2.0	−0.8	50.5
Middle-income countries	3.1	4.3	35.6
Subtotal (excl. OPEC)	2.4	2.7	86.1
OPEC members	4.0	5.0	13.9
Total developing countries	2.8	3.0	100.0

Source: World Bank.

1968–1972; their exports had also been growing most slowly (1.8 percent per annum); the pressure of their populations on the food supply was most acute; they generally lacked a capacity to generate increased diversified exports; they depended more heavily on concessional aid and lacked large foreign-exchange reserves and access to private capital markets. They contained half the population of the developing noncommunist world; that is, almost a billion human beings.

Table III-76 exhibits one estimate of the terms-of-trade movement experienced by these categories of nations in 1973–1975.[241] It will be noted that the oil exporters had already enjoyed by 1973 an increase of one-third in their terms of trade above the 1967–1969 level. Of the other groups, the least advantaged in 1973 were, again, those under $200 per capita. In 1974 all other groups suffered in varying degree as the terms of trade of the oil-exporting countries increased in a way without precedent in economic history.

In terms of the transfer of resources, the gain by the oil exporters of (say) $70 billion in the price environment of 1974–1975 was accompanied by an annual loss, as compared to 1973, of about $13 billion by other developing countries, a figure which rises substantially when the effect of the recession on their export earnings is taken into account.

In the course of 1974–1975, the international community took some measures to alleviate the palpable inequity involved in throwing a disproportionate burden of adjustment on the poorest and most economically defenseless men, women, and children on the face of the planet. There was no master plan; but individual nations, the World Bank, and the International Monetary Fund did some useful things, as the summary in Table III-77 indicates. The oil producers with excess funds made some of that surplus, beyond their current import capacity, available to their less fortunate (mainly Moslem) brethren: perhaps $4.6 million in 1974.[242] An additional $200 million was disbursed by the U.N. Emergency

TABLE III-76. *Terms of Trade: Categories of Developing Countries, 1973–1975 (1967–1969 = 100)*

	1973	1974	1975
1. Oil-exporting countries	134	313	308
2. Other-minerals exporters	95	90	79
3. Other developing countries by per capita income groups:			
a. Above $375	104	97	90
b. $200–375	101	94	88
c. Below $200	99	84	83
Total, excluding oil exporters	102	94	89

Source: Wouter Tims, "The Developing Countries," Chapter 5 in Fried and Schultze (eds.), *Higher Oil Prices and the World Economy*, p. 178.

Operation. The World Bank accelerated disbursements under existing loans to the nations under $200 per capita. The IMF created (with some support from the oil producers) an emergency oil fund permitting nations to cover, in the short run, deficits created by the rise in oil prices. But, as of the close of 1976, these measures, some of which were short-term, were clearly insufficient to maintain even low pre-1973 growth rates. The prospects for all the developing countries except the oil producers for the rest of the 1970's remained rather dim and greatly dependent on the pace of growth in the OECD world as well as longer-run aid and trade policies still to be agreed upon.

The longer-term problems and prospects for the world economy are dealt with in Part Six. But one final question, highly relevant to trend-period analysis, should be posed here: Was the price revolution of 1972–1976 a transient event, or the opening of the fifth protracted period of relatively high food and raw-material prices in the past two centuries?

As of 1976 the case could be argued either way. Raw-material prices had fallen during the recession of 1974–1975; food prices had eased with the good harvests of 1974, hardened somewhat with the Soviet crop failure of 1975, then relatively softened again. OPEC was struggling to hold its prices (relative to import prices) by cutting production, against a background of enormous stocks in the industrialized world and idled oil tankers. Some analysts could—and did—envisage a quick return to pre-1972 relative price relationships.

TABLE III-77. *Net Capital Flows to Developing Countries, 1973–1975*[a] *(in Billions of U.S. Dollars)*

		Recipient Country Groups			Total	Total in U.S. $, 1974[b]
		Low-Income Countries	Middle-Income Countries	Oil-Exporting Countries		
1973	Official capital	3.59	6.84	0.95	11.38	16.01
	Private capital	0.79	11.12	1.95	12.78	17.92
	Total	4.38	17.96	2.90	24.16	33.98
1974	Official capital	5.55	9.48	1.14	16.17	16.17
	Private capital	1.42	17.98	1.04	20.44	20.44
	Total	6.97	27.47	2.18	36.61	36.61
1975	Official capital	7.43	12.41	1.43	21.27	20.07
	Private capital	0.94	21.95	1.75	24.64	23.24
	Total	8.37	34.36	3.18	45.91	43.31

[a] Flows to all developing countries, received from bilateral and multilateral sources, but excluding technical assistance and flows without specified destinations.

[b] Deflated by the index of developing countries' import prices.

Source: World Bank.

On the other hand, one could view the price softening of 1974–1976 as the product of transient circumstances: the industrialized world was in stagnation; progress in most of the developing world had slowed down or halted; the world's food stocks had not been rebuilt; the winter of 1974–1975 in the north had been blessedly mild and energy-saving, a circumstance not to be counted upon regularly; the world's population continued to expand at not much less than the pre-1972 rate; the measures envisaged in 1975–1976 to expand agricultural, raw-material, and energy production (and to conserve energy) appeared to have built into them frictions and lags perhaps as great as those required to open up new regions and countries in the trend-period upswings of the pre-1914 era. One could, thus, argue that the relative prices of basic materials were likely to remain high for some time.

Which view proves correct will depend greatly, of course, on whether the industrialized nations of the world have the wit and will to avoid the kind of protracted stagnation which marked inter-war Britain, to make the necessary structural adjustments, and to resume relatively steady growth on a somewhat altered sectoral basis. It will also depend on whether the early- and late-comers to industrialization translate the descent from the rhetorical confrontation of 1974 to the more temperate negotiations of 1975–1976 into viable collective policies. It is still not clear whether the world community faces a protracted neomercantilist struggle for resources, or whether it will find the stable terms of partnership its members rationally require. What is involved in these two questions we shall consider in Part Six.

But if the answers to these questions are positive, if reasonably orderly progress is resumed at rates like those of the 1960's, I would guess—no more is justified—that the inexorable pressure of excessive population increase in the developing world, the tendency of the poor to spend increases in income disproportionately on food, the rising demand for grain-expensive proteins, the pace of industrialization among those catching up, and the strains of the energy crisis will persist. Given these powerful and sustained demands operating on food, energy, and raw-material prices and the costs we shall have to incur to achieve and maintain clean air and water, I believe we are in for a long period when the prices of these basic inputs to the economy will remain relatively high, despite transient intervals of abundance.

Under hopeful assumptions about the rationality of economic and political policy, then, the extraordinary changes in the world economy during 1972–1976 may emerge as the first phase in what might be called the fifth Kondratieff upswing.*

* As of the spring of 1977, as this book goes to press, I am even more confident than when these lines were drafted that the world economy confronts a protracted period of relatively high energy, food, and raw-material prices, despite the failure thus far of the OECD world to reattain the growth rates of the 1960's.

19

Trend Periods Summarized

How can we summarize briefly this long analysis of trend-period phenomena over the past 185 years? We have tried to explain upward and downward phases in prices, relative prices, interest rates, real wages, income distribution, and patterns of investment in terms of two major variables: the relative abundance or scarcity of various foodstuffs and raw materials; and the character of the leading sectors in the major economies. Population movements (international and domestic), housing construction, and the rate of expansion of urban infrastructure have been seen, essentially, as functions of these two interacting major variables, although the enlarged role of public housing policies after the First World War introduced a special new element into the equation. Wars affected the way these variables moved and, to a lesser extent, the flow of gold from the mines.

One way to look back and to summarize the story is to ask, for each trend period, whether the pace at which the leading sectors in the various economies moved forward was constrained or accelerated by the abundance or scarcity of foodstuffs and raw materials, war, or gold mining.

1. *1790–1815.* Here, clearly, war and the necessity for expanding agriculture in Britain (and protecting, at high cost, imports of food and raw materials) damped the pace at which the major leading sector, cotton textiles, would otherwise have expanded. This was notably true after 1802. On the other hand, war conditions may have somewhat accelerated the expansion of the modern British iron industry. In the United States, war provided the new nation with an initial phase of high prosperity, based on the prices of its food and raw-material exports, foreshadowing the "new-country dynamics" later to be observed in many other parts of the world. After 1806 war forced a phase of import substitution in manufactures which helped prepare the way for the post-1815 New England take-off. Some areas on the Continent experienced similar forward movement in cotton textiles; but overall the British industrial lead as of 1793 had increased by 1815.

2. *1815–1848*. The postwar abundance of grain and, after 1818, of cotton set a framework of relatively cheap foodstuffs and raw materials for the next phase. Cotton textile manufacture, railway building, the steamship on the rivers, and the diffusion of the steam engine to industry could proceed more rapidly in this environment because basic commodities were relatively cheap—except, of course, in the 1830's. The pace of cotton industry expansion in the previous decade yielded a price explosion in 1833–1835. This made profitable the diversion of large U.S. and British capital flows to the expansion of acreage in the American South; and the West, too, absorbed substantial capital for infrastructure to make its products more marketable in the East. As after 1818, these developments overshot the world market needs at existing prices; and prices, interest rates, etc. resumed their post-1815 trends in the 1840's. The economic environment of that decade made it attractive for capital to flow into the emerging new leading sector complex: the railways and all connected with them. This happened in the American Northeast and in Britain, Belgium, Germany, and France. This period experienced no significant diversions or distortions due to wars. But in the 1840's (notably in Ireland) there were signs that the food-population balance was going awry, signs similar to the cotton warning signals of the late 1820's. The potato crisis of 1845–1847 yielded a population push from land pressed too hard into European cities and across the Atlantic to the New England mills.

3. *1848–1873*. The trends reversed sharply in this trend period. The balance between food and population increase yielded a substantial rise in grain prices in the 1850's. Capital flowed in a big way to open up the Middle West. Cotton, after a decade's slack, also moved up in price, and acreage pushed west as far as Texas. Urban real wages came under severe pressure. For the first time the new leading sector converged with food and raw-material requirements, providing the means for bringing new acreage into production. These agricultural demands did not, however, prevent Western Europe from also moving forward rapidly with the railroad sectoral complex down to 1873. The American Civil War set back the United States and imposed transient constraints on the world's cotton supply as well as stimulating cotton production in regions beyond the American South. The 1850's and the post–Civil War period saw large flows of population from European agriculture to the European cities and across the Atlantic. The trans-Mississippi railroad extension after 1865 again drew large flows of British (and U.S. eastern) capital, yielding in time enormous increases in grain exports, further cheapened by falling shipping rates. The course of prices, interest rates, terms of trade, income distribution, and flows of capital were distorted in this period by a series of minor wars and, for the first time, by the attractions of gold mining.

4. *1873–1896*. Once again, in an interval of relative peace and abundance of foodstuffs and raw materials, the leading industrial

sectors were driven forward in an uninhibited way. The railways peaked out as a leading sector in the more industrialized countries, holding up until the 1880's in the United States; but out of the railways had come steel in all its nonrail uses, machine tools, ships and more efficient steam engines for ships, while electricity and new forms of chemicals began to move from the stage of invention to an early phase of innovation. But the railroad was not finished. In Canada and Australia, India, Argentina, Brazil, and Russia it was beginning to transform the agricultural sectors, and not a moment too soon. For the limits of the American frontier were formally reached in the 1890's; and the pull of the American agricultural and industrial economy in the post–Civil War period generated increases in population and urbanization which were to limit U.S. grain-exporting capacity. In the 1870's Sweden, in the 1880's Japan, and in the 1890's Russia and Italy moved into take-off at rates which began to close some of the ground between themselves and the earlier-comers to industrialization.

As between 1815 and 1850, the trends in prices and interest rates were down, and real-wage movements and income distribution favored the urban worker in industrial societies; but, as in the 1830's, there was a break in the continuity of these trends. The Argentine boom of the late 1880's drew capital and stimulated the world economy, along with concurrent movements elsewhere, to produce a brief inflationary interval. But in the first half of the 1890's the post-1873 trend phenomena reasserted themselves.

5. *1896–1920.* Relative shortages of foodstuffs and raw materials again emerged in an environment of small wars, enlarged military outlays, and then a great war. This was a period bearing a family resemblance to that of 1850–1873, including increased gold mining. Large flows of capital to redress the balance in the world economy flowed this time not to the United States but to Australia, Argentina, Canada, and Russia, the latter two enjoying rapid industrial as well as agricultural expansion. Industrial real wages came under pressure, as in the 1850's; but those drawing income from agriculture and profits did relatively well.

The diversion of resources to agricultural expansion (and to wider purposes in agricultural nations), to gold mining, to increased arms outlays, and to war exacerbated a transitional phase in the leading sectors of the more advanced industrial nations of the Atlantic world. Railroads had, by the late 1890's, fallen away as a leading sector. Steel and all its related subsectors were decelerating. Electricity, certain new chemicals, and the automobile sectoral complex were moving forward rapidly, but not at a rate sufficient to compensate for the decline in momentum and productivity of the older leading sectors. The net result of this tension between various diversionary capital outlays and the leading sector transition was not uniform among the major industrial nations. It was most marked in Britain, where the Boer War was quite expensive, and it was followed by hitherto unprecedented levels of capital exports. It was a clear but less marked phenomenon in Germany and the United States, where the momentum of steel and all related to it, while decelerating, was sustained better than in Britain. In France, whose progress in the three preceding decades had been relatively slow, there was some acceleration as the coming of electricity helped compensate for the lack of a Ruhr and the loss of Alsace-Lorraine in the age of steel.

In Europe, the First World War, on balance, accentuated and distorted the pattern of this trend period; that is, the character of the military conflict created artificially high requirements for steel and other heavy-industry products of the aging leading sectors, while also inducing further expansion of agriculture in non-European areas not sustainable under normal peacetime circumstances. The United States and Canada shared, of course, the latter phenomenon; but it was during the First World War that the United States moved solidly into the age of the mass automobile, with Canada in line astern. In 1920, the prices of agricultural products and raw materials broke sharply, absolutely and relatively, shifting the terms of trade favorably to industrial societies, lifting the real income of urban families, but reducing the incomes and purchasing power of those dependent on the production and sale of basic commodities.

6. *1920–1936.* Excepting the United States, where the new leading sectors of high mass-consumption carried the economy forward at a rate consistent with the high levels of employment, the more advanced industrial nations of Europe did not fully recover in the 1920's. France from 1925 to 1929 did best, aided by a currency devaluation which strengthened its relative export position. But, in general, the weakness of Europe's traditional pre-1914 export markets and the lower level of income per capita than in the United States converged to produce a situation where the new leading sectors of high mass-consumption (e.g., the automobile and durable consumers' goods) did not move forward rapidly enough to bring the major economies back to full employment. Then came the Great Depression, with catastrophic consequences in both industrial and basic commodity sectors.

There were many features unique to this trend period, but, as compared to its predecessors (1815–1850 and 1873–1896), its central characteristic was that relatively cheap prices for basic commodities did not, in themselves, encourage a sufficiently accelerated diffusion of the new leading sectors to avoid a retardation of overall growth in the most advanced economies.

7. *1936–1951.* Here, again, was a time of relatively high-priced basic commodities and the distortions of war. Recovery came in the 1930's against a background of reduced output of basic commodities which, at last, had yielded a reduction of the large stocks which overhung the markets in the 1920's and early 1930's. From about

1936 rearmament accelerated. The war reduced agricultural production in most of Europe, increased it in overseas areas. Relative shortages persisted, however, down to 1951, affected by the pace of recovery and the Korean War. Then, as in 1920, prices broke, relatively as well as absolutely.

8. *1951–1972*. But this time the outcome was quite different from what it had been between the wars. The leading sectors moved forward rapidly in North America, Western Europe, and Japan, strengthened by cheap energy, food, and raw materials. And there was another difference: despite weakened prices for basic commodities (especially in the 1950's), Asia, the Middle East, Africa, and Latin America also moved forward in earlier stages of growth, with appropriately different leading sectors. Their capacity to do so, in what might otherwise have been adverse circumstances, was strengthened by the extraordinary and sustained boom in the advanced industrial nations and the provision of a substantial official flow of capital for development purposes, on concessional terms, quite aside from flows of private capital.

In the United States from the late 1950's, the automobile and durable consumers' goods sectoral complexes (embracing also the movement to suburbia, massive road building, etc.) began to lose their momentum. They were superseded by a rapid expansion of private and public outlays for education, health, travel, and other services.

As the 1960's wore on, it was evident, beneath the surface, that the rapid global expansion in food and energy requirements was altering the balance which had existed since the price turn in 1951. One region after another moved into a food-deficit position, leaving the United States, Canada, and Australia virtually alone as food-surplus nations. Grain reserves as a proportion of annual global consumption fell away. The Indian food crisis of 1965–1967 (like the Irish crisis 120 years earlier) was a significant warning of what was to come. Similarly, the pace of energy consumption in the United States converged with an attenuation of American gas and oil reserves to require a rapid increase in U.S. oil imports. In 1972 the food situation came to crisis; in 1973 OPEC, perceiving its monopolistic leverage, moved to exploit it by a fourfold increase in oil prices.

9. *1972–1976*. The price revolution of 1972–1976, like its four predecessors, shifted the terms of trade, income distribution, the rate of inflation, and the patterns of both investment and world trade. Its effects on real income, income distribution, and the balance-of-payments position of the industrial world also set in motion a severe recession, bringing to an end the great post-1945 boom. It struck directly at the leading sectors: the automobile, durable consumers' goods, and a new range of chemicals (e.g., plastics and synthetic textiles). All were energy-intensive. The recession also struck at tax revenues on which the continued expansion of key

public services depended. In the developing world, the direct impact was most severe among the poorest nations; but virtually all, except the oil monopolists, were hit by the stagnation of the advanced industrial world; and even they were not wholly exempt from the shock.

In short, the first phase of the trend period which began in 1972 saw a sharp but not historically unique clash between the movements of basic prices and the forward momentum of the leading-sector complexes in the world economy. In 1975 recovery began; but as of the close of 1976 it was by no means clear that the old leading sectors were capable, in the new environment of relative prices, of bringing the advanced industrial world promptly back to the low unemployment and high growth rates of the previous two decades.

Part Four

Business Cycles

20

Cycles: Another Result of Unbalanced Growth

In Part Three we took as our initial focus changes in the relative prices of foodstuffs and raw materials; and we traced out how their movements, interweaving with forces set in motion by the sequence of leading sector complexes, imparted a special cast to a series of nine trend periods over the past 185 years, during which national economies and world markets sought a dynamic sectoral equilibrium never quite attained.

Putting aside public policies toward the building of roads, canals, and railroads (and toward open frontier land, in certain nations), this effort was carried on down to 1914 and, in many nations and sectors, down to the present, primarily by private investment decisions designed to maximize private profit in an uncertain world. And even where governments intervened on the demand side of the market, the supply of resources was generated in competitive private capital markets. That institutional framework for adjusting sectoral capacity to requirements, plus the multiple lags inherent in the investment process, resulted not merely in the sequence of trend movements examined in Part Three but also in the more or less regular business cycles which are the subject of Part Four.

Business cycles, unlike trend periods, consist in fluctuations in employment and output or, after 1945, in the rate of increase in output. In the case of both trends and cycles, however, irregularity in the pattern of growth derives from lags and from distortions in the process of investment away from its optimum sectoral paths. To repeat the earlier argument, these distortions arise from three factors: Investment decisions tend to be determined by current indicators of profitability rather than by rational long-range assessments; these indicators tend to make many investors act in the same direction, without taking into account the total volume of investment in particular sectors that is being induced by current profit expectations; and, beyond these technical characteristics of the investment process, there is, psychologically, a follow-the-leader tendency, as waves of optimism and pessimism about the profits to be earned in particular sectors sweep the capital market and industries where profits are (or are not) being plowed back in the expansion of plant. In both trend periods and business cycles the result is phases where capacity exceeds current requirements or falls short of them.

In the historical analysis of business cycles, it is essential to begin with these forces tending to cause overshooting and undershooting of sectoral optimum levels of capacity, because each business cycle has its own character, and both expansion and contraction are bound up with what happens in major sectors of the economy. The sectoral character of investment changes from one cycle to the next.

With the notable exception of Robert A. Gordon,[1] most modern business-cycle theorists set out their central propositions not in sectoral terms but in terms of the aggregate volume of investment, income, consumption, and employment (or output). They deal not with the relation of the current rate and pattern of investment to the appropriate level of capacity in particular sectors but with the relation of the total level of investment to the size of the total capital stock "that is needed."[2] There is an important element of legitimacy in such aggregation. This arises from the fact that an expansion (or contraction) of investment in a particular sector leads via the multiplier to a diffuse expansion (or contraction) of income. In turn, an expansion (or contraction) of income can lead via the accelerator (or stock-adjustment principle) to an expansion or contraction of investment over a wide front.

Historically, then, business-cycle expansions are a mixture of exaggerated surges of investment in particular directions which overshoot the sectoral optima of their time, accompanied by more general expansions in investment, output, income, and employment.

The upper and lower turning points of cycles are simple in aggregative theory, complex in practice. In theory, during a business expansion the interaction of the multiplier and accelerator proceeds in a cumulative, self-reinforcing process until full employment of labor or some other physical bottleneck is reached. This sets a ceiling on the level of output. The accelerator, which gears investment to the rate of increase in output, then turns investment downward. Through the multiplier, income and output fall. Through the accelerator, investment declines further. And so on. A theoretical floor is reached when gross fixed investment falls to zero. Investment and income cease to decline. The excess capital stock has been worked off. The continued rise in population and continued flow of technological possibilities with the passage of time now make investment and the expansion of the capital stock profitable again; investment expands; and the interaction of the multiplier and the accelerator yields a new cumulative cyclical expansion.

There are, indeed, some cycles which proceed to a peak of very low unemployment and acute physical bottlenecks. The British cyclical peak of September 1872 was, for example, of this character. In the only such year between 1851 and 1914, unemployment among trade unionists was less than 1 percent in 1872. The average level of money wages rose by 12 percent between 1871 and 1873. There was also a bottleneck in coal which caused its export price to more than double between 1871 and 1873, its domestic price to increase by two-thirds. Short-term interest rates began to rise in the spring of 1872. As the peak approached, the expected rate of return over cost for investment in many directions was thus reduced by a sharp rise in wages, raw materials, intermediate products, and working capital.

The British peak of 1872 illustrates another complexity. Britain was, of course, part of a lively, interconnected international economy. Full employment in Britain at the peak was the product of rapid expansion elsewhere, notably in the United States and Germany. British capital exports played a part in those expansions, notably to the United States; and they had their major impact on Britain's export industries. Aside from an exaggerated expansion in those industries, the sectoral distortions which brought on the downturn were primarily abroad rather than in Britain. In short, one must examine the sectoral pattern of expansions and the mechanism of upper turning points on an international as well as a national basis.

But there are also cycles in which the downturn occurs without any such dramatic arrival at a full-employment ceiling. The expected rate of return over cost in key sectors declines not because of a rise in costs but because it is perceived that the prior expansion in investment has brought capacity beyond the optimum level in those sectors; the expected rate of return on further expansion thus declines, without significant pressure from rising costs. (In R. C. O. Matthews' vocabulary, we observe at a sectoral level that investment is "a diminishing function of the stock of capital.") The British boom reaching its peak in December 1882 was of this type, as were minor (inventory) cycles in general. A rather famous case of a sectoral decline occurring for this reason was the peaking of the American housing boom in 1925–1926, well before the general downturn of the economy in 1929.

A disaggregated, sectoral view of the lower turning point is similarly complex. Declines do not usually proceed until gross investment is zero. Sectors where overshooting did not occur in the previous boom (or where overshooting was mild), plus the more or less steady flow of new technical possibilities and population increase, can pull economies out of the slump before the theoretical floor in multiplier-accelerator analysis is reached. This cushioning was aided, in the pre-1945 world, by declines in costs which helped raise the expected rate of return over cost in those sectors. And there is one well-studied case of an economy promptly cushioning the downturn after the peak by shifting to a new sectoral investment pattern; i.e., the prompt British shift from capital exports to domestic-housing and urban-infrastructure investment in the period 1874–1877.

The length and intensity of business-cycle upswings—and the

extent of overshooting they yield—are partially determined by the time lags involved in the particular leading sectors of the boom. If the lag between the inception of investment and its completion is relatively long in a particular sector, the flow of investment in that direction may continue for a longer time than if the lag were relatively short. It takes more time to reveal that overshooting has occurred. The degree of sectoral overshooting in a boom helps determine not only its length and intensity but also the length and intensity of the subsequent slump.[3]

The shortest cycle, therefore, has been the inventory cycle. The lag between a decision to build (or reduce) inventories and the fulfillment of that decision is relatively short; and the judgment about the appropriate level of inventories in relation to current and expected output is somewhat less complex than in the case of fixed capital stock.[4] The shortness of the inventory cycle is related to another inherent characteristic of this form of investment: inventories have a short life. Unlike a factory, a road, or a house, they are used up rather promptly in the production process. Inventory overshooting, therefore, tends to be capable of correction fairly soon. Housing stands at the other extreme: houses last a generation, and their replacement (relative to inventories or even machinery) is more postponable. Moreover, when a housing deficit occurs, due, for example, to a war, the annual rate of construction during a postwar housing boom is a low proportion of the capital stock. The adjustment of the housing stock to its optimum level is, therefore, generally slow, and housing cycles are generally much longer than those in other forms of capital construction.

Against this brief background we turn to summarize the character and timing of cyclical patterns in four periods: the eighteenth century; 1783–1914; the interwar years; and post-1945.

21

Cycles in the Eighteenth Century: 1700–1783

Britain is the only country where business fluctuations in the eighteenth century have been examined in a reasonably systematic, if still exploratory, way.[5] Ashton's chronology of British turning points in business fluctuations is given in Table IV-1, with the peaks and troughs in building cycles noted in parentheses.

At first sight, one is tempted to treat these fluctuations as cycles

TABLE IV-1. *British Business Fluctuations, 1700–1783*

Trough	Length of Cycle (Trough to Trough)	Peak	Length of Cycle (Peak to Peak)
1700	—	1701	—
1702	2	1704 (1705?)	3
1706	4	1708	4
1712 (ca. 1711)	6	1714	6
1716	4	1717–1718	3.5
1722	6	1724–1725 (1724)	7
1727 (1727)	5	1728	3
1730	3	1733	5
1734	4	1738 (1736)	5
1742	8	1743	5
1746 (1744)	4	1746	3
1748	2	1751 (1753)	5
1755	7	1761	10
1763 (1762)	8	1764	3
1769	6	1771–1772	7.5
1775	6	1777 (1776)	5.5
1781 (1781)	6	1783	5
	Av. 5.1		Av. 5.0

Source: T. S. Ashton, *Economic Fluctuations in England, 1700–1800*, pp. 172–173; John Parry Lewis, *Building Cycles and Britain's Growth*, p. 14.

Note: Dates in parentheses are peaks and troughs of building cycles, from Lewis.

of a kind continuous with those of the pre-1914 century. For example, in setting turning points for British cycles from 1788 to 1913, one emerges with an average duration of 5.25 years, just about the average for the eighteenth century;[6] and the building cycle in Table IV-1 averages 17.4 years, close enough to the modern twenty-year building cycle of our textbooks again to suggest a continuity reaching back to 1700. But, as nearly as we can discern, domestic harvests and war played a larger role in these fluctuations before 1783 than they did later, although they were not absent from the world of 1783–1914; technological change and industrial investment certainly played a lesser role. There are, thus, significant differences between pre-1783 fluctuations and post-1783 cycles, as well as some elements of continuity.

The building fluctuations of the eighteenth century, for example, cannot be understood without reference to the major periods of conflict: 1701–1714; 1739–1748; 1756–1763; 1775–1783.[7] Through high interest rates (or the rationing of credit within the limit of the Usury Laws) the periods of most intense government expenditures for war, as later, damped building activity. Putting aside the uncertain case of the building expansion peaking in 1705, all the other expansions took place during intervals of peace; while the major periods of stagnation or contraction (including that with a trough at about 1711) were, in one way or another, connected with war.[8] Demographic factors and internal migration, however, also left a clear mark on indicators of the trend of building construction, with a lift in the scale of activity from about mid-century to 1793, reflecting both the expansion of the population and the accelerated urbanization which accompanied the quickening in the tempo of industrial life.

As for the shorter fluctuations, four characteristics of the English economy of the eighteenth century make it difficult to identify a regular cyclical process:

—the large role played by the harvests in determining the level of effective demand, the distribution of income, and the pressure on the foreign balance via the scale of grain exports or, as the century wore on, grain imports;[9]

—the immobility of the labor supply and the possibility of wide variation in regional economic circumstances, making generalization about the state of the national economy uncertain;

—the lack of major industrial innovations for most of the period and the relatively minor role of industrial investment;

—the impact on the British economy not merely of the wars but also of other international traumas, including those transmitted via Amsterdam, which remained Europe's financial center.

On the other hand, there is evidence that woven into the other determinants of foreign trade were elements, at least, of an inventory cycle.[10] And the role of outlays on canals and turnpikes, as well as on housing, provides evidence of a longer rhythm of expansion and contraction, even if their timing was closely connected with the arbitrary coming of war and peace. There is even some evidence of tension in the demand for both labor and capital between the demands of export industries and those of housing and infrastructure investment, foreshadowing a characteristic of the period 1870–1914 in the Atlantic economy.[11] Moreover, one has an impression, at least, that certain of the fluctuations in the eighteenth-century British economy at times of relative peace foreshadow, as a whole, the more shapely and consistent cycles after 1783; e.g., 1722–1727, 1748–1755.

I conclude that the pre–take-off British economy contained within it the major elements that were later to yield modern business cycles, except for major industrial innovation. Moreover, the process of capital stock adjustment to requirements and possibilities did occur in transport; and, given the rise in output down to 1783, there was evidently considerable industrial expansion without major technological change. The arbitrary requirements of war altered, of course, the composition of output and capital away from optimum peacetime paths; e.g., stimulating output of ships, cannon, and uniforms, depressing construction of houses. But the responsiveness of the British economy to wartime needs itself indicates that the capital-stock-adjustment principle was at work. In a predominantly agricultural economy, the impact of the harvests was relatively greater. In an economy marked by a large volume of partially unemployed labor, one can find only occasional references to demand so intense as to yield labor shortage (e.g., 1760–1761); and total unemployment, in the modern sense, was probably low, certainly unmeasurable on present evidence.

If we had the evidence, we could probably trace out similar erratic but suggestive fluctuations in the French and other Continental economies; and one would expect to find reasonably strong inventory cycles in the Dutch economy, given its predominant financial and large commercial role in the eighteenth-century world economy. I would guess that, given the time and distance involved and the role of credit, there was also an element of inventory fluctuation in the foreign trade of the American colonies down to 1775.

22

Cycles in the Classic Era: 1783–1914

We come now to the classic era of business cycles. We shall proceed by first considering cycles in the British economy, which remained throughout a central, if not wholly dominating, force in the world economy. We shall then consider divergences from the British pattern in the timing and character of business cycles in some other major economies.

Table IV-2 presents turning-point dates for British business cycles from 1783 to 1914, with building-cycle peaks noted (annually) in parentheses.

The first point to be made about the cycles dated in Table IV-2 is that they were not uniform in character and amplitude. An asterisk indicates that the cyclical expansion thus marked was characterized by substantial long-term investment, at home and/or abroad; and that conditions of virtually full employment were reached. Of these, the most ambiguous case is that of 1907, where capital exports occurred, during expansion, on a considerable scale, but home investment was not sufficient to create conditions of full employment. In the case of most cycles not marked by an asterisk (e.g. 1796, 1806, etc.), the primary impulse toward expansion lay in foreign trade. The cycle marked by a peak in 1800, a trough in 1801, is to be regarded as an interruption in the expansion from 1797 to 1802, rather than as a minor cycle confined to foreign trade. Similarly, the setback of 1861–1862 is to be regarded rather as an interruption in a major cycle expansion than as a minor cycle contraction, being affected by the outbreak of the American Civil War.

Chart IV-1 underlines the distinction between major and minor cycles by juxtaposing two sets of figures: a cyclical index, derived from the full range of data available on the British economy, covering the period 1784–1850, before general unemployment estimates were available; and unemployment among members of British trades unions, from 1850 to 1914.[12]

Because of Britain's central role in the world economy, its cyclical fluctuations over the period 1783–1914 deserve particular atten-

TABLE IV-2. *British Business Cycles: Cyclical Turning Points, 1783–1917*

Monthly		Annual	
Peak	Trough	Peak	Trough
—	—	1783	1784
—	—	1787	1788
1792 Sept.*	1794 June	1792* (1793)	1793
1796 May	1797 Sept.	1796	1797
1800 Sept.	1801 Oct.	1800	1801
1802 Dec.*	1804 Mar.	1802*	1803
1806 Aug.	1808 May	1806	1808
1810 Mar.*	1811 Sept.	1810* (1811)	1811
1815 Mar.	1816 Sept.	1815	1816
1818 Sept.*	1819 Sept.	1818* (1819)	1819
1825 May*	1826 Nov.	1825* (1825)	1826
1828 Jan.	1829 Dec.	1828	1829
1831 Mar.	1832 July	1831	1832
1836 May*	1837 Aug.	1836* (1836, 1840)[a]	1837
1839 Mar.	1842 Nov.	1839	1842
1845 Sept.*	1846 Sept.	1845* (1847)[a]	1848
1847 Apr.	1848 Sept.		
1853 III*	1854 Dec.	1854*	1855
1857 Sept.	1858 Mar.	1857	1858
1860 Sept.	1862 Dec.	1860	1862
1866 Mar.*	1868 Mar.	1866*	1868
1872 Sept.*	1879 June	1873* (1876)	1879
1882 Dec.*	1886 June	1883*	1886
1890 Sept.*	1895 Feb.	1890*	1894
1900 June*	1901 Sept.	1900* (1898–1899)	1901
1903 June	1904 Nov.	1903	1904
1907 June*	1908 Nov.	1907*	1908
1912 Dec.*	1914 Sept.	1913*	1914

* Major cycle peaks.

[a] The 1840 and 1847 peaks are, to some significant extent, related to railway construction rather than merely to housebuilding.

Sources: 1783–1787, Ashton, *Economic Fluctuations in England*, p. 173; 1788–1848, A. D. Gayer et al., *The Growth and Fluctuation of the British Economy, 1790–1850* (Oxford: Clarendon Press, 1953), vol. 1, p. 348; 1854–1914, Arthur F. Burns and Wesley C. Mitchell, *Measuring Business Cycles* (New York: National Bureau of Economic Research, 1946), p. 79. The hiatus in monthly turning-point dates between Gayer and Burns-Mitchell is filled in from J. R. T. Hughes, *Fluctuations in Trade, Industry and Finance* (Oxford: Clarendon Press, 1960), p. 29. Hughes observes: "The downswing began with the depression in textiles in the fourth quarter of 1853." See also Hughes' persuasive reservations on 1854 as a peak year (pp. 27–28).

tion. But precisely because of Britain's role they cannot be fully understood except as part of an interacting process in which Britain both reflected forces at work in other economies and acted upon them. Table IV-3, based on both statistical and qualitative evidence, is meant to suggest somewhat impressionistically how the major cycles of these 130 years involved, on the one hand, the progressive absorption of new technologies within the British economy and, on the other hand, a shifting pattern of expansion in foreign trade and capital exports.

The major capital-export booms were those peaking in 1825, 1836, 1854, 1873, 1890, and 1913. In each case they left their mark clearly on the pattern of British exports. But, of course, increases in British exports were also determined by the more or less autonomous movements of nations into industrialization; e.g., the United States, Western Europe, Scandinavia, Japan, Russia. And periods of relatively rising or high foodstuff and raw-material prices were reflected in increased British exports to the producing regions, whether or not British capital exports were also flowing to them concurrently.

The minor cycles are distinguished here by the fact that they involved increases in production and employment arising preponderantly, but not exclusively, from increases in exports. In the first half of the nineteenth century textiles and other consumers' goods constituted the dominant element in British exports. Against the back-

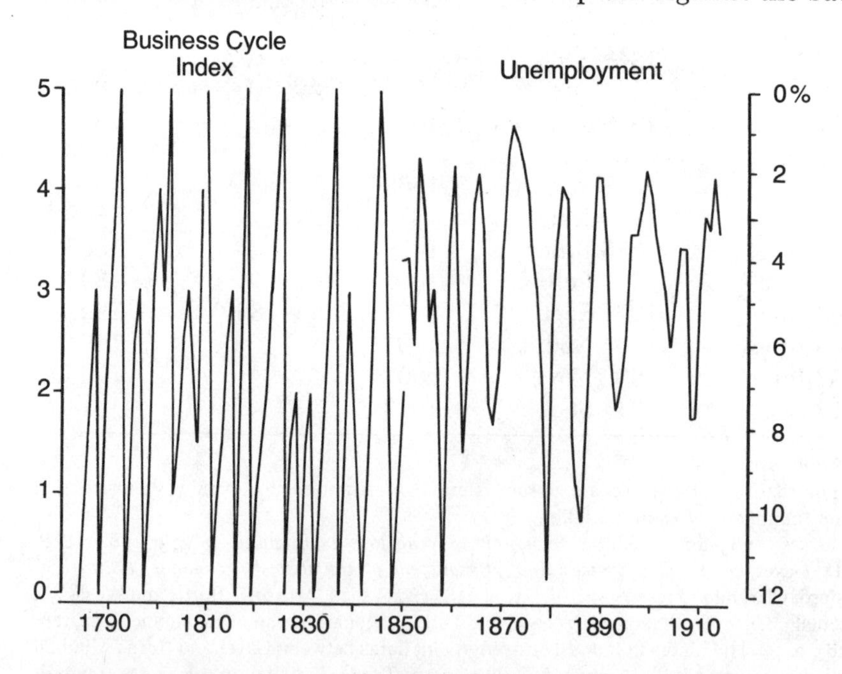

CHART IV-1. *Great Britain: Business-Cycle Index, 1784–1850; Unemployment Percentage (Inverted), 1850–1914*

Source: See note 12.

TABLE IV-3. *British Major Cycles, 1784–1914: Principal Directions of Enterprise*

Major Cycle Expansion with Peak in:	Major Directions of Domestic Investment	Major Directions of Export Expansion	Major Directions of Capital Export Expansion
1792	Canals, turnpikes, housing, textile and iron industries	United States	—
1802	Agriculture, ships, docks, textile and iron industries	Germany, United States	Large loans and subsidies to allies supporting export and re-export trade via Hamburg
1810	Agriculture, transport infrastructure	Latin America[a]	Large outlays for British armies abroad; short-term financing of Latin American trade
1818	Housing	Latin America, Italy, Russia	First peacetime flotation of foreign government bonds (Russia, France, Prussia, Austria)
1825	Massive general investment boom: housing, factory construction, ships, gaslighting, etc.	Latin America	Latin America
1836	Massive general industrial investment boom, with railways emerging as a substantial sector	United States, Southern Europe	Large: United States, Spain, Portugal
1845	British railway investment dominant with attendant expansion in iron and coal industries, steamships, first foreign railways built by British contractors	United States, China	Relatively low
1854[b]	Shipbuilding, iron, coal, textiles, agriculture	Australia, United States	Large: United States

TABLE IV-3. (*continued*)

Major Cycle Expansion with Peak in:	Major Directions of Domestic Investment	Major Directions of Export Expansion	Major Directions of Capital Export Expansion
1866	Shipbuilding, iron, coal, housing, railroads	Western Europe, United States (1865–1866), India, China, Egypt, Brazil, Colombia, New Zealand	Moderately substantial but diffuse, with Indian railways a major outlet
1873	Shipbuilding, iron, coal, telegraph, but not housing, which revived after the downturn (1874–1877)	United States, Canada, Western Europe (except France), Argentina, Chile, Peru, India, South Africa, Australia, New Zealand	Very large: United States, Latin America, Europe
1883	Steel, shipbuilding, electricity	Western and Southern Europe, United States (1879–1880), Mexico, Argentina, Chile, India, South Africa, Canada, Australia	Modest expansion: to Europe, United States, Asia, with large countercyclical increase to Australia, 1883–1886
1890	Shipbuilding, machinery, coal	Argentina, other Latin America, France, Germany, Spain, United States, Scandinavia, Russia, India	Large: Argentina, South Africa, North America
1900	Housing, other construction (including large local authorities' expenditures), shipbuilding, bicycles	Russia, Western Europe, Southern Europe, Japan, Argentina, Canada, Australia	Capital-exports decline during boom
1913	Shipbuilding, electrical engineering, motor vehicles, chemicals	Canada, Western Europe, Russia, Japan, Latin America, India, Australia	Greatest capital export boom of the century: Canada, Argentina, Australia

[a] Includes non-British West Indies.

[b] British fluctuations in the 1850's were complicated by the coming of the Crimean War (1854–1856) which cushioned the economy after the peak in the third quarter of 1853. The war was followed by a boom in exports (but not in domestic investment) which ended with the international crisis of 1857.

ground of a rising world population and real income, and cheapened real costs of production and transport, the amounts capable of being sold in world markets increased year after year: the demand curve for British exports shifted more or less steadily to the right, and the supply curve as well. The markets through which British exports were sold abroad, however, were speculative in the sense that more or less was sent abroad, by individual merchants, depending on their information and judgments concerning stocks and prices in foreign markets at future times. In addition, because time lags were involved at various stages in the process of trade, current and expected conditions with respect to the price and the availability of credit in Britain entered the calculation.

Acting, in fact, on similar or identical intelligence, British merchants tended to behave in roughly the same manner. When inventories fell off and prices rose abroad, word was received from overseas agents and fully circulated; and more goods were shipped from Britain. Such actions, individually taken, tended to reverse the conditions in foreign markets which had justified the increased shipments in the first instance; and the reversal could not be reported instantaneously, nor the production decisions which stemmed from it instantaneously executed within Britain.

The rhythm of this inventory cycle was, of its nature, relatively short;[13] and, for a time of peace and normal market relationships, the amplitude of its movement was relatively mild. There are several reasons why this should have been so:

First, the period of time between a change in market conditions and the receipt of intelligence in London was not very great, even before the introduction of the cables.

Second, the flow of exports could be altered quickly and sensitively, with changed knowledge and judgment about future market conditions; a commitment to build a railway is binding over a number of years; commitments to manufacture and to ship textiles are capable of review and alteration in a matter of weeks or months.[14]

Finally, the demand for consumers' goods from peoples abroad was under fairly steady impulse to enlargement; the purchases of foreign merchants were, of course, sensitive to changes in British prices and to general movements of demand within their own market regions; but behind them were enlarging populations, with increasing real incomes.[15]

From the late 1780's, however, this rhythm was woven into the longer and deeper rhythm of fluctuations in long-term investment. In the latter stages of the boom reaching its peak in 1792, for example, there was an expansion in canal and road building, agricultural enclosures, and an increased building of ships, houses, and factories. This element of long-term investment grew relatively as the economy became increasingly industrialized; and it grew notably after the ending of the French wars had lifted the burdens and removed the distorting pressures which war had imposed. Until the

1860's, however, the short cycle not only can be detected, but, based on the judgments which entered the compilation of Table IV-2, had sufficient power to produce distinguishable general movements in total production and employment.

As the railway age came, abroad as well as within Britain, and the metallurgical and engineering industries began to play an increased proportional role in the economy, the long-term investment cycle became increasingly dominant. This was the trend not only for Britain, but also for certain key British markets on the Continent and in the United States; and thus the longer rhythm—the nine-year average—suffused not only British domestic activities but foreign trade as well.

The net effect of the British and world-wide transition toward capital development and industrialization was to overwhelm, in a sense, the minor cycle as an independent cyclical phenomenon. Its rhythm, however, can still be detected in the export figures for British textiles. Whereas, between 1848 and 1914, ten business cycles can be marked off, there are some fifteen cycles which can be detected in the value of exports of cotton goods and yarn, with an average duration of somewhat over four years. In the early decades of the nineteenth century the movement of textile exports might have been decisive to the contour of fluctuations in the economy as a whole; in the latter years it was simply one determinant of general fluctuations, and by no means the most powerful. But the short rhythm of its movement persisted.

The two types of fluctuations—the minor and major cycles—did not pursue their course in separate and discrete channels. They were linked in at least four ways:

First, both partially depended, in their timing, on the state of the London capital market; and their course related to conditions in the interwoven complex of credit markets in London and the provinces.

Second, and more broadly, the consumers' goods industries and capital goods industries competed for labor and raw materials in common markets; cost calculations which affected decisions in both stemmed from partially identical data.

Third, a part of British exports of both consumers' and capital goods depended on the export of capital.

Fourth, among the sources of the confidence and the funds for long-term investment were the increases in profits and in income derived directly and indirectly from prior increases in the export trade.

For these reasons, among others, fluctuations within the British economy must ultimately be studied and understood as a whole, no matter how useful the distinction may be between minor and major cycles.

The shift in the balance and structure of the British and world economies, and thus the changed character of cyclical fluctuations, had consequences for the relative impact of the business cycle on the economy and the society as a whole. At the beginning of the era Britain was, in agriculture, virtually self-sufficient, with only minor capital industries and a foreign trade mainly in consumers' goods. By the end of the era Britain was heavily deficit in agriculture, with its industries closely tied, in both their domestic and their foreign markets, to long-term capital development. Undoubtedly a larger proportion of the population felt the impact of the business cycle on their lives and fortunes in 1910 than in 1790.

There is, further, good evidence for concluding that the amplitude of business cycles, in both their expansion and their contraction phases, increased after the French wars. From 1819 to 1848, however, covering the three great major cycles of the 1820's, 1830's, and 1840's, there appears to have been no clear trend increase in the amplitude of cyclical movements. And, if one regards the post-1850 unemployment figures as a uniformly representative sample, one is led to the conclusion that, while the business cycle undoubtedly affected an increasing proportion of the population, the relative amplitude of cyclical movements in employment did not change in a systematic and significant way from 1850 to 1914.

For the period to 1850, clearly, and probably to the 1870's, the domestic harvests played a significant part in British business fluctuations, as they had in the eighteenth century. And one can trace quite clearly how the harvests operated through the foreign balance and the money market. A good harvest reduced the requirements for imports of grain; a bad harvest increased those requirements. The orders of magnitude of the outlays in a poor harvest year, as opposed to those in a time of domestic abundance, were very considerable. And an increase in grain imports served to put pressure on the money markets, to raise interest rates, and thus to discourage other forms of foreign trade, domestic commerce, and long-term investment. In addition, it set in motion strong forces in the labor market making for higher wages. A good harvest, on the other hand, tended to reduce the pressure on the foreign balance, to ease the money markets, to lower interest rates, and to free funds for other purposes.

The good harvests of 1797–1798, 1820–1823, 1832–1835, 1843–1844, and 1850–1852 undoubtedly helped foster the major cycle expansions which were set in motion in those years; conversely, the high wheat prices and increased imports of 1795–1796, 1800–1801, 1810, 1817–1818, 1824–1825, 1836–1837, and 1846–1847 undoubtedly contributed to the pressure on the money market in those years of strain or crisis. The evidence, however, does not justify the conception of a business cycle detonated into its upward phase by a good harvest, operating through the foreign balance and the monetary mechanism, and brought to its close by an inadequate harvest and monetary stringency. Nevertheless, the harvests must be accounted, to the 1870's, a significant permissive and contributory factor, which affected the timing of recovery, and which counted among the various strains within the economy which helped bring on the downswing. As Britain's harvest came to contribute a decreasing proportion of the total food supply, however, and foodstuffs were drawn from an increasingly large number of sources, this factor appears to have diminished in importance.

One of the most consistent cyclical phenomena, throughout this era, was the tendency in Britain for long-term investment decisions to concentrate in the latter stages of the upswing of the major cycles. This appears to have been true, not only of formal flotations in the capital markets, but to a considerable extent of other forms of investment also; e.g., housing, shipbuilding, and industrial investment. On the whole, the impression one receives is that the industrial revolution, regarded as a process of plant expansion and the installation of new industrial methods and techniques, lurched forward in a highly discontinuous way, with a relative concentration of decisions to expand, or to improve technique, occurring in the latter stages of the major cycle.

There are, of course, exceptions to this general pattern, some of considerable importance. The modern iron industry in Scotland, for example, based on Nielson's hot-blast, was founded in 1828 and grew steadily, for a considerable time, with apparently little relevance to the trade cycle. Moreover, in several instances the result of the withdrawal from the capital market of the high-yield new investment, which had dominated the latter stages of expansion, and which had been discredited in the course of the turning point and crisis, was to bring promptly into the market investment of lower expected yield which had been, as it were, starved out in the course of expansion. Moreover, the period of gestation of many types of investment was such that projects undertaken in the boom were not completed until some time after the turning point. And, as a result, the impact of depression, in its early stages, was cushioned by the necessity for completing projects earlier begun. A notable, but by no means unique, instance of this was the period 1845–1847. The mileage of new railway lines actually opened reached its peak in 1848, although the cyclical downturn came, clearly, in 1845. This element of lag at the peak is quite generally typical of brick production and of shipbuilding.

As for the monetary system, the early stages of revival were normally marked by easy money conditions and by falling rates of interest, short- and long-term, inside and outside the Bank of England. To this tendency, as noted earlier, abundant British harvests contributed in several important instances. Credit advanced in all forms outside the Bank probably increased mildly in most such early stages; but the falling tendency of prices made it possible to finance an increased volume of transactions with a given supply of money. Within the Bank, bullion increased, bills and notes discounted decreased, and the Bank rate fell, or remained steady at a low level.

In the latter stages of expansion there was a gradual tightening in the market, and a tendency first for the market and then for the Bank rate to rise. Credit advanced outside the Bank rose sharply, and an increased amount of business came to the Bank as well, as other credit resources became more fully employed.

After the peak, interest rates continued to rise, but credit advances outside the Bank fell off. The Bank's discounts rose, often rapidly, as it fulfilled more or less adequately its role as last resort. Up to the turning point the Bank had been gradually coming to share a proportion of the burden of financing expansion; after the turning point it was meeting a crisis in confidence, an increase in liquidity preferences. The great financial crises of this era occurred, almost without exception, after the downturn of the cycle; and in fact they resulted largely from the change in expectations which can be taken, analytically if not statistically, to define the beginnings of the downturn. The nature of financial crisis, with its hasty liquidations and spreading of panic, accelerated the course of the decline in production and employment. It would, however, be incorrect to regard the financial crises of nineteenth-century Britain as the mechanism by which prosperity was turned into depression.

The question still remains, nevertheless, as to whether the gradual tightening of the money markets and the rise in interest rates in the latter stages of expansion, well before financial crisis, played a decisive part in causing a changed view of the future, and the downturn. The evidence suggests that rising interest rates, like rising prices, symbolized an approach to an unstable position of full employment in the major cycles. They made cost conditions different from those which had been expected when various investment commitments were undertaken, and they carried psychological overtones as well. Meanwhile, the situation was also being altered by the completion of acts of investment previously undertaken. From these basic alterations in the complex of forces determining the volume of investment, rather than from a short-term credit shortage, the turning point appears to have occurred. Like the supply of labor or commodities or fixed capacity, the short-term money supply set a limit to the extent to which expansion could proceed. But that limit was certainly more elastic than for other factors of production, so long as confidence prevailed.

Table IV-4 sets out the National Bureau of Economic Research monthly reference-cycle turning points for the United States, France, and Germany alongside those already given for Britain, for the differing periods when data are available;[16] for earlier periods, annual turning points are given from indicated sources.

For our limited purposes, the central fact about Table IV-4 is that, despite evident deviations, the major cycles of this period identified in the British evidence and, quite often, the minor cycles as well are also roughly reflected in the turning-point dates for the United States, France, and Germany. In broad terms there is no doubt that the rhythm of cyclical fluctuations was international.

TABLE IV-4. *Cyclical Turning Points: United States, France, Germany, and Great Britain Compared, Pre-1914 Era*

	Great Britain	United States	France	Germany
Peak	1792	—	—	—
Trough	1793	—	—	—
Peak	1796	1796	—	—
Trough	1797	1798	—	—
Peak	1802	1801	—	—
Trough	1803	1803	—	—
Peak	1806	1806	—	—
Trough	1808	1808	—	—
Peak	1810	1811	—	—
Trough	1811	1812	—	—
Peak	1815	1815	—	—
Trough	1816	1816	—	—
Peak	1818	1818	—	—
Trough	1819	1820	—	—
Peak	1825	1825	—	—
Trough	1826	1826	—	—
Peak	1828	1828	—	—
Trough	1829	1829	—	—
Peak	1831	1831	—	—
Trough	1832	1833	1831	—
Peak	1836	1836	1836	—
Trough	1837	1837	1837	—
Peak	1839	1839	1838	—
Trough	1842	1843	1839	—
Peak	1845	1845	1846	—
Trough	1846	1846	—	—
Peak	1847	1847	—	—
Trough	1848	1848	1848	—
Peak	1854	—	1853	1852
Trough	Dec. 1854	Dec. 1854	1854	1855
Peak	Sept. 1857	June 1857	1857	1857
Trough	Mar. 1858	Dec. 1858	1858	1858
Peak	Sept. 1860	Oct. 1860	1864	1860
Trough	Dec. 1862	June 1861	Dec. 1865	1861
Peak	Mar. 1866	Apr. 1865	Nov. 1867	1863
Trough	Mar. 1868	Dec. 1867	Oct. 1868	1866

TABLE IV-4 continued

	Great Britain	United States	France	Germany
Peak	—	June 1869	Aug. 1870	1869
Trough	—	Dec. 1870	Feb. 1872	1870
Peak	Sept. 1872	Oct. 1873	Sept. 1873	1872
Trough	—	—	Aug. 1876	—
Peak	—	—	Apr. 1878	—
Trough	June 1879	Mar. 1879	Sept. 1879	Feb. 1879
Peak	Dec. 1882	Mar. 1882	Dec. 1881	Jan. 1882
Trough	June 1886	May 1885	Aug. 1887	Aug. 1886
Peak	—	Mar. 1887	—	—
Trough	—	Apr. 1888	—	—
Peak	Sept. 1890	July 1890	Jan. 1891	Jan. 1890
Trough	—	May 1891	—	—
Peak	—	Jan. 1893	—	—
Trough	Feb. 1895	June 1894	Jan. 1895	Feb. 1895
Peak	—	Dec. 1895	—	—
Trough	—	June 1897	—	—
Peak	June 1900	June 1899	Mar. 1900	Mar. 1900
Trough	Sept. 1901	Dec. 1900	Sept. 1902	Mar. 1902
Peak	June 1903	Sept. 1902	May 1903	Aug. 1903
Trough	Nov. 1904	Aug. 1904	Oct. 1904	Feb. 1905
Peak	June 1907	May 1907	July 1907	July 1907
Trough	Nov. 1908	June 1908	Feb. 1909	Dec. 1908
Peak	—	Jan. 1910	—	—
Trough	—	Jan. 1912	—	—
Peak	Dec. 1912	Jan. 1913	June 1913	Apr. 1913
Trough	Sept. 1914	Dec. 1914	Aug. 1914	Aug. 1914

Sources: U.S. annual turning points, 1796–1832, estimated from a combination of data in Willard L. Thorp, *Business Annals* (New York: National Bureau of Economic Research, 1926), pp. 113–121, and W. B. Smith and A. H. Cole, *Fluctuations in American Business, 1790–1860* (Cambridge, Mass.: Harvard University Press, 1935), pp. 3–84. French annual turning points, 1831–1848, estimated from François Crouzet, "Essai de construction d'un indice annuel de la production industrielle française au XIXe siècle," *Annales, Economies, Sociétés, Civilisations*, no. 1 (January–February 1970). German annual turning points, 1850–1866, estimated from Walther G. Hoffmann, *Das Wachstum der Deutschen Wirtschaft seit der Mitte des 19. Jahrhunderts* (Berlin: Springer-Verlag, 1965). Otherwise, dates are taken from Burns and Mitchell, *Measuring Business Cycles*, pp. 78–79.

Using different evidence for a shorter time period (but including three additional countries), Gottfried von Haberler devised a method for exhibiting visually the degree of concordance and deviation in national cyclical fluctuations reproduced in Chart IV-2.[17]

Analytically, of course, the deviations in timing and intensity of cyclical fluctuations are of equal or greater interest than the agreements.

As between the United States and Great Britain, the differential impact of wartime conditions largely accounts for the deviations of 1801–1802, 1811–1812, 1860–1865, and 1897–1903. The most

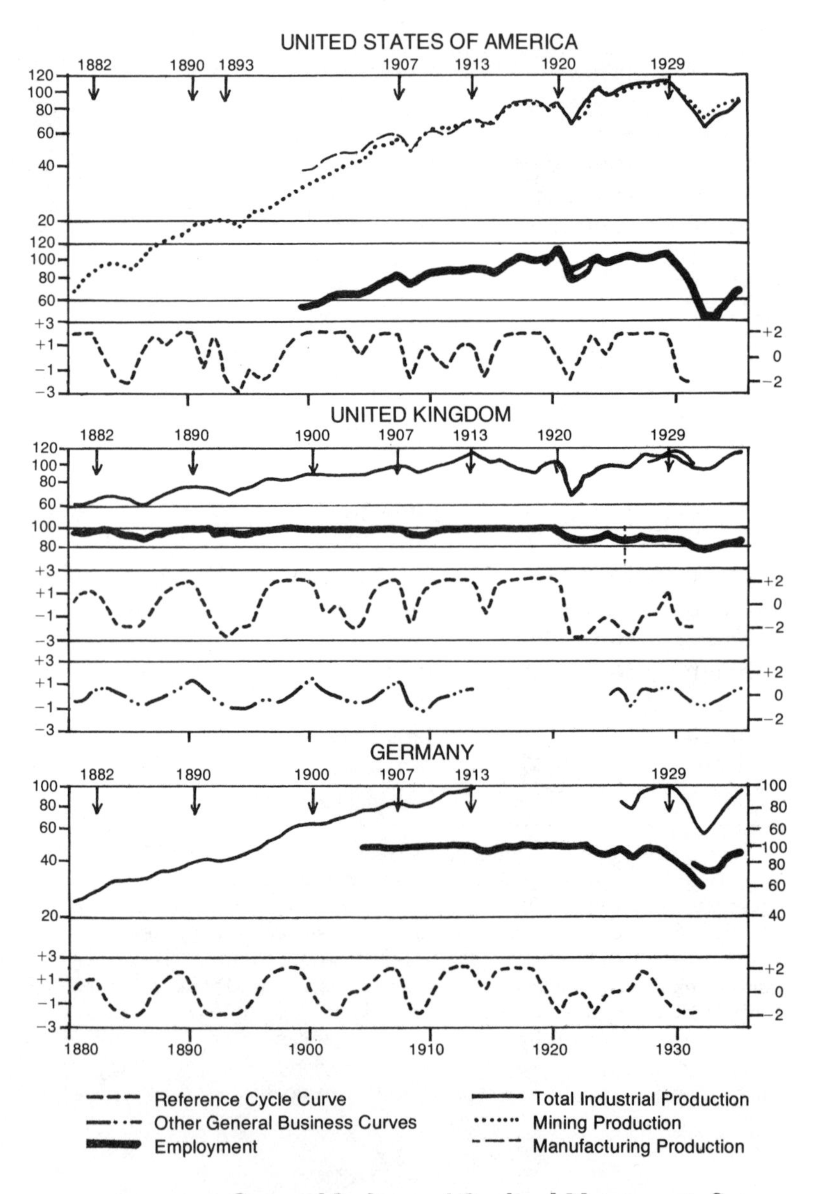

CHART IV-2. *General Indices of Cyclical Movement: Seven Countries, 1880–1935*

marked difference, however, is the greater number of minor cycles in the American experience from 1867 to 1914. When these are analyzed more closely they appear to stem from several different causes:[18]

—The extremely mild contraction of June 1869–December 1870 may have been touched off by a brief panic caused by the attempt of Jay Gould and Jim Fisk to corner the gold market; and there may have been an element of inventory contraction related to the gold panic.

—The contraction of March 1887–April 1888 was also extreme-

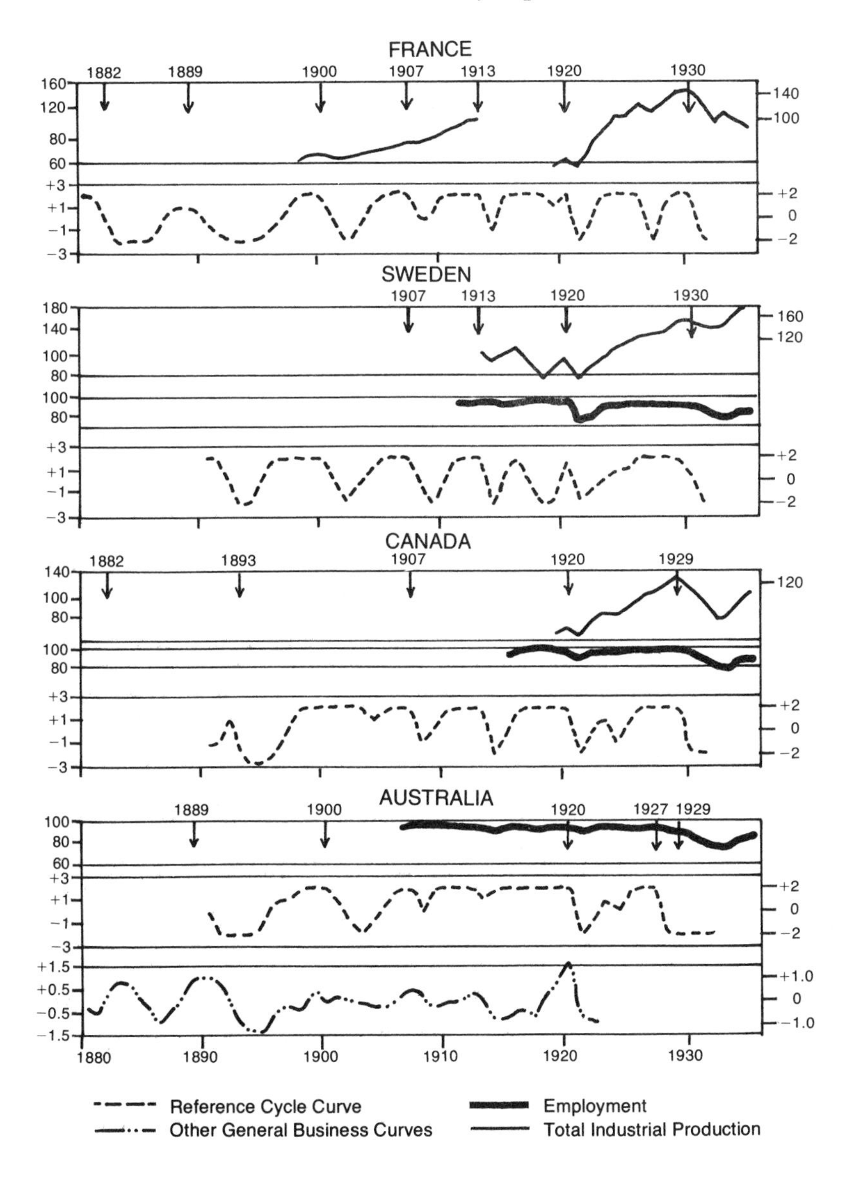

Source: Gottfried von Haberler, *Prosperity and Depression*, pp. 170–171, with method explained on p. 347.

ly mild. Here we have more forces capable of inducing a recession than we need: poor crops and a hard winter; an unfavorable shift in the trade balance and a brief passage of monetary stringency; a decline in housing construction, possibly related to higher interest rates; a falling off of orders for railway equipment; a possible net deflationary impulse from the federal government's various fiscal and monetary activities; and, even, uncertainty about the effects of the Interstate Commerce Act. Without attempting to arbitrate this matter, the most persuasive general force operating which might have touched off a general recession, after almost two full years of prior expansion, was a poor harvest, with its attendant psychological, income, balance-of-payments, and monetary effects.

—The expansion of May 1891–January 1893 is probably linked to a good American harvest at a time when European harvests, notably in the Ukraine, were generally bad. Its multiple effects were capable of temporarily reversing the downturn which had begun in Britain as well as the United States in 1890. But an American expansion running counter to strong contractions elsewhere tended to develop an adverse trade balance.

—The expansion from June 1894 to December 1895[19] and the subsequent contraction to June 1897 are, despite considerable analysis, still somewhat obscure. With railroads gone as a leading sector, and immigration declining, it is difficult to identify why recovery in the United States should have begun a year earlier than in Europe, although the shift to the use of steel in construction and as tinplate was under way. The downturn and a revival, delayed until the good harvest of 1897 (again with poor European crops), are usually associated with U.S. monetary problems, including the anxieties created by the debate over the monetization of silver which came to a head in the presidential campaign of 1896. But the real and monetary problems of the severely depressed mid-1890's have not yet been satisfactorily sorted out.

—The mild contraction of January 1910 to January 1912 may be an inventory cycle, perhaps triggered by a weakening in the trade balance in 1910.[20]

The deviations in the American business-cycle pattern remain, in my view, still to be fully explained. Several features of the scene nevertheless emerge. First, the multiple role of the harvests: good American harvests, accompanied by poor harvests abroad and greatly expanded exports; and bad harvests which could, again by various routes, impart both real and monetary deflationary impulses to the U.S. economy. Second, the peaking of railway construction in the late 1880's and the structural adjustment of the American economy to a new set of leading sectors during the abnormally depressed 1890's. Third, the peculiar instabilities of the American monetary and fiscal system, lacking a central bank. Finally, the significant and systematic difference in the cyclical behavior of the U.S. and British trade balances over the period 1880–1914, carefully analyzed by Ilse Mintz.[21]

It appears from quarterly data that the American trade balance behaved countercyclically; that is, general business expansion depressed and contraction improved the trade balance. This was due not merely to a large rise in imports during U.S. business expansions but also to an average tendency for the quantity of exports to decline in the second half of expansion:

> In the first half of American expansions [1879–1913] export prices were stable; but they begin to climb as the rising domestic demand gradually overtook the growth in production. This price rise must have hampered export sales. In addition, the pressure of domestic demand may also reduce exports directly as delivery periods are stretched, credit is harder to get and more expensive, and producers' interest in exports lags. Thus, the large rise in export quantities typical for the first half of expansion may be turned into a decline during the second half. . . . The depressing effect of the late stages of American expansions on exports was particularly strong in the case of raw cotton exports.[22]

The British trade balance differed from the American in its cyclical behavior in two major respects: it conformed positively to business cycles, and it was less volatile. The disproportionate expansion of exports in the latter stages of expansion was in some cases related to British capital exports; the deterioration of the British balance in the early stages of contraction was, as in earlier times, sometimes linked to the increased value of food imports due to high prices.[23]

The lesser amplitude of cyclical fluctuations in the British trade balance raises the question of whether American business cycles in general were more violent phenomena in this period than those of Britain and the other industrialized nations. It has been conventional to assume that they were;[24] and there is some evidence to support the hypothesis.

The major international economies were, evidently, closely linked through the transmission of income effects, short- and long-term capital markets, and the impact of harvests on internationally determined prices. Moreover, the United States and Western Europe were absorbing, essentially, the same set of technologies from the coming of the railway age forward. But neither the amplitude nor the timing of their fluctuations was identical. Differences in geography, natural-resource endowments, rates of population increase, proportions of population in agricultural life, degrees of protection, and organization of financial and business institutions all affected cyclical patterns. It was at times of international financial crisis that the advanced industrial economies were most closely bound together.[25] The American cyclical pattern was, among this group, the most idiosyncratic, mainly because of its extra cycles. Britain, France, and Germany appear more closely linked. Nevertheless, French and German turning points also deviate from the British, as

Table IV-4 reveals. The Franco-Prussian War, for example, threw both countries out of phase, with the Germans moving on to the great boom peaking in 1872, the French experiencing a more muted expansion but enjoying a lesser slump thereafter. The bad French harvests of 1910 and 1911 again pulled France out of phase. And even when the timing of turning points was in rough concordance, there were significant differences in amplitude, with France generally experiencing milder cycles than Germany. In the pre-1914 era it appears to have been true that the amplitude of cyclical fluctuations was related to the trend rate of industrial growth.

When the perspective is widened to embrace fluctuations in preindustrial as well as industrial economies, there is, as one would expect, a high degree of conformity between British and world fluctuations;[26] but before 1914 there is a marked tendency for world imports, with a strong upward trend, to lag in their cyclical movement at peaks and to lead at cyclical troughs. This characteristic is shared by the index of world manufacturing production, which is also marked by a strong upward trend. Chart IV-3 summarizes these relationships as well as the deviant behavior of the United States with its extra minor cycles.

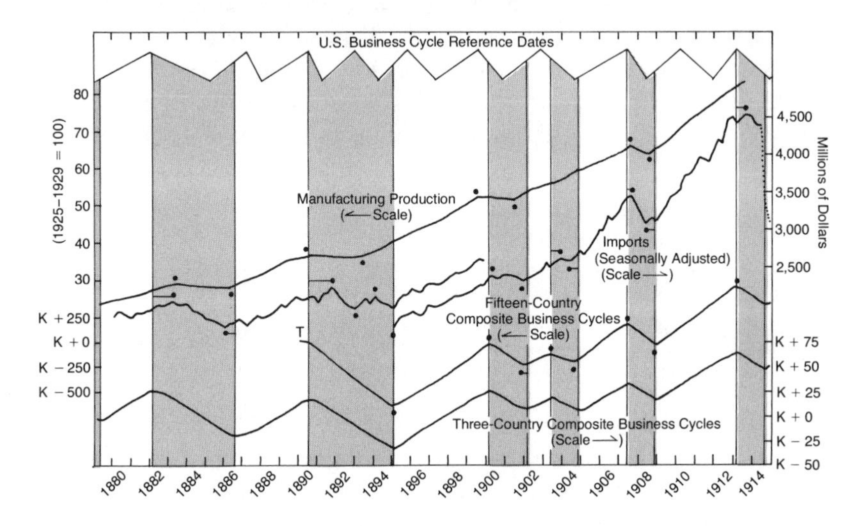

CHART IV-3. *Four Types of Cycles: World* ex *United States, 1879–1914*

Shaded periods are contractions in three-country composite business cycles. Turns in other series are indicated by dots, tentative turns by T.

Series for manufacturing production, annual; all other series, quarterly.

Imports for 1914 interpolated without German data, which are not available.

Source: Ilse Mintz, *Trade Balances during Business Cycles*, p. 65.

23

Interwar Cycles: 1919–1939

The broad pattern of cyclical fluctuations during the interwar period has already been considered in the context of the analysis of this interval as a trend period (see above, Chapter 15). The National Bureau of Economic Research reference-cycle turning-point dates for the four major economies are given in Table IV-5. Chart IV-4 shows the relation between the U.S. turning points and various indicators of cyclical fluctuations in the rest of the world.

Despite the differences in cyclical turning points, the broadly shared cyclical movements of the period emerge in Chart IV-4. After about six months of postwar reconversion, an intense, typical postwar boom occurred, peaking (except for Germany) in 1920. The recession was also short, giving way to the prolonged expan-

TABLE IV-5. *Business-Cycle Turning Points: United Kingdom, United States, France, and Germany, 1919–1939*

	United Kingdom	United States	France	Germany
Trough	Apr. 1919	Apr. 1919	Apr. 1919	June 1919
Peak	Mar. 1920	Jan. 1920	Sept. 1920	May 1922
Trough	June 1921	Sept. 1921	July 1921	Nov. 1923
Peak	Nov. 1924	May 1923	Oct. 1924	Mar. 1925
Trough	—	—	June 1925	—
Peak	—	—	Oct. 1926	—
Trough	July 1926	July 1924	June 1927	Mar. 1926
Peak	Mar. 1927	Oct. 1926	—	—
Trough	Sept. 1928	Dec. 1927	—	—
Peak	July 1929	June 1929	Mar. 1930	Apr. 1929
Trough	Aug. 1932	Mar. 1933	July 1932	Apr. 1932
Peak	—	—	July 1933	—
Trough	—	—	Apr. 1933	—
Peak	Sept. 1937	May 1937	June 1937	—
Trough	Sept. 1938	May 1938	Aug. 1938	—

Source: Burns and W. C. Mitchell, *Measuring Business Cycles*, pp. 78–79.

sion of the 1920's, which the four principal economies shared in different degree and with differing minor cycle fluctuations. The cyclical downturn leading to the Great Depression began in the spring and summer of 1929 (earliest in Germany), well before the October stock market crash in New York, except in France, which continued in prosperity until March 1930. Recovery began in the summer of 1932, except in the United States, where it was delayed by about nine months. The United States led the way in both the recession of 1937–1938 and the recovery from it. The difference in movement during the 1930's between world manufacturing production and trade in Chart IV-4 reflects the power of the protectionist policies which framed most recovery programs.

Oskar Morgenstern has examined in some detail the degree of concordance and difference in these cyclical fluctuations, comparing the pre-1914 with the interwar experience.[27] Chart IV-5 exhibits

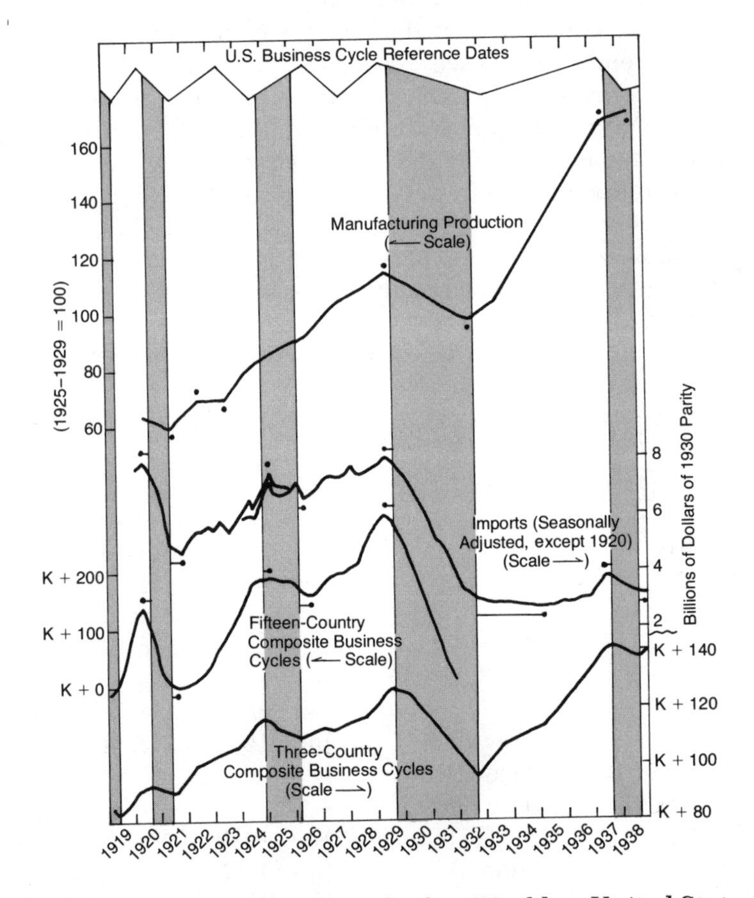

CHART IV-4. *Four Types of Cycles: World* ex *United States, 1919–1938*

Shaded periods are contractions in three-country composite business cycles. Turns in other series are indicated by dots.

Series for manufacturing production, annual; all other series, quarterly.

Source: Mintz, *Trade Balances during Business Cycles*, p. 66.

visually the reference cycles marked off in Table IV-6; Table IV-6 compares, for the two periods, behavior during phases of expansion and contraction. There was clearly an increase in the proportion of time when the three European countries were out of phase with each other; a decline in occasions when all four countries were in the same phase; but a decline also in the proportion of time when the three European countries were in the same phase, the United States in the opposite phase. Morgenstern concludes: "The three European countries became less in step with each other but more in step (as a group) with the United States."[28]

What these numbers reflect, of course, are a variety of unique, traumatic events and experiences which bore on individual European countries; e.g., the French occupation of the Ruhr, the German hyperinflation of 1922–1923, the British general strike of 1926, the post-1930 political as well as economic vicissitudes of France, when British devaluation reversed the French exchange advantage of the previous six years, its effects compounded by the American devaluation of 1933. After 1929 they also reflect the increasingly nationalist cast of economic policy.

These aberrations relate to three major factors. Down to 1929 they are quite directly linked to the aftermath of the First World War: the peculiar position of Germany, its reparations burden, and

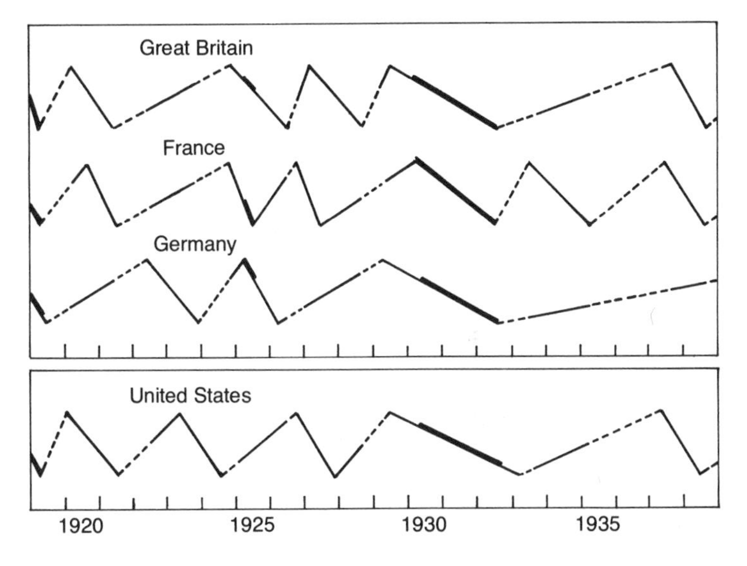

CHART IV-5. *Interwar Cyclical Turning Points: Three European Economies and the United States*

For the three European countries, the heavy solid line represents correspondence between the three countries in contraction; the dashed line, correspondence in expansion; and the fine solid line, no correspondence.

For the United States, the three types of lines indicate correspondence or no correspondence between the United States and all three European countries.

Source: Oskar Morgenstern, *International Financial Transactions and Business Cycles*, p. 43.

TABLE IV-6. *Phase Comparison of Reference Cycles: Three European Countries and the United States*

	Pre-1914 Period[a] (% of Total)	Interwar Period[b] (% of Total)
Three European countries		
1. All three expand	47.5	25.5
2. All three contract	35.6	19.7
3. All three in same phase (1 + 2)	83.1	45.2
4. In different phase	16.9	54.8
Total	100.0	100.0
Four countries		
5. Three European countries expand, United States expands	31.3	17.8
6. Three European countries expand, United States contracts	16.2	7.7
7. Three European countries contract, United States expands	13.4	1.9
8. Three European countries contract, United States contracts	22.2	17.8
9. Three European countries in same phase, United States in opposite phase (6 + 7)	29.6	9.6
10. Four countries in same phase (5 + 8)	53.5	35.6
11. Four countries in different phase (4 + 6 + 7)	46.5	64.4
Total	100.0	100.0

[a] September 1879–August 1914, 419 months.
[b] June 1919–July 1932, 157 months.
Source: Morgenstern, *International Financial Transactions and Business Cycles*, p. 45.

the French effort to exact meaningful reparations; the effort of a weakened Britain to return to the pre-war sterling exchange rate which, in turn, as we have emphasized elsewhere, required a wage policy that helped trigger the coal strike and the subsequent general strike. Second, they relate to the character of the trend period which began with the disproportionate decline of foodstuff and raw-material prices in 1920–1921. Third, they relate to the underlying shift in economic power from Britain to the United States, a shift already under way before 1914 but much accelerated by the differential impact of the First World War. The trend-period alteration in the terms of trade helps account for the change in the cyclical behavior of the British trade balance, which shifted from a positive to a negative correlation to cyclical fluctuations.[29] As noted earlier (see above, pp. 227–229), it is the failure of the United States fully to accept its new central position in the world monetary and trade system which helps account for the depth of the world depression and, in particular, for the fact that the depression brought on a protectionist breakdown in that system.

Despite these powerful structural elements at work on the contours of interwar cyclical fluctuations, there was, in a narrow sense, considerable continuity with a longer past. The immediate postwar pattern of readjustment, boom, and slump (1918–1921) echoed the sequence after the Napoleonic Wars a century earlier (1815–1819) and anticipated the sequence after the Second World War (1945–1949).[30] In a fashion familiar since the eighteenth century, peace brought a powerful wave of residential building. In conventional business-cycle terms, the major interwar peaks (1920, 1929, 1937) came at intervals which gave them a rough and ready continuity with the major cycles of the era that began in 1783. The minor cycles, in the United States at least, continued to occur in the shorter rhythm their inventory character would suggest. The tools of business-cycle analysis generated to explain the sequence from 1783 to 1914 therefore remain relevant to the interwar years despite their special pathology.

But there were two new elements which anticipated to a degree the thirty years after the Second World War. First, the role of the automobile and durable consumers' goods, the latter related to the concurrent expansion of electricity production and consumption. This factor has already been explored in the context of the trend-period analysis in Chapter 15 but is worth underlining here.

For the United States, Robert A. Gordon's account of the 1920's is sharply focused on the role of the new consumer-oriented leading sectors.

> The most important stimulus to investment and to expansion of total output in the 1920's was the automobile. Like electric power, this was a prewar innovation. But its full impact on the American economy was not felt until the 1920's. . . .
>
> The effect of the automobile on aggregate demand came

> from two sources—the expansion in the *production* of cars and trucks and the enormously increased *use* of motor vehicles. . . .
>
> . . . Motor vehicle production nearly trebled between 1919 and 1929, but the increase in registrations—the number of cars and trucks on the road—was even larger. And steadily greater use was made of each vehicle. The result was an enormous expansion in employment in oil refining, filling stations and garages, truck and bus driving, selling of supplies and accessories, and construction and repair of roads. . . .
>
> Another prewar innovation, electric power, was a highly important stimulus to investment. Electric power production more than doubled between 1920 and 1929, and generating capacity increased in proportion. Use of this power in turn required electrical equipment and opened up methods of reducing costs that involved other types of new machinery. Value added by the electrical machinery industry also more than doubled between 1919 and 1929, compared to an increase of about 30 percent for manufacturing as a whole. Along with the growth of electric power production and the use of electrically driven machinery and handling equipment in industry went rapid expansion in the telephone industry (again a prewar innovation), the growth of radio (entirely a postwar development), and the rapid electrification of the home.[31]

Gordon is clearly conscious in this passage of the links of the automobile to various service sectors and to residential construction as well as to a wide range of industries. On the other hand, in dealing with the depth of the post-1929 depression and the incomplete American recovery down to 1937, he adduces a much more general "overinvestment" and "exhaustion of investment opportunities."[32] For example, in explaining the downturn of 1937 he points to the rise in wage rates from the end of 1936 to the middle of 1937, concluding: "Under more favorable conditions, the increase in costs could have been absorbed by an expanding demand fed by a rising volume of private investment. In 1937 the depressing effect of the rise in costs was not offset by continued expansion in demand."[33] In analyzing the boom of the 1920's, then, Gordon sees clearly the role of the leading sectors and the accelerator (broadly defined), stimulating investment through the expansion of incomes; in dealing with the unsatisfactory boom of the 1930's, he is back in the world of the multiplier, looking for autonomous investment opportunities that were not there. As the post-1945 experience of the United States, Western Europe, and Japan was to demonstrate, the sectoral complexes which carried forward the American economy of the 1920's were far from exhausted, once an environment of steady full employment and rising incomes was re-created and maintained. It was the lack of sufficient stimulus to effective demand, not exhausted investment opportunities, that caused the chronic high levels of unemployment of the 1930's.

It was precisely in this direction that a second aspect of the interwar cyclical experience foreshadowed later events; that is, the effort of governments to counter the post-1929 depression. In no case were those efforts wholly successful, with the possible exceptions of Nazi Germany and Japan. From 1936 at least, rearmament played a large role in the former case; and military outlays played a decisive role in the latter after 1931; but the German recovery from 1932 to 1936 was closely linked to the rapid expansion in automobile production and road building. It was during the depression of the 1930's that governments in the advanced industrial world began to assume political responsibility for the level of employment. Cyclical analysis can no longer be conducted without taking account of the conscious efforts of public authorities to use fiscal, monetary, and trade policy to achieve higher levels of national income, output, and employment. These efforts were by no means wholly successful. And, in some cases, whatever their intent, they were counterproductive; e.g., the NRA in the United States and some of the experiments of the Blum government in France. From the perspective of the historical analysis of business fluctuations, however, a probably irreversible watershed had been passed. It was, somewhat ironically, during the Second World War, in a context of policy designed to control inflation rather than to reduce unemployment, that the statistical tools of national income analysis were refined, notably in Britain and the United States, and absorbed within the central government bureaucracies.

24

Cycles in Growth Rates: 1945–1973

From 1945 to the recession of 1974–1975—for almost thirty years—cyclical fluctuations assumed a new form in the more advanced economies of the noncommunist world; and they have generated a new literature of cyclical analysis.[34] Cycles became primarily systematic fluctuations in the rate of growth, rarely broken by the absolute declines in output which marked off the classical cycles of the past. Put another way, the average level of unemployment declined markedly, as compared to the pre-1914 era as well as with the inter-war years. Even for the still abnormally volatile United States, GNP in real terms declined only three times between 1947 and 1973: in 1954, 1958, and 1970. And those brief declines averaged less than 1 percent. Unemployment averaged only 4.7 percent for these twenty-seven years, just about the average level for the prosperous 1920's.

Tables IV-7 and IV-8 capture clearly the character of this profound change for the United Kingdom, for which detailed comparative measurements with past experience have been made.[35]

The following points are to be noted:

—As compared to cycles in earlier periods, those from 1951 to 1964 were shorter and marked by more equal phases of expansion and contraction. The latter characteristic flows in part from the method of measurement. Peaks and troughs are calculated as deviations from the trend rate of growth and, by definition, reflect roughly equivalent variations on both sides of the trend.[36] Periods of rising output, at rates slower than the trend average, become part of the downswing.

—The average length of cycles as a whole was less than in previous periods, approximating the typical short rhythm of inventory cycles.

—Both upswings and downswings were marked by increases in GDP, the difference being greater in constant than in current prices because of the persistence of inflation even during cyclical downswings.[37]

TABLE IV-7. *United Kingdom: Average Duration and Amplitude of Cycles, Selected Periods, 1872–1964*

	Average Duration (in Years)		Annual Growth Rates (%)			Duration Factor	Amplitude
	Downswing (1)	Upswing (2)	Downswing (3)	Upswing (4)	Difference (4 − 3) (5)	(6)	(7)
Constant prices:							
1951–1964	2.0	2.3	1.2	4.8	3.6	0.49	1.8
1920–1937	2.0	6.5	−6.6	3.2	9.8	0.69	5.8
1872–1914	3.8	4.4	−0.4	2.7	3.1	0.91	2.5
Current prices:							
1951–1964	2.0	2.3	6.9	7.8	0.9	0.49	0.5
1920–1937	2.0	6.5	−13.2	1.6	14.8	0.69	8.5
1872–1914	3.8	4.4	−1.4	3.7	5.1	0.91	4.2

Source: R. C. O. Matthews, "Postwar Business Cycles in the United Kingdom," p. 103.

TABLE IV-8. *United Kingdom: Average Amplitude of Fluctuations in Unemployment and Gross Domestic Product (GDP), Selected Periods, 1872–1964*

	GDP	Employment
1951–1964	1.8	0.3[a]
		0.7[b]
1920–1937	5.8	5.1
1872–1913	2.5	3.2

[a] Reference cycles.
[b] Employment cycles.
Source: Matthews, "Postwar Business Cycles in the United Kingdom," p. 123.

—The amplitude of fluctuations in GDP and employment was notably less. A comparison of the amplitude of fluctuations in GDP and employment indicates a reduced sensitivity of employment to changes in output, a fact mainly attributable to the chronically high pressure of demand for labor, "labor hoarding" by firms, etc. The average level of unemployment in the United Kingdom from 1950 to 1965 was 1.48 percent, a level approximated in peacetime only during a few intense cyclical peak years since 1850.

The structural change in postwar British growth cycles is suggested in Table IV-9, showing the amplitude of cyclical movement in the major components of GDP.

The following are the major changes as compared to the past:

—The stability of the world economy and a reduced proportion of British exports flowing to producers of primary products radically reduced the absolute and relative role of export fluctuations in British cycles.

—The relative contribution of domestic fixed capital formation to the amplitude of GDP fluctuation increased, although its absolute amplitude of movement slightly declined as compared to past experience.

—Fluctuations in outlays of public authorities, dominated by changes in defense expenditures, moved on balance inversely with cycles, although there was a large rise in the wake of the Korean War (1950–1953) and a subsequent rapid subsidence (1953–1958), unconnected with cycles.

—Although the absolute amplitude of fluctuations in consumers' durables (including automobiles) declined as compared to the interwar years, their movement became a major factor in postwar growth cycles because of their increased importance in the economy as well as their increased relative contribution to GDP fluctuations. They exhibited a systematic tendency to lead other types of expenditure at peaks and troughs; and their control was a major objective of government policy through restricting or easing installment credit terms. The extent to which their fluctuations were a function of government policy as opposed to an inherent tendency to overshoot and undershoot an optimum level of consumers' durables holdings remains moot.[38]

—Inventory fluctuations contributed a major and increased relative element to the amplitude of changes in GDP.

—The extreme sensitivity of imports to phases of rapid British growth increased markedly their negative contribution to the amplitude of GDP fluctuations; but, by weakening the balance-of-payments position, their rapid expansion phases set the stage for the stop-and-go policies which were the central feature of British postwar cyclical behavior: in D. H. Robertson's memorable description, "a biennially recurrent oscillation between exchange panic and fools' paradise."[39]

TABLE IV-9. *United Kingdom: Amplitude of Fluctuations in Components of Gross Domestic Product (GDP) at Constant Market Prices, Selected Periods, 1872–1964*

	Exports[a]	GDFCF[b]	PACE[c]	Consumption			Stockbuilding	Imports[a]	GDP
				Total	Durables[d]	Nondurables			
Amplitude									
1951–1964	1.8	3.4	−0.9	1.6	4.2	1.0	7.0	4.2	1.8
1920–1937	14.3	4.1	3.6	2.8	6.5	2.0	(49.4)	7.1	5.8
1872–1914	5.5	4.1	1.8	1.2	—	—	—	3.4	2.5
Amplitude relative to GDP									
1951–1964	0.4	0.5	−0.2	1.0	0.5	0.5	1.0	0.9	1.8
1920–1937	2.8	0.5	0.4	2.2	0.9	1.3	(1.3)	1.3	5.8
1872–1914	1.3	0.3	0.1	1.0	—	—	—	0.8	2.5
Percentage contribution to amplitude of GDP									
1951–1964	20	27	−9	57	28	29	57	−52	100
1920–1937	48	9	7	38	16	22	(22)	−22	100
1872–1914	52	12	4	40	—	—	—	−32	100

[a] Exports and Imports include both goods and services.
[b] Gross Domestic Fixed Capital Formation.
[c] Public Authorities' Current Expenditure on Goods and Services.
[d] Consumers' durables include the goods placed in this category in the National Income *Blue Books* (motor cars and cycles, furniture and floor coverings, and radio and electrical goods) together with clothing, footwear, and household textiles.

Source: Matthews, "Postwar Business Cycles in the United Kingdom," p. 106.

Note: In 1872–1914 the constituents in the second and third panels do not add to the total, because GDP has been calculated to include a stockbuilding figure estimated at 40 percent of annual change in national income.

Postwar growth cycles differed considerably among the various advanced economies. For example, Table IV-10 presents gross and net instability coefficients calculated by Erik Lundberg for thirteen countries over the period 1950–1964: the gross coefficient is the sum of the annual average variations of six GNP components (private consumption, fixed investment, inventory investment, government demand for goods and services, exports, and imports); the net coefficient is simply the average variation of the growth of total GNP. They are arrayed in the table in order of the variation in the net instability coefficient. Excepting Japan, with its uniquely high but variable rate of growth, the gross coefficient is largest in the smaller countries, where foreign trade is often a high proportion of GNP, but where export and import fluctuations tend to be mutually offsetting. The net coefficient differs over a significant but narrower range and indicates a much lesser instability than in earlier periods.

Despite these and other distinctions, several features of British structural change in cyclical behavior can be generalized: low average levels of unemployment; a stable international environment permitting rapid expansion in exports to other industrialized countries; an increased relative role for fluctuations in durable consumers' goods and inventories; endemic inflation; and, above all, a tendency for rapid growth phases to be brought to a halt via balance-of-payments pressures.[40]

The dates for turning points in postwar growth cycles are set out in Table IV-11,[41] and, for part of the period, presented visually in Chart IV-6.

There are, evidently, considerable variations in cyclical turning points among these economies. But some major movements are

TABLE IV-10. *Gross and Net Instability Coefficients for Selected Countries, 1950–1964*

	Net Coefficient	Gross Coefficient	Ratio of Gross to Net Coefficient
Japan	4.5	10.6	2.4
Canada	2.7	6.8	2.6
United States	2.6	5.0	1.9
Denmark	2.5	8.8	3.5
Austria	2.4	8.3	3.4
Netherlands	2.3	10.9	4.7
Germany	1.9	5.0	2.7
Switzerland	1.8	6.9	3.8
Sweden	1.5	6.0	4.0
United Kingdom	1.4	4.6	3.2
Norway	1.4	6.3	4.5
France	1.4	4.5	3.3
Italy	1.4	4.8	2.4

Source: Erik Lundberg, "Postwar Stabilization Policies," Chapter 15 in Bronfenbrenner (ed.), *Is the Business Cycle Obsolete?*, p. 482.

widely shared; e.g., the trough of 1954 (excepting the United Kingdom); the trough of 1958 or early 1959; the peak of 1969–1970; the virtually universal boom of 1972–1973. The most substantial discrepancies occur in the period 1962–1966.

Table IV-12 confirms the generality of these movements. It establishes the contours of an international growth cycle from 1954 to 1973 by averaging the performance of eight countries, excluding the United States, and comparing their average cyclical behavior with that of the United States.

The United States emerges, once again, as a somewhat more volatile economy than the median of the other eight, with a lower average rate of growth. But still, its average growth rate was slightly higher over these twenty years than for the decade before 1929. For a full generation Americans never suffered more than a series of D. H. Robertson's "slumplets"[42]—five, in fact, including the exceedingly mild setbacks of 1960, 1963, and 1967. For the whole advanced industrial world this was a unique passage in economic history.

Within this framework, however, there is much familiar from the longer past about the minor fluctuations that did occur: the various sensitive business-cycle indicators continued to lead and lag in their old ways; the short rhythm of inventory fluctuations could still be detected and measured; the various other components of investment remained volatile and still accounted substantially for business fluctuations as a whole, although the economies of

TABLE IV-11. *Business-Cycle Turning Points: Six Major Economies, 1945–1974*

	United States	United Kingdom	Germany	France	Japan	Italy
Trough	Oct. 1945	[1947]	—	—	—	—
Peak	Nov. 1948	—	—	I 1949	—	—
Trough	Oct. 1949	—	—	II 1950	—	—
Peak	—	1951	Apr. 1951 (P)	—	June 1951	—
Trough	—	1952	—	—	Oct. 1951	—
Peak	July 1953	—	—	I 1952	Jan 1954	—
Trough	Aug. 1954	—	Jan. 1954	II 1954	Nov. 1954	1954
Peak	July 1957	Dec. 1955	Jan. 1956	II 1957	June 1957	II 1957
Trough	Apr. 1958	Nov. 1958	Mar. 1959	I 1959	June 1958	III 1958
Peak	May 1960	Nov. 1960	Jan. 1961	—	Dec. 1961	—
Trough	Feb. 1961	Feb. 1963	Feb. 1963	—	Oct. 1962	—
Peak	[Apr. 1962]	Aug. 1965	—	II 1964	Oct. 1964	III 1963
Trough	[Apr. 1963]	—	—	I 1965	Feb. 1965	I 1965
Peak	[June 1966]	—	Dec. 1965	II 1966	—	—
Trough	[Oct. 1967]	Dec. 1968	Aug. 1967	II 1968	—	—
Peak	[June 1969]	II 1969	May 1970	III 1970	Mar. 1970	II 1969
Trough	Nov. 1970	Feb. 1972	July 1972	II 1971	Mar. 1972	II 1971
Peak	Oct. 1973	IV 1973	Feb. 1973	II 1973	I 1973	II 1974

Sources: See note 41.
Note: Roman numerals refer to quarters of relevant years.

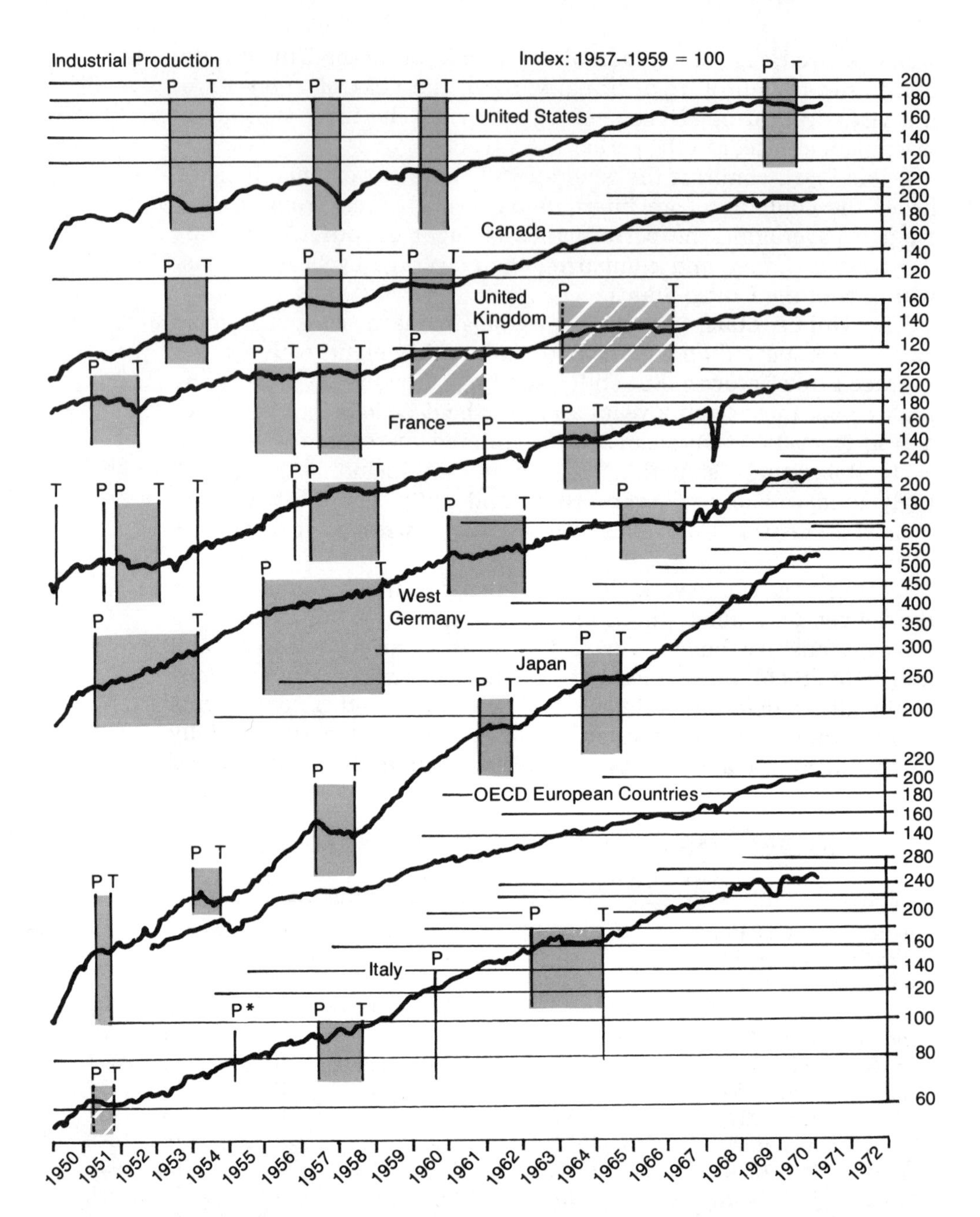

CHART IV-6. *Business-Cycle Turning Points and Index of Industrial Production: Seven Market-Oriented Economies, 1950–1970*

P: Peak.

T: Trough.

* J. C. R. Dow notes the period 1954–1957 as "flat" in terms of growth cycles ("Cyclical Developments in France, Germany, and Italy since the Early 1950's," pp. 178–179).

Source: Philip A. Klein, *The Management of Market-Oriented Economies*, p. 153.

Western Europe and Japan now joined North America in experiencing the short-run sensitivity of fluctuations in durable consumers' goods. Still, most analysts considering the period 1945–1973 would echo Robert A. Gordon's dictum about the American economy: "The business cycle, although in a gratifyingly attenuated form, still exists."[43]

The postwar rapid growth experience with damped cycles of economies with large private enterprise sectors and the concurrent existence of a number of socialist economies in Eastern Europe, as well as in the Soviet Union, have led to a new literature of comparison between the kinds of fluctuations in growth rates that occur in the two types of systems.[44] There are considerable unresolved problems of both data and analysis; but the following tentative conclusions can be drawn.

—Eight socialist economies exhibited total output fluctuations which, in the 1950's, averaged higher than those of eighteen nonsocialist economies.[45] The USSR was the least volatile, slightly below the level of France and Scandinavia. The average greater volatility of the planned economies was most marked in agriculture, but significant in construction as well. Differences were least marked in industry. Whatever the ambiguities or appropriateness of the method of measurement, the existence of substantial fluctuations in growth rates in socialist economies is beyond question.

—In the case of the USSR and other socialist economies, harvest fluctuations have had and continue to have significant pervasive economic effects, including balance-of-payments consequences; but the harvest factor does not appear systematically cyclical.

—In the USSR there were several episodes, of which 1929–1933 is the extreme prototype, in which the political authorities opted for investment programs which, in scale, composition, or both, brought about maladjustments requiring correction. These distortions could take the form of an inappropriate technical balance among the sectors or of allocations as between investment and consumption judged politically to require correction because of popular discontent. These elements are clearly evident in the economic history of the USSR, but they are not sufficiently systematic to permit identification of a regular political cycle. Moreover, phases of greater or lesser allocations to armaments and such special events as the Great Purge of the 1930's, Stalin's death, and Khrushchev's removal have also left their mark on the data.

—The degree of instability varies considerably among the various Eastern European economies, depending on their degree of industrial sophistication, natural-resource endowments, and reliance on foreign trade. In the cases of Hungary and Czechoslovakia there is some evidence, at least, of cycles derived from either structural distortions in the allocation of investment to the various sectors (Hungary) or phases of excessive investment in projects with long gestation periods accompanied by rapid increases in inventories

(Czechoslovakia). In the case of both economies, phases of overinvestment could lead to balance-of-payments pressures arising from increased import requirements.

Josef Goldmann has generalized his image of growth cycles in socialist economies in these terms:

> In a relatively small, industrially developed socialist country, there is a tendency for the raw-material base to lag behind the growth of manufacturing industries whenever the rate of growth exceeds a certain optimum level. This is due to tendencies toward underfulfillment of production (and investment) plans in the extractive and raw-material industries and toward overfulfillment of such plans in the higher-stage manufacturing industries, resulting in the formation of what has come to be known as the raw-material barrier.

TABLE IV-12. *Growth Rates in the United States and Eight Other Countries, 1953–1973*

	Median Percentage Change, Eight Countries, *ex* United States				
	Industrial Production (1)	Real GNP (2)	Value of Imports (3)	Value of Exports (4)	Consensus of Peaks and Troughs (5)
1953–1954	9.2 P	4.4	3.8	11.2	
1954–1955	8.4	7.0 P	12.3	15.1 P	P
1955–1956	7.5	4.8	16.6 P	12.3	
1956–1957	4.6	4.1	10.6	10.4	
1957–1958	0.4 T	2.4 T	−9.2 T	0.4 T	T
1958–1959	8.2	5.4	9.4	10.4	
1959–1960	9.8 P	6.7 P	17.2 P	15.8 P	P
1960–1961	5.4	5.2 T	7.4	5.0 T	T
1961–1962	5.2 T	6.0 P	6.6 T	5.7	
1962–1963	6.4	4.8 T	11.8	9.2	
1963–1964	8.7 P	6.7 P	14.9 P	16.2 P	P
1964–1965	4.6 T	4.6	4.4 T	11.0	
1965–1966	6.2 P	4.2 T	12.4 P	9.8	
1966–1967	2.9 T	4.5	5.8 T	7.4 T	T
1967–1968	6.6	6.1	12.2	15.0	
1968–1969	10.7 P	6.3 P	18.8 P	17.8 P	P
1969–1970	5.8	5.5	16.8	17.2	
1970–1971	2.4 T	4.0 T	12.1 T	14.6 T	T
1971–1972	7.0	4.2	19.9	20.2	
1972–1973	8.4 P	6.1 P	34.7 P	32.5 P	P
Averages, 1955–1972					
Peak years		6.6			
Trough years		3.8			
All years		5.1			

Source: Geoffrey H. Moore, "The State of the International Business Cycle," *Business Economics*, vol. 9, no. 4 (September 1974), p. 24.

This in turn will bring about additional imbalances in foreign trade. That barrier, likewise, is bound to slow down economic growth, particularly in a small country with a limited raw-material endowment.

In the given context, agriculture is playing a similar role, in view of the economic and institutional factors making for slow agricultural growth. This relatively slow development will cause additional strain whenever the over-all growth rate exceeds the rate of balanced growth.

The results of economic disequilibrium, ensuing from a growth rate in excess of the rate of balanced growth, will be intensified by the well known effect of overinvestment, induced or necessitated by the planned rate of growth. Overinvestment, consequently, is not an independent cause of the subsequent

Percentage Change, United States

Industrial Production (6)	Real GNP (7)	Value of Imports (8)	Value of Exports (9)	Consensus of Peaks and Troughs (10)
−5.3 T	−1.4 T	−5.6 T	4.2 T	T
12.7 P	7.6 P	11.3 P	11.6	P
4.4	1.8	11.1	21.7 P	
1.3	1.4	3.8	11.4	
−6.5 T	−1.1 T	−2.6 T	−16.1 T	T
11.9 P	6.4 P	18.6 P	0.3	P
2.2	2.5	−3.6 T	19.4 P	
0.8 T	1.9 T	−1.5	2.3 T	T
8.2 P	6.6 P	11.9 P	3.3	P
6.0 T	4.0 T	4.8 T	7.2	T
6.8	5.5	9.7	14.5 P	
9.2	6.3	15.0	3.8 T	
9.8 P	6.5 P	18.5 P	10.8 P	P
2.1 T	2.6 T	5.4 T	4.6 T	T
5.7 P	4.7 P	22.8 P	9.7 P	P
4.7	2.7	8.5 T	8.2 T	
−3.7 T	−0.4 T	11.1	15.3 P	T
0.2	3.2	14.3	1.9 T	
7.9	6.1	22.5	14.0	
9.8 P	6.2 P	27.9 P	45.4 P	P
	6.3			
	2.8			
	4.5			

Note: The eight countries are Belgium, Canada, France, West Germany, Italy, Japan, Netherlands, and the United Kingdom.

decline in the rate of growth, but one of the factors accompanying excessive growth.[46]

The time period for which systematic data are available is too short to yield firm evidence of systematic growth cycles in socialist economies. What is clear is that centrally planned economies share with those with large private-enterprise sectors the same fundamental problem: how to allocate resources among the sectors as well as between investment and consumption to achieve a viable economic and political balance. The economic and political processes determining the outcome differ radically, of course; but in both cases institutional and human imperfections decree overshooting and undershooting the investment patterns required for balanced growth; both kinds of economies face the problem of lags between the initiation and completion of investment projects; and even powerful central-political-control systems cannot wholly suppress in safety the desire of consumers for rising real income per capita. It is not difficult to construct, therefore, pure logical theories of growth cycles for socialist economies if one assumes (correctly) imperfect foresight among planners and their political authorities. And elements, at least, of such cycles can be perceived in the limited data thus far analyzed.

25

Inflation: The Price of Full Employment

As noted in Chapter 8 (see above, pp. 87–88), the nations with large private-enterprise sectors paid a considerable price for the rapid growth they enjoyed from 1945 to 1973. The price was a rate of inflation unique in the peacetime history of the modern world economy, which accelerated dangerously as the period drew to a close.

For the United States, for example, the consumers' price index declined by 1 percent in the recession of 1949, by 0.4 percent in 1955. In every other year it rose. The increase, of course, was not uniform among the components of the cost of living, nor did inflation proceed at a uniform rate. Table IV-13 shows the average annual rate of increase for the cost of living and some major components. Evidently, the prices of manufactured consumers' goods, led by durables, rose least; services, led by medical care, rose most. For all commodities except food, the average annual rate of increase

TABLE IV-13. *U.S. Cost-of-Living Indexes: Average Annual Rate of Increase, 1945–1973 (%)*

All items	3.3
Food	3.7
Housing (total)	3.0
Rent	2.7
Apparel and upkeep	2.6
Transportation	3.6
Medical care	4.3
Personal care	3.0
Reading and recreation	2.5
Other goods and services (total)	3.0
Durable consumers' goods	1.9

Source: Consumer price indexes for urban wage earners and clerical workers, *Economic Report of the President* (Washington, D.C.: Government Printing Office, February 1975), pp. 300 and 301 (durable consumers' goods).

was 2.4 percent; for all services except rent, 4.2 percent. Average (spendable) weekly earnings in private nonagricultural industries rose at an annual average rate of 4.1 percent over this period, in constant dollars at 1.4 percent.[47]

The phases of post-1945 inflation can be roughly distinguished as follows, with annual average rates of U.S. consumers' price increase given in parentheses after each time period:

1948–1952 (2.5 percent). Brief recession followed by recovery and Korean War period, including a rise of 7.9 percent in 1950–1951.

1952–1956 (0.6 percent). Post-Korean recession and recovery, accompanied by a net decline in food and other commodity prices, a slow continued rise in prices of services.

1956–1961 (1.9 percent). After a 3.6 percent rise at peak of boom (1957), prices continue to rise slowly in subsequent sluggish and erratic phase of growth, due to wage-push inflation.

1961–1965 (1.3 percent). Price increases low as economy revives, controlled in part by wage-price guideposts, against background of modest commodity price increases.

1965–1968 (3.3 percent). Rate of inflation rises with effects of 1964 tax reduction, increased military outlays, break in wage guideposts (1966), and beginning of significant commodity price increases.

1968–1972 (4.7 percent). Rate of increase accelerates with abandonment of wage-price guideposts (1969) despite decline in military expenditures. Inflation in commodity prices increases.

1972–1974 (8.6 percent). Rate of increase accelerates further with price revolution starting at the end of 1972.

Table IV-14, covering the period 1955–1974, shows consumer price indexes for a number of the major industrial economies as well as the United States.[48] In different ways all shared the immediate postwar inflationary boom as well as the Korean War boom and subsequent retardation. The annual inflation rates for the decade after 1955 varied from 0.6 percent in the United States, damped by low growth rates and then wage-price guideposts, to 4.9 percent in France, which suffered severe inflation in the late 1950's, as well as two currency devaluations. The Japanese inflation rate was also high in this decade (3.8 percent); but its balance-of-payments consequences were cushioned by rapid productivity increases and subsidies in its major export sectors. Japanese export prices followed a course quite different from the consumers' price index. Among the Western European countries, the German performance was best (2.3 percent), the Italian worst (3.4 percent), excepting France. From 1965 to 1972 inflation rates increased in virtually all cases.[49] For the United States the acceleration began in 1966; for the others, more nearly 1969. Britain and the Netherlands experienced the most severe inflation, Germany the least. The American inflation rate increased by two and a half times. The price

TABLE IV-14. *Consumer Price Indexes in the United States and Other Major Industrial Countries, 1955–1974 (1970 = 100)*

	United States	Average Annual Rate of Increase (%)	Canada	Average Annual Rate of Increase (%)	Japan	Average Annual Rate of Increase (%)	France	Average Annual Rate of Increase (%)
1955	69.0		69.9		52.6		50.4	
1956	70.0		70.9		52.8		51.4	
1957	72.5		73.2		54.4		53.2	
1958	74.5		75.0		54.2		61.2	
1959	75.1		75.9		54.7		65.0	
1960	76.3	1.5	76.7	1.7	56.7	3.8	67.3	4.9
1961	77.0		77.1		59.7		69.5	
1962	77.9		78.0		63.8		72.9	
1963	78.8		79.4		69.2		76.4	
1964	79.9		80.8		71.9		79.0	
1965	81.3		82.8		76.7		81.0	
1966	83.6		85.9		80.6		83.2	
1967	86.0		88.9		83.8		85.4	
1968	89.6	4.1	92.6	3.8	88.3	5.5	89.3	4.7
1969	94.4		96.8		92.9		95.0	
1970	100.0		100.0		100.0		100.0	
1971	104.3		102.9		106.3		105.5	
1972	107.7		107.8		111.5		111.7	
1973	114.4	8.6	116.0	8.9	124.5	16.9	119.9	10.4
1974	127.0		127.9		152.4		135.5	

TABLE IV-14. *(continued)*

	Germany	Average Annual Rate of Increase (%)	Italy	Average Annual Rate of Increase (%)	Netherlands	Average Annual Rate of Increase (%)	United Kingdom	Average Annual Rate of Increase (%)
1955	70.1		62.2		57.8		59.0	
1956	71.9		64.3		58.9		61.9	
1957	73.3		65.2		62.7		64.2	
1958	75.0		67.0		63.8		66.2	
1959	75.7		66.7		64.3		66.5	
1960	76.7	2.3	68.2	3.4	66.4	3.1	67.2	3.1
1961	78.5		69.7		67.0		69.5	
1962	80.9		72.9		68.3		72.5	
1963	83.3		78.3		70.9		73.9	
1964	85.2		83.0		74.8		76.3	
1965	88.1		86.7		78.7		80.0	
1966	91.2		88.8		83.3		83.1	
1967	92.5		91.6		86.0		85.2	
1968	93.9	3.4	92.8	3.6	89.1	5.7	89.2	5.6
1969	96.4		95.2		95.8		94.0	
1970	100.0		100.0		100.0		100.0	
1971	105.3		105.0		107.5		109.5	
1972	111.1		110.9		115.9		117.0	
1973	118.8	6.8	122.4	12.4	125.2	8.6	126.7	11.7
1974	126.8		140.0		136.6		145.9	

Source: *Economic Report of the President* (February 1975), p. 359.

revolution of 1972–1974 was marked by a doubling or worse in inflation rates over those of the previous period, except for the Netherlands, which was already experiencing the most severe inflation in 1965–1972.

The analysis of inflation in its post-1945 setting is an exceedingly complex art. It involves the interweaving and interaction of three major elements: (1) the intensity of effective demand for labor in relation to supply, including, on the side of demand, fiscal and monetary policy; on the side of supply, the potentialities for drawing labor from rural areas and abroad (demand-pull); (2) the extent to which foodstuffs, raw materials, and energy are scarce or abundant on a world basis, and a nation's relative dependence on imported supplies (raw-materials push); and (3) the degree to which implicit or explicit disciplines within societies link money-wage increases to the average level of productivity increase (wage-push). The leverage of labor unions in wage bargains is obviously related to the tightness of the labor market. Demand-pull and wage-push inflation cannot be wholly separated. On the other hand, there are significant differences among nations in the response of wages to degrees of unemployment and changes within nations over periods of time. Phillips curves—charting annual levels of unemployment against price changes—have not been stable or internationally uniform.[50] In addition, the pace of inflation has been affected by currency revaluations. These reflected, in part, the prior relative success of the various nations in controlling inflation on a national basis; but, in altering the relative prices of exports and imports, they affected in turn the subsequent course of inflation. Germany, for example, was thus doubly rewarded for its capacity to constrain domestic wage-push inflation better than most: its domestic price increases were less, and the upward revaluation of its currency relatively reduced the cost of its imports, making the control of inflation easier. On the other hand, Britain was doubly punished by its difficulties in controlling inflation and the effect of its series of devaluations in raising import prices. There was even an element of triple jeopardy for Britain vis à vis Germany. The necessity for stop-and-go policies imposed by relatively high inflation rates lowered the level of domestic industrial investment and may have caused lower rates of increase in productivity (and, therefore, export competitiveness) relative to Germany.

The role of these elements in the story of post-1945 inflation, and the interactions among them, varied.

For example, all three types of inflationary pressure were involved in the initial phase of readjustment and reconversion, down to 1948: tight labor markets, high raw-material prices, and (in the United States, at least) wage increases in excess of the average productivity increase, raising unit labor costs. By 1948–1949, the initial postwar readjustment was about completed in Western Europe (excepting Germany) as well as in the United States. The latter experienced a sharp recession in 1949 which cut wage increases sufficiently to lower unit labor costs. Then came the Korean War boom which involved a brief passage of demand-pull, raw-materials push, and (with a typical lag) wage-push inflation. From 1951, however, foodstuff and raw-material prices entered a protracted phase when they were relatively low. This background eased the problem of inflation over the following fifteen years in the advanced industrialized areas of the world. Nevertheless, excepting the period 1961–1965 in the United States, when reasonably effective wage-price guideposts operated, the element of wage-push inflation was present, as well as a demand-pull inflation, generally more acute in Western Europe and Japan than in the United States.[51]

The acceleration of inflation from the mid-1960's involved in the United States both demand-pull inflation, as unemployment fell below 4 percent in the period 1966–1969, and a not unrelated weakening of wage guideposts. Unit labor costs averaged a 3.7 percent annual increase in the last three years of the Johnson administration and surged to 7.1 percent in 1969 when wage-price guideposts were formally abandoned. The movement of foodstuff and raw-material prices exacerbated the problem in the sense that, by this time, they had generally ceased their relative decline. The American farm parity ratio had, for example, fallen from 107 in 1951 to 76 in 1964. It averaged 75.6 for the period 1965–1969. At the same time real wages in the nonagricultural sector came under pressure, averaging a small net decline (0.1 percent per annum) when spendable weekly earnings are calculated in constant dollars. This heightened the natural thrust of the unions to increase wage rates in negotiated settlements.

The acceleration of inflation in the United States after 1965 is fairly well analyzed and understood.[52] But there is no solid consensus on the reasons for its acceleration elsewhere from 1969 to 1972. F. W. Paish describes the origins of this phase in Britain, and its subsequent course down to 1974, in terms which justify quotation at length:

> Up to the end of the third quarter of 1969 there is a clear relationship . . . between the level of unemployment and the rise of incomes from employment. After the third quarter of 1969, however, this relationship disappears, and between then and 1972 the main cause of the faster rise of employment incomes was the use of their monopoly power by the trade unions. The reason for this change seems to have been the success of the government's policy between 1967 and 1969 of holding down real disposable personal incomes in order to divert resources from consumption to exports. It is tragic that, just as this policy had been successful and it was becoming possible to allow consumption to resume its rise, the trade unions felt obliged to adopt a more militant policy in order to raise the real disposable incomes of their members. . . .

> Towards the end of 1972, the already large effects on the rate of rise of prices of the over-rapid rise of wage rates were reinforced by a rapid rise of import prices, especially of food, feedingstuffs and industrial raw materials. For most of the period between the collapse of the Korean war boom in 1951 and the third quarter of 1972, import prices had risen much more slowly than home costs, so that the effect of imports was to slow down the rate of rise of total prices. . . . In the last quarter of 1973, the rise of total import prices was greatly accelerated by the monopolistically-imposed quadrupling of prices of imported oil, so that between the second quarter of 1972 and the second quarter of 1974 average import prices of all goods and services rose by nearly 90 per cent, causing British internal prices to rise faster than home costs for the first time since 1952.
>
> The faster rise in consumption prices in turn caused the trade unions to increase their wage demands further, so that, although the rise of import prices greatly slowed down after the second quarter of 1974, mainly as the result of a fall in the prices of many industrial raw materials, the rise of consumption prices has continued to accelerate, and may well accelerate further.[53]

Paish's fear of further acceleration was justified: in the late spring of 1975, British inflation was thoroughly out of hand and proceeding at an annual rate of 40 percent, a momentum broken to a degree in the second half of the year by a strong deflationary government policy executed with belated support from the labor-union leaders.

What Paish captures is a sequence in which demand-pull inflation, accompanied by some wage constraint, set off a subsequent phase of determined wage-push inflation, which then was reinforced by the almost universal boom of 1972–1973 and, in particular, by the dramatic rise in the relative prices of basic materials, starting at the end of 1972, which, in turn, exerted severe pressure on real wages. The British case proved to be extreme, in that wage-push inflation resisted the cyclical downturn of 1974–1975 with its softening of food and raw-material prices. But Table III-73, above, makes clear the universality of a doubling or more of inflation rates as between 1960–1973 and 1974–1975 in the OECD world. The sequence described by Paish for Britain has several special features; but, in catching the convergence in the latter years of all three types of inflation, it is generally illuminating.

The problem of inflation was perceived from the early postwar years to be a potential time bomb in an era of relatively steady, rapid growth. Summing up the papers written for a conference at Oxford in September 1952, D. H. Robertson posed the issue well:

> What of . . . the tendency of wage-rates to climb steadily up-

> wards, even . . . in face of temporary flickerings of demand? Is this also a potential cause of "an industrial depression of the traditional form"? Or is it rather . . . a potential cause of something quite different—a complete break-down of monetary stability, leading to a naked choice between totalitarianism and chaos? Has this result been hitherto prevented . . . by the occurrence of the mild price and employment recessions of 1949 and 1951? And if so, can we rely on an indefinite succession of these beneficent slumplets, not severe enough to generate widespread distress but sufficient to prevent the reputation of money as a store of value from being irretrievably undermined? Or does anybody know of a "wages policy" which will purge a "full employment" regime, not of its manifold inefficiencies and injustices—that is too much to hope—but of its propensity to ultimate suicide? [54]

The best analysts of Western European growth in the 1960's noted the penalties high growth rates and low unemployment levels exacted in political democracies and also expressed their anxiety for the future.[55] The governments themselves were not wholly passive. In the United States the control of inflation was part of the national agenda from the Truman administration forward.[56] And virtually all the Western European governments experimented with versions of incomes policy which would, by negotiation, constrain money wages and the bargaining power of unions in the face of chronically tight labor markets.[57] For brief periods these policies appear to have had some benign effect; e.g., in the Netherlands down to 1963, the United States from 1961 to 1966 and 1971–1972, and, generally, in Germany, where for most of this period the unions exercised self-restraint out of old memories of inflation and a lively sense of the connection between wage increases and their nation's capacity to export.

The fact is, however, that over the whole span of the postwar boom of 1946–1974, the political and social task of constraining money wages became increasingly difficult. In part, perhaps, the reasons are technical: the labor surpluses to be drawn into the urban working-force pool from the countryside or from abroad have diminished; and the post-1951 damping effect of relative raw-material and foodstuff prices ceased to operate as the 1960's wore on and then gave way to a mighty inflationary push. In part, the reason is psychological: the tendency of inflation to accelerate set up expectations of further inflation which led union leaders to try, in their current negotiations, not merely to correct for past pressures of inflation on real wages, but to achieve settlements which would hedge their clients' real incomes against expected future inflation. In a sense, failure bred failure: the breakdown of successive incomes-policy efforts consolidated inflationary expectations in business and labor. And so these rich, comfortable, and rapidly expanding economies became—so far as wages and prices were concerned—like a dog chasing its tail. The process was chronically exacerbated by wage drift among nonunion workers, achieving in tight labor markets greater increases than those negotiated by unions; and it was virtually always complicated by varying degrees of fragmentation among the unions, leading to competition in wage settlements by the various contending union leaders as well as difficulties in getting the rank and file to accept the deals their leaders negotiated.

But deeper questions are involved, which we shall only note here but develop further in Part Six. The willingness and ability of various societies to implement successfully a social contract governing price and wage behavior are a measure of their political cohesion and sense of common purpose. As an American analyst of the European experience of the 1950's observed, a wage policy cannot be effective except as "part of a coordinated effort to achieve a clearly defined national objective in which the relation between national interests and trade union wage action may be given unambiguous and measurable significance."[58] When the relatively easy phase of postwar growth down to 1972 gave way to the more constrained environment of the new trend period, none of the advanced industrial countries—nor all of them together—had yet defined their interests and objectives in ways that made wage restraint acceptable, except by policies which slowed down the rate of growth or raised the level of unemployment. Inflation decelerated in most but not all OECD countries in 1974–1975; but this old-fashioned remedy was not proving sufficient to bring the powerful momentum of wage-push inflation to a halt, despite the effect of recession on raw-material prices. The prospects for the OECD in 1976 appeared to be a rate of growth which would leave unemployment relatively high, combined with an average inflation rate of about 8 percent. The temperature of a quite sick patient was being lowered at great economic and social cost; but no cure was in sight. And this was still the case as the disappointing revival of 1975–1976 promised to make 1977 the fourth successive year of stagflation.

26

Stagflation: 1974–1976

The price revolution of 1972–1976 brought not only an exacerbated phase of inflation to the industrialized market economies but also the sharpest recession since the end of the Second World War. Chart IV-7 vividly shows how the OECD world fell off its curve by plotting industrial production as deviations from the 1955–1973 trend. The causes and character of that recession raise the question of whether growth cycles of the kind experienced since 1945 will persist. Certainly, the short-run problem of moving from recession to full recovery is different from any encountered in the previous thirty years.[59]

There is nothing new about a cyclical recession brought about by balance-of-payments pressures arising from excessive imports during a period of rapid growth. Indeed, a recession in 1974 was foreshadowed by a deceleration in industrial production and by other leading indicators in the second half of 1973, before the major increase in oil prices of November had significant balance-of-payments effects.[60] It is, of course, the scale, persistence, and character of the balance-of-payments effects of the oil price increase which complicate the task of recovery, while the energy crisis in its wider sense is posing domestic problems—notably, pressure on real income per capita—which may well alter the structural character of recovery in the short run, and of resumed growth in the long run.

In the short run, the central fact is that recession is not significantly decreasing the net foreign-exchange outlays for oil imports. Therefore, relief from balance-of-payments pressure must be found in other directions. By and large, the recycling problem proved in 1974–1975 more manageable than was at first thought; that is, increased OPEC imports and foreign aid, the lending resources of the Euro-dollar market, and various other measures providing short-term credits to hard-pressed oil importers reduced the expected size of OPEC's capital exports to selected oil importers and the problem of compensating for distortions in those capital flows. But the various nations exhibited quite unequal capacities to reduce their current-account deficits by expanded exports. Germany, Benelux, and Japan did relatively well; Britain, Italy, and France, quite poorly. Thus, the prospects for particular countries differ considerably in conventional stop-go cyclical terms. Germany, at one end of the spectrum—with its inflation rate relatively low, its currency appreciated, and its balance-of-payments surplus—is in a vastly better position to conduct expansionary domestic fiscal and monetary policies than Britain or Italy. Their high inflation rates and large continuing current balance deficits mean that further radical measures of constraint may be necessary before reasonably stable policies of expansion can be launched—measures which might include wage freezes, devaluation, further increases in taxation, and reductions in public outlays.

But there is a second problem which will confront Japan and Germany, as well as Britain, Italy, and the United States. The rise in the oil price has had two structural effects on real incomes. It has reduced real incomes in the industrialized, oil-importing parts of the world; and it has increased the real incomes of oil exporters. To some extent the industrialized nations can move back toward full

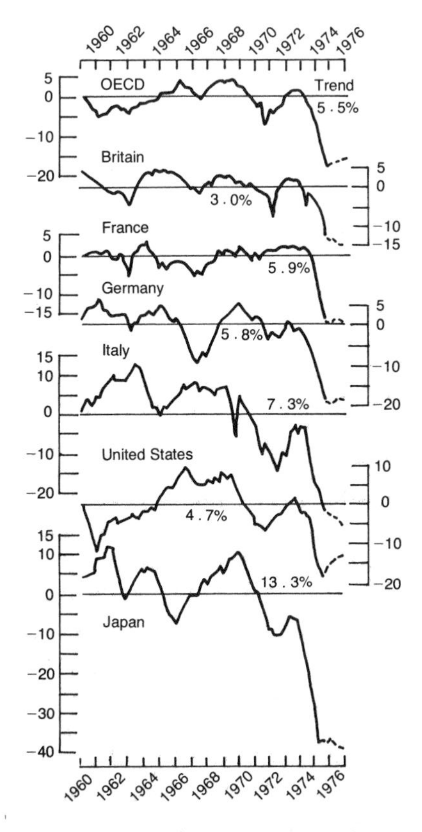

CHART IV-7. *Industrial Production: OECD and Major Countries, 1960–1976 (Percentage Deviation from 1955–1973 Trend)*

Source: London *Economist*, 20–26 December 1975, p. 72.

employment by exporting relatively less to each other, relatively more to those now richer. But increased exports to oil exporters are not likely to prove a sufficient compensation, in terms of employment, for the weakening of the leading sectors which carried forward Western European and Japanese growth in the period down to 1972. Those sectors (automobiles, durable consumers' goods, etc.) are energy-intensive. With higher energy prices a rise in incomes is likely to yield a lesser increase in demand for such products. In addition, public policy may frown on and formally constrain a simple return to previous consumer expenditure patterns in the light of current and prospective energy prices and dependence on imports.

Meanwhile, in one country after another, a sense is emerging that limits are being approached or have been exceeded to levels of social services provided by public authorities. The expansion of such services was an important source of increased demand and employment in the 1960's, as Table IV-15 suggests. Outlays for education,

TABLE IV-15. *Social Welfare Expenditures as a Percentage of GNP: Eleven Countries, 1950–1972*

	Sweden	Denmark	Finland	
1950	7.7	5.2	—	
1955	8.5	6.3	9.6	
1960	11.5	7.5	8.9	
1965	12.6	11.1	9.4	
1969	14.3	14.5	9.5	
1972	16.4	18.2	9.3	
	Austria	Netherlands	Norway	Belgium
1950	5.7	5.2	3.1	—
1953	8.5	5.3	3.6	—
1955	6.8	5.5	3.7	—
1957	7.7	6.2	4.3	6.1
1960	8.0	6.5	3.9	9.0
1965	9.7	8.3	4.8	9.3
1969	10.1	9.9	6.7	10.1
1972	10.3	10.9	9.2	11.9
	Switzerland	Spain	Portugal	United States
1950	1.4	—	—	—
1955	0.9	1.0	3.0	3.1 (1956)
1960	0.9	1.3	3.6	4.3
1965	1.5	1.7	2.8	4.8
1969	2.2	2.9	3.6	6.5
1972	2.4	3.3	—	8.8

Source: Joseph E. Pluta, "National Defense and Social Welfare Budget Trends in Ten Nations of Postwar Western Europe," *International Journal of Social Economics*, June 1977; and (for U.S.), idem, "Growth and Patterns in U.S. Government Expenditures, 1956–1972," *National Tax Journal*, vol. 27, no. 1 (March 1974), p. 92.

public health, and other welfare services are, to be sure, financed through taxation; but their expansion not only reflected an important aspect of the income elasticity of demand in rich societies during the 1960's, it also had spreading effects (notably in education and health) similar to those of other leading sectors. Schools and hospitals were built and supplied with equipment. Their continued expansion provided increased employment indirectly as well as directly.

Surely, the automobile and durable consumers' goods sectors will remain large, as will the level of outlays flowing through public budgets to various kinds of social services. But they are unlikely to expand as they did in the 1950's and 1960's; and they may well contract to a degree. Therefore, the question is: What are the sectors whose expansion will bring the OECD economies back to relatively full employment in the short run and to sustained growth at high levels over the longer pull? Put another way, there is a danger not of a great depression like that of 1929–1933 but of the advanced industrial nations' being caught in a protracted phase of chronically high unemployment and low growth rates, like Britain between the wars. Between the wars a sharp favorable shift in the terms of trade helped bring on a need for structural adjustment in patterns of investment. The price revolution of 1972–1976 poses a similar problem due to an unfavorable shift in the terms of trade.

A part of the answer can be perceived in micro-terms; for example, the shift in United States steel manufacture from strip steel for automobiles to oil pipelines and offshore drills and the drift of workers from Detroit to the expanding coal mines of West Virginia, a process which began promptly (but weakly) to assert itself in the United States in the months after the oil price rise, as Table IV-16 reveals. Increased investment in non-OPEC energy sources is, evi-

TABLE IV-16. *Changes in Employment in the Private Nonfarm Economy: Total and Selected Energy-Related Industries, November 1973–March 1974 (Seasonally Adjusted)*

Industry	Change in Employment Number (Thousands)	Percentage
Total private nonfarm	−8	0.0
Energy-using:		
Motor vehicles and equipment	−114	−12.2
Gasoline service stations	−67	−10.4
Motor vehicle dealers, retail	−57	−6.7
Other transportation	−23	−14.3
Hotel and other lodging places	−21	−2.3
Substitutes for imported oil:		
Oil and gas extraction	9	3.2
Coal mining	2	1.2

Source: Department of Labor, Bureau of Labor Statistics, in *Economic Report of the President* (February 1975), p. 59.

dently, one potentially major compensatory avenue for increased employment. Similarily, investment in various kinds of energy conservation is potentially important; e.g., insulated housing and (especially in the United States) new mass-transport facilities. In a number of OECD countries there was evidence before the price revolution of 1972–1976 that citizens and public authorities were increasingly conscious that rapid growth based on the leading sectors of high mass-consumption had yielded environmental degradation which required correction in the time ahead. Investment to clean the air and the water and otherwise to improve the quality of urban life is another potential source of increased employment.

Looking further ahead, research and development on an increased scale will be required to create new renewable forms of energy as oil reserves run down; and if industrial growth proceeds in the world economy at anything like the average rate it sustained between 1948 and 1971 (5.6 percent), there will be parallel problems in a wide range of raw materials. Certainly, if the populations scheduled to expand over the next generation are to be fed, research and development in agriculture will have to expand.

These are issues central to Part Six. But they bear also on the nature of cycles and growth in the wake of the recession of 1974–1975. Full recovery in the OECD world is not likely to come by a simple expansion in effective demand accompanied by further diffusion of the amenities of high mass-consumption through the private sector and additional public services. Both resumed growth at high levels of employment and balanced growth now require enlarged investment in the sectors necessary to sustain industrial civilizations with the inputs of energy, raw materials, food, air, and water they need. As we know from Part Three, this is the fifth time since 1790 that such changes in patterns of investment have been required by food or other shortages in basic materials. In the past, those changes in the composition of investment were brought about primarily by the international price system and by the changing directions of profitability private investors could perceive. And surely in the 1970's this kind of market adjustment is playing and will play a major role. But it is equally true that, given the nature of the compensatory sectors involved, the role of the public authorities will have to expand. The pace and efficacy of that transition will largely determine, along with success or failure in mastering wage-push inflation, whether the OECD world will be able to resume the mild growth cycles of the previous three decades or whether it will find itself in a protracted phase of frustrated growth and higher average levels of unemployment.

Part Five

Stages of Economic Growth: Twenty Countries

27

Aggregate and Sectoral Analysis of Growth

We have thus far looked at the dynamics of economic growth from the perspective of the world economy, introducing special regional and national features of the story in an ancillary way. In this section, we turn the subject around. I shall try, with extreme brevity, to present patterns of national growth for twenty countries, introducing as a secondary theme only the impact on them of the trends and cycles, wars and other traumatic events generated in the world outside. The world economy has followed a path determined by the interaction between the forces operating within the international economic, political, and military arena and these (and other) national histories of modernization and failure to modernize. In turn, the stories of national growth are rooted in aspects of geography, natural-resource endowments, culture, and noneconomic history which are, in each case, unique. The purpose of Part Five is to capture some of these elements of uniqueness as well as certain broad uniformities in aggregate and sectoral patterns of economic growth. It is also designed to make clear a fundamental characteristic of the 1970's; namely, that the world economy contains nations at quite different points in the unfolding process of absorbing efficiently the pool of modern technology. There is a transition to affluence related to the demographic transition; and the nations and regions of the world stand at quite different points in that transition. In the end I shall try to give this notion some rough quantitative meaning as a prelude to Part Six.

In these exercises in compressed national economic history I shall use as an expository device the concept of stages of economic growth. In each of the four previous sections I have from time to time made reference to the movement of national economies through the stages of economic growth. The concept of stages of growth as I developed it in the 1950's was the subject of some controversy in the 1960's. I responded fully to that debate and absorbed the further relevant evidence accumulated over a decade in an appendix to a second edition in 1971.[1] In terms of historical analysis, a good deal of the debate turned out to be a matter of vocabulary. There is, for example, no question among specialized students of national economies about the approximate timing of the entrance of Great Britain, the United States, Germany, Sweden, Italy, Russia, Argentina, Turkey, Mexico, Taiwan, South Korea (and many other countries) into sustained industrial growth. One may choose to call that crucial watershed the coming of the industrial revolution, the beginnings of modern growth, the take-off, or by some other congenial phrase; but, leaving scope for inevitable and appropriate debate over refinements in dating, there is a high degree of consensus about these intervals of general economic acceleration when modern technologies began systematically to be absorbed into the various national economies with reasonable efficiency.[2] And, for those who have gone deeply into national economic histories for later stages of development, the range of debate about when key technologies of greater sophistication were efficiently absorbed is also narrow. Kazushi Ohkawa and Henry Rosovsky, for example, have proposed a somewhat different vocabulary to date the stages of Japanese economic growth in the century following the Meiji Restoration;[3] but the fact is, our dating is virtually identical, and we are evidently talking about the same phenomena.

More fundamental for our present purposes is the central analytic issue which lies behind the debate about the stages of economic growth. That issue is whether growth should be analyzed in terms of broad aggregates (like GNP, the proportion of income invested, the proportion of GNP generated in primary, manufacturing, and service sectors, etc.), or whether changes in these aggregates must be linked to movements in the sectors and subsectors within which new technologies are actually absorbed efficiently into an economy. Historians, by the nature of their profession, are driven toward disaggregated analyses. They know movements in the aggregates sum up what actually happened in particular sectors and regions or even in particular shops and factories. They are instinctively uncomfortable until they can identify where and when crucial events occurred in the past which caused these abstract index numbers to move as they did. Economists and statisticians, however, have sometimes conducted their analyses solely at much higher levels of aggregation. They have opted for these broad aggregates for converging reasons of convenience and theoretical bias. The data most easily available for purposes of international comparison were in highly aggregated form. This was the case because data collection had been stimulated by the Keynesian revolution and the development of national income analysis at a highly aggregated level. Thus, as often in the past, prevailing theory helped determine, with a lag, the kind of data gathered by public authorities. With these data the comparative analysis of growth has, to a degree, certainly been advanced; but, without greater disaggregation, it remains incomplete.

There is an important initial agreement among us all that transcends, but bears upon, this problem of method. The agreement is that modern economic growth, at its core, consists in the progressive generation and diffusion of new technologies linked, in one way or another, to the prior build-up of the stock of basic science. New technologies, however, are not introduced into GNP, agriculture, manufacturing, or services: they are introduced into particular sectors or subsectors of the economy; e.g., new wheat strains in certain regions, cotton spinning, steamboats on certain rivers, or whatever. Conceptually, then, there is agreement that the economic growth of a national economy ought to be analyzed on a highly disaggregated basis related to the effective absorption of new technologies.[4] But, despite this conceptual agreement, economists and statisticians with an aggregative bent have a second line of defense. If technological change takes place simply by "a large number of small advances over a wide front,"[5] then one can average the increase in productivity for an economy as a whole attributable to the absorption of new technology and stay at a theoretically and statistically high and comfortable level of aggregation.[6] One can insert into conventional income analysis an overall variable measuring the rate of technological change and proceed with familiar neo-Keynesian manipulations. And this is often done.

Now there is, indeed, a great deal of technological change that takes place by small advances over a wide front. It takes place in minor sectors and in large but slowly growing sectors; and it takes place also in the evolution of the great leading sectoral complexes which, in my view, have played a major role in economic history. Any serious historical analysis of technological change would underline the fact that since the eighteenth century such change has been the work of many minds and hands operating in a cultural, a social, an economic, and sometimes a political setting that attached a high premium to this kind of human creativity. But this does not mean that all inventions are created equal and are of equal economic significance. Historians and analysts of growth have for long identified certain inventions and innovations of particular power and consequence; and their lists have been reasonably uniform: for example, cotton spinning machinery, Watt's more efficient steam engine, Cort's puddling process for making good wrought iron with coke, the steamboat, the railroad, cheap steel, a range of specific chemicals, the internal combustion engine, electricity and its major applications beyond the supply of power (the telegraph, telephone, radio, television, computers, etc.). Again, these were not once-for-all inventions. From the initial break-throughs, each with a long prior history of incremental effort and achievement, there was a subsequent process of progressive refinement. But without recognizing the reality of such discontinuous creative changes, both economic theory and economic history are grossly incomplete. The economic stage is not empty if one drops cotton, iron, and the steam engine from the story of Britain between 1783 and 1830; the railroad from the story of Britain, the United States, and Western Europe between 1830 and 1870; steel from the story of the Atlantic world between 1870 and 1914, electricity and the internal combustion engine since 1900; but one is presenting *Hamlet* without the Prince.

In any case, the concept of the stages of economic growth is a form of analysis which would insist on the central role of these (and other) major technological innovations without in any way deprecating the role of lesser refinements in method which, in modern societies, proceed unceasingly but unevenly over a broad front in agriculture, industry, and what we lump together under the awkward rubric of "services."

Having adopted that view of the contours of modern growth, one immediately confronts a problem of measurement to which I alluded earlier;[7] i.e., it is impossible to measure accurately the full scale of a leading sector complex, including all its ramified linkages and spreading effects. Perhaps the most complete estimate available is that for the automobile industry in the United States. It illustrates the complexity and difficulties of any such measurement as well as the extraordinary scale of a fully developed leading sector which, as of the 1970's, has passed its peak role and whose proportionate scale in the economy may now be in decline.

In attempting to measure the American motor vehicle sectoral complex, three approaches have been applied: employment generated in automobile manufacture and directly related production and service sectors; the number of business establishments related to the production and use of motor vehicles; and the proportion of GNP accounted for by highway transport expenditures. Details of these calculations are presented in Appendix C.

Each of these calculations involves problems of both data and conception. Taken together, however, they justify the view that the motor vehicle sectoral complex may have constituted something like a sixth of the American economy as of the early 1970's, with a high sensitivity to fluctuations in consumers' real income.[8] It should be underlined, however, that the order of magnitude we are trying to approximate here for illustrative purposes is not that which is directly relevant to leading sector complexes in growth analysis. What we are concerned with historically is the contribution to overall growth made by a leading sector complex as it comes into the economic system and rapidly expands. A leading sector complex at full maturity or beyond, like the automobile sectoral complex of the United States in the mid-1970's (or like British cotton textiles in the late nineteenth century or the American railroads in the 1920's), can be very big without making a major contribution to the economy's expansion, although its rapid retardation, stagnation, or absolute decline can damp significantly the overall rate of growth.

We evidently lack the data to make systematic estimates of the full scale of leading sector complexes in the historical past, although we have had a certain amount of sport arguing about the scale of the railroad sectoral complex in the nineteenth century. But we do know that the major leading sector complexes ramified out in many directions: generating inputs from other industries (and agriculture); accelerating the growth of related services; increasing the rate of urbanization in new regions and old, with all manner of playback effects on the overall pace of economic growth. *It should be borne in mind, therefore, that the sectoral data charted in Part Five of this book stand as proxies for complexes which far transcend their narrow, literal scope.*

There is a further point to be made about the role of leading sectors in growth analysis. They entered and rapidly expanded within economies that had already attained a considerable scale. All modern (and premodern) economies have allocated a large proportion of the working force and physical resources to activities other than those directly affected by the leading sectors; e.g., agriculture, food and leather processing, housing construction, government services. What we are focusing on, therefore, is not the proportionate scale of a leading sector in the structure of the economy but the role of leading sectors in the growth of an economy. Growth is a marginal increment to an existing base. Rapid expansion in a leading sector complex can, therefore, contribute much more to growth than its proportionate scale in the economy would suggest.

There is a final aspect of growth analysis to be noted that transcends straightforward sectoral measurement. The absorption of technologies took place in the past and apparently takes place at present in a sequence related, on the one hand, to the degree of complexity of the technology and, on the other, to the income elasticity of demand for final products. Hollis B. Chenery and Lance Taylor captured the resultant sequence in an analysis that related levels of GNP per capita to the proportionate role of twelve standard industrial groups in a number of contemporary nations at different stages of growth. They categorize these industrial groups under three headings, as follows, in conclusions reflected in Chart V-1:

> *Early Industries*: The early industries are those which (1) supply essential demands of the poorest countries, (2) can be carried on with simple technology, and (3) increase their share of GNP relatively little above income levels of $200 [U.S., 1960] or so. They consist of food, leather goods, and textiles. . . . These industries have income elasticities of domestic demand of 1.0 or less and exhaust their potentials for import substitution and export growth at fairly low income levels. The group as a whole maintains a fairly constant share of GNP; it declines from 56 per cent to 23 per cent of manufacturing as per capita income rises from $100 to $1,000. . . .

> *Middle Industries*: We define the middle industries as those which double their share of GNP in the lower income levels but show relatively little rise above income levels of $400–$500. These characteristics are shown . . . by nonmetallic minerals, rubber products, wood products, and chemicals and petroleum refining. This group of industries accounts for 40 per cent of the increase in the industrial share in large countries from $100 to $400 but contributes considerably less thereafter.
>
> The finished goods produced by these industries (roughly half their output) typically have income elasticities of 1.2–1.5. The early rise of this group is due to a considerable extent to import substitution, which is exhausted at fairly low income levels.
>
> The share of the middle group in total manufacturing does not vary much above the level of $200 per capita. . . .
>
> *Late Industries*: The late industries are those that continue to grow faster than GNP up to the highest income levels; they typically double their share of GNP in the later stages of industrialization (above $300). This group includes clothing, printing, basic metals, paper, and metal products. Taking an income of $300 as the half-way mark in the process of industrialization, the late industries account for 80 per cent of the subsequent increase in the share of industry in large countries.
>
> This group includes consumer goods with high income elasticities—durables, clothing, printing—as well as investment goods and the principal intermediate products used to produce them.[9]

Broadly speaking, Chenery and Taylor's "early industries" are similar to the typical leading sectors of take-off.[10] Their "middle industries" embrace capital-deepening sectors typical of the drive to technological maturity. Their "late industries," including consumers' durables (automobiles are subsumed in "metal products"), embrace the sectors whose rapid expansion characterizes the stage of high mass-consumption.

Given the broad industrial categories measured by Chenery and Taylor, their linkage to the leading sector complexes used here can only be rough and suggestive. But their analysis incorporates an important point: there are batches of technologies that tend to be absorbed at about the same time in the sequence of growth. A nation manufacturing for the first time its cotton textiles in substitution for imports is also likely to be absorbing a range of other relatively simple technologies; e.g., in food processing, shoe manufacture, and other light fabricated consumers' goods. In the contemporary world, as in the past, the absorption of wood and rubber fabrication and certain basic chemical processes is likely to come at about the same time and, I would add, to be accompanied by the emergence of a light engineering sector capable, for example, of

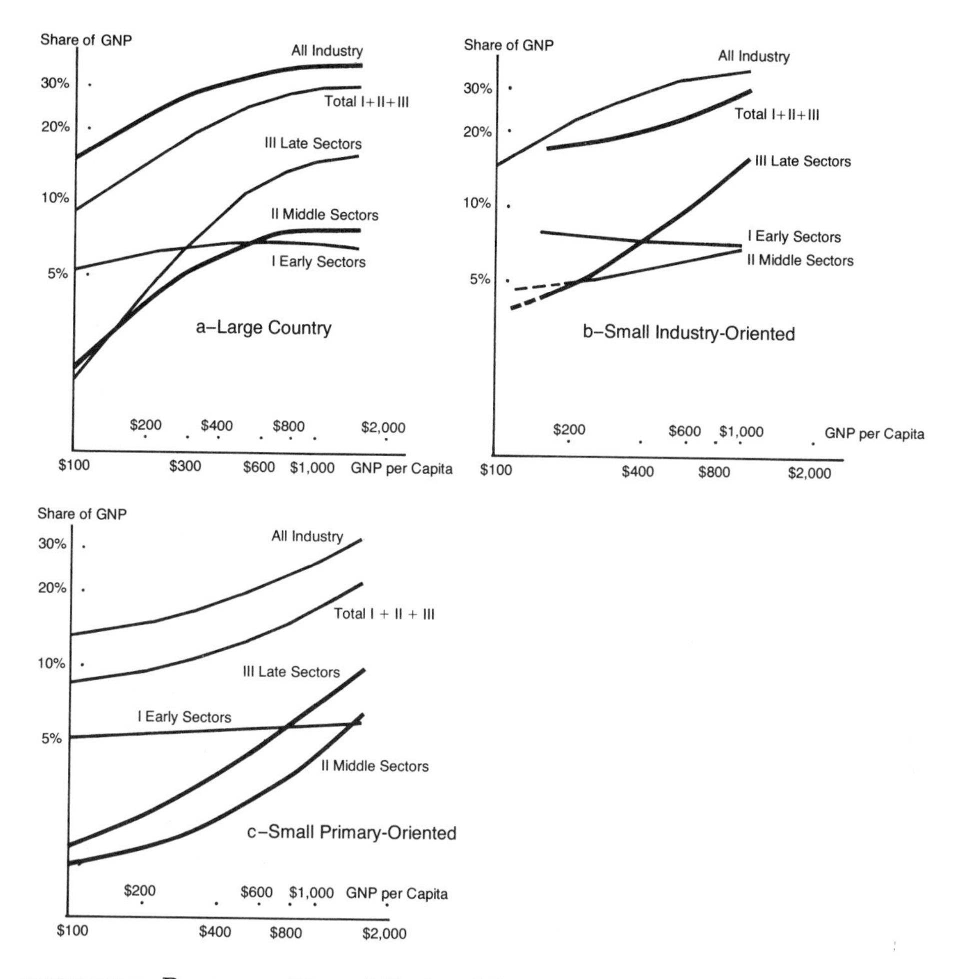

CHART V-1. *Decomposition of Sectoral Patterns*

Source: Hollis B. Chenery and Lance Taylor, "Development Patterns: Among Countries and over Time," p. 413.

manufacturing sewing machines and bicycles. Heavy engineering and advanced metal fabrication are likely to come at levels of income per capita when the automobile and durable consumers' goods begin to constitute a mass market and, I would add, to be accompanied by the emergence of a light electronics industry. As Chenery and Taylor's distinction among types of countries and the scale of domestic markets suggests (Chart V-1), there is no simple uniformity here; but the rough reality of "early," "middle," and "late" technologies emerges quite clearly.

Against this background, we turn to examine in a compressed and stylized way the patterns of growth of twenty national economies which entered take-off between the 1780's and the 1960's, using both conventional aggregate measures and sectoral data which symbolize the sequence of leading sector complexes. Nations which have not yet experienced sustained modern growth are excluded; but a good many which have experienced take-off have not been included. Those chosen are judged important either intrinsically because of their size or because their experience is representative of others. The countries covered contained as of 1976 about two-thirds of the world's population, perhaps 80 percent of global GNP. The aggregate data used are real income per capita; industrial production; and the proportion of income invested. The sectoral data are cotton consumption (or yarn or cloth production); railroads (miles or kilometers built); and pig iron, steel, electricity, and motor vehicle production. With respect to chemicals it is necessary to present several types, since the industry is extremely heterogeneous with respect to both technology and the determinants of demand. Petroleum refining and rubber manufacture are excluded because of their close connection with motor vehicle production and use. I have chosen sulphuric acid, with its wide range of industrial uses, to represent the older generation of chemicals; nitrogen, plastics, and synthetic fibers to capture movement in more modern subsectors of this industry. While each of these branches of the chemical industry is too small to be judged a leading sector complex, the chemical industry as a whole is, of course, a major component in economies which have moved beyond take-off. In these and other cases where particular sectors are not judged to have been full-scale leading sectors in growth, the time when their growth rates ceased to exceed that of industrial production as a whole is, nevertheless, indicated.

The data presented in the charts accompanying the text are five-year moving averages or rates of change in such averages.[11] A five-year moving average smooths inventory cycles and other short-term fluctuations but does not eliminate the longer (say, nine-year) business cycle. For our purposes it was judged a better device than, say, overlapping decadal averages, which wash out too much economic history.

I have tried to let the aggregate and sectoral data presented in these sketches tell as much of the story as possible. The brief texts are meant to indicate how the various national economies made their way into modern economic growth and to define certain special features of their subsequent experience. They are, in one sense, a minimum supplement to the charts, although the texts are also designed to convey the story to those for whom charts are a distraction rather than an aid.

Evidently, one great unfulfilled common task for analysts of growth is to combine and relate aggregative and sectoral methods of analysis. I believe progress in this direction is required not only for a better understanding of the past but also for the making of effective economic policy, now and for the future. I trust this section makes a constructive contribution to that objective.

28

Great Britain

Since Great Britain was the first country to experience an industrial revolution, its prior economic history has received a great deal of scholarly attention. But when I began to work on this book I found that the deceptively familiar story of how Britain managed to generate the first industrial revolution is neither simple nor agreed upon among historians and analysts of growth. Before I felt I had solved the puzzle reasonably well for myself, I found I had written a separate book, *How It All Began*. All we deal with under the headings of mercantilism, the commercial revolution, and the scientific revolution, between the fifteenth and eighteenth centuries, bears on the story, as well as the manner in which the religious conflicts of the period were resolved in the various European states. Moreover, this passage in the early modern history of Europe and the Atlantic is the matrix which prepared the way not only for the British take-off but also for those that followed. The preparation was quite direct in North America and Europe of the seventeenth and eighteenth centuries, more derivative in the regions beyond.

Narrowly, however, the surge of industrial expansion that began in Britain after 1783 was preceded by a set of prior economic developments that quite technically prepared the way:

—improvements in agricultural method which were not quite sufficient to permit Britain to remain a grain exporter, in the face of the population increase in the second half of the eighteenth century, but which did permit a growing and urbanizing population to be fed with a manageable level of grain imports;

—a marked acceleration in the scale of inventive effort, from the 1760's forward, including significant improvements in cotton textile manufacture, iron manufacture with coke as the fuel, and the efficiency of the steam engine—all critical for the British take-off;

—a wave of enterprise in canal and road building, which rendered Britain a more tightly knit and efficient national market;

—an environment of expanding international commerce which ultimately permitted Britain's precocious break-through in cotton textile manufacture to be translated promptly into an expansion in the scale of production far transcending the demands of the home market;

—an answering response in the American colonies in 1793, in the form of Eli Whitney's cotton gin, cheapening the price of an essential raw material.

The aggregate data (Chart V-2, parts 1 and 2) show the more than doubling in the rate of increase of total real output per capita that occurred during the initial phase of the British take-off (1783–1802).[12] The industrial production index exhibits a 1.0 percent average annual rate of growth from 1700 to 1783, 3.4 percent from 1783 to 1802. The sectoral data (Chart V-2, part 3) capture the extraordinary acceleration in the production of cotton textiles and the marked acceleration of pig iron output in those two critical decades. Related to both was the availability of Watt's improved steam engine.

It is generally agreed that the proportion of British national income invested rose during take-off; but the order of magnitude of the increase is still a matter for indecisive debate and further research.[13] The rate of capital formation almost certainly rose further at the peak of the railway age (say, 1830–1860).[14] Gross capital formation may have fluctuated in the range of 10–13 percent from 1860 to 1914 (Chart V-2, part 2). As we know from Part Three the relative scale of domestic and foreign investment varied significantly within these proportions. The interwar years saw a decline, the post-1945 years a recovery in the net capital formation rate. The proportion of investment resources required to maintain the British capital stock rose over the past century from, say, one-fifth to about one-half of gross investment. Thus, gross capital formation in fixed assets plus net foreign investment was about 10.2 percent in the 1860's, 15.6 percent in the 1950's.

The average annual rate of growth of total real output of GNP from 1780 to 1972 was about 1.2 percent (13 percent per decade), with variations in per capita rates per decade indicated in Table V-1.[15] The latter are also exhibited for shorter periods in Chart V-2, part 2.

The rather puzzling deceleration for the period 1831–1841 to 1861–1871 in Table V-1 resulted, as Chart V-2, part 2, shows, from the depth of the depression of the late 1830's and early 1840's and then from the damping effect of the American Civil War on the British cotton textile industry. The latter resumed expansion thereafter at a markedly reduced rate. British cotton consumption, which had been increasing at an average annual rate of about 4 percent over the previous twenty years, declined absolutely during the 1860's and reachieved its 1860 level in 1870. Its annual average growth rate over the subsequent decade was only 2.4 percent. This peaking out of what had been a major leading growth sector was certainly significant, given the scale it had attained in the economy. It oc-

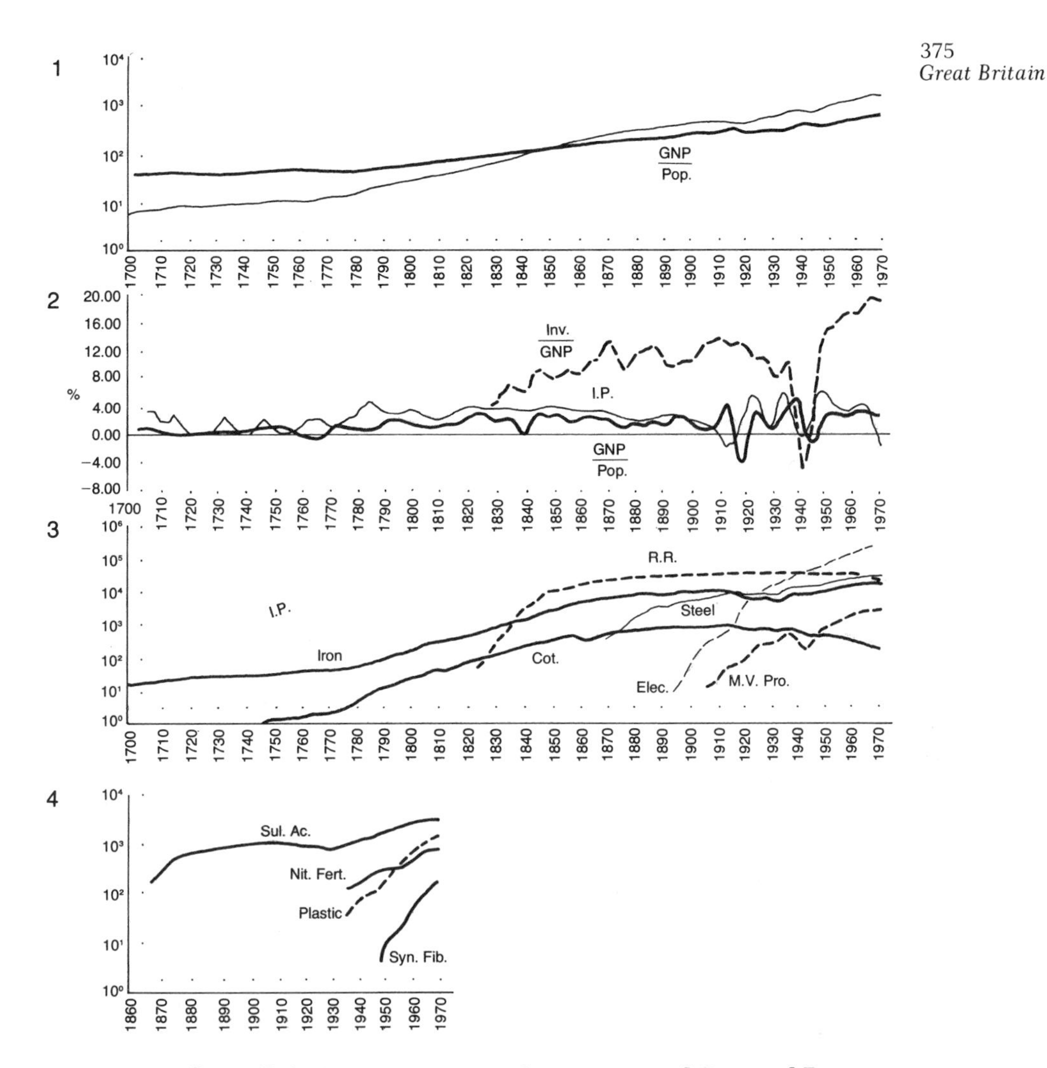

CHART V-2. *Great Britain, 1700–1972: Aggregate and Sectoral Data (Smoothed)*

1. GNP per capita ($\frac{\text{GNP}}{\text{Pop.}}$); industrial production index (I.P.).
2. Gross investment as % of GNP ($\frac{\text{Inv.}}{\text{GNP}}$); rate of change, GNP per capita ($\frac{\text{GNP}}{\text{Pop.}}$); rate of change, industrial production (I.P.).
3. Six major sectors: railroads (miles) (R.R.); raw cotton consumption (Cot.); production of iron (Iron); steel (Steel); electricity (Elec.); and motor vehicles (M.V. Pro.).
4. Production of four major chemicals: sulphuric acid (Sul. Ac.); nitrogen fertilizer (Nit. Fert.); plastics and resins (Plastic); and synthetic fibers (Syn. Fib.).

Sources: See Appendix D.

curred at a time of rapid decline in new mileage added to the British railroad net (see Chart V-3, part 3). The high rate of per capita increase in real product for the period 1861–1871 to 1891–1901 is a result of relatively falling import prices and favorable terms of trade rather than a surge in domestic production and productivity. Hoff-

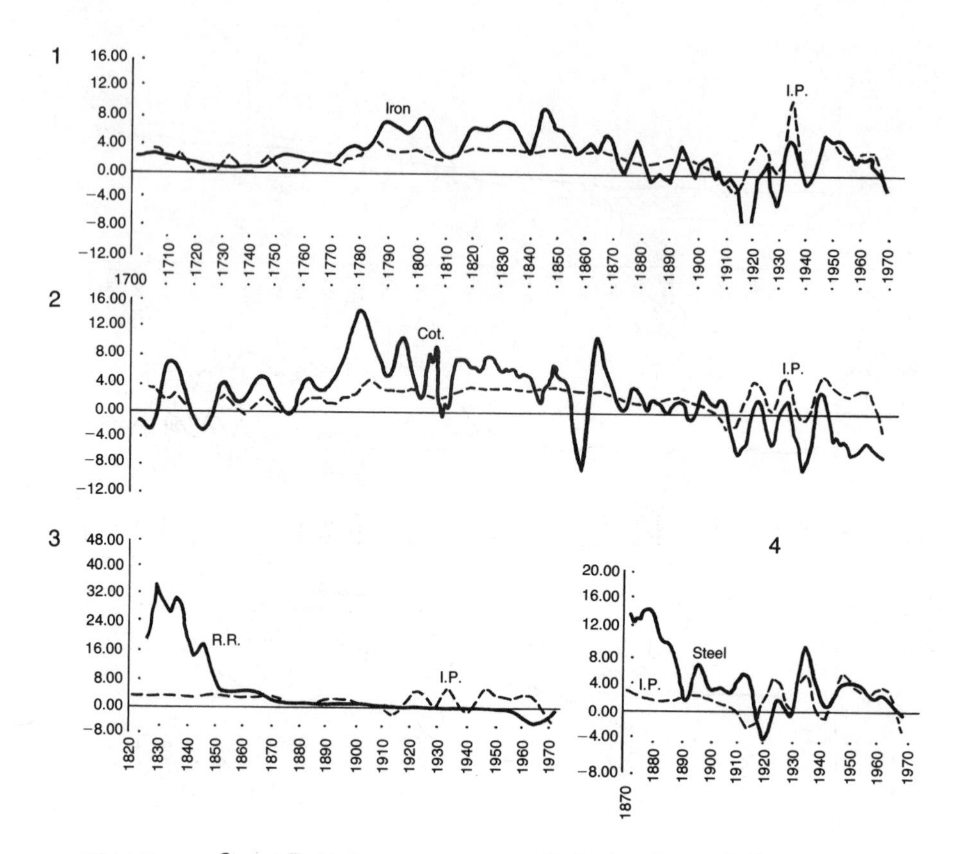

CHART V-3. *Great Britain, 1700–1972: Relative Growth Rates—Major Sectors and Industrial Production (Smoothed)*

1. Iron production (Iron).
2. Raw cotton consumption (Cot.).
3. Railroads (miles) (R.R.).
4. Steel production (Steel).

Sources: See Appendix D.

mann's index of industrial production (including building) moves as follows for these decades when measured between major cycle peaks (annual average percentage growth rates):

1802–1810	2.3
1810–1818	2.2
1818–1825	3.5
1825–1836	3.3
1836–1845	3.2
1845–1854	3.3
1854–1866	3.1
1866–1873	2.9
1873–1882	1.8
1882–1890	1.5

The acceleration after the Napoleonic Wars and the retardation from the 1870's emerge clearly.

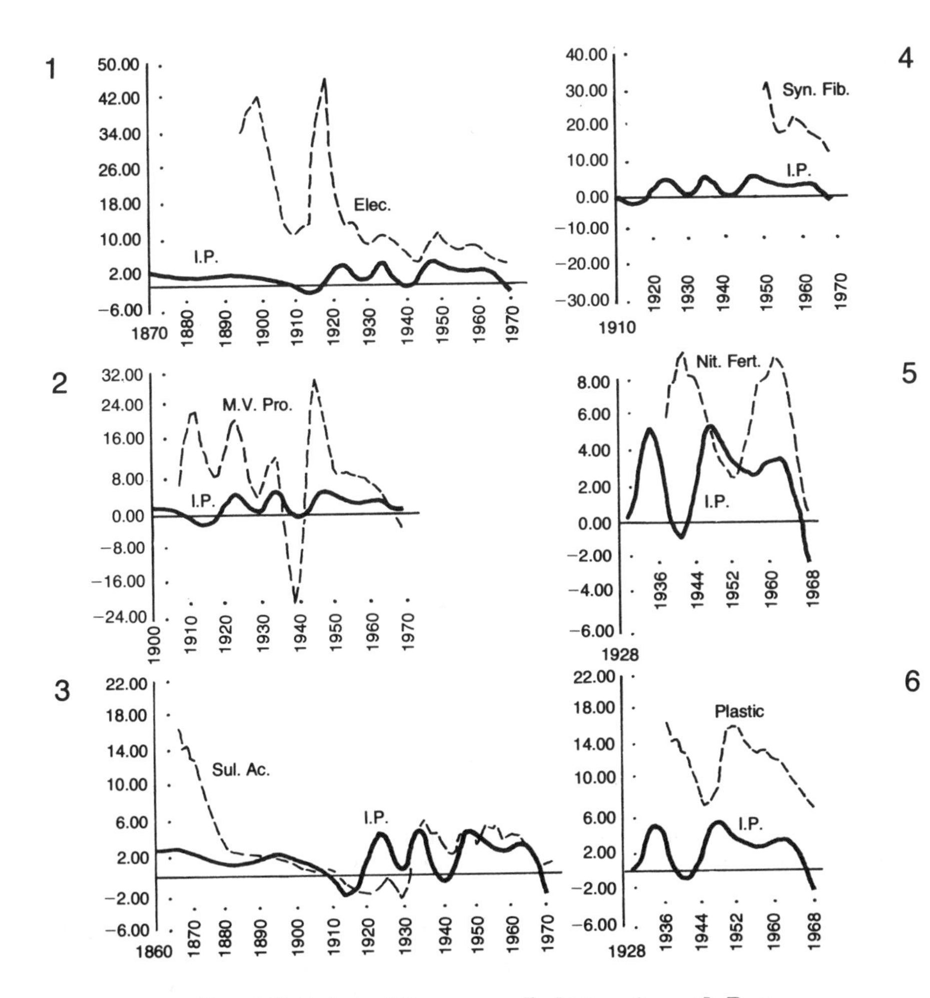

CHART V-4. *Great Britain, 1860–1972: Relative Growth Rates—Major Sectors and Industrial Production (Smoothed)*

1. Electricity (Elec.).
2. Motor vehicles (M.V. Pro.).
3. Sulphuric acid (Sul. Ac.).
4. Synthetic fibers (Syn. Fib.).
5. Nitrogen fertilizer (Nit. Fert.).
6. Plastics and resins (Plastic).

Sources: See Appendix D.

The other major features of Table V-1 are already familiar from Parts Three and Four: the deceleration in product per capita in the pre-1914 trend period; the limited recovery of the 1920's; the rather vigorous post-1931 lift from depression; the high post-1945 rate of growth, weakening in the course of the 1960's.

Turning now to the story of the major leading sectors, in Chart V-2, part 3, the outstanding features, of course, are two major characteristics of the process of growth: the inherently decelerating path of these sectors; and the fact that they proceed in a historical sequence, with new leading sectors emerging out of the interplay of

TABLE V-1. *Rates of Growth: Total Product, Population, and Product per Capita, Great Britain and United Kingdom, 1760–1967*

	Duration of Period (Years)	Rates of Growth per Decade (%)		
		Total Product	Population	Product per Capita
Great Britain				
1760–1770	10	7.2	—	0.8
1770–1780	10	2.7	—	−4.1
1780–1790	10	25.2	—	13.7
1790–1800	10	22.2	—	10.5
1801–1811 to 1831–1841	30	32.1	15.4	14.5
1831–1841 to 1861–1871	30	23.8	12.2	10.3
1861–1871 to 1891–1901	30	38.6	12.4	23.3
United Kingdom				
1885–1894 to 1905–1914[a]	20	23.8	11.1	11.4
1885–1894 to 1925–1929[a]	37.5	14.0	8.4	5.2
1925–1929 to 1950–1954	25	16.3	4.5	11.3
1950–1954 to 1963–1967	13	34.9	5.6	27.8

[a] Excluding Ireland.

Sources: 1760–1800, Phyllis Deane and W. A. Cole, *British Economic Growth, 1688–1959*, p. 78, note 1, indexes excluding government sector and adjusted; 1801–1967, Simon Kuznets, *Economic Growth of Nations: Total Output and Production Structure*, p. 38.

Note: Annual average rates of growth run slightly less than one-tenth of rates per decade. For example, a 10 percent rate of increase for a decade equals an annual average growth rate of 0.96 percent.

science, invention, and the requirements of the market as the older leading sectors decelerate.[16] This sequence is most widely spaced in the case of Britain, because it pioneered the early stages of technology in the industrial revolution. The British lead (vis-à-vis the United States, France, and Germany) was most substantial in cotton textiles; Britain also led substantially in pig iron; the lead narrowed with railroads. The age of steel came in virtually concurrently, as did electricity, motor vehicles, and the various modern chemicals, although, in the case of motor vehicles, the United States moved into the lead in the mass diffusion of the private automobile in the second decade of the twentieth century.[17]

The late-comers of the nineteenth century (e.g., Sweden, Japan, Italy, and Russia) could draw from the cumulative pool of technology created by those who had already moved into take-off. The late-comers of the twentieth century could draw from a still larger pool; but, as the data developed by Chenery and Taylor indicate, as well as the patterns of national growth we shall examine later in this part of the book, the imperatives of modernization and of the income elasticity of demand still, in most cases, decree a sequence of absorption which bears a family relation to those of the historical past; that is, cotton and other light consumers' goods precede steel and heavy engineering, while the manufacture of motor vehicles on

TABLE V-2. *Approximate Timing of Leading Sectors: Great Britain, 1783–1972*

Sector	Maximum Rate of Expansion	Estimated Time Sector Became Leading Sector	Estimated Time Sector Ceased to Lead	Comments
Cotton textiles	1780's	1780's	1860's	—
Pig iron	1790's	1780's	1880's	—
Railroads	1830's[a]	1830's	1870's	Marked slowdown in railway construction in 1850's, some revival in 1860's.
Steel	1870's[b]	1870's	1920's	—
Electricity	1900–1910	1900–1910	—	As in other advanced industrial countries, the high energy prices of the 1970's may bring electricity's role as a leading sector to a close.
Motor vehicles	1900–1910	1920–1929	1960's	—
Sulphuric acid	1870's	[c]	1890's	From 1890's sulphuric acid production fluctuated at rates approximating industrial index.
Nitrogen	1940's	[c]	—	—
Plastics and resins	1940's	[c]	—	—
Synthetic fibers	1920's	[c]	—	—

[a] Figures for mileage added in each decade are as follows: 1825–1830, 71; 1830–1840, 1,400; 1840–1850, 4,586; 1850–1860, 2,985; 1860–1870, 4,493; 1870–1880, 2,001; 1880–1890, 1,718.

[b] Estimate begins in 1871 with 329,000 tons. Maximum growth rate may have come earlier, at very low levels of production.

[c] Industry not on sufficient scale to be regarded, in itself, as a leading sector.

a substantial scale and durable consumers' goods in general, electronics, and the modern chemicals generally come still later.

Table V-2 shows the approximate timing of the absorption of the major leading sectors in Great Britain.

The periods of maximum rate of expansion emerge from a reasonably straightforward statistical calculation and can be seen in Charts V-3 and V-4, where sectoral growth rates are plotted against the overall rate of industrial growth. Similarly, the period when a sector is judged no longer a leading sector (or ceases to lead) is generally defined in statistical terms; that is, when the trend rate of growth in the sector approximates or falls below the trend rate of increase of industrial production as a whole. The estimate of when a rapidly growing sector becomes a leading sector is a more difficult matter. In concept a leading sector is defined as emerging in the period when it attains not merely a high rate of growth but a significant scale in the economy and when its ramified potential spreading effects are also being exploited within the economy.[18] If the sector involves a new product (not merely a new way of producing an existing product), the maximum rate of growth is likely to come in its first years, when output rises from zero. The scale of the sector may, therefore, be too small and its spreading effects too limited to justify designation as a leading sector. This would be the case, for example, if railroads were measured by the rate of increase in mileage in the second half of the 1820's, or if steel were measured before 1871. It is the case for motor vehicles as measured here in the period before, say, 1910. When, on the other hand, new technology transforms a substantial existing sector (e.g., cotton textiles and pig iron in the 1780's), it can be judged a leading sector when or even before it attains its maximum rate of growth. On balance, I would estimate the expansion of the British railways as sufficient in the 1830's to constitute a leading sector, even though the peak expansion in mileage came, of course, in the 1840's. But this is a marginal and debatable judgment.

As for spreading effects, they are not automatic. They represent the response of a society and its institutions to the pressures and possibilities set up by the bringing in of a new technology. For example, the initial response of China, India, and Argentina to the laying of large railway nets was, in my view, not sufficient to lift those economies into take-off, although the railroads had significant economic effects, notably in the commercialization of agriculture. For another example, Venezuela and Iran enjoyed the foreign-exchange benefits of their respective oil enclaves for some time before oil-generated resources were geared effectively to development programs suffusing the economies as a whole. And it was still later that their economies achieved the sophistication to exploit some of the other potential spreading effects; e.g., petrochemical production. Therefore, in conception, there must be both attainment of a sufficient scale in the sector itself (not merely a high rate of growth) and evidence that multiple spreading effects are, in fact, occurring, before a sectoral complex is designated as "leading."

If historical economic data were regularly organized in such ways as to capture not merely the scale of the leading sector in the economy (e.g., in terms of value added and/or proportion of the working force engaged) but also the scale of its backward and lateral linkages, we could reduce the problem from one of judgment, on the basis of imperfect quantitative and qualitative evidence, to one of straightforward, if arbitrary, measurement. This is precisely what we cannot do. Therefore, the judgment of when a rapidly growing sector becomes a leading sector is a matter of rough estimation. It yields, for example, with respect to take-off, the problem of the "preceding decade"; that is, should the French take-off be dated from the 1830's or the 1840's; the German, from the 1840's or the 1850's; the Russian, from the 1880's or the 1890's.[19] There are similar problems with the dating of other stages.

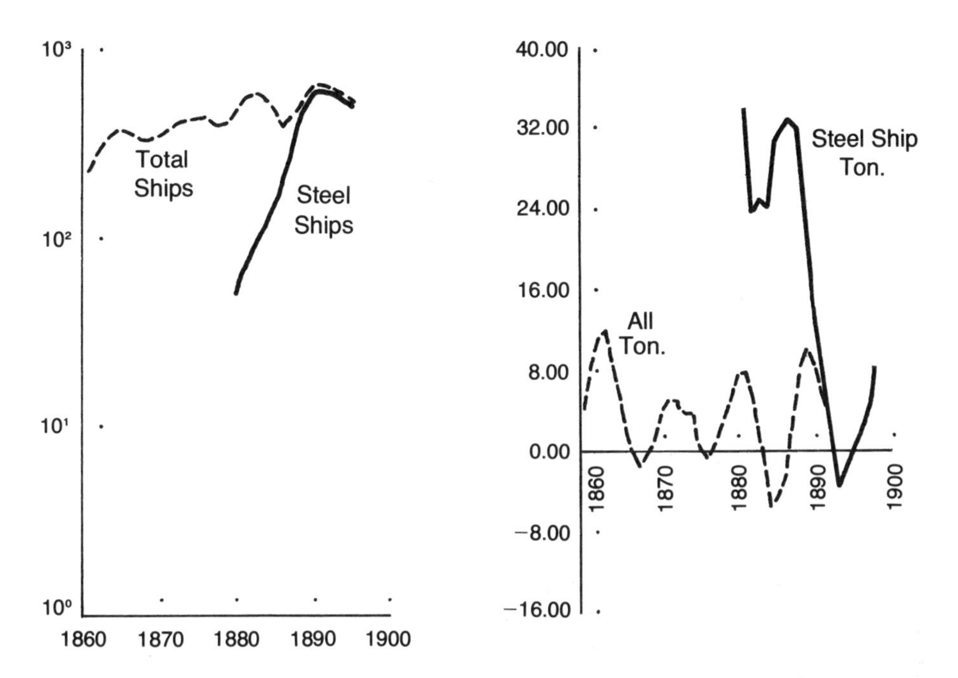

CHART V-5. *The Revolution in Steel Ships:* Left, *Total and Steel Tonnage, United Kingdom, 1860–1900;* Right, *Rates of Growth of Total and Steel Tonnage, United Kingdom, 1860–1900*

Sources: See Appendix D.

The British economy was characterized in the pre-1914 century by two features that justify special comment: shipbuilding and coal production.

Shipbuilding was, of course, a large sector throughout, given Britain's large proportionate role in world trade. Shipbuilding underwent, in effect, three technological revolutions: the transitions from sail to steam; from wood to iron; from iron to steel.[20] The surge of steamship building in the 1860's brought total tonnage close to that of sail. In the 1870's, steam came to predominate. In the 1860's, also, iron began to surpass wood in sailing tonnage, as it always had in steamships. In the 1880's, steel moved in to dominate ship construction. There was a surge of steel sailing as well as steam ships in the 1880's; but from the 1890's the sailing ship faded away. The transition to steel ships in the 1880's was a true leading sector for the period, cushioning the effects of the decline in British exports of rail and railway equipment and, at last, making the steamship efficient in long-distance haulage. This transition was thus a major result for Britain and the world of the steel revolution, along with the use of steel in railroads, construction, machine building, etc. (See Chart V-5.)

TABLE V-3. *Value of Coal Exports as a Percentage of Total Value of British Exports, 1830–1913 (Current Values)*

1830	0.5
1840	1.2
1850	1.8
1860	2.5
1870	2.8
1873	5.2
1880	3.7
1890	7.2
1900	13.3
1910	8.7
1913	10.2

Source: B. R. Mitchell, with the collaboration of Phyllis Deane, *Abstract of British Historical Statistics* (Cambridge: At the University Press, 1971), pp. 282–284 and 302–306.

As for coal, its availability in large quantities was a historic national asset with significant effects before the coming of the industrial revolution.[21] It was a major source of national economic strength throughout the period from 1783 to the present. It should also be noted, however, that coal gradually became a significant source of foreign exchange, as the railways and the steamship combined with an expanding global demand for energy to increase the role of coal sales in the total value of British exports (Table V-3). The figures for 1873 and 1900 suggest Britain's gain from the two "energy crises" of the period. The rate of increase in the volume of U.K. coal exports was consistently higher than the rate of increase in industrial production from the 1830's to the eve of the First World War. The increase in the role of coal exports, notably between 1880 and 1913, was fortunate for Britain. Its role as a raw-materials exporter cushioned the competitive pressures it faced in international markets in something like the way the American role as an agricultural (and also coal) exporter has cushioned its balance-of-payments position in recent years, as it faced Western European and Japanese competition.

I would now date the British stages of growth in a somewhat different way than I have in the past, linked more explicitly to the sequence of leading sector complexes. The problem of dating the British stages has always been dual: its precocious movement into sustained industrial growth on the basis of cotton textiles, with a vast export market, along with its pioneering of iron manufactured with coal and an efficient steam engine; the subsequent catching up in the new technologies by Western Europe and the United States, during the railway age, so that when steel came in during the 1870's the major industrial countries of the Atlantic world were roughly together, where (with uneven pace and timing) they have subsequently remained. In the past I have taken 1851, the date of the Crystal Palace Exposition, as a symbolic benchmark for British arrival at technological maturity. And, indeed, by that time Britain had pretty well worked through the first round of modern technologies: the rate of increase in cotton textiles was beginning to come down toward the average rate of industrial growth; the great railway boom of the 1840's represented the mature fruition of iron and steam.

The problem posed by this dating is that France, Germany, and the United States, whose take-offs came later than Britain's and were based primarily on the railroads and related technology, arrived at technological maturity, by my initial definition, in the period 1900–1910, at which time their leading sector patterns were, broadly, similar to Britain's.

The most straightforward way to deal with Britain's early start and the later catching up of the others is to present the British drive to technological maturity in two phases: the first embracing the railroad age (say, 1830–1870); the second, steel and all its works (say, 1870–1910). What is unique about the British case then stands out clearly; that is, its early and unique movement into take-off on the basis of cotton textiles; for, while Britain did move into railways somewhat ahead of France and Germany, by and large the railway age was a concurrent phenomenon in Western Europe and the United States, bringing a sustained modern economic growth which Britain had already attained on the basis of its initial lead and the scale of its export markets in factory-manufactured cotton textiles.

I would, therefore, set out the British stages of growth as follows.

Take-off:

1783–1830. The initial surge of 1783–1802; then a phase of deceleration down to 1815; with the cotton textile revolution brought to fruition during the 1820's.

Drive to Technological Maturity, Phase 1:

1830–1870. The railway age, during the first two decades of which cotton textiles remained still a leading sector, while the railroads moved toward a central role in the economy in the 1840's.

Drive to Technological Maturity, Phase 2:

1870–1913. Steel, including a special role for steel ships, as well as the early phase of electricity, motor vehicles, and modern chemicals.

High Mass-Consumption:

1920–. Leading sectors of high mass-consumption (automobiles, durable consumers' goods, electricity, plastics, synthetic fibers, etc.) moving forward rather weakly during the interwar years, rapidly in the post–World War II generation, accompanied by sharply increased relative outlays for education and medical care. The British deceleration of the late 1960's is more marked than for most of the other major industrial economies, and the subsequent impact of the price revolution of 1972–1977 more acute.

29

The United States

The preconditions for American industrialization lay in the kinds of men and women who began to move across the Atlantic in the seventeenth century. They were drawn in goodly proportion from the Nonconformists who played a disproportionate role in generating the interaction among scientists, inventors, and innovators which ultimately yielded the industrial revolution in Britain; and those who were of the Church of England found themselves in a setting quite different from the established society they had left. Some fifteen citizens of the North American colonies became members of the Royal Society, among them Cotton Mather and Benjamin Franklin. Increase Mather led a group that set up as early as 1683 a short-lived American counterpart, the Boston Philosophical Society. Franklin's Junto, formed in 1727, directly led on to the setting up in Philadelphia of the American Philosophical Society sixteen years later, "for Promoting Useful Knowledge among the British Plantations in America." And Boston responded competitively in 1780 with the American Academy of Arts and Sciences, looking rather more to the model in Paris.[22] There was no lack of modernizing ferment in colonial America; and, as Thomas Jefferson's scientific and gadgeteering bent suggests, it was not confined to the North. This ferment occurred within an economy with a lively commercial and banking sector and an agriculture particularly oriented to foreign as well as domestic markets.

But the economic potentialities and constraints of American resources and geography postponed the generation of an American industrial revolution for some time: comparative advantage lay strongly in the production of agricultural products and raw materials, and there were massive transport problems to be overcome before an effective national market could be created.

As we have already seen in Part Three, industrialization came to the United States against a background of territorial and agricultural expansion, interwoven with price and other impulses from the international economy. These gave the first seven decades of national life a particular cast. In the end—with the expanded international demand for American wheat and the related attractiveness of extending the railway lines to the West—the impulses for agricultural and industrial expansion fully converged. But before the 1850's there was a kind of alternating rhythm between extensive agricultural expansion and industrialization, both contributing to increases in output, both requiring relatively high levels of investment.

The key phases of industrialization have for long been familiar:

—the mainly abortive efforts during the years of embargo and war (say, 1807–1815);

—the sturdy expansion centered around textiles in New England launched after 1816;

—the wider-based industrialization of the 1840's and 1850's, centered in the 1840's on the railroadization of the East, in the 1850's on the railroadization of the Midwest, accompanied by heavy-industry expansion.[23]

In a kind of counterpoint, however, there were phases when the expansion of agricultural acreage, production, and exports was more nearly at the center of American enterprise. Thus:

—the export boom of the 1790's (which survived the vicissitudes of the Peace of Amiens and continued to 1806), frustrating Alexander Hamilton's desire to launch America promptly into industrialization;

—the brief postwar export boom (to 1817), accompanied by a surge of movement into new land beyond the Appalachians and in the Southeast;

—the massive westward expansion of cotton land and production of the 1830's, accompanied also by the expansion of land and infrastructure in the Midwest, supported by heavy capital imports;

—the great agricultural (as well as industrial) expansion of the 1850's.

The coming of industrialization to the United States poses sharply a problem to be observed in a good many other nations down to contemporary China, India, and Brazil; that is, the uneven regional pace of modernization within national societies. The problem existed and exists even within smaller national units; e.g., Britain, France, Germany, Italy. As we know, growth proceeds forward by sectors whose spreading effects suffuse the national market structure; but the various regions are unequally affected. Especially in early stages of growth, some may be only slightly affected and left as quasi-traditional backwaters while growth proceeds rapidly in regional industrial enclaves.[24]

In the United States the issue first arises with respect to the surge of cotton textile production in New England, after the severe postwar setback in 1816. As Robert Brooke Zevin's figures indicate (see above, p. 138, and Table N-11), the industry expanded without a year of absolute decline from 1816 to 1842. In 1816 some 5,000 people were employed in large-scale manufacturing enterprises in New England, slightly more than 1 percent of the working force; in 1840, about 100,000, one-seventh of the working force.[25] Annual

TABLE V-4. *Rate of Growth of Proportion of Urban Population to Total Population: New England and the Middle Atlantic, 1790–1860 (%)*

	1790–1800	1800–1810	1810–1820	1820–183(
New England	0.68	1.87	0.44	3.47
Middle Atlantic	1.51	1.27	−0.18	2.95
United States	0.94	1.19	−0.07	1.57

Source: Jeffrey G. Williamson, "Urbanization in the American Northeast, 1820–1870 Chapter 32 in Robert W. Fogel and Stanley L. Engerman (eds.), *The Reinterpretation* *American Economic History*, p. 429. Originally published in *Journal of Economic Histor* December 1965.

average growth rates in New England cotton cloth production decelerated from very high levels down to 1833, then fluctuated about high but more conventional rates (Chart V-7, part 2).

The rise of the cotton textile industry in New England had all the familiar spreading effects, including an accelerated rate of urbanization, as Table V-4 reveals. The surge of urbanization in New England at rates far above the national average (strengthened in the 1840's by the flow of Irish immigrants) emerges clearly, as does that of the Middle Atlantic states in the 1840's, when railroadization and accelerated industrialization came to the whole Northeast. In interpreting pre-1860 American economic history in terms of stages of economic growth, I have chosen to regard the industrialization of New England as a regional take-off and dated the national take-off from the 1840's and 1850's, when the railroads definitively solved the problem of creating an efficient national market, although the canals, turnpikes, and steamboats on the rivers had earlier contributed significantly to improving the market linkages.

The issue of regionalism also arises, of course, with respect to the antebellum South. This book is not an appropriate place to add to the voluminous debate on the economics, sociology, and psychology of slavery and on the life of human beings in a society dominated by the production of cotton with slave labor.[26] There is no doubt that the comparative advantage of the South lay in cotton production in the pre-1860 world economy; and, like plantation production of a commercial crop at many times and places, it was profitable. One can argue, as do Robert William Fogel and Stanley L. Engerman, that income per capita in the South, while lower than in the North, was relatively high; and that it was expanding quite respectably between 1840 and 1860 when compared to that of other countries in the world.[27] The South also had acquired a considerable railway net and a modest industrial base. The comparison is particularly favorable with countries which had not yet entered take-off. The same argument can be made for other pre–take-off nations well endowed with land, climate, and world markets; e.g., pre-1896 Canada, pre-1901 Australia, pre-1914 Argentina. But income per capita is an insufficient measure of a society's degree of modernization or stage of growth. Specifically, this line of thought does not capture fully the

30–1840	1840–1850	1850–1860
0	9.34	7.87
5	7.41	9.88
5	4.47	4.49

long-term limits to the expansion in income imposed by excessive reliance on a single high-value crop and the structural transformation required before diversified industrialization can get under way at high momentum. Like the American South, a good many nations, notably in Latin America, have had difficulty with that transition, in part because of the heritage left by a protracted period when economic life was focused on the production and export of one or a few export commodities. Put another way, there is a great difference between attaining reasonably high levels of income per capita, through favorable resource endowments, and modernizing a society in ways which permit regular and efficient absorption of the new technologies required for sustained growth. Fogel and Engerman's preliminary conclusion makes *prima facie* sense: ". . . slavery both retarded industrialization and increased per capita income [for the South as a whole]."[28] What they fail to add is that the full complex heritage of slavery—with its consequences for whites as well as blacks—continued to retard the industrialization of the South long after Appomattox; and that among the long-run costs of building a society around a single crop are the suggestive figures of the educational level for whites, by regions, for 1861 given in Table V-5. As Albert

TABLE V-5. *Educational Level, Public Facilities: United States, by Regions, 1861*

Region	Enrollment Rate (%) (1)	Average Daily Attendance Rate (%) (2)	Average Length of School (Days) (3)	Number of Days of School per White Person, 5–19[a] (4)
New England	62.8	74.9	135	63.5
Middle Atlantic	61.4	53.0	157	51.1
North Central	75.9	56.7	116	49.9
South	29.5	45.0	80	10.6
U.S. Total	57.4	56.2	124	40.0

[a] Column 1 times column 2 times column 3.

Source: Albert Fishlow, "The American Common School Revival: Fact or Fancy?" in Henry Rosovsky (ed.), *Industrialization in Two Systems: Essays in Honor of Alexander Gerschenkron by a Group of His Students*, p. 62.

Fishlow makes clear, the detailed data do not justify a simple inverse correlation between the relative prevalence of slavery, state by state, and the educational level of the white population.[29] The connection between the acceptance of slavery and the relative lower priority for education in the South is complex; but a connection there must certainly be.

I would conclude that the South's long delay in moving from relative prosperity, as the slave-based Cotton Kingdom, to diversified self-sustained growth must take into account the inherently difficult transition from a single-crop economy to full modernization; the specific heritage of slavery, its ending by defeat in war, Reconstruction and its aftermath, including the distortions of southern political life imposed by the intent to maintain Jim Crow; the social as well as economic advantages of the North attained before 1860, reinforced after 1865 by its relative resource endowments in the age of steel; and the weakness of the cotton price down to 1898. The widening of the North-South gap in income per capita ceased at about that time; but the Sunbelt only moved forward strongly to narrow the gap from about the mid-1930's, as it acquired belatedly a sophisticated industrial base and a high-productivity agriculture.

Looking at the sweep of American growth as a whole, the aggregate data (Chart V-6, parts 1 and 2) move forward at steeper slopes than those for Britain, as one would expect, given the higher rate of population increase. Kuznets' calculations of decadal per capita increases in national product for the nineteenth century fall, broadly, in a range similar to those for Britain; but, excepting the 1950's and 1960's, the British rates are lower in the twentieth century (Table V-6). And, as we shall see, other nations, coming later into take-off, have sustained higher rates of per capita growth than either Britain or the United States. What is unique about the economic history of the United States is not its average rate of increase in product per capita but that it managed to sustain, down to the early 1970's, its

TABLE V-6. *Rates of Growth: Total Product, Population, and Product per Capita, United States, 1800–1967; Product per Capita, United Kingdom, 1800–1967*

	Duration of Period (Years)	Rates of Growth per Decade (%)			
		Total Product, U.S.	Population, U.S.	Product per Capita, U.S.	Product per Capita, U.K.
1800 to 1840	40	52.3	34.1	13.5	14.5
1839 to 1859	20	59.1	35.7	17.3	10.3
1834–1843 to 1868–1878	35	49.7	31.5	13.9	10.3
1869–1878 to 1889–1898	20	50.0	24.7	20.3	23.3
1885–1894 to 1905–1914	20	44.7	20.5	20.1	11.4
1900–1909 to 1925–1929	22.5	36.7	17.4	16.5	5.2
1925–1929 to 1950–1954	25	33.2	11.8	19.2	11.3
1950–1954 to 1963–1967	13	42.1	17.6	20.8	27.8

Source: Kuznets, *Economic Growth of Nations*, p. 40.

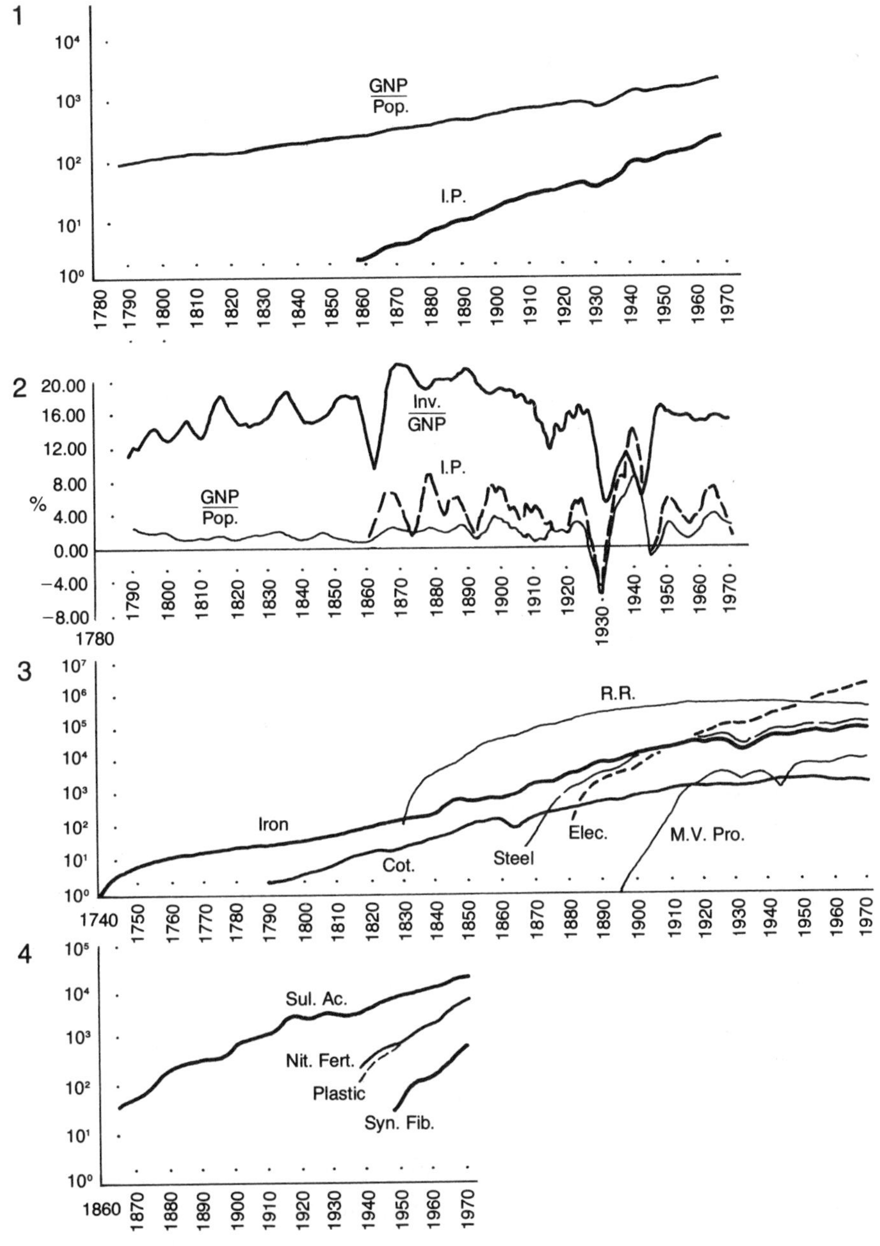

CHART V-6. *United States, 1740–1972: Aggregate and Sectoral Data (Smoothed)*

1. GNP per capita ($\frac{\text{GNP}}{\text{Pop.}}$); industrial production index (I.P.).
2. Gross investment as % of GNP ($\frac{\text{Inv.}}{\text{GNP}}$); rate of change, GNP per capita ($\frac{\text{GNP}}{\text{Pop.}}$); rate of change, industrial production (I.P.).
3. Six major sectors: railroads (miles) (R.R.); raw cotton consumption (Cot.); production of iron (Iron); steel (Steel); electricity (Elec.); and motor vehicles (M.V. Pro.).
4. Production of four major chemicals: sulphuric acid (Sul. Ac.); nitrogen fertilizer (Nit. Fert.); plastics and resins (Plastic); and synthetic fibers (Syn. Fib.).

Sources: See Appendix D.

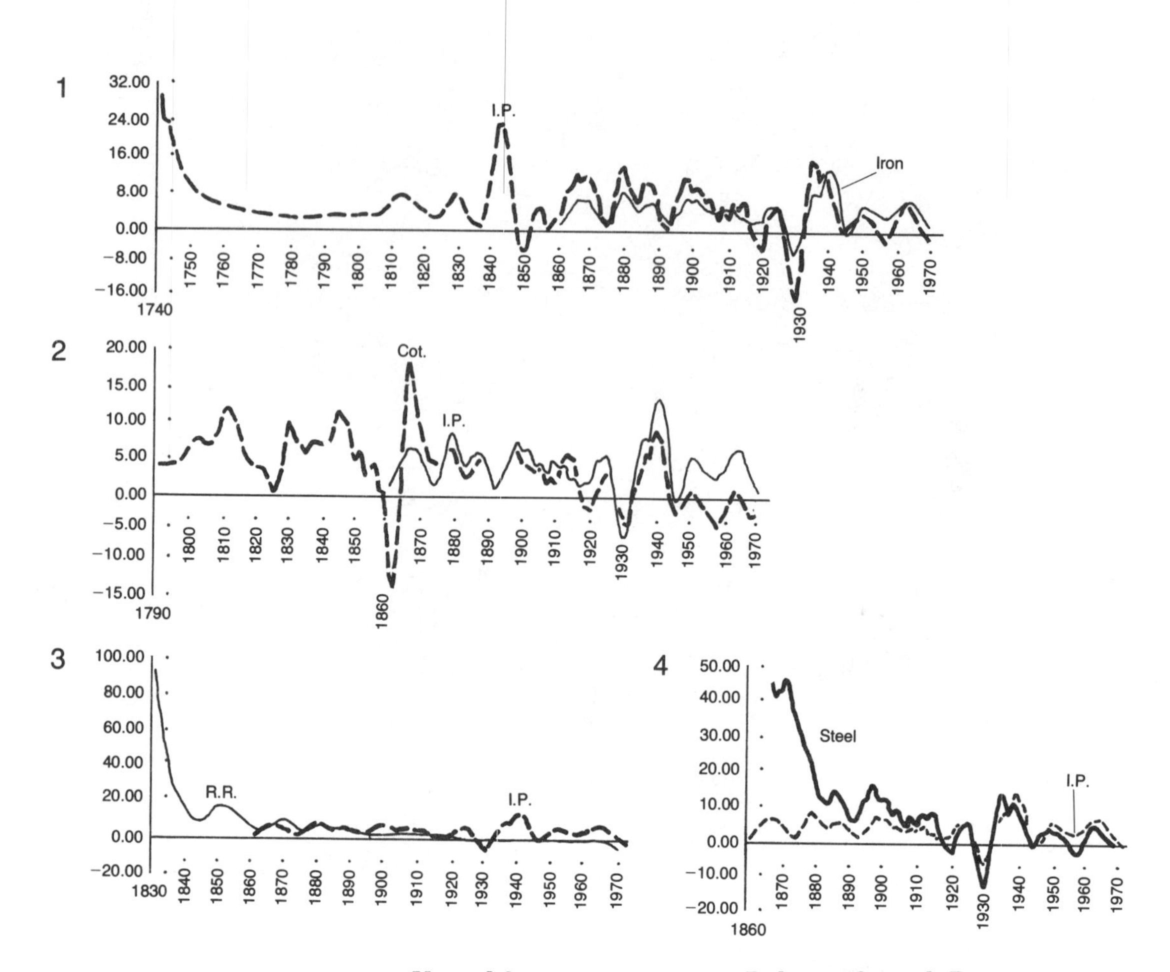

CHART V-7. *United States, 1740–1972: Relative Growth Rates—Major Sectors and Industrial Production (Smoothed)*

1. Iron production (Iron).
2. Raw cotton consumption (Cot.).
3. Railroads (miles) (R.R.).
4. Steel production (Steel).

Sources: See Appendix D.

initial advantage in product per capita, while absorbing for much of the period a large flow of immigration and opening up a continent, a process which made it both affluent for the individual and the largest national economic unit in the world economy.

Pre-1839 American national product is difficult to calculate by conventional methods. An imaginative effort to do so on an annual basis has been made by Thomas S. Berry, bringing to bear rates of change in a variety of economic series related to the course of real product.[30] His calculations are used for GNP per capita and the proportion of GNP invested in Chart V-6, parts 1 and 2.

By all accounts and estimates, the American national product rose sharply in the 1790's, responding to the high prices of the country's agricultural products and its large profits in foreign trade. From

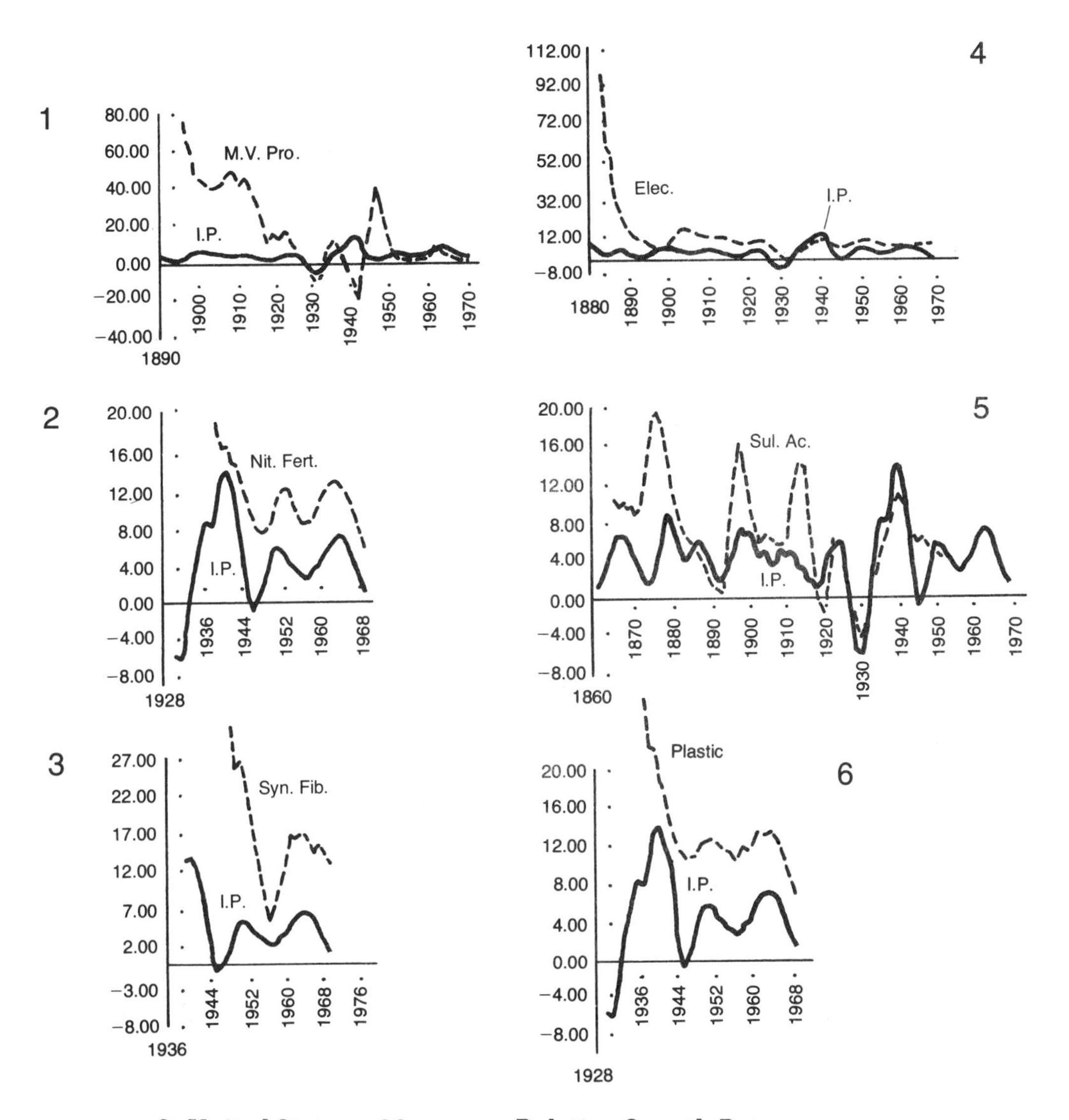

CHART V-8. *United States, 1860–1972: Relative Growth Rates—Major Sectors and Industrial Production (Smoothed)*

1. Motor vehicles (M.V. Pro.).
2. Nitrogen fertilizer (Nit. Fert.).
3. Synthetic fibers (Syn. Fib.).
4. Electricity (Elec.).
5. Sulphuric acid (Sul. Ac.).
6. Plastics and resins (Plastic).

Sources: See Appendix D.

1789 to 1802, per capita product may have increased at an annual average rate of about 2 percent (24 percent per decade), a rate not exceeded until after the Civil War.[31] This phase of expansion continued at perhaps half that rate down to about 1806, after which the period of trade obstruction and war began. Industrialization in New

England in the 1820's and the agricultural boom of the first half of the 1830's yielded a second major surge in overall per capita growth. There was a severe setback from 1839 down to about 1843, a period of relative industrial stagnation, accompanied by low agricultural prices. But the average rate of real growth from 1843 to 1860 was high, with industry radically increasing its share in national product in the 1840's, the period I would identify as the first decade of the national take-off. The increase in the share of value added by industry, as compared to agriculture, between 1839 and 1849, from 22 percent to 36 percent in constant prices, is by far the largest relative shift in the structure of the American economy between 1839 and 1949.[32] Agriculture as well as industry expanded rapidly in the 1850's.

Real product per capita was, of course, hard hit by the Civil War; but a high rate of growth was resumed in the following two decades. The severe depression of the 1890's gave way to a strong recovery and then a phase of retardation in the decade before the First World War. The boom of the 1920's, the Great Depression, the wartime recovery, and high postwar rates of growth have all left their mark on these figures.[33]

Conventionally measured, gross investment (excluding inventories) rises from 9 percent to 14 percent of GNP measured from 1834–1843 to 1849–1858. Berry's comparable figures (17 percent and 18 percent) appear too high; but, given the role of agricultural investment at this time, in an economy rapidly expanding its acreage, one cannot be certain.[34] In all estimates, a higher investment ratio emerges after the Civil War (above 20 percent). On the basis of the experience of other nations, I would associate this shift with the massive scale of post–Civil War railroadization, although other interpretations have been offered.[35] The gross investment rate declines in the twentieth century, the net ratio still more sharply with the rise in depreciation allocations required to maintain an enlarged capital stock.

Chart V-6, parts 3 and 4, presents the sequence of leading sectors; Charts V-7 and V-8, the relation between their respective growth rates and the average rate of industrial growth. Table V-7 shows the approximate timing of the movement of the leading sectors.

The American stages of growth emerge, then, as follows.

New England Regional Take-off:

1815–1850. Cotton textiles.

Take-off of American North:

1843–1870. Railroadization, heavy industry, and continental expansion.

Drive to Technological Maturity:

1870–1910. Steel, early stage of electricity, etc.

High Mass-Consumption:

1910–. Interrupted by depression of 1930's and Second World

TABLE V-7. *Approximate Timing of Leading Sectors: United States, 1790–1972*

Sector	Maximum Rate of Expansion	Estimated Time Sector Became Leading Sector	Estimated Time Sector Ceased to Lead	Comments
Cotton textiles	1805–1815	1820's	1870's	—
Pig iron	1840's	1840's	1910–1920	—
Railroads	1830's	1830's	1890's	—
Steel	1870's	1870's	1920's	—
Electricity	1880's	1900–1910	—	—
Motor vehicles	1900–1910	1910–1920	1950's	Production set back severely in 1930's, even relative to industrial index.
Sulphuric acid	1870's	[a]	1920's	—
Nitrogen	1940's	[a]	—	—
Plastics	1940–1945	[a]	—	—
Synthetic fibers	1950–1955	[a]	—	—

[a] Not judged, by itself, a leading sector.

War, with rapidly increased outlays on education and health care, electronics, aerospace, and travel compensating in the 1960's for deceleration of automobile sectoral complex in the 1950's.

30

France

The preconditions for the French take-off, which I date from the 1830's, lay, of course, in the forces that germinated within Europe from the fifteenth century forward, which laid the basis also for the first stage of modern growth in Britain and elsewhere in the West.[36] In the seventeenth century, Britain and France lagged behind the Dutch Republic in commerce, shipping, and financial virtuosity; both made up ground, the British earlier than the French. Under Colbert's leadership, the French made considerable industrial and commercial progress from 1665 to 1685. The period of war that then followed set France back more severely than Britain until the end of the War of the Spanish Succession. From about 1715 to 1783, France gained relative to Britain; but it did not match the British after 1760 in generating new technologies and, especially, in bringing them efficiently into the economy. There was progress, notably in cotton textiles, but not on the scale achieved by the British. The French Revolution and the Revolutionary Wars set France back in the 1790's, when the British continued to forge ahead, achieving a virtual monopoly in international commerce and maintaining extraordinary momentum in cotton textiles, as well as in iron production and the diffusion of the steam engine. Between 1800 and 1812, the French economy recovered and expanded, under the aegis of Napoleon, exploiting after 1806 the British difficulties in exporting manufactured goods to the Continent. But, when the wars ended, the British lead over France was greater than it had been a generation earlier.

Jan Marczewski estimates that French industrial output increased at an average annual rate of just under 2 percent from the mid-1780's to the average for the best Napoleonic years (1803–1812).[37] The equivalent British figure, from Hoffmann's index, is 3 percent. But these aggregate measures do not catch the critical point: the British lead in cotton textiles in international markets was so well established by 1815 that subsequent French expansion, which was considerable, had to proceed mainly on the basis of the domestic market; and the scale of the industry in France did not, in my view, generate the spreading effects sufficient to bring the French economy as a whole into take-off. Britain led also in the coke-based production of iron and in the diffusion of steam power. As of 1840 Britain had installed some 620,000 horsepower in steam; France, 90,000.

Turning to the aggregate measures of French growth, there is a certain drama in the British-French comparison. As of 1973, French per capita gross domestic product was 37 percent higher than British —a figure distorted by international monetary factors and other measurement problems, but reflecting some real differential.[38]

Long-term comparisons of real national income are beset with difficulties of conception as well as uncertainty about the quality of the data. The first such estimate, made by Gregory King toward the close of the seventeenth century, put French per capita income 22 percent below that of England.[39] The gap may have been somewhat narrowed down to 1783, with the rapid French recovery from about 1720. In the decade after 1783, both nations progressed, Britain more rapidly; but the gap widened during the war years and down to the beginning of the French take-off in the 1830's. Then the two nations seesawed: France moved ahead faster down to about 1870; slower to the mid-1890's; more rapidly in the pre-1914 generation and in the recovery of the 1920's. Britain did somewhat better in the 1930's and, of course, suffered less in the Second World War. In the 1950's and 1960's, however, superior French economic management opened a substantial gap between the two economies. As a matter of long-term trend, the gap began to narrow significantly with the coming of the technologies of electricity, the internal combustion engine, and modern chemicals (from, say, the 1890's), when French resource deficiencies in coal and iron, relative to Britain and Germany, diminished in importance.

The French aggregate data exhibit these significant phases of acceleration and retardation, as the Kuznets calculations suggest (Table V-8; for more detail, Chart V-9, parts 1 and 2). Comparable British data are included in Table V-8 for purposes of comparison;

TABLE V-8. *Rates of Growth: Total Product, Population, and Product per Capita, France, 1831–1966; Product per Capita, United Kingdom, 1831–1966*

	Duration of Period (Years)	Rates of Growth per Decade (%)			
		Total Product, France	Population, France	Product per Capita, France	Product per Capita, U.K.
1831–1840 to 1861–1870	30	26.3	3.9	21.6	10.3
1861–1870 to 1891–1900	30	15.7	1.9	13.5	23.3
1896 to 1929	33	18.4	2.0	16.1	5.2
1929 to 1950–1954	23	11.5	1.3	10.0	11.3
1950–1954 to 1963–1966	12.5	61.0	11.7	44.1	27.8

Source: Kuznets, *Economic Growth of Nations*, p. 38.

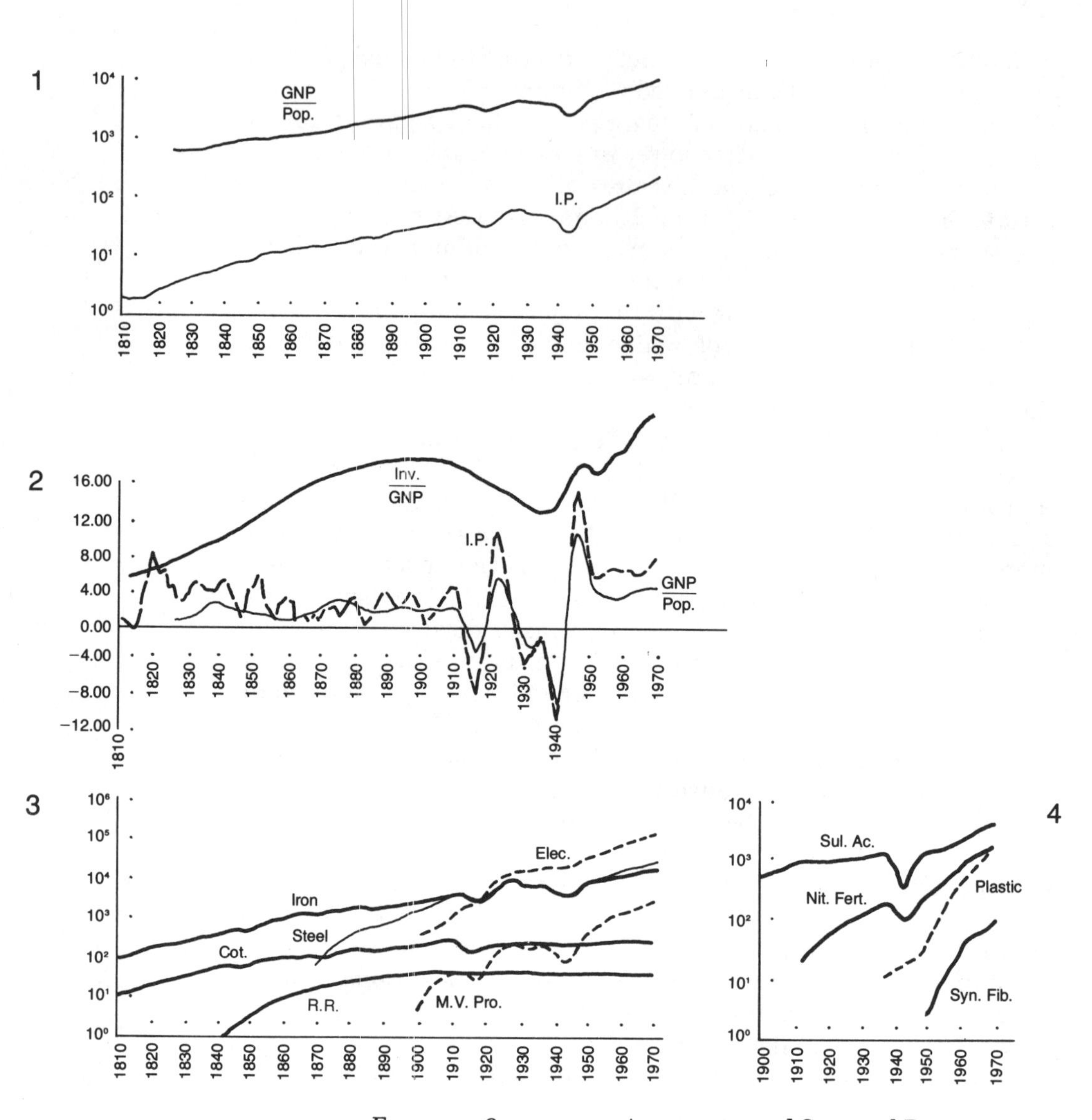

CHART V-9. *France, 1810–1972: Aggregate and Sectoral Data (Smoothed)*

1. GNP per capita ($\frac{\text{GNP}}{\text{Pop.}}$); industrial production index (I.P.).

2. Gross investment as % of GNP ($\frac{\text{Inv.}}{\text{GNP}}$); rate of change, GNP per capita ($\frac{\text{GNP}}{\text{Pop.}}$); rate of change, industrial production (I.P.).

3. Six major sectors: railroads (kilometers) (R.R.); raw cotton consumption (Cot.); production of iron (Iron); steel (Steel); electricity (Elec.); and motor vehicles (M.V. Pro.).

4. Production of four major chemicals: sulphuric acid (Sul. Ac.); nitrogen fertilizer (Nit. Fert.); plastics and resins (Plastic); and synthetic fibers (Syn. Fib.).

Sources: See Appendix D.

they exhibit clearly the phases when one or the other economy gained or lost ground relative to the other.

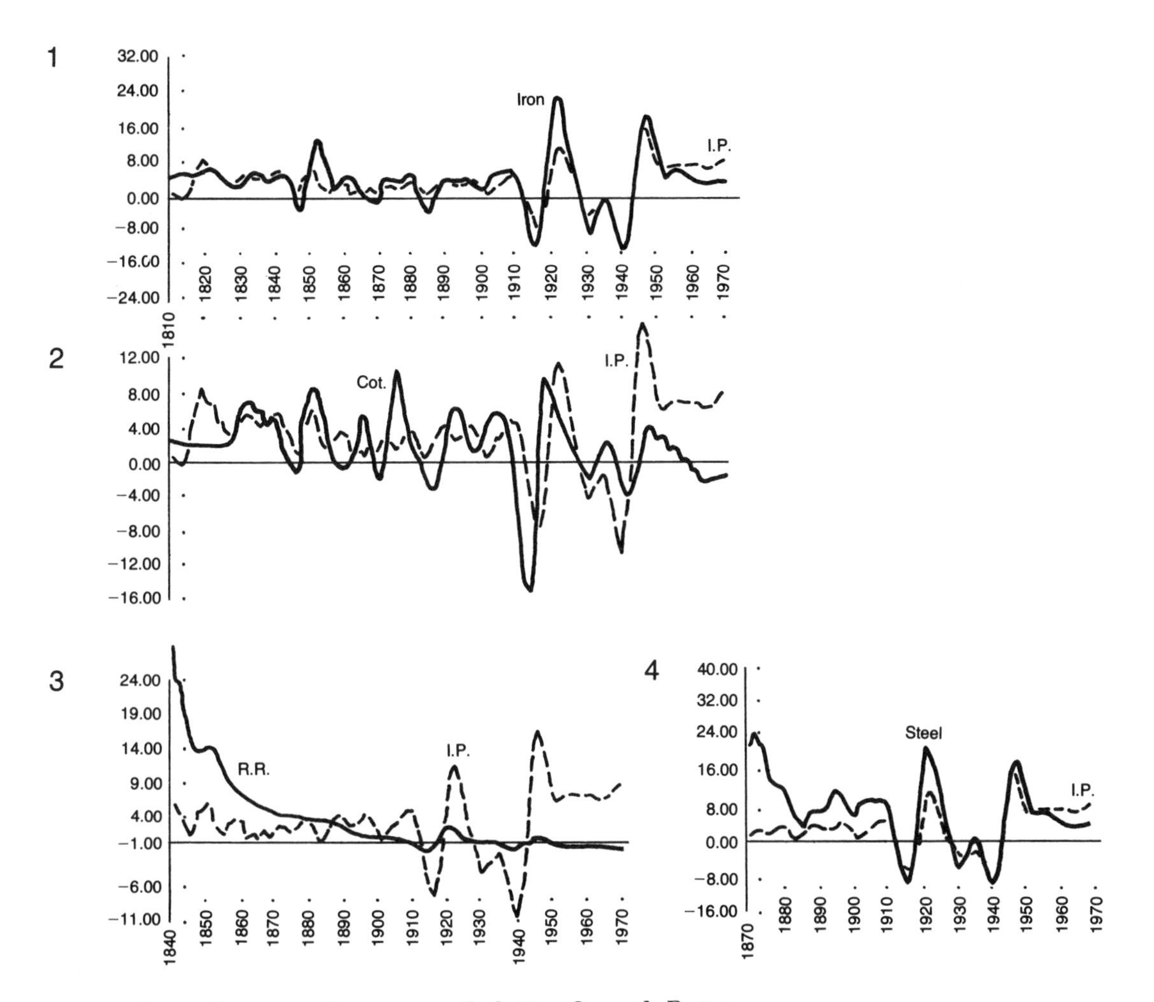

CHART V-10. *France, 1810–1972: Relative Growth Rates—Major Sectors and Industrial Production (Smoothed)*

1. Iron production (Iron).
2. Raw cotton consumption (Cot.).
3. Railroads (kilometers) (R.R.).
4. Steel production (Steel).

Sources: See Appendix D.

By Marczewski's calculations, the pre–take-off annual average percentage rate of increase in French product per capita was 0.44 percent.[40] It moved up as follows:

1825–1834	0.70
1835–1844	1.43
1845–1854[41]	0.98
1855–1864	1.23
1865–1874	1.69

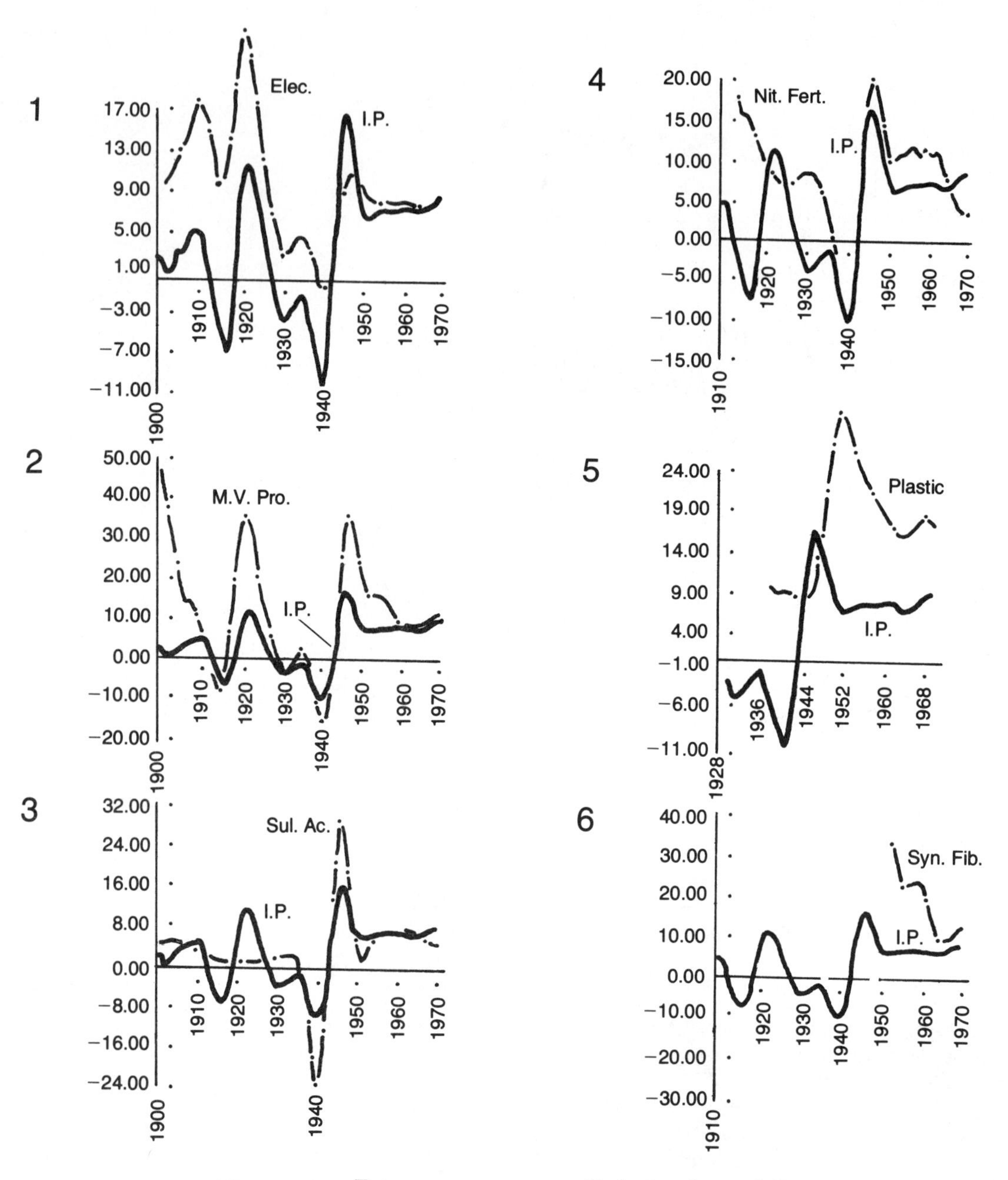

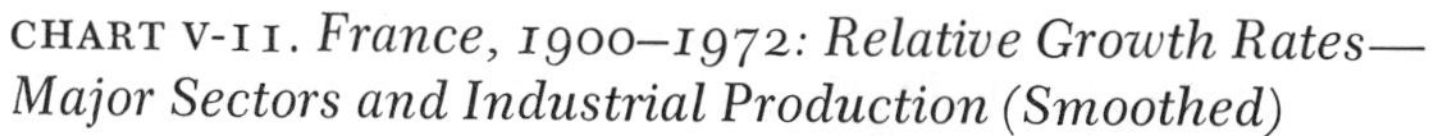

CHART V-11. *France, 1900–1972: Relative Growth Rates—Major Sectors and Industrial Production (Smoothed)*

1. Electricity (Elec.).
2. Motor vehicles (M.V. Pro.).
3. Sulphuric acid (Sul. Ac.).
4. Nitrogen fertilizer (Nit. Fert.).
5. Plastics and resins (Plastic).
6. Synthetic fibers (Syn. Fib.).

Sources: See Appendix D.

There is a phase of retardation, reflected in Table V-8, down to the 1890's and then a second acceleration:

1875–1884	0.48
1885–1894	0.85
1895–1904	1.65
1905–1913	1.82

The acceleration of the French economy in the pre-1914 generation had multiple roots. There was the rapid expansion of industries based on new technologies (see above, pp. 182–183); notably, motor vehicles, rayon, aluminum, electricity, calcium carbide. There was also rapid expansion in minette ore production and in steel production as the Thomas-Gilchrist process was applied. The interwar years saw, as noted in Chapter 4, a sturdy recovery in the 1920's, a particularly unyielding stagnation in the following decade. Then came the remarkable postwar growth of per capita income of 44.1 percent per decade (Table V-8, 1950–1954 to 1963–1966), which compares with a British rate of only 27.8 percent for that period.

The acceleration of the French economy in the take-off period, 1830–1870, can be observed not only in aggregate measures of product per capita and industry but also in the proportion of income invested (Table V-9).[42] From mid-century these figures are in the same range as those of Britain. In the post-1945 years, the French proportion was somewhat higher, as was the apparent productivity of domestic investment outlays, measured as the incremental capital-output ratio. Between 1949 and 1962, for example, British gross domestic product increased at 2.5 percent per annum, and gross fixed capital formation averaged 16.1 percent of domestic product, yielding a high capital-output ratio of 6.7. The equivalent French figures were 4.8 percent, 20.6 percent, and 4.6 percent.[43]

The sectoral map of French economic growth is presented in Chart V-9, parts 3 and 4, with sectoral growth rates and their relation to

TABLE V-9. *Gross and Net Capital Formation Proportions: France, 1788–1912*

	Gross Private Capital Formation as Percentage of Gross Domestic Product	Net Capital Formation as Percentage of Net Domestic Product
1788 to 1839	5.8	3.0
1839 to 1852	11.2	8.0
1852 to 1880	17.0	12.1
1880 to 1892	19.7	12.9
1892 to 1902–1903	20.0	12.4
1902–1903 to 1912	19.9	12.2

Source: Jan Marczewski, "The Take-off Hypothesis and French Experience," p. 121.

TABLE V-10. *Approximate Timing of Leading Sectors: France, 1700–1972*

Sector	Maximum Rate of Expansion	Estimated Time Sector Became Leading Sector	Estimated Time Sector Ceased to Lead
Cotton textiles	Post-1815	[a]	1880's
Pig iron	1850's	1830's	1950's
Railroads	1840's	1840's	1880's
Steel	1870's	1870's	1950's
Electricity	1920's	1900–1910	1960's
Motor vehicles	1900–1910	1920's	—
Sulphuric acid	1945–1950	[b]	1950's
Nitrogen	1945–1950	[b]	Late 1960's
Plastics	1950's	[b]	—
Synthetic fibers	1950's	[b]	—

[a] Sector not judged sufficiently large to move the French economy as a whole into self-sustained growth.
[b] Not judged, by itself, a leading sector.

the average rate of industrial expansion in Charts V-10 and V-11. Table V-10 summarizes some of the timing features of this story.

Dates for the French stages of growth are judged to be as follows.

Take-off:

1830–1870. Based on coal, iron, engineering, and, from 1840's on, railroad leading sector complex.

Drive to Technological Maturity:

1870–1913. Relatively damped down to the mid-1890's, accelerating somewhat in the pre-1914 generation.

High Mass-Consumption:

1920–. Set back severely in the 1930's and during the Second World War; rapid in the 1950's and 1960's.

31

Germany

Although it clearly conforms to the general Western European pattern, the story of modern French growth contains special elements, associated as it is with indifferent resource endowments in the critical age of iron, coal, and steel, and with low rates of population and working-force increase for most of the past two centuries.[44] The modern growth of the German economy is a more straightforward story. Unification came late; but the German states, notably Prussia, had shared in the preindustrial process of modernization in Europe after the end of the Thirty Years' War in 1648.[45] And when Germany's take-off began in the 1840's or 1850's (at the time of the *Zollverein*, but before political unification), Germany had made up some ground lost vis-à-vis Britain since the 1780's; but its GNP per capita was probably somewhat below that of France, well below that of Britain.[46]

I originally set the German take-off dates as 1850–1873. On the basis of the argument of Walther Hoffmann,[47] I am now inclined to set them a decade earlier. The issue is still debatable, and the nature of the argument may be worth exposing here because it is a classic example of the problem of "the preceding decade."

Hoffmann regards the end of the preconditions as 1830–1835, coinciding with the coming of the *Zollverein* (1834). He would date the period 1830–1835 to 1855–1860 as the take-off, with sustained growth firmly established by the latter date. As that of a true pioneer in stage analysis related to sectoral patterns and rates of growth, and the master of German historical statistics, his judgment deserves great weight. The case for the 1850's as the beginning of take-off is the fact that pig iron production accelerated rapidly at that time, after marked retardation from the mid-1830's;[48] but coal production accelerated in the 1830's, and, most important of all, railroad expansion in Germany during the 1840's was on a larger scale than that in France. Hoffmann notes Arthur Spiethoff's observation that the first modern business-cycle fluctuation came in the 1840's, with the railroad boom of 1843–1847. There was also, by 1850, considerable progress in the mechanization of the textile industry, whose high growth rates also ran back to the 1830's; but, as in France, I would not judge textile expansion a sufficiently large and pervasive phenomenon to justify, in itself, designating the period as a take-off.

Hoffmann sums up the evidence on this period with a table comparing the relative sectoral progress of Germany and the United Kingdom from 1820 to 1880 (Table V-11). At a much lower level, Germany kept pace with Britain's expansion of coal output in the period 1830–1850, gaining only in the 1850's, when the potentialities of the Ruhr began to be seriously exploited. Pig iron, still imported in substantial quantities from Belgium, lost ground until the 1850's. Cotton gained a bit, at low relative levels, in the 1840's, wool more substantially from 1830; but the rapid decline in hand spinning came only after 1855, rapid acceleration in mechanical weaving only in the 1850's and 1860's. Nevertheless, the pace at which the railway net was laid down in the 1840's, at the time of the maximum rate of expansion in the British system, remains impressive.[49] If one were so inclined, one could argue, on a sectoral basis, that, until the Ruhr began to be systematically exploited, Germany remained in a pre–take-off stage, despite the lively goings-on after the mid-1830's. And in steam power installed, Germany in 1850 had only 40,000 horsepower in fixed engines, 200,000 in locomotives, 20,000 in steamboats, versus the following figures for France in these categories: 67,000, 291,000, and 22,000.[50] Total steam power installed was at 68 percent of the French level. But, with a railway net twice the mileage of the French in 1850, and pig iron production at 71 percent of the French level, it is difficult to deny Hoffmann's judgment that the 1840's should be included in the take-off.

A firm resolution of this question would be aided by the existence of reasonably firm aggregate data for pre-1850 Germany; but such estimates exist on an annual basis only from mid-century. I now conclude, on balance, that, if the 1830's should be embraced in the take-off dates for France, the 1840's should be embraced in Germany's case.

TABLE V-11. *Production and Consumption Standards per Head of Population in Germany Compared with the United Kingdom (U.K. = 100)*

	Consumption of Coal	Production of			Length of Railway Lines
		Pig Iron	Cotton Yarn	Woolen Yarn	
1820	6	—	—	—	—
1830	7	10	—	15	—
1840	7	8	5	26	24
1850	7	6	7	29	35
1860	10	9	11	34	45
1870	17	16	13	39	53
1880	22	23	13	48	80

Source: Walther G. Hoffmann, "The Take-off in Germany," p. 118.

TABLE V-12. *Rates of Growth: Total Product, Population, and Product per Capita, Germany and Western Germany, 1850–1967; Product per Capita, United Kingdom, 1850–1967*

	Duration of Period (Years)	Rates of Growth per Decade (%)			
		Total Product, Germany	Population, Germany	Product per Capita, Germany	Product per Capita, U.K.
1850–1859 to 1880–1889	30	26.7	8.9	16.4	23.3
1880–1889 to 1905–1913	24.5	32.9	13.5	17.0	11.4
1895–1904 to 1925–1929	27.5	17.7	9.7	7.3	5.2
1925–1929 to 1950–1954	25	26.5	12.5	12.5	11.3
1950–1954 to 1963–1967	13	83.2	12.2	63.3	27.8

Source: Kuznets, *Economic Growth of Nations*, pp. 38–39.

Table V-12 presents Kuznets' decadal rates of movement for the German aggregate growth from 1850 to 1967 for long periods, along with approximately comparable per capita British rates; Chart V-12, part 2, exhibits fluctuations in rates of change in national product per capita for shorter periods.

What Table V-12 tells us, essentially, is that during take-off and in the drive to technological maturity, down to the eve of the First World War, Germany sustained an increase in total product per capita at first slower and then more rapid than that of Britain; that the interwar years as a whole produced for both the deceleration with which we are familiar from Chapter 14; and that in the 1950's and 1960's West Germany sustained the highest rate of growth among the major European states. German increase in product per capita significantly exceeded the British from the 1880's to 1914 and in the post-1950 period.[51]

Looked at more closely (Chart V-12, part 2), it is clear that German product per capita was strongly affected by the business cycles of the period. In particular, after the heroic boom of the early 1870's, there was a full decade of marked retardation. In terms of the trend periods analyzed in Part Three, the pre-1914 retardation emerges clearly. Product per capita moved at an average annual rate as follows: 1850–1854 to 1870–1874, 1.91 percent; 1870–1874 to 1895–1899, 1.52 percent; 1895–1899 to 1910–1913, 0.94 percent. The rather successful German recovery of the 1930's yielded an average annual increase of 2.2 percent from 1925 to 1934–1938. From 1950–1954 to 1960–1964, product per capita increased at the historically unexampled average annual rate (for Germany or any other nation in Western Europe) of 5.6 percent.

Hoffmann's estimates of the proportion of national income invested begin in the 1850's at 7.4 percent for 1851–1855, rising to 8.4 percent in the second half of the decade. He assumes as reasonable a rate of 5 percent for the period 1831–1855. Chart V-15 shows how the ratio, marked by the extraordinary cyclical peak of the early 1870's, subsequently varied down to 1914. It averaged 15.7 percent

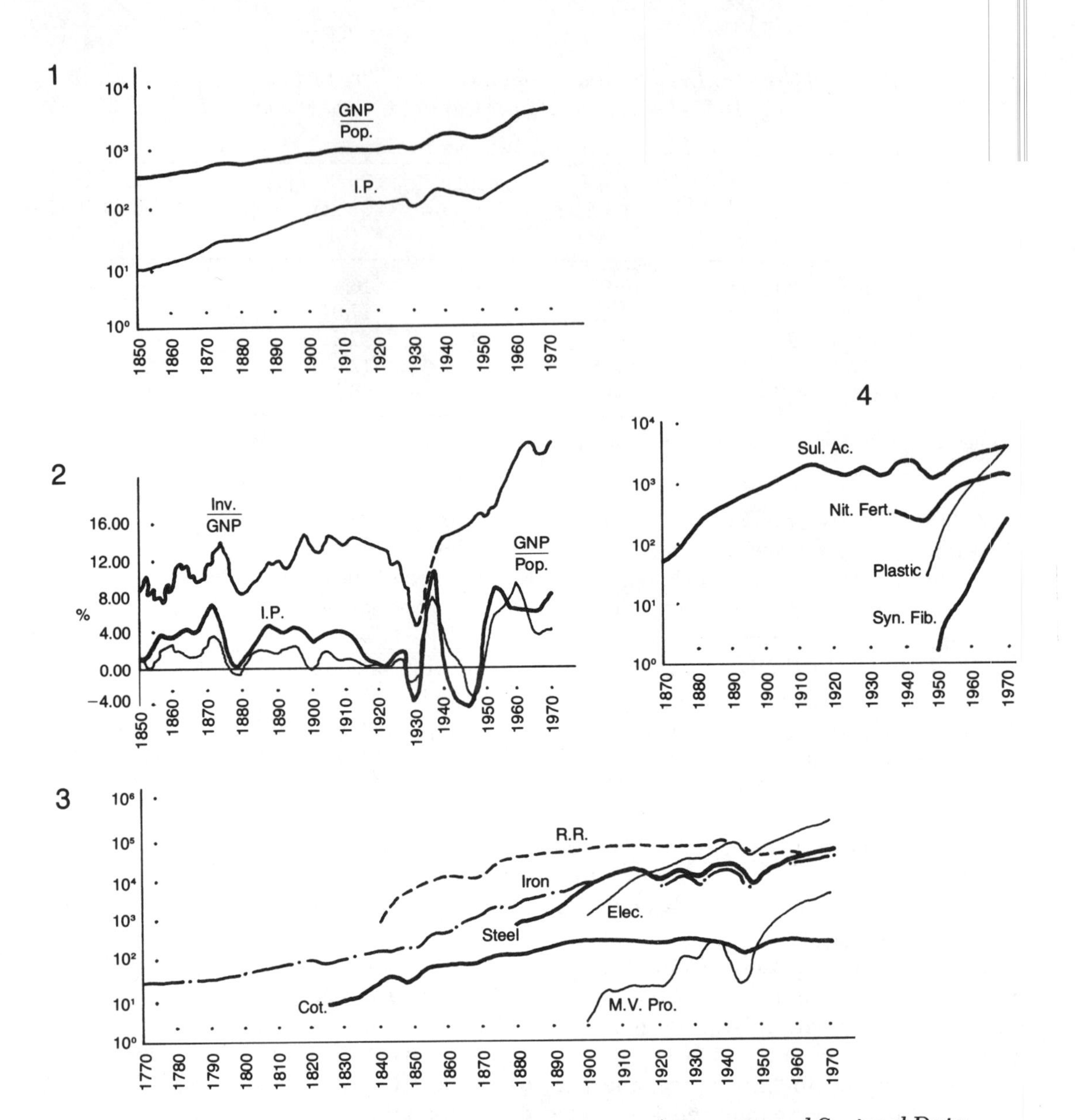

CHART V-12. *Germany, 1770–1972: Aggregate and Sectoral Data (Smoothed)*

1. GNP per capita ($\frac{\text{GNP}}{\text{Pop.}}$); industrial production index (I.P.).

2. Gross investment as % of GNP ($\frac{\text{Inv.}}{\text{GNP}}$); rate of change, GNP per capita ($\frac{\text{GNP}}{\text{Pop.}}$); rate of change, industrial production (I.P.).

3. Six major sectors: railroads (kilometers) (R.R.); raw cotton consumption (Cot.); production of iron (Iron); steel (Steel); electricity (Elec.); and motor vehicles (M.V. Pro.).

4. Production of four major chemicals: sulphuric acid (Sul. Ac.); nitrogen fertilizer (Nit. Fert.); plastics and resins (Plastic); and synthetic fibers (Syn. Fib.).

Sources: See Appendix D.

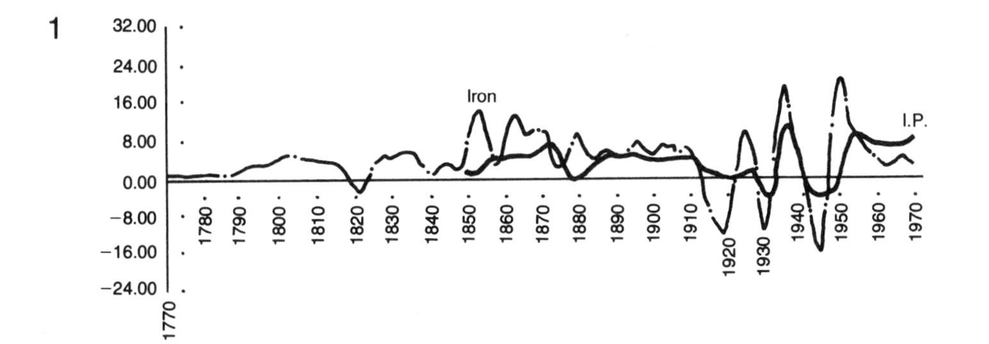

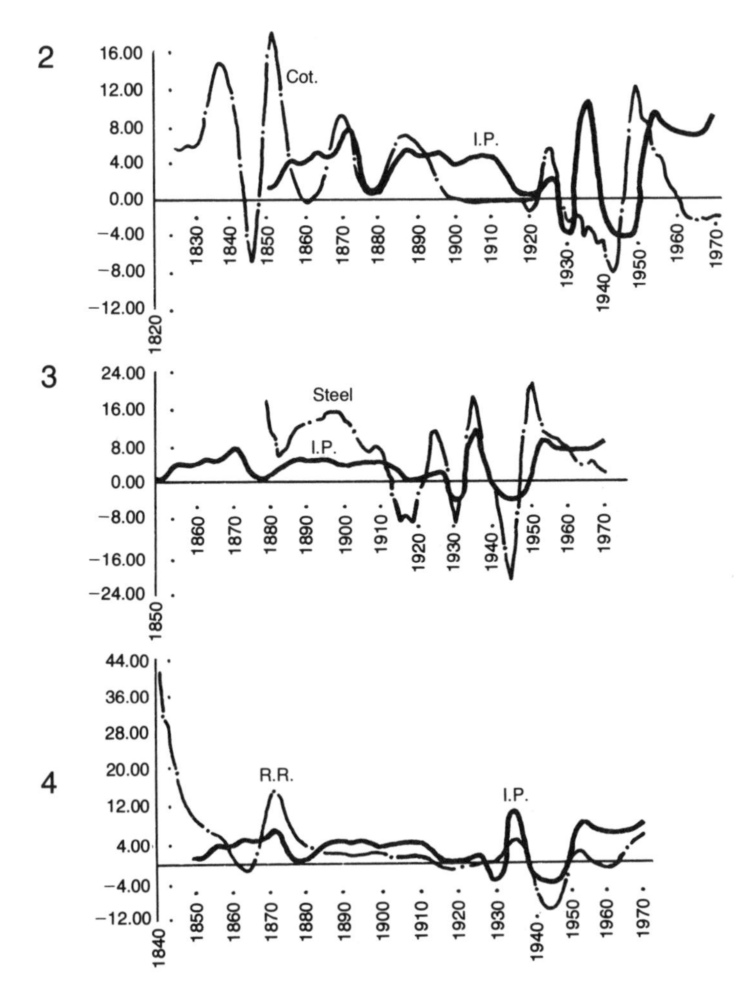

CHART V-13. *Germany, 1770–1972: Relative Growth Rates— Major Sectors and Industrial Production (Smoothed)*

1. Iron production (Iron).
2. Raw cotton consumption (Cot.).
3. Steel production (Steel).
4. Railroads (kilometers) (R.R.).

Sources: See Appendix D.

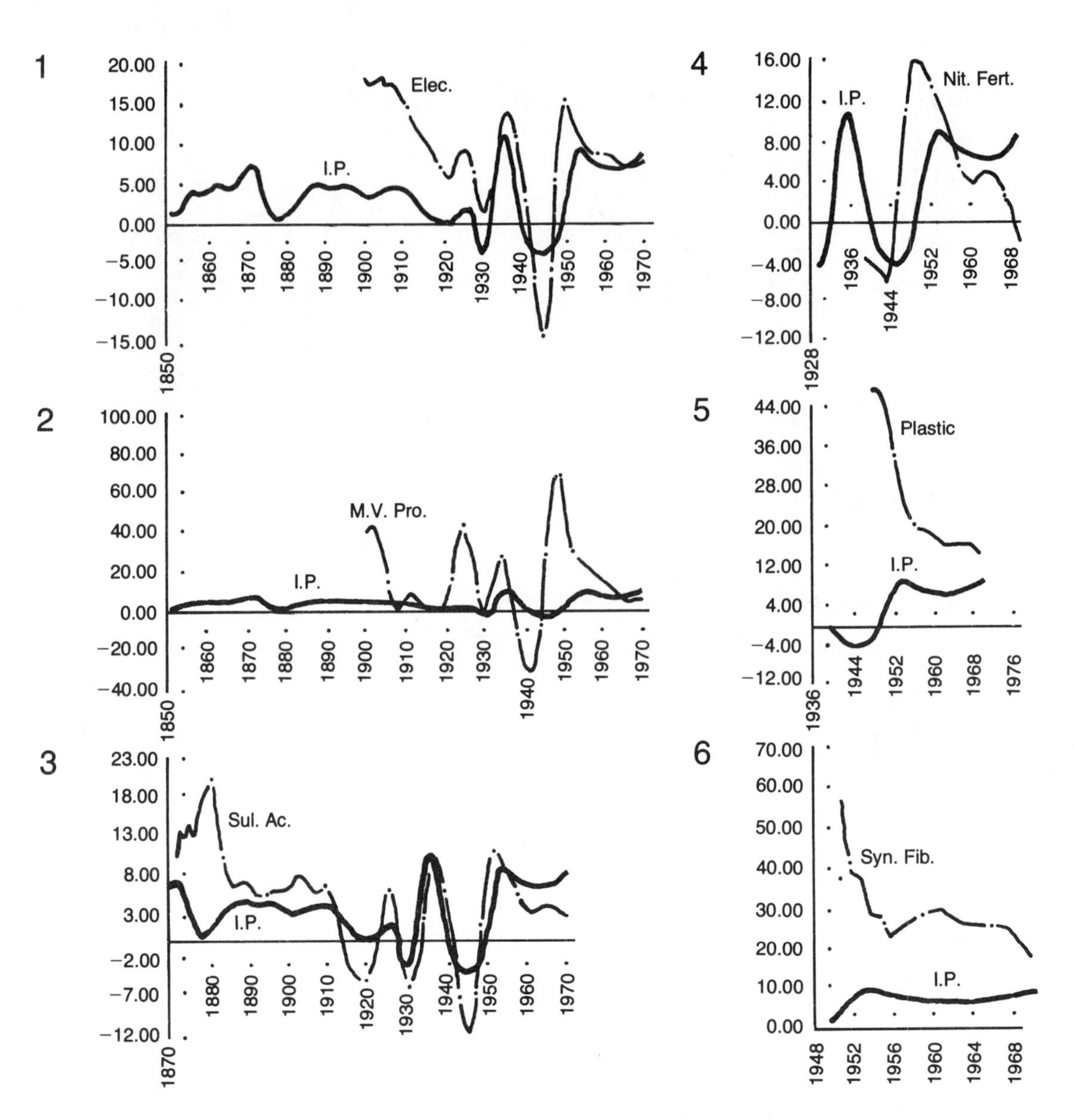

CHART V-14. *Germany, 1850–1972: Relative Growth Rates—Major Sectors and Industrial Production (Smoothed)*

1. Electricity (Elec.).
2. Motor vehicles (M.V. Pro.).
3. Sulphuric acid (Sul. Ac.).
4. Nitrogen fertilizer (Nit. Fert.).
5. Plastics and resins (Plastic).
6. Synthetic fibers (Syn. Fib.).

Sources: See Appendix D.

for 1906–1910.[52] The rise and subsidence of the capital coefficient in the second half of the nineteenth century reflects, probably, the time required for the enormous outlays on railroads to yield their full benefits to the economy. Railway investment was over 20 per-

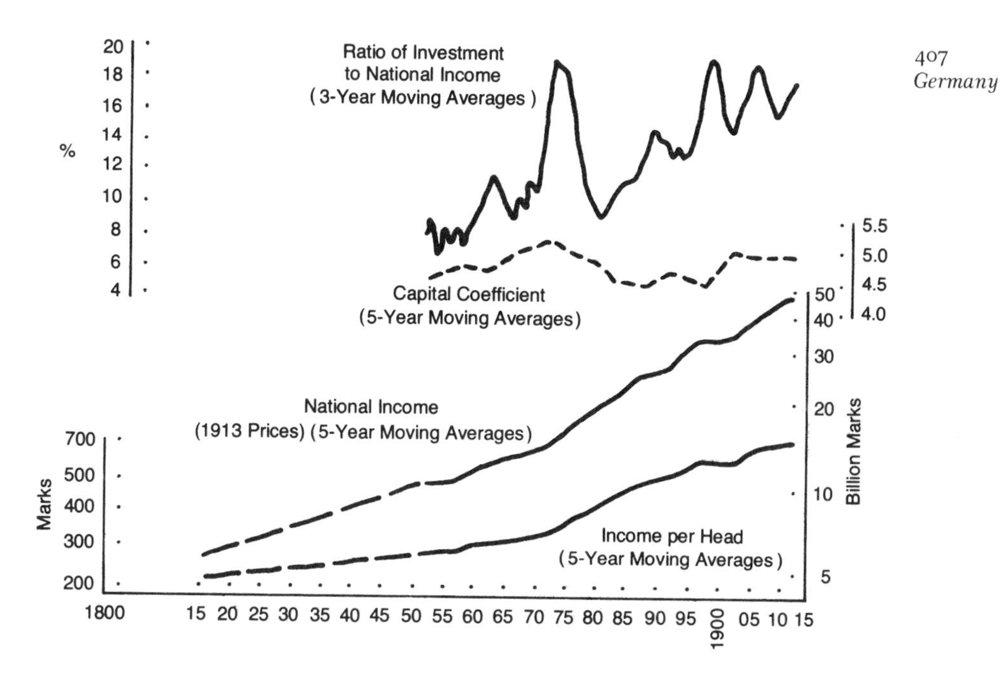

CHART V-15. *Income, Investment, and Capital Coefficient: Germany, 1850–1914*

Source: Hoffmann, "The Take-off in Germany," p. 114.

cent of total investment in Germany in 1851–1855, almost 17 percent in 1856–1860.

The sectoral patterns of German growth are set out in Chart V-12, parts 3 and 4; the relation of their growth rates to the average increase in industrial production, in Charts V-13 and V-14. Table V-13 summarizes certain key conclusions from the sectoral data.

One has a choice in dating the end of German iron and steel as a leading sector between, say, the 1920's and the 1950's. In prosperous periods the rate of increase of both series exceeded that of the industrial production index as a whole; e.g., the latter part of both the 1920's and the 1930's. They also led in post–World War II recovery. But the setbacks of both war and depression were also more extreme than for the industrial index. One could conclude that iron and steel were simply more volatile than industrial production as a whole, but not a leading sector from the 1920's forward. But, given the role of steel both in rearmament in the late 1930's and in post-1945 reconstruction, I am inclined to postpone dating its end as a leading sector to the 1950's, as in the case of France.

The German stages of growth emerge as follows.

Take-off:

1840–1870. Based on railroads, exploitation of Ruhr, heavy industry.

Drive to Technological Maturity:

1870–1913. Steel, etc.

TABLE V-13. *Approximate Timing of Leading Sectors: Germany, 1830–1972*

Sector	Maximum Rate of Expansion	Estimated Time Sector Became Leading Sector	Estimated Time Sector Ceased to Lead	Comments
Cotton textiles	1830's	[a]	1890's	—
Pig iron	1850's	1850's	1950's	See text.
Railroads	1840's	1840's	1880's	—
Steel	1870's	1870's	1950's	See text.
Electricity	1900–1910	1900–1910	Late 1960's	—
Motor vehicles	1900–1910	1920's	Late 1960's	—
Sulphuric acid	1870's	[a]	1930's	—
Nitrogen	1945–1910	[a]	—	—
Plastics	1950's	[a]	—	—
Synthetic fibers	1950's	[a]	—	—

[a] Not judged, by itself, a leading sector.

High Mass-Consumption:

1925–. Interrupted severely after the First World War, by depression, 1929–1933, and by the Second World War. Resumed strongly about 1950.

32

Sweden

Sweden was an active force in the military, political, and economic arena of the seventeenth and eighteenth centuries, although its political role diminished after the Battle of Poltava in 1709 and its economic role diminished after 1717, when it started to limit the number and output of its iron forges and thus its exports. Nevertheless, eighteenth-century Swedish society was based on a vigorous mercantilist economy that held its own in the trading arena down to 1780. Like the rest of the European continent, it fell, relatively, behind Britain during the Revolutionary and Napoleonic Wars.

There was some slow absorption of the new technologies after 1815; but it was not until the British market for timber was opened round about mid-century and the steam saw brought into use that a foundation for rapid growth emerged.[53] There was also a slow modernization of the iron industry on the basis of British methods and the gradual removal of deeply embedded mercantilist regulations, accomplished by 1859. Iron output may have doubled between 1830 and 1860. Railroads came slowly, with only 375 miles in 1860 and 1,090 miles a decade later, as compared to more than three times that mileage by 1880. Despite the developments between 1815 and 1870, Sweden, as of the latter date, still had 72 percent of its population engaged in agriculture. In terms of stages of growth, I would conclude that the pace of industrial progress picked up from about mid-century and that the Swedish take-off began with the expansion of the early 1870's, sustained by rapid railroadization and, down to 1877, by the British housing boom. Table V-14 suggests the scale of the expansion as reflected in total trade and trade with the United Kingdom. The pace of the great lift of the early 1870's was not maintained; but it left Sweden on a new course of self-sustained growth.

This image derived from foreign trade data is confirmed by Kuznets' calculations of growth rates for long periods and by calculations of per capita national product at five-year intervals in constant prices here carried forward to the 1960's (Tables V-15 and V-16 and Chart V-16, part 2).

TABLE V-14. *Sweden and Norway: Total Trade and Trade with the United Kingdom, 1854–1880 (Current Values, Annual Averages)*

	Total Exports (in Million Kronor)	Exports to U.K. (in £ Millions)	Total Imports (in Million Kronor)	Imports from U.K. (in £ Millions)
1854–1858	—	3.2	—	0.9
1859–1864	95.8 (1861–1864)	4.1	101.2 (1861–1864)	1.2
1865–1869	125.0	6.0	126.0	1.6
1870–1874	218.2	9.5	255.6	3.6
1875–1877	249.7	10.0	279.7	4.3
1878–1880	233.3	9.5	237.3	2.8

Sources: Swedish and Norwegian imports and exports from A. J. Youngson, *Possibilities of Economic Progress*, pp. 187–188; trade with United Kingdom, from William Page (ed.), *Commerce and Industry: Statistical Tables* (London: Constable, 1919), pp. 104–105.

TABLE V-15. *Rates of Growth: Total Product, Population, and Product per Capita, Sweden, 1861–1967*

	Duration of Period (Years)	Rates of Growth per Decade (%)		
		Total Product	Population	Product per Capita
1861–1869 to 1885–1894	24.5	28.5	6.5	20.7
1885–1894 to 1905–1914	20	38.8	7.1	29.6
1905–1914 to 1925–1929	17.5	28.6	6.2	21.1
1925–1929 to 1950–1954	25	45.5	6.5	36.6
1950–1954 to 1963–1967	13	49.9	6.5	40.8

Source: Kuznets, *Economic Growth of Nations*, p. 39.

TABLE V-16. *Per Capita Gross Domestic Product: Sweden, 1861–1969 (Annual Average Percentage Rate of Growth between Average Levels for Indicated Years)*

1861–1864	—	1915–1919	1.7
1865–1869	0.25	1920–1924	0.5
1870–1874	4.9	1925–1929	4.2
1875–1879	1.1	1930–1934	0.7
1880–1884	1.0	1935–1939	4.2
1885–1889	1.4	1940–1945	1.9
1890–1894	2.1	1946–1949	5.4
1895–1899	3.0	1950–1954	3.3
1900–1904	2.2	1955–1959	2.9
1905–1909	2.9	1960–1964	3.6
1910–1914	2.7	1965–1969	3.1

Sources: 1861–1864 to 1950–1954, Östen Johansson, *The Gross Domestic Product of Sweden and Its Composition, 1861–1955* (Stockholm: Almqvist and Wiksell, 1967), Table 60, pp. 160–161; 1950–1954 to 1960–1969, official Swedish estimates published in *United Nations Statistical Yearbooks*.

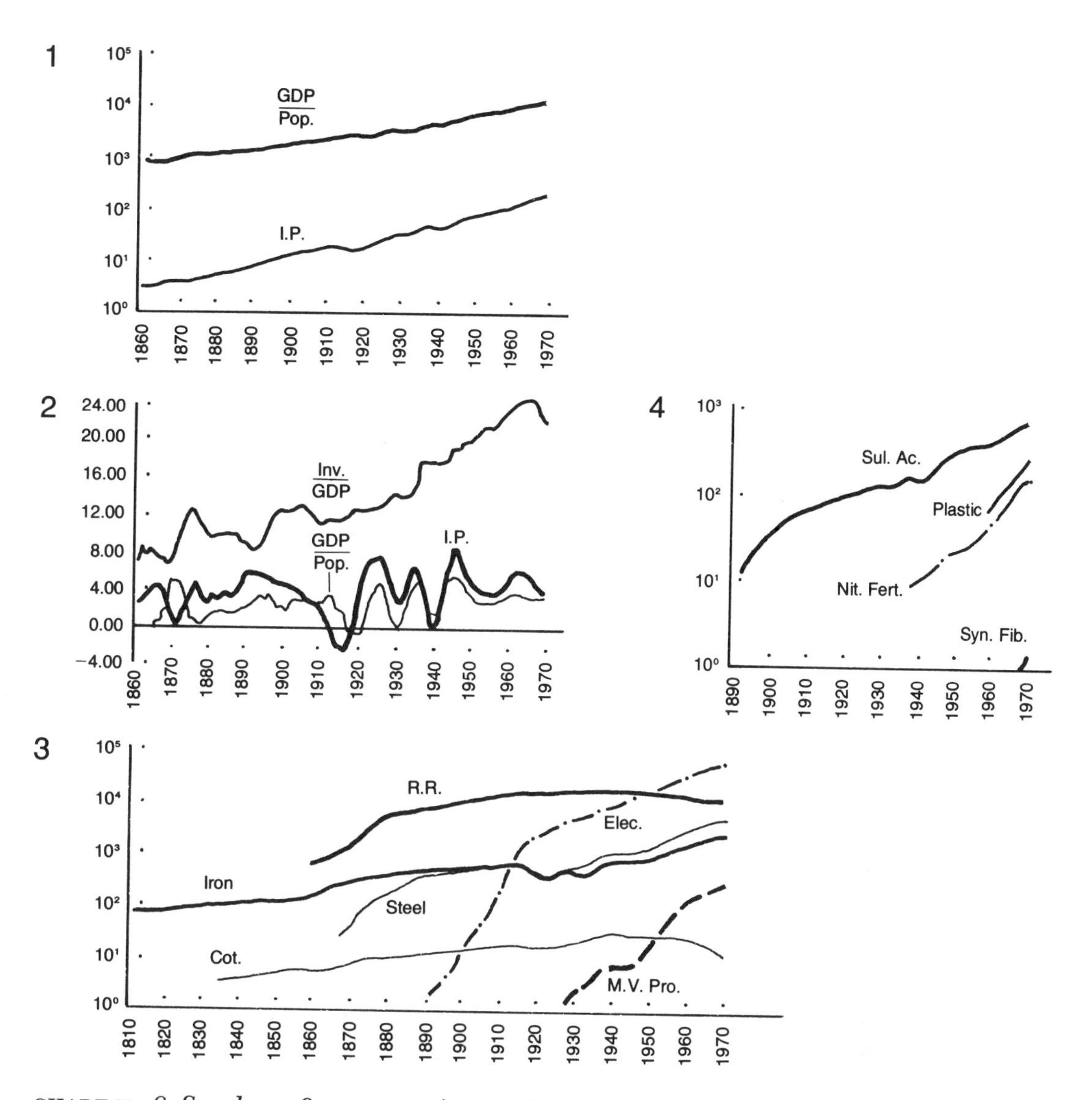

CHART V-16. *Sweden, 1810–1972: Aggregate and Sectoral Data (Smoothed)*

1. GDP per capita ($\frac{\text{GDP}}{\text{Pop.}}$); industrial production index (I.P.).

2. Gross investment as % of GDP ($\frac{\text{Inv.}}{\text{GDP}}$); rate of change, GDP per capita ($\frac{\text{GDP}}{\text{Pop.}}$); rate of change, industrial production (I.P.).

3. Six major sectors: railroads (kilometers) (R.R.); raw cotton consumption (Cot.); production of iron (Iron); steel (Steel); electricity (Elec.); and motor vehicles (M.V. Pro.).

4. Production of four major chemicals: sulphuric acid (Sul. Ac.); nitrogen fertilizer (Nit. Fert.); plastics and resins (Plastic); and synthetic fibers (Syn. Fib.).

Sources: See Appendix D.

After the great boom of the early 1870's and subsequent retardation in the 1880's, the pace of growth picked up again in the 1890's, as Sweden moved beyond timber and railroads to the exploitation of more sophisticated technologies. Lennart Jörberg's is a classic de-

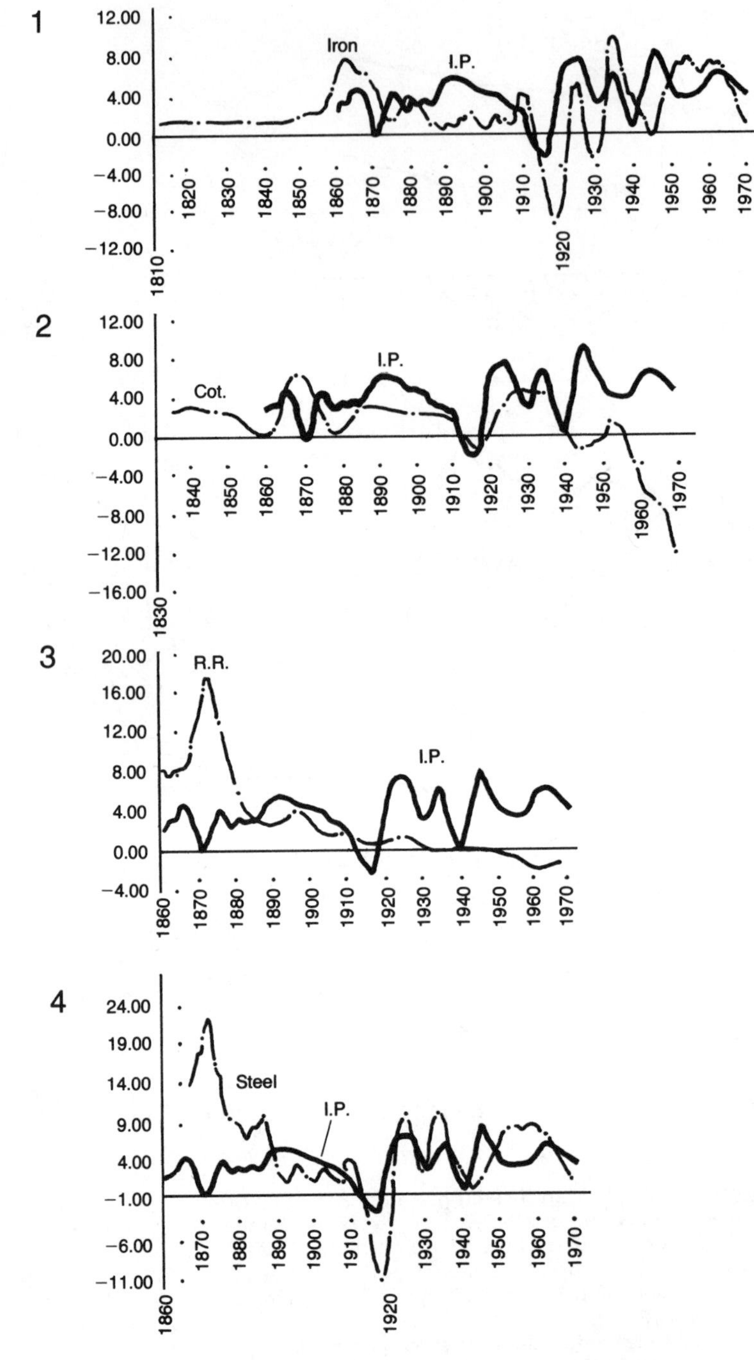

CHART V-17. *Sweden, 1810–1972: Relative Growth Rates—Major Sectors and Industrial Production (Smoothed)*

1. Iron production (Iron).
2. Raw cotton consumption (Cot.).
3. Railroads (kilometers) (R.R.).
4. Steel production (Steel).

Sources: See Appendix D.

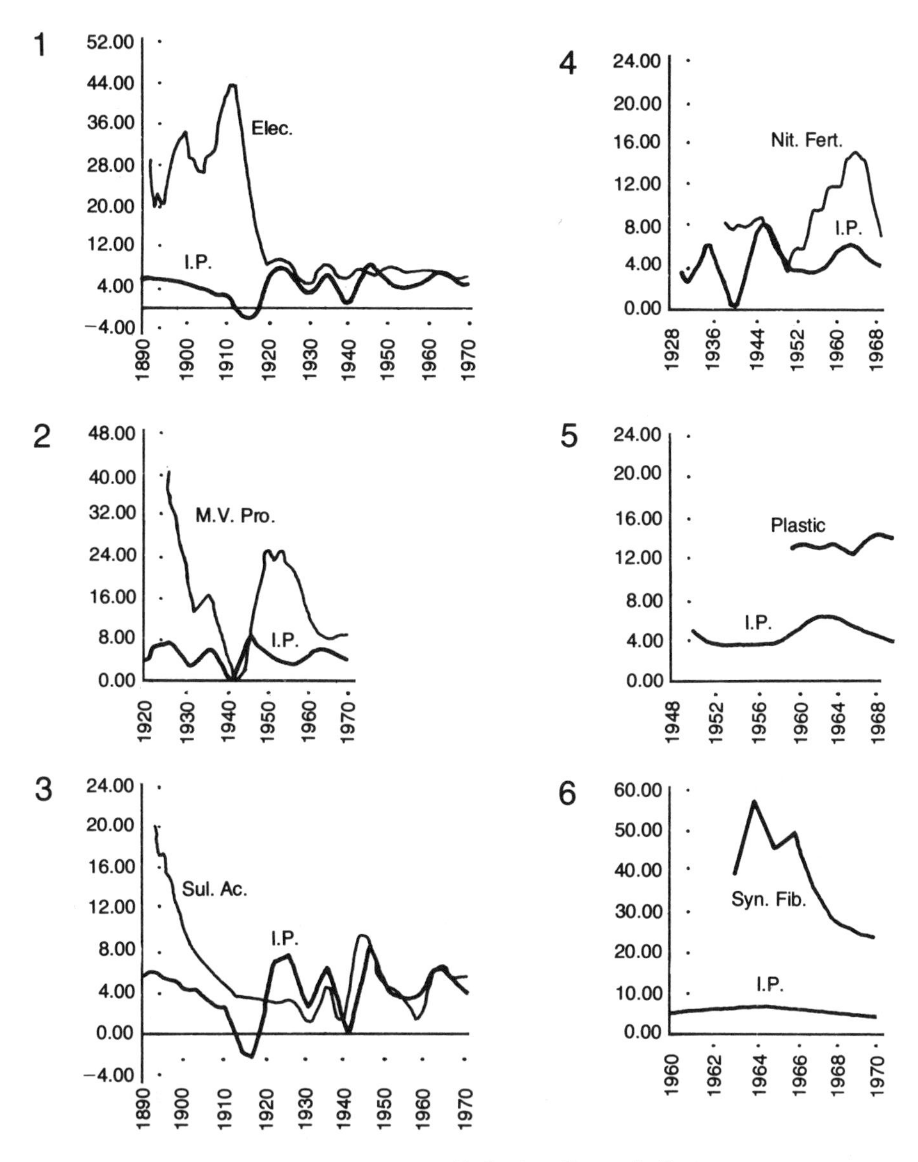

CHART V-18. *Sweden, 1890–1972: Relative Growth Rates—Major Sectors and Industrial Production (Smoothed)*

1. Electricity (Elec.).
2. Motor vehicles (M.V. Pro.).
3. Sulphuric acid (Sul. Ac.).
4. Nitrogen fertilizer (Nit. Fert.).
5. Plastics and resins (Plastic).
6. Synthetic fibers (Syn. Fib.).

Sources: See Appendix D.

scription of the transition from take-off to the drive to technological maturity in the context of a particular mixture of raw-materials endowments and technological possibilities:

The expansion of the 1890's is to some extent reminiscent of

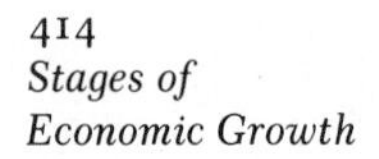

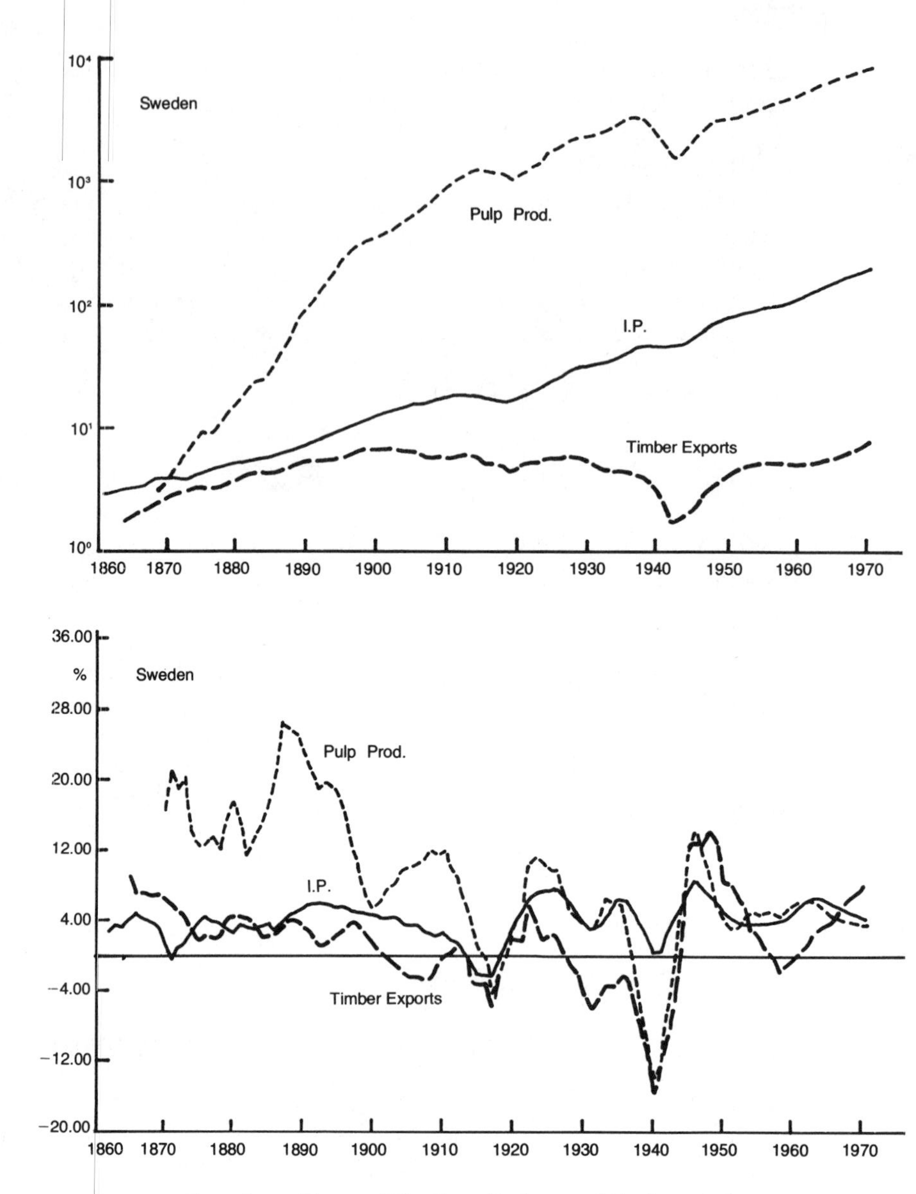

CHART V-19. *Sweden:* Above, *Timber, Pulp, and Industrial Production, 1860–1972 (Smoothed);* Below, *Growth Rates of Timber, Pulp, and Industrial Production, 1860–1972 (Smoothed)*

Sources: See Appendix D.

that of the 1870's. . . . [but] the starting position in the 1890's was more diversified—industrialization had been extensive during the 1880's, i.e., more and more industries had commenced activities, thereby creating a basis for the expansion of the 1890's. . . . [which] led to a greater structural change in industry than in the 1870's. The domestic market gained increasing importance for industry. The export industry became diversified, exports being split up among a greater number of products,

> and the previously dominating export goods—wood and steel—were extended with more processed products. But at the same time there was also an increase in exports of industrial raw materials, especially iron ore. . . .
>
> Several of the industrial groups developed by leaps and bounds as from the middle of the 1890's. The leather industry doubled, the metal industry more than doubled, the paper and pulp industry doubled and the mining industry almost doubled the value of production during the cycle. The number of workers in the manufacturing industry increased by 67%, and the value of production by 95%.[54]

The relative roles of timber exports and pulp production symbolize and are a significant part of Sweden's transition from take-off to the drive to technological maturity. Chart V-19 shows the initial surge and rapid deceleration of timber exports, balanced and more by the emergence of the pulp sector, incorporating a more sophisticated technology.

The proportion of Swedish net national product invested (Chart V-16, part 2) moved above 10 percent in the boom of the 1870's and in the pre-1914 expansion. It rose from the 1930's into the range of 20 percent in the 1950's and 1960's.

The timing of sectoral movements is given in Table V-17.

Sweden's stages of economic growth can be dated as follows.

Take-off: 1868–1890.

Drive to Technological Maturity: 1890–1925.

High Mass-Consumption: 1925–.

TABLE V-17. *Approximate Timing of Leading Sectors: Sweden, 1860–1972*

Sector	Maximum Rate of Expansion	Estimated Time Sector Became Leading Sector	Estimated Time Sector Ceased to Lead
Cotton consumption	1870's	[a]	1880's
Railroads	1870's	1870's	1880's
Iron	1860's	1870's	1960's
Steel	1870's	1870's	1960's
Electricity	1890's	1890's	—
Motor vehicles	Late 1920's	1950's	—
Sulphuric acid	—	[a]	—
Nitrogen	1930's	[a]	—
Plastics	1960's	[a]	—
Synthetic fibers	1960's	[a]	—

[a] Not judged, by itself, a leading sector.

33

Japan

Japanese economic growth after the Second World War has generated a fresh literature of historical and statistical analysis reaching back to the Meiji Restoration and even to the dynamics of the Tokugawa era.[55] Having closed themselves off substantially from the external world in the seventeenth century, except for the small window at Nagasaki, the Japanese did not share the complex European ferment of the premodern industrial era and of the first seventy years after the British take-off, although some members of the Japanese elite knew what was transpiring.

But the essentially self-contained Tokugawa economy and society were not static. The required presence of the nobles in Edo (Tokyo) stimulated the rapid growth of the city, with all its attendant requirements for food, handicraft manufactures, and services. The maintenance of peace and unity encouraged a classical expansion of population and output, with premodern technologies, which came under a degree of Malthusian strain in the late eighteenth and early nineteenth centuries which is still a matter of debate among scholars of the period. This was also a society which encouraged a significant amount of popular education and literacy. Although the European scientific revolution did not generate in the two Tokugawa centuries the kind of attitudes and strivings that emerged in the West, the Japan on which Commodore Perry descended was a vigorous and sophisticated, if still traditional and feudal, society.

The enforced opening of Japan to external trade in 1853–1854 set in motion a turbulent period of inner debate on Japan's future course, climaxed in early 1868 by the Meiji Restoration and the Emperor's Charter Oath. That oath expressed the conclusion at which the victorious Western clans had arrived: a decision actively to seek and apply the fruits of modern science and technology to protect and enhance the power of the Japanese nation in the contentious world arena which had emerged around it and which threatened its independence and dignity. The samurai statesmen, in particular, were determined to avoid the humiliation and travail visited upon China since the early 1840's. In the next sixteen years, the Japanese established the technical conditions for sustained industrial growth, despite passages of civil war and acute inflation. The Japanese government led the way with:

—a land reform scheme which gave the former owners national bonds, the peasants strong incentives, and the government a vital flow of revenue available for infrastructure and industrial investment over the period until a wider tax base emerged from growth itself;

—creation of a technical school, banks, insurance companies, railways, steamshipping, postal and telegraph services, and factories, many linked to the military establishment;

—creation of the Kobu Sho (Department of Industrial Matters) which, in the critical preconditions years 1870–1885, "served as an indispensable midwife of almost all the industrial projects including the task of rounding out social overhead capital";[56]

—a remarkable financial and currency stabilization in the early 1880's, ending inflation and providing an adequate monetary base for the take-off.

The preconditions process was aided (as in England) by the relatively low requirements for transport expenditure in a small island nation, with coastal shipping available, and by the fact that housing outlays in the expanding cities were modest.[57]

Social, institutional, and structural changes marked the pre–take-off period in Japan, as well as civil conflict, inflation, and its rigorous taming by Matsukata. Statistical data before the 1880's are sparse. They exhibit some erratic expansion of investment, notably in government construction and production of durable equipment.[58] Ohkawa's national income and sectoral data, beginning with 1878–1882 averages, can only tell us that there was some momentum prior to the rapid and steady expansion which is clearly marked across the board from the mid-1880's.[59]

The pragmatism that marked these initial two decades of modern Japan led the government to sell to a rapidly emerging private enterprise some of its inefficient factories and to leave the new dynamic textile industry in private hands.

The broad headings of Japanese public policy in the preconditions period are familiar, although their context, like that of other nations, had particular features. Policy toward popular education, however, was unique among the Eurasian cases of the nineteenth century.

The preamble to the new school regulations of 1872 read: "Henceforth, throughout the land, without distinctions of class and sex, in no village shall there be a house without learning, in no house an ignorant individual." Although Japanese educational policies and institutions did not evolve smoothly in this Jeffersonian, almost Emersonian, spirit, the initial dispositions of the Meiji period yielded by 1910 a situation in which 98 percent of the total population aged six to thirteen was registered in primary schools, while technical and advanced education flourished.[60]

Once begun, in the mid-1880's, Japanese economic growth proceeded at a high average rate, even before its unique pace of growth from the 1950's to the early 1970's. In this Japan resembled Sweden, which was also a relative late-comer to take-off, with a literate, energetic, and resourceful population capable of absorbing rapidly the accumulated backlog of available technologies as well as the flow of new technologies relevant to its rather special resource endowments and needs. Chart V-20, part 3, shows the fluctuations in the Japanese growth rate per capita. There is a sharp jump during the take-off (say, 1880–1884 to 1895–1899), then a phase of deceleration in the first decade of the twentieth century. This was related to both the Russo-Japanese War (and a sharp rise in the claims of the military budget) and the transition from the leading sectors of the take-off to the more complex and differentiated sectors of the drive to technological maturity.[61] A second phase of accelerated growth followed down to the end of the First World War. The Japanese economy decelerated in the first half of the 1920's, adjusting to the rather troubled postwar environment, and then shared in the prosperous years down to 1929. There was a third slowdown in the early 1930's, followed by rapid expansion geared to Japanese military requirements. Then, as we have already seen, came postwar recovery and the super-growth rates down to 1973 marked, as elsewhere, by phases of acceleration and deceleration.

Kuznets' decadal growth rates for comparable periods for the United Kingdom, Sweden, and Japan indicate not only the uniqueness of the Japanese postwar boom but also how the latter two latecomers made up ground on the pioneer once their take-offs began (Table V-18).

Unlike the United Kingdom, Sweden and Japan both escaped direct involvement in the First World War, and they moved forward

TABLE V-18. *Growth Rates: Product per Capita, United Kingdom, Sweden, and Japan, 1885–1967 (Percentage Growth Rates per Decade)*

	U.K.	Sweden	Japan
1885–1894 to 1905–1914	11.4	29.6	25.5
1905–1914 to 1925–1929	5.2	21.1	32.8
1925–1929 to 1952–1954	11.3	36.6	9.9
1925–1929 to 1963–1967	16.6	38.0	38.4
1952–1954 to 1963–1967	27.8	40.8	128.4

Source: Kuznets, *Economic Growth of Nations*, pp. 38–40.

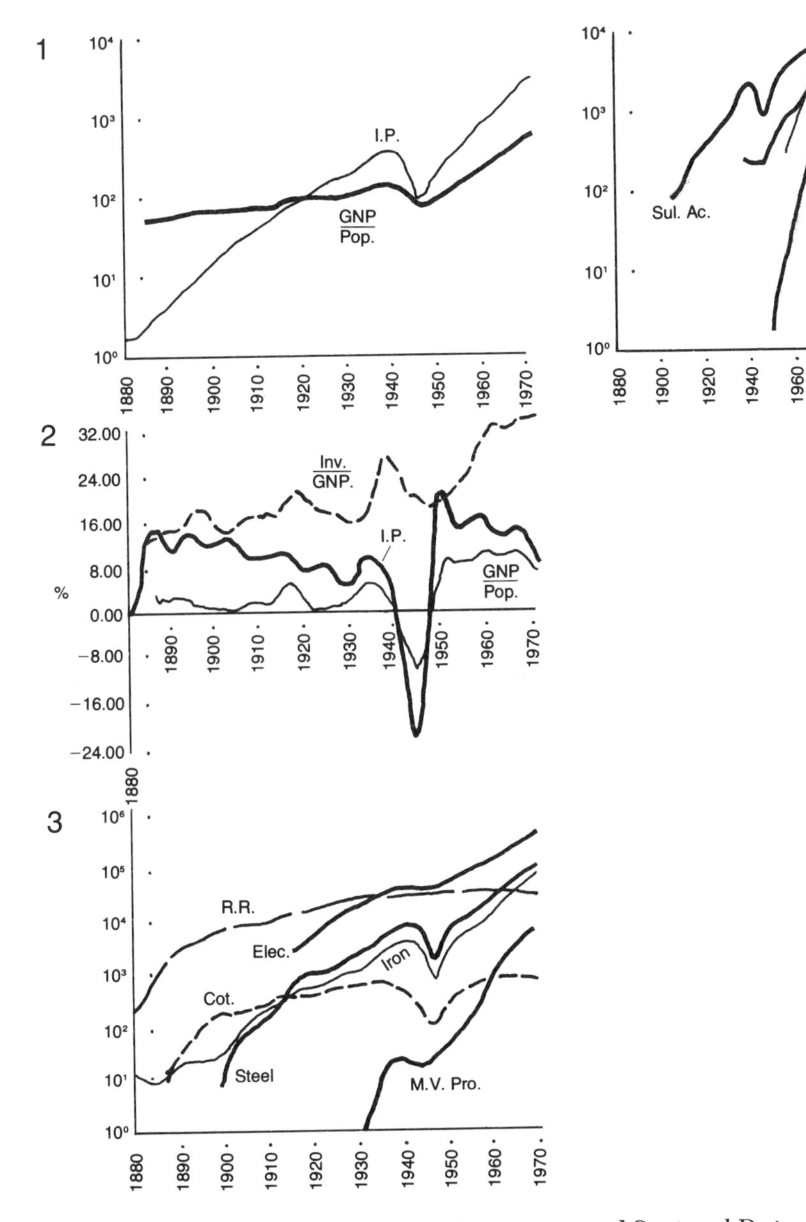

CHART V-20. *Japan, 1880–1972: Aggregate and Sectoral Data (Smoothed)*

1. GNP per capita ($\frac{\text{GNP}}{\text{Pop.}}$); industrial production index (I.P.).

2. Gross investment as % of GNP ($\frac{\text{Inv.}}{\text{GNP}}$); rate of change, GNP per capita ($\frac{\text{GNP}}{\text{Pop.}}$); rate of change, industrial production (I.P.).

3. Six major sectors: railroads (kilometers) (R.R.); raw cotton consumption (Cot.); production of iron (Iron); steel (Steel); electricity (Elec.); and motor vehicles (M.V. Pro.).

4. Production of four major chemicals: sulphuric acid (Sul. Ac.); nitrogen fertilizer (Nit. Fert.); plastics and resins (Plastic); and synthetic fibers (Syn. Fib.).

Sources: See Appendix D.

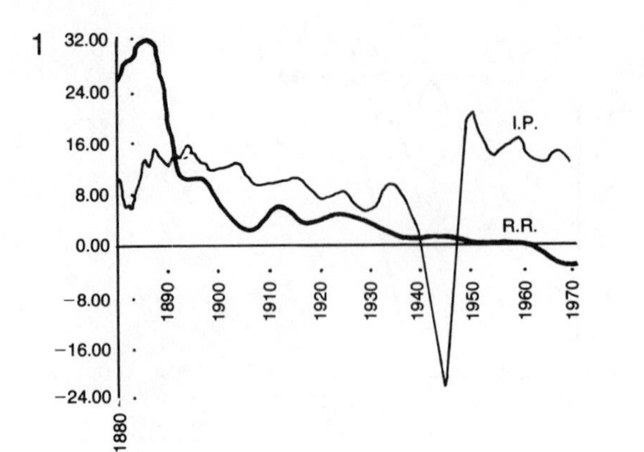

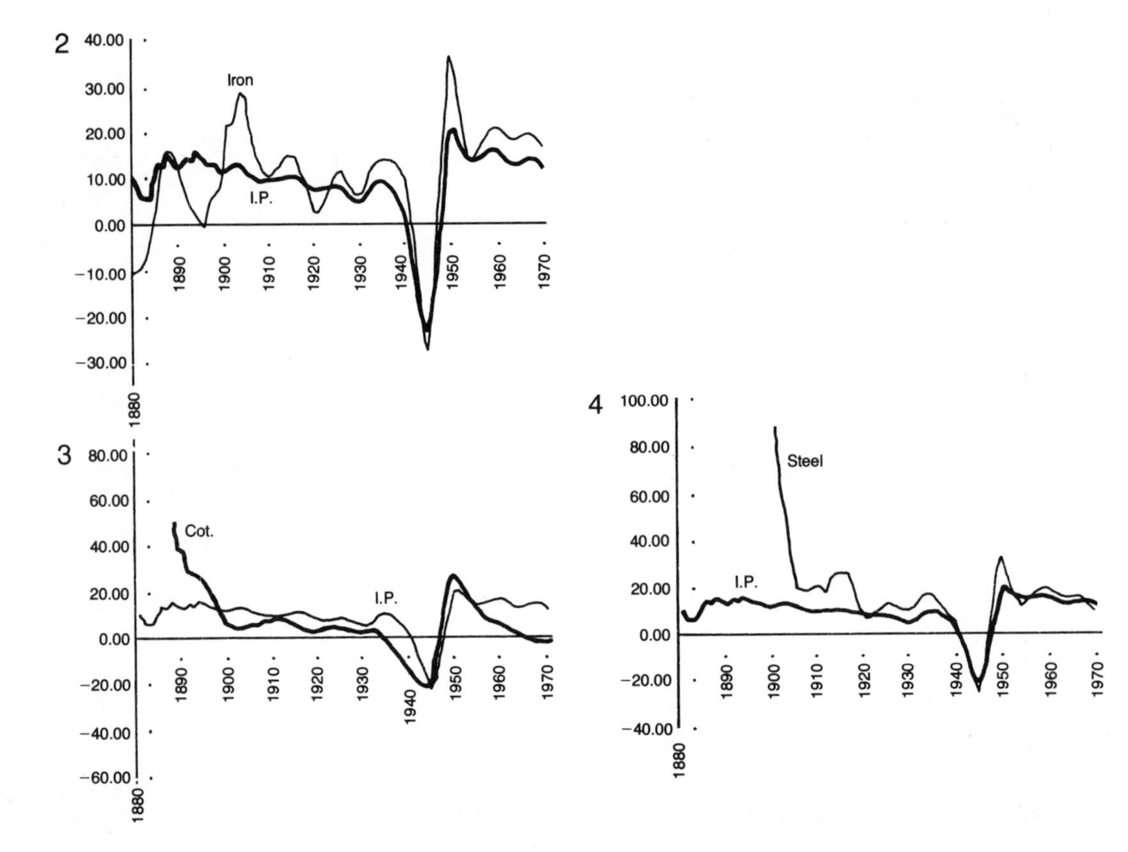

CHART V-21. *Japan, 1880–1972: Relative Growth Rates—Major Sectors and Industrial Production (Smoothed)*

1. Railroads (kilometers) (R.R.).
2. Iron production (Iron).
3. Raw cotton consumption (Cot.).
4. Steel production (Steel).

Sources: See Appendix D.

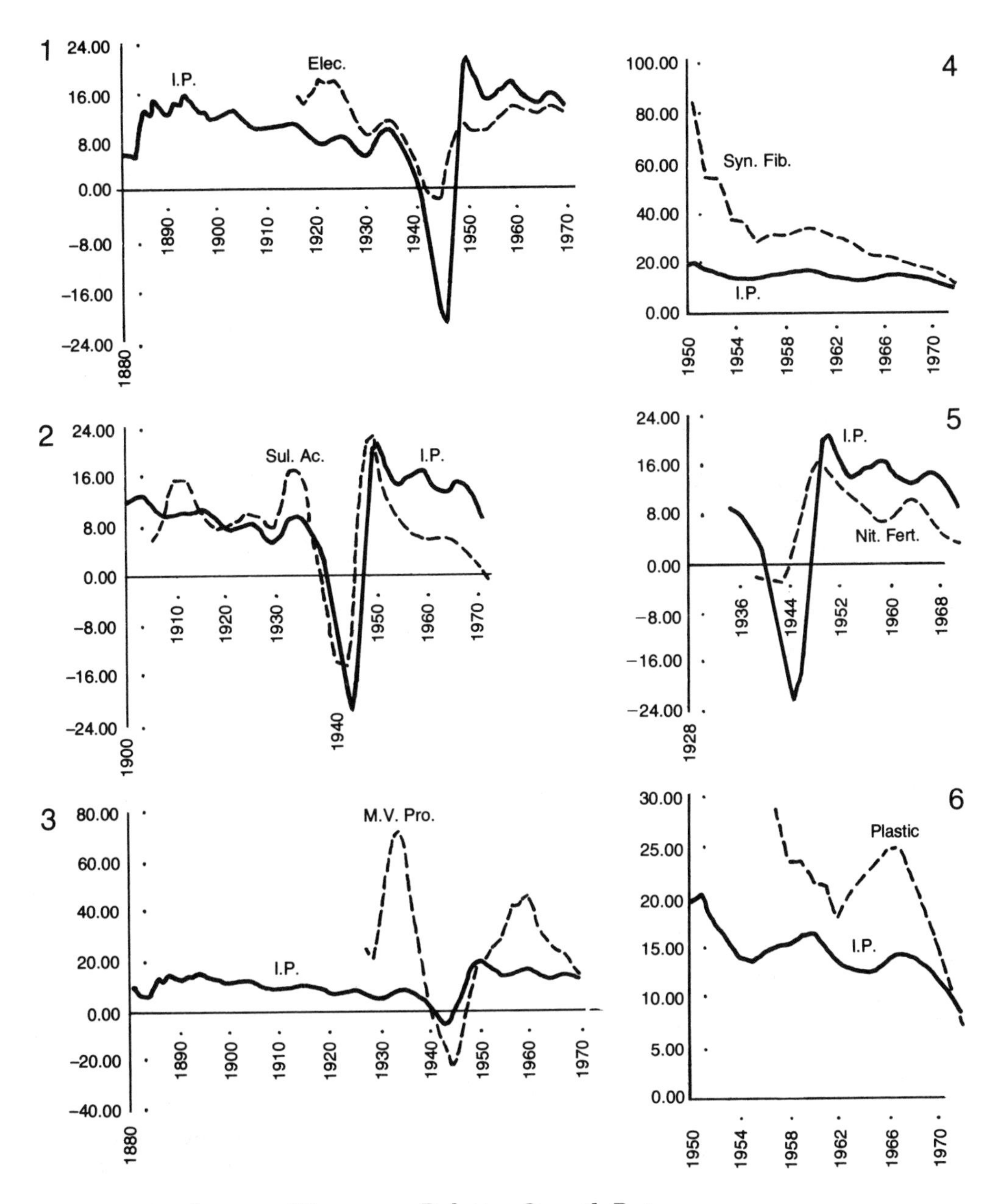

CHART V-22. *Japan, 1880–1972: Relative Growth Rates—Major Sectors and Industrial Production (Smoothed)*

1. Electricity (Elec.).
2. Sulphuric acid (Sul. Ac.).
3. Motor vehicles (M.V. Pro.).
4. Synthetic fibers (Syn. Fib.).
5. Nitrogen fertilizer (Nit. Fert.).
6. Plastics and resins (Plastic).

Sources: See Appendix D.

relatively well during the interwar years, while the impact of the Second World War was, of course, much more severe on Japan than on Britain. Leaving these matters aside, what emerges is the consistently higher rates of Japanese and Swedish than British growth, rates which also exceed those for France and Germany for comparable periods, excepting the 1950's and 1960's, when only the Japanese growth rate exceeds those of the Western European leaders.

Chart V-20, part 2, shows the typical take-off investment rates of the 1880's, rising to successively higher levels, with a virtually unique rate of over 30 percent sustained in the great expansion of the 1950's and 1960's.

The Japanese sectoral pattern is presented in Charts V-20, parts 3 and 4, V-21, and V-22. Table V-19 sets out the timing of the major sectoral complexes.

The broad sectoral evolution of the Japanese economy follows a now familiar sequence; but, like others, it contains distinctive features. Among the major economies, Japan shares with Britain the experience of a take-off based squarely on the production and export of textiles. In the case of Japan, however, silk as well as cotton was of major importance, as Table V-20 indicates. By 1910 Japan

TABLE V-19. *Approximate Timing of Leading Sectors: Japan, 1880–1972*

Sectors	Maximum Rate of Expansion	Estimated Time Sector Became Leading Sector	Estimated Time Sector Ceased to Lead	Comments
Cotton yarn	1885–1890	1885–1890	1900–1910	—
Railroads	1880's	1880's	1900–1910	—
Pig iron	1900–1910	1900–1910	—	—
Steel	1900–1910	1900–1910	—	—
Electricity	1920's	1920's	1950's	—
Motor vehicles	1930's	1930's	—	Mass manufacture and diffusion of private automobile beginning in the 1950's.
Sulphuric acid	1930's	[a]	—	Post-1945 surge in production ruled out.
Nitrogen	1950's	[a]	—	—
Plastics	1955–1960	[a]	—	—
Synthetic fibers	1950's	[a]	—	—

[a] Not judged, by itself, a leading sector.

TABLE V-20. *Silk Worm Culture and Japanese Silk Exports, 1874–1917*

	Silk Worm Culture (in Million Yen: Constant 1874–1876 Prices)	Raw Silk Exports as Percentage of Total Exports
1874	32	37.7 (1873–1877)
1879	43	—
1884	50	37.7 (1883–1887)
1889	51	36.8 (1888–1892)
1894	77	32.6 (1893–1897)
1899	106	27.8 (1898–1902)
1904	121	26.2 (1903–1907)
1909	152	29.3 (1908–1912)
1914	183	24.9 (1913–1917)

Source: Kamekichi Takahashi, *The Rise and Development of Japan's Modern Economy*, translated by John Lynch (Tokyo: The Jiji Press, 1969), pp. 293 and 325.

was exporting three-fourths of its silk production. About 7 percent of total exports was in the form of silk manufactures. The experience of expanding silk production and successfully meeting competition in international markets helped modernize rural life and generate a virtuosity in foreign trade later exhibited in other fields. Although machine methods were gradually introduced, notably for exports, the industry remained essentially rural and small-scale. It was an important source of supplementary income in the countryside, where almost a third of farm households came to be involved in it before 1914. Nevertheless, significant improvements in quality were introduced both in cocoon raising and in the reeling industry. Perhaps most important, the concept of quality control was introduced on a mass basis to the Japanese working force.

In cotton textiles Japan initially faced even more severe competition than in silk. It first succeeded in supplanting imports and then made inroads (against India and Britain), notably in the Chinese market. On the eve of the First World War about 20 percent of total exports were cotton goods. During the First World War Japan greatly extended its export domain: the volume of cotton cloth exported almost tripled between 1913 and 1918.

As in Britain, shipbuilding played a disproportionate role in the development of modern Japan. In 1870 Japan had 35 steamships of 15.5 thousand tons; in 1905, at the end of take-off, 1,988, totaling 939.5 thousand tons; at the end of the First World War, in 1920, the figures were 5,810 ships and 3,047 thousand tons. The annual average growth rate of tonnage during the take-off (1885–1905) was 15 percent; in the first fifteen years of the drive to technological maturity (1905–1920), 8 percent. A sharp decline followed in the first half of the 1920's, which gave way to two great surges, broken,

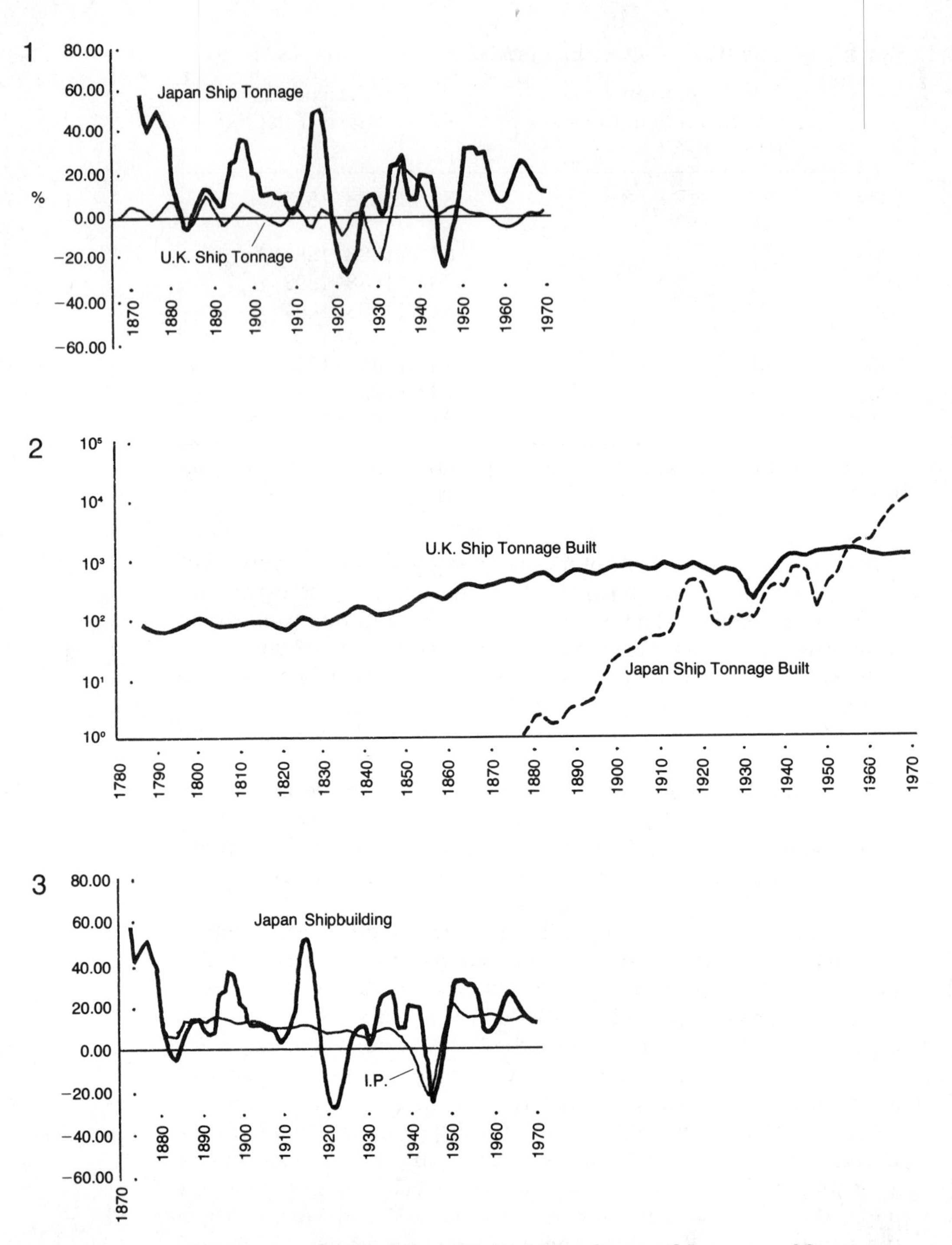

CHART V-23. *Shipbuilding: United Kingdom and Japan, 1788–1972*

1. Relative growth rates, United Kingdom and Japan.
2. Annual tonnage built, United Kingdom and Japan.
3. Relative growth rates, Japan: industrial production and shipbuilding.

Sources: See Appendix D.

of course, by the decline in the worst years of the Second World War. The sweep of Japanese shipbuilding over the whole modern period can be observed in Chart V-23. The comparative levels of shipbuilding of Britain and Japan are also given in Chart V-23 with the dramatic crossing of the curves at the end of the 1950's.

Japanese stages of growth can be dated as follows.

Take-off: 1885–1905.

Drive to Technological Maturity: 1905–1941.

High Mass-Consumption: 1955–.

34

Russia-USSR

The long, slow build-up of the preconditions for take-off in Russia reach far back into the early modern history of Europe. At the minimum, one must begin in the sixteenth century, when purposeful efforts to acquire the technologies of Western Europe were undertaken.[62] From about 1630 the setting up of new factories, most with the aid of foreign entrepreneurs and technicians, accelerated. Then came the remarkable effort to narrow the gap under Peter the Great, including the exploitation of the iron and charcoal potential of the Urals. The process of industrialization with premodern technology proceeded steadily, if less dramatically, in post-Petrine Russia of the eighteenth century; but Russia's momentum was broken by the trading and physical impact of the Napoleonic Wars, as well as by the coming of the new methods of iron production pioneered in Britain. After 1815 Russia proceeded laboriously to absorb the new technologies in textiles and the steam engine, but it lost ground in relation to Western Europe. As in China of the late nineteenth century, the rulers had to overcome grave reservations about setting in motion the social and political changes railroadization might bring.

It is conventional to date a new phase of pre–take-off economic dynamism from the decision of 1861 to free the serfs and the construction in the 1860's of some six thousand miles of railroads, after the traumatic experience of the Crimean War; but there was considerable industrial expansion in the two preceding decades. For example, Donets coal output increased at an annual average rate of 8.8 percent between 1845 and 1860; in the 1850's cotton spinning moved ahead at 8.7 percent per annum, cotton weaving at 5.2 percent; the Moscow–St. Petersburg railway link opened for business in November 1851.[63] Mulhall's calculations of steam power installed in Russia from 1840 to the eve of take-off (1888) capture both the reality of pre-1860 progress and its modest level compared both to Britain and to later decades in Russia (Table V-21).

The fall in agricultural prices in the 1870's and 1880's bore heavily on the Russian economy; and the freeing of the serfs, in fact,

TABLE V-21. *Steam Power Installed in Russia and the United Kingdom, 1840–1888 (in Units of Horsepower)*

	Russia				United Kingdom
	Fixed	Locomotives	Steamboats	Total	Total
1840	10,000	10,000	10,000	30,000	620,000
1860	60,000	100,000	40,000	200,000	2,450,000
1880	237,000	1,400,000	100,000	1,737,000	7,600,000
1888	300,000	1,800,000	140,000	2,240,000	9,200,000

Source: Michael G. Mulhall, *The Dictionary of Statistics*, p. 548.

moved slowly. There was, nevertheless, a gathering sense of purpose in Russian economic policy. Specifically, the Russian state:

—built up its gold reserves as the basis for a stable currency and international credit-worthiness, and generated budget surpluses for direct investment and industrial subsidy;

—encouraged and undertook foreign borrowing;

—directly stimulated industry through orders to meet government requirements;

—shifted gradually, beginning in 1877, from a liberal to a protectionist tariff policy, climaxed by the high duties of 1891;

—purposefully generated foreign exchange by forced grain exports;

—encouraged industry through the policy of the state-owned banks;

—provided direct and indirect government financing of the railways, of which there were some eighteen thousand miles by 1890.

In the 1890's, the Russian take-off clearly took place, its contours described well by the Soviet historian Peter Lyashchenko:

> During the last decade of the nineteenth century . . . Russian industry outstripped nearly all countries. The smelting of pig iron during this ten-year period, for example, increased in England by 18 per cent, in Germany by 72, in the United States by 50, and in Russia by 190, as a result of which Russia became the seventh ranking power in 1880, sixth in 1890, fifth in 1895, and fourth in 1900. The production of iron during this period increased in England by 8 per cent, in Germany by 78, in the United States by 63, and in Russia by 116. The coal industry of Great Britain expanded by 22 per cent, that of Germany by 52, of the United States by 61, and that of Russia by 131. Finally, in number of spindles operating in the cotton industry, England made a gain of 3.8 per cent in the course of the same decade, the United States, 25.6, the European continent, 33, and Russia, 76. By virtue of this number of spindles, Russia in 1890 owned 4 per cent of the world's total number of spindles and 14 per cent of the total spindles in use on the European conti-

nent, while by 1899 it accounted for 6 per cent of the world total and 18 per cent of the European total number of spindles. . . . the 1890's definitely brought the national economy of Russia into the world system of capitalist economy as a major national-capitalist entity with vast natural possibilities for development and with capitalist institutions penetrating deeply into the nation's economy.[64]

There was a period of industrial stagnation early in the new century, then a second surge down to 1914, firmly launched by 1908. The latter saw a more diversified industrial expansion, marking the beginnings of the Russian drive to technological maturity. It also saw a definitive completion of the freeing of the serfs, an accelerated increase in agricultural output, greatly enlarged allocations to education, and a diminished relative role for foreign capital and entrepreneurship.

Evidently Soviet total output per capita did not move at the same rate as the increase in industrial production; but the estimates for the former are available only in rough approximation for long periods. Table V-22, showing (by two independent calculations) the rate of increase in industrial output for shorter intervals, catches the irregular phases of Russian expansion from 1860 to 1913 with greater sensitivity. The acceleration of the 1890's emerges clearly, as does the subsequent stagnation and then the resumption of rapid growth in the pre-1914 decade.

Later Soviet industrial growth was also marked by phases of acceleration and deceleration (Table V-23). The 1913 overall level of output was reattained by about 1928; then came Stalin's two five-year plans, which rapidly carried forward the heavy-industry sectors of the drive to technological maturity to the eve of the German at-

TABLE V-22. *Russian Industrial Growth Rates, 1860–1913 (Index: 1913 = 100)*

	Borenstein-Goldsmith Index	Annual Average Rate of Increase (%)		Nutter Index	Annual Average Rate of Increase (%)	
1860	8.8			5.7		
1865	7.5	−3.1		4.3	−5.5	
1870	11	8.0		6.4	8.3	
1875	14	4.9	4.4	9.9	9.1	5.2
1880	18	5.2		13	5.6	
1885	24	5.9		19	7.9	
1890	32	5.9		25	5.6	
1895	44	6.6		39	9.3	
1900	63	7.4		59	8.6	
1905	61	−0.6	5.1	60	0.3	6.4
1910	86	7.1		78	5.4	
1913	100	5.2		100	8.6	

Source: G. Warren Nutter, *The Growth of Industrial Production in the Soviet Union* (Princeton: Princeton University Press, 1962), p. 164. For a discussion of these indexes and their weighting systems, see ibid., pp. 343–345.

TABLE V-23. *Soviet Industrial Production, 1913–1972 (Average Annual Percentage Rate of Growth)*

1913–1928	0.1
1928–1940	9.9
1940–1955	4.6
1956–1960	8.9
1961–1965	6.9
1966–1970	6.8
1971	6.2
1972	5.0

Sources: 1913–1955, Nutter, *The Growth of Industrial Production in the Soviet Union*, p. 163; 1956–1972, Rush V. Greenslade and Wade E. Robertson, "Industrial Production in the USSR," in *Soviet Economic Prospects for the Seventies*, Papers Submitted to the Joint Economic Committee, Congress of the United States (Washington, D.C.: Government Printing Office, 1973), p. 271.

tack on Russia in 1941. The Soviet economy recovered quickly, enjoying a high rate of growth in the 1950's, which decelerated in the next decade and into the 1970's.

The aggregate data on Russian and Soviet real product per capita, presented in Chart V-24, part 3, show a marked acceleration from 1885 to 1900 as compared to the previous fifteen years. The average rate of growth is somewhat less from 1900 to 1913, due to the relative stagnation of the early years of the century. From 1928 to the present, putting aside the terrible setback of the Second World War, Soviet output per capita has moved forward at high but decelerating rates.

Taking the aggregate performance of Russia-USSR over the whole sweep of its industrialization, its economy belongs in the family of the late-comers of the nineteenth century; e.g., Sweden and Japan. Averaged over long periods, its rate of growth in output per capita is higher than that of countries which entered take-off earlier (Table V-24).

Estimates of gross investment rates are available only since 1928. They show a rise (in 1937 prices) from 12.5 percent in 1928 to 26 percent in 1937. The ratio then fell with the rise in pre-1941 defense expenditures. A further increase occurs in the postwar years to levels over 30 percent in the 1960's, accompanied by a sustained decline in the productivity of investment outlays.

Despite certain special features, including wars and revolution, the sectoral pattern of Russian economic growth is reasonably straightforward:

—Cotton textile production has a long history; it led the way between 1815 and 1860. As in continental Western Europe, modernization of textile production did not generate sufficient spreading effects to lift the economy as a whole into take-off.

—The clearly marked take-off of the 1890's bore a family relationship to the American surge of the 1850's; that is, accelerated

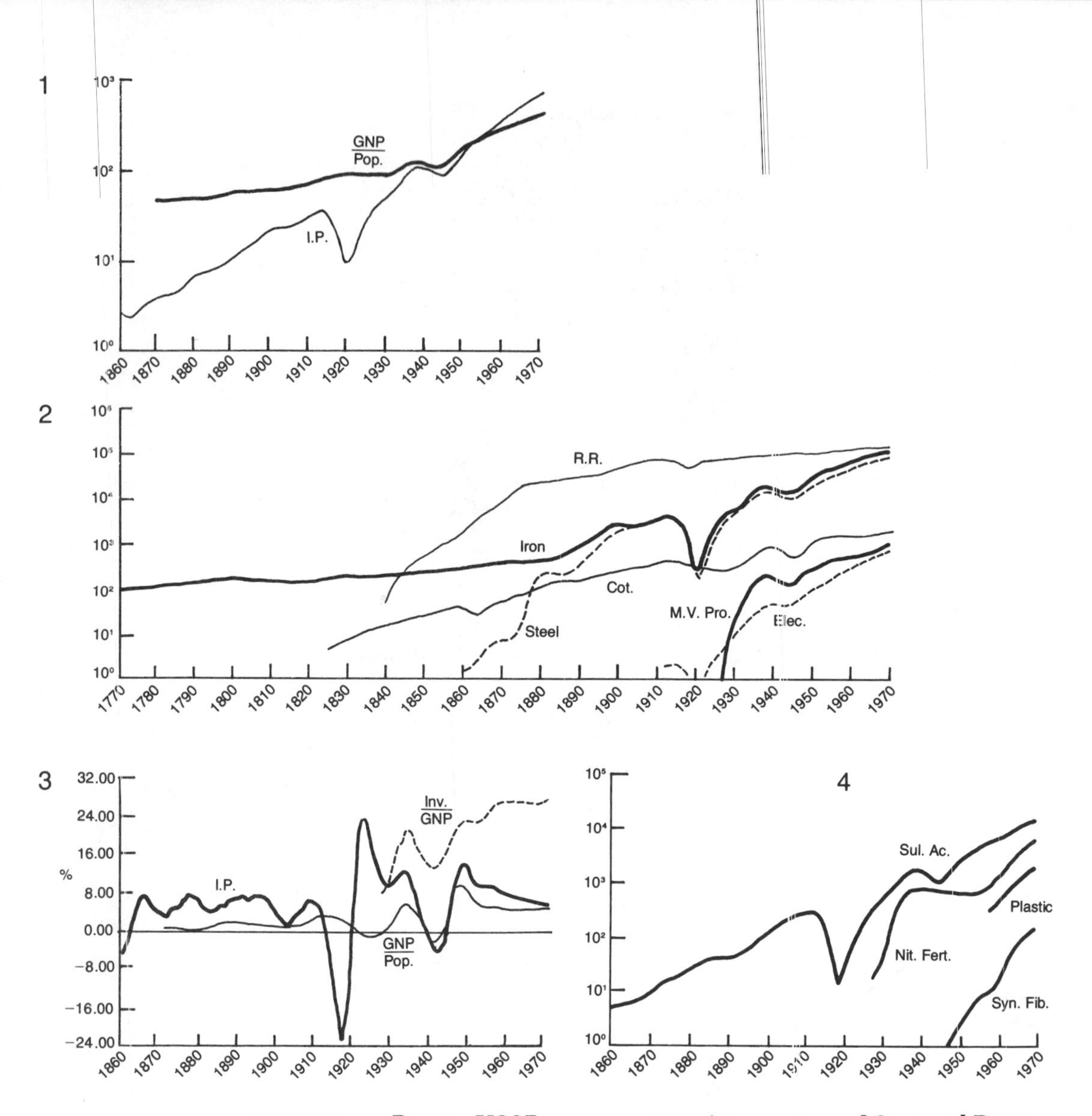

CHART V-24. *Russia-USSR, 1770–1972: Aggregate and Sectoral Data (Smoothed)*

1. GNP per capita ($\frac{\text{GNP}}{\text{Pop.}}$); industrial production index (I.P.).

2. Six major sectors: railroads (kilometers) (R.R.); raw cotton consumption (Cot.); production of iron (Iron); steel (Steel); electricity (Elec.); and motor vehicles (M.V. Pro.).

3. Gross investment as % of GNP ($\frac{\text{Inv.}}{\text{GNP}}$); rate of change, GNP per capita ($\frac{\text{GNP}}{\text{Pop.}}$); rate of change, industrial production (I.P.).

4. Production of four major chemicals: sulphuric acid (Sul. Ac.); nitrogen fertilizer (Nit. Fert.); plastics and resins (Plastics); and synthetic fibers (Syn. Fib.).

Sources: See Appendix D.

railroadization, with evident industrial spreading effects, accompanied by an expansion of agricultural production and acreage in an international environment of rising agricultural prices, after the mid-1890's.

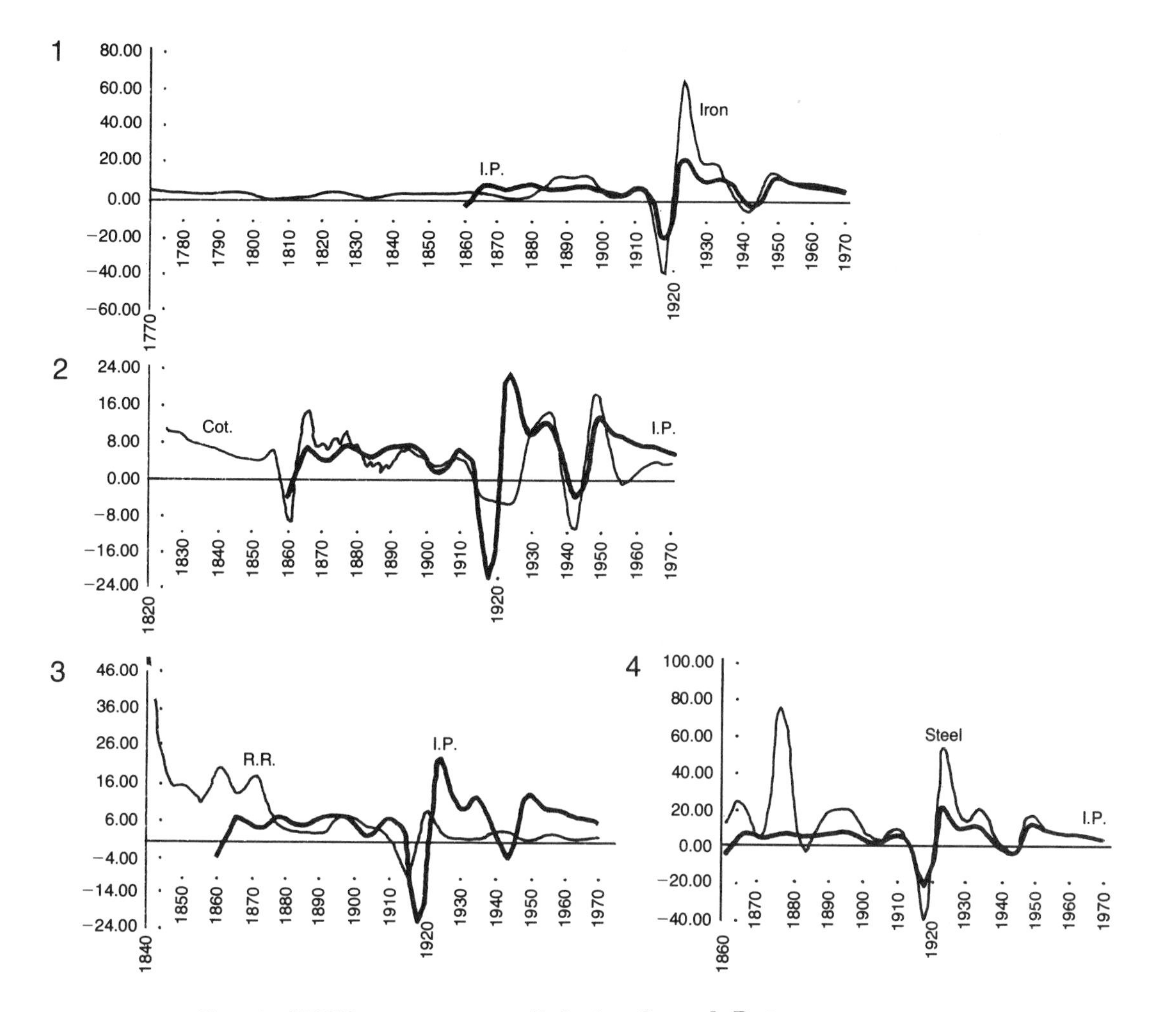

CHART V-25. *Russia-USSR, 1770–1972: Relative Growth Rates—Major Sectors and Industrial Production (Smoothed)*

1. Iron production (Iron).
2. Raw cotton consumption (Cot.).
3. Railroads (kilometers) (R.R.).
4. Steel production (Steel).

Sources: See Appendix D.

—The story of pig iron is, of course, distinctive, with the decline from eighteenth-century pre-eminence, based on the ore and charcoal of the Urals. The industry there was considerably modernized in the course of the nineteenth century. But there is also an analogy with the German take-off; that is, the exploitation of the Ruhr, in the one case, the linking of Krivoi Rog iron ore and Donets coal, in the other, which brought the Ukraine to primacy over the Urals in iron and steel production in the 1890's.

—Electricity, the various chemicals, and the internal combustion engine were absorbed with something of a lag, as compared with the United States and Western Europe. As of 1913, the lag in certain of

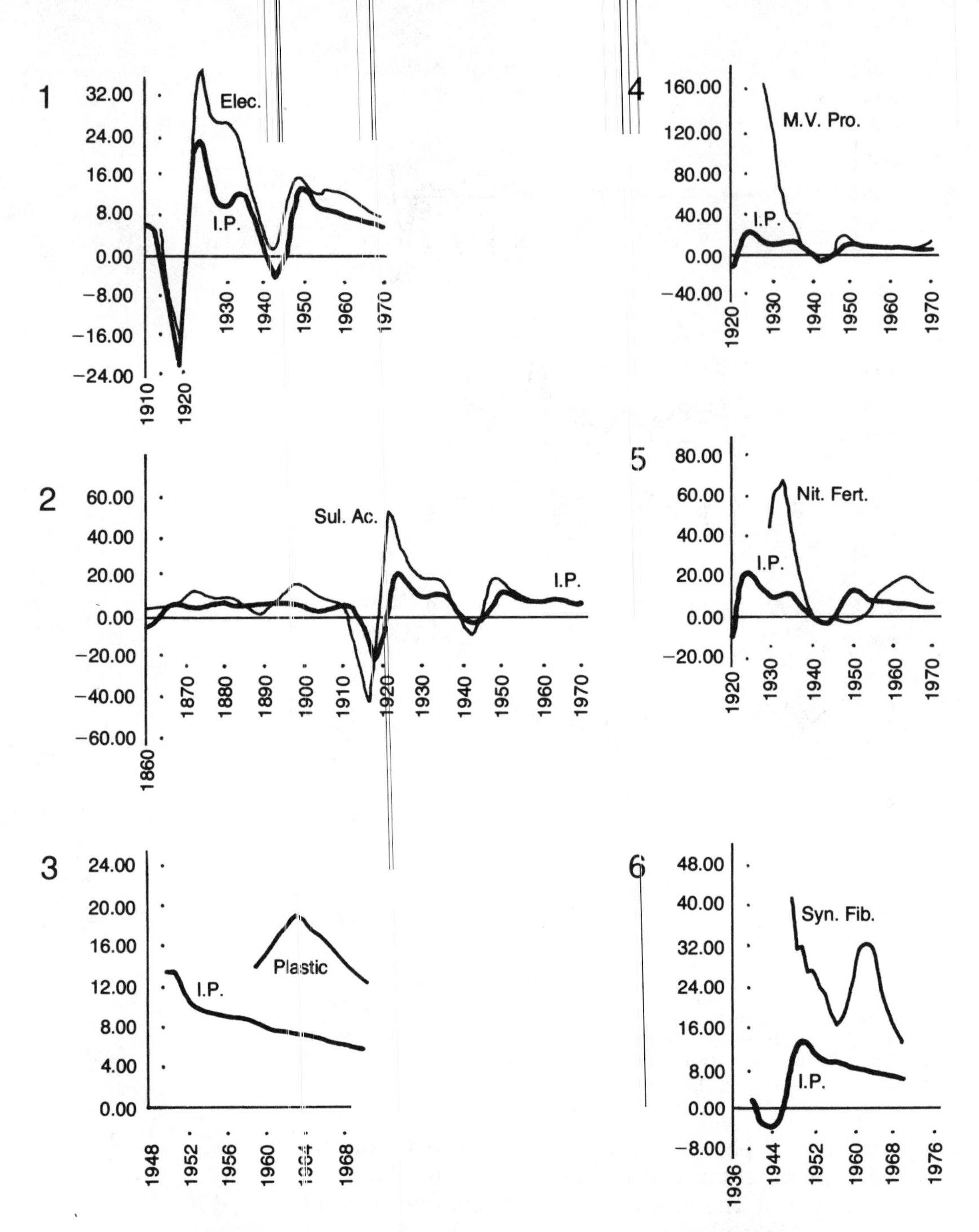

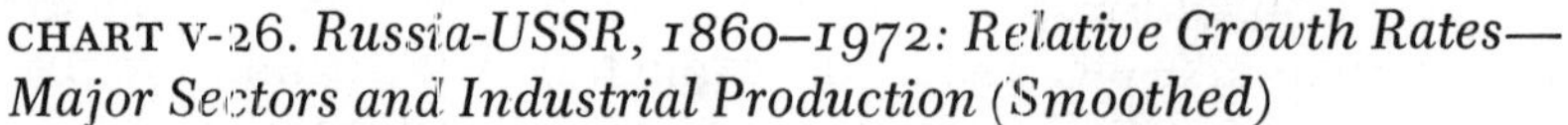

CHART V-26. *Russia-USSR, 1860–1972: Relative Growth Rates—Major Sectors and Industrial Production (Smoothed)*

1. Electricity (Elec.).
2. Sulphuric acid (Sul. Ac.).
3. Plastics and resins (Plastic).
4. Motor vehicle (M.V. Pro.).
5. Nitrogen fertilizer (Nit. Fert.).
6. Synthetic fibers (Syn. Fib.).

Sources: See Appendix D.

TABLE V-24. *Growth of National Product per Capita in Constant Prices, Long Periods: Selected Countries*

	Rate of Growth per Decade (%)
Russia-USSR	
1860 to 1913	14.4
1913 to 1958	27.4
Sweden	
1861–1865 to 1960–1962	28.3
Japan	
1879–1881 to 1959–1961	26.4
United Kingdom	
1780 to 1881	13.4
1855–1859 to 1957–1959	14.1
France	
1841–1850 to 1960–1962	17.9
Germany–West Germany	
1851–1855 to 1871–1875	9.2
1871–1875 to 1960–1962	17.9
United States	
1839 to 1960–1962	17.2

Source: Simon Kuznets, *Modern Economic Growth* (New Haven and London: Yale University Press, 1966), pp. 64–65.

these new sectors, vis-à-vis the United States, was less than for the older textile, heavy-industry, and railway-associated sectors. In Table V-25, compare, for example, the lags in cotton and woolen fabrics, pig iron, steel, rails, and railroad cars with those for electric power, petroleum, synthetic dyes, motor vehicle tires, and rayon fabrics.

After 1913 the gap widened down to 1928, as the United States moved easily through the First World War and the 1920's, while Russia suffered war devastation and slow recovery from the revolution. From 1928 the gap in heavy-industry sectors tended to narrow, as well as that in electric power and in most chemicals, although the trend was temporarily interrupted by the relative economic impact on the two countries of the Second World War. Large gaps persist in certain items of consumption, of which the late introduction of the privately owned automobile is the most dramatic case, a result which is, of course, largely a matter of Soviet policy.

Table V-26 sets out conclusions drawn from data presented by Charts V-25 and V-26.

Cotton manufacture expanded rapidly at a decelerating rate after 1815, as Table V-27 indicates. By the 1840's, it had attained roughly the scale of the French cotton industry during the 1820's.[65] As Chart

TABLE V-25. *Lag of Soviet Union behind United States in per Capita Output: Benchmark Dates, Forty-seven Industries*

	Lag (Number of Years) as of						
	1913	1928	1937	1955	1958	1960 Plan	1965 Plan
Iron ore	73	88+	52	54	55	51	46
Pig iron	48	84	52	56	57	55	53
Steel ingots	30	46	40	49	49	47	39
Rolled steel	28+	43+	50	52	50	47	39
Copper	52	69	57	65	n.a.	65	n.a.
Lead	105+	120+	109	76	n.a.	75	n.a.
Zinc	53	68	57	59	n.a.	56	n.a.
Electric power	14	27	26	25	20	20	18
Coal	66	80	69	69	64	63	68
Coke	36	53	49	56	57	n.a.	n.a.
Crude petroleum	27	40	34	41	38	39	32
Natural gas	33	45	52	69	49	n.a.	23
Soda ash	27	40	43	45	n.a.	33	n.a.
Caustic soda	19	34	40	35	n.a.	30	n.a.
Sulphuric acid	26	38	32	34	35	n.a.	n.a.
Mineral fertilizer	43+	58+	40	16	17	15	—
Synthetic dyes	14+	12	20	18	n.a.	n.a.	n.a.
Paper	54+	69+	67	71	70	70	71
Motor vehicle tires	13	26	31	42	44	n.a.	n.a.
Cement	30	45	38	47	38	10	—
Construction gypsum	17	43	36	49	n.a.	n.a.	n.a.
Construction lime	33+	48+	57+	75+	n.a.	n.a.	n.a.
Lumber	114+	129+	102	111	113	115	116
Rails	63	78+	77	84	n.a.	n.a.	n.a.
Window glass	34+	44	−2	15	11	—	—
Railroad freight cars	33+	48+	57+	75+	78+	80+	n.a.
Railroad passenger cars	30	48+	57	69	71	66	n.a.
Flour	—	—	—	—	n.a.	n.a.	n.a.
Butter	30	46	50	58	49	49	44
Vegetable oil	16	28	40	44	43	37	38
Meat slaughtering	33+	48+	57+	75+	78+	80+	85+
Sausages	24+	39+	48+	59	54	n.a.	n.a.
Fish catch	33+	48+	57+	19	10	—	—
Soap	34+	49+	58+	76+	79+	n.a.	n.a.
Salt	33+	43	46	58	n.a.	n.a.	n.a.
Raw sugar consumption	43+	58+	66	79	68	60	49
Canned food	43+	58+	62	60	58	56	n.a.
Beer	43+	58+	67+	85+	n.a.	n.a.	n.a.
Cigarettes	0	11	16	23	23	n.a.	n.a.
Boots and shoes	23+	38+	47+	65+	68+	70+	75+
Rubber footwear	14+	29+	38+	56+	n.a.	n.a.	n.a.
Cotton fabrics	43+	58+	67+	85+	88+	87	95+

TABLE V-25. *Lag of Soviet Union behind United States in Per Capita Output: Benchmark Dates, Forty-seven Industries (Continued)*

	Lag (Number of Years) as of						
	1913	1928	1937	1955	1958	1960 Plan	1965 Plan
Pure silk and nylon fabrics	38	58+	64	82	n.a.	n.a.	n.a.
Rayon and mixed fabrics	14+	29+	38+	23	n.a.	n.a.	n.a.
Woolen and worsted fabrics	43+	58+	67+	85+	88+	90+	95+
Bicycles	14+	29+	38+	7	—	—	n.a.
Sewing machines	14+	29+	38+	—	—	—	n.a.
Median	—	—	—	56	52	51	44

Source: Nutter, *The Growth of Industrial Production in the Soviet Union*, p. 274, where notes and detailed sources are provided.

TABLE V-26. *Approximate Timing of Leading Sectors: Russia-USSR, 1820–1972*

Sector	Maximum Rate of Expansion	Estimated Time Sector Became Leading Sector	Estimated Time Sector Ceased to Lead	Comments
Cotton consumption	1820's	[a]	1880's	Periods of rapid recovery after U.S. Civil War and First and Second World Wars set aside.
Railroads	1880's	1890's	—	—
Pig iron	1890's	1890's	1950's	Post–World War I recovery rate set aside.
Steel	1870's	1890's	1950's	Post–World War I recovery rate set aside.
Electricity	1920's	1920's	1950's	—
Motor vehicles	1930's	1950's	—	Passenger vehicles expanded rapidly only from 1950's.
Sulphuric acid	1920's	[a]	—	Growth exceeded average growth in industrial production throughout.
Nitrogen	1930's	[a]	—	—
Plastics	1960's	[a]	—	—
Synthetic fibers	1945–1950	[a]	—	—

[a] Not judged, by itself, a leading sector.

TABLE V-27. *Cotton Textile Manufacture: Russia, 1821–1887*

Period	Cotton Consumed (Tons)	Average Annual Growth Rate (%)	Cloth Made (Miles)
1821–1830	50,000		300,000
1831–1840	130,000	10.0	750,000
1841–1850	240,000	6.3	1,400,000
1851–1860	360,000	4.1	2,100,000
1861–1870	320,000	−1.2	1,800,000
1871–1880	820,000	9.9	4,600,000
1881–1887	890,000	0.9	5,150,000

Source: Mulhall, *The Dictionary of Statistics*, p. 160.

V-25, part 2, reveals, there were strong surges in cotton textile manufacture not only in the period of post-1865 recovery (and after the First and Second World Wars), but also in the cyclical expansions of the 1890's and the pre-1914 years. The iron and steel series reflect the exceedingly high priority for heavy-industry production in the 1930's and the 1950's. In fact, the Russian drive to technological maturity is best viewed as comprising the following four distinct phases:

1. 1906–1914. Industrialization proceeded between recovery from the 1905 revolution to the First World War on a wider, more differentiated basis than in the 1890's.
2. 1920–1929. Although overall production only approximated the 1913 level in 1928, considerable progress was made in the 1920's in electricity and in educating the working force, managers, and administrators. The 1920's was an important phase in the modernization of Russian society as well as the period of consolidation of Soviet rule.
3. 1930–1941. Heavy industry expanded rapidly and, toward the end of the period, was diverted to increased armament production.
4. 1945–1956. Reconstruction was accomplished and the drive to technological maturity completed.

Since about 1956 the Soviet Union has moved some distance in the broad direction of high mass-consumption; but, with a low-productivity agriculture and continuing large military and space outlays, its momentum in the relevant leading sectors has been less than that of Western Europe and Japan. The marked deceleration of growth rates in the past two decades is judged to be mainly the result of four factors: the failure to move forward vigorously (like Western Europe and Japan) in the technologies of high mass-consumption; the necessity to allocate increased investment resources to an inherently low-productivity agriculture; the need to rely on increasingly distant and expensive raw-materials sources;

alue (£ Millions)		
otton	Manufactures	Net
4	24	20
0	45	35
4	56	42
2	69	47
0	75	35
2	138	76
4	123	69

and the continued allocation of its best scientific, engineering, and entrepreneurial talent to military production.

The stages of Russian growth emerge, then, as follows.

Take-off: 1890–1905.

Drive to Technological Maturity: 1905–1956.

High Mass-Consumption: 1956–.

35

Italy

Although Italy was, relatively, a late-comer to take-off, it played, as we all know, a significant role in certain aspects of the early modern history of Europe which led to the first industrial revolution. Scientific institutions were set up in Italy as early as the sixteenth century. Copernicus was trained in Bologna for astronomy, in Padua for medicine as well as canon law; and Galileo, of course, was a pathfinder in experimental science. William Harvey, too, was a product of Padua as well as Cambridge; and one of his distinguished successors was Marcello Malpighi of Bologna. The voyages of discovery which led to the commercial revolution also owed a great deal to Italy and Italians who helped orient Spain and Portugal to the Atlantic in the wake of their frustrations in the eastern Mediterranean; and the Dutch Republic learned much about commerce and banking from the northern Italian cities. Above all, perhaps, the forty years of almost unbroken peace in the second half of the fifteenth century, ending with the invasion of Charles VIII in 1494, permitted the Italian Renaissance, in all its dimensions, which provided a philosophic and psychological as well as artistic base for much in the modern world.

But Italian creativity did not produce an industrial revolution. It can be argued that the thrust of the early Italian scientists was to modernize the Church rather than to accelerate material progress; that Italy was denied the political unity and nationalism which harnessed the new science and technology to the mercantilist struggle for power and profit in northern Europe; that its resources and geography were against it. Nevertheless, Italy participated in the expansion of international trade in the eighteenth century and experienced the accelerated population increase which marked many European nations after 1750. It was, however, relatively slow to acquire the new technologies in textiles, iron, and steam which moved Britain into modern growth at the end of the eighteenth century, the United States and northwestern Europe in the first half of the nineteenth century.

Aggregate and sectoral data tell us clearly that the Italian take-off came in the pre-1914 generation. Per capita product increased at an average annual rate of less than 0.2 percent between the early 1860's and the late 1890's. From the latter date to the period 1910–1914 it increased at an annual average rate of more than 2 percent By League of Nations calculations, the pace of industrialization during the take-off was sufficient for Italy substantially to increase its percentage of world manufacturing production: from 2.4 percent in 1881–1885 to 3.1 percent in 1906–1910.

The figure for 1881–1885 is significant, however, because it suggests that Italy was not wholly bypassed in the diffusion of industry during the earlier decades of the nineteenth century. It did not begin at the extremely low levels of, say, Turkey and Iran in the 1920's. As Table V-28 shows, Italy lagged behind France in the nineteenth century; and, down to the 1880's, it lagged behind Spain as well in cotton and iron consumption, although its railroadization began a bit earlier. Given the substantially larger Italian population, the lag in what might be called per capita industrialization was greater, although both Italy and Spain were still overwhelmingly rural in the 1890's, with less than 20 percent of the people living in cities or towns with population over ten thousand. In the late 1880's Italy and Spain lagged behind France by twenty-five to fifty years, according to these rough measures; but, even before the Italian take-off, the gap was being narrowed. As of the mid-1890's, Mulhall estimated Italian and Spanish average income per capita at about half that of France.

The unification of Italy in 1870 permitted the government to turn to the tasks of internal development; and the pace of progress accelerated from that time. But more than Italian political unity was involved. Here the Spanish figures are instructive, illustrating as they do that the technologies generated in the industrial revolution from northwestern Europe generally took some time before they took root in the south. And this was true, of course, within Italy itself.[66] In 1871 the illiteracy rate was 59 percent in the north, 84 percent in the south. The north was not only closer, in geography as in culture and social structure, to the vital centers of western Europe, but it also contained better supplies of iron ore and moved more quickly into cotton textiles, machinery, and the production of railway equipment. And when, during the take-off, electricity became available, it was the north that could exploit its hydroelectric power resources. The new central government tried to act in compensatory ways; for example, in 1871 only 7 percent of Italy's railroads were in the south, by 1875 the proportion had risen to 32 percent. But the first phase of Italian industrialization (as in other countries) tended to heighten a regional differential which the long sweep of Italy's fragmented history had already created.

The movement of Italy into sustained and accelerated industrial growth between 1881 and 1913 has been well mapped.[67] The basic data are set out in Table V-29, as well as in Chart V-27.

TABLE V-28. *Comparative Economic Indicators: France, Italy, and Spai 1830–1894*

	1830	1840	1850	1860	18
Cotton consumption (millions of lbs.)					
France	68	116	140	226	22
Italy	4	8	16	26	2
Spain	6	14	34	52	5
Iron consumption (tons)					
France	250,000	—	600,000	—	1,350,00
Italy	20,000	—	50,000	—	100,00
Spain	40,000	—	80,000	—	150,00
Railroads (mileage)					
France	—	360	1,890	5,880	9,77
Italy	—	13	270	1,120	3,83
Spain	—	—	80	1,190	3,20
Steam power (horsepower)					
France	—	87,000	380,000	1,148,000	1,853,00
Italy	—	—	—	—	330,00
Spain	—	—	—	—	241,00
Earnings per capita (£ British)					
France	—	—	—	—	-
Italy	—	—	—	—	-
Spain	—	—	—	—	-

Sources: 1830–1888, Mulhall, *The Dictionary of Statistics*, pp. 156 (cotton); 333 (iron 495 (railroads); 545 (steam); 1894 data from Michael Mulhall, *Industries and Wealth Nations*, pp. 119, 193, and 204 (cotton); 189, 201, 545 (steam power); 391 (earnings p

TABLE V-29. *Total and Sectoral Industrial Growth Rates: Italy, 1861–1913, by Subperiods (Annual Average Percentag Rates of Change)*

	Total Industrial Production	Textile Production	
		Raw Cotton Production	Raw Wool Consumptio
1861–1888	1.7	6.9	0.6
1888–1896	0.0	5.3	1.0
1896–1908	5.1	5.2	6.9
1908–1913	1.5	−0.5	4.4
1861–1913	2.2	5.5	1.9

[a] Initial figure exceedingly low.

Source: B. R. Mitchell, *European Historical Statistics, 1750–1970* (Londo Macmillan, 1975), pp. 355 and 357 (index of total industrial production); p 429–430 (raw cotton consumption); pp. 444–445 (raw wool consumption

1880	1888	1894
200	310	363
64	152	231
88	105	143
—	1,900,000	—
—	290,000	—
—	300,000	—
14,500	20,900	—
5,340	7,830	—
4,550	5,930	—
3,024,000 (1878)	—	4,515,000 (1895)
414,000 (1877)	830,000	1,370,000
—	816,000	1,130,000
—	—	31.2
—	—	14.0
—	—	15.5

pita).

Note: As of 1894 Mulhall estimated the population of France at 3.4 million; Italy, 31.2; Spain, 17.6.

Ietals and Metalworking Production

inc	Iron Ore	Pig Iron	Crude Steel	Sulphuric Acid	Beer	Electricity
5.2[a]	2.8	2.0	58.2[a] (1880–1888)	—	—	—
3.4	1.8	−6.5	−7.0	—	−6.0	—
2.1	8.4	41.6[a]	30.0	13.8	14.6	27.8[a]
0.8	2.3	30.5	11.7	4.2	3.5	16.0
3.7	3.9	22.6	11.7	10.9	5.4	24.2

. 379 and 381 (zinc ore production); pp. 387 and 389 (iron ore production); pp. 393 and 395 (pig iron production); pp. 399–400 (crude steel production); pp. 460 and 462 (sulphuric acid production); pp. 472 and 475 (beer oduction); p. 480 (output of electricity).

The total industrial index suggests the slow preliminary expansion between 1861 and 1888, from a low initial base, and the subsequent deceleration. Then came the take-off of 1895–1913 and the pre-1914 deceleration Italy shared with other European states. The leading sectors of take-off lay in the metalworking and engineering, chemicals, and electricity sectors. Italian electricity production in 1913 approximated that of France and Britain, although it was far below that of Germany. The availability of hydroelectric power was peculiarly important for Italy, accounting for about three-quarters of the increase in electricity output, compensating to a degree for its poor coal endowment. Although Italian coal production expanded at a rate of 6 percent in the period 1861–1913, coal imports expanded at 7.6 percent. The exploitation of some indigenous deposits of petroleum and gas helped a bit to enlarge the energy base. The older textile industries also moved forward, and Italy acquired a modern beer industry and exploited its rather meager mineral resources. Italian aluminum production began as early as 1907.

The aggregate rate of growth in per capita product moved as shown in Table V-30 and Chart V-27, part 2.

If these figures are to be credited, the industrial surge of 1881–1888 was not of sufficient weight to lift real product per capita by counterbalancing a sluggish agriculture and a high rate of population increase. Taking the whole sweep, from take-off in the 1890's to the 1960's, Italy clearly belongs among the late-comers who gained ground on those who entered modern growth in the first half of the nineteenth century. Its average annual rate of growth in per capita product, damped by the sluggish south, was 2.8 percent from 1895–1899 to 1963–1967, somewhat lower than that for Sweden and Japan over a comparable period, but much higher than that for Britain, France, Belgium, and Germany.[68] Over shorter periods, per capita product moved in ways now familiar: rapid but decelerating growth in the pre-1914 generation; a relatively mild setback during the First World War; a strong expansion in the 1920's; again a relatively mild setback in the early 1930's; a reasonably strong recovery down to the eve of the Second World War; a severe setback during that war; and then a postwar phase of growth at about twice the rate of Italy's best previous performance.

There was an interesting break in momentum during the mid-1960's. Italian per capita product expanded at about 5 percent per annum from 1953 to 1963. It then slowed down to about half that rate in 1964–1965. This deceleration was linked to the rather sudden appearance of a relative labor shortage, increased labor bargaining power, and a rise in real wages, bringing with it, among other things, large meat imports which suddenly burdened the balance of payments. Up to that point the flow of labor from the Italian south had kept the labor market soft despite the large flow of Italian labor to Western Europe. In a sense, the long era of excess labor supply

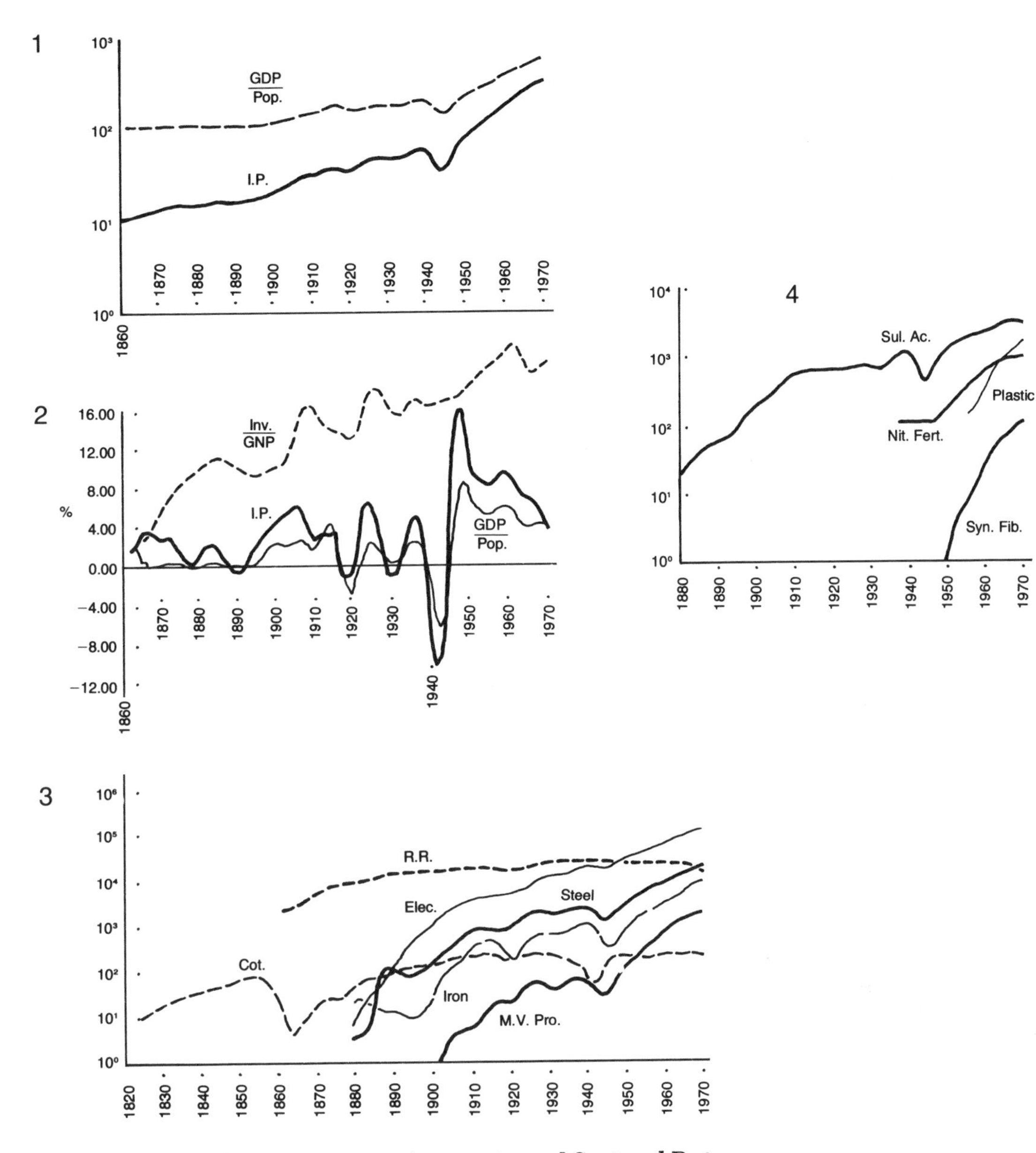

CHART V-27. *Italy, 1825–1972: Aggregate and Sectoral Data (Smoothed)*

1. GDP per capita ($\frac{\text{GDP}}{\text{Pop.}}$); industrial production index (I.P.).

2. Gross investment as % of GNP ($\frac{\text{Inv.}}{\text{GNP}}$); rate of change, GDP per capita ($\frac{\text{GDP}}{\text{Pop.}}$); rate of change, industrial production (I.P.).

3. Six major sectors: railroads (kilometers) (R.R.); raw cotton consumption (Cot.); production of iron (Iron); steel (Steel); electricity (Elec.); and motor vehicles (M.V. Pro.).

4. Production of four major chemicals: sulphuric acid (Sul. Ac.); nitrogen fertilizer (Nit. Fert.); plastics and resins (Plastic); and synthetic fibers (Syn. Fib.).

Sources: See Appendix D.

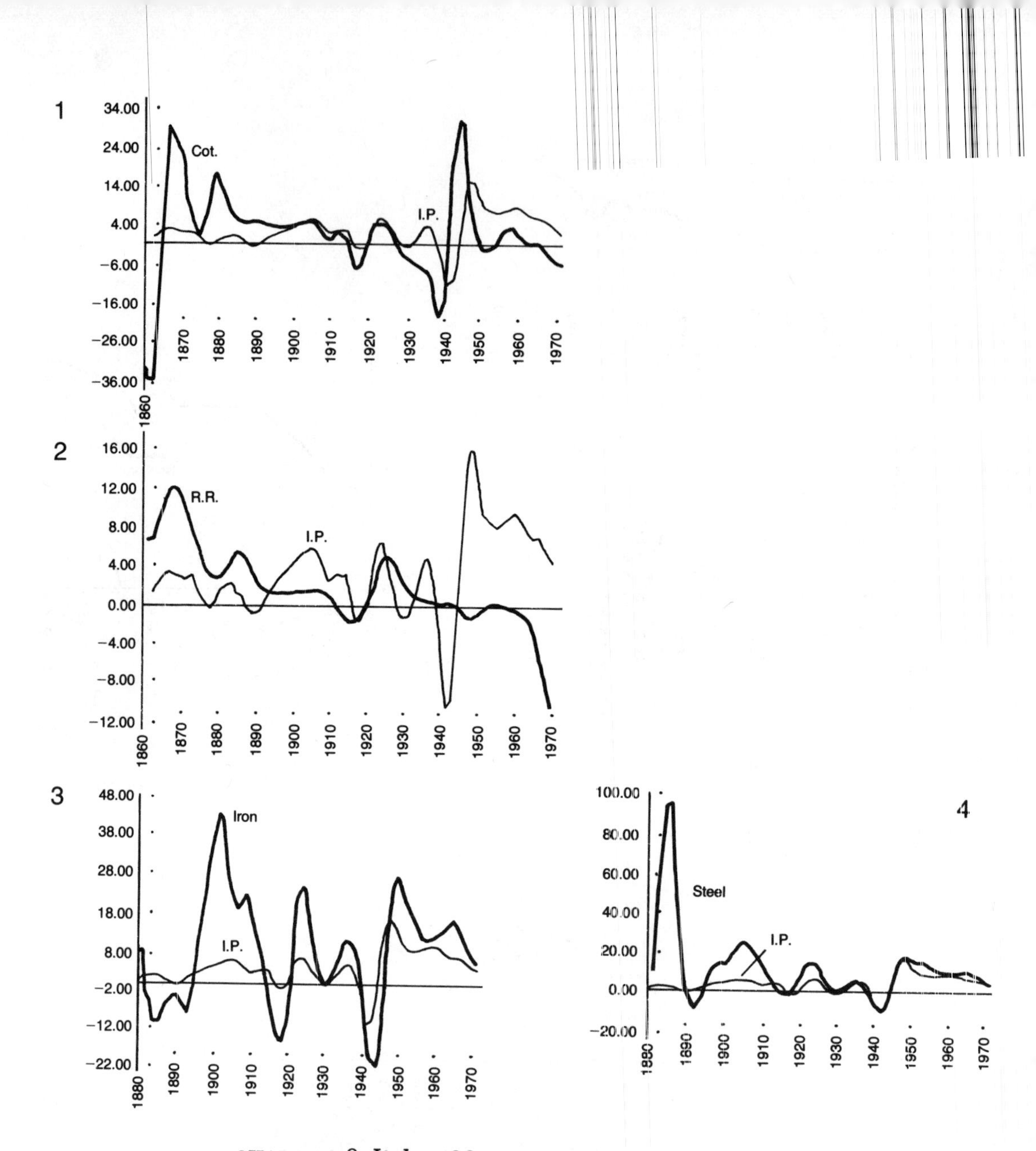

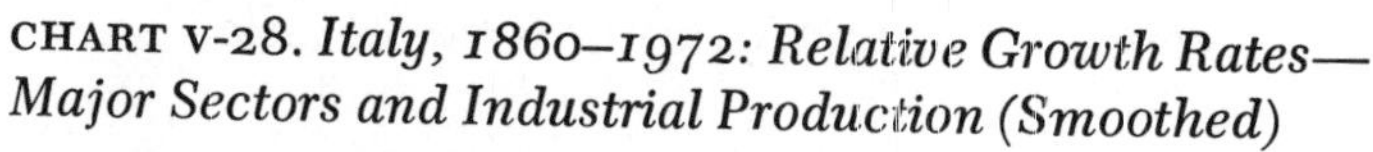

CHART V-28. *Italy, 1860–1972: Relative Growth Rates—Major Sectors and Industrial Production (Smoothed)*

1. Raw cotton consumption (Cot.).
2. Railroads (kilometers) (R.R.).
3. Iron production (Iron).
4. Steel production (Steel).

Sources: See Appendix D.

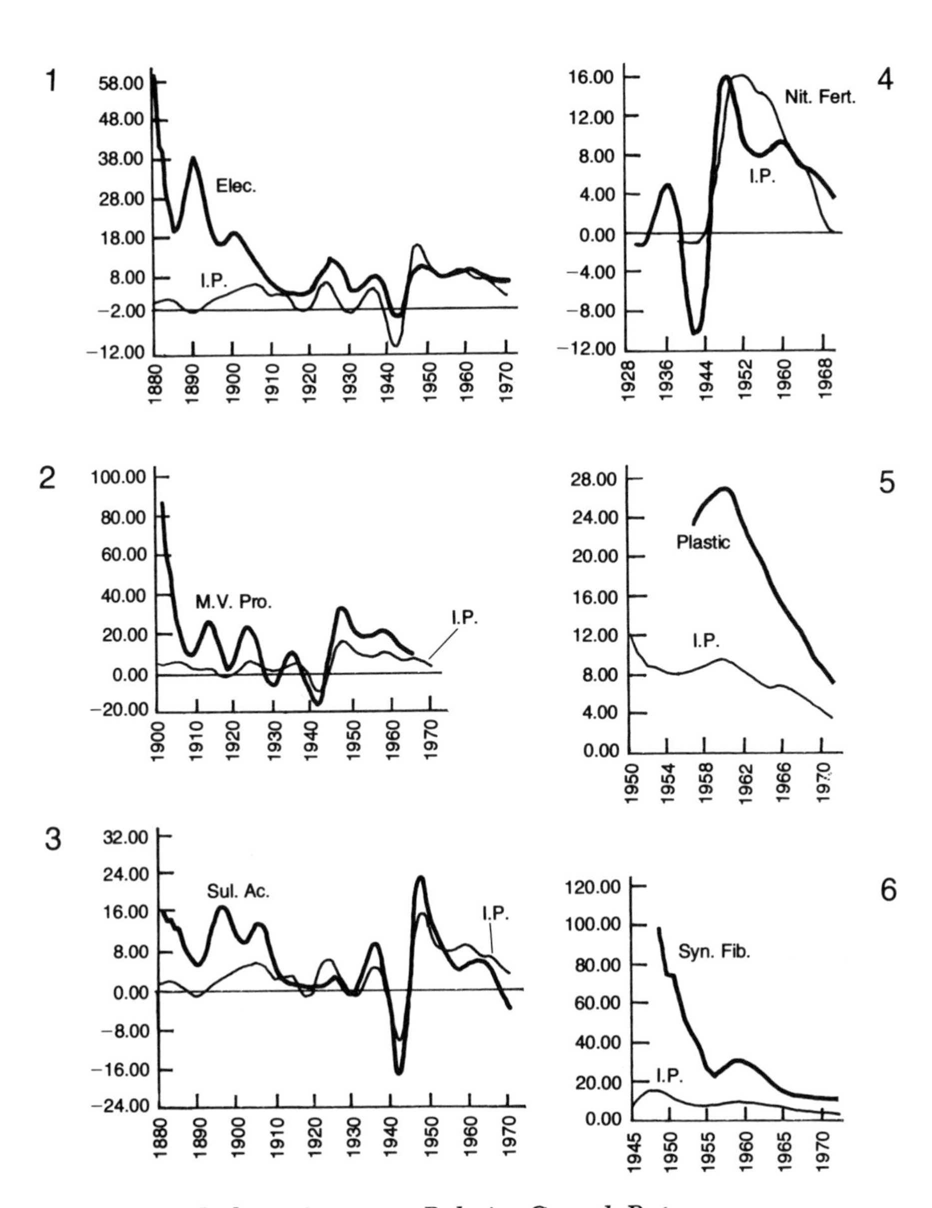

CHART V-29. *Italy, 1880–1972: Relative Growth Rates—Major Sectors and Industrial Production (Smoothed)*

1. Electricity (Elec.).
2. Motor vehicles (M.V. Pro.).
3. Sulphuric acid (Sul. Ac.).
4. Nitrogen fertilizer (Nit. Fert.).
5. Plastics and resins (Plastic).
6. Synthetic fibers (Syn. Fib.).

Sources: See Appendix D.

TABLE V-30. *Rate of Growth of Product per Capita: Italy, 1861–1970 (Annual Average Percentage Rate of Growth)*

1861–1864 to 1865–1869	0.5	1915–1919 to 1920–1924	1.8
1865–1869 to 1870–1874	0.1	1920–1924 to 1925–1929	2.4
1870–1874 to 1875–1879	0.4	1925–1929 to 1930–1934	−0.5
1875–1879 to 1880–1884	0.04	1930–1934 to 1935–1939	2.3
1880–1884 to 1885–1889	0.16	1935–1939 to 1940–1945	−4.3
1885–1889 to 1890–1894	0.2	1940–1945 to 1946–1949	2.1
1890–1894 to 1895–1899	0.1	1946–1949 to 1950–1954	5.6
1895–1899 to 1900–1904	2.3	1950–1954 to 1955–1959	4.9
1900–1904 to 1905–1909	2.2	1955–1959 to 1960–1964	5.7
1905–1909 to 1910–1914	1.9	1965 to 1970	5.3
1910–1914 to 1915–1919	0.04		

Sources: To 1950–1954, Instituto Centrale di Statistica, "Indogine statistica sullo sviluppo del reddito nazionale dell' Italia dal 1861 al 1956," *Annali di Statistica*, Series 8, vol. 9 (Rome, 1957), Table 37, pp. 251–252. Later data from official sources in *United Nations Statistical Yearbooks*, annual.

TABLE V-31. *Approximate Timing of Leading Sectors: Italy, 1870–1972*

Sector	Maximum Rate of Expansion	Estimated Time Sector Became Leading Sector	Estimated Time Sector Ceased to Lead	Comments
Cotton consumption	—	[a]	—	—
Railroads	1870's	[b]	1890's	—
Pig iron consumption	1900–1910	1900–1910	Late 1960's	—
Steel production	1880's	1895–1905	1960's	—
Electricity	1880's	1890's	1950's	—
Motor vehicles	1900–1910	1920's	Late 1960's	—
Sulphuric acid	1880's	[a]	1920's	Post-1945 surge in production ruled out.
Nitrogen	1950's	[a]	1960's	—
Plastics	1950's	[a]	—	—
Synthetic fibers	1945–1950	[a]	—	—

[a] Not judged, by itself, a leading sector.
[b] Spreading effects not sufficient to be judged a leading sector.

from southern Italy ended in those years, and Italy became a more normal Western European economy, although the north-south differential could still, of course, be detected in other indicators.

As Chart V-27, part 2, shows, the Italian gross investment rate rose in rather classical style during take-off; moved up again during the interwar years; and then sustained still higher levels, in the range of 20 percent during the great expansion of the 1950's and 1960's.

Against this background, the sectoral pattern of Italian growth set out in Charts V-28 and V-29 yields the conclusions summarized in Table V-31.

The Italian stages of growth emerge as follows.

Take-off: 1895–1913.

Drive to Technological Maturity: 1920–1940.

High Mass-Consumption: 1950–.

36

Canada

Like Australia, the United States, and Argentina, Canada moved into modern industrial growth only after overcoming through the railroad certain critical transport problems and, in a sense, overcoming also the attractiveness of concentrating on the exploitation of its rich natural resources.[69] Further, it shared with these nations a high level of income per capita in preindustrial times due to the balance between its population and its resource endowments. But it confronted a special circumstance: proximity to a dynamic United States which, at different times, drew off its workers and men of talent, provided a creative challenge, and, ultimately, offered a vital flow of agricultural and industrial technology, entrepreneurship, and capital as well as highly diversified trade.

The early economic history of Canada has been charted, under the inspiration of Harold Innis, in terms of furs, timber for shipbuilding, and, from about the mid-nineteenth century, sawn timber. Canadian development was also shaped by the hope of serving as an entrepôt for overseas exports from the American Middle West. This prospect stimulated canal building along the St. Lawrence and the early phase of railway building which peaked in the 1850's. The Erie Canal and then the American railway lines laid out to the Middle West in the 1850's frustrated this hope. Nevertheless, Canadian ties to the United States intensified in the 1850's and, to a degree, during the Civil War, when American markets absorbed a substantial flow of Canadian agricultural products. For a time the United States seemed to offer an alternative link at a time when Britain had moved toward a free-trade policy which appeared to cast Canada loose in the world economy, affecting its timber exports in particular. Thus, the U.S.-Canadian Reciprocity Treaty of 1854. But that treaty was abrogated by the United States in 1866, and the Canadian Confederation was created in 1867. It was clear that post–Civil War America would generate its own agricultural resources, and its dynamism might run against Canadian interests unless Canada took its destiny into its own hands. The confederation looked to the opening up of new lands and resources, a full east-west transcontinental railroad system, and a Canadian industry protected by tariffs. As indicated in Chapter 14, the three decades that followed were, on balance, disappointing. Prices of Canadian exports were falling, and there was substantial net emigration to the United States. Nevertheless, much constructive change was brought about, and the transport, agricultural, and industrial foundations were laid for the post-1896 Canadian take-off, rooted in a rapid expansion of wheat production in the prairie provinces, but with much wider repercussions for Canadian growth.

The aggregate data set out in Chart V-30, parts 1 and 2, capture the rapid but uneven pace of Canadian growth since confederation. Table V-32 sets out, for key intervals, the movement of GNP per capita in terms of constant dollars, which can be seen in greater detail also in Chart V-30, part 2.

O. J. Firestone confirms that the turning point in the acceleration of overall Canadian growth came after the trough of 1896, a watershed interval for which good national product data are not available.[70] The figure for 1900–1910 catches the high momentum of Canada's take-off, which continued down to the eve of the First World War. Despite the wartime boom of 1914–1918, the decade as a whole was one of marked deceleration; but Canada shared the American boom of the 1920's. The Second World War lifted Canada, like the United States, from an incomplete recovery during the 1930's to full employment and rapid expansion in output. After an initial postwar readjustment and decline, postwar Canadian growth resumed at a high rate, generally following the phases of acceleration and retardation to be observed in the United States.

As one would expect in a nation laying out an exceedingly expensive transport infrastructure in a thinly populated land, the Canadian proportion of gross investment to GNP was relatively high in the pre–take-off period, 1870–1890: over 15 percent (Chart V-30, part 2). Supported by large capital imports, the proportion was 26.5 percent in 1910. The figure was slightly lower in the boom of the 1920's and in the post-1950 generation of rapid growth, averaging about 23 percent in both periods, with a slightly declining trend in the 1960's.

TABLE V-32. *Rate of Change: Real GNP per Capita, Canada, 1867–1970 (Average Annual Percentage Rate of Growth)*

1867–1870	1.3	1920–1929	2.0
1870–1880	1.5	1929–1939	−0.5
1880–1890	1.8	1939–1945	7.3
1890–1900	1.7	1945–1950	−0.5
1900–1910	2.4	1950–1953	2.7
1910–1920	0.2	1960–1970	3.5

Sources: 1867–1953, O. J. Firestone, *Canada's Economic Development, 1867–1953*, p. 66; 1953–1970, *United Nations Statistical Yearbooks*, annual.

The development of Canada's modern industrial structure clearly dates from the pre-1914 boom launched in the 1890's. Canada belongs among the cases of take-off in which there was convergence between agricultural and industrial expansion; as, for example, in the United States of the 1850's, Russia after 1890, São Paulo in the period 1900–1920, Australia after 1901.[71] Nevertheless, Canadian industrial development proceeded after the mid-1890's from a considerable manufacturing base which had been expanding rapidly since the middle of the nineteenth century. Table V-33 captures the scale of this expansion and its changing composition from 1851 to 1900. Canadian manufactures in this "pioneering stage," to use Firestone's phrase, were "the simpler types of manufacturing . . . carried on to process natural products for export and to serve the more urgent needs of the community for the bare necessities of life: food, clothing, and shelter."[72] In a high-income-per-capita economy, engaged in raw-materials processing and export, the proportionate contribution of this kind of manufacturing can be quite high (18.3 percent in 1851, 20.8 percent in 1900). The processing of wheat and timber led the way throughout, with meat packing and dairy products emerging during the 1890's. Manufacturing was generally conducted in small units, using simple technology. There was no significant increase in industrial productivity over this period. The market served by Canadian industrial plants was small; and entrepreneurial skill and ambition were generally modest. This was the kind of manufacturing activity which dominated the American industrial structure as a whole until the big New England textile mills emerged, post-1815, and a modern metallurgical and engineering industry, between 1843 and 1860. By the turn of the century, however, all this was changing, as Canada moved into a phase of truly modern industrial development reflected in the sectoral patterns of Chart V-30, parts 3 and 4.

The steel industry as well as modern cotton textiles expanded rapidly after 1900, as did pulp and paper, farm machinery, motor vehicles and sectors linked to them. Despite the retardation in real GNP during the First World War, the absorption of new industrial technologies continued and in certain sectors (e.g., shipbuilding and aircraft construction) accelerated. Diversification proceeded rapidly down to 1929, backed by large direct industrial investments from the United States. The Canadian drive to technological maturity was brought toward completion by forced-draft industrial development during and immediately after the Second World War, symbolized in Chart V-32 by the emergence of plastics and synthetic fiber production on a large scale.

The sectoral data in Charts V-31 and V-32 yield the sequence set out in Table V-34.

The Canadian stages of economic growth may be set out as follows, reflecting the fact that a high-income-per-capita nation can achieve high mass-consumption before technological maturity; that

TABLE V-33. *Ten Leading Industries, by Value of Output: Canada, Selected Years, 1851–1900*

	Gross Value of Production ($ Millions)	Gross Value of Production (% of Total)		Gross Value of Production ($ Millions)	Gross Value of Production (% of Total)
1851[a]			1890		
Flour and grist mill products	24	13.1	Log products	54	11.5
Log products	10	13.0	Flour and grist mill products	52	11.1
Shipbuilding	7	9.1	Clothing	34	7.2
Boots and shoes	5	6.5	Boots and shoes	19	4.0
Carding, pulling, and woolens	4	5.2	Foundry products	17	3.6
Tanned leather	2	2.6	Bread, biscuits, and confectionery	15	3.2
Carriages and wagons	2	2.6	Lumber products	15	3.2
Alcoholic beverages	1	1.3	Refined sugar	12	2.6
Laundry products	1	1.3	Tanned leather	12	2.6
Furniture	1	1.3	Butter and cheese	11	2.3
Total	57	74.0	Total	241	51.3
Total, all manufacturing industries	77	100.0	Total, all manufacturing industries	470	100.0
1870[a]			1900		
Flour and grist mill products	39	17.6	Log products	59	10.1
Log products	31	14.0	Flour and grist mill products	54	9.3
Boots and shoes	16	7.2	Slaughtering and meat packing	30	5.1
Clothing	12	5.4	Butter and cheese	29	5.0
Tanned leather	9	4.1	Boots and shoes	28	4.8
Laundry products	7	3.1	Clothing	22	3.8
Alcoholic beverages	6	2.7	Bread, biscuits, and confectionery	21	3.6
Woolen goods	6	2.7	Foundry products	16	2.7
Carriages and wagons	5	2.2	Tanned leather	14	2.4
Shipbuilding	4	1.8	Refined sugar	13	2.2
Total	135	60.8	Total	286	49.0
Total, all manufacturing industries	222	100.0	Total, all manufacturing industries	584	100.0

[a] For four provinces only.

Source: O. J. Firestone, "Development of Canada's Economy, 1850–1900," p. 237.

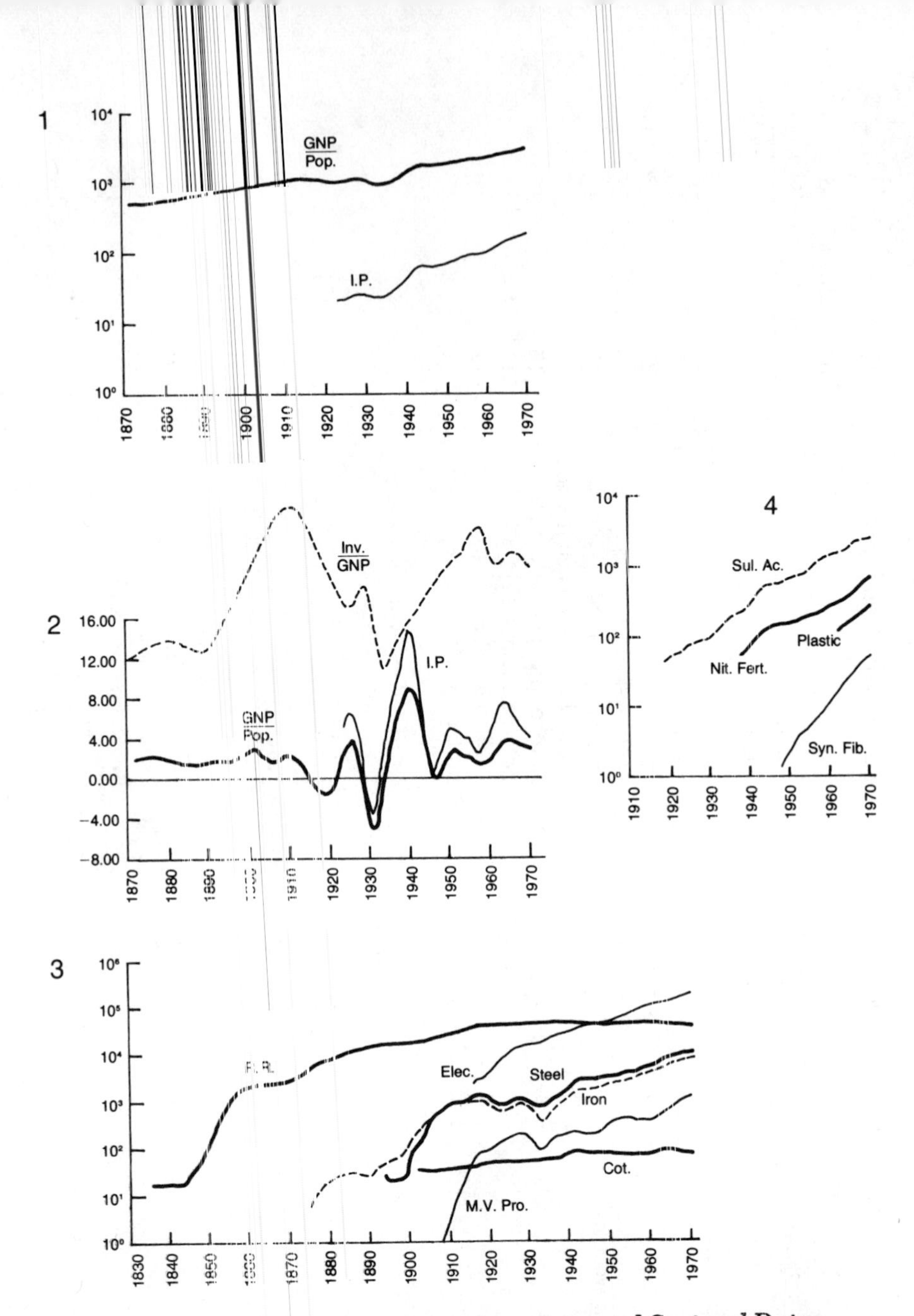

CHART V-30. *Canada, 1835–1972: Aggregate and Sectoral Data (Smoothed)*

1. GNP per capita ($\frac{\text{GNP}}{\text{Pop.}}$); industrial production (manufacturing production index) (I.P.).

2. Gross investment as % of GNP ($\frac{\text{Inv.}}{\text{GNP}}$); rate of change, GNP per capita ($\frac{\text{GNP}}{\text{Pop.}}$); rate of change, industrial production (manufacturing production index) (I.P.).

3. Six major sectors: railroad mileage (R.R.); raw cotton consumption (Cot.); production of iron (Iron); steel (Steel); electricity (Elec.); and motor vehicles (M.V. Pro.).

4. Production of four major chemicals: sulphuric acid (Sul. Ac.); nitrogen fertilizer (Nit. Fert.); plastics and resins (Plastics); and synthetic fibers (Syn. Fib.).

Sources: See Appendix D.

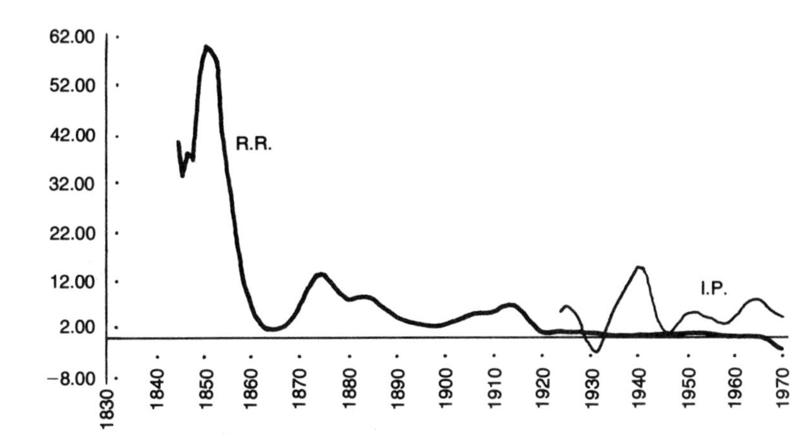

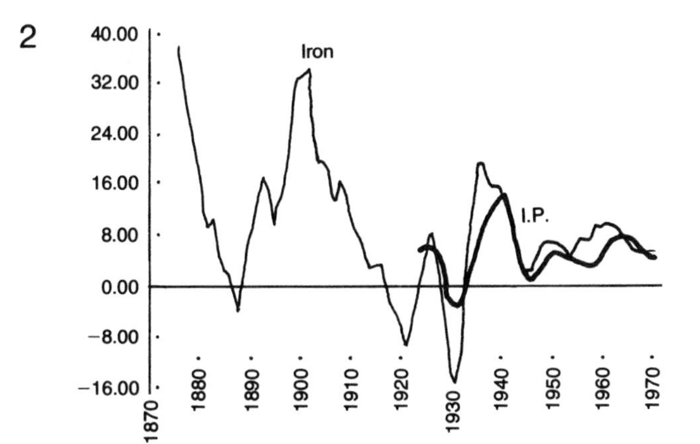

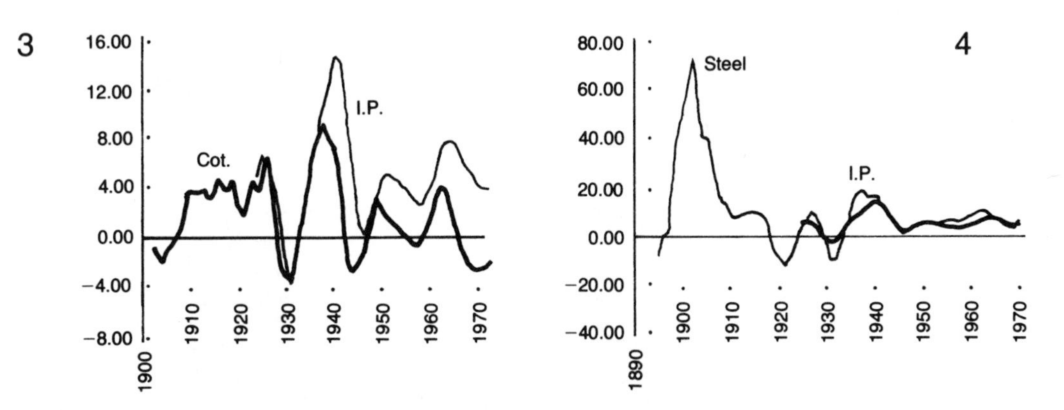

CHART V-31. *Canada, 1845–1972: Relative Growth Rates—Major Sectors and Industrial Production (Smoothed)*

1. Railroad mileage (R.R.).
2. Iron production (Iron).
3. Raw cotton consumption (Cot.).
4. Steel production (Steel).

Sources: See Appendix D.

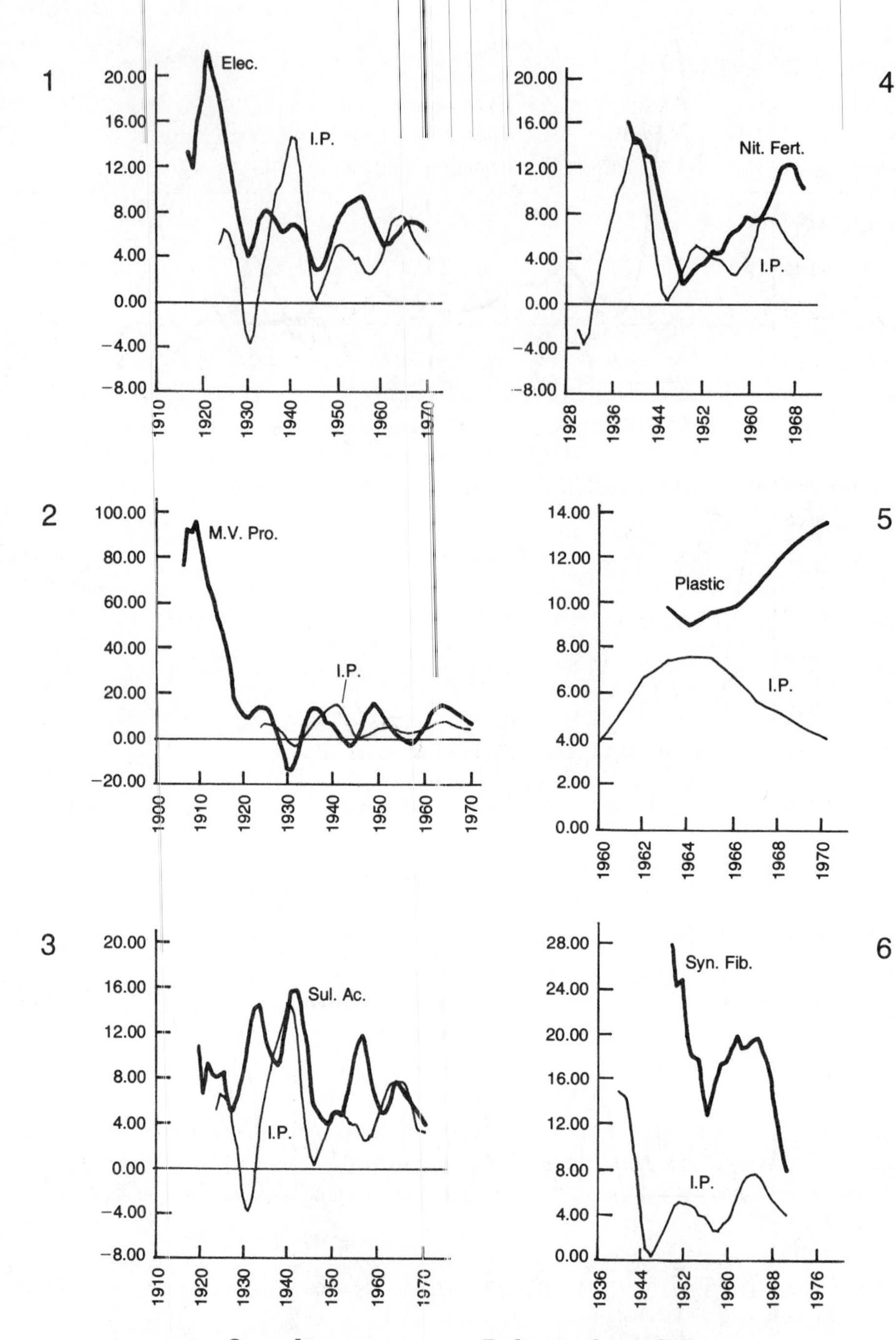

CHART V-32. *Canada, 1910–1972: Relative Growth Rates—Major Sectors and Industrial Production (Smoothed)*

1. Electricity (Elec.).
2. Motor vehicles (M.V. Pro.).
3. Sulphuric acid (Sul. Ac.).
4. Nitrogen fertilizer (Nit. Fert.).
5. Plastics and resins (Plastic).
6. Synthetic fibers (Syn. Fib.).

Sources: See Appendix D.

TABLE V-34. *Approximate Timing of Leading Sectors: Canada, 1835–1972*

Sector	Maximum Rate of Expansion	Estimated Time Sector Became Leading Sector	Estimated Time Sector Ceased to Lead	Comments
Railroads	1850's	1896–1914	—	Without an industrial index, accelerated railroad expansion in pre-1914 decade cannot be compared with overall industrial growth.
Cotton textiles	1910–1920	[a]	1920's	Rate during recovery from depression of 1930's ruled out.
Iron	Late 1870's	1890's	Late 1960's	—
Steel	1900–1910	1900–1910	Late 1960's	—
Electricity	1920's	1920's	—	—
Motor vehicles	1900–1910	1910–1920	—	—
Sulphuric acid	1920's	[a]	—	—
Nitrogen	1940's	[a]	—	—
Plastics	1960's	[a]	—	—
Synthetic fibers	Early 1950's	[a]	—	Low rate for 1970 may be a temporary phenomenon.

[a] Sector too small to be judged, in itself, a leading sector.

is, Canada in the 1920's and subsequently lagged only mildly behind the U.S. pattern of consumption outlays, but it did not achieve a fully diversified industrial structure until during and after the Second World War.

Take-off: 1896–1914.

Drive to Technological Maturity: 1915–1929, 1933–1950.

High Mass-Consumption: 1919–.

37

Australia

The first century of Australia's economic history is a story of sheep, gold, railroads, sheep again, wheat, meat, and dairy products.[73] It begins with John Macarthur's insight, toward the close of the eighteenth century, that if Australia was to flourish it required an export that would exploit the abundance of land with little labor and yield a raw material in considerable demand that could bear the expense of a long sea voyage. He decided wool fulfilled these requirements, and by 1797 he was launched on his first experiment in wool growing with imported merino sheep. A decade later the first commercial shipment of wool arrived in London. From about 1813 the industry began a phase of expansion, which accelerated markedly from the late 1820's.[74]

Mulhall offers the data in Table V-35 on the progress of Australian wool production over the next seven decades. An annual average increase of over 8 percent per annum was maintained down to the 1880's, when some deceleration evidently occurred.

Between mid-century and 1890 the sheepherding industry was transformed, accelerating notably with the pastoral investment boom of the 1870's (see Chart V-33, part 2). The number of sheep in eastern Australia rose from about 17 million in 1862 to some 90 million in 1892.[75] Noel G. Butlin describes clearly the change between the largely nomadic sheepherding industry of the first half of the century and the highly capitalized sheep station of, say, 1890, with its functional buildings, fences, water conservation measures, wagons, tools, steam engines, and stocks of working capital.[76] Gold had dominated the 1850's, railroad and residential construction the 1860's, although gold remained the leading export. But, as the investment rate in Chart V-33, part 2, suggests, "It was in the twenty years from 1871 that the big surge of rural investment occurred";[77] and sheep were at its center. The great capital import boom of the 1880's permitted this expansion to proceed concurrently with the creation of the bone structure of the nation's railroad system. By 1890 some ten thousand miles of track had been laid in Australia; and, although

TABLE V-35. *Wool Production: Australia, 1821–1887*

	Production (Equivalent in Thousand Washed Tons)	Average Annual Rate of Growth (%)	Proportion of World Production (%)	Value (in £ Millions)
1821–1830	10	—	0.5	4
1831–1840	30	11.6	1.4	10
1841–1850	40	7.2	2.2	23
1851–1860	140	8.8	4.5	45
1861–1870	330	8.9	8.6	102
1871–1880	730	8.3	14.8	184
1881–1887	680	3.4	17.8	124

Source: Mulhall, *The Dictionary of Statistics*, p. 599.

TABLE V-36. *Rate of Change in Product per Capita: Australia, 1861–1969 (Annual Average Percentage Rate of Growth)*

1861–1864 to 1865–1869	0.82	1910–1913 to 1914–1919	−2.57
1865–1869 to 1870–1874	1.63	1914–1919 to 1920–1924	2.34
1870–1874 to 1875–1879	2.66	1920–1924 to 1925–1929	−0.75
1875–1879 to 1880–1884	0.81	1925–1929 to 1930–1934	−1.86
1880–1884 to 1885–1889	1.12	1930–1934 to 1935–1938	2.80
1885–1889 to 1890–1894	−1.93	1935–1938 to 1948–1949	1.56
1890–1894 to 1895–1899	−2.29	1948–1949 to 1950–1954	1.80
1895–1899 to 1900–1904	1.81	1950–1954 to 1955–1959	1.78
1900–1904 to 1905–1909	3.19	1955–1959 to 1960–1964	2.07
1905–1909 to 1910–1913	1.9	1960–1964 to 1965–1969	2.99

Sources: 1861–1938, calculated by Simon Kuznets from Noel G. Butlin, *Australian Domestic Product, Investment and Foreign Borrowing, 1861–1938/39*, pp. 10–11, 460–461; 1938–1949, from unpublished revisions of Butlin estimate by Bryan D. Haig, of the Research School of Social Sciences, The Australian National University, supplied by Simon Kuznets; 1950–1969, official figures from *United Nations Statistical Yearbooks*, annual.

the 1890's were severely depressed, the foundation had been established for Australia to move forward in the pre-1914 years on the basis of higher export prices, wheat, and the meat (and butter) exports permitted by the refrigerated ship.[78] In the thirty years between the 1860's and the 1890's, Australian population, reinforced by irregular flows of immigration, expanded at an annual rate of more than 3 percent.

Table V-36 and Chart V-33, part 2, exhibit fluctuations in the rate of change in Australian real per capita product.

The acceleration of the 1870's and the high but lesser rate of growth in the 1880's gave way to the deep setback of the 1890's,[79] exacerbated by a protracted drought from 1895 to 1903. Growth then resumed at a high rate down to the First World War. After a wartime setback, Australia recovered; but relatively low prices, Brit-

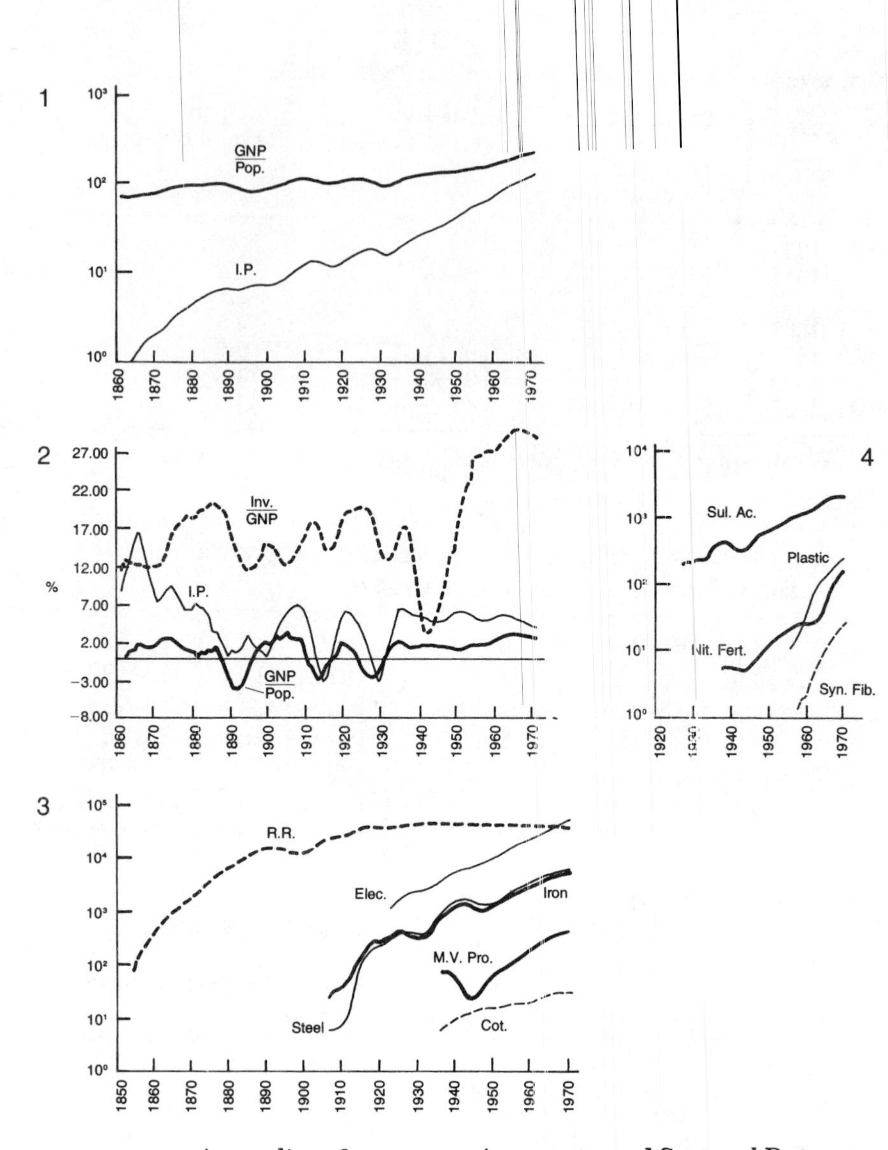

CHART V-33. *Australia, 1855–1972: Aggregate and Sectoral Data (Smoothed)*

1. GNP per capita ($\frac{\text{GNP}}{\text{Pop.}}$); industrial production (manufacturing production index) (I.P.).

2. Gross investment as % of GNP ($\frac{\text{Inv.}}{\text{GNP}}$); rate of change, GNP per capita ($\frac{\text{GNP}}{\text{Pop.}}$); rate of change, industrial production (manufacturing production index) (I.P.).

3. Six major sectors: railroads (kilometers) (R.R.); raw cotton consumption (Cotton); production of iron (Iron); steel (Steel); electricity (Elec.); and motor vehicles (M.V. Pro.).

4. Production of four major chemicals: sulphuric acid (Sul. Ac.); nitrogen fertilizer (Nit. Fert.); plastics and resins (Plastics); and synthetic fibers (Syn. Fib.).

Sources: See Appendix D.

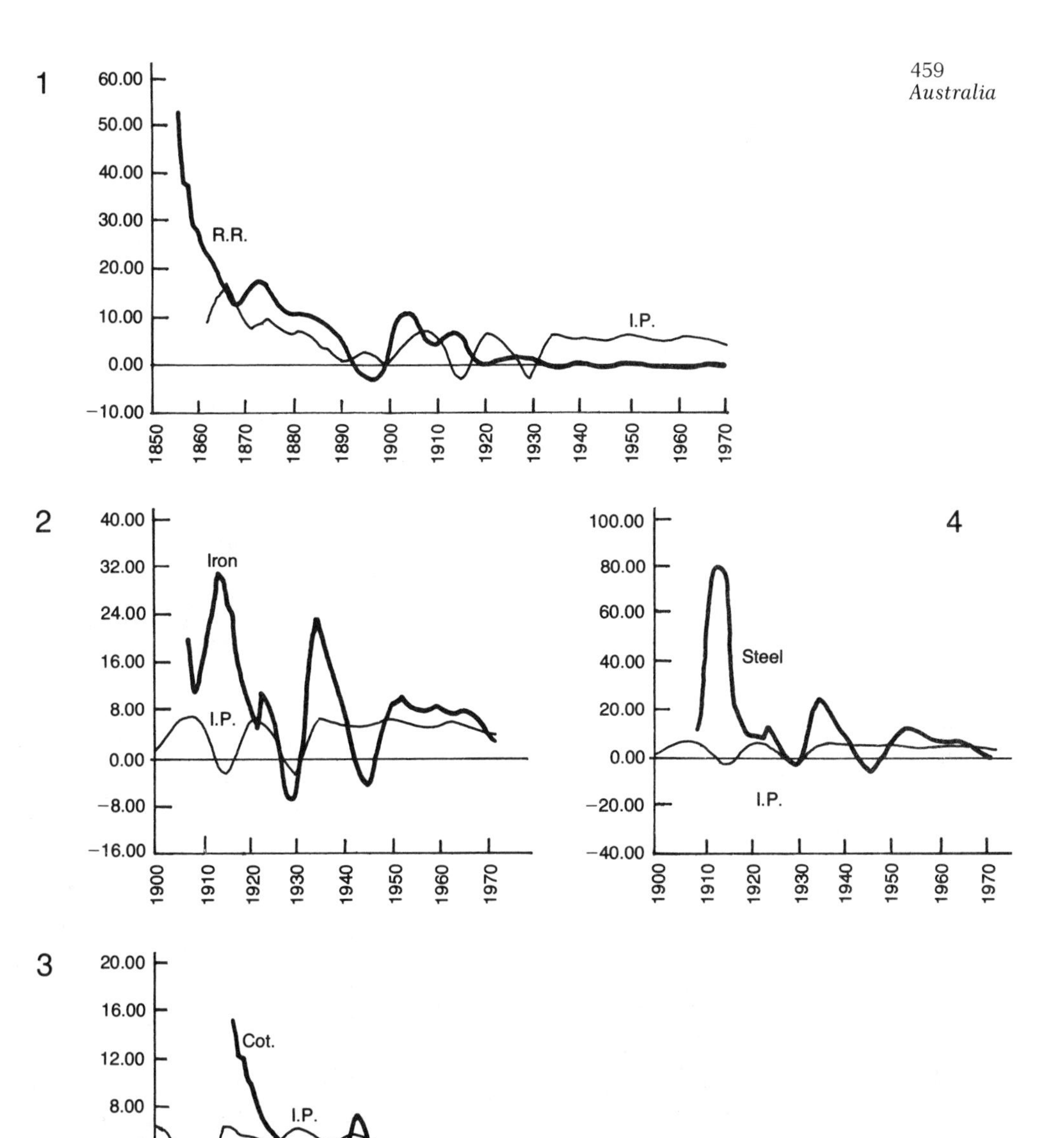

CHART V-34. *Australia, 1855–1972: Relative Growth Rates—Major Sectors and Industrial Production (Smoothed)*

1. Railroads (kilometers) (R.R.).
2. Iron production (Iron).
3. Raw cotton consumption (Cot.).
4. Steel production (Steel).

Sources: See Appendix D.

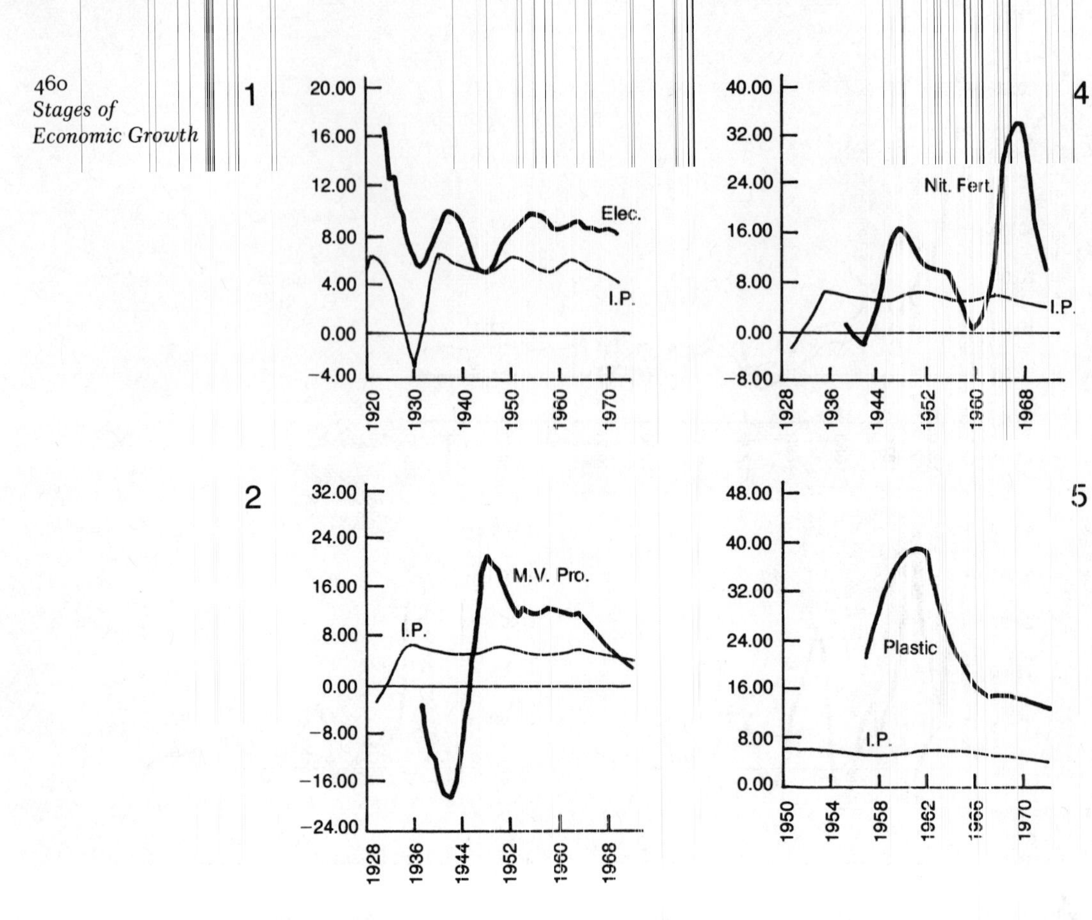

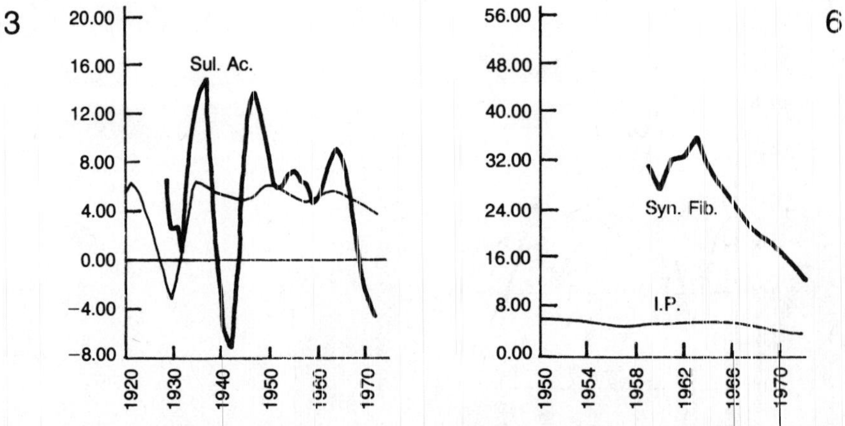

CHART V-35. *Australia, 1920–1972: Relative Growth Rates—Major Sectors and Industrial Production (Smoothed)*

1. Electricity (Elec.).
2. Motor vehicles (M.V. Pro.).
3. Sulphuric acid (Sul. Ac.).
4. Nitrogen fertilizer (Nit. Fert.).
5. Plastics and resins (Plastic).
6. Synthetic fibers (Syn. Fib.).

Sources: See Appendix D.

ain's incomplete revival in the second half of the 1920's, and the depression of the early 1930's again reduced real per capita product. On the eve of the Second World War, despite a considerable revival, real per capita product was below the average level of 1910–1913. After the Second World War, Australia, now equipped with a modern, diversified industrial establishment and rapidly exploiting its rich mineral resources, sustained better than a 2 percent average annual increase in per capita product, the rate rising in the late 1960's. In the course of that decade (1966–1967), Japan succeeded Britain as Australia's largest export market; and in 1968–1969, exports to the United States also slightly surpassed those to Britain.

Given Australia's high rate of population growth, its extraordinary requirements for social overhead capital, and its erratic but substantial access to capital imports, the proportion of gross national product invested was relatively high (as in Canada) from 1861 forward. The periods of great capital imports in the 1880's and in the quarter-century after 1945 emerge clearly in Table V-37 and Chart V-33, part 2. These data reflect the phases in Australian economic history

TABLE V-37. *Investment as a Percentage of GNP: Australia, 1861–1969*

Period	Percentage
1861 to 1865	15.7
1866 to 1870	13.9
1871 to 1875	13.9
1876 to 1880	19.1
1881 to 1885	22.2
1886 to 1890	23.5
1891 to 1895	13.9
1896 to 1900	14.3
1901 to 1910	13.2
1911 to 1913	16.6
1914–1915 to 1919–1920	14.1
1920–1921 to 1928–1929	18.3
1929–1930 to 1931–1932	12.9
1932–1933 to 1938–1939	14.3
1939–1940 to 1944–1945	8.5
1945–1946 to 1949–1950	24.0
1950–1951 to 1954–1955	23.2
1955–1956 to 1959–1960	24.0
1960–1961 to 1964–1965	25.2
1965–1966 to 1968–1969	26.7

Sources: 1861–1900, proportion of investment to gross domestic product, from Noel G. Butlin, *Investment in Australian Economic Development, 1861–1900*, p. 51; 1901–1969, from E. A. Boehm, *Twentieth Century Economic Development in Australia*, p. 79, where sources are indicated. Boehm's figures are for gross fixed investment as a proportion of gross national product and, for the 1880's and 1890's, are 2–3 percent lower than Butlin's estimates cited here.

with which we are already familiar, notably the surge of the 1870's and 1880's, the subsequent setback and pre-1914 revival, the inter-war doldrums and the great post-1945 boom.

What of the Australian take-off?

Clearly, it did not come before the federation of the Australian states in 1901:

> During the nineteenth century the Australian market for manufactured goods—spread through six autonomous colonies—was too small for cheap production. The pre-federation market was strongly divided by tariff barriers through the protectionist policies of Victoria, South Australia, and Tasmania while New South Wales was solidly free trade. The market was also hampered by inadequate, expensive transport over the long distances between the colonies. Furthermore, it was isolated from the world's main industrial centres and the demand in Europe and North America.
>
> The smallness and fragmentation of the Australian market contributed to a tendency for techniques and capital equipment in Australia to be simple and primitive. Manufacturing was largely restricted to production for domestic requirements of goods using basic local or imported materials. . . .
>
> . . . Thus manufacturing activity was concentrated in the production of the following industrial groups: food and drink from local products, the manufacture of clothing and textiles (mainly from imported materials), bricks, printing, the preliminary treating of agricultural and pastoral products (such as wool scouring and washing and flour milling), and metal works and machinery (especially for repairs and maintenance).[80]

These typical industrial activities of a society in the preconditions for take-off expanded rapidly between 1861 and the mid-1880's and then virtually stagnated down to the turn of the century.[81] In 1891 about 20 percent of the occupied population in Victoria was engaged in these small, labor-intensive manufacturing activities, about a sixth in Queensland and South Australia, about 15 percent in New South Wales. Although Australia was a high-income-per-capita nation, due to its population-resource balance, these manufacturing proportions are typical in the contemporary world of a nation at, say, $200 (1964) or less (see above, pp. 56–57).

Putting the pre-1901 era aside, the first candidate for the take-off is the period between 1901 and the end of the First World War. The unified domestic market permitted larger-scale and more efficient industrial plants to be introduced. Metalworks and machinery led the way, with an average annual increase of 6.9 percent in the working force in that sector between 1903 and 1913, as compared to an annual increase of 5.5 percent for manufacturing as a whole.[82] Between 1912 and 1920–1921 the manufacturing work force increased at a rate of only 1.8 percent; but the 1921 census showed the proportion of the working force classified as industrial (excluding construction) as 28.5 percent in Victoria, 25 percent in New South Wales, 21 percent in Queensland, 23.9 percent in South Australia. These are proportions associated in the contemporary world with countries at or above $400 (1964) per capita, beyond take-off. The problem here is that, while the aggregated data, including the industrial production index, suggest a take-off after 1901, the sectoral data I have been able to mobilize are not adequate to confirm it.

If one takes the view that the modernization of Australian light industries on the basis of a national market after 1901 constituted a take-off, there is a good case for dating the drive to technological maturity from about 1920. It was foreshadowed by the opening in 1915 of the substantial steelworks at Newcastle. In the 1920's and in the recovery phase of the 1930's, Australian industrialization continued at a modest rate but on a more diversified basis. E. A. Boehm's description includes sectors generally associated with the drive to technological maturity: "Leading manufacturing activity [1921–1939] included iron and steel, some non-ferrous metals, machinery and engineering, electrical and electronic equipment, motor vehicle assembly and parts, chemicals and fertilizers."[83]

The First World War did not greatly stimulate Australian industrial development. Australia was far from the theaters of action, and its industrial plant was insufficiently developed. The battles were closer in the Second World War; and Australian industrial capacity became more diversified and mature. The result was an annual average increase in the industrial work force of 4.7 percent in the decade after 1938–1939. As Chart V-33, part 3, shows, iron and steel production surged forward, as did the manufacture of motor vehicles. By the end of the war Australia's drive to technological maturity was about complete; and it was in a position to supply a quite high proportion of the industrial underpinning for the stage of high mass-consumption its citizens had for some time enjoyed on the basis of imported manufactured goods. In the period 1948–1949 to 1967–1968, the proportion of both the working force and the value of production declined in all sectors except industrial metals, machines, conveyances, and chemicals. Within the former, the rise of the motor vehicle industry dominated, along with electrical and electronic equipment, and iron and steel, as Table V-38 exhibits.

Like Canada, then, Australia has managed to acquire and apply efficiently virtually all the major modern industrial technologies while still paying its way in the world mainly through the sophisticated exploitation of its land and other natural resources. Australian exports of wool, wheat, meat, and minerals, along with lesser products of agriculture, constituted 71 percent of total exports in the second half of the 1960's. Unlike Canada, Australia enjoyed no proximate industrial neighbor with which it could also share the market for motor vehicles and other sophisticated manufactured products; but its industrialization has been maintained, notably in the post-

TABLE V-38. *Classification of the Major Industry Group "Industrial Metals, Machines, Conveyances": Australia, Selected Years, 1948–1949 to 1967–1968*

	Iron and Steel	Transport Equipment		Plant, Machine and Engineeri
		Motor Vehicles, Parts and Repairs	Other[a]	
	(1)	(2)	(3)	(4)
Average Employment (% of Col. 8)				
1948–1949	3.5	7.1	7.8	9.6
1953–1954	3.8	9.2	7.8	10.2
1958–1959	5.0	10.6	6.4	10.3
1963–1964	5.4	12.0	5.4	11.3
1967–1968	5.3	12.3	5.2	12.0
Value of production (% of Col. 8)				
1948–1949	4.4	6.2	6.5	9.5
1953–1954	4.5	8.5	6.0	10.0
1958–1959	6.8	9.1	4.6	9.8
1963–1964	7.0	9.8	3.7	10.6
1967–1968	6.6	9.9	3.8	11.1

[a] Comprises tramcars and railway rolling stock, horse-drawn vehicles, aircraft, cycl and ship and boat building and repairing.

Source: Boehm, *Twentieth Century Economic Development in Australia*, p. 131.

TABLE V-39. *Approximate Timing of Leading Sectors: Australia, 1860–1972*

Sector	Maximum Rate of Expansion	Estimated Time Sector Became Leading Sector	Estimated Time Sector Ceased to Lead
Cotton consumption	1940's	a	1950's
Railroads	1860's	b	1920's
Iron	1910–1920	1920's	—
Steel	1910–1920	1920's	—
Electricity	1920's	1920's	—
Motor vehicles	1945–1950	1950's	—
Sulphuric acid	1930's	a	—
Nitrogen	1960's	a	—
Plastics	Early 1950's	a	—
Synthetic fibers	1960's	a	—

[a] Not judged, by itself, a leading sector.

[b] Spreading effects not sufficient to be judged a leading sector

lectrical and lectronic Equipment	Processing and Refining of Other Metals	Total of Industry Group (Cols. 1–6)	Total Manufacturing Industries
)	(6)	(7)	(8)
			Thousands
5	5.5	38.0	877
8	5.1	40.8	974
2	5.3	43.8	1,071
4	5.7	46.3	1,194
8	5.9	47.6	1,315
			$ Millions
1	7.5	38.1	1,106
7	5.9	39.6	2,386
7	5.6	41.7	3,532
7	6.3	43.1	5,042
7	7.2	44.3	7,132

1945 years, by large flows of capital imports accompanied by the acquisition of new technology and supportive entrepreneurial skills. The timing of Australia's acquisition of modern technologies is suggested in Table V-39, based on Charts V-34 and V-35.

Australia's stages of growth can be dated as follows, with some question in my mind as to whether the take-off may be a bit early, despite the nation's high income per capita.

Take-off: 1901–1920.

Drive to Technological Maturity: 1920–1945.

High Mass-Consumption: Approx. 1925–.

38

Argentina

The early economic history of Argentina belongs rather more with that of Canada and Australia than with that of most other Latin American nations, although its post-1945 failure to move forward to full-scale industrialization has distinctively Latin American economic and noneconomic features.[84]

The story of Argentine economic modernization can be arbitrarily dated from the liberalization of trade within the empire permitted by the Spanish government, starting in 1776. Argentina's economy, ruled from Lima, was then oriented primarily toward the supply of the mining center of Potosí. The interior provinces (notably, Tucumán, Córdoba, and Salta) produced agricultural goods, handicraft textiles, and simple manufactured goods, and raised mules for the miners; the Cuyo region provided wines, liquors, and dried fruit. These provinces also supplied the small coastal settlement at Buenos Aires, which conducted a busy contraband trade, importing slaves, tobacco, wines, and textiles from Brazil and Europe in exchange for locally generated hides and salted meat as well as Peruvian silver. The population of Buenos Aires rose from about nine thousand in 1720 to twenty-three thousand a half-century later. The frustrations of this dynamic community and its region helped bring about the limited trading reforms of the 1770's, which accelerated the process of systematically exploiting Argentina's comparative advantage in pastoral products. By 1809 Buenos Aires was a city of ninety-two thousand. The rural population in its hinterland may have expanded at an annual rate of 6 percent between 1781 and 1798. Hide exports increased at an annual rate of 10 percent between 1778 and 1796, as the size of domesticated cattle herds rose rapidly. The process was carried forward when events during the Napoleonic Wars permitted the British firmly to install themselves commercially in the River Plate region. Wartime circumstances also permitted, from 1810, de facto independence for the viceregal and successor governments centered there. Formal independence came in 1816; but external and internal struggles only subsided with the coming to power in 1880 of General Julio Roca.

Meanwhile, however, Argentina moved forward as a producer and exporter of pastoral products. The more distant interior provinces (e.g., Jujuy and Salta) deteriorated or stagnated in response to the decline of the Potosí mines. Those closer to Buenos Aires were sustained by its role as part of the rapidly expanding Atlantic economy. Hides, tallow, and salted beef were initially the major exports, although the wool industry was put on a new and firmer base when in 1813 the United States consul, Thomas Halsey, imported one hundred merino sheep. Wool production moved up rapidly to become Argentina's leading export by 1860 (Table V-40). Nevertheless, hides, salted meat, and tallow grease continued to earn a substantial proportion of Argentina's foreign exchange. The structural change brought about between the early 1880's and the eve of the First World War by the railroads, the opening of wheat and corn lands, and the refrigerated ship is suggested in Table V-41.

As of 1894, at a period of cyclical depression, but in the wake of the great railroad expansion of the late 1880's, Mulhall calculated that Argentine income per capita was quite high: £24 per capita. This compared with his estimates of £44 for the United States, £36 for the United Kingdom and Canada, £31 for France, £25 for Germany, £14 for Italy, £9.5 for Russia.[85]

Modern estimates of Argentine national income begin only with the turn of the century; but it is from the mid-1890's that one can date an acceleration in real product per capita (Table V-42).

After the great surge in the first decade of the century, there was deceleration and a severe setback during the First World War. The recovery of the 1920's, while real enough, yielded only a mild net annual average rate of increase between 1910–1914 and 1924–1929: 0.5 percent. After the setback of the early 1930's, however, Argentina moved ahead quite rapidly during the Second World War and in its immediate aftermath. Subsequent successive phases of retardation and acceleration are broadly reflected in Table V-42 and Chart V-36, part 2. From 1945–1949 to 1965–1969 Argentina aver-

TABLE V-40. *Wool Production: Argentina, 1821–1887*

	Production (Equivalent in Thousand Washed Tons)	Average Annual Rate of Growth (%)	Proportion of World Production (%)	Value (in £ Millions)
1821–1830	20	—	1.0	4
1831–1840	30	4.1	1.4	6
1841–1850	40	2.9	1.5	7
1851–1860	60	4.1	1.9	10
1861–1870	170	11.0	4.4	26
1871–1880	340	7.2	6.9	46
1881–1887	330	1.6	8.6	39

Source: Mulhall, *The Dictionary of Statistics*, p. 599.

TABLE V-41. *Estimates of Quantum of Exports: Argentina, 1880–1884 and 1910–1914 (Annual Averages, in Million Gold Pesos at 1910–1914 Prices)*

	1880–1884 (Million Pesos)	1910–1914 (Million Pesos)	Change (%)
Wool	41.3	51.9	26
All hides	22.5	44.0	86
Salted and jerked meat	3.6	1.1	−69
Chilled and frozen mutton and lamb	0	8.9	—
Frozen beef	0	49.7	—
Chilled beef	0	4.3	—
Canned meat	0	3.0	—
Wheat	1.2	78.1	651
Corn	1.3	72.4	603
Linseed	1.2	41.0	342
Oats, barley, and rye	[a]	14.6	—
Quebracho extract	0	4.9	—
Quebracho logs	0	5.0	—
Total	71.1	378.9	533

[a] Value less than 0.1 million.

Source: Carlos F. Díaz Alejandro, *Essays on the Economic History of the Argentine Republic*, p. 5.

TABLE V-42. *Rate of Increase in Product per Capita: Argentina, 1900–1969 (Annual Average Percentage Rate of Change)*

Period	Rate	Period	Rate
1900–1904 to 1905–1909	4.4	1935–1939 to 1940–1944	1.2
1905–1909 to 1910–1914	0.4	1940–1944 to 1945–1949	2.7
1910–1914 to 1915–1919	−4.3	1945–1949 to 1950–1954	−0.3
1915–1919 to 1920–1924	3.3	1950–1954 to 1955–1959	1.8
1920–1924 to 1925–1929	3.3	1955–1959 to 1960–1964	0.96
1925–1929 to 1930–1934	−3.1	1960–1964 to 1965–1969	2.3
1930–1934 to 1935–1939	1.5		

Sources: 1900–1959, based on estimates of the Economic Commission for Latin America, *El desarollo económico de la Argentina*; 1954–1969, *United Nations Statistical Yearbooks*, annual.

aged an annual increase of only 1.2 percent in real product per capita, as compared to something like twice that rate for Australia and Canada. It was in this period that it fell definitively behind.

The relatively modest average rate of growth that emerged from Argentina's erratic post-1945 path of economic progress was accompanied by a quite high rate of gross investment, averaging about 20 percent of GNP when measured in terms of current prices; but this figure drops to 13 percent when measured in 1935–1938 prices.[86] There was a sharp relative rise in Argentine capital goods prices, produced under heavy protection for a small market.

The course of Argentine economic growth and its somewhat pathological post-1945 experience can only be understood in terms of a

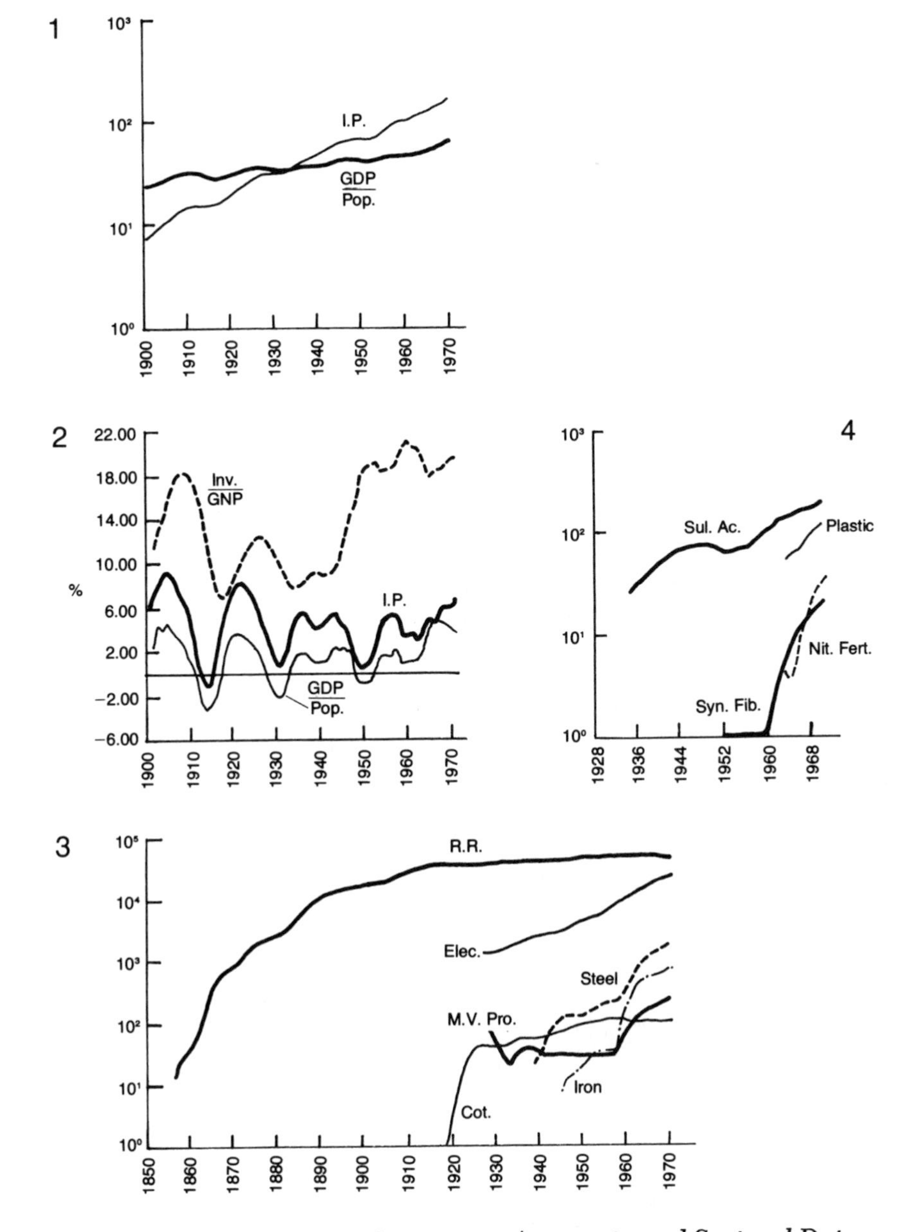

CHART V-36. *Argentina, 1855–1972: Aggregate and Sectoral Data (Smoothed)*

1. GDP per capita ($\frac{\text{GDP}}{\text{Pop.}}$); industrial production (manufacturing production index) (I.P.).

2. Gross investment as % of GNP ($\frac{\text{Inv.}}{\text{GNP}}$); rate of change, GDP per capita ($\frac{\text{GDP}}{\text{Pop.}}$); rate of change, industrial production, manufacturing production index (I.P.).

3. Six major sectors: railroads (kilometers) (R.R.); raw cotton consumption (Cot.); production of iron (Iron); steel (Steel); electricity (Elec.); and motor vehicles (M.V. Pro.).

4. Production of four major chemicals: sulphuric acid (Sul. Ac.); nitrogen fertilizer (Nit. Fert.); plastics and resins (Plastic); and synthetic fibers (Syn. Fib.).

Sources: See Appendix D.

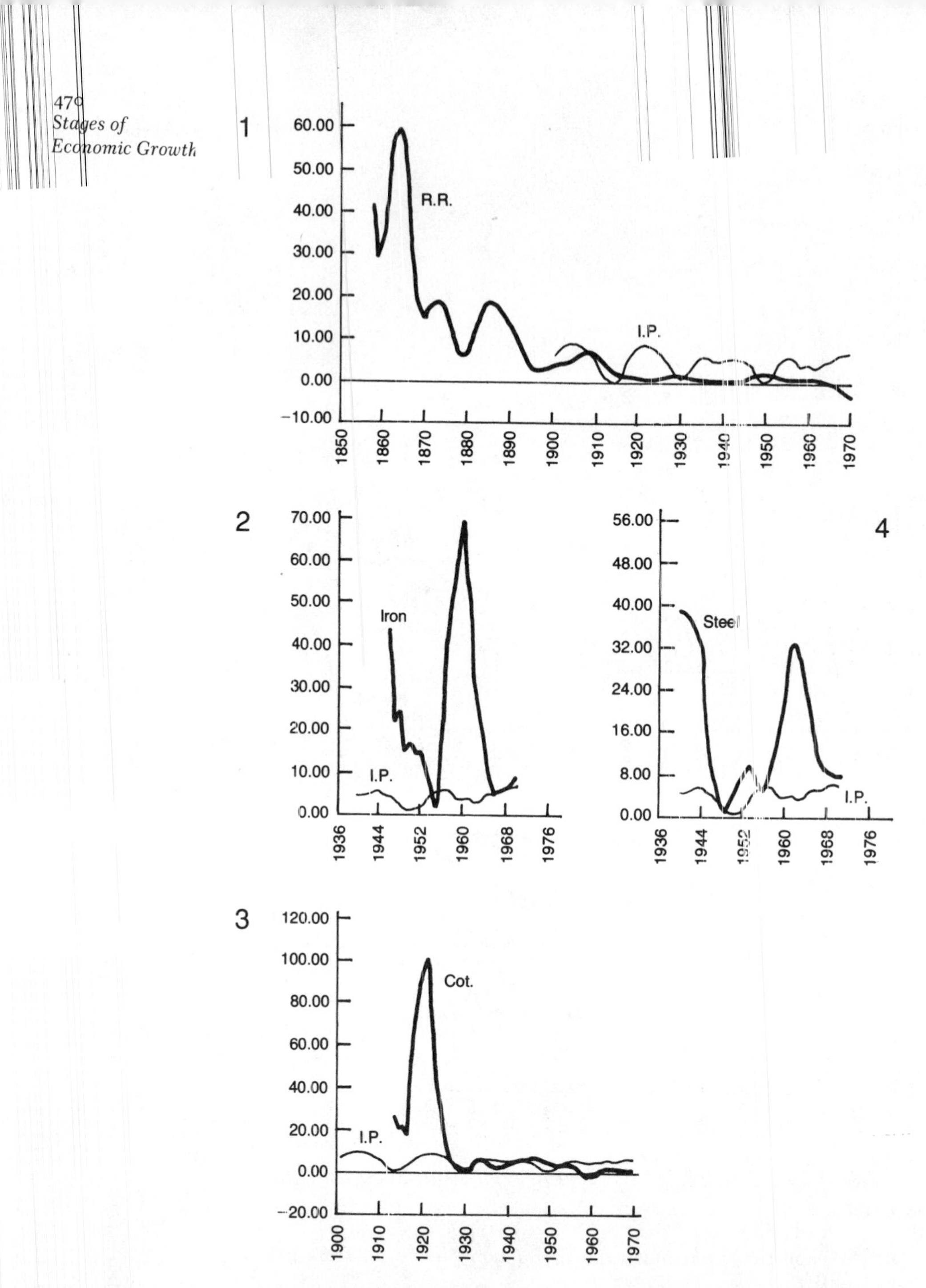

CHART V-37. *Argentina, 1855–1972: Relative Growth Rates—Major Sectors and Industrial Production (Smoothed)*

1. Railroads (kilometers) (R.R.).
2. Iron production (Iron).
3. Raw cotton consumption (Cot.).
4. Steel production (Steel).

Sources: See Appendix D.

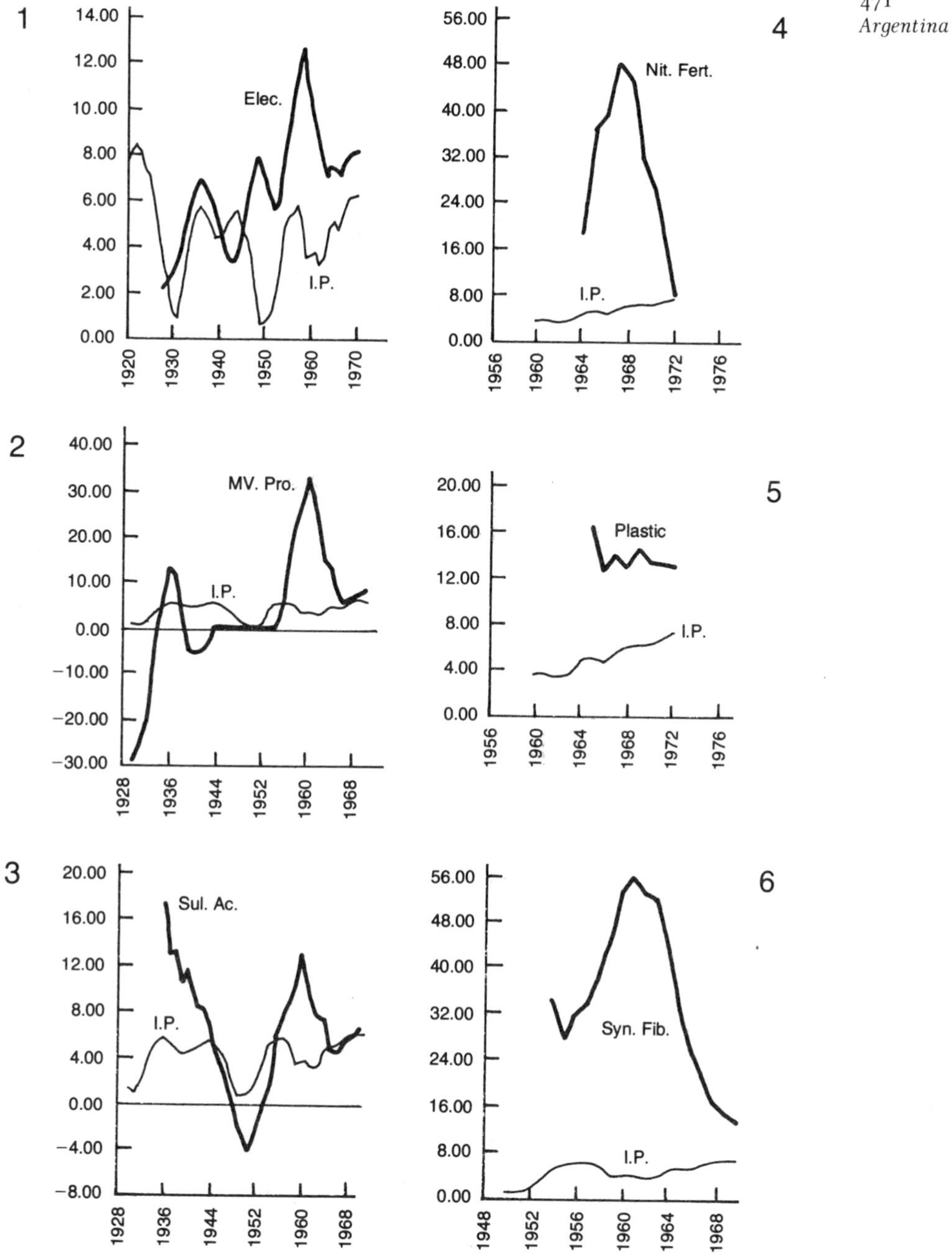

CHART V-38. *Argentina, 1920–1972: Relative Growth Rates—Major Sectors and Industrial Production (Smoothed)*

1. Electricity (Elec.).
2. Motor vehicles (M.V. Pro.).
3. Sulphuric acid (Sul. Ac.).
4. Nitrogen fertilizer (Nit. Fert.).
5. Plastics and resins (Plastic).
6. Synthetic fibers (Syn. Fib.).

Sources: See Appendix D.

disaggregated sectoral analysis. Down to about 1930, Argentina imported the bulk of its high-quality consumers' goods, including textiles. There was, nevertheless, a considerable local industry supplying low-quality textiles, wine, beer, sugar, flour, and nontropical foodstuffs.[87] There was also a substantial industrial complex which supported Argentine exports: meat-packing plants, the processing of dairy products, wool-washing establishments, and the maintenance of the railroad system. These did not lead to the progressive absorption of new technologies; and I would characterize them as pre–take-off industrial activities.

In the 1930's, under the pressure of foreign-exchange constraints and purposeful public policy, Argentina moved into a phase of rapid industrialization based on import-substitution consumers' goods industries. This phase, which I would designate as the Argentine take-off, ended with the setback in 1949 and the relative sluggishness of the early 1950's. In the course of the 1950's and 1960's, Argentina proceeded to absorb the typical technologies of the drive to technological maturity: metalworking and engineering, electrical machinery, and chemicals. These stages emerge with reasonable clarity in Table V-43 as well as in Chart V-36, parts 3 and 4.[88]

The erratic character of this familiar structural transformation and the relatively slow average rate of increase in product per capita enjoyed by Argentina while it was taking place can be attributed mainly to these four factors:

TABLE V-43. *Structure of the GDP at Factor Cost in Manufacturing: Argentina, 1925–1965 (% of Total)*

	1925–1929	1937–1939	1948–1950	1959–1961	1963–1965
Foodstuffs and beverages	36.6	37.3	25.4	19.2	18.7
Tobacco	0.8	0.7	0.7	0.6	0.6
Textiles	2.9	7.4	11.7	8.4	7.8
Clothing	6.9	5.4	5.9	3.4	2.9
Wood products	3.2	2.1	2.1	1.9	1.7
Paper and cardboard	1.9	1.3	1.6	1.8	1.8
Printing and publishing	9.8	6.3	4.0	3.6	3.4
Chemical products	5.7	4.4	5.8	7.1	8.0
Petroleum refining	1.6	4.9	5.3	7.2	8.4
Rubber products	—	0.8	1.0	1.4	1.4
Leather products	6.5	4.2	4.7	4.1	2.6
Stone, glass, and ceramics	6.9	4.3	5.1	4.6	4.3
Metals	4.5	6.4	6.5	8.8	10.1
Vehicles and machinery	2.9	5.6	9.6	14.1	16.5
Electrical machinery and appliances	—	1.1	2.0	6.6	5.8
Other manufacturing and handicrafts	9.6	7.9	8.7	7.3	6.1

Source: Díaz Alejandro, *Essays on the Economic History of the Argentine Republic*, p. 224.

—the purposeful neglect of Argentina's agricultural sector, including a failure to absorb the new high-productivity agricultural and pastoral technologies generated and diffused in the United States, Canada, and Australia;[89]

—a consequent chronic shortage of foreign exchange, as agricultural and pastoral exports declined;

—the maintenance of an excessively protectionist environment for the emerging new industries, which, along with the limited size of the Argentine market, made the prices of their products excessive at home, noncompetitive abroad;

—endemic inflation, which, in conjunction with chronic foreign-exchange shortage, led to stop-and-go policies which slowed the average rate of real growth.

A wider analysis would have to include, of course, the political and social forces and the reactive nationalism which led Argentina, in the 1940's, to turn its back on its agricultural and pastoral resources and which have also yielded the political fragmentation and instability that have marked Argentine life over the past forty years.

There are, evidently, uniquely Argentine aspects in this array of problems which damped and rendered erratic its passage through the drive to technological maturity; but, with appropriate variation, they apply to a good many small and medium-sized Latin American countries over the past quarter-century. In particular, the small size

TABLE V-44. *Approximate Timing of Leading Sectors: Argentina, 1860–1972*

Sector	Maximum Rate of Expansion	Estimated Time Sector Became Leading Sector	Estimated Time Sector Ceased to Lead	Comments
Railroads	1860's	[a]	—	—
Cotton yarn	1920's	[b]	—	—
Iron	1940's	Early 1960's	—	—
Steel	1940's	Early 1960's	—	—
Electricity	1950's	1950's	—	—
Motor vehicles	1960's	1960's	—	—
Sulphuric acid	Late 1930's	[b]	—	—
Nitrogen	Late 1960's	[b]	—	Decline in growth rate may be temporary.
Plastics	Late 1960's	[b]	—	—
Synthetic fibers	Early 1960's	[b]	—	—

[a] Spreading effects insufficient to be judged a leading sector.
[b] Not judged, in itself, a leading sector.

of the Argentine domestic market has made it difficult to absorb efficiently the modern capital-intensive technologies and to sustain high momentum for protracted periods in the key sectors of the drive to technological maturity. Like other Latin American nations (excepting Brazil and Mexico), Argentina awaits the emergence of an effectively enlarged regional common market.

Conclusions to be drawn from the sectoral patterns set out in Charts V-37 and V-38 are presented in Table V-44.

Argentina's stages of growth emerge as follows.

Take-off: 1933–1950.

Drive to Technological Maturity: 1950–.

As in Canada and Australia, Argentina's high income per capita, based on its population–natural-resource balance, permitted it increasingly to enjoy the amenities of high mass-consumption—perhaps from the end of the Second World War—before technological maturity was attained.

39

Turkey

As in many traditional societies, the early stages of Turkish modernization were dominated by the interplay between external military and political pressures and internal political and social change. In the Turkish case this inherently painful process was complicated because Turkey was a substantial empire dealing with assertive nations that had entered the industrial revolution earlier, generating thereby relatively greater military power.[90] Political and administrative reform and efforts at economic modernization were systematically linked to prior military or diplomatic setbacks, while the internal modernizers were driven on, as in many other cases, by a desire to recapture national dignity in the face of a technologically more advanced external world. Although there were earlier precedents, the rule of Selim III (1789–1807) is conventionally taken as the beginning of the process of Turkish modernization. His reforms were undertaken in the wake of military setbacks at the hands of the Hungarians and Russians.

By the 1860's the Turkish government was prepared to contract foreign loans and permit foreign companies to construct railway lines and public utilities, and to expand port facilities. Some eight hundred miles of railways had been laid down by 1880. Under the influence of the Young Turks, a Law for the Encouragement of Industry was passed in 1909; but in 1913 there were in the whole of Ottoman Turkey only 269 establishments working with machines, employing about seventeen thousand workers.[91] It was not until 1923 that the coming of peace permitted Kemal Ataturk to turn wholeheartedly to domestic development. There was some progress down to 1929; but the depression set back the economy. In 1933 a first five-year plan was launched, with the state the principal entrepreneur. Backed by two large state banks, the government controlled the chemical, ceramics, iron and steel, paper and cellulose, sulphur and copper-mining, cotton, woolen, hemp, and sponge industries, all on a modest scale. As in Japan, the way was left open to transfer ownership and management to private entrepreneurship as capable men emerged. Aided by the recovery in the world economy after 1933, Turkish industry expanded. It is from this period that the take-off can be dated, based on import substitution in light industries and the less sophisticated heavy industries. As the aggregate data in Chart V-39, parts 1 and 2, show, progress was thwarted by conditions during the Second World War; but the first phase of Turkish industrialization was completed in the 1950's. After an awkward period of adjustment late in the decade, Turkish development accelerated from 1961, moving forward on a more diversified basis with a range of industries leading the way which were typical of the early phase of the drive to technological maturity. Steel production accelerated; nitrogen fertilizer and synthetic fiber production came in, as well as the assembly and then manufacture of motor vehicles, radios, and television receivers. The investment rate rose to about 20 percent from its typical take-off level of about 15 percent.

The course of aggregate growth in Turkey emerging from this sequence is approximately as set out in Table V-45. The proportionate contribution of industry to Turkish gross domestic product rose from 13 percent in 1939 to 18 percent in 1965, 23 percent in 1970. As the discussion below (pp. 501–503) indicates, Turkey has been the hard-working plodder as compared to Egypt and Iran. Its modernization was less advanced than Egypt's when Ataturk came to power, but it has moved relatively ahead in the subsequent half-century. On the other hand, it has not enjoyed the benefits of oil export which permitted Iran to come from behind and outstrip Turkey and Egypt in the past two decades.

TABLE V-45. *Annual Average Aggregate Real Growth Rates: Turkey, 1935–1971*

	Total (%)	Per Capita (%)	Industry (%)
1935–1939	6.4	4	—
1939–1945	−3.1	−4.5	—
1938–1950	—	0.04	4.7
1950–1955	5.2[a]	3.4	12.0
1955–1960	6.2[b]	3.2	5.6
1960–1965	5.3	2.1	8.6
1965–1970	6.6	4.1	9.4

[a] 1948–1956.
[b] 1956–1960.

Sources: 1935–1939 to 1960–1965, Z. Y. Hershlag, *Turkey: The Challenge of Growth*, pp. 280, 342, 343, 361; 1965–1970, *United Nations Statistical Yearbook, 1973*, except for industry for 1965–1970, from State Institute of Statistics, *Turkey: An Economic Survey* (Istanbul: Turkish Industrialists' and Businessmen's Association, April 1977), p. 65.

Note: The total figure is for GNP at constant prices; the per capita figure is for net national product at factor cost; the figure for industry is for gross industrial production.

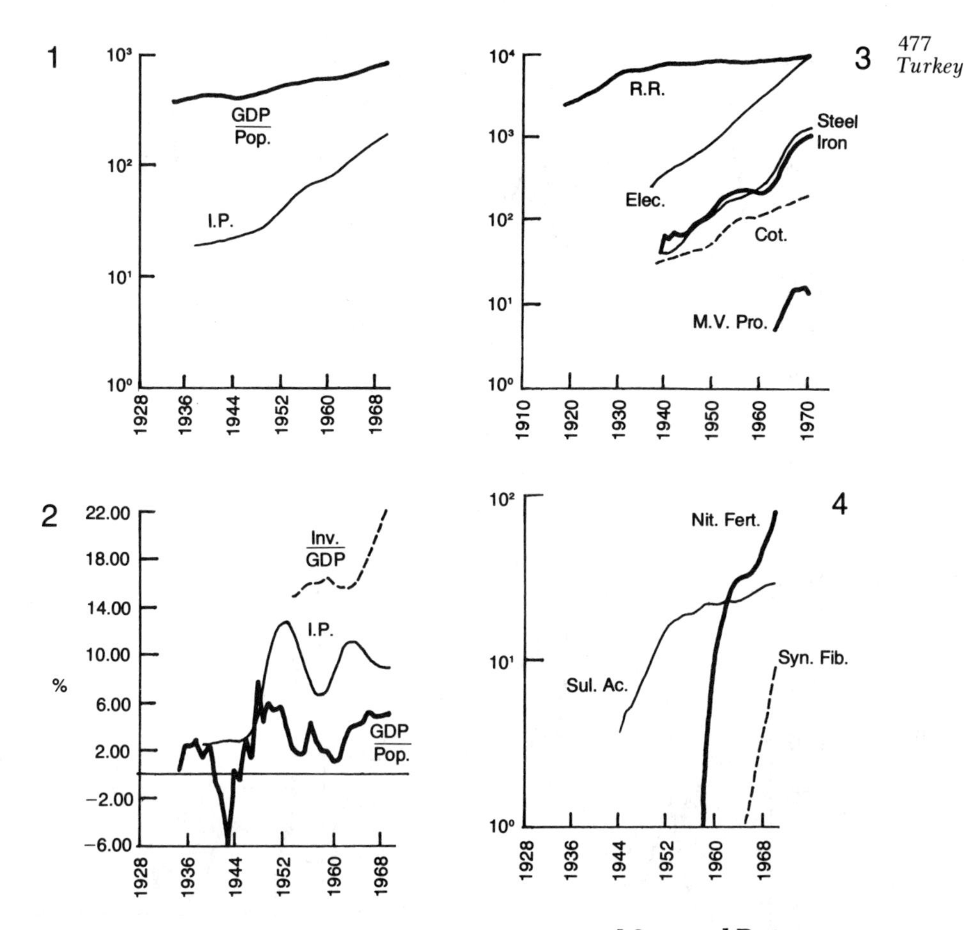

CHART V-39. *Turkey, 1920–1972: Aggregate and Sectoral Data (Smoothed)*

1. GDP per capita ($\frac{\text{GDP}}{\text{Pop.}}$); industrial production (manufacturing production index) (I.P.).

2. Gross investment as % of GDP ($\frac{\text{Inv.}}{\text{GDP}}$); rate of change, GDP per capita ($\frac{\text{GDP}}{\text{Pop.}}$); rate of change, industrial production (manufacturing production index) (I.P.).

3. Six major sectors: railroads (kilometers) (R.R.); raw cotton consumption (Cot.); production of iron (Iron); steel (Steel); electricity (Elec.); and motor vehicles (M.V. Pro.).

4. Production of three major chemicals: sulphuric acid (Sul. Ac.); nitrogen fertilizer (Nit. Fert.); and synthetic fibers (Syn. Fib.).

Sources: See Appendix D.

The sectoral pattern of Turkish economic growth is presented in Charts V-39, parts 3 and 4, V-40, and V-41; its timing, in Table V-46.

The Turkish stages of economic growth can be dated approximately as follows.

Take-off: 1933–1961.

Drive to Technological Maturity: 1961–.

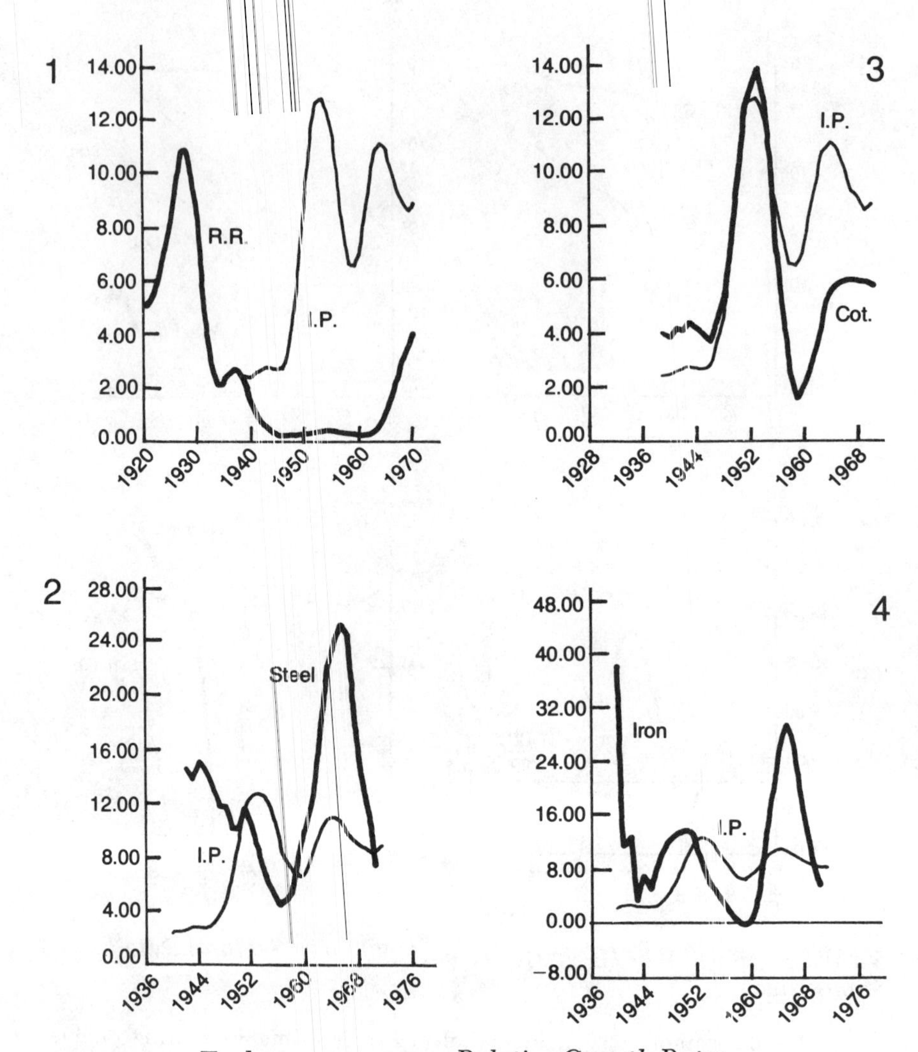

CHART V-40. *Turkey, 1920–1972: Relative Growth Rates—Major Sectors and Industrial Production (Smoothed)*

1. Railroads (kilometers) (R.R.).
2. Steel production (Steel).
3. Raw cotton consumption (Cot.).
4. Iron production (Iron).

Sources: See Appendix D.

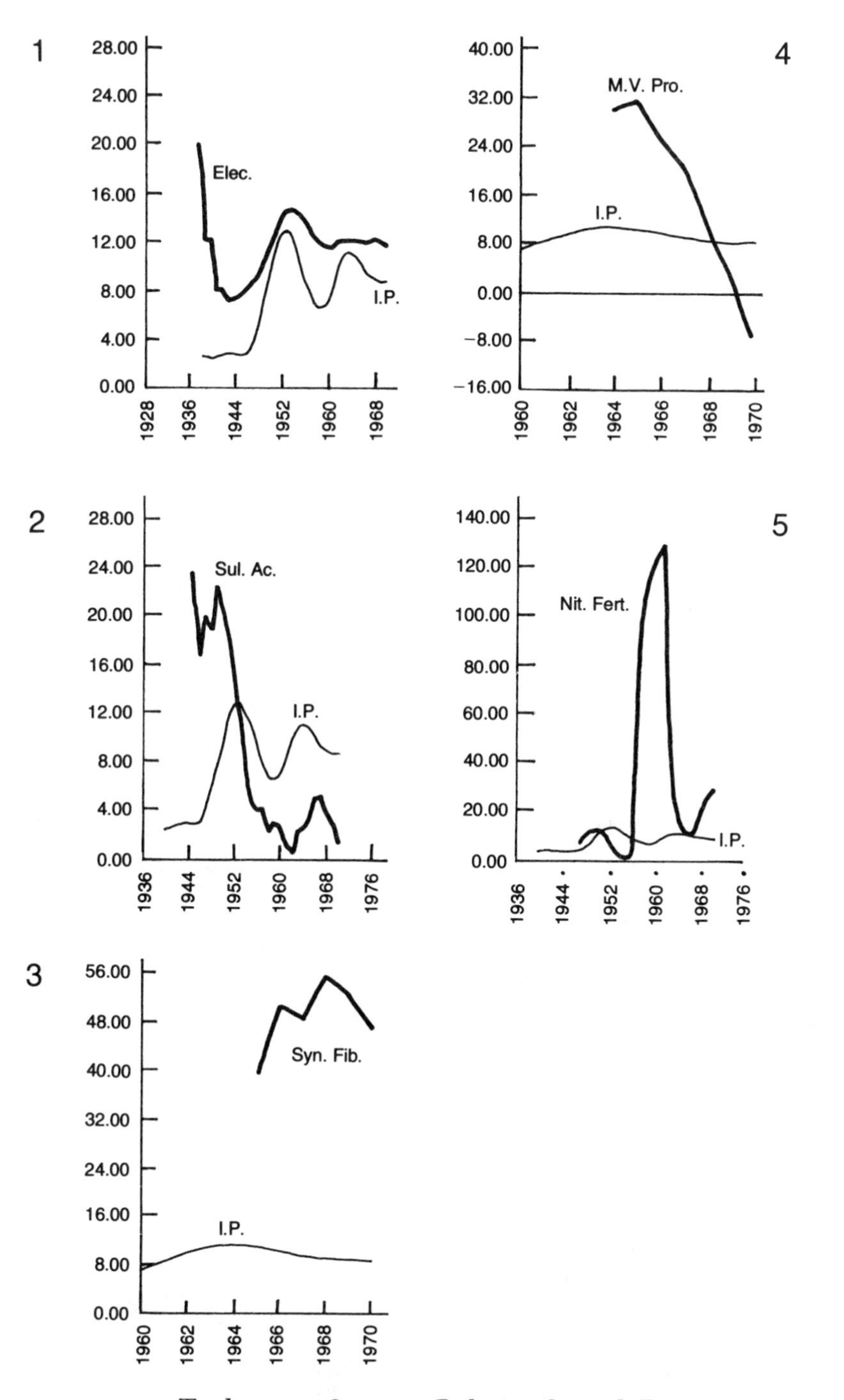

CHART V-41. *Turkey, 1936–1972: Relative Growth Rates— Major Sectors and Industrial Production (Smoothed)*

1. Electricity (Elec.).
2. Sulphuric acid (Sul. Ac.).
3. Synthetic fibers (Syn. Fib.).
4. Motor vehicles (M.V. Pro.).
5. Nitrogen fertilizer (Nit. Fert.).

Sources: See Appendix D.

TABLE V-46. *Approximate Timing of Leading Sector Complexes: Turkey, 1920–1972*

Sector	Maximum Rate of Expansion	Estimated Time Sector Became Leading Sector	Estimated Time Sector Ceased to Lead
Railroads	1920's	[a]	1930's
Cotton yarn	Late 1940's–early 1950's	[b]	—
Iron	1940's	—	—
Steel	1960's	1960's	—
Electricity	Late 1930's	1950's	1960's
Motor vehicles	1960's	1960's	—
Sulphuric acid	1940's	[b]	1950's
Nitrogen	Early 1960's	[b]	—
Synthetic fibers	Late 1960's	[b]	—

[a] Spreading effects not sufficient to be judged leading sector.
[b] Not judged, by itself, a leading sector.

40

Brazil

Down to the 1930's, and to a diminishing degree beyond, Brazil was a classic example of an economy oriented toward the export of foodstuffs and raw materials. As a colony Brazil initially exported a tropical timber (Brazilwood) used to produce a dye for textiles; then, for something over the century beginning in 1550, sugar from the northeast dominated; in the eighteenth century gold from Minas Gerais helped break the depression caused by low sugar prices and the protected mercantilist markets in Europe for West Indian sugar. Nevertheless, sugar exports remained important, especially after the gold ran out from about 1760. The subsequent sequence is set out in Table V-47. Coffee emerged by the 1830's and maintained its preeminence, although hard hit by the relative price decline of the 1930's. Sugar was the highest-value export in the 1820's, but fell away rapidly from the 1860's, in part due to the rise of the sugar beet in Europe. Cotton fluctuated in its relative position, falling away in competition with the American South from the 1830's, reviving during the Civil War, again in the 1930's and, to a lesser degree, in the years of the Second World War. Rubber had a great period in the bicycle boom of the 1890's and the early decades of the automobile age, but it lost out to the Far East rubber producers, who started their plantations with smuggled Brazilian seedlings.

Although Brazilian national income estimates until recent years are notably uncertain, average annual exports may have approximated 12 percent of national income in 1889, 14 percent in 1919.[92] These are, relatively, high proportions but possibly exaggerated by the method of calculation. Nevertheless, the fortunes of Brazil before the 1930's fluctuated with both the demand for its various export products and their prices relative to import prices. The capacity to import (value of exports divided by import prices) increased at an annual average rate of 2.8 percent per capita in the period 1822–1849; 1.6 percent, for 1850–1896; 2.5 percent in the pre-1914 boom, when the terms of trade were particularly favorable, as Table V-48 shows.[93] Donald Coes concludes that the quantity of Brazilian exports

TABLE V-47. *Value of Eight Export Commodities, in Percentage of Tot Exports: Brazil, 1821–1945*

Year	All Eight	Coffee	Sugar	Cocoa	M
1821–1830	85.8	18.4	30.1	0.5	n.
1831–1840	89.8	43.8	24.0	0.6	0.
1841–1850	88.2	41.4	26.7	1.0	0.
1851–1860	90.9	48.8	21.2	1.0	1.
1861–1870	90.3	45.5	12.3	0.9	1.
1871–1880	95.1	56.6	11.8	1.2	1.
1881–1890	92.3	61.5	9.9	1.6	1.
1891–1900	95.6	64.5	6.0	1.5	1.
1901–1910	95.2	51.3	1.2	2.8	2.
1911–1920	85.5	53.0	3.0	3.6	3.
1921–1930	88.6	69.6	1.4	3.2	2.
1931–1940	77.5	50.0	0.5	4.2	1.
1941	57.2	30.0	0.1	4.7	0.
1942	47.3	26.2	0.6	2.9	1.
1943	48.2	32.1	0.2	3.9	0.
1944	54.9	36.2	1.1	2.9	0.
1945	54.9	35.5	0.4	1.9	0.

Source: Henry William Spiegel, *The Brazilian Economy* (Philadelphia: Blakeston C pany, 1949), p. 123. From *Anuário Estatístico do Brasil, 1930–40*, p. 1380; *Bole Estatístico*, passim.

TABLE V-48. *Net Barter Terms of Trade: Brazil, Selected Periods, 1826–1910 (1826–1830 = 100)*

Period	Index
1826–1830	100
1851–1855	206
1866–1870	127
1881–1885	183
1906–1910	244

Source: Nathaniel H. Leff, "Tropical Trade and Development in the Nineteenth Century: The Brazilian Experience," p. 682.
Note: Leff's Brazilian export price index is constructed with shifting weights which reflect the changing composition of Brazil's exports. British export prices are used to measure import prices.

increased at an annual average rate of 2.9 percent between 1878–1882 and 1911–1915, their value at 3.5 percent.[94] Population increased at an average annual rate of more than 2 percent. On the basis of uncertain evidence it may be concluded that per capita real income may have increased at something like 1 percent per annum, with stagnation or decline in the northeast, higher than average rates in the south.[95]

bacco	Cotton	Rubber	Hides and Skins
5	20.6	0.1	13.6
9	10.8	0.3	7.9
3	7.5	0.4	8.5
6	6.2	2.3	7.2
0	18.3	3.1	6.0
4	9.5	5.5	5.6
7	4.2	8.0	3.2
2	2.7	15.0	2.4
4	2.1	28.2	4.3
6	2.0	12.1	6.2
1	2.4	2.6	4.6
5	14.2	1.1	4.4
6	15.0	1.4	4.5
7	8.6	2.0	5.3
3	4.7	2.2	3.5
5	6.2	3.4	2.8
1	8.7	2.9	2.5

There was more to this phase of growth than the expansion in the value of its exports. That expansion was made possible by Brazil's acquisition of a railroad network starting in the late 1850's. As in a good many nations, railroadization stimulated the commercialization of agriculture; but it did not promptly generate spreading effects in heavy industries, as, for example, it did in Belgium, France, Germany, Russia, and the United States. It did, however, galvanize the region centered on Rio and São Paulo. South central Brazil (like Canada after 1896) managed to combine rapid export expansion with a rapid pace of industrialization. Here railroads did, indeed, play a part in making possible the expansion of coffee production and export,[96] the expansion of the port of Santos, the rapid growth of São Paulo itself, and an environment of expanding real income in the region as a whole. The relevant chapter in one of the major studies of this period is entitled simply "Coffee and Rails."[97] But the key to the transition was the emergence of a generation of entrepreneurs who, behind increasingly high tariff barriers, set the process of industrialization going. Its initial focus was consumers' goods production in substitution for imports.

Cotton textiles had a history in Brazil reaching back to mid-century. Two textile mills existed in Brazil in 1850; forty-four in 1881, engaging only some three thousand workers. Brazil imported the bulk of its factory-manufactured textiles. The process which permitted Brazil to supply 90 percent of the domestic textile market by 1927 dates from the shift of the cotton textile industry from Bahia to Rio, São Paulo, and Minas Gerais between the 1860's and the 1880's (Table V-49). The movement to Rio was aided by the railroad links to Minas Gerais and São Paulo and by the use of steam power fueled with imported coal.[98]

The subsequent rise and distribution of the cotton textile industry is suggested in Table V-50. The four areas shown in the table, accounting for two-thirds or more of the cotton industry, contained in 1900 and 1920 only 43 percent of the country's population. By 1920 the state of São Paulo, with 15 percent of the population, contained a quarter of the Brazilian cotton industry.

The annual average rate of increase in Brazilian spindles and looms of about 7 percent between 1905 and 1915 is impressive. The marked retardation during the First World War emerges clearly.[99] These tables also exhibit the relative rise of São Paulo. Both Rio de Janeiro and São Paulo were aided in this period by the cheaper energy available after 1905 from hydroelectric power plants. Although Rio initially led the way in introducing modern industry on a significant scale, the story of São Paulo has been the object of special attention because of its relative rise in the period 1900–1920 and its later industrial pre-eminence.[100] The growth rates for textiles in the pre-1914 decade were high, as they were for shoes and hats; and São Paulo fared reasonably well even during the war years (Table V-51).[101]

Given the rapid pace of urbanization in the region and the swift growth of electricity consumption (Chart V-42, part 3), one can assume a rapid expansion of production of building materials and other necessary inputs for the creation of a modern infrastructure. There was a high but somewhat erratic rate of increase in São Paulo's

TABLE V-49. *Estimated Geographical Distribution of Brazilian Cotton Mills, 1866, 1875, 1885*[a]

Province	1866	1875	1885
Maranhão	—	1	1
Pernambuco	—	1	1
Alagoas	1	1	1
Bahia	5	11	12
Rio (city, province)	2	5	11
São Paulo	—	6	9
Minas Gerais	1	5	13
Total	9	30	48

[a] Since the data are incomplete, these statistics merely indicate the general trend.

Source: Stanley J. Stein, *The Brazilian Cotton Manufacture*, p. 21, where detailed sources are indicated.

TABLE V-50. *Growth of Brazilian Cotton Mills, 1905–1921*

	Area	Mills		Spindles		Looms		Workers	
		Number	%	Number	%	Number	%	Number	%
1905	Brazil	110	100	734,928	100	26,420	100	39,159	100
	Federal District	10		209,200		7,360		8,216	
	State of Rio	11		115,560		3,776		6,024	
	State of São Paulo	18		110,996		3,907		6,269	
	State of Minas	30		45,382		2,295		3,098	
		69	63	481,138	65	17,338	66	23,607	60
1915	Brazil	240	100	1,512,626	100	51,134	100	82,257	100
	Federal District	23		338,326		11,562		16,045	
	State of Rio	23		176,610		5,405		8,280	
	State of São Paulo	51		378,138		12,743		18,338	
	State of Minas	53		131,486		4,321		9,028	
		150	63	1,024,560	68	34,031	67	51,691	63
1921	Brazil	242	100	1,521,300	100	59,208	100	108,960	100
	Federal District	14		411,000		13,000		19,000	
	State of Rio	23		180,000		6,000		12,500	
	State of São Paulo	55		415,900		14,700		25,000	
	State of Minas	60		130,000		5,800		18,000	
		152	63	1,136,900	75	39,500	67	74,500	68

Source: Stein, *Brazilian Cotton Manufacture*, p. 101, where detailed sources are indicated.

TABLE V-51. *Annual Cumulative Growth Rates in Output of Selected Commodities in São Paulo State, 1905–1920*

	Cotton Cloth (%)	Shoes (%)	Hats (%)
1905–1910	15.5	12.7	0
1910–1915	9.9	6.2	12.0
1915–1920	8.9	6.8	−1.0

Source: Nathaniel H. Leff, "Long Term Brazilian Economic Development," p. 476.

industrialization during the interwar years, accompanied by relatively little diversification. Iron and steel production was, for example, based on the melting down of scrap or used charcoal until the emergence of a modern steel industry during the Second World War. Annual average rates of increase in industrial production and population in the state of São Paulo for this formative period are given in Table V-52. These are rates which do, indeed, suggest that the São Paulo region experienced a take-off between, say, 1900 and 1920, proceeding thereafter in somewhat irregular but sustained economic growth. Sharp setbacks were experienced (as elsewhere) in 1921 and in the period 1929–1932. Brazilian industrial produc-

TABLE V-52. *Industrial Production and Population Increase: São Paulo, 1900–1940*

	Population (%)	Industrial Production (%)
1900–1907	5.4	11.4
1907–1920	2.6	7.4
1920–1940	2.3	6.3

Source: Warren Dean, *The Industrialization of São Paulo*, p. 106, where detailed sources are indicated.

tion as a whole increased at an annual rate of 7 percent between 1932 and 1940.[102]

As with a good many other nations, the initial development of a substantial textile and light consumers' industry in substitution for imports was not sufficient to lift the national economy into take-off. But against the background of the recovery from depression after 1932, developments during the Second World War launched Brazil into the diversified pattern of growth reflected in Charts V-42, parts 3 and 4, V-43, and V-44. Wartime conditions not only encouraged import substitution in producers' goods but also permitted Brazil to become a significant exporter of textiles. The proportion of national product contributed by industry rose from 17.4 percent in 1939 to 21.7 percent in 1947; and between those dates industry expanded at an average annual rate of 6.6 percent.[103] Evidently, progress since 1945 has been uneven. There was deceleration in the early 1950's, partially caused by a sharp unfavorable shift in the terms of trade; and what might be called the Goulart crisis occurred in the 1960's, compounded of uncontrolled inflation and political disarray. After 1965 a course was set which yielded after 1967 extraordinarily high rates of expansion down to 1974, when the quadrupling of oil prices and world recession caused, as elsewhere, a sharp deceleration in growth rates. The high if erratic course of aggregate progress in Brazil since the second half of the 1930's emerges in Table V-53.

We unfortunately lack Brazilian investment rates earlier than the post-1945 years, when Brazil was already generating fixed capital formation at levels compatible with sustained economic growth.

Table V-54 sets out the timing of the leading sectors.

Against this background, the Brazilian stages of economic growth can be set out as follows.

São Paulo Regional Take-off: 1900–1928.

National Take-off: 1933–1950.

Drive to Technological Maturity: 1950–.

With a per capita income perhaps twice that of the northeast, south central Brazil may be in the early phase of high mass-consumption as of the early 1970's, although the momentum of the economy was broken, for the time at least, by the events of 1974–1976.

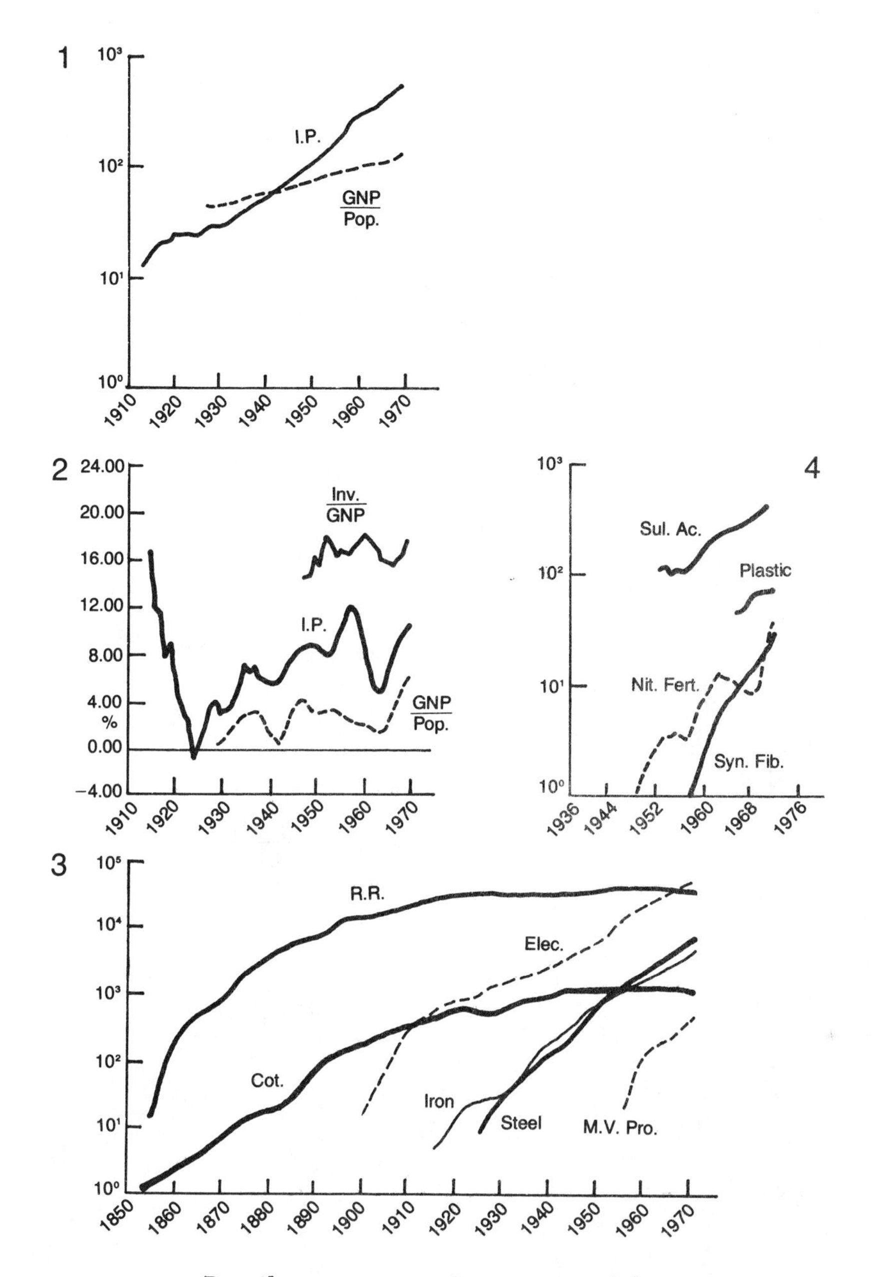

CHART V-42. *Brazil, 1950–1972: Aggregate and Sectoral Data (Smoothed)*

1. GNP per capita ($\frac{\text{GNP}}{\text{Pop.}}$); industrial production index (I.P.).

2. Gross investment as % of GNP ($\frac{\text{Inv.}}{\text{GNP}}$); rate of change, GNP per capita ($\frac{\text{GNP}}{\text{Pop.}}$); rate of change, industrial production (I.P.).

3. Six major sectors: railroads (kilometers) (R.R.); production of cotton cloth (Cot.); iron (Iron); steel (Steel); electricity (Elec.); and motor vehicles (M.V. Pro.).

4. Production of four major chemicals: sulphuric acid (Sul. Ac.); nitrogen fertilizer (Nit. Fert.); plastics and resins (Plastic); and synthetic fibers (Syn. Fib.).

Sources: See Appendix D.

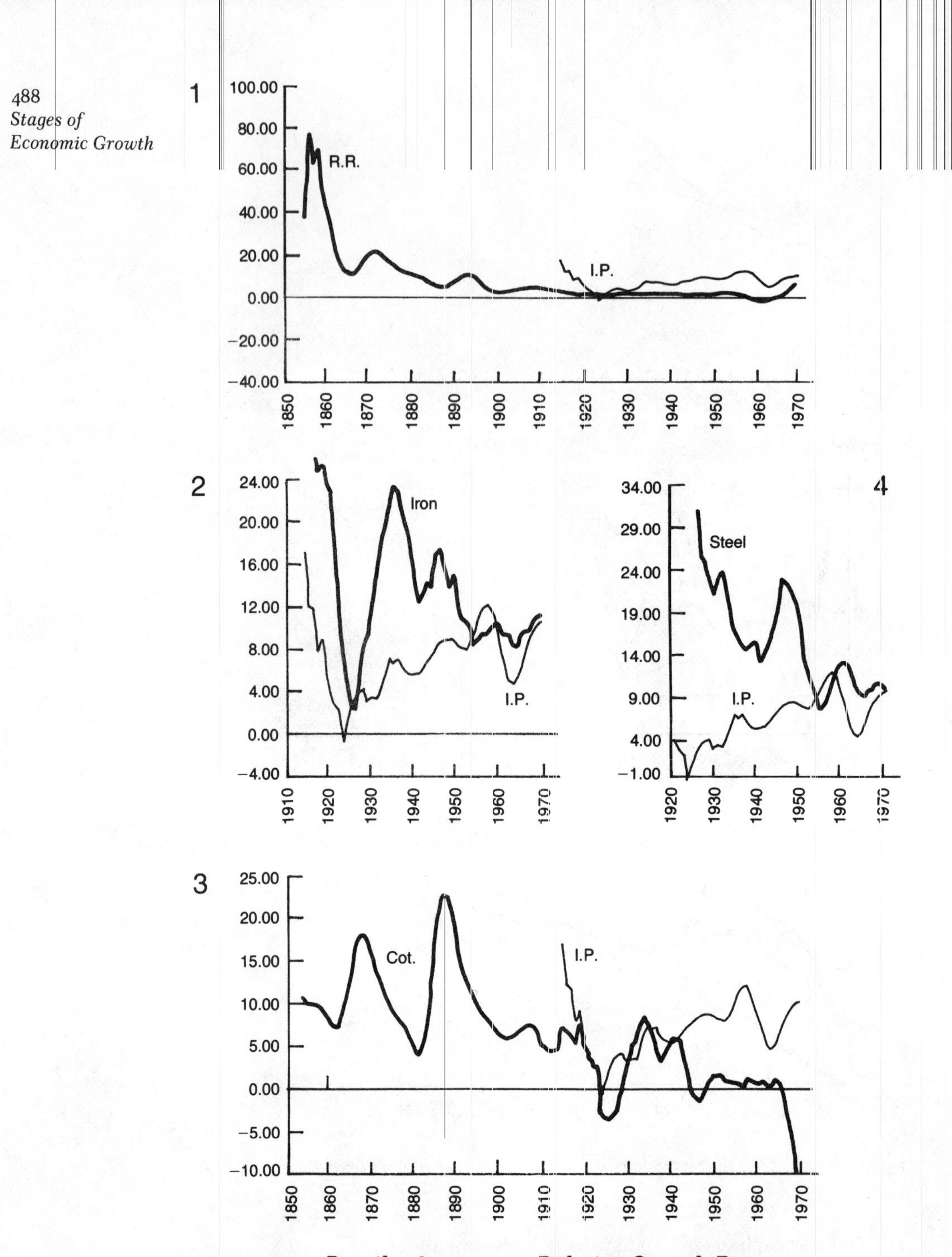

CHART V-43. *Brazil, 1850–1972: Relative Growth Rates—Major Sectors and Industrial Production (Smoothed)*

1. Railroads (kilometers) (R.R.).
2. Iron production (Iron).
3. Cotton cloth production (Cot.).
4. Steel production (Steel).

Sources: See Appendix D.

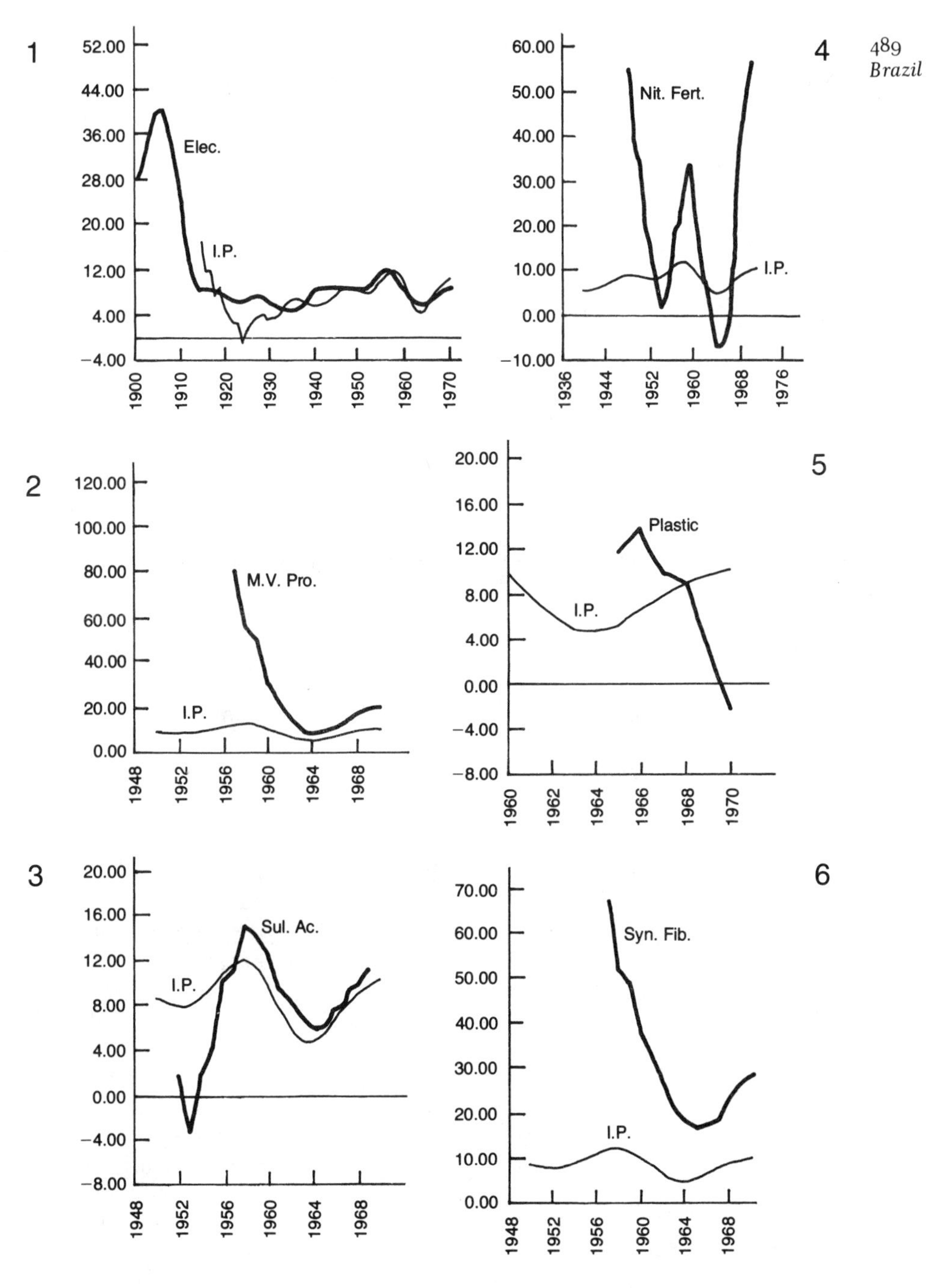

CHART V-44. *Brazil, 1900–1972: Relative Growth Rates—Major Sectors and Industrial Production (Smoothed)*

1. Electricity (Elec.).
2. Motor vehicles (M.V. Pro.).
3. Sulphuric acid (Sul. Ac.).
4. Nitrogen fertilizer (Nit. Fert.).
5. Plastics and resins (Plastic).
6. Synthetic fibers (Syn. Fib.).

Sources: See Appendix D.

TABLE V-53. *Gross Domestic Product per Capita in Constant Prices: Brazil, 1925–1929 to 1965–1970 (1925–1929 = 100)*

		Annual Average Rate of Growth (%)
1925–1929	100	
1930–1934	97.5	−0.5
1935–1939	110.2	2.5
1940–1944	116.2	1.1
1945–1949	123.5	1.2
1950–1954	143.2	3.0
1955–1959	162.1	2.5
1960–1964	186.23	2.8
1965–1970	204.44	1.9
[1960–1963]	—	[2.4]
[1963–1967]	—	[0.7]
[1967–1970]	—	[5.8]

Sources: 1925–1929 to 1950–1954, ECLA sources; 1955–1959 to 1965–1970, *United Nations Statistical Yearbooks*, annual.

TABLE V-54. *Approximate Timing of Leading Sectors: Brazil, 1853–1972*

Sector	Maximum Rate of Expansion	Estimated Time Sector Became Leading Sector	Estimated Time Sector Ceased to Lead	Comments
Railroads	1860's	[a]	1880's	—
Cotton	1900–1905	1930's	1940's	First World War surge in cotton textile production excluded.
Iron	1920's	1950's	—	—
Steel	1920's	1950's	—	Modern steel industry began with Volta Redonda launched during Second World War.
Electricity	1900–1910	1920's	1960's	—
Motor vehicles	1960's	1960's	—	—
Sulphuric acid	1950's	[b]	—	—
Nitrogen	1960's	[b]	—	—
Plastics	Late 1960's	[b]	—	—
Synthetic fibers	Late 1960's	[b]	—	—

[a] Spreading effects not sufficient to justify designation as leading sector complex; but note connection with regional take-off in São Paulo (pp. 483–485, above).

[b] Not judged, by itself, a leading sector.

41

Mexico

The passage of Mexico from independence in 1810 to the beginning of take-off round about 1940 is one of the most complex and troubled passages in modern history.[104] Behind some twenty formal constitutional documents, chronic civil and international strife, and the rise and fall of a gallery of picturesque and passionate leaders was a former Spanish colony, split three ways on racial lines, finding its way to nationhood and modernity by solving a sequence of basic problems: the appropriate degree of centralization for republican government; the relative status of *mestizos* versus *criollos* in the structure of political power; the role of the Church; the system of land ownership; the role of the labor unions; the place of foreign capital in the economy; a viable, nationalist stance toward the overbearing but inescapable presence of the United States; and an appropriate ideology for an industrializing modern Mexico.

The issues unfolded in the following rough sequence, once formal independence was attained by the victory of the *criollos* over the eighty thousand or so European-born *gachupines* who had dominated Mexican colonial life:

—The 1824 Constitution, which settled the question of monarchy versus republicanism, but provided for a federal structure of diffuse power, unrealistic in the disorganized condition of Mexican state governments; it represented a transient victory of liberal *mestizo* forces over the more conservative *criollo*-dominated party.

—The 1836 Constitution, sanctioning central and more conservative rule.

—The Juárez Constitution of 1857, formally restricting the power of the army and the Church as landowners; seeking to establish a secular nation-state, with all under civil law, land for the peasant, and the *mestizo* majority dominant.

—The modernizing dictatorship of Porfirio Díaz (1877–1911), who came to power on the battle cry 'No Re-election and Effective Suffrage' to rule for thirty-four years, carrying Mexico through an important phase of building the preconditions for take-off but at the cost of converging discontents (centered on the *hacienda* system, excessive foreign ownership, and the limitation of democratic political rights) which produced the revolutionary explosion of 1910–1920.

—The Constitution of 1917, with its vesting of ownership of land and other natural resources in the nation, laying the basis for both agrarian reform and, later, oil expropriation, and including a chapter specifying in detail the rights of labor.

—The emergence of the National Revolutionary Party (1928–1929), embracing left, right, and center groups within the broad ambiguous consensus represented by the Mexican Revolution.

—The Cárdenas-Toledano flirtation with international communism of the 1930's, constrained at critical moments by a profound Mexican nationalism, the setting of limits on the power of the labor unions, and the oil expropriation of March 1938.

—The coming to power of the quiet, pragmatic Manuel Avila Camacho in December 1940, launching a period of national unity and industrialization.

Technically, a good deal of Mexico's preparation for modern growth occurred in the long dictatorship of Porfirio Díaz. Railways and electric power plants were built, oil resources and mines developed with foreign capital. A commercial banking system developed, and the first generation of light industries typical of the preconditions period; for example, textiles, shoes, beer, tobacco, soap, sugar refining, and flour milling.[105]

The prolonged revolution of the second decade of the twentieth century set back the economy severely. The pre–take-off generation unfolded as follows:

—A modest recovery from the period of revolution, from 1920 to 1929, marked by an increase of GNP by perhaps 20 percent and of manufacturing output by perhaps one-third.

—1929–1933, depression years, severely felt in Mexico as elsewhere.

—1934–1940, a concentration of public enterprise in land reform, agricultural improvement, highway construction, irrigation projects, electrification, and school construction. Important in its own right and a symbol of this period was the founding in 1934 of the Nacional Financiera, which, along with three other major institutions (the Bank of Mexico, the National Bank for Agricultural Credit, and the National Bank for Urban Mortgages and Public Works), provided Mexico for the first time with strong centralized credit institutions, sensitive to government policy. Mexican recovery from the bottom of the depression proceeded strongly in tolerable order; and, with a final dramatic expression of Mexican nationalism in the oil nationalization of 1938, the country was ready for a new political and economic phase of development.

From 1940, Mexican growth continued for thirty-five years with a stability matched by few, if any, developing nations of the contemporary world.

The aggregate data presented in Chart V-45, parts 2 and 3, capture something of Mexico's experience with modern growth: the quite rapid pre-1910 advance of GNP per capita at low absolute levels of industrial output; the resumption of forward movement in the 1920's, broken by the Great Depression; the recovery of the 1930's; and then the uneven acceleration from about 1940 in industrial production accompanied by high, well-sustained, but fluctuating increase in GNP per capita.

The movement of the investment rate from 1940, rising in typical style from about 6 percent to 14 percent during take-off and moving up again in the drive to technological maturity, can also be observed in Chart V-45, part 3.

In an imaginative exercise in the reconstruction of historical estimates, Clark Reynolds concludes that pre-independence levels of real per capita income (1800–1810) were only reattained in the 1930's: ". . . if the earlier figures are correct, then either there was little or no increase in per capita income over the course of the nineteenth century, or per capita income actually declined over much of the nineteenth century despite the gains of the Porfiriato. In either case growth from 1900 to 1930 simply reflects a recovery of pre-Independence levels of productivity."[106]

Mexico's growth rates, aggregate and in broad sectors, are given in Table V-55 for the three major phases of the nation's twentieth-century experience. The annual average per capita growth rate for the period 1965–1970 was 3.4 percent.

Table V-56 shows the changing structure of production in the Mexican economy since 1900, with its sharp relative rise in manufacturing and the usual relative decline in agriculture, accompanied in the Mexican case also by a relative decline in the contribution of mining.

The sectoral data in Chart V-45, parts 3 and 4, suggest the kind of technologies whose progressive absorption brought about the sharp rise in the role of manufacturing after 1940. They are summarized with respect to timing in Table V-57, based on Charts V-46 and V-47.

We observe, as in a good many contemporary developing nations, a long lag between the installation of a railroad system and sustained economic growth. Again cotton textiles were an insufficient basis for take-off. Iron, steel, and simple forms of metalworking (as well as a wide range of light import-substitution industries) came in during the 1940's and 1950's; in the 1960's Mexico moved into a more diversified industrial development, here symbolized by motor vehicle production on a significant scale and the modern branches of the chemical industry.

The Mexican stages of economic growth can, then, be dated as follows.

Take-off: 1940–1960.

Drive to Technological Maturity: 1960–.

TABLE V-55. *Growth Rates of the Mexican Economy, 1900–1965 (Compound Annual Rates of Growth)*

	Porfiriato	Revolution and Reform	
	1900–1910	1910–1925	1925–1940
1. Gross domestic product	3.3	2.5	1.6
2. Population	1.1	0.1	1.6
3. Per capita product	2.2	2.4	0.0
4. Agricultural production[a]	1.0	0.1	2.7
5. Manufacturing production	3.6	1.7	4.3
6. Mining and petroleum production	7.2	5.6	−1.9

[a]"Agricultural production" in this table includes crop production, animal husbandry, forestry, and fishing.

Source: Clark W. Reynolds, *The Mexican Economy*, p. 22, where detailed sources and methods are indicated.

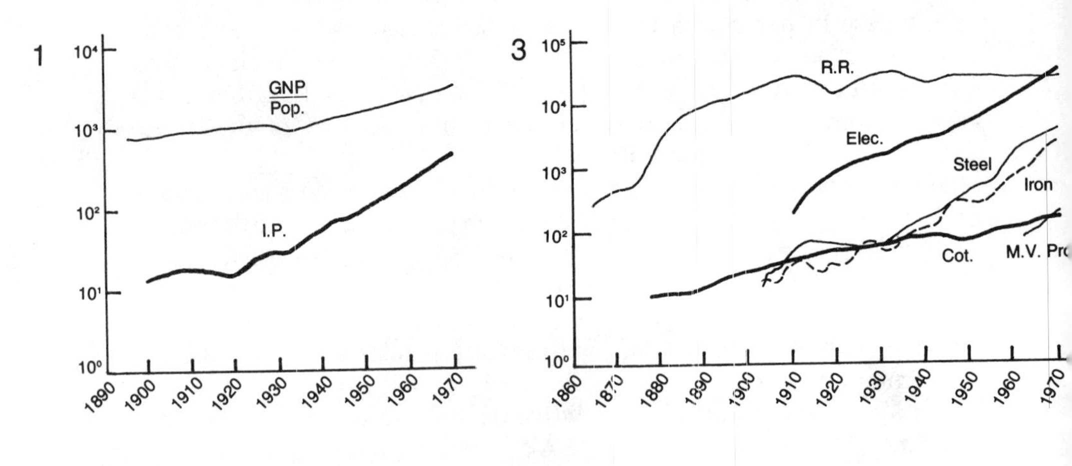

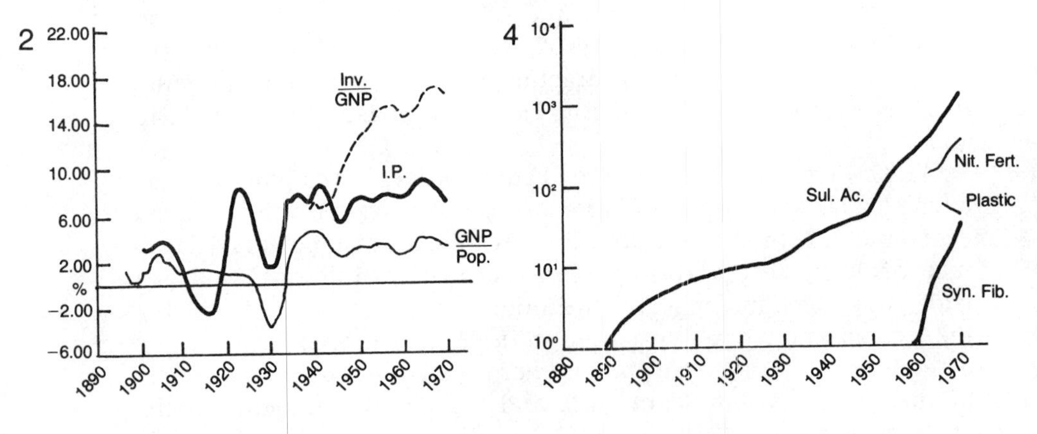

)evelopment

940–1950	1950–1960	1960–1965	1925–1965
.7	6.1	6.1	4.5
.8	3.1	3.4	2.6
.9	3.0	2.7	1.9
.8	4.3	4.3	4.2
.1	7.3	8.1	6.4
.5	5.3	4.2	1.7

:HART V-45. *Mexico, 1865–1972: Aggregate and Sectoral Data Smoothed)*

1. GNP per capita ($\frac{GNP}{Pop.}$); industrial production (manufacturing produc-ion index) (I.P.).
2. Gross investment as % of GNP ($\frac{Inv.}{GNP}$); rate of change, GNP per capita $\frac{GNP}{Pop.}$); rate of change, industrial production (manufacturing production ndex) (I.P.).
3. Six major sectors: railroads (kilometers) (R.R.); raw cotton consump-ion (Cot.); production of iron (Iron); steel (Steel); electricity (Elec.); and notor vehicles (M.V. Pro.).
4. Production of four major chemicals: sulphuric acid (Sul. Ac.); nitrogen ertilizer (Nit. Fert.); plastics and resins (Plastics); and synthetic fibers Syn. Fib).

Sources: See Appendix D.

TABLE V-56. *Structure of Production: Mexico, 1900–1965 (%)*

	Porfiriato		Revolution and Reform	Development			
	1900	1910	1930	1940	1950	1960	1965
Gross domestic product	100.0	100.0	100.0	100.0	100.0	100.0	100.0
Agriculture	—	—	—	24.3	22.5	18.9	17.4
Crop production	14.3	11.4	13.1	12.6	14.6	12.3	—
Livestock	15.6	12.8	10.6	10.4	7.1	6.1	—
Forestry	—	—	—	1.2	0.6	0.3	—
Fishing	—	—	—	0.1	0.2	0.2	—
Manufacturing	13.2	13.7	16.7	18.0	20.5	23.0	25.3
Mining	6.4	8.8	9.8	5.6	3.0	2.2	1.7
Electric energy	—	—	—	1.0	0.9	1.2	1.4
Petroleum	—	0.3	3.7	2.9	2.7	3.2	3.2
Construction	—	—	—	3.6	3.1	3.5	3.5
Transportation	3.1	2.8	5.3	4.5	4.8	4.9	4.3
Commerce	—	—	15.8	24.0	26.2	25.7	—
Government	—	—	3.6	3.1	3.2	2.7	2.7
Unclassified activities	47.4	50.3	21.4	13.0	13.1	14.8	40.5[a]

[a] Includes commerce for 1965.

Source: Reynolds, *The Mexican Economy*, p. 61, where detailed source data are indicated.

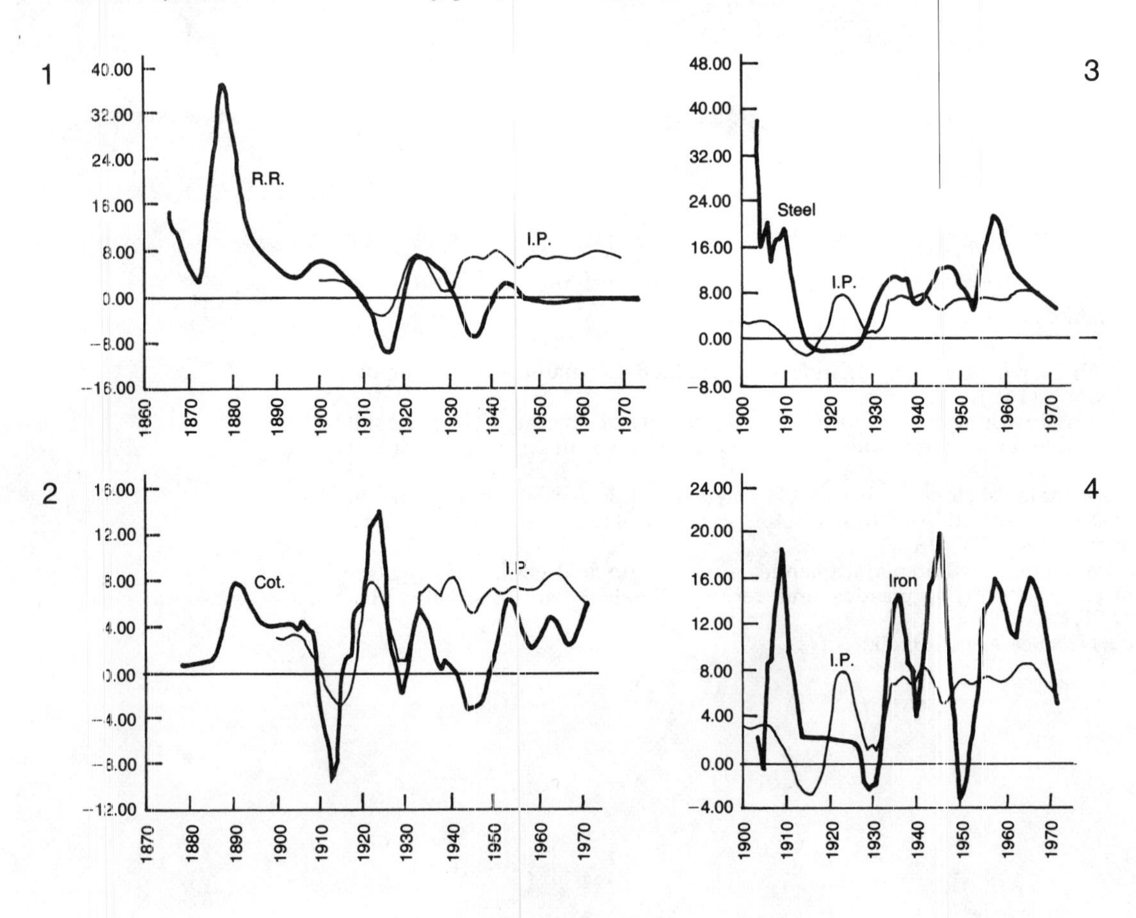

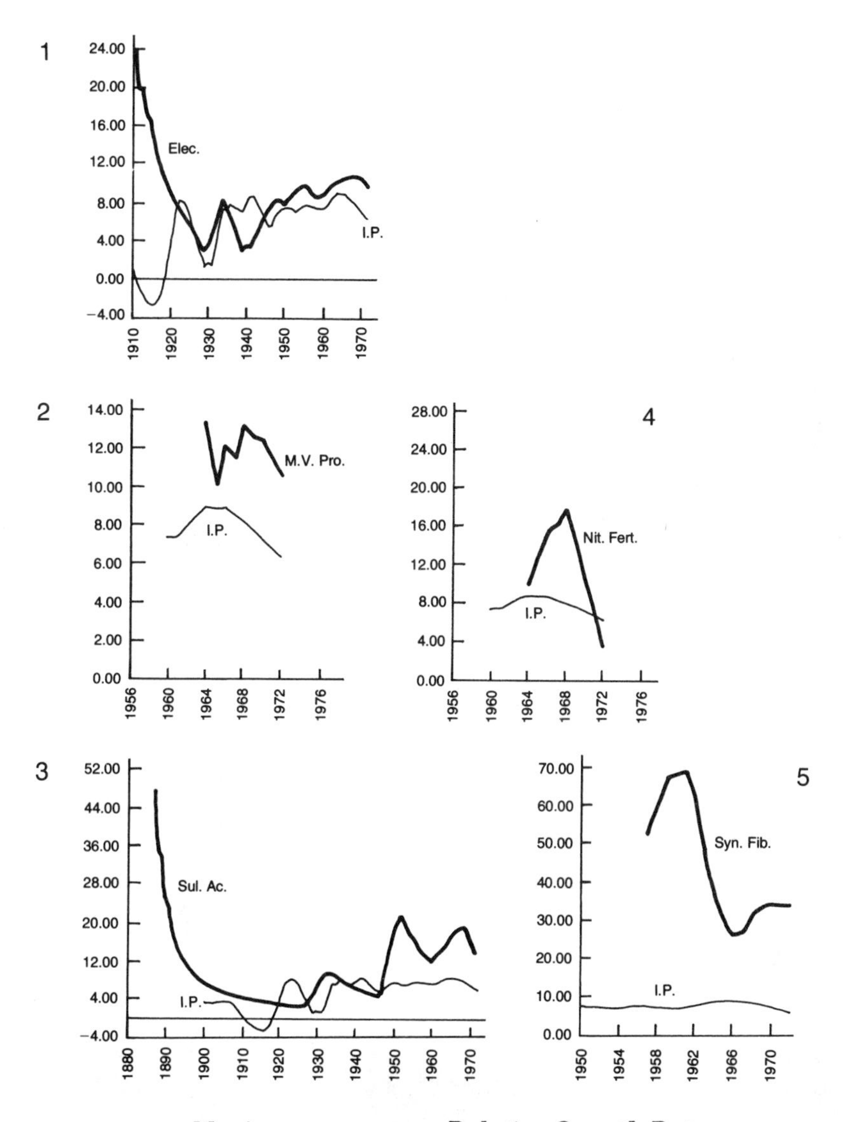

CHART V-47. *Mexico, 1910–1972: Relative Growth Rates—Major Sectors and Industrial Production (Smoothed)*

1. Electricity (Elec.).
2. Motor vehicles (M.V. Pro.).
3. Sulphuric acid (Sul. Ac.).
4. Nitrogen fertilizer (Nit. Fert.).
5. Synthetic fibers (Syn. Fib.).

Sources: See Appendix D.

ART V-46. *Mexico, 1865–1972: Relative Growth Rates—ajor Sectors and Industrial Production (Smoothed)*

. Railroads (kilometers) (R.R.).
. Raw cotton consumption (Cot.).
. Steel production (Steel).
. Iron production (Iron).
ources: See Appendix D.

TABLE V-57. *Approximate Timing of Leading Sectors: Mexico, 1860–1972*

Sector	Maximum Rate of Expansion	Estimated Time Sector Became Leading Sector	Estimated Time Sector Ceased to Lead	Comments
Railroads	Late 1870's–early 1880's	[a]	Post-1910	Railway recovery after Revolution set aside.
Cotton consumption	Mid-1920's–Mid-1930's	[b]	1950's	—
Iron	1900–1910	1940's	—	—
Steel	1900–1910	1940's	—	—
Electricity	1910–1920	1940's	—	—
Motor vehicles	1960's	1960's	—	—
Sulphuric acid	1890's	[b]	—	—
Nitrogen	1960's	[b]	—	—
Plastics	1960's	[b]	—	—
Synthetic fibers	1960's	[b]	—	—

[a] Spreading effects insufficient to justify designation as a leading sector.
[b] Not judged, by itself, a leading sector.

We have for Mexico an index of poverty constructed for the period 1900–1960 by James Wilkie.[107] Its rate of decline in relation to the rise in per capita product emerges as shown in Table V-58.

The relative rates of movement suggest that the rise in per capita product, especially since 1940, is related to the decline in poverty; but the link is not rigorous. Rapid industrialization based on the progressive absorption of new and more sophisticated technologies has contributed to the decline in poverty by drawing workers to new urban jobs and also providing increased public revenues for social purposes. But the high rate of population increase and the uneven development of agriculture have left large numbers of Mexicans relatively untouched by the aggregate average rise in real income per capita.

TABLE V-58. *A Comparison of Poverty Reduction and per Capita Growth: Mexico, 1910–1960*

	1910–1925	1925–1940	1940–1950	1950–1960
1. Cumulative annual percentage *decline* in the poverty index	0.7	0.8	1.5	1.8
2. Cumulative annual percentage *rise* in per capita product	2.4	0.0	3.9	3.0

Source: Reynolds, *The Mexican Economy*, p. 47.

42

Iran

As of 1977, Iran was evidently one of the economic success stories of the developing world. As Chart V-48 shows, it had been moving forward at an extremely high aggregate rate of growth in product per capita and, more important, absorbing rapidly the classic technologies of the drive to technological maturity: steel and metalworking, electricity and light electronics, and the modern chemicals. The surge of additional oil revenues after 1973 evidently expanded the scope for pressing forward with this stage. The Fifth Iranian Development Plan (1973–1978) was revised upward in the summer of 1974. Projected investment levels were doubled. An annual industrial growth rate of 18 percent is now envisaged, 7 percent in agriculture, GNP per capita, 22 percent. But the acceleration in Iranian growth, from already high rates, can be dated from the second half of the 1960's.

The story of how Iran came to this ebullient, perhaps excessively ebullient, phase in its long history is, as for many other nations, one which involves the overcoming of severe geographical and resource constraints; an inhospitable international environment, aggravated by the relative lateness of its modernization; and a cultural, social, and political heritage that required much painful change before sustained modern growth could begin.[108]

Iran is a mountainous country, about the size of all of Western Europe. It is, generally, arid; and at its center is a huge desert. Its rivers afford neither easy navigational routes nor major sources of irrigation. Its traditional society had a strong nomadic element. Central government was weak, compared with most traditional systems.

Its location led to embroilment with stronger and more assertive external powers, from the Greeks, Arabs, and Mongols, down to the Russian-British rivalry of the nineteenth and first half of the twentieth centuries. Nevertheless, a continuity of culture was maintained, although the Persians adapted much from their various invaders.

As the industrial revolution came to the Western world, at the end of the eighteenth century, Iran was recovering from a series of exhausting wars in which Afghan, Russian, and Turkish invaders were repulsed. Civil conflict followed which ended only with the coming of Qajar rule in 1796. Despite brief humiliating wars with Russia in 1813 and 1826, the subsequent 118 years were a period of modernization; but this process moved much more slowly than in Turkey and other parts of the Middle East. Issawi sets out the reasons and consequences:

> Iran's geographical position was . . . , in the nineteenth century context, distinctly unfavorable. Unlike Egypt, Syria, and Iraq, it did not lie on Britain's direct route to India, and therefore offered far less attraction to railway and canal builders. Until the opening of the Suez Canal, it lay more than 11,000 miles from Western Europe. Its productive regions were shut off from the sea by high mountain ranges. And its richest part, the northern, was still farther removed from the center of world activity. Moreover, the fact that Iran was adjacent to India meant that the British authorities inevitably thought of it as a glacis, to be kept denuded of any facilities which might make it easier for the Russians to advance through it to the subcontinent, while the Russians were most reluctant to expose their southern flank to British economic or political penetration.
>
> The combined result of all these factors was the comparative neglect of Iran by European capital and enterprise and its far slower rate of development. Whereas Egypt alone had some 250,000 European residents in 1914, those in Iran were numbered in hundreds. Foreign capital investment was negligible until the turn of the century and even in 1914 was below £30 million ($150 million), including the national debt. Not one modern port had been built, and there were less than a dozen miles of railways. The banking system was still rudimentary. And although trade did increase considerably, its rate of growth was far smaller than that of Egypt, Lebanon, and Syria and below that of Turkey and Iraq.[109]

Nevertheless, there was an expansion of foreign trade, of internal and external communications, and, from 1901 forward, Iran became caught up in the story of oil production. The increased British interest in Persian oil in the south and the concurrent dynamism of Russia pressing from the north helped trigger the revolution of 1906; but the revolution also yielded the Anglo-Russian agreement of 1907, partitioning the country into explicit spheres of influence.

Out of the post-1918 turmoil, including the Russian Revolution and civil war, Iran emerged by 1925 with a strong nationalist, modernizing ruler in Reza Shah, who pressed forward in the style of his neighbor Kemal Ataturk from a less advanced base.

Table V-59 shows how Iran, from an initially lower level, had caught up with or surpassed Egypt and Turkey by 1968 in terms of a variety of measures of modernization.

TABLE V-59. *Comparative Modernization Data: Iran, Egypt (U.A.R.), and Turkey, 1925, 1938, 1950, 1968*

	1925	1938	1950	1968
Population (millions)				
Iran	12.5	15	19.3	27.3
Egypt	14	16.4	20.4	31.7[a]
Turkey	13.1	17.1	20.9	33.5
Per capita GDP (U.S. $)				
Iran	—	—	—	299
Egypt	—	—	—	161[a]
Turkey	—	—	—	338
Per capita energy consumption (coal equivalent, kilos)				
Iran	—	103	234	478
Egypt	—	125	217	298[a]
Turkey	—	127	258	450
Electricity output (million kWh)				
Iran	—	—	200	5,008
Egypt	—	—	642	6,735[a]
Turkey	—	—	676	6,886
Per capita steel consumption (kilos)				
Iran	—	—	—	63
Egypt	—	—	—	21[a]
Turkey	—	—	—	26
Per capita textile consumption (kilos)				
Iran	—	—	—	4.2
Egypt	—	—	—	4.0[a]
Turkey	—	—	—	5.4
Per capita sugar consumption (kilos)				
Iran	—	—	—	24
Egypt	—	—	—	15[a]
Turkey	—	—	—	18
Imports ($ millions)				
Iran	88	55	191	1,386
Egypt	250	184	564	690[a]
Turkey	246	119	286	770
Railways (kilometers)				
Iran	250	1,700	3,180	3,645
Egypt	4,555	5,606	6,092	5,500[a]
Turkey	4,700	7,324	7,634	8,162
Automobiles (thousands)				
Iran	4	15	38	238
Egypt	18	34	78	143[a]
Turkey	8	11	33	223

TABLE V-59. *Comparative Modernization Data: Iran, Egypt (U.A.R.), and Turkey, 1925, 1938, 1950, 1968 (continued)*

	1925	1938	1950	1968
Cement production (thousand metric tons)				
Iran	—	65	54	2,000
Egypt	90	375	1,022	3,147[a]
Turkey	59	287	396	4,733
Refined sugar output (thousand metric tons)				
Iran	—	22	69	458
Egypt	109	238	218	414[a]
Turkey	5	247	186	700
Cereals output (million metric tons)				
Iran	—	3.09	3.09	5.05
Egypt	—	3.63	3.72	5.55[a]
Turkey	—	6.46	6.74	13.98
Cotton output (thousand metric tons)				
Iran	—	34	26	127
Egypt	—	400	364	479[a]
Turkey	—	52	99	356
Students in schools (thousands)				
Iran	74	234	743	3,613
Egypt	635	1,309	1,597	4,947[a]
Turkey	413	810	1,798	5,610
Annual average growth rate, GNP per capita, 1960–1970 (%)				
Iran	—	—	—	4.9
Egypt	—	—	—	1.2
Turkey	—	—	—	3.4

[a] U.A.R.

Sources: Annual average growth rates, 1960–1970, World Bank sources; all other data, Charles Issawi, *The Economic History of Iran, 1800–1914*, pp. 375 (1925), 379 (1938), 381 (1950), 382 (1965), where original sources are given.

The following specific points in Table V-59 are worth noting:

—The evolution of population in all three countries has been quite similar, with the Turkish figure for 1925 abnormally low due to the long period of military struggle ending only in 1923.

—By every modernization measure available for 1925, Iran was the least advanced and, excepting railway mileage, Egypt the most advanced of the three countries. The railroadization of Iran (1925–1950) evidently came late.

—Iran gained, relatively, down to 1938 but still remained the least modernized of the three countries. Turkey also gained relatively; but, in general, Egypt maintained its lead.

—Between 1938 and 1950, Iran gained relatively in education, while still far behind; but it registered little or no net gain except in refined sugar output, where its production was still extremely low. Turkey gained significantly on Egypt only in education and cotton production.

—Between 1950 and 1968, there was marked progress for all three countries. Iran acquired industrial production capacity in sectors where it had long lagged (e.g., cement, electricity); its school population moved close to the range of Egypt and Turkey; its oil revenues permitted much higher levels of imports. Its rapidly increasing GDP per capita had surpassed that of Egypt and was closing rapidly on Turkey, which in almost all categories (including education) had now surpassed Egypt.

As of 1974, per capita income for the three countries may have been: Iran, $1,340; Turkey, $690; Egypt, $280. Iran's figure reflects, of course, the impact of the oil price increases since October 1973. The quite dramatic surge of postwar Iran before that date was also closely related to its oil revenues and their utilization. Briefly, Reza Shah had used his relatively modest revenues to buy military equipment; from 1941 to 1955 the bulk of the revenues were used to support the national budget; since 1955 they have been geared with increasing sophistication to national development programs, despite large allocations to modernize the Iranian armed forces. One can date an authentic take-off from about 1955, on the basis of all the data available. In the second half of the 1960's the diversification of Iranian industry became increasingly marked, with a shift away from light consumers' goods into the classic sectors of the drive to technological maturity; e.g., metalworking, engineering, and electrical equipment.[110] This was accompanied by a rise in the proportion of large-scale manufacturing units.[111] Table V-60 shows the pace of the transition between 1962 and 1967.

The gross investment rate rose during the 1960's from a typical take-off level (15 percent) to 20 percent (Chart V-48, part 2).

Table V-61 summarizes the highly compressed timing of Iran's absorption of modern technologies.

The stages of economic growth for Iran can, then, be dated as follows.

Take-off: 1955–1965.

Drive to Technological Maturity: 1965–.

As of 1976, real income per capita in Iran would place it statistically in the stage of high mass-consumption; but it is not yet clear how the surge in resources flowing from increased oil revenues will, in fact, be disposed between increased consumption and accelerated investment and whether income distribution will become more equitable. In 1973 the poorest 40 percent of the Iranian population commanded only 12.5 percent of GNP. This figure compares favorably with those of some Latin American countries; e.g., Colombia and Peru (8.6 percent), Brazil (9.8 percent), Mexico (10.5 percent). It

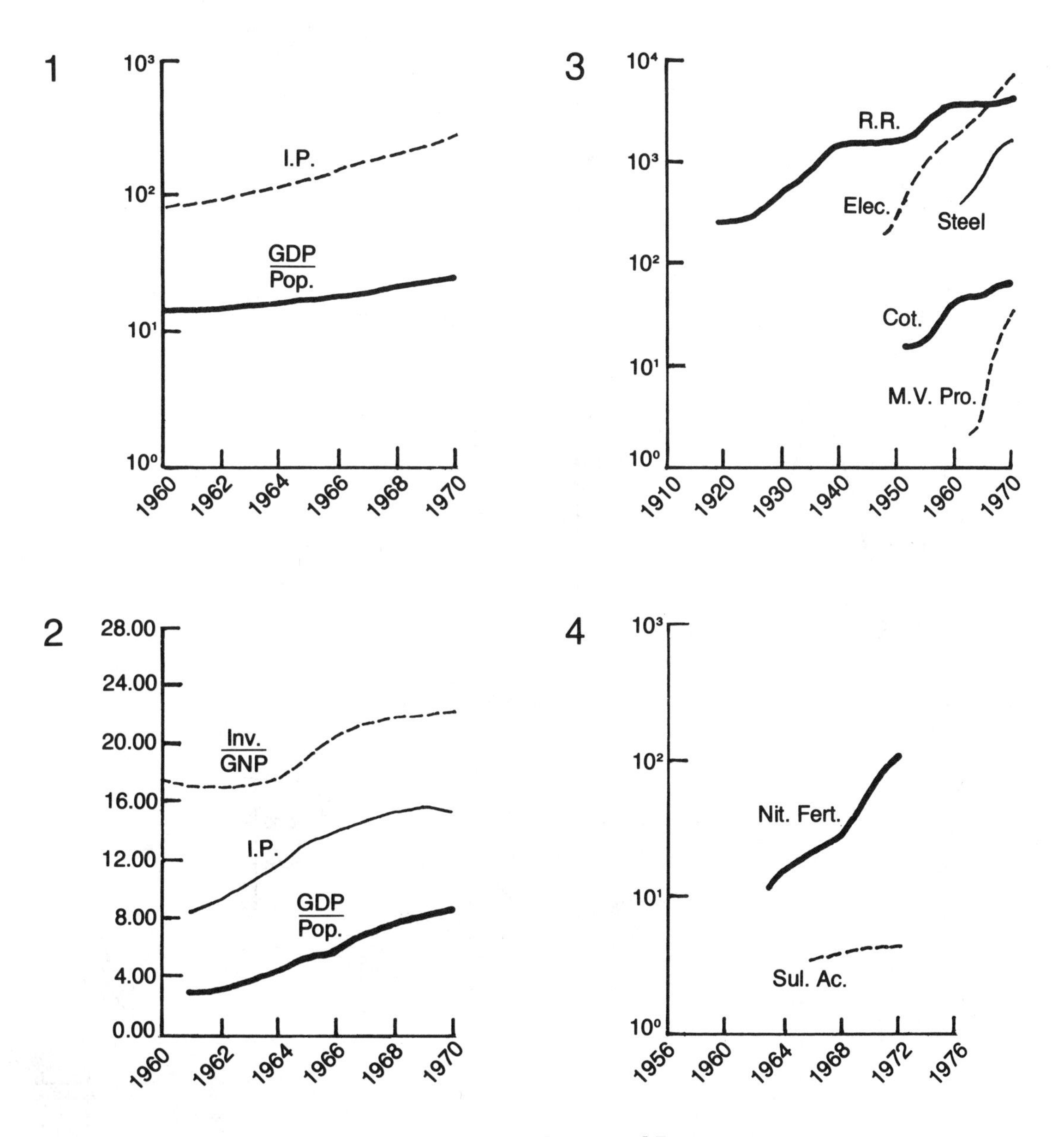

CHART V-48. *Iran, 1920–1972: Aggregate and Sectoral Data (Smoothed)*

1. GDP per capita ($\frac{\text{GDP}}{\text{Pop.}}$); industrial production index (I.P.).
2. Gross investment as % of GNP ($\frac{\text{Inv.}}{\text{GNP}}$); rate of change, GDP per capita ($\frac{\text{GDP}}{\text{Pop.}}$); rate of change, industrial production (I.P.).
3. Five major sectors: railroads (kilometers) (R.R.); raw cotton consumption (Cot.); steel (Steel); electricity (Elec.); and motor vehicles (M.V. Pro.).
4. Production of two major chemicals: sulphuric acid (Sul. Ac.) and nitrogen fertilizer (Nit. Fert.).

Sources: See Appendix D.

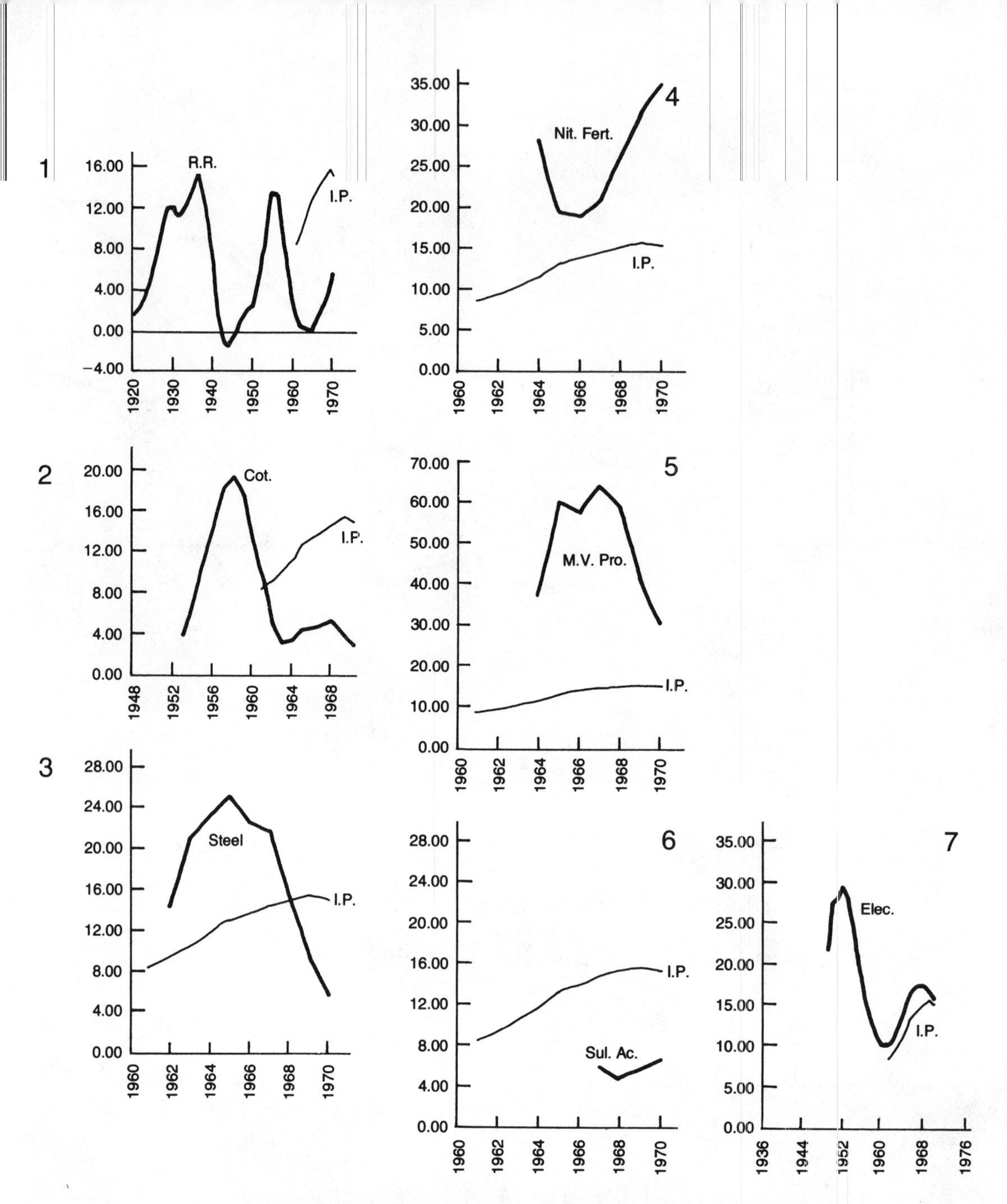

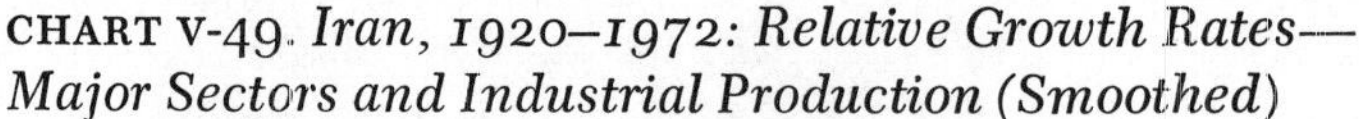

CHART V-49. *Iran, 1920–1972: Relative Growth Rates—Major Sectors and Industrial Production (Smoothed)*

1. Railroads (kilometers) (R.R.).
2. Raw cotton consumption (Cot.).
3. Steel production (Steel).
4. Nitrogen fertilizer (Nit. Fert.).
5. Motor vehicles (M.V. Pro.).
6. Sulphuric acid (Sul. Ac.).
7. Electricity (Elec.).

Sources: See Appendix D.

TABLE V-60. *Changes in Value Added in Iranian Manufacturing, 1962, 1967*

	Distribution of Value Added			Share of Growth	Value-Added Growth Rate per Annum (%)
	1962	1967	Change (%)		
Total value added (million rials)	34,087	68,489	—	34,402	14.9
Analysis (%)	100.0	100.0	0.0	100.0	14.9
Nondurable consumers' goods	68.1	62.8	−5.3	57.6	13.1
Food	21.9	20.7	−1.2	19.5	13.6
Beverages	2.1	1.0	−1.1	−0.2	−1.4
Tobacco	12.3	8.0	−4.3	3.8	5.6
Textiles	24.6	19.5	−5.1	14.4	9.8
Apparel	3.4	10.0	+6.6	16.6	43.0
Wood products	2.3	3.2	+0.9	4.0	22.0
Leather	1.5	0.4	−1.1	−0.7	−11.3
Intermediate goods	22.2	25.6	+3.4	29.0	18.4
Paper	0.7	1.0	+0.3	1.3	23.0
Printing	0.6	1.1	+0.5	1.7	32.0
Rubber	0.8	2.2	+1.4	3.6	40.0
Chemicals	4.2	4.4	+0.2	4.6	16.1
Oil and coal products	—	0.5	+0.5	0.9	21.0[a]
Basic metals	0.3	2.0	+1.7	3.6	65.8
Metal products	7.3	5.7	−1.6	4.2	9.5
Nonmetallic minerals	8.3	8.7	+0.4	9.1	16.1
Durable and capital goods	8.9	10.3	+1.4	11.7	18.5
Machinery (nonelectric)	0.2	0.6	+0.4	1.0	42.0
Electrical machinery	0.7	3.9	+3.2	7.0	61.7
Transport equipment	8.0	5.8	−2.2	3.7	8.1
Miscellaneous industries	0.8	1.2	+0.4	1.6	24.0

[a] Growth rate is calculated on the base of 1963 oil and coal value added.

Source: Robert E. Looney, *The Economic Development of Iran*, p. 108. From Ministry of Economy, *Annual Industrial Survey*, 1965, 1967.

is much higher than that of Iraq (6.8 percent). But it is below the level in societies which have experienced high mass-consumption, where the range is from, say, 14.0 percent (Sweden) to 20.0 percent (Canada).

As noted earlier, Iran's economic and social development plans have been greatly accelerated since its acquisition of vastly increased foreign-exchange resources in 1973–1974. The government evidently intends to use what may be a transient phase of abundant access to imports to move Iran rapidly through the drive to technological maturity so that when its oil reserves are run down (or command less favorable relative terms in world markets) it can stand on its feet as a highly diversified, rich, industrial economy. Its first three years of pursuing this policy are not reassuring. It is by no means clear that Iran's absorptive capacity can match the flow of resources it seeks to mobilize from abroad; agriculture appears still to be omi-

TABLE V-61. *Approximate Timing of Leading Sectors: Iran, 1920–1972*

Sector	Maximum Rate of Expansion	Estimated Time Sector Became Leading Sector	Estimated Time Sector Ceased to Lead	Comments
Railroads	Mid-1920's–Mid-1930's	[a]	—	—
Yarn production	1950's	[b]	1960's	—
Iron	—	—	—	—
Steel	Early 1960's	1960's	—	Relative decline in steel growth rate for late 1960's may be temporary.
Electricity	1950's	1950's	—	—
Motor vehicles	Late 1960's	1960's	—	Relative decline in motor vehicle growth rate for late 1960's may be temporary.
Sulphuric acid	Late 1960's	—	—	—
Nitrogen	Early 1960's	[b]	—	—
Plastics	—	—	—	—
Synthetic fibers	—	—	—	—

[a] Spreading effects insufficient to justify designation as a leading sector.
[b] Not judged, by itself, a leading sector.

nously neglected; and it is possible that the profligate effort is creating considerable social tension marked by an accentuation rather than narrowing of income-distribution differentials.

43

India

There is a legitimate sense in which the industrialization of the West can be said to have been triggered by the import substitution policies of Britain in the face of Indian superiority in the manufacture of cotton textiles. It was the restriction on Indian cotton imports starting in 1700 which set up the incentive to match with machines the skill Indian hands had developed in a tradition reaching back over two thousand years. Coarser fustians, a mixture of linen and cotton, did not satisfy the European consumer once she had come to know Indian cottons. The search for a pure cotton cloth capable of manufacture in Europe went on. British inventors and innovators broke through with the response which set modern industry into rapid motion in the 1780's.

The India which generated this challenge was a vast traditional society, poorly integrated both politically and economically. The unity achieved at the peak of Mogul rule gave way progressively with the coming to power of Aurangzeb in 1658. Internal conflict was compounded in the eighteenth century by Persian and Afghan invasions. When the Mogul emperor regained his throne in 1764, internal unity was nominal, and the British had triumphed over the French in the initially mercantile struggle which had been going on among the European states over the previous century and a half in counterpoint to India's internal and other external difficulties. Some sixty further years of instability and war followed until the East India Company consolidated its rule and India experienced, except for the mutiny of 1857–1859, a century and a quarter of unity and relative tranquillity under an imperial regime.

Chart V-50 summarizes something of India's economic experience from 1860 to the early 1970's. In broad historical terms it tells us three things:

—There may have been a mild net upward drift in real per capita income: a fairly rapid rise in the 1870's and 1880's; a setback to the turn of the century; progress again to 1929; some net decline to 1952, under the impact of the depression, with postwar difficulties canceling out the mild recovery during the Second World War; and then the beginnings of somewhat higher rates of advance with the launching of the First Indian Five Year Plan in the 1950's. India's investment rate moved into the range associated with sustained growth only in the 1950's. Table V-62 presents calculations showing these phases of relative advance and retardation.

The annual average rate of increase in per capita income over the ninety-year span from 1860 to 1950 was low: 0.51 percent. Indian average per capita income begins and ends within the lowest range we know (say $40–60 per capita, U.S., 1962).

—Along the way India acquired a large railway net, a large factory-based cotton textile (and jute) industry, a modest iron and steel industry. Industrial production accelerated and diversified after 1952.

—As in the case of China, we face the problem of explaining why a century of piecemeal modernization occurred before take-off began.

TABLE V-62. *Average per Capita National Income of India at 1948–1949 Prices for Overlapping Nine-Year Periods, 1860–1955*

Period (1)	Centering (2)	Per Capita Income in 1948–1949 Rs. (3)	Average Annual Rate of Growth (%) (4)
1857–1863 (7 years)	1860	169	
1861–1869	1865	169	
1866–1874	1870	172	
1871–1879	1875	177	0.55
1876–1884	1880	197	
1881–1889	1885	216	
1886–1894	1890	204	
1891–1899	1895	201	−0.55
1896–1904	1900	199	
1901–1909	1905	203	
1906–1914	1910	220	
1911–1919	1915	241	1.09
1916–1924	1920	253	
1921–1929	1925	261	
1926–1934	1930	260	
1931–1939	1935	260	
1936–1944	1940	265	−0.12
1941–1949	1945	225	
1946–1954	1950	253	
1952–1958 (7 years)	1955	275	1.68

Source: M. Mukherjee, *National Income of India: Trends and Structure* (Calcutta: Statistical Publishing Society, 1969), p. 61. It should be noted that, on the basis of estimates that farm output per head may have fallen in the first half of the twentieth century, Angus Maddison tentatively concludes that there was probably no net increase in per capita real income in the years 1900–1946 (*Class Structure and Economic Growth: India and Pakistan since the Moghuls* [New York: W. W. Norton, 1971], pp. 67 and 166–181).

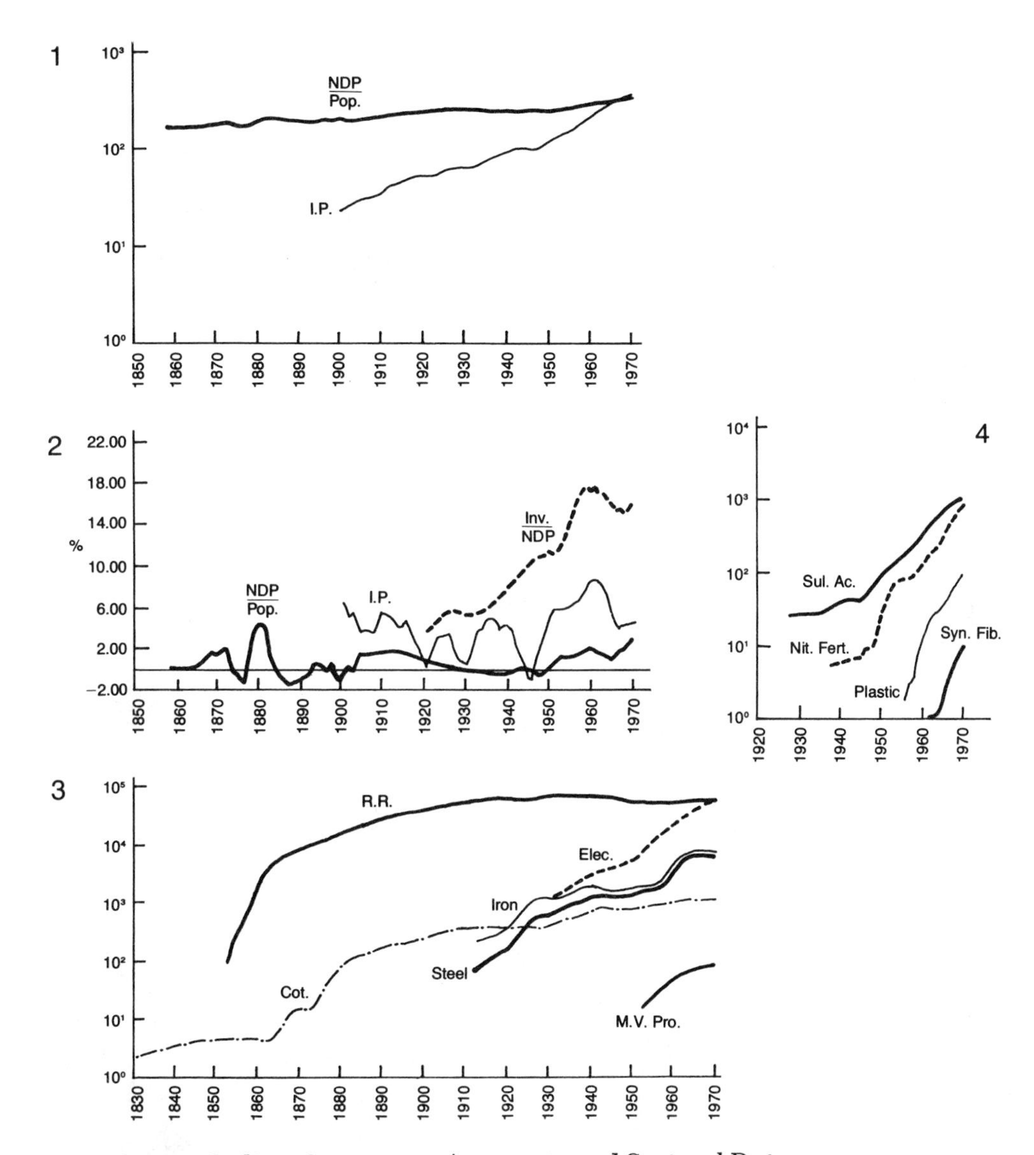

CHART V-50. *India, 1830–1972: Aggregate and Sectoral Data (Smoothed)*

1. NDP per capita ($\frac{\text{NDP}}{\text{Pop.}}$); industrial production index (I.P.).

2. Gross investment as % of NDP ($\frac{\text{Inv.}}{\text{NDP}}$); rate of change, NDP per capita ($\frac{\text{NDP}}{\text{Pop.}}$); rate of change, industrial production (I.P.).

3. Six major sectors: railroads (kilometers) (R.R.); raw cotton consumption (Cot.); production of iron (Iron); steel (Steel); electricity (Elec.); and motor vehicles (M.V. Pro.).

4. Production of four major chemicals: sulphuric acid (Sul. Ac.); nitrogen fertilizer (Nit. Fert.); plastics and resins (Plastic); and synthetic fibers (Syn. Fib.).

Sources: See Appendix D.

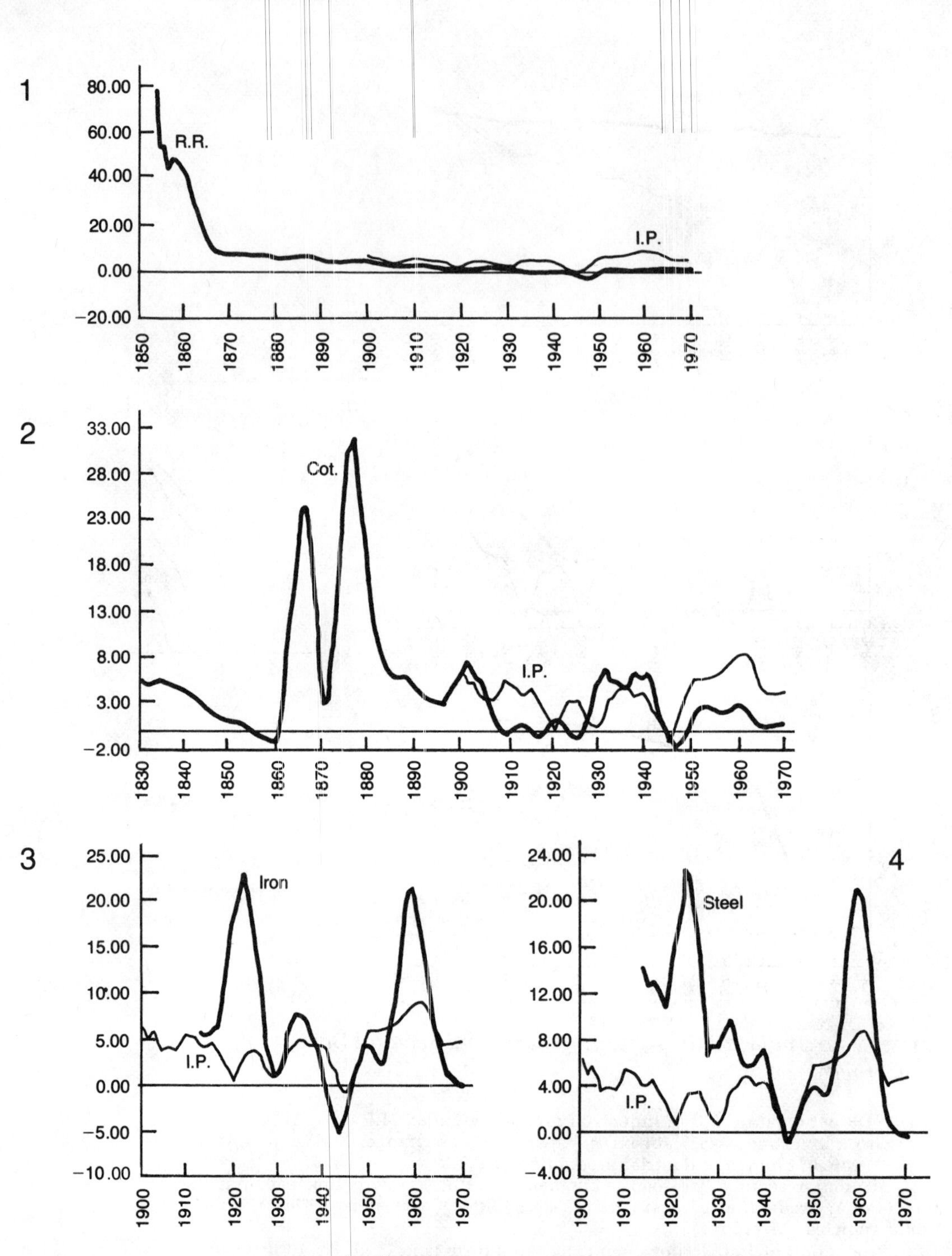

CHART V-51. *India, 1830–1972: Relative Growth Rates—Major Sectors and Industrial Production (Smoothed)*

1. Railroads (kilometers) (R.R.).
2. Raw cotton consumption (Cot.).
3. Iron production (Iron).
4. Steel production (Steel).

Sources: See Appendix D.

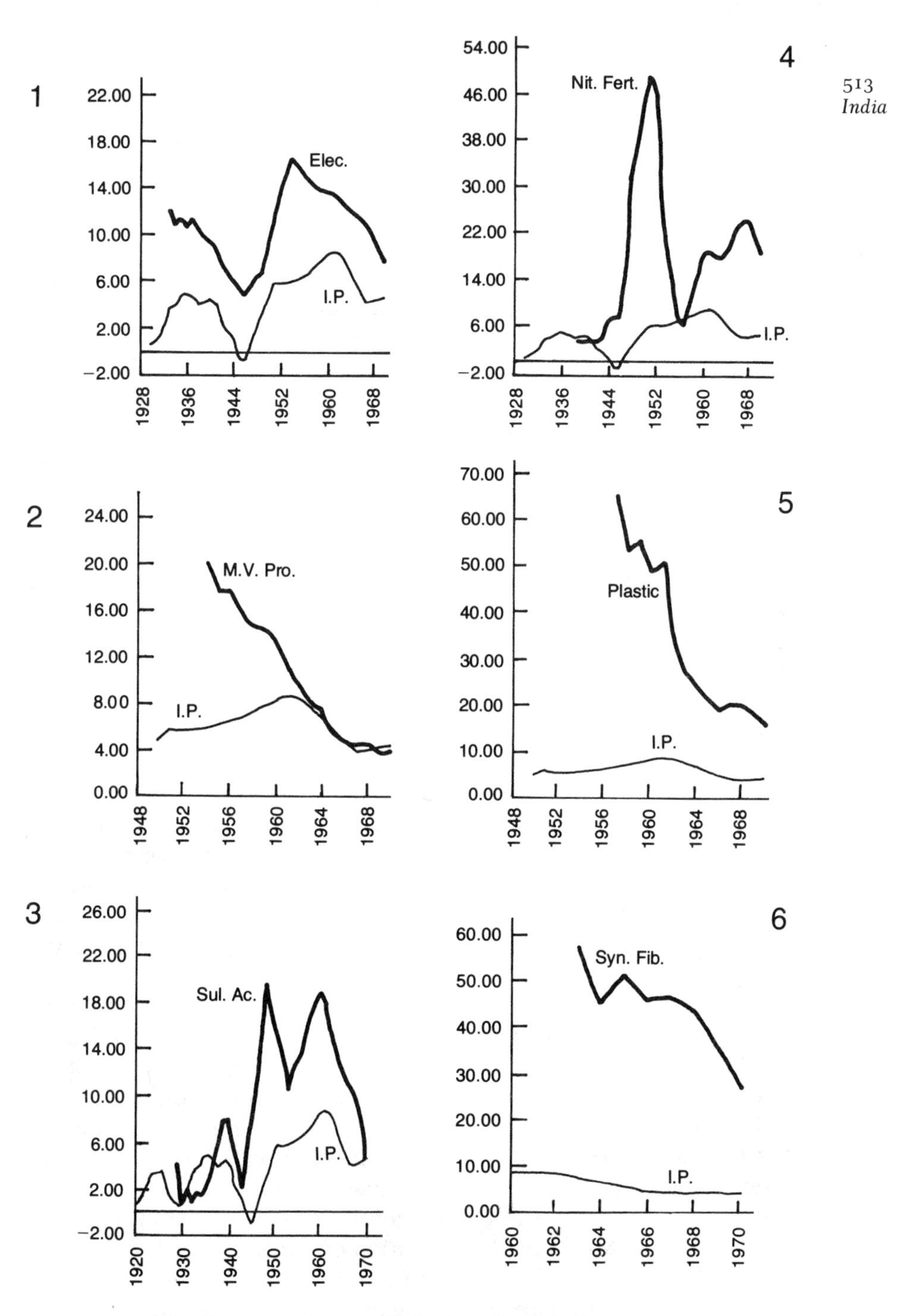

CHART V-52. *India, 1920–1972: Relative Growth Rates—Major Sectors and Industrial Production (Smoothed)*

1. Electricity (Elec.).
2. Motor vehicles (M.V. Pro.).
3. Sulphuric acid (Sul. Ac.).
4. Nitrogen fertilizer (Nit. Fert.).
5. Plastics and resins (Plastic).
6. Synthetic fibers (Syn. Fib.).

Sources: See Appendix D.

The latter issue has, of course, been the subject of protracted and even impassioned controversy, woven as it is into the question of whether British rule accelerated or postponed the modernization of Indian society.[112] It also involves, as in the case of China, technical questions of some interest. For example, why were the industrial spreading effects of the laying of the Indian rail network so limited? What was the net impact on the Indian economy of the availability to Indian handloom weavers of cheap manufactured British cotton yarn? Why did generally improving terms of trade not lead to more rapid economic growth?[113]

With respect to the delay in the Indian take-off, I would hazard two observations. First, whatever British rule provided in the way of internal unity, relative peace, competent administration, external markets, and access to western technology, it never set sustained Indian economic growth as a purposeful goal. It did not perform for India the task undertaken and successfully executed by, say, the Meiji administrators in Japan after 1868 or Sergei Witte, his predecessors and successors, in pre-1914 Russia. Some things which occurred under British rule undoubtedly contributed to the piecemeal modernization of India, e.g., the building of the railway net, the generation of coal mining to fill its needs, as well as toleration of a modern cotton textile industry from the 1850's forward. Others, notably British financial policy, may have slowed things up.[114] But it is palpable that the modernization of Indian industry and agriculture, except for the restoration and expansion of irrigation works, was not a purposeful objective of British rule. Things might have gone even slower without British rule; but the fact is that Britain did assume the responsibility for ruling India. Second, the nature of Indian society—the values of its elites, its social structure and land tenure system—certainly contributed to the delay in the Indian take-off. British rule was sufficiently flexible to permit enterprising Indians, usually from lesser castes, to make of Gujarat something of an Indian São Paulo and to set in motion an iron and steel industry. But the scale of the problem of modernizing the Indian economy was such that Indian leaders would have had to address themselves to the task in a unified and concentrated way to move India into take-off while under British rule. That never happened.

It has been argued that British political policy within India, notably after the Mutiny (e.g., the elevation of the native princes), made it difficult or impossible to focus Indian leaders around the goal of modernization.[115] Perhaps more important, the fact of alien rule led the literate Indian middle class to concentrate a great deal of its creative energy, starting in the last quarter of the nineteenth century, on politics and what became the struggle for independence. Significant elements in economic modernization went forward; but, as in China during the same period, the leadership of a succession of generations addressed its talents to problems of politics and power rather than economics and welfare. Included in the latter were the problems arising from India's own heritage that had to be overcome before the rapid modernization of the economy could take place. Without dogmatism, I suspect the greatest delaying consequence of British rule arose from its becoming the primary target for the energies of literate and competent Indians. Creation of the preconditions for take-off from a base in a traditional society requires great energy and purposefulness in both public policy and among the inevitably thin ranks of well-trained private leaders. British policy and Indian reaction to it combined to make that stage peculiarly protracted.

Nevertheless, as Chart V-50, parts 3 and 4, demonstrates, some of the Indian modern sectors were set in motion after 1850. Between the end of the Napoleonic Wars and 1850, a new pattern of Indian trade had emerged, set against the background of a rapid increase in both value and volume.[116] Table V-63 shows the relative rise of raw cotton, opium, and sugar as against indigo, cotton piece goods, and raw silk. Such data are generally taken to symbolize the transformation of India "from a manufacturing country into a country exporting raw produce."[117] But by the 1850's modern manufactures and railway building had begun in India. The factory textile industry is conventionally dated from 1854, when C. N. Davar's mill began production in Bombay.[118] The rapid subsequent expansion and marked deceleration from the 1890's can be observed in Table V-64.

The opening of the Suez Canal was a benchmark in Indian economic history, reducing the distance from London by almost four thousand miles. The great surge in cotton spinning evidently came in the 1870's and 1880's, in weaving during the 1880's and 1890's. Somewhat more than half the industry was located in Bombay in the early decades of growth. Meanwhile, Indian raw cotton production, which had expanded at an annual average rate of 1 percent from 1791 to 1840, increased over the next half century at about three times that rate, with 70 percent going to the local market around 1890.

As of 1890, the Indian cotton industry was the sixth largest in the world, outranked only by those of Britain, the United States, France, Germany, and Russia. But the subsequent rise of the Japanese and Chinese industries restricted its export possibilities. A decade of Job-

TABLE V-63. *The Commodity Composition of India's Exports, 1814–1815, 1857–1858 (Percentage Share in Total Value)*

	Indigo	Cotton Piece Goods	Raw Silk	Raw Cotton	Opium	Sugar
1814–1815	20.0	14.3	13.3	8.0	—	3.0
1857–1858	6.1	2.9	2.9	15.6	32.7	4.3

Source: K. N. Chaudhuri (ed.), *The Economic Development of India under the East India Company, 1814–58*, p. 26.

Note: Sugar exports rose to 7 percent in 1839–1840, 10 percent in 1850–1851; raw cotton exports had reached a level of 20–21 percent in the 1830's.

TABLE V-64. *The Growth of the Indian Cotton Textile Industry, 1854–1953*

	Mills[a]	Spindles	Looms	Workers[b]	Average Annual Rate of Growth (%)	Workers in Bombay
1854	1	30,000	—	500	—	—
1869	17	393,000	4,600	10,000	22.1	7,857
1880	58	1,471,000	13,000	40,000	13.4	29,417
1889	108	2,667,000	22,000	92,000	9.7	52,490
1901	190	4,933,000	41,000	156,000	4.9	82,162
1913	259	6,597,000	94,000	251,000	4.0	110,033
1923	292	7,732,000	143,000	344,000	3.2	148,771
1933	344	9,580,000	189,000	435,000[c]	2.4	129,213
1943	398	10,200,000	198,000	625,000	3.7	210,735
1953	407	11,876,000	199,000	732,000[d]	1.6	—

[a] Mills in French possessions excluded.
[b] Estimated numbers up to and including 1869.
[c] Adjusted for employment on second shift.
[d] Adjusted for employment on second and third shifts.
Sources: Except Bombay workers, all data from S. D. Mehta, *The Cotton Mills of India, 1854 to 1954* (Bombay: Textile Association [India], 1954), p. 233. Bombay workers (average daily employment) from Morris David Morris, *The Emergence of An Industrial Labor Force in India: A Study of the Bombay Cotton Mills, 1854–1947*, pp. 213–214.

like vicissitudes then occurred;[119] but the underlying fact was that India could have continued its prior rate of expansion only if it had been able successfully to supplant its major competitors in international markets. And this proved impossible. Except for the opportunities offered by the two world wars, the Indian cotton industry thus followed the typical path of a decelerating leading sector whose limits are set by the effective size of the domestic market. As in many other cases, the industry was not sufficiently large to lift the nation into self-sustained growth; and its spreading effects were limited by reliance until recent times on imported equipment. Nevertheless, the repair and maintenance of textile equipment was an important basis for India's later capacity to move forward into the manufacture of engineering products.

The exact impact of large British cotton imports and then the emergence of an indigenous modern textile industry on the handloom weaver remains (as in China) a subject of controversy.[120] There is agreement that the handloom weavers survived and that there may have been an increase in their absolute numbers from 1800 to, say, 1950. There is also agreement that (as in China) they shifted substantially to the use of cheaper manufactured yarn. What is at issue is mainly whether this survival was achieved only at the cost of a reduced per capita income or whether they shared the slow increase in the nation's per capita income. On this point the data appear inconclusive, requiring more regional studies.

The effects of the railroadization of India were also real, but in-

TABLE V-65. *Railroad Statistics: India, 1855–1920*

	Route Mileage	Average Annual Rate of Change (%)	Net Ton-Miles Carried	Average Annual Rate of Change (%)
1855	169	—	—	—
1860	838	38	—	—
1865	3,363	32	—	—
1870	4,771	7	—	—
1875	6,541	6	—	—
1880	8,995	2	—	—
1882	9,982	5	2,450,100,000	—
1885	11,950	6	3,299,100,000	10
1890	15,845	6	3,440,900,000	1
1895	18,713	3	4,861,000,000	7
1900	23,628	5	6,491,000,000	6
1905	26,955	3	8,815,800,000	6
1910	30,572	3	11,772,000,000	6
1912	31,955	2	15,283,700,000	14
1914–1915	33,756	4	14,833,500,000	−1
1919–1920	35,199	1	19,855,400,000	6

Source: Michelle Burge McAlpin, "Railroads, Prices, and Peasant Rationality: India, 1860–1900," *Journal of Economic History*, vol. 34, no. 3 (September 1974), p. 682. From an unpublished paper by Morris David Morris, later published as "Selected Railway Statistics for the Indian Subcontinent (India, Pakistan and Bangladesh), 1853–1946–47," *Artha vijnana*, vol. 17, no. 3 (September 1975).

sufficient to move the country into take-off. The pace of railroadization is set out in Table V-65 and can be seen in Chart V-51, part 1. In absolute terms, India's railway net, like its cotton industry, was large. By 1890 only Britain, the United States, France, Germany, Russia, and Austria had laid down more mileage. Moreover, as a comparison of the relative growth rates in mileage and traffic carried indicate, it was used with increased intensity over the period 1882–1920. It undoubtedly contributed to the expansion of grain and cotton production and exports over these years.[121] It stimulated coal mining, an industry whose existence, in turn, stimulated the search for iron ore and the emergence in the pre-1914 years of an iron and steel industry. It reduced, as it was partially designed to do, the human cost of famine in hitherto isolated regions. And it accelerated urbanization. But India was a huge subcontinent. Despite its large railway net, its economy continued to suffer from exceedingly poor communications. And the railroads did not promptly induce or accelerate the emergence of an Indian iron, steel, and engineering industry.[122]

But, as Charts V-50, parts 3 and 4, and V-51, parts 3 and 4, show, an Indian iron and steel industry did develop before independence. By 1900 some iron was being produced by modern methods, using coal rather than charcoal. The Tata family established a modern integrated mill at Jamshedpur from which the first iron emerged in 1911, steel in 1913. The industry expanded rapidly during the First World War but faced difficult times after the collapse of prices in 1921. Its major customer was initially the railroads, although there was slow movement toward diversification during the interwar years, including the manufacture of locomotives and tin plate.[123]

There was diversification in other directions as well before 1952; e.g., sulphuric acid production was begun (Chart V-50, part 4). On the eve of the First Indian Five Year Plan the nation had accumu-

TABLE V-66. *Indicators of Comparative Levels of Development in Mainland China and India*

	Units
Gross national product	$ Billions (U.S., 1952)
GNP per head	U.S. $, 1952
Population	Millions
Crude birth rate	Per thousand
Crude death rate	Per thousand
Proportion in agriculture and fishing	Per thousand
Agriculture	
Number of persons dependent on agriculture per acre of cultivated land	Persons per acre
Paddy rice yield	Metric quintals per hecta
Wheat yield	Metric quintals per hecta
Industry	
Coal	Total in million metric ton
	Kilograms per capita
Pig iron	Total in million metric ton
	Kilograms per capita
Crude steel	Total in million metric ton
	Kilograms per capita
Finished steel	Total in million metric ton
	Kilograms per capita
Generating capacity of electric power	Total in thousand kilowat
	Kilowatts per capita
Cotton spindleage in industry	Total in thousands
	Units per capita
Cement	Total in million metric ton
	Kilograms per capita

Source: Compiled by Alexander Eckstein, in W. W. Rostow et al., *The Prospects Communist China* (New York: John Wiley and Technology Press of M. I. T., 1954), 258–259, where detailed sources are indicated.

lated an industrial base of considerable absolute size—in fact, just about the size of that of China, as Table V-66 reveals; but industrial progress was not at a pace capable of regularly raising real income per capita; while the agricultural sector was, essentially, still traditional, with lower productivity per hectare, due mainly to China's greater use of irrigation and double cropping.

From this base the Indian economy has moved erratically forward in sustained economic growth at higher average rates of industrial expansion than in the past, and a higher investment rate (Chart

dia nount	Year	China Amount	Year
22.00	1950	$ 30.00	1952
60.00	1950	60.00	1952
358.00	1950	582.00	1953
38.00	1949	40.00	1930–1935
24.00	1949	34.00	1930–1935
68.00	1931	80.00	1952
0.60	1931	1.90	1953
13.30	1934–1938	25.30	1931–1937
6.80	1937–1939	10.80	1931–1937
34.90	1951	53.00	1952
97.00	1951	91.00	1952
1.90	1951	1.60	1952
5.00	1951	2.75	1952
1.50	1951	1.20	1952
4.00	1951	2.00	1952
		0.70	1952
		1.20	1952
2,409.00	1951	2,850.00	1952
0.01	1951	0.005	1952
0,144.00	1952	5,000.00	1952
0.03	1952	0.01	1952
3.20	1951	2.30	1952
9.00	1951	4.00	1952

V-50, part 2). As Table V-67 shows, there have been three periods of retardation or setback in product per capita since 1960: 1961–1963, 1965–1967, and 1972–1975.

Movements of national product have been extremely sensitive to harvest fluctuations, as one would expect in a nation where agriculture contributes almost half of total product. But the slowdown of 1972–1974 was also caused in part by bottlenecks in electric power and raw-materials supply to industry. In 1973–1974, Indian industry was operating at only 70 percent of capacity. With a good harvest and a purposeful effort to deal with shortages, the Indian economic situation markedly improved in 1975–1976. Real net national product rose by 8.8 percent. Industrial production was running, in 1976, 14 percent above its 1974–1975 level. Net domestic capital formation was 16.2 percent in 1975–1976, as opposed to 14.7 percent a year earlier. Both foreign exchange and grain reserves were high. In 1977, momentum slowed, responding in part to poor monsoons and reduced harvests.

Despite the modest increase in real national income per capita since independence, the structure of the Indian economy has been significantly transformed. The heavy-industry, chemical, and engineering sectors expanded and diversified in the 1950's and 1960's. The average annual rate of increase of industrial production between 1960 and 1973 was 6 percent; but production of stationary diesel engines and power-driven pumps moved at an average rate of 9 percent; radio receivers, 15 percent; sulphuric acid, 10 percent; nitrogen fertilizers, 20 percent; automobile tires, 9 percent; electricity generation, 11 percent. These dynamic sectors contrast, for example, with a 1.2 percent increase in cotton cloth production. Despite its periodic setbacks, then, India was moving forward in the familiar pattern of the drive to technological maturity. And these are the directions in which India plans to go in its Fifth Five Year Plan (1974–1979). The average annual projected increase in mining and manufacture is 8 percent; but the figure for fertilizers is 14 per-

TABLE V-67. *Per Capita Net National Product: India, 1960–1961 to 1975–1976 (1960–1961 = 100)*

1960–1961	100.0	1968–1969	108.5
1961–1962	101.2	1969–1970	112.2
1962–1963	100.8	1970–1971	115.2
1963–1964	104.1	1971–1972	114.0
1964–1965	109.6	1972–1973	110.4
1965–1966	101.7	1973–1974	111.3
1966–1967	100.8	1974–1975	109.4
1967–1968	107.4	1975–1976	116.7

Source: 1960–1974, Government of India, *Economic Survey, 1974–1975*, p. 59; 1974–1976, Supplement to *Reserve Bank of India Bulletin*, December 1976.

cent; iron and steel, 12 percent; machine tools, 16 percent; electronics, 12 percent; electricity, 11 percent.[124]

The Indian government now recognizes that a higher rate of increase in agricultural output and an expanded program of family planning are essential to the success of the next phase of Indian development. A 4.67 percent annual rate of increase in agricultural output is projected in the current Five Year Plan, as opposed to the 3.0 percent achieved (in grain) between 1960–1962 and 1969–1971. The latter figure was accompanied by a 3.4 percent annual increase in grain consumption. The achievement of the new target will depend critically on the planned expansion in fertilizer production.

As noted in Chapter 3, the Indian crude birth rate per thousand is officially estimated to be about 35, having dropped four points during the Fourth Five Year Plan. The target for the Fifth Plan is 30 for 1978–1979, with a further reduction to 25 by 1983–1984.

Looking back over the sweep of India's modern economic history the timing of the coming in of the major technologies is suggested in Table V-68, based on Charts V-51 and V-52.

The Indian stages of economic growth may be dated as follows.

Take-off: 1952–1963.

Drive to Technological Maturity: 1963–.

TABLE V-68. *Approximate Timing of Leading Sectors: India, 1850–1972*

Sector	Maximum Rate of Expansion	Estimated Time Sector Became Leading Sector	Estimated Time Sector Ceased to Lead	Comments
Cotton consumption	1870's	[a]	1945–1950	—
Railroads	1850's	[b]	1900–1910	Lack of industrial production index before 1900 precludes earlier comparison of growth rates.
Iron	1920's	1950's	1965–1970	Relative decline of iron and steel in late 1960's may prove temporary.
Steel	1920's	1950's	1965–1970	—
Electricity	1950's	1950's	—	—
Motor vehicles	1950's	1950's	—	—
Sulphuric acid	1950's	[a]	—	—
Nitrogen	Early 1950's	[a]	—	—
Plastics	1955–1960	[a]	—	—
Synthetic fibers	1960's	[a]	—	—

[a] Not judged, by itself, a leading sector.

[b] Spreading effects not sufficient to justify designation as a leading sector.

44

China

Like India under colonialism, China had acquired a not insignificant modern industrial establishment in the turbulent century that began with the opium wars of the early 1840's. Aside from an extensive railroad net, China contained in the 1940's a substantial modern cotton textile industry, considerable coal, cement, flour, and sugar production, and the foundations, at least, for an iron, steel, and engineering industry (see Table V-69).

Its modern sectors were centered in the coastal cities, largely devoted to the management of foreign trade as well as the manufacture of light industrial products; and in Manchuria, where capital goods production had expanded after 1931 under Japanese occupation.[125] The two structures had evolved in, roughly, the following sequence:

—1840–1895: trade expansion centered in the coastal cities, largely under foreign pressure and auspices, with little industrialization except the building of government arsenals and armament works in the 1860's and 1870's.

—1860–1931: rapid expansion of population and agricultural production in Manchuria, accelerated in the first decade of the twentieth century by railroadization and the opening of new ports.

—1895–1914: first phase of import-substitution consumers' goods industries, including modern textiles, launched by rights granted in treaty ports to foreigners under the Treaty of Shimonoseki, as well as foreign development of railroads and mines.

—1914–1931: rapid expansion of light industry in coastal cities in the face of import shortages during the First World War, continued thereafter under protectionist policies, with a shift from Western to Japanese and Chinese entrepreneurship and ownership.

—1931–1945: rapid development of Manchurian heavy-industry capacity by the Japanese, on the basis of considerable industrial expansion in the previous decade.

At no time between the 1840's and 1949 were the Chinese free to concentrate wholeheartedly on the tasks of economic and social modernization. As with many late-comers to modern economic

TABLE V-69. *Selected Industrial Production Indicators: China, 1933–1952*

Product	Unit of Measurement	1933	1949	1952	Precommunist Peak Output	Year
Electric power	Billion kWh	2.07	4.31	7.26	5.95	1943
Coal	Million MT	28.38	32.43	66.49	64.86	1942
Crude oil	Thousand MT	89.00	—	871.00	842.00	1942
Pig iron	Thousand MT	609.00	252.00	1,929.00	1,889.00	1943
Steel	Thousand MT	Negl.	158.00	1,349.00	923.00	1943
Cement	Thousand MT	784.00	660.00	2,860.00	2,300.00	1942
Cotton yarn	Million bales	2.45	1.80	3.62	2.45	1933
Machine-made paper	Thousand MT	45.00	108.00	372.00	165.00	1943

Source: Alexander Eckstein, *China's Economic Development* (Ann Arbor: University of Michigan Press, 1975), p. 171, where sources are indicated. It will be noted that Eckstein revised upward his earlier calculations for Chinese 1952 production of coal, iron, steel, and cement which appear in Table V-66, above.

growth, the political life of the nation was dominated by a counterpoint between various forms of external intrusion and inner debate and struggle over the appropriate form of political and social organization for a modern China.

The early phase of China's reaction to external intrusion interwove with the period of domestic unrest, centered in the Taiping Rebellion. Western thought and religion contributed obliquely to the banners and concepts of that rebellion; Western power, joined with the Manchu dynasty and elements of the Chinese gentry, helped suppress it. The subsequent negotiation with the British might, conceivably, have established a livable equilibrium within which China could have found its way slowly forward to modernization in dignity. This effort failed in part because the British merchants in China did not accept the Alcock Convention (1869). The more intrusive agreement of 1858 continued to prevail. The 1858 agreement and the so-called Tientsin Massacre of 1870 set the stage for a period of progressive internal Chinese disintegration and increasingly hardhanded intrusions. In 1895 Japan, in the midst of take-off, defeated the Chinese decisively; and the Boxer Rebellion occurred in 1900.

The Chinese, under these pressures, cast about in many directions for a formula to restore unity, self-respect, and a path to modernization. After 1868 they looked to the Japanese model among others. There were in 1898 the hundred days of reform, during which a monumental series of edicts was issued; but there was no effective means, as there had been thirty years earlier in Japan, to implement those reforms; no samurai to serve as a purposeful modernizing group; no effective central government.

Power fell back, as often when dynasties were failing, into the hands of regional warlords. The effort of Sun Yat-sen's Revived China Society, begun in 1894, led to the overthrow of the Manchu dynasty in 1911 and the formation of the National People's Party in 1912. Its principles were nationalism (that is, the reassertion of China's dignity); democracy; and the people's livelihood. But Sun

Yat-sen could not organize effective government in the face of the warlords; and in the decade after 1911 such reform and innovation as took place occurred piecemeal and regionally. The First World War initially gave China a chance to breathe, since the Western states were preoccupied elsewhere; and there was some significant industrial development. The Japanese, however, were able to press their expansion into China, in an effort to supplant German extraterritorial status, evoking strong, widespread nationalist reactions, symbolized by the 1917 demonstrations and the boycott of Japanese imports.

With the Russian Revolution of 1917 the Chinese reformers turned to a new model. They were impressed not by communism as a whole but by the success of the Leninist party structure in bringing effective unity to Russia after the First World War. In effect, they decided that national dignity could not be achieved and economic progress could not take place until China was unified.

The two major contenders for power, the Kuomintang and the Chinese Communist Party, were both built on the Leninist party model. They worked in uneasy collaboration in the early 1920's; and then Chiang Kai-shek, from a southern base, moved out to unify China under his leadership in 1927. With victory in the KMT grasp, the left and right wings within the KMT split; and the possibility of effective consolidation of unitary rule was lost. The KMT won out temporarily over the communists; but China faced twenty years of civil war, combined, after 1931, with Japanese aggression against it. The communists were never crushed; the difficulties with the warlords persisted. During the Second World War the Chinese Nationalist government, driven back into the interior at Chunking, lost its cohesion and vitality; and, although Chiang Kai-shek came back in 1945 with great prestige, he failed in his military and political struggle with the Chinese communists, who took over in 1949.

The Chinese communists hold a special place in the sequence of revolution in modern China. We can place Sun Yat-sen as among the first generation of modern Chinese revolutionaries. Born in 1866, he had ties and memories that went back directly to the aftermath of the Taiping Rebellion. Sun's generation defined China's revolutionary problem, experimented with reform, but never solved the primary problem of establishing a foundation of national authority capable of achieving its purposes. It was a generation more concerned with ends than means.

In these terms, the men who came to power on the mainland, and also those who went in defeat to Taiwan in 1949, belonged to a second generation. They were initially technicians in the problem of power, concerned primarily with the means for controlling societies rather than with the ends a modern China should pursue. It is only since 1949 that they, and those they brought within the framework of political power, have focused sharply on the working tasks of economic and social development.

The process of economic modernization that proceeded piecemeal as China struggled to shape its political destiny was framed by its underlying demographic position. Eighteenth-century China had been, within the limits of its technology, prosperous and at peace. As noted in Chapter 3, population expanded, and it continued to expand in the first half of the nineteenth century, pressing down the average arable acreage per capita available in rural areas. The economic and political setting of China in the second half of the century, including the bloody Taiping Rebellion, yielded no net population increase; but expansion resumed and then accelerated, as elsewhere, in the twentieth century.

Population pressure and the fear of Russian penetration into a relatively empty Manchuria combined in 1860 to launch a period of accelerated Chinese settlement, a process rendered more attractive by the Sino-Russian agreement to open a treaty port at Newchwang.[126] Manchurian population expanded over the subsequent eighty years at an average annual rate of about 3 percent, half of which may have represented Chinese migration.[127] The proportion of population to arable acreage was, of course, much more favorable in Manchuria than in the rest of China. The region initially prospered on the basis of exports of soybeans, bean cake, and bean oil. Large additions to acreage were permitted by the completion of the Chinese Eastern and South Manchurian railways in 1901 and 1903. The role of Japan and Japanese capital in the area increased after the Russo-Japanese War. In 1907 the commercial possibilities of Manchuria were expanded by the opening up of three additional ports at Antung, Dairen, and Tatungkow.

As Alexander Eckstein and his colleagues pointed out, the development of Manchuria followed a pattern not unlike that of "countries of new settlement"; e.g., Canada, Australia, and Argentina. A period of rapid agricultural and export expansion, accompanied by large immigration, supported by railroadization, gave way in time to general industrial development. The shift toward industry began in the 1920's and accelerated sharply after 1936, under Japanese auspices. In effect, Manchuria experienced a regional take-off: in the early 1930's its per capita product was about 16 percent higher than that of China; in the 1940's, the gap was 74 percent. The rate of gross investment in fixed capital was 9 percent in Manchuria in 1924, over 17 percent in 1934, 23 percent in 1939. As in the case of other "countries of new settlement," capital imports (from Japan) helped bring about the elevation of the investment rate in Manchuria. The pre-1949 investment rate in China was about 5 percent. As a united China launched its First Five Year Plan in 1953, Manchuria, containing 9 percent of the nation's population, contributed about 14 percent to national product, almost a third to its manufacturing output.

The industrial development outside Manchuria took place against the background of a much harder-pressed rural sector and less ample relative endowments in coal and iron ore, and in a setting more closely interwoven with the political and bureaucratic life of regional and central governments.

By 1912 there were some 20,749 "factories" in China; but only 363 of these employed mechanical power and only 235 employed more than five hundred workers.[128] Eighty-eight percent, in fact, employed less than thirty workers. The array of modern economic ac-

TABLE V-70. *Companies Registered with the Ministry of Agriculture, Industry, and Commerce: China, 1904–1908*

Type of Business	Authorized Capital (in Taels)		
	100,000 and Below	100,001–500,000	500,001–1,000,000
Cotton spinning and weaving	9	7	2
Silk reeling	4	4	0
Dyeing	4	0	0
Railroads	0	0	0
Steamships and steam launches	6	1	1
Electricity and other utilities	4	4	0
Pottery and glass	8	2	1
Soap and candles	8	0	0
Mining and smelting[a]	7	3	0
Matches	1	1	0
Leather	0	1	0
Cement	0	0	1
Paper	0	1	0
Machinery	0	1	0
Miscellaneous manufacturing	8	0	0
Flour milling and rice husking	9	5	1
Tobacco and cigarettes	9	1	0
Oil pressing, bean-cake	4	4	0
Sundry food manufacturing	6	0	0
Modern-type banks	0	2	2
Native banks	4	2	0
Insurance	0	1	2
Pawnshops	18	0	0
Wholesale and retail commerce	25	3	0
Agriculture and fishery	10	1	0
Land reclamation and river dredging	1	3	0
Building contractors	4	2	0
Publishing, booksellers, stationers	6	0	1
Totals	155	49	11

[a]This includes as a single unit the Han-Yeh-P'ing Coal and Iron Corporation, consisting (three companies whose total authorized capital was $20,000,000 (Chinese).

Source: Albert Feuerwerker, *China's Early Industrialization*, p. 3.

tivities which had been generated toward the end of the Manchu dynasty is suggested by Table V-70. In both its content and its weighting, the list is typical of a pre–take-off modernizing society.

Why the early absorption of Western technologies failed to generate self-sustained industrial growth in China, while Japan moved briskly through its take-off and beyond, is a question much discussed among historians of modern Asia. In broad historical terms the an-

,000,001– ,000,000	2,000,001 and Over	Totals
	0	21
	0	8
	0	4
	3	4
	0	8
	0	8
	0	11
	0	8
	1[a]	12
	0	2
	0	1
	0	1
	0	1
	0	1
	0	8
	0	15
	0	10
	0	8
	0	6
	1	7
	0	6
	0	3
	0	18
	0	28
	0	11
	0	4
	0	6
	0	7
	5	227

swer lies in the failure of China to generate an equivalent to the Meiji Restoration of 1868, with its purposeful new leadership prepared to reorganize the old society so that it could move forward in a single-minded way on a modernizing path. And behind that failure lay China's size, its majestic tradition, and the capacity of the old regime and the old ways to survive for a time the buffeting which began in the 1840's. There was, thus, a transitional character to these early Chinese efforts at modernization. On the basis of a detailed study of some of the major enterprises sponsored by the government but partly financed and managed by merchants (*kuan-tu shang-pan* industries), Albert Feuerwerker attributes the relative sterility of this phase of Chinese economic modernization to five major factors which reflect the transition:

> 1. The close relationship of the *kuan-tu shang-pan* industries to the regional foci of political power which developed after the Taiping Rebellion;
> 2. The dependence of these enterprises on capital and, to a lesser degree, personnel from the merchants of China's treaty ports;
> 3. The role of officials and traditional bureaucratic methods in their management, and the corollary deficiency in rationalized business practices;
> 4. The vulnerability of this modern sector of China's economy to official exactions;
> 5. The importance of the grant of officially protected monopoly privileges.[129]

There was, in effect, a carrying over to modern industry of public-private relationships and methods that had grown up in a society where the concept of regular economic growth was unknown and where the central issue was how a relatively fixed pool of resources was to be divided. The immediate model for the *kuan-tu shang-pan* industries was the management of the production, distribution, and taxation of salt. The new industries were managed with an eye to short-run advantage, including political power and graft, rather than to the maximizing of long-run growth. This was not an industrial system capable of generating rapid expansion through the plowing back of profits or of moving promptly and effectively into the export of manufactures. But Chinese potentialities were suggested, at least, by the expansion of the cotton spinning industry in the wake of the defeat by Japan in 1895, and the sanction, in the Treaty of Shimonoseki, of foreign-owned manufacturing establishments on Chinese soil. As of 1895 there were some 174,500 modern cotton spindles in six plants operating with monopoly privileges granted by the government. By 1913 there were about 822,700, of which 41 percent were foreign-owned, reflecting an annual average rate of increase of 9 percent over these eighteen years.[130] The modern cotton industry had acquired a base by 1914 from which it could rapidly expand during the First World War, maintaining its momentum in the 1920's. The proportion of Chinese ownership in the spinning industry remained somewhat over 50 percent, with the Japanese rising from 14 percent to 44 percent among foreign owners from 1913 to 1936.

The evolution of the Chinese textile industry as a whole, which dominated the early phase of the country's modern development, was marked by a special characteristic: the survival of a sturdy and efficient handicraft weaving industry. Despite the growth in factory-manufactured cotton yarn and cloth, a large part of Chinese cloth output continued to be produced by families in rural areas, using factory-manufactured yarn.[131] Such cloth found a market not only within China but also in other parts of Asia. Down to 1927, China was a net importer of yarn for this purpose.

Tables V-71, V-72, and V-73 reflect the rise of the factory system, the role of yarn imports, and the continued vitality of the handicraft weaving industry. Estimates of the proportion of cotton cloth produced in the handicraft sector as late as the 1930's center around 70 percent.[132] The capacity of this sector to survive flowed from the fact that in rural areas, where there was a labor surplus, it paid the family to engage in this activity, supplementing earnings from agriculture, so long as the net marginal return was above zero. Put another way, a family, unlike a factory, could calculate its net profit without taking wages into account. After 1949 the communist regime shifted radically toward the use of power looms in weaving. The proportion of total cotton cloth output produced in the handicraft sector (mainly in cooperatives rather than families) had fallen to 21 percent by 1956.[133]

TABLE V-71. *Factory Production of Cotton Yarn and Cloth: China, 1890–1936*

Period	Cotton Yarn		Cotton Cloth	
	Average Output (Thousand Bales)	Increase over Preceding Period (%)	Average Output (Million Sq. Yds.)	Increase over Preceding Period (%)
1890–1894	38.7	—	23.9	—
1895–1899	188.7	38	39.1	63
1900–1904	276.6	47	40.9	4
1905–1909	340.9	23	40.9	0
1910–1914	439.0	29	63.4	55
1915–1919	698.1	59	123.1	94
1920–1924	1,293.5	85	249.0	102
1925–1929	2,263.2	75	531.8	113
1930–1934	2,725.0	20	965.5	81
1935–1936	2,786.8	2	1,294.7	34

Source: Kang Chao, "The Growth of a Modern Cotton Textile Industry and the Competition with Handicrafts," p. 172.

TABLE V-72. *Export and Import of Cotton Yarn: China, 1922–1932 (Thousand Bales)*

Year	Export	Import	Year	Export	Import
1922	13	406	1928	117	95
1923	30	254	1929	115	78
1924	49	188	1930	110	53
1925	22	216	1931	206	16
1926	64	153	1932	116	32
1927	113	98			

Source: Kang Chao, "The Growth of a Modern Cotton Textile Industry and the Competition with Handicrafts," p. 172.

TABLE V-73. *Implied Annual Growth Rates of the Handicraft Weaving Industry in Selected Localities: China, 1903–1937*

Locality	Boom Period(s)	Rate (%)	Indicator
Hopei			
Ting hsien	1903–1915	13	Sales to other areas, 1903–1915
	1910–1915	15	Sales to other areas, 1910–1915
Kao-yang	1915–1920	15	Number of ordinary looms, 1915–1926
	1926–1930	37	Number of Jacquard looms, 1915–1929
	1934–1937	24	All looms combined, 1912–1926
Shantung			
Wei hsien	1926–1933	32	Number of looms, 1926–1933
	1915–1933	31	Number of looms, 1915–1933
Nan-liu	1929–1936	20	Yarn consumption, 1929–1933
Kwangsi			
Yū-lin	1931–1933	52	Yarn consumption, 1931–1933

Source: Kang Chao, "The Growth of a Modern Cotton Textile Industry and the Competition with Handicrafts," p. 175, where detailed sources are indicated.

Chart V-53, parts 1 and 2, exhibits the aggregate data available on the evolution of the Chinese economy since 1912. The index of industrial production reflects the high rates of growth (dominated by cotton textiles) during the First World War and the lower but still high rate of expansion in the 1920's. The rate of increase declined as the weight of the Japanese attack on China extended, to become negative in the worst years of the war after 1937; but production in Manchuria continued to expand. The communist period was marked by a phase of reconstruction (1949–1952) and then the expansion down to the failure of the Great Leap Forward in 1959–1960, exacerbated by the withdrawal of Soviet aid and by bad harvests. The subsequent recovery was set back more mildly during the Cultural Revolution (1965–1969), after which a period of steady, modest rate of growth persisted.

Rates of increase in GDP per capita reflect this same sequence less dramatically.

The extrapolated investment rate in Chart V-53, part 2, consists of the figures for specific years given in Table V-74, usefully compared by Dwight H. Perkins with those for three other Asian coun-

TABLE V-74. *Capital Formation and per Capita Gross Domestic Product: China and Selected Countries, 1933–1970*

China	1933	1952	1957	1970
(1) Per capita GDP (U.S. $, 1957)	62	58	74	109
(2) GDCF/GDP (%)				
1933 prices	5	16	17	23–24
1957 prices	—	—	21	28–29
1952 prices	7	19.5	23.5	31–32
Japan	1886	1905	1930	1938
(3) Per capita GDP (U.S. $, 1960)	63	98	264	333
(4) GDCF/GNP (%)	11.1	13.9	18.8	21.7
South Korea	1960	1963	1967	1970
(5) Per capita GDP (U.S. $, 1960)	99	107	139	190
(6a) GDCF/GNP (%)	10.5	15.3	23.3	27.3
(6b) GDI—Foreign Saving/GNP (%)	2.2	6.9	11.8	15.4
Taiwan	1953	1958	1966	1969
(7) Per capita GDP (U.S. $, 1960)	84	98	152	185
(8) GDCF/GNP (%)	14.0	18.0	23.2	25.3
Average of less-developed nations	Per capita GDP ranges			
(9) Per capita GDP (U.S. $, 1958)	under 100	100–199	200–349	350–574
(10) GDCF/GNP (%)	15.2	16.4	16.9	20.9

Source: Dwight H. Perkins (ed.), *China's Modern Economy in Historical Perspective*, p. 134, where detailed sources and methods of calculation are presented. For much lower net capital formation figures see Subramanian Swamy, "Economic Growth in China and India, 1952–1970," *Economic Development and Cultural Change*, vol. 21, no. 4, part 2 (July 1973), pp. 65–68, where Indian prices are used as a basis for comparison. The capital-output ratio for China emerges as 3.3 for China, 3.2 for India from Swamy's calculations—quite conventional figures.

tries which have experienced high post-1945 rates of growth. The rise of the Chinese investment rate after 1949 is quite typical of take-off. Its calculation is sensitive to the price structure used but it falls in the higher bracket among developing countries, similar to that of Taiwan, although the latter has experienced a higher growth rate. The capital-output ratio in China, a rough measure of the productivity of investment, emerges as high; that is, high investment rates have yielded untypically low rates of increase in output. This may indicate, simply, that the gross investment rates are overestimated.

The sectoral data in Chart V-53, parts 3 and 4, reflect the early expansion of the cotton industry, the rise of the heavy industry sector in the 1930's in Manchuria under Japanese auspices, and relatively high rates of heavy-industry growth sustained since 1949 despite the severe setback after 1958 and the milder retardation during the most acute difficulties of the Cultural Revolution.

Table V-75 summarizes conclusions that can be drawn from the Chinese sectoral pattern, which can be observed in Charts V-54 and V-55.

As in the case of India, the dating of Chinese stages of economic growth is reasonably straightforward. In neither case is there serious doubt about when sustained (if erratic) economic growth set in on a national basis. The Chinese take-off occurred in the 1950's, after reconstruction had been achieved and pre-war peak levels of output reattained: 1952 is a good benchmark date. And there is no difficulty in defining the leading sectors of the take-off: they were heavy-industry sectors related quite explicitly in government pronouncements of the 1950's to the modernization of the Chinese armed forces. Moreover, it is possible to note in the 1960's a transition which would now place China among the nations passing through the drive to technological maturity. After the failure of the Great Leap Forward, the withdrawal of Soviet assistance, and the sharp setback of the early 1960's, there was a period of consolidation, after which China's industrial expansion proceeded on a more diversified basis. This was notably true of chemicals (e.g., petroleum, fertilizers) and metalworking in increasingly sophisticated products.[134] The latter may have been related to a thrust for increased self-reliance in military hardware after the definitive break with the Soviet Union. In the early 1970's, the Chinese authorities set their central objective as developing "basic industries, particularly petrochemicals, machinery and metallurgy," an objective requiring, at this early phase of the drive to technological maturity, expanded imports of sophisticated capital goods still beyond the reach of the Chinese economy.[135]

Against this background the stages of Chinese economic growth may be set out as follows.

Regional Take-off, Manchuria: 1930's.

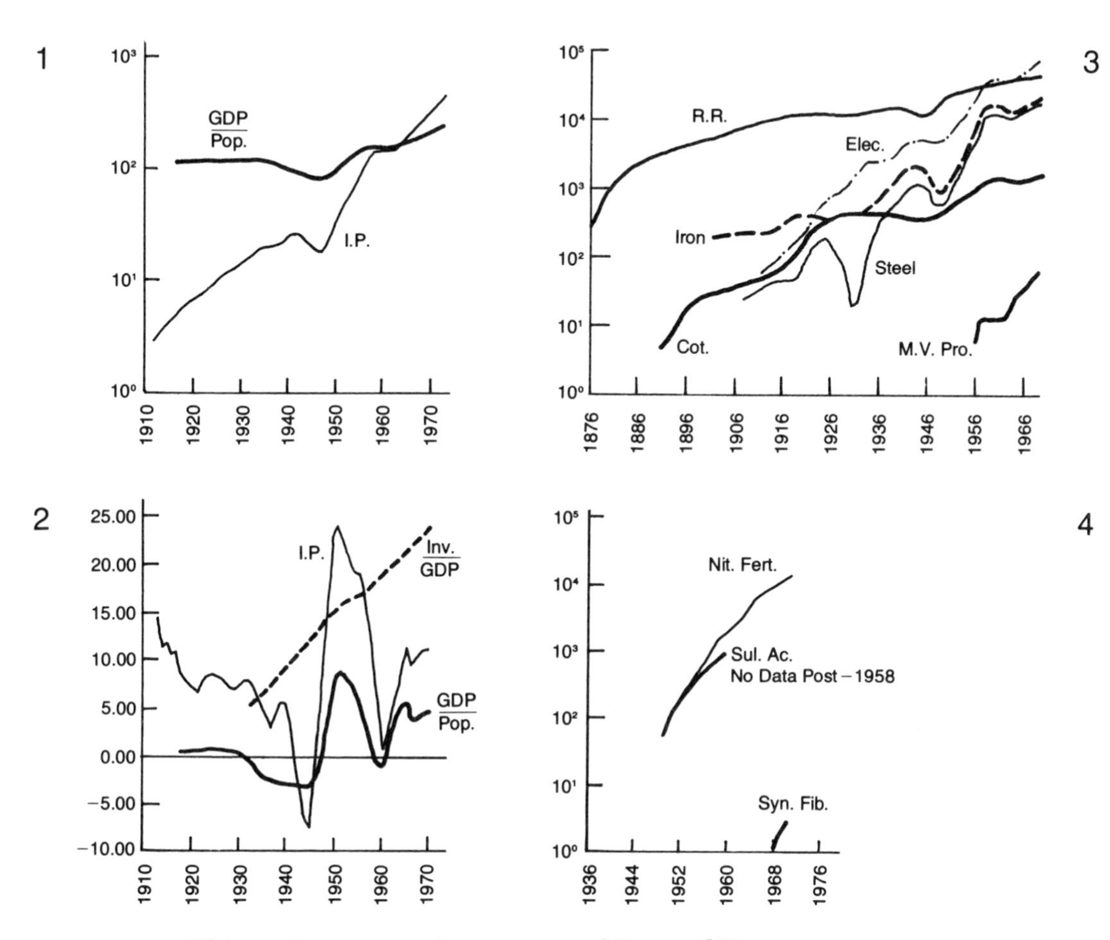

CHART V-53. *China, 1875–1972: Aggregate and Sectoral Data (Smoothed)*

1. GDP per capita ($\frac{\text{GDP}}{\text{Pop.}}$); industrial production index (I.P.).
2. Gross investment as % of GDP ($\frac{\text{Inv.}}{\text{GDP}}$); rate of change, GDP per capita ($\frac{\text{GDP}}{\text{Pop.}}$); rate of change, industrial production (I.P.).
3. Six major sectors: railroads (kilometers) (R.R.); cotton yarn production (Cot.); production of iron (Iron); steel (Steel); electricity (Elec.); and motor vehicles (M.V. Pro.).
4. Production of three major chemicals: sulphuric acid (Sul. Ac.); nitrogen fertilizer (Nit. Fert.); and synthetic fibers (Syn. Fib.).

Sources: See Appendix D.

Take-off: 1952–1967, embracing the rapid expansion down to 1958, the severe setback of the early 1960's, the milder setback during the Cultural Revolution.

Drive to Technological Maturity: 1968–.

Two features of the Chinese experience of economic modernization should be underlined. First, there was the acquisition before 1949 of a rather substantial economic transport infrastructure, light industry in the coastal cities, heavy industry in Manchuria. This

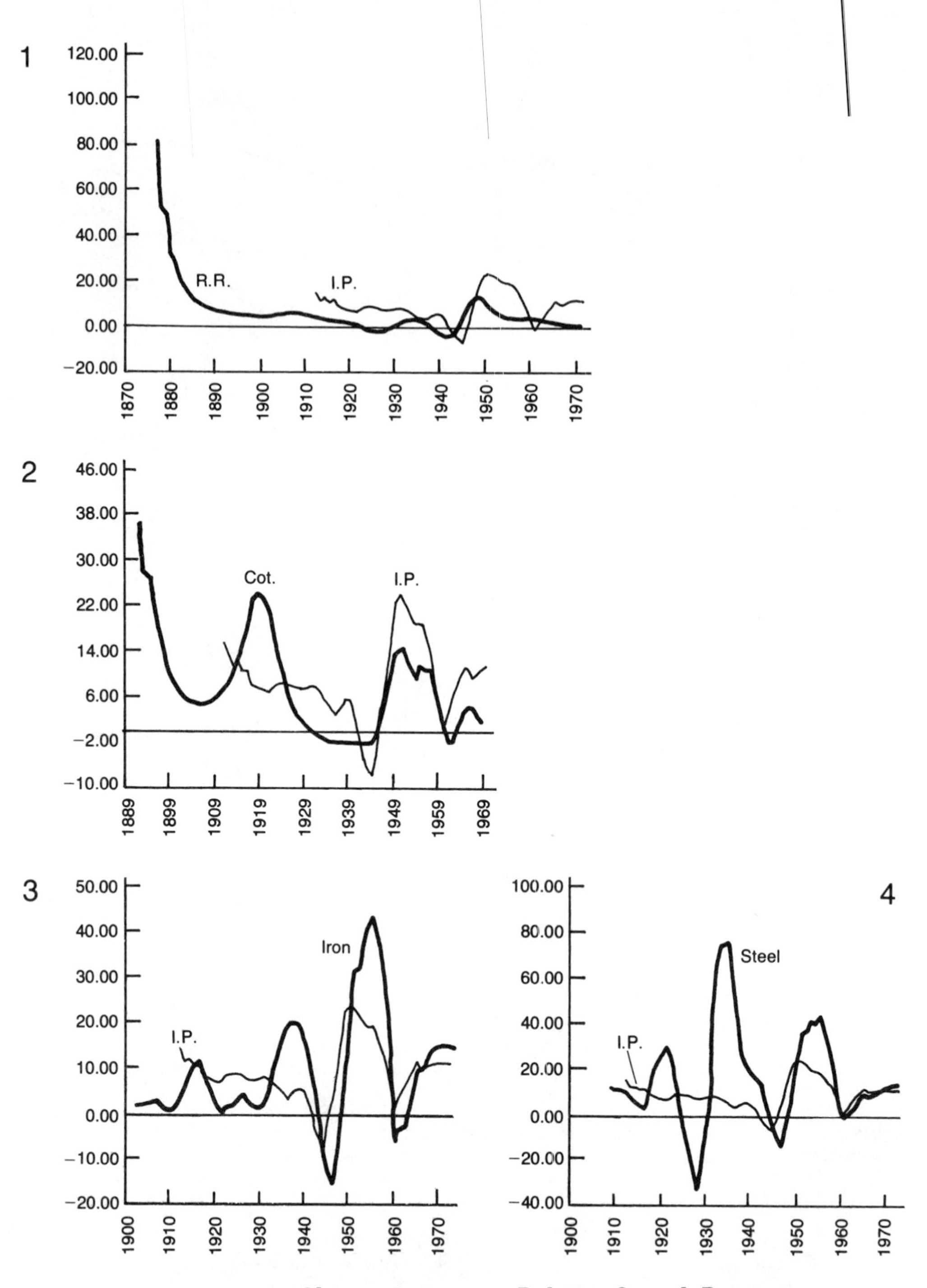

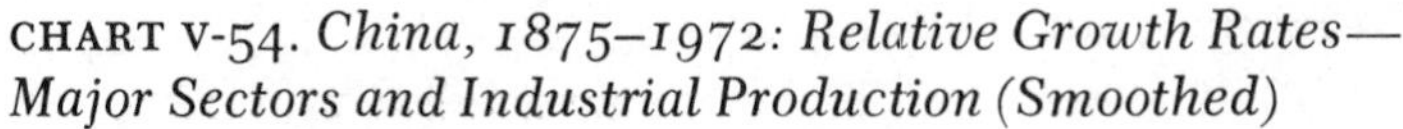

CHART V-54. *China, 1875–1972: Relative Growth Rates—Major Sectors and Industrial Production (Smoothed)*

1. Railroads (kilometers) (R.R.).
2. Cotton yarn production (Cot.).
3. Iron production (Iron).
4. Steel production (Steel).

Sources: See Appendix D.

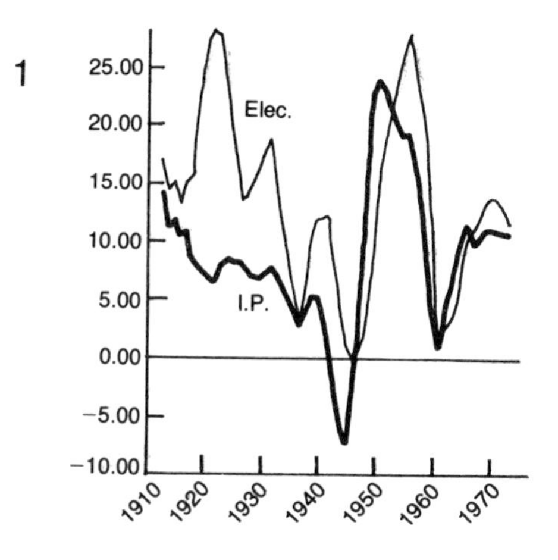

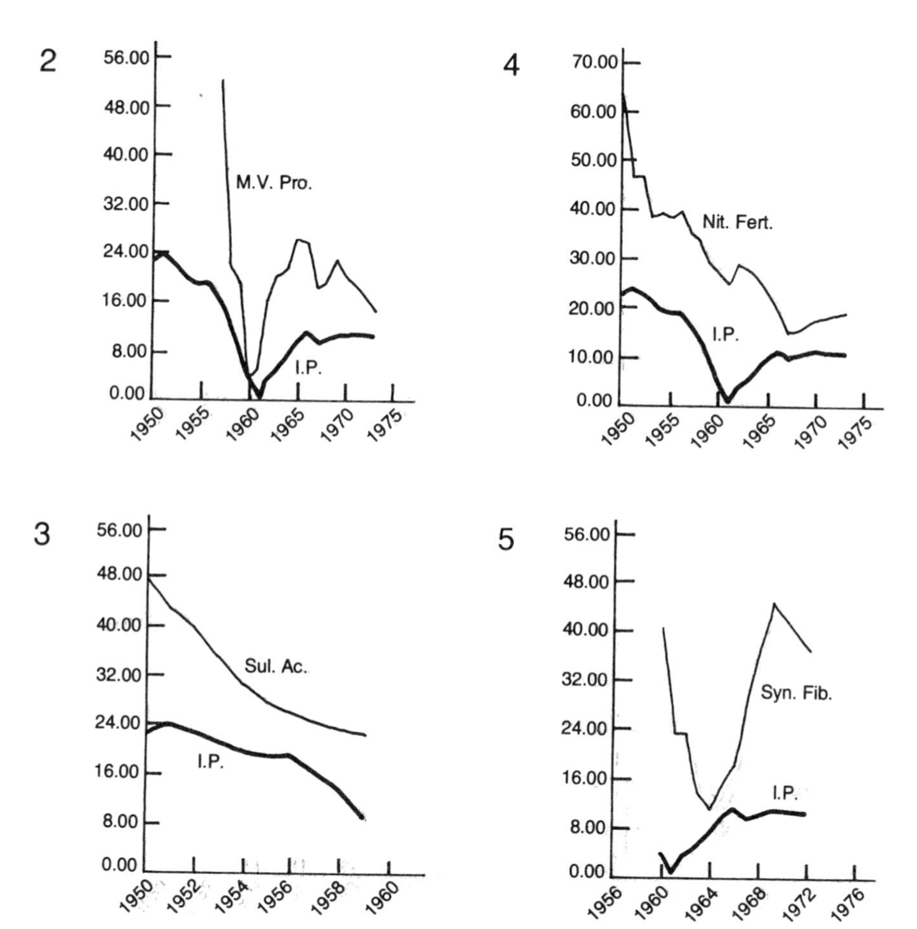

CHART V-55. *China, 1915–1972: Relative Growth Rates—Major Sectors and Industrial Production (Smoothed)*

1. Electricity (Elec.).
2. Motor vehicles (M.V. Pro.).
3. Sulphuric acid (Sul. Ac.).
4. Nitrogen fertilizer (Nit. Fert.).
5. Synthetic fibers (Syn. Fib.).

Sources: See Appendix D.

TABLE V-75. *Approximate Timing of Leading Sectors: China, 1870–1970*

Sector	Maximum Rate of Expansion	Estimated Time Sector Became Leading Sector	Estimated Time Sector Ceased to Lead	Comments
Railroads	1870's	[a]	—	—
Cotton yarn	1890's	[b]	1950's	—
Iron	1950's	1950's	—	Peak growth in 1950's may reflect exaggerated figures during Great Leap Forward.
Steel	1930's	1950's	—	—
Electricity	1920's	—	—	—
Motor vehicles	1950's	1960's	—	—
Sulphuric acid	1950's	[b]	—	—
Nitrogen	1950's	[b]	—	—
Synthetic fibers	Early 1960's	[b]	—	—

[a] Spreading effects insufficient to justify designation as leading sector.
[b] Not judged, by itself, a leading sector.

process was accompanied by the emergence of a considerable number of vigorous Chinese industrial entrepreneurs, technicians, and skilled workers. Under conditions of domestic political order and external tranquillity, these assets might have been sufficient to induce a movement into sustained modern economic growth; but, of course, a technical counterfactual statement of that kind is without much meaning. The acquisition of a modern industrial sector was interwoven inextricably with foreign intrusion, including the Japanese takeover of Manchuria after 1931. As in India, the literate leaders of China had to focus obsessively on problems of politics and power rather than economics and welfare. Second, the impressive urban enclaves of modern industrial activity in China are surrounded by an agriculture (and a vast agricultural population) in which modernization proceeds more slowly. Within the limits of relatively fixed arable land, China had pushed irrigation and double cropping quite far before 1949. Output per acre was relatively high by international standards. Although the pace of industrial expansion has been relatively rapid since 1949, it has not been sufficient to reduce significantly the proportion of the population in the countryside. Indeed, the government has adopted a rather strong policy of discouraging movement to the cities. China remains, therefore, a land-poor, labor-intensive, agricultural country. Increase in agricultural output must come primarily through productivity increases stemming from increased application of fertilizers, improved seeds, etc. Despite high levels of investment in agriculture, output has increased slowly, at about 2 percent per annum between 1957 and the early 1970's. Therefore, we are observing a vast nation, containing perhaps 20 percent of the human race, with an increasingly sophisticated industrial sector embedded within a society still dominated by an agriculture yielding low income per capita. Average real income per capita is, therefore, low and expanding at only a modest rate.

On the other hand, if political stability is sustained and the farmer provided with adequate incentives, the enlarged foreign-exchange resources China's oil production may provide could move its economy into a phase of more rapid advance than that achieved in the past quarter-century.

45

Taiwan

The early history of Formosa is surrounded with obscurity. Aboriginal tribes still live in the eastern mountains, probably stemming from Malaysia, Indonesia, and, perhaps, from parts of mainland China. The first substantial wave of Chinese immigration may have arrived in the thirteenth century as the Mongols pressed down on the waning Sung dynasty.[136] The Hoklos, from Fukien, came to dominate the rich western plain, the Hakkas occupying the lower foothills to the east.

The Ming dynasty (1368–1644) left the island pretty much to itself. By the seventeenth century it had developed as part of a rather remarkable piratical trading network, centered in Fukien, reaching throughout southeast Asia and as far north as Japan. Formosa briefly became a place of importance under the dual pressures of the Manchu dynasty's takeover from the Ming and the probing intrusions of the Portuguese, Spanish, Dutch, and Japanese. The latter dropped out of contention for more than two centuries when the Tokugawa rulers made the decision substantially to cut off contacts with the outer world in 1640. In a complex passage, the Dutch consolidated their position on Formosa between 1623 and 1636. Their primacy lasted until 1661, when the extraordinary Japanese-born Cheng Ch'eng-kung (Koxinga) landed an army from Amoy. He succeeded in laying siege to the Dutch garrison, which finally surrendered and withdrew. His dual objective was to drive out the Dutch and to establish a base from which he could contest the Manchu dynasty, whose takeover from the Ming was not yet complete. It was in the context of a dynasty in defeat that large-scale immigration from the south of China to Formosa began. The quasi-independent Cheng dynasty on Formosa—still remembered on both sides of the straits as a golden moment in Chinese history—lasted until 1683, when Cheng's successors made their terms with the now fully triumphant Manchu rulers in Peking. For two centuries the island, full of inner contention, was loosely administered as a county of Fukien province. Despite some fifteen major rebellions against the government and innumerable minor clashes and feuds, it emerged as a fertile, food-surplus area.

The Chinese population of Formosa, which had risen to, say, 150,000 by 1683, was over 2.5 million two centuries later.[137] At that time the island was designated a province and acquired in Liu Ming-ch'uan an energetic, modernizing administration. Over the four previous decades Formosa, like the mainland, had felt the increased weight of British and American diplomacy and trading contacts. By the 1870's the ambitious Meiji administration began to envisage Formosa as part of the Japanese empire. In this contentious setting, heightened by conflict with the French expanding north from Indo-China, Peking called on Liu, an able soldier, to take over and defend the newly created island province.

Liu did more than assure the physical integrity of Formosa. His brief rule was a second brief golden interval in the island's history. He established a new modern capital at Taipei, built railroads, roads, and a telegraph system, and threw the switch in 1887 which brought electricity for the first time to a Chinese city. He paid for all this with enlarged exports (notably, camphor) and improved methods of tax collection. By 1891, after only seven years, his string had run out. Ill health and opposition in Peking to his aggressive modernizing policies led to his removal. Four years later, despite a defiant declaration of independence by a Republic of Taiwan, Japan took over the island against some armed resistance under the terms of the Treaty of Shimonoseki.

As in Korea, the forty years of Japanese colonial rule saw elements of modernization as well as hard-handed frustration. Transport and communications were developed, agricultural production and exports increased; notably, sugar, rice, sweet potatoes, and bananas. There was some industrialization during the First World War and in the 1930's. Before the end of Japanese rule Taiwan manufactured, on a small scale, modern textiles as well as cement, sulphuric acid, and superphosphates. Elementary education expanded; but, excepting certain types of technical training, Formosans were generally denied higher education. Population was almost 5 million in 1935, including some 270,000 Japanese. Resistance to Japanese rule was endemic, including a rising movement for independent statehood.

The coming of Nationalist administration in 1945 was initially greeted with enthusiasm. But inefficient and corrupt rule led to a brief bloody revolt in February 1947. The war-damaged economy was permitted further to run down. Discontent was heightened in 1949, when the defeated army, administration, and refugees came from the mainland. Despite these unpromising beginnings and chronic discontent among the Formosans, the island economy has moved in the past quarter-century into take-off and beyond.

As Chart V-56, part 2, shows, after abnormally high rates of expansion in the period of reconstruction (say, 1949–1953), industrial growth continued at average rates exceeded by few developing nations: over 10 percent per annum for the period 1953–1960; 16 percent for the 1960's. This surge was accompanied by a classic rise in the investment rate and by per capita rates of increase in gross domestic product of about 3.8 percent in the 1950's, over 7 percent in the 1960's. As the sectoral data show (Chart V-56, part 4), the 1960's saw rapid movement into modern sophisticated chemicals. Shipbuilding, automobile assembly and component production, and the manufacture of radio and television receivers also reflect the swift diversification of the economy. The expansion was led by rapid increases in light-industry exports progressively supported by import-substitution in the capital goods sectors. The resultant change in economic structure is suggested in Table V-76. This process was aided by a vigorous expansion of exports, large flows of foreign aid down to the mid-1960's, and substantial private capital imports. Taiwan's total foreign trade (imports and exports) was, in the early 1970's, at about the same level as that of the People's Republic of China. Taiwan's growth since the early 1950's was conducted, however, in the face of an extremely high allocation of resources for military purposes and, down to the second half of the 1960's, a much more rapid growth of total population than population in its economically active component. Between 1952 and 1965–1968, the economically active population fell from about 36 percent to 31 percent of the total.[138]

Behind this remarkable pace of economic modernization were two phenomena. First, there was an extremely successful land reform, conducted in stages between 1949 and 1953. Agricultural output expanded over this period at rates fluctuating around 5 percent per annum, helping produce a remarkably equitable income distribution on the island. Second, there was, as in South Korea, an explosive expansion of education, as a largely literate population at last gained access to secondary schools and institutions of higher learning.

The timing of Taiwan's sectoral pattern is summarized in Table V-78.

The stages of economic growth for Taiwan can, then, be viewed as follows.

Take-off: 1953–1960.

Drive to Technological Maturity: 1960–.

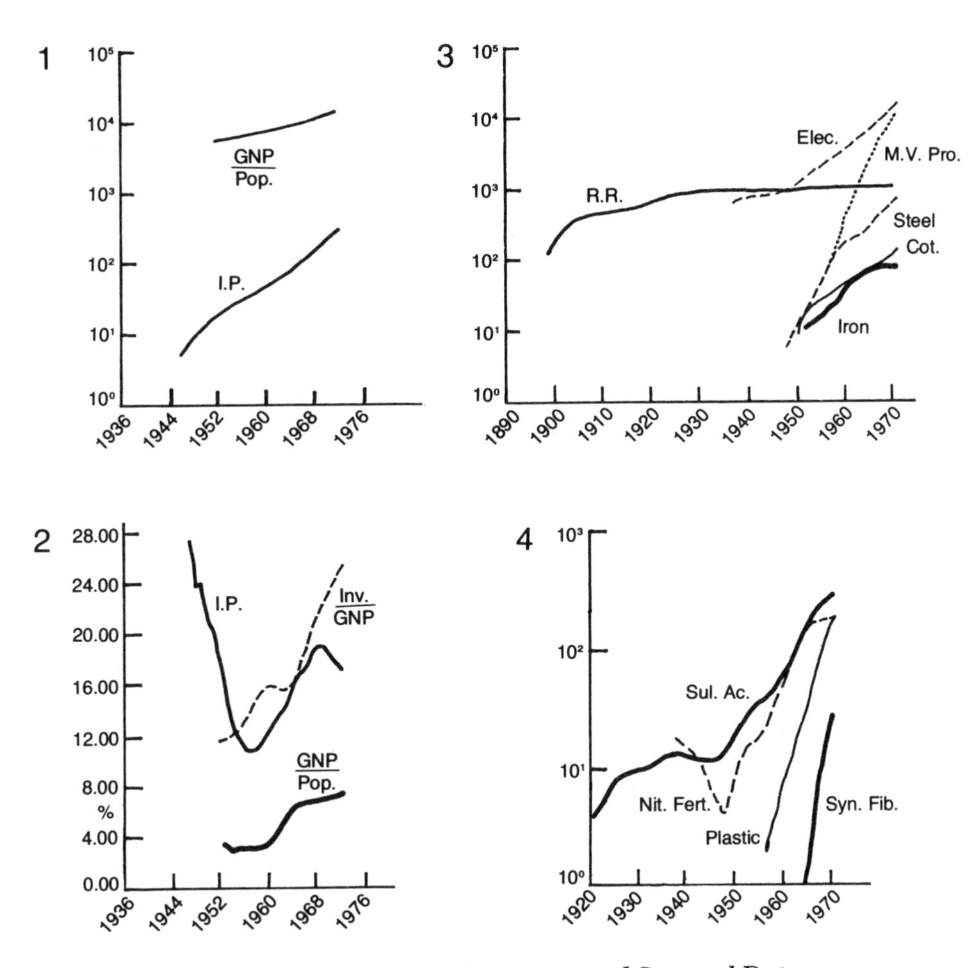

CHART V-56. *Taiwan, 1900–1972: Aggregate and Sectoral Data (Smoothed)*

1. GNP per capita ($\frac{\text{GNP}}{\text{Pop.}}$); industrial production index (I.P.).

2. Gross investment as % of GNP ($\frac{\text{Inv.}}{\text{GNP}}$); rate of change, GNP per capita ($\frac{\text{GNP}}{\text{Pop.}}$); rate of change, industrial production (I.P.).

3. Six major sectors: railroads (kilometers) (R.R.); raw cotton consumption (Cot.); production of iron (Iron); steel (Steel); electricity (Elec.); and motor vehicles (M.V. Pro.).

4. Production of four major chemicals: sulphuric acid (Sul. Ac.); nitrogen fertilizer (Nit. Fert.); plastics and resins (Plastic); and synthetic fibers (Syn. Fib.).

Sources: See Appendix D.

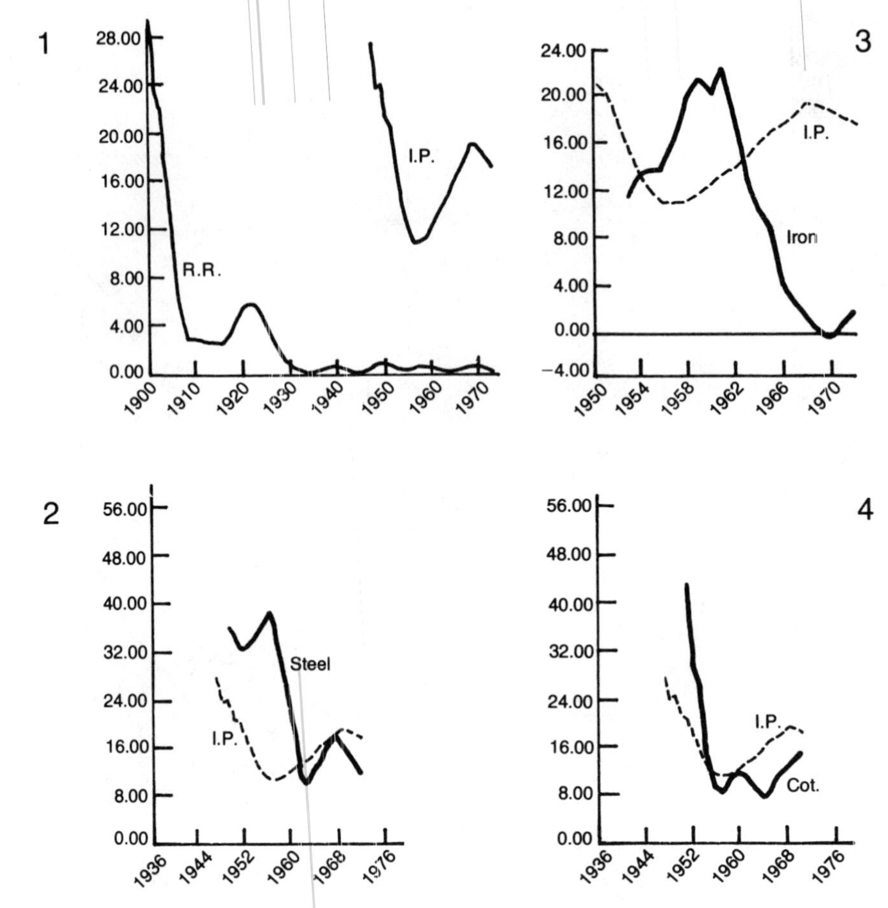

CHART V-57. *Taiwan, 1900–1972: Relative Growth Rates—Major Sectors and Industrial Production (Smoothed)*

1. Railroads (kilometers) (R.R.).
2. Steel production (Steel).
3. Iron production (Iron).
4. Raw cotton consumption (Cot.).

Sources: See Appendix D.

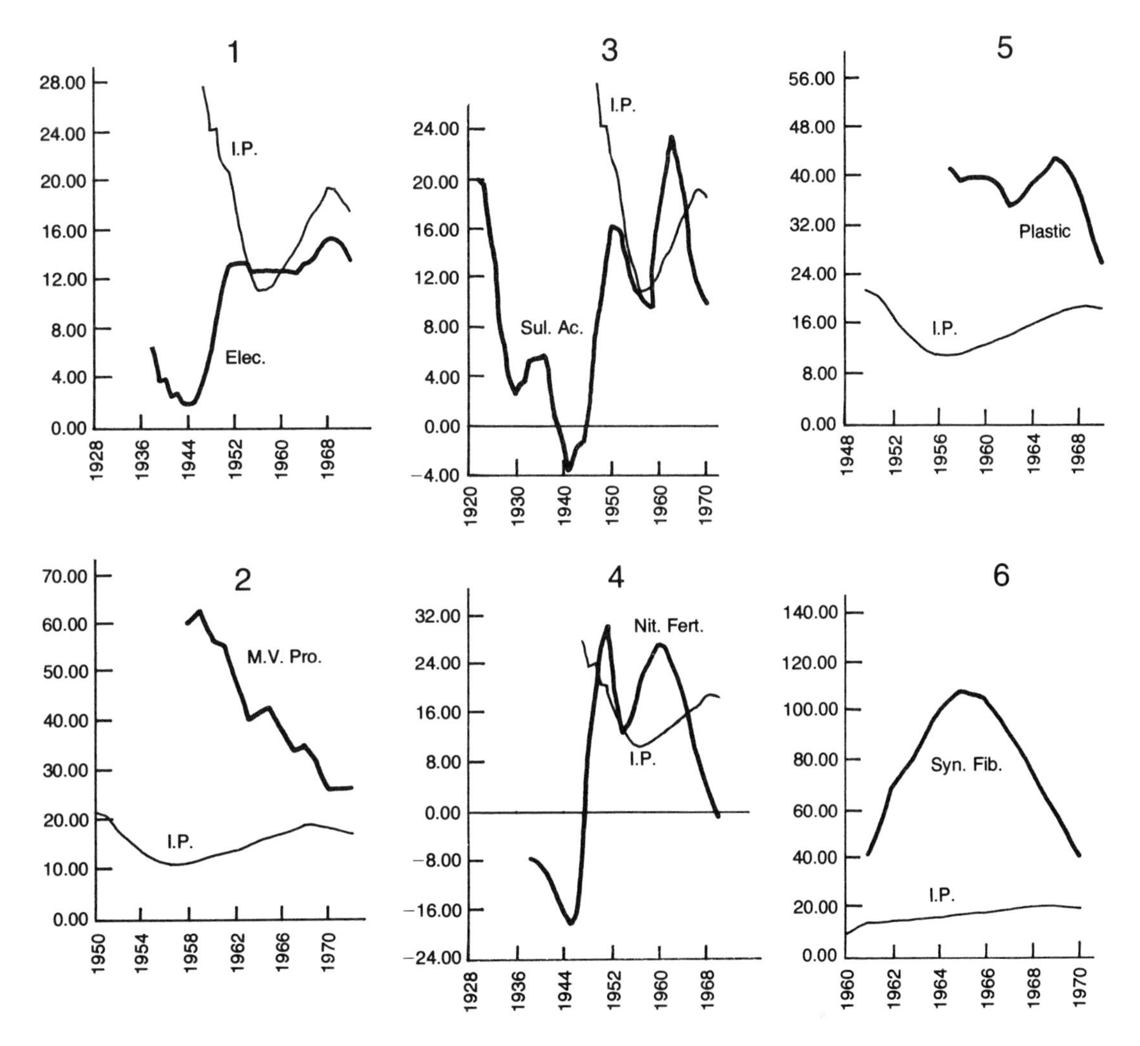

CHART V-58. *Taiwan, 1920–1972: Relative Growth Rates— Major Sectors and Industrial Production (Smoothed)*

1. Electricity (Elec.).
2. Motor vehicles (M.V. Pro.).
3. Sulphuric acid (Sul. Ac.).
4. Nitrogen fertilizer(Nit. Fert.).
5. Plastics and resins (Plastic).
6. Synthetic fibers (Syn. Fib.).

Sources: See Appendix D.

TABLE V-76. *Growth Rates and Percentage Distribution of Industrial Gross Product at Constant Prices: Taiwan, 1953–1956 to 1965–1968 (Annual Averages)*

	Food	Textiles	Wood and Wood Products	Paper	Chemicals and Chemical Produc
Growth rates					
1953–1956	25.84	13.63	−1.84	23.41	3.00
1957–1960	12.34	8.86	11.59	9.64	10.75
1961–1964	−0.04	18.05	30.48	18.14	31.42
1965–1968	2.47	13.97	−4.74	6.29	17.78
Percentage distribution					
1952	32.08	13.53	6.24	5.14	8.96
1953–1956	43.89	16.71	3.46	5.08	6.45
1957–1960	48.31	12.13	2.81	6.20	5.66
1961–1964	35.12	12.10	5.35	6.07	8.61
1965–1968	13.41	14.10	3.87	6.89	10.66

Source: Mo-Huan Hsing, "Taiwan: Industrialization and Trade Policies," in *Industry and Trade in So Developing Countries: The Philippines and Taiwan* (London: Oxford University Press, published for the Develo ment Centre, OECD, Paris, 1971), p. 168.

TABLE V-77. *Expansion of Education: Taiwan, 1950, 1967, 1973 (Thousands)*

	1950	1967	1973
Primary school enrollment	892	2,348	2,43
Secondary school enrollment	115	785	1,37
Higher-education enrollment	6[a]	141	27
(a) Total school population	1,013	3,274	4,07
(b) Total population	7,554	13,000	15,55
(a) as % of (b)	13	25	2

[a] 1949.

Sources: 1950, Fred W. Riggs, *Formosa under Chinese Nationalist Rule* (New Yor Macmillan, 1952), pp. 139–141; 1967, *United Nations Statistical Yearbook, 1969*, p. 71 1973, *China Yearbook*, 1974, p. 247.

Petroleum and Coal Products	Nonmetallic Mineral Products	Metals and Metal Products	Electrical Products	Others
13.57	12.80	25.13	32.81	−17.99
13.57	26.82	28.67	15.89	16.05
12.18	21.13	13.45	20.44	26.82
30.48	8.88	23.02	63.98	5.65
4.95	3.26	4.10	0.84	20.90
5.82	3.32	4.74	1.19	9.34
4.97	4.52	8.45	1.59	5.36
5.26	6.32	10.08	1.89	9.20
7.70	6.21	15.23	6.68	9.25

Annual Average Increase, 1950–1967 (%)	Annual Average Increase, 1967–1973 (%)
5.9	0.6
12.0	9.8
19.2	11.5
—	—
—	—
—	—

TABLE V-78. *Approximate Timing of Leading Sectors: Taiwan, 1950–1972*

Sectors	Maximum Rate of Expansion	Estimated Time Sector Became Leading Sector	Estimated Time Sector Ceased to Lead	Comments
Railroads	—	[a]	—	As text notes, railroads built pre-1949.
Cotton	Late 1960's	Late 1960's	—	Export-led expansion emerged in 1960's.
Steel	Late 1950's	Late 1950's	—	—
Electricity	1965–1970	1960's	—	Electrification begun pre-1950.
Motor vehicles	Late 1960's	Late 1960's	—	—
Sulphuric acid	Early 1950's	[b]	—	—
Nitrogen	Early 1950's	[b]	—	—
Plastics	Early 1960's	[b]	—	—
Synthetic fibers	Mid-1960's	[b]	—	—

[a] Spreading effects insufficient for designation as leading sector.
[b] Not judged, by itself, a leading sector.

46

Thailand

As compared to most of the developing nations considered in Part Five, the Thai transition from traditional to modern life has been relatively placid. From the fourteenth-century creation of the monarchy of Siam at Ayutthaya to its overthrow by the Burmese in 1767, the Thais enjoyed continuity of rule. The Ayutthaya monarchy initially accepted trading contacts with the Portuguese, British, French, and Dutch; but in 1688, in reaction against French intrusion, ties with the West were severed or attenuated for some 160 years. Meanwhile, the Burmese were driven out, and the founder of the present Thai dynasty established his capital at Bangkok in 1782.

Modernization began with King Mongkut's mid-nineteenth-century decision that Thailand would have to learn from the West to survive, and that the learning process justified concessions to foreign traders as well as the acceptance of foreign technicians and administrators. Under him and his successors the development of the country's resources began, railways and irrigation works were built, and a more modern administration was created.

Unlike that in China, this process of slow-moving absorption of Western methods proceeded without major internal disruption down to the multiple coups of 1932. These left the monarch a figurehead and put power in the hands of a sequence of military leaders leagued with an increasingly competent bureaucracy whose major figures were Western-trained.[139] In contrast to the situation in Japan, entrepreneurship outside government administration lay mainly in the hands of foreigners and the vigorous Chinese minority. Nevertheless, Thailand's rice, teak, tin, and rubber moved into the world's markets. The railroad system and the port of Bangkok expanded; but virtually no modern industry developed in Thailand before the Second World War.

During that war Thailand made the best terms it could with Japan on the basis of a neutrality favorable to the latter. The immediate postwar years were difficult both economically and politically. Thailand had to accept international control over the distribution of its rice surplus. By the end of 1947, however, the country had recovered from the disruptions of war and resumed a normal place in the international community under the leadership of Luang Pibul Songgram. He exercised power from 1938 to 1957, except for the three immediate postwar years. The 1950's saw considerable government effort to foster import-substitution industries. These were often run by Chinese protected by Thai officials,[140] but they generated little momentum. Working with experts from the World Bank, the ablest economic administrators threw their weight into development programs which aimed to build up the nation's transport, power, and irrigation systems and to increase output and productivity in its major export products. These resulted, *inter alia*, in a diversification of agricultural exports, including a remarkable expansion of corn production and export for the Japanese market. In effect, the 1950's can be regarded as the completion of the preconditions for take-off in Thailand.

A new phase of the country's development began with the coming to power in 1958 of Field Marshal Sarit Thanarat—an intelligent, corrupt, charismatic, Rabelaisian figure. He backed the new generation of economist-administrators led by the strong-minded, austere Puey Ungphakorn, dean of the faculty at Thammasat University in Bangkok, governor of the Central Bank and, at various times, holder of other official posts. This partnership of power and expertise, held together by a shared conviction that Thai industrial development was required for the nation's survival, brought about a marked acceleration in Thailand's growth. The government accepted increased reliance on foreign firms to expand industry. But investment resources were also allocated to maintain the momentum of productivity in agriculture as well as to assure its continued diversification. The effort was guided by successive five-year plans, begun in 1961, framed by a sophisticated, stabilizing monetary policy.[141] The latter was rendered easier by Thailand's export capacity, ample foreign aid, and the accretion of foreign exchange from U.S. military expenditures in the area.[142]

TABLE V-79. *Thailand: The Acceleration of the 1960's (in U.S. $ Millions, 1966 Prices)*

	1953	1960	Rate of Growth (%)	1968	Rate of Growth (%)
Gross domestic product	1,845	2,581	4.9	5,205	9.2
Value added in manufacturing	236	302	3.6	808	13.1
Exports	43	41	−0.7	62	5.3
Imports	314	412	4.0	1,000	11.7
Energy production (million kWh)	158	804[a]	26.2	4,406[b]	18.5

[a] 1963.
[b] 1970.
Source: Asian Development Bank, *Southeast Asia's Economy in the 1970's*, p. 248, except energy production, which is from *United Nations Statistical Yearbooks*, annual.

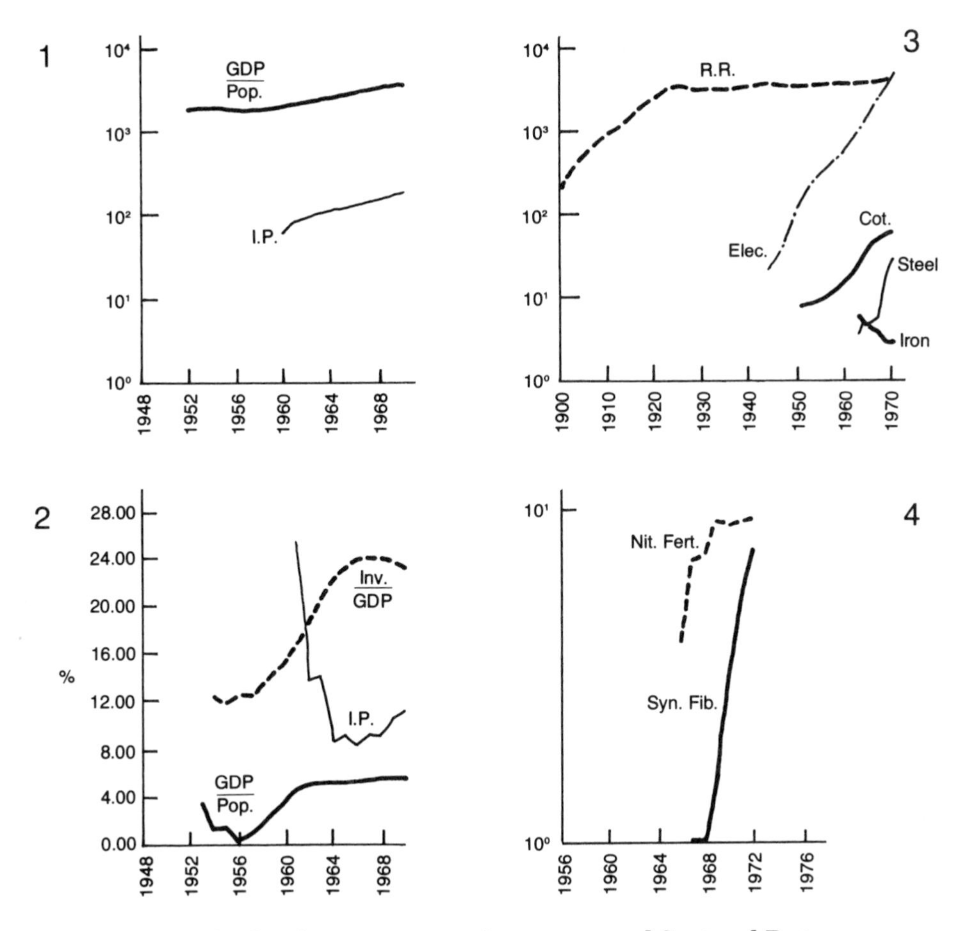

CHART V-59. *Thailand, 1900–1972: Aggregate and Sectoral Data (Smoothed)*

1. GDP per capita ($\frac{\text{GDP}}{\text{Pop.}}$); industrial production index (I.P.).

2. Gross investment (domestic fixed capital formation) as % of GDP ($\frac{\text{Inv.}}{\text{GDP}}$); rate of change, GDP per capita ($\frac{\text{GDP}}{\text{Pop.}}$); rate of change, industrial production (I.P.).

3. Five major sectors: railroads (kilometers) (R.R.); raw cotton consumption (Cot.); production of iron (Iron); steel (Steel); and electricity (Elec.).

4. Production of two major chemicals: nitrogen fertilizer (Nit. Fert.) and synthetic fibers (Syn. Fib.).

Sources: See Appendix D.

Table V-79 sets out some indicators of the accelerated expansion of the Thai economy in the 1960's. Between 1960 and 1971 the proportion of gross domestic product contributed by industry rose from 14 percent to 20 percent, while agriculture declined from 40 percent to 29 percent. Thailand sustained in the 1960's an annual average increase in real product per capita of 4.6 percent. As Chart V-59, part 2, shows, its gross investment rate rose from an average of 14 percent to over 25 percent.

In terms of Thai social as well as economic history, the decisive shift in the 1960's was toward the encouragement of foreign invest-

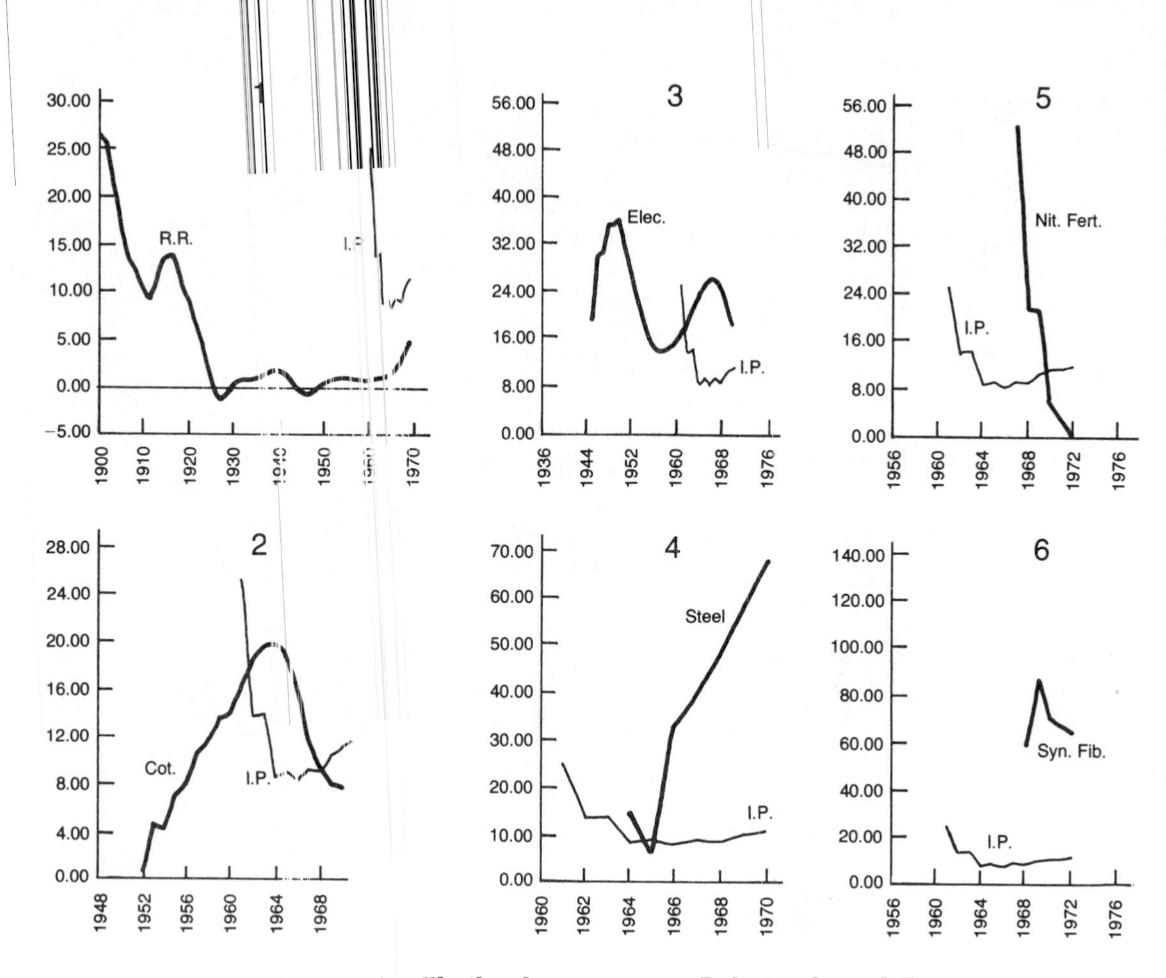

CHART V-60. *Thailand, 1900–1972: Relative Growth Rates—Major Sectors and Industrial Production (Smoothed)*

1. Railroads (kilometers) (R.R.).
2. Raw cotton consumption (Cot.).
3. Electricity (Elec.).
4. Steel production (Steel).
5. Nitrogen fertilizer (Nit. Fert.).
6. Synthetic fibers (Syn. Fib.).

Sources: See Appendix D.

ment accompanied by an increased entrepreneurial role for Thais as well as Chinese. Of the 607 firms registered under the Promotion of Industrial Investment Act between 1959 and 1969, 42 percent were wholly owned by Thai nationals, 4 percent wholly owned by foreign subsidiaries, and 54 percent jointly owned by Thais and foreign nationals.[143] A new Thai industrial (as opposed to bureaucratic and commercial) elite was beginning to emerge.

The bulk of the industrial activity was in light consumers' goods designed to substitute for imports and supply a rapidly expanding domestic market. Toward the end of the 1960's, however, there was an expansion of Thai manufactured exports. In structure Thai industry is typical for a nation entering self-sustained growth through import-substitution: about two-thirds consists of the production of consumers' goods; about a quarter, of intermediate goods, including the processing of raw materials; only 12 percent (1968), of capital and durable consumers' goods.[144] In 1970 Thailand produced, for example, only forty thousand tons of steel.

In terms of stages of economic growth, then, Thailand entered take-off in the 1960's. Among contemporary developing nations it has been almost unique in maintaining its agricultural export position despite a high rate of population increase. It has done so by combining a quite high rate of acreage expansion with increases in productivity: annual rates of 4.2 percent and 1.4 percent, respectively, in the early 1960's.[145] Although it is estimated that only half of Thailand's agricultural acreage is under cultivation, it is expected that these proportions will shift in the 1970's to, say, 1.3 percent and 2.7 percent, respectively.[146] Thailand will continue to earn foreign exchange from some of its raw materials, notably tin. It lacks the basis for a substantial steel industry using local resources, but, as elsewhere, the search is on for oil, some of which has been found and is locally refined. Like the small and medium-sized Latin American countries, Thailand's capacity to move forward beyond a take-off based on the manufacture of consumers' goods in substitution for imports may depend on the success or failure of its region in developing effective common-market arrangements.

47

South Korea

Part of a split nation, under de facto and then formal Japanese rule for some forty years, subjected to a war in which there were almost a million civilian and 320,000 military casualties, South Korea transformed itself to sustain from 1962 to 1972 an average rate of increase in real GNP per capita of 7.3 percent (102 percent per decade), 17 percent in industrial production. South Korean exports were $55 million in 1962, $1.6 billion in 1972. In terms of stages of economic growth, the country moved from enclaves of modern economic activity within a basically premodern society in 1945 through the take-off into the drive to technological maturity.

The large flow of American economic aid and dollar outlays within South Korea in the twenty years after 1945 undoubtedly helped make this transformation possible. It sustained the level of imports during a period when the country was incapable of earning sufficient foreign exchange to support its people, its defense, and its growth. Foreign aid bought time. But the swift emergence of a modern South Korea can be understood only in terms of a process of modernization which began, at the latest, in 1876. In that year Korea entered a treaty of commerce with Japan, having successfully faced down intruding French, German, and American expeditions over the previous decade. The treaty reflected a convergence of Japanese pressure and reforming groups in Korea that wished to end its long isolation. Over the next decade, similar treaties were entered into with the United States and the major European states, including Great Britain and Russia. The thirty-year period from 1876 to Korea's takeover by Japan in 1904–1905 is a counterpoint between external buffeting, as Russia, Japan, China, and Britain contended for power and profit, and Korea's domestic striving for a modernization evidently required if the nation was to recover its independence and dignity. Indeed, the first of the modernization movements, the Taewongun Reform of 1864, predated the Japanese treaty, responding to the forces unleashed in Asia by the Western intrusions into China of the 1840's, Japan of the 1850's.[147] As in China of the same period, the thrust for modernizing change came from many directions within this essentially feudal society:[148] the bureaucratic elite, the long-repressed peasantry, Western-oriented intellectuals. In all cases, there was a strand of nationalism reacting against intrusion, as well as some tendency to orient toward one or another external power. But these diverse efforts failed to unite. Their failure left Korea to a painful passage of colonial rule from 1895.

Under these circumstances, Korean thought and feeling focused primarily around the aspiration for independence. A protracted military struggle for independence was repressed by the Japanese only with great difficulty in the period 1907–1910. Rioting and open rebellion broke out in March 1919. The prestige and aura of legitimacy of Syngman Rhee dates from this period. After escaping to Hawaii from a period of underground struggle against the Japanese, he formed in 1919 a Korean government in exile which campaigned for independence over the next quarter-century.

The degree of harshness of Japanese rule varied over the colonial period;[149] but, in general, opposition was ruthlessly repressed, Korean participation in public affairs narrowly circumscribed, education beyond the elementary level extremely limited in a purposeful effort to restrict Korean capabilities. Japanese was installed, in effect, as a second language, and from 1937 the teaching of Korean was prohibited. As of 1935, there were only nineteen public secondary schools in Korea, with a total enrollment of 10,278, for a population of about 22 million.[150] Perhaps twice that number were enrolled in the twenty-one private secondary schools operating in Korea in that year. A good deal of Korean intellectual talent, frustrated in other directions, devoted itself to private education during the Japanese occupation.

Economically, the modernization of Korea proceeded slowly and in piecemeal fashion under Japanese rule, reflecting, as in similar situations, the interests of the colonial power. There was some emigration of Japanese to Korea, where they acquired land and dominated international trade. Foodstuffs and fertilizers were exported in return for manufactured goods. A system of rail lines and bridges, linking Korea to Manchuria, was completed in 1928; a system of centralized finance and banking was created, as well as some urban infrastructure; and certain industrial activities were begun, mainly with Japanese capital, in mining, ore smelting, cotton ginning, gas and electricity, rice cleaning, tobacco manufacture, brewing, and tanning. After 1931, during the period of war with China, Japanese interests in exploiting Korean resources intensified, notably in minerals. This period left as one legacy the great Yalu River dam and the power station at Suiho. In general, Japan, like other colonial powers, took its colony into economic activities which provided some typical elements of the preconditions for take-off; but the degree of economic modernization was, by 1945, uneven and limited. Korea was still some distance from take-off, notably in the mainly agricultural south.

With the liberation and then division of the country, South Korea experienced a generation of traumatic changes: a massive flow of refugees from the north; a period of war and mass population movements, as the battle swept up and down the peninsula; a sequence of inner political struggles climaxed by the overthrow of Rhee in April 1960, the young officers' coup of May 1961, and the emergence of a period of stable, more or less constitutional rule in December 1963. Beneath these events two related processes were under way which substantially explain South Korea's subsequent rapid and sustained economic and social modernization. First was the remarkable expansion of education depicted in Table V-80. The South Korean passion for education, reinforced by a compulsory public education system, wholly transformed in a single generation the capacity of the nation to absorb modern technology. The proportion of the population in school was higher in South Korea than in Japan in 1971; and 45 percent were female students. Along with land reform, the necessities of war and defense, and political change, the educational explosion also opened the way for talent to rise in both the public and private sectors. There was a true social revolution in post-1945 Korea.

The second phenomenon, derived from these profound alterations in the society, was the emergence of a generation of young leaders and technicians, civil and military, to whom the economic modernization of the country became an almost obsessive goal: a route to independence of all the surrounding major powers, a foundation for resisting pressure from the north, and a way of expressing human and national capacities long frustrated by history. Trained at home as well as abroad, they quickly absorbed what the teaching of economics, engineering, business management, and public administration could supply; and they took over, from about 1961, the operation of the Korean economy. Working with foreign experts, they soon ac-

TABLE V-80. *Increase in School Population: South Korea, 1935–1971 (Thousands)*

	1935[a]	1945	1955	1964	1971	Annual Average Rate of Growth, 1945–1971 (%)
Elementary	840	1,382	2,959	4,744	5,807	5.7
Secondary	38	85	748	1,066	2,201	13.3
Higher	5	8	87	143	206	13.3
(a) Total school population	883	1,475	3,794	5,953	8,214	—
(b) Total population	22,000	16,000	21,500	28,000	32,000	—
(a) as % of (b)	4	9	18	21	26	—

[a] All Korea.

Sources: 1935 (all Korea), from a Japanese source quoted in W. D. Reeve, *The Republic of Korea: A Political and Economic Study*, p. 87; 1945, 1955, 1964, from Hahn-Been Lee, *Korea: Time, Change, and Administration*, p. 49, where source is cited; 1971, from *United Nations Statistical Yearbook, 1972*.

quired the skills necessary for sophisticated economic planning.[151]

Chart V-61 exhibits the upshot for certain measures of aggregate and sectoral growth in the South Korean economy. The post-1945 years break quite sharply from 1961, when the military government took over and the first Five Year Plan was launched. Down to that time, Korean economic development proceeded at a reasonably high but uneven aggregate rate, accompanied by rapid inflation, in a setting of high unemployment, excessive population increase, and dependence to an extraordinary degree on foreign aid and U.S. military outlays within the country. There was rapid rehabilitation and expansion of transport facilities and of coal and iron mining, and some increase in the fishing industry. The textile industry also expanded. But there was no coherent development plan, an excessive dependence on foreign aid to sustain a rather modest rate of investment, no sense of solid progress, and a slackening off in the rate of growth between 1958 and 1960, when the increase in production barely matched the rate of population increase (see Table V-81). All this contributed to the environment of frustration which yielded the successive coups of 1960 and 1961. Nevertheless, in retrospect the economic (as well as social) developments of this period helped bring toward completion the preconditions for the South Korean take-off.

The transition to accelerated and sustained economic growth after 1961 was, of course, not instantaneous. Inflation, for example, was not brought under effective control until 1964–1965 by a series of measures which also promptly and substantially increased the volume of domestic savings.[152] Nevertheless, real per capita product increased between 1960 and 1965 at 3.4 percent, industrial production at 12 percent. After 1965 there was a marked acceleration, including an average gross investment rate of 29 percent for 1965–1970. The Korean take-off into self-sustained growth was, by that time, evidently under way. Charts V-61, V-62, and V-63 capture the statistical contours of this story; Table V-82, the timing of the major sectors.

What we observe in Table V-82 is an extraordinary compression in time of the absorption of the backlog of existing technologies. Cotton consumption expanded rapidly in the early 1950's, but its capacity to lead in the small South Korean market was soon exhausted. The take-off of the early and mid-1960's was reflected in the rapid expansion of elecricity, iron, steel, and sulphuric acid production; but by the late 1960's South Korea had already moved on to the drive to technological maturity, symbolized by its absorption of the modern chemicals and the capacity to produce motor vehicles. It also became in these years the producer of large tankers.

The South Korean stages of growth can, thus, be dated roughly as follows.

Take-off: 1961–1968.

Drive to Technological Maturity: 1968–.

Like other developing economies, that of South Korea was hit hard by the rise in the international oil price of 1973–1974 and the recession in the OECD world of 1974–1975. Its dependence over the pre-

TABLE V-81. *Some Economic Indicators: South Korea, 1954–1960*

	(1) Per Capita Product at Constant Prices (1953 = 100)	(2) Gross Investment as % of Total Available Resources	(3) Electricity Production (Million kWh)	(4) Coal Production (Million Metric Tons)
1954	103	11.5	899	0.9
1955	109	11.2	897.3	1.3
1956	106	10.8	1118.3	1.8
1957	112	15.3	1328	2.4
1958	117	12.1	1520	2.7
1959	119	10.0	1741	4.1
1960	118	9.6	1758	5.4

Sources: Cols. 2, 4, and 5, Hahn-Been Lee, *Korea*, pp. 86, 83, 82, from official Korean sources; cols. 1, 3, 6, and 7, *United Nations Statistical Yearbooks*, annual. Imports, exports, and electricity, 1954–1960, *United Nations Statistical Yearbook, 1962*.

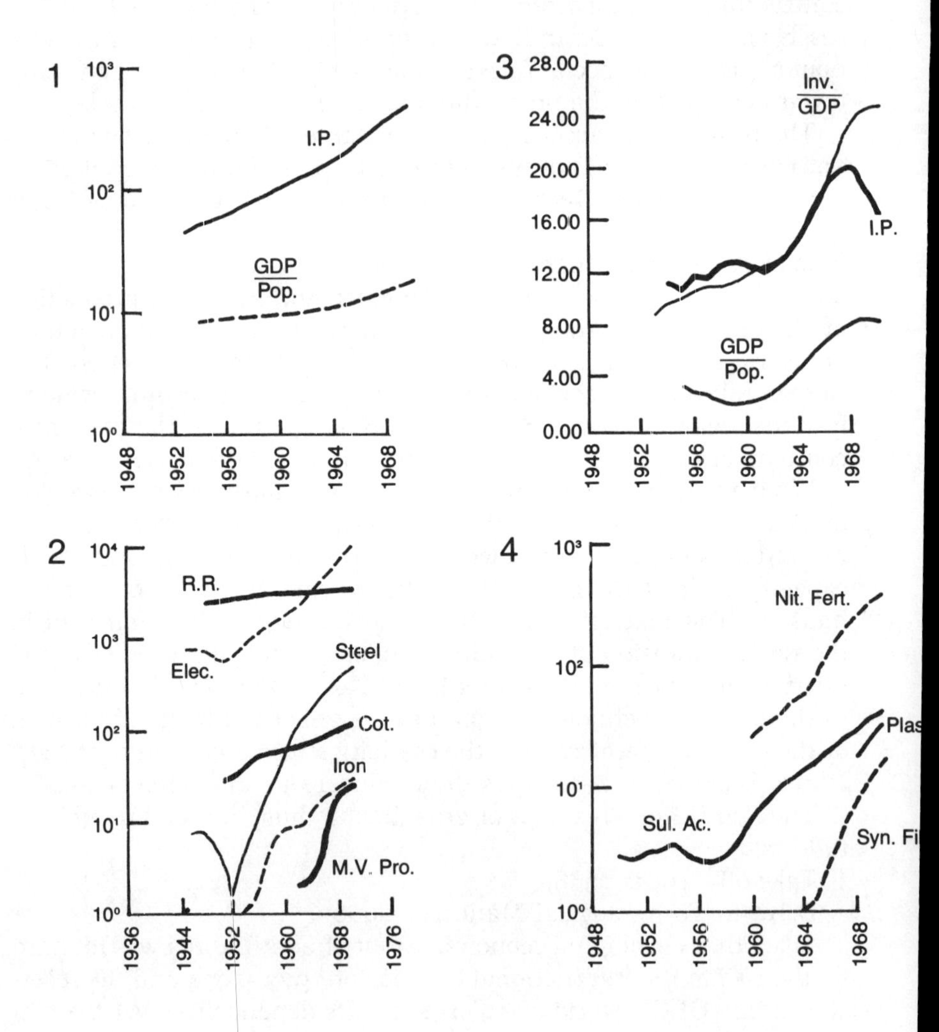

(5) Index of Industrial Production (1960 = 100)	(6) Imports ($ Millions)	(7) Exports ($ Millions)
43.0	243	24
51.4	341	18
62.9	386	25
72.6	422	22
80.0	378	17
91.8	304	19
100	344	33

:HART V-61. *South Korea, 1945–1972: Aggregate and Sectoral Data Smoothed)*

1. GDP per capita ($\frac{GDP}{Pop.}$); industrial production index (I.P.).
2. Six major sectors: railroads (kilometers) (R.R.); raw cotton consumpion (Cot.); production of iron (Iron); steel (Steel); electricity (Elec.); and notor vehicles (assembly) (M.V. Pro.).
3. Gross investment (fixed capital formation) as % of GDP ($\frac{Inv.}{GDP}$); rate f change, GDP per capita ($\frac{GDP}{Pop.}$); rate of change, industrial production I.P.).
4. Production of four major chemicals: sulphuric acid (Sul. Ac.); nitrogen ertilizer (Nit. Fert.); plastics and resins (Plastic); and synthetic fibers Syn. Fib.).

Sources: See Appendix D.

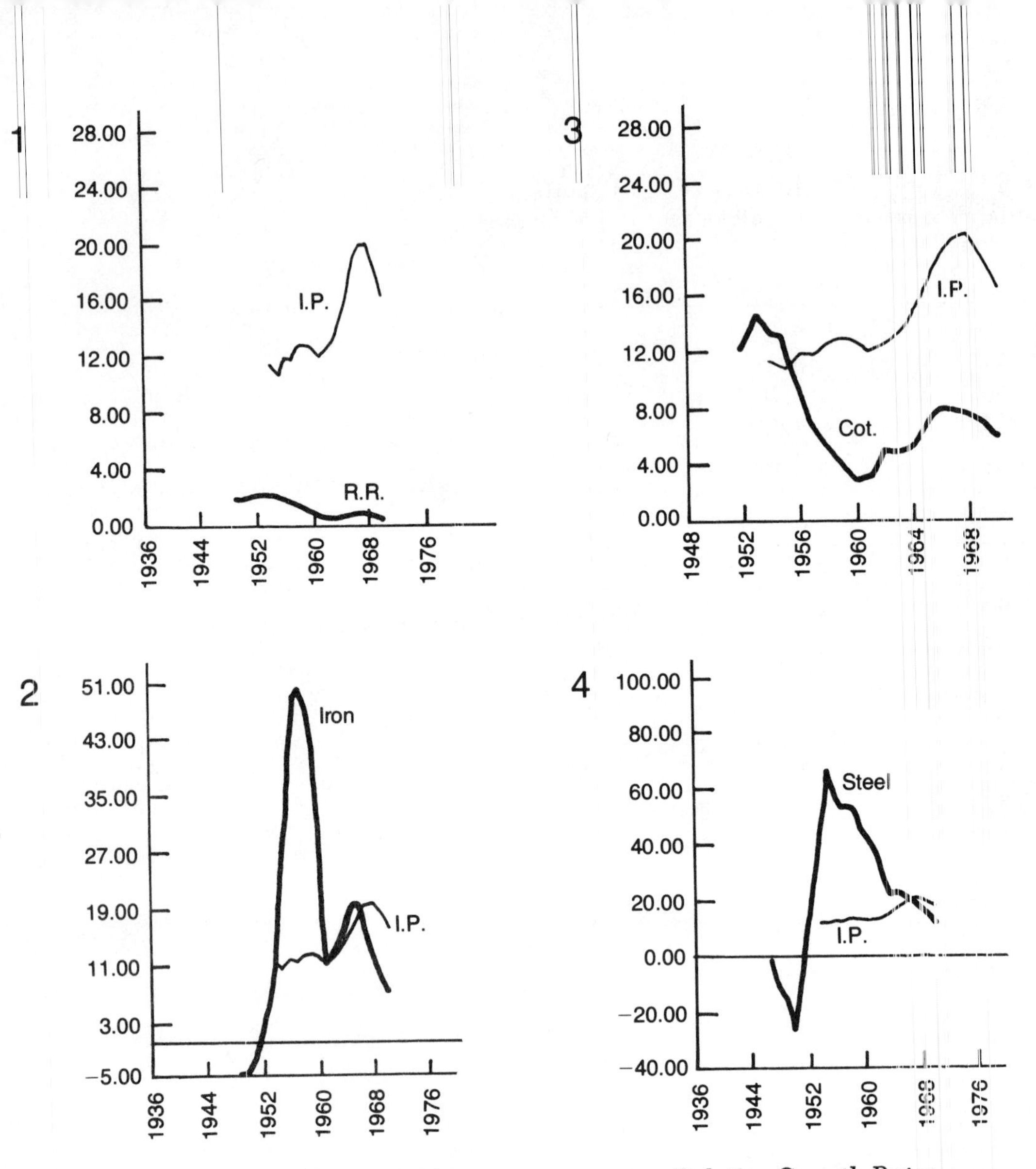

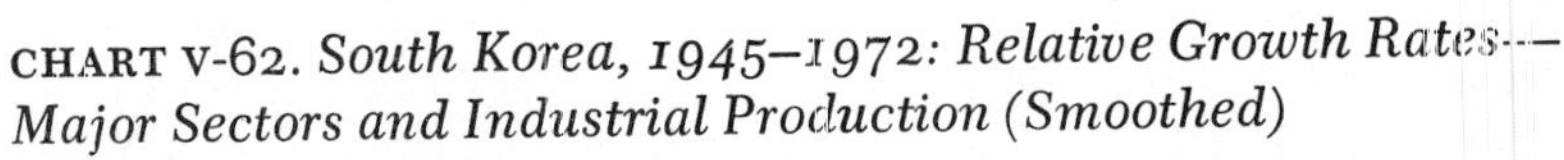
CHART V-62. *South Korea, 1945–1972: Relative Growth Rates—Major Sectors and Industrial Production (Smoothed)*

1. Railroads (kilometers) (R.R.)
2. Iron production (Iron).
3. Raw cotton consumption (Cot.).
4. Steel production (Steel).

Sources: See Appendix D.

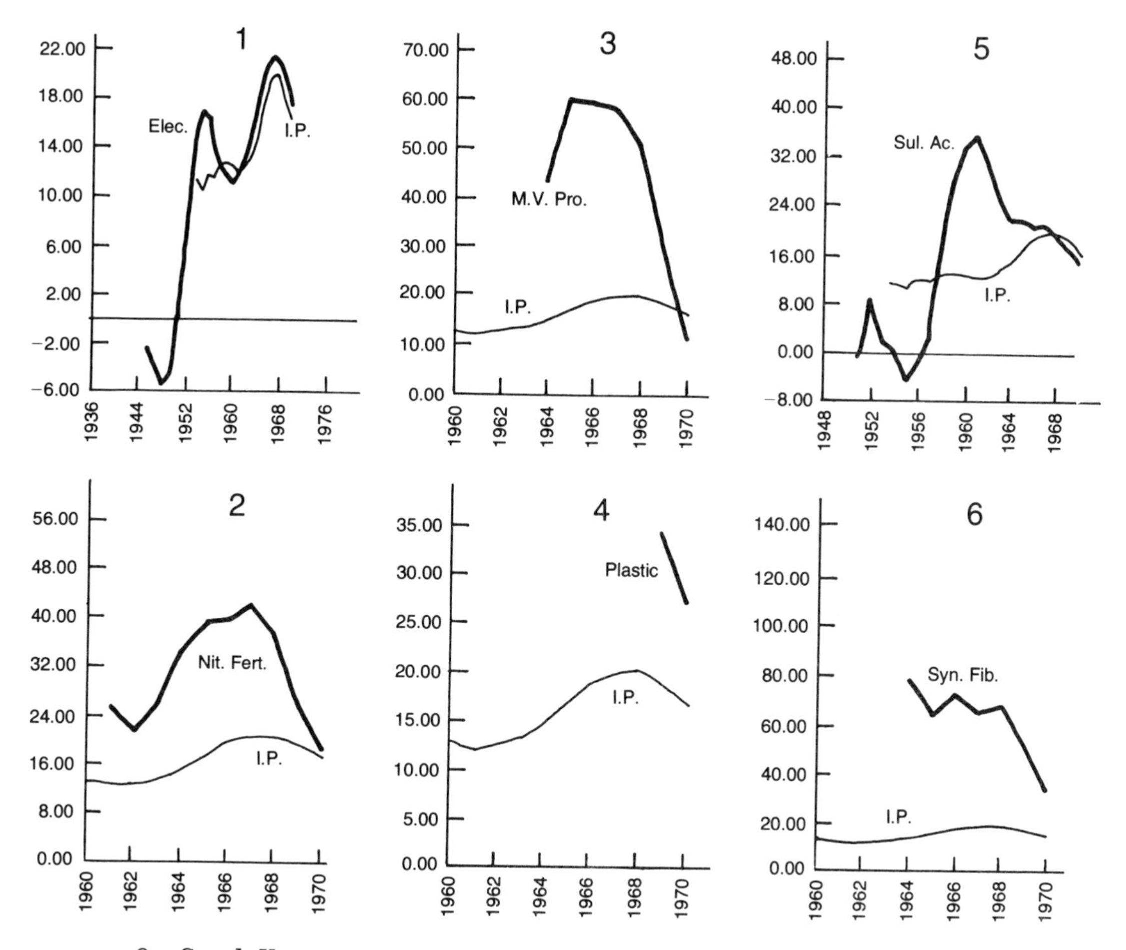

CHART V-63. *South Korea, 1945–1972: Relative Growth Rates—Major Sectors and Industrial Production (Smoothed)*

1. Electricity (Elec.).
2. Nitrogen fertilizer (Nit. Fert.).
3. Motor vehicles (M.V. Pro.).
4. Plastics and resins (Plastic).
5. Sulphuric acid (Sul. Ac.).
6. Synthetic fibers (Syn. Fib.).

Sources: See Appendix D.

TABLE V-82. *Approximate Timing of Leading Sectors: South Korea, 1900–1972*

Sector	Maximum Rate of Expansion	Estimated Time Sector Became Leading Sector	Estimated Time Sector Ceased to Lead
Cotton consumption	Early 1950's	[a]	Late 1950's
Railroads	1900–1910	[b]	1910–1920
Iron	1950's	1960's	—
Steel	1950's	1960's	Late 1960's
Electricity	1960's	1960's	—
Motor vehicles	Late 1960's	Late 1960's	—
Sulphuric acid	Late 1960's	[a]	Late 1960's
Nitrogen	1960's	[a]	—
Plastics	Late 1960's	[a]	—
Synthetic fibers	Mid-1960's	[a]	—

[a] Not judged, by itself, a leading sector.
[b] Spreading effects not sufficient to justify designation as a leading sector.

vious decade on a rapid increase in exports to Japan and the United States rendered its balance of payments vulnerable, and this vulnerability was compounded by dependence on a high level of capital imports, public and private. As of early 1977 South Korea appeared to be making considerable progress toward an adjustment, in part based on expanded exports and other economic relations with OPEC countries.

48

Four Conclusions

There are four major conclusions that can be drawn from these stylized surveys of growth in twenty economies which bear on the prospects for the world economy to be examined in Part Six.

First, late-comers to take-off command the potentiality, at least, of catching up with those whose take-offs came earlier. Continental Western Europe and the United States narrowed or closed the initial gap with Great Britain in command over modern technologies and income per capita in the course of the nineteenth century. The late-comers of the nineteenth century (e.g., Sweden, Japan, Russia, Canada, and Italy) narrowed or closed the gap with Western Europe and the United States in the first three-quarters of the twentieth century. Some, at least, of the nations which entered take-off in the second and third quarters of the twentieth century (e.g., Brazil, Iran, South Korea, Taiwan) exhibited in the 1960's a capacity to absorb technologies and to increase income per capita at rates which are narrowing the gap with all those who entered modern growth in the nineteenth century except, perhaps, Japan.

The rule is not, of course, universal. There are countries whose size, geography, resource endowments, culture, social structure, or politics, in various combinations, have thus far prevented take-off (e.g., Burma, Yemen, some of the smaller African nations); and some which entered modern growth have, for similar reasons, moved forward erratically (e.g., Argentina, Uruguay, Chile), at average rates which are not narrowing the gap with North America, Western Europe, and Japan. The vicissitudes of both groups which have not excelled in growthmanship need not be permanent. In many cases, for example, they might well move forward in a more rapid and sustained way if they were to become part of larger regional and subregional economic units, although more than economic problems are involved in this transformation, and history offers no guarantee that this acceleration of growth will happen.

The historical evidence for the gap-narrowing process is confirmed by the recent experience of countries at different levels of income per capita, as Tables V-83 and V-84 indicate. In the 1960's, countries at the lowest levels of income per capita moved forward relatively more slowly than the average. This group was heavily weighted, of course, by the Indian and Chinese cases; but it also contained a good many pre–take-off countries with indifferent natural-resource endowments. In most nations which had acquired a capacity to absorb rapidly diversified technologies, that is, the "Middle Income Countries," the pace quickened; it decelerated among the richest nations as a whole; and within that group the richest went forward more slowly than the less rich; that is, the rate for Europe (average GNP per capita, $1,620) was higher (3.7 percent per annum) than for North America and Oceania ($3,450, 3.2 percent).[153] The relatively lower rates of growth for the richest nations can be seen as the result of their rather full exploitation of the pool of existing technologies and their greater dependence on the effective absorption of new technologies rather than an unexploited backlog. It is also possible that the shift of the income elasticity of demand at high income-per-capita levels to certain services which do not incorporate new high-productivity technology (e.g., education, medical services, travel) may help account for this deceleration among the most affluent.

But the central point here is that both historical and contemporary patterns of growth rates suggest that forces are at work which can narrow and ultimately close the income-per-capita gap among nations.

A second conclusion is that the cases of India and China should be viewed in somewhat special terms. They dramatize a now familiar distinction; that is, between average national income per capita and a nation's capacity to absorb efficiently the pool of modern technology. Both countries now command a quite high proportion of the basic technologies of the modern world. The modern industrial sectors within their economies are, in absolute terms, reasonably large. The rapid diversification of their industries indicates that they are in the drive to technological maturity. On the other hand, average national income per capita is low; their average rates of growth in per capita income over the past quarter-century have been below

TABLE V-83. *Growth Rates in the 1960's: High-, Middle-, and Low-Income Countries*

	Average GNP per Capita (U.S. $, 1967)	Annual Growth 1960–1970 (%)
High-income countries	2,420	3.5
Middle-income countries	650	5.4
Low-income countries	100	2.0
Average for total	610	3.2

Source: Adapted from Thorkil Kristensen, *Development in Rich and Poor Countries* (New York: Praeger, 1974), p. 30.

those of the most advanced countries; and they still face the task of modernizing the life of most of the 80 percent or so of their populations living in rural areas. The problem they confront is, of course, not historically unique. Russia on the eve of the First World War faced something like this dichotomy. To a degree, it is to be observed in Mexico and some other Latin American countries where substantial modern industrial sectors coexist with large regions of low-productivity, labor-intensive agriculture. Regional disparities were also faced in the southern regions of the United States, France, and Italy, as well as in Quebec and northeast Brazil. Indeed, there is a large literature on economic development under dualistic conditions; and, since economic growth always proceeds unevenly in terms of sectors and regions, we are talking about a problem that is, in an important sense, universal. But, as one looks to the future, the problem is worth underlining; for the scale of the Indian and Chinese problems is unique. We are talking about two nations which contained perhaps 35 percent of the world's population in 1976, a proportion not likely to decline over the next quarter-century. A good deal of history, economic and otherwise, will flow from the pace and manner in which rural life is modernized in India and China. If China maintains political stability and continuity in a reasonably rational economic policy, its increased oil revenues may permit it to modernize its rural sector quite rapidly and move toward a regime of more rapid growth. Although India's energy prospects now seem less substantial than China's, the attainment and maintenance of the investment rate of 20 percent now planned could also accelerate the modernization of its countryside if the priority of the agricultural sector is raised. In any case these two large countries are likely to be capable of managing highly sophisticated technologies over a wide front long before they achieve the levels of income per capita associated with high mass-consumption.

Third, this survey dramatizes in a particular way a familiar but central fact about the contemporary world economy. It contains nations at quite different stages of economic growth; differing, that is, in the degree to which they have effectively exploited modern technologies. It may, therefore, be useful to suggest the extent to which the various regions of the world have achieved some arbitrary standard of affluence. The reason for such play with numbers is, to a degree, serious. In Part Six we shall address ourselves to the question of the limits to growth. Virtually all futurologists, optimists and pessimists alike, assume that, at some point in human history, the level of the world's population will level off (or decline); and we have, in the concepts of the demographic transition and net reproduction rates, measurable devices for assessing how far toward population stability particular nations and regions have moved.

We cannot predict arrival at some equivalent ceiling for affluence, assuming history permits the human race as a whole to achieve that state, somehow defined. We simply do not know at what levels of income per capita, as we arbitrarily measure that concept, human beings will decide, on average, that enough is enough and diminishing relative marginal utility will set in for real income itself.

In seeking to indicate how far through the transition to affluence we had come, as of the early 1970's, I have, therefore, made two arbitrary calculations set out in Table V-84. Column A estimates how long it would take, if the growth rates and patterns of the 1960's were recovered and sustained, for each of seven groups of countries, arrayed by income per capita, to achieve U.S. income per capita as of 1967; Column B estimates how long it would take, if, say, the universal target turned out to be $20,000 per capita at U.S. 1967 prices.

In fact, we do not know what $20,000 per capita (in 1967 U.S. prices) would look like in a world of future technologies, tastes, resource constraints, taxes, etc.[154] But the more or less serious point of such speculation is to ask this question: Roughly how long will it take for the various nations of the world to achieve some meaningful level of affluence? The answer appears to be at various times between now and a century from now, if the U.S. 1967 level is defined as the target (average, the year 2024); between the fourth decade of the twenty-first century and the middle of the twenty-second, if the target of $20,000 per capita is chosen (average, the year 2078). This kind of exercise tells us, in effect, that compound interest is powerful if we can sustain it, and that meaningful levels of affluence, as we now define it, are conceivable on a more or less universal basis in a relatively short time period, by historical standards, if the growth process is not frustrated by resource, technological, political, or other constraints.

It should be noted that, if past experience is a guide, net reproduc-

TABLE V-84. *GNP per Capita, 1967, and Future Prospects: Selected Countries*

	Population 1967 (Millions)	GNP per Capita, 19[illegible] (U.S. $)
United States	199	3,670
Group 1 ($1,750–3,670)	307	3,120
Group 2 ($1,000–1,750)	238	1,490
Group 3 ($700–1,000)	444	930
Group 4 ($400–700)	161	550
Group 5 ($200–400)	299	270
Group 6 ($100–200)	376	130
Group 7 ($50–110)	1,580	90
World	3,391	610

Source: Calculated from World Bank data as organized by Kristensen, *Development Rich and Poor Countries*, pp. 156–159 and 30.

tion rates of one would be achieved before an affluence ceiling; for, as we saw in Part One (p. 17), such rates were reached or approached around 1970 in the industrialized countries with far lower levels of per capita income than the United States. Thus, if U.S. per capita GNP as of 1967 is taken as an affluence norm, the world average is 17 percent, whereas it was estimated (p. 39) that the world had passed by 1960 43.5 percent through the demographic transition. The expansion in global production implied by the notion that all nations will seek to achieve high per capita income levels immediately raises the question of the limits to growth, an issue addressed in the first chapter of Part Six.

A fourth major question raised by the twenty country analyses of Part Five is more proximate and urgent: What are likely to be the leading sectors in the future growth of the presently most advanced industrial societies? One of the striking aspects of the charts exhibiting sectoral growth rates in relation to industrial growth rates for the United States, Canada, Western Europe, and Japan is the declining rate of increase in motor vehicle production in the 1960's. Quite aside from the increase in petroleum prices after October 1973, with its income and price effects on the demand for motor vehicles, it was likely that automobile ownership would peak at lower levels in relation to population size in Europe and Japan than in the United States and Canada. This result flowed from geography, as well as from public policies with respect to mass transport and gasoline taxes. It is clearly suggested by the relative patterns of automobile registration and their decelerating rates of change in the 1960's set out in Chart V-64. The pace of diffusion of the private automobile in the Soviet Union is, of course, a matter of public policy rather than a

% of U.S.	Average Annual Growth Rates, 1960–1970 (%)	(A) No. Years to Attain U.S. 1967 Level	(B) No. Years to Attain $20,000 per Capita (U.S., 1967), Assuming 3.2% Growth Rate Continues
100	3.2	—	70
85	3.4	5	75
41	3.5	29	99
25	6.5	39	109
15	4.4	50	120
7	2.9	71	141
4	2.6	98	168
2	1.7	114	184
17	3.2	57	111

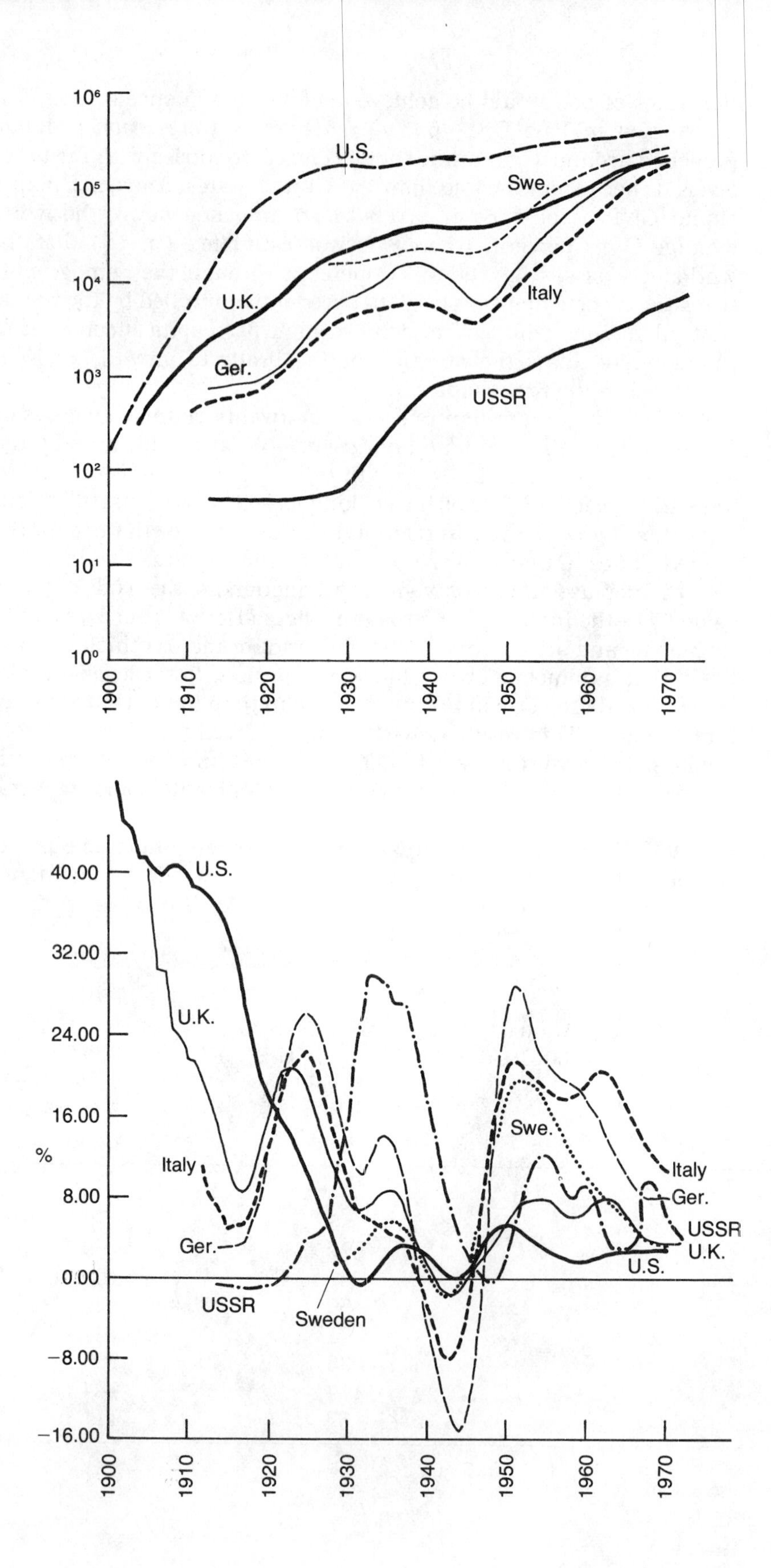
U.S.
Swe.
U.K.
Italy
Ger.
USSR
10⁶
10⁵
10⁴
10³
10²
10¹
10⁰
1900
1910
1920
1930
1940
1950
1960
1970
40.00
32.00
24.00
16.00
8.00
0.00
−8.00
−16.00
%
U.S.
U.K.
Italy
Ger.
USSR
Sweden
Swe.
Italy
Ger.
USSR
U.K.
U.S.
1900
1910
1920
1930
1940
1950
1960
1970

more or less free market phenomenon.[155]

As for other consumers' goods, since about 1950 the standard package was being quickly if not universally diffused in Western Europe and Japan; that is, television, electric refrigerators, vacuum cleaners, etc. In short, the leading industrial sectors of high mass-consumption were rapidly (but not uniformly) decelerating in the 1960's in the most advanced industrial nations; and the natural prospect was for their further deceleration in the 1970's even without the multiple blows struck at these sectors by the rise in energy prices and, for some countries, a decline in real income per capita. Under these circumstances, the phenomenon noted by an analyst of the German economy in 1976 is likely to be quite general throughout the advanced industrial world: "For most [durable] consumers goods there are now unmistakable *signs of saturation* (in housing, cars, and electrical household appliances). The growing volume of first-time purchases is now substituted by replacement orders which make for a stagnating and highly vulnerable market."[156]

The question then arises: were there other leading sectors emerging which compensated in the 1960's for this deceleration which we did not include in our sectoral charts? After all, the OECD world enjoyed one of its strongest surges of growth in the boom which peaked in 1973–1974. The answer is that the prosperity of the advanced industrial countries was also sustained by a rapid expansion of certain services in real terms; e.g., education, travel, and medical care. In the United States, for example, between fiscal year 1950 and fiscal year 1975 total health expenditures rose from 4.5 percent to 8.3 percent of GNP, with the federal share in those outlays increasing from 12 percent to 29 percent.[157] There was also a significant upgrading in the amount and quality of housing and, in some countries, an increased proportion of protein in the diet.

The service leading sectors were also struck hard by the price revolution of 1972–1977. Travel fell off in response to rising energy costs and the decline in real incomes caused by both unfavorable terms of trade and the recession. The increases in education and medical-care outlays in real terms, which may have been decelerating toward some natural limits, were further decelerated by the need for budget-

HART V-64. Top, *Automobile Registration per Million Population: ix Countries, 1900–1972 (Smoothed)*; Bottom, *Rates of Change in utomobile Registration per Million Population: Six Countries, 900–1972 (Smoothed)*

Sources: For all countries, excepting Sweden, 1900–1958, W. W. Rostow, *he Stages of Economic Growth*, pp. 168–171, where detailed sources are in-icated. Sweden from 1930 and all other countries, 1958–1975 (except the SSR), *Automobile Facts and Figures*, published annually by the Automobile Ianufacturers Association, Detroit (name changed to Motor Vehicle Manu-acturers Association in 1972). USSR, post-1957, from *World Motor Vehicle ata* (Detroit: Motor Vehicle Manufacturers Association, 1974), p. 113 (U.S. epartment of Commerce figures), and earlier editions.

ary restraint at a time of reduced real revenues (caused by recession), acute balance-of-payments pressure, and exacerbated inflation. Moreover, in an environment of stagnant or declining private real income, a strong political reaction set in throughout the OECD world against increased government outlays for welfare purposes.

The specific circumstances of 1974–1977 need not, of course, prevail over the next generation. A resumption of growth should in time take place; and new technologies may emerge to enlarge the consumers' range of choice. This will, almost certainly, be the case with respect to communications. Moreover, as argued in Part Six, there is no lack of tasks to be undertaken in the advanced industrial nations capable of employing the working force. The gradual waning of the growth rates in the automobile, durable consumers' goods, and certain key service sectors does not, in itself, decree a protracted phase of high unemployment, quite aside from the increased real resources (in the form of expanded exports) required to purchase OPEC oil. What is clear is that the return to regular full employment in the OECD world must be based on a somewhat different pattern of consumption and investment outlays than in the great quarter-century postwar boom. There were inklings of this transition even before the price revolution of 1972–1977 in the increased concern about air, water, and the environment in general—a concern that was already leading to a significant shift in the allocation of investment resources. Public policy had begun to reflect an awareness that the inputs to sustain a viable industrial civilization ought to be enlarged. Prosperity and growth could not be built indefinitely merely on the progressive expansion at high rates of conventional consumers' goods and services per capita. The price revolution of 1972–1977 and its causes dramatized the fact that, for a protracted period, the inputs required to sustain industrialized societies would have to be expanded; and this expansion would constitute not only the base for necessary structural adjustments in the world economy but also the foundation for a return to high levels of employment and resumed steady growth.

Part Six

The Future of the World Economy

49

Are There Limits to Growth?

The previous five parts of this book each ended by posing problems which shadow the prospects for future economic and social progress in important regions of the world economy or in its workings as a whole. Taken together, Chapters 4 and 9 raised the question of whether the populations scheduled to emerge in the next quarter-century and beyond can be fed. Chapter 5, taken in conjunction with the country analyses of Part Five, raised a second basic question: Do the resources exist which would permit the advanced societies, whose take-offs occurred from 1783 to the 1890's, to continue to grow while the late-comers to modern growth of the twentieth century go forward to fulfill their dreams of affluence? Chapter 18 brought these issues into short- and medium-term focus by viewing the price revolution of 1972–1977 as the initial explosive stage of the fifth Kondratieff upswing confronted in a world economy which has experienced four marked, if irregular, cycles since 1790 in the relative scarcity or abundance of foodstuffs and raw materials. Against this background, the concluding passages of Chapter 26 asked, in effect: Are we at the end of a thirty-year phase when the cyclical mechanism, familiar since 1783 at least, assumed the benign form of mild undulations in a high average rate of growth? Must we expect in the advanced industrial societies much higher average levels of unemployment and lower average rates of growth than we have known since 1945? Chapter 26 also questioned whether the citizens and institutions of advanced industrial societies are capable of the kind of equitable cooperation, for perceived common purposes, necessary to contain wage-push inflation, which stubbornly persisted in the recession of 1974–1975.

I have come at these issues by trying to tell the story of the world economy over the past two centuries in a particular way. Others have come to a somewhat similar view of man's agenda over the next few generations by a related but different route. Starting with the kinds of population and industrial growth rates experienced in the world economy over recent decades, they ask: For how long can such rates continue on a physically finite planet? In answering that question, there are pessimists and optimists. The best known pessimistic analysis is that of Dennis L. Meadows and his colleagues in *The Limits to Growth*, elaborating methods pioneered by Jay Forrester.[1] They came to an apocalyptic conclusion: "If the present growth trends in world population, industrialization, pollution, food production, and resource depletion continue unchanged, the limits to growth on this planet will be reached sometime within the next one hundred years. The most probable result will be a rather sudden and uncontrollable decline in both population and industrial capacity."[2] They arrived at this result by setting up a computerized model which sought to interrelate the key variables: population, food availability, industrial raw-materials requirements, and pollution. The model treated the world as a single economic unit and predicted the future by projecting forward past movements of the variables and assumed relations among them. The "World Model Standard Run" came out of the computer with a crisis in agriculture and industry early in the twenty-first century, population and pollution peaking later, due to inherent lags (Chart VI-1).

The Meadows team then ran its model on assumptions which differed from their measurement of, or hypotheses about, past relationships:

—If natural-resource reserves are doubled, the crisis, brought on by their estimates of pollution level, is merely delayed.

—If "unlimited resources" are assumed, due to break-throughs in renewable energy and recycling techniques for raw materials, again pollution brings the system down.

—If successful pollution control is added to "unlimited resources," limits on arable land and the increased diversion of investment to higher-cost agriculture set the limits to growth and yield a downturn—a result postponed but not avoided by population limitations brought about by an increase in the effectiveness of birth control.

—If average land yields, in the 1970's, are doubled, under the "unlimited-resources" and pollution-control assumptions, the system can expand to higher levels, but the scale of industrial production again brings on a pollution crisis during the next century.

—If radical improvements are simultaneously assumed in resource availabilities, pollution control, land yields, and birth control, a period of transient opulence results (at, say, U.S. 1970 income per capita levels), which gives way to decline when the scale of industrialization again depletes resources, generates excessive pollution, and forces a reduction in food production.

Out of these exercises *The Limits to Growth* analysts commend the earliest possible achievement of a stable equilibrium state in the world economy in which capital plant and population are maintained at constant levels, as are food and industrial production per capita, while pollution is contained at low and manageable levels. This requires both the acceptance by the more advantaged of radical income redistribution and the acceptance by all of a standard of living less dependent on industrial output. In short, they argue that the world

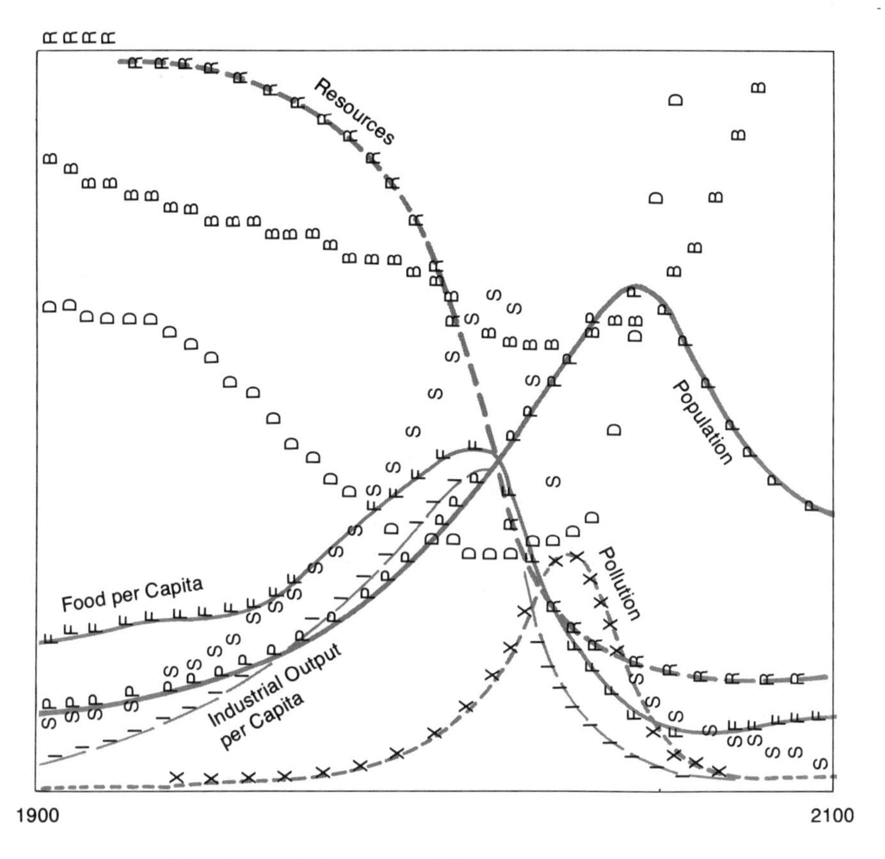

CHART VI-1. *World Model Standard Run, 1900–2100*

The "standard" world model run assumes no major change in the physical, economic, or social relationships that have historically governed the development of the world system. All variables plotted here follow historical values from 1900 to 1970. Food, industrial output, and population grow exponentially until the rapidly diminishing resource base forces a slowdown in industrial growth. Because of natural delays in the system, both population and pollution continue to increase for some time after the peak of industrialization. Population growth is finally halted by a rise in the death rate due to decreased food and medical services.
Source: Donella H. Meadows et al., *The Limits to Growth*, p. 124.

community should quickly abandon the concept of progress and the pursuit of affluence as they have come historically to be defined; radically alter the social values of modern life, as it has emerged; and make all the necessary adjustments required to achieve soon and maintain an egalitarian steady state on a global basis. As one reads these passages in *The Limits to Growth*, one cannot avoid a sense that the authors regard this outcome as good as well as necessary. Thus, there are some unstated value judgments embedded in the book.[3]

The Meadows study has been examined carefully and subjected to the acute criticism appropriate to so fundamental a theme.[4] In my view, *The Limits to Growth* has the virtue of posing and dramatizing effectively a real set of problems. Moreover, its emphasis on the interconnections among the problems of population, food, energy, raw materials, and pollution is salutary in a world where specialization is the reigning intellectual, professional, and bureaucratic mode. But it suffers from five serious weaknesses.

First, the calculations are global. In fact, of course, the world economy consists of national or closely interconnected regional units. Among the advanced noncommunist states there are the intimate ties among the Western European economies and between the United States and Canada, with Japan closely linked to North America, Australia, and the developing nations of Southeast Asia. By and large, it is not unrealistic to conceive of what might be called an OECD economy. China is virtually self-sufficient. The USSR and most of Eastern Europe are closely linked, with modest but expanding ties to the OECD world. The developing nations, however, are at quite different stages of growth, with limited ties to each other and generally close but widely varying relations to the OECD world. Among them, India is an economy so large, with its external links so limited, that its destiny must be considered in primarily national terms despite the critical marginal role of foreign trade and external assistance. There are, of course, forces operating more or less pervasively in the world economy; e.g., the price of grain and oil and, perhaps, certain types of pollution. But an analysis aggregated in global terms is highly abstract and its conclusions potentially misleading.[5] Acute limits-to-growth crises can occur—indeed, are occurring—in some parts of the world while others go forward. The nature of our current situation and tasks can be obscured by focusing on a relatively distant global crisis. Again, we must disaggregate if we are to understand and to make useful policy.

Second, the factual basis for the system model is exceedingly weak. Only the population equation is reasonably satisfactory, but it is subject to the kind of common ignorance suggested at the close of Chapter 4. The data on pollution, which plays a critical role in frustrating growth if other limits are expanded and population constrained, are fragmentary. From the incomplete evidence now available, the containment or even rollback of air and water pollution is an expensive but economically manageable task.

Third, the handling of technological and resource constraints is misleading. In *The Limits to Growth* exercises these constraints are usually relaxed by assuming once-over expansions in, say, acreage, productivity, or resource availabilities. In fact, productivity changes and the bringing in of additional resources or the creation of new resources are an incremental process whose limits we cannot predict. A once-over expansion in limits will merely postpone a crisis when confronted with a geometric increase in requirements. An incremental expansion of both resources and technology, of the kind to be observed over the past two centuries, need not yield a crisis.[6] This problem is compounded in *The Limits to Growth* by acceptance of one of the oldest propositions in economics, reaching back to *The Wealth of Nations*: the assumption of a high rate of technological progress in industry and of diminishing returns in agriculture and raw materials. Over the past century this assumption has not proved true, although increases in agricultural productivity may not continue automatically at their previous pace.[7] In certain of Meadows' computer runs the assumption of diminishing returns to agriculture and raw-materials acquisition helps cause the system's downturn by requiring more and more investment to maintain a given flow of food and mineral supplies, thus starving the flow of investment in other necessary directions.

Fourth, there is in this model no price system to increase incentives to invent or discover, to constrain consumption of scarce items, or to find substitutes. As Part Three makes clear, the relative price mechanism was, for two centuries and more, a powerful engine for setting in motion compensatory action in the face of resource constraints.

Finally, there is no evidence that the Meadows prescription is politically, socially, and psychologically viable. On the contrary, the thrust for affluence of less advantaged groups and nations is one of the most powerful forces operating on the world scene; and so is the determination of advantaged nations and social groups to sustain and even improve their material status. Thus far the tensions generated by these ambitions have been softened because the pie to be divided was expanding. It is one thing to quarrel about fair shares when all are gaining in real income: the struggle for fair shares is a more dour matter in the face of a static or low growth rate in income per capita. It is wholly possible, even certain, that, with the passage of time, man's perceptions of affluence will change. Almost two decades ago, in writing *The Stages of Economic Growth*, I raised the question of what would happen in the richer societies when "diminishing relative marginal utility sets in, on a mass basis, for real income itself."[8] The problem was much discussed in the 1960's. A margin of the most affluent young went into revolt against the values of material progress and the consequences of those values as they perceived them.[9] They sought nonmaterial objectives. But that is not a majority view. The fact is that we must count, among both the early- and late-comers to industrialization, on a protracted period of effort to continue to grow. Right or wrong, the odds are that the effort will be made; and serious policy-making should be based on that probability. As a black colleague of mine once said, the disadvantaged of this world are about to buy tickets for the show; they are quite unmoved by the affluent emerging from the theater and pronouncing the show bad; they are determined to find out for themselves.

Among the critics of *The Limits to Growth* is a spectrum of relative optimists about the prospects for the world economy over the next century. The optimists recognize the reality of present and prospective problems of population pressure, food and energy supply, as well as certain environmental dangers. They also recognize that at some time in the future not only population but income per capita will level off. But they hold that the technological performance over the past two centuries, present scientific capacity, and future prospects all justify faith that man can find or create the new resources, the methods of conservation and of pollution control to continue to go forward. No doubt with many vicissitudes and setbacks, they foresee the achievement of a plateau of more or less universal affluence, achieved at different times for different nations, as a possible and statistically more likely outcome of industrial civilization than either a great convulsive global crisis and decline or an early and purposeful adoption of a no-growth, income-redistribution strategy. The tone of the relative optimists is caught well in this Hudson Institute summary statement:

> While we accept the need for much reassessment and change, we are inclined largely to reject much of the current negativism, at least as it applies to the next century or so, and almost certainly for the next ten to twenty years. We feel that technological growth and economic progress will be able to make all reasonably rich, and that with advancements in technology itself, along with self-restraint, proper policies and designs, and the allocation of sufficient resources (mostly money), we will be able to cope with the various problems. Indeed, under today's political and economic conditions, more money and more technology seem essential in order to meet many of the most urgent and potentially most disastrous problems.[10]

The relative optimists, too, tend to have an ideological bias, captured in the following diary report by a Canadian diplomat of a dinner conversation in wartime London—a useful reminder that the tension between the quality of life as perceived by the comfortable and the values of mass material progress is not new:

> 7 September 1940.
>
> Dinner with R. B. McCallum, my former tutor at Oxford, at the National Liberal Club. . . . He began by saying that he had that day been motoring through the industrial suburbs off the Great West Road. "A cheering sight," he said. I suppose I may have winced at this description of that nondescript waste of dreary characterless little houses. "You," he went on, "and other lovers of the picturesque may lament the green fields and pretty villages which once stretched about London, but remember that those villages housed a desperately poor population of agricultural labourers. You may say that the factory workers' houses which now stand there are ugly and depressing, but remember that the fathers and grandfathers of these workers lived four or five in a room in some filthy slum where misery, dirt, gin and incest flourished. Now these people have attained respectability,

> the dearest craving of the working classes. That is a great achievement. You with your apocalyptic talk of the spiritual deadness of the babbitry ignore all this, but it is the triumph of our civilisation, and we are too slow to praise it. You talk to me of our failure to turn the Industrial Revolution to good account in human terms, but when war broke out we were busily engaged in doing just that, although I admit that the pace was slow and that there was still a great deal of slack to be taken up."[11]

Anyone who has examined carefully, for example, the quality of life as it has been transformed since 1945 in Western Europe for most citizens, must side with McCallum. This is so whether the measure is diet, housing, education, social security, or vacations on the Mediterranean rather than, say, Blackpool.

And, despite the intellectual fashion of pessimism about the fruits of the scientific revolution, there are some, at least, who hold with undiminished faith to the old optimism about the constructive and humane possibilities which will be opened up in the future by the further development of science:

> When one looks at the components of the optimistic prediction, one sees as their most important and common base a belief in the infinite power of reason, in the unlimited comprehensibility of the world. In our day, epistemological optimism has become not only a result but a condition of and a factor in the acceleration of scientific, technical, economic, and social progress . . . ; namely, the idea of infinite knowledge, of transformation, clarification, and particularization of valid concepts of the world. . . . The three basic developments—atomic energy, electronics, and cybernetics—have now reached their own, if one may put it this way, economic maturity.[12]

Meadows and his colleagues have reacted constructively to the debate stimulated by their elaboration of Forrester's method. In further studies, they have, notably, introduced the concept of continuous, incremental improvements in technology.[13] The time of possible crisis and collapse for industrial civilization is extended, thereby, down to the end of the next century. There are even rates of technological adaptation which can be assumed which postpone crisis indefinitely. There is also, in this later work, a tendency to shift the emphasis from inescapable physical limitations to growth toward the need for changes in social attitudes and policies.[14] This is, after all, what the demographic transition is all about as it relates to family size, as well as the notion that, at some point, diminishing relative marginal utility sets in for real income per capita. Moreover, Meadows has always acknowledged that the bases for predicting the scale of pollution and the costs of its containment are exceedingly weak; and, as we noted earlier, pollution levels are exceedingly important in some of *The Limits to Growth* computer runs. Clearly, the sharpness of the confrontation between the Meadows team and its critics has diminished.

In the end, this debate takes its place with four previous debates, each occurring during a Kondratieff upswing; that is, at times of pressure on food and/or raw-materials supplies and relatively high or rising prices for basic products. The first was triggered by Malthus' pessimism about the consequences of Britain's population increase and Ricardo's pessimism about the productivity prospects in agriculture.[15] Both views, generated by population-food tension during the French Revolutionary and Napoleonic Wars, were ultimately rooted in the concept of diminishing returns to investment in agriculture. The second debate centered on the future of Britain's coal supply, especially the most easily accessible seams: an issue raised with some force by W. S. Jevons in the 1860's. He projected forward the then-current rate of increase in consumption (3.5 percent); emerged with palpably impossible levels of British coal requirements; and, like Meadows, concluded "our motion must be reduced to rest."[16] A more general subject of debate at this time might have been the question of the population-food balance, in the wake of the Irish famine and Europe's problems of the early 1850's; but the potentialities of the American Middle West and the railroads were obvious. The third occasion for concern arose out of the relative rise of foodstuff and raw-materials prices in the pre-1914 generation and the consequently unfavorable shift in the British terms of trade. In 1912 Keynes, looking at relative export and import prices, re-evoked the classic specter: "There is now again a steady tendency for a given unit of manufactured product to purchase year by year a diminished quantity of raw product. The comparative advantage in trade is moving sharply against industrial countries."[17] D. H. Robertson, using A. L. Bowley's terms-of-trade calculations, strongly reinforced Keynes' anxiety: ". . . the normal tendency for the ratio of exchange to alter against the manufacturing and in favor of the agricultural communities was in force in the seventies, was suspended in the eighties and nineties, and is now once more on the whole triumphing. This is perhaps the most significant economic fact in the world today."[18] This was the anxious view of the position of the industrial nations which Keynes took to the Versailles Peace Conference and which strongly shaped Chapter 2 in his *Economic Consequences of the Peace* (1919). But just as the wheat price tumbled after the Napoleonic Wars and the coal price after 1873, so, as we saw in Chapter 15, the British terms of trade turned so favorably after 1920 as to impoverish export markets and contribute to Britain's chronic interwar unemployment. A fourth period of anxiety came after the Second World War when food and raw-materials prices continued to rise relatively. In the United States the apparent scarcity stimulated the massive report in 1952 by the President's Materials Policy Commission, chaired by William S. Paley. The commission was luckier than some of its predecessors in this field. Relative prices broke favorably for the industrial nations in 1951, and the commission's final report (*Resources for Freedom*, 1952) was written in the altered price setting. It took the temperate view that resources should be viewed in terms of the cost of acquisition rather than in terms of absolute depletion, and that the unfolding of technology was a powerful force in fending off classical diminishing returns. In its wake, a permanent institution to monitor the problem was created, Resources for the Future, Inc., which continues to do authoritative studies in this field.

It is worth noting that the debate about resource constraints was opened for the fifth time in the past two centuries before the publication of *The Limits to Growth* and before the price revolution of 1972–1977. In October 1970 the U.S. Congress passed the National Materials Policy Act. Its primary underlying concern at the time was not pressure on supplies of food, energy, or raw materials, but the pressure of the American economy on the environment: "It is the purpose of this title to enhance environmental quality by developing a national materials policy to utilize present resources and technology more efficiently, to anticipate the future materials requirements of the Nation and the world, and to make recommendations on the supply, use, recovery, and disposal of materials." A National Commission on Materials Policy was created in the wake of this legislation. It reported shortly before the explosive rise in the oil price (June 1973). The title of its report reflects its focus: "Material Needs and the Environment." This perspective began to suffuse public and intellectual life in the OECD world during the 1960's and early 1970's. And, of course, clean air and water, as well as land preserved for recreation and against corrosive use, are as real resources as food, energy, and raw materials, and, in fact, more finite.

There is, then, nothing new about anxieties stimulated by the projection of geometric increases in demand against absolutely limited or arithmetically expanding supplies, shadowed by diminishing returns. In each case, prior to the 1970's, they were belied by the coming in of new supplies or the development of new technologies. That fact is no cause for complacency now. But the undulating sequence of scarcity and oversupply traced out in Part Three does raise the question of how useful long-run projections of current situations and trends really are.

I believe they are of some use. After all, most public policy is made in response to immediate pressures on the political process. It is rare for governments to act with even a five- or ten-year horizon in view, except with respect to weapons systems. For just this reason, the attempt to predict or even to speculate systematically about the world fifty or seventy-five years from now is not an empty intellectual exercise. It may force governments to think and act now with a longer time perspective in view. This is necessary because there are significant lags at work in some of the critical problems faced in the world economy. The lag between the achievement of a net reproduction rate of one and a constant population is long, given population age structures inherited from the past. The lag is also long in creating and diffusing new technologies in energy, agriculture, and other fields that may urgently be required by the end of this century. Above all, attitudes must change and suffuse the net judgments of the majority before measures even the optimists regard as necessary (e.g., resource conservation) can be effectively carried out in democratic societies; and here the lag can be long, indeed. There is another, more human reason for taking the middle of the next century seriously. It is not all that far away: children now born in the advanced parts of the world have a good statistical chance of living until 2050. When we talk of what may transpire between now and then, we are talking about what will or will not be achieved in the span of a single lifetime; in short, the world our children and grandchildren will experience. We owe them a bit of farsightedness.

There are, then, good reasons to look ahead a half-century and more, to identify palpably dangerous problems, and to begin to act now to mitigate or solve them.

But diminishing returns set in rather early in the refinement of long-range projections. No matter how much the data base and the equations of interaction are improved by mobilizing additional historical or contemporary evidence, errors compound as the computer hums into the future. The potentialities for a crisis in the industrial civilization built since the eighteenth century are clear enough: the challenges of feeding the populations scheduled to be born, of providing the energy and raw materials for the industrial structures scheduled to emerge are real; the tasks of maintaining a viable environment of air and water will certainly be expensive and can be ignored only at considerable risk; and, in confronting these challenges, it is evident that significant changes in policy and ways of doing things will be required both within national societies and among them. Long-run projections, pessimistic and optimistic, have helped create an intellectual consensus that such tasks must be faced if industrial civilization is to survive. And that has been an important contribution. In both science and public policy the correct identification of the problem is a considerable part of its solution.

Having said all that, the critical question still remains: How do we get from here to there? What must we begin doing now to maximize the chance that these challenges can be overcome and the optimists' vision of the twenty-first century come to pass?

The next quarter-century will prove critical in answering these questions. By the year 2000, if we are wise and lucky, we will have achieved the following:

—Gross birth rates in the developing world will have been brought down from their present explosive level, at or close to 40 per thousand, to 20 or less.

—The level and productivity of agriculture, notably in the developing regions, will have increased enough so that the expanded populations can be decently fed and gross Malthusian crises avoided in the most vulnerable parts of the world.

—The scientific and technical problems involved in creating a new energy source, based on renewable or essentially infinite sources, will have been solved.

—Air and water pollution will be under control.

—Expanded production, substitution, economy, and recycling will provide, at reasonable costs, sufficient raw materials to permit industrialization to continue to proceed.

—In order to accomplish the above results, patterns of investment will have been restructured, including the scale and directions of research and development, and new technologies generated in agriculture and raw materials (as well as energy), which will permit growth to proceed in the next century.

—High and steady rates of growth will have been reconciled with price stability.

—The developing nations, taken as a whole, will have about doubled their present income per capita and acquired another quarter-century's experience of modernization, as well as competence in a much widened range of technologies. They will be much more capable of adjusting to changing circumstance and solving their problems in the century beyond.

There is, of course, no guarantee that humanity will prove wise and lucky. As nearly as we can perceive through the mists of the future, with imperfect data and imperfect understanding, the hardest part of the transition before us is that on which we are now embarked. It is in the next quarter-century that we shall make or fail to make major changes in technology, public policy, and attitudes of mind that will significantly determine the character of the century beyond.

I turn now to some major implications of this proposition. I shall first try to answer the question: Is a favorable outcome technically feasible? Second: If solutions are technically feasible, what is the character and order of magnitude of the economic problems they pose? I shall conclude by probing at what I judge to be the ultimate question: What are the changes in public policy and in social and psychological attitudes required for a favorable outcome?

The objective here is not to present detailed policy recommendations. It is to develop, from the historical perspective this book aims to provide, a framework for policy.

50

Population and Food

Like all the other problems on the international agenda, population and food are closely interrelated. At one extreme, there is the possibility that unmanageable food shortages will produce starvation and other increases in deaths on a scale sufficient to decimate population in certain vulnerable regions. Putting Malthusian catastrophes aside, there are more subtle links between the rate of population increase and the availability of food supplies. Desired family size, for example, is partially related to expected rates of survival among infants and young children. These rates, in turn, are sensitive to the scale and nutritional value of food supplies over periods of time sufficiently long to affect the expectations of parents. Improved food supplies take their place, therefore, with education, health services, and other forms of economic and social improvement which help create a setting in which parents choose to have fewer children.

As for population, the conventional arithmetic yields figures of about 6.5 billion for the year 2000. This assumes the average annual rate of increase will fall only slightly below 2 percent in the next quarter-century. Chart VI-2 exhibits the sensitivity of estimates for the year 2000 to various assumed rates of growth over the intervening period. The lags between a reduction in family size and the rate of population increase are, as noted earlier, significant. The sensi-

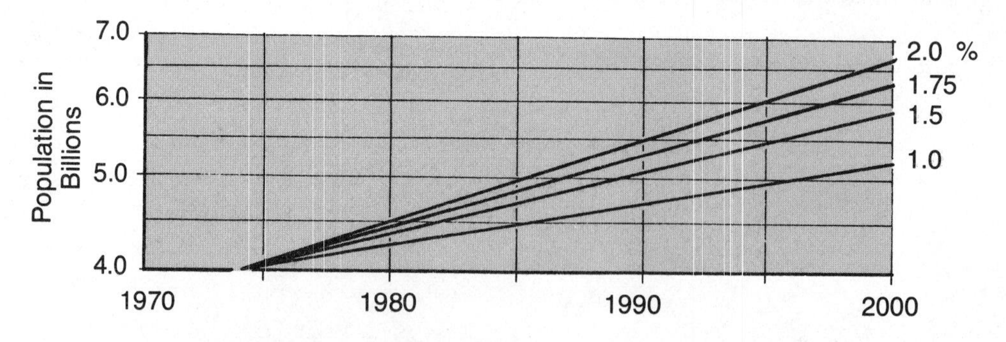

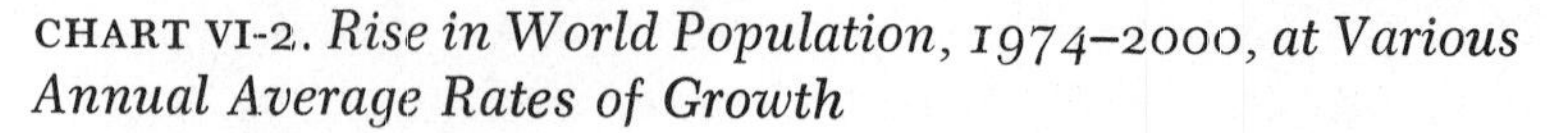

CHART VI-2. *Rise in World Population, 1974–2000, at Various Annual Average Rates of Growth*

tivity of the population problem in the twenty-first century to what transpires in the next quarter-century can be suggested by carrying forward the data in Chart VI-2. In that chart alternative assumptions about the rate of population increase over the next quarter-century yield a spread of estimates for the year 2000 from 5.2 billion, associated with an annual average rate of 1.0 percent, to 6.7 billion, associated with 2.0 percent. If those rates are extended for an additional half-century, world population in 2050 would be, at the lower margin (growth rate 1.0 percent) 8.5 billion, at the upper margin (growth rate 2.0 percent) 18.0 billion. A population range of 1.3 to 1 becomes, with the passage of an additional half-century, 2.1 to 1.

Two operational conclusions emerge from this kind of play with global numbers. So far as the ultimate problem of population is concerned, looking beyond the year 2000, a great deal hinges on the pace at which birth rates are reduced in the next quarter-century. So far as agriculture is concerned, there is a virtually inescapable task of feeding a population rising to about 6.5 billion. Eighty percent of that population (say, 5.2 billion) will live in the presently less developed regions of the world—Asia (*ex* Japan), Africa, and Latin America. About 90 percent of the population increase is likely to be in these regions, which, as of 1975, contained about 2.7 billion human beings. The central task in agriculture is, therefore, to expand production in the developing countries sufficiently to feed all these people at levels appropriate to the higher per capita incomes they are then likely to command.

As for birth rates, there is no reputable method for predicting how fast they will, in fact, be reduced in the developing regions over the next quarter-century. If the typical correlations of the 1960's between income per capita and birth rates hold for the next quarter-century, only a mild mitigation in the rate of population increase can be expected in the developing world between 1975 and 2000, even if real income per capita resumes its movement forward at an annual average rate of 2.5 percent. Put another way, it will take a remarkable change from the pattern of the 1960's in government policies and human attitudes toward family size to reduce greatly the rate of population increase in the developing world between now and the year 2000. But it is a cheering fact that, at some point in the mid-1970's, the global rate of population increase reached its historic peak and began slowly to subside.

Looking beyond the year 2000, and assuming substantial and steady increases in real income per capita (with accompanying increases in urbanization, education, food consumption, and social services), the prospects improve; that is, round about $400 (U.S., 1964) the presently developing regions will be coming into levels of real income per capita where the decline in the birth rate normally accelerates and the decline in the death rate decelerates. By very rough calculation, half the population of what we call the developing world could attain this level (or better) round about the year 2000, the balance about a third of a century later, if per capita annual increases of the kind achieved in the 1960's can be recovered and sustained.[19] Stripped of inflammatory rhetoric, what the spokesmen for developing nations generally argue at international population meetings is for the rich to act to accelerate the rise in income per capita of the poor in order to bring down birth rates. The spokesmen for the rich tend to argue for government policies in the developing world which would break the average statistical linkage of birth rates and real income per capita—as, say, in Taiwan and South Korea.

What about these "miracles"? What are the chances of bringing birth rates down more rapidly than death rates before average real income per capita reaches something like the $400 (U.S., 1964) per capita mark? The fact is that population experts do not yet know how to convert the "miracle" case into the "normal" case. I would hazard two observations. First, aside from a background of expected rising real income per capita, successful programs not only are backed with political conviction and resources, but also are multidimensional. They strike at an interacting complex problem at many points, setting in motion a self-reinforcing process. In this connection, the fifteen-point checklist quoted in Part One, note 25, Table N-3 (applied to China), and the elements delineated in the South Korean case (pp. 31–34) appear relevant. There is, in short, no one route to an accelerated decline in birth rates. One must seek simultaneously to move every accessible variable relevant to the choice of family size in the same direction. Second, there is scope for a major contribution from the more advanced nations. It is now conventional to stress the importance of creating in the developing world an improved social environment as an inducement to limit family size. I would not quarrel with this prescription if the diversion of resources from other aspects of modernization is not excessive; for, historically, the great additions to welfare flows have been the product of high rates of growth in income per capita and consequently enlarged public revenues. But there is still a need for birth control devices that are cheap, efficient, longer-lasting, and psychologically easier to accept. A totalitarian state can use its political and social powers to induce a later average age for marriage. But, if human beings are fortunate, few governments will command such controls over individual choice. And it is apparent, from the vicissitudes of India and others, that imperfections in birth control technology have played a significant part in frustrating family planning programs. Here is a task which deserves exceedingly high priority on the research and development agenda of the scientific world.

As for agricultural production, the bulk of the increase to match the rise in population must evidently come from an expansion of production in the developing world. The first question is, therefore: Is an expansion on this scale technically and economically feasible?

Agricultural experts, like others, have areas of disagreement; but they do agree that expansion on the requisite scale is technically possible.[20] The basic reasons for this optimistic view are implicit in Table VI-1. Between 1960–1962 and 1969–1971 the developing countries demonstrated that they could sustain a 3.5 percent annual growth rate in grain production at a time when population was increasing at 2.6 percent. But effective demand increased at a slightly higher rate than grain production: 3.7 percent. Therefore, dependence of the developing regions on imports increased. Nevertheless, the first source of optimism is the actual performance of the 1960's. It was not quite sufficient to match the increase in demand, and a substantial proportion of the populations in the developing world suffered from chronic malnutrition, probably more than 20 percent. But performance in the 1960's came close enough to what was required to indicate that, with increased effort and priority, the overall objective of grain self-sufficiency is not grossly unrealistic.

The question then arises as to whether arable land is sufficient. The consensus appears to be that at least twice as much land is physically available for crop production as is presently used. Table VI-1 indicates that acreage expansion in the developing countries in the 1960's was 1.4 percent annually. If that rate persisted, arable acreage would be available for another half-century. But the performance of the developed countries indicates that, as agriculture evolves in a setting of progressive modernization, dependence on land diminishes. The area under grain in developed countries declined slightly in the 1960's. Increases in yield carried the full burden of expansion and more. One can expect that kind of transformation in the developing countries with the passage of time; that is, yield-raising techniques will increasingly be the basis for the expansion of output except in developing regions where large amounts of good arable land are still available, notably, parts of Latin America and Africa.

Yield-raising techniques include irrigation, the use of new seeds, increased application of fertilizers and pesticides. Of these, fertilizers are a key component. In the developing countries, chemical fertilizer consumption in the 1960's increased at an extraordinary annual average rate of over 13 percent, slowing somewhat in the latter part of the decade. The increase in cereal yields between 1961 and 1972 was from 2.1 to 3.1 metric tons per hectare; in the developing countries, from 1.1 to 1.3. These figures indicate that the upper limit in agricultural productivity is still rising and there is, even with existing technologies, an enormous margin of yield increase possible in the developing world.

In short, rough calculations of the technical potentialities indicate that the great population increase in the developing world over the next quarter-century can be matched or substantially exceeded by increases in food production.

TABLE VI-1. *Growth Rates in Factors Affecting Grain Production and Consumption, 1960–1962 to 1969–1971*

Country	Area	Yield	Production	Consumption	Population	Income[a]
Compound rate of growth, 1960–1962 to 1969–1971						
Developed countries	−0.1	2.8	2.7	2.5	1.1	4.4
United States	−1.0	3.4	2.4	2.1	1.3	3.9
Canada	0.0	3.3	3.3	2.9	1.8	4.0
EC	0.7	2.5	3.2	2.2	0.7	3.7
EC 6	−0.2	3.3	3.2	2.2	0.8	4.2
EC 3	2.1	1.3	3.4	2.1	0.5	2.6
Other West Europe	0.2	3.5	3.8	3.5	0.9	5.1
South Africa	3.2	1.1	4.2	4.5	3.0	5.7
Japan	3.5	1.3	−2.2	3.3	1.1	9.8
Australia and New Zealand	3.6	0.2	3.7	3.9	2.0	4.2
Centrally planned countries	0.0	3.0	3.0	3.4	1.4	5.2
East Europe	−0.6	3.7	3.0	2.9	0.6	4.5
USSR	−0.1	3.4	3.3	4.3	1.3	6.5
China (PRC)	0.5	2.2	2.7	2.6	1.8	2.7
Developing countries	1.4	1.9	3.5	3.7	2.6	4.6
East Asia	1.6	3.1	4.8	5.6	2.4	4.3
Indonesia	1.3	2.0	3.6	3.7	2.5	2.0
Southeast Asia	1.3	2.2	3.6	5.0	2.6	3.9
South Asia	1.3	2.2	3.2	3.1	2.6	3.4
India	1.0	2.0	3.0	3.4	2.6	3.3
North Africa/Middle East	0.6	2.4	3.1	3.9	2.7	6.2
Central Africa	3.5	−0.5	3.0	4.4	2.4	2.9
East Africa	5.0	+0.5	5.6	5.7	2.5	4.1
Mexico/Central America	2.7	3.0	5.7	5.6	3.3	6.5
Venezuela	4.9	0.6	5.5	7.8	3.0	5.4
Brazil	5.0	0.0	5.0	4.3	2.9	7.0
Argentina	2.6	1.7	4.4	3.2	1.5	4.1
Other South America	0.2	1.8	2.1	3.2	2.8	3.8
World	0.4	2.6	3.1	3.3	2.0	4.6

[a] Private consumption expenditures calculated for 1960–1970 in constant 1970 dollars.

Source: *The World Food Situation and Prospects to 1985*, p. 18, from U.S. Department of Agriculture, Foreign Agricultural Service and Economic Research Service for area, yield, production, and consumption data; United Nations for population and income data.

The task looks somewhat more difficult if one examines some of the technical and economic problems more closely, and if one disaggregates from the developing countries as a whole to key regions and countries.

Particular technological break-throughs in agriculture follow a path similar to that of the leading industrial sectors examined in Parts Three and Five. New technologies do not go on indefinitely yielding constant rates of increase in productivity. They decelerate. If the average rate of yield increase in potential agricultural output is to be sustained at the level of the period since about 1950, an endless creative effort in research and development will be required. That effort may now be inadequate. This was the central message of the cautionary 1975 report of the National Academy of Sciences.[21]

The need for an adequate flow of economically efficient new techniques and the rapid diffusion of unapplied existing techniques has been significantly complicated in two ways since 1973 by the relative rise in energy prices: the relative prices of fertilizers and pesticides have thereby risen; and balance-of-payments limitations constrict the level of fertilizer imports. Moreover, the sequence of events in the 1960's led to a shortage of fertilizer capacity, now being made good; but predictions of reduced effective farmers' demands and, therefore, possible future fertilizer surpluses, could cut back the level of investment in fertilizer capacity in the second half of the 1970's. Somewhat conflicting estimates of fertilizer supply in the decade ahead have been developed by the World Bank and the U.S. Department of Agriculture.[22] But both assume no significant increase in the rate of growth of effective fertilizer demand over that which prevailed in the latter part of the 1960's when there was a slowdown. Clearly, the problem of increasing fertilizer production, notably in developing countries, and of finding ways to finance its application at a much higher rate than in the late 1960's is central to whether the technical possibilities open to the developing nations in agriculture will, in fact, be exploited.

Then, it is necessary to disaggregate. In a useful breakdown, the authors of *The World Food Situation and Prospects to 1985* distinguish five categories among the developing nations:

—Those where the Green Revolution is under way but where economic and other problems limit the rate of diffusion (e.g., India, Indonesia, Pakistan, the Philippines, etc.).

—Those which have been slow to make the most of potentialities which would be relatively easy to exploit (e.g., a good many Latin American countries).

—Countries with serious economic or technical production constraints which will require a major purposeful international effort to exploit potentialities (e.g., Bangladesh and the Sahelian countries in Africa).

—Countries which have traditionally produced food surpluses but which are not now fully exploiting their potential (e.g., Kenya, Rhodesia, Thailand, Burma, Mexico, Brazil).

—Deficit countries that can afford to purchase food imports (e.g., South Korea, Taiwan, the OPEC countries, etc.).

In the most constructive of the generally contentious and sterile international gatherings of 1974, the governments reached a significant degree of consensus at the World Food Conference held in Rome on 5–16 November. The central agreement was that food production in the developing countries would have to increase rapidly "within the wider framework of development." Responsibilities for the developed nations were also outlined: to maintain reserves, generate new technologies, provide capital as well as technological assistance, and conduct supportive trade policies. But it is only a little less true of agricultural than of population policy that the critical tasks lie within the developing nations themselves.

The elevation of priority for agricultural production poses serious political, even ideological, problems. In Mexico, for example, it raises the searching issue of how to transform the *ejidos* into efficient production units. Here are institutions deeply embedded in the political and social life of the country, hallowed by their link to the Mexican Revolution. In the short run, it is easier for politicians to accept the cost of low-productivity agriculture than to confront and solve the difficulties of their transformation. Something of the same is true of agricultural institutions in the USSR and some Eastern European countries which provide inadequate incentives for high productivity; and, of course, in India and elsewhere there are forms of land tenure in parts of the country which inhibit the full exploitation of the potentialities for increased agricultural production. Whether or not the developing nations in fact produce the increases in output required to avoid Malthusian disasters in the next quarter-century will depend, in my view, at least as much on the political courage of governments as on the technical or economic problems involved. But the developing nations are not alone in facing technical and economic issues where political courage—the will to act in new ways—will be decisive to the outcome.

The generation of political courage at home, however, can be rendered substantially easier if domestic decisions are taken against a background of effective international cooperation. Therefore, a great deal hinges on whether or not, how well and how soon, the November 1974 resolutions from Rome are translated into a working agricultural system. Will the bottlenecks in fertilizer production and in the financing of its distribution at an appropriate rate be broken? Will the pace of research and development be so maintained as to sustain the rate of increase in yield potentials experienced over the past generation? Will the regional economic organizations in Latin America, Africa, and Asia generate effective pressure on their members to raise the priority of agriculture and to encourage the exploitation of potentialities which palpably exist within most developing nations?

A transformation in the perception of the development process is also needed. The insistence of the developing nations on inserting at Rome the phrase "within the wider framework of development" has a long history. It stems from the economic, almost ideological, view that development is primarily a matter of industry and the transfer of labor from agriculture to industry. A neocolonial taint still, to a degree, suffuses agriculture in the developing world. The most underdeveloped ministry in developing countries is usually the agriculture ministry. Agricultural technicians are expensively trained, often abroad, but find their way to offices in the capital cities. They rarely see a farm.

All this is understandable; but almost all of it is based on inadequate development theory. It is true that, in any given year, investment allocations to agriculture compete with allocations to industry, physical infrastructure, education, etc. But dynamically, over time, the modernization of agriculture wholly converges with the building of a modern industrial society. That is the lesson of the economic history of North America and Australia, Western Europe and Japan. It has become increasingly apparent to the rulers of the communist states of Eastern Europe and in the USSR, although they have confronted certain painful political dilemmas in acting effectively on this perception. A modernized agriculture is necessary to feed the cities, provide raw materials to industry, provide a mass market to industry, earn (or conserve) foreign exchange, raise the level of nutrition and the physical and intellectual quality of the working force, create a setting where a decline in birth rates is more easily induced, and, as agricultural productivity increases, provide a flow of workers for urban pursuits. An acceptance of this lesson of convergence, palpable from history and the contemporary scene, could increase significantly the chance that the population-food challenge of the next quarter-century will be surmounted.

Looking beyond the year 2000, it is difficult to calculate the extent to which an expansion of acreage and the further diffusion of existing technologies will be able to provide sufficient food to support the levels world population may attain. The problem is complicated because the possibilities of acreage expansion vary; Latin America and Africa command, for example, greater potential arable acreage than, say, South Asia. Therefore, the pursuit of new technologies in food production is more urgent than a global perspective would suggest.

Some of the fruitful directions for such research and development are already clear.[23] For example, the earth's atmosphere is rich in nitrogen; but only a few species of plants have the capacity to fix and use that source. Research to extend that capacity is under way and could, evidently, be of immense value, notably in a world where nitrogen fertilizer has become relatively expensive. Similarly, promising work is going forward on the crossing of widely different grains; e.g., wheat and rye (tricale). One list of further agricultural frontier possibilities includes:

> . . . new strategies for pest control . . . increasing the photosynthetic efficiency and inhibiting photorespiration of plants genetically, physically, and chemically; water and fertilizer management (trickle irrigation, foliar application, and timely placement of nutrients); improved grain quality (especially amino acid balances in foodgrains); protected cultivation; carbon dioxide enrichment; multiple and intensive relay cropping (which has especially great potential for the tropics and for developing countries); plant growth regulants; treatments of plant substances, such as cotton seed meal, for human consumption; use of nonprotein nitrogen in ruminant rations; use of crop residues, animal wastes, and other methods for optimal utilization of crop acreages for livestock feeding; livestock crossbreeding; and increased fertility and disease control in livestock.[24]

In short, like the expansion of agricultural production since 1950, the creation and sustaining of an adequate agricultural base may require for some nations soon and for all beyond the year 2000 the generation and application of new technologies. The prospects seem reasonably promising; but evidently the world as a whole will have to change the perspective which led the United States National Science Board of the National Science Foundation to omit agriculture in 1973 from its list of problems warranting greater research and development efforts. It is comforting to know that in the United States, at least, the scale, in real terms, and the proportion of federal research and development resources allocated to agriculture were substantially increased between 1973 and 1977.

51

Energy

Dr. Samuel Johnson once observed: "Depend upon it, Sir, when a man knows he is to be hanged in a fortnight, it concentrates his mind wonderfully." The quadrupling of international oil prices in 1973 certainly had the effect of concentrating the minds of public servants, energy experts, and economists. The result is a mountainous literature of analysis and prescription. The amount of purposeful action that was taken by governments to deal with the energy crisis, while not negligible, was on a much lesser scale; for the actual hanging proved a bit less imminent than some at first thought. In the United States, the Congress failed to act effectively on proposals presented by Presidents Nixon and Ford in the period 1974–1976. As this book goes to press, the Congress is seized of President Carter's proposals of 20 April 1977. The continued availability of OPEC oil, even at high prices, permitted a time for analysis and debate, while governments felt their way toward new dispositions, in an awkward environment of stagflation, foreign-exchange constraint, and understandable public resistance to changing patterns of behavior built up in a protracted period of relatively cheap energy. Meanwhile, the relative rise in the price of energy gave governments an opportunity to observe the extent to which the price system, to the degree it was permitted to operate, would bring about restraints on consumption, measures to increase economy in use, and measures to expand production.

As considered toward the close of Chapter 17, the energy crisis of 1973–1977 was not the result of an immediate global shortage of energy supplies. There was no true equivalent to the wiping out of world grain reserves due to the bad harvests of 1972. The crisis arose, essentially, from a convergence of four factors:

—a high global rate of increase of energy consumption in the 1960's (about 5 percent per annum);

—an arbitrary price structure for petroleum (and, in the United States, natural gas) which led to increased reliance on these attractive sources of energy as opposed to coal and atomic energy;

—the peaking out of United States gas and petroleum production in 1970–1971 (against a background of waning reserves), and increased United States dependence on oil imports, all of which dramatized the market leverage available to the OPEC nations;

—and OPEC's successful exploitation of the opportunity thus presented both to quadruple oil prices, and, for the Arab members, to apply an oil embargo for strategic purposes in the context of the Arab-Israeli war of 1973. It is fair to add that OPEC's initiative was also colored by a growing awareness that its members' oil reserves were, in different degree, limited, and that the time available for their exploitation was inherently transient.

OPEC's actions set in motion a review by many groups of the demand-and-supply energy position: past and current, medium-term, and long-term. Such reviews have been conducted from national, regional, and global perspectives and accompanied by recommendations for virtually every dimension of national and international economic policy.[25]

To begin, it may be useful to pose a question embedded in those reviews and often left implicit. The question is: Why should the oil importers reduce their reliance on OPEC oil and avoid "excessive" OPEC imports? The problem of "excessive" dependence on OPEC oil is complex. It arises, in the first instance, from the possibility of another oil embargo like that of late 1973 or of a Middle East conflict on a scale and of a character such as to reduce access to the region's petroleum. Since Japan and Western Europe as a whole have more limited possibilities than the United States for expanding energy production, a good deal of the responsibility for reducing the collective dependence of the OECD world on OPEC imports comes to rest on the United States as, for example, Table VI-8 suggests. The responsibility of the United States in this respect is heightened by its military responsibilities as the major nuclear-weapons power of the OECD world, whose diplomatic and military freedom of action is essential to maintain the security of Western Europe, Japan, and Oceania. There are, of course, cooperative as well as simply American actions that can contribute to this end. The collective build-up of oil stockpiles and the kind of collective agreements which now exist for sharing energy shortages at a time of crisis are significant insurance measures and, perhaps, deterrents to another oil embargo.

There is a second sense in which dependence on OPEC oil could be judged "excessive"; that is, if the scale and cost of oil imports so burden the OECD balance-of-payments position as to cause chronic unemployment and international financial chaos. Here, again, collective action has mitigated and can mitigate the dangers, notably under circumstances of a rapid expansion in OPEC imports from OECD countries. Insight into this range of problems was obscured by the impact of recession and good weather in 1974–1975, which damped the level of imports from OPEC. It was difficult to separate these factors from longer-run economies in oil imports. The limited but still substantial revival of the world economy in 1975–1977, plus a cold winter in 1976–1977, brought about a resumed sharp expansion in imports from OPEC. If OECD growth resumes at rapid rates and longer-run measures to enlarge non-OPEC energy production and to economize energy use are not taken, "excessive dependence" in strictly economic as opposed to strategic terms might emerge.

A third meaning of "excessive dependence" might arise from the long-run prospects for world oil and gas reserves. If the judgment is correct that these reserves will begin to run down in a decade or so, current reliance on OPEC oil could be "excessive" if sufficient time were not allowed to generate additional energy resources from coal, shale, atomic power, solar energy, etc. As of the late spring of 1977 that is the central concern of many energy experts.

Finally, and most urgent, reliance on OPEC oil could be judged "excessive" if OECD energy production and conservation policy failed to generate the bargaining position necessary to achieve a stable and mutually satisfactory agreement between oil producers and consumers.

Against this background, there are, in effect, three energy questions to pose and seek to answer in the special context of this chapter:

—Looking ahead, to the year 2000 and beyond, are there energy resources in sight or likely, capable of supporting for the long pull a fully industrialized and affluent global population at the level the latter may well attain? Evidently this question may come to rest on finding some renewable or virtually infinite source of energy and vindicating the "unlimited" energy assumption in certain of Meadows' computer runs.

—Over the next quarter-century, are there energy resources and methods of economy and conservation in sight to support the continued expansion of the world economy at, roughly, the rates attained in the 1960's, without a reliance on OPEC oil that is in some meaningful sense excessive? Technically, for the OECD nations the answer here lies primarily in the potentialities of expanded production of non-OPEC oil and gas and on the effective utilization of coal resources and atomic power, as well as on new measures of economy and efficiency in power use. For the hardest-hit developing nations, the answer appears to lie in such production and economy measures, where they are available, plus international actions which would mitigate balance-of-payments pressures arising from high oil prices.

—Finally, can the oil importers generate promptly sufficient bargaining position to achieve a stable and reasonable agreement with OPEC? The problem here is that, for the present and immediate future (say, 1977–1985), lags in both policy-making and investment processes decree continued heavy reliance on OPEC oil combined with methods of restraint and conservation that can quickly be applied. But persuasive movement in the directions outlined above for the medium term would maximize the chance that the oil-producing and major importing states will come together around policies which reconcile their respective interests and recognize their common responsibilities to the least affluent.

As in the case of population and food production, there are, then, long lags at work here. They stem from the inherently time-consuming processes of science, invention, innovation, and diffusion. They are heightened because it is only since 1974 that creative minds have turned, on a large scale, to the array of new problems thrown up by the various dimensions of the energy crisis. The decisions made or not made in the mid-1970's will, therefore, strongly affect the options open from, say, the year 2000, as well, of course, as those available in the 1980's. We know already that the delay in formulating a national energy policy in the United States between 1974 and 1977 will prove costly to the United States and other nations in the constrained oil supply environment almost universally predicted for the 1980's. The cost of further delay is likely to increase.

First, then, the crude order of magnitude of energy requirements over the longer future. Tables VI-2 and VI-3 offer a lucid view of the path and distribution of energy consumption in recent decades. The pre-1973 world economy was increasing energy consumption at about 5.6 percent per annum, over 3.6 percent per capita. For the United States, the figures were 4.2 percent and 2.9 percent, respectively. The proportionate U.S. share was, therefore, declining, as Western Europe and Japan moved into high mass-consumption and a rapid expansion of industry proceeded there and elsewhere in the world. In the 1960's there was a reasonably close, but by no means rigid, connection between rates of increase in energy consumption and increase in real income.[26] If we assume continued rapid economic growth and a stable relationship between energy consumption and real income, global energy requirements for the year 2000 could be 4.25 times the 1972 level; for the year 2050, 56 times. These are, evidently, formidable figures. Three factors provide comfort to some analysts: the lower apparent rates of growth in energy consumption per capita in earlier times before the coming of the automobile, durable consumers' goods, and the ubiquitous use of electricity;[27] the decelerating trend of consumption per capita in the United States; and possibilities of increased economy and efficiency in energy use, which might alter past relationships between GNP per capita and per capita energy consumption. President Carter's target, for example, is to bring the annual rate of U.S. energy consumption under 2 percent, from the 3 percent which would otherwise prevail. The latter figure already reflects a deceleration brought about by circumstances since the rise of the OPEC oil price in 1973. But, if the optimists' vision of the future is broadly vindicated, global energy consumption must mightily increase; that is, if one assumes that the

TABLE VI-2. *World Energy Consumption and Population, Selected Years, 1925–1972*

	Total Energy Consumption (10^{12} BTU)	Population (Millions)	Energy Consumption per Capita (10^6 BTU)
1925	44,249	1,890.1	23.4
1950	76,823	2,504.5	30.7
1955	99,658	2,725.6	36.6
1960	124,046	2,989.9	41.5
1965	160,722	3,281.2	49.0
1968	189,737	3,484.5	54.5
1970	214,496	3,608.6	59.4
1971	223,522	3,678.3	60.8
1972	237,166	3,747.2	63.3
	Average annual percentage rates of change		
1925–1950	2.2	1.1	1.1
1950–1955	5.3	1.7	3.6
1955–1960	4.5	1.9	2.5
1960–1965	5.3	1.9	3.4
1965–1970	5.9	1.9	3.9
1970–1972	5.2	1.9	3.2
1950–1960	4.9	1.8	3.1
1960–1970	5.6	1.9	3.6
1960–1972	5.5	1.9	3.5
1950–1970	5.3	1.8	3.4
1950–1972	5.3	1.8	3.4

Source: J. Darmstadter and S. H. Schurr, "World Energy Sources and Demand," p. 414, where sources are indicated.

gap between the early- and late-comers to industrialization is to be narrowed over the next quarter-century, moving toward some more or less universal affluence in the twenty-first century. Charles A. Zraket, for example, sets out a gap-narrowing table by way of a bold hypothesis under the assumption of moderately rapid economic progress with decelerating rates of increase in energy consumption per capita (Table VI-4).

Despite the assumed decline in rates of per capita increase, one still emerges with an increase of energy consumption of something like 5.6 times between 1970 and 2000 and about 11 times over the subsequent century.

Such figures are, of course, useful only for limited purposes. One purpose is to pose the question of whether energy use on this scale, if otherwise feasible, could raise the average surface temperature of the earth with potentially catastrophic global effects. The answer appears to be that we do not understand the complex processes at work which determine climate; but that whatever risks may be involved are reduced progressively in degree as one moves from fossil fuels to nuclear fission to nuclear fusion to solar energy as a power

TABLE VI-3. *World Energy Consumption and Population, by Major Regions: Percentage Distribution, 1950, 1960, 1970, and Average Annual Percentage Rates of Change, 1960–1970*

Region	Percentage Distribution			
	1950		1960	
	Energy Consumption	Population	Energy Consumption	Populatio
North America	48.0	6.6	39.3	6.6
Canada	3.5	0.5	3.1	0.6
United States	44.5	6.1	36.1	6.0
Western Europe [a]	22.8	12.1	21.0	10.9
Oceania	1.2	0.5	1.1	0.5
Latin America	3.1	6.5	4.0	7.1
Asia (excl. communist)	5.0	32.2	6.6	32.5
Japan	2.3	3.3	3.0	3.1
Other Asia [a]	2.7	28.9	3.7	29.4
Africa	1.7	8.7	1.7	9.2
USSR and communist Eastern Europe	16.7	10.8	20.9	10.5
USSR	11.0	7.2	14.4	7.2
Eastern Europe [a]	5.7	3.6	6.5	3.3
Communist Asia	1.6	22.8	5.3	22.7
World	100.0	100.0	100.0	100.0

[a] Yugoslavia is included in Western Europe throughout these tables; Turkey appears in Other Asia.
Source: Darmstadter and Schurr, "World Energy Sources and Demand," p. 415.

TABLE VI-4. *World Population and per Capita Power Consumption, 1970, 2000 2100*

	Global Population (Billions)	Average Annual Rate of Increase (%)	Global Energy Consumption (in Quads)	Average Annu Rate of Increase (%)
1970	3.6	—	218	—
2000	6.0	1.7	1,223	5.9
2100	12.0	0.7	13,394	2.42

Source: Charles A. Zraket, *Energy Resources for the Year 2000 and Beyond*, supplemented private communication from the Mitre Corporation. The Mitre Corporation calculations for glo energy consumption in thermal watts have been converted into quads of BTU's for purposes of cc parison with other estimates used later in this chapter. A quad is 10^{15} (a quadrillion) of Brit thermal units. The conversion is as follows: 1,000 thermal watts = 1 thermal kWh = 3.413 BT

'0		Average Annual Percentage Rates of Change, 1960–1970		
ergy nsumption	Population	Energy Consumption	Population	Energy Consumption per Capita
4.7	6.3	4.3	1.3	3.0
3.3	0.6	6.1	1.8	4.2
1.4	5.7	4.2	1.3	2.9
2.3	9.9	6.3	0.9	5.3
1.1	0.5	5.8	2.2	3.5
4.3	7.8	6.3	2.9	3.4
9.7	34.1	9.7	2.4	7.1
5.2	2.9	11.9	1.0	10.7
4.5	31.3	7.7	2.5	5.0
1.7	9.7	5.4	2.4	3.0
0.9	9.7	5.6	1.1	4.5
4.9	6.7	6.0	1.2	4.7
6.0	2.9	4.7	0.7	4.0
5.3	22.0	5.6	1.6	3.9
0.0	100.0	5.6	1.9	3.6

er Capita Power Consumption (Thermal Watts)					
nited tates	Average Annual Rate of Increase (%)	Other Developed Countries	Average Annual Rate of Increase (%)	Developing Countries	Average Annual Rate of Increase (%)
1,000	—	4,000	—	600	—
0,000	2.0	12,000	3.7	4,000	6.5
0,000	0.9	50,000	1.4	32,000	2.1

r hour or 29,898 BTU's per annum. It should be noted that global energy consumption is sensitive
t only to assumptions about population increase in the various parts of the world, but also to
sumed rates of economic growth and the assumed linkage between economic growth and energy
nsumption. The Mitre Corporation has projected both higher and lower figures for 2100 under
fferent assumptions.

source.[28] This is a matter pursued in Chapter 53, where environmental issues are examined.

A second reason for projecting such energy requirements is to ask whether they can be matched from known or likely fossil fuel reserves, or from known or likely new technologies of energy production.

The answer appears to be that, at current or even somewhat damped rates of usage, oil reserves (including new finds) are likely to run down rather quickly, in a generation or two; gas reserves could last somewhat longer; while coal remains, still, relatively abundant. One can attach numbers to such estimates; for example, at 1970 rates of utilization, known global coal reserves could last 2,300 years; at a 4.1 percent annual growth rate of coal consumption, 111 years.[29]

But knowledge of actual global reserves, of possibilities of increased efficiency of use and conservation, and of new technologies that bear on the finding and exploitation of energy reserves is uncertain. It justifies only this broad and almost universally acccepted generalization: we have ample fossil fuel reserves, if supplemented by some expansion of nuclear power from existing technology, to cover requirements down to about the 1990's; but the energy base of industrial civilization will then have to include increasingly some new energy source. Chart VI-3 presents one version of that process.

This conclusion is strengthened by environmental and other constraints on exploiting fully, with existing technologies, the still large potential of coal. One estimate, for example, is that over the next thirty years coal, constituting 80 percent of the world's fossil fuel reserves, will supply only some 22 percent of the world's energy, while more attractive oil and gas, constituting some 7 percent of world fossil fuel reserves, will supply about 67 percent of world energy.[30] Among the candidates to supersede significantly fossil fuels, solar energy, breeder fission, and fusion power generation are now seen as the three most promising. Indeed, the commercial application of the breeder reactor may be quite close in some countries. But geothermal energy, fuels from waste and biomass, methanol, hydroelectric and tidal energy, and wind could play significant lesser roles. In terms of physics, there is no foreseeable long-run shortage of energy resources.[31]

One can conclude, then, that, theoretically, essentially infinite sources of energy exist; that, for practical purposes, we must envisage a running down over the next generation of oil and then gas and their phasing out during the next century; that coal could remain a significant major source of energy for a longer time; and that the state of scientific and technological ignorance about the relative virtues and potentialities of the various successor candidates is such as to justify urgent research and development efforts, from the present forward. The chances of success in creating a new energy base appear reasonably good; but the length of time available and the scale of resources devoted to the task will help determine the outcome.

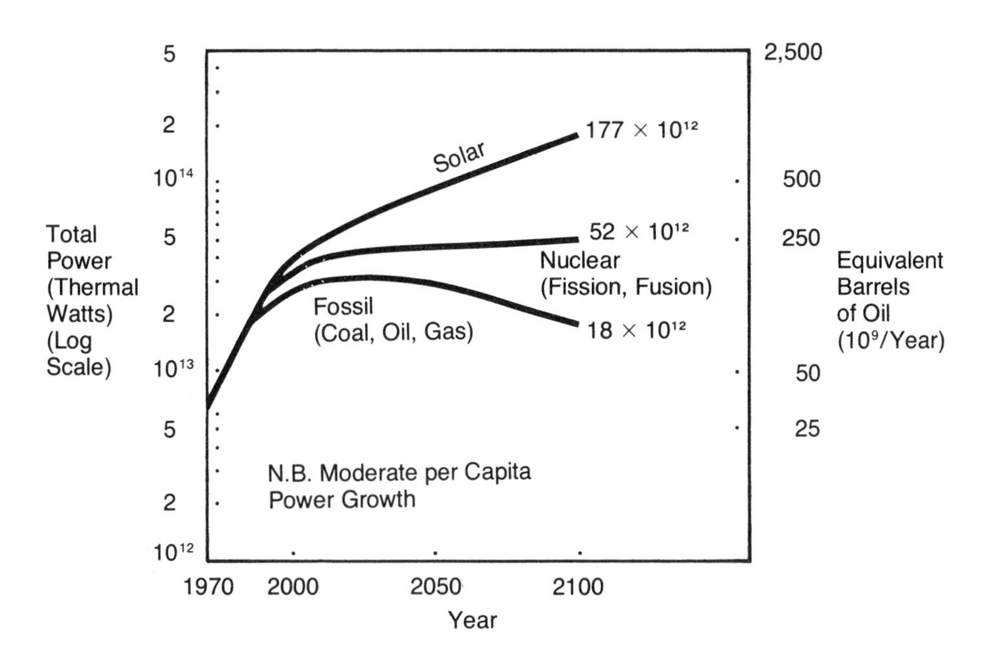

CHART VI-3. *Projected Decline in Reliance on Fossil Fuels, 1970–2100*

Source: Mitre Corporation, Report M74-82, September 1974, reprinted in Zraket, *Energy Resources for the Year 2000 and Beyond*, p. 19.

As one turns to the tasks of the next quarter-century, the agenda is technologically simpler, economically and politically more complex. Ample energy sources exist to cover even rapidly expanding requirements down to the year 2000: not only coal, gas, oil, and nuclear power conventionally exploited, but also shale oil, tar sands, synthetic oil and gas derived from coal, with some modest contributions possible from solar, geothermal, biomass, and solid-waste energy sources. The breeder reactor should also emerge over this time span; and there are substantial possibilities of increased economy and efficiency in energy use.

The energy programs envisaged by the OECD nations vary, of course, with their special circumstances, from Norway's export surplus to Japan's extreme energy deficit. But these programs generally look to some combination of continued OPEC imports at levels lower than estimated before the price increase of 1973, increased economy, and improved efficiency.

Possible variations in this general pattern can be illustrated from the American case. Tables VI-5 and VI-6 array for the United States six different estimates of energy demand and supply by use and by source, plus President Carter's plan of 20 April 1977. It should be noted that the Teller study is unique among American prescriptions in envisaging by 1985 a shift to an energy export position at the level of 15 quads. For purposes of comparison, in examining these 1985 estimates, it should be recalled that United States energy con-

TABLE VI-5. *United States: 1985 Estimates of Domestic Energy Supplies (Rounded to Nearest 0.1 Quad per Year)*

	Oil	Natural Gas	Coal	Nuclear	Other[a]	Net Energy Imports	Totals
FEA[1]—Maximum Production Levels							
Oil at $11 per barrel							
Business as Usual	31.8	23.4	24.8	7.0	4.6	n.e.	92
Accelerated Development	42.4	29.3	47.3	8.2	8.7	n.e.	136
Ford Foundation[2]							
Historical Growth							
High Domestic Oil and Gas	32	29	25	10	9	11	116
High Nuclear	32	29	23	12	9	11	116
Technical Fix							
Self-Sufficiency	30	27	16	8	4	7	92
Environmental Protection	29	26	14	5	4	14	92
CED[3]	28.5	26.5	21.5	10	8.5	10	105
NAE[4]	27.8	33.1	21.2	17.6	4.7	0	104
Edward Teller[5]	35	28	33	12	8	−15	116
Carter plan (20 April 1977)[6]	22	19	31	8	5	14	98

[a] Includes shale oil, synthetic oil and gas, hydroelectric, geothermal, solid waste, solar, etc.

Source: Elaborated from Edward Teller, "Energy—A Plan for Action," p. 27. Specific sources as follows:

[1] Federal Energy Administration, *Project Independence Report*, p. 67.

[2] Ford Foundation Energy Policy Project, *A Time to Choose*, pp. 28 and 76.

[3] Committee for Economic Development, *Achieving Energy Independence*, p. 16.

[4] National Academy of Engineering, *U.S. Energy Prospects: An Engineering Viewpoint* (Washington, D.C., 1974), pp. 86–88 (maximum production, net 1985 demand after conservation and efficiency measures).

[5] Teller, "Energy," p. 27.

[6] The balance sheets for the Carter plan are to be found in *The National Energy Plan* (Executive Office of the President, Energy Policy and Planning, 29 April 1977), pp. 95 and 96. The figures are here converted into quads per year from million barrels of oil equivalent (m.b.o.e.) per day at 1 quad = 0.472 m.b.o.e. Due to rounding, the components of the Carter target add to 99 quads. Actual total is 98.31 quads (46.4 m.b.o.e.), deducting for 2.54 quads of coal exports.

sumption in 1973 was 77.6 quads (gross). The average annual rates of increase vary, therefore, between a high of 3.4 percent (Ford Historical Growth) and 1.4 percent (Ford Technical Fix) in which large investments in energy conservation and efficiency are envisaged.[32]

In terms of supply, all these energy balance sheets envisage a radical expansion in nuclear power from the 1973 level of 0.9 quad;[33] and all but the Ford Foundation Technical Fix scenario envisage a radical expansion in coal from its 1973 level of 15.0 quads. All except FEA's Business as Usual and Ford's Historical Growth scenarios envisage significant measures of conservation and improved efficiency, including radical reductions in the rate of growth of energy consumption in transport, which absorbed 18.8 quads in 1973. The con-

TABLE VI-6. *United States: 1985 Estimates of Domestic Energy Demand (Rounded to Nearest 0.1 Quad per Year)*

	Electricity	Residential and Commercial	Industry[a]	Transportation	Gross	Net[b]
FEA[1]—Accelerated Supply with Conservation						
Oil at $7 per barrel						
Primary energy sources	37.7	16.7	25.0	20.4	99.7	—
Including electricity	—	23.7	29.3	20.4	—	73.4
Oil at $11 per barrel						
Primary energy sources	35.6	16.0	24.4	20.0	96.0	—
Including electricity	—	23.1	28.2	20.0	—	71.3
Ford Foundation[2]						
Historical Growth						
Primary energy sources	37.5	18.1	34.5	26.0	116.1	—
Including electricity	—	24.9	40.6	26.0	—	91.5
Technical Fix						
Primary energy sources	23.2	17.8	30.7	19.6	91.3	—
Including electricity	—	22.6	33.9	19.6	—	76.1
CED[3]						
Primary energy sources	31.0	15.5	33.5	25.0	105.0	—
Edward Teller[4]						
Primary energy sources	33	18	30	22	103	—
Including electricity	—	24	35	22	—	81
Carter plan[5]						
Primary energy sources	33	14	29	22	98	—
Including electricity	—	32	44	22	—	—

[a] Includes nonenergy.

[b] The figures in this column represent the energy used. They differ from the previous column by the energy wasted in generating electricity. The difference is substantial, but it must be realized that other energy uses also are connected with some waste—a fact not evident in the table.

Source: Elaborated from Teller, "Energy—A Plan for Action," pp. 18–19. Specific sources as follows:

[1] Federal Energy Administration, *Project Independence Report*, pp. 195–198.

[2] Ford Foundation Energy Policy Project, *A Time to Choose*, p. 46.

[3] Committee for Economic Development, *Achieving Energy Independence*, p. 16.

[4] Teller, "Energy," pp. 18–19.

[5] Converted as for Table VI-5.

sensus is strong that smaller, more efficient automobiles are required, used in less energy-profligate ways.

President Carter's plan of 20 April 1977 assumes less domestic oil and gas production than the others and continued large oil imports. Only the Ford Foundation Environmental Protection option carries with it as high a 1985 import level as the Carter plan. The plan's other targets fall in intermediate ranges when compared with earlier calculations. As of the late spring of 1977 it is the virtually unanimous judgment of energy experts that the price and other policies incorporated in the Carter plan are not consistent with the fulfillment of its production targets.

When the possible situation in 1985 is extended down to the year 2000, analysts generally project their 1985 calculations with continued (or even increased) restraint on transport energy expenditures and with somewhat enlarged contributions from such quite likely technologies as solar energy for household purposes, the production of synthetics from coal, and the exploitation of oil from shale.[34]

This is not an appropriate setting in which to try to arbitrate in detail among these visions and recommendations for the American future. They involve, among other differences, varying degrees of continued reliance on imports, on coal and atomic energy exploitation, on investment in conservation and efficiency. Although the potentialities for substitution for OPEC imports are greater in the United States than in Western Europe as a whole and in Japan, atomic energy and the potentialities of conservation are available throughout the OECD world, and coal is available in Western Europe, in addition to OPEC oil. The point to be made here is, simply, that, in terms of existing known resources and technologies, a physical energy shortage need not prevent the continued growth of the United States, the OECD world, and the world economy as a whole over the next quarter-century.

If this technical conclusion is accepted, the operational question becomes: Is the world economy, and notably the OECD world, on a path consistent with a combination of production and economy policies that would reconcile continued economic growth with diminished reliance on OPEC oil? Here three related points should be made:

—The United States and the OECD world generally made exceedingly slow progress along these possible paths of expanded production, increased economy and efficiency down to the spring of 1977. High energy prices and general economic recession did, indeed, set in motion trends in the right directions; but, as recession gave way to even a modest recovery, OPEC imports rose. It was most uncertain that the envisaged reductions in reliance on OPEC imports would soon be achieved. Indeed, United States reliance on imports was still rapidly rising three and a half years after the initial OPEC price increase.

—Virtually all analyses agree that large increases in capital investment will be required in energy production and conservation to move along any of these paths; and, with greater or less anxiety, most analyses envisage a rise in the proportion of total investment going, in one way or another, to the energy sector. The conclusion of the 1974 OECD Report on Energy is representative:

> The realisation of *full* physical and technological potential from reducing energy consumption and expanding indigenous production, would make the OECD almost self sufficient in energy by 1985 [as shown in Table VI-7, case (c)]. But it seems highly improbable since, as production is pushed up, there is growing risk of conflict between high indigenous production and other objectives of government policy concerning income distribution, industrial structure and policies aimed at combating inflation. Even in the $9 case, cumulative capital requirements for indigenous energy production including replacement and investment in conversion, transportation and distribution amount to about $1,100 billion (1972 $) between 1974 and 1985 excluding the necessary infrastructure, e.g., harbours for coal export and import. This is about 13.5 per cent of all gross fixed asset formulation by 1985 as against 7.7 per cent in the early 1970's.
>
> The sum is divided as follows:
>
> - $500 billion for oil and gas
> - $40 billion for coal
> - $550 billion for electricity.
>
> To increase self sufficiency beyond that point would entail an investment of roughly $1,800 billion for both conservation and realising full production potential. This would represent a large shift of financial resources into the energy sector, particularly for the energy rich countries [notably, the United States]. There would likely be difficulties in making this shift in allocation of resources as well as in financing the necessary investments in the energy sector.[35]

TABLE VI-7. *Annual Energy Investments**: *OECD, Early 1970's–1985, Alternative Assumptions (as a Share in Gross Fixed Asset Formation)*

Early 1970's (%)		1977 (%)	1980 (%)	1985 (%)	Import Dependence (%)
7.7% (import dependence, 36%)	(a)	8.9	9.1	10.9	—
	(b)	9.4	10.2	13.5	21
	(c)	10.2	12.9	18.5	2–7

* Including replacement of existing facilities.
(a) $6 per barrel oil price.
(b) $9 per barrel oil price.
(c) Potential.
Source: "Energy Prospects to 1985," *OECD Observer*, no. 73 (January–February 1975), p. 19.

Despite three and one-half years of the $9 case, the level of energy investment in the OECD world was not expanding on a scale capable of achieving the projected 1980 and 1985 figures.[36] And when the OECD countries took stock of 1985 prospects late in 1976, they found themselves budgeting for a level of oil imports 72 percent higher than the earlier figure for 1985.[37] The increase appeared particularly ominous in the light of the emerging consensus that total world oil production would peak out during the 1980's.

—Thus, while a good many energy analysts were concerned about the potentially excessive claims of energy investment on total economic resources, the OECD economies, as of 1975–1977, experienced a slow recovery, with the highest unemployment rates since the end of the Second World War, large idle industrial capacity, and low levels of investment. Some conventional measures to cushion the decline in consumers' demand were being taken; but each nation was looking to expansion elsewhere to permit its own recovery to proceed with exports as a leading sector—a procedure unlikely to succeed, as the London *Economist* of 12 July 1975 pointed out in an article, "You Can't All Export at Once."[38] Put another way, no major OECD economy was moving persuasively back to full employment and resumed high growth rates by the rapid expansion of investment in energy production and conservation. We shall return to this paradoxical situation in Chapter 54. It should be noted, however, that three and one-half years is a short period for a complex world economy to respond to a radical shift in relative energy prices; and the pace of a structural adjustment that still may emerge has been slowed by a variety of political problems. There have been, for example, controversies with respect to government-private roles in the exploitation of the North Sea; the environment in the case of offshore United States possibilities; safety, waste disposal, and nuclear proliferation in the exploitation of atomic energy; labor and environmental issues in the exploitation of coal; oil and gas pricing in the United States. In addition to what might be called such negative issues, energy investment (in conservation as well as production) awaits certain positive actions by government. There are production projects so large and experimental projects carrying such risk that they cannot be undertaken by private industry without some form of government assistance or guarantee. There is also the need for legislation to encourage the better insulation of buildings and to make the most of possibilities for solar energy which even existing technologies provide. This is particularly striking in the case of the United States. Whether one leans on balance (as does Edward Teller) toward programs of radically expanded production or (as does the Ford Foundation report) toward maximum exploitation of the possibilities of economy and efficiency, one ends with long lists of positive government actions required to make it attractive for private investment to increase rapidly in appropriate directions.[39]

In terms of the historical perspective provided by Part Three, what is involved in the energy problem over the next ten to twenty-five years is not unlike the challenge faced in the world economy of the 1850's and 1890's; that is, shortage of a basic commodity whose redress requires a radical shift in the direction of investment. In the past, those shifts were achieved primarily by changes in relative prices and, thereby, changes in relative profitability among the various sectors of the world economy. And, surely, now the change in the relative price of energy is operating to a degree and will remain an essential instrument to produce the changed patterns of investment and consumption required for movement toward the new energy balance governments seek. But, as in the case of population and food production, the energy sector is so intertwined with public policy, in every nation, that political action will be required as well as the workings of the market system. The failure of policy to move swiftly to produce this change in the direction of investment was a major cause of the high level of unemployment in the OECD world of 1974–1977 for, while relatively high energy prices were slow to yield a surge of investment in new directions, they contributed promptly to a decline or radical deceleration in the automobile and durable consumers' goods sectoral complexes, which had for thirty years been so vital to growth in the OECD world. And in their impact on real public revenues, through accelerated inflation and recession, high energy prices also constrained outlays for certain social expenditures whose previous high rates of expansion had helped sustain the rate of growth.

Thus, just as the problem of the food-population balance came to rest in the short and medium run not on resource limitations but on the difficult economics of fertilizer production and distribution and the difficult politics of expanding domestic food production in developing countries, so the short- and medium-run problems of energy supply come to rest on the question of how to induce in the OECD world a rapidly altered pattern of investment. And this turns out to be, as well, a substantial part of the key to a return to full employment, a resumed high rate of growth, and expanded public revenues.

As for the non-OPEC developing nations, their energy problems and prospects vary over a wide range. Some (e.g., Mexico and India) contain energy resources capable of reasonably rapid development with existing technologies. China has moved already to an oil export position with prospects some (but not all) judge to be extremely promising over the longer run.[40] But most developing nations will continue to be borne down by high energy prices unless, as considered in Chapters 54 and 55, enlarged external assistance is provided in one form or another.

Now, finally, the question of energy prices; for it is the price of energy rather than its physical availability that is in question over the next decade. Is it appropriate to assume we shall live down to 1985 and, perhaps, down to the end of the century in a world of relatively high energy prices? Or, will the price of Middle East oil, the temporarily abundant and cheaply produced source of residual supply, break sharply downward?

Here, again, the world economy faces a paradoxical situation. From the side of supply it is apparent that the oil importers need high energy prices to render profitable the expansion of energy resources with present technologies. The dotted line in Chart VI-4, for example, suggests that something above a $10 (1974) per barrel price is required, except for United States coal, to produce profitably all the ready alternatives, including offshore and Arctic oil and gas. (A more conventional figure for the minimum oil price necessary to make profitable the exploitation of such resources is $7.50 per barrel in 1974 prices; say, $10.50 in 1977 prices.) Chart VI-4 also underlines the much greater investment costs per unit of output involved in the United States than in the Middle East. The exact figures are, of course, debatable as well as subject to both inflation and the possibilities of incremental improvement in existing technologies. But the general thrust of Chart VI-4 would be widely accepted by energy experts; that is, excepting the perhaps transient case of coal, the natural selling price of non-OPEC sources of energy is at or higher than the OPEC oil price.

The situation leads to a dilemma in policy: for short-run balance-of-payments reasons, a reduction in the OPEC oil price is highly desirable; but a price floor is necessary to induce the reduced dependence on OPEC oil desired in the longer run, via both reduced rates of increase in consumption and expanded alternative supplies.

On the other hand, a vigorous expansion of non-OPEC energy production, combined with energy economy, could conceivably break the OPEC price, for a time at least. This possibility emerges clearly in studies which attempt to bring together price analysis with global projections of supply and demand.[41] Before the 1973 rise in oil prices, an increase in global energy requirements at an annual rate of 5.5 percent was predicted down to 1985.[42] In 1974 an international group of experts predicted energy requirements would increase down to 1985 at only 4.8 percent. For oil, however, the predicted rate of increase declines from 5.6 percent to 3.8 percent as other forms of energy are evoked and special efforts to conserve petroleum are undertaken. Since oil importers are assumed to be pressing to the limit their own oil-producing capacity, as well as practicing conservation, the projected change in the volume of oil imports is much more dramatic: the expected annual rate of increase falls from 5.5 percent to 1.5 percent (Table VI-8).

If, in fact, the oil importers met the production and conservation targets implicit in Table VI-8, they could pose a serious problem for OPEC, which comprises three groups of countries with quite differing economic requirements:[43]

—Countries which need all the oil revenues they can get and are, therefore, inclined to push production to its physical limits; e.g., Venezuela, Indonesia, Algeria, Nigeria, Iraq.

—Countries which generate revenues in substantial excess of development requirements and which have imposed restrictions on oil

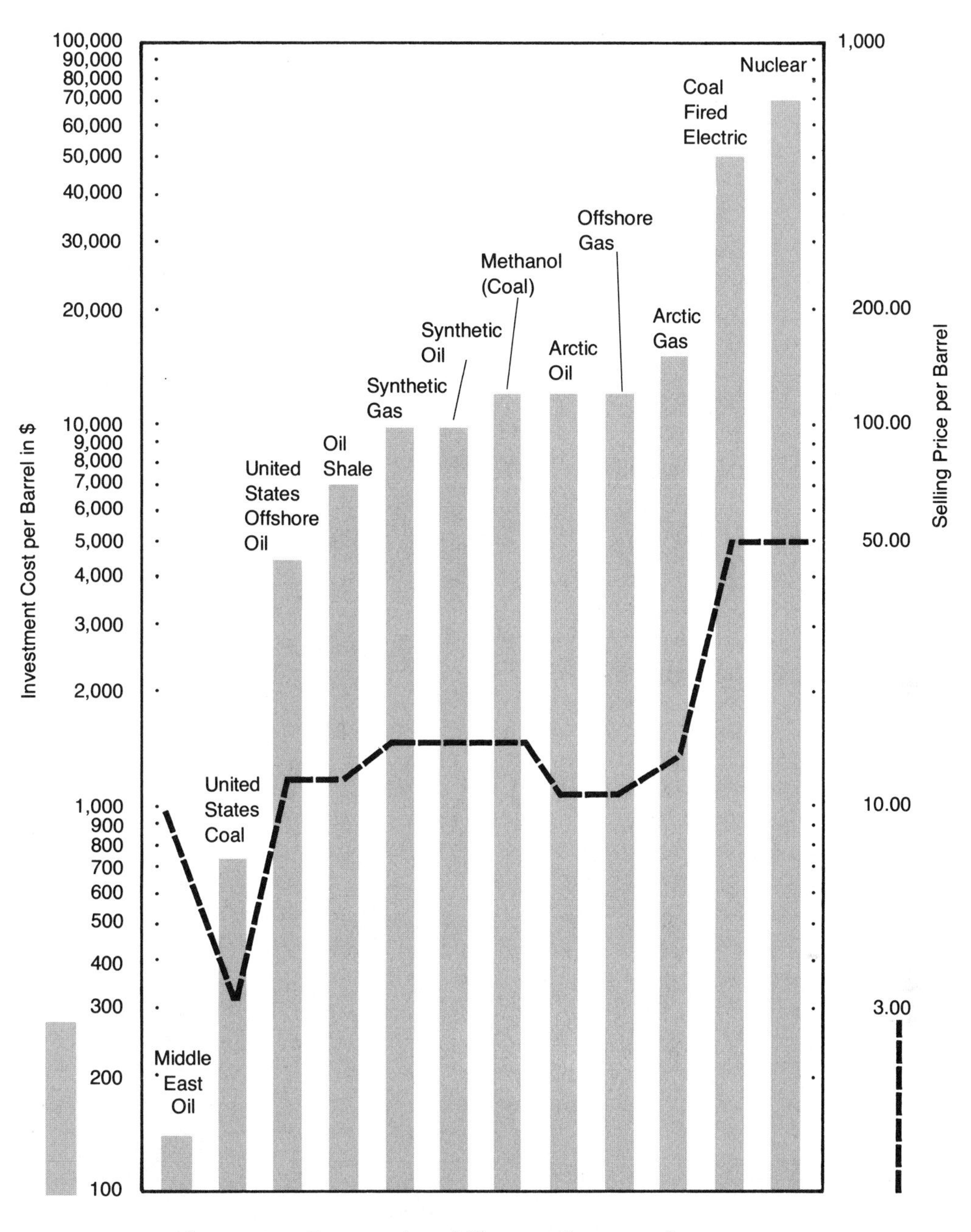

CHART VI-4. *Alternative Conventional Energy Sources: Investment Costs and Break-Even Selling Prices*

Source: Zraket, *Energy Resources for the Year 2000 and Beyond*, p. 5.

TABLE VI-8. *Oil Import Requirements of Net Oil-Importing Countries, Actual for 1972 and Projections for 1985 (Millions of Barrels per Day)*

Country	Actual, 1972	Pre–October 1973 Projection, 1985	Revised Projection, 1985
United States	5	13	2[a]
Western Europe	14	23	18
Japan	5	11	9
Other industrial countries	1	—	—
Developing countries	3	9	5
Total net imports	28	56	34[a]

[a] It should be noted that President Carter's plan of 20 April 1977 calls for 7.6 m.b.o.e. gas and oil imports in 1985, rather than 2; while OECD estimated in March 1977 that, without radical changes in policy, OECD imports in 1985 would approximate 40 m.b.o.e., rather than 34.

Source: Brookings Institution, *Cooperative Approaches to World Energy Problems*, p. 49, where sources are indicated. For purposes of comparison with energy tables presented earlier, it should be noted that 1 quad per year equals 0.472 million barrels of oil per day.

production to conserve resources for the long run. Only Libya and Kuwait are now in this category.

—Countries which are potentially in the position of Libya and Kuwait and which might in the future restrict oil production to sustain oil prices and the cohesiveness of OPEC. Saudi Arabia is the principal country that might assume the role of residual supplier for these purposes. But the smaller states on the Persian Gulf are also in a position to support such a reduction. Iran, with large development objectives and a substantial population, belongs basically in the first category; but its oil resources are so large that it might, to a degree, constrain production to sustain the international oil price and maintain OPEC unity.

If the OECD nations were to achieve the relatively reduced imports in Table VI-8, these differences among the OPEC countries could become significant. Pre–October 1973 projections suggested that oil available for export might reach the level of 63 million barrels per day, as opposed to 28 in 1972. The revised figure for oil available for export in 1985 is of the order of 55; but this figure compares with actual oil import requirements of only 34. Thus, there is a potential "surplus" of 21 million barrels per day. Oil available from the countries tending to maximize production alone could reach, say, 30 in 1985. Thus, theoretically, the oil producers conserving oil resources and residual oil suppliers could be virtually driven from the market. The problem could be even more acute if the major oil importers continue to experience low growth rates. This vast theoretical surplus will not, of course, emerge: oil prices will fall and/or OPEC oil production will be reduced. But the point is worth elaborating for two reasons. First, the bargaining power of the OECD countries vis-à-vis OPEC hinges greatly on their actually moving forward rapidly to expand production and conserve energy use.

Here the role of the United States is critical, as Table VI-8 makes clear. Second, the proper medium-term relationship between the OECD countries and OPEC should be one of cooperation rather than confrontation. That cooperation ought to center on the following four common objectives: to assure resumed high rates of growth in the OECD world; to assure an oil price sufficient to induce continued measures to expand energy production and conserve consumption in the OECD world; to assure a "fair" and predictable price to oil producers and an assured flow to oil importers; to assure by joint OECD-OPEC measures that relatively high energy prices do not continue to damp food production and overall economic growth in the most vulnerable developing regions, which now encompass perhaps a billion human beings.

If OECD and OPEC representatives come to grips objectively with the dilemma, they will discover that, in effect, three different oil prices are conceptually desirable: a price sufficiently high in importing countries to stimulate necessary economies and to induce the necessary expansion of alternative energy resources; an intermediate price for oil imports to industrialized nations that would not burden excessively their balance of payments and frustrate their resumption of high growth rates; and a subsidized low price for the low-income developing countries to reduce balance-of-payments pressure on them and to permit rapid increases in fertilizer production and in other inputs necessary for an accelerated expansion of agricultural production. If there were complete political confidence between OPEC and the major industrialized importing nations, the first two prices could be reconciled, perhaps, by an initially lowered but then gradually rising price geared to the generation of alternatives to imported oil over a longer time period than now envisaged in various plans. Alternatively, if the international oil price were lowered, OECD import taxes could maintain internal prices required to provide incentives to expand energy resources and to economize. In either case, long-term, reliable increases in aid from OPEC could substitute for a special reduced price for the low-income developing nations.

There are various ways to reconcile these three criteria. But a rational examination of them may await a sufficiently persuasive OECD energy policy to induce the cooperation with OPEC that ultimate mutual interests and responsibilities would make desirable. As of the spring of 1977, the prospects for such a policy appeared exceedingly slim in the light of the unpersuasive plan presented to the Congress by President Carter. The most likely outcome, therefore, was for further increases in the OPEC price, intensified balance-of-payments problems among the oil importers, and a later confrontation with the realities of the energy problem, after more exceedingly precious time had been wasted.

52

Raw Materials

There is some symmetry between the long- and medium-term problems of raw materials and energy, as well as significant differences. In both cases, the theoretical long-term supply capacity to sustain industrialization (say, 2000–2100) is very great, if not infinite. In both, large and perhaps expanded efforts in science, invention, and innovation will be required to evoke that capacity on the requisite scale. Just as prospective energy costs appear to require measures of increased economy and efficiency, it may well be necessary to put raw-materials supply and use on an increasingly efficient and renewable resource basis via recycling and other methods. In both cases, ample supplies appear available for the medium term (1976–2000); but their location raises potential balance-of-payments problems for the importing nations. There is also some debate on whether medium-term prospects are for relatively high raw-materials prices or for levels like those experienced from 1951 to the late 1960's. Major differences between the energy and raw-materials situations are that there is no equivalent in raw materials to the foreseeable end of the petroleum age and that no effective group of producers' cartels now controls raw-materials prices. Those prices softened considerably in response to the recession of 1974–1975, after their sharp rise of 1972–1974 (see, above, pp. 288–289). Therefore, governments are somewhat less anxious about raw materials than about energy, and the new literature on raw-materials problems and prospects, while ample, is not on the scale of that which poured forth on energy.[44] Technically, raw materials also differ in a number of ways from energy: they serve a wide variety of special purposes, although there is considerable substitutability among some of them; they are subject to significant recycling; and they are diffused in the earth's crust and under the sea as the result of a less special geological history than oil and gas. There is a general consensus that larger relative reserves of minerals exist (and are likely still to be found) than additional reserves of gas and oil. Historically, "known reserves" have been an essentially economic rather than geological figure; that is, resources have been invested in finding new mineral sources in response to current prices and expected future demand. There is every reason to believe that physical shortages of minerals are not likely to be a restraint on future industrial development.[45]

But, of course, that is not the point. In the cataclysmic *Limits to Growth* projections, it was the classic assumption of diminishing returns in the mining of minerals (as well as in agriculture) which helped bring on crisis by diverting increasing amounts of investment resources in a losing effort to sustain the inputs required for continued industrial growth. Here, as in agriculture, historical experience suggests, on balance, an optimistic view of the combined potentialities of nature's resources and man's technological ingenuity; but past trends will not continue automatically. Technological creativity and intelligent public policy will be required to prove that diminishing returns can continue to be overcome.

The bases for optimism lie in curves like those presented in Charts VI-5 and VI-6. These charts record two related facts: excepting timber, productivity in mining as in agriculture increased fairly steadily between 1870 and 1960; the relative prices of farm products and minerals varied, as we know from Part Three, with cycles, wars, and trend periods, but the long-term trend in minerals was quite stable from 1880, and, depending on how one constructs the trend curve, steady or only slightly rising for farm products. The case of timber emerges as a significant exception: the failure to generate productivity increases comparable to those elsewhere in the world economy and the consequent rise in its relative price induced invention and innovation which successfully substituted for timber in many uses.

Despite this impressive record of holding diminishing returns at bay, there are pessimists about the possibility of continuing to do so. R. V. Ayres and A. V. Kneese, for example, produce these five arguments, which strongly influenced the judgment of the Meadows team on this matter:

—Lower quality ores in some important materials do not necessarily exist in exploitable quantities.

—There are few new geographic areas left to explore, except for seabeds.

—Social (e.g., environmental) costs will probably be reflected in future mineral prices, and could rise disproportionately as output increases.

—The effort and investment required to achieve productivity gains in the future will probably be much greater than has been true in the past.

—It is not unlikely that raw-material exporters (upon whom rich countries are becoming dependent) will increasingly band together to multiply their bargaining power and increase their revenues.[46]

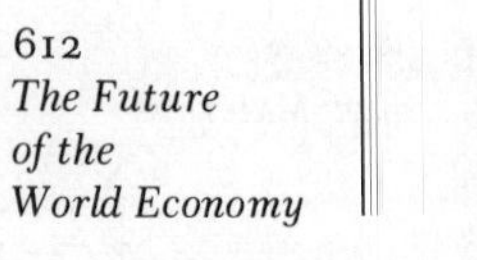

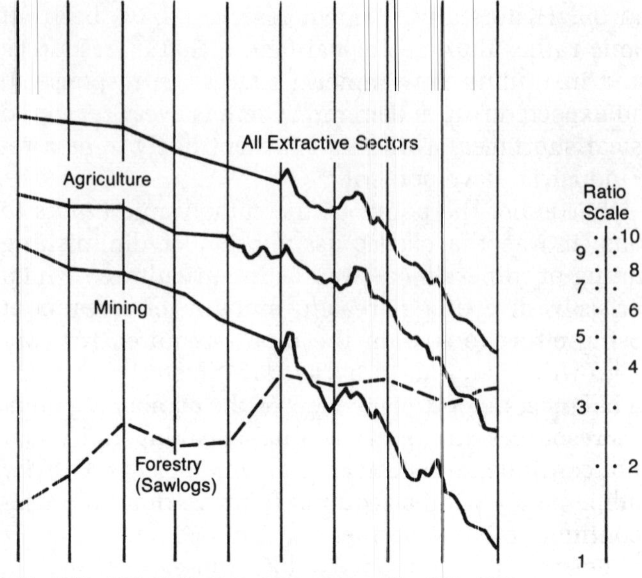

CHART VI-5. *Relative Trends in Ratio of Employment to Output in Resource Sectors: United States, 1870–1960*

Source: Hans Landsberg et al., *Resources in America's Future*, p. 13.

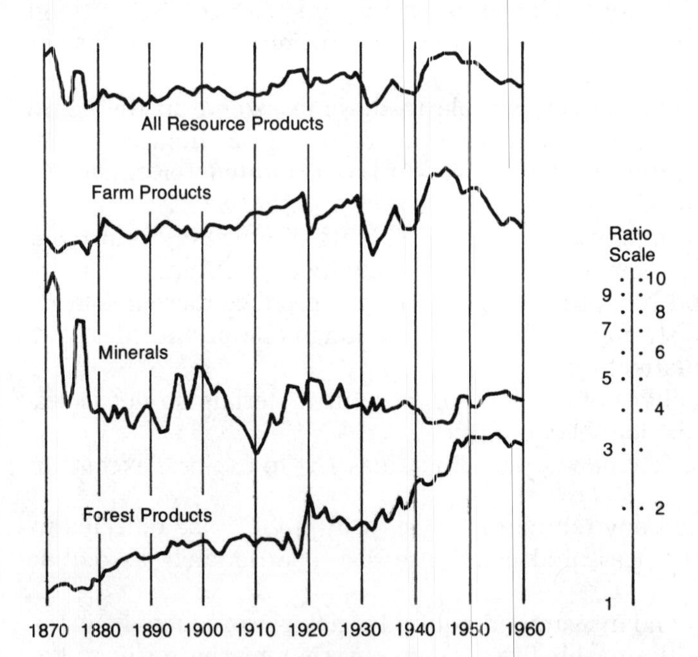

CHART VI-6. *Relative Fluctuations in Deflated Prices of Resource Products: United States, 1870–1960*

Source: Landsberg et al., *Resources in America's Future*, p. 13.

Putting the last point aside for later discussion, the relative optimists would respond to these points along the following lines. The history of the past century has seen remarkable technical progress in profitably processing increasingly lean ores. There is no reason that trend cannot continue. The exploration of the earth's crust is incomplete, even in the United States, and new technologies for discovering mineral deposits are available and rapidly evolving. The social costs of maintaining the environment are limited and manageable without endangering the economy, although they are a cost-raising factor. The prospects for increased substitution of capital and machines for labor remain substantial, despite considerable mechanization in the past.

The projected scale of increased raw-materials requirements and the evident need to continue to overcome diminishing returns with invention and innovation suggest, however, that large investments in raw-materials production, technology, and economy are likely to be required in both the medium and the long run. Rough estimates of future minerals demand are set out in Table VI-9 for the United States and the rest of the world.[47]

As with food and energy, the key problems over this medium-term period emerge as economic and political rather than as problems of resource limitation in the physical sense. The degree of American dependence on imports will increase, on these projections; and this raises, as with the problem of energy, balance-of-payments questions as well as the possibility of producers' cartels and the cut-off, for political or strategic purposes, of the flow of essential imports.

The scale of the United States' increased dependence on imports and the order of magnitude of the balance-of-payments pressures which may be set up by its expanded requirements down to the year 2000 is suggested in Table VI-10. Increased import requirements for aluminum, iron, and copper account for 66 percent of the estimated deficit in that year. Jamaica, Surinam, Canada, and Australia are the present and prospective major sources for bauxite and aluminum; Canada, Venezuela, Japan, and the EEC, for iron ore and manufactured iron; Canada, Peru, and Chile, for copper.

The potentialities for mitigating this increased degree of dependence, should it be judged desirable, are substantial: through new mineral discoveries, technologies which permit the efficient exploitation of lower-grade domestic ores, changes in product design and substitution, and recycling. As in the case of energy, the degree to which these potentialities are exploited will depend on how political relations evolve between producers and consumers; but it will depend also on the future course of raw-materials prices.

The price position for raw materials is, of course, quite different than for oil, for which a fixed (money) price was maintained from the end of 1973 until it was raised by 10 percent in September 1975 and again (to an uncertain extent) in December 1976. In constant dollars (1973 = 100), the prices of metals, minerals, and ores

TABLE VI-9. *Projected Minerals Demand: United States and the Rest of the World, 1972–2000*

	United States			
	1972	2000	Increase, 1972–2000	% pe[r] Year
Chromium (thousand tons)	506	1,090	584	2.7
Iron (million tons)	83	153	70	2.2
Manganese (thousand tons)	1,366	2,360	994	2.0
Molybdenum (million lbs.)	51	188	137	4.7
Nickel (thousand tons)	172	385	213	2.9
Silicon (thousand tons)	561	1,000	439	2.1
Tungsten (million lbs.)	14	74	60	6.1
Aluminum (million tons)	5	26	21	6.1
Copper (thousand tons)	1,951	5,400	3,449	3.7
Lead (thousand tons)	970	1,430	460	1.4
Tin (thousand tons)	49	90	41	2.2
Zinc (thousand tons)	1,489	3,100	1,611	2.6
Vanadium (thousand tons)	7	31	24	5.3

Source: U.S. Bureau of Mines, *Mineral Facts and Problems* (Bulletin 650, 1970; u[p]dated 11 January 1974), reprinted in Commission on Critical Choices for Americans, *Vi[tal] Resources*, Reports on Energy, Food, and Raw Materials, Critical Choices for America[ns], vol. 1 (Lexington, Mass., and Toronto: D.C. Heath and Company, 1977), pp. 140–141.

TABLE VI-10. *Value of U.S. Primary Minerals Gap, 1950, 1972, 2000 (Millions of 1972 Dollars)*

	Primary Mineral Production		
	1950	1972	2000[a]
Chromium	0	0	0
Iron	4,126	3,760	4,497
Manganese	33	2	0
Molybdenum	52	193	338
Nickel	2	47	116
Silicon	110	161	318
Tungsten	5	21	6
Aluminum	239	215	320
Copper	691	1,698	3,574
Lead	207	186	312
Platinum group	3	1	3
Tin	0	0	0
Zinc	312	172	361
Vanadium	12	28	58
Total of 62 minerals	7,877	10,080	17,418

[a] Assumes past twenty-year production trend continues.
Source: Commission on Critical Choices for Americans, *Vital Resources*, p. 152.

est of World				United States as % of World, 1972–2000
72	2000	Increase, 1972–2000	% per Year	
678	3,800	2,122	2.9	22.9
396	780	384	2.4	16.5
646	18,300	9,654	2.7	12.3
107	345	238	4.2	32.6
353	915	562	3.4	30.6
284	3,800	2,516	3.9	24.4
65	125	60	2.4	28.0
8	49	41	6.7	36.5
270	18,300	13,030	4.5	24.5
083	5,000	1,917	1.7	23.1
191	270	79	1.2	23.0
551	9,200	4,649	2.5	25.2
18	33	15	2.2	40.0

Primary Mineral Demand			Surplus or Deficit		
1950	1972	2000	1950	1972	2000
52	75	149	−52	−75	−149
4,737	6,030	11,965	−611	−2,270	−7,468
143	73	150	−110	−71	−150
37	89	323	+15	+104	+15
184	481	1,178	−182	−434	−1,063
120	168	335	−10	−7	−17
9	35	226	−4	−14	−220
585	2,338	15,312	−346	−2,123	−14,992
967	1,990	7,452	−276	−292	−3,878
335	291	543	−128	−105	−231
44	86	219	−41	−85	−216
283	194	560	−283	−194	−560
574	536	1,860	−262	−364	−1,499
8	39	167	+4	−11	−109
10,423	17,150	57,629	−2,546	−7,070	−40,211

TABLE VI-11. *Intensity of Raw-Materials Use: World, 1951–2000 (Units per $ Billion Gross Domestic Product)*

	World		
	1951–1955	1966–1969	2000
Crude steel (thousand mt)	124	152	135
Iron ore (thousand tons)	87	106	94
Copper (mt)	1,980	1,968	1,713
Aluminum (mt)	1,398	2,560	4,068
Zinc (mt)	1,335	1,372	1,170
Fluorspar (mt)	683	1,031	1,381
Sulfur (mt)	7,993	8,931	8,736
Energy (equivalent of thousand mt of coal)	1,759	1,781	1,830

mt: metric tons.
Source: Wilfred Malenbaum, "Resources Shortages in an Expanding World," in *Growth and Its Implications for the Future*, Part 2, p. 1143. (See note 48 below for publication data.)

moved as follows on a world basis from 1971 to 1975, according to World Bank calculations:

1971	85
1972	79
1973	100
1974	115
1975	93

Recession in the OECD world thus reduced mineral prices in real terms by 24 percent, not quite back to their 1972 trough. They lifted again quite strongly in the limited revival of 1976–1977.

The future of raw-materials prices will evidently remain in part a function of the rate of growth in the OECD world. Experts exhibit a proper uncertainty about their course down to the end of the century. On the one hand, minerals taken as a whole are not shadowed by an adjustment like that assumed to be required as oil and gas reserves begin to run down over the next generation. Moreover, the rate of raw-materials use in relation to increases in real income is likely to continue to decline in the more advanced industrial nations; and that decline is not fully outweighed by the rise in relative raw-materials use as the present developing nations move forward in industrialization (Table VI-11). This is the vista which leads Wilfred Malenbaum, for example, to conclude: "Such a *deceleration* from past rates of growth of supply of resource output (with a relative decline in the share of resource output to total domestic product) portrays a future where relative prices for nonrenewable resources can be expected to fall."[48] But a declining rate of increase in demand may not be the only variable at work. From the side of supply a great deal of investment and new technology must be generated to continue to overcome diminishing returns; and, above all, there are uncertainties about public policy. Thus, an international group of experts concludes as follows:

ich Lands			Poor Lands		
)51–1955	1966–1969	2000	1951–1955	1966–1969	2000
140	167	138	48	77	121
101	114	92	21	72	107
300	2,240	1,850	441	649	1,026
650	2,920	4,550	145	852	1,744
553	1,500	1,195	283	749	1,043
775	1,170	1,530	255	380	610
350	9,550	8,950	1,490	5,875	7,638
830	1,860	1,845	872	1,425	1,760

A more realistic constraint on mineral supplies than resource depletion could be insufficient investment—the factor that transforms mineral occurrences into marketable supplies. Not only will mining and processing have to compete with other claims on capital for expansion, but there are also uncertainties about public policy on ownership rights, taxation, environmental protection, and price controls that introduce risks for potential investors in mineral development.

These considerations apply to the industrial countries as well as the developing world. Quite generally, mineral-exporting countries have been demanding larger shares of the economic rents associated with mining and refining activities. These demands have taken a number of forms: higher taxes and royalties on mineral production; partial or total nationalization of foreign mineral firms; and coercion of mining companies to smelt, refine, and process minerals in the exporting countries, even where the additional processing may be uneconomic. When these forms of economic nationalism tilt the terms of investment excessively in favor of the host country, investment in exploration and in capital facilities could be discouraged. This is not likely to bring about an immediate withdrawal of foreign firms, since their investment in plant and equipment is fixed and they would find partial recovery better than none. But the result could be a tendency to redirect operations and investments toward safe areas even though the deposits cost more to extract, leaving more favorable deposits to go undeveloped—to the mutual disadvantage of countries with high quality deposits and mineral consumers.[49]

As of 1977, nationalism in South America and political unrest in Africa were operating to damp the investment level in raw materials in areas which contained rich ore deposits.

Among the forms of economic nationalism most canvassed, debated, and feared has been an extension of producers' cartels, like OPEC, to other raw materials. Efforts in this direction were undertaken in 1973–1974 among some producers of phosphates and bauxite, in the latter case with considerable success. And they may be attempted in other commodities. The particular mixture of conditions which has made OPEC possible and thus far unified is not generally present in other cases—notably, the existence of major residual suppliers who can afford large fluctuations in foreign-exchange earnings. But the impulse to emulate OPEC could create both economic and political circumstances leading to higher costs for raw materials.

Thus, in raw materials, as with food and energy, economic rather than resource problems in the narrow sense are critical to the outcome. These economic problems, in turn, are heavily dependent on the cast of public policy, national and international. If the OECD world recovers and sustains the high growth rates of the 1960's, the odds are strong, in my view, that relatively high raw-materials prices will prevail over the next quarter-century. This is likely to be true even if the North-South negotiations discussed in Chapter 55 yield price-stabilizing agreements between producers and importers of raw materials.

53

Pollution and the Environment

As noted earlier, the serious public examination of environmental problems raised by the expansion of industry antedates acute concern about energy, food, and raw materials. Perhaps the publication of Rachel Carson's *Silent Spring* in 1962 is a useful benchmark, although discussions in the 1950's of the consequences of atmospheric atomic explosions may have stimulated thought in this direction. They, too, were an exercise in global welfare economics. In the course of the 1960's, concern about the future of the environment was translated into various forms of governmental action, at national and local levels; and the issue was dramatized at the 1972 Stockholm Conference on the Human Environment, sponsored by the United Nations.

In talking about the human environment and its problems, one is, of course, dealing with a spectrum including potential dangers to human life on a massive, even global, scale; serious dangers for particular communities; substantial dangers which raise mortality and illness rates in particular regions to a limited degree; progressive degradation of the physical and aesthetic environment in which human beings live; and failures to exploit opportunities to create a more agreeable setting for human life. On an ascending scale, the spectrum has been broadly defined as follows:

> Class 1 in which the amenities and aesthetic qualities of life are violated.
>
> Class 2 in which there is injury or death to individuals from environmental contamination.
>
> Class 3 in which whole species are threatened with extinction from disturbances in ecological interrelationships.
>
> Class 4 in which fundamental cycles in the biologic pyramid and its natural environment are distorted or destroyed to such a degree that life for whole series of living forms becomes impossible over wide areas and possibly over the globe as a whole.[50]

Just as momentum was gathering to deal with this spectrum of concerns, the world economy was struck by the price convulsion of

1972–1974, the acute recession it set in motion in the OECD world, and the consequent retardation in most of the non–oil-producing developing countries. The upshot was a decline or reduction in the increase of real public resources available for all purposes. From a budgetary point of view, this has sharpened the inevitable conflict between claims for resources to improve the environment and other urgent tasks. In a setting of continued inflation, with long-run prospects for relatively high energy, food, and, perhaps, raw-materials costs, the limited but real cost increases associated with environmental control and improvement have weighed more heavily on governments than when they were initially calculated in the ebullient pre-1973 setting of the world economy. In a larger perspective, the budgetary calculus should not be decisive. As we shall see, up to a point outlays to improve the air and water are a form of productive investment which, if enlarged, could both pay their way and hasten the return of high growth rates in the OECD world.

In the developing regions, there has been a tendency to regard environmental concern as a luxury only rich nations can afford. Nevertheless, the tasks remain. Nations, acting individually and collectively, will have to decide the priority they should enjoy. And to some degree they can be made to converge with tasks laid on the common agenda by other forces that have come into play; that is, the environment should be improved by efforts to damp the rate of population increase, to reduce the size and energy consumption of automobiles, and to find a new, essentially infinite, relatively nonpolluting energy base.

As for the dangers, the greatest remains the most obscure; that is, the possibility of man's economic activities so altering the climate as to produce a major catastrophe. The concern centers on two contrary possibilities.

> Theories and speculations of the global effects of pollution have included assertions that the build-up of CO_2 from fossil fuel combustion might warm up the planet and cause the polar ice to melt, thus raising the sea level several hundred feet and submerging coastal cities. Equally foreboding has been the warning of the possibility that particles emitted into the air from industrial, energy, and transportation processes might prevent some sunlight from reaching the earth's surface, thus lowering global temperature and beginning a new ice age.[51]

These anxieties come to rest on the possibility of inducing, respectively, a contraction or an expansion of the polar ice pack, with consequences for the weather which we do not yet understand but which, conceivably, could be catastrophic. These anxieties arise, in turn, from the apparently delicate balance in nature by which the arctic ice is maintained, its possible vulnerability to melting with the rise of a few degrees centigrade in temperature, and the probability that, once melted, it would not again freeze over. The possibility of controlling excessive emission of particles into the atmosphere, by electrostatic precipitation, has tended to focus anxieties on a heating of the atmosphere rather than a cooling, on a dissipation of arctic ice rather than its enlargement.

It should be noted, parenthetically, that, quite independent of the weather changes that an enlarged industrial civilization might bring about, some sober students of weather cycles believe that we are due for a protracted period of cooler temperatures in the northern hemisphere of a kind not known since the end of the seventeenth century. By these calculations, a mini–ice age (1400–1700) gave way to a warming period which, conceivably, may have begun to reverse about 1940.

For our purposes, three conclusions suffice:

—the scale and intensity of energy generation on the earth are not likely to raise this possible problem until the next century, although energy emissions can have (and are having) narrower local and regional effects;

—large increases in knowledge are required before we can confidently predict what effects even vastly expanded industrial activity might have on the equations of nature which determine climate;

—but, as noted earlier, these concerns increase the relative desirability of fusion power or, even more, solar energy as ultimate solutions to the energy problem.

In terms of resources, the costs of enlarged research on man's impact on the climate, including increased monitoring of temperature changes, etc., will be substantial, but not a significant economic burden.

In the spectrum of danger, the next level down from irreversible change in the climate is the array of problems thrown up by the use of nuclear fission to generate electric power. They include, at one extreme, the problem of increasing the likelihood of additional nations deciding to produce explosive devices from materials generated by atomic energy plants—an inefficient but possible method. There is the possibility of theft of nuclear materials from power plants and the manufacture and use of weapons for purposes of terror. There is also the possibility of a major, if localized, disaster caused by a technical failure; for example, the rupture of a main pipe carrying cooling water in the reactor, combined with a failure of the backup cooling system. The chance of a pipe rupture is estimated narrowly between one chance in ten thousand per reactor per year and one chance in twenty thousand. If there were one thousand reactors operational, this means the emergency cooling system would be called upon to perform every decade or two. If the backup system also failed and the overheated reactor melted down and breached, the result would be not an explosion but the release of radiation, which could be dangerous if the unlikely double failure occurred near a densely populated area. The radiation could cause deaths from acute exposure, cancer, and gastric defects for up to five generations.

The breeder reactor (LMFRB) also carries with it serious problems of waste disposal and a different kind of potential danger. A critical mass of fissionable material could conceivably assemble, leading to a low-grade nuclear explosion (say, equivalent to less than a ton of TNT). But the prospects are for a breeder reactor at least as safe as present nuclear plants. There is also the problem of endlessly and securely disposing of the radioactive wastes generated by atomic energy plants and avoiding, for example, leakage from the underground storage of such wastes. However low one may rate the statistical likelihood of the dangers that flow from the generation of electricity by nuclear reactors with existing technology, their reality suggests to many the priority in the short run of expanding energy production, where possible, by other means, and, in the longer run, the priority of achieving efficient fusion or solar power. We can limit the scale of the risks associated with atomic power, but we cannot eliminate them. Atomic energy plants now operate in many parts of the world. Many more are building or will be built. From every current indication, nuclear energy will be not a last resort but a massive energy sector over the next generation. These facts of life require of us endless care and vigilance, as well as efforts to contain nuclear weapons proliferation at its present amply dangerous limits.

As the focus shifts, from a possible Faustian tragedy brought on by man's altering irreversibly his climate or not controlling adequately the possible by-products of atomic energy, to dirty water and impure air, one confronts less danger and more expense. This is an area where the health and mortality rates of citizens in particular regions are involved and, perhaps, the survival of certain species of animals, birds, or fish. The amenities and aesthetic quality of the environment are also at stake. One is up against a grandiose version of the textbook case of external diseconomies: How do you take into account and correct for "harmful effects on other people that result from one man's production"—or other economic activity?[52] How do you measure and decide the desirability of outlays to reduce or eliminate external diseconomies against other uses of scarce resources?

The evidence is that, even with existing technologies, the objectives of reasonably clean air and water are attainable at a real but moderate price; that is, a price that does not damp significantly or absolutely reduce real income per capita so long as a reasonably high overall growth rate is maintained. The benefits of such outlays, althought difficult to measure in conventional income accounting, are real and substantial, quite aside from the aesthetic objectives achieved; e.g., reduced metal corrosion, crop losses, work days lost through illness, etc. In the United States, for example, it was estimated that damage from air pollution could reach a level of $24 billion in 1977, of which $9 billion would be damage to health.[53]

The effects on British cities of the Clean Air Act of 1956 are widely cited, as is progress achieved in reducing pollution in the Thames and Hudson rivers, as well as in the Great Lakes. The costs of achieving various environmental goals evidently depend, in part, on the standards set and the time period allowed for their achievement. Costs tend to rise disproportionately as one seeks the very highest standards of purity. For example, it was estimated in 1972 that to remove 85–90 percent of major pollutants from water in the United States would cost in 1980 $23–$27 billion (1971 dollars) in capital, operating, and maintenance costs.[54] To remove 95–99 percent of major pollutants would raise the 1980 cost to $60–$70 billion. The order of magnitude of the total costs involved (under the first assumption about water) is suggested by the estimate that some $40 billion would be required to meet United States air and water standards in 1980 as opposed to outlays of $4 billion in 1970.[55] These are not trivial figures; and the United States would have to allocate a significant proportion of its increment of real income to pay this bill. Just what the proportion of antipollution expenditures to GNP in fact proves to be depends on a good many variables, including the manner in which capital costs are accounted for. Such estimates as are now available for OECD countries suggest new programs of pollution control may rise to levels of 1.5–2.0 percent of annual GNP in the second half of the 1970's, to about twice that level in Japan.[56]

The building into our economic life of regular outlays expanding in this way is bound to have substantial effects. Pollution control has, for example, increased costs and prices; and it will continue to make the rate of inflation somewhat higher than it would otherwise be. Pollution control has also become a big enough enterprise to affect the level of employment. In the sharp recession of 1974–1975, outlays for pollution control in the United States, at least, somewhat cushioned the decline in output and employment; but if we sustain relatively full utilization of labor and industrial capacity over the next decade, the increase in gross national product is likely to be somewhat less than it would be without pollution control expenditures—perhaps as much as 2.2 percent lower in 1984 than it would otherwise be. The capital requirements for pollution control are now a significant element in capital requirements for the future; and they may lead to somewhat higher interest rates than would otherwise prevail. Moreover, the problems posed by pollution control have an uneven impact on various industries. They are particularly important in pulp and paper, metalworking, electric utilities, chemicals, iron and steel. In a period of rapid general expansion of the economy, this uneven impact could contribute to the emergence of capacity bottlenecks which could bring the boom to a premature end.

On the other hand, there are two reasons why calculations of this kind are an insufficient measurement of the impact of pollution control on the economy. First, our traditional measurements of gross national product have not embraced the serious capital depreciation imposed upon air, water, and other aspects of the environment by growth in the sectors which are measured. There is no doubt that if gross national product had been correctly measured in the past, to take account of environmental damage, its rate of increase would be lower than we now calculate. Second, an improvement in the quality of air and water will have certain quite straightforward positive economic effects. They are real enough, although difficult to measure with precision. For example, an improvement in air quality will not only reduce the incidence of certain diseases but also enlarge the effective amount of work a labor force of a given size can contribute. For another example, an improvement in air quality will reduce the amount of damage done to buildings and other structures and thereby reduce the costs of repair and repainting. Similar straightforward economic benefits derive from cleaner water—for example, an enlarged commercial supply of fish. Moreover, in affluent nations where an increasing proportion of the population can afford to travel to beaches, parks, and lakes, these amenities take on an economic as well as an aesthetic significance. In the 1960's, for example, visitors to national parks increased at an average rate of 8 percent, more than twice the rate of increase in gross national product.

In short, the real costs of pollution control are substantially unavoidable if we are not to run down irretrievably certain basic natural resources; and the results of effective pollution control contribute positively to the nation's income, even if those contributions are difficult to measure with precision. If excessively high standards of air and water purity are not sought, the control of pollution is likely to prove cost-effective in conventional economic as well as in aesthetic terms.

The politics of pollution control, notably in the case of water, is complex. Rivers, lakes, and oceans do not neatly conform to the structure and jurisdiction of the political units which have emerged over time. Even within a state or county, different communities will feel the impact of water pollution in differing ways and apply quite different standards in calculating the costs and benefits of outlays to reduce pollution. Many major water pollution problems in the United States require detailed agreement on courses of action among several states. In Europe, problems of the Rhine, the Baltic, and the Mediterranean are, inherently, international as are, of course, problems of the Atlantic and Pacific. Thus, once again, problems that start with concern over the pressure of an expanding industrial civilization on scarce resources emerge, in the first instance, as economic, but ultimately as political. In this case, the political problem takes a double form: the will of political units to accept the costs (and seek the benefits) of maintaining a safe, healthy, and aesthetically satisfying environment, and the necessity of creating new forms of domestic and international cooperation.

54

Political Economy in the Fifth Kondratieff Upswing

The burden of the argument is, then, that history has brought us to a time when, for a protracted period, the relative prices of food and energy, air and water, and perhaps raw materials in general will be higher than we have known them to be over the past generation; and, in dealing with this situation, political action will be critically important. What broad implications for policy and politics flow from these judgments? What actions will be required if the world community is to transit successfully the next quarter-century and open the way for relatively easier times in the century ahead?

In this and the subsequent chapter I shall consider in sequence policies which might achieve the following results:

—necessary changes in patterns of investment;

—the return to full employment and regular growth in the OECD world;

—the return to high growth rates in the developing world;

—required patterns of international cooperation;

—an appropriate role for the United States;

—and the changes in public attitudes within societies required to sustain appropriate policies, including the effective control of inflation.

A special and unifying characteristic of this book is its insistence on the central role of changing patterns of investment as opposed to a more conventional emphasis on the aggregate scale of investment in relation to GNP. This perspective suffused the treatment of trends, cycles, and growth in Parts Three, Four, and Five. It is also, in my mind, the most fundamental way to approach the tasks of public policy that lie ahead.

The first proposition that flows from the review of major problems in this chapter concerns a kind of investment usually separated from others; that is, investment in science, invention, and the initial acts of innovation. These activities are usually given short shrift in conventional expositions of economic theory. It seems to me evident that two things are true: the total volume of investment (including first-rate human talent) in science, research, and development, as a proportion of total investment, must be increased; second, the pattern of investment in research and development must shift in new directions. In part, changing relative prices can be counted upon to bring about these shifts; but public policy is critically involved.

As for the total scale of outlays in science, invention, and innovation, our statistics are imperfect. Private sector R&D outlays are particularly difficult to assemble, even in a field of such heightened priority as energy.[57] The best approximations we have are the estimates of total outlays for research and development for twenty OECD countries. These exhibit some leveling off or decline after a peak in the mid-1960's for the larger nations (Chart VI-7). Nevertheless, as one sums up the major issues in this chapter, one can conclude with some confidence that R&D outlays ought to increase rather sharply as a proportion of GNP (or total investment) in the years ahead. The list of essential tasks is quite formidable: improved birth control technology, new methods to maintain the momentum of productivity increase in agriculture, the increased priority for conservation and new sources of supply in both energy and raw materials, and the desirability of new technologies to control air and water pollution.

The energy case poses again, in narrower form, the recurrent theme of aggregated versus disaggregated analysis. The task in energy R&D has not been merely to enlarge outlays; it has been to change the pattern of those outlays in a quite particular way. Down to the coming of the oil crisis in 1973, government R&D outlays in energy were overwhelmingly concentrated on atomic power; and, in the United States, 40 percent of the total for energy was assigned in a single direction—the liquid metal fast breeder reactor. Evidently, a great enlargement of total energy R&D outlays is required if the full range of promising short-, medium-, and long-run measures to constrain consumption and expand energy output is to be explored. And this is so, even if priority for the breeder reactor is reduced. In the United States the process is under way: total federal R&D expenditures on energy almost quadrupled, in real terms, between 1969 and 1977, and those enlarged allocations were increasingly diversified. A similar transition in R&D energy outlays is occurring among other OECD nations, as well as in less developed nations which contain potential energy sources.

The pattern of R&D outlays in the private energy sector must also change. In 1972, for example, two-thirds of private R&D funds in the United States were for oil and gas: its discovery; equipment for its exploration; and its transmission. Less than 0.5 percent was for coal. The energy industry had geared its research priorities to the world of artificially cheap energy prices and, within it, to the acquisition of gas and oil. Past priorities for research and development

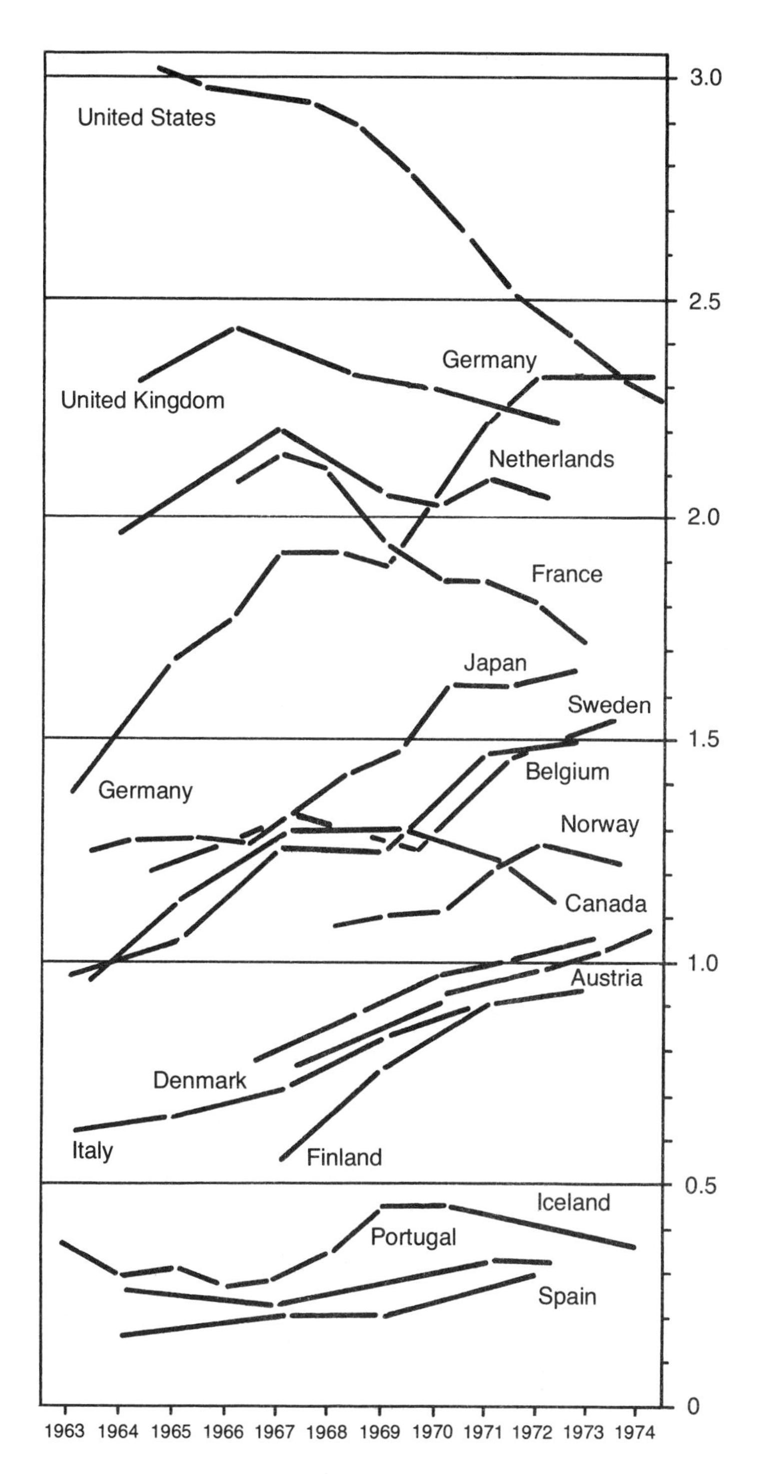

CHART VI-7. *Gross Expenditures in Research and Development as Percentage of GDP: Twenty OECD Countries, 1963–1974*

Source: *OECD Observer*, no. 76 (July–August 1975), p. 31.

in the automobile and other industries have similarly been rendered out of date.

It is the market of politics (combined with intellectual fashion and bureaucratic inertia) that determines public allocations of R&D resources. It is instructive to see the directions in which public resources were shifting in the 1960's (Table VI-12). On the eve of the rise in oil prices, the direction of shift was away from military R&D and "Big Science" (that is, aviation, new transport technology, nuclear science, and data processing) toward problems of health, environmental protection and research into urban life. Now, in the mid-1970's, of course, the directions are shifting again.[58]

The change in direction of R&D priorities and the need to expand the relative volume of resources devoted to such purposes raise questions about three important matters which can be dealt with only briefly here: the criteria for the public role in R&D; the scope for international cooperation; and problems of national planning of R&D.

J. Herbert Holloman and his colleagues have attempted to draw the appropriate general lines justifying the allocation of public resources for R&D in the field of energy.[59] Where the government is the owner of energy resources, they believe it should "try to maximize the returns on its holdings" and "assume *the same tax and regulatory circumstances* as would a private owner." As an overseer of

TABLE VI-12. *Rank of Major Groups in Government Research and Development Funding during the 1960's: Twelve Countries*

	(1) National Security and Big Science	(2) Economic Development	(3) Community Services	(4) Advancement of Science
Belgium	2 → 4	3	4 → 2	1
Canada	1 → 2	2 → 1	4 → 3	3 → 4
France	1	3	4	2
Germany	1 → 2	3	4	2 → 1
Italy	1 → 2	3	4	2 → 1
Japan	3	2	4	1
Netherlands	3 → 2	2 → 3	4	1
Norway	3	2	4	1
Spain	2	1	4	3
Sweden	1	3	4	2
United Kingdom[a]	1	2	4	3
United Kingdom[b]		3		2
United States	1	3	2	4

[a] Research Councils distributed.
[b] Research Councils grouped in "Advancement of Research."
Arrows indicate change of rank during 1960's.
Source: *OECD Observer*, no. 72 (October–November 1974), p. 12.

the private energy supply system, the government should intervene only when noneconomic values are at stake (e.g., national security, foreign policy, public welfare, equity) or when "the market may fail to allocate resources in a socially optimal way."

They identify three types of market failure. First, externalities, "where the relevant decision-making unit is unable to fully perceive or to compute all the costs or benefits associated with its activities. There are strong economic arguments for the government to support R&D in this instance." Second, "where the costs of carrying out specific research tasks would be significantly lowered if supported by the government on a nationwide basis." Third, where "the product of such research possesses the characteristics of what economists term 'public goods' " and "the decision of how much to supply to each unit or individual . . . must be made by the political system."

It will be necessary to arrive at consensus on some such criteria in the time ahead over a much wider range of activity than R&D. But the fact is that the sectors of American and other national industries vary a great deal in their capacity to generate and apply new technologies. Cost-benefit analysis in private profit terms does not wholly explain these variations. For reasons going deep into their origins, structure, and executive personalities, the chemical, electricity and electronic, and aerospace industries in the United States have been much more comfortable in allocating resources to and using promptly the results of R&D than, say, the steel, automobile, and metalworking industries. The latter have been exceedingly sluggish despite the goad of international competition. In part, this is a matter of when they became leading sectors in economic growth: the older industries (e.g., railroads, textiles, steel) have generally been less oriented to modern R&D methods than newer industries (e.g., chemicals, electricity, electronics). Institutional analysis must buttress prima facie application of welfare economics in this field.

If, in fact, R&D resources emerge as scarce over the next generation, the case for international cooperation is inherently strong. Truly international research institutions have, in some cases, yielded striking results; e.g., the wheat strains developed in Mexico, the rice strains in the Philippines. And these examples have led to an enlargement of international efforts focused on specific agricultural problems.[60] In Europe there is well-coordinated or integrated work going forward on coal technology and the possibility of nuclear fusion.[61] On the other hand, integrated or international R&D institutions are not easy to build and sustain at the highest levels of excellence. They should be used sparingly on a restricted range of carefully identified problems of wide international interest and high priority. Moreover, there is considerable virtue as well as inevitability in the likelihood that national programs will draw the bulk of R&D resources. The priority tasks of particular nations differ with their resource endowments and deficiencies, their stage of development, and their economic and social priorities. Areas of comparative advantage might naturally emerge, where a group within a particular country appears to be forging ahead and its progress justifies the international community in throwing behind its effort an enlarged flow of talent and resources.

Finally, there is the question of how governments should organize themselves to guide and nurture the R&D sector. In democratic societies this requires the orchestration of direct government action with incentives to a diffuse private sector to approximate, in the end, a desired national result. There is no simple administrative formula for doing this. What is required in each major dimension of R&D is a central point in government with an intelligent overview of the resources available; the building of a public-private consensus on appropriate priorities; the use of direct and indirect government influence to approximate those priorities; and a system of constant evaluation of results combined with a willingness to shift priorities as the living processes of science and technology development unfold.

There is a subtle supply side to this equation. It is not merely a matter of governments' supplementing the incentives of the market to make necessity more efficiently the mother of invention. Science is not wholly a malleable body of knowledge supporting equally invention in one desired direction or another. It has evolved in a sequence related to ease of observation and the availability of tools for experiment and measurement.[62] At any period of time it has a life and set of directions of its own. As within an economy, certain sectors of scientific endeavor are rising rapidly, full of excitement as they unfold the implications of new basic insights; others are elaborating second- or third-order refinements, rooted in germinal concepts generated further in its past. These new directions in science do not yield automatically new practical inventions, any more than cotton textile machinery, the manufacture of iron from coke, and Watt's steam engine flowed directly from the labors of the great sequence of pioneers stretching from Copernicus to Newton. In the mid-1970's we live in a world where the entire body of knowledge may have doubled in the past twenty years; more than half the research and development ever conducted has occurred in the past ten years; 90 percent of all scientists and engineers ever professionally trained are now alive.[63] The scale, momentum, and new directions of basic science are already yielding potential results (through, for example, microbiology and the laser) which could transform technologies in industry and agriculture in ways we do not know. Therefore, one aspect of public policy is to nurture and remain alert to the paths basic scientific knowledge may take, out of its own inner life, and to foreshorten the time when these insights are put to use.

An active concern with the specific directions science, invention, and innovation take is simply one facet of a general task of public policy: to assume responsibility, over a significant range, for the pattern of investment as well as its aggregate scale. This requires changes in modes of thought and in the organization of government in democratic societies.

The dominating intellectual framework for public policy evolved since the 1930's has been income analysis; that is, the analysis of the major broad components of national income in terms that permitted public authorities to act, through fiscal and monetary policy and by other devices, to maintain relatively full employment without causing the society to experience excessive inflation. Putting aside the mobilization and dispersal of public funds for welfare and other social purposes, national income analysis had little concern for how individuals and firms in the private sector spent or invested their scarce resources. The tests of private taste and private judgments about profitability sufficed. Evidently, this mode of thought and the policies that flowed from it were insufficient to control wage-push inflation; but they did serve tolerably well in a time when the OECD world was diffusing the automobile and durable consumers' goods on a mass basis, while increasing public (as well as private) allocations to education, health, and other welfare purposes. Built into this system were important implicit assumptions: an increasing population could be provided with jobs and fed; the scale and directions taken by R&D (except for military purposes and space) could be left mainly to private judgments and incentives; relative price and profit movements would generate appropriate patterns of investment and adequate inputs of energy, raw materials, and food; environmental problems could be ignored or dealt with, as minor matters, under the heading of public policy designed to correct for external diseconomies.

This is, evidently, an inadequate intellectual framework for a protracted period when problems of population, food, energy, raw materials, and the environment have marched to the center of the stage and require something more than the price system and modest adjustments in public policy. If the portrait of the world economy and its prospects developed here is roughly correct, economists and governments must be concerned with the structure of output as well as its level, the composition of investment as well as its aggregate adequacy to the requirements of relatively full employment. The advanced industrial nations will live, if they are successful, in a setting somewhere between a mixed Keynesian welfare economy and a war economy. The latter analogy is relevant because now, as during a war, the composition of output matters. In a war one must set targets, with reasonable precision, for the number of uniforms, guns, ships, planes, the direction of R&D, etc. The analogy is not exact because the legitimate concerns of government are now much narrower and, generally, less detailed than during a war. Private tastes and investment decisions can continue to prevail over a much wider front. Perhaps the best analogy is the kind of indicative sectoral planning pioneered by Jean Monnet in France after the Second

World War. At its core was close but flexible public-private cooperation to assure levels of investment in key sectors appropriate to the requirements for the modernization of the economy.

For those, like myself, who would prefer to see the competitive market system operate to the maximum consistent with the public interest and who believe public intervention involves costs as well as potential benefits, the question arises: What is it, precisely, that requires a significant degree of sectoral planning of investment? The answer is twofold. First, governments are already deeply embedded in agricultural, energy, raw-materials, and environmental policy. In fact, by somewhat different routes, both the food crisis at the end of 1972 and the energy crisis begun a year later were products of prior governmental policy. As a practical matter, it seems most unlikely that governments will, in fact, remove themselves from these fields. Second, there are aspects of each of these four fields (as well as of family planning) where government participation appears technically necessary if public purposes are to be more or less fulfilled. To use the vocabulary quoted earlier with reference to energy R&D, all these fields are touched with "noneconomic values" (including national security) and affected by private markets subject to "externalities" and "indivisibilities," which, in varying degree, "fail to allocate resources in a socially optimal way"; and, in some cases, these fields involve products which are "public goods" (e.g., clean air and water).

In short, the governments, in a disjointed way, are in the sectoral planning business; they are likely to stay there; to a degree they ought to stay there; and the objective, therefore, is to do the best job intelligence and a sense of proportion permit.

This is no trivial conclusion. It is, in fact, similar to the empirical conclusion at which Keynes arrived which led to his revolutionary reshaping of classical economics. His central insight was that, in his time, money wages had become inflexible downward. A decline in the effective demand for labor did not yield the fall in money wages which, in classical theory, would have cleared the labor market and maintained full employment. Therefore, to maintain the level of employment, governments had to act to maintain the level of effective demand for labor. The conclusion here is that, for good or ill, governments are so inextricably enmeshed in the sectors on which both full employment and structural adjustment depend that the necessary alternations in the pattern of investment will not occur without conscious government policy. The last four Kondratieff upswings were (more or less) transited by the redirection of private investment resources in response to changes in relative prices and evolving technological possibilities. We shall have to think our way through the fifth Kondratieff upswing. Relative price changes are a necessary but not sufficient condition for the appropriate change in investment patterns. But to arrive at this conclusion is the beginning, not the end, of the matter.

Governments face tasks as basic as new forms of data collection and as difficult as coordinating the policies of their various departments and guiding the private sectors on to the right patterns of investment without frustrating them and destroying their powers of initiative. There is, evidently, a great deal for governments to do. With respect to energy, for example, the Teller report concludes with fourteen substantive recommendations for federal action under the heading of conservation; nine bearing on energy in relationship to the environment; seven with respect to oil and gas production; four with respect to coal; seven with respect to nuclear reactors; two with respect to electricity; twenty-two with respect to R&D; five bearing on demonstration plants; one concerning underground nuclear plants; three with respect to highly specific forms of international cooperation; and four general and institutional recommendations, including the creation of a National Resource Mobilization Corporation, a recommendation to which the Ford administration (but not the Congress) promptly responded.[64] Every one of these seventy-eight recommendations involves technical and/or policy complexities, including legislation in some cases. The Ford Foundation report on energy concludes with almost as long a list.[65] Studies of family planning, agriculture, raw materials, and the environment emerge with similar catalogues of recommended public action, national and international.

Without accepting or rejecting any of these prescriptions, we can see that they all reflect a simple fact: in the modern political world the price system will not suffice to bring about the kinds of structural adjustment, the changed patterns of investment the situation requires. This is why the OECD economies are likely to move toward sectoral planning and intensified public-private cooperation in the time ahead.

The lack of a firm grasp on the sectors contributes to an inability of economists and the governments they advise to answer persuasively an important aggregate question about the future: Do the nations of the OECD world require higher levels of investment than, say, those of the 1960's? I shall have something to say about this in the context of recovery from the recession of 1974–1975. In longer-run terms, neither the data nor the techniques exist to project overall investment requirements because, to be helpful, they must emerge from detailed analyses of sectoral requirements and assumed public policies toward the sectors. Such estimates must also allow for the changing sectoral structure of economies. Highly aggregated analyses (covering, say, consumption, investment, and public outlays) simply do not suffice.

Nevertheless, six observations on this question are possible, reflecting major variables that will determine the outcome.

—Whether higher investment rates will be required will vary considerably within the OECD world, because the new trend period opened with considerable variation in those rates. For example, in

1970 the proportion of gross investment to GNP was 41 percent in Japan, 30 percent in Germany, 29 percent in France, 23 percent in Italy, 20 percent in the United Kingdom, 18 percent in the United States. It is from something like those figures that each nation will have to redispose its investment patterns in the new trend period. One's instinctive feeling is, of course, that it is more likely that the United Kingdom and the United States will have to raise their investment rates than, say, Japan, Germany, and France.

—The outcome will be partially determined by the extent to which the state of the economy and public policy encourage or constrain the further diffusion of automobiles, durable consumers' goods, and other energy-intensive forms of private consumption. If these are sharply constrained, investment requirements in the relevant sectoral complexes will be reduced, freeing resources for investment in other directions. The size these complexes had attained in the various OECD economies by the early 1970's makes the degree of their reduction (or retardation) a significant element in determining whether enlarged investment proportions will be necessary to meet other needs.

—The extent of available alternative energy resources available and public policies toward energy production and economy will affect the level and proportion of energy-related investment possible and actually undertaken. For example, there is greater scope for enlarged energy-related investment in the United States than in Japan. In the extreme case, the setting of an objective that the United States become an energy exporter by 1985 would require more investment than settling for, say, a 50 percent dependence in petroleum on OPEC imports. But even here the calculation is complex, since 50 percent dependence means that large outlays, including investment outlays, will be required to sustain the necessary level of exports to OPEC countries with (probably) unfavorable United States terms of trade.

—The outcome will also depend on the targets set and the policies actually pursued toward pollution control, housing (including insulation and investment in solar heating and cooling), research and development, etc.

—Similarly, the resources available for additional investment will depend on welfare policy: whether governments continue to expand real outlays on education, medical care, etc.; whether transfer payments for welfare purposes are expanded or leveled off; and whether such changes affect private consumption or resources available for investment.

—Finally, the outcome will depend on the rate of growth of the economy itself and the degree to which public policy (including, especially, tax policy) encourages the plowing back of profits as opposed to their flow to public authorities or stockholders. This factor may prove to be critical to the real rate of growth of the OECD countries, because three forces are at work tending to reduce the productivity of investment (raising the marginal capital-output ratio): the higher cost of energy; the tendency for productivity increases to decelerate in the older leading sectors (e.g., automobiles); and those allocations to the improvement of the environment which are not cost-effective in conventional national income accounting terms. Taken together, they make it likely that a higher proportion of GNP will have to be invested than in the past two decades to sustain a given rate of growth. They also justify in advanced industrial societies special efforts to accelerate productivity increases throughout the economy, for what is at stake here is not merely the formal statistical performance of the OECD economies in some abstract growthmanship race. The rate of productivity increase (as well as high, sustained levels of employment) will also help determine whether the real wages of labor can continue to rise despite chronically unfavorable terms of trade and enlarged allocations of resources to strengthen the foundations of industrial civilization. In each of the other four Kondratieff upswings examined in Part Three, real wages came under pressure.

Barry Bosworth and his colleagues have attempted to calculate investment requirements in their study of the United States, *Capital Needs in the Seventies*.[66] Their finding that a slight increase in the investment rate is necessary is considered below. But the general debate on whether the OECD world faces a capital crunch remains indecisive and impressionistic because the data available and the theoretical concepts most generally applied do not permit us to deal with the problem in a systematic way.

As often in history, the long-run issue will be settled by a sequence of short-run decisions; in particular, the decisions taken or not taken to bring the OECD world back to relatively full employment.

The link between short-run and long-run problems is illustrated by the debate about investment conducted between high-level protagonists in the United States, Republican and Democrat, conservative and liberal. In the summer of 1975, Walter Heller, for example, challenged the tax prescriptions of President Ford and his Secretary of the Treasury, William Simon, for generally stimulating investment.[67] Heller argued that the aggregate level of investment in relation to GNP had remained stable over the past decade; that a high rate of economic growth would generate the savings and investment to meet the needs of the next decade; and that the United States required increased general stimulus to consumption and a closing of tax loopholes rather than regressive tax changes to stimulate investment at a time of large idle industrial capacity. As a debating matter, Professor Heller scored some good points; but this was because the Ford administration had posed the problem in an overaggregated way, permitting Heller to reply in similar terms. What was then required in the United States and in other OECD countries was not an undifferentiated expansion of investment but a rapid expansion in certain particular directions: energy, energy conservation, housing, pollution control programs, etc.

The Heller-Simon debate, with both missing the central point, continued to suffuse American politics in different forms over the two subsequent years. The Carter administration pressed forward with neo-Keynesian measures while responding to public pressure to constrain federal deficits. The Republicans continued to argue for undifferentiated tax stimulus to investment. No effective political voice argued that the key to sustained high growth rates lay in expanded investment in energy, energy conservation, and effective action on other major structural problems of the fifth Kondratieff upswing.

Why is it that the prescriptions for reducing unemployment through stimulus to consumers' demand are not now sufficient? The short answer is that higher energy prices and, for some advanced industrial countries, a sharp unfavorable shift in the terms of trade have cut into real income or sharply decelerated its expansion; against this background and the combination of inflation and recession, governments do not command the tax resources to compensate by rapidly expanding outlays for social services (e.g., education and health care). Meanwhile, increased deficit financing confronts the fact that budgets are already severely unbalanced, and there is a quite general political revolt in the OECD world against increasing government welfare outlays at previous rates. The rapid expansion of exports to the OPEC countries constitutes an insufficient compensation for these reduced private and public outlays.

The rise in energy prices has thus weakened the viability of the leading sectors in North American, Western European, and Japanese growth, which were also the basis for the high level of international trade within the OECD world among industrialized countries. As in the 1850's and 1890's, resumed prosperity and growth require a massive shift in investment in new directions toward generating the output the movement of relative prices has signaled as necessary. A revival of international trade, in somewhat different patterns, will follow these shifts in patterns of investment and a return to high OECD growth rates.

Put another way, it is the multiplier (expanding income and employment through new forms of investment) rather than the accelerator (expanding investment through the increase in income) that primarily will be required to pull the OECD world out of recession and back to sustained growth. In a sense, the world economy is returning in a degree to the dynamics of the pre-1914 world as opposed to the environment which has existed since the 1920's, when the leading sectors of high mass-consumption emerged.

This proposition relates to a marginal shift in the relative role of the two mechanisms, not to a complete reversal. Surely, various built-in supports to the level of income and consumption cushioned the recession of 1974–1975 in the OECD world, as did government deficits and a liberalization of monetary policies; and this cushioning prevented even greater declines in investment levels than those which in fact occurred. Surely, fiscal and monetary policy must contribute further to the return to full employment, as they have to the limited but still real OECD revival of 1975–1977. Nevertheless, the marginal shifts in the pattern of investment outlays required are of significant orders of magnitude. They have been given rough quantitative form by Barry Bosworth and his colleagues,[68] who estimate, for example, a rise of energy investment (in real terms) at an average annual rate of 8 percent, with a shift from 24.6 percent to 32.6 percent of energy to total investment between 1973 and 1980. Public and private investment to control pollution and to expand mass transport facilities are also assumed to increase rapidly. Bosworth and his colleagues foresee, further, the need for enlarged investment in a number of raw-materials processing industries, in which capacity shortages would assert themselves if unemployment were reduced to the 4 percent norm they assume and commend. Overall, the gross investment rate (public and private) would, in their calculations, rise from 17.5 percent of GNP in the period 1970–1973 to 18 percent in 1974–1980. This modest net movement assumes absolute declines in public outlays (in real terms) for education and highway construction (notably, the interstate system), outweighed by increases in energy, environmental, and mass-transport investment. These authors do not take into account a possible rise in R&D investment, which has, in fact, occurred. Residential construction would exhibit a slight net decline from its 1973 peak level even if public policy encourages housing investment considerably beyond demographic requirements. This study does not explore shifts in the pattern of private investment outlays, aside from its emphasis on material processing industries. In particular, it does not deal with the automobile sectoral complex, in which investment may have declined by a third in the recession of 1974–1975 and which is likely to play a somewhat diminished role in the American economy in the years ahead.

In effect, what the Bosworth analysis asserts is that the leading sector in the next U.S. cyclical expansion will be enlarged fixed investment (in energy, pollution control, public transport, etc.), with other categories declining or increasing only slightly in their relative role in the economy (Table VI-13). The purpose of the study was not to consider how the United States could get back to relatively full employment, but rather whether at 4 percent annual growth estimated capital requirements could be met without excessive strain. Nevertheless, the conclusions dramatize the critical role of a rapid expansion in energy and environmental investment in achieving full employment, notably at a time when investment in the automobile sectoral complex will relatively diminish in its role in the economy. Of their nature, these new, expanding sectors have important direct and indirect public components. Therefore, much

TABLE VI-13. *Gross National Product and Major Components: United States, Selected Years, 1960–1973, and Projected to 1980 (in Billions of 1973 Dollars)*

Component	Actual			Projected	Percentage Distribution		
	1960	1970	1973	1980	1960	1973	1980
Gross national product	758.0	1,118.4	1,289.1	1,730.2	100.0	100.0	100.0
Consumption	458.4	693.6	804.0	1,058.9	60.5	62.4	61.2
Nonresidential investment	74.0	119.3	144.2	215.6	9.8	11.2	12.5
Fixed investment	69.1	113.7	136.2	199.9	9.1	10.6	11.6
Inventory accumulation	4.9	5.6	8.0	15.7	0.6	0.6	0.9
Residential construction	37.3	37.9	58.0	56.3	4.9	4.5	3.3
Net exports	4.9	0.1	5.8	9.7			0.6
Federal government purchases	97.0	120.5	106.6	129.6	12.8	8.3	7.5
State and local government purchases	86.4	146.7	170.5	231.8	11.4	13.2	13.4
Unallocated resources	0	0	0	28.3	—	—	1.6

Source: Barry Bosworth, James S. Duesenberry, and Andrew S. Carron, *Capital Needs in the Seventies*, p. 38, where sources are indicated. The $28.3 billion in "unallocated resources" is, in these calculations, the consequence of a budget surplus achieved due to the shift of taxpayers to higher income brackets with the continued process of inflation assumed. It is the authors' judgment that if excessive rates of inflation are to be avoided, or a "capital market crunch," a surplus in the federal budget of this order of magnitude will have to be retained.

Note: Due to rounding, totals do not always equal sums of components.

more will be required of governments than conventional Keynesian remedies if the United States and other OECD countries are to resume the growth rates of the 1960's. They will have to turn their minds and policies to the task of nurturing the appropriate levels of investment in the key sectors of the economy required both by the need to return to relatively full employment and by the imperatives of structural balance in the world economy.

The return of the OECD world to regular growth is, of course, necessary for the social as well as economic well-being of its national societies: to generate increased public resources for welfare and investment purposes; to enlarge the resources available for private investment; and to expand the volume of trade, which has been overwhelmingly among the countries of this group (78 percent in 1970, although recession and the increase in OPEC imports have recently lowered that proportion). The full and sustained recovery of the OECD world is also one essential condition for the resumption of high growth rates in the less developed regions of the world. The linkage between OECD growth rates and the import capacity of developing nations is threefold: it affects the volume of sales to OECD nations, the terms of trade of developing countries, and the political and psychological willingness of OECD countries to envisage enlarged assistance to developing countries and trade policies that would assist those countries in earning more foreign exchange.

Putting aside for the moment the question of development assistance and trade policy, the powerful effects of alternative assumptions of OECD growth rates on the fortunes of two groups of developing countries can be seen in Table VI-14.[69] Average OECD growth of 3.5 percent per annum from 1975 to 1980 as opposed to 4.9 percent would reduce by half per capita growth rates in developing countries as a whole; and in the lower-income developing countries, embracing perhaps a billion human beings, it would reduce a

TABLE VI-14. *Projected Effects of Alternative OECD Growth Assumptions on the Developing Countries, 1975–1980*[a] *(% per Annum)*

	Lower-Income Countries		Middle-Income Countries		All Sample Panel Countries	
OECD growth	4.9	3.5	4.9	3.5	4.9	3.5
Developing countries' growth rates						
Volume of exports	5.8	4.6	8.6	6.6	8.2	6.4
Exports, capacity to import	6.5	4.8	8.4	6.1	8.1	5.9
Volume of imports	4.4	3.2	6.0	4.0	5.8	3.9
Gross domestic product	3.8	2.8	5.3	4.1	4.9	3.8
GDP per capita	1.2	0.2	2.6	1.4	2.3	1.2

[a] Assumes oil price constant at $9.40 per barrel in 1974 dollars.
Source: World Bank.

modest rate of progress (1.2 percent per capita) to virtual stagnation. It should be noted that the OECD growth rate was 4.9 percent from 1960 to 1970, −0.4 percent for 1974, −2.0 percent for 1975; per capita GDP increased for all developing countries at an average rate of 2.8 percent for 1961–1970, 3.0 percent for 1971–1974; but there was regression over the latter period (−0.8 percent) for the low-income countries. The middle-income countries (aside from OPEC) fared reasonably well down to 1974, but were hard hit by the OECD recession of 1974–1975, even though they enjoyed a higher capacity to sustain their level of imports from reserves and short-term borrowing.

Resumed high growth rates in the OECD world are evidently a necessary condition for resumed momentum in the non-OPEC developing world. But they are insufficient; that is, the 2.3 percent average per capita growth rate in the more optimistic projection in Table VI-14 compares with 2.8 percent for 1961–1970, 3.0 for the boom period 1971–1974. The 1975–1980 projections are, of course, damped by the fact that the initial year was one of depressed growth rates. The average performance for 1976–1980 is, therefore, assumed to be higher. But, by any accounting, the rate of progress in the lower-income developing countries in the 1960's (2 percent per capita) was inadequate. There are obvious human and ethical reasons for seeking higher rates of growth in the low-income developing nations, but the linkage of economic and social progress to declining birth rates makes this a major objective from the special perspective of this chapter, for it is in those regions that population pressure is most acute and the demographic transition least advanced.

A second potential source of acceleration in the developing world would be a decline of the oil price in real terms. The quadrupling of the oil price affected the developing world indirectly through its role in the OECD recession but also directly in shifting the terms of trade adversely for many developing countries and thus reducing their capacity to expand imports at a pace consistent with desirable rates of growth. Table VI-15 shows the substantial effect of a 20 percent decline in the oil price, notably on the growth per capita of the lower-income developing countries. The responsibility here lies not merely, or perhaps mainly, with OPEC; for that group of developing countries can be expected to try to maximize its market position. A real price decline in oil awaits a demonstration by the major oil importers of their seriousness about reducing their dependence on OPEC oil supplies, a demonstration still to be made.

A third potential source of resumed high growth rates in the developing world is an expansion in capital imports from governments and private sources. Table III-77 showed the scale of estimated net capital flows for the period 1973–1975. But the 44 percent rise in official aid to non-OPEC countries in 1974 barely matched the rise in import prices for developing countries; and, of course, it did not

TABLE VI-15. *Projected Effects of Alternative Oil Price Assumptions on the Developing Countries, 1975–1980 (% per Annum)*[a]

	Lower-Income Countries		Middle-Income Countries		All Sample Panel Countries	
Oil price[b]	9.40	7.50	9.40	7.50	9.40	7.50
Developing countries' growth rates						
Volume of exports	5.2	4.9	7.6	7.5	7.3	7.2
Exports, capacity to import	5.6	6.0	7.3	7.6	7.1	7.5
Volume of imports	3.8	4.3	5.0	5.4	4.9	5.3
Gross domestic product	3.3	3.8	4.7	5.0	4.4	4.7
GDP per capita	0.7	1.2	2.0	2.3	1.8	2.1

[a] Assumes medium OECD growth of 4.2 percent per year.
[b] Dollars per barrel (constant 1974 prices).
Source: World Bank.

fully cushion the total rise in import costs. The developing nations ran down their reserves and resorted, where access was available, to private capital markets, a process reflected in a 79 percent increase in private capital flows. The terms on which such loans were available sharply raised the burden of debt payment for a good many developing countries, while the willingness of OPEC countries to commit themselves to long-term aid programs is uncertain.

The prospect for OPEC aid is shadowed by the extent to which the sudden acquisition of additional resources has led to accelerated development programs in the oil-exporting countries, which may be difficult to sustain for the long pull. Some of the OPEC countries also face exacerbated inflationary situations, like regions which struck it rich in cotton, wheat, and gold in the pre-1914 world. Estimates of the surplus OPEC countries might generate by 1980 originally ran as high as $650 billion. Depending on the OECD growth rate and the vigor of its energy programs, current estimates fall in the range of $120–245 billion (U.S., 1974). The OPEC countries have spent more of their foreign-exchange increase on imports than estimates of their absorptive capacity had suggested was likely. Their share in world trade bounded up from 6.3 percent in 1970 to an astonishing 16.8 percent in 1974. The only equivalents for this shift in modern history were interwoven with the effects of major wars: the rise in the British trade proportion caused by the cotton textile revolution and the trade distortions of the French Revolutionary and Napoleonic Wars (12 percent in 1780; 22 percent in 1800); and the rise in the U.S. trading proportion between 1938 and the immediate post–World War II period (10 percent, 1938; 16 percent, 1948).

As noted earlier (Chapter 18), the OPEC countries provided substantial cushioning aid flows in 1974–1975; but, if the foreign-exchange availabilities of the developing world are to be sustained, the aid policies of the OECD world will remain critically important. In the context of the Second Development Decade, the OECD countries agreed to a target of 0.7 percent of gross national product for their levels of development assistance. In fact, the aggregate proportion for 1973 was 0.3 percent, due to the aid policies of the larger OECD countries, most notably the United States. As of 16 September 1975, the OECD countries formally recommitted themselves in the special session of the United Nations to achieve the 0.7 percent target by the end of the decade, although the United States, at least, quickly took its distance from the resolution. Before that formal and dilute recommitment, a realistic estimate was for a further decline to 0.24 percent by 1980. Rough calculations suggest that, if development assistance from the OECD world were, in fact, to move up to the 0.7 percent target, an average 6 percent per annum growth in real GNP (say, 3.5 percent per capita) could be achieved in the developing world.

As a matter of arithmetic, it is evident that the flows of official aid derived from the 0.7 percent target are sensitive to the rate of growth in the OECD economies. As a matter of politics, the flows of aid generated from the OECD nations will be even more sensitive to their prosperity. Democratic nations bedeviled by chronic high unemployment are unlikely to increase their aid allocations substantially even if they remain relatively affluent—a fact demonstrated by the limited and cautious commitment to expanded aid made in the May 1977 meetings in Paris. But something more than renewed high OECD growth will be required, for the proportion of OECD resources allocated to aid was falling even in the prosperous pre-1974 years. As suggested in Chapter 55, an authentic sense of common objectives and partnership will have to be generated between the OECD world and the developing countries, so real that it penetrates the consciousness of voters and their representatives, before the fragile commitment of 16 September 1975 to 0.7 percent becomes a reality.

Much the same can be said for the fourth major potential source of renewed growth in the developing world: an enlargement of developing countries' exports and, especially, exports of manufactures. If the OECD countries would dismantle their systems of subsidies, tariffs, and nontariff barriers on agricultural and forestry products, exports from developing countries might increase by as much as $[illegible]2 billion by 1980, notably in sugar and forestry products. There is also scope for greatly enlarged exports of manufactures to advanced industrial countries if these are diversified and do not press excessively on a few sensitive industries (e.g., textiles and shoes). Indeed, in a politically homogeneous world, maximizing its income per capita, the OECD nations might permit such industries to decline rapidly, rely on imports, and concentrate capital and employment in high-productivity sectors, as New England surrendered a good deal of its textile industry to the American South. Table VI-16 exhibits the order of magnitude of the improvement in the status of developing

TABLE VI-16. *Projected Effects of Alternative Manufactured Export Growth Assumptions on the Developing Countries, 1975–1980 (% per Annum)*[a]

	Lower-Income Countries		Middle-Income Countries		All Sample Panel Countries	
Manufactured export growth	15.0	20.0	15.0	20.0	15.0	20.0
Developing countries' growth rates						
Volume of exports	5.2	5.5	7.6	8.9	7.3	8.4
Exports, capacity to import	5.6	6.0	7.3	8.4	7.1	8.1
Volume of imports	3.8	4.1	5.0	6.0	4.9	5.8
Gross domestic product	3.3	3.6	4.7	5.3	4.4	4.9
GDP per capita	0.7	1.0	2.0	2.6	1.8	2.3

[a]Assumes mid-point OECD growth rate at 4.2 percent per annum; constant oil price at $9.40 per barrel in 1974 dollars.

Source: World Bank.

countries that might come about if the annual average rate of growth of manufactured exports was raised from 15 percent to 20 percent. Movement in such directions depends on a sufficiently high rate of growth within the OECD world to provide ample alternative employment opportunities for the working force and, perhaps even more, on a sense of political reliability and confidence between the OECD and developing nations.

But in trade, as in population policy and agriculture, the developing countries themselves also bear a major responsibility if the potentialities for expanded trade are to be fully exploited. The high average rate of growth in manufactured exports is the result of extremely uneven performances among the developing nations. Some have shown an extraordinary ability to study foreign market possibilities, gear their production to those possibilities, and absorb the disciplines of quality control and salesmanship; e.g., South Korea and Taiwan. Others have moved only sluggishly in these directions; e.g., a good many Latin American countries. Market opportunities transcend the OECD world. There are large possibilities for expanded exports to the OPEC nations and to other developing nations, as they move forward and their import requirements become more diversified. Here a good deal hinges on the further development of regional and subregional economic cooperation in Latin America, Africa, Asia, and the Middle East.

It is not impossible, then, to envisage a revival of momentum in the developing nations after their sharp setback of 1974–1975. That revival depends, however, on public policies which would lead to a rapid return of the OECD world to full employment; serious and sustained cooperation toward this objective by OPEC; increased aid; and liberalized trade. Above all, it hinges on a new sense of political solidarity and mutual confidence within the whole international community.

55

Tasks of International Cooperation

The political agenda that flows from this view of where we are and what we face poses, then, a challenge to nations in their domestic dispositions and, equally, to their capacity for cooperation. Within the OECD world, the problems of cooperation are real enough. The resource endowments among them vary, as do their perceptions of vulnerability. Norway, for example, must weigh its possible contribution to easing the European energy position by expanding its production at a maximum rate against distortions in the composition of its working force and other costs to its national life. British policy is strongly colored by expectations of an enlarged oil flow from the North Sea. Australia and Canada are so greatly endowed with natural resources (aside from oil) that they may feel a temptation to join with less-developed raw-materials producers in OEPC-type organizations in other fields. The three major OECD agricultural food exporters (the United States, Canada, and Australia) face the conflict between a desire to maximize foreign-exchange earnings in a world close to the margin of food scarcity and domestic pressure on the cost of living in societies which are overwhelmingly urban. On the other hand, Japan and Italy, notably, but others as well, live with a heightened sense of vulnerability; and they are tempted to seek secure flows of essential supplies by special bilateral agreements rather than through OECD or global arrangements. These and other inner tensions and differences in endowments and interests complicate the tasks of effective cooperation.

But they are likely to be overridden to a significant degree. The convergence of security and political interests with a mature knowledge of the virtues of economic cooperation and the large costs of economic confrontation tends to pull the OECD countries together. Despite initial uncertainty in the field of energy cooperation, the OECD has moved toward a consensus on appropriate technological, economic, and political lines of action. While useful and stabilizing, this broad consensus has thus far had a mainly negative result, important as it is: it has avoided a mercantilist tearing apart of

OECD's political cohesion. Energy, energy-conservation, and energy-efficiency programs remain essentially national, although information about them is exchanged. The major changes required to increase OECD's bargaining position vis-à-vis OPEC lie substantially in the hands of the United States, which has not yet decided how to use its rich resource potential and to constrain effectively its basic rate of energy utilization, aside from the impact of recession. Working cooperation in R&D within OECD has hardly begun. There is, moreover, no coherent OECD agricultural and raw-materials policy; and antipollution policies remain mainly confined to actions within each nation. Above all, there is profound intellectual confusion and, therefore, no effective policy consensus on how the OECD economy as a whole can return to high and stable rates of growth.

There is, of course, a particular reason for the limited scale of OECD cooperation: its problems inherently transcend the OECD world. The global energy problem was, after all, pressed inescapably on the world community by OPEC's quadrupling of oil prices; the dangerous underlying global food-population balance was forced on the world's attention by the bad harvests of 1972 in Russia, India, China, and Africa; the terms of trade which have struck nations in such disparate ways are the related results of changes in global energy and agricultural prices and the OECD recession. Evidently, it is in North-South relations that the greatest challenges to statesmanship lie. Indeed, the momentum of serious cooperation within OECD is closely linked to progress made in North-South cooperation.

In this respect, 1974 was not a good year. For many intellectuals and politicians in the developing world, the success of OPEC in asserting its power in the autumn of 1973 was a memorable and heartening event. Here were nations—mostly small, in some cases poor, in all cases not fully modernized—using their control over a basic raw material to shake the foundations of the rich and comfortable societies which, to a degree, had based their prosperity on cheap energy. Hitherto weaker states successfully asserted their capacity to divert more resources to themselves. At last, the late-comers could feel that the unfair allocation of the benefits that their raw materials had provided in the past was redressed. Whether that allocation was, in fact, fair or unfair, OPEC's action was a demonstration of power through a disciplined cooperation the developing nations had never before been able to generate.

As the brief accounts of some of the late-comers in Part Five indicate, the problems in many parts of the developing world are less the result of prior colonial or quasi-colonial relationships than of the lateness with which they got themselves into sustained industrial growth. That lateness can only be explained in terms of their histories and their cultures, which, with all their richness, lacked initially the capacity rapidly to absorb the expanding pool of technology the early-comers were generating. In fact, with all their inequities and humiliation, the contacts with more advanced nations, even colonial contacts, on balance accelerated the process of modernization rather than forestalled it. From Alexander Hamilton's *Report on Manufactures* to the 1791 Congress to the present, a driving impulse within developing nations was the perception that their independence, as well as their prosperity, was involved in industrialization. Although welfare benefits evidently played a part (as Hamilton acknowledged), the desire to industrialize has been substantially rooted in a reactive nationalism flowing from the intrusions or feared intrusions of more advanced on less advanced nations. Of course, I would not defend all the relationships that grew up in the eighteenth, nineteenth, and twentieth centuries between the more and less advanced nations and peoples; but moralizing is not the point. What we are dealing with is a problem of early-comers and late-comers to modern economic growth, with the problems and sentiments of vulnerability and dependence that can be noted from at least the seventeenth century, when Britain and France reacted to the commercial and financial dominance of the Dutch Republic.

Against this background, it is not difficult to reconstruct the enflamed hopes which led some developing nations to believe that they could emulate OPEC by organizing in ways which would also divert resources from the rich to the poor. And it is not difficult to understand why politicians in the developing world chose in 1974—and still, to a degree, choose—to posture in ways which suggest the desire for a systematic North-South confrontation.

If one reviewed the major international conferences of 1974, one might guess that North-South relations had already polarized and that we faced inevitably a protracted neomercantilist struggle. There was the acrimonious United Nations General Assembly debate of April 1974; the population meeting at Bucharest; the food conference at Rome; and the sterile session on the law of the seas at Caracas. In all of them, the air was filled with rhetoric about imperialism; with claims for the unilateral transfer of resources from the rich to the poor; and with the ardent assertion of national sovereignty by the less developed nations, combined with equally ardent demands that the more developed states surrender sovereignty and behave in terms of the requirements of the international community.

In the face of this verbal and political onslaught, the more developed nations mainly reacted defensively. It was not difficult to envisage all this yielding a neomercantilist fragmentation of political, economic, and military affairs—and disaster for the human race—as men and nations squabbled meanly for scarce resources in a nuclear age.

In fact, the state of North-South diplomacy was not quite as precarious as a superficial view of the rhetoric of 1974 would suggest. Beneath the surface these conferences generated considerable mutual understanding. The participants listened to each other, even if they did not finally act in concert. More important, North-South bilateral relations were marked in many cases by a good deal of continued hard-headed pragmatism based on a recognition of mutual interests. And, in the case of the Rome conference on food, a consensus of far-reaching importance was defined; namely, that the rise in agricultural production in the developing nations had to be the principal instrument for dealing with the expansion of population and food requirements.

The special United Nations session of September 1975 was, in tone and substance, distinctively different and less contentious than those of 1974. Three factors appear to account for the change. First, the United States laid out at length both a doctrine of reconciliation and a working agenda for North-South cooperation. Second, the OECD recession over the previous year had badly damaged prospects in many parts of the developing world, demonstrating in a rather painful way the reality of North-South interdependence. In 1974, close to the peak of the previous boom, there had been much talk from the South about the North's excessive consumption of raw materials: in 1975 the South was concerned because the North was not buying enough raw materials. Third, the damage done the developing world by OPEC's oil price increase was better understood, and the somewhat artificial 1974 unity of the developing nations was thereby strained.

The upshot was the package of resolutions agreed to on 16 September 1975. In substance, it covers almost the full array of problems which emerge from the agenda outlined here: trade, aid, the transfer of science and technology, accelerated industrialization, food and agriculture. Two subjects were left out: family planning, which was, essentially, left in the hands of national governments by the Bucharest resolutions of August 1974; and the problem of the oil price, much on the mind of most delegates but not brought to consensus.[70]

By normal standards of international performance, the resolutions of 16 September 1975 represent a considerable achievement. An array of complex problems was identified, and broad courses of action to deal with those problems were verbally agreed upon. The scene then shifted to Paris, where detailed discussions to implement these resolutions were launched. A new international organization was created: the Conference on International Economic Co-operation and Development, in which eight countries represented the industrialized North and nineteen represented the developing South, including OPEC. After some eighteen months of laborious work in committees and subcommittees, the major issues were brought to negotiation at the level of foreign ministers in May–June 1977. Included among them was one whose importance had greatly increased since September 1975; that is, the heavy debt burden contracted by some of the more advanced developing countries, with access to private capital markets, in an effort to sustain their growth rates in the face of high oil import prices and the slowdown of growth in the OECD world. The developing countries had developed a debt burden of some $180 billion by 1977, with more than 40 percent owed to private institutions.

The demands made by the developing nations came to rest on these four points:

—a $6 billion common fund to support commodity prices by financing buffer stocks;

—a generalized debt moratorium;

—a commitment from the developed countries to double aid levels (from less than 0.4 percent to 0.7 percent of GNP);

—a commitment by the developed countries to link raw-materials export prices to the rise in import prices paid by developing nations caused by inflation.

The outcome was a limited success for the developing nations: a promise to raise a special $1 billion fund to aid the most hard-pressed poorer nations; a commitment to consider at a later time the creation and financing of buffer stocks and commodity price stabilization; a commitment to consider debt roll-overs on a case-by-case basis; the offer of long term support for transport and communication development in Africa. Evidently, sufficient progress had been made to justify continuation of the dialogue.

Behind the failure to make more far-reaching progress lay three unresolved problems, interwoven in complex ways.

The first was the failure of the conference to bring under common examination and negotiation the questions of OPEC oil pricing and aid. Both technically and ideologically the impetus for the new North-South dialogue had arisen from OPEC's action in 1973. Technically, it was that action which threw the advanced industrial countries into a phase of reduced growth and exacerbated inflation. At the same time it bore down heavily on the economies of the oil-importing developing nations both directly and through its impact on the North. In a world governed by simple, direct economic interests, the oil-importers, developed and developing, would have united to press OPEC to moderate its prices and to make large compensatory contributions to aid the other developing nations. That was not what happened. Psychologically, the sympathy of the governments of the developing nations lay with OPEC. That instinct was, no doubt, strengthened by certain oblique economic considerations: the hope that the OPEC example could be extended to other commodities or that the threat of its extension could force the industrialized North to make concessions with respect to the stabilization of other commodity prices; OPEC's use of development aid as an instrument for holding the developing nations together; the belief that the overall bargaining position of the developing nations would be enhanced by having OPEC representatives among them; the lack of effective bargaining position versus OPEC of either the industrialized or the developing nations. Whatever the rationale, the fact is that the North-South dialogue is significantly diminished and lacking in reality so long as energy prices and policy are excluded.

Second, the document of September 1975 and subsequent negotiations were too one-sided for the good of the developing nations themselves. Liberalized trade agreements and measures of price and/or income stabilization for raw material exporters are thoroughly legitimate objectives of potential mutual advantage to all parties. The North can benefit from cheaper and more abundant imports and from less volatile incomes in (and thus exports to) the relevant nations of the South. But to be effective, the South must commit itself to maintain a regular flow of supplies, uninterrupted by political or quasi-OPEC considerations. The agreement negotiated in February 1975 between the European Common Market and forty-six developing nations (the Lomé Treaty) is a potential model for such arrangements. It includes a fund to compensate exporters in case their prices fall below a stated percentage of the average for the three previous years, and duty-free access to the Common Market for all manufactured products and most farm exports. It is significant that the Lomé Treaty had a particular political background: its participants were African and a few other nations, most of which were former colonies which had maintained aid and other amicable political ties with the former metropolitan powers. There was a reasonable basis for mutual confidence. That political element was useful, perhaps essential, for a pioneering effort; but a more solid political base, embracing a wider group of nations, will be required if such methods are to be expanded in trade and other fields. That political base must, moreover, include understandings about the role of private as well as public capital in expanding raw-materials production in developing areas. As noted in Chapter 52, the attenuation of such capital flows is a force likely not only to raise raw-materials prices but also to force developed nations to develop raw-materials production in their own or politically hospitable territories. It is a sign of immaturity and evasiveness that this real and serious issue cannot yet be temperately addressed in global gatherings and is left to more pragmatic bilateral negotiations.

Similarly, there is an aura of unreality over much of the debate about the transfer of technology. There are, of course, types of external assistance which can increase a developing nation's scientific and technological base; for example, the education abroad of individuals, the strengthening of local educational institutions, the setting up of specialized research institutions. And there is legitimate scope for re-examining the potentialities for transferring technologies controlled by governments as well as for reviewing private patent arrangements for elements of monopoly and other inequities. But the central fact is that the bulk of new technologies have been absorbed in developing nations by the creation of business firms which incorporate them in their production. Local, foreign, or joint entrepreneurship capable of putting the technology to work efficiently in the production process has been the critical factor rather than the transfer of the technology itself since, say, Francis Cabot Lowell in 1814 set up his mill in Massachusetts on the basis of British technology. Some developing nations have generated cadres of domestic entrepreneurs capable of bringing into effective use new technologies drawn from abroad. In other cases, foreign firms and entrepreneurs are initially required. And there is a wide spectrum of local capacities and external needs in between, including the possibility of management contracts. Thus, for the flow of technology to be accelerated, what is required in many cases is a stable resolution within developing countries of the criteria for accepting foreign firms or managers and stable rules of the game for their profitable survival on terms economically and politically acceptable to host governments. This is extremely important, for example, if chemical fertilizer capacity is to be expanded rapidly in many developing countries which now lack management and technological skills on a requisite scale. One can explain psychologically and politically why this issue periodically becomes enflamed within developing countries; but one can explain equally why such reactive nationalism produces, in turn, grave reactions in the parliaments, congresses, and board rooms of developed countries. These reactions, in turn, limit the possibilities of generating political support for increased aid and liberalized trade. By discouraging private investment from abroad, they also reduce the flow of new technology and the building of badly needed industrial capacity.

This is a tough and complex set of issues; but it is capable of rational resolution. No North-South partnership will be truly serious until it is faced and resolved. This judgment is not only a recognition that any partnership must be a two-way street; it is rooted in the narrower circumstance that the most efficient arrangements for the progress of developing nations must be based on the realities of economic interdependence, including the absorptive capacity of developing nations with respect to new technologies.

The third unresolved problem which has limited the possibilities of North-South negotiations is that addressed at the close of Chapter 54, that is, the failure of the OECD world to deal with the changed contours of the fifth Kondratieff upswing and recapture the momentum of the 1960's. As the World Bank calculations set out in Chapter 54 made clear, there is some combination of high OECD growth, easement by OPEC, liberalized trade, and expanded aid that could permit the developing nations to move forward more rapidly in the 1970's than they did in the 1960's. But when one moves from the realm of economic calculation to politics, they all hinge on OECD growth rates. It is simply beyond the capacity of democratic legislative bodies to liberalize trade in manufacture and radically to expand aid unless their economies are experiencing low levels of unemployment and rapid growth. And, if the analysis developed in this book is roughly correct, this will not happen unless the United States, notably, and the OECD in general pursue much more vigorous policies of energy production as well as conservation. Such policies, in turn, offer the only likely route to a serious OECD-OPEC negotiation, which should include an enlarged OPEC contribution to the developing nations either through special reduced prices or much enlarged, long-term compensatory aid.

But in the end a true North-South partnership, rather than endless diplomatic fencing with the language of resolutions, requires more, even, than renewed, rapid OECD growth and the more generous policies which might then commend themselves to the several OECD electorates. A stable and effective partnership must be based on a fresh, shared vision of the common task. The common task is to preserve industrial civilization as a whole by bringing forward to full modernization the late-comers of the South, while permitting the early-comers of the North to continue to grow and to evolve societies of higher quality and equity. This requires, in turn, that all parties address themselves jointly to the generation of the additional resources, the measures of resource conservation, and the creation and diffusion of new technologies required to make that vision viable.

The articulation of some such vision will probably not soon supplant the rhetoric of aggrieved dependency and the waving of the imperialist bloody shirt in United Nations councils and defensive reactions to such talk. But it would be useful for all parties to take rhetoric more seriously. What government representatives say in public, in response to domestic constituencies, can be costly or helpful to working diplomacy. Soon or late, the full exploitation of the potentialities of interdependence requires a mature and explicit acceptance of the extent to which the progress and fate of each nation, North and South, is bound up with the fate of all. Without the spread of this necessary and healing doctrine down from the pronouncements of politicians and diplomats to the grass-roots of societies, the political foundations for North-South partnership will remain uncertain.

The United States has, I believe, a special responsibility in trying to move the world in this direction, despite the decline of its relative power over the past thirty years. Since 1948, when the Marshall Plan was accepted by the Congress and Tito split with Stalin, the central underlying process going forward in the world arena has been a diffusion of power away from both Washington and Moscow.[71] The primacy of the United States in the immediate post-1945 years was the product of inherently transient circumstances: the war-induced weaknesses of Western Europe and Japan, and the full recovery of the United States during the Second World War from the depression of the 1930's. Putting aside strategic matters, there is every reason to believe that the diffusion of economic power will continue over the long term. The trends in world production and trade foreshadow a relative decline in the American position in the world economy as the late-comers to take-off move forward into the drive to technological maturity and beyond.

But the special character of the economic issues that have

emerged on the world agenda since the end of 1972 has increased, for a time at least, the capacity of the United States to influence how well and how promptly those issues are dealt with.

First, the United States alone commands sufficient alternative energy resources to reduce sharply OECD dependence on OPEC oil and, thereby, set the stage for well-balanced agreement between oil producers and consumers, including special provisions for the hardest-hit developing nations.

Second, the United States, if it continues to nurture its agricultural base, should remain the dominant source of food exports, including exports to certain developing nations until their own production can be expanded at a higher pace. The United States agricultural export capacity is also a significant cushioning factor in its balance of payments, strengthening the relative position of the dollar among the major currencies.

Third, the energy and energy-related investment requirements in the United States are so large that it should be relatively easy for the United States to return quickly to full employment and thereby help lead the OECD world in that direction.

Fourth, the United States has special advantages and responsibilities in the R&D sector as a whole. The proportion of United States GNP spent on R&D has fallen, but the absolute level still towers over that of the other major industrial nations, excepting the USSR, whose R&D remains extraordinarily concentrated on military tasks.

Finally, the United States has a special responsibility for political leadership. This is not a matter of higher virtue. It is the case because, if the United States fails to lead, there is, as yet, no nation to fill the gap: Western Europe is insufficiently unified, Japan too vulnerable, the Soviet Union too constricted by its ideological commitments to lead comfortably a heterogeneous mixture of polities, China similarly constricted and at a stage of development when its inner problems and border anxieties dominate its energies. Leadership in this context in no way implies dominance. It requires a mixture of three elements: a national capacity to act significantly with respect to the major issues; a capacity to define common objectives in ways that are not excessively self-serving; and, then, the capacity to help translate those objectives into a working agenda, and to help move it forward with dogged stubbornness. These are assets the United States potentially commands.

Whether the United States will fully use its potentiality for leadership remains to be seen. Here there is legitimate scope for optimists and pessimists. For what it is worth, I would guess that the inner strength and resilience of American society will reassert themselves in politics and diplomacy after recent vicissitudes. But, objectively, the exercise of America's potentialities depends on an altered view within its political life of the world and the American relationship to it, a change in perspective which, in the end, will be required of all nations, big and small, North and South, East and West.

The central concluding theme of this book, then, is that industrial civilization—germinated in Europe between the fifteenth and the eighteenth centuries, operationally launched in the 1780's, now diffused in varying degree to all the continents—is now endangered, that the next quarter-century is of critical importance to the outcome, that neither physical-resource limitations nor economic problems pose insurmountable obstacles to fending off those dangers, but that quite substantial changes in politics and policy are required if the world economy is to get through to easier times. For example, since the 1930's the underlying assumption of the more advanced societies was that resources were abundant. The central task was to put them to work. After 1945 they were put to work. Rapid and, by historical standards, remarkably steady rates of growth resulted, as high mass-consumption spread across the North, including, in a delayed, modified, and straitened way, the USSR and some of the European states with communist governments. Moreover, the steadily rising real resources available to governments, which resulted from such growth rates, permitted major expansions in welfare expenditures, notably in education and health services. Some economists and political scientists taught the young during the 1960's that the problem of scarcity was behind us. The argument ran that, if outdated institutional arrangements and policies could be removed, the rich societies of the North could devote themselves wholly to improving the quality of life, and individuals, to the satisfaction of private tastes and senses.

Now we come to a time when scarcity, in the form of relatively high prices for basic products, has asserted itself in a rather old-fashioned way. Over the next generation, societies will have to make somewhat sharper choices than in the previous generation. The further diffusion of the automobile and durable consumers' goods will have to be measured against their energy requirements. The further expansion in welfare expenditures will have to be measured against outlays to control pollution and expand energy production. In general, somewhat more investment will be needed to expand the inputs required to sustain industrial civilization, somewhat less to expand its outputs as conventionally measured. These are, statistically, marginal shifts. They should not prevent a steady rise in private income per capita in the OECD world, nor need they prevent significant progress in the developing regions. But they are of significant orders of magnitude and will require and impose changes in attitude and perspective.

If the OECD world adjusts wisely to the new environment, two things will happen. There will be a new priority for certain virtues regarded by many over the past generation as of waning relevance; for example, technological ingenuity, imaginative entrepreneurship, even hard work. But, if all goes reasonably well, the pursuit of a higher quality of life will be carried forward. I have in mind the expansion of investment not merely in the control of air and water pollution, but also in continued schooling of an increasingly well-educated citizenry (for example, through Open University methods), in expanded support for the arts, in the beautification of cities and towns. If one looks at the outlays of society in a disaggregated way, it is not inevitable that increased allocations to deal with the energy problem necessarily impose reductions across the board.

A successful response to the new agenda should bring with it another change: a heightened sense of community within nations. The stage of high mass-consumption is, inherently, a time when laissez-faire individualism can have reasonably free play. Private sectors are competent at producing and selling automobiles, durable consumers' goods, and suburban houses. And they produce them for individual families which have moved up to income levels which permit them to enjoy these real amenities as a matter of private taste and choice. The essential tasks of government at this stage are supplementary; for example, to build the roads and the suburban infrastructure to support the migration from central cities. Calvin Coolidge's much mocked dictum was not wholly irrelevant to the United States of the 1920's or even to the other societies enjoying this lively but transient stage: "The business of the government is business."

In the phase we entered at the close of 1972, things are somewhat different. The role of communal problems and communal action has expanded. A serious energy or food policy, a serious R&D program must be geared to national and international issues which make sense only if framed by attitudes of solidarity and agreed common purpose.

Solidarity and common purpose, both within societies and on the world scene, require, however, a heightened sensibility to problems of equity. In the past generation many OECD countries acted in ways which diminished inequalities of opportunity within their societies. This was done by the normal interplay of special interest groups, heightened occasionally by enlightened statesmanship; for example, in avoiding, up to the present, at least, in Canada a French-Canadian separation; in widening the educational base in British society; in bringing forward nonwhites toward social equality and political power in America. But all this was accomplished when resources available for private consumption per capita were rapidly expanding. It will be not quite so easy when investment requirements for communal purposes damp the rate of increase in private consumption in the forms which have become conventional. But the need for equity is fundamental, notably because the rise in energy and food prices strikes hardest at the least advantaged groups within advanced industrial societies as well as the least advantaged nations on the world scene.

It is in this setting that the OECD nations have an opportunity to bring under control the pathology of wage-push inflation which has marred the extraordinary prosperity of the past generation and which gravely complicates successful action on the new agenda. I quoted earlier the dictum of Mark Leiserson that disciplined wage-price policies must be, if they are to be accepted, "part of a coordinated effort to achieve a clearly defined national objective" (see above, p. 357). The appropriate objective of the OECD nations should be clear enough: to resume regular growth in ways which maximize the chance that their own societies and the larger civilization of which they are a part will remain viable. This is a challenge which ought to be capable of pulling the political life of the OECD nations, individually and collectively, toward unity. It is a challenge to which every nation has the opportunity to make a meaningful response. But to build that kind of consensus will require that political leaders explain and dramatize the issue and advocate courses of action which will give it meaning. That has not yet happened.

If such a consensus does emerge, it ought to be possible to achieve stable social contracts relating money wages to increases in productivity, and to do so in ways which do not result in an excessive surge in profits. My own preferred formula is radical by the standards of contemporary neo-Keynesian economists but, perhaps, more understandable to readers of Part Three, notably, the passages on the periods 1815–1848 and 1873–1896. That formula is: a protracted wage freeze, accompanied by strong, credible measures to ensure that increases in productivity are passed along to the consumer in lower prices.[72] Ultimately, what is involved, however, is not a technical formula, but a coming together of labor, business, and government to achieve a common goal. And, in this case, the common goal reflects the authentic long-run interests of business and labor, since both groups suffer severely, on balance, from the multiple consequences of wage-push inflation. It is, evidently, not easy to create a negotiating framework in which authentic long-run interests triumph over even chimerical short-run interests. The mediocre record of efforts in this direction by OECD nations underlines the psychological, institutional, and political difficulties involved.[73] But, in a time when a higher sense of communal purpose will be, in any case, required to deal successfully with national and international problems, the chances of instituting more stable social contracts, capable of disciplining wage-push inflation to common advantage, should be enhanced.

It is proper to place great emphasis on the changes of attitude within the OECD world because, over the next quarter-century, it will remain, if things go reasonably well, still the dominating force in the world economy. The countries of the South should continue to gain some ground relatively; but the bulk of the resources, technology, and international initiative required to restore balance and momentum in the world economy will have to come from the North. On the other hand, two of the most fundamental tasks of adjustment within the world economy lie overwhelmingly in the hands of the southern states: the creation of an environment in which birth rates rapidly decline, and an accelerated expansion in agricultural output. In both cases, northern resources and technology can have significant marginal influence on the outcome. But, essentially, the changes in attitude and priority must take place within the southern societies.

Beyond those fundamental observations, generalization is difficult. There is, despite conventional phrases like "the third world" and "the developing nations," much greater heterogeneity among the southern nations than within the amply variegated OECD world. They differ not only in size, history, and cultural setting but also in resource endowments, income per capita, and stage of growth. Many are still struggling to generate a sense of nationhood transcending family and clan, tribe, region, and class. What they now share is an assertive nationalism and, related to it, a sense of lagging behind the more affluent and technically proficient North. As in the past, nationalism and a will to close the gap with those ahead will remain essential springs for the effort at modernization that will be required.

But there is a lesson incorporated in the story this book tries to tell which could, if accepted, soften the harshness of the transitions through which these nations must pass; ease, perhaps, the North-South tension; and make more natural that North-South partnership which the facts of economic life suggest is rational. The lesson is that, in the end, late-comers to modern growth can, indeed, catch up with early-comers. Rich and poor nations there certainly are, viewed in cross section as of 1977. But, dynamically, the world economy is made up of nations that entered modern growth at different times over the past two centuries. Those that experienced take-off between the 1780's and 1890's have already come close to equality in stage, in real income per capita, and in passage through the demographic transition. The problems of population and food complicate the task for some who experienced take-off in the twentieth century; but it is not an impossible dream to envisage their coming to a recognizable version of mass affluence at different times over the next century or so.

That was the concluding theme of *The Stages of Economic Growth*, which first appeared in 1960. Some regard that book as excessively optimistic, somehow belied by the experiences of the subsequent decade. In fact, it underlined, before it was the conventional wisdom, the dangers to development inherent in the pace of population increase and the neglect of agriculture.[74] It did not present economic growth as an easy automatic process, but as an endless struggle to generate new leading sectors as the old ones waned, a struggle engaging the political and social life of societies as well as the economy in the narrow sense.

Taken overall, the performance of the developing nations down to 1974–1975 vindicates the possibilities of growth at rates which promise, in time, to narrow the gap in affluence. The non-OPEC developing nations, as a group, would settle gladly for a resumption of those rates, although it would be better for all if they set and achieved higher targets. Evidently, their performance was not uniform. There are nations so small and so poorly endowed with natural resources that it is hard to envisage how they can move forward in modernization unless they become states within larger economic and political groupings. Then there are India and China, facing the task of modernization with 80 percent of vast populations in rural areas which modernization has reached only irregularly and imperfectly. No one looking at the inescapable tensions between population and food supply over the next quarter-cenutry can regard the prospects for development complacently; but there is no reason to judge it beyond the capacity of the human race to struggle through to a time when adequate food, shelter, clothing, education, and the considerable amenities a mature industrial civilization can provide are available for the overwhelming proportion of the world's men, women, and children.

There are, evidently, values to be cherished beyond material progress: the joys of family, the arts, religion, and the full expression of unique personalities. And these deserve cultivation, in the South as well as the North, as governments and their citizens struggle through the challenging agenda of the next quarter-century. But only those who do not know what the round of life is like in an impoverished village or an overcrowded urban slum, whether in eighteenth-century Europe or contemporary developing regions, will fail to appreciate how material progress has improved the quality of life and can continue to do so.

In the end, then, despite the inevitable parochialism of our attachments to national societies and cultures, the change most required is the gradual acceptance of the reality of a common experience, common dangers, and a common goal. It is a wholesome fact that individual cultures have great survival power. The process of modernization does bring important changes; but the uniqueness of the longer past is not washed away. But, in part of our beings, all of us are now children of the revolutionary insight of seventeenth-century Europe. Man, by the scientific understanding of nature and its laws, can manipulate the physical world to his advantage. The systematic application of this insight has made the life of the average citizen better over the past three centuries, by standards the overwhelming majority of mankind would accept. It has also yielded Faustian dangers: in the weapons created, the greater ease of reducing death rates than birth rates, the pollution of air and water, and the old mercantilist temptation to make science and technology an instrument for a narrow national pursuit of profit and power. These dangers have already distorted the paths of economic and social progress. They could destroy us. But it is also possible that the benign side of the scientific revolution will triumph; that the ecumenical spirit of constructive adventure which inspired the line of men from Copernicus to Newton will prevail; and that gradually the common goal of preserving this industrial civilization and the diverse cultures within it, unfolding its possibilities on all the continents and exploring together what lies beyond, will come increasingly to suffuse the minds of men as well as the policies of governments.

As often in the past, I am driven finally back to these lines of Walt Whitman:

> One thought ever at the fore—
> That in the Divine Ship, the World,
> breasting Time and Space,
> All peoples of the globe together sail,
> sail the same voyage,
> Are bound to the same destination.

Appendix A

Index of World Industrial Production, 1700–1971

This index splices together three separate calculations for the period 1820–1971: Michael Mulhall's estimate of the value in pounds sterling of total manufacturing output for the years 1820, 1840, 1860, and 1894 (*Industries and Wealth of Nations* [London, New York, and Bombay: Longmans, Green, 1896], p. 32); Folke Hilgerdt's annual index of world manufacturing production, 1913=100, covering the period 1870–1938 (Folke Hilgerdt, *Industrialization and Foreign Trade* [New York: League of Nations; distributed by Columbia University Press, 1945], pp. 132–134); and the United Nations world index of manufacturing production, 1963=100, covering the period 1938–1971 (*United Nations Statistical Yearbook, 1972* [New York, 1973], p. 43).

The linking of Mulhall's to Hilgerdt's estimates presented three difficulties. First, Mulhall supplies no clear and satisfactory account of how his index is constructed. One is left with an impression (pp. 28–33) that the weight assigned textiles might be excessive and the index not sufficiently inclusive; but, in fact, one must, as often in using Mulhall's figures, rely on his rather high and demonstrated record for good sense and judgment. Nevertheless, the figures drawn from Mulhall must be taken as rougher approximations than those after 1870.

Second, Mulhall's data had to be converted from current value figures to a volume index. This was first done by correcting them with Albert H. Imlah's price index for British exports, on the assumption that, over the period covered, the Imlah index roughly reflected the prices of world manufactures. Given the abnormal role of cotton textile manufactures in British exports (and total industrial production), since no other nation generated so large an export market, the Imlah export price index disproportionately reflects movements of cotton prices. The extraordinary fall in cotton prices between 1820 and 1840 distorts the rise in Mulhall's estimate for the value of world manufacturing production from 1820 to 1840 when it is corrected with Imlah's British export price index (Albert H. Imlah,

"The Terms of Trade of the United Kingdom, 1798–1913," *Journal of Economic History*, vol. 10, no. 2 [November 1950], pp. 178–181). Therefore, a composite British price index was used to correct Mulhall from Walter T. Layton and Geoffrey Crowther, *An Introduction to the Study of Prices* (London: Macmillan, 1938), p. 237. Only the Mulhall figures for 1820 and 1840 differed significantly from those which emerged from the Imlah correction.

Third, the only year of direct overlap between Mulhall's calculations and Hilgerdt's is 1894. Mulhall's price-corrected estimates and Hilgerdt's volume index were equated at 1894, and Mulhall's figures calculated backward from that overlap, thus converting them onto a 1913=100 base. Mulhall's data for the period 1860–1894 yield an annual average growth rate of 3.15 percent; Hilgerdt's, for the period 1870–1894, 3.27 percent. The trends were sufficiently close to justify, for present rough purposes, linking the two series. In fact, given the American deceleration of the 1860's, one would expect Mulhall's figure, embracing that decade, to be slightly lower than Hilgerdt's.

Mulhall's figures thus converted onto a volume index of 1913=100 are:

1820	4.16
1840	7.40
1860	14.7
1894	42.2

The linkage of Hilgerdt's series to that of the United Nations is facilitated by the overlapping estimates for 1938. The United Nations figures were then put on to the 1913=100 base.

Mulhall's data cover only "the nations of Christendom," that is, Europe, the United States, and the British colonies. Hilgerdt includes Japan, India, and China. For the pre-1860 period, for which Mulhall was used, this difference is not significant.

To provide some feel, at least, for the course of manufacturing output in the period 1700–1820, British and French indexes have been exploited. The task here is to link Walther G. Hoffmann's and Jan Marczewski's volume indexes of British and French industrial production, beginning in the first decade of the eighteenth century, to Mulhall's value calculations for the years 1820–1840.

British annual data are to be found in Walther G. Hoffmann, *British Industry, 1700–1950*, translated by W. H. Chaloner and W. O. Henderson (Oxford: Basil Blackwell, 1955), end tables. The French calculations for selected years are those of Jan Marczewski, "Some Aspects of the Economic Growth of France, 1660–1958," *Economic Development and Cultural Change*, vol. 9, no. 3 (April 1961), p. 375.

The Marczewski value data, for industry and handicrafts, in millions of francs at 1905–1913 value, and Hoffmann's industrial production index (excluding building) for equivalent years are set out below.

	France: Marczewski (Millions of Francs at Fixed Value)	Great Britain: Hoffmann (Annual Average, 1913=100)
1701–1710	133	1.262
1781–1790	604	3.260
1803–1812	931	6.247
1825–1834	1730	12.112

If Mulhall's figures for Britain and France are averaged for 1820 and 1840 and equated with Hoffmann's and Marczewski's figures for 1825–1834, (all centered on 1830) the data can be recalculated back to the beginning of the eighteenth century as follows:

	Great Britain	France
1830	339	285
1803–1812	190	153
1781–1790	99	96
1701–1710	38	22

In broad historical terms these figures are not unpersuasive. They exhibit the initial advantage of Britain in the early eighteenth century, after the more acute difficulties of France in the 1690's and during the War of the Spanish Succession; the relative recovery of France down to the 1780's; Britain's leap ahead during its take-off, but also the recovery of France under Napoleon, in the first decade of the nineteenth century; the continued momentum of Britain in the period 1815–1830 and the postwar revival of France at a slightly higher rate, from a lesser initial base.

To fit these figures to the world manufacturing index it is necessary to put them onto a 1913=100 base. The price-corrected world average as calculated by Mulhall for 1820–1840 is 5.78, when put onto a 1913=100 basis, as described above. Britain represents 23.1 percent of Mulhall's world total at that time, France 19.5 percent. If one assumes arbitrarily that the proportion of British plus French manufacturing output to the world total was constant over the whole period 1700–1830, one can derive a very crude 1913=100 figure for the total, as well as for Britain and France, reaching back to 1701–1710, as follows:

	World Total	Britain and France	Britain	France
1830	5.78	2.46	1.33	1.13
1802–1812	3.18	1.35	0.75	0.60
1781–1790	1.81	0.77	0.39	0.38
1701–1710	0.55	0.23	0.15	0.08

The composite index emerges, then as follows:

World Industrial Production, 1700–1971 (1913=100)

1701–1710	0.55
1781–1790	1.81
1802–1812	3.18
1820	4.16
1830[a]	5.78
1840	7.40
1860	14.7
1870	19.5
1880	26.9
1890	41.1
1894[b]	42.2
1900	58.7
1913	100.0
1929	153.3
1938[c]	182.7
1948	274
1971	950

[a] Average for 1820 and 1840, for linkage of Mulhall to Marczewski-Hoffmann estimates.

[b] Overlapping date for linkage of Mulhall-Hilgerdt estimates.

[c] Overlapping date for linkage of Hilgerdt–United Nations estimates.

Appendix B

The Volume and Distribution of World Trade, 1720–1971

Making an index of the volume of world trade covering the period 1720–1971 involves three problems. Starting at the end, the United Nations data in *United Nations Statistical Yearbook, 1972* (New York, 1973), pp. 40–43, or some variant, must be linked with the Folke Hilgerdt series in *Industrialization and Foreign Trade* (New York: distributed by Columbia University Press, 1945), pp. 157–167, or some variant. The task is facilitated by the provision in United Nations data of an overlapping year, 1938, although there is some difference of view about the 1948 trade level in relation to that of 1938.

Various linkages of these data (including refinements of them) have been made: W. Arthur Lewis, "World Production, Prices and Trade, 1870–1960," *Manchester School*, vol. 20, no. 2 (May 1952); Ingvar Svennilson, *Growth and Stagnation in the European Economy* (Geneva: United Nations, 1954), p. 292 (Table A.58); Paul Lamartine Yates, *Forty Years of Foreign Trade* (London: George Allen and Unwin, 1959), Chapter 2 and Appendix, Section 1; Karl W. Deutsch and Alexander Eckstein, "National Industrialization and the Declining Share of the International Economic Sector, 1890–1959," *World Politics*, vol. 13, no. 2 (January 1961), p. 290; Angus Maddison, "Growth and Fluctuation in the World Economy, 1870–1960," *Quarterly Review* (Banca Nazionale del Lavoro), no. 61 (June 1962), pp. 166–195; and Simon Kuznets, *Modern Economic Growth* (New Haven and London: Yale University Press, 1966), pp. 304–310, and idem, "Quantitative Aspects of the Economic Growth of Nations, X, Level and Structure of Foreign Trade: Long Term Trends," *Economic Development and Cultural Change*, vol. 15, no. 2, part 2 (January 1967), pp. 2–10.

Although problems exist in the 1870–1938 and 1945–1971 data and in their linkage—notably problems of coverage and price correction—for our broad purposes the problems are evidently manageable. The best discussion of the sources and discrepancies is to be found in Angus Maddison's paper, pp. 166–176.

The second problem concerns the use of Michael G. Mulhall's data from 1800 to 1860 (*The Dictionary of Statistics* [London: George Routledge, 1892], p. 128) and its linkage to the Hilgerdt data from 1870 onward. Mulhall, as usual, does not supply sources. It appears that from 1720 through 1800 (for which year he took the 1801 data) Mulhall used British official values for exports, re-exports, and imports, not including specie movements. With minor variations, his estimates down to that point conform to those in other sources. Official values are, of course, volume figures. From 1860 onward he used declared values in current prices, which also conform to data in other sources. The problem lies, therefore, between 1800 and 1860. For the years 1820, 1830, 1840, and 1850, Mulhall used figures which, in varying degrees, are below both official values and declared values, as follows:

British Domestic Exports, Re-exports, and Imports (in £ Millions)

	Mulhall	Official Values[a]	Declared Values[a]
1800	67	73.7 (1801 fig., 67.1)	114.7
1820	74	81.4	101.0
1830	88	116.0	99.8
1840	114	184.0	152.6
1850	169	297.8	186.4
1860	375	(end in 1853)	375.0

[a] From B. R. Mitchell, with the collaboration of Phyllis Deane, *Abstract of British Historical Statistics* (Cambridge: At the University Press, 1971), pp. 279–284).

The discrepancies are sufficiently large to affect estimates of the scale of world trade as well as the British proportion of the total. Mulhall's shift to current values in 1860 also yields an excessive increase in the value of British trade between 1850 and 1860. The fact that Mulhall's total world trade figure combines current values for others with an apparently underestimated volume figure for Britain raises the question of the legitimacy of applying a price correction to his total for world trade as, for example, Kuznets does (*Modern Economic Growth*, p. 308, in discussion of sources for Panel A, on p. 306).

In the period of overlap of Mulhall and Hilgerdt (or similar) estimates, 1870–1889, the behavior of Mulhall's series conforms pretty well. Here, for example, are Mulhall's and Maddison's value data for world trade over comparable years, with the conversion to U.S. dollars at $5 per British pound, which Mulhall used.

	Mulhall	Maddison	Difference
	(in Millions of Current U.S. Dollars)		
1870	$10,955	$10,836	+1%
1880	$15,165	$13,975	+8%
1889	$16,885	$15,845	+7%

The discrepancies would, of course, be less if the pound were taken at $4.866.

Mulhall's total figures conform closely enough in the period of overlap to justify the correction of the British data from 1800 to 1860 to declared values (current prices), the calculation of new world trade value figures, and then price correction which permits linkage to the data from 1870 forward. For price correction, the Rousseaux (overall) index is used (reprinted in Mitchell, with Deane, *Abstract*, pp. 471–473). This is the index used also by Kuznets for correction of the Mulhall value data. It is well to minimize diversity in these matters, except for substantial reasons, although the abnormally low prices of 1850 may exaggerate the volume increase in international trade between 1840 and 1850 and underestimate the increase over the next decade. The Rousseaux index is converted here onto a 1913=100 base, to conform to the price-correction procedures used by Hilgerdt, Maddison, and others. Rousseaux's index is weighted, however, for 1865 and 1885.

Table B-1 shows the resultant new British value data for the period 1800–1850, the new world trade value totals, and the volume data from 1800 to 1889, when Mulhall's corrected data are put onto a 1913=100 basis. The link between the price-corrected data in column 6 to the 1913=100 index has been made in 1889, on the basis of Maddison's figure 45.3, which conforms closely to other such estimates round about 1889. Maddison gives no figure for 1880, but his 1881 index number is 34.5, which fits quite well the price-corrected Mulhall figure for 1880 (33.5). The Mulhall figure for 1870 is 22.4, the Maddison, 23.8. For broad-brush purposes, then, we can regard a linkage of the Mulhall and post-1870 data as possible and legitimate.

The Hilgerdt and United Nations data yield the following series when linked at 1938 and put onto a 1913=100 basis. Svennilson's calculations for the period 1876–1880 to 1948 are given in parentheses.

1876–1880	32	(30)	1936–1938	107	(106)
1881–1885	39	(38)	1938	103	(103)
1886–1890	45	(44)	. . . . .	. . .	. . .
1891–1895	49	(48)	1948	100	(103)
1896–1900	56	(57)	1953	138	[142]
1901–1905	68	(67)	1958	182	[187]
1906–1910	81	(81)	1963	261	[269]
1911–1913	96	(96)	1964	308	[317]
1913	100	(100)	1965	332	[342]
. . . . .	. . .	. . .	1967	351	[361]
1921–1925	82	(82)	1968	395	[407]
1926–1929	110	(110)	1969	437	[450]
1930	112	(113)	1970	476	[480]
1931–1935	95	(93)	1971	505	[520]

TABLE B-1. *British and World Trade Recalculated, 1800–1889*

	(1) Mulhall Original British Data	(2) Mulhall Original World Value Total	(3) Recalculated British Value Data
1800	67	302	114.7
1820	74	341	101.0
1830	88	407	99.8
1840	114	573	152.6
1850	169	832	186.4
1860	—	—	—
1870	—	—	—
1880	—	—	—
1889	—	—	—

[a] Mulhall figures converted to 1913 = 100 base.

Both Svennilson and Maddison have reworked the pre-1938 figures to take account of trade flows excluded in the Hilgerdt calculations; and Maddison (p. 173) has also recalculated the U.N. data for the period 1948–1960 to take into account both Sino-Soviet trade and intra-German trade, while making other lesser adjustments. These recalculations yield a total world trade figure about 15 percent higher for the year 1960 than the United Nations total. To preserve continuity with the regularly available U.N. series, I have only accepted the Svennilson adjustments. But Maddison's most important point should be underlined; that is, the U.N. world trade total excludes the communist states, except Yugoslavia. If Svennilson's judgment is accepted, and the 1948 world trade figure is taken at the same level as that of 1938 (rather than slightly below), the bracketed index numbers emerge from the U.N. data, 1953–1971.

This leaves the third problem: whether and how to link the Mulhall estimates for the eighteenth century to data covering the next two centuries. In one sense, the problem is easier than the linkage of Mulhall's series to the post-1870 estimates; that is, there is no ambiguity about what his British data are. They are the conventional official value (volume) figures. The other data used are almost certainly current value estimates; e.g., the French figures. Mystery surrounds the method by which Mulhall derived most of his other reasonably persuasive figures; but they must also be presumed to be value data.

Kuznets has used these Mulhall estimates by correcting the world trade totals with the Rousseaux index for 1820–1889, extrapolating back to 1720, 1750, and 1780 by linking the Rousseaux index to that of Elizabeth Schumpeter and Elizabeth Gilboy (reprinted in Mitchell, with Deane, *Abstract*, p. 468). Kuznets accords a weight of 0.8 to the Schumpeter-Gilboy consumers' goods index, 0.2 to that

(4) Recalculated World Value Total	(5) Rousseaux Index (1913 = 100)	(6) Column 4, World Trade Price, Corrected	(7) Volume Index (1913 = 100)
350	165.1	212	2.3
368	124.5	296	3.1
419	102.8	408	4.3
612	120.7	507	5.4
849	89.6	947	10.1
,489	113.7	1,310	13.9
,191	103.8	2,111	23.8 (22.4)[a]
,033	96.2	3,153	— (33.5)[a]
,377	79.2	4,264	45.3

for producers' goods. Aside from the flaw involved in treating a volume series (British official values) as representing current values, the calculation yields the anomalous result of a decline in the volume of British foreign trade between 1780 and 1800 which we know did not happen. There was an evident increase in both the volume and value of foreign trade between those two dates.

Perhaps for that reason, Kuznets skipped the Mulhall 1800 figure, averaged the Mulhall price-corrected data for 1720, 1750, and 1780, and emerged with some sense of the growth in the volume of world trade from the mid-eighteenth century to the average for 1820 and 1830 (*Modern Economic Growth*, p. 306). Since he was interested primarily in demonstrating the accelerated expansion of world trade in the nineteenth as compared to the eighteenth century, his procedure sufficed.

If we wish to produce a more continuous series from 1720 forward, capable of linkage to the revised 1800 Mulhall figure, we must somehow correct the British official value data for pre-1800 price changes, because we do not have the benefit of declared values for the eighteenth century. This can be done, after a fashion, by first calculating British trade figures on the assumption that there was no price change in the eighteenth century, but linking the official and declared values at 1800; then correcting the resultant series with the Rousseaux–Schumpeter-Gilboy price index, adjusted to a 1913=100 base. Revised British and world value data can then be calculated and the latter can be converted onto the 1913=100 index base as in Table B-2.

The only major change brought about in Mulhall's value figures of world trade by this procedure is to dramatize the price rise between 1780 and 1800, inflating the British and world value figures for 1800 as compared to 1780. The question then arises: Does the

TABLE B-2. *British and World Trade Recalculated, 1720–1800*

	(1) Mulhall Original World Total	(2) Mulhall Original British Data	(3) Column 2 Adjusted to Base 114.7[a] = 67	(4) Rousseaux–Schumpeter-Gilboy Price Index Adjusted to 1800 = 100
1800	302	67	114.7	100
1780	186	23	39.4	56
1750	140	21	35.9	47
1720	88	13	22.2	50

[a] Declared value of imports, domestic exports, and re-exports, 1800, = £ 114.7 million.

Schumpeter-Gilboy index, as weighted by Kuznets' method, project an excessive increase in prices entering into British and world trade between 1780 and 1800? The critical period is 1790–1800, since British prices were relatively steady (or may have fallen) during the 1780's. The Schumpeter-Gilboy index rises by 65 percent in the 1790's, when weighted by the Kuznets method; Kondratieff's index by 47 percent; Silberling's by 59 percent; Jevons' by 62 percent; the Gayer domestic price index by 97 percent (heavily weighted with grain), the import price index by 49 percent, from January 1790 to December 1800. These indexes are to be found in A. D. Gayer et al., *The Growth and Fluctuation of the British Economy, 1790–1850* (Oxford: Clarendon Press, 1953), vol. 1, pp. 468–470 (Gayer); p. 521 (Jevons); p. 524 (Silberling); p. 526 (Kondratieff). If the Schumpeter-Gilboy price index for consumers' goods other than cereals is weighted at 0.8 and used, instead of the general consumers' goods price index, the rise between 1790 and 1800 is 47 percent. On the whole, I am inclined to conclude that the price correction between 1780 and 1800 is somewhat excessive; that is, there was probably a greater rise in the volume of world trade than that exhibited by these calculations. But, for present purposes, refinement is not justified. The major historical fact, however, does emerge; namely, that there was a radical shift in the proportion of world trade conducted by Britain between 1780 and 1800.

The figures finally used to represent the approximate volume of world trade, exhibited in Chart II-3 and from which the growth rates in Table II-7 were calculated, are, then, those shown in Table B-3.

The adjustments to the Mulhall data described here and the availabilty after 1860 of more or less agreed world trade data in current values permit the distribution of world trade, by country and regions, to be calculated, as presented in Table II-8. I used Mulhall's data, as corrected, for the period 1720–1889. Rather surprisingly, his breakdown is more complete than in the League of Nations (Folke Hilgerdt) series, used for 1891–1895 and 1901–1905, as

5) Column 3 Corrected by Column 4 (Approximate British Value Data)	(6) Revised Mulhall World Value Data	(7) Column 6 Price Corrected, 1913 = 100	(8) Volume Index, 1913 = 100
14.7	350	212	2.3
22.0	185	201	2.18
17.0	136	175	1.90
11.0	86	104	1.13

TABLE B-3. *Volume of World Trade, 1720–1971 (1913 = 100)*

1720	1.13	1921–1925	82
1750	1.90	1926–1929	110
1780	2.18	1930	113
1800	2.3	1931–1935	93
1820	3.1	1936–1938	106
1830	4.3	1938	103
1840	5.4	1948	103
1850	10.1	1953	142
1860	13.9	1958	187
1870	23.8	1963	269
1876–1880	30	1964	317
1881–1885	38	1965	342
1886–1890	44	1967	361
1891–1895	48	1968	407
1896–1900	57	1969	450
1901–1905	67	1970	490
1906–1910	81	1971	520
1911–1913	96		
1913	100		

presented in Kuznets, *Modern Economic Growth*, p. 307. For 1913, 1928, and 1937, Kuznets' table, ibid., p. 308, is used, built up from sources described, ibid., p. 309. The year 1938 is included, from U.N. sources, because it provides a pre–World War II detailed breakdown matching the United Nations postwar figures. There is, however, an exception. The United Nations gives no figure for pre-war Germany. The 1938 German trade total, taken from Maddison, is used here, with the U.N. world trade total appropriately expanded.

Appendix C

The Size of the United States Motor Vehicle Sectoral Complex, Early 1970's

TABLE C-1. *Motor Vehicle Industry Employment and Payrolls, 1972*

SIC (Standard Industrial Classification) No.	Employees	Payroll ($ Millions)
Motor vehicle industry	5,111,285	42,396.3
Manufacturing	907,200	10,691.9
371 Motor vehicle and motor vehicle equipment	806,600	9,447.1
2911 Petroleum refining	100,600	1,244.8
Wholesaling	580,022	4,947.2
501 Automotive wholesale	382,469	3,239.2
517 Wholesale petroleum and petroleum products	197,553	1,708.0
Retailing	1,641,515	10,375.4
551 New and used motor vehicle dealers	732,158	6,273.7
552 Used motor vehicle dealers	42,110	259.3
553 Auto and home supply stores	169,140	1,103.9
554 Gasoline dealers	698,107	2,738.5
556 Recreational vehicle dealers	n.a.	n.a.
Selected services	405,567	2,480.9
751 Automotive rental, leasing without driver	66,538	533.3
752 Automobile parking	37,136	176.0
753 Automotive repair shops	235,901	1,557.6
754 Automotive service except repair	65,992	214.0
1611 Highway and street construction	219,659	1,867.3
Transportation	1,357,322	12,033.6
41 Local passenger transportation	368,649	2,598.5
421 Trucking, local and long-distance	986,019	9,411.7
423 Trucking terminal facilities	2,654	23.4

Sources: Manufacturing, U.S. Bureau of the Census, *1972 Census of Manufacturers*; wholesaling, retailing, selected services, highway construction and transportation, U.S. Bureau of the Census, *Country Business Patterns, 1972.*

Table C-1 summarizes the categories of employment of 5.1 million workers who could be identified as of 1972 as involved in the motor vehicle industry. If some 8 million truck drivers employed by private not-for-hire enterprises are added, the total automotive-generated employment would approximate 13 million, or about 15 percent of the civilian working force, 6 percent if truck drivers are excluded.

Wassily Leontief has translated this set of interconnections into a powerful marginal calculation. Using input-output tables adjusted for employment, he estimated in December 1974 that a $1 billion reduction of automobile sales results in a loss of about 56,000 jobs, as shown in Table C-2.

Leontieff's calculations are reported in the *New York Times* (December 8, 1974), Section 3, p. 1, in an article by Leonard Silk. They are based, in turn, on calculations for the year 1947 published in Leontieff's "Domestic Production and Foreign Trade: The American Capital Position Re-examined," *Proceedings of the American Philosophical Society*, vol. 97, no. 4 (September 28, 1953), pp. 333–335. The key table is Table C-3.

Perhaps 40 percent of the decline in total employment in the United States between November 1973 and November 1974 could thus be accounted for by an $11 billion decline in auto sales in constant dollars. The high income elasticity of demand for private automobiles, combined with the rise in gasoline prices, made automobile sales peculiarly sensitive to the recession of 1973–1974.

TABLE C-2. *Estimate of Employment Reduction Associated with a Decline of $1 Billion in U.S. Automobile Sales, 1973–1974*

Industry	Employment Decline
Motor vehicle manufacturing	22,900
Other industries:	
Iron and steel	4,600
Fabricated metal products	4,170
Nonelectrical machinery	2,650
Textiles	1,900
Electrical machinery	1,840
Rubber	1,340
Glass	760
Wholesale and retail trade	4,420
All other	11,360
Total, other industries	33,040
Total, all industries	55,940

Source: Wassily Leontief, reported in the *New York Times*, December 8, 1974.

TABLE C-3. *Capital and Labor Requirements for the Final Output of One Million Dollars' Worth of Motor Vehicles*

Industry	Output Requirements ($ Thousands)[a]	Requirements per $ Million of Output of Industry Listed at Left		Requirements per $ Million of Final Output of Motor Vehicles	
		Capital ($ Thousands)	Labor (Man-Years)	Capital ($ Thousands)	Labor (Man-Years)
(1)	(2)	(3)	(4)	(5)	(6)
26. Motor vehicles (145)	1,457.45[b]	565.8	60.340	824.6	87.942
15. Iron and steel	235.14	1,026.3	77.777	241.3	18.288
19. Other fabricated metal products	118.25	713.5	95.335	84.5	11.273
16. Nonferrous metals	78.69	1,001.6	55.715	78.8	4.384
25. Other electrical machinery	75.50	551.1	102.638	41.6	7.749
22. Other nonelectric machinery	60.70	775.7	96.579	47.1	5.862
10. Chemicals	57.95	592.7	49.779	34.3	2.885
12. Rubber products	56.19	493.1	90.172	27.7	5.067
31. Railroad transportation	50.18	3,343.3	153.640	167.8	7.710
11. Products of petroleum and coal	46.85	1,397.2	29.843	65.5	1.398
4. Textile mill products	39.29	493.6	110.563	19.4	4.344
14. Stone, clay, and glass products	33.64	1,026.3	128.539	34.5	4.324
8. Paper and allied products	31.95	564.1	64.805	18.0	2.071
34. Trade	31.82	984.9	165.876	31.3	5.278
30. Coal, gas, and electric power	29.50	2,222.6	99.318	65.6	2.930
1. Agriculture and fisheries	27.53	2,524.4	82.025	69.5	2.258
21. Metalworking machinery	27.48	1,246.9	130.705	34.3	3.592
33. Other transportation	23.88	928.3	121.576	22.2	2.903
9. Printing and publishing	19.72	436.0	114.038	8.6	2.249
38. Business services	18.44	144.5	97.543	2.7	1.799
39. Personal and repair services	18.10	681.8	183.503	12.3	3.321
6. Lumber and wood products	15.98	537.9	141.540	8.6	2.262
5. Apparel	13.74	262.2	108.795	3.6	1.495
29. Miscellaneous manufacturing	11.26	439.4	100.364	4.9	1.130

2. Food and kindred products	9.98	361.9	43.143	3.6	0.431
36. Finance and insurance	9.83	28.2	92.242	0.3	0.907
35. Communications	6.21	4,645.4	163.097	28.8	1.013
44. Eating and drinking places	6.02	688.0	125.365	4.1	0.755
27. Other transportation equipment	5.11	759.0	122.419	3.9	0.626
13. Leather and leather products	5.06	264.0	109.629	1.3	0.555
23. Motors and generators	4.99	404.3	117.7 '1	2.0	0.588
24. Radios	4.65	449.0	124.097	2.1	0.577
7. Furniture and fixtures	4.28	485.1	116.923	2.1	0.500
18. Fabricated structural metal products	3.79	441.9	83.300	1.7	0.316
20. Agriculture, mining, and construction machinery	3.65	838.6	87.794	3.1	0.320
17. Plumbing and heating supplies	2.67	509.9	99.388	1.4	0.265
40. Medical, educational, and nonprofit organizations	2.05	2,689.5	253.044	5.5	0.519
3. Tobacco manufactures	0.53	557.6	40.539	0.3	0.021
41. Amusements	0.10	1,082.9	166.899	0.1	0.017
		Total requirements in all industries per million dollars of final output of motor vehicles		2,104.8	201.476

[a] The output required from each industry in order to produce $1 million worth of motor vehicles for export or domestic consumption. See W. Duane Evans and Marvin Hoffenberg, "The Interindustry Relations Study for 1947," *The Review of Economics and Statistics*, vol. 34, no. 2 (May 1952), Table 6, following p. 142.

[b] This figure includes the "back feed" within this industry, i.e., the automotive industry's purchases from itself, as well as the million dollars' worth of motor vehicles going to final consumers and the amounts needed by the various other industries to meet their output requirements. For detailed explanation of the technical point involved, see Evans and Hoffenberg, "Interindustry Relations," pp. 137–140.

Source: Leontief, "Domestic Production and Foreign Trade," p. 334.

For a somewhat different estimate of the rise of the automobile sectoral complex, see Simon Kuznets, *Economic Growth of Nations: Total Output and Production Structure* (Cambridge, Mass.: the Belknap Press of Harvard University Press, 1971), pp. 314–322. By 1948, Kuznets estimates this complex represented 19.4 percent of U.S. manufacturing output, 22.6 percent of capital in manufacturing.

Although intellectually less satisfactory, a measurement of U.S. business establishments dependent on manufacture, distribution, servicing, and use of motor vehicles can yield estimates of over 800,000, as shown in Table C-4. This figure embraces perhaps 16 percent of all U.S. business establishments. One would, of course, have to assume that the average size of the establishments included in the automobile sector approximated the average size of U.S. business establishments as a whole for this figure to be meaningful.

A further approach to estimating the scale of the motor vehicle sector, via road transport expenditures entering into GNP calculations, yields the estimates in Table C-5, accounting for 16–18 percent of GNP for 1969–1972.

TABLE C-4. *U.S. Businesses Dependent on Motor Vehicles*

Automotive manufacturing	3,526
Automotive wholesaling	65,698
Automotive retailing	307,271
Automotive services and miscellaneous	197,018
Highway and street construction contractors	14,713
Motor freight transportation and related services	234,549
	822,775

Source: *Automobile Facts and Figures, 1973–74* (Detroit: Automobile Manufacturers Association), p. 52.

TABLE C-5. *Estimated U.S. Highway Passenger and Freight Transportation Expenditures (in $ Billions)*

	1969	1970	1971	1972[a]
Highway passenger transportation expenditures				
Auto				
New and used cars	37.3	33.0	41.7	46.4
Tires, tubes, accessories	6.1	6.7	7.4	8.3
Gasoline and oil	24.6	26.1	27.7	30.0
Tolls	0.6	0.6	0.7	0.7
Insurance	3.5	4.1	5.1	5.4
Interest on debt	5.5	5.7	5.9	6.5
Auto registration fees	1.5	1.7	1.7	1.8
Operator's permit fees	0.2	0.2	0.2	0.3
Repair, greasing, washing, parking, storage, rental	9.4	10.3	11.3	12.3
Total	88.8	88.4	101.7	111.6
Local				
Bus and transit[b]	0.8	0.8	0.8	0.8
Taxi	1.4	1.4	1.5	1.6
School bus	1.1	1.2	1.4	1.5
Total	3.2	3.5	3.7	4.0
Intercity				
Bus	0.7	0.8	0.8	0.8
Total highway passenger transportation expenditures	92.7	92.6	106.3	116.4
Highway freight transportation expenditures				
Truck, intercity				
ICC-regulated	13.9	14.6	16.7	18.7
Non-ICC-regulated	17.4	19.0	20.9	23.0
Truck, local	30.4	35.5	41.7	50.5
Bus	0.1	0.1	0.1	0.1
Total highway freight transportation expenditures	61.9	69.2	79.4	92.3
Total highway freight and passenger expenditures	154.7	161.8	185.0	208.7
Percentage of GNP	16.6	16.6	17.5	18.0

[a] Preliminary.
[b] One-half of amount shown by source for "bus and transit."
Source: Transportation Association of America, *Transportation Facts and Trends*, eleventh edition (December 1974), pp. 4 and 5; sources given, pp. A-2–A-5.
Note: Due to rounding, total may not equal sum of components.

Appendix D

Sources for Charted Data, Part Five

Chapter 28. *Great Britain*

1. *GNP per capita (1958 pounds)*
   A. *GNP at factor cost*
      1700–1821* Phyllis Deane and W. A. Cole, *British Economic Growth, 1688–1959*, second edition (Cambridge: Cambridge University Press, 1969), Table 19, p. 78; Table 72, p. 282.
      1830–1869. Phyllis Deane, "New Estimates of Gross National Product for the United Kingdom, 1830–1914," *The Review of Income and Wealth*, Series 14, no. 2 (June 1968).
      1870–1965. C. H. Feinstein, *National Income, Expenditure and Output of the United Kingdom, 1855–1965* (Cambridge: At the University Press, 1972), Table 5, pp. T14–T17.
      1966–1971. Central Statistical Office, *Annual Abstract of Statistics* [*AAS*], 1972, Table 318, p. 297.
   B. *Population*
      1701, 1751, 1791. Deane and Cole, *British Economic Growth*, Table 2, p. 6.
      1712, 1754, 1780. Michael G. Mulhall, *The Dictionary of Statistics* [*DS*] (London: George Routledge and Sons, 1892), p. 444.

* Linkage Procedures: For the period 1700–1821, GNP per capita estimates were derived from a GNP index (1958=100) created from the following sources: *1700–1821*, Deane and Cole, *British Economic Growth*, Table 19, p. 78, and Table 72, p. 282. Linkage year 1801 was derived from Table 19, assuming an annual rate of growth of 2.82 percent for total real output during the decade 1790–1800. *1830–1912*, Deane, "New Estimates," Table B, pp. 106–107. Deane's estimates were transformed into index numbers and the data were linked in 1831 with the GNP index derived from Deane and Cole, *British Economic Growth*, Table 72, p. 282. *1913–1965*, Feinstein, *National Income, Expenditure and Output*, Table 6, Compromise Estimate, pp. T18–T20. All index numbers were standardized to base year 1958=100. GNP estimates for 1700–1821 were calculated by multiplying the yearly index number by Feinstein's 1958 estimate for GNP at factor cost (20,396; see Table 5, p. T17).

1801–1939. B. R. Mitchell, with the collaboration of Phyllis Deane, *Abstract of British Historical Statistics*, (Cambridge: At the University Press, 1962), pp. 8–10.
1940–1952. *AAS*, 1952, Table 6, p. 7.
1951–1972. Ibid., 1972, Table 6, p. 7.

2. *Industrial production index (including building)* (1958=100)
1700–1912. Walther G. Hoffmann, *British Industry, 1700–1950*, translated by W. H. Chaloner and W. O. Henderson (Oxford: Basil Blackwell, 1955), Tables 54A and 54B, p. 331.
1913–1937. B. R. Mitchell, with Deane, *Abstract*, Lomax Index, p. 272.
1938–1952. *United Nations Statistical Yearbook* [*UNSY*], 1953, p. 99.
1953–1957. Ibid., 1958, p. 108.
1958–1964. Ibid., 1965, p. 166.
1965–1972. Ibid., 1973, p. 152.
(Linkage years: 1913, 1938, 1952, 1957, 1958.)

3. *Gross investment as % of GNP (current prices)*
1830–1914. Deane, "New Estimates," Table A, pp. 104–105 [(GFDC + NFI) ÷ GNP_{fc}].
1920–1959. Deane and Cole, *British Economic Growth*, Appendix 3, Table 91, pp. 332 and 333.
1960–1966. *United Nations Yearbook of National Account Statistics* [*UNYNAS*], 1967, p. 697.
1967–1971. Ibid., 1973, vol. 3, Table 2A, p. 52.

4. *Railroads (miles)*
1825–1847. Henry G. Lewin, *Early British Railways*, cited in B. R. Mitchell, with Deane, *Abstract*, p. 225.
1848–1938. B. R. Mitchell, with Deane, *Abstract*, pp. 225–227.
1939–1965. B. R. Mitchell and H. G. Jones, *Second Abstract of British Historical Statistics* (Cambridge: At the University Press, 1971), pp. 104–105.
1966–1971. *AAS*, 1972, Table 255, p. 228. (Figures from 1948 onward refer to British railways only.)

5. *Raw cotton consumption (thousand metric tons)*
1695–1795. Deane and Cole, *British Economic Growth*, Table 15, p. 51 (retained imports).
1800–1938. B. R. Mitchell, with Deane, *Abstract*, p. 179.
1939–1965. B. R. Mitchell and Jones, *Second Abstract*, p. 90.
1966–1972. *UNSY*, 1973, p. 504.

6. *Production of pig iron (thousand metric tons)*
1700–1818. W. W. Rostow, *How It All Began* (New York: McGraw-Hill, 1975), Table 12, p. 165.
1823–1938. B. R. Mitchell, with Deane, *Abstract*, pp. 131–133.
1939–1952. *UNSY*, 1953, p. 228.
1953–1960. Ibid., 1962, p. 256.
1961–1969. Ibid., 1970, p. 307.

1970–1973. Ibid., 1973, p. 296.

7. *Steel production (thousand metric tons)*
   1871–1938. B. R. Mitchell, with Deane, *Abstract*, pp. 136–137.
   1939–1947. *UNSY*, 1948, p. 239.
   1948–1952. Ibid., 1953, p. 231.
   1953–1961. Ibid., 1962, p. 257.
   1962–1966. Ibid., 1967, p. 300.
   1967–1972. Ibid., 1973, p. 297.
8. *Electricity—electrical energy production (million kWh)*
   1895–1927. B. R. Mitchell and Jones, *Second Abstract*, pp. 71 and 72.
   1928–1947. *UNSY*, 1948, p. 262.
   1948–1949. Ibid., 1949–1950, p. 284.
   1950–1952. Ibid., 1954, p. 262.
   1953–1959. Ibid., 1962, p. 318.
   1960–1962. Ibid., 1963, p. 345.
   1963–1972. Ibid., 1973, p. 367.
9. *Motor vehicle production (thousands)*
   1907–1973. *World Motor Vehicle Data* [WMVD] (Detroit: Motor Vehicle Manufacturers Association, 1974), pp. 8–9.
10. *Sulphuric acid (thousand metric tons, 100% pure)*
   1867–1925. Ingvar Svennilson, *Growth and Stagnation in the European Economy* (Geneva: United Nations, 1954), Tables A48a and A48b, pp. 286–287.
   1928–1947. *UNSY*, 1948, p. 213.
   1948–1952. Ibid., 1953, p. 204.
   1953–1957. Ibid., 1958, p. 214.
   1958–1966. Ibid., 1967, p. 274.
   1967–1972. Ibid., 1973, p. 265.
11. *Nitrogen fertilizer production (thousand metric tons)*
   1938. *UNSY*, 1948, p. 216.
   1939–1945. Mirko Lamer, *The World Fertilizer Economy* (Stanford: Stanford University Press, 1957), Table 8, p. 650.
   1947–1951. *UNSY*, 1953, p. 210.
   1952–1957. Ibid., 1958, p. 219.
   1958–1960. Ibid., 1962, p. 242.
   1961–1966. Ibid., 1967, p. 280.
   1967–1972. Ibid., 1973, p. 271.
12. *Plastics and resins (thousand metric tons)*
   1937, 1947–1951. Svennilson, *Growth and Stagnation*, Table A55, p. 291 (plastics only).
   1956–1957. *UNSY*, 1965, p. 288.
   1958–1965. Ibid., 1967, p. 281.
   1966–1972. Ibid., 1973, p. 272.
13. *Synthetic fibers (noncellulosic continuous fibers, thousand metric tons)*
   1948–1955. *UNSY*, 1959, p. 209.

1956–1962. Ibid., 1965, p. 272.
1963–1972. Ibid., 1973, p. 249.

14. *Shipbuilding (total and steel, tonnage)*
1860–1900. B. R. Mitchell, with Deane, *Abstract*, pp. 221–224.
1900–1938. Ibid. (total tonnage).
1939–1965. B. R. Mitchell and Jones, *Second Abstract*, p. 102.
1966–1972. *UNSY*, 1973, p. 308.

Chapter 29. *United States*

1. *GNP per capita (1929 dollars)*
1789–1973. Thomas S. Berry, "U.S. Product and Income Accounts since 1789: Revised Annual Estimates" (unpublished manuscript), Table 38B, p. 22.

2. *Industrial production index (1958=100)*
1860–1914. Edwin Frickey, *Production in the United States, 1860–1914* (Cambridge, Mass.: Harvard University Press, 1947), Table 6, p. 54.
1919–1929. *Historical Statistics of the United States: Colonial Times to 1957* [*HSUS*] (Washington, D.C.: U.S. Bureau of the Census, 1960), Series W24, pp. 600–601.
1930–1971. *Economic Report of the President* (Washington, D.C.: Government Printing Office, 1972), Table B-35, p. 235.
(Linkage years: 1914, 1929.)

3. *Gross investment as % of GNP (current dollars)*
1789–1973. Berry, "U.S. Product and Income Accounts," Table 5B, p. 3.

4. *Railroads (miles)*
1830–1890. *HSUS*, Series Q15, p. 427.
1891–1957. Ibid., Series Q49 and Q50, p. 429.
1958–1959. U.S. Department of Commerce, *Statistical Abstract of the United States* [*SAUS*], no. 177 (Washington, D.C.: Bureau of the Census, 1962), p. 572 (First Main Track and Other Main Tracks).
1960–1962. Ibid., no. 813 (1965), p. 580.
1969–1971. Ibid., no. 923 (1973), p. 557.

5. *Raw cotton consumption (thousand metric tons)*
1790–1859. M. B. Hammond, *The Cotton Industry: An Essay in American Economic History* (New York: Macmillan, 1897), Appendix 1, p. 358.
1860–1957. *HSUS*, Series P197, p. 414.
1958–1964. *UNSY*, 1965, p. 504.
1965–1972. Ibid., 1973, p. 503.

6. *Production of pig iron (thousand metric tons)*
1740, 1790, 1800. *DS*, 1899, p. 332.
1810–1956. *HSUS*, Series M207, pp. 365–366.
1957–1962. *UNSY*, 1963, p. 282.
1963–1972. Ibid., 1973, p. 296.

7. *Steel production (thousand metric tons)*
   1867–1955. G. Warren Nutter, *The Growth of Industrial Production in the Soviet Union* (Princeton: Princeton University Press, 1962), Table E1, Series 103, pp. 582–583; Table E2, Series 103, p. 609.
   1956–1964. *UNSY*, 1965, p. 306.
   1965–1972. Ibid., 1973, p. 297.
8. *Electricity—electrical energy production (million kWh)*
   1882–1955. Nutter, *Growth*, Table E1, pp. 584–585.
   1956–1957. *UNSY*, 1958, p. 268.
   1958–1960. Ibid., 1962, p. 312.
   1961–1962. Ibid., 1963, p. 340.
   1963. Ibid., 1965, p. 366.
   1964–1972. Ibid., 1973, p. 367.
9. *Motor vehicle production (thousands)*
   1895–1899. *Automobile Facts and Figures* [*F&F*] (Detroit: Motor Vehicle Manufacturers Association, 1924), p. 9.
   1900–1973. *WMVD*, 1974, pp. 8–9.
10. *Sulphuric acid (thousand metric tons, 100% pure)*
   1865–1926. *The American Fertilizer Handbook* (Philadelphia: Ware Bros., 1927), Table 7, D-9.
   1929–1946. *UNSY*, 1948, p. 212.
   1947–1951. Ibid., 1953, p. 203.
   1952–1953. Ibid., 1958, p. 213.
   1954–1961. Ibid., 1963, p. 262.
   1962. Ibid., 1965, p. 282.
   1963–1969. Ibid., 1972, p. 275.
   1970–1972. Ibid., 1973, p. 265.
11. *Nitrogen fertilizer production (thousand metric tons)*
   1938, 1947–1950. *UNSY*, 1953, p. 210.
   1951–1956. Ibid., 1958, p. 219.
   1957–1961. Ibid., 1965, p. 287.
   1962–1964. Ibid., 1970, p. 285.
   1965–1972. Ibid., 1973, p. 270.
12. *Plastics and resins (thousand metric tons)*
   1937, 1947–1951. Svennilson, *Growth and Stagnation*, Table A55, p. 291 (plastics only).
   1956–1963. *UNSY*, 1965, p. 288.
   1964–1972. Ibid., 1973, p. 272.
13. *Synthetic fibers (noncellulosic continuous fibers, thousand metric tons)*
   1952–1956. *UNSY*, 1958, p. 201.
   1957–1964. Ibid., 1965, p. 272.
   1965–1972. Ibid., 1973, p. 249.

Chapter 30. *France*

1. *GNP per capita (1959 million francs)*
   A. *GNP (1959 million francs)*
      1825–1898. *Annuaire Statistique de la France: Résumé Rétro-*

spectif [ASFR] (Paris: Institut National de la Statistique et des Etudes Economiques, 1966), Table 13, p. 555.
1901–1958, 1960–1964. Ibid., Table 14, p. 556. (Sauvy's estimates).
1959. Ibid., Table 8, p. 553.
1966–1971. *UNYNAS*, 1972, vol. 1, p. 353.
(Linkage years: 1959, 1963.)

B. *Population*
1821–1936. *ASFR*, 1966, Table 1, p. 22 (existing territory).
1946–1965. Ibid., Table 2, p. 23.
1972. *UNSY*, 1973, p. 71.

C. *Price index (general)*
1825–1898. *ASFR*, 1966, Table 1, p. 373 (decade average), and Table 3, p. 375 (1935–1940 average). For the period 1825–1898, GNP estimates were inflated to 1938 francs before converting the annual GNP estimates to 1959 francs.

2. *Industrial production index (1959=100)*
1705, 1785. Jan Marczewski, "The Take-Off Hypothesis and French Experience," Chapter 7 in W. W. Rostow (ed.), *The Economics of Take-off into Sustained Growth* (New York: St. Martin's Press, 1963), pp. 123–125.
1815–1913. François Crouzet, "Essai de construction d'un indice annuel de la production industrielle française au XIXe siècle," *Annales, Economies-Sociéties-Civilisations*, vol. 25, no. 1 (January–February 1970), Table 8b.
1919–1964. *ASFR*, 1966, Table 1, p. 561.
1965–1972. *UNSY*, 1973, p. 149.
(Linkage years: 1913, 1963.)

3. *Gross investment as % of GNP (current prices)*
1813–1908. Marczewski, "Take-off Hypothesis," Table 2, p. 121.
1938. *ASFR*, 1961, Table 4, p. 356.
1949–1959. Ibid., 1966, Table 8, p. 553.
1960–1971. *UNYNAS*, 1973, vol. 3, p. 47.

4. *Railroads (kilometers)*
1841–1965. *ASFR*, 1966, Table 1A, p. 319; Table 1B, p. 321.
1970–1971. *Annuaire Statistique de la France* (Paris: Institut National de la Statistique et des Etudes Economiques, 1973), p. 401.

5. *Raw cotton consumption (thousand metric tons)*
1700, 1750. *DS*, 1899, p. 160.
1785–1829. B. R. Mitchell, *European Historical Statistics, 1750–1970* (London: Macmillan, 1975), pp. 427–428.
1831–1850. David Landes, *The Unbound Prometheus* (Cambridge: At the University Press, 1969), Table 3, p. 165.
1855, 1865, 1875, 1884. B. R. Mitchell, *European Historical Statistics*, p. 429.
1869, 1873, 1876, 1887–1914. J. H. Clapham, *The Economic Development of France and Germany, 1815–1914* (Cambridge: At the University Press, 1921), p. 247.

1922–1925. International Institute of Agriculture, *The Cotton Growing Countries, Present and Potential* (London: P. S. King and Sons, 1926), pp. 280–281.
1928–1935. International Institute of Agriculture, *World Cotton Production and Trade* (Rome: International Institute of Agriculture, 1936), p. 382.
1938, 1947–1950. *UNSY*, 1953, p. 279.
1951–1957. Ibid., 1958, p. 286.
1958–1964. Ibid., 1965, p. 504.
1965. Ibid., 1970, p. 529.
1966–1972. Ibid., 1973, p. 503.

6. *Production of pig iron (thousand metric tons)*
1700–1820. *DS*, 1899, p. 332.
1824–1913, 1919–1938, 1946–1965. *ASFR*, 1966, Table 1, p. 240; Table 2, p. 241.
1918. B. R. Mitchell, *European Historical Statistics*, p. 393.
1939–1945. *UNSY*, 1948, p. 236.
1966–1972. Ibid., 1973, p. 296.

7. *Steel production (thousand metric tons)*
1870–1881. B. R. Mitchell, *European Historical Statistics*, p. 399.
1882–1913, 1921–1938, 1946–1950. Svennilson, *Growth and Stagnation*, Table A29, p. 260; Table A31, pp. 262–263.
1918–1920, 1939–1945. B. R. Mitchell, *European Historical Statistics*, p. 400.
1951–1957. *UNSY*, 1958, p. 237.
1958–1964. Ibid., 1965, p. 306.
1965–1972. Ibid., 1973, p. 297.

8. *Electricity—electrical energy production (million kWh)*
1901–1965. *ASFR*, 1966, Table 1, p. 210 (prior to 1923, electric consumption).
1966–1972. *UNSY*, 1973, p. 362.

9. *Motor vehicle production (thousands)*
1900–1972. *WMVD*, 1974, pp. 8–9.

10. *Sulphuric acid (thousand metric tons, 100% pure)*
1900–1929. Svennilson, *Growth and Stagnation*, Tables A48a and A48b, pp. 286–287.
1938–1946. *UNSY*, 1948, p. 212.
1947–1952. Ibid., 1953, p. 203.
1953–1957. Ibid., 1958, p. 213.
1958–1964. Ibid., 1965, p. 282.
1965–1972. Ibid., 1973, p. 264.

11. *Nitrogen fertilizer production (thousand metric tons)*
1913–1937. Svennilson, *Growth and Stagnation*, Table A51, p. 289.
1938–1945. Lamer, *World Fertilizer Economy*, Table 25, p. 659.
1947–1950. *UNSY*, 1953, p. 210.
1951–1956. Ibid., 1958, p. 219.
1957–1963. Ibid., 1965, p. 287.

1964. Ibid., 1970, p. 285.
1965–1972. Ibid., 1973, p. 271.
12. *Plastics and resins (thousand metric tons)*
1937, 1947–1951. Svennilson, *Growth and Stagnation*, Table A55, p. 291.
1956–1964. *UNSY*, 1965, p. 288.
1965–1972. Ibid., 1973, p. 272.
13. *Synthetic fibers (noncellulosic continuous fibers, thousand metric tons)*
1948. *UNSY*, 1958, p. 201.
1950–1951. Ibid., 1957, p. 235.
1952–1955. Ibid., 1958, p. 201.
1956–1962. Ibid., 1965, p. 272.
1963–1972. Ibid., 1973, p. 249.

Chapter 31. *Germany*

1. *GNP per capita (1913 million marks)*
A. *GNP*
1850–1959. Walther G. Hoffmann, *Das Wachstum der Deutschen Wirtschaft seit der Mitte des 19. Jahrhunderts* (Berlin: Springer-Verlag, 1965), Table 249, pp. 827–828.
1960–1964. *UNYNAS*, 1965, p. 124.
1966–1971. Ibid., 1972, p. 385.
(Linkage years: 1959, 1963.)
B. *Population*
1817–1959. Hoffmann, *Das Wachstum*, Table 1, pp. 172–174.
1961, 1963. *UNSY*, 1967, p. 83.
1964. Ibid., 1965, p. 93.
1969. Ibid., 1970, p. 84.
1972. Ibid., 1973, p. 71.
(Beginning in 1945, data are for West Germany.)
2. *Industrial production index (1913 = 100)*
1850–1959. Hoffmann, *Das Wachstum*, Table 101, pp. 451–452.
1960–1965. *UNSY*, 1967, p. 161.
1966–1972. Ibid., 1973, p. 149.
(Linkage year: 1958.)
3. *Gross investment as % of GNP*
A. *Investment*
1850–1956. Hoffmann, *Das Wachstum*, Table 248, pp. 825–826.
1957–1966. *UNYNAS*, 1967, p. 238.
1967–1971. Ibid., 1972, vol. 1, p. 384.
B. *GNP*
1850–1956. Hoffmann, *Das Wachstum*, Table 248, pp. 825–826.
1957–1966. *UNYNAS*, 1967, p. 240.
1967–1971. Ibid., 1972, vol. 1, p. 384.
(Beginning in 1960, figures include Saar and West Berlin.)

4. *Railroads (kilometers)*
   1840, 1850, 1860. *DS*, 1899, p. 495.
   1867–1966. Arthur S. Banks, *Cross-Polity Time Series Data* (Cambridge, Mass.: M. I. T. Press, 1971), Segment 3, pp. 112–113.
   1970. Henry Sampson (ed.), *Jane's World Railways, 1970–1971* (New York: McGraw-Hill, 1970), p. 186.
   (Beginning in 1949, data are for West Germany.)
5. *Raw cotton consumption (thousand metric tons)*
   1825, 1845, 1855, 1865, 1875, 1883. *DS*, 1899, p. 160.
   1848, 1868, 1873, 1895. Clapham, *Economic Development*, pp. 295–297.
   1922–1925. International Institute of Agriculture, *Cotton Growing Countries*, pp. 280–281.
   1928–1935. International Institute of Agriculture, *World Cotton Production and Trade*, Table 30, p. 388.
   1938, 1947–1950. *UNSY*, 1953, p. 279.
   1951–1956. Ibid., 1965, p. 504.
   1965. Ibid., 1967, p. 503.
   1966–1972. Ibid., 1973, p. 503.
   (Beginning in 1947, data are for West Gemany.)
6. *Production of pig iron (thousand metric tons)*
   1700–1820. *DS*, 1899, p. 332.
   1823–1944. Hoffmann, *Das Wachstum*, Table 68, pp. 352–354.
   1946–1956. *UNSY*, 1957, p. 269.
   1957–1961. Ibid., 1965, p. 305.
   1962–1964. Ibid., 1973, p. 296.
   (For the period 1823–1944, data were derived from Hoffmann's index, base year 1913=100, and Svennilson's 1913 estimate of German pig iron production [*Growth and Stagnation*, Table A27, p. 257].)
   (Beginning in 1946, data are for West Germany, including Saar.)
7. *Steel production (thousand metric tons)*
   1879–1913. Simon S. Kuznets, *Secular Movements in Production and Prices* (Boston and New York: Houghton Mifflin, 1930), Table 36, p. 473.
   1914–1944. Hoffmann, *Das Wachstum*, Table 68, p. 354.
   1946–1956. *UNSY*, 1958, p. 237.
   1957–1963. Ibid., 1965, p. 306.
   1964–1972. Ibid., 1973, p. 297.
   (Linkage year: 1913.)
   (Beginning in 1946, data are for West Germany, including Saar.)
8. *Electricity—electrical energy production (million kWh)*
   1900–1929. Hoffmann, *Das Wachstum*, Table 75, p. 388.
   1930–1938. *UNSY*, 1948, p. 260.
   1939–1943. Ibid., 1949–1950, p. 283.
   1946–1948. Ibid., 1948, p. 260.
   1951–1955. Ibid., 1957, p. 305.
   1956–1962. Ibid., 1965, p. 361.
   1963–1972. Ibid., 1973, p. 362.

(Linkage year: 1930.)
(Beginning in 1946, data are for West Germany.)

9. *Motor vehicle production (thousands)*
1900–1973. *WMVD*, 1974, pp. 8–9.

10. *Sulphuric acid (thousand metric tons, 100% pure)*
1871–1929. Hoffmann, *Das Wachstum*, Table 70, pp. 361–362.
1930–1944. *UNSY*, 1948, p. 212.
1949–1952. Ibid., 1953, p. 203.
1953–1957. Ibid., 1958, p. 213.
1948, 1958–1962. Ibid., 1965, p. 282.
1963–1972. Ibid., 1973, p. 264.
(For the period 1871–1929, data are derived from Hoffmann's index, base year 1913, and Svennilson's 1913 estimate of German sulphuric acid production [*Growth and Stagnation*, Table A48a, p. 286].)
(Beginning in 1948, data are for West Germany, including Saar after 1960.)

11. *Nitrogen fertilizer production (thousand metric tons)*
1938, 1947–1952. *UNSY*, 1953, p. 210.
1957–1964. Ibid., 1965, p. 287.
1965–1972. Ibid., 1973, p. 271.
(Beginning in 1938, data are for West Germany.)

12. *Plastics and resins (thousand metric tons)*
1947–1951. Svennilson, *Growth and Stagnation*, Table A55, p. 291.
1956–1963. *UNSY*, 1965, p. 288.
1964–1965. Ibid., 1967, p. 281.
1966–1972. Ibid., 1973, p. 272.
(Beginning in 1947, data are for West Germany.)

13. *Synthetic fibers (noncellulosic continuous fibers, thousand metric tons)*
1950–1955. *UNSY*, 1957, p. 235.
1956–1964. Ibid., 1965, p. 272.
1965–1972. Ibid., 1973, p. 249.

Chapter 32. *Sweden*

1. *GDP per capita*
A. *GDP at market prices (1959 million kronor)*
1861–1954. Östen Johansson, *The Gross Domestic Product of Sweden and Its Composition, 1861–1955*, (Stockholm: Almqvist and Wiksell, 1967), Table 56, pp. 152–153.
1955–1965. *UNYNAS*, 1967, p. 628.
1966–1971. Ibid., 1972, vol. 2, p. 454.
(Linkage years: 1955, 1965.)
B. *Population*
1861–1955. Johansson, *Gross Domestic Product*, Table 58, pp. 156–157.
1958, 1961. *UNSY*, 1962, p. 35.
1963, 1966. Ibid., 1967, p. 84.

1972. Ibid., 1973, p. 72.

2. *Industrial production index (1959=100)*
   1861–1949. Johansson, *Gross Domestic Product*, Table 17, pp. 72–73.
   1950–1954. *UNSY*, 1957, p. 138.
   1955–1961. Ibid., 1962, p. 88.
   1962–1964. Ibid., 1967, p. 163.
   1965–1972. Ibid., 1973, p. 151.
   (The index to 1949 is the value of the output of manufactures and handicrafts. Linkage years: 1950, 1955, 1961, 1965.)
3. *Gross investment as % of GDP (current prices)*
   1861–1969. B. R. Mitchell, *European Historical Statistics*, pp. 782, 789, 795.
   1970–1972. *UNSY*, 1973, p. 565.
4. *Railroads (kilometers)*
   1860–1965. Banks, *Cross-Polity Time Series Data*, Segment 3, pp. 128–129.
   1966–1972. *Statistical Abstract of Sweden* (Stockholm: National Central Bureau of Statistics, 1973), Table 149, p. 169.
5. *Raw cotton consumption (thousand metric tons)*
   1835–1883. *DS*, 1899, p. 161.
   1913, 1929, 1939. W. S. Woytinsky and E. S. Woytinsky, *World Population and Production* (New York: Twentieth Century Fund, 1953), Table 452, p. 1075.
   1922–1925. International Institute of Agriculture, *Cotton Growing Countries*, p. 280.
   1938, 1947–1950. *UNSY*, 1953, p. 279.
   1951–1955. Ibid., 1957, p. 323.
   1956. Ibid., 1960, p. 317.
   1957–1958. Ibid., 1965, p. 504.
   1959–1965. Ibid., 1967, p. 503.
   1966–1972. Ibid., 1973, p. 504.
6. *Production of pig iron (thousand metric tons)*
   1812–1860. *DS*, 1899, pp. 333–336.
   1867–1879. Lennart Jörberg, *Growth and Fluctuations of Swedish Industry, 1867–1912* (Stockholm: Almqvist and Wiksell, 1961), Table 34, p. 405.
   1880–1938. Svennilson, *Growth and Stagnation*, Table A27, pp. 257–258. (Beginning in 1920, data include ferroalloys.)
   1939–1955. *UNSY*, 1957, p. 271.
   1956–1963. Ibid., 1965, p. 305.
   1964–1972. Ibid., 1973, p. 296.
7. *Steel production (thousand metric tons)*
   1867–1912. Jörberg, *Growth and Fluctuations*, Table 34, p. 405.
   1920–1936. Svennilson, *Growth and Stagnation*, Table A31, p. 262.
   1937–1955. *UNSY*, 1957, p. 272.
   1956–1962. Ibid., 1965, p. 306.
   1963–1972. Ibid., 1973, p. 297.

8. *Electricity—electrical energy production (million kWh)*
   1891–1912. Jörberg, *Growth and Fluctuations*, Table 36, p. 406 (million watts.)
   1920–1927. Landes, *Unbound Prometheus*, Table 40, p. 441.
   1928–1947. *UNSY*, 1948, p. 262.
   1948. Ibid., 1960, p. 300.
   1950–1956. Ibid., 1957, p. 306.
   1957–1963. Ibid., 1965, p. 365.
   1964–1972. Ibid., 1973, p. 367.
9. *Motor vehicle production (thousands)*
   1925–1973. *WMVD*, 1974, p. 10.
10. *Sulphuric acid (thousand metric tons, 100% pure)*
   1892, 1912. Thomas H. Norton, "Chemical Industries of Belgium, Netherlands, Norway, and Sweden," *Special Agent Series, No.* 65, Department of Commerce and Labor (Washington, D.C.: Government Printing Office, 1912), p. 73.
   1913. Woytinsky and Woytinsky, *World Population and Production*, Table 490, p. 1188.
   1928–1947. *UNSY*, 1948, p. 213.
   1948. Ibid., 1953, p. 204.
   1950–1956. Ibid., 1957, p. 248.
   1957–1963. Ibid., 1965, p. 282.
   1964–1971. Ibid., 1973, p. 265.
11. *Nitrogen fertilizer production (thousand metric tons)*
   1938, 1947–1948. *UNSY*, 1953, p. 210.
   1949–1956. Ibid., 1957, p. 253.
   1957–1964. Ibid., 1965, p. 287.
   1965–1972. Ibid., 1973, p. 271.
12. *Plastics and resins (thousand metric tons)*
   1959–1960. *UNSY*, 1965, p. 288.
   1961–1965. Ibid., 1970, p. 287.
   1966–1971. Ibid., 1973, p. 271.
13. *Synthetic fibers (noncellulosic continuous fibers, thousand metric tons)*
   1961. *UNSY*, 1965, p. 272.
   1963–1972. Ibid., 1972, p. 249.
14. *Timber exports (thousand metric tons)*
   1864–1967. B. R. Mitchell, *European Historical Statistics*, pp. 346–350.
   1970–1973. *Statistical Abstract of Sweden*, 1974, p. 158.
15. *Wood pulp production (thousand metric tons)*
   1869–1968. B. R. Mitchell, *European Historical Statistics*, pp. 464–465.
   1969–1972. *UNSY*, 1973, pp. 253–254.

Chapter 33. *Japan*

1. *GNP per capita (1963 billion yen)*
   A. *GNP*
      1885–1904. Kazushi Ohkawa et al., *Estimates of Long Term*

Economic Statistics of Japan since 1868 (Tokyo: Toyo Keizai Shinpo Sha, 1974), Table 18, p. 213.

1905–1962. Kazushi Ohkawa and Henry Rosovsky, *Japanese Economic Growth*, (Stanford: Stanford University Press, 1973), Table 6, pp. 288–289.

1963–1973. World Bank, "Basic Economic Data Sheet, World Table I," *1975 World Tables* (Washington, D.C.: World Bank, 1976), p. 12.

(Linkage Years: 1905, 1963.)

B. *Population*

1872–1970. *Japan Statistical Yearbook, 1970* (Tokyo: Bureau of Statistics, Office of the Prime Minister, 1970), p. 10.

1972. *UNSY*, 1973, p. 73.

2. *Industrial production index (1963=100)*

1880–1964. Bank of Japan, *100 Years Statistics of the Japanese Economy* (Tokyo: Statistics Department of the Bank of Japan, 1966), pp. 94, 397.

1965–1972. *UNSY*, 1973, p. 147.

(Linkage years: 1927, 1963.)

(For Charts V-21 and V-22, 1965=100.)

3. *Gross investment as % of GNP (current prices)*

1885–1904. Ohkawa et al., *Estimates*, Table 1, p. 178 (col. 3 ÷ col. 7).

1905–1970. Ohkawa and Rosovsky, *Japanese Economic Growth*, Table 5, pp. 286–287, (col. 3 ÷ col. 6).

1971–1973. World Bank, "Basic Economic Data Sheet," p. 12.

4. *Railroads (kilometers)*

1872–1964. Bank of Japan, *100 Years Statistics*, p. 114–117.

1972. *Japan Statistical Yearbook, 1973/74* (Tokyo: Bureau of Statistics, 1974), p. 262.

5. *Raw cotton consumption (thousand metric tons)*

1888–1911. Sung Joe Koh, *Stages of Industrial Development in Asia* (Philadelphia: University of Pennsylvania Press, 1966), Table 1-1, pp. 325–326.

1912–1913. Y. Takenob, *The Japan Yearbook 1915* [*JY*] (Tokyo: Japan Yearbook Office, 1915), p. 394.

1915–1920. Sung Joe Koh, *Stages*, Table 1–6, p. 334.

1923–1934. *JY*, 1936, p. 554.

1946–1950. Ibid., 1949–1952, p. 496.

1956–1958. *UNSY*, 1958, p. 286.

1959–1965. Ibid., 1965, p. 504.

1966–1967. Ibid., 1967, p. 503.

1970–1973. Ibid., 1973, p. 503.

6. *Production of pig iron (thousand metric tons)*

1895–1911. Hirooto Saegusa and Kenichi Iida, *Nihon Kindai Seitesu Gyiutsu Hattatsu Shi* (Tokyo: Toyo Keizai Shinpo Sha, 1957), p. 654. (*Note*: Pre-1900 approximations for Japanese iron and steel production [Charts V-20 and V-21] are included;

but the data are not judged of sufficient reliability to be placed in the data bank.)

1912–1964. Bank of Japan, *100 Years Statistics*, pp. 100–101.
1965–1972. *UNSY*, 1973, p. 296.

7. *Steel production (thousand metric tons)*
1900–1916. Saegusa and Iida, *Nihon Kindai Seitesu*, p. 655.
1917–1964. Bank of Japan, *100 Years Statistics*, pp. 100–101.
1965–1972. *UNSY*, 1973, p. 297.

8. *Electricity—electrical energy production (million kWh)*
1916–1964. Bank of Japan, *100 Years Statistics*, pp. 124–125.
1965–1973. *UNSY*, 1973, p. 364.

9. *Motor vehicle production (thousands)*
1927–1932. *F&F*, 1932, p. 65.
1933–1934. Ibid., 1935, p. 78.
1935–1936. Ibid., 1937, p. 96.
1937–1938. Ibid., 1939, p. 53.
1946–1973. *WMVD*, 1974, p. 9.

10. *Sulphuric acid (thousand metric tons, 100% pure)*
1905–1908. Bank of Japan, *100 Years Statistics*, p. 102 (strength not reported).
1918–1919. *JY*, 1921–1922, p. 477.
1926–1964. Bank of Japan, *100 Years Statistics*, pp. 102–103.
1965–1972. *UNSY*, 1973, p. 264.

11. *Nitrogen fertilizer production (thousand metric tons)*
1938, 1947–1948. *UNSY*, 1953, p. 210.
1949–1955. Ibid., 1957, p. 253.
1956. Ibid., 1962, p. 242.
1957–1964. Ibid., 1965, p. 287.
1965–1972. Ibid., 1973, p. 270.

12. *Plastics and resins (thousand metric tons)*
1956–1964. *UNSY*, 1965, p. 288.
1965–1972. Ibid., 1973, p. 272.

13. *Synthetic fibers (noncellulosic continuous fibers, thousand metric tons)*
1950–1955. *UNSY*, 1957, p. 235.
1956–1961. Ibid., 1962, p. 229.
1962–1966. Ibid., 1967, p. 264.
1967–1972. Ibid., 1973, p. 249.

14. *Ship tonnage built (metric tons)*
1870–1964. Bank of Japan, *100 Years Statistics*, pp. 106–107.
1965–1972. *UNSY*, 1973, p. 308.

Chapter 34. *Russia-USSR*

1. *GNP per capita (1937 million rubles)*
A. *GNP*
1870–1913. Raymond W. Goldsmith, "The Economic Growth of Tsarist Russia, 1860–1913," *Economic Development and Cultural Change*, vol. 9, no. 3 (April 1961), pp. 441–475.

1928–1965. Angus Maddison, *Economic Growth in Japan and the USSR* (New York: W. W. Norton and Company, 1969), Appendix C, Table B-1, p. 155.

1966–1969. Stanley Cohn, "General Growth Performance of the Soviet Economy," in Joint Economic Committee, *Economic Performance and the Military Burden in the Soviet Union* (Washington, D.C.: Government Printing Office, 1970), Section D-31, Table 1, p. 17.

1970–1972. *UNYNAS*, 1973, vol. 11, p. 639.

(Linkage years: 1913, 1965, 1969.)

(The GNP estimates were derived from an index [1937=100] and multiplied by Richard Moorsteen and Raymond Powell's GNP estimate for 1937. See Moorsteen and Powell, *The Soviet Capital Stock, 1928–1962* [Homewood, Ill.: Richard D. Irwin, 1966], Table 1, p. 622.)

B. *Population (thousands)*

1851, 1863. Peter I. Lyashchenko, *History of the National Economy of Russia to the 1917 Revolution*, translated by L. M. Herman (New York: Macmillan, 1949), p. 273.

1858–1910. Nutter, *Growth*, Table C-3, p. 519.

1920–1950. Roy A. Clarke, *Soviet Economic Facts, 1917–1970* (London: Macmillan, 1972), pp. 3–4.

1960–1973. Frederick A. Leedy, "Demographic Trends in the USSR," in *Soviet Economic Prospects for the Seventies*, Papers Submitted to the Joint Economic Committee, Congress of the United States (Washington, D.C.: Government Printing Office, 1973), p. 432.

2. *Industrial production index (1937=100)*

1860–1912. Goldsmith, "Economic Growth," Table 7, pp. 462–463.

1913–1955. Nutter, *Growth*, Table 47, p. 185; Table 53, pp. 196–197.

1956–1972. Rush V. Greenslade and Wade E. Robertson, "Industrial Production in the USSR," in *Soviet Economic Prospects for the Seventies*, Table A-2, p. 280.

(Linkage years: 1913, 1955.)

3. *Gross investment as % of GNP (1937 prices)*

1928–1967.* B. R. Mitchell, *European Historical Statistics*, pp. 788, 794.

1967–1972. *UNSY*, 1973, p. 569.

1973. *UNSY*, 1974, p. 620.

1967–1973.* Unpublished U.S. government calculations.

4. *Railroads (kilometers)*

* Linkage procedures: For the period 1955–1967, estimates were obtained in 1937 prices using 1955 linkage year index from B. R. Mitchell, *European Historical Statistics*, p. 794. For the period 1967–1973, the United Nations current figures and U.S. Government gross investment estimate in 1969 prices were transformed into index numbers, and the data were linked in 1967 with the 1937 transformed prices above. The Soviet consumer price index is con-

1840–1850. *DS*, 1899, p. 495.
1860–1966. Banks, *Cross-Polity Time Series Data*, Segment 3, pp. 131–132.
1970. Sampson (ed.), *Jane's World Railways*, p. 224.

5. *Raw cotton consumption (thousand metric tons)*
1825–1855. *DS*, 1899, p. 160.
1860–1956. Nutter, *Growth*, Table B-1, p. 414 (ginned cotton consumption); Table B-2, p. 430.
1957–1963. *UNSY*, 1965, p. 504.
1964–1965. Ibid., 1967, p. 503.
1966–1972. Ibid., 1973, p. 504.

6. *Production of pig iron (thousand metric tons)*
1710–1860. William L. Blackwell, *The Beginnings of Russian Industrialization, 1800–1860* (Princeton: Princeton University Press, 1968), Table A, p. 421; Table C, p. 423.
1870–1890, 1905. Woytinsky and Woytinsky, *World Population and Production*, Table 465, p. 1117.
1900, 1903. Lyashchenko, *History*, p. 688.
1913–1959. Nutter, *Growth*, Table B-2, p. 420.
1960–1965. *UNSY*, 1967, p. 299.
1966–1972. Ibid., 1973, p. 296.

7. *Steel production (thousand metric tons)*
1860–1927. Nutter, *Growth*, Table B-1, p. 411; Table B-2, p. 420.
1928–1937. *UNSY*, 1948, p. 239.
1938–1956. Ibid., 1957, p. 272.
1957–1958. Ibid., 1965, p. 306.
1959–1965. Ibid., 1967, p. 300.
1966–1972. Ibid., 1973, p. 297.

8. *Electricity—electrical energy production (million kWh)*
1913–1958. Nutter, *Growth*, Table B-2, p. 421.
1959–1966. *UNSY*, 1967, p. 363.
1967–1972. Ibid., 1973, p. 367.

9. *Motor vehicle production (thousands)*
1927–1931. *F&F*, 1932, p. 65.
1932. Ibid., 1934, p. 80.
1933–1934. Ibid., 1935, p. 78.
1935–1936. Ibid., 1937, p. 39.
1937–1938. Ibid., 1940, p. 53.
1946–1973. *WMVD*, 1974, p. 10.

10. *Sulphuric acid (thousand metric tons, 100% pure)*
1860–1959. Nutter, *Growth*, Table B-1, p. 412; Table B-2, p. 424.
1960–1966. *UNSY*, 1967, p. 274.
1967–1972. Ibid., 1973, p. 265.

---

stant. Although it is not an adequate index for the prices of capital goods, I have judged it legitimate to assume capital goods prices essentially constant over these years. The investment proportions which emerge by this method differ only marginally from those to be derived for 1970–1973 from Central Statistical Board of the Council of Ministers, *The USSR in Figures for 1973* (Moscow: Progress Publishers, 1975), pp. 144, 175.

11. *Nitrogen fertilizer production (thousand metric tons)*
1928–1938. Lamer, *World Fertilizer Economy*, Table 42a, pp. 667–668.
1955–1958. *UNSY*, 1960, p. 242.
1959–1964. Ibid., 1967, p. 280.
1965–1972. Ibid., 1973, p. 271.
12. *Plastics and resins (thousand metric tons)*
1958–1962. *UNSY*, 1967, p. 280.
1963–1964. Ibid., 1965, p. 288.
1965–1968. Ibid., 1970, p. 287.
1969–1972. Ibid., 1973, p. 272.
13. *Synthetic fibers (noncellulosic continuous fibers, thousand metric tons)*
1948, 1956–1957. *UNSY*, 1965, p. 272.
1953. Ibid., 1960, p. 217.
1958–1966. Ibid., 1967, p. 264.
1967–1972. Ibid., 1973, p. 249.

Chapter 35. *Italy*

1. *GDP per capita (1954 market prices, million lira)*
A. *Gross domestic product*
1861–1964. Giorgio Fia, *Notes on Italian Economic Growth, 1861–1964* (Milan: Editore Guiffie, 1965), Table 3, pp. 60–63; Table 4, p. 64.
1966–1972. *UNYMAS*, 1972, vol. 1, p. 581.
(Linkage years: 1952, 1960.)
B. *Population*
1862, 1867. Instituto Centrale di Statistica, "Indogine statistica sullo sviluppo del reddito nazionale dell'Italia dal 1861 al 1956," *Annali di Statistica*, Series 8, vol. 9 (Rome, 1957), Table 37, pp. 251–252.
1870–1938. Angus Maddison, *Economic Growth in the West* (New York: Twentieth Century Fund, 1964), Appendix B, p. 205.
1946–1955. Organization for European Economic Cooperation (OEEC), *Industrial Statistics, 1900–1955* (Paris: OEEC, 1955), p. 146.
1956–1960. Maddison, *Economic Growth in the West*, Appendix B, p. 206.
1963, 1972, *UNSY*, 1973, p. 71.
(Maddison's index linked with OEEC statistics in 1920, 1955.)
2. *Industrial production index (1954=100)*
1861–1947. *Annali di Statistica*, Series 8, vol. 9 (cited in B. R. Mitchell, *European Historical Statistics*, pp. 355, 357).
1948–1954. B. R. Mitchell, *European Historical Statistics*, p. 357–358.
1955–1960. *UNSY*, 1962, p. 86.
1961–1964. Ibid., 1967, p. 162.
1965–1972. Ibid., 1973, p. 150.

(Linkage years: 1913, 1953, 1960.)

3. *Gross investment as % of GNP (current prices)*
   1865. Shepard B. Clough, *The Economic History of Modern Italy* (New York: Columbia University Press, 1964), Appendix Table 7, p. 372; Table 10, p. 375.
   1875–1959. Maddison, *Economic Growth in the West*, Appendix I, pp. 239–240.
   1960–1971. *UNYNAS*, 1972, vol. 1, p. 580.
4. *Railroads (kilometers)*
   1861–1966. Banks, *Cross-Polity Time Series Data*, Segment 3, pp. 116–117.
   1970. Sampson (ed.), *Jane's World Railways*, p. 198.
5. *Raw cotton consumption (thousand metric tons)*
   1825, 1835, 1845, 1855. *DS*, 1899, p. 161.
   1861–1947. B. R. Mitchell, *European Historical Statistics*, pp. 429–430.
   1948–1953. *UNSY*, 1954, p. 279.
   1954–1956. Ibid., 1957, p. 323.
   1957–1963. Ibid., 1965, p. 504.
   1964–1965. Ibid., 1967, p. 503.
   1966–1972. Ibid., 1973, p. 503.
6. *Production of pig iron (thousand metric tons)*
   1880–1913, 1920–1950. Svennilson, *Growth and Stagnation*, Table A27, p. 257; Table A28, p. 258.
   1914–1919, 1940–1945. *ASFR*, 1966, Table 11, p. 67.
   1951–1952. *UNSY*, 1953, p. 228.
   1953–1955. Ibid., 1962, p. 256.
   1956–1962. Ibid., 1965, p. 305.
   1963–1972. Ibid., 1973, p. 296.
7. *Steel production (thousand metric tons)*
   1880–1938, 1946–1950. Svennilson, *Growth and Stagnation*, Table A29, p. 260; Table A31, p. 262.
   1939–1945. *ASFR*, 1966, p. 69.
   1951–1956. *UNSY*, 1957, p. 272.
   1957–1964. Ibid., 1965, p. 306.
   1965–1972. Ibid., 1973, p. 297.
8. *Electricity—electrical energy production (million kWh)*
   1880–1920. Clough, *Economic History*, p. 97.
   1923–1929. League of Nations, *International Statistical Yearbook* [*ISY*], 1929, (Geneva, 1930), Table 57, p. 107.
   1930. Clough, *Economic History*, p. 97.
   1931–1949. *UNSY*, 1949–1950, p. 284.
   1950–1952. Ibid., 1953, p. 260.
   1953–1957. Ibid., 1962, p. 317.
   1958–1962. Ibid., 1965, p. 362.
   1963–1972. Ibid., 1972, p. 363.
9. *Motor vehicle production (thousands)*
   1901–1973. *WMVD*, 1974, pp. 8–9.
10. *Sulphuric acid (thousand metric tons, 100% pure)*

1881–1913. Alexander Gerschenkron, *Economic Backwardness in Historical Perspective* (New York: Frederick A. Praeger, 1962), p. 396.
1928–1947. *UNSY*, 1948, p. 212.
1948–1949. Ibid., 1953, p. 203.
1950–1955. Ibid., 1957, p. 247.

11. *Nitrogen fertilizer production (thousand metric tons)*
1938, 1947–1948. *UNSY*, 1953, p. 210.
1949–1953. Ibid., 1957, p. 253.
1954–1957. Ibid., 1962, p. 242.
1959–1964. Ibid., 1967, p. 280.
1965–1972. Ibid., 1973, p. 271.

12. *Plastics and resins (thousand metric tons)*
1956–1957. *UNSY*, 1965, p. 288.
1958–1965. Ibid., 1967, p. 281.
1966–1972. Ibid., 1973, p. 272.

13. *Synthetic fibers (noncellulosic continuous fibers, thousand metric tons)*
1950–1955. *UNSY*, 1957, p. 235.
1948, 1956–1961. Ibid., 1962, p. 229.
1962–1965. Ibid., 1967, p. 264.
1966–1972. Ibid., 1973, p. 249.

Chapter 36. *Canada*

1. *GNP per capita (1961 million dollars)*
A. *GNP*
1870–1925. Maddison, *Economic Growth in the West*, Table A-2, pp. 201–202.
1926–1971. Minister of Industry, Trade, and Commerce, *Canadian Statistical Review: Historical Summary* [*CSRHS*] (Ottawa: Information Canada, 1972), Section 3, Table 1.3, p. 16.
(Linkage Year: 1929.)
B. *Population*
1867–1961. M. C. Urquhart and K. A. H. Buckley, *Historical Statistics of Canada* (Toronto: Macmillan, 1965), Series A1, p. 14.
1962–1971. *CSRHS*, Section 2, Table 1, p. 7.
1972. *UNSY*, 1973, p. 68.

2. *Manufacturing production index (1961 = 100)*
1923–1954, 1956–1957, 1959–1960. Urquhart and Buckley, *Historical Statistics*, Series Q138, and Q139, p. 475.
1955, 1961. Statistical Office of the United Nations, *The Growth of World Industry, 1938–1961* (New York, 1963), p. 105.
1958, 1963–1972. *UNSY*, 1973, p. 144.
(Linkage years: 1955, 1958.)

3. *Gross investment as % of GNP*
1870–1913. Maddison, *Economic Growth in the West*, p. 238.
1926–1960. Ibid., p. 240.

1961–1971. *CSRHS*, 1970, Section 3, Table 1.2, p. 15.

4. *Railroads (miles)*
   1836–1874. Urquhart and Buckley, *Historical Statistics*, Series 28, p. 528.
   1875–1906. Ibid., Series 24, p. 528.
   1907–1960. Ibid., Series 78 and 79, p. 532.
   1961. *Canada Year Book* [*CYB*], 1965 (Ottawa: Dominion Bureau of Statistics, 1965), p. 763.
   1962–1965. Ibid., 1967, p. 791.
   1966–1970. Ibid., 1972, p. 875.
5. *Raw cotton consumption (thousand metric tons)*
   1902–1925. *CYB*, 1926, p. 463.
   1926–1935. Ibid., 1940, p. 533.
   1936–1945. Ibid., 1946, p. 556.
   1946–1950. Ibid., 1954, p. 1005.
   1951–1956. *UNSY*, 1958, p. 286.
   1957–1958. Ibid., 1960, p. 317.
   1959–1965. Ibid., 1967, p. 503.
   1966–1972. Ibid., 1973, p. 503.
   (For the years 1902–1950, import of raw cotton and linters used in manufacturing was indexed, base year 1950, and linked with the U.N. data in 1951.)
6. *Production of pig iron (thousand short tons)*
   1875–1903. Department of Agriculture, *The Statistical Yearbook of Canada*, 1904 (Ottawa: S. E. Dawson, 1905), p. 195.
   1904–1908. *CYB*, 1909, p. 411.
   1909–1925. Ibid., 1926, p. 351.
   1926–1971. *CSRHS*, 1970, Table 1, p. 89.
7. *Steel production (thousand short tons)*
   1894–1908. Urquhart and Buckley, *Historical Statistics*, Series 283, p. 486.
   1909–1925. *CYB*, 1926, Table 26, p. 351.
   1926–1971. *CSRHS*, Table 15, p. 83.
8. *Electricity—electrical energy production (million kWh)*
   1916–1918. *CYB*, 1919, p. 499.
   1919–1920. Ibid., 1921, p. 521.
   1921–1922. Ibid., 1924, p. 374.
   1923–1925. Ibid., 1926, p. 365.
   1926–1971. *CSRHS*, 1970, Table 1, p. 89.
9. *Motor vehicle production (thousands)*
   1905–1973. *WMVD*, 1974, pp. 8–9.
10. *Sulphuric acid (thousand metric tons)*
   1919–1952. Urquhart and Buckley, *Historical Statistics*, Series 305, p. 485.
   1953–1954. *UNSY*, 1957, p. 247.
   1955–1957. Ibid., 1961, p. 227.
   1958–1960. Ibid., 1967, p. 274.
   1961–1967. Ibid., 1968, p. 280.
   1968–1972. Ibid., 1973, p. 264.

11. *Nitrogen fertilizer production (thousand metric tons)*
  1938, 1947–1950, *UNSY*, 1953, p. 210.
  1951–1956. Ibid., 1958, p. 219.
  1957–1960. Ibid., 1965, p. 287.
  1961–1964. Ibid., 1969, p. 259.
  1965–1972. Ibid., 1973, p. 270.
12. *Plastics and resins (thousand metric tons)*
  1962–1967. *UNSY*, 1969, p. 260.
  1968–1972. Ibid., 1973, p. 272.
13. *Synthetic fibers (noncellulosic continuous fibers, thousand metric tons)*
  1948, 1950–1955. *UNSY*, 1959, p. 209.
  1956–1957. Ibid., 1962, p. 229.
  1958–1964. Ibid., 1967, p. 264.
  1965–1972. Ibid., 1973, p. 249.

Chapter 37. *Australia*

1. *GNP per capita (1966 million pounds)*
  A. *GNP*
    1861–1937. Noel G. Butlin, *Australian Domestic Product, Investment, and Foreign Borrowing, 1861–1938/39* (Cambridge: At the University Press, 1962), Table 269, pp. 460–461.
    1938, 1948. B. D. Haig, "National Income Estimates," *Australian Economic History Review*, vol. 7, no. 2 (September 1967), p. 180.
    1949–1956. Commonwealth Bureau of Census and Statistics, *Australian National Accounts: National Income and Expenditure* (Canberra: Australian Government Publishing Service, 1963), Table 10, p. 32.
    1957–1959. *UNYNAS*, 1967, p. 10.
    1960–1971. Ibid., 1972, vol. 1, p. 12.
    (Linkage years: 1960, 1957, 1948, 1938.)
  B. *Population*
    1861–1945. Commonwealth Bureau of Census and Statistics, *Demography*, 1945, Bulletin no. 63 (Canberra: Commonwealth Government Printer, 1947), pp. 146–147.
    1946–1971. Commonwealth Bureau of Census and Statistics, *Official Yearbook of the Commonwealth of Australia*, [*OYCA*], 1972 (Canberra: Commonwealth Government Printer, 1972), p. 1031.
    (1961–1971 includes aborigine population.)
2. *Manufacturing production index (1966=100)*
  1861–1936, 1938. Butlin, *Australian Domestic Product*, Table 91, pp. 175–176; Table 267, pp. 455–456.
  1937, 1948. J. A. Dowie, "The Service Ensemble," in C. Forster (ed.), *Australian Economic Development in the Twentieth Century* (London: George Allen and Unwin, 1970), p. 260

(Haig's estimates of the value of manufacturing output at constant prices).
1958–1966. *UNSY*, 1967, p. 164.
1967–1972. Ibid., 1973, p. 152.
(For the period 1861–1948, the value of manufacturing output at constant prices was indexed, base year 1960, and linked with the U.N. industrial index. Linkage years: 1937, 1960.)

3. *Gross investment as % of GNP (current prices)*
A. *Investment*
1861–1937. Butlin, *Australian Domestic Product*, Table 1, pp. 6–7, (gross domestic capital formation).
1938–1952. Ibid., Table 272, p. 468; Table 273, p. 469 (gross private investment plus gross public investment).
1953–1963. *UNYNAS*, 1965, p. 6.
1964–1971. Ibid., 1972, vol. 1, p. 11.
B. *GNP*
1861–1938. Butlin, *Australian Domestic Product*, Table 1, pp. 6–7 (gross domestic product at factor cost).
1953–1964. *UNYNAS*, 1965, p. 7.
1965–1971. Ibid., 1972, p. 14.

4. *Railroads (kilometers)*
1855, 1861, 1871, 1881, 1891. *OYCA*, 1901–1918, p. 634.
1901–1913. Banks, *Cross-Polity Time Series Data*, Segment 3, p. 100.
1915–1918. *OYCA*, 1901—1918, p. 634.
1919–1939. Banks, *Cross-Polity Time Series Data*, Segment 3, p. 100.
1940–1945. *OYCA*, 1946–1947, p. 150.
1946–1966. Banks, *Cross-Polity Time Series Data*, Segment 3, pp. 100–101.
1967–1971. *OYCA*, 1972, p. 347.

5. *Raw cotton consumption (thousand metric tons)*
1936, 1938, 1948. *The Australian Encyclopaedia* (Sydney: Halstead Press, 1958), vol. 3, p. 68.
1951–1957. *UNSY*, 1958, p. 286.
1958–1961. Ibid., 1962, p. 334.
1962–1964. Ibid., 1967, p. 503.
1965. Ibid., 1968, p. 505.
1966–1972. Ibid., 1973, p. 503.

6. *Production of pig iron (thousand metric tons)*
1907–1919. Helen Hughes, *The Australian Iron and Steel Industry, 1848–1962* (Carlton South, Victoria: Melbourne University Press, 1964), Table 3, p. 197.
1920–1927. *ASFR*, 1966, Table 10, p. 66.
1928–1936. *UNSY*, 1948, p. 237.
1937–1955. Ibid., 1958, p. 236.
1956–1962. Ibid., 1965, p. 305.
1963–1972. Ibid., 1973, p. 296.

7. *Steel production (thousand metric tons)*
   1907–1924. Hughes, *Australian Iron and Steel*, Table 3, p. 197.
   1925–1927. *ASFR*, 1966, Table 11, p. 68.
   1928–1936. *UNSY*, 1948, p. 239.
   1937–1956. Ibid., 1957, p. 272.
   1957–1962. Ibid., 1965, p. 306.
   1963–1972. Ibid., 1973, p. 297.
8. *Electricity—electrical energy production (million kWh)*
   1923–1927. *ISY*, 1929, Table 57, p. 107.
   1928–1947. *UNSY*, 1948, p. 262.
   1948–1952. Ibid., 1953, p. 261.
   1953–1955. Ibid., 1958, p. 272.
   1956–1962. Ibid., 1965, p. 359.
   1963–1972. Ibid., 1973, p. 360.
9. *Motor vehicle production (thousands)*
   1937–1947. *UNSY*, 1949–1950, p. 270.
   1948, 1953–1957. Ibid., 1962, p. 264.
   1958–1962. Ibid., 1967, p. 312.
   1963–1972. Ibid., 1973, p. 309.
10. *Sulphuric acid (thousand metric tons, 100% pure)*
   1928–1945. *UNSY*, 1948, p. 213.
   1946–1952. Ibid., 1953, p. 204.
   1953–1955. Ibid., 1958, p. 214.
   1956–1962. Ibid., 1965, p. 282.
   1963–1972. Ibid., 1973, p. 264.
11. *Nitrogen fertilizer production (thousand metric tons)*
   1939–1945. Lamer, *World Fertilizer Economy*, Table 9, p. 650.
   1938, 1947–1950. *UNSY*, 1953, p. 210.
   1951–1956. Ibid., 1958, p. 219.
   1957–1964. Ibid., 1965, p. 287.
   1965–1972. Ibid., 1973, p. 271.
12. *Plastics and resins (thousand metric tons)*
   1956–1961. *UNSY*, 1965, p. 288.
   1962–1964. Ibid., 1968, p. 287.
   1965–1972. Ibid., 1973, p. 272.
13. *Synthetic fibers (noncellulosic continuous fibers, thousand metric tons)*
   1958–1962. *UNSY*, 1965, p. 272.
   1963–1972. Ibid., 1973, p. 249.

Chapter 38. *Argentina*

1. *GDP per capita (1960 billion pesos)*
   A. *Gross domestic product*
      1900–1934. Carlos F. Díaz Alejandro, *Essays on the Economic History of the Argentine Republic* (New Haven: Yale University Press, 1970), Table 19, pp. 418–420.
      1935–1965. Ibid., Table 11, pp. 407–408.
      1966–1971. *UNYNAS*, 1972, vol. 1, p. 6.
      (Linkage years: 1935, 1965.)

B. *Population*
1797–1965. Díaz Alejandro, *Essays*, Table 20, p. 421.
1972. *UNSY*, 1973, p. 69.

2. *Manufacturing production index (1960=100)*
1900–1934. Díaz Alejandro, *Essays*, Table 41, p. 449.
1935–1966. Ibid., Table 39, p. 443.
1967–1972. *UNSY*, 1973, p. 145.
(Linkage years: 1935, 1966.)

3. *Gross investment as % of GNP (current prices)*
1902–1932. United Nations Economic Commission for Latin America, *Análisis y proyecciones del desarrollo económico*, vol. 5, *El desarrollo económico de la Argentina* (Mexico City, 1959), part 1, Table 85, p. 71.
1935–1963. Díaz Alejandro, *Essays*, Table 3, pp. 398–399; Table 1, p. 395.
1964–1973. World Bank, "Basic Economic Data Sheet, World Table 1," p. 81.
(Linkage years: 1937, 1950, 1964.)

4. *Railroads (kilometers)*
1857–1917. Alejandro Bunge, *Ferrocarriles argentinos* (Buenos Aires, Imprenta Mercatali, 1918), pp. 119–121.
1919–1939. Banks, *Cross-Polity Time Series Data*, Segment 3, p. 100.
1940–1945. Congreso Panamérica de Ferrocarriles, *Boletín de la Asociación Internacional Permanente*, no. 94 (January–February 1946), p. 39.
1946–1966. Banks, *Cross-Polity Time Series Data*, Segment 3, p. 100.
1970. Sampson (ed.), *Jane's World Railways*, p. 450.

5. *Raw cotton consumption (thousand metric tons)*
1913, 1921. Adolfo Dorfman, *Historia de la industria argentina* (Buenos Aires: Solar/Hachette, 1970), p. 378.
1925–1948. United Nations, *Economic Survey of Latin America* [*ESLA*], 1949 (New York, 1949), Table 28, p. 142.
1949–1950.*UNSY*, 1953, p. 279.
1951–1953. Ibid., 1957, p. 323.
1954–1961. Ibid., 1962, p. 334.
1962–1963. Ibid., 1965, p. 504.
1964–1965. Ibid., 1968, p. 505.
1966–1972. Ibid., 1973, p. 503.

6. *Production of pig iron (thousand metric tons)*
1945–1956. *UNSY*, 1956, p. 237.
1957–1962. Ibid., 1965, p. 305.
1963–1972. Ibid., 1973, p. 296.

7. *Steel production (thousand metric tons)*
1939–1944. *ESLA*, 1949, Table 53, p. 182.
1946–1955. *UNSY*, 1958, p. 237.
1956–1964. Ibid., 1965, p. 306.
1965–1972. Ibid., 1973, p. 297.

8. *Electricity—electrical energy production (million kWh)*
   1927. United Nations Economic Commission for Latin America, *Análisis y proyecciones*, vol. 5, part 1, p. 34.
   1932. Raul C. Migone (ed.), *Inter-American Statistical Yearbook, 1942* (New York: Macmillan, 1942), p. 274.
   1935–1947. *UNSY*, 1949–1950, p. 281.
   1948–1950. Ibid., 1953, p. 258.
   1951–1957. Ibid., 1958, p. 268.
   1958–1960. Ibid., 1962, p. 313.
   1961–1962. Ibid., 1965, p. 359.
   1963–1972. Ibid., 1973, p. 360.
9. *Motor vehicle production (thousands)*
   1929, 1932, 1938–1940. Adolfo Dorfman, *Evolución industrial argentina* (Buenos Aires: Editorial Losada, 1942), p. 159.
   1957–1961. *UNSY*, 1962, p. 264.
   1962–1973. *WMVD*, 1974, p. 11.
10. *Sulphuric acid (thousand metric tons, 100% pure)*
   1935–1952. *UNSY*, 1953, p. 203.
   1953–1957. Ibid., 1958, p. 213.
   1958–1962. Ibid., 1965, p. 282.
   1963–1972. Ibid., 1973, p. 264.
11. *Nitrogen fertilizer production (thousand metric tons)*
   1963–1967. *UNSY*, 1968, p. 286.
   1968–1972. Ibid., 1973, p. 270.
12. *Plastics and resins (thousand metric tons)*
   1964–1965. *UNSY*, 1968, p. 287.
   1966–1972. Ibid., 1973, p. 272.
13. *Synthetic fibers (noncellulosic continuous fibers, thousand metric tons)*
   1953. *UNSY*, 1968, p. 270.
   1957–1962. Ibid., 1965, p. 272.
   1963–1972. Ibid., 1973, p. 249.

Chapter 39. *Turkey*

1. *GDP per capita*
   A. *Gross domestic product (1948 million Turkish lira)*
      1933–1962. Oktag Yenal, "Development of the Financial System," in Frederick C. Shorter (ed.), *Four Studies on the Economic Development of Turkey* (New York: Augustus M. Kelley, 1967), Table 4, p. 103.
      1963–1964. *UNYNAS*, 1965, p. 369.
      1966–1970. Ibid., 1972, vol. 2, p. 563.
      (Linkage years: 1962, 1963.)
   B. *Population*
      1927, 1929, 1935–1939. W. W. Rostow, *Politics and the Stages of Growth* (Cambridge: At the University Press, 1971), Table 5, p. 93.
      1930, 1946–1950. OEEC, *Industrial Statistics*, p. 146.
      1951–1965. Z. Y. Hershlag, *Turkey: The Challenge of Growth*,

second edition (Leiden: E. J. Brill, 1968), Table 20, p. 343.
1968. *UNSY*, 1969, p. 61.
1972. Ibid., 1973, p. 71.

2. *Manufacturing production index (1963=100)*
   1938, 1948, 1950, 1955–1963. Hershlag, *Turkey*, Table 47, p. 361.
   1964–1973. World Bank, "Basic Economic Data Sheet, World Table 1," p. 79.
   (Linkage year: 1963.)
   (For the period 1964–1973, estimates of the value of manufacturing output were deflated with a wholesale price index, 1963 prices, and converted to an index, 1963=100.)
3. *Gross domestic fixed capital formation as % of GDP (current prices)*
   A. *Gross domestic fixed capital formation*
      1953, 1955, 1957–1966. *UNYNAS*, 1967, p. 684.
      1954, 1956. Hershlag, *Turkey*, Table 24, p. 345.
      1967–1970. *UNYNAS*, 1972, p. 561.
   B. *Gross domestic product at factor cost*
      1938, 1948, 1956. Hershlag, *Turkey*, Table 16, p. 685.
      1953, 1955, 1957–1966. *UNYNAS*, 1967, p. 685.
      1967–1970. Ibid., 1972, vol. 2, p. 562.
4. *Railroads (kilometers)*
   1919–1966. Banks, *Cross-Polity Time Series Data*, Segment 3, p. 131.
   1970. Sampson (ed.), *Jane's World Railways*, p. 548.
5. *Raw cotton consumption (thousand metric tons)*
   1938, 1947–1950. *UNSY*, 1953, p. 279.
   1951–1956. Ibid., 1958, p. 286.
   1957–1959. Ibid., 1965, p. 504.
   1960–1965. Ibid., 1968, p. 506.
   1966–1972. Ibid., 1973, p. 504.
6. *Production of pig iron (thousand metric tons)*
   1939–1955. *UNSY*, 1958, p. 235.
   1956–1962. Ibid., 1965, p. 305.
   1963–1973. Ibid., 1973, p. 296.
7. *Steel production (thousand metric tons)*
   1940–1957. *UNSY*, 1958, p. 235.
   1958–1964. Ibid., 1965, p. 305.
   1965–1972. Ibid., 1973, p. 296.
8. *Electricity—electrical energy production (million kWh)*
   1940–1957. *UNSY*, 1958, p. 237.
   1958–1964. Ibid., 1965, p. 306.
   1963–1973. Ibid., 1973, p. 297.
9. *Motor vehicle production: motor vehicle assembly (thousands)*
   1963–1972. *UNSY*, 1973, p. 311.
10. *Sulphuric acid (thousand metric tons, 100% pure)*
    1944–1947. *UNSY*, 1949/50, p. 227.

1948–1952. Ibid., 1953, p. 203.
1953–1955. Ibid., 1957, p. 247.
1956–1962. Ibid., 1965, p. 282.
1963–1972. Ibid., 1973, p. 265.

11. *Nitrogen fertilizer production (thousand metric tons)*
1938, 1947–1952. *UNSY*, 1953, p. 210.
1953–1957. Ibid., 1958, p. 219.
1958–1964. Ibid., 1965, p. 287.
1965–1972. Ibid., 1973, p. 270.

12. *Synthetic fibers (noncellulosic continuous fibers, thousand metric tons)*
1964–1972. *UNSY*, 1973, p. 249.

Chapter 40. *Brazil*

1. *GNP per capita*
A. *GNP (1953 million cruzieros)*
1927–1937. Alexander Ganz, "Problems and Uses of National Wealth Estimates in Latin America," in Raymond Goldsmith and Christopher Saunders (eds.), *The Measurement of National Wealth* (London: Bowes and Bowes, 1959), p. 225.
1939–1954. United Nations Economic Commission for Latin America, *Análisis y proyecciones del Desarrollo Económico*, vol. 2, *El desarrollo económico del Brasil* (Mexico City, 1956), Table 1, p. 12.
1955–1966. *UNYNAS*, 1967, p. 71.
1967–1973. World Bank, "Basic Economic Data Sheet, World Table 1," p. 84.
(Linkage years: 1942, 1953, 1966.)
B. *Population*
1808, 1823, 1830, 1854, 1872, 1890. T. Lynn Smith, "Demographic Factors Related to Economic Growth in Brazil," in Simon Kuznets et al., *Economic Growth: Brazil, India, Japan* (Durham, N.C.: Duke University Press, 1955), Table 8, p. 242.
1900–1949. *ESLA*, 1949, Table 4A, p. 211.
1950, 1951. *United Nations Demographic Yearbook* [DY], 1953, p. 107.
1952, 1953. Ibid., 1954, p. 102.
1957. *UNSY*, 1958, p. 28.
1960. *DY*, 1961, p. 108.
1958, 1964. *UNSY*, 1965, p. 87.
1963, 1969. Ibid., 1970, p. 82.
1972. Ibid., 1973.

2. *Industrial production index (1950 = 100)*
1914–1958. Jean-Marie Martin, *Processus d'industrialisation et développement énergétique du Brésil* (Paris: Institut des Hautes Etudes de l'Amérique Latine, 1966), Table 99, p. 333.
1959–1962. *UNSY*, 1965, p. 161.

1963–1970. Ibid., 1973, p. 145.
(Linkage year: 1958.)

3. *Gross investment as % of GNP (current prices)*
1948–1959. Statistical Office of the United Nations, *Growth of World Industry, 1938–1961*, p. 63.
1960–1969. *UNYNAS*, 1972, vol. 1, p. 106.
1970–1973. World Bank, "Basic Economic Data Sheet, World Table 1," p. 84.

4. *Railroads (kilometers)*
1854–1855. J. F. Normano, *Brazil: A Study of Economic Types* (Chapel Hill: University of North Carolina Press, 1935), p. 213.
1856–1859. Bureau of Information, *Economical Notes on Brazil* (Rio de Janeiro: Villas Boas, 1921), p. 76.
1860–1966. Banks, *Cross-Polity Time Series Data*, Segment 3, p. 103.
1970. Sampson (ed.), *Jane's World Railways*, pp. 450–454.

5. *Cotton cloth production (million meters)*
1853, 1866, 1882, 1895, 1905, 1911–1947. Stanley J. Stein, *The Brazilian Cotton Manufacture: Textile Enterprise in an Underdeveloped Area* (Cambridge, Mass.: Harvard University Press, 1957), pp. 191–192.
1948, 1955–1958. *UNSY*, 1962, p. 222.
1965–1970. Ibid., 1973, p. 240.

6. *Production of pig iron (thousand metric tons)*
1916–1929. Werner Baer, *The Development of the Brazilian Steel Industry* (Nashville: Vanderbilt University Press, 1969), Table 15, p. 61.
1930–1932. *UNSY*, 1949–1950, p. 255.
1933–1952. Ibid., 1953, p. 228.
1953–1960. Ibid., 1962, p. 256.
1961–1962. Ibid., 1968, p. 304.
1963–1972. Ibid., 1973, p. 296.

7. *Steel production (thousand metric tons)*
1925. Baer, *Development*, Table 20, p. 87.
1926–1929. *ESLA*, 1949, Table 16A, p. 250.
1930–1948. *UNSY*, 1949–1950, p. 257.
1949–1955. Ibid., 1957, p. 271.
1956–1960. Ibid., 1962, p. 257.
1961–1964. Ibid., 1968, p. 305.
1965–1972. Ibid., 1973, p. 297.

8. *Electricity—electrical energy production (million kWh)*
1900–1952. Martin, *Processus*, Table 103, pp. 345–346.
1953–1955. *UNSY*, 1962, p. 314.
1956–1962. Ibid., 1965, p. 359.
1963–1972. Ibid., 1973, p. 360.
(Linkage year: 1952.)

9. *Motor vehicle production (thousands)*
1956. *UNSY*, 1962, p. 264.

1957–1972. *WMVD*, 1974, p. 11.

10. *Sulphuric acid (thousand metric tons, 100% pure)*
   1951–1952. *UNSY*, 1958, p. 213.
   1953–1957. Ibid., 1962, p. 237.
   1958. Ibid., 1965, p. 282.
   1959–1962. Ibid., 1968, p. 280.
   1963–1969. Ibid., 1973, p. 264.
11. *Nitrogen fertilizer production (thousand metric tons)*
   1947–1952. *UNSY*, 1953, p. 210.
   1954–1956. Ibid., 1958, p. 219.
   1957–1963. Ibid., 1965, p. 287.
   1964. Ibid., 1968, p. 286.
   1965–1972. Ibid., 1973, p. 270.
12. *Plastics and resins (thousand metric tons)*
   1964–1969. *UNSY*, 1971, p. 265.
   1970. Ibid., 1973, p. 272.
13. *Synthetic fibers (noncellulosic continuous fibers, thousand metric tons)*
   1956–1961. *UNSY*, 1965, p. 272.
   1962–1970. Ibid., 1971, p. 243.
   1971–1972. Ibid., 1973, p. 249.

Chapter 41. *Mexico*

1. *GNP per capita (1950 million pesos)*
   A. *Gross national product*
      1895–1910. Enrique Pérez López, "The National Product of Mexico: 1895 to 1964," in *Mexico's Recent Economic Growth*, translated by Marjory Urquidi, Latin American Monographs, no. 10, Institute of Latin American Studies (Austin: University of Texas Press, 1970), Table 2, p. 28.
      1921–1939. Ibid., Table 3, p. 29.
      1938–1965. Clark W. Reynolds, *The Mexican Economy* (New Haven: Yale University Press, 1970), Table D5B, pp. 371–373.
      1966–1970. *UNYNAS*, 1972, vol. 2, p. 100.
      (Linkage years: 1939, 1963.)
   B. *Population*
      1895, 1910, 1921, 1929, 1934. Pérez López, "National Product," Table 1, p. 26.
      1900, 1930, 1940–1962. Reynolds, *Mexican Economy*, Table E1, p. 384.
      1964. *UNSY*, 1965, p. 85.
      1963, 1972. Ibid., 1973, p. 69.
2. *Manufacturing production index (1950 = 100)*
   1900–1965. Reynolds, *Mexican Economy*, Table E11, pp. 403–404.

1966–1972. *UNSY*, 1973, p. 144.
(Linkage year: 1965.)

3. *Gross investment as % of GNP (current prices)*
1939–1965. Reynolds, *Mexican Economy*, Table D1A, pp. 345–347.
1966–1970. *UNYNAS*, 1972, vol. 2, p. 99.

4. *Railroads (kilometers)*
1864–1966. Banks, *Cross-Polity Time Series Data*, Segment 3, pp. 120–121.
1970. Sampson (ed.), *Jane's World Railways*, p. 342.

5. *Raw cotton consumption (thousand metric tons)*
1878, 1889, 1894, 1901, 1907. Daniel Cosío Villegas, *Historia moderna de México*, vol. 7, part 1 (Mexico City: Editorial Humes, 1955), p. 341.
1910–1924. Alston H. Garside, *Cotton Year Book of the New York Cotton Exchange, 1930* (New York: Van Rees Press, 1930), p. 17.
1925–1946. *ESLA*, 1949, Table 11A, p. 425.
1947–1952. *UNSY*, 1953, p. 279.
1953–1956. Ibid., 1958, p. 286.
1957–1962. Ibid., 1965, p. 504.
1963–1965. Ibid., 1968, p. 506.
1966–1972. Ibid., 1973, p. 504.
(For the period 1910–1946, the data were indexed and linked with the U.N. estimates; linkage years: 1947, 1925.)

6. *Production of pig iron (thousand metric tons)*
1903–1909. Cosío Villegas, *Historia Moderna*, vol. 7, part 1, p. 236.
1930–1949. *UNSY*, 1949–1950, p. 255.
1950–1955. Ibid., 1957, p. 269.
1956–1962. Ibid., 1965, p. 305.
1963–1972. Ibid., 1973, p. 296.

7. *Steel production (thousand metric tons)*
1903–1909. Cosío Villegas, *Historia moderna*, vol. 7, part 1, p. 237.
1911. Alfredo Navarrete R., "The Financing of Economic Development," in *Mexico's Recent Economic Growth*, p. 107.
1930. Ernesto Fernández Hurtado, "Private Enterprise and Government in Mexican Development," in *Mexico's Recent Economic Growth*, p. 63.
1937–1956. *UNSY*, 1957, p. 271.
1957–1963. Ibid., 1965, p. 306.
1964–1972. Ibid., 1973, p. 297.

8. *Electricity—electrical energy production (million kWh)*
1911. Navarrete R., "Financing," p. 107.
1926–1935. Ernesto Galarza, *La industria eléctrica en México* (Mexico City: Fondo de Cultura Económica, 1941), p. 48.

1936–1949. *UNSY*, 1949–1950, p. 281.
1950–1955. Ibid., 1957, p. 302.
1956–1962. Ibid., 1965, p. 363.
1963–1972. Ibid., 1973, p. 364.

9. *Motor vehicle production (thousands)*
1963–1972. *UNSY*, 1973, p. 309.

10. *Sulphuric acid (thousand metric tons, 100% pure)*
1886. Cosío Villegas, *Historia moderna*, vol. 7, part 1, p. 369.
1930. Fernández Hurtado, "Private Enterprise," p. 63.
1950–1955. *UNSY*, 1957, p. 247.
1956–1964. Ibid., 1965, p. 282.
1965–1972. Ibid., 1973, p. 264.

11. *Nitrogen fertilizer production (thousand metric tons)*
1963–1964. *UNSY*, 1971, p. 263.
1965–1972. Ibid., 1973, p. 270.

12. *Plastics and resins (thousand metric tons)*
1964–1965. *UNSY*, 1968, p. 287.
1966–1972. Ibid., 1973, p. 272.

13. *Synthetic fibers (noncellulosic continuous fibers, thousand metric tons)*
1956–1962. *UNSY*, 1965, p. 272.
1963–1972. Ibid., 1973, p. 249.

Chapter 42. *Iran*

1. *GDP per capita*
A. *Gross domestic product at factor cost (1959 billion rials)*
1959–1970. Jahangir Amuzegar and M. Ali Fekrat, *Iran: Economic Development under Dualistic Conditions* (Chicago: University of Chicago Press, 1971), Table 1.5, p. 96.
B. *Population*
1925, 1938, 1950. Charles Issawi (ed.), *The Economic History of Iran, 1800–1914* (Chicago: University of Chicago Press, 1971), Table 2, p. 375; Table 3, p. 379; Table 4, p. 381.
1958–1968. United Nations, *Statistical Yearbook for Asia and the Far East* [*SYAFE*], 1969 (Bangkok, 1969), p. 162.
1972. *UNSY*, 1973, p. 70.

2. *Industrial production index (1963=100)*
1960–1968. *SYAFE*, 1970, p. 147.
1969–1972. *UNSY*, 1973, p. 146.

3. *Gross investment as % of GNP (1959 constant prices)*
1959–1970. Amuzegar and Fekrat, *Iran*, Table 4.1, p. 82.

4. *Railroads (kilometers)*
1919–1966. Banks, *Cross-Polity Time Series Data*, Segment 3, p. 116.
1967–1970. *SYAFE*, 1972, p. 148.

5. *Raw cotton consumption (thousand metric tons)*
1951–1956. *UNSY*, 1957, p. 323.

1957–1964. Ibid., 1965, p. 504.
1966–1972. Ibid., 1973, p. 503.
6. *Steel consumption (thousand metric tons)*
1961–1970. *SYAFE*, 1972, p. 148.
1971–1972. *UNSY*, 1973, p. 507.
7. *Electricity—electrical energy production (million kWh)*
1948. Issawi, *Economic History*, Table 4, p. 381.
1964–1972. *UNSY*, 1973, p. 363.
8. *Motor vehicle production (assembly, passenger cars only)*
1963–1972. *UNSY*, 1973, p. 310.
9. *Sulphuric acid (thousand metric tons, 100% pure)*
1966–1972. *UNSY*, 1973, p. 264.
10. *Nitrogen fertilizer production (thousand metric tons)*
1963–1964. *UNSY*, 1968, p. 286.
1965–1972. Ibid., 1973, p. 270.

Chapter 43. *India*

1. *NDP per capita*
A. *Net domestic product (1948 million rupees)*
1857–1945. M. Mukherjee, *National Income of India: Trends and Structure* (Calcutta: Statistical Publishing Society, 1969), Table A 2.13, p. 98; Table 2.5, p. 61.
1946–1966. Angus Maddison, *Class Structure and Economic Growth: India and Pakistan since the Moghuls* (New York: W. W. Norton, 1971), Table B-2, p. 169.
1967–1970. *UNYNAS*, 1972, vol. 1, p. 514.
(Linkage years: 1950, 1966.)
B. *Population*
1800, 1834, 1845, 1855. Kingsley Davis, *The Population of India and Pakistan* (Princeton: Princeton University Press, 1951), Table 6, p. 25.
1856–1951. Mukherjee, *National Income*, Table A 2.14, p. 99.
1961. *UNSY*, 1962, p. 30.
1963, 1972. *UNSY*, 1973, p. 70.
2. *Industrial production index (1948=100)*
1900–1951, K. Mukerji, *Levels of Economic Activity and Public Expenditure in India* (Bombay: Asia Publishing House, 1965), Table 4, p. 88, col. 8.
1952–1957. Statistical Office of the United Nations, *Growth of World Industry*, p. 385.
1958–1964. *SYAFE*, 1969, p. 133.
1965–1972. *UNSY*, 1973, p. 146.
(Linkage years: 1952, 1960.)
3. *Gross investment as % of NDP (billion current rupees)*
1921, 1926, 1931, 1936. Mukherjee, *National Income*, Table A 10.2, p. 369.
1948, 1961. Ibid., Table 9.1, p. 330.

1962–1973. World Bank, "Basic Economic Data Sheet, World Table 1," p. 51.

(Linkage year: 1962.)

4. *Railroads (kilometers)*

1853–1961. J. Johnson, *The Economics of Indian Rail Transport* (London: Allied Publishers, 1963), p. 404–406.

1962–1971. *SYAFE*, 1972, p. 115.

5. *Raw cotton consumption (thousand metric tons)*

1830, 1845, 1855, 1865, 1869, 1875, 1880, 1884, 1887, 1889. *DS*, 1899, p. 156, 157.

1901–1922, 1926. Sung Joe Koh, *Stages of Industrial Development in Asia*, Table 3-3, p. 367, p. 368.

1927–1931. International Institute of Agriculture, *World Cotton Production and Trade*, Table 40, p. 441.

1932–1944. Sung Joe Koh, *Stages of Industrial Development in Asia*, Table 3-5, p. 369.

1951–1957. *UNSY*, 1958, p. 286.

1958–1964. Ibid., 1965, p. 504.

1965. Ibid., 1967, p. 503.

1966–1972. Ibid,, 1973, p. 503.

6. *Production of pig iron (thousand metric tons)*

1913, 1920. *ISY*, 1926, p. 86.

1921–1929. *ASFR*, 1966, Table 10, p. 66.

1930–1931. *ISY*, 1935–1936, p. 144.

1932–1936. *UNSY*, 1948, p. 236.

1937–1955. Ibid., 1958, p. 235.

1956–1963. Ibid., 1965, p. 305.

1964–1972. Ibid., 1973, p. 296.

7. *Steel production (thousand metric tons)*

1913. *ISY*, 1926, p. 87.

1920–1927. Ibid., 1929, p. 111.

1928–1936. *UNSY*, 1948, p. 238.

1937–1955. Ibid., 1958, p. 237.

1956–1962. Ibid., 1965, p. 306.

1963–1972. Ibid., 1973, p. 297.

8. *Electricity—electrical energy production (million kWh)*

1932. *UNSY*, 1953, p. 252, 258.

(*Note*: The 1932 estimate of electrical energy production was derived by assuming the 1937 rate of capacity utilization.)

1939–1962. *ASFR*, 1966, p. 58.

1963–1972. *UNSY*, 1973, p. 363.

9. *Motor vehicle production (thousands)*

1953–1955. *UNSY*, 1962, pp. 264–265.

1956–1962. Ibid., 1965, p. 318.

1963–1972. Ibid., 1973, p. 309.

(1953, assembly only.)

10. *Sulphuric acid (thousand metric tons, 100% pure)*

1928–1946. *UNSY*, 1948, p. 212.

1947. Ibid., 1949–1950, p. 227.
1948, 1953–1955. Ibid., 1962, p. 237.
1950–1952. Ibid., 1957, p. 247.
1956–1962. Ibid., 1965, p. 282.
1963–1972. Ibid., 1973, p. 264.

11. *Nitrogen fertilizer production (thousand metric tons)*
1938, 1947–1951. *UNSY*, 1953, p. 210.
1952–1956. Ibid., 1958, p. 219.
1957–1962. Ibid., 1965, p. 287.
1963–1970. Ibid., 1971, p. 263.
1971–1972. Ibid., 1972, p. 270.

12. *Plastics and resins (thousand metric tons)*
1956–1961. *UNSY*, 1965, p. 288.
1962–1965. Ibid., 1970, p. 287.
1966–1972. Ibid., 1973, p. 272.

13. *Synthetic fibers (noncellulosic continuous fibers, thousand metric tons)*
1962. *UNSY*, 1970, p. 269.
1963–1967. Ibid., 1973, p. 249.

Chapter 44. *China*

1. *GDP per capita (1957 million yuan)*
A. *Gross domestic product*
1916, 1933, 1957. Dwight H. Perkins, "Growth and Changing Structure of China's Twentieth Century Economy," in idem (ed.), *China's Modern Economy in Historical Perspective* (Stanford: Stanford University Press, 1975), Table 1, p. 117.
1949–1956, 1958–1973. Arthur G. Ashbrook, Jr., "China: Economic Overview, 1975," in *China: A Reassessment of the Economy*, A Compendium of Papers Submitted to the Joint Economic Committee, Congress of the United States (Washington, D.C.: Government Printing Office, 1975), Table 5, pp. 42–43.
(For the period 1949–1973, gross domestic product estimates were derived by multiplying Ashbrook's GNP index, 1957 = 100, with Perkins' 1957 estimate of GDP.)
B. *Population*
1916, 1933. Perkins, "Growth and Changing Structure," Table 3, p. 122.
1949–1973. Ashbrook, "China," Table 5, pp. 42–43.

2. *Industrial production index (1957 = 100)*
1912–1948. John K. Chang, *Industrial Development in Pre-Communist China* (Chicago: Aldine Publishing Company, 1969), Table 14, pp. 60–61.
1949–1973. Robert Michael Field, "Civilian Industrial Production in the People's Republic of China: 1949–1974," in *China: A Reassessment of the Economy*, Table 1, p. 149.
(Linkage year, 1949.)

3. *Gross investment as % of GDP*
   1933, 1952, 1957, 1970. Perkins, "Growth and Changing Structure," Table 6, p. 134.
4. *Railroads (kilometers)*
   1876–1966. Banks, *Cross-Polity Time Series Data*, Segment 3, pp. 105–106.
   1970–1971. Phillip W. Vetterling and James J. Wagy, "China: The Transportation Sector, 1950–1971," in *People's Republic of China: An Economic Assessment*, A Compendium of Papers Submitted to the Joint Economic Committee, Congress of the United States (Washington, D.C.: Government Printing Office, 1972), Table 1, p. 178.
5. *Cotton yarn production (thousand metric tons)*
   1892, 1897, 1902, 1907, 1912, 1917. Kang Chao, "The Growth of a Modern Cotton Textile Industry and the Competition with Handicrafts," in Perkins (ed.), *China's Modern Economy*, Table 2, p. 172.
   1919–1931. Bruce Lloyd Reynolds, "The Impact of Trade and Foreign Investment in Industrialization: Chinese Textiles, 1875–1931" (Ph.D. dissertation, University of Michigan, 1975), Table B-4, p. 254.
   1933, 1949, 1952–1960. *ASFR*, 1966, Table 20, p. 77.
   1963–1969. *UNSY*, 1973, p. 238.
6. *Production of pig iron (thousand metric tons)*
   1902, 1907, 1912, 1917. Thomas G. Rawski, "The Growth of Producer Industries, 1900–1971," in Perkins (ed.), *China's Modern Economy*, Table 1, p. 214.
   1913, 1920–1925. *ISY*, 1928, p. 100.
   1926–1944. *ASFR*, p. 66.
   1949–1973. Field, "Civilian Industrial Production," Table B-2, p. 166.
7. *Steel production (thousand metric tons)*
   1908, 1912, 1917. Rawski, "Growth," Table 1, p. 214.
   1920–1927. *ISY*, 1928, p. 101.
   1928–1944. *UNSY*, 1948, p. 238.
   1949–1973. Field, "Civilian Industrial Production," Table B-2, p. 166.
   (1928–1935 excludes Manchuria.)
8. *Electricity—electrical energy production (million kWh)*
   1912–1948. Chang, *Industrial Development*, Table A-2, pp. 122–123.
   1949–1973. Field, "Civilian Industrial Production," Table B-2, p. 166.
9. *Motor vehicle production (units)*
   1956–1973. Field, "Civilian Industrial Production," Table B-1, p. 165.
10. *Sulphuric acid (thousand metric tons, 100% pure)*

1949–1950. Nai-Ruenn Chen, *Chinese Economic Statistics* (Chicago: Aldine Publishing Company, 1967), Table 4.6, p. 186.
1951. *UNSY*, 1960, p. 226.
1952–1959. Ibid., 1961, p. 227.

11. *Nitrogen fertilizer production (thousand metric tons)*
1949–1973. Field, "Civilian Industrial Production," Table B-2, p. 166.

12. *Synthetic fibers (noncellulosic continuous fibers, thousand metric tons)*
1959–1962. *UNSY*, 1968, p. 270.
1963–1972. Ibid., 1973, p. 249.

Chapter 45. *Taiwan*

1. *GNP per capita (1966 million N.T. dollars)*
A. *GNP*
1952–1970. Lin Shu-ting et al. (eds.), *China Yearbook* [CY], 1972–1973 (Taipei: China Publishing Company, 1973), p. 207.
1971–1972. *Statistical Abstract of the Republic of China* [*SARC*], 1973 (Directorate General of Budget, Accounting and Statistics Executive, Yuan, Republic of China, 1974), Table 257, p. 672.
B. *Population*
1905–1943. *Statistical Summary of Taiwan Province for the Past Fifty-one Years* (Compiled by the Statistics Section of the Office of the Chief Administrator of Taiwan Province, Republic of China, 1946), p. 76.
1947. *UNSY*, 1948, p. 24.
1952–1968. *Taiwan Statistical Data Book* [*TSDB*], 1969, (Council for International Economic Cooperation and Development Executive, Yuan, Republic of China, 1969), Table 2-2, p. 4.
1969–1972. *SARC*, 1973, Table 12, p. 38.

2. *Industrial production index (1966 = 100)*
1946–1972. *SARC*, 1973, Table 65, p. 169.

3. *Gross investment as % of GNP (current prices)*
1952–1960. *TSDB*, 1969, Table 3-7a, p. 19.
1961–1972. *SARC*, 1973, Table 256, pp. 658–659.

4. *Railroads (kilometers)*
1899–1945. *Statistical Summary of Taiwan Province for the Past Fifty-One Years*, Table 430, p. 1154.
1946, 1950, 1956–57, *SARC*, 1973, Table 138, p. 417.
1969–1972.
1958–1968. *SYAFE*, 1969, p. 99.

5. *Raw cotton consumption (thousand metric tons)*
1950–1956. *UNSY*, 1957, p. 323.
1957–1962. Ibid., 1965, p. 504.

1963–1970. Ibid., 1971, p. 514.

6. *Production of pig iron (thousand metric tons)*
   1952–1968. *TSDB*, 1969, Table 5-6c, p. 56.
   1969–1972. *SARC*, 1973, Table 67, p. 218.
7. *Steel production (thousand metric tons)*
   1948-1957. *UNSY*, 1958, p. 237.
   1958–1968. *SYAFE*, 1969, p. 98.
   1969–1971. *CY*, 1972–1973, p. 251.
8. *Electricity—electrical energy production (million kWh)*
   1937–1938. *UNSY*, 1957, p. 303.
   1948–1952. Ibid., 1953, p. 258.
   1953–1956. Ibid., 1962, p. 315.
   1957–1972. *SARC*, 1973, Table 70, p. 249.
9. *Motor vehicle production (private automobile production, units)*
   1957–1972. *SARC*, 1973, Table 67, p. 237.
10. *Sulphuric acid production (thousand metric tons, 100% pure)*
   1921–1942. *Statistical Summary of Taiwan Province for the Past Fifty-One Years*, Table 282.
   1948, 1953–1955. *UNSY*, 1962, p. 237.
   1956–1961. Ibid., 1965, p. 282.
   1962–1970. Ibid., 1971, p. 258.
11. *Nitrogen fertilizer production (thousand metric tons)*
   1948. *UNSY*, 1953, p. 210.
   1937, 1949–1953. Ibid., 1957, p. 253.
   1954–1956. Ibid., 1962, p. 242.
   1957–1962. Ibid., 1965, p. 287.
   1963–1970. Ibid., 1971, p. 263.
12. *Plastics and resins (thousand metric tons)*
   1956–1961. *UNSY*, 1965, p. 288.
   1962–1970. Ibid., 1971, p. 265.
13. *Synthetic fibers (noncellulosic continuous fibers, thousand metric tons)*
   1960–1961. *UNSY*, 1968, p. 270.
   1962–1970. Ibid., 1971, p. 243.

Chapter 46. *Thailand*

1. *GDP per capita*
   A. *GDP* (1962 million baht)
      1951–1959. Statistical Office of the United Nations, *Growth of World Industry*, p. 729.
      1960, 1963–1971. *UNYNAS*, 1972, vol. 2, p. 528.
      (Linkage year: 1960.)
   B. *Population*
      1901–1919. *Statistical Yearbook of the Kingdom of Siam*, 1919 (Bangkok: Department of Commerce and Statistics, Ministry of Finance, 1919), p. 14.
      1929, 1937, 1970. Ralph Thomlinson, *Thailand's Population:*

Facts, Trends, Problems, Policies (Bangkok: Thai Watana Press, 1971), Table III-1, p. 23.

1920, 1925, 1930, 1935, 1942, 1947–1950. Central Statistical Office, *Statistical Yearbook, Thailand* [SYT], 1952 (Bangkok: National Economic Council, 1952), Table A-1, p. 1.

1957. *SYAFE*, 1968, p. 262.

1958–1968. Ibid., 1969, p. 342.

2. *Industrial production index (1962 = 100)*

1960–1973. World Bank, "Basic Economic Data Sheet, World Table 1," p. 47.

(Estimates of the value of manufacturing output were deflated with the GDP price deflator, 1962 prices, and converted to an index, 1962 = 100.)

3. *Gross domestic fixed capital formation as % of GDP (current prices)*

A. *Gross domestic fixed capital formation (current market prices)*

1953–1958. *UNYNAS*, 1965, p. 355.

1959–1968. *SYAFE*, 1970, p. 344.

1969–1971. *UNYNAS*, 1972, vol. 2, p. 527.

(Linkage years, 1959, 1969.)

B. *Gross domestic product (current market prices)*

1950–1952. *UNYNAS*, 1957, p. 211.

1953–1958. Ibid., 1965, p. 355.

1959–1968. *SYAFE*, 1970, p. 344.

1969–1971. *UNYNAS*, 1972, vol. 2, p. 527.

(Linkage years: 1953, 1959, 1969.)

4. *Railroads (kilometers)*

1898–1918. *Statistical Yearbook of the Kingdom of Siam*, 1919, pp. 106, 182.

1919–1939. Banks, *Cross-Polity Time Series Data*, Segment 3, p. 130.

1940–1958. *SYT*, 1956–1958, p. 376.

1959–1969. *SYAFE*, 1970, p. 349.

1970–1971. Ibid., 1972, p. 385.

5. *Raw cotton consumption (thousand metric tons)*

1951–1956. *UNSY*, 1958, p. 286.

1957–1964. Ibid., 1965, p. 504.

1966–1972. Ibid., 1973, p. 504.

6. *Production of pig iron (thousand metric tons)*

1963–1971. *UNSY*, 1973, p. 296.

7. *Steel production (thousand metric tons)*

1963–1971. *UNSY*, 1973, p. 297.

8. *Electricity—electrical energy production (million kWh)*

1944–1949. *SYT*, 1952, Table N 13, pp. 360–361.

1959–1960. *SYAFE*, 1969, p. 348.

1961–1971. Ibid., 1972, p. 383.

9. *Nitrogen fertilizer production (thousand metric tons)*

1966–1972, *UNSY*, 1973, p. 270.

10. *Synthetic fibers (noncellulosic continuous fibers, thousand metric tons)*
   1967–1972. *UNSY*, 1973, p. 249.

Chapter 47. *South Korea*

1. *GDP per capita*
   A. *GDP (1960 billion won)*
      1953–1964. *UNYNAS*, 1965, p. 212.
      1965–1972. *UNSY*, 1973, p. 550.
      (Linkage year: 1963.)
   B. *Population*
      1920, 1925, 1930, 1935, 1940, 1944, 1949, 1955–1958. *Korea Statistical Yearbook* [KSY], 1961 (Republic of Korea: Economic Planning Board, 1961), Table 27, p. 18.
      1959–1969. *SYAFE*, 1970, p. 191.
      1972. *UNSY*, 1973, p. 70.
2. *Industrial production index (1960 = 100)*
   1960–1965. *SYAFE*, 1970, p. 200.
   1953, 1958, 1966–1972. *UNSY*, 1973, p. 147.
   (Linkage year: 1965.)
3. *Gross domestic fixed capital formation as % of GDP*
   A. *Gross domestic fixed capital formation (current prices)*
      1953–1958. *UNSY*, 1965, p. 212.
      1959–1968. *SYAFE*, 1970, p. 197.
      1969–1971. *UNSY*, 1972, vol. 1, p. 685.
      (Linkage years: 1959, 1969.)
   B. *Gross domestic product (current prices)*
      1953–1958. *UNSY*, 1965, p. 212.
      1959–1968. *SYAFE*, 1970, p. 195.
      1969–1971. *UNSY*, 1972, vol. 1, p. 685.
4. *Railroads (kilometers)*
   1948–1966. Banks, *Cross-Polity Time Series Data*, Segment 3, p. 118.
   1967–1971. *SYAFE*, 1972, p. 205.
5. *Raw cotton consumption (thousand metric tons)*
   1951–1957. *UNSY*, 1958, p. 286.
   1958–1965. Ibid., 1966, p. 510.
   1966–1972. Ibid., 1973, p. 504.
6. *Production of pig iron (thousand metric tons)*
   1948. *UNSY*, 1965, p. 305.
   1958–1960. *SYAFE*, 1969, p. 210.
   1961–1970. Ibid., 1972, p. 202.
7. *Steel production (thousand metric tons)*
   1946–1956. *UNSY*, 1957, p. 271.
   1957–1960. Ibid., 1962, p. 257.
   1961–1969. Ibid., 1970, p. 308.
   1970–1971. Ibid., 1972, p. 305.

8. *Electricity—electrical energy production (million kWh)*
   1945–1957. *KSY*, 1961, Table 169, p. 199.
   1958–1960. *UNSY*, 1964, p. 355.
   1961–1962. Ibid., 1970, p. 373.
   1963–1961. Ibid., 1972, p. 370.
9. *Motor vehicle assembly (thousands)*
   1962–1964. *UNSY*, 1966, p. 314.
   1965–1972. Ibid., 1973, p. 310.
10. *Sulphuric acid (thousand metric tons, 100% pure)*
   1950–1960. *KSY*, 1961, Table 134, p. 170.
   1961–1971. *SYAFE*, 1972, p. 202.
11. *Nitrogen fertilizer production (thousand metric tons)*
   1960–1964. *UNSY*, 1967, p. 280.
   1965–1972. Ibid., 1973, p. 270.
12. *Plastics and resins (thousand metric tons)*
   1968–1972. *UNSY*, 1973, p. 272.
13. *Synthetic fibers (noncellulosic continuous fibers, thousand metric tons)*
   1963–1970. *UNSY*, 1973, p. 249.

Notes

Part One. The Demographic Transition

CHAPTER 1. *Two Centuries of Expansion in World Population*

1. For the broad-brush purposes of Table I-1 and Chart I-1, I have used the calculations of John D. Durand, "The Modern Expansion of World Population," *Proceedings of the American Philosophical Society*, vol. 111, no. 3 (June 22, 1967), p. 137. These are reprinted accessibly in E. A. Wrigley, *Population and History* (New York and Toronto: McGraw-Hill Book Company, 1969), pp. 205 and 207. Durand's estimates do not exactly conform to those of others, used in later portions of the text; but they capture adequately the sweep and prospects for population on a global and regional basis. Reflecting the lack of adequate data for early periods, Durand provides "high," "medium," and "low" estimates (p. 138). Table I-1 is his "medium" estimate. The "low" estimate yields a quadrupling in world population between 1750 and 1950. (It should be noted that Durand provided slightly different "medium" estimates in his paper for the 1965 World Population Conference: "World Population Estimates, 1750–2000," in *Proceedings of the World Population Conference, 1965* [New York: United Nations, 1967], vol. 2, pp. 17–22.) The greatest doubts relate to the figures for Africa, China, and India. On Africa, the issue is whether there was stagnation or slow increase between 1650 and 1850. For a discussion of alternative views, see, especially, D. V. Glass and E. Grebenik, "World Population, 1800–1950," Chapter 2 in M. M. Postan and H. J. Habakkuk (eds.), *The Cambridge Economic History of Europe*, vol. 6, part 1, *The Industrial Revolutions and After* (Cambridge: At the University Press, 1966), pp. 57–59. Alternative estimates for population in Africa are: for 1800, 90 and 100 million; for 1850, 95 and 100 million; for 1900, 120 and 141 million. On China, Ping-ti Ho has estimated population at 150 million for 1700, 313 million for 1794 (*Studies on the Population of China, 1368–1953* [Cambridge, Mass.: Harvard University Press, 1958], pp. 264, 266, 268–270). For the role of early-ripening rice (and double-cropping) in the long-term expansion of Chinese population, see Ping-ti Ho, "Early-Ripening Rice in Chinese History," *Economic History Review*, Second Series, vol. 9, no. 2 (December 1956). Dwight H. Perkins calculates a range of 200–250 million for 1750 (*Agricultural Development in China, 1368–1968* [Chicago: Aldine Publishing Company, 1969], pp. 16 and 216). On India, there is the basis only for imaginative estimation before the census of 1871. Kingsley Davis counseled that a figure of about 125 million should be taken for 1600; that a constant population should be assumed down to 1750; and that a gradual increase should then be assumed, accelerating down to 1870 (*The Population of India and Pakistan* [Princeton: Princeton University Press, 1951], p. 26). The 1871

census, corrected by Davis for under-enumeration, yields a figure of 255 million (p. 27). For a discussion of global population estimates before 1920, see, notably, *The Determinants and Consequences of Population Trends* (New York: United Nations, 1953), pp. 5–20, as well as the appendix to Durand's paper (pp. 145–159).

2. Durand, "Modern Expansion," p. 139. Projections for the year 2000 made by the United Nations have been consistently rising. For example, the 1973 estimate is 6.5 billion (*The Determinants and Consequences of Population Trends* [New York: United Nations, 1973], vol. 1, p. 564). A figure of 6.4 billion for the year 2000 is projected in "Recent Population Trends and Future Prospects," Document E/Conf. 60/3, prepared by the United Nations Secretariat for the United Nations World Population Conference, Bucharest, 19–30 August 1974.
3. Data from *Population Index*, vol. 39, no. 2 (April 1973), pp. 285–292, as well as vol. 40, no. 2 (April 1974); vol. 41, no. 2 (April 1975); and vol. 42, no. 2 (April 1976).
4. See, notably, the predictions of Frank W. Notestein et al. in *The Future Population of Europe and the Soviet Union: Population Projections, 1940–1970* (Geneva: League of Nations, 1944), especially pp. 53–71.

CHAPTER 2. *Population Dynamics among the Early-Comers to Industrialization*

5. Glass and Grebenik, "World Population, 1800–1950," pp. 68–69. The use of crude birth and death rates here and elsewhere in this chapter presents difficulties which are well stated and illustrated by Glass and Grebenik, especially pp. 90–105. In particular, crude birth rates may fail to catch accurately the timing of a change in family size, since they average the fertility behavior of a series of generations whose size, in each case, may depend on past death as well as birth rates. For purposes of international comparison over long periods of time, however, crude birth and death rates are the only data available; and, for present limited analytic purposes, they are adequate. It should be noted, however, that efforts are now under way to provide more sophisticated historical measures of population movements capable of cross-comparison. Ansley J. Coale, for example, has sought to separate the role of Malthusian and neo-Malthusian factors in reducing birth rates in a number of countries ("Factors Associated with the Development of Low Fertility: An Historic Summary," in *Proceedings of the World Population Conference, 1965* [New York: United Nations, 1967], vol. 2, pp. 205–209). He first establishes a maximum norm, based on the fertility of married Hutterite women for the period 1921–1930. Malthusian deviations from the norm reflect, essentially, later marriages than the norm. Neo-Malthusian deviations reflect, essentially, birth control, including abortion. The resulting table for a selected group of countries over the period 1870–1960 presents his findings on the relative role of the two types of influences on overall fertility (Table N-1).

   Coale notes that marriage ages tend to decline (and the proportion of fertile women married to rise) in countries where birth control has been widely adopted: "The development of neo-Malthusian fertility reduction seems to have released a propensity to marry in populations that had long practiced substantial Malthusian limitation" (p. 207).

   For summary of new insights into the complexities and variations in the demographic transition, see Coale's paper, "The Demographic Transition," in *Proceedings of the International Population Conference* (Liège, 1973), vol. 1, pp. 53–71, published by the International Union for the Scientific Study of Population.
6. Countries included in the sample for the early-comers of northern and western Europe are Belgium, Denmark, Finland, France, Germany, Netherlands, Norway, Sweden, Switzerland, England and Wales, and Scotland. For the late-comers of eastern and southern Europe the sample includes Austria, Bulgaria, Hungary, Italy, Poland, Rumania, Spain, and Yugoslavia. Within these two categories it should be noted that there are considerable ranges. Birth rates in the more advanced parts of Europe in the period 1906–1910 range from 31.6 for Germany to 20.2 for France; death rates from 19.1 for France to 13.7 for Denmark

TABLE N-1. *Fertility Indexes for Selected Populations*

Population	Index of Overall Fertility				Index of Marital Fertility (Neo-Malthusian)				Index of Proportion Married (Malthusian)			
	1870	1900	1930	1960	1870	1900	1930	1960	1870	1900	1930	1960
Western Europe:												
Norway	0.33	0.33	0.17	0.22	0.76	0.73	0.38	0.32	0.40	0.42	0.42	0.66
Sweden	0.33	0.30	0.15	0.17	0.71	0.64	0.30	0.24	0.42	0.41	0.42	0.63
England and Wales	0.37	0.27	0.15	0.22	0.68	0.54	0.29	0.29	0.51	0.48	0.50	0.71
Ireland	0.29	0.23	0.24	0.29	0.67	0.74	0.66	0.60	0.42	0.31	0.35	0.47
France	0.28	0.24	0.19	0.22	0.48	0.38	0.30	0.31	0.54	0.57	0.58	0.67
Eastern Europe:												
European Russia	—	0.55	0.42	0.24	—	0.77	0.65	0.35	—	0.70	0.63	0.62
Bulgaria	—	0.52	0.31	0.20	—	0.70	0.41	0.24	—	0.73	0.75	0.78
Overseas European:												
United States	0.37	0.29	0.20	0.28	—	0.49	0.31	0.36	—	0.58	0.63	0.75
Australia	—	0.29	0.19	0.28	—	0.58	0.33	0.38	—	0.47	0.54	0.71
Hutterites	—	—	0.70	—	—	—	1.00	—	—	—	0.70	—
Asia:												
Japan	—	—	0.37	0.17	—	—	0.51	0.29	—	—	0.68	0.58
Taiwan (1956)	—	—	0.54	0.50	—	—	0.66	0.68	—	—	0.78	0.72
India	—	—	—	—	—	—	—	—	—	0.80	0.83	0.88
Latin America:												
Mexico	—	—	—	0.50	—	—	—	0.76[a]	—	—	—	0.61[b]

[a] Illegitimate births assumed to occur to consensual unions.
[b] Includes consensual unions.
Source: Coale, "Factors Associated with the Development of Low Fertility," p. 209.

and Norway. Among the less advanced regions, the range in birth rates is from 42.1 for Bulgaria to 32.6 for Italy; for death rates, from 26.0 for Rumania to 21.1 for Italy. Italy, with distinctively different economic and demographic patterns in north and south, is statistically on the border between the two groups, as of 1906–1910. On regional patterns in Italian demographic data, see Annali di Statistica, Anno 94, Serie VIII, vol. 17, *Sviluppo Della Popolazione Italiana del 1861 al 1961* (Rome: Instituto Centrale di Statistica, 1965), especially pp. 401 and 461. To take two polar cases, in 1871 death and birth rates in Piedmont and Puglia were 35 and 28 per 1,000 in the former case, 41 and 34 in the latter. In 1951, the equivalent figures were 11 and 12; 27 and 10.

7. *United Nations Demographic Yearbook, 1971* (New York, 1972), p. 111.
8. Frank Lorimer, *The Population of the Soviet Union: History and Prospects* (Geneva: League of Nations, 1946), p. 87. Glass and Grebenik, "World Population, 1800–1950," p. 97, cite sources for prerevolutionary crude birth rates. For a more recent analysis of reasons for higher fertility rates in the Asian republics of the Soviet Union, see especially D. Peter Mazur, "Fertility among Ethnic Groups in the U.S.S.R.," *Demography*, vol. 4, no. 1 (1967), pp. 172–195.
9. Lorimer, *The Population of the Soviet Union*, pp. 130–131.
10. Ibid., p. 34.
11. Table I-10 is from A. M. Carr-Saunders, *World Population: Past Growth and Present Trends* (London: Oxford University Press, 1936), p. 49; Chart I-3 from ibid., p. 51. Table I-10 represents rough, gross movements, calculated independently from emigration and immigration data. As Carr-Saunders notes (p. 50): "In view of the very unsatisfactory nature of the material, the failure of the account to balance need cause no surprise; indeed it is remarkable that the totals should be so close." Efforts have been made in some cases to estimate net immigration. For example, for the period 1801–1935, gross immigration in the United States has been calculated as 38.5 million, net immigration as 26.5. Net immigration to Brazil for the period 1821–1945 may have been only half the gross total of about 5 million; net immigration to Australia for the period 1788–1946, 1.3 million, or less than half. See *The Determinants and Consequences of Population Trends* (New York: United Nations, 1953), pp. 102–103, where sources are given.
12. Warren S. Thompson and P. K. Whelpton, *Population Trends in the United States* (New York: McGraw-Hill Book Company, 1933), p. 303.
13. Ibid., p. 304 n. 1.
14. Ibid.
15. Ibid., pp. 308–311. For an indecisive examination of the Franklin-Walker hypothesis, see also J. J. Spengler, "Effects Produced in Receiving Countries by Pre-1939 Immigration," Chapter 2 in Brinley Thomas (ed.), *Economics of International Migration* (London: Macmillan and Company, 1958). On the inherently interacting nature of the process causing international migration in the nineteenth-century Atlantic economy (including Australia), see Brinley Thomas' rebuttal to critics, *Migration and Urban Development* (London: Methuen, 1972), especially Chapter 1, pp. 1–16.
16. The relation between net immigration and the natural increase in population for three overseas countries of recent settlement is given in Table N-2.
17. See, for example, Glass and Grebenik, "World Population, 1800–1950," p.112.
18. Carr-Saunders, *World Population*, p. 53.
19. See, notably, Evarts B. Greene and Virginia D. Harrington, *American Population before the Federal Census of 1790* (New York: Columbia University Press, 1932). Also, Thompson and Whelpton, *Population Trends*, p. 1. The changing content of U.S. vital statistics is discussed in Thompson and Whelpton, pp. 228–230 and 262, as well as in *Historical Statistics of the United States: Colonial Times to 1957* (Washington, D.C.: Department of Commerce, 1960), pp. 17–21.
20. See, notably, Thompson and Whelpton, *Population Trends*, pp. 262–264. For the gap in life expectation of whites and black slaves in 1850, see

TABLE N-2. *The Contribution of Immigration to the Growth of Population in Canada, New Zealand, and Australia*

Period	Population at Beginning of Period (Millions)	Annual Natural Increase (%)	Annual Net Immigration (%)	Annual Total Net Gain (%)
Canada				
1901–1911	5.37	1.59	1.82	3.41
1911–1921	7.21	1.60	0.60	2.20
1921–1931	8.79	1.51	0.30	1.81
New Zealand[a]				
1871–1881	0.26	3.92	4.58	8.50
1881–1891	0.49	2.69	0.10	2.79
1891–1901	0.63	1.87	0.45	2.32
1901–1911	0.77	1.95	1.06	3.01
1911–1921	1.01	1.65	0.44	2.09
1921–1931	1.24	1.31	0.50	1.81
1931–1932	1.44	0.91	−0.20	0.71
1932–1933	1.46	0.87	−0.15	0.72
Australia[a]				
1871–1881	1.70	2.30	1.26	3.56
1881–1891	2.31	2.30	1.72	4.02
1891–1901	3.24	1.82	−0.02	1.80
1901–1911	3.83	1.62	0.34	1.96
1911–1921	4.57	1.71	0.33	2.04
1921–1931	5.51	1.37	0.55	1.92
1931–1932	6.55	0.82	−0.05	0.77

[a] The population figures for Australia and New Zealand exclude aborigines and Maoris.
Source: Carr-Saunders, *World Population*, p. 163.

Robert William Fogel and Stanley L. Engerman, *Time on the Cross*, vol. 1, *The Economics of American Negro Slavery* (Boston and Toronto: Little, Brown and Company, 1974), pp. 123–126. They estimate the life expectation of slaves as 12 percent less than that of all whites in 1850, but higher than that of whites in the still dangerous cities, or about the level of France as a whole in the 1850's.

21. For a description and analysis of early Japanese population data, see Irene B. Taeuber, *The Population of Japan* (Princeton: Princeton University Press, 1958), pp. 40–55. For a revisionist view of Japanese population (and the Japanese economy) in the Tokugawa era, see Kozo Yamamura, "Toward a Reexamination of the Economic History of Tokugawa Japan," *Journal of Economic History*, vol. 33, no. 3 (September 1973), including footnote references to other revisionist studies.
22. Taeuber, *The Population of Japan*, pp. 40–55.

CHAPTER 3. *Population Dynamics among the Late-Comers to Industrialization*

23. Ping-ti Ho, *Studies on the Population of China*, p. 278.
24. Ibid., p. 96.
25. See, notably, Leo A. Orleans, "China's Population: Can the Contradictions Be Resolved?" in *China: A Reassessment of the Economy*, A Compendium of Papers Submitted to the Joint Economic Committee, Congress of the United States (Washington, D.C.: Government Printing Office, July 10, 1975), pp. 69–80. For earlier estimates, see John S. Aird, "Population Policy and Demographic Prospects in the People's Republic of China," in *People's Republic of China: An Economic Assessment*, A Compendium of Papers Submitted to the Joint Economic Committee, Congress of the United States, May 18, 1972 (Washington, D.C., 1972), pp. 220–326. For an exposition of his more optimistic view of the Chinese demographic transition, see Leo A. Orleans, *Every Fifth Child: The Population of China* (Stanford: Stanford University Press, 1972), especially pp. 43–56. Orleans' "informed guess" in 1972 was that the crude birth rate fell from 43 per 1,000, just before 1949, to 38 at the end of the 1950's, to 32 in 1969. With respect to the death rate, Orleans rejects the official Chinese figure for a death rate of 17 per 1,000 in 1953. He believes the death rate was "in the low thirties" on the eve of the Communist takeover; fell to 22 per 1,000 by 1958; a rise in the death rate followed in the crisis period during and after the Great Leap Forward; the death rate then slowly subsided from 22 in 1964 to 17 in 1970. For a further thoughtful study by Orleans, based on a visit to China, see *China's Experience in Population Control: The Elusive Model*, prepared for the Committee on Foreign Affairs, United States House of Representatives (Washington, D.C.: Government Printing Office, September 1974). Orleans checks out China's policy against fifteen criteria in Table N-3. Orleans does not believe the Chinese government itself knows firmly the rate of population increase, and he ventures no new quantitative estimate of his own; but he regards the Chinese family planning program as serious and, within limits, effective, although not capable of transference to other societies and political systems. For a discussion of Chinese birth control technology and policy, see also Carl Djerassi, Victor Li, and Ling-lu Wang, "Birth Control in the People's Republic of China," *Bulletin of the American Academy of Arts and Sciences*, vol. 27, no. 8 (May 1974), pp. 36–46. Lester R. Brown reviews Chinese population estimates in *World Population Trends: Signs of Hope, Signs of Stress*, Worldwatch Paper 8 (October 1976), pp. 34–37, providing an estimate for 1975 of a birth rate as low as 19 per 1,000, a death rate of only 8 per 1,000. These are based on a scattered sample of provinces, cities, and communes and should be regarded with some reserve until more solid evidence emerges.
26. Arthur G. Ashbrook, Jr., "China, Economic Overview, 1975," in *China: A Reassessment of the Economy*, p. 43.
27. Aird, "Population Policy and Demographic Prospects," p. 317, from an interview of Li Hsien-nien in November 1971 with a Cairo journalist.

TABLE N-3. *Evaluating China's Family Planning Program*

Criteria[a]	Availability	Comment
1. Fertility reduction included in official planning policy.	Yes	Particularly since 1970; some earlier periods policy not clearly defined.
2. Favorable public statements by political leaders.	Yes	The program to plan births is promulgated in the name of Chairman Mao Tse-tung.
3. Contraception readily and easily available, publicly and commercially throughout the country.	Yes	Distributed free of charge through the health system.
4. Customs and legal regulations allow importation of contraceptives not manufactured locally.	NA	Although imported in earlier years, supply of Chinese-manufactured contraceptives now appears adequate for current needs.
5. Vigorous effort to provide family planning services to all married women of reproductive age.	Yes	Broadly based and wide-reaching.
6. Adequate family planning administration structure.	Yes	Responsibility for family planning assumed by public health and by a variety of mass organizations.
7. Training facilities available and utilized.	Yes	Primarily through the public health system.
8. Full-time home visiting field workers.	Yes	Usually locally recruited and trained.
9. Postpartum information, education, and service program.	Yes	Readily available to all.
10. Abortion services openly and legally available to all.	Yes	But not encouraged as a substitute for contraception.
11. Voluntary sterilization services (male and female) openly and legally available to all.	Yes	In some areas performed by specially trained paramedical personnel.
12. Use of mass media on a substantial basis.	Yes	Main emphasis, however, on personal approach and group study.
13. Government provides substantial part of family planning budget from its own resources.	Yes	Manufacture and free distribution of contraceptives, for example.
14. Recordkeeping systems for clients at clinic level and program service statistics.	Yes	Program service statistics more limited.
15. Serious and continuous evaluation effort.	No	Probably limited to sample areas.

[a]Criteria suggested by Robert J. Lapham and W. Parker Mauldin, "National Family Planning Programs: Review and Evaluation," *Studies in Family Planning*, vol. 3, no. 2, March 1972.

Source: Orleans, *China's Experience*, p. 44.

28. Government of India, Planning Commission, *Draft Fifth Five Year Plan 1974–79* (New Delhi, n.d.), vol. 2, p. 240. For U.N. Indian estimates, see *United Nations Demographic Yearbook, 1974*, p. 122.
29. Ibid., p. 233.
30. Demographic patterns in India vary regionally as well as between urban and rural populations (see, for example, *Measures of Fertility and Mortality in India*, Sample Registrar System Analytic Series No. 2, 1972, Vital Statistics Division, Office of the Registrar General, India, Ministry of Home Affairs, New Delhi). As Table N-4 indicates, birth and death rates (and rates of population increase) tend to be lower in the southern part of the country.

TABLE N-4. *Crude Birth Rate and Death Rate by States, Rural, 1968 and 1969*

State	Period	Crude Rate per 1,000 Population	
		Birth Rate	Death Rate
Andhra Pradesh	1968	36.6	15.8
	1969	35.4	17.2
Assam	1968	45.5	20.0
	1969	40.8	17.4
Gujarat	1968	45.4	17.7
	1969	42.3	20.7
Haryana	1968	N.A.	N.A.
	1969	39.5	11.7
Jammu and Kashmir	1968	41.2	17.5
	1969	39.5	14.4
Kerela	1968	33.2	10.0
	1969	31.1	9.0
Maharashtra	1968	36.9	13.9
	1969	32.9	15.5
Mysore	1968	33.7	13.3
	1969	34.1	15.4
Punjab	1968	33.6	12.0
	1969	33.6	11.6
Rajasthan	1968	46.0	18.4
	1969	44.0	24.0
Tamil Nadu	1968	N.A.	N.A.
	1969	33.8	18.8
Uttar Pradesh	1968	45.4	23.5
	1969	45.6	25.6
Pooled estimates	1968[a]	39.0	16.8
	1969[b]	38.8	19.1

[a] Includes Bihar, Orissa, West Bengal, Delhi, and Manipur.
[b] Includes Delhi, Manipur, and excludes Bihar (data under verification), Orissa, and West Bengal (due to nonavailability of adequate data).
Source: *Measures of Fertility and Mortality in India*, p. 46.

For an effort to establish by regression analysis the relative effectiveness of family planning programs in sixteen Indian states (as opposed to degrees of economic and social modernization), see World Bank Staff Report (Timothy King, coordinating author), *Population Policies and Economic Development* (Baltimore: Johns Hopkins Press, 1974), pp. 149–163.

See also David G. Mandelbaum, *Human Fertility in India* (Berkeley: University of California Press, 1974), for a general survey of India's population policy and (Chapter 3) for an analysis of social, cultural, and other birth-rate differentials.

31. Government of India, Planning Commission, *Draft Fifth Five Year Plan, 1974–79*, vol. 2, Chapter 10, pp. 232 ff.
32. Embassy of India, Washington, D.C., *India: Questions and Answers* (1975).
33. Durand's method is explained, "Modern Expansion," pp. 150–151, although he concludes that an examination of the limited evidence is mainly useful "in showing the wide ranges of uncertainty."
34. The two great pioneers in estimating global population, A. M. Carr-Saunders (*World Population*) and W. Willcox ("Population of the World and Its Modern Increase," in Imre Ferenczi [ed.], *International*

Migrations [New York: National Bureau of Economic Research, 1929], vol. 2), have differed over the evolution of Africa's population. Their estimates are given in Table N-5. Carr-Saunders (pp. 34–35) accepts Willcox's benchmark of 100 million for 1650, but argues that slave raiding and the impact of European diseases must have reduced population down to 1800 and that evidence on Egypt and scattered evidence on other parts of Africa suggest expansion after 1800. For discussion of this debate, see also Glass and Grebenik, "World Population, 1800–1950," pp. 58–59, and Durand, "Modern Expansion," pp. 152–153, where Durand explains his independent estimates for North Africa and "the remainder of Africa" (see Table I-1). For a review of evidence on African population over the period 1900–1960, see, notably, *World Population Prospects as Assessed in 1963*, Department of Economic and Social Affairs Population Studies, No. 41 (New York: United Nations, 1966), pp. 93–102. For a detailed assembly of the unsatisfactory population data on that part of Africa under British colonial rule, see R. R. Kuczynski, *Demographic Survey of the British Colonial Empire*, vol. 1, *West Africa* (1948), vol. 2, *East Africa* (1949), etc. (London, New York, Toronto: Oxford University Press).

35. Carr-Saunders, *World Population*, pp. 303–304.
36. Ibid., pp. 280–284.
37. *United Nations Demographic Yearbook, 1971*, p. 111.
38. Ibid., pp. 635 and 690. Large urban-rural differences exist in Rhodesian birth rates for the Asiatic and European populations: 20–44 and 16–24, respectively. The gap is insignificant for the colored population: 34–35. With respect to death rates, there is a reversal of historical experience. In the past, urban death rates were typically higher than rural, due to the impact on concentrated populations of infectious diseases, under existing conditions of sanitation, water supply, etc. In more recent times, the improvement in public services, combined with the greater availability of medical care, has reversed that pattern. In Rhodesia urban-rural death rates for the Asiatic population in 1968, for example, were 4.4 versus 12.9; for the colored population, 4.0 versus 12.0. The gap was much less for the European population: 7.1 versus 8.1. Presumably, Europeans living in rural areas have adequate access to medical services.
39. For the derivation of these figures, see Durand, "Modern Expansion," pp. 156–159. Population censuses for Mexico, Brazil, and some of the Caribbean islands reach back to the late eighteenth century; but they involve, as usual, problems of under-enumeration which various scholars have sought to correct. In this connection, Durand's footnote citations are useful. See also citations in the bibliography of *Determinants and Consequences*, pp. 319–394; *The Future Growth of World Population* (New York: United Nations, 1958), p. 55; *World Population Prospects as Assessed in 1963*, pp. 107–118. O. Andrew Collver has attempted a sophisticated reconstruction of Latin American birth rates from 1850–1854 to 1955–1959 (*Birth Rates in Latin America: New Estimates of Historical Trends and Fluctuations*, Research Series No. 7 [Berkeley: Institute of International Studies, University of California, 1965]). Appendixes to this study present valuable country-by-country summaries and evaluations of population data and analyses of

TABLE N-5. *Population of Africa (in Millions)*

	Willcox	Carr-Saunders
1650	100	100
1750	100	95
1800	100	90
1850	100	95
1900	141	120

Sources: Willcox, "Population"; Carr-Saunders, *World Population*.

them. With respect to birth rates, Collver concludes that by the end of the 1950's only three Latin American countries had made a permanent transition to low birth rates: Uruguay, Argentina, and Cuba. In the other cases, one can observe fluctuations in birth rates, responding primarily to economic conditions, but rates remain over 40 per 1,000 down to the end of his period of study, excepting Chile. Chile shows some symptoms of the demographic transition, but less sharply marked than in the cases of Uruguay, Argentina, and Cuba (see, especially, pp. 25–36). For a bibliographical review of recent work on Latin American population, see Michael E. Conroy, "Recent Research in Economic Demography Related to Latin America: A Critical Survey and an Agenda," *Latin American Research Review* (Summer 1974), pp. 3–27.

40. *World Population Prospects as Assessed in 1963*, p. 138. The decline in the rate of increase in temperate South America in the 1930's reflects a falling off of immigration and, perhaps, other depression-induced phenomena.

41. See, for example, Kuczynski, *Demographic Survey*, vol. 3, *West Indian and American Territories* (1953), pp. 48–51, for summary data, as well as more detailed analyses elsewhere.

CHAPTER 4. *The Contemporary Scene: A Preliminary View*

42. Lee-Jay Cho, "Estimated Refined Measures of Fertility for all Major Countries of the World," *Demography*, vol. 1 (1964), pp. 359-374; key data reprinted in Donald J. Bogue, *Principles of Demography* (New York: John Wiley and Sons, 1969), Table 18-4, pp. 664–668.

43. Bogue, *Principles of Demography*, p. 672. Bogue measures the degree of demographic transition completed as the median percent of each continent. The definition of the median flows from a breakdown of the demographic transition into ten equal stages or steps. There is obviously a wide distribution of steps within each nation and continent. The median is computed as the step which 50 percent of the population lies above, on the way through the demographic transition.

44. For a visual sense of the range which Chart I-7 summarizes, the reader may consult the scattergram of per capita gross domestic product plotted against percentage of demographic transition completed in Bogue, *Principles of Demography*, p. 675. See also Bogue's scattergrams relating the demographic transition to percentage of urban population (p. 672), percentage of population illiterate (p. 673), percentage of population dependent on agriculture (p. 674), infant mortality rate (p. 676), and expectation of life at birth for females (p. 677).

45. The World Bank Staff Report, *Population Policies and Economic Development*, presents a somewhat different picture of birth rates in relation to economic development as of 1973, using a coarser breakdown of levels of GNP per capita (pp. 12–15). The major conclusion drawn is the following (p. 15): "The birth rate distribution is highly bimodal, falling in two distinct groups. Countries with a per capita Gross National Product (GNP) below $600 [1973] have an average birth rate of 39.2 . . . ; in countries with a per capita GNP above $600, the birth rates . . . are half this average. . . . no country with a per capita GNP below $600 has a birth rate below 30. Few countries have a birth rate in the intermediate range; most have birth rates above 40 or below 25. Of 150 countries with available data, only fifteen have birth rates in the range 25–34; eighty-two have birth rates of 40 or above; and forty-one have rates of 20 or below.

"Apparently, when fertility begins to fall and the birth rate reaches a level of about 35, the fertility decline gathers momentum and the birth rate falls sharply until it drops below 25."

If this generalization holds for India and China, the world's population prospects may prove somewhat more hopeful than presently estimated.

46. See, for example, my discussion in W. W. Rostow, *How It All Began* (New York: McGraw-Hill Book Company, 1975), pp. 66–81.

47. See above, note 5, for a comment on the limitations of crude birth- and death-rate statistics. It should also be noted that, even with respect to the recent behavior of death rates in developing regions, there are ambiguities and uncertainties. See, for example, Harold Frederiksen, "Determinants and Consequences of Mortality Trends in Ceylon," *Public Health Reports*, vol. 76, no. 8 (August 1961), pp. 659–663, reprinted in David M. Heer (ed.), *Readings on Population* (Englewood Cliffs, N.J.: Prentice-Hall, 1968), Chapter 6.
48. See, for example, Stanley Friedlander and Morris Silver, "A Quantitative Study of the Determinants of Fertility Behavior," *Demography*, vol. 4, no. 1 (1967), who examine, *inter alia*, the relation between family size and social reform, social mobility, overcrowded housing, religion, culture, the achievement motive, the social position of women, diet, and communist versus noncommunist governments.
49. Some examples of correlation analysis bearing on this problem are: Robert Weintraub, "The Birth Rate and Economic Development: An Empirical Study," *Econometrica*, vol. 40, no. 4 (October 1962), pp. 812–817; Irma Adelman, "An Econometric Analysis of Population Growth," *American Economic Review*, vol. 53, no. 3 (June 1963), pp. 314–339; David M. Heer, "Economic Development and Fertility," *Demography*, vol. 3, no. 2 (1966), pp. 423–444; Friedlander and Silver, "A Quantitative Study," pp. 30–70; Llad Phillips, Harold L. Votey, Jr., and Donald E. Maxwell, "A Synthesis of the Economic and Demographic Models of Fertility: An Econometric Test," *Review of Economics and Statistics*, vol. 51, no. 3 (August 1969), pp. 298–309; and William Rich, *Smaller Families through Social and Economic Progress*, Monograph No. 7 (Washington, D.C.: Overseas Development Council, 1973). These and other studies are pulled together and summarized in Julian L. Simon, *The Effects of Income on Fertility* (Chapel Hill: Carolina Population Center, University of North Carolina at Chapel Hill, 1974), and in the World Bank Staff Report, *Population Policies and Economic Development*. See also Bogue, *Principles of Demography*, especially pp. 663–679; and, for the application of correlation analysis to the cases of Colombia, Puerto Rico, and Taiwan, Richard R. Nelson, T. Paul Schultz, and Robert L. Slighton, *Structural Change in a Developing Economy: Colombia's Problems and Prospects* (Princeton: Princeton University Press, 1971), especially Chapter 2, pp. 8–44, where education and child health and survival are judged the critical explanatory variables with respect to the birth rate. Donald J. O'Hara has produced a formal model of the demographic transition in terms of household decision-making, which emphasizes the role of mortality rates (and survivors-to-maturity) in the calculation of family size ("Microeconomic Aspects of the Demographic Transition," *Journal of Political Economy*, vol. 83, no. 6 [February–December 1975], pp. 1203–1216).
50. The World Bank Staff Report, *Population Policies and Economic Development*, gives special emphasis to the role of income distribution in determining the pace of decline in fertility rates. See pp. 47–49 and Appendix A, pp. 141–148 (by Robert Repetto).
51. This spectrum is well presented in ibid., pp. 60–78.
52. Ibid., p. 75.
53. *Plan of Action*, August 30, 1974, par. 14. For a thoughtful assessment of the results of the Bucharest Conference, see Philander P. Claxton, Jr., "The World Population Conference: An Assessment," *Department of State Bulletin*, vol. 71, no. 1846 (November 11, 1974), pp. 649–654. For an effort to articulate an acceptable synthesis of the positions reflected at Bucharest, see Michael S. Teitelbaum, "Population and Development: Is a Consensus Possible?" *Foreign Affairs* (July 1974), pp. 742–760. For a survey of post-Bucharest population developments, see Lester R. Brown, *World Population Trends*.

Part Two. Growth since the Eighteenth Century: An Overall View

CHAPTER 5. *Industrial Growth and Its Diffusion*

1. Michael G. Mulhall, *The Dictionary of Statistics* (London: George Routledge, 1892), p. 156.
2. Ibid., p. 332.
3. Simon S. Kuznets, *Secular Movements in Production and Prices* (Boston and New York: Houghton Mifflin, 1930), p. 3.
4. The dating which Chart II-2 roughly records and the underlying rationale are presented in Chapters 28–47 of Part Five.
5. Unlike the case of the industrial production index whose rate of movement is presented in Table II-1, it has not been found possible to reconcile satisfactorily Michael Mulhall's distribution calculations for 1820, 1840, 1860 (*Industries and Wealth of Nations* [London, New York, and Bombay: Longmans, Green, 1896], p. 32) with those of Folke Hilgerdt for the period 1870–1936/1938 (*Industrialization and Foreign Trade* [New York: League of Nations, 1945], p. 13). The following major differences emerge when the two sets of calculations are compared for roughly comparable periods:

   —Mulhall appears to assign to Austria a higher level than Hilgerdt, which results in the United Kingdom, France, and Germany representing a higher percentage of total European production in Hilgerdt's than in Mulhall's estimates.

   —The gap between the United Kingdom and France is greater in Hilgerdt's than in Mulhall's calculations.

   —Hilgerdt takes account of industrial production in India, Japan, China, and Canada, which Mulhall does not do. Evidently, conclusions can only be drawn within each estimator's calculations, not between them. Therefore, a double line separates the estimates at 1860. United Nations figures for 1963 are from *The Growth of World Industry* (New York: United Nations, 1968), vol. 1, pp. 388–390. They are the weights assigned to build the world industrial production index. Albania, the People's Republic of China, North Korea, and North Vietnam are not included.

   To give some impression of further developments in the 1960's, energy consumption data for 1968 and 1971 are added (*United Nations Statistical Yearbook, 1972* [New York, 1973], pp. 353–356. The relatively higher proportion of energy consumed than industrial output for the United States (and reciprocal differences for the USSR) almost certainly represents the greater use of private motor cars and electricity-consuming durable consumers' goods in the United States.

CHAPTER 6. *Growth and Structural Change*

6. Politics will not be dealt with in any systematic way in the present volume. For my view of the interconnections of economic growth and politics, see W. W. Rostow, *Politics and the Stages of Growth* (Cambridge: At the University Press, 1971).
7. Hollis B. Chenery and Moises Syrquin, assisted by Hazel Elkington, *Patterns of Development, 1950–1970* (London: Oxford University Press [for the World Bank], 1975), pp. 20–21. This table summarizes, in the form of averages, post-1945 data covering 100 countries over the period 1950–1970. The structural characteristics of countries are averaged against GNP per capita in U.S. 1964 dollars.
8. A considerable literature of controversy surrounds this matter, in which Simon Kuznets and I were major protagonists, although Arthur Lewis is, in fact, the intellectual father of the notion that a doubling of the investment rate is to be expected in the early stage of modern growth. The controversy can be traced in W. W. Rostow, *The Stages of Economic Growth* (Cambridge: At the University Press, 1960 and 1971),

pp. 39–46; idem (ed.), *The Economics of Take-off into Sustained Growth* (New York: St. Martin's Press, 1963), pp. 30–55 (Kuznets); pp. xiv–xvi and 320–322 (Rostow); and pp. 189–195 and 233–237 of the second (1971) edition of *Stages of Economic Growth*, Appendix B. For a summary of historical evidence, which generally fails to catch the take-off transition in investment rates because of lack of data, see Simon Kuznets, *Modern Economic Growth* (New Haven and London: Yale University Press, 1966), pp. 234–240 (for gross investment rates); pp. 248–251 (for net investment rates). In general, I would regard the whole thrust of Table II-3, not merely the saving and investment data, as confirming my view of the take-off as the definitive structural transition into sustained modern growth.

9. See Rostow, *Politics and the Stages of Growth*, Chapter 4, especially pp. 141–160 and 176–183.

10. See Table N-6 for more detailed data on government expenditures than are reflected in Table II-5.

11. The German data are from Andic and Veverka, "Growth of Government Expenditure," pp. 206 and 209. The British data are from B. R. Mitchell with the collaboration of Phyllis Deane, *Abstract of British Historical Statistics* (Cambridge: At the University Press, 1971), pp. 367–368, 397–398, 417–418, and 420–421. The U.S. data are calculated from *Historical Statistics of the United States: Colonial Times to 1957* (Washington, D.C.: Department of Commerce, 1960), pp. 139, 209, and 723. As shown in Table N-7, Albert Fishlow has calculated for the pre-1900 period somewhat different proportions for four countries ("Levels of Nineteenth-Century American Investment in Education," Chapter 20 in Robert W. Fogel and Stanley L. Engerman [eds.], *The Reinterpretation of American Economic History* [New York: Harper and Row, 1971], pp. 270–271). By Fishlow's calculations public outlays in the United States rose from 47 percent of total outlays for formal education in 1840 to 79 percent in 1900 (p. 266). For present purposes the essential point is that only by about 1913 did educational expenditures in these four of the most advanced countries of the period begin to approximate the proportion of GNP allocated in recent times by nations with GNP per capita of less than $100.

On the pre-1860 period in the United States, see also Fishlow's "The American Common School Revival: Fact or Fancy?" in Henry Rosovsky (ed.), *Industrialization in Two Systems: Essays in Honor of Alexander Gerschenkron by a Group of His Students* (New York: John Wiley, 1966), pp. 40–67.

The most systematic historical study of allocations to education in terms of stages of economic growth is O. J. Firestone, *Industry and Education: A Century of Canadian Development* (Ottawa: University of Ottawa Press, 1969), especially Chapter 17. His aggregative analysis is summarized in Table N-8.

The astonishing expansion of Canadian educational expenditures, notably for higher education, is not untypical of advanced industrial countries in the quarter-century after the end of the Second World War. The proportion of public education outlays to GNP increased by 2–3 times (or more) over this period in Sweden, Denmark, Austria, Netherlands, Norway, Belgium, Switzerland, and Spain (Joseph Pluta, "National Defense and Social Welfare Budget Trends in Ten Nations of Postwar Western Europe," unpublished paper presented to Western Economic Association Meetings, San Diego, June 1975, Table 7).

12. Kuznets, *Modern Economic Growth*, p. 389, line 12. British data from Roger Schofield, "Dimensions of Illiteracy, 1750–1850," *Explorations in Economic History*, vol. 10, no. 4 (Summer 1973); U.S. data from *Historical Statistics of the United States*, p. 214. The gap between British male and female nonsigners, about 25 percent in 1750 (when 65 percent of the women marrying did not sign) gradually narrowed to 1850 (when the gap was 30 percent versus 45 percent), and then rapidly narrowed, virtually to disappear by 1890. The illiteracy rate for American nonwhites was systematically higher than for whites, as follows: 1870, 80 percent; 1900, 45 percent; 1920, 23 percent; 1952, 10 percent. The relatively high rate of literacy in Tokugawa Japan is

TABLE N-6. *Government Expenditures as a Percentage of GNP or National Income: Five Countries*

Great Britain		France		Germany		Japan		United States	
Year	%	Year	%	Year	%	Year	%	Year	%
		1788–1790	15						
1792	11								
1800	24								
1814	29								
1822	19								
		1825–1874	15						
1831	16								
1841	11								
1850	12								
1860	11								
1870	9								
				1872	9[a]				
		1875–1884	21						
1880	10					1880	10		
				1881	10				
		1885–1913	20						
1890	9					1890	12	1890	7
				1891	13				
1900	14					1900	21		
				1901	15				
				1907	16				
1910	13					1910	47		
1913	12			1913	18			1913	9
1920	26	1920–1924	31			1920	30		
								1922	13
		1925–1934	24	1925	25				
								1927	12
1929	24			1929	31				
						1930	40		
1931	29								
				1932	37			1932	21
1934	25								
		1935–1938	39						
1938	30			1938	43				
						1940	45	1940	22
1947	44								
								1948	23
1950	39	1950–1954	46	1950	41	1950	55		
1955	37	1955–1958	47						
								1957	29
				1958	44				
						1960	33		
								1961	30
								1968	33
1970	44					1970	21[b]	1970	35

[a] Central government expenditures only.

[b] From U.N. sources, central government expenditures only.

Sources: For Great Britain, Alan T. Peacock and Jack Wiseman, assisted by Jindrich Veverka, *The Growth of Public Expenditure in the United Kingdom* (London: George Allen and Unwin, 1967 edition), p. 37 (1792–1880); p. 166 (1890–1955); *United Nations Statistical Yearbook, 1973*, pp. 579 and 700 (1970). For France, Jan Marczewski, "Some Aspects of the Economic Growth of France, 1660–1958," *Economic Development and Cultural Change*, vol. 9, no. 3 (April 1961), p. 372. For Germany, Supan Andic and Jindrich Veverka, "The Growth of Government Expenditure in Germany since the Unification," *Finanzarchiv*, vol. 23, no. 2 (January 1964), pp. 244–245. For Japan, Koichi Emi, *Government Fiscal Activity and Economic Growth in Japan,*

1868–1960 (Tokyo: Kinokuniya Bookstore Company, 1963), p. 16. For the United States, Richard A. Musgrave, *Fiscal Systems* (New Haven and London: Yale University Press, 1969), p. 94 (1890–1957); W. W. Rostow, *The Diffusion of Power* (New York: Macmillan, 1972), pp. 148, 327, and 540 (1961–1970). For comparative government expenditures on goods and services as a proportion of GNP for fourteen countries over the period 1870–1965 (selected years), see Angus Maddison, *Economic Growth in Japan and the USSR* (London: George Allen and Unwin, 1969), pp. 13–14. With respect to Japan, it should be noted that the recent upward revision of GNP estimates for the early Meiji period would reduce the proportion of government expenditures to GNP. If, for example, the Ohkawa-Rosovsky 1973 GNP estimates are used, Emi's proportion of 44 percent for 1905 declines to 33 percent; his figure of 31 percent for 1911 to 26 percent (Kazushi Ohkawa and Henry Rosovsky, *Japanese Economic Growth* [Palo Alto: Stanford University Press, 1973]).

TABLE N-7. *Educational Expenditures*

	United States, Public and Private Expenditures (% GNP)	France (% GDP)	United Kingdom (% GNP)	Germany (% NNP)
1840	0.6	—	—	—
1850	0.7	—	—	—
1860	0.8	0.4	—	1.0
1870	1.3	—	—	—
1880	1.1	0.9	0.9	1.6
1890	1.5	—	—	—
1900	1.7	1.3	1.3	1.9

Source: Fishlow, "Levels of Nineteenth-Century American Investment," pp. 270–271.

TABLE N-8. *Canadian Stages of Economic Growth and Allocations for Education*

	Expenditures on Formal Education (% GNP)	Annual Average Rate of Increase (%) Real GNP	Real School Revenues
Preconditions (1867–1896)	1±[a]	2.3	4.8
Take-off (1896–1914)	1.25±[a]	3.7	6.3
Drive to technological maturity (1914–1950)	2±[a]	3.0	3.7
High mass-consumption (1950–1967)	2.6[a]	4.5	9.5
1967	7.3		

[a] Beginning of period.
Source: Firestone, *Industry and Education*, pp. 185, 191.

suggested by the approximation of Ronald P. Dore, *Education in Tokugawa Japan* (Berkeley and Los Angeles: University of California Press, 1965), pp. 317–322. Dore estimates that in 1868 about 43 percent of boys and 10 percent of girls attended elementary school. If all emerged literate and the proportion had been stable for some time, the figure for males would approximate that for contemporary developing nations in the $100–200 (1964) range and for Britain round about 1815.

13. Ernst Engel, *Die Lebenkosten Belgischer Arbeiter-Familien Früher und Jetzt* (Dresden: C. Heinrich, 1895).
14. The classic analysis of the changing structure of production (and the working force) as income per capita expands is in Colin Clark's pioneering study, *The Conditions of Economic Progress* (London: Macmillan Company, first edition, 1940, second edition [completely rewritten], 1951).

15. See, for example, Simon Kuznets, *Economic Growth of Nations: Total Output and Production Structure* (Cambridge, Mass.: The Belknap Press of Harvard University Press, 1971), pp. 144–147, exhibiting the post-1945 rise in the service share of gross domestic product for thirteen of the richest countries of the world. Kuznets notes: "The range of its coverage [the service sector] is from unskilled services to highly professional activity; from services engaged in distribution and finance to those engaged in public defense; from business services to education and recreation" (p. 271). The problem is compounded by the disorganized state of data in the various service categories. For a significant challenge to the view that the productivity increase in services is grossly less rapid than in the production of commodities and, especially, that past patterns can be projected into the future, see Edward F. Denison, "The Shift to Services and the Rate of Productivity Change," Technical Series Reprint T-003 (Washington, D.C.: The Brookings Institution, 1973), reprinted from *Survey of Current Business*, vol. 52, no. 10 (October 1973).
16. For an exhaustive analysis of labor and product shares on a historical as well as cross-sectional basis, and the implications of comparisons between them, see Kuznets, *Economic Growth of Nations*. Kuznets' conclusions are summarized in his Chapter 7, pp. 303–314.
17. This point is developed in ibid., pp. 312–314.
18. World Bank Staff Report (Timothy King, coordinating author), *Population Policies and Economic Development* (Baltimore: John Hopkins Press, 1974), pp. 144–145. As of the mid-1960's, the highest proportion among nations under $250 per capita was Taiwan (20.4 percent), the lowest, Iraq (6.8 percent).

CHAPTER 7. *International Trade and Its Changing Distribution*

19. The rate of growth of trade for the period 1840–1850 is exaggerated and that for 1850–1860 abnormally damped because the Rousseaux price index, used for correcting the value of world trade, was extremely low in 1850: 95, as opposed to 128 in 1840, 120 in 1860. There was a brief interval of relatively low prices in the period 1848–1852, reflecting both cyclical depression and relatively good harvests.
20. See, notably, L. Katus, "Economic Growth in Hungary during the Age of Dualism (1867–1913)," in E. Pamlenyi (ed.), *Social-Economic Researches on the History of East Central Europe*, no. 62 (Budapest: Hungarian Academy of Sciences, 1970). Katus dates the Hungarian take-off as from 1887 to 1913, with a period of active preconditions for take-off beginning in 1867.
21. Kuznets (*Modern Economic Growth*, p. 308) calculates a 1913 figure for the area now covered by the "Communist Bloc" as engaging in 12.8 percent of the world's trade. If the Russian proportion is taken at 4 percent and an allowance of about 1 percent made for the trade of presently communist Asia, the Eastern European figure would emerge as about 8 percent.
22. See note 19 above.
23. Kuznets, *Modern Economic Growth*, p. 314. The proportion of trade to national product varies if estimates are made in current or constant prices. Kuznets provides both estimates. Later and higher estimates of Japanese national output for this period would somewhat lower these proportions.
24. These and following data are drawn from Stanley L. Engerman, "The Slave Trade and British Capital Formation in the Eighteenth Century: A Comment on the Williams Thesis," unpublished paper presented at the New Economic History Conference, Cambridge, England, September 1970. At its eighteenth-century peak, Engerman estimates British profits from the slave trade at about 0.5 percent of national income. See also Robert P. Thomas and Richard N. Bean, "The Fishers of Man: The Profits of the Slave Trade," *Journal of Economic History*, vol. 34, no. 4 (December 1974), pp. 885–914. For the beginning of African modernization and the rapid increase in exports of tropical

products in the pre-1914 era, see, notably, W. Arthur Lewis (ed.), *Tropical Development, 1880–1913* (London: George Allen and Unwin, 1970).

CHAPTER 8. *Prices*

25. Phyllis Deane and W. A. Cole, *British Economic Growth, 1688–1959*, second edition (Cambridge: At the University Press, 1969), following p. 350. For a discussion of the limitations of these price indexes, see pp. 12–18.
26. *United Nations Statistical Yearbook*, 1972, p. 571. For an imaginative and persuasive effort to measure the rate of concealed inflation in the Soviet Union and other Eastern European countries, see W. P. Culbertson, Jr., and R. C. Amacha, "Inflation in the Planned Economies: Some Estimates for Eastern Europe," unpublished manuscript, 1977. The authors calculate the de facto inflation rate in the Soviet Union as 8.6 percent per annum for the period 1960–1970.
27. The best analysis of fluctuations in this period is that of T. S. Ashton, *Economic Fluctuations in England, 1700–1800* (Oxford: Clarendon Press, 1959).
28. E. H. Phelps Brown and Sheila V. Hopkins, "Seven Centuries of the Prices of Consumables, Compared with Builders' Wage-Rates," *Economica*, n.s., vol. 23, no. 92 (November 1956), reprinted in Peter H. Ramsey (ed.), *The Price Revolution of the Sixteenth Century* (London: Methuen and Company, 1971), pp. 23 and 26.
29. Douglass C. North and Robert Paul Thomas, *The Rise of the Western World* (Cambridge: At the University Press, 1973), p. 105, cite the following figures for England and Wales: 1600, 4.8 million; 1630, 5.6 million; 1670, 5.8 million; 1700, 6.1 million. They note these estimates are probably too high, but suggestive of the trend. The trend decelerates sharply after 1630.
30. See ibid., pp. 71–119, for a useful summary of European evidence as a whole.
31. Phelps Brown and Hopkins "Seven Centuries," p. 30.
32. The Gayer combined index of domestic and imported prices (annual, 1821–1825 = 100) rises from a pre-war trough of 88.0 in 1792 to 107.9 in 1798 to 155.7 in 1801. It is heavily weighted with the wheat price. The wartime peak is 168.9 for 1813. Thus 59 percent of the wartime increase comes in the period 1798–1801. The Schumpeter-Gilboy consumers' goods price index shows 66 percent of the total wartime price increase between 1798 and 1801. The role of the extraordinary increase in the wheat price between those years is suggested by the fact that the Schumpeter-Gilboy consumers' goods index exclusive of cereals exhibits only 30 percent of the wartime rise in the period 1798–1801.
33. Comparable annual average rates of inflation for the United States (consumers' price index) were: 1946–1956, 3.36 percent; 1956–1966, 1.79 percent; 1966–1972, 4.32 percent. Overall, the average annual rate of British price increase over the period was 4.25 percent, as opposed to 2.97 percent in the United States.
34. W. W. Rostow, *The Process of Economic Growth*, second edition (Oxford: Clarendon Press, 1960), pp. 197–200 and 359 (for statistical data).

CHAPTER 9. *Relative Prices and the Terms of Trade*

35. Adam Smith, *Wealth of Nations* (London: George Routledge, 1890), p. 196. The tendency to group commodities according to "foodstuffs and raw materials" on the one hand and "industrial manufactures" on the other proceeds from three sources: the classical distinction, referred to in the text, between long-run productivity prospects in the two forms of economic activity; the empirical fact that there have been protracted periods of relative depression and relative prosperity in agriculture; and the empirical fact of relative inelasticity of short-

period supply in "foodstuffs and raw materials," particularly in foodstuffs.

36. For an analysis of the case of increasing returns in the economic literature of the past two centuries, see W. W. Rostow, "Technology and the Price System," Chapter 5 in William Breit and William Patton Culbertson, Jr. (eds.), *Science and Ceremony: The Institutional Economics of C. E. Ayres* (Austin: University of Texas Press, 1976), pp. 75–113.
37. The complexity of the forces operating on import and export prices in this period is suggested in A. D. Gayer et al., *The Growth and Fluctuation of the British Economy, 1790–1850* (Oxford: Clarendon Press, 1953), vol. 1, pp. 10–11, 27–31, 61–66.
38. Albert H. Imlah, *Economic Elements in the Pax Britannica* (Cambridge, Mass.: Harvard University Press, 1958), p. 105, and discussion, pp. 103–106. See, also, Rostow, *Process of Economic Growth*, pp. 201–207 for an effort to assess the net effect of the fall in raw cotton prices on British import and export indexes, as well as the relative role of improvements in technology in both yarn production and cotton goods.
39. For detailed discussion, see Rostow, *Process of Economic Growth*, pp. 213–218. Also, C. P. Kindleberger, *The Terms of Trade: A European Case Study* (Cambridge, Mass.: The Technology Press of M.I.T., and New York: John Wiley, 1956), pp. 150–175.
40. See, notably, Kindleberger, *Terms of Trade*, pp. 16–28, where current account indexes for eight European countries are presented, dramatizing, notably for the interwar years, the extent to which they diverge from the merchandise terms-of-trade indexes in the cases of Britain, France, Netherlands, Sweden, and Switzerland.
41. For a discussion of this calculus, see Rostow, *Process of Economic Growth*, pp. 187–188.
42. Kindleberger, *Terms of Trade*, pp. 26–27.
43. The relation between the B curve and the British terms of trade altered after 1945. The shift in favor of primary products versus manufactures was about 50 percent between 1938 and 1948. The unfavorable shift in the British terms of trade was only 17 percent. The subsequent short-run movements of the two series roughly conform. Table N-9 exhibits the pre-1938 conformity and post-1945 divergence of Hilgerdt's B series and the British terms of trade.

TABLE N-9. *Relation between Hilgerdt B Series and British Terms of Trade (1913 = 100)*

	Hilgerdt B Series: Relative Prices of Manufactured Goods as Percentage of Prices of Primary Products	British Terms of Trade
1921–1925	124	129
1926–1929	113	119
1930	130	128
1931–1935	148	143
1936–1938	133	137
1948	80	121
1953	81	128
1958	87	141
1960	92	144
1965	94	145
1970	97	154
1972	102	163

Sources: Hilgerdt, *Industrialization and Foreign Trade*, and Imlah, *Economic Elements in the Pax Britannica*, updated from *Statistical Abstract of the United Kingdom*.

44. In a set of imaginative calculations, W. Arthur Lewis has sought to systematize our knowledge of the terms of trade between manufactures and various categories of primary products ("World Production, Prices and Trade, 1870–1960," *Manchester School*, vol. 26, no. 2 [May 1952]; Professor Lewis was good enough to make available to me a pedagogi-

cal note, "The Terms of Trade," August 1974, prepared for his classes in Princeton University, which extends his analysis down to 1972). He demonstrated a close trend correlation between world production of manufactures and the quantity of primary products traded between 1870 and 1950. In cycles, fluctuations in trade are less than in manufactures, as one would expect, given the inelasticity of demand for foodstuffs, which figure substantially in the former. In the depression of the 1930's, however, the increased degree of autarchy lowered the relation between manufacturing output and trade in primary products during the expansion of the latter part of the decade.

Turning to the terms of trade between manufactures and raw materials, Lewis finds a good conformity between fluctuations in manufacturing output and raw-material prices if it is assumed that capacity in raw-material output normally increases at a steady rate, through booms and slumps. Price thus varies as actual supply rises or falls relative to "normal," increasing capacity.

With respect to the terms of trade in food, he assumes that short-run supply fluctuates relatively little with booms or slumps, or, indeed, with prices. Lacking an index of real income, he then links fluctuations in the price of food to the relation between world manufacturing production (as a surrogate for real income) and food production.

In this kind of system, it is the rate of growth of manufactures which determines the required level of production in both raw materials and food, with the level of investment (or disinvestment, through wars) determining whether appropriate levels of primary capacity and output are forthcoming and whether the terms of trade move favorably or unfavorably to manufactures. In his 1952 article Lewis used his simple but powerful set of equations to approximate raw-material price movements from 1870 to 1938 and food prices from 1913 to 1950. He also speculated about where the terms of trade would stand in 1960.

In his 1974 "pedagogical note," he extends the analysis down to 1972, on the basis of five-year moving averages, eliminating short-run movements. He finds his basic relationships hold, when economies in raw-material use in manufacturing are taken into account. He also

TABLE N-10. *Basic Data (1963 = 100)*

	Production		Prices				
	Manufactures	Food	Manufactures	Food	Raw Materials	Tropical Crops	Cereals
1953	62	76	92	108	107	97	119
1954	62	79	91	108	107	107	106
1955	70	79	91	104	109	99	103
1956	72	81	95	103	111	109	102
1957	75	86	98	106	111	98	99
1958	72	86	97	103	103	88	97
1959	80	91	96	96	102	83	95
1960	86	94	98	94	103	86	94
1961	89	97	99	92	101	82	94
1962	95	97	99	94	98	79	99
1963	100	100	100	100	100	100	100
1964	108	102	101	105	102	103	103
1965	116	106	103	103	103	89	99
1966	125	107	105	105	104	91	103
1967	128	112	107	104	99	89	105
1968	137	116	107	102	99	87	100
1969	148	120	110	106	102	97	98
1970	151	123	117	111	105	108	96
1971	154	125	124	117	115	112	100
1972	165	129	135	132	129	127	111

Source: Lewis, "Terms of Trade."

introduces the terms of trade for tropical products. He finds, tentatively, an intriguing competitive relation between the terms of trade for tropical products and cereal production: the terms of trade for tropical products improve when the relative terms of trade for cereals deteriorate and vice versa. In the depression of the 1930's, of course, both were low.

For our purposes, Lewis' analysis is important not so much for his specific econometric findings but because it is one of the few formal efforts to supply a formal, dynamic mechanism to explain major trend fluctuations in the world economy, the subject matter of Part Three.

The basic data used by Lewis in his "pedagogical note" are shown in Table N-10.

Part Three. Trend Periods

CHAPTER 10. *Balanced and Unbalanced Growth*

1. The concept of optimum sectoral requirements in relation to economic growth is elaborated in W. W. Rostow, *The Process of Economic Growth*, second edition (Oxford: Clarendon Press, 1960), Chapter 4; fluctuations about these optimum paths longer in duration than conventional business cycles are considered in Chapter 6 as well as in my *Essays on the British Economy of the Nineteenth Century* (Oxford: Clarendon Press, 1948), Chapter 1.
2. Kondratieff's work was first presented in English in an article entitled "The Long Waves in Economic Life," *The Review of Economic Statistics*, vol. 17, no. 6 (November 1935). Kondratieff acknowledged two predecessors in his pioneering essay. A useful but incomplete bibliography (e.g., Kondratieff is missing) is provided in Richard A. Easterlin's *Population, Labor Force, and Long Swings in Economic Growth* (New York: National Bureau of Economic Research, 1968), pp. 275–287.
3. For an analytic critique of the long-cycle (or trend-period) literature, see W. W. Rostow, "Kondratieff, Schumpeter, and Kuznets: Trend Periods Revisited," *Journal of Economic History*, vol. 35, no. 4 (December 1975), pp. 719–753.
4. For a summary of forces making for deceleration in leading sectors, see Rostow, *Process of Economic Growth*, pp. 101–103. It is impossible to chart the transition in leading sectors with precision for two reasons. First, conceptually, what we need are data embracing the whole leading sector complex; that is, the sector incorporating the new technology plus its backward and lateral linkages to the rest of the economy. Appendix C tries to approximate such an estimate for the automobile sectoral complex in the United States in recent times; but those estimates are incomplete as well as rare. Second, there are narrower data problems. The traditional industrial classifications derive from institutional rather than technological history, embracing subsectors with neither uniform price nor income elasticities of demand nor uniform technological influences nor, even, uniform short-run elasticities of supply. Without further disaggregation, these categories leave us often in the position of having no analytic grip on the statistical movements they describe. Thus, Kuznets' despairing conclusion: "Since the high and accelerated rate of technological change is a major source of the high rates of growth of per capita product and productivity in modern times and is also responsible for striking shifts in production structure, it is frustrating that the available sectoral classifications fail to separate new industries from old, and distinguish those affected by technological innovations" (*Economic Growth of Nations: Total Output and Production Structure* [Cambridge, Mass.: The Belknap Press of Harvard University Press, 1971], p. 315). Nevertheless, some

useful propositions about leading sectors are possible short of satisfactory measurement. And, as I have argued on other occasions, I believe it wiser to get at leading sectors with such data as we can muster than to confine our study to over-aggregated data which conceal from view variables critical to growth, trend, and cyclical analysis. (See, for example, W. W. Rostow, *The Stages of Economic Growth*, second edition [Cambridge: Cambridge University Press, 1971], especially pp. 183–189.)

5. For a brief discussion of inventions as an induced phenomenon, and science and technology as sectors of the economy, see Rostow, *Process of Economic Growth*, pp. 22–24 and 83–86. The issue is well canvassed in a number of the essays contained in *The Rate and Direction of Inventive Activity: Economic and Social Factors*, National Bureau of Economic Research (Princeton: Princeton University Press, 1962).
6. I have here taken conventional single-year turning points. When various series are analyzed formally, on an international basis, there is a spread. For example, in Kondratieff's initial exposition he dated his long cycles as follows: troughs at 1790, 1844–1851, and 1890–1896; peaks at 1810–1817, 1870–1875, and 1914–1920.
7. Simon Kuznets, in measuring long cycles, used overlapping ten-year averages ("Long Swings in the Growth of Population and in Related Economic Variables," *Proceedings of the American Philosophical Society*, vol. 102, no. 1 [1958]). Strictly speaking, therefore, his peaks are in the intervals 1875–1885 to 1880–1890; 1895–1900 to 1900–1910; 1915–1925 to 1920–1930. Other analysts have added peaks in the 1830's, 1850's, and 1950's. See, notably, Moses Abramovitz, "The Nature and Significance of Kuznets Cycles," *Economic Development and Cultural Change*, vol. 9, no. 3 (April 1961) (for 1830's and 1850's); Easterlin, *Population, Labor Force, and Long Swings*, for the 1950's, a movement believed to stem from the postwar baby boom in the United States.

CHAPTER 11. *1790–1815*

8. For a discussion of various estimates, starting in 1801, see A. D. Gayer et al., *British Basic Statistical Data* (Ann Arbor, Mich.: University Microfilms), pp. 145–156 (supplement to idem, *The Growth and Fluctuation of the British Economy, 1790–1850* [Oxford: Clarendon Press, 1953]). Most production estimates were made by estimating a figure for average per capita grain consumption and deducting grain imports. See also Mancur Olson, Jr., *The Economics of the Wartime Shortage* (Durham, N.C.: Duke University Press, 1963), Chapter 3, "The Wars with France, 1793–1814," especially pp. 67–72, where estimates of the scale of enclosure and the increase in wheat production are given. For the period 1800–1814 Olson regards an annual average rate of increase of 2.3 percent as a minimum—a rate evidently higher than the rate of increase of population.
9. Gayer et al., *British Basic Statistical Data*, Table 124, p. 397, from R. S. Tucker, "Real Wages of Artisans in London, 1729–1935," *Journal of the American Statistical Society* (March 1936), pp. 73–84.
10. See, notably, John Parry Lewis, *Building Cycles and Britain's Growth* (London: Macmillan; New York: St. Martin's Press, 1965), especially pp. 10–15. Lewis draws a good deal of his eighteenth-century analysis from the work of T. S. Ashton, *Economic Fluctuations in England, 1700–1800* (Oxford: Clarendon Press, 1959), especially pp. 84–105.
11. J. P. Lewis, *Building Cycles*, p. 14. The weak expansion of the 1730's may be the result of the population stagnation or decline of that decade, often associated with the gin mania. See, for example, the array of population estimates in B. R. Mitchell, with the collaboration of Phyllis Deane, *Abstract of British Historical Statistics* (Cambridge: At the University Press, 1971), p. 5.

12. On the rise in the rate of investment in this period, see Phyllis Deane and W. A. Cole, *British Economic Growth, 1688–1959*, second edition (Cambridge: At the University Press, 1969), pp. 259–263, and my comments in *Stages of Economic Growth*, second edition, pp. 205–207. Total public revenues may have risen from (say) 10 percent of GNP in 1792 to, say, 23 percent in 1810. For public finance data for this period, see Mitchell, with Deane, *Abstract*, pp. 388, 391, 392, 396, 402, 405.
13. J.-C. Toutain, "La Population de la France de 1700 à 1959," *Cahiers de l'Institut de Science Economique Appliquée*, Série AF, no. 3, suppl. no. 133 (January 1963). Jacques Dupâquier's calculations yield, for the period 1780–1788, a slightly lower rate, 0.35 percent per annum ("French Population in the 17th and 18th Centuries," a chapter in Rondo Cameron [ed.], *Essays in French Economic History* [Homewood, Ill.: Richard D. Irwin, 1970], p. 164).
14. See, for example, Michel Morceneau, "Was There an Agricultural Revolution in 18th Century France?" a chapter in Cameron (ed.), *Essays.*
15. Jan Marczewski, "Some Aspects of the Economic Growth of France, 1660–1958," *Economic Development and Cultural Change*, vol. 9, no. 3 (April 1961), p. 375. A feeling that this estimate may be excessive is reinforced by Tihimor V. Markovitch's estimate that food industries actually declined between 1781–1790 and 1803–1812 ("The Dominant Sectors of French Industry," a chapter in Cameron [ed.], *Essays*, Table VI, item 21).
16. Marczewski, "Some Aspects," p. 378. Marczewski's price indexes are obtained by dividing estimates of product in current prices by corresponding estimates in constant prices. The periods chosen for comparison bypass the worst phase of wartime inflation in the 1790's.
17. François Crouzet, "Wars, Blockade, and Economic Change in Europe, 1792–1815," *Journal of Economic History*, vol. 24, no. 4 (December 1964).
18. Markovitch, "Dominant Sectors," Table VI, first statistical column; Marczewski, "Some Aspects," p. 375.
19. Markovitch, "Dominant Sectors," Table VI, items 20 and 23.
20. *Historical Statistics of the United States: Colonial Times to 1957* (Washington, D.C.: Department of Commerce, 1960), p. 116 (Warren and Pearson indexes).
21. W. B. Smith and A. H. Cole, *Fluctuations in American Business, 1790–1860* (Cambridge, Mass.: Harvard University Press, 1935), p. 17.
22. Douglass C. North, *The Economic Growth of the United States, 1790–1860* (Englewood Cliffs, N.J.: Prentice-Hall, 1961), p. 31.
23. See, for example, ibid., p. 58.
24. See, notably, Robert Brooke Zevin, "The Growth of Cotton Textile Production after 1815," Chapter 10 in Robert William Fogel and Stanley L. Engerman (eds.), *The Reinterpretation of American Economic History* (New York: Harper and Row, 1971). Zevin's table indicates the relative continuity of the expansion of the industry from 1808 forward as well as the sharp, temporary setback of 1816 (Table N-11).
25. Smith and Cole, *Fluctuations*, p. 22.
26. Ibid., p. 23.
27. Lennart Jörberg, *A History of Prices in Sweden, 1732–1914* (Lund: CWK Gleerup, 1972), 2 vols., especially vol. 2, part 4 (by Göran Ahlström), pp. 127 ff.
28. Ibid., p. 175.

CHAPTER 12. *1815–1848*

29. See, for example, Jörberg, *History*, vol. 2, pp. 194 and 196. As Chart III-5 shows, there was a sharp rise in the British wheat price in 1816–1817. The rise was much greater on the Continent. John D. Post analyzes the weather conditions that produced this brief but nearly universal dearth and its consequences in "A Study in Meteorological and Trade Cycle History: The Economic Crisis Following the Napoleonic Wars," *Journal of Economic History*, vol. 34, no. 2 (June 1974), pp. 315–349. The expansion in agricultural acreage induced by this brief price convulsion may have exacerbated the adjustment that, in any case,

TABLE N-11. *New England Cotton Industry Output, 1805–1860*

	Yards of Cloth (Thousands)	Value Added ($ Thousands)		Annual Increase (%)	
		Cloth	Total	Cloth	Total
1805	46	2	16	—	—
1806	62	3	22	a	34.6
1807	84	4	29	a	35.9
1808	181	10	64	a	121.0
1809	255	13	90	a	40.6
1810	648	34	228	a	153.0
1811	801	42	282	a	23.7
1812	1,055	55	372	a	31.9
1813	1,459	77	515	a	38.4
1814	1,960	103	691	a	34.2
1815	2,358	124	831	a	20.3
1816	840	44	—	−64.4	—
1817	3,883	204	—	362.0	—
1818	7,216	379	—	85.8	—
1819	9,941	522	—	37.8	—
1820	13,874	728	930	39.6	—
1821	22,292	1,170	1,394	60.7	49.9
1822	30,171	1,584	1,820	35.3	30.6
1823	41,459	2,177	2,424	37.4	33.2
1824	55,771	2,928	3,186	34.5	31.4
1825	69,677	3,658	3,928	24.9	23.3
1826	84,349	4,429	4,710	21.1	19.9
1827	95,005	4,988	5,281	12.6	12.1
1828	111,187	5,837	6,142	17.0	16.3
1829	128,779	6,761	7,078	15.8	15.2
1830	141,616	7,435	7,765	10.0	9.7
1831	161,566	8,482	8,817	14.1	13.5
1832	205,836	10,806	11,238	27.4	27.4
1833	231,486	12,153	12,639	12.5	12.5
1834	238,260	12,509	13,009	2.9	2.9
1835	250,773	13,166	13,692	5.3	5.3
1836	283,182	14,867	15,472	12.9	13.0
1837	308,079	16,174	16,858	8.8	9.0
1838	315,440	16,561	17,290	2.4	2.6
1839	317,605	16,674	17,436	.7	.8
1840	323,000	16,958	17,762	1.7	1.8
1841	353,111	18,538	19,465	9.3	9.6
1842	373,895	19,629	20,660	5.9	6.1
1843	369,565	19,402	20,469	−1.1	−.9
1844	395,762	20,778	21,969	7.1	7.3
....					
1850	596,867	31,336	33,567	—	—
....					
1855	634,200	33,296	36,165	—	—
....					
1860	857,225	45,004	48,464	—	—

[a]Cloth output not computed separately from total output before 1816.
Source: Zevin, "The Growth of Cotton Textile Production after 1815," pp. 123–124.

would have been faced in moving from war to peacetime international market circumstances.

30. For a recent effort to settle this still contentious matter, see M. W. Flinn, "Trends in Real Wages, 1750–1850," *Economic History Review*, Second Series, vol. 27, no. 3 (August 1974), pp. 395–411.

31. Another effort to approximate French real-wage movements in Paris during the nineteenth century is that of Jacques Roughie, "Remarques

sur l'histoire des salaires à Paris au XIXe siècle," *Le Mouvement Social*, no. 63 (April–June 1968), pp. 71–108. During the post-1815 recovery of France there was, as elsewhere in Europe, a marked decline in the cost of living down to 1825. It was accompanied by a sharp rise in money wages. In the second half of the 1820's, both movements reversed, suggesting a decline in real wages. The first half of the 1830's was again a good time for real wages, but a rise in living costs in the second half of the decade with relatively constant money wages again set back real wages until living costs fell sharply away as the 1840's began. In that decade some rise in money wages barely held its own down to the bad years, 1845–1847, when, as elsewhere in Europe, the poor harvests produced a convulsive rise in living costs. As in all other calculations, the sharp price increase of 1852–1854 set back real wages. These figures suggest a rise in real wages from 1817 to 1847; a unique high point in 1825; only a slight increase if any between the first half of the 1830's and the first half of the 1840's.

32. Jörberg, *History*, pp. 378, 382.
33. Joel Mökyr, *Industrialization in the Low Countries, 1795–1850* (New Haven: Yale University Press, 1976), pp. 165–202. Wage movements between 1819 and 1846 show considerable dispersion. There are substantial increases in textiles, paper, metallurgy, and mining; substantial declines in leather, apparel, wood, and foodstuffs. If the average increase of wages in the linen industry is set aside, since most linen workers were omitted from the 1846 survey, the result is only a slight net increase (2.8 percent).
34. Ibid., pp. 44, 339.
35. By decades, French potato production increased as follows (in million quintals): 1815–1824, 25.30; 1825–1834, 42.16; 1835–1844, 63.26; 1845–1854, 49.79; 1855–1864, 68.77. (*Cahiers de l'Institut de Science Economique Appliquée*, Série AF, no. 2, quoted in Alan S. Milward and S. B. Saul, *The Economic Development of Continental Europe, 1780–1870* [London: George Allen and Unwin, 1973], p. 355).
36. Marczewski, "Some Aspects," p. 376.
37. See, notably, Douglass C. North, "Ocean Freight Rates and Economic Development, 1750–1913," *Journal of Economic History*, vol. 18, no. 4 (December 1958), p. 542.
38. Ibid., p. 541.
39. The controversy over cotton prices and production in the 1830's took its start with the data presented in Smith and Cole, *Fluctuations*, on fluctuations in land sales and their linkage to price movements, in particular, pre-1860 business cycles in general (see, notably, pp. 51–58 and 114–115). Douglass C. North brought the argument into sharp focus by his exposition of how the periodic surges in cotton prices, expansions in acreage, and further expansions in production came about (*Economic Growth*, pp. 71–74). In essence, his position was that a fairly continuous increase in demand for cotton confronted a supply curve that shifted to the right discontinuously. Discontinuity was triggered when the movement of demand intersected an inelastic portion of the supply curve; the price rose; a surge of movement into new land occurred; and, with a time lag, the supply curve for cotton shifted outward excessively, yielding a subsequent sharp reduction in price.

In an essentially confirmatory analysis (on the supply side) Jeffrey G. Williamson (*American Growth and the Balance of Payments, 1820–1913* [Chapel Hill: University of North Carolina Press, 1964], pp. 38–43) calculates indexes of excess or insufficient supply and relates them to movements of the cotton price. He does this by measuring the difference between five-year moving averages of rates of change of United States cotton produced and annual rates of change in British cotton textile production and exports. The latter exhibit no fluctuations to match the gross behavior of the cotton price. When the two series are brought together, the result is a curve indicating a relative surplus of supply from the middle to the late 1820's; a shortage until the mid-1830's; a period of surplus down to the mid-1840's; a shortage emerging in the late 1840's; another surplus in the early 1850's; a brief deficit in the mid-1850's; a surplus toward the end of the decade. These fluctuations match well the cotton price movements of the period; that is, the periods of surplus are associated with low or declining prices, of deficit, with high or rising prices. The line of argument developed by North and Williamson would have been strengthened if they had introduced the evidence on British cotton stocks and their proportion to British cotton consumption included in Table III-14.

The North-Williamson doctrine has been challenged by Peter Temin ("The Causes of Cotton-Price Fluctuations in the 1830's," *The Review of Economics and Statistics*, vol. 49, no. 4 [November 1967], pp. 463–470). Temin sets aside the discontinuities in U.S. acreage and supply by a simple, arbitrary device: he makes the long-run U.S. cotton supply a direct function of the steadily increasing population of the South, extrapolated between census years. For the short run, he recognizes the role of weather and the size of the cotton harvest. He then turns to examine the narrow time period 1833–1841. His method is to calculate deviations from trend for a number of factors he judges as determining the supply and demand for American cotton. He concludes that the good British harvests of 1833–1834 were the decisive factor in the rise of the cotton price of the 1830's, yielding a surge of demand in Britain for cotton goods. On the side of supply, the only factor he recognizes as operative is the short-run fluctuation in the American harvest. He then grandly administers the *coup de grâce* to North, Williamson, and others who share their view: "First there is no evidence—either in the steady growth of cotton production itself or in the other data available—of an exhaustion of cotton-growing capacity in the ante-bellum period, much less of a *periodic* exhaustion. The hypothesis of price rises based on periodic exhaustion of capacity accordingly should be abandoned. With it goes the explanation of 'long swings' in American cotton prices generated by the changing elasticity of the supply of cotton" ("Causes," p. 470).

There is a good deal to question in Temin's analysis. First, there is no way to test the North-Williamson hypothesis without examining the whole sequence from 1815 to 1860. One cannot assess whether and why there were periods of relative abundance or scarcity relative to the demand-supply trend by studying the years 1833–1841. For example, as I have pointed out on another occasion (W. W. Rostow, "The Strategic Role of Theory: A Commentary," *Journal of Economic History*, vol. 31, no. 1 [March 1971], pp. 79–80), if one examines the period 1828–1832, before the good British harvests arrived, one finds the price of cotton and of slaves beginning to move up from their trough levels of the 1820's, British cotton stocks declining, and sales of land in the cotton states increasing. The boom of 1833–1836 in the Atlantic world evidently occurred against the background of growing pressure of demand on the cotton supply. The existence of this process is reinforced by calculations done after the publication of Temin's work, presented in Robert William Fogel and Stanley L. Engerman, *Time on the Cross*, vol. 1, *The Economics of American Negro Slavery* (Boston and Toronto: Little, Brown and Company, 1974), especially pp. 86–94. They calculate and compare indexes of cotton demanded and supplied between 1829 and 1861 (see chart, ibid., p. 92). Both fluctuate erratically around a virtually identical long-term trend; but periods of relative oversupply (late 1830's, early 1840's, early and then late 1850's) clearly emerge and correlate well with cotton price fluctuations. Unfortunately, Fogel and Engerman did not push their supply-demand analysis back to 1815.

Second, the link between good and bad harvests and the British demand for raw cotton is not as simple as Temin's analysis would suggest. The British harvest bears in this period a systematic and rather complex relation to real wages, the course of the business cycle, the level of income, and the effective demand for textiles. Year-by-year movements in the level of employment and real income are required to "explain" the cotton demand, not merely the British harvest. The rate of growth of British cotton exports is relevant; for example, the expansion in cotton yarn and twist produced between 1831 and 1836 was 44 percent for the export market, 14 percent worked up for the British market. The absolute increases were similar for the two markets (£27 million and £30 million, respectively). And, given the pace of productivity increase in the cotton industry of this period, the movement of supply as well as demand curves is also relevant to the industry's raw-material requirements. Fluctuating British harvests are, then, an insufficient basis for analyzing shifting British demand for cotton.

Third, as Table III-14 indicates, it is not the case that American cotton production expanded smoothly in some simple relation to the trend in southern population. Between 1816 and 1860 the rates of increase in cotton production over five-year periods varied from 77 percent to 13 percent. Moreover, if one examines Tables N-12 and N-13, showing the percentage distribution of cotton production and the percentage rates of increase by states, it is palpable that the three great post-1815 surges into new land left their mark on the total level of output as well as on its regional distribution.

Compare, for example, the percentage shares for 1811 and 1821 in the case of Alabama, Mississippi, Louisiana, and Tennessee. Compare the figures for 1834 and 1839 in the case of Georgia, Mississippi, and Louisiana. Note the declines and increases when 1849 and 1859 are compared. More generally, one cannot examine these disaggregated figures without knowing that the unfolding of cotton production in the antebellum south was not the smooth application of a gradually increasing scarce factor (labor) to an abundant surplus factor (land), a process fluctuating only with the vagaries of the weather. It was, both among the states and within the states, an extremely uneven process in which acreage was extended at different times and places in response to fluctuating market forces. While the land itself was cheap, there was substantial expense and difficulty in moving, settling, purchasing equipment, and actually bringing the land into cultivation. There is nothing in modern econometric analysis that, in fact, alters the weight of historical evidence that this process proceeded in waves of optimism related to the cotton price and its believed prospects. Fogel and Engerman (*Time on the Cross*, vol. 1, pp. 103–106) show how these expectations affected not only movement into new cotton lands but also the price of slaves in the thirty antebellum years.

Gavin Wright, also using econometric tools, has re-examined the problem analyzed by Temin ("An Econometric Study of Cotton Production and Trade, 1830–1860," *The Review of Economics and Statistics*, vol. 53, no. 2 [May 1971], pp. 111–120). He notes that Temin's use of population increase rules out, by definition, any long-run price elasticity of supply. Addressing himself to the relation between price movements and cotton supply, he establishes that "All of the land-sales demand equations show significant elasticity with respect to the cotton price" (p. 116); and the price elasticity is higher as the lag is lengthened between price movements and land sales (p. 115). He finds it "unreasonable" not to link the large crops and low prices of 1837–1838 and 1839–1840 to the large earlier land sales of the decade.

Although Wright's data do not permit him to deal with the period, I dare say the same conclusion would emerge about the large crops and low prices of the early 1820's in relation to the large land sales of 1817–1819. Wright devotes a good deal of his effort to demonstrating that the price elasticity for cotton and cotton goods was relatively low and concludes: "The picture of the cotton markets which emerges from this study is not one of supply shifting out along a highly elastic demand curve, but of supply and demand curves which are rather inelastic (at least in the short-term), but shifting rapidly and unsteadily over time" (p. 119).

But on this matter Wright acknowledges that his analysis is incomplete: ". . . we simply have no variables which adequately indicate shifts in the world demand curve" (p. 118). Nothing less than a global

TABLE N-12. *United States Cotton Production; Percentage Share of Individual States, 1791–1859*

State	1791	1801	1811	1821	1826	1833	1834	1839	1849	1859
North Carolina	—	10.0	8.7	5.7	3.1	2.3	2.1	6.5	3.0	3.2
South Carolina	75.0	50.0	50.0	28.2	21.2	16.7	14.3	7.8	12.2	6.9
Georgia	25.0	25.0	25.0	25.4	22.7	20.0	16.4	20.7	20.2	15.4
Florida	—	—	—	—	0.6	3.4	4.4	1.6	1.8	1.5
Alabama	—	—	—	11.3	13.6	14.8	18.6	14.8	22.9	21.7
Mississippi	—	—	—	5.7	6.0	15.9	18.6	24.3	19.7	26.4
Louisiana	—	—	2.5	5.7	11.5	12.5	13.5	19.5	7.2	15.4
Texas	—	—	—	—	—	—	—	—	2.3	1.0
Arkansas	—	—	—	—	0.1	0.1	0.1	0.8	2.6	0.8
Tennessee	—	2.5	3.8	11.3	13.6	11.3	9.8	3.5	7.8	6.5
All other states	—	12.5	10.0	6.7	7.6	3.0	2.2	0.5	0.2	1.2

Source: S. W. Bruchey, *Cotton and the Growth of the American Economy, 1790–1860* (New York: Harcourt, Brace and World, 1967), Table D, statistical introduction, p. 19.

TABLE N-13. *Percentage Increases in the Cotton Production of Individual States: Selected Years, 1791–1859*

State	1791	1801	1811	1821	1826	1833	1834	1839	1849	1859
North Carolina	—	—	75.0	42.8	0.0	0.0	−5.0	446.3	−43.2	119.0
South Carolina	—	1,233.3	100.0	25.0	40.0	4.3	−10.3	−5.8	94.5	17.5
Georgia	—	200.0	100.0	125.0	66.7	17.3	−17.3	117.9	22.1	56.5
Florida	—	—	—	—	—	650.0	−33.3	−39.5	48.8	66.1
Alabama	—	—	—	—	125.0	44.4	30.8	37.8	92.4	65.3
Mississippi	—	—	—	—	100.0	250.0	21.4	127.3	0.4	175.8
Louisiana	—	—	—	400.0	250.0	44.7	12.7	148.2	−53.6	335.5
Texas	—	—	—	—	—	—	—	—	—	727.5
Arkansas	—	—	—	—	—	60.0	−37.5	1,100.0	330.0	524.5
Tennessee	—	—	200.0	566.6	125.0	11.1	−10.0	38.5	180.9	69.6
All other states	—	—	60.0	50.0	108.5	−48.0	−23.1	−55.0	−64.5	1,443.8

Source: Bruchey, *Cotton and the Growth of the American Economy*, Table E, statistical introduction, p. 19.

analysis is required because of the role of British exports in the total demand for cotton. Michael G. Mulhall supplies a table for the distribution of cotton consumption by countries from 1830 to 1860 (Table N-14).

The average annual rates of increase (6.13 percent, 4.20 percent, 5.86 percent) far exceed the global rate of population increase (0.5 percent) and any likely increase in real income per capita. What was happening was a bit more complicated than conventional demand elasticity analysis takes into account, a process not quite captured by Wright's conclusion: "It now appears that the rise in world income (or the steady shift of world population from subsistence agriculture into the market economy) must have provided the continually expanding market for British cloth" (p. 119). What, in fact, was happening was that rapidly cheapening manufactured cotton textiles (British imports and local manufactures) were substituting for handicraft textile manufactures over widening areas, a process additional to that set in motion by the conventional forces of price and income elasticity of demand. There is an important element of substitution at work here, but a substitution made possible by the falling price of manufactured cottons due to improvements in technology and, to some extent, the declining price trend for raw cotton. In the case of the United States, for example, Zevin concludes that the "largest portion" of the explanation for the remarkable expansion of New England cloth production in the period 1815–1824 (see Table III-16) is "due to a change in the composition of total production between home and factory" ("Growth," pp. 136–137). In addition, of course, the introduction of "a new product with a very rapidly declining relative price" (Zevin, "Growth," p. 135) could be expected to yield, in the early stages of its appearance, rapid expansion of sales. Drawing his evidence from a period when this early revolutionary phase had passed in Britain and almost passed in the United States, Wright emerges with a conclusion of doubtful generality: "The price elasticity is low, and the income-elasticity is high" (p. 117). In many parts of the world where British cotton exports were being introduced in the pre-1860 period and where local factory production was emerging, that early phase—of substitution for household manufacture and

TABLE N-14. *World Consumption of Cotton, 1830–1860 (Millions of Lbs.)*

	1830	1840	1850	1860
United Kingdom	250	454	588	1,140
France	68	116	140	226
Germany	16	26	46	140
Russia	4	14	48	87
Austria	20	34	58	94
Italy	4	8	16	26
Spain	6	14	34	52
Sweden	1	2	8	16
Holland	2	4	5	6
Belgium	8	16	22	29
Switzerland	9	18	24	30
Europe	388	707	988	1,847
United States	77	135	288	390
India	—	—	—	26
Various	5	10	10	10
Total	470	852	1,286	2,273
Annual average rate of increase		6.13%	4.20%	5.86%

Source: Michael G. Mulhall, *The Dictionary of Statistics* (London: George Routledge, 1892), p. 156.
Note: Due to rounding, totals may not equal sum of components.

high price elasticity of demand—had not yet passed. On a world basis the gradual transit of that phase yielded a marked deceleration in world cotton consumption even after the recovery from the American Civil War. The annual average growth in world cotton consumption, according to Mulhall's data, moved as follows: 1860–1869, 0.9 percent; 1869–1880, 4.05 percent; 1880–1888, 3.6 percent. Gavin Wright explores the implications for the postbellum American South of this retardation in British cotton consumption in "Cotton Competition and the Post-Bellum Recovery of the American South," *Journal of Economic History*, vol. 34, no. 3 (September 1974), pp. 610–635.

40. It should be noted that U.S. production in the 1850's included the bringing of Texas into the cotton economy on a substantial scale, a fact not reflected in the land sale figures put together by Cole. The population of Texas increased between 1850 and 1860 from 212,592 to 604,215; slaves, from 58,161 to 182,566; cotton production from 58,072 to 431,463 bales (Lewis C. Gray, *History of Agriculture in the Southern United States to 1860*, 2 vols. [Washington, D.C.: Carnegie Institution of Washington, 1939], vol. 2, p. 907). In 1860, cotton production in Texas was a small proportion of total U.S. output (0.9 percent); but Texas supplied a sizeable proportion of the increment to U.S. output between 1850 and 1860 (14.8 percent). The Cole figures for the period 1848–1860 are incomplete for another reason: they exclude land purchased with military land warrants and scrip. (See Paul W. Gates, "Charts of Public Land Sales and Entries," *Journal of Economic History*, vol. 24, no. 1 [March 1964], pp. 22–28.)

41. Ulrich B. Phillips, *American Negro Slavery* (New York and London: D. Appleton, 1918), pp. 370–375. M. B. Hammond quotes figures indicating a similar trend rise, in a somewhat lower range: $200 in 1798, a figure which had been stable for some time; an average of about $1,400 in 1860 (*The Cotton Industry* [New York: Macmillan, 1897], vol. 1, pp. 50–52).

42. The best account and analysis of British fluctuations in construction for this period is that of J. P. Lewis, *Building Cycles*, pp. 29–38, 61–87. See also E. W. Cooney, "Long Waves in Building in the British Economy of the Nineteenth Century," *Economic History Review*, Second Series, vol. 13, no. 2 (December 1960), pp. 257–267.

43. J. P. Lewis, *Building Cycles*, p. 37.

44. Ibid., pp. 61–63. Also Gayer et al., *Growth and Fluctuation*, vol. 1, pp. 284–285.

45. J. P. Lewis, *Building Cycles*, pp. 66–70. The regional differences in British building patterns, which can be traced (via bricks) from 1832 to 1849 and (via building permits, etc.) from 1850, exhibit particularly wide divergences in the 1850's.

46. J. R. Riggleman compiled a building index for the period 1830–1935 from building-permit data drawn from an increasing number of U.S. cities ("Building Cycles in the United States, 1830–1935," thesis, Johns Hopkins University, Baltimore, n.d.). Riggleman converted the value figures in which the building permits were expressed into dollars of 1913 purchasing power. He also corrected the figures for population, in effect clearing the series for trend, given the linkage between population and housing construction.

CHAPTER 13. *1848–1873*

47. See Mitchell, with Deane, *Abstract*, p. 397 (for military expenditures); p. 367 (for national income); p. 373 (for level of investment).

48. Mulhall's total figure for world wheat production in 1888 (2,271 million bushels) is in the same range as the later calculation of Wilfred Malenbaum, who estimates world production for 1885–1889 at 2,391 million bushels (*The World Wheat Economy, 1885–1939* [Cambridge, Mass.: Harvard University Press, 1953], p. 238). Figures for certain individual countries differ in the two sources due to the boundary definitions chosen.

49. Indian wheat exports moved as follows (annual averages): 1873–1876, 72,000 tons; 1877–1881, 190,000 tons; 1882–1885, 900,000 tons; 1886–1888, 950,000 tons (Mulhall, *Dictionary of Statistics*, p. 56). As in the United States, Russia, Canada, Australia, and Argentina, this development was closely tied to the railroadization of India. (See, for example, Michelle Burge McAlpin, "Railroads, Prices, and Peasant Rationality: India 1860–1900," *Journal of Economic History*, vol. 34, no. 3 [September 1974], pp. 662–684.)
50. Williamson, *American Growth*, p. 256.
51. Smith and Cole, *Fluctuations*, p. 100; North, *Economic Growth*, pp. 236 and 244.
52. See, for example, Rostow, *Process of Economic Growth*, p. 217.
53. For a discussion of the views of those who have tended to deprecate the importance of the railroads in American economic growth, see Rostow, *Stages of Economic Growth*, second edition, pp. 223–229. It should be noted that the debate on this matter was put on the wrong path from the beginning. R. W. Fogel set out to prove that, at some higher cost, the United States might have been rendered an integrated national market via roads, horses, wagons, and canals. Thus Fogel could hold that, in some sense, the railroads in America were not "indispensable" or "necessary"—contributing, by Fogel's debatable calculations, less than 5 percent to 1890 gross national product, as opposed to the alternative modes of transport. This proposition in no way diminishes the judgment that, in fact, railroadization had the multiple revolutionary effects imputed to it here—and by other economic historians. Fogel, unlike some of his disciples, was quite aware of this fact, as the following passage suggests: "The most important implication of this study is that no single innovation was vital for economic growth during the nineteenth century. Certainly if any innovation had title to such distinction it was the railroad. Yet despite its dramatically rapid and massive growth over a period of a half century, despite its eventual ubiquity in inland transportation, despite its devouring appetite for capital, despite its power to determine the outcome of commercial (and sometimes political) competition, the railroad did not make an overwhelming contribution to the production potential of the economy" ("Railroads and American Economic Growth," Chapter 14 in Fogel and Engerman [eds.], *Reinterpretation*, p. 202). There are two critical words involved in this (incomplete) tribute to the powerful role of the railroad in nineteenth-century American economic history: *vital* and *overwhelming*. Behind their evocative use for debating purposes are interesting technical economic issues. By *vital* Fogel means that in fact there was a range of technological solutions available to deal with the American transport problem; and the railroad was, in a sense, adventitious. This notion flows, presumably, from the production possibility curves we draw in expounding elementary economic theory showing a given level of output produced by different combinations of labor and capital (or land), the optimum combination depending on their relative prices. And, in real life, one can find such differences in technique flowing from such differences in factor endowments and prices, e.g., between techniques used in Japanese versus U.S. or Canadian agriculture. But, of course, human ingenuity does not provide smooth, incremental production possibility curves. The technological possibilities generated are notably discontinuous. It has, for example, been difficult to generate the kind of less-capital-intensive technologies that would fit relative factor prices in the industrial sectors of the less-developed nations of the contemporary developing world. Fogel does the best he can in debating horses, wagons, roads, and canals versus railroads as the second-best option in the United States. But on close examination it turns out to be a poor second best; and worse still if applied to the geography of France, Germany, Russia, Canada, Argentina, etc. It takes, then, a special, literal definition of *vital* to assert that the nineteenth-century railroads were not "vital." The various economies would not have died without railroads; but their economic history

would have been strikingly different, their economies substantially less productive.

As for *overwhelming*, again Fogel has in mind a lucid technical point. Railroads were big business indeed within the American and other economies that fully absorbed them; but no sector in a large differentiated, modernizing economy is "overwhelming." Agriculture, food and leather processing, construction, and government and private services absorb, for example, large proportions of the working force. In a cross-section analysis of sectoral contributions to gross domestic product for fifty-seven countries at different levels of development in 1958, agriculture declines from 54 percent to 9 percent with the rise in income, manufacturing peaks out at about 31 percent, construction at 7.5 percent, public utilities at about 3 percent, transport and communication at 9 percent, trade at 15 percent, public administration and defense at about 15 percent (Kuznets, *Economic Growth of Nations*, p. 104). By using the word *overwhelming*, Fogel is setting up, in a familiar revisionist ploy, a straw man. There is no such thing as an overwhelming sector. In so doing, he misses a critical point. Growth is a marginal process taking place on a big, complex, differentiated base with many overhead activities built into its structure. A high proportion of current investment must flow to maintain and expand that structure as population and urbanization increase; e.g., houses must be built, and roads, and urban infrastructure. In developed economies, industrial investment, for example, is, except under rare circumstances, a smaller proportion of total investment (say, 19 percent) than social overhead capital (say, 31 percent) or housing (say, 25 percent). When, therefore, gross U.S. railroad investment accounts for more than 15 percent of U.S. gross capital formation in 1849–1858 (almost 25 percent in 1854), we are in the face of an extraordinary phenomenon. Although calculations have not been made, I would guess that it was generally true that the proportionate concentration of investment in railroads was unique in the history of a number of countries at the peak of the process of railroadization. What was necessary, of course, in the United States and elsewhere, was the building of effectively integrated markets, with lowered transport costs. The railroads were the optimum technique available. Their diffusion was the central factor in economic growth in this trend period and, in certain regions, in the following two trend periods. The issue both has philosophic implications and relates to the inadequacy of neoclassical economic theory as a framework for the analysis of economic development, as Stefano Fenoaltea perceives ("The Discipline and They: Notes on Counterfactual Methodology and the 'New' Economic History," *Journal of European Economic History*, vol. 2, no. 3 [Winter 1973], pp. 729–746). See also Peter D. McClelland, "Railroads, American Growth, and the New Economic History: A Critique," *Journal of Economic History*, vol. 28, no. 1 (March 1968); Paul A. David, "Transport Innovation and Economic Growth," *Economic History Review*, Second Series, vol. 22, no. 3 (December 1969); and Stanley Lebergott, "United States Transport Advance and Externalities," *Journal of Economic History*, vol. 26, no. 4 (December 1966).

54. Albert Fishlow, *American Railroads and the Transformation of the Ante-Bellum Economy* (Cambridge, Mass.: Harvard University Press, 1965). My marginal differences with Fishlow's analysis centering on his interpretation of the 1840's and his failure to take into account the lateral spreading effects of railroadization, are set out in *Stages of Economic Growth*, second edition, pp. 225–229. See also Jan Kmenta and Jeffrey G. Williamson, "Determinants of Investment Behavior: United States Railroads, 1872–1941," *Review of Economics and Statistics*, vol. 48 (1966), pp. 172–181. Kmenta and Williamson note that during the years 1870–1895 railroads accounted for 13 percent of aggregate gross U.S. investment, declining to about 7 percent over the period 1896–1914, 3 percent for 1920–1940. They make an interesting effort to establish the determinants of investment in the industry's stages

of "adolescence," "maturity," and "senility"—stages which fit well the life cycle of a leading sector complex. Presumably, they would regard railroadization in the United States in the period 1840–1860 as part of the industry's vigorous adolescence. On data problems in calculating U.S. railroad investment pre-1860, see E. R. Wicker, "Railroad Investment before the Civil War," a chapter in *Trends in the American Economy in the Nineteenth Century: Studies in Income and Wealth*, vol. 24, Conference on Research in Income and Wealth (Princeton: Princeton University Press for the National Bureau of Economic Research, 1960), pp. 503–545.

55. G. R. Hawke, *Railways and Economic Growth in England and Wales, 1840–1870* (Oxford: Clarendon Press, 1970), especially pp. 187–196 and 401–411. Like Fishlow, Hawke does not take into account what I call the lateral effects of this leading sector.

56. Taking the average annual rate of growth of real product in Great Britain for the period 1831–1841 to 1861–1871 as 2.2 percent (Deane and Cole, *British Economic Growth*, p. 170) the increase over twenty-five years would be 72 percent. If the end-year figure was rendered 10 percent higher than it would otherwise have been by railroad innovation, 24 percent of the expansion can be attributed to this source. The figure is credible. Hawke (*Railways and Economic Growth*, p. 209) cites figures indicating that railway investment averaged 23 percent of gross domestic capital formation in the period 1856–1865. The figure for the 1840's would probably be somewhat higher, certainly in the second half of the decade. The returns on railway investment ran generally higher than the average for the period (Hawke, *Railways and Economic Growth*, pp. 405–408).

57. Hawke, *Railways and Economic Growth*, p. 407.

58. See, notably, ibid., pp. 283–312. By Fishlow's calculations total factor productivity rose much more promptly during the 1840's, when U.S. railroad building was concentrated in the Northeast, linking existing commercial centers and mining resources close to them (as in Pennsylvania), than in the 1850's, when the rail net expanded into the Middle West (A. Fishlow, "Productivity and Technological Change in the Railroad Sector, 1840–1910," *Studies in Output, Employment, and Productivity in the United States after 1800*, vol. 30 [New York: National Bureau of Economic Research, 1966], p. 626).

59. An index of industrial real wages for Germany can be constructed from data in B. R. Mitchell, *European Historical Statistics* (London: Macmillan, 1975), pp. 184–185 (gross weekly wages) and 742–743 (cost of living). The amplitude of fluctuation in the cost-of-living index, however, is so great as to give some improbable results on a year-to-year basis; and its construction changes in 1871. One can, nevertheless, observe certain features common to other real-wage movements in Europe: 62 percent of the money-wage increase between 1845 and 1873 comes in the years 1852–1856 and 1870–1873; the pressure on real wages in 1845–1847 and in the early 1850's is clearly marked; and the average increase in real wages from 1845 to the peak level for both countries in the mid-1870's is approximately the same as between the German data and Jean Lhomme's calculations for France. But over shorter intervening intervals the trend rise in German real wages appears less than that in France.

60. B. R. Mitchell presents scattered industrial money wages for France (Paris and the provinces) and a continuous cost-of-living index from 1840 (*European Historical Statistics*, pp. 184–185 (money wages); pp. 742–743 (cost of living). In Table N-15, these uncertain figures are converted on to a base of 1850 = 100, yielding a real-wage comparison with Lhomme's calculations in Table III-23. The provincial data follow the path of Lhomme's estimates quite closely. The Paris data exhibit a net rise from 1842 to 1880 quite similar to the British and American calculations in Table III-23; and, except for the explicable difference in the early 1870's, are similar to the British estimates throughout.

61. For a comparison of Alvin H. Hansen's real-wage estimates with his own and four others for the years 1860, 1870, 1875, and 1880, see

TABLE N-15. *Real Wages in France, 1842–1880: Three Estimates (1850 = 100)*

	Mitchell: Paris	Mitchell: Provinces	Lhomme
1842	89	—	97
1852	100	—	95
1853	—	85	87
1856	97	—	76
1857	—	89	86
1862	109	—	103
1873	104	105	105
1880	132	116	119

Clarence D. Long, *Wages and Earnings in the United States, 1860–1890* (Princeton: Princeton University Press, 1960), p. 63. These various estimates exhibit quite sharp differences, but all show a decline from 1860 to 1865, a rise to 1870; and all but Wesley Mitchell's, a net increase over the subsequent decade.

62. Jörberg, *History*, vol. 2, pp. 301–308, 349–355.
63. J. P. Lewis, *Building Cycles*, pp. 66–139, for the period 1850–1880 treated in regional terms.

CHAPTER 14. *1873–1920*

64. From the perspective of the food-population balance and the price level in general, the mid-1890's is an appropriate designation for the end of one trend period, the beginning of another. From a trough in 1894, the price of wheat begins its secular rise to the eve of the First World War and beyond—to 1920. More general price indexes are at a trough in 1895–1896 for Britain; 1895 for Germany; 1897 for the United States. From a different perspective, however, the trend period can be viewed as ending only with the coming of the Spanish-American War in 1898 and the Boer War in 1899. Price increases from the troughs of the decade are exceedingly modest until 1898; and many of the Great Depression patterns persist until the last two years of the century, when war and a British coal bottleneck (like that of the early 1870's) produce a general price convulsion.
65. For a useful account of the lively international wheat market in this period see Morton Rothstein, "America in the International Rivalry for the British Wheat Market, 1860–1914," a chapter in Harry N. Scheiber (ed.), *United States Economic History: Selected Readings* (New York: Alfred A. Knopf, 1964), pp. 290–308 (reprinted from *The Mississippi Valley Historical Review*, vol. 47 [December 1960], pp. 401–408). On the complex factors determining profitability in a single wheat-growing region in the United States, see James F. Shepard, "The Development of Wheat Production in the Pacific Northwest," *Agricultural History*, vol 49, no. 1 (January 1975), pp. 258–271.
66. C. P. Kindleberger, "Group Behavior and International Trade," *Journal of Political Economy*, vol. 59, no. 1 (February 1951), p. 37. For a view of post-1873 British agriculture that emphasizes the relatively successful compensatory shift from grain to cattle and dairy products, see T. W. Fletcher, "The Great Depression of English Agriculture, 1873–1896," *Economic History Review*, vol. 13, no. 3 (April 1961).
67. Mulhall, *Dictionary of Statistics*, p. 13. Mulhall (ibid., p. 15) estimates an increase in British meat consumption from 87 pounds per head in 1871–1880 to 98 pounds in 1881–1887.
68. Noel G. Butlin, *Investment in Australian Economic Development, 1861–1900* (Cambridge: At the University Press, 1964), pp. 320–322 and p. 29.
69. For example, see *Economist, Review of 1885*, p. 8, according to which some £ 16.6 million in Australian loans were floated at 3.5 or 4 percent.

70. Quoted by Malenbaum, *World Wheat Economy*, p. 141.
71. See especially A. R. Hall, *The London Capital Market and Australia, 1870–1914* (Canberra: The Australian National University, 1963), facing p. 88 and Appendixes II and IV.
72. See A. G. Ford, *The Gold Standard, 1880–1914, Britain and Argentina* (Oxford: Clarendon Press, 1962). For general economic background and data, see pp. 81–89; for capital import statistics, in the form of annual U.K. issues for Argentina, p. 195. See also John H. Williams, *Argentine International Trade under Inconvertible Paper Money, 1880–1900* (Cambridge, Mass.: Harvard University Press, 1920); and H. S. Ferns, *Britain and Argentina in the Nineteenth Century* (Oxford: Clarendon Press, 1960).
73. See especially Williams, *Argentine International Trade*, pp. 223–226.
74. Malenbaum, *World Wheat Economy*, p. 137.
75. W. T. Easterbrook and Hugh G. J. Aitken, *Canadian Economic History* (Toronto: Macmillan Company of Canada, 1956), p. 483. For the convergence of factors which led to the Canadian wheat boom after 1896, see K. H. Norrie, "The Rate of Settlement of the Canadian Prairies, 1870–1911," *Journal of Economic History*, vol. 35, no. 2 (June 1975), pp. 410–427.
76. Kenneth Buckley, *Capital Formation in Canada, 1896–1930* (Toronto: University of Toronto Press, 1955), pp. 14 and 64.
77. Malenbaum, *World Wheat Economy*, p. 145.
78. Jacob Metzer, "Railroad Development and Market Integration: The Case of Tsarist Russia," *Journal of Economic History*, vol. 34, no. 3 (September 1974), p. 545.
79. Herbert Feis, *Europe: The World's Banker, 1870–1914* (New Haven: Yale University Press, 1930), pp. 210–211. See also Rondo Cameron, *France and the Economic Development of Europe, 1800–1914*, second edition (Chicago: Rand McNally, 1961), pp. 300–301.
80. A. K. Cairncross, "Investment in Canada, 1900–1913," reprinted in A. R. Hall (ed.), *The Export of Capital from Britain, 1870–1914* (London: Methuen and Company, 1968), p. 157, from Cairncross's *Home and Foreign Investment, 1870–1913* (Cambridge: At the University Press, 1953).
81. Roland Wilson, *Capital Imports and the Terms of Trade* (Melbourne: Melbourne University Press in association with Macmillan Company, 1931).
82. See above, pp. 139 and 149.
83. For a fuller exposition of the balance sheet for Britain, see Rostow, *British Economy of the Nineteenth Century*, pp. 26–28.
84. For discussion of the relatively sluggish British performance in steel, see, notably, D. L. Burn, *The Economic History of Steelmaking, 1867–1939* (Cambridge: At the University Press, 1940); Ingvar Svennilson, *Growth and Stagnation in the European Economy* (Geneva: United Nations, 1954), pp. 120–124; David S. Landes, *The Unbound Prometheus* (Cambridge: At the University Press, 1969), pp. 249–269; Peter Temin, "The Relative Decline of the British Steel Industry, 1880–1913," in Henry Rosovsky (ed.), *Industrialization in Two Systems: Essays in Honor of Alexander Gerschenkron* (New York: John Wiley, 1966), pp. 140–155; and Donald N. McCloskey, "International Differences in Productivity—Coal and Steel in America and Britain before World War I," in idem (ed.), *Essays on a Mature Economy: Britain after 1840* (Princeton: Princeton University Press, 1971), pp. 285–304 and discussion, pp. 305–309.
85. Svennilson (*Growth and Stagnation*, p. 123) presents the estimates in Table N-16.
86. Aside from D. L. Burn's price data, in Chart III-33, see also Svennilson, *Growth and Stagnation*, pp. 128–129; Walther G. Hoffmann, *Das Wachstum der Deutschen Wirtschaft seit der Mitte des 19. Jahrhunderts* (Berlin: Springer-Verlag, 1965), p. 607 (col. 7); and William Page (ed.), *Commerce and Industry: Statistical Tables* (London: Constable, 1919), p. 218 (pig iron).
87. E. H. Phelps Brown, with Sheila V. Hopkins, "The Course of Wage-Rates

TABLE N-16. *Rates of Increase in Steel Production in Europe, 1880–1913 (Average Annual Percentage Rates of Increase)*

	United Kingdom	Germany	France	Belgium-Luxembourg
1880–1882 to 1895–1897	5.70	11.50	6.75	9.05
1895–1897 to 1911–1913	3.60	8.50	8.75	9.50
1880–1882 to 1911–1913	4.60	9.95	7.80	9.30

in Five Countries, 1860–1939," *Oxford Economic Papers*, vol. 2, no. 2 (June 1950), especially pp. 238–239; E. H. Phelps Brown, with S. J. Handfield-Jones, "The Climacteric of the 1890's: A Study in the Expanding Economy," *Oxford Economic Papers*, vol. 4, no. 3 (October 1952); E. H. Phelps Brown and B. Weber, "Accumulation, Productivity, and Distribution in the British Economy, 1870–1938," *Economic Journal*, vol. 63, no. 250 (June 1953); Bernard Weber and S. J. Handfield-Jones, "Variations in the Rate of Economic Growth in the U.S.A., 1869–1939," *Oxford Economic Papers*, vol. 6, no. 2 (June 1954). For earlier speculation on retardation in older sectors, compensated (to an unmeasured extent) by rapid growth in sectors incorporating new technology, see Arthur F. Burns, *Production Trends in the United States since 1870* (New York: National Bureau of Economic Research, 1934), especially pp. 276–281. Also G. T. Jones, *Increasing Return* (Cambridge: At the University Press, 1933). Phelps Brown updates his calculations in "Levels and Movements of Industrial Productivity and Real Wages Internationally Compared, 1860–1970," *Economic Journal*, vol. 83, no. 329 (March 1973), pp. 58–71.

88. The sharp decline in French real wages late in the period derives from a particularly rapid increase in cost of living due to poor French harvests. In a chart of product wage rates, Phelps Brown, with Handfield-Jones, "Climacteric of the 1890's," p. 268, shows Belgium sharing the relative stagnation of real wages after 1900. Paul Douglas' classic study of real wages in the United States showed no increase in real full-time earnings between the period 1890–1899 and 1914 (*Real Wages in the United States, 1890–1926* [Boston: Houghton Mifflin Company, 1930], p. 582). In effect, Douglas concluded that rising real hourly wages were taken in the form of shorter work hours. Mainly on the basis of revised cost-of-living indexes this conclusion is challenged by Albert Rees, assisted by Donald P. Jacobs, in *Real Wages in Manufacturing, 1890–1914* (Princeton: Princeton University Press, 1961), especially pp. 120–127. Rees concludes that up to 77 percent of the increase in real hourly earnings was taken in the form of increased consumption of goods and services. Combining Long's conclusions (*Wages and Earnings*) and Rees', a marked retardation if not stagnation of real earnings nevertheless emerges in the first decade of the new century. The rate of increase of real earnings (yearly) was 1.65 percent per annum in the depressed 1870's; 3.25 percent in the 1880's; 1.23 percent (daily) for the 1890's, much affected by the severe depression; and 1.09 percent from 1900 to 1910, years of generally low unemployment.

89. See, for example, Lennart Jörberg, *Growth and Fluctuations of Swedish Industry, 1868–1912* (Stockholm: Almqvist and Wicksell, 1961).

90. The trend rate of growth of Japanese GNP apparently rises from a trough in 1902 to a peak in 1916. See Kazushi Ohkawa and Henry Rosovsky, Chapter 1, in Lawrence Klein and Kazushi Ohkawa (eds.), *Economic Growth: The Japanese Experience since the Meiji Era* (Homewood, Ill.: Richard D. Irwin, 1968), p. 8. On the diversification of Japanese industry in this period, based as in Sweden on the absorption of more sophisticated technologies, see Yuichi Shionoya, Chapter 3, ibid., especially pp. 74–77. On the sharp rise of real consumption expenditure per capita, after a brief setback during the period 1904–1908 (embracing the Russo-Japanese War), see Simon Kuznets, Chapter 7,

ibid., especially p. 198. In Ohkawa and Rosovsky's *Japanese Economic Growth* (Palo Alto: Stanford University Press, 1973), p. 25, they date the period of accelerated growth from a trough in 1901 to a peak in 1917.

91. Jan Marczewski, "Some Aspects of the Economic Growth of France, 1660–1958," *Economic Development and Cultural Change*, vol. 9, no. 3 (April 1961), especially pp. 382 and 386, as well as Tables 5, 7, and 9; Francois Crouzet, "Essai de construction d'un indice annuel de la production industrielle française au XIXe siècle," *Annales, Economies, Sociétés, Civilisations*, no. 1 (January–February 1970), especially pp. 71–73, 78–81, and Tables 6, 10b, 11a, and 11b in the statistical annex.

92. Burns, *Production Trends*, especially Chapter 5. For retardation in productivity after 1899 see John W. Kendrick, *Productivity Trends in the United States* (Princeton: Princeton University Press, 1961), Chapter 3, especially the five-year-moving-average chart of total factor productivity, p. 67.

93. Solomon Fabricant, with the assistance of Julius Shiskin, *The Output of Manufacturing Industries, 1899–1937* (New York: National Bureau of Economic Research, 1940). William Howard Shaw's *Value of Commodity Output since 1869* (New York: National Bureau of Economic Research, 1947) also supplies highly disaggregated data permitting isolation of rapidly growing new sectors.

94. Fabricant, with Shiskin, *Output*, p. 296.

95. Ibid., p. 102.

96. R. Wagenführ, "Die Industriewirtschaft Entwicklungstendenzen der deutschen und internationalen Industrieproduktion 1860–1932," Sonderheft 31, *Vierteljahreschrifte zur Konjunkturforschung* (Berlin, 1933), p. 18; Hoffmann, *Das Wachstum*, pp. 451–452. The two indexes oi industrial production move by decades as shown in Table N-17

TABLE N-17. *Wagenführ and Hoffmann Indexes of Industrial Production, by Decades (1913 = 100)*

	Wagenführ	Annual Average Growth Rate (%)	Hoffmann	Annual Average Growth Rate (%)
1860	14.1		12.7	
1870	17.4	2.1	18.8	4.0
1880	24.8	3.6	26.1	3.3
1890	40.5	5.0	38.9	4.1
1900	64.5	4.5	61.4	4.7
1910	88.4	3.2	85.5	3.4

97. Hoffmann, *Das Wachstum*, pp. 392–393.

98. Ibid., pp. 361–362.

99. See, for example, Landes, *The Unbound Prometheus*, especially pp. 287–290.

100. Hoffmann, *Das Wachstum*, p. 388.

101. Ibid., p. 358.

102. Phelps Brown, with Handfield-Jones, "The Climacteric of the 1890's," p. 283.

103. In sulphuric acid, for example, the British loss of leadership is suggested by Table N-18.

104. Penelope Hartland, "Canadian Balance of Payments since 1868," in *Trends in the American Economy in the Nineteenth Century: Studies in Income and Wealth*, vol. 24, Conference on Research in Income and Wealth (Princeton: Princeton University Press for the National Bureau of Economic Research, 1960), pp. 719–721, footnote 5.

105. O. J. Firestone, *Canada's Economic Development, 1867–1953*, Income and Wealth Series VII (London: Bowes and Bowes, 1958), pp. 100–101.

TABLE N-18. *World Production of Sulphuric Acid, 1867–1913 (Thousands of Tons of 100 Percent Acid)*

Country	1867	1878	1900	1913
United Kingdom	155	600	1,000	1,082
Germany	75	112	950	1,686
France	125	200	500	900
Italy	—	—	200	600
Belgium	20	30	165	420
United States	40	180	940	2,250
Rest of world	(85)	(165)	(475)	(1,362)
Total world	(500)	(1,300)	(4,200)	(8,300)

Source: Svennilson, *Growth and Stagnation*, p. 286.
Note: Svennilson says figures in parentheses are tentative, less reliable than other figures in the table.

In current dollars the proportion (averaging the years 1870, 1890, and 1900) was 12.6 percent; in constant dollars, 13.6 percent.

106. Hartland, "Canadian Balance of Payments," pp. 717–719.
107. Buckley, *Capital Formation in Canada*, pp. 45–47.
108. Arthur I. Bloomfield, *Patterns of Fluctuation in International Investment before 1914*, Princeton Studies in International Finance, no. 21 (Princeton, 1968), p. 25.
109. Brinley Thomas, *Migration and Economic Growth* (Cambridge: At the University Press, 1954), especially pp. 56–63, 67–70, 113–116, 202–204.
110. Butlin, *Investment in Australian Economic Development*. Butlin states his general thesis, which pervades his study, as follows: "Britain had an important role in sustaining general expansion. But, specifically, the critical decisions in capital formation and in the orientation of the economy were taken in Australia, by Australians and in the light of Australian criteria" (p. 5).
111. The boom in New Zealand capital formation and immigration started earlier than that of Australia in the 1870's and peaked (for migration) as early as 1874, capital imports in 1882. See especially J. A. Dowie, "Inverse Relations of the Australian and New Zealand Economies, 1871–1900," *Australian Economic Papers*, vol. 2, no. 2 (December 1963), pp. 151–179. Also, on New Zealand, C. G. F. Simkin, *The Instability of a Dependent Economy* (Oxford: Clarendon Press, 1951), especially pp. 40–52.
112. Thomas, *Migration and Economic Growth*, pp. 113–114.
113. Australia was among the more respectable and secure borrowers from the London capital market. It was able to float its issues at low rates in the 1870's, at a time when British lenders were smarting from their disappointments in the wake of the crisis of 1873. See, for example, Rostow, *British Economy of the Nineteenth Century*, pp. 191–201. See also Butlin, *Investment in Australian Economic Development*, pp. 334–336. The attraction of Argentina in the period 1888–1890 may well help account for the Australian peak as early as 1885 in capital imports and 1888 in immigration. In the wake of the Baring Crisis, Australia came back strongly into the London market as a borrower in 1891.
114. The linkage of these variables now constitutes a large literature on so-called Kuznets long cycles. These are analytically quite different from the long cycles analyzed by Simon S. Kuznets in his *Secular Movements in Production and Prices* (Boston and New York: Houghton Mifflin Company, 1930). For a discussion of this distinction and long cycles in general, see Rostow, "Kondratieff, Schumpeter, and Kuznets: Trend Periods Revisited," pp. 719–730. Some of the key initial insights were developed by: Walter Isard, "A Neglected Cycle: The Transport-Building Cycle," *Review of Economic Statistics* (November 1942);

Norman J. Silberling, *The Dynamics of Business* (New York and London, McGraw-Hill, 1943), especially pp. 175–238; Cairncross, *Home and Foreign Investment*, especially pp. 187–221; Thomas, *Migration and Economic Growth*, especially pp. 102–113; Kuznets, "Long Swings in the Growth of Population and in Related Economic Variables," pp. 25–52. The subsequent work in this field is well listed in the bibliography of Easterlin's *Population, Labor Force, and Long Swings*, pp. 275–287.

115. Kuznets, "Long Swings in the Growth of Population and in Related Economic Variables," especially pp. 33–34.
116. Robert E. Gallman and Edward S. Howle, "Trends in the Structure of the American Economy since 1840," Chapter 3 in Fogel and Engerman (eds.), *Reinterpretation*, p. 26.
117. Stanley Lebergott, *Manpower in Economic Growth: The American Record since 1800* (New York: McGraw-Hill, 1964), p. 510.
118. See, notably, J. P. Lewis, *Building Cycles*, pp. 184–210, for the forces at work on British housing construction between 1870 and 1913.
119. For a discussion of these proportions, see especially Deane and Cole, *British Economic Growth*, pp. 266–267. The range over which the investment rate fluctuated during business cycles varied a good deal: there was a marked decline from the peak in 1873 (14.2 percent) to the severely depressed year, 1879 (9.7 percent). There was also a considerable decline from the peak in 1890 (12.6 percent) to the 1894 trough (9.3 percent). On the other hand, there was no decline from 1883 (10.4 percent) to the trough in 1886 (10.8 percent); nor from 1900 (11.3 percent) to 1904 (11.2 percent). There were significant and well-established increases in unemployment during these latter recessions: from 2.1 percent to 6.9 percent and from 2.5 percent to 6.0 percent, respectively. The insensitivity of the capital formation proportion could result from the exclusion of stocks (and, therefore, inventory fluctuations) or from other flaws in the data.
120. The best recent calculations are those presented in Deane and Cole, *British Economic Growth*, pp. 299–303, and in the estimates of C. H. Feinstein, *National Income, Expenditure and Output of the United Kingdom, 1855–1965* (Cambridge: At the University Press, 1972), pp. T4–T5. Contemporary views and the conclusions of A. L. Bowley are presented in Rostow, *British Economy of the Nineteenth Century*, pp. 103–107. In his *Wages and Income in the U.K. since 1860* (Cambridge: At the University Press, 1937), p. 92, Bowley calculated the shift from 1880 to 1913 as follows:

	Property (%)	Labor (%)
1880	37.5	62.5
1900	35–36	64–65
1913	37.5	62.5

121. London *Economist, Review of 1903*, p. 5. Giffen estimated the war's cost at £ 220 million, the annual "surplus income" at about £ 240 million.
122. For military outlays, see Mitchell, with Deane, *Abstract*, p. 398; for capital formation, p. 374; for net national income at current prices, p. 367.
123. For military outlays, see *Historical Statistics of the United States*, 1960 ed., p. 718; for gross capital formation and gross national product, p. 143.
124. For German military expenditures, see Supan Andic and Jindrich Veverka, "The Growth of Government Expenditure in Germany since the Unification," *Finanzarchiv*, vol. 23, no. 2 (January 1964), p. 269.
125. Mitchell, *European Historical Statistics*, pp. 398 and 368.
126. Burn, *Economic History of Steelmaking*, pp. 385–402.
127. See A. C. Pigou, *Aspects of British Economic History, 1918–1925* (London: Macmillan, 1947), pp. 95–106, for wartime developments and postwar vicissitudes in Britain's cotton textile export markets.
128. James J. Flink, *America Adopts the Automobile, 1895–1910* (Cambridge, Mass.: M. I. T. Press, 1970), pp. 275–278. On the transition of the automobile to a mass phenomenon, see also John B. Rae, *The Road*

and the Car in American Life (Cambridge, Mass.: M. I. T. Press, 1971), especially pp. 40–73.

129. Svennilson, *Growth and Stagnation*, pp. 21–22.
130. George Maxey and Aubrey Silverston, *The Motor Industry* (London: George Allen and Unwin, 1959), p. 13.
131. Firestone, *Canada's Economic Development*, p. 211.
132. Buckley, *Capital Formation in Canada*, pp. 64–67. Buckley estimates capital inflows as $1,515 million for 1911–1915, $262 million for 1916–1920.
133. Ibid., p. 63.
134. For the parallel dating (with different vocabularies) of Japanese growth by Ohkawa-Rosovsky and Rostow, see W. W. Rostow, *Politics and the Stages of Growth* (Cambridge: At the University Press, 1971), pp. 378–379, footnote 31.
135. Ohkawa and Rosovsky, *Japanese Economic Growth*, p. 191.
136. Ibid., p. 185.
137. Imre Ferenczi (ed.), *International Migrations* (New York: National Bureau of Economic Research, 1929), vol. 1, p. 231.
138. Svennilson, *Growth and Stagnation*, p. 63.
139. Ibid.
140. Buckley, *Capital Formation in Canada*, p. 141.
141. Ibid., p. 41.
142. Mitchell, *European Historical Statistics*, p. 239.
143. Feinstein, *National Income, Expenditure and Output*, p. T108.
144. Clarence D. Long, *Building Cycles and the Theory of Investment* (Princeton: Princeton University Press, 1940), pp. 209–211.

CHAPTER 15. *1920–1936*

145. C. P. Kindleberger summarizes usefully the forces at work on each of the major commodities over this period and their significance in *The World in Depression, 1929–1939* (Berkeley and Los Angeles: University of California Press, 1973), Chapter 4, pp. 83–107. For a detailed analysis of wheat production and prices over this period, see especially W. Malenbaum, *World Wheat Economy*, pp. 154–191. Malenbaum traces out not only the role of increasing carry-over stocks in depressing wheat prices but also the efforts of governments to shield their economies from the impact of falling prices by protectionist policies.
146. Mitchell, with Deane, *Abstract*, p. 332.
147. *Historical Statistics of the United States*, 1960 ed., p. 283.
148. See, notably, Svennilson, *Growth and Stagnation*, pp. 82–101, for a survey of interwar European agriculture.
149. Ibid., p. 90.
150. Automobile Manufacturers Association, *Automobile Facts and Figures* (New York, 1939), p. 39. For only slightly lower proportions for 1958 and contemporary scale of plastics consumption in automobiles, see *Automobile Facts and Figures* (Detroit, 1959), p. 60. See also John B. Rae's assessment of the scale of the automobile sectoral complex (*The Road and the Car*, pp. 45–49) and Appendix C in the present volume.
151. See, for example, R. S. Sayers, "The Springs of Technical Progress in Britain, 1919–1939," *Economic Journal*, vol. 60, no. 238 (June 1950). Writing of the 1920's in Britain, A. J. Youngson (*The British Economy, 1920–1957* [Cambridge, Mass.: Harvard University Press, 1960], p. 47) describes the backward linkages of the automobile industry as follows: "This scale of production, like the rate of growth, was far slower than in the United States. But the contribution which the car industry made to economic development was very substantial. The industry demanded not only such things as high speed machine tools, ferrous alloys, glass, magnetos and rubber tyres, but also roads and petrol. No very reliable computation can be made of the amounts spent on roads, bypasses and bridges in the 'twenties, but certainly

a lot was done; the Watford bypass, the Edinburgh-Glasgow motor road, and the two great bridges on A.1 over the Tyne at Newcastle and the Tweed at Berwick were all built at that time. Oil—'this most speculative of industries'—was a big new field of investment, with world consumption increasing, it was estimated, by about 10 per cent per annum. Petroleum refining employed fewer than 6,000 people in 1930, but the capital investment was very heavy and net output per head—£ 1,016—was higher in this industry than in any other in Britain."

152. Harold G. Vatter has challenged the notion of a consumers' durables revolution in the twentieth century ("Has There Been a Twentieth-Century Consumers Durables Revolution?" *Journal of Economic History*, vol. 27, no. 1 [March 1967], pp. 1–16). Using highly aggregated data, he asserts (p. 15): "There has been no significant secular rise in the importance of real expenditures on durables relative to total consumption expenditures or to disposable income." He does allow, however, for two striking facts: First, the proportion of outlays on consumers' durables rose relative to outlays on housing ("The net stock of consumers durables increased much faster than total wealth, all nonbusiness private wealth, and all business wealth, in the half century between 1900 and 1949. In regard to this phenomenon . . . it may be possible to speak of a consumers durables revolution" (p. 15). Second, at a time when consumers' outlays on services (or "intangibles") were relatively on the rise, durable tangible goods (by his measurement) remained an "approximately constant proportion of total consumer outlays," thus increasing their role vis à vis semi-durable and perishable consumers' products.

Vatter makes no reference to the useful disaggregated data bearing on this matter mobilized in Shaw's *Value of Commodity Output since 1869*. Shaw concluded, in general: "Differences in rates of growth among the commodity groups are reflected by appreciable changes in the composition of total finished commodities. Especially striking was the increase in the share of consumer durable commodities. From an average of some 10 percent during the early decades it reached an average of almost 20 percent during the recent [decades]. . . . The extraordinary increase in durable commodities can be credited largely to the automotive and electrical industries" (p. 28).

Table N-19 indicates how and when the role of durables changed among the commodities purchased by American consumers.

After fluctuating in the range of 10.5–12.8 percent from 1869 to 1909, consumers' durables as a proportion of total consumers' commodities rose to 19 percent in 1919 and to almost 25 percent in 1929. Over the critical years of the consumers' durable revolution (1909–1929) the total real value of consumers' commodities increased at an average annual rate of 4.0 percent; consumers' durables at 7.7 percent;

TABLE N-19. *Value of Finished Commodities Destined for Domestic Consumption (1913 Prices in Billions of Dollars)*

	Finished Consumers' Commodities						
	Total	Perishables	Semidurables	Consumers' Durables, of Which:			
				Total	Motor Vehicles	Motor Vehicle Accessories	Electrical Househol Supplies and Radio
1869	1.72	1.1	0.4	0.220	—	—	—
1879	3.47	2.3	0.8	0.365	—	—	—
1889	5.11	3.3	1.2	0.609	—	—	—
1899	7.71	5.1	1.7	0.905	0.003	—	—
1909	10.94	7.1	2.5	1.34	0.109	0.015	—
1919	14.87	8.8	3.2	2.87	1.33	0.292	0.045
1929	24.13	12.5	5.7	5.93	3.40	0.542	0.307
1939	24.11	14.5	4.2	5.41	3.50 (1937)	0.938 (1939)	0.314

Source: Shaw, *Value of Commodity Output since 1869*, pp. 70–75.

TABLE N-20. *Value of Finished Commodities Destined for Domestic Consumption (Current Prices in Billions of Dollars)*

	Total Consumers' Durables	Electrical Household Appliances and Supplies	% of Total Durables	Radios	% of Total Durables
1919	4.076	0.065	1.6	0.014	0.3
1929	6.312	0.177	2.8	0.366	5.8
1937	5.742	0.333	5.8	0.218	3.8

Source: Shaw, *Value of Commodity Output since 1869*, p. 68.

motor vehicles at 18.8 percent; electrical household appliances and radios at 14.1 percent.

Electrical household supplies and radios only emerge, in Shaw's data, from 1919 (Table N-20). In current values, excepting motor vehicles and accessories, they are the only two types of durable consumers' goods exhibiting rapid growth in value over this period among Shaw's sixteen categories. Some exhibited modest rates of growth between 1919 and 1937: nonelectrical household appliances, house furnishings, china and household utensils, books, pleasure craft. Some declined: musical instruments, jewelry, silverware, clocks and watches, luggage, motorcycles and bicycles, monuments and tombstones.

The critical point to be made, in terms of leading sector analysis, is that the motor vehicle, electrical appliances, and the radio were linked to new industrial technologies. The other categories included some commodities also subject to technical change, but in no case as rapid or with such powerful spreading effects in the economy.

It should also be noted that among the spreading effects from the internal combustion engine and electricity were a good many rapidly growing activities which emerged under the category of services rather than commodity production, e.g., roadside restaurants, the moving picture industry, radio stations.

The changed character of the commodities involved in the durable consumers' goods revolution is suggested by Table N-21, showing cyclical behavior before and after World War I.

With respect to prices, it should be noted that the new (postwar) consumers' durables rose much less in business expansions than the old (pre-war) (3.2 versus 26.2). This undoubtedly reflected the rapid productivity increase in these leading sector industries. No similar distinction emerges for perishables or semidurable consumers' goods. In contractions, prices fell somewhat less (8.9 versus 9.6), despite the fact that the acute depression of 1929–1933 is included. This anomaly, present also in producers' durables, may reflect the more oligopolistic nature of the new consumers' durables industries.

With respect to output (value in 1913 prices), there is strikingly greater amplitude in both expansions (21.2 versus 51.9) and contractions (5.2 versus 41.1). Post–World War I consumers' durables, in fact, behave much like producers' durables. Clearly, Vatter's treatment of the older and newer consumers' durables as a single analytic category is not satisfactory.

153. For a measure of increased agricultural productivity in Europe between 1909–1913 and 1934–1938, by countries, see Svennilson, *Growth and Stagnation*, p. 97.

154. As Svennilson points out, there were important technological changes during the interwar years in two older industries: ship construction and cement manufacture, where the large rotary kiln took over (ibid., pp. 152–160).

155. In a footnote commenting on this hypothesis, C. P. Kindleberger observes: ". . . it is not self-evident that durable [consumers'] goods behave differently from investment in plant, equipment or inventories in producing the upturn" (*World in Depression*, p. 194). As I see it, the difference is the following: Investment outlays are determined by the

TABLE N-21. *Value of Finished Commodities and Price Indexes (Major Commodity Groups, Producers' Current and 1913 Prices; Averages of Specific Cycle Relatives for Cycles before and after World War I)*[a]

	Pre-war Cycles Average				Postwar Cycles Average			
	No.	Rise	Fall	Total Swing	No.	Rise	Fall	Total Swing
Value in producers' current prices								
Consumer perishable	5	26.7	6.6	33.3	3	25.5	19.9	45.4
Consumer semidurable	4	29.7	6.2	35.9	5	17.5	18.7	36.2
Consumer durable	3	50.3	11.1	61.4	4	44.0	39.8	83.8
Producer durable	5	42.3	21.5	63.8	4	51.9	42.2	94.1
All finished commodities	4	33.3	10.0	43.3	4	27.1	23.2	50.3
Price indexes								
Consumer perishable	6	8.4	4.8	13.2	4	10.2	16.8	27.0
Consumer semidurable	4	8.6	5.1	13.7	3	15.1	22.8	37.9
Consumer durable	2	26.2	9.6	35.8	3	3.2	8.9	12.1
Producer durable	3	12.7	3.3	16.0	3	2.8	12.3	15.1
All finished commodities	6	6.9	3.8	10.7	3	6.4	12.5	18.9
Value in producers' 1913 prices								
Consumer perishable	5	21.7	4.4	26.1	2	20.4	6.8	27.2
Consumer semidurable	6	15.4	2.4	17.8	4	21.8	14.6	36.4
Consumer durable	6	21.2	5.2	26.4	4	51.9	41.1	93.0
Producer durable	5	39.9	20.4	60.3	4	54.5	39.7	94.2
All finished commodities	3	32.0	6.6	38.6	4	24.4	14.4	38.8

[a] The war year cycles are excluded from the averages.
Source: Shaw, *Value of Commodity Output since 1869*, p. 23.

expected rate of return over costs. That rate of return is automatically raised by certain cost-reducing depression phenomena: e.g., a fall in raw-material costs, interest rates, and, possibly, money wages. If the rate of return is geared to long-run expectations about the profitability of, say, opening up new areas, cost reduction during a depression could set in motion an increase in investment, raising income via the multiplier. In the stage of high mass-consumption, investment becomes more dependent on the accelerator, that is, on the rate of increase of income itself. This is so because the leading sectors are geared to the diffusion of the automobile, the suburban house, and durable consumers' goods. Behind them lie large capital goods industries from which they draw support and service sectors which depend on their momentum. An expansion in investment thus requires a prior increase in consumers' demand and expectations among consumers sufficiently sanguine to increase purchases of such postponable goods.

156. Firestone, *Canada's Economic Development*, p. 74.
157. Noel G. Butlin, *Australian Domestic Product, Investment, and Foreign Borrowing, 1861–1938/9* (Cambridge: At the University Press, 1962), pp. 18–19.
158. Carlos F. Díaz Alejandro, *Essays on the Economic History of the Argentine Republic* (New Haven: Yale University Press, 1970), pp. 43 and 52.
159. Ibid., p. 70.
160. Ibid.
161. J. P. Lewis (*Building Cycles*, pp. 224–233) summarizes the story of British interwar housing and housing policy. For a detailed analysis, see Marian Bowley, *Housing and the State, 1919–1944* (London: Allen and Unwin, 1944).
162. Mitchell, with Deane, *Abstract*, p. 418.
163. Brinley Thomas (*Migration and Economic Growth*, p. 177) would date the beginning of inverse building movements as far back as 1847; but the role of the Crimean War in the 1850's and the American Civil War in the 1860's makes the notion of inverse movement somewhat forced before 1865.

164. Feinstein, *National Income, Expenditure and Output*, p. T108.
165. W. Arthur Lewis quotes estimates that show long-term international capital movements of $1.97 billion for 1928 (*Economic Survey, 1919–1939* [London: Allen and Unwin, 1949], p. 49). Of this sum, 51 percent went to Germany; 10 percent to Australia; 9 percent to Argentina; 8 percent to Canada; 6 percent to Poland. A high proportion of the lending outside Germany was also for nonagricultural purposes in the 1920's. For the whole period 1924–1929, Kindleberger quotes estimates for U.S. and British foreign lending by destination (*World in Depression*, p. 56). Capital flows from these two countries probably accounted for 85 percent of the world total at this time, with the United States accounting for about twice the level of the United Kingdom. The average annual total for the six years was $1.62 billion, of which 38 percent went to Europe; 22 percent to Latin America; 21 percent to Asia and Oceania; 15 percent to Canada; 4 percent to Africa.
166. Kindleberger, *World in Depression*.

CHAPTER 16. *1936–1951*

167. Mitchell, with Deane, *Abstract*, p. 332. It should be noted that the recession of 1938 yielded a sharp, temporary improvement in the British terms of trade.
168. The period 1951–1955 was an interval of retardation in Japanese investment and growth. Manufacturing and mining, for example, increased at 29.3 percent per annum from 1946 to 1951, 11.2 percent from 1951 to 1955. For a discussion of this interval, see, notably, Myohei Shinohara, "Patterns and Some Structural Changes in Japan's Postwar Industrial Growth," Chapter 9 in Klein and Ohkawa (eds.), *Economic Growth*, pp. 278–283.
169. Feinstein, *National Income, Expenditure and Output*, p. T97. These calculations are at 1958 replacement cost for gross reproducible capital stock. See also M. M. Postan, *An Economic History of Western Europe, 1945–1964* (London: Methuen, 1967), p. 23: "As a result of the war, the United Kingdom, the U.S.S.R., the U.S.A., and Germany acquired new technologies, leadership and cadres in a number of industries with great potentialities for future growth.

    "More significant, though less understood, are the great additions which both the United Kingdom and Germany made to their productive capital during the years of rearmament and war. In conventional discussions of war economies the tragic years of 1939–45 are commonly referred to as years of 'disinvestment': a period when nations allowed their productive capital to run down. In actual fact, these were years of steadily growing capacity. In Britain government investment in fixed capital of industries serving the production of munitions probably approached £ 1,030 millions between 1936 and 1945, some 80 percent of which was invested after 1938. In addition, at least £ 500 and possibly as much as £ 800 million may have been invested by private firms into munitions factories, and both by the Government and private firms into equipment serving civilian as well as military needs. The combined net investment—probably in excess of £ 1,500 millions—was more than the nation had added to the capital of its industries and utilities in comparable periods before 1935.

    "The accretions were even greater and more remarkable in Germany."

    Tables N-22 and N-23 roughly measure the increase in industrial capacity brought about in certain European countries during the war years.
170. Svennilson, *Growth and Stagnation*, p. 304.
171. See ibid., pp. 242 (housing construction), 253 (coal), 262–263 (steel), 278–279 (motor vehicle registrations).
172. Economic Commission for Europe, *Economic Survey*, pp. 239–242.
173. Ibid., p. 248.
174. Ibid., pp. 243 and 269.

TABLE N-22. *Motive Power Installed in Industry (End of Year)*

Country	Thousand H.P. 1938	1945
Denmark[a]	555	712
Finland[b]	1,110	1,198
Hungary	991	—
Netherlands[c]	782	—
Norway[d] (A)	1,095	1,248
(B)	2,159	2,367
Sweden	2,782	3,785
Switzerland[e]	917	1,362

[a] Pre-war: 1939.
[b] Changing territory.
[c] All industries are not included.
[d] (A) excluding and (B) including plant for smelting, electrolysis, etc.
[e] Electric motors in 1937 and 1944. In 1949, the capacity was 1,797 thousand H.P.
Source: Economic Commission for Europe, *Economic Survey of Europe since the War* (Geneva: United Nations, 1953), p. 2.

TABLE N-23. *Machine-Tool Inventory (Thousand Units)*

	1938	1940	1945
Germany			
Metal-cutting	900	1,178	1,737–1,233[a]
Metal-cutting and metal-forming	1,281	1,577	2,316–1,776[a]
All metal-working	1,614	—	2,594–2,143[a]
United Kingdom			
Metal-cutting and metal-forming	—	700	800
France			
All metal-working	550	—	600
Italy			
All metal-working	207[b]	—	290
USSR			
Metal-cutting	—	423	500
All metal-working	—	710	—
United States			
Metal-cutting	—	942	1,883

[a] Maximum and minimum estimates respectively.
[b] 1939.
Source: Economic Commission for Europe, *Economic Survey*, p. 3.

175. Ibid., pp. 274–275.
176. Díaz Alejandro, *Essays*, pp. 463 and 477. These calculations are for merchandise exports and imports at 1950 prices.
177. Svennilson, *Growth and Stagnation*, pp. 176–177. In 1938 61 percent of Europe's exports went to European countries; 50 percent of its imports were of European origin. In 1950 the figures were 53 percent and 46 percent, respectively.
178. Economic Commission for Europe, *Economic Survey*, pp. 39 and 42–43. Abram Bergson calculated the gross national product of the Soviet Union in 1950 at about 24 percent higher than in 1940 (*The Real National Income of Soviet Russia since 1928* [Santa Monica, Calif.: RAND, October 1961], p. 227). By that time Bergson estimated that it was moving ahead at 7.6 percent per annum (p. 228).
179. Janet G. Chapman, *Real Wages in Soviet Russia since 1928* (Santa

Monica, Calif.: RAND, October 1963), p. 166. It should be noted that by Chapman's computations there was a decline of perhaps 10 percent in Soviet real wages between 1937 and 1940.

180. The average decline in exports to Europe for Czechoslovakia, Hungary, Poland, Rumania, and Bulgaria between 1938 and 1950 was from 86 percent to 54 percent; for imports, from 80 percent to 49 percent (Svennilson, *Growth and Stagnation*, pp. 171 and 173).
181. Economic Commission for Asia and the Far East, *Economic Survey of Asia and the Far East, 1953* (Bangkok: United Nations, 1954), p. 118.
182. Economic Commission for Europe, *The European Housing Problem: A Preliminary Review* (Geneva: United Nations, October 1949), Appendix I, Table 19, Sheet 1.
183. Ibid., Sheet 2.
184. Economic Commission for Europe, *Economic Survey*, p. 5.
185. B. R. Mitchell and H. G. Jones, *Second Abstract of British Historical Statistics* (Cambridge: At the University Press, 1971), pp. 117–118.
186. J. P. Lewis, *Building Cycles*, p. 238.
187. For a discussion of the technological backwardness of the French construction industry down to the 1950's, see C. P. Kindleberger, *Economic Growth in France and Britain, 1851–1950* (Cambridge, Mass.: Harvard University Press, 1964), pp. 302–309.
188. Brinley Thomas (ed.), *Economics of International Migration* (London: Macmillan and Company, 1958), p. 73.
189. Ibid., p. 201.
190. Ibid., p. 216.
191. *Historical Statistics of the United States*, 1960 ed., p. 56. The rate of net alien immigration per 1,000 in the total U.S. population was as follows for these intervals: 1925–1930, 1.84; 1931–1945, 0.10; 1946–1950, 1.01 (Easterlin, *Population, Labor Force, and Long Swings*, pp. 208–209).
192. Easterlin, *Population, Labor Force, and Long Swings*, pp. 154–157 and 70.
193. *Historical Statistics of the United States*, 1960 ed., p. 393.

CHAPTER 17. *1951–1972*

194. Food and Agriculture Organization, "International Agricultural Adjustment," Secretariat paper C 73/15, August 1973, prepared for the Seventeenth Session of the FAO, Rome, 10–29 November 1973, p. 17.
195. A useful summary of the background to the energy crisis is the following passage from *Exploring Energy Choices*, A Preliminary Report of the Ford Foundation's Energy Policy Project (Washington, D.C.: The Ford Foundation, 1974), pp. 8–9:

    "The roots of the current crisis lie in the gap between consumption and domestic production of energy, which began to increase in the early 1960s and continued until shortages appeared and forced emergency curtailments of energy use. Consumption grew virtually unchecked while domestic production of fuels has actually been stable since 1970. A major reason that energy consumption has grown so rapidly is that until a year ago it was a bargain compared to most other items. The price of energy, relative to the prices of other goods and services, actually declined during the 1960s. But there were other reasons on the consumption side:

    "(a) Rate structures for natural gas and electricity promoted more consumption by offering large-volume users a significantly lower price per Btu than small users.

    "(b) Promotional advertising encouraged the use of energy-consuming goods such as autos, air conditioners, home appliances, electric heating systems, color televisions, and petrochemical products (such as plastics, which require large amounts of energy in their manufacture).

    "(c) Construction of the interstate highway system with the billions of dollars from the Highway Trust Fund brought a rapid increase in intercity, high-speed auto travel.

"(d) Subsidies to truck and air transportation encouraged a shift in freight away from rail transport. Public expenditures for road and airport construction plus military development of aircraft later used for freight and passenger travel were among these subsidies.

"(e) Passenger air fares dropped in comparison with bus and rail fares, and stimulated air traffic. While air fares increased 8 percent between 1950 and 1970, bus and rail fares increased 90 percent and 47 percent respectively.

"(f) Investment tax incentives and steadily rising wage rates encouraged industry to expand with energy-intensive capital equipment.

"(g) The growth in suburbia, encouraged by federal income tax breaks and federally guaranteed loans for homeowners, has resulted in the soaring use of gasoline for commuting and other energy for the single-family homes that were built.

"At the same time, federal government policies worked to curb growth in production of energy:

"(a) The foreign tax credit, which permits oil companies to subtract the payments to host governments from their U.S. income taxes, became a greater incentive to oil production abroad—rather than at home—during the 1950s and 1960s. Ironically, while the import quota system was trying to boost domestic oil production, the foreign tax credit was effectively stimulating oil production abroad by U.S. oil companies.

"(b) FPC regulation of natural gas prices and reductions in the oil and gas depletion allowances in 1969 from 27½ percent to 22 percent were also viewed by industry and others as a deterrent to development.

"(c) Price controls imposed in 1971 on fuels (as well as on other goods and services) distorted normal marketplace actions to balance supply and demand.

"(d) Offshore oil and gas lease sales were virtually halted after 1969 for a year and a half.

"(e) Implementation of the Coal Mine Health and Safety Act of 1969 resulted in lower productivity in underground coal mines.

"(f) The National Environmental Policy Act of 1969, requiring detailed environmental impact assessments of major federal projects, caused delays in the Trans-Alaska Pipeline, offshore lease sales, and nuclear power plants, while government agencies learned to comply adequately with its requirements.

"(g) The Clean Air Act of 1970 caused industrial and power plant operators to turn away from coal to natural gas and oil to meet the sulfur oxide standards as well as automobile manufacturers to build cars with reduced fuel economy to meet emission requirements."

196. See, notably, Fred M. Howell and H. A. Merklein, "Joint Association Survey Aids in U.S. Hydrocarbon Finding Cost Study," *World Oil*, vol. 175 (July–December 1972), pp. 91–101.

197. See, notably, Economic Commission for Europe, *Some Factors in Economic Growth in Europe during the 1950's* (Geneva: United Nations. 1964); Angus Maddison, *Economic Growth in the West* (New York: Twentieth Century Fund, 1964); C. P. Kindleberger, *Europe's Postwar Growth: The Role of Labor Supply* (Cambridge, Mass.: Harvard University Press, 1967); Postan, *Economic History*; A. J. Youngson, *The British Economy, 1920–1965* (Cambridge, Mass.: Harvard University Press, 1968); Edward F. Denison, *Why Growth Rates Differ* (Washington, D.C.: Brookings Institution, 1967); Ohkawa and Rosovsky, *Japanese Economic Growth*; Edward F. Denison, *Accounting for United States Economic Growth, 1929–1969* (Washington, D.C.: Brookings Institution, 1974). Of these studies, Postan's quite purposefully and Youngson's to a significant degree are sufficiently disaggregated to capture the role of the leading sectors in post-1945 growth.

198. Postan, *Economic History*, especially Chapters 5, 6, 8 and 11. On these critical linkages in more general terms, see, for example, Fabricant, with Shiskin, *Output of Manufacturing Industries*, p. 120: "Technological progress induces growth, and growth leads to lower costs and

thereby to further growth which may stimulate additional technological advances, and so on. If any factor has been taken as prime it is technological progress in the early stages of an industry's growth—particularly as the consequence of invention. This consideration suggests, in turn, that a more or less typical chronological pattern of the cost and price of an industry's output may be followed during an industry's growth and maturity. Since growth is most rapid in the early stages of an industry's life, declines in unit costs and prices also tend to be greatest at that time. As the industry approaches maturity, its unit costs and values decline less rapidly and tend to become subject to influences more important, at that stage, than technological progress."

Daniel Creamer, S. P. Dobrovsky, and Israel Borenstein conclude (*Capital in Manufacturing and Mining* [Princeton: Princeton University Press, 1960], p. 106): "Industries having the highest relative rates of growth or the lowest relative declines in output, as the case may be, are those in which worker-output and capital-output ratios declined the most. In other words, intensive use of capital and of labor is positively correlated with higher rates of growth in production."

With respect to British industrial growth and productivity, K. S. Lomax draws a similar conclusion ("Production and Productivity Movements in the United Kingdom since 1900," *Journal of the Royal Statistical Society*, Series A [General], vol. 122, part 2 [1959], p. 203): "The rates of change have risen quite markedly in the most recent post-war period. The well known phenomenon of productivity advance being closely associated with production growth is again apparent. The period of most rapid growth of productivity has also been that during which output has most increased. Productivity rarely seems to rise when the economy is stagnant or in recession. Performance in the individual groups has mostly been as expected although there is much scope for analysing and explaining individual industry movements in a detail which would be out of place here. The new developing industries and those in which there have been important technological changes show up in the most favourable light. The consistently high rate of productivity growth in Vehicles and also, to a rather lesser extent, in Paper and Printing are examples. The rapidly accelerating movement in Chemicals and, again, in the Utilities group are striking cases of productivity in newer industries following the production growth pattern."

For a general discussion of this point, see W. W. Rostow, "The Past Quarter-Century as Economic History and the Tasks of International Economic Organization," *Journal of Economic History*, vol. 30, no. 1 (March 1970), especially pp. 171–176.

199. Postan, *Economic History*, p. 128. See also pp. 163–166.
200. Denison, *Why Growth Rates Differ*, pp. 236–237. A quite similar ad hoc perception briefly breaks through in Denison's aggregative analysis of Japanese growth rates, when he notes the extraordinary expansion of consumers' durables, automobiles, etc., as the foundation for the "leading-sector" role of manufacturing (Edward F. Denison and William K. Chung, *How Japan's Economy Grew So Fast: The Sources of Postwar Expansion* [Washington, D.C.: The Brookings Institution, 1976], pp. 12–16.
201. Denison, *Why Growth Rates Differ*, p. 253, including note 62.
202. Kindleberger, *Europe's Postwar Growth*, p. 3. Kindleberger acknowledges his debt in this mode of analysis to the 1964 report of the Economic Commission for Europe, *Some Factors in Economic Growth in Europe during the 1950's*.
203. W. Arthur Lewis, "Development with Unlimited Supplies of Labor," *The Manchester School*, vol. 22, no. 2 (May 1954).
204. Maddison, *Economic Growth in the West*, p. 43.
205. Kindleberger, *Europe's Postwar Growth*, especially pp. 11–12 and 132–147.
206. Ibid., p. 229. The high income elasticity of demand for automobiles makes a brief earlier appearance on p. 56, in connection with Austrian sheet steel exports.

207. Postan, *Economic History*, p. 25.
208. R. C. O. Matthews, "Why Has Britain Had Full Employment since the War?", *Economic Journal*, vol. 78, no. 311 (September 1968), pp. 555–569. See also G. B. Stafford's "Comment" and Matthews' "Reply," ibid., vol. 80, no. 317 (March 1970), pp. 165–176. For other discussions of the reasons for postwar full employment, see, notably, Postan, *Economic History*, Chapter 2 (pp. 22–51), and J. R. Sargent, "Recent Growth Experience in the Economy of the United Kingdom," *Economic Journal*, vol. 78, no. 309 (March 1968), pp. 19–42.
209. Denison, *Why Growth Rates Differ*. See also his later study, *Accounting for United States Economic Growth, 1929–1969*, where slightly different U.S. real national income figures are given, p. 13, and the data are extended down to 1969, capturing the acceleration of the 1960's.
210. Denison, *Why Growth Rates Differ*, pp. 301–302.
211. Denison, *Accounting for United States Economic Growth, 1929–1969*, p. 124. The slowdown in the 1950's and the acceleration of the 1960's become even clearer if shorter periods are taken for the growth of U.S. GNP in 1958 dollars: 1948–1953, 4.98 percent; 1953–1957, 2.32 percent; 1957–1961, 2.38 percent; 1962–1964, 5.34 percent; 1964–1969, 4.54 percent.
212. Ibid., p. 138.
213. V. R. Fuchs, *The Service Economy* (New York: National Bureau of Economic Research, 1968), p. 1.
214. Ibid., pp. 75–76.
215. Ibid., pp. 84–85.
216. H. S. Houthakker and L. D. Taylor, *Consumer Demand in the United States, 1929–1970* (Cambridge, Mass.: Harvard University Press, 1966), Chapters 4 and 5. See especially the summary on pp. 154 ff.
217. Ben J. Wattenberg, *The Real America* (Garden City, N.Y.: Doubleday, 1974), p. 85.
218. From data in *Economic Report of the President* (Washington, D.C.: Government Printing Office, January 1969), pp. 227, 234, and 301.
219. For method of calculation, see Rostow, *Politics and the Stages of Growth*, pp. 386–387.
220. Real output in Japan increased, for example, at an annual rate of 9.97 percent from 1960 to 1965, at 10.87 percent from 1965 to 1972; industrial production at the rates of 11.38 percent and 13.43 percent, respectively (*United Nations Statistical Yearbooks*). See also the figures in Ohkawa and Rosovsky, *Japanese Economic Growth*, p. 25, showing an acceleration for the period 1962–1969 versus 1956–1962, and their comment on page 33. Accelerated inflation and balance-of-payments pressures might well have forced some deceleration in 1973–1974, however, even without the shock of the energy crisis.
221. Ohkawa and Rosovsky, *Japanese Economic Growth*, pp. 71–77.
222. Ibid., p. 154 note 6. Even more precisely, see Hisao Kanamori, "Economic Growth and Exports," Chapter 10 in Klein and Ohkawa (eds.), *Economic Growth*, p. 319: "Among the 55 industries studied . . . , those in which fixed capital formation increased sharply during 1955–64 comprise many of the new industries such as organic medicines, metal-processing machinery, automobiles, business machinery, and radios and TV. A number of traditional industries such as electric bulbs, cotton yarn and textiles, woolen yarn and textiles, lumber, porcelain, wood products, and footwear showed a low rate of increase."
223. Ohkawa and Rosovsky, *Japanese Economic Growth*, p. 157–160.
224. Ibid., p. 160.
225. Ibid., p. 182.
226. Shinohara, "Patterns and Some Structural Changes," pp. 278–302. See also Kanamori, "Economic Growth and Exports."
227. Shinohara, "Patterns and Some Structural Changes," pp. 283–288.
228. Ibid., pp. 296–297. Alfred Maizels has calculated the income elasticity of demand for major industrial categories and for the composition of exports (*Growth and Trade* [Cambridge: At the University Press, 1970], pp. 51–65). He exhibits the high degree to which "the pattern of industrial growth has consisted . . . of a shift towards chemicals, metals, and engineering" (p. 52), accompanied by an enlargement of

exports in these sectors. But his categories are too "heterogeneous" to isolate the role of leading sectors.

229. Shinohara, "Patterns and Some Structural Changes," p. 293.

230. For a more precise statistical specification of the sources of Japanese export increase by time periods, see Kanamori, "Economic Growth and Exports," pp. 311–312.

231. Ohkawa and Rosovsky, *Japanese Economic Growth*, p. 293.

232. Ibid., p. 96.

233. *OECD Observer*, no. 59 (August 1972), pp. 4–5.

234. Soviet sectoral targets for 1970, suggesting the new priority for durable consumers' goods and automobiles, as well as increased agricultural investment, are given in Table N-24, from *The European Economy in 1966* (Geneva: United Nations Economic Commission for Europe, 1967), Chapter 2, p. 48.

235. The role of motor vehicle assembly and production in the more advanced of the contemporary developing nations is somewhat different than in Western Europe and Japan. It usually begins on a small scale as an assembly operation to cut down the foreign exchange burden of automobile imports by the relatively rich. The production of some components follows, e.g., tires, batteries, etc. Quite often progress is impeded because the assembly of too many models is initially permitted, denying the advantages of economies of scale. As the domestic market enlarges, the proportion of components locally produced increases, and (as in Iran) the number of passenger and truck types licensed for production is reduced to increase efficiency. Although the proportion of the population owning automobiles remains low by standards of the more advanced nations, occasionally levels of output are attained which permit efficient production of a whole vehicle; e.g., Volkswagen in Brazil. In general, motor vehicle production, even when inefficient, has proved one route for the absorption of the technologies of metalworking, light electronics, and certain branches of the chemical industry in the drive to technological maturity in the contemporary developing world.

236. The "military transactions" item in the U.S. balance of payments (net of sales of military equipment) rose to about $2 billion during the Korean War, fluctuating subsequently between $2.1 billion and a peak of $3.6 billion (1972). In real terms and as a proportion of the U.S. balance of payments it thus declined. It represented a real burden on the U.S. international monetary position but not an expanding burden.

CHAPTER 18. *The Price Revolution of 1972–1976*

237. The Gayer index for Great Britain is used for the measurement over the period 1792–1813; Sauerbeck-Statist indexes for the two other trend periods with rising price trends. These indexes are to be found accessibly in Mitchell, with Deane, *Abstract*, pp. 470 and 474–475, respectively.

238. The terms-of-trade data in this paragraph are from *Economic Report of the President* (Washington, D.C.: Government Printing Office, February 1975), p. 358.

239. OECD 1973 GNP is estimated at about $3,133 billion; the cost of zero net growth in 1974 (as against previously normal 5 percent average growth) is about $156 billion.

240. Edward R. Fried and Charles L. Schultze (eds.), *Higher Oil Prices and the World Economy: The Adjustment Problem* (Washington, D.C.: Brookings Institution, 1975). This study distinguishes the following six sources of impact flowing from the rise in oil prices (pp. 6–7):

"The additional cost of imported oil. . . .

"The increase in exports from countries of the Organisation for Economic Co-operation and Development (OECD) to the oil-exporting countries because of the improvement in the financial position of the latter. . . .

"The reduction in OECD exports to the oil-importing (or nonoil) developing countries. . . .

"Changes in the trade of the OECD countries with each other in-

TABLE N-24. *Selected Output Targets of Soviet Industry*

	1958	1965	Annual Average Rate of Growth (%)	1970[a]	Annual Average Rate of Growth (%)
Electric power (billion kWh)	235.0	507.0	11.6	830–850	10.6
Oil (million tons)	110.0	243.0	11.6	345–355	7.6
Gas (billion cubic meters)	29.9	129.0	23.2	225–240	12.5
Coal (million tons)	493.0	578.0	2.3	665–675	3.0
Steel (million tons)	54.9	91.0	7.5	124–129	6.8
Passenger cars and trucks (thousands)	511.0	615.0	2.7	1,360–1,510	18.5
Tractors (thousands)	220.0	355.0	7.1	600–625	11.5
Mineral fertilizers (in conventional units, million tons)	12.4	31.3	14.1	62–65	15.2
Textile fabrics (billion square meters)	5.8	7.5	3.7	9.5–9.8	5.2
Leather footwear (million pairs)	356.0	486.0	4.6	610–630	5.0
Granulated sugar (million tons)	5.2	8.9	8.0	9.8–10	2.2
Radio receivers (millions)	3.9	5.2	4.2	7.5–8.0	8.3
Television sets (millions)	1.0	3.7	20.6	7.5–7.7	15.5
Refrigerators (millions)	0.4	1.7	23.0	5.3–5.6	26.2

[a] 1965–1970 planned growth rates calculated from midpoints.
Source: Directives of the 23rd Congress of the CPSU for the Five-Year Economic Development Plan of the Soviet Union for 1966–1970 and Mr. Kosygin's introductory statement.

TABLE N-25. *Selected Factors Affecting the Magnitude of the Initial Economic Impact of Higher Oil Prices in 1974 (Percentage of GDP)*

	Increase in Oil Import Bill	Increase in Exports to Oil-Exporting Countries	Increase in Payments to Domestic Oil Producers	Loss of Exports to Oil-Importing Developing Countries	Total
United States	−1.03	+0.18	−0.86	−0.03	−1.74
Western Europe	−2.28	+0.35	—	−0.03	−1.96
Japan	−2.67	+0.49	—	−0.06	−2.24

Note: Signs indicate direction of effect on aggregate demand.

duced by the internal effects of higher oil prices in reducing gross national product (GNP).

"The impact of higher oil costs and the oil-induced reductions in world GNP on the trade and income of the developing countries, as modified by offsetting or aggravating changes in capital movements.

"Increased prices paid in the importing countries for domestically produced oil and other primary sources of energy."

The effect of four of these factors is roughly measured in Table N-25 (p. 19).

241. Wouter Tims, "The Impact of Increased Oil Prices on Developing Countries," Chapter 5 in Fried and Schultze (eds.), *Higher Oil Prices and the World Economy*, p. 178.

242. See, notably, Maurice J. Williams, "The Aid Program of the OPEC Countries," *Foreign Affairs*, vol. 54, no. 2 (January 1976), especially pp. 317–324. The commitments made in 1974 and actual disbursements were as shown in Table N-26.

TABLE N-26. *Transfer of Resources from OPEC Members to the Third World in 1974 (in Millions of U.S. Dollars)*

Country	Concessional Aid		Financial Transfers		Total Disbursements
	Commitments	Disbursements	Commitments	Disbursements	
Algeria	117	35	22	5	40
Iran	1,270	400	990	309	709
Iraq	415	235	275	—	235
Kuwait	796	384	525	246	630
Libya	377	95	482	32	127
Nigeria	12	11	240	240	251
Qatar	148	50	156	27	77
Saudi Arabia	1,456	810	1,534	993	1,803
UAE	573	135	499	134	269
Venezuela	111	60	865	405	465
TOTAL	5,275	2,215	5,588	2,391	4,606

Source: OECD, *1975 Review of Development Cooperation*, Report by the Chairman of the Development Assistance Committee, November 1975.

Part Four. Business Cycles

CHAPTER 20. *Cycles: Another Result of Unbalanced Growth*

1. See, notably, Robert A. Gordon, *Business Fluctuations*, second edition (New York: Harper and Row, 1961). Although Gordon commands fully the modern theoretical apparatus of income and cycle analysis, it is significant that he dedicates his book to Wesley C. Mitchell, whose exploratory analysis of cycles was eclectic and disaggregated, and to Joseph Schumpeter, who focused sharply on what are here called leading sectors in growth. Broadly speaking, William Fellner's analysis of cycles belongs also under the same general disaggregated rubric as Gordon's (see *Trends and Cycles in Economic Activity* [New York: Henry Holt, 1956]).

2. I take this formulation from R. C. O. Matthews, *The Trade Cycle* (Cambridge: At the University Press, 1959, 1970), p. 7. Matthews' lucid exposition of modern aggregative business-cycle theory is systematically linked to growth via the concept of overshooting and undershooting the "needed," "desired," or "appropriate" total level of the stock of capital. He elaborates the mechanism of the cycle in a modification of familiar multiplier-accelerator terms, which he calls "the capital stock adjustment principle . . . , viz., that investment is an increasing function of income and a diminishing function of the stock of capital . . ."

(p. 49). Matthews' exposition has the virtue of dealing with the multiplier-accelerator interaction not merely in conventional mechanistic terms but also in terms of its meaning for expected profits as seen by the individual firm. For my general formulation of cycle theory in relation to growth, including reservations on the adequacy of the multiplier-accelerator mechanism (which would apply also to the aggregate stock-adjustment principle), see W. W. Rostow, *The Process of Economic Growth*, second edition (Oxford: Clarendon Press, 1960), Chapter 5, "Growth and Business Cycles." See also W. W. Rostow, *Essays on the British Economy of the Nineteenth Century* (Oxford: Clarendon Press, 1948), Chapter 2, "Cycles in the British Economy: 1790–1914."

3. See, for example, Arthur F. Burns, *Production Trends in the United States since 1870* (New York: National Bureau of Economic Research, 1934), especially pp. 248–249, where Burns considers how a "sharp divergence of production trends" and "the strain and loss of industrial balance" can cause a protracted phase of readjustment and recovery of balance.
4. Nevertheless, the modern inventory cycle is by no means a simple phenomenon, as Moses Abramovitz' study reveals (*Inventories and Business Cycles* [New York: National Bureau of Economic Research, 1950]). In general, there is a high degree of conformity of manufacturing inventories in current prices to business-cycle fluctuations in general; and, as one would expect, there is a lag (of three to six months), suggesting an adjustment of inventories to expected business conditions. But there is considerable variation in behavior as among the components of manufacturing (ibid., p. 86). The lag is somewhat greater if inventories are measured in constant prices (ibid., p. 98). Still more heterogeneous cyclical behavior emerges if one compares the cyclical behavior of inventories in manufactures with that in trade, transportation and public utilities, agriculture, or mining and quarrying (ibid., pp. 104–105). Other complexities surround differences in behavior of stocks of finished goods, goods in process, and raw materials, and the fact that inventory-output ratios are not constant (see especially ibid., pp. 461–462).

CHAPTER 21. *Cycles in the Eighteenth Century: 1700–1783*

5. The most systematic effort is T. S. Ashton's *Economic Fluctuations in England, 1700–1800* (Oxford: Clarendon Press, 1959). As noted earlier (see above, pp. 115–116 and 737 n. 10) John Parry Lewis extends Ashton's work and usefully surveys English building fluctuations in *Building Cycles and Britain's Growth* (London: Macmillan; New York: St. Martin's Press, 1965), Chapter 2. See also J. D. Gould, "Agricultural Fluctuations and the English Economy of the Eighteenth Century," *Journal of Economic History*, vol. 22, no. 3 (1962).
6. See Rostow, *British Economy of the Nineteenth Century*, pp. 32–39.
7. The timing of the impact of wars on the eighteenth-century English economy cannot be read off simply from the dates given in history books for their formal opening and conclusion. As Ashton's account makes clear, the economy could be affected by an anticipatory pre-war heightening of tensions; the intensity of war outlays varied within their duration; and peacemaking was often a slow process, with the weight of hostilities lifting before the signing of peace itself. Year-by-year public expenditures and the numbers of men under arms are reasonably sensitive indicators of the burden (and, in some sectors, stimulus) of military activities.
8. The decline of 1724–1727 may at least equally be considered as continuing to 1729 (J. P. Lewis, *Building Cycles*, p. 14). It is connected with the brief (1727–1729) war of Britain and France against Spain, ending with the Treaty of Seville (November 1729). Although we still have much to learn about this period, there may also have been an element of more conventional cyclical decline after the considerable expansion of the first half of the 1720's.
9. The question of how good and bad harvests affected the British economy in the eighteenth century from year to year has been a matter of anal-

ysis and debate since Adam Smith at least. Given the inelasticity of the demand for grain, one would assume that a bad harvest (and a disproportionate increase in price) would be good for the agricultural community. And, on the face of it, a good harvest (and a disproportionate decline in food costs) would be good for urban consumers and good for industry, since consumers could allocate more for purchases of manufactured goods. In a predominantly agricultural society one could, nevertheless, draw the conclusion that the national advantage was served by lean harvests. The debate on this issue is footnoted and discussed in Gould, "Agricultural Fluctuations," pp. 313–322. The issue is complicated, as always in agriculture, by variations among the regions and by long-period changes in methods and productivity, well delineated in E. L. Jones (ed.), *Agriculture and Economic Growth in England*, 1650–1815 (London: Methuen, 1967).

So far as short-run business fluctuations are concerned, it is my net judgment that good harvests were, on balance, good for both rural and urban communities and a general stimulus to the national economy—the view taken most notably by Ashton (*Economic Fluctuations*, pp. 27–48). This assessment arises from the following three major factors:

—Large numbers of farmers produced mainly for their own consumption and their livestock. Abundance meant an expansion in their consumption and in their capacity to maintain livestock and also to sell for cash any surplus, even at relatively low prices.

—Good harvests increased both the supply of agricultural raw materials used in industry and the demand for industrial products; e.g., beer, candles, soap, and leather.

—Good harvests increased grain exports or lowered imports (in the second half of the century), contributing to strain or ease in the London money market and the banking system.

These factors appear to outweigh the possible net advantage to large farming units, producing predominantly for a commercial grain market, which might gain, on balance, from lean harvests and high prices. Large landlords with political influence certainly pressed Parliament for protection in periods of abundance and low prices.

Gottfried von Haberler summarizes well the literature on agriculture and the business cycle for later, more modern periods in Chapter 7 of *Prosperity and Depression* (Geneva: League of Nations, 1937), pp. 142–157. The routes of impact he explores are also mainly germane to the eighteenth century.

10. See, notably, Ashton, *Economic Fluctuations*, p. 174. In the eighty years from 1701 to 1781, twenty-one cycles in British export volume (official value) can be marked off, averaging 3.8 years, a shorter rhythm than for Ashton's cycles as a whole. In the period after 1783 I found minor cycles averaged four years in length, attributing them primarily to inventory fluctuations in foreign trade (*British Economy of the Nineteenth Century*, pp. 38–42).

11. See, for example, Ashton, *Economic Fluctuations*, pp. 138–139.

CHAPTER 22. *Cycles in the Classic Era: 1783–1914*

12. The data for 1784–1850, Chart IV-1, are drawn from A. D. Gayer et al., *The Growth and Fluctuation of the British Economy, 1790–1850* (Oxford: Clarendon Press, 1953), vol. 1, p. 356, where the construction of the index is explained. The following figures were added on the basis of Ashton, *Economic Fluctuations*, and the data in the Gayer study:

1784	0	1787	3
1785	1	1788	0
1786	2	1789	2

The trade-union unemployment data are to be found in B. R. Mitchell, with the collaboration of Phyllis Deane, *Abstract of British Historical*

Statistics (Cambridge: At the University Press, 1971), pp. 64–65. For a discussion of the inadequacies and biases of the trade-union unemployment series, see Rostow, *British Economy of the Nineteenth Century*, pp. 33–35, including footnote 1, p. 35. It should be noted that among the data available before 1850, used to establish the business-cycle pattern in the Gayer study, are figures from 1831 forward on the percentage unemployed in the Friendly Society of Iron-Founders. That series conforms sensitively to cyclical fluctuations in general over the period 1831–1850 and reflects as well the relative intensity of major and minor cycles, as one would expect in a series linked so closely to domestic investment (Gayer et al., *Growth and Fluctuation*, vol. 2, pp. 967–968). Down to 1856 the iron-founders are the only group covered in the unemployment series.

13. Thomas Tooke's *History of Prices* (London: Longman, 1838) is the best source of data on the course and the mechanics of short cycles in British foreign trade, his account deriving vitality and authority from a long merchant's experience. The institutional arrangements, with their time lags, credit arrangements, and dependence on expectations, are described by Norman S. Buck, *The Development of the Organization of Anglo-American Trade, 1800–1850* (New York: Greenwood Press, 1925, 1968); for the system of credit advances on consignments and the "interlacing of credits" and speculation with foreign trade operations, see especially pp. 12–14, 23, and 39; for reference to the inventory nature of the foreign-trade crises of 1816 and 1831, see pp. 138–139. For a further analysis of the nature and possible causes of inventory fluctuations, partially relevant to this problem, despite its application to a closed economy, see L. A. Metzler, "The Nature and Stability of Inventory Cycles," *Review of Economic Statistics*, vol. 23 (August 1941), and idem, "Factors Governing the Length of Inventory Cycles," ibid., vol. 29 (February 1947).

14. Buck, *Anglo-American Trade*, p. 102, notes: "As it generally took from a month to six weeks to manufacture the goods and prepare them for shipment, merchants, who purchased from the manufacturers, were required to place their orders for goods fairly early." To establish what Metzler, in his articles cited above, calls "the planning period," one would, presumably, have to take into account the length of time from the placing of the order by the merchant to the receipt of the manufactured goods. This would include the period from transmission to receipt of orders from overseas, as well as the period for shipment and delivery of the finished British products. In fact, shipments from Britain to the United States tended to be concentrated in two periods of the year: "There were the spring shipments, from the middle of January until the middle of April, and the fall shipments, during the months of July and August" (Buck, *Anglo-American Trade*, p. 102). It is not unlikely that "the planning period," fully analyzed in this trade, would work out to something close to six months.

15. The economies to which Britain sold its exports were themselves subject to fluctuations, as well as to secular growth: fluctuations in harvests, in their income from exports, and in their domestic industry. These fluctuations undoubtedly affected the demand for British exports; and the fluctuations both were affected by and influenced the course of British cycles. What is essential to the argument here, however, is that, until about the 1850's, British exports were dominated by consumers' rather than capital goods.

The year 1860 in no sense constitutes a sharp analytic line of demarcation with respect to the relative role of the two types of cycles; although there is a marked deceleration of cotton-goods exports in the 1860's, a low rate of growth in the 1870's. The coming of the railway on a very large scale in Britain in the 1840's affords a sharper conceptual breaking point. Indeed, the minor cycle of the late 1840's is so slight a manifestation that it is not recorded in the annual turning points; and that of the 1850's (peak 1857) would, perhaps, not have stood out so strongly but for the distortions imposed on the pattern of the decade by the Crimean War.

16. Arthur F. Burns and Wesley C. Mitchell, *Measuring Business Cycles* (New York: National Bureau of Economic Research, 1946), pp. 78–79.
17. Haberler, *Prosperity and Depression*, pp. 170–171. Oskar Morgenstern provides a diagram of reference cycles, 1879–1938, for the United States, Great Britain, France, and Germany in his *International Financial Transactions and Business Cycles* (Princeton: Princeton University Press, 1959), pp. 42–43. See also Wesley C. Mitchell's comparative annals of business fluctuations for the United States, Britain, Germany, and France from 1889 to 1911 in *Business Cycles* (Berkeley: University of California Press, 1913), summarized, p. 88, and described, pp. 44–87.
18. See, notably, Rendigs Fels, *American Business Cycles, 1865–1897* (Chapel Hill: University of North Carolina Press, 1959). The extent to which the United States was odd-man-out in pre-1914 business cycles is roughly measured by the fact that the three major European economies were in the same cyclical phase for 83.1 percent of the months from September 1879 to August 1914, whereas the United States was in phase with all three for 53.5 percent of the period (Morgenstern, *International Financial Transactions*, p. 45).
19. Fels, *American Business Cycles*, pp. 197–198, argues that the downturn began one or more months earlier than December 1895, when it is often associated with the crisis over Venezuela.
20. Milton Friedman and Anna Jacobson Schwartz suggest the following sequence as explaining the recession of January 1910–January 1912: a very substantial net gold inflow in the wake of the panic of 1907; a disproportionate subsequent rise in U.S. prices, accompanied in 1909–1910 by large capital imports; a decline in capital imports in 1911 and a subsidence in the U.S. relative price level imposed by monetary restraint (*A Monetary History of the United States, 1867–1960* [Princeton: Princeton University Press, 1963], pp. 173–174). W. C. Mitchell (*Business Cycles*, p. 85) adduces business apprehensions about public policy and poor grain harvests as damping factors in 1911. For a detailed factual analysis, leaning heavily on monetary factors, see William Charles Schluter, *The Pre-War Business Cycle* (New York: Columbia University, 1923), pp. 56–104.
21. Ilse Mintz, *Trade Balances during Business Cycles: U.S. and Britain since 1880*, Occasional Paper 67 (New York: National Bureau of Economic Research, 1959).
22. Ibid., pp. 35–36.
23. For a discussion of the British trade balance in the period 1801–1848 in relation to wheat imports, see Gayer et al., *Growth and Fluctuation*, vol. 2, pp. 797–798. In this period, for which only annual data are available, the British trade balance systematically deteriorated in the latter stages of expansion, improving in all other stages. It thus conformed more nearly to American than British cyclical behavior for the period 1880–1914.
24. See, for example, ibid., p. 40, including footnote 2, with its quotation from an unpublished manuscript of Wesley C. Mitchell. In his *Business Cycles: The Problem and Its Setting* (New York: National Bureau of Economic Research, 1927), Mitchell assembled some data which suggest, at least, the likelihood that the average amplitude of American cycles was greater than those in Britain and Germany (pp. 273–280). He measured standard deviations of the relative deviations of original data from lines of secular trend, corrected when necessary for seasonal variations. Roughly comparable standard deviations emerge, as shown in Table N-27.

    Variations in the proportion of the nonagricultural working force unemployed in the course of business cycles would constitute the most satisfactory measure of relative amplitude. Unfortunately, German (and French) data do not exist. Moreover, the British data on percentage of trade-union members unemployed (B. R. Mitchell, with Deane, *Abstract*, pp. 64–65) are not comparable with the U.S. data (from 1890) on the proportion of the total civilian labor force unemployed (Stanley Lebergott, *Manpower in Economic Growth: the Amer-*

TABLE N-27. *Amplitude of Cycles: Deviations from Secular Trend*

	United States		United Kingdom		Germany	
Pig iron	(1879–1896)	19.30	(1865–1913)	8.77	(1882–1914)	6.64
	(1897–1913)	15.65				
Stock prices	(1879–1896)	11.91	(1903–1914)	4.3	(1900–1914)	8.45
	(1897–1913)	11.94				
Provincial bank clearings	(1879–1896)	12.03	(1887–1913)	5.25	(1898–1914)	6.83
	(1897–1913)	7.98				
Bank clearings (New York)	(1879–1896)	24.55	(1903–1914)	13.3	—	
	(1897–1913)	18.21				

Source: W. C. Mitchell, *Business Cycles: The Problem and Its Setting*, pp. 273–280.

ican Record since 1800 [New York: McGraw-Hill, 1964], pp. 177–184 and 522). From 1900 Lebergott (p. 512) calculates unemployment among nonfarm employees. A comparison of these figures with those for British trade-union unemployment for the period 1900–1914 (Table N-28) suggests, somewhat indecisively, greater volatility in the American data as well as a higher average unemployment level in the United States. The data for the proportion of the total civilian labor force unemployed are included from 1890, although they are distorted by the peculiarly severe U.S. depression of the 1890's.

TABLE N-28. *Percentage Unemployment: United States and United Kingdom, 1890–1914*

	United Kingdom Trade-Union Membership (%)	United States Civilian Labor Force (%)	Nonfarm Employees (%)
1890	2.1	4.0	—
1891	3.5	5.4	—
1892	6.3	3.0	—
1893	7.5	11.7	—
1894	6.9	18.4	—
1895	5.8	13.7	—
1896	3.3	14.4	—
1897	3.3	14.5	—
1898	2.8	12.4	—
1899	2.0	6.5	—
1900	2.5	5.0	12.6
1901	3.3	4.0	10.1
1902	4.0	3.7	8.6
1903	4.7	3.9	9.0
1904	6.0	5.4	12.0
1905	5.0	4.3	9.5
1906	3.6	1.7	3.9
1907	3.7	2.8	6.0
1908	7.8	8.0	16.4
1909	7.7	5.1	10.3
1910	4.7	5.9	11.6
1911	3.0	6.7	13.0
1912	3.2	4.6	9.0
1913	2.1	4.3	8.2
1914	3.3	7.9	14.7

Sources: B. R. Mitchell, with Deane, *Abstract*, pp. 64–65; Lebergott, *Manpower in Economic Growth*, p. 512.

25. Mintz, *Trade Balances*, pp. 80–81.
26. Ibid., pp. 76–78. Ilse Mintz applies four measures of cyclical fluctuations, *ex* United States: a composite of British, French, and German cycles; a fifteen-country composite based on Willard Thorp's annals, weighted by each country's role in world trade; Folke Hilgerdt's index of world manufacturing production; and a series for world imports (ibid., pp. 60–68). The three- and fifteen-country cyclical indexes conform closely to each other as well as to the British turning points.

CHAPTER 23. *Interwar Cycles: 1919–1939*

27. Morgenstern, *International Financial Transactions*, pp. 40–53.
28. Ibid., p. 48.
29. Mintz, *Trade Balances*, pp. 55–56. The U.S. trade balance maintained its generally inverse correlation with business cycles except for the decline during the post-1949 depression.
30. The British immediate postwar experience is well described and analyzed in A. C. Pigou, *Aspects of British Economic History, 1918–1925* (London: Macmillan, 1947). For the United States, see Thomas Wilson, *Fluctuations in Income and Employment* (London: Isaac Pitman, 1942), pp. 93–113, and Gordon, *Business Fluctuations*, pp. 401–406. For an interesting comparison and explanation of the parallel behavior of the U.S. trade balance in the years immediately following the First and Second World Wars see Mintz, *Trade Balances*, pp. 22–23. See also J. A. Dowie, "1919–20 Is in Need of Attention," *Economic History Review*, Second Series, vol. 28, no. 3 (August 1975). pp. 429–450. Dowie emphasizes the effect of the coming of the eight-hour day in 1919, yielding a disproportionate British rise in costs and prices and consequent reduction in competitive position.
31. Gordon, *Business Fluctuations*, pp. 410–411. For the role of the automobile in British interwar cyclical fluctuations see, notably, H. W. Richardson, *Economic Recovery in Britain, 1932–9* (London: Weidenfeld and Nicolson, 1967), especially pp. 82–99, 104–107, 119–123, 129–141, 266–279; for its role in the German recovery after 1932, R. J. Overy, "Cars, Roads, and Economic Recovery in Germany, 1932–8," *Economic History Review*, Second Series, vol. 28, no. 3 (August 1975), pp. 466–483.
32. Gordon, *Business Fluctuations*, pp. 442–446.
33. Ibid., p. 442.

CHAPTER 24. *Cycles in Growth Rates: 1945–1973*

34. Some of the major efforts to delineate, measure, and analyze postwar cyclical behavior are the following: Erik Lundberg (ed.), *The Business Cycle in the Post-war World* (proceedings of a conference held by the International Economic Association) (London: Macmillan, 1955); Mintz, *Trade Balances*; Ilse Mintz, *American Exports during Business Cycles, 1879–1958* (New York: National Bureau of Economic Research, 1961); Gordon, *Business Fluctuations*, especially pp. 451–504; Miyohei Shinohara, *Growth and Cycles in the Japanese Economy* (Tokyo: Kinokuniya Bookstore Co., 1962); Erik Lundberg, *Instability and Economic Growth* (New Haven: Yale University Press, 1968); Martin Bronfenbrenner (ed.), *Is the Business Cycle Obsolete?* (based on a conference of the Social Science Research Council Committee on Economic Stability) (New York: John Wiley, 1969); Ilse Mintz, *Dating Postwar Business Cycles: Methods and Their Application to Western Germany, 1950–67* (New York: National Bureau of Economic Research, 1969); Arthur F. Burns, *The Business Cycle in a Changing World* (New York: National Bureau of Economic Research, 1969); Philip A. Klein, *The Management of Market-Oriented Economies* (Belmont, Calif.: Wadsworth Publishing Co., 1973), especially Chapters 8 and 9; Geoffrey H. Moore, "The State of the International Business

Cycle," *Business Economics*, vol. 9, no. 4 (September 1974), pp. 21–29; Ilse Mintz, *Dating United States Growth Cycles* (New York: National Bureau of Economic Research, 1974). For the analysis of a sector which showed cyclical fluctuations in absolute as well as relative terms during Swedish postwar growth cycles, see Lars Vinell, *Business Cycles and Steel Markets*, translated by Roger Tanner (Stockholm: Beckmans, 1973).

35. R. C. O. Matthews, "Postwar Business Cycles in the United Kingdom," Chapter 4 in Bronfenbrenner (ed.), *Is the Business Cycle Obsolete?*, pp. 103 and 123.
36. Matthews notes (ibid., p. 102, note 5) the alterations in historical cyclical turning points as compared to those that flow from Burns and Mitchell's dates when deviations from trend rather than changes in absolute values are used. In some cases the turning points, on an annual basis, come a year earlier when the method of deviations from trend is employed; e.g., for cyclical peaks, 1856–1857, 1865–1866, 1872–1873, 1889–1890.
37. In the case of Britain, from 1952 to 1965, prices increased markedly more during growth-cycle downswings—more than twice as fast. For Matthews' measurement and discussion of this phenomenon, see ibid., pp. 124–126.
38. Ibid., pp. 117–120.
39. D. H. Robertson, "An Introductory Note," in Lundberg (ed.), *The Business Cycle in the Post-war World*, p. 8.
40. At the other end of the growth spectrum from Britain, one can observe these elements operating also in Japanese postwar growth cycles. See, notably, Shinohara, *Growth and Cycles in the Japanese Economy*.
41. Sources for Table IV-11: United States, 1945–1961, Burns, *Business Cycle*, pp. 16–17; bracketed cycles, 1962–1969, from Mintz, *Dating United States Growth Cycles*, p. 59, are growth cycles not reflected in "classical" reference-cycle dates; the October 1973 peak is the lowest month for unemployment, seasonally corrected, in this cycle (*Economic Report of the President* [February 1974], p. 279). On a growth-cycle basis, Philip A. Klein dates the 1973 peak as early as March (*Business Cycles in the Postwar World* [Washington, D.C.: American Enterprise Institute, February 1976], p. 24). United Kingdom annual dates, 1951–1952, Matthews, "Postwar Business Cycles in the United Kingdom," p. 99; 1947 taken as initial postwar trough on the basis of unemployment data cited by E. A. G. Robinson, "Industrial Fluctuations in the United Kingdom, 1946–1952," in Lundberg (ed.), *Business Cycle*, p. 37; monthly dates, 1955–1968, are growth-cycle turning points from Geoffrey H. Moore and Philip A. Klein, *International Economic Indicators*, Final Report on Phase I (New York: National Bureau of Economic Research, 30 June 1974); 1972 trough, Klein, *Business Cycles*, p. 24. Klein does not include the mild cycle included here on the basis of fluctuations in industrial production and effective demand with a peak in II 1969 and trough in IV 1971 (trough not shown here), from *OECD Observer* (January–February 1975), p. 33. The peak in IV 1973 is added from the latter source on the basis of unemployment data, p. 34. German turning points, 1951–1967, Mintz, *Dating Postwar Business Cycles*, p. 53, with reference to a tentative downturn in 1951 running to 1954, p. 49; 1967–1973 monthly dates, Klein, *Business Cycles*, p. 25. French dates, 1949–1965, J. C. R. Dow, "Cyclical Developments in France, Germany, and Italy since the Early 1950's," Chapter 5 in Bronfenbrenner (ed.), *Is the Business Cycle Obsolete?*, p. 148; 1966–1973 turning points, *OECD Observer* (January–February 1975), pp. 33–34. Japanese dates, 1951–1965, Miyohei Shinohara, "Postwar Business Cycles in Japan," Chapter 3 in Bronfenbrenner (ed.), *Is the Business Cycle Obsolete?*, p. 73; 1966–1972 dates, Klein, *Business Cycles*, p. 25; 1973 peak, *OECD Observer* (January–February 1975), pp. 33–34. Italian turning points, 1954–1965, Dow, "Cyclical Developments," p. 179; 1969–1974 dates, *OECD Observer* (January–February 1975), pp. 33–34.
42. Robertson, "Introductory Note," p. 9. For a "rate-of-change" approach to

Canadian growth from 1953 to 1973, exhibiting characteristics similar to those of the U.S. economy, see Charles Schwartz, *The Cyclical Momentum of Economic Activity in Canada, 1953–1973*, Working Paper of Macro-Economic Analysis Group (Ottawa: Department of Industry, Trade, and Commerce, May 1974).

43. Robert A. Gordon, "The Stability of the U.S. Economy," Chapter I in Bronfenbrenner (ed.), *Is the Business Cycle Obsolete?*, p. 28.
44. This literature is well reflected in Bronfenbrenner (ed.), *Is the Business Cycle Obsolete?*, Chapters 9, 10, and 11, including commentary papers, and Bronfenbrenner's account of the discussions they generated, pp. 531–540.
45. George Staller, "Fluctuations in Economic Activity: Planned and Free Market Economies, 1950–1960," *American Economic Review*, vol. 54, no. 4, part 1 (June 1964), pp. 385–395. Staller's "index of total output fluctuations" measures absolute deviations from the trend in growth. If fluctuations were measured as percentages of the trend value, they would appear less volatile, as Francis Seton points out in a comment on Josef Goldmann, "Fluctuations in the Growth Rate in a Socialist Economy and the Inventory Cycle," Chapter 11 in Bronfenbrenner (ed.), *Is the Business Cycle Obsolete?*, p. 351. This point could also be made about the volatility of the Japanese economy (see above pp. 342–343).
46. Goldmann, "Fluctuations," p. 333.

CHAPTER 25. *Inflation: The Price of Full Employment*

47. *Economic Report of the President* (Washington, D.C.: Government Printing Office, February 1975), p. 285.
48. Klein (*Management of Market-Oriented Economies*, p. 200) sets out relative inflation rates for a somewhat different grouping of advanced industrial economies over the period 1950–1970, as shown in Table N-29, with 1973, 1974, and estimated 1975 rates added from *OECD Economic Observer*, no. 16 (December 1974).
49. France appears an exception; but if the French performance for 1965–1972 is compared with the six years 1959–1965, the inflation rate also rises from 3.7 percent to 4.7 percent.
50. For the United States, see, for example, the chart in W. W. Rostow, *The Diffusion of Power* (New York: Macmillan, 1972), p. 325. Klein (*Management of Market-Oriented Economies*, p. 202) produces an interesting chart constituting a kind of international Phillips curve (Chart N-1). It does show the expected rough inverse conformity between rates of unemployment and consumers' price increases. But the deviations are significant; e.g., the abnormally "bad" performance of Italy, abnormally "good" performances of West Germany and the Netherlands. In fact, putting the Italian case aside, one could argue that annual price increases of 2–3 percent could be associated with average annual unemployment rates of anywhere from 1 to 5+ percent; and that unemployment rates of 1–2 percent could be associated with annual price increases of anywhere from 2+ to almost 6 percent. For a discussion of some of the more fundamental forces determining these differences, see C. P. Kindleberger, *Europe's Postwar Growth: The Role of Labor Supply* (Cambridge, Mass.: Harvard University Press, 1967), pp. 217–220.
51. In the United States, unit labor costs increased at an average rate of 4.9 percent in the two boom years, 1956–1957; 1.4 percent in the three years of setbacks and limited recovery, 1958–1960; 0.4 percent in the four years of recovery, 1961–1965.
52. See, for example, the brief account in Rostow, *Diffusion of Power*, pp. 537–540.
53. F. W. Paish, "Inflation, Personal Incomes and Taxation," *Lloyds Bank Review*, no. 116 (April 1975), pp. 2–3. For a quantitative estimate of the factors producing the price increase in Britain from 1972 to 1974, also emphasizing the increased role of wage-push inflation in 1973–

TABLE N-29. *Average Annual Percentage Change in Consumer Prices: Eleven Market-Oriented Economies, 1950–1975*

	1950–1955	1955–1960	1960–1965	1965–1968	1969	1970	1973	1974	1975 (est.)
United States	2.2	1.9	1.3	3.3	5.4	5.9	5.5	11.5	11
Canada	2.9	2.1	1.6	3.8	4.5	3.4	6.1	10	11.5
Japan	—	—	6.0	4.8	5.2	7.7	11.7	25	16
France	6.1	6.2	3.8	3.3	6.4	5.2	7.1	13.8	13
West Germany	2.5	1.8	2.8	2.3	2.7	4.7	7.0	7.5	7
Italy	4.5	4.3	4.9	2.3	2.6	5.0	10.8	19.3	20.3
United Kingdom	2.0	2.7	3.6	3.7[b]	5.5	6.4	8.6	14.8	18
Belgium	0.05[a]	1.3	2.5	3.2	3.8	3.9	7.0	12.5	11.5
Denmark	3.6	2.0	5.5	7.4[b]	3.5	5.6	9.3	14.5	14.5
Netherlands	3.2	2.4	3.5	4.3	7.5[b]	4.4	9.0	10.5	10.5
Sweden	5.1	3.0	3.6	4.2	2.7	7.0	6.7	10	11

[a] 1953–1955 only.
[b] Figures for these years were seriously inflated by changes in indirect taxes and other measures directly affecting consumer prices.

Sources: 1950–1970, Klein, *Management of Market-Oriented Economies*, p. 200; 1950–1960 computed from OECD, *Statistics of National Accounts, 1950–61* (Paris: OECD, 1964), reports by country; 1960–1969 from OECD, *Inflation: The Present Problem* (Paris: OECD, December 1970), Table 4; 1970 computed from OECD, *Main Economic Indicators* (Paris: OECD, May 1971), reports by country; 1973–1975, *OECD Economic Observer*, no. 16 (December 1974).

TABLE N-30. *Contributions to Six-Monthly Percentage Increases in Index of Market Prices: United Kingdom, 1972–1974*

Period	Calculated Contributions				Residual Error	Overall Increase over 6 Months (%)
	Employment Income per Unit of Output	Gross Profits, Etc., per Unit of Output	Net Indirect Tax Rates	Import Prices of Goods and Services		
(1) Q2 to Q4, 1972	+2.4	+1.5	−0.1	+0.9	—	4.7
(2) Q4, 1972, to Q2, 1973	+2.35	+0.25	−0.6	+2.2	—	4.2
(3) Q2 to Q4, 1973	+2.9	+0.8	+0.3	+2.8	+0.4	7.2
(4) Q4, 1973, to Q2, 1974	+4.7	−0.9	+1.35	+5.5	+0.65	11.3
(5) Q2 to Q4, 1974	+6.9	+2.0	−1.3	+1.6	−0.3	8.9

Source: Allen, "Immediate Contributors," p. 610.

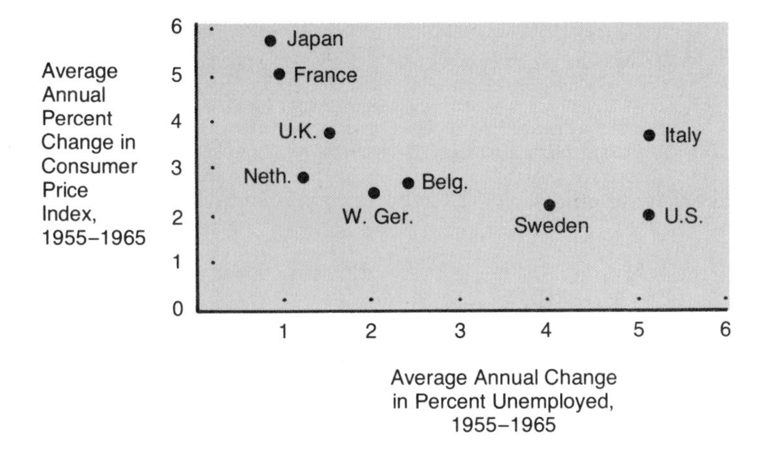

CHART N-1. *Average Annual Percentage Change in the Consumer Price Index and in the Percentage of the Civilian Labor Force Unemployed: Nine Market-Oriented Economies, 1955–1965*

Source: Klein, *Management of Market-Oriented Economies*, p. 202.
Note: Data for Netherlands, 1955–1964; for Japan, 1960–1965.

1974, see R. G. D. Allen, "The Immediate Contributors to Inflation," *Economic Journal*, vol. 85, no. 339 (September 1975), pp. 607–611. Allen's conclusions are summarized in Table N-30.

54. Robertson, "Introductory Note," p. 9.
55. See, for example, Kindleberger, *Europe's Postwar Growth*, especially pp. 214–227, and M. M. Postan, *An Economic History of Western Europe, 1945–1964* (London: Methuen, 1967), especially pp. 52–89.
56. See, notably, Craufurd D. Goodwin (ed.), *Exhortation and Controls: The Search for a Wage-Price Policy, 1945–1971* (Washington, D.C.: Brookings Institution, 1975).
57. See, for example, Kindleberger, *Europe's Postwar Growth*, pp. 214–220.
58. Mark W. Leiserson, *A Brief Interpretative Survey of Wage-Price Problems in Europe*, Study Paper No. 11 for Consideration of the Joint Economic Committee, 86th Congress, 1st session (Washington, D.C.: Government Printing Office, 1959), p. 55.

CHAPTER 26. *Stagflation: 1974–1976*

59. One might argue that the situation of Western Europe and Japan in the immediate postwar years parallels that of 1973–1975. In both cases the terms of trade were unfavorable and import levels could only be sustained by capital imports. In the latter case, of course, there was no Marshall Plan. In fact, one could view OPEC's policy as an effort to impose a reverse Marshall Plan.
60. See, especially, Moore, "State of the International Business Cycle," pp. 27–28.

Part Five. Stages of Economic Growth: Twenty Countries

CHAPTER 27. *Aggregate and Sectoral Analysis of Growth*

1. See W. W. Rostow, *The Stages of Economic Growth*, second edition (Cambridge: At the University Press, 1971), Appendix B, pp. 172–241. See

also my earlier reply to critics of the take-off concept, W. W. Rostow (ed.), *The Economics of Take-off into Sustained Growth* (New York: St. Martin's Press, 1963), especially pp. xiii–xxvi and Chapter 1, pp. 1–21.

2. The area of pragmatic agreement on the timing of take-off, the industrial revolution, or entrance into modern growth is suggested by the dates offered by Simon Kuznets for "the beginning of modern growth" set out against my original (1960) "tentative, approximate take-off dates" (Table N-31).

Kuznets' time periods are shorter than mine because he is seeking to date "the beginning" of modern growth, while I was seeking to date the whole take-off period, which, in the pre-1914 world, tended to last about twenty years by my calculations.

Kuznets' operational criterion for dating "the beginning" in this particular context was an accelerated rate of urbanization. (Kuznets' full criteria for modern growth are: the application of modern scientific thought and technology to industry; a sustained and rapid increase in real product per capita, usually associated with high rates of population growth; a shift of the working force out of agriculture to industry and services; significant contacts with the outside world.) My view of what lies at the heart of take-off and the beginning of modern growth is the effective absorption of a limited range of modern technologies, yielding a high rate of expansion and significant scale in an identified leading sector complex, with evidence of spreading effects, bringing about in the usual case an acceleration of increase in GNP per capita, a rise in the investment rate, and an acceleration of the pace of urbanization. I regard accelerated urbanization as evidence of the "lateral spreading effects" of leading sectors.

The similarity of the two sets of dates is striking; but the differences deserve brief comment.

I would not regard the British urbanization data as sufficiently reliable in the eighteenth century either to serve as a unique criterion or to justify pushing the take-off back to 1765. There was an acceleration in the British economy between the end of the Seven Years' War and the beginning of the American War of Independence; but it was only after 1783 that a marked and sustained acceleration began. In addition, there is firm evidence that the new technologies—in cotton, iron, and the efficient steam engine—were rapidly absorbed only after 1783. As for the United States, there is evidence of marked acceleration in urbanization rates in the 1820's in New England (see Chapter 29) during its regional take-off. I should think the real choice in dating "the beginning of modern growth" in the United States is between the 1820's and the 1840's, depending on one's evaluation of the New England take-off.

The difference with respect to Sweden is a case of "the preceding decade." I would not judge our difference here as significant, although

TABLE N-31. *"Beginning of Modern Growth" and "Take-off" Dates: Eight Countries*

	Kuznets	Rostow
Great Britain	1765–1785	1783–1802
France	1831–1840	1830–1860
Belgium	1831–1840	1833–1860
United States	1834–1843	1843–1860
Germany	1850–1859	1850–1873
Sweden	1861–1869	1868–1890
Japan	1874–1879	1878–1900
Canada	1870–1874	1896–1914

Sources: Simon Kuznets, *Economic Growth of Nations: Total Output and Production Structure* (Cambridge, Mass.: The Belknap Press of Harvard University Press, 1971), p. 24; W. W. Rostow, *The Stages of Economic Growth*, first edition (Cambridge: At the University Press, 1960), p. 38.

the decline in real product per capita between 1861–1864 and 1865–1869, followed by an annual average rate of increase of 3 percent for the next decade, suggests the later dating is more appropriate. The evidence is quite strong (p. 409 & Table V-16) that it was with the great boom of the early 1870's that Sweden moved unambiguously into self-sustained growth, after an active period of preparation from about 1850.

I would now regard both Kuznets' dating and mine (as of 1960) as wrong on Japan. Later research makes it reasonably clear that sustained industrial growth in Japan began only after the end of the Matsukata deflation in 1885 (see, for example, Henry Rosovsky, "Japan's Transition to Modern Economic Growth, 1868–1885," in idem [ed.], *Industrialization in Two Systems: Essays in Honor of Alexander Gerschenkron by a Group of His Students* [New York: John Wiley, 1966], p. 132). And, as explained at the beginning of Chapter 31, I am now, on balance, inclined to follow Walther Hoffmann's suggestion and include the 1840's in the period of the German take-off.

On Canada, following the conventional wisdom of economic historians of Canada and the full range of statistical data, I would still hold that it was from the mid-1890's, and the rise in the wheat price, that Canada entered into modern economic growth, although, as noted in Part Three, pp. 185–186, the preceding period was not unfruitful.

Kuznets' reason for seeking dates for "the beginning of modern growth" is worth noting. He was concerned with a statistical rather than a strictly historical problem. If one extrapolates backward from average rates of growth of product per capita in modern times, for which reasonable data are available, it is clear that at some point in the past product per capita will fall so low as to cease to be credible. Therefore, there must have been some (usually long) period in the past of each country in which GNP per capita was constant (or fluctuated about a low average level) or increased much more slowly than in modern times. Kuznets approximated these periods of acceleration in the rate of growth of GNP per capita by reference, primarily, to periods of accelerated urbanization—a not unreasonable measure if one seeks a single criterion.

3. See W. W. Rostow, *Politics and the Stages of Growth* (Cambridge: At the University Press, 1971), pp. 378–379, for a comparison of the two sets of stages.
4. See, for example, the quotation from Simon Kuznets, in Part Three, note 4.
5. The quotation is from Donald F. Gordon, in a review of my *How It All Began*, *Business Week*, 19 May 1975, p. 23. The full context of Gordon's observation indicates its relevance to the question of leading sector analysis: "Economic growth has not been the result of a small number of spectacular inventions and leading sector industries, but rather it appears as a result of a large number of small advances over a wide front."
6. For the long history of difficulty economic theory has had with the problem of dealing with major technological change, from Adam Smith to the present, see W. W. Rostow, "Technology and the Price System," Chapter 5 in William Breit and William Patton Culbertson, Jr. (eds.), *Science and Ceremony: The Institutional Economics of C. E. Ayres* (Austin: University of Texas Press, 1976).
7. See Part Three, note 4. For occasional years it is possible to estimate value added in particular branches of production—a quite different measurement than the full impact of a leading sector complex. Nevertheless, such calculations are useful in illustrating both the large continuing role of sectors not affected by major new innovations (e.g., building) and the rise and fall of the sequence of leading sectors. See, for example, Walther G. Hoffmann's calculation of weights in his index of British industrial production, *British Industry, 1700–1950*, translated by W. H. Chaloner and W. O. Henderson (Oxford: Basil Blackwell, 1955), pp. 16–23. These are calculated for selected years when censuses of production, of various degrees of reliability, are available: 1740, 1783, 1812, 1850, 1881, 1907, 1924.

8. Estimates of the price elasticity of demand for automobiles in the United States range from −0.6 to −1.5; income elasticity, from +1.5 to +4.3.
9. Hollis B. Chenery and Lance Taylor, "Development Patterns: Among Countries and over Time," *The Review of Economics and Statistics*, vol. 50, no. 4 (November 1968), pp. 409–412. For an earlier, historical analysis of the relation between industrial growth and industrial structure see Walther G. Hoffmann, *The Growth of Industrial Economies*, translated by W. O. Henderson and W. H. Chaloner (Manchester: Manchester University Press, 1958).
10. Chenery made this connection between "early sectors" and the take-off in his "Patterns of Industrial Growth," *American Economic Review*, vol. 50, no. 4 (September 1960), p. 651.
11. The smoothing technique used is the following: each smoothed value is obtained by evaluating the least squares polynomial of degree 1 relevant to the five successive points. In effect, the smoothed values are the product of a moving fitted curve rather than simple arithmetic averages. Rates of change are calculated from those curves.

CHAPTER 28. *Great Britain*

12. For alternative measures of British real output (and output per capita) in the eighteenth century, see Phyllis Deane and W. A. Cole, *British Economic Growth, 1688–1959*, second edition (Cambridge: At the University Press, 1969), pp. 75–82. They conclude (p. 281): "The acceleration in the rate of growth found for the last two decades of the century is in accordance with what now seems to be the generally accepted view among economic historians." If the volatile government and defense sector is removed from the Deane and Cole estimates of real national output (and the weights of industry and agriculture correspondingly increased), the annual average growth rates are as follows: 1740–1750, 0.85 percent; 1750–1760, 1.08 percent; 1760–1770, 0.71 percent; 1770–1780, 0.27 percent; 1780–1790, 2.27 percent, 1790–1800, 2.03 percent.
13. For a review of the debate on investment rates and the British take-off, see my discussion in the 1971 edition of *Stages of Economic Growth*, pp. 205–207; and for results of further research, see François Crouzet (ed.), *Capital Formation in the Industrial Revolution* (London: Methuen, 1972). Later research has suggested a more marked increase in the proportion of income invested than originally estimated by Deane and Cole.
14. Deane and Cole, *British Economic Growth*, pp. 259–277, trace out the course of British capital formation down to 1959.
15. Kuznets (*Economic Growth of Nations*, p. 41) states that his calculations for Britain (and twelve other nations, similarly presented) "do not provide support for W. W. Rostow's 'take-off' theory which suggests an initial rapid acceleration in the rate of growth of per capita product. . . ." In the case of Britain, this is evidently the case because he chose not to include the Deane and Cole estimates for the pre–take-off decades, included here, which exhibit clearly the expected rapid acceleration. In the case of France, Belgium, Germany, and Italy, Kuznets similarly begins during or after the take-off. In the case of Japan, his initial period (1874–1879 to 1895–1904) blankets the pre–take-off and take-off periods, also making a test of the take-off hypothesis impossible in terms of this criterion.
16. Although they are not rigidly linked, there are historical connections of some significance in this sequence of leading sectors. The expanded use of steam engines and the expanded requirements for textile machine building, in the first generation of modern technology, helped create the engineering capacity necessary to build efficient railroad engines. Moreover, the expanded requirements for transport to and from cotton factories helped create (but did not uniquely determine) the incentives for lower transport costs, to which the railways responded; e.g., the Manchester-Liverpool line. The requirement for rails

with lower rates of obsolescence than iron certainly increased the incentive to make cheap steel. Rail requirements dominated the first phase of the modern steel industry. The full development of the potentialities of steel certainly played a large role in making possible an efficient internal combustion engine. The development of petroleum chemistry helped set the stage for the emergence of certain modern new chemicals, etc.

17. Britain's initial technological lead and the subsequent closing of the technological gap raised questions about the definition and dating of the stage of Britain's technological maturity discussed in Rostow, *Stages of Economic Growth*, pp. 67–70, and in this book, pp. 382–383.
18. These issues are discussed, in the context of the 1960 debate at Konstanz on the take-off, in Rostow (ed.), *Economics of Take-off into Sustained Growth*, pp. xvi–xx, 1–9, 22–43 (Kuznets), 315–324 (summary of discussion).
19. For further discussion of this point, see Rostow, *Stages of Economic Growth*, second edition, pp. 195–196.
20. There were major expansions in ship construction in the cyclical expansions peaking in 1802 and 1810, the peak in ship construction lagging a year in the latter case. 1815 was also a peak year in British ship construction.
21. For a summary of the debate on the possible link between the early British use of coal and Britain's pioneering of the industrial revolution, see W. W. Rostow, *How It All Began* (New York: McGraw-Hill, 1975), pp. 178–180.

CHAPTER 29. *The United States*

22. On this early ferment, see, notably, Ralph S. Bates, "Scientific Societies in Eighteenth Century America," in idem, *Scientific Societies in the United States*, second edition (New York: Columbia University Press, 1958), pp. 1–27.
23. The course of pig iron production in the 1850's, an industry undergoing a technological transformation to more modern methods, does not adequately capture the heavy-industry surge of that decade. The proportion of value added in manufacturing contributed by fabricated metal, nonelectrical machinery, and transport equipment rose from 11.4 percent in 1849 to 16.3 percent in 1859. For computations and analysis emphasizing this feature of the pre–Civil War decade see Albert W. Niemi, "Structural and Labor Productivity Patterns in United States Manufacturing," *Business History Review*, vol. 46 (Spring 1972), pp. 69–84.
24. For the persistence of regional differentials in advanced industrial countries see, for example, O. J. Firestone, *Regional Disparity: United States, United Kingdom, Australia, and Canada*, Research Paper No. 7515, University of Ottawa (Ottawa, July 1975). For the tendency of regional differentials to increase in "early development stages" and to diminish in "the more mature stages of national growth and development," see Jeffrey G. Williamson, "Regional Inequality and the Process of National Development," *Economic Development and Cultural Change*, vol. 13, no. 4. (July 1965), pp. 3–84.
25. Robert Brooke Zevin, "The Growth of Cotton Textile Production after 1815," Chapter 10 in Robert William Fogel and Stanley L. Engerman (eds.), *The Reinterpretation of American Economic History* (New York: Harper and Row, 1971), p. 123.
26. With respect to Robert William Fogel and Stanley L. Engerman, *Time on the Cross*, vol. 1, *The Economics of American Negro Slavery*; vol. 2, *Evidence and Methods—A Supplement* (Boston: Little, Brown and Company, 1974), I regard the book's title as a misnomer. Economic analysis of the kind used by Fogel and Engerman cannot capture the inherent nature of a slave's situation; and the authors did not reach beyond the conventional box of neoclassical economists' tools in deal-

ing with their subject matter, as, for example, Gunnar Myrdal did in *An American Dilemma.* What, for example, is one to make of the extraordinary chart (vol. 1, p. 145) showing the distribution of whippings over a two-year period on a Louisiana plantation? With some apparent satisfaction, the authors note: "The record shows that over the course of two years a total of 160 whippings were administered, an average of 0.7 whippings per hand per year. About half the hands were not whipped at all during the period." After some brief references to whipping, from the Scriptures forward, they note the acceptance of the custom in interviews with ex-slaves, and the fact that whippings were meant to increase efficiency "with minimum impairment to the human capital which the master owned" (p. 147). But, quite aside from the linkage of welfare theory and Paretan optimality to freedom of choice for the individual (elaborated by Paul A. David and Peter Temin, "Slavery: The Progressive Institution?" *Journal of Economic History*, vol. 34, no. 3 [September 1974], pp. 739–783), what of the psychological effects on a man, his wife, his children, of living under a system where whipping was an accepted part of his round of life? To deal with this dimension of slavery—and all its other inherently demeaning characteristics—requires a framework of concepts far transcending conventional economics. One can approach the heart of the matter by speculating (*Time on the Cross*, vol. 1, pp. 236–238) on the "large nonpecuniary disadvantages" of gang labor on plantations; but one comes then merely to the edge of what time on the cross was really like. One is saying something—but nothing very new to a reader of Lewis C. Gray's *History of Agriculture in the Southern United States to 1860*, first edition, 2 vols. (Washington, D. C.: Carnegie Institution of Washington, 1933)—by proving that slaves were fed and cared for in about the way one would expect pieces of rather expensive capital equipment to be maintained. It should also be noted that there is no reference in *Time on the Cross* to the level of literacy among slaves or to opportunities for education, beyond those available through artisan labor and the occasional emergence of men of erudition (vol. 1, pp. 149–153). Even a narrow economic analysis of slavery would have to deal with the fact that in the 1870 census 80 percent of nonwhites in the United States were still illiterate.

27. Fogel and Engerman, *Time on the Cross*, vol. 1, pp. 247–257.
28. Ibid., p. 257. This dictum is thrown in almost as an afterthought and not fully developed. For an observation on Fogel and Engerman's analysis in the same vein, see Gavin Wright, "Slavery and the Cotton Boom," *Explorations in Economic History*, vol. 12, no. 4 (October 1975), pp. 439–450.
29. Albert Fishlow, "The American Common School Revival: Fact or Fancy?" in Henry Rosovsky (ed.), *Industrialization in Two Systems: Essays in Honor of Alexander Gerschenkron* (New York: John Wiley, 1966), pp. 60–62.
30. Prof. Berry described his "consensus" method and published his initial findings in Thomas S. Berry, *Estimated Annual Variations in Gross National Product, 1789 to 1909* (Richmond, Va.: The Bostwick Press, 1968). He later modified his calculations and kindly made available to me his latest unpublished data. These are used for GNP per capita and the proportion of income invested in Chart V-6, parts 1 and 2. The pre-1839 trends which emerge from Berry's calculations conform well with those of Paul David in "The Growth of Real Product in the United States before 1840: New Evidence, Controlled Conjectures," *Journal of Economic History*, vol. 27, no. 2 (June 1967). (See note 31 below.) Although Berry made his calculations for the whole period 1789–1973, for the period 1889–1920 he used the Kendrick-Kuznets series; for 1929–1973, the revised U.S. Department of Commerce estimates are used for GNP per capita and the proportion of GNP invested in Chart V-6, parts 1 and 2. While based on imperfect data, Berry's figures conform in a rough and ready way to what we know from all kinds of evidence about the course of the American economy from the

1790's forward; and his method yields approximations for later years, when better data are available, that conform quite well to more conventional national-income estimates.

For longer periods, Berry's calculations yield an annual average rate of growth of 1.35 percent from 1789 to 1863, which compares with David's figure of 1.31 percent for 1790–1860. For 1800–1835 the two figures are, respectively, 1.27 percent and about 1.28 percent; for 1835–1855, 1.19 percent and 1.30 percent. For comparison with Table V-6, 1.35 percent per annum yields a decadal growth of 14.35 percent.

31. Berry's current calculations of growth rates in GNP per capita for overlapping decadal intervals (eleven years) for the pre–Civil War period are as follows (annual average percentage rate of growth):

1790–1800	1.91
1795–1805	1.70
1800–1810	1.03
1805–1815	1.01
1810–1820	1.24
1815–1825	1.08
1820–1830	1.45
1825–1835	1.73
1830–1840	1.78
1835–1845	0.98
1840–1850	1.46
1845–1855	1.13
1850–1860	0.62

32. Robert E. Gallman and Edward S. Howle, "Trends in the Structure of the American Economy since 1840," Chapter 3 in Fogel and Engerman (eds.), *Reinterpretation of American Economic History*, p. 26.
33. For Kuznets' measurements over shorter periods, permitting fluctuations in product-per-capita growth rates to be more precisely identified, see his "Notes on the Pattern of U.S. Economic Growth," Chapter 2 in Fogel and Engerman (eds.), *Reinterpretation of American Economic History*, p. 18.
34. Gallman and Howle, "Trends," pp. 30–32.
35. See, notably, Jeffrey G. Williamson, "Watersheds and Turning Points: Conjectures on the Long-Term Impact of Civil War Financing," *Journal of Economic History*, vol. 34, no. 3 (September 1974), pp. 636–661.

CHAPTER 30. *France*

36. For a summary of the debate on the French take-off, see Rostow, *Stages of Economic Growth*, second edition, pp. 207–214. For a comparison of British and French economic growth in the eighteenth century and an assessment of the reasons for the earlier British take-off, see Rostow, *How It All Began*, especially pp. 167–189.
37. Jan Marczewski, "The Take-Off Hypothesis and French Experience," Chapter 7 in Rostow (ed.), *Economics of Take-off into Sustained Growth*, p. 124. As Franklin F. Mendels has emphasized, the scale and momentum of industrialization in early phases of modern growth are sensitive to whether traditional handicraft manufactures are included in statistical measurements ("Proto-industrialization: The First Phase of the Industrialization Process," *Journal of Economic History*, vol. 32, no. 1 [March 1972], pp. 241–261; the French case is cited on pp. 257–260).
38. *OECD Observer*, no. 74 (March–April 1975), pp. 22–23. These calculations are in current prices and exchange rates, reflecting the greater depreciation of the pound than the franc vis-à-vis the U.S. dollar since 1970. A painstaking study sponsored by the United Nations and the World Bank suggests that, as of 1970, British gross domestic product per capita was about 80 percent of the French level; consumption, 92 percent; capital formation, 55 percent; government, 98 percent. (Ir-

ving Kravis et al., *A System of International Comparisons of Gross Product and Purchasing Power* [Baltimore: Johns Hopkins University Press, 1975]).

39. Gregory King's famous calculation for 1688 was: England £7 18s.; France £6 3s. His estimate for Holland, leading the pack, was £8 1s. 4d., 2 percent above the English level (George E. Barnett [ed.], *Two Tracts by Gregory King* [Baltimore: Johns Hopkins Press, 1936], p. 55). Extrapolating backward on the basis of growth rates, Kuznets (*Economic Growth of Nations*, pp. 24–27) exhibits British and French per capita GNP in 1965 dollars (U.S.) for "the beginning of modern growth" and for 1895 (pp. 25–26, note 7), using Mulhall data, which conform fairly well to the Kuznets calculations.

40. Marczewski, "Take-off Hypothesis," p. 135. From the mid-nineteenth century, C. P. Kindleberger has analyzed in detail the comparative economic performance of France and Britain in *Economic Growth in France and Britain, 1851–1950* (Cambridge, Mass.: Harvard University Press, 1964). His useful summary table (p. 13) of phases of acceleration and retardation should be read with an awareness that he misses the real cyclical expansion of Britain from 1879 to 1882, which France shared.

41. As Crouzet has pointed out, decadal averages of the kind used by Marczewski and others mask the rapid growth of the 1840's because of the abnormal decline in output caused by the revolution of 1848 (François Crouzet, "Essai de construction d'un indice annuel de la production industrielle française au XIXe siècle," *Annales, Economies, Sociétés, Civilisations*, no. 1 [January–February 1970], especially pp. 76 and 87–88).

42. Tihimur V. Markovitch has calculated for shorter periods gross capital formation as a proportion of gross national product (less imports) in *L'Industrie française de 1789 à 1964—Conclusions générales, Histoire quantitative de l'économie française*, no. 7, Cahiers de l'Institut de Science Economique Appliquée, no. 179 (November 1966), Chapter 4, pp. 88–117. The most satisfactory of his three methods yields the following percentages of gross capital formation to GNP (p. 99):

1781–1790	8.6
1803–1812	8.1
1815–1824	7.1
1825–1834	7.0
1835–1844	9.2
1845–1854	11.0
1855–1864	13.9
1865–1874	13.8
1875–1884	14.9
1885–1894	15.0
1895–1904	16.4
1905–1913	16.9
1920–1924	23.5
1925–1934	17.9
1935–1938	16.3

43. M. M. Postan, *An Economic History of Western Europe, 1945–1964* (London: Methuen, 1967), p. 115.

CHAPTER 31. *Germany*

44. For an argument on the special leisurely character of the French experience with modern growth, see especially Maurice Levy-Leboyer, "Croissance économique en France au XIXe siècle," *Annales, Economies, Sociétés, Civilisations*, vol. 23, no. 4 (July–August 1968), pp. 788–807. See also Claude Fohlen, "The Industrial Revolution in France," in Rondo Cameron (ed.), *Essays in French Economic History* (Homewood, Ill.: Richard D. Irwin, 1970), pp. 201–225.

45. See especially Chapter 2 in Rostow, *How It All Began*.
46. See Michael Mulhall's data on relative German and French national income and wealth per capita, *Industries and Wealth of Nations* (London, New York, and Bombay: Longmans, Green, 1896), pp. 128–132 (France) and 151–154 (Germany).
47. Walther G. Hoffmann, "The Take-off in Germany," Chapter 6 in Rostow (ed.), *Economics of Take-off into Sustained Growth*, pp. 95–118.
48. Ibid., p. 107.
49. In the discussion of his paper at Konstanz, Hoffmann noted, however, that "The spreading effects of the railways were not great before 1848, but the railways did unify the country by bringing the regions together for the first time" (in Rostow [ed.], *Economics of Take-off into Sustained Growth*, p. 352).
50. Michael G. Mulhall, *The Dictionary of Statistics* (London: George Routledge, 1892), p. 547.
51. C. P. Kindleberger analyzes thoughtfully the relative pre-1914 progress of Britain and Germany in "Germany's Overtaking of England, 1806–1914," parts 1 and 2, *Weltwirtschaftliches Archiv*, vol. 3, nos. 2 and 3 (1975), pp. 253–281 and 477–504.
52. Ibid., pp. 114 and 116.

CHAPTER 32. *Sweden*

53. The development of the Swedish economy between 1815 and 1870 is analyzed in G. A. Montgomery, *The Rise of Modern Industry in Sweden* (London: P. S. King, 1939); Eli Heckscher, *An Economic History of Sweden*, translated by Goran Ohlin (Cambridge, Mass.: Harvard University Press, 1954), especially Chapter 6, pp. 209–266; and A. J. Youngson, *Possibilities of Economic Progress* (Cambridge: At the University Press, 1959), Chapter 9, "The Acceleration of Economic Progress in Sweden, 1850–80," pp. 146–190.
54. Lennart Jörberg, *Growth and Fluctuations of Swedish Industry, 1868–1912* (Stockholm: Almqvist and Wiksell, 1961), pp. 304–305.

CHAPTER 33. *Japan*

55. For my views on the origins and unfolding of Japanese industrialization, see Rostow, *Politics and the Stages of Growth*, pp. 71–72, 88–89, 128–132, 149–152. The revisionist literature on the Tokugawa era, which would emphasize premodern industrial and commercial progress before 1868, is well reflected in Kozo Yamamura, "Toward a Reexamination of the Economic History of Tokugawa Japan, 1600–1867," *Journal of Economic History*, vol. 33, no. 3 (September 1973), pp. 509–541. For a brief but valuable essay on the preconditions for take-off after the Meiji Restoration, see Rosovsky, "Japan's Transition," pp. 91–139.
56. S. Tsuru, "The Take-off in Japan, 1868–1900," Chapter 8 in Rostow (ed.), *Economics of Take-off into Sustained Growth*, p. 144.
57. Most recent research has modified the earlier judgment that the Japanese investment rate was abnormally low during its take-off. See, for example, James I. Nakumura, *Agricultural Production and the Economic Development of Japan, 1873–1922* (Princeton: Princeton University Press, 1966). Nakumura argues that the level of agricultural production in the early Meiji years was understated in official valuation, but that understatement progressively declined. Therefore, the rate of agricultural expansion (and of expansion in real GNP) is conventionally overstated for the early phases of modern Japanese growth. He also finds Japanese investment probably underestimated. He concludes, in consequence, that the proportion of Japanese investment to GNP was higher and the productivity of investment (capital-output ratio) more conventional than suggested in previous analyses (see especially his pp. 170–174).

58. Henry Rosovsky, *Capital Formation in Japan, 1868–1904* (Glencoe, Ill.: Free Press, 1961), especially pp. 164, 204, 207, 321.
59. Kazushi Ohkawa et al., *The Growth Rate of the Japanese Economy since 1878* (Tokyo: Kinokuniya Bookstore Company, 1957), pp. 16–34.
60. Robert E. Ward and Dankwart A. Rustow (eds.), *Political Modernization in Japan and Turkey* (Princeton: Princeton University Press, 1964), p. 188. Rosovsky, "Japan's Transition," pp. 105–107, summarizes the evidence for a relatively high educational base in Tokugawa Japan. See also Angus Maddison, *Economic Growth in Japan and the USSR* (London: George Allen and Unwin, 1969), p. 17, where Table N-32 is provided, from data made available by the research section, Ministry of Education, Tokyo.

TABLE N-32. *Enrollment Ratios in Japanese Education, 1880–1963*

	Primary and Two Secondary Levels, Enrollment as Percentage of Population Aged 5–19	Upper Secondary Enrollment as Percentage of Population Aged 15–19	Higher Education Enrollment as Percentage of Population Aged 20–24
1880	31	1	0.3
1915	63	21	1.3
1950	86	71	5.2
1963	94	92	10.2

Source: Maddison, *Economic Growth in Japan and the USSR*, p. 17.

61. Allen C. Kelley and Jeffrey G. Williamson properly emphasize the role of military outlays in this phase of retardation (*Lessons from Japanese Development* [Chicago: University of Chicago Press, 1974], pp. 114–115). Their highly aggregated model, however, permits them to deal with the pace and character of the absorption of technology only in exceedingly general terms.

CHAPTER 34. *Russia-USSR*

62. For a short account, see Rostow, *How It All Began*, especially pp. 55–60, 208–211. See also idem, *Politics and the Stages of Growth*, pp. 87–88.
63. If the expansion in cotton weaving is measured from 1851 to the peak in 1859, the annual average rate of increase was 7.3 percent. For annual data on the 1840's and 1850's, see S. Strumlin, "Industrial Crises in Russia, 1847–67," translated by Malcolm E. Falkus, in François Crouzet, W. H. Chaloner, and W. M. Stern (eds.), *Essays in European Economic History, 1789–1914* (New York: St. Martin's Press, 1969), pp. 155–178. The point of Strumlin's essay appears to be to insist (in a review article criticizing a Soviet study entitled *World Economic Crises, 1848–1935*) that Russia was caught up in the cyclical rhythm of the international economy from at least the crisis of 1847. He argues the point convincingly. But he introduces along the way a good deal of evidence on the expansion of Russian industrial production in those mid-century decades. In fact, his concluding theme (p. 178) is the unexampled pace of mechanization, from an initially low level, in the quarter-century from 1845 to 1870.

    On the early history of the Russian railroads, see especially J. N. Westwood, *A History of Russian Railways* (London: George Allen and Unwin, 1964), pp. 17–58. Some who opposed the railroads in Russia called them "this modern sickness" which would, among other things, "ruin morality" (pp. 28–29). By 1860, however, a thousand miles were open.
64. Peter Lyashchenko, *History of the National Economy of Russia to the 1917 Revolution*, translated by L. M. Herman (New York: Macmillan, 1949), pp. 563–564.
65. Mulhall, *Dictionary of Statistics*, p. 160.

66. For a perceptive historical essay on north-south differences in Italian economic development, see Shepard B. Clough and Carlo Levi, "Economic Growth in Italy: An Analysis of the Uneven Development of North and South," *Journal of Economic History*, vol. 16, no. 3 (September 1956), pp. 334–349. On Italy's economic difficulties in the 1860's, including north-south differences, see G. Luzzatto, "The Italian Economy in the First Decade after Unification," translated by Anna Hearder, in Crouzet, Chaloner, and Stern (eds.), *Essays in European Economic History*, pp. 203–225.
67. See notably, Alexander Gerschenkron, "Notes on the Rate of Industrial Growth in Italy, 1881–1913," *Journal of Economic History*, vol. 15, no. 4 (December 1955), pp. 360–375; and Jon S. Cohen, "Financing Industrialization in Italy, 1894–1914: The Partial Transformation of a Late-Comer," *Journal of Economic History*, vol. 27, no. 3 (September 1967), pp. 363–382. On the linkages between the Italian take-off and the Balkans, see Angelo Tambora, "The Rise of Italian Industry and the Balkans (1900–1914)," *Journal of European Economic History*, vol. 3, no. 1 (Spring 1974), pp. 87–120.
68. Kuznets, *Economic Growth of Nations*, pp. 11–13.

CHAPTER 36. *Canada*

69. The rich literature on Canadian economic development includes the following: Kenneth Buckley, *Capital Formation in Canada, 1896–1930* (Toronto: University of Toronto Press, 1955); W. T. Easterbrook and Hugh G. J. Aitken, *Canadian Economic History* (Toronto: Macmillan Company of Canada, 1956); O. J. Firestone, *Canada's Economic Development, 1867–1953*, Income and Wealth Series VII (London: Bowes and Bowes, 1958); Harold A. Innis, *The Fur Trade in Canada* (New Haven: Yale University Press, 1930); idem, *Problems of Staple Production in Canada* (Toronto: Ryerson Press, 1933); W. A. Mackintosh, *The Economic Background of Dominion-Provincial Relations* (study prepared for the Royal Commission on Dominion-Provincial Relations) (Ottawa, 1939); John A. Stovel, *Canada in the World Economy* (Cambridge, Mass.: Harvard University Press, 1959).
70. Firestone, *Canada's Economic Development*, pp. 38–39. Firestone has generalized and sharpened the general findings of his research on Canadian economic growth in *Industry and Education: A Century of Canadian Development* (Ottawa: University of Ottawa Press, 1969), especially Chapters 2–4 and 10–13. He provides a table of Canadian growth rates broken out in terms of the stages of economic growth (Table N-33).

    Firestone speculates about the possible reason for the lower per capita growth rate for the take-off than for the period of preconditions. He cites, in particular, the extraordinary pace of immigration and the large outlays required for infrastructure and housing, which normally are associated with high capital-output ratios. If one exam-

TABLE N-33. *Canadian Growth Rates by Stages (Annual Average Percentage Rates of Change of Real GNP)*

	Total	Per Capita	Per Person Working
Preconditions: 1867–1896	3.3	2.0	1.6
Take-off: 1896–1914	3.7	1.3	0.7
Drive to technological maturity: 1915–1950	3.0	1.5	1.5
High mass-consumption: 1950–1967	4.5	2.1	2.1
1867–1967	3.5	1.7	1.5

Source: Firestone, *Industry and Education*, p. 123.

ines the annual data for per capita national product (ibid., Appendix A, pp. 261–263) during take-off, its annual rate evolved as follows: 1896–1903 (beginning of take-off to end of Boer War, which inhibited capital flows from London), 1.7 percent; 1903–1913 (period of maximum capital imports and expansion, broken by recessions of 1904, 1907, and 1912), 2.0 percent. Firestone's figure for 1896–1914 (1.3 percent) is strongly affected by the 10 percent decline in GNP per capita in the year 1914. The overall per capita growth rate for 1896–1913 is 1.9 percent; for total growth, 4.4 percent. And if one measures from the cyclical trough of 1897 to 1913, the two figures are 2.95 percent and 5.56 percent, respectively. In short, the comparison of growth rates during the Canadian preconditions and take-off is quite sensitive to the particular years chosen for measurement. One can firmly conclude only that the overall rate of Canadian real growth was higher in the take-off, the per capita figure perhaps slightly lower at a time when the Canadian population was increasing at an annual rate of 2.4 percent, as opposed to 1.4 percent in the period 1867–1896. So far as stages-of-growth analysis is concerned, however, the critical factor in defining the take-off is not an acceleration in GNP per capita but Canada's efficient absorption of a new range of modern industrial technologies—a process which palpably did occur in the pre-1914 generation.

71. Edward J. Chambers and Donald F. Gordon dramatize by indirection the significance of this convergence in their "Primary Products and Economic Growth: An Empirical Measurement," *Journal of Political Economy*, vol. 74, no. 4 (August 1966), pp. 315–332. They argue that the impressive rise in Canadian real income per capita between 1900 and 1910 (23 percent) could be attributed in only very small measure to the expansion of prairie agriculture (5.20 percent–8.40 percent). They conclude (p. 328) that "other factors" must account for the rapid rise in real income per capita. Their use of comparative statics denies them, however, a lucid perspective on the complex interconnections among the wheat boom, railroadization, capital imports, immigration, urbanization, and industrial expansion required to explain the Canadian take-off. By the turn of the century Canada was an economy and a society prepared, with the aid of U.S. technology and entrepreneurship, to exploit the potential spreading effects of a process which did, indeed, have at its center the rising world price of wheat and the exploitation of the Canadian prairies.

72. O. J. Firestone, "Development of Canada's Economy, 1850–1900," in *Trends in the American Economy in the Nineteenth Century*, Studies in Income and Wealth, vol. 24 (Princeton: Princeton University Press, 1960), p. 236.

CHAPTER 37. *Australia*

73. Noel G. Butlin has merged, in a rare synthesis, regional, institutional, and disaggregated analysis with calculations of total investment and national income in *Australian Domestic Product, Investment and Foreign Borrowing, 1861–1938/9* (Cambridge: At the University Press, 1962), and *Investment in Australian Economic Development, 1861–1900* (Cambridge: At the University Press, 1964). On early Australian economic development, see, especially, in the latter work, pp. 3–110. See also Alan Barnard, *The Australian Wool Market, 1840–1900* (Carlton: Melbourne University Press, 1958); E. A. Boehm, *Twentieth Century Economic Development in Australia* (Victoria: Longman, 1971); T. A. Coghlan, *Labour and Industry in Australia from the First Settlement in 1788 to the Establishment of the Commonwealth in 1901*, 4 vols. (London: Oxford University Press, 1918); A. R. Hall, *The London Capital Market and Australia, 1870–1914* (Canberra: The Australian National University, 1963); E. Shann, *An Economic History of Australia* (Cambridge: At the University Press, 1930); Roland Wilson, *Capital Imports and the Terms of Trade* (Melbourne: Melbourne University Press in association with Macmillan Company, 1931).

74. See, notably, F. J. A. Broeze, "The Cost of Distance: Shipping and the Early Australian Economy, 1788–1850," *Economic History Review*, vol. 28, no. 4 (November 1975), pp. 582–597. Broeze argues persuasively that the greater proportional decline in freight rates than in the wool price lowered the proportion of the freight factor in the wool price between 1827 and 1831; and this reduction, along with the reduction in the bulk of wool made possible by the wool press, rendered Australian wool profitable at European prices.
75. Butlin, *Investment in Australian Economic Development*, p. 67.
76. Ibid., pp. 59–60.
77. Ibid., p. 61; see also pp. 47–48.
78. On wheat and the railroads, see above, Chapter 14.
79. Butlin examines in detail the anatomy of the depression of the 1890's in *Investment in Australian Economic Development*, pp. 407–450.
80. Boehm, *Twentieth Century Economic Development*, pp. 125–126. See also Butlin, *Investment in Australian Economic Development*, pp. 201–210.
81. Butlin, *Investment in Australian Economic Development*, p. 18. Butlin's estimates for the value of manufactures in constant prices exhibit the following annual average percentage rates of growth (*Australian Domestic Product*, pp. 460–461):

1861 to 1871	12.2
1871 to 1881	7.7
1881 to 1891	3.9
1891 to 1900–1901	0.3
1900–1901 to 1912–1913	5.7
1912–1913 to 1920–1921	–1.23
1920–1921 to 1928–1929	5.6
1928–1929 to 1931–1932	–9.3
1931–1932 to 1938–1939	6.4

The argument here is that the rapid growth of manufacturing from an initially very low base in the period 1861–1881 was a part of the Australian preconditions for take-off; the take-off occurred in the surge from 1900 to 1913; the drive to technological maturity occurred between 1920 and 1945; and, on the foundations thus established, Australia was subsequently in a position to support substantially the stage of high mass-consumption. My doubt about this argument stems from uncertainty, from the data available to me, about the character of the industrial expansion during the pre-1914 decade. Did it involve sufficient absorption of modern industrial technology to justify designation as a take-off period? Or, did take-off in Australia come only in the 1920's, when a diversified modern industrial structure clearly did emerge?
82. Boehm, *Twentieth Century Economic Development*, p. 127.
83. Ibid., pp. 129–130.

CHAPTER 38. *Argentina*

84. Among the studies of Argentine economic history relevant to the present analysis are: Carlos F. Díaz Alejandro, *Essays on the Economic History of the Argentine Republic* (New Haven: Yale University Press, 1970); H. S. Ferns, *Britain and Argentina in the Nineteenth Century* (Oxford: Clarendon Press, 1960); A. G. Ford, *The Gold Standard, 1880–1914, Britain and Argentina* (Oxford: Clarendon Press, 1962); Thomas F. McGann, *Argentina: The Divided Land* (Princeton: Princeton University Press, 1966); James R. Scobie, *Revolution on the Pampas: A Social History of Argentine Wheat, 1860–1910* (Austin: University of Texas Press, 1964); Arthur Smithies, "Argentina and Australia," *American Economic Review*, vol. 55, no. 2 (May 1965); Guido di Tella and Manuel Zymelman, *Las etapas del desarrollo económico argentino* (Buenos Aires: Editorial Universitaria de Buenos Aires, 1967); United Nations Economic Commission for Latin America, *El desarrollo económico de la Argentina*, 3 vols. (Mexico City, 1959); John H. Williams, *Argentine International Trade under Inconvertible Paper Money*,

1880–1900 (Cambridge, Mass.: Harvard University Press, 1920). On the early phase of Argentina's economic history see especially Jonathan Brown, "The Commercialization of Buenos Aires: Production and Trade of Pastoral Products in the River Plate to 1860" (Ph.D. dissertation, University of Texas at Austin, 1975).

85. Mulhall, *Industries and Wealth of Nations*, pp. 52 and 377.
86. Díaz Alejandro, *Essays*, pp. 309–310. For a full analysis of this problem, see ibid., Chapter 6, "Relative Prices, Industrialization, and Capital Formation," pp. 309–350.
87. For detailed data on Argentine industry in its first phase, see Ernesto Tornquist and Company, *The Economic Development of the Argentine Republic in the Last Fifty Years* (Buenos Aires, 1919), pp. 34–113.
88. Díaz Alejandro summarizes this structural change in relation to apparent Argentine income elasticities of demand for various manufactures (*Essays*, pp. 227–230): "During 1937–39/1948–50 it was primarily the lighter branches of manufacturing that showed output-growth elasticities greater than the apparent income elasticities of demand. Such was the case for foodstuffs and beverages, tobacco, textiles, clothing, wood products, printing and publishing, and leather products. On the other hand, such key branches as electrical machinery and appliances, vehicles and machinery, metals, petroleum refining, rubber products, and chemicals grew at relative rates lower than the income elasticity of demand for their products. . . . Although import-substitution advanced during this period in the lighter branches, it lagged in those producing mainly capital goods and heavy intermediate products. Further disaggregation of the somewhat heterogeneous categories used would strengthen this conclusion.

"The lag was not noticed during the immediate postwar years, when plentiful foreign exchange made possible the importation of these goods. But beginning around 1949, Argentina was faced with severe exchange difficulties. . . . By that time, the light branches had nearly exhausted their import-substitution possibilities, thus eliminating a possible source of exchange savings. To obtain the capital and intermediate goods required for economic expansion, exportables had to be encouraged and/or the lagging industrial sectors had to be given greater stimulus. The gap between the output-growth elasticities and the income elasticities of demand was reduced or eliminated during 1948–50/1959–61 for metallurgical industries, as well as in other branches producing intermediate goods. Even then, high income elasticities of demand for the output of these activities and special needs for capital goods maintained great pressure on imports, generating periodic payments crises. On the other hand, industries that had expanded vigorously during 1937–39/1948–50 stagnated after 1950.

"Two well-defined stages may then be seen in post-1930 manufacturing growth, cutting across political regimes. . . . During 1925–29/1948–50, textiles, foodstuffs, and beverages accounted for between 34 and 42 percent of the total expansion; after 1948–50, the same branches represented between 11 and 9 percent of output growth. On the other hand, the metallurgical sector (metals, vehicles, all machinery, and electrical appliances), which during the first stage contributed only between 24 and 30 percent of the overall expansion, after 1948–50 provided between 53 and 62 percent of it. Other light branches whose relative contribution during 1925–29/1948–50 exceeded substantially their post 1948–50 participations include clothing, leather products, and other manufacturing and handicrafts. The opposite was the case with such relatively complex activities as chemicals and petroleum refining."
89. Ibid., especially pp. 167–207.

CHAPTER 39. *Turkey*

90. For a brief account of Turkey's political and economic modernization, see Rostow, *Politics and the Stages of Growth*, pp. 74–75, 81–82, 92–93,

135–136, 153–155. For more detailed accounts, see Ward and Rustow (eds.), *Political Modernization in Japan and Turkey*, and Z. Y. Hershlag, *Turkey: The Challenge of Growth*, second edition (Leiden: E. J. Brill, 1968).

91. Hershlag, *Turkey*, p. 52.

CHAPTER 40. *Brazil*

92. Henry William Spiegel, *The Brazilian Economy* (Philadelphia: Blakeston Company, 1949), p. 117. Nathaniel H. Leff points out that the gross undervaluation of the milreis led to an export proportion to GNP of 15.5 percent in 1920; but on a purchasing-power parity basis the proportion might be as low as 8.8 percent ("Long Term Brazilian Economic Development," *Journal of Economic History*, vol. 29, no. 3 [September 1969], p. 482, note).
93. Nathaniel H. Leff, "Tropical Trade and Development in the Nineteenth Century: The Brazilian Experience," *Journal of Political Economy*, vol. 81, no. 3 (May–June 1973), pp. 681–682.
94. Donald Coes, "Brazil," Chapter 4 in W. Arthur Lewis (ed.), *Tropical Development, 1880–1913* (Evanston: Northwestern University Press, 1970), pp. 100–127. The referenced export table is on page 103.
95. Ibid., pp. 123–125. For an interesting, reflective analysis on the deeper reasons for Brazil's slow growth and late acceleration, see Nathaniel H. Leff, "Economic Retardation in Nineteenth Century Brazil," *Economic History Review*, Second Series, vol. 25, no. 3 (August 1972), pp. 489–507.
96. On the railroads and coffee, see O. G. de Bulhões' discussion of "an agricultural take-off" in Rostow (ed.), *Economics of Take-off into Sustained Growth*, pp. 229–231.
97. Richard Graham, *Britain and the Onset of Modernization in Brazil, 1850–1914* (Cambridge: At the University Press, 1968), Chapter 2, pp. 51–72. Graham analyzes in detail the multiple British roles in the Brazilian economy of this period and how they both stimulated and damped the Brazilian movement towards modern industrial growth.
98. Stanley J. Stein, *The Brazilian Cotton Manufacture: Textile Enterprise in an Underdeveloped Area* (Cambridge, Mass.: Harvard University Press, 1957), p. 21.
99. There is some difference of view among experts on the impact of the First World War on industrial output. Following Warren Dean, Leff ("Long Term Brazilian Economic Development," pp. 475–476) emphasizes the net decelerating effects on industry of the lack of imported raw materials and capital goods. He does allow for some stimulus through import substitution. Werner Baer (*Industrialization and Economic Development in Brazil* [Homewood, Ill.: Richard D. Irwin, 1965], pp. 16–19) emphasizes the "great opportunity for Brazilian infant industries" offered by the restriction of manufactured imports; an increase of perhaps 150 percent in real industrial output; and the creation of 5,936 new industrial establishments between 1914 and 1919. He also notes, however, the considerable postwar setback to some of the war babies when manufactured imports were again available in the early 1920's. Resolution of these different but not necessarily inconsistent perspectives is hindered by the lack of adequate comparable pre- and postwar statistical data.
100. See, especially, Warren Dean, *The Industrialization of São Paulo, 1880–1945*, Latin American Monographs, no. 17 (Austin: University of Texas Press, 1969). Dean traces vividly the immigrant roots of the new industrial entrepreneurs, the tensions and convergences of interest with the older elite, based on the coffee plantations (pp. 49–80).
101. See, notably, Stein, *Brazilian Cotton Manufacture*, and Leff, "Long Term Brazilian Economic Development," p. 477.
102. Baer, *Industrialization*, p. 21, where detailed sources are indicated. The annual industrial production index for São Paulo runs only to 1933.
103. Ibid., p. 27.

CHAPTER 41. *Mexico*

104. For a discussion of Mexico's problems in the preconditions for take-off, see Rostow, *Politics and the Stages of Growth*, pp. 75–77, 82–83, and 93–94.
105. See, for example, W. P. Glade, Jr., and Charles W. Anderson, *The Political Economy of Mexico* (Madison: University of Wisconsin Press, 1963), p. 81.
106. Clark W. Reynolds, *The Mexican Economy* (New Haven: Yale University Press, 1970), p. 313. Reynolds' reconstruction of pre-independence per capita income is in his Appendix A, pp. 311–314.
107. James W. Wilkie, *The Mexican Revolution: Federal Expenditure and Social Change since 1910* (Berkeley: University of California Press, 1967). Wilkie's poverty index pierces the veil of income-per-capita calculations by averaging the percentage of population reporting itself in censuses as: (1) illiterate, (2) speaking only Indian languages, (3) dwelling in communities of under 2,500 inhabitants (items 1–3 for years 1910–1940), (4) regularly going barefoot, (5) regularly wearing sandals, (6) regularly eating tortillas rather than wheat bread, (7) lacking sewage disposal. Wilkie's poverty index, by regions, is shown in Table N-34.

TABLE N-34. *A Poverty Index for Mexico by Region (1940 = 100)*

	1910	1921	1930	1940	1950	1960
Total Mexico	124	115	109	100	86	72
North Pacific	131	121	107	100	87	74
North	131	122	112	100	88	76
South Pacific	111	108	103	100	90	82
Gulf	129	122	110	100	87	76
Center (less Federal District)	118	113	107	100	91	78
Federal District	179	145	126	100	79	79

Source: Wilkie, *Mexican Revolution*, p. 234.

CHAPTER 42. *Iran*

108. For Iran's long road to economic modernization, see notably, Charles Issawi (ed.), *The Economic History of Iran, 1800–1914* (Chicago: University of Chicago Press, 1971). Issawi includes (pp. 391–399) a rather full bibliography. For the more recent period, the relations between oil revenues and economic growth in aggregate terms are traced out down to 1969 in Jahangir Amuzegar and M. Ali Fekrat, *Iran: Economic Development under Dualistic Conditions* (Chicago: University of Chicago Press, 1971).
109. Issawi, *Economic History*, p. 16.
110. See, for example, Robert E. Looney, *The Economic Development of Iran* (New York: Praeger, 1973), Chapter 6, pp. 106–125.
111. Ibid., pp. 11 and 107, describes as follows this transformation of industrial structure associated with the early stage of the drive to technological maturity: "Development has not taken place at a uniform rate in the various branches of the industrial sector. Within the durable consumer goods group, refrigerators and motor vehicles made the biggest contributions. Intermediate goods, or inputs into production of final products, owed their growth mainly to chemicals, nonmetallic minerals, and metal products. Within chemicals the dynamic products were plastic articles, paints, cosmetics, pharmaceuticals, and washing powder. These products grew at rates ranging from almost 20 percent to nearly 100 percent a year. Nondurable consumer goods continued to contribute the bulk of Iran's industrial growth. Here, the majority was contributed by food and beverages, textiles, footwear, and apparel.

However, output of foodstuffs and textiles—the two largest industries in Iran—rose at a slower rate than did the general index of industrial production. . . . In 1962 nondurable consumer goods represented nearly 69 percent of the total value added. By 1967, this had fallen to 62.8 percent. The rising importance of producer goods industries in the late 1960s is again evident, indicating the direction of recent industrial expansion."

CHAPTER 43. *India*

112. A useful presentation of the issues in this debate as of the 1960's, including references to early defenders and critics of the economic impact of British rule, is Morris David Morris et al., *Indian Economy in the Nineteenth Century: A Symposium* (Delhi: Delhi School of Economics, 1969). Angus Maddison's *Class Structure and Economic Growth: India and Pakistan since the Moghuls* (New York: W. W. Norton, 1971) provides a fresh appraisal based on a rare combination of economic and social analysis (Part Three, pp. 35–70). His imaginative quantitative estimates of social structure in relation to income distribution between the Mogul Empire and the end of British rule should especially be noted (pp. 33 and 69).
113. B. M. Bhatia, "Terms of Trade and Economic Development: A Case Study of India—1861–1939," *Indian Economic Journal*, vol. 16, nos. 4–5 (April –June 1969), pp. 414–433.
114. See, for example, Morris et al., *Indian Economy*, pp. 12–13 and 167–168 (Morris D. Morris).
115. See, for example, B. L. Grover and R. R. Sethi, *Studies in Modern Indian History* (Delhi: S. Chand and Company, 1963), p. 187.
116. In value terms, Indian merchandise exports increased at an average annual rate of 2.5 percent between 1814–1815 and 1854–1855; imports, at 6 percent (K. N. Chaudhuri [ed.], *The Economic Development of India under the East India Company, 1814–58* [Cambridge: At the University Press, 1971], p. 25). It is impossible to correct these value figures for price changes, but the decline in the British terms of trade over this period (see p. 93, above) suggests that the Indian terms of trade may well have been moving favorably. K. N. Chaudhuri estimates a 17 percent favorable shift in the Indian terms of trade between 1828–1829 and 1839–1840 ("India's Foreign Trade and the Cessation of the East India Company's Trading Activities," *Economic History Review*, Second Series, vol. 19 [1966], p. 351).
117. Quoted from Parliamentary Papers, 1840, vol. 7, Special Committee on the Petition of the East India Company for Relief, 2 June 1840, Question 191, in Chaudhuri (ed.), *Economic Development*, p. 27.
118. See, notably, Morris David Morris, *The Emergence of an Industrial Labor Force in India: A Study of the Bombay Cotton Mills, 1854–1947* (Berkeley and Los Angeles: University of California Press, 1965), pp. 22–24. Morris notes earlier efforts reaching back to 1817.
119. S. D. Mehta (*The Cotton Mills of India, 1854 to 1954* [Bombay: Textile Association (India), 1954], p. 64) describes vividly this "decade in which disasters repeated themselves with a regularity that refused to be monotonous only on account of the diversity of causes from which they sprang":

    "From 1892 to 1901, an amazing variety of unfortunate circumstances made its appearance and cast its shadow over the fortunes of the mill industry. In 1893 a currency muddle caused a major setback by drastically curtailing the yarn market in China and Japan; and to make matters worse, communal riots brought the industry in Bombay City to a standstill, engendering communal antipathies which did not completely subside with the suppression of the more violent forms. In 1894 Manchester succeeded in securing the levy of an excise duty on yarn produced in Indian mills above count 20s, and while the agitation was pending, brought uncertainties to the trade in yarn and piece-goods. Hardly had the industry made some inevitable adjustments in 1895 when a violent epidemic of plague broke out in Bombay and, to a lesser extent, in Ahmedabad and other centers. Simultaneously, the China market found itself glutted with stocks of yarn which could not be liquidated even at fantastically low prices. Once again, only two years after its last victory, Manchester succeeded in inflicting an injustice against the entire mill industry, an excise duty on all cloth produced—an injustice which had no parallel even in its successful agitation of the past. Famines further aggravated the difficulties only too obviously inherent in the situation. Plague continued to take its heavy toll in 1897, and in the last few months of the same year the China market once again faced a glut in stocks of unusual dimensions. This state of affairs continued in 1898, once again interrupted by a Government policy in the field of currency which resulted in a financial stringency which badly hurt even the best mills. In the closing years of the century Japanese and Chinese competition brought home to the industry a sense of impending crisis, and prices that were often below the costs of production. 1901 was a year of famine, although the difficulties did not last beyond the first few months."

120. See, notably, Morris et al., *Indian Economy*, especially pp. 8–11 (Morris); 20–22 (Toru Matsui); 52–63 (Bipan Chandra); 93–94 (T. Rarjchaudhuri); 159–165 (Morris' reply to the debate).
121. In an imaginative analysis, Michelle Burge McAlpin argues that the expanded absolute production of Indian agriculture for commercial markets in this period did not cause a shift in the proportion of output devoted to food grains, because the peasant, conscious of the possibility of famine, resisted price incentives in the interest of the security of his family's food supply ("Railroads, Prices, and Peasant Rationality: India, 1860–1900," *Journal of Economic History*, vol. 34, no. 3 (September 1974), pp. 662–684.
122. Later in the development of the Indian subcontinent, however, the great Indian railway repair facility at Lahore, incorporating a high level of skills and a long experience, helped greatly in the emergence of an engineering industry in Pakistan.
123. See, for example, D. A. Gadgil, *The Industrial Evolution of India in Recent Times, 1860–1939* (Bombay: Oxford University Press, 1971), pp. 282–290.
124. Government of India, Planning Commission, *Draft Fifth Five Year Plan, 1974–79* (New Delhi, n.d.), vol. 1, pp. 34–35.

CHAPTER 44. *China*

125. Rostow, *Politics and the Stages of Growth*, p. 90.
126. The complexities of the Ch'ing dynasty's Manchurian settlement policy and its failure are analyzed in Robert H. G. Lee, *The Manchurian Frontier in Ch'ing History* (Cambridge, Mass.: Harvard University Press, 1970), and summarized in Alexander Eckstein, Kang Chao, and John Chang, "The Economic Development of Manchuria: The Rise of a Frontier Economy," *Journal of Economic History*, vol. 34, no. 1 (March 1974), pp. 240–241.
127. Eckstein, Kang Chao, and Chang, "Economic Development," p. 246.
128. Albert Feuerwerker, *China's Early Industrialization* (Cambridge, Mass.: Harvard University Press, 1958), p. 5.
129. Ibid., p. 30.
130. Ibid., p. 222.
131. See, notably, Kang Chao, "The Growth of a Modern Cotton Textile Industry and the Competition with Handicrafts," in Dwight H. Perkins (ed.), *China's Modern Economy in Historical Perspective* (Stanford: Stanford University Press, 1975), pp. 167–201. Also, Bruce Lloyd Reynolds, "The Impact of Trade and Foreign Investment on Industrialization: Chinese Textiles, 1875–1931" (Ph.D. dissertation, University of Michigan, 1975).
132. Kang Chao, "Growth of a Modern Cotton Textile Industry," pp. 196–197.

133. Ibid., p. 198. For Kang Chao's evaluation that the Chinese communist contraction of the handicraft sector may have been economically "premature," see p. 201.
134. The evolution of capital goods industries in China is well traced out by Thomas G. Rawski, "The Growth of Producer Industries, 1900–1971," in Perkins (ed.), *China's Modern Economy*, pp. 203–234.
135. Ibid., p. 233.

CHAPTER 45. *Taiwan*

136. For a romantic account of pre-fifteenth-century Formosa, see W. G. Goddard, *Formosa: A Study in Chinese History* (East Lansing: Michigan State University Press, 1966), Chapter 1, "The Beginnings," pp. 1–34.
137. For estimates of Formosa's population and its racial constitution between 1661 and 1935, see Shinkichi Eto, "An Outline of Formosan History," a chapter in Mark Mancall (ed.), *Formosa Today* (New York: Praeger, 1964), p. 53.
138. Mo-Huan Hsing, "Taiwan: Industrialization and Trade Policies," in *Industry and Trade in Some Developing Countries: The Philippines and Taiwan* (London: Oxford University Press, 1971), p. 155.

CHAPTER 46. *Thailand*

139. For an analytic account of the transformation and modernization of the Thai bureaucracy see, notably, Fred W. Riggs, *Thailand: The Modernization of a Bureaucratic Polity* (Honolulu: East-West Center Press, 1966), especially Chapter 4, pp. 110–131. Riggs distinguishes five stages in this sequence: 1851–1873, Western influences introduced without structural change in the traditional bureaucracy; 1873–1891, some new functional departments created with the help of Western advisers (e.g., foreign affairs, post office); 1892–1900, sweeping reorganization of government in the form of twelve conventional ministries; 1900–1932, consolidation, readjustment, and expansion of the new governmental structure; 1932–, acceleration and deepening of functional specialization.
140. See ibid. on Chinese "pariah entrepreneurship," pp. 251–254.
141. The emergence of national economic planning in Thailand is well described by T. H. Silcock, "Promotion of Industry and the Planning Process," Chapter 11 in idem (ed.), *Thailand* (Canberra: Australian National University Press [in association with Duke University Press], 1967), especially pp. 260–288.
142. See, notably, Paul B. Trescott, *Thailand's Monetary Experience* (New York: Praeger, 1971). For Thai direct receipts from U.S. foreign-defense expenditure, see Asian Development Bank, *Southeast Asia's Economy in the 1970's* (London: Longman, 1971), Part 7, pp. 628–643 (Emile Benoit).
143. Asian Development Bank, *Southeast Asia's Economy*, p. 410.
144. Ibid., pp. 244–246.
145. Ibid., p. 132.
146. Ibid.

CHAPTER 47. *South Korea*

147. The Korean modernization movements of this period are briefly summarized in Hahn-Been Lee, *Korea: Time, Change, and Administration* (Honolulu: East-West Center Press, University of Hawaii, 1968), pp. 43–45.
148. A British commentator, writing in 1903, described the typical Korean as follows: "He is more set in his ancestor worship than the Chinese, more Confucianist than Confucius, more stereotyped in his dress than

even the blue-skirted Celestial, and belongs to a social structure whose limitations are adamantine. If it seems a hopeless task to lift the Chinaman out of his groove, it is a hundred times more difficult to change the habits of the Korean" (H. J. Whigham, quoted in W. D. Reeve, *The Republic of Korea: A Political and Economic Study* [London: Oxford University Press, 1963], pp. 5–6).

149. See, for example, the account of Reeve in ibid., pp. 17–21.

150. Quoted, Hahn-Been Lee, *Korea*, p. 195, note 21. The Japanese source used for 1935 educational data in Table V-80 gives a somewhat higher figure.

151. See, notably, Ronald I. McKinnon, *Money and Capital in Economic Development* (Washington, D.C.: Brookings Institution, 1973), pp. 105–111, 136–137, and 161–166.

152. See, notably, Irma Adelman, *Practical Approaches to Development Planning: Korea's Second Five-Year Plan* (Baltimore: Johns Hopkins Press, 1969). See also David C. Cole and Princeton N. Lyman, *Korean Development* (Cambridge, Mass.: Harvard University Press, 1971), Chapter 9, "The Significance of Economic Planning," pp. 203–221. This study contains a rather full account of South Korean economic and political development down to 1968. Chapter 8 in Paul Kuznets, *Economic Growth and Structure in the Republic of Korea* (New Haven: Yale University Press, 1977), describes the increasing sophistication of the three South Korean five-year plans. It also includes (pp. 221–232) a full bibliography on South Korean economic development.

CHAPTER 48. *Four Conclusions*

153. Thorkil Kristensen's interesting analysis of this phenomenon (*Development in Rich and Poor Countries* [New York: Praeger, 1974], pp. 24–36) is not set out explicitly in terms of stages of economic growth. But his emphasis on the pace at which nations can absorb and apply technologies is compatible with stages-of-growth analysis as used in this book. The highest rates of growth occur in countries I would designate as in the drive to technological maturity and in the early phases of high mass-consumption. I examine this subject as a whole in detail in "Growth Rates at Different Levels of Income and Stage of Growth: Reflections on Why the Poor Get Richer and the Rich Slow Down," *Research in Economic History*, vol. 3, January 1978.

154. While we do not know what future consumers' tastes and choices will be, nor the options new technologies may offer the consumer, we do know something about how families at different income levels in one industrial society disposed of their resources in the early 1960's and, to a lesser degree, a decade later. In February 1965 the Bureau of Labor Statistics of the U.S. Department of Labor published the results of a detailed survey of this field: *Consumers' Expenditures and Income, Total United States, Urban and Rural, 1960–61*, BLS Report No. 237-93. The partial results of a 1972–1973 sample survey of consumers' expenditures were released on 16 April 1975 (USDL:75-212).

The more complete 1960–1961 survey does not show expenditure patterns in detail for families with incomes (after taxes) of over $15,000. There is, simply, a category, "$15,000 and over," whose income before taxes averages $28,399, after taxes, $22,144.

When adjusted for price changes since 1961–1962 and for average family size, we are dealing with gross per capita income in 1975 U.S. dollars of almost $14,000 ($8,200 in 1967 dollars).

Table N-35, adapted from the February 1965 report (p. 16), exhibits the average disposition of gross family income for the population as a whole, and for families with incomes of $2,000–2,999 and over $15,000. I have set aside those with family incomes under $2,000 because they generally represent disproportionately older persons with small families and expenditure patterns affected by variables other than income. This, to a degree, is still true of the $2,000–2,999 category.

TABLE N-35. *Summary of Family Expenditures, Income, and Savings, by Income Class (All Urban and Rural Families and Single Consumers: United States, 1961)*

	Total	Money Income after Taxes $2,000–2,999	$15,000 and O
Family Characteristics			
Estimated number of families in universe (thousands)	55,306	6,077	1,100
Percentage of families	100.0	11.0	2.0
Average			
Family size	3.2	2.7	3.9
Number of children under 18	1.2	0.9	1.3
Total disbursements (in Dollars)	7,579	3,624	28,922
Increase in assets	1,493	594	10,370
Decrease in liabilities	473	125	1,527
Personal insurance	298	89	1,151
Gifts and contributions	277	137	1,601
Expenditures for current consumption	5,038	2,679	14,273
Percentage distribution, expenditures for current consumption	100.0	100.0	100.0
Food, total	24.4	28.4	19.2
Food prepared at home	19.6	23.6	13.1
Food away from home	4.8	4.8	6.1
Tobacco	1.8	2.3	1.0
Alcoholic beverages	1.5	1.0	1.7
Housing, total	28.9	31.5	29.8
Shelter	13.1	15.3	12.5
Rented dwelling	5.3	9.7	1.6
Owned dwelling	7.1	5.2	8.7
Other shelter	0.7	0.4	2.2
Fuel, light, refrigeration, water	5.0	6.7	3.7
Household operations	5.7	5.3	8.7
House furnishings and equipment	5.2	4.3	5.1
Clothing, clothing materials, services	10.4	8.4	12.6
Personal care	2.9	3.2	2.4
Medical care	6.8	8.6	6.2
Recreation	4.0	2.7	4.7
Reading	0.9	0.9	0.8
Education	1.1	0.4	2.8
Transportation	15.1	10.8	14.1
Automobile	13.6	9.2	10.3
Other travel and transportation	1.5	1.6	3.8
Other expenditures	2.2	1.9	4.7

Note: Due to rounding, totals may not equal sums of components.

The first conclusion to be derived from this table, borne out by more detailed breakdowns, is that as families get richer they spend more on every category of consumption. Their absolute outlays for insurance and gifts also rise. There is a shift (not shown in this table) from a net negative to a net positive annual change in assets and liabilities at a 1961–1962 family income level of $4,000–4,900. In relative terms, the most striking difference at various income levels is the rise in the proportion of gross income allocated to increasing the family's assets: up to 18 percent for those $15,000 and over, as opposed to 4 percent for the average. There is only a modest percentage increase in the proportion of disbursements for gifts and contributions, and relative stability in proportions allocated to personal insurance.

With respect to consumption, the proportionate outlays between the average and affluent families fall significantly with the rise in income for food, tobacco, and utilities. The proportions rise for food away from home, "other shelter" (presumably hotels), household operations, clothing, education, and nonautomotive (presumably air) travel. This pattern was roughly borne out by the manner in which American families disposed of their rising real incomes in the 1960's. (See above, p. 271).

We can conclude, then, that, if consumers' tastes prevail and the U.S. pattern of 1961–1962 proves a rough general reflection of those tastes:

—Up to a point, there is ample scope for families to spend higher incomes than they now enjoy on more or higher-quality food, drink, housing, clothing, medical care, education, travel, etc.

—Within those categories, there is an impulse to spend relatively less on food as a whole, more on eating out, hotels, higher-quality clothing, education, and long-distance travel.

—There is a marked tendency, as higher levels of family income are attained, to build up assets rather than to consume.

155. Hiroya Uneo and Hiromachi Muto suggest that the pace of diffusion of the automobile accelerates at about $500 per capita national income, decelerates at about $1,300. They do not specify the period for which these dollar measurements would apply; but their hypothesis appears quite reasonable for income per capita measured, say, in U.S. dollars of the late 1950's ("The Automobile Industry of Japan," *Japanese Economic Studies*, vol. 3, no. 1 [Fall 1974], pp. 22–24).

156. Dieter Schröder, "Structural Problems of the Next Few Years," *Intereconomics*, August 1976, p. 232.

157. *Economic Report of the President*, January 1976, pp. 117–118.

Part Six. The Future of the World Economy

CHAPTER 49. *Are There Limits to Growth?*

1. Donella H. Meadows, Dennis L. Meadows, Jørgen Randers, and William W. Behrens III, *The Limits to Growth* (New York: Universal Books, 1972). This study was sponsored by the Club of Rome. Their analysis, in turn, is a more elaborate and empirical extension of that developed by Jay W. Forrester, *World Dynamics* (Cambridge, Mass.: Wright Allen Press, 1971).
2. Meadows et al., *Limits to Growth*, p. 23.
3. The underlying values and ideals of the Meadows team and of other supporters of the no-growth view are perceptively analyzed by Harvey Simmons in Chapter 13 of H. S. D. Cole (ed.), *Thinking about the Future* (London: Chatto and Windus for Sussex University Press, 1973, pp. 203–207). Simmons identifies a mood of "pessimism and despair" about the consequences of material progress among certain intellectual groups in advanced industrial societies, combined with increasing concern about the environment. These lead to "the notion that quality of life (however vaguely defined) is more important than such things as increased material goods. . . . Moreover, . . . the pessimists argue that the result of carelessness will not be merely a loss of certain amenities in life but disaster on a global scale" (p. 204). To this view of the values suffusing no-growth positions, the Hudson Institute analysts add an element of special interest among members of the upper middle class: "There is increasing recognition, both conscious and unconscious, that in many ways the quality of life for the upper middle class goes down when the GNP per capita goes up. That is, the rich do very well (they always do well), the middle class does well, and the poor do well, but the upper middle class does not do well except for those members who have recently changed their status from poor or middle to upper middle. This failure to do well is one reason for their recent intense opposition to economic growth. It may turn out

in the long run, however, that even the upper middle class will find itself benefited by general economic growth, but at the moment this is an open question" (Hudson Institute, *1973 Synoptic Context on the Corporate Environment: 1973–1985*, vol. 2, *Prospects for Mankind, the Role of "Futurology" Ideologies, and the Current Hudson Institute Paneqole Study* [Croton-on-Hudson, New York, 1973], p. 10). For the definitive statement by the Hudson Institute of its view on the limits to growth, see Herman Kahn, William Brown, and Leon Martel, with the assistance of the staff of the Hudson Institute, *The Next 200 Years* (New York: William Morrow, 1976). See also W. W. Rostow, *Politics and the Stages of Growth* (Cambridge: At the University Press, 1971), pp. 248–266.

4. The most complete critique of *The Limits to Growth* is that of H. S. D. Cole (ed.), *Thinking about the Future*. This volume is a product of the Science Policy Research Unit of Sussex University and contains contributions by thirteen members of that unit. It contains useful references to other critics of *The Limits to Growth*. See also the excellent counter-polemic: Wilfred Beckerman, *In Defence of Economic Growth* (London: Jonathan Cape, 1974).
5. Presumably in awareness of this weakness in the Forrester-Meadows world models, the Club of Rome has sponsored the study of Mihajlo Mesarovic and Eduard Pestel, *Mankind at the Turning Point*, Second Report to the Club of Rome (New York: E. P. Dutton/Reader's Digest Press, 1974). This work seeks to disaggregate its analysis of particular problems (notably, population, food, and energy) into ten regions. It was carried out in the midst of the price revolution which began toward the close of 1972 and is more focused on near-term problems than *The Limits to Growth*. Its central recommendation is for international co-operation to overcome problems which, while different in their regional impact, are inherently global.
6. This point is lucidly put in H. S. D. Cole (ed.), *Thinking about the Future*, pp. 10–11 and 37–42.
7. See, notably, *Agricultural Production Efficiency* (Washington, D.C.: National Academy of Sciences, 1975), especially pp. 3–15, on "some warning signals" now apparent and other possible limitations on productivity increase.
8. W. W. Rostow, *The Stages of Economic Growth* (Cambridge: At the University Press, 1960 and 1971), p. 91. For discussion of the limits and ultimate objectives of affluence, see pp. 90–92, 156, and 166–167.
9. This issue is discussed at some length in Rostow, *Politics and the Stages of Growth*, Chapter 6, "The Politics of the Search for Quality."
10. Hudson Institute, *1973 Synoptic Context*, vol. 2, p. 10.
11. Charles Ritchie, *The Siren Years* (Toronto: Macmillan of Canada, 1974), p. 65.
12. Boris Kuznetsov, "Nonclassical Science and the Philosophy of Optimism," translated by Allen M. Hegland with the assistance of Russell McCormmach, in Russell McCormmach (ed.), *Historical Studies in the Physical Sciences*, Fourth Annual Volume (Princeton: Princeton University Press, 1975), pp. 197, 220–221.
13. Dennis L. Meadows et al., *The Dynamics of Growth in a Finite World* (Cambridge, Mass.: Wright-Allen Press, 1973), especially pp. 522–527. Here two cases are examined: exponential changes in technology indefinitely put off a downturn in industrial civilization; adaptive changes at 5 percent per annum postpone a crisis beyond the year 2000, although food per capita begins to decline in the second half of the next century.
14. Ibid., especially pp. 543–549. Here a combination of changes in social policies and technological adaptations of a highly productive kind, promptly undertaken, yield stable equilibrium in the twenty-first century.
15. One could, of course, find earlier examples of anxiety and debate about raw materials: for example, those induced by the believed pressure on Swedish timber resources by iron manufacture, leading to the restric-

tion of iron exports in 1730, and the pressure on British timber supplies in the eighteenth century, leading to shifts in cost which heightened efforts to use coal efficiently in iron manufacture.

16. W. S. Jevons, *The Coal Question*, second edition (London: Macmillan, 1866), p. vii. In an evocative chapter ("Concluding Reflections," pp. 370–376), Jevons poses the general problem of limits to growth in terms not unlike the current debate. He asks (in a Meadows mood) if there are not values in British history, culture, and society which transcend material progress; he then asks if these values are not linked to progress since the days of Elizabeth and Bacon, and concludes, on the basis of the limits of easily accessible coal: *"We have to make the momentous choice between brief greatness and longer continued mediocrity"* (p. 376).
17. J. M. Keynes, "Return of Estimated Value of Foreign Trade of United Kingdom at Prices of 1900," *Economic Journal*, vol. 22, no. 88 (1912), pp. 630–631.
18. D. H. Robertson, *Industrial Fluctuations* (London: P. S. King, 1915; reprinted 1945), p. 169, note.

CHAPTER 50. *Population and Food*

19. This broadly hopeful conclusion was arrived at by extending data organized by Thorkil Kristensen (*Development in Rich and Poor Countries* [New York: Praeger, 1974], p. 157). The less developed countries (less than $400 per capita, U.S., 1967) are grouped in three categories:

    —a group containing 13 percent of the population in developing countries, averaging $270 per capita, with a 2.9 percent average annual per capita growth rate during the 1960's;

    —a group containing 17 percent of the relevant population, averaging $130 per capita, growing at 2.6 percent per capita;

    —a group containing 70 percent of the relevant population (including China and India), averaging $90 per capita, growing at 1.7 percent per capita.

    The first group will attain $400 per capita by 1981, if the growth rate of the 1960's is sustained.

    The second group will attain $270 by 1995, $400 by 2009, if the growth rates associated with the respective groups are sustained.

    The third group will attain $130 by 2019, $400 by 2033, if the pattern of growth rates persists.

    Evidently, only the roughest and most general conclusions can be drawn from this kind of arithmetic. It should be noted that the U.S. GNP deflator for 1967 was 8 percent higher than for 1964, the year in which the $400 per capita benchmark is measured. For present broad purposes, the change in base year is not significant.
20. The most cogent case for this proposition is *The World Food Situation and Prospects to 1985* (Washington, D.C.: Economic Research Service, U.S. Department of Agriculture, Foreign Agricultural Economic Report No. 98, December 1974). This study usefully presents demand and supply estimates other than its own, indicating the ranges of disagreement among experts.
21. *Agricultural Production Efficiency*, especially pp. 20–39, 56–88. See, also, *World Food Situation*, pp. 67–71.
22. *World Food Situation*, pp. 62–64. The problem of assuring a steady and high rate of increase in fertilizer applications in developing countries is complex. On the side of demand, the local fertilizer price must be sufficiently low, in relation to agricultural prices, to make it attractive for farmers to buy fertilizers. In 1974–1975, for example, prices were so high, due in part to high oil prices, that some fertilizer plants in developing countries were operating short of full capacity. On the other hand, the expectation of reasonably high fertilizer prices is necessary to induce the large investments necessary to build new plants at the required rate; and expectations matter because of the three- to five-year lead time between the decision to build a plant and its coming on

stream. The surge in food prices begun in 1972 has induced large increases in investment in fertilizer capacity, including large additions to capacity in developing countries. The fear among experts is that forecasts of a deceleration in fertilizer applications, due to current high prices in relation to farmers' net returns, will cause surpluses of capacity in the latter part of the 1970's; and these projected surpluses will, in turn, cut down the rate of investment in fertilizer capacity. A variety of policy devices is being explored to bridge this gap and to encourage investors, public and private, in both developed and developing countries, to sustain high levels of investment in fertilizer capacity:

—temporary concessional financing to permit foreign-exchange-deficit developing countries to continue to increase their imports, accompanied, if necessary, by domestic concessional financing to farmers to sustain their level of effective demand at otherwise excessive prices;

—government guarantees to investors in fertilizers to purchase and stockpile surpluses, should they develop;

—concessional financing for certain publicly owned plants in exporting countries, to be operated only when additional fertilizer is needed to avoid a rise in prices so severe as to cut down the rate of increase in fertilizer applications.

Evidently, OPEC members generating excess foreign exchange could contribute substantially to the process of sustaining a high rate of increase in fertilizer application in developing countries by devices of the following kind:

—providing fertilizer feedstocks at concessional prices for periods long enough to justify expanded fertilizer capacity in developing countries;

—providing loans at concessional rates to assist developing countries to maintain their fertilizer import levels;

—expanding their own fertilizer production and exporting to developing countries on long-run concessional terms.

23. See, notably, *Agricultural Production Efficiency*, especially pp. 14–19 and 150–185.

24. Commission on Critical Choices for Americans, vol. 1, *Vital Resources*, Reports on Energy, Food & Raw Materials (Lexington, Mass., and Toronto: Lexington Books, D. C. Heath and Company, 1977), pp. 116–117.

CHAPTER 51. *Energy*

25. Among the major reviews of the energy position are: Brookings Institution, *Cooperative Approaches to World Energy Problems* (a tripartite report by fifteen experts from the European Community, Japan, and North America) (Washington, D.C., 1974); Committee for Economic Development, *Achieving Energy Independence* (Washington, D.C., December 1974); J. Darmstadter and S. H. Schurr, "World Energy Resources and Demand," *Philosophical Transactions of the Royal Society of London*, Series A, vol. 276 (1974); Federal Energy Administration, *Project Independence Report* (Washington, D.C., November 1974); Ford Foundation Energy Policy Project, *A Time to Choose* (New York, 1974); OECD, *Energy Prospects to 1985: An Assessment of Long Term Energy Developments and Related Projects* (Paris, 1975); Edward Teller, "Energy—A Plan for Action," in *Power and Security*, Critical Choices for Americans, vol. 4 (Lexington, Mass.: Lexington Books, 1976); Charles A. Zraket, *Energy Resources for the Year 2000 and Beyond*, MTP-401, Revision 2 (McLean, Va.: Mitre Corporation, March 1975); Executive Office of the President, Energy Policy Planning, *The National Energy Plan* (Washington, D.C.: Government Printing Office, 29 April 1977); Workshop on Alternative Energy Strategies, A Project Sponsored by the Massachusetts Institute of Technology, Carroll L. Wilson, Project Director, *Energy: Global Prospects, 1985–2000* (New York: McGraw-Hill, 1977). Several of these reports generated a body of specialized analyses of particular technical and/or economic aspects of the energy problem.

26. Darmstadter and Schurr present the estimates of the elasticity of demand for energy in relation to GNP given in Table N-36. For a scatter diagram illustrating this linkage for 1968, on a cross-sectional basis, see Meadows et al., *The Limits to Growth*, p. 70. For a careful analysis of the determinants of differences in energy use in advanced industrial society, see, notably, Joel Darmstadter, Joy Dunkerley, and Jack Alterman, *How Industrial Societies Use Energy: A Comparative Analysis* (Washington, D.C.: Resources for the Future, April 1977).

27. John C. Fisher has produced some interesting historical calculations of energy consumption per capita reaching back to 1850 (*Energy Crises in Perspective* [New York: John Wiley, 1974], especially pp. 19–25 and appendix tables, pp. 157–172). Fisher estimates that energy consumption per capita declined slightly from 1855 to 1885; rose slowly, then rapidly from about the turn of the century through the boom of the 1920's, as the use of electricity expanded and the mass use of the automobile occurred; fell away sharply during the depression of the 1930's; recovered to a higher but not increasing level in the postwar years, down to 1960; and increased rapidly in the 1960's (see Chart N-2). As the chart indicates, even before the energy crisis of 1973–1975, Fisher predicted a sharp deceleration of U.S. energy consumption per capita from the 1960's annual rate of 2.7 percent to an average of 1.1 percent, from 1970 to 2000.

Historically, as Chart N-3 indicates, the American energy base altered radically over these 120 years, with coal and then oil and gas taking over from fuel wood and work animals.

For calculations of total and per capita energy consumption in 1840 and 1895 in "the nations of Christendom," see also Michael Mulhall, *Industries and Wealth of Nations* (London, New York, and Bombay: Longmans, Green, 1896), pp. 19–21. Combining hand, horse, and steam power, Mulhall (in terms of foot-tons) shows an annual average per capita increase of 1.1 percent per annum for the United States; 1.4 percent for the total of the nations included. The rise of steam power (6.6 percent annually for the total) was, of course, the major factor at work in this period. In more detailed calculations for the United States

TABLE N-36. *Energy Consumption Growth Relative to GNP Growth: Selected Countries, 1960–1971*

	1960–1965: Average Annual Rate of Change (%)			1965–1971: Average Annual Rate of Change (%)		
	(1) Energy Consumption	(2) Real GNP	(3) Elasticity: (1)/(2)	(1) Energy Consumption	(2) Real GNP	(3) Elasticity: (1)/(2)
United States	3.9	4.8	0.81	4.5	3.1	1.45
Canada	6.2	5.6	1.11	6.1	4.8	1.27
United Kingdom	2.5	3.3	0.76	1.6	2.5	0.64
France	5.5	5.8	0.95	5.7	5.7	1.00
West Germany	5.8	5.0	1.16	4.2	4.6	0.91
Italy	9.1	5.3	1.72	7.8	5.2	1.50
Sweden	5.8	4.9	1.18	6.1	3.3	1.85
Switzerland	6.8	5.3	1.28	6.0	3.9	1.54
Spain	5.8	8.6	0.67	8.9	6.0	1.48
Belgium-Luxembourg	6.1	4.8	1.27	4.9	4.6	1.06
Netherlands	7.8	5.0	1.56	7.9	5.3	1.49
Denmark	8.6	5.2	1.65	5.2	4.4	1.18
Japan	10.0	10.0	1.00	11.8	11.2	1.05
Australia	6.3	5.0	1.26	4.6	5.1	0.90
India	7.0	3.3	2.12	3.5	4.2	0.83
Venezuela	5.7	7.7	0.74	2.6	4.2	0.56
Mexico	4.6	7.0	0.66	7.9	6.3	1.25

Source: Darmstadter and Schurr, "World Energy Resources and Demand," p. 422.

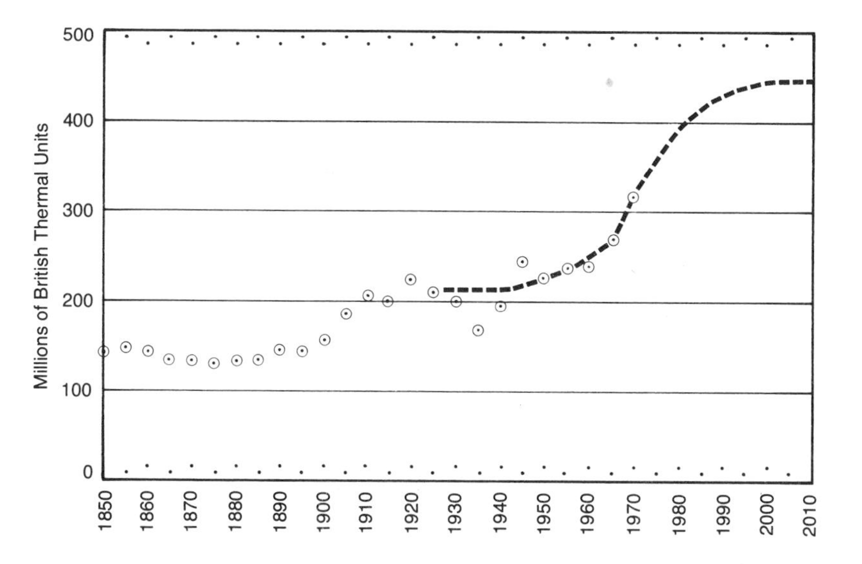

CHART N-2. *Per Capita Energy Consumption in the United States, 1850–1970, and Projected to 2010*

Annual energy consumption is projected to level off at about 450 BTU per person by the end of the century.

Source: Fisher, *Energy Crises*, p. 24.

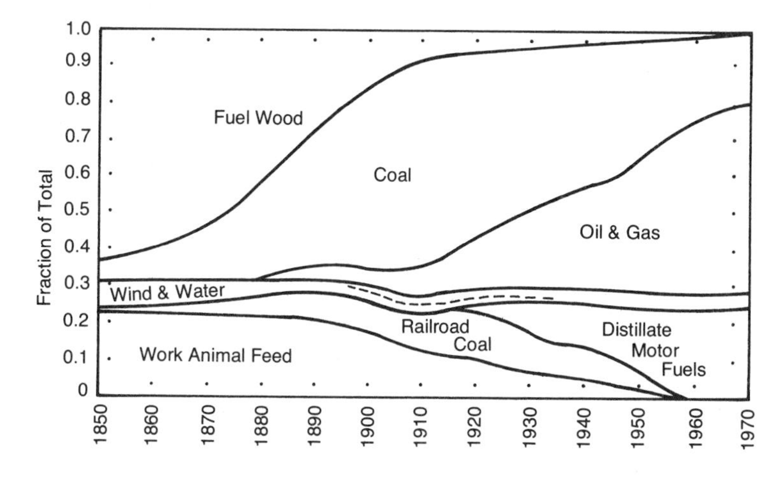

CHART N-3. *Segmentation of Fuel Input to the United States, 1850–1970*

Five great energy substitutions have occurred during the past 120 years. Fuel wood, used primarily for heating, was largely replaced by coal between 1850 and 1910. Coal has since been progressively replaced by gas and oil. Work animal feed was partially replaced by railroad coal in the late 1800's and early 1900's. Then, with a shorter time constant, animal feed and railroad coal both were replaced by distillate motor fuels between 1920 and 1950. Direct wind and water power were replaced by hydroelectricity in the years 1890–1940. A sixth substitution, not explicitly shown in the chart, is a steady increase in the proportion of fossil fuel converted to electricity prior to consumption.

Source: Fisher, *Energy Crises*, p. 14.

(p. 285), Mulhall separates out his three components, permitting rates to be calculated for horse and steam power alone. He also provides his estimate for 1860. Per capita U.S. consumption of horse and steam power increased at an annual average rate of 1.03 percent from 1840 to 1860; 1.23 percent from 1860 to 1895.

28. The manner in which doubts on this matter affect the view of sober analysts is illustrated by the following observation of Zraket (*Energy Resources*, p. 20): "It is important to reiterate here the influence on climate caused by the use of 'stored' energy, e.g., fossil fuels, fission, and fusion. This stored energy, burned at a rate approximating 1 per cent of the solar energy absorbed by the earth's surface, may produce a 2 to 3° Centigrade rise in average global temperature and a 10° Centigrade or more rise at the poles. This temperature increase would be in addition to that caused by carbon dioxide if fossil fuels were used. Therefore, it probably will be prudent to limit the use of stored fuels to less than one percent of the solar input until we know much more about climate effects from the use of energy." Such anxieties lead to a bias toward the development of solar energy, although the latter also contributes to the atmospheric heat burden when converted to useful form. The underlying analysis of this problem is contained in *Understanding Climatic Change: A Program of Action* (Washington, D.C.: National Academy of Sciences, September 1974). For a more reassuring view, even if the polar ice cap melts, see William W. Kellogg, "Mankind as a Factor in Climate Change," in Edward W. Erickson and Leonard Waverman (eds.), *The Energy Question: An International Failure of Policy* (Toronto and Buffalo: University of Toronto Press, 1974), vol. 1, pp. 241–255. On weather changes of economic significance not related to energy use, see *Report of the Ad Hoc Panel on the Present Interglacial* (Washington, D.C.: National Science Foundation, August 1974).
29. Meadows et al., *Limits to Growth*, p. 56.
30. Zraket, *Energy Resources*, p. 4. See also Workshop on Alternative Energy Strategies, *Energy*, especially pp. 167–188 and 241.
31. Zraket, for example, concludes as follows (*Energy Resources*, p. 11): "In contrast to the dwindling supplies of currently preferred fuels, there are six sources of energy which can be considered to be essentially infinite: nuclear fission; nuclear fusion; geothermal; hydrologic runoff; tidal dissipation; and solar. . . . The solar input to the earth is over 5×10^{21} BTU per year. If a small fraction of this energy could be economically converted to electricity or fuel, a major fraction, if not all, of the world energy needs could be satisfied for the indefinite future. The fusion of deuterium (a naturally occurring isotope of hydrogen) in one cubic mile of water could provide over 10^{20} BTU. Since there are over 300 million cubic miles of water in the world, the potential energy in the fusion reaction likewise could support a very high rate of use for millions of years. If the breeder reactor concept proves to be economically viable, one million tons of uranium ore could generate over 10^{19} BTU. Since the earth's crust contains thousands if not a million times a million tons of uranium and since thorium can also be used in a breeder reactor (thorium is even more abundant than uranium), this, too, is an energy source potentially capable of supplying the world indefinitely.

    "The heat from the interior of the earth flows outward; this 'geothermal flux' can be tapped to provide a continuing flow of energy until the earth cools off millions of years from now. Smaller sources of energy that are essentially 'infinite' are hydrological (rain) runoff and tidal power. Although probably only about 10 percent of potential sources of geothermal, hydrological, and tidal power will be economically practicable to exploit, together they could supply up to 3/5 of the world's energy at current use rates.

    "We can, therefore, assume that there are more than sufficient potential energy resources to maintain world supplies indefinitely."
32. The Ford Foundation Energy Policy Project report (*A Time to Choose*) contains a third scenario in which the United States moves, by the

1990's, to Zero Energy Growth. This objective is attained by a mixture of investments in energy efficiency and economy combined with a redirection of consumption to less energy-intensive goods and services. The average annual rate of growth of consumption would, under this scenario, be about 1.3 percent down to 1985, 0.9 percent between 1985 and 2000 (p. 111).

33. There are increasing questions about the future role of conventional (fission) nuclear power in the U.S. energy base, as well as about the future of the breeder reactor. These stem from a mixture of anxieties about safety, waste disposal, and other environmental resistances plus altering evaluations of relative costs of nuclear versus fossil-fuel electricity-producing units. On a world basis, concern about nuclear proliferation in relation to atomic power stations has risen. See, for example, Mitre Corporation, *Alternatives to the Project Independence Blueprint* (McLean, Va., 21 February 1975). On the other hand, all serious energy balance sheets for the OECD world down to the year 2000 require for their viability a greatly expanded role for atomic energy.

34. See, for example, Teller, "Energy," p. 33, and Ford Foundation Energy Policy Project, *A Time to Choose*, pp. 21 and 28 (for Historical Growth) and 46–47 (Technical Fix). The range of disagreement is suggested by these differences in estimates for the year 2000; Teller assumes U.S. production of 200 quads, of which 30 would be exported; Ford Historical Growth assumes an even higher level of domestic consumption (187); Ford Technical Fix assumes that intensive investment in conservation and economy would require consumption of only 124.

35. "Energy Prospects to 1985," summarized in *OECD Observer*, no. 73 (January–February 1975), pp. 18–19.

36. Although the scale and pace of expansion of investment in energy, energy conservation, and energy economy are evidently critical variables for the OECD world, the data are not yet systematically organized in ways which permit easy comparison between current investment levels and those required to fulfill national objectives. There are, nevertheless, some data on the United States, whose energy adjustment is critically important for the energy importers as a whole and their common bargaining position vis-à-vis OPEC. The Economics Department of McGraw-Hill Publications Company has, for example, made the estimates of recent and prospective investment levels in certain key subsectors of the energy complex found in Table N-37.

Although the projected expansion in electric utilities investment lifts the estimated total in the course of the 1970's at a quite high rate, even when corrected for probable inflation rates, the simple fact is that outlays now envisaged for expanding the flow of new oil and gas (excepting Alaska) are not likely to reverse the overall decline in U.S. output and reserves. To reachieve the combined gas and oil production levels of 1976—or slightly exceed them, as envisaged in President Carter's plan of 20 April 1977—would require a doubling of drilling rates over the 1976 level. The rate of increase of coal investment will also, as estimated, be high even if price-corrected; but the rise in coal capacity and output appears unlikely to compensate for declining oil and gas production and reduce U.S. energy imports in the period 1975–1980.

Historical estimates of American energy investment in new plant and equipment and projections under alternative energy policy assumptions down to 1985 are provided in Federal Energy Administration, *National Energy Outlook, February 1976* (Washington, D.C.: Government Printing Office, 1976), pp. 293–323.

President Carter's plan of 20 April 1977 is estimated to require, at the minimum, energy investments of $645 billion (1976 dollars). For details of this calculation, see E. Victor Niemeyer, "U.S. Energy Investment, 1977 to 1985," appendix to W. W. Rostow, William Fisher, and George Kozmetsky, "The National Energy Plan: An Overview," in *Preliminary Assessment of the President's National Energy Plan* (Austin: University of Texas at Austin, 11 May 1977), pp. 36–41. It is the judgment of the *Preliminary Assessment* that the price, tax, and rebate

TABLE N-37. *U.S. Capital Spending: Energy, 1973–1979*

	Current Dollars ($ Billions)	Price Corrected[a]	Capacity Increase
Petroleum			
1973	12.4	—	
1974	19.5	17.7	
1975	23.9	—	Continued decline
1976[b]	29.8	—	
1977–1979[c]	27.7	—	
Coal			
1973	0.53	—	
1974	0.83	0.75	
1975	1.32	—	
1976[b]	1.89	—	15%, 1975–1978
1977–1979[c]	2.17	—	
Electric utilities			
1973	16.0	—	
1974	17.6	15.9	
1975	17.0	—	
1976[b]	20.1	—	30%, 1975–1978
1977[b]	22.7	—	
1978[b]	25.8	—	
1979	28.2	—	
Gas utilities			
1973	—	—	
1974	2.9	—	
1975	3.4	—	
1976[b]	4.5	—	Continued decline in gas supply
1977[b]	4.4	—	
1978[b]	4.2	—	
1979[b]	4.5	—	

[a] Corrected by GNP price deflator for producers' durable equipment.
[b] Estimated.
[c] Estimated annual averages.
Source: McGraw-Hill Publications' Economics Department Special Table on Capital Spending Plans of the Energy Industry, May 7, 1976.

policies in the Carter plan are inconsistent with its production and investment targets.
37. "The World Energy Outlook for the Next Ten Years," *OECD Observer*, no. 85 (March 1977), p. 4.
38. "You Can't All Export at Once," *Economist*, 12 July 1975, p. 68.
39. See, for example, Teller, "Energy," pp. 40–46; Ford Foundation Energy Policy Project, *A Time to Choose*, pp. 325–333.
40. See, notably, Selig S. Harrison, "Time Bomb in East Asia," and Choon-ho Park and Jerome Alan Cohen, "The Politics of the Oil Weapon," *Foreign Policy*, no. 20 (Fall 1975), pp. 3–49. A less sanguine view of China's future oil export capabilities is stated in the CIA Report, "The International Energy Outlook for 1985" (April 1977), p. 13. The CIA estimates that difficulties with coal production and domestic oil needs will reduce Chinese oil exports by 1985 to "a negligible level."
41. See, notably, Brookings Institution, *Cooperative Approaches to World Energy Problems*.
42. Ibid., pp. 48–49, where sources are indicated.
43. Ibid., pp. 8–9.

44. See, notably, *Material Needs and the Environment Today and Tomorrow*, Final Report of the National Commission on Materials Policy (Washington, D.C.: Government Printing Office, June 1973). Footnote references (pp. 2-29 and 2-30) include titles of significant supplementary studies generated by the commission, including W. Malenbaum, *Materials Requirements in the United States and Abroad in the Year 2000* (Wharton School, University of Pennsylvania, March 1973). Also, Brookings Institution, *Trade in Primary Commodities: Conflict or Cooperation?* (A tripartite report by fifteen economists from Japan, the European Community, and North America) (Washington, D.C., 1974). Also, *Government and the Nation's Resources*, Report of the National Commission on Supplies and Shortages (Washington, D.C.: Government Printing Office, December 1976). As background, a basic study is Hans Landsberg et al., *Resources in America's Future* (Baltimore: Johns Hopkins Press for Resources for the Future, Inc., 1963).
45. See, for example, Beckerman, *In Defense of Economic Growth*, pp. 222–235.
46. R. V. Ayres and A. V. Kneese, "Economic and Ecological Effects of a Stationary Economy," *Annual Review of Ecology and Systematics*, no. 2 (1971). The chapter in H. S. D. Cole (ed.), *Thinking About the Future*, examining the Meadows-Ayres-Kneese argument is a useful summary of the issue: Chapter 3 by William Page, "The Non-renewable Resources Sub-system," pp. 33–42.
47. It should be noted that there is considerable disagreement among experts projecting U.S. requirements for particular minerals in the year 2000. In particular, Bureau of Mines projections, as of January 11, 1974, differ in several significant respects from the range of estimates generated by Resources for the Future analysts in their contribution of 1972 to the Commission on Population and Growth and the American Future. In the cases of chromium, manganese, tin, and zinc, the two sets of estimates are more or less consistent. The 1974 Bureau of Mines projections exceed the maximum estimates of Resources for the Future with respect to molybdenum, aluminum, and copper. They are lower with respect to iron ore, vanadium, lead, and platinum.
48. Wilfred Malenbaum, "Resource Shortage in an Expanding World," *Wharton Quarterly*, Winter 1973, reprinted in *Growth and Its Implications for the Future*, Part 2, Hearing Appendix for the Subcommittee on Fisheries and Wildlife, Conservation and the Environment of the Committee on Merchant Marine and Fisheries, House of Representatives, Ninety-third Congress, *The Effects National Growth Will Have on Resources, the Environment, and Food Supply in the Future*, Serial No. 93-28 (Washington, D.C.: Government Printing Office, 1974), p. 1144.
49. Brookings Institution, *Trade in Primary Commodities*, p. 17. See also C. Fred Bergsten, *A New OPEC in Bauxite* (Washington, D.C.: Brookings Institution, 1976).

CHAPTER 53. *Pollution and the Environment*

50. H. S. D. Cole (ed.), *Thinking about the Future*, p. 179. The Hudson Institute provides a more vivid list of environmental anxieties (*1973 Synoptic Context*, vol. 2, p. 12):

"A. Radioactive debris from various peaceful nuclear issues

"B. Possible greenhouse or other effects from increased CO_2 in the atmosphere, or new ice age because of dust in stratosphere, etc.

"C. Other special dangerous wastes—methyl, mercury, DDT, etc.

"D. Waste heat

"E. Other less dangerous but environment degrading wastes such as debris and garbage

"F. Noise, ugliness and other annoying by-products of many modern activities

"G. Excessive urbanization
"H. Excessive overcrowding
"I. Excessive tourism
"J. Insecticides, fertilizers, growth 'chemicals,' food additives, plastic containers, etc."

51. *Man's Impact on the Global Environment*, Report of the Study of Critical Environmental Problems (SCEP) (Cambridge, Mass.: M. I. T. Press, 1970), reproduced in *Growth and Its Implications for the Future*, Part 2, pp. 1268–1303, quotation from p. 1275. See also *Inadvertent Climate Modification*, Report of the Study of Man's Impact on Climate (SMIC) (Cambridge, Mass.: M. I. T. Press, 1971), reproduced in *Growth and Its Implications for the Future*, Part 2, pp. 1304–1330; and *Understanding Climatic Change*, previously cited.
52. I take this definition from Paul Samuelson's *Economics*, seventh edition (New York: McGraw-Hill, 1967), p. 451. Evidently, "one man's production" is an excessively narrow definition of the source of "external diseconomies," given the role of automobile pollution and poor public waste-disposal systems as well as factories. For useful textbook elaborations of this mode of analysis, see, for example, Robert Dorfman and Nancy S. Dorfman (eds.), *Economics of the Environment: Selected Readings* (New York: W. W. Norton, 1972); Donald T. Savage et al., *The Economics of Environmental Improvement* (Boston: Houghton Mifflin, 1974). For a sophisticated approach to the trade-offs inevitably involved in environmental policy in terms of special-interest politics rather than cost-benefit analysis for the community, see, notably, Robert Dorfman and Henry D. Jacoby, "A Public-Decision Model Applied to a Local Pollution Problem," Chapter 14 in Dorfman and Dorfman (eds.), *Economics of the Environment*, pp. 205–249.
53. For a useful review of environmental progress, problems, costs, and benefits, see, notably, Beckerman, *In Defense of Economic Growth*, Chapters 5–7. Cost and benefit estimates are examined on pp. 190–213.
54. Ivars Gutmanis, "The Environment," in Charles L. Schultze et al., *Setting National Priorities: The 1973 Budget* (Washington, D.C.: Brookings Institution, 1972), p. 374. For a detailed breakdown yielding a similar result for 1981, see the table on U.S. Pollution Control Expenditures in U.S. Council on Environmental Quality, *Environmental Quality: The Fourth Annual Report* (Washington, D.C.: Government Printing Office, 1973), p. 93, and discussion in subsequent annual reports.
55. Schultze et al., *Setting National Priorities*, p. 375. For more detailed discussion of these estimates, see, especially, Allen V. Kneese and Charles L. Schultze, *Pollution, Prices, and Public Policy* (Washington, D.C.: Brookings Institution, 1975), especially pp. 69–84.
56. Table N-38 suggests, at least, the substantial order of magnitude of the increases planned in outlays for pollution control in seven OECD coun-

TABLE N-38. *The Cost of Pollution Control: Total Expenditure on New Programs of Pollution Control after Adjustments as a Percentage of Total GNP over the Program Period*

	1971–1975	1976–1980	1971–1980
Germany	0.8	—	—
Italy	0.4	1.3	0.9
Japan	3.0–5.5	—	—
Netherlands	0.42	1.3	0.9
Sweden	0.5–0.9	—	—
United Kingdom[a]	—	—	0.3–0.5
United States	0.8	1.7	1.4

[a] These numbers have been adjusted upward to allow for operating costs on the basis of the relation between operating costs and investment in other countries. They are also adjusted upward by 15 percent to allow for solid waste disposal.
Source: *OECD Observer*, no. 71 (August 1974), p. 35.

tries. See also the discussion of such estimates in Beckerman, *In Defense of Economic Growth*, pp. 190–197.

CHAPTER 54. *Political Economy in the Fifth Kondratieff Upswing*

57. See, for example, J. Herbert Holloman et al., and Michel Grenon, *Energy Research and Development*, papers prepared for the Energy Project of the Ford Foundation (Cambridge, Mass.: Ballinger, 1975), including the roughness of U.S. private sector outlays and the significant gaps in knowledge of R&D energy expenditures outside the United States in the country summaries, pp. 129–257. The best available estimates of the scale, sources of finance, and allocation of R&D in the United States are to be found in three National Science Foundation publications: *National Patterns of R&D Resources*, NSF 76-310 (Washington D.C., April 1976); *Research and Development in 1974*, NSF 76-322 (September 1976); and *An Analysis of Federal R&D Funding by Function*, NSF 76-325 (September 1976). For a discussion of U.S. energy R&D priorities and a brief appendix on R&D expenditures elsewhere (pp. C1–C3), see Energy Research and Development Administration, *A National Plan for Energy Resource and Development: Creating Energy Choices for the Future*, vol. 1, *The Plan*, ERDA-48 (Washington, D.C.: Government Printing Office, 28 June 1975).
58. For an early and incomplete assessment of the shift, see *OECD Observer*, no. 76 (July–August 1975), pp. 30–32.
59. Holloman et al., *Energy Research and Development*, pp. 11–16. See also the criteria set out by the Energy Research and Development Administration, *National Plan for Energy Resource and Development*, vol. 1, *The Plan*, pp. VII-1–4.
60. For an account of the eight major international institutes for research in agriculture now at work, see Consultative Group on International Agricultural Research, *International Research in Agriculture* (New York, 1974). The sponsors of the Consultative Group are the FAO, the United Nations development program, and the World Bank.
61. See Michel Grenon's survey in Holloman et al., *Energy Research and Development*, pp. 129–141.
62. W. W. Rostow, *How It All Began* (New York: McGraw-Hill, 1975), pp. 139–140.
63. Quoted from statement of Richard Lesser of NASA in Charles A. Zraket, "Some Relationships between Technology and Productivity" (unpublished manuscript, August 1975), p. 4.
64. Teller, "Energy," pp. 40–46.
65. Ford Foundation Energy Policy Project, *A Time to Choose*, pp. 325–343.
66. Barry Bosworth, James S. Duesenberry, and Andrew S. Carron, *Capital Needs in the Seventies* (Washington, D.C.: Brookings Institution, 1975). See also the summary of a somewhat similar study within the U.S. government in *Economic Report of the President*, January 1976, pp. 41–47. The latter concludes more flatly than the former that a rise in the U.S. investment rate will be required to meet the nation's energy and environmental objectives as well as overall growth and employment targets between 1975 and 1980.
67. Walter Heller, "Taxes and the 'Capital Shortfall'," *Wall Street Journal*, 19 August 1975.
68. Bosworth, Duesenberry, and Carron, *Capital Needs*, especially Chapter 2. For a critique of the Bosworth estimates and a less sanguine view of the U.S. capital supply problem, see, for example, "Capital Crisis," *Business Week*, 22 September 1975, pp. 42–48. Also see "Getting Enough Money for Modernization and Growth," *Nation's Business*, December 1975, pp. 16–20 (an interview with Reginald H. Jones). Albert T. Sommers examines the tension between economic growth and other public objectives in "Social Goals and Economic Growth—The Policy Problem in Capital Formation," *Conference Board Record*, December 1975, pp. 17–26. A thoughtful review of the whole capital shortage question is Eli Shapiro and William L. White (eds), *Capital for Pro-*

ductivity and Jobs, The American Assembly, Columbia University (Englewood Cliffs, N.J.: Prentice-Hall, 1977).

69. Unless otherwise indicated, statistical data used in this section are from World Bank sources and estimates.

CHAPTER 55. *Tasks of International Cooperation*

70. The major directions of apparent agreement in the United Nations resolutions of 16 September 1975 were these.

International Trade

—The developing countries should expand and diversify their exports, increase productivity, and thereby improve their foreign-exchange position and their real terms of trade.

—Special emphasis should be given to the expansion of manufactured exports and to processing raw materials increasingly within developing countries.

—With respect to raw materials, stable and "equitable" prices and export earnings should be sought through stockpiling agreements, compensatory financing to cushion price declines, and improved marketing and transport arrangements for such commodities within developing countries. The possibility of linking raw-materials export prices to the prices of manufactured imports should be explored.

—Developed countries should act to reduce or remove, where feasible, nontariff barriers to imports from developing countries and to extend existing generalized trade preferences.

—Restrictive private business practices limiting exports of developing countries should be eliminated.

Increased Aid

—Aid from developed to developing countries should be expanded and, as a general rule, be untied. As noted earlier, the target of 0.7 percent of gross national product in official development assistance by 1980 was reaffirmed, with significant reservation.

—The IMF was urged to consider linking special drawing rights (SDR's) to development assistance, by allocating a portion of the proceeds of gold sales and through voluntary donations of a portion of their SDR holdings by developed nations. SDR's should increasingly supplant gold as the central reserve asset of the international monetary system.

—Contributions to the United Nations Special Fund for assistance to countries hardest hit by the economic crisis should be expanded.

—The role of developing nations in the IMF and World Bank should be increased.

Transfer of Science and Technology

—Support by developed countries for the expansion of science and technology in developing countries should be significantly increased.

—The possibility of an international energy institute should be explored promptly.

—Work on an international code for the transfer of technology, including revision of conventions on patents and trademarks, with special attention to the interests of developing countries, should be pressed to conclusion by 1977.

Accelerated Industrialization

—The transfer of less competitive industries from developed to developing countries should be accelerated.

—International cooperation should be intensified to accelerate industrial development, including regional and subregional associations among developing countries.

Food and Agriculture

—The doctrine of the 1974 Rome Conference was reaffirmed: "The solution to world food problems lies primarily in increasing rapidly food production in the developing countries."
—Developed countries should facilitate agricultural exports from developing countries.
—Post-harvest losses of food in developing countries should be improved by better arrangements for marketing and distribution.
—The developed countries should insure a stable and sufficient supply of fertilizers to developing countries at reasonable prices.
—The International Fund for Agricultural Development should be brought into being by the end of 1975 by voluntary contributions of developed countries with initial resources of one billion SDR's.
—Food aid should be built up with a target of ten million tons for grains for the 1975–1976 season; a world food reserve should be created large enough to cover foreseeable major production shortfalls; ad interim, stocks or funds of not less than 500,000 tons should be earmarked by developed countries and placed at the disposal of the World Food Program.

The United Nations

—The United Nations should support subregional and interregional cooperation among developing countries and, in general, consider ways to restructure its work in economic and social development so as better to support this array of recommended policies.

71. See, for example, Rostow, *Stages of Economic Growth*, pp. 123–128.
72. The proposal of fixed money wages with prices falling with the average increase of productivity requires some elaboration. The policy should be set in motion for, say, five years to permit expectations of inflation to change and adjustments to be made in fiscal and monetary policy and the wage structure, all of which have built-in lags.

Here are the advantages of such a proposal: It would end inflation in ways that would increase pensions and other provisions for the future, raise the real income of the poor and unorganized as well as the well-organized, and force all elements in the community to focus on the role of productivity increases as the critical engine of economic and social progress. It would also deal with the problem of wages in public service sectors, whose adjustment, in an environment of inflation, has raised severe political and social difficulties in many countries.

What about the problems?

John Maynard Keynes carefully and sympathetically examined this proposal in his *General Theory* (New York: Harcourt Brace, 1936), pp. 269–271. He compared it with a regime of constant prices with wage rates rising with productivity. He noted four difficulties with fixed money wages and falling prices. Three related to the greater ease of sustaining full employment with a regime of gently rising wages. These, I believe, can now be set aside. In his time, the problem of expanding effective demand through the use of fiscal, monetary, and public investment policy appeared formidable. If the basic argument of Part Six of this book is correct, the task is thoroughly manageable once governments seize on the role of increased investment in the inputs industrial societies now require.

The fourth difficulty Keynes posed remains real enough. With falling prices, the burden of debts fixed in money terms would slowly increase. It would be compensated for by a fall in interest rates and by a rise in the real value of savings, insurance policies, pensions, etc.

But Keynes did not deal with the major difficulty. While a regime of constant money wages and falling prices is the optimal situation for labor, how could labor unions and their leaders be persuaded that industry would actually pass along productivity increases in lower prices? How could an excessive shift of national income to profits be avoided? This critical element, common to all serious wage-price agreements, requires credible public commitments from all parties and effective monitoring arrangements by governmental authorities.

73. These difficulties of OECD countries with wage-price policy are well summarized in the *OECD Observer*, no. 76 (July–August 1975), pp. 16–19.
74. See, notably, *Stages of Economic Growth*, pp. 140–141.

Author Index

Subject Index